HANDBOOK OF DISTANCE EDUCATION

HANDBOOK OF DISTANCE EDUCATION

Edited by

Michael Grahame Moore
The Pennsylvania State University

William G. Anderson
Massey University

LAWRENCE ERLBAUM ASSOCIATES, PUBLISHERS
2003   Mahwah, New Jersey   London

Director, Editorial:	Lane Akers
Editorial Assistant:	Jason Planer
Cover Design:	Kathryn Houghtaling Lacey
Textbook Production Manager:	Paul Smolenski
Full-Service Compositor:	TechBooks
Text and Cover Printer:	Hamilton Printing Company

This book was typeset in 10/12 pt. Times, Italic, Bold, Bold Italic. The heads were typeset in Helvetica, Helvetica Italic, and Helvetica Bold.

Lawrence Erlbaum Associates, Inc., Publishers
10 Industrial Avenue
Mahwah, New Jersey 07430

Library of Congress Cataloging-in-Publication Data

Handbook of distance education / edited by Michael Grahame Moore,
    William Anderson.
        p.   cm.
    Includes bibliographical references and indexes.
    ISBN 0-8058-3924-0 (casebound : alk. paper)
    1. Distance education—Handbooks, manuals, etc.   I. Moore, Michael G.
    II. Anderson, William (William George)
    LC5800.H36   2003
    371.3′58—dc21
                                                        2002152189

Books published by Lawrence Erlbaum Associates are printed on
acid-free paper, and their bindings are chosen for strength and durability.

Printed in the United States of America
10 9 8 7 6 5 4 3 2 1

Contents

v

VII: INTERNATIONAL PERSPECTIVES

Preface

Michael G. Moore

The Handbook of Distance Education has been developed in recognition of the need for an authoritative compilation reflecting the state of the art in what is arguably the most significant development in education in the past quarter century. Distance education, which encompasses all forms of learning and teaching in which those who learn and those who teach are for all or most of the time in different locations, dominates the discussion agendas of policymakers, administrators, faculty, and students across the educational spectrum. Its importance and its potential are now generally and widely accepted, as much by professors in universities and community colleges as by trainers of teachers and members of the armed forces and by those responsible for the continuing professional education of physicians and nurses, public accountants and pharmacists, managers in the corporate board-room and workers seeking new skills on the factory floor.

What has brought about this sudden explosion of interest and the recent frenzy of activity? Although there is no simple answer to this question, there can be no denying that the emergence and spread of new computer-based communications technologies is one of the principal reasons. As will be seen in more than one chapter of this book, the idea of using communications technologies to deliver instruction at a distance is at least as old as the invention of universal postal systems at the end of the 19th century, and the idea that education provided in this way would open doors of opportunity to people who were otherwise disadvantaged by conventional institutions of education and training is just as old. Until recently, however, these ideas have rarely, if ever, found acceptance among mainstream educational administrators, faculty, or educational theorists (the reason for this neglect is itself an interesting phenomenon that I hope will be the subject of research in future). Now, the first years of the new century have seen a new, unparalleled willingness to consider the benefits of teaching outside of the classroom and beyond the campus. The idea of distance learning seems to have finally entered the educational mainstream. Nonetheless, few commentators or policymakers have yet come to recognize the implications of the shift of focus from where the teacher is to where the learner is—implications for how education is conceptualized, how it is organized, what roles teachers should assume, and how financial and other resources are to be distributed.

To open up the imagination of readers to these new possibilities by providing a comprehensive and detailed account of the current state of the art—an account that includes information about the wide variety of contemporary practices as well as the foundations on which these practices are built—is the purpose of this handbook. Here we have assembled a compendium of new, specially commissioned work from all the leading thinkers and practitioners of distance education in the United States, supplemented with chapters by some of the most distinguished of their foreign peers. The book aims to provide a broad and exhaustive review of the research on such topics as the best way to practice distance education at the teacher level and the administrator level, the public policy implications of shifting a greater proportion of educational resources to this method, and the implications of the expansion of distance education for the theory of education and the practice of educational research.

In undertaking the compilation of the book, I have been driven by a single passion, a passion that has two roots. This passion is to produce a work of enlightenment about this field. What I mean by that will become clearer if I describe the two roots of my motivation. First, in my practice as the editor of the *American Journal of Distance Education* and as adviser of doctoral students facing the challenge of preparing a dissertation, I have become very concerned at the common, indeed almost universal assumption that research is nothing more than mere empiricism. This is expressed by an attitude that the beginning and end of the research process is gathering, analyzing, and reporting data. The "literature review" that typically is the second chapter in a dissertation or comprises the opening section of a research article is widely regarded as a chore imposed by convention that has to be got through as quickly as possible before getting to the "real thing," which is to gather and report the results of a survey or experiment. Very often the research design can be described most kindly as a one-shot case study and is little more than an account of what a particular teacher did in a particular program, with little general value beyond the context of the particular case (but that is another issue!). What is so sad is to see many young researchers asking questions that have already been answered, or at least answered in part, or asking questions that are beyond being answered given the present state of knowledge, or delivering well-organized data that, were they theoretically grounded, might make a significant contribution to knowledge. New knowledge cannot be created by people who do not know what is already known, yet what characterizes a great deal of what is presented as research in distance education today consists of data that have no connection with what is already known. In this regard, the enthusiasm for new technology is a problem, because what is known about education at a distance—its organization, philosophies, and issues—are not technologically specific. People whose starting point is the technology of the Internet cut themselves off from knowing what is known about distance education, for obviously the Internet is so new a communications channel that what is known in that context is minimal.

Beginning with the technology leads to the invention of terms like *e-learning* and *asynchronous learning*, terms that make good sense if one knows the broader context of all that came before the new technology but become serious impediments when they encourage potential researchers to confuse the particular technology (i.e., the species) with the genus of distance education itself. Researchers suffering from this confusion tend to compose research questions that are truly new when applied to the new technology, although their answers are well known within the larger field. More must be done in our teaching and by those who control the research review process, including the review of articles for publication, to help and indeed to require authors and researchers to base their inquiries and the data they gather and report on a solid foundation of knowledge and exposition of what is already known!

The second root of the motivation for this collection is closely related to the first, and I will state it only briefly. My experience as a consultant to a wide range of institutions, states, national governments, and international agencies over several decades has led me to conclude that an impatience for moving to action without adequate comprehension of previous experience characterizes not only the research but virtually all American practice in this field.

Just as it is hard to imagine that in any other field of inquiry researchers could set out to gather data without full knowledge of what research had previously been undertaken, so it is hard to imagine that other professionals would build programs, train teachers, invest millions of dollars, make appearances before Congressional committees, and so on, without a substantial review of previous practice in their field—without a review of what had succeeded and what had failed and the reasons for the successes and failures. Yet in distance education, it happens all the time. Ask a university professor to design a course for teaching distance learners online and fail to explain, train, or in other ways bring that person to study how courses have been successfully designed for individual learners at a distance using textual communications in hard copy, or fail to introduce that person to the research and experience of building learning communities through audio and video teleconferencing, (not to suggest that the online procedures are identical, but there is knowledge that is transferable), and the result will be a chaos of misdirected, naive, costly, and wasteful initiatives—a fair summary of the state of the art at many institutions today.

Thus, this book will be a source of enlightenment if students, researchers, practitioners, and policymakers turn to it as a key for *knowing what is known* before they begin to search for new knowledge or begin to design and deliver new programs. It should be noted, especially by researchers, that it is a key only and does not, obviously, pretend to supply the whole body of knowledge. My recommendation to students interested in doing research is, after deciding on an area to focus on, to look at the relevant chapter or chapters as the starting point for identifying the main body of literature in that area. The next step is to study each of the references listed in those chapters. No author in the handbook is able to communicate through synthesis or summary of other people's research the knowledge provided by that research itself. Each of the chapters merely points the way to the literature, thorough study of which is the essential first step to avoiding waste and gaining confidence in a particular direction to go, in both research and practice.

In the handbook, we have attempted to bring together the most respected authorities in the field, mostly well-established authors but some who are regarded as "rising stars." In extending our invitations, we aimed to deal with another common problem encountered in advising students and in reviewing research. This is the problem of *authority*. Along with my plea for more attention to building a solid theoretical foundation for research and practice (i.e., knowing what is known), I would like students to appreciate that not all that is published is of equal value. Students and others must learn who are the authors and which the publications that have greater authority and which have less, and they must also learn the criteria to apply in making evaluative judgments. As regards this issue, the reader can be sure the authors in this book have considerable authority. At a minimum, every one has been published at least once in the *American Journal of Distance Education*, itself the result of considerable competition and a rigorous review process. Most are veterans of many years of research, writing, practice, and study, the authors of all the main books and principal articles in the field. I owe an enormous debt, not so much for myself, but on behalf of the field of distance education, to these authors. As "authorities," each of them is in great demand in a field that is now insatiable in its search and need for true expertise, and each made a significant sacrifice of time and other opportunities to contribute to the book. I might have flinched from asking for so much from such persons were it not for the fact that I have worked to a greater or lesser extent with every one of them on previous projects and anticipated that I could depend on their goodwill and commitment to the field. I am delighted to acknowledge that I was not disappointed and to thank them all for the high quality of their work, their patience with the editors, and above all for their continued friendship and collegiality.

In particular, I wish to express my thanks to Bill Anderson, Lecturer in New Zealand's Massey University, who spent much of his time when working on his doctorate at Penn State University in assisting with the administrative aspects of this enterprise, doing this with great dependability and much tact as well as offering insights from his own impressive scholarship. I would also thank other members of staff at the American Center for Study of Distance Education, particularly Joe Savrock, who assisted enormously with editing. Finally, I thank Lawrence Erlbaum and his staff, particularly Lane Akers, for their initiation of the project and their encouragement and support throughout its implementation.

This Book in Brief: Overview

Michael G. Moore

The 55 chapters that make up this handbook provide overviews and summaries of the research and practice of distance education in the United States. As was pointed out in the Preface, the last 3 to 5 years have seen a rapid and explosive development of interest in and discussion about distance education, driven by excitement among educators and other professionals about the potential applications of interactive computer-based technology. In varying degrees all authors in this handbook discuss or at least make reference to the impact of this new technology. However, technology, whether new or old, is only part of the distance education system—and a relatively simple part by comparison with the pedagogical, organizational, and policymaking components. The handbook is not about technology but about the consequences of separating learners and teachers, one of which is the need to use technology. Thus, the handbook is made up of several sets of reviews and analyses of the research that deals with the history and theory of distance education, learning and learners, design and instruction, management, administration and policy, the characteristics of different audiences, the issues of costs, and finally some international dimensions.

In commissioning these chapters, we asked each author to adopt what may be described as a bibliographic essay style, charging each to give an overview and synthesis of the research and scholarly literature of the subject being treated, supported by an extensive list of references. We also asked the authors to consider three specific questions, our intention being to provide a similar focus and structure for all the chapters and give harmony to the style of the handbook as a whole. These common questions were as follows:

1. What is the current state of your special research area in contemporary distance education in America?
2. What knowledge about this is based on empirical research evidence?
3. What further research is needed in light of the changes that are occurring?

A minority of the authors invited to contribute have established themselves as researchers in fields adjacent to distance education rather than in distance education itself, and they were invited because I believe distance education should be enriched by such cross-fertilization. Authors outside the field do not always locate their area of study within the broad field of distance education itself. Some of the terms that will be found in the handbook (e.g. *tele-learning* and *e-learning*) emphasize the use of a particular communications technology, others (*distributed learning* and *distant learning*) focus on the location of learners, others (*open learning* and *flexible learning*) point out the relative freedom of distance learners to exercise more control over their learning than is normal in conventional education. By emphasizing a particular feature of distance education, such terms are valuable, but the reader should keep in mind that these terms are not synonyms for distance education itself. These are all different aspects of distance education, defined as "all forms of education in which all or most of the teaching is conducted in a different space than the learning, with the effect that all or most of the communication between teachers and learners is through a communications technology." Thus *distance education* is the generic term, and other terms express subordinate concepts.

ORGANIZATION AND CONTENTS

This handbook is divided into seven parts, as follows:

Part I. Historical and Conceptual Foundations
Part II. Learning and Learners
Part III. Design and Instruction
Part IV. Policies, Administration, and Management
Part V. Different Audiences in Distance Education
Part VI. The Economics of Distance Education
Part VII. International Perspectives

Part I. Historical and Conceptual Foundations

In Part I, nine authors review the history, theory, and philosophy of the field. First, Farhad (Fred) Saba, in my view the most sophisticated theorist of distance education writing today, summarizes the classical theories of distance education before discussing how contemporary changes in practice give rise to new questions of a theoretical nature. In concluding his chapter, he proposes a new theoretical position, one based on the philosophy of pragmatism, and advocates the application of a systems approach. This opening chapter introduces many of the field's core ideas (such as the "centrality and individuality of the learner") and mentions the names of some of the leading contributors to distance education theory, most of whom are authors of later chapters of this book.

V. Von Pittman remains, as he has been for more than a quarter century, America's leading historian of distance education. In his chapter, he reviews the current state of historiography, discusses unpublished and fugitive resources, expresses his opinion on the value of doctoral dissertations, and concludes with a list of topics meriting research by the historian. Von Pittman builds his contribution on the foundation of the chapter he wrote for *Contemporary Issues in American Distance Education*. This book, which I edited in 1990, was in fact the first compilation of American scholars in this field. It is perhaps of interest that the idea for producing the current handbook was inspired by the success of that book and the suggestion from various quarters that it was time for an update. A considerable number of authors in this handbook were, like Von Pitman, contributors to *Contemporary Issues*.

Charles (Chuck) Feasley is one of them. Like Von Pittman, a scholar of many years' standing in the field, including a long involvement with the University Continuing Education Association, Feasley is highly qualified to describe the history of distance education from the perspective of the national organizations. He gives a typology of such organizations, classifying them as pioneering organizations, curriculum organizations, technology organizations, and regional universities. One of Feasleys messages—a message discernible in almost every chapter of the handbook—is that the problems faced by organizations and institutions in the past are similar to the challenges faced by their counterparts today.

By contrast to the first authors, the next is a relative newcomer to the field. Ellen Bunker, one of my ex-students, accepted my invitation to write a chapter based on her doctoral dissertation, in which she provided a unique analysis of more than a half-century of papers presented at conferences of the International Council for Distance Education. In her chapter, she draws on the data she gathered for her dissertation to show how a commitment to strong educational values and the sharing of good practice are long-standing characteristics of distance education in the international arena and that these have been maintained in the face of recurring waves of excitement about new technologies, a phenomenon that by no means began with the Internet!

Donald Hanna's chapter on emerging organisational models in higher education is the first that looks specifically at the university. It helps us focus on what is, in my view, one of the principal reasons distance education has not been able to progress further and faster than it has—and is still being restrained more than I would like. The central issue introduced by Hanna is organizational change. To understand why higher educational institutions do not do distance education better than they do, the best place to look is neither technology nor pedagogy but rather the internal dynamics of the institutional culture. Wherever there is demand for social change of any kind, it is the culture and the propensity for innovation within the culture that determines the extent to which change occurs, and generally the American higher education culture has been and remains resistant to significant organizational restructuring, which is necessary for fully implementing distance education pedagogies.

One of the few Europeans invited to contribute to the handbook is Börje Holmberg, a past president of ICDE and one of the pioneer theorists mentioned by Saba in Chapter 1. Holmberg expands on his previously published ideas about the importance of empathy between distant learner and the instructing agency and the concept of teaching as a guided didactic conversation, explaining how he feels these can be applied in the context of the technologies that have emerged since he began writing on these issues nearly half a century ago.

The thoughts of fellow European Otto Peters, like those of Holmberg, are of special interest because both these writers hold globally recognized positions among the founding fathers of scholarship in distance education. Peters has the added distinction of being the founding rector of Germany's distance teaching university, the FernUniversität. In his chapter, he reflects on changes in this field that he has studied for many decades—and on the new world based on digitalization, along with the pedagogical gains he believes it brings as students interact with adaptive teaching programs, worldwide databases, and, of course, each other.

Changes resulting in understanding of learning and its support online are further considered by Randy Garrison, Terry Anderson, and Walter Archer as they outline a theoretical framework that uses the concepts of cognitive presence, social presence, and teaching presence as the basis for an understanding of the development of online communities of inquiry. They discuss some of the technological and organizational issues related to the creation of these communities.

Terry Anderson is sole author of the next chapter, in which he elaborates further on the central and vital concept of interaction. Building on what I can describe as a very simple (since I wrote it!) three-part typology, Anderson proposes three additional types of interaction and suggests areas of and approaches to research that should expand our understanding and competence when using these tools and approaches. He comments that the challenge issued to distance educators some 20 years ago by Daniel and Marquis—to "get the mix right"—is still valid today.

Part II. Learning and Learners

In Part II the common primary focus of each chapter is on learning and learners, although a significant part of several chapters deal with how learning at a distance should be supported by institutions and instructors. Opening Part II, adult education professor Chère Gibson discusses the distant learner and introduces the focus on learning from the perspective of the theoretical framework popularized by Boyd and Apps in their contribution to the 1980 *Handbook of Adult Education*. Using the three dimensions of the framework—transactional mode, client focus, and system—and the facets of each dimension, Gibson provides a conceptual tool for exploring existing research and identifying theoretical gaps and overlaps. She concludes by noting the importance of recognizing the different contexts within which learning occurs.

In the second chapter of Part II, Randy Garrison focuses on one of the key, perhaps even defining, characteristics of learning associated with distance education, self-directed learning (it is noteworthy that distance education was once widely known in the United States as *independent study*). Garrison suggests that in the new era of distance education, when it is easier than ever to create communities of learners, even at a distance, the concept of self-directed learning needs to be reconsidered to allow for changing motivational and metacognitive aspects of learning.

Then the issue of "context," as raised by Gibson, is featured in the chapter by Daniel Granger and Maureen Bowman, who note the challenge faced by distance educators of working beyond the foundation of good centrally prepared packages to ensure their applicability to each individual learner. For Granger and Bowman, the key to successful distance teaching lies in recognizing and responding to learner differences and providing for each individual's construction of knowledge.

Picking up the theme of individualization, Rob Curry's chapter deals with the critically important practice of academic advising. For better or worse (and personally I think there should be more investment in specialist student support services that are separate from the faculty's teaching role), most advising is undertaken by faculty—the same people responsible for developing course content and facilitating interaction. Curry helps us consider what further research is needed on the advisor-student relationship, and how to support the kind of individual approach to each student discussed in previous chapters.

Next, Don Winiecki puts the focus sharply on computer-mediated communication (CMC), in particular, its use in facilitating instructional discussion in online distance education. Using accounts by practitioners as well as the results of research, Winiecki identifies the characteristics of what he calls conversational interactions as conducted in various situations, and he attempts to classify the discussions that occur in instructional dialogue as a way of helping instructors improve their facilitation of online discussion.

Kayleigh Carbajal, Deborah La Pointe, and Charlotte Gunawardena also discuss learning online, picking up on some of the themes introduced by Garrison with their focus on development of learning communities. They first briefly analyze the interplay of social and task dimensions described by most group development theories, then provide an overview of group development models. Next they discuss the impact of technological variables, and they end by considering a framework based on social, task, and technological dimensions.

Connie Dillon and Barbara Greene continue the discussion of learner differences introduced by Granger and Bowman with a closer examination of the meaning and treatment of individual differences. They argue that the current approach to research on learner differences in distance education is unproductive and suggest that questions about learner differences need to be reconceptualized and considered through a focus on the learner's approach to study. This would inform teacher-student interaction in a way that will help students be more successful in learning how to learn. That, I might add, would further strengthen the student's propensity for self-management of the learning process.

Cognitive and other learning factors are further considered in Chapter 17, by Michael Hannafin, Janette Hill, Kevin Oliver, Evan Glazer, and Priya Sharma. Reviewing research in Web-based distance learning, the authors divide their report into two sections. The first focuses on cognitive factors (those that initiate or stimulate an individual's mental processing) whereas the second focuses on learning factors (those that cause students to engage in particular ways with specific concepts, content, or skills to be learned). The authors conclude by setting out a framework for further research into Web-based distance learning based around six areas: learners and learning, instructors and teaching, domain and task factors, course organization and sequence, community and communication, and assessment.

In the last chapter of Part II, Cheris Kramarae discusses a range of issues that women students working online have reported as having a strong impact on their studies. These issues include the amount of time involved in study, the online curriculum (what's available and how it is taught), cost, and the use of information technologies. Kramarae concludes by pointing to areas for further research that might help ensure that the new technologies in distance education do not reproduce the inequities women have faced in on-campus higher education.

Part III. Design and Instruction

Rick Shearer opens Part III with a chapter on the decision-making processes used by instructional and course designers as they select among the various technologies available for distance education. He explains why it is crucial for designers to understand and take into account the strengths and weaknesses of each technology. He also reminds us that distance educators must consider how their decisions about which technologies they use will impact the interacting parts of a distance education delivery system.

Diane Davis, a long-time expert in the design of instructional text, after acknowledging the significance of the expansion of Web-based instruction, points out that most of the material on the Web is in the form of text (reminding us once again that in distance education there is a hundred years of experience in teaching by text). Her chapter examines the literature related to the use of online text and explores how research and practice can inform our use of electronic text for instruction. Included are strategies related to the broad design features of purpose, structure, and interactivity that should guide the development of instructional online text.

Chute's review of distance learning at AT&T, Lucent Technologies, and Avaya Inc. might have been placed in Part V, where we present research on a number of different audiences. It is located here because we felt it would help complete the focus on design issues as seen from the perspective of the different technologies used. Chute's review moves from audioconferences to audio graphics to videoconferencing and then to use of the Internet. Among the ideas introduced is that there is a need to develop a range of knowledge management tools and also a need to examine the implications of the new technologies in terms of costs and return on investment—a theme returned to later in the book.

In Chapter 22, Robert Wisher and Christina Curnow review findings on the impact on learning of video-based instruction. Their chapter is presented in four parts in a roughly temporal (and technological) sequence: a review of research conducted up to 1945; a review of audiovisual instruction and educational television prior to the introduction of the desktop computer; a review of CD-ROM and videodisc use prior to the common availability of the Internet; and a review of research on the use of digital video in Web-based learning.

Web-based instruction is the focus of the next three chapters. First, Curtis Bonk and Vanessa Dennen provide five pedagogical frameworks that they believe may be used to create variety in Web-based instruction. These frameworks relate to the psychological justification for online learning, interaction among participants, levels of technology integration, instructor and student roles, and pedagogical strategies. The authors suggest that these frameworks can lead to initiatives related to research agendas, tool development, instructional design benchmarks, instructor training, and development of pedagogical guidelines and material.

Staying with the theme of online delivery, the next two chapters, by Som Naidu and by Richard Hall, Steve Watkins, and Vicky Eller, address the subject of course design. First, using the currently popular term *e-learning*, Naidu presents a variety of different instructional models—distributed problem–based learning, critical incident–based learning, goal-based learning, learning by designing, and web-based role simulation—that he believes should inform the design of instruction in the online learning environment.

Hall, Watkins, and Eller also present a model to serve as a framework for the design of Web-based learning. Their model consists of seven components: directionality, usability, consistency, interactivity, multimodality, adaptability, and accountability. These authors see design as requiring a balance of simplicity (represented by consistency and usability), complexity (represented by interactivity), multimodality, adaptability, and evaluation (represented by accountability).

A modern system of distance education must include library services, whether the information comes in hard-copy or electronic form. In her chapter, Sue McKnight brings an Australian perspective on the role of library services in distance education and then considers the link between libraries and teaching and learning and how that link is becoming more explicit. She points to the blurring of the boundary between the curriculum and the kind of information provided by library support services. Anticipating a new kind of problem, one that more and more American institutions will have to deal with, she discusses the demands placed on libraries as they attempt to service a growing number of overseas students.

In the final chapter in Part III, Morris Sammons returns us to the discussion of the relationship of the learner to the distant teacher as he sets out an argument for Web-based technology as a means of achieving the more learner centered conception of teaching and learning that we have met in earlier chapters. Use of Web-based technology is seen as offering one way to make the requisite adjustments in teaching and learning. Sammons notes that it will require time for educators to gain the experience to work effectively in such an environment.

Part IV. Policies, Administration, and Management

Opening the set of chapters that deal with policy issues, Lucille Pacey and Erin Keough describe the general policy context for distance education and then briefly consider a small selection of public policies and their intended outcomes. The focus then moves to institutions and their planning strategies as they relate to changing public policy. The chapter ends with recommended research in the policy arena that might help the distance education community close the gap between what it wants and what is being achieved.

Michael Simonson and Tamara Bauck complement the (Canadian) perspective of Pacey and Keough with an introduction to policy issues at the state level in the United States. They distinguish seven policy categories, discuss each of these, and note related policy issues. Simonson then provides a sample of policy statements based on his work with the South Dakota Department of Education.

A vitally important policy area at both national and state levels is discussed in Amy Lezburg's chapter on accreditation. Beginning with a brief historical overview of accreditation, Lezburg then considers accreditation in distance education specifically. She discusses the role of the Distance Education and Training Council (formerly the Home Study Council) and explains how the regional accrediting agencies have begun to extend their range of interest beyond on-campus education to include distance education.

Closely related to the theme of accreditation is that of quality assurance. In Chapter 31, Annette Sherry indicates some of the methods used to obtain information about the quality of distance education programs. She also reports on some of the guidelines and principles that are emerging from a range of state and national organizations and gives her own summary of recommendations for maximizing quality.

Peter Dirr, who wrote the final important chapter of *Contemporary Issues in American Distance Education*, takes a look "Towards 2010" in reviewing a set of specific policy areas beginning with quality. Other policy areas summarized here include equity and access, collaboration and communication, globalization, intellectual property rights, the role of technology, faculty, students, research, and evaluation. Dirr ends with a set of questions related to each of the above policy areas, questions that could well be seen as constituting a research agenda for those interested in policy issues that affect distance education.

One of Dirr's policy areas, intellectual property, is the subject of Tomas Lipinski's chapter. Here are presented some of the legal issues arising from the development and use of copyrighted material in Web-based distance education. The author explains how using Web sites as vehicles for content delivery has increased the complexity of copyright issues and notes some recent developments brought about by court decisions.

In a chapter that addresses some issues that are also dealt with in the design section of the book, Roger Kaufman and Ryan Watkins explain the importance of institutions basing their distance education policy on a sophisticated understanding of their potential student market. Recommending that any institution do a needs assessment prior to moving to develop a distance education program, their framework outlines a process that aligns strategic, tactical, and operational planning. They suggest that the institutions that succeed will be those that are involved in change proactively, working to create their own educational market. (A number of interesting questions may come to mind by recalling the discussion of institutional culture in Chapter 5.)

Achieving good policy is impossible without good leadership, and leadership—or rather the absence of studies of leadership in distance education—is the subject of Michael Beaudoin's chapter. Beaudoin reviews the literature in this area and postulates a number of attributes he believes are needed for successful leadership, noting the importance of a macro-level view on the part of institutional leaders and an understanding of the wider strategic implications of adopting new technology for distance education.

Moving to the related theme of institutional management, Andrew Woudstra and Marco Adria begin with a discussion of the ways in which traditional patterns of management are likely to be disrupted by the need to deliver programs by the Internet. Organizations are becoming networks, and managing a network requires skills and organizing processes that will be new to managers as well as to faculty and support staff. The chapter discusses some of the particular contingencies that managers must consider as they reorganize their structures and operations.

Obviously one of the greatest challenges facing educational leaders and managers is how to deal with faculty members acculturated into a world of academic practice that is fast disappearing. Linda Wolcott has specialized in this area, and in her chapter she provides a review of research on the motivations and barriers related to faculty participation. How faculty participation and motivation are affected by institutional policies is one of the areas in which further research is suggested.

Part IV ends with a chapter by Melody Thompson and Modupe Irele on program evaluation. The authors discuss the context of and rationale for rigorous, well-supported evaluation; the purposes of such evaluation; new trends in this area, especially new guidelines for practice; and changing standards of effectiveness.

Part V. Different Audiences in Distance Education

In this part, nine separate chapters report on applications of the distance education method in the principal sectors of the educational and training fields. (Let me acknowledge here that our organization of chapters into discrete parts is far from exact! Throughout this book, each author, understandably and inevitably, addresses questions of learning, teaching, policy, management, and often theory, as well as, on occasion, such issues as globalization. The integration of many themes dealt with elsewhere is particularly noticeable in Part V.)

In the first chapter of Part V, Diana Oblinger and Sean Rush describe the roles of corporations. Corporations are both consumers and suppliers of distance education. Their entry into the market as major suppliers is a relatively recent phenomenon, and after explaining the nature of corporate universities, the authors consider what it is that motivates corporations to become involved in this area. They draw attention particularly to benefits such as productivity improvements, staff retention, competitiveness, and cost savings in training. They also note the range of areas in which corporations are involved in supplying services to educational institutions. These areas include admissions, library services, procurement, content development, testing, and advising and tutoring.

Zane Berge in the next chapter, considers the training needs of contemporary organizations and the capabilities required to meet these needs. He looks at distance training in the light of these needs and capabilities and presents a framework to help managers chose the most appropriate kind of distance training programs.

Moving the focus from corporate training to continuing professional education (CPE), Kathy Perdue addresses questions related to the motivation of professionals to use distance learning and the deterrents to their participation in Web-based CPE. She discusses three trends that she believes will make an impact, namely, the globalization of the professions, the redefinition of CPE, and the changing nature of the population making up the professional sector.

The chapters on the corporate and continuing professional education sectors are followed by three chapters on distance education in the armed forces. As with distance education in other sectors, it is not generally realized what a long tradition there is of distance education in the armed forces, nor is the contribution of the armed forces to the wider development of distance education well enough known. (Just to illustrate, Charles Wedemeyer, the founder of distance education scholarship, acquired his first experience of designing programs for distance teaching when serving as a naval officer in World War II. I well remember in the early 1970s accompanying Wedemeyer on visits to the U.S. Armed Forces Institute (USAFI), in Madison, Wisconsin, where he maintained his support of military training by distance methods, including some of the earliest applications of the computer. USAFI, with around half a million students, was the largest distance teaching agency in the world at that time and would still dwarf most programs today.)

Each of three chapters briefly presents the author's view of the history and extent of distance education within a branch of the armed forces and then moves to consider how that branch is responding to the challenges of today's military environment. Philip Westfall discusses the Air Force's Advanced Distributed Learning Initiative; Steven Jones, Larry Blevins, Wanda Mally, and James Monroe, the Marine Corps' Training and Education Modernization initiative; and Michael Freeman, the Army Distance Learning Plan. The chapters all note the importance of systematic approaches to the task of providing appropriate training and the ways in which advanced technologies are enhancing the provision of that training.

Another very important player in distance education, the community college (which has probably done as much as, if not more than, the university in developing the use of video technology, in particular), is discussed by Christine Dalziel. In her chapter, she discusses some previously encountered issues—including accreditation, support services, the digital divide, faculty training, and copyright—from the community college perspective, as well as the key issue of collaboration between colleges.

Finally, Tom Clark reviews the role of distance education in the education of children, primarily in the high school sector. If distance education has been marginal in higher and continuing education, it has been even more marginal in the education of children. Clark reviews historical trends from the 1920s through to the development of today's virtual schools, including the evolution of audio- and video-based K-12 courses as well as professional development for school teachers. A review of research in this sector covers topics such as persistence, academic achievement, and participation.

Part VI. The Economics of Distance Education

This part, on the economics of distance education, comprises only three chapters. Instead of incorporating these chapters into Part IV, on policy, administration, and management (an option that would be conceptually defensible), we decided to allow these chapters to stand alone in recognition of the special importance of and great interest in this topic. Probably no question is more frequently asked about distance education than whether it is cost-effective (a question asked far less frequently about on-campus education, unfortunately), and there are few issues in the field that are subject to more misunderstandings. Further, I am convinced that the benefits of distance education cannot be fully realized unless and until our managers and leaders fully understand the economic implications and prerequisites. It is simply not possible to design and deliver distance education programs of quality without understanding and applying such basic economic concepts as division of labor and specialization, relationship of labor to capital, economies of large-scale production, and return on investment.

The opening chapter of this part is by one of the most highly regarded authorities on the subject, Greville Rumble, another of our European contributors. Rumble reviews several models used for costing distance education and points out the difficulties that arise with each of them. He examines the factors that are driving costs in distance education, saying that despite the difficulties with the models, it can be shown that distance education is typically, but not necessarily, more cost-efficient than classroom-based systems. The chapter concludes by noting that new computer-based or virtual classroom systems have new cost variables that are not well understood and that call for new research.

Insung Jung's chapter, which further investigates the issue of cost-effectiveness, focuses on online delivery. After giving her perspective on the cost-effectiveness of earlier forms of distance education, Jung reviews some of the individual cost-drivers, such as the number of students in a course, the number of courses offered, the type of software platform used, and the choice of synchronous or asynchronous online interaction.

Finally, repeating and complementing some of the points raised by Rumble and Jung, Alistair Inglis compares online delivery costs and the costs of some alternative distance delivery methods. Setting out several models of course delivery that claim or promise reduced costs per student, Inglis also discusses some of the difficulties of comparing the costs of different forms of distance education delivery. He provides a brief summary of the possible conclusions that can be made through a cost-comparison process and points to further aspects of the relative costs of online education that it would be useful to understand.

Part VI. International Perspectives

Although the *Handbook of Distance Education* is designed primarily for use by educators in the United States, contributors include nationals of a number of other countries, reflecting the fact that distance education, since its inception, has been more international than conventional education (partly because of the continuing stimulus of the ICDE, as described in Chapter 4). Part VI of this book is a good place to look for clues to the direction that the field will take in the years ahead, for in the view of many it is likely that, as the world's economy becomes increasingly global, so too will the design, delivery, and support of learning.

This subject, the impact of globalization on today's universities, is introduced by Robin Mason, from the Open University. She reviews the links between the following factors: the drivers behind globalization itself, the threatened "commodification" of education, the organisational structures of the early online providers, and the ways people who are currently nonparticipants may react to the changing context.

Charlotte Gunawardena, Penne Wilson, and Ana Nolla focus on the meaning and significance of culture. Building on research conducted in the fields of cross-cultural psychology, intercultural communication, and intercultural computer-mediated communication, they explore theoretical constructs that explain how culture influences perception, cognition, the teaching-learning process, and the diffusion of online education. The chapter includes a discussion of research issues in cross-cultural studies and the implications for future research related to distance education online.

In the next chapter, Australian scholars Terry Evans and Darryl Nation review historical precedents to provide a perspective from which to consider the trend toward globalization. Echoing themes stated in earlier chapters, they stress the importance of the trend toward greater interaction between learners and the need to account for the individual contexts within which students are learning—contexts that are increasingly variable as the catchment area for any course becomes global. Evans and Nation's chapter could almost as well be placed in the first part but is located here because of the attention they give to globalization and because they present an Australian view of the issues. I suggest the reader might return to some of the chapters in Part I, particularly that of Saba, and compare and contrast some of the ideas there with those of Evans and Nation.

Jan Visser looks at global issues and the relationship of distance education to the international development agenda from the unique position of one who has spent many years in leadership positions in UNESCO (United Nations Educational, Scientific and Cultural Organization), where he was director of the massive Learning Without Frontiers initiative. Visser provides a critique of established practices in distance education based on his view that learning should help people meet the demands of their lives. He also discusses the implications of his critique for institutions, society at large, and individuals engaged in learning.

In the following chapter, John Daniel, who is now at UNESCO as director of education and was previously vice chancellor of the Open University, teams up with Wayne McIntosh of the University of South Africa to address three questions: What is the state of tertiary education around the world? Why have the large open learning systems used by the mega-universities been so successful? And what have we learned from the mega-university experience regarding the future of the university? Concentrating on the large single-mode distance teaching universities, such as the Open University and the University of South Africa, these authors show how they are meeting the challenges of the "eternal triangle"—improving quality, cutting costs, and serving more students.

The final chapter of the book is on an important and often overlooked development in the field, namely the distance education work of the international agencies. In this chapter, Michael Foley discusses the World Bank's Global Development Learning Network, including the design of the system and the range of factors impacting its implementation on an international scale. Issues such as access, technology choices, target audience, economics, and pedagogy are considered. I can think of no more interesting topic to round out the story of this field of practice and study, which began with John Foster, a newspaper editor in Scranton, New Jersey, in the late 1890s and William Rainey Harper, first president of the University of Chicago, than the creation of a learning network by an institution funded by all the wealthiest nations of the world with the intent of opening opportunity for personal, community, and national development across the globe.

It is the vision and the mission of opening access and bringing greater equality of opportunity that has inspired and driven distance educators for a hundred years—and will, I hope, continue to do so. In passing, though, I would note that the need for opportunity is no longer, if it ever was, confined to the economically and socially disadvantaged. To put it one way, any person who wishes to learn and is not able to access the means of supporting learning is in a sense "disadvantaged" and deserves the consideration of those who work in the field.

CONCLUSION

Clearly, as this short review of the chapters of this book shows, distance education is not to be identified with communications technology. Certainly those who think that distance education is merely adding such technology to the existing tools and procedures of the classroom miss the point completely. In truth, distance education encompasses a commitment to open opportunity and level inequalities, a pedagogy that redirects some of the control and authority that conventionally lies with teachers toward the learners, a set of instructional design principles and methods of facilitating interaction, special leadership and managerial practices, a rethinking of educational policy, and a way of organizing resources that changes the balance of capital (technology) and labor (teachers) to create a more efficient system. Thus, distance education holds out the promise of better teaching, better quality of learning, and far better returns to public and private institutions for money invested in education and training. None of this can happen without careful and deliberate planning, without a vision and clear policy—and without courageous leadership. Leadership is needed not only to motivate and explain but to tackle the resistance of those entrenched interests that, while readily willing to adopt new technology, nevertheless do not take kindly to changes in the roles of teachers or the reapportionment of human and financial resources. It is essential that the opportunities for distance education be carefully evaluated within the framework of national, state, and institutional development plans in general and educational and training policies in particular.

In undertaking the evaluation of opportunities, it would be wise to keep in mind not only the promise of technology but its limitations and the hard policy decisions that have to be made if technology is not to disappoint. I would echo the words of a report from UNESCO:

> It is widely acknowledged that the past ten years have seen ... intense development of distance education experiences. They gave birth to a surprising change of vision, and rhetoric to express the hopes and promises attached to concepts of modern technologies. Oddly enough buzzwords and catchy ideas were adopted and replaced well-known definitions of distance learning ... too many experts or gurus jumped on the idea, without considering the hard facts such as the costs and uses of modern technologies. (*Distance Education*, 2001, p. 5)

If anything threatens the potential success of distance education more than the rejection and neglect it has received in the past, it is the danger of overenthusiasm about technology leading to underfunded, undermanned, poorly designed, and poorly managed programs. If the present volume serves to temper some of the more impetuous enthusiasm and replace it with well-grounded understanding of the costs involved and of the need for substantial investment, training, reorganizing of administrations, monitoring and evaluation of learning, and support of learners—of the need, that is to say, for careful and long-term planning and development of new and different delivery systems—the authors jointly will have made an extremely valuable contribution.

REFERENCE

Distance education in E-9 countries. 2001. Paris: United Nations Educational, Scientific and Cultural Organization.

I

Historical and Conceptual Foundations

1

Distance Education Theory, Methodology, and Epistemology: A Pragmatic Paradigm

Farhad Saba
San Diego State University
fsaba@mail.sdsu.edu

INTRODUCTION

America's approach to distance education has been pragmatic and atheoretical. With the notable exception of contributions made by Charles A. Wedemeyer, theories of distance education have been primarily conceptualized and developed by Europeans, Australians, and Canadians. The practice of distance education in the United States traces back to the late 1800s, but the first scholarly journal on the subject did not appear until 1987. Publication of the *American Journal of Distance Education* and symposia of the American Center for the Study of Distance Education organized by its director, Dr. Michael G. Moore, have brought the question of theory to the forefront of discourse in the United States and have highlighted the contribution of American scholars to research and practice within the discipline.

Today, traditional American pragmatism is evident in the search for "best practices" and the establishment of methodological benchmarks. A broad look at the American scene indicates there is a quest for practical solutions and a neglect of theory. This chapter contains a comprehensive review of theoreticians who have contributed to the conceptual development of distance education. It examines unresolved theoretical issues and demonstrates that the philosophy of pragmatism (as explicated by William James) could be of immense utility in resolving such theoretical issues by offering a solid epistemological foundation and a robust methodology. American pragmatism is in fact presented as one possible foundation for the development of distance education paradigms in the foreseeable future.

Theorists of distance education have addressed the main issues in the field from a holistic perspective. Special areas of synergy have emerged, with the result that the core concepts and building blocks of the field are understood with exceptional clarity. These areas of synergy are explored and analyzed in the first section. Then, contemporary changes that have introduced several theoretical issues and seemingly dichotomous concepts to the field are explored. Finally, the pragmatic school of philosophy is shown to provide a possible framework for a new interpretation of distance education.

DISTANCE EDUCATION THEORISTS

Theorists are model builders. They observe a segment of the world around them and search for order in the realm of experience, which is often confusing, if not outright bewildering, because of its inherent complexity (Dubin, 1978). In their attempts to improve our understanding of distance education, several theorists have presented significant models, each of which explains an important aspect of the field. An overview shows that these theorists have approached the discipline from a broad perspective and have treated it holistically. Their conceptualization of the field addresses overarching issues, such as how to define its characteristics and how to distinguish distance education from other forms of education. This is to be expected from a relatively young area of study, one that, compared with similar disciplines in the humanities and sciences, is still in its infancy.

In looking at distance education from a broad perspective, the leading theorists of the field have developed conceptual synergies. For example, Börje Holmberg, Charles A. Wedemeyer, and Michael G. Moore put the learner and his or her interaction with others at the center of the education process. The centrality of the learner is one of the distinguishing features of distance education, and understanding this fact is essential for discerning why it is essentially different from other forms of education.

Another example of synergy is presented by the theories and models of Desmond Keegan, Otto Peters, Randy Garrison, and John Anderson, which are primarily concerned with how the field is organized and how it functions. Although these theorists do not lose sight of the centrality of the learner, they concentrate on structural issues (e.g., industrialization) and how such issues might affect the process of teaching and learning.

THE CENTRALITY AND INDEPENDENCE OF THE LEARNER

Holmberg (1995) clearly placed the learner in the center when he stated, "A basic general assumption is that real learning is primarily an individual activity and is attained only through an internalizing process" (p. 47). Unmistakably, Holmberg's focus here is on the learner and the learner's responsibility for learning. Nevertheless, learner accountability is not unilateral and finds its full expression in relation to the teacher's contribution to the process of education. Holmberg termed the learner-teacher relationship "guided didactic conversation." He presented seven postulates to clarify this concept. In these postulates, Holmberg emphasized the importance of a "personal relation" between learner and teacher. This theme is often lost in the midst of the discussion of current lay views of distance education, where it is represented as a "delivery system" or a "technology" or in some other similarly misguided way.

The independence of the learner is the conceptual attractor to which seminal thinkers in the field point, including Wedemeyer (1981), the premier American theorist. Wedemeyer recognized the independence of the learner and posited that such independence would be afforded to learner by a variety of means and strategies, including anytime and anywhere learning and learner control over the pacing of the learning process. Wedemeyer also acknowledged the necessity for the learner to take more responsibility for learning, freeing the instructor of the "custodial" duties of teaching. But the real impact of Wedemeyer's contribution to the theory and practice of distance education is yet to be realized.

For Wedemeyer, distance education is a distinct "nontraditional" type of education. In his book *Learning at the Back Door*, Wedemeyer (1981) stated, "As Moore pointed out, learning apart (physically separated) from a teacher by means of communications through print, mechanical, or electronic devices implies quite a different concept of learning from that acquired in school" (p. 111). Thus Wedemeyer put into motion an essential concept for a revolutionary approach to learning that is just beginning to be noticed by administrators and program planners in higher education as well as those in government, business, and industry.

Building on Wedemeyer, Moore (1983) introduced the concept of "transactional distance," which defined the relationship of instructor and learner in more precise terms. He stated, "There is now a distance between learner and teacher which is not merely geographic, but educational and psychological as well. It is a distance in the *relationship* of the two partners in the educational enterprise. It is a 'transactional distance'" (p. 155).

Moore's concept of transactional distance is important because it grounds the concept of *distance* in education in a social science framework and not in its usual physical science interpretation. This is a significant paradigm shift of the kind described by Kuhn (1970).

As significant as the individual learner is to distance education, this type of education invariably involves institutional structures as well. Structural and institutional concepts in distance education are reviewed in the next section.

ORGANIZATIONAL STRUCTURES

Peters (1994) made a major contribution to the theory of distance education by recognizing and explicating the industrialization of education—the use of technology to reach a mass audience. Industrialization has been a feature of distance education for many years. In fact, it is hard to imagine distance education without some elements of industrialization. To the extent that correspondence education relies on the mass production of instructional materials and involves a division of labor, it is an industrial enterprise. The course team as originally conceptualized by the British Open University is another example of the division of labor in distance education.

Keegan (1993) presented a typology of "distance teaching systems" in which he classified the organizational structures of institutions involved in the field. He presented two general categories: autonomous institutions and mixed institutions. Autonomous institutions, which are free-standing organizations, encompass (a) public and private correspondence schools and (b) distance teaching universities. Mixed institutions encompass (a) independent study divisions of extension colleges (these exist mostly in the United States and Canada); (b) consultation systems, in which students are assigned both to a distant university or college, from which they receive their degree, and to a nearby "consultation" institution, from which they receive instructional services (these systems exist mostly in Europe); and (c) integrated systems, in which an academic department, supported by administrative staff, provides the same curriculum to both on-campus, and remote students (these were first established in Australia).

The picture of distance education that has emerged thus far in this review of the field's theorists is of a complex set of relationships between learners and teachers within various types of industrially structured organizations. Although our goal is theoretical parsimony, we still must address contemporary sources of complexity in the field in addition to those discussed above if we are to achieve a clear understanding of distance education. This is the task of the next section.

EMERGENCE OF POSTINDUSTRIAL EDUCATION

The introduction of the Internet, with its potential for a postindustrial form of education, has led to a critique of industrialization. Garrison and Anderson (1999), drawing on a distinction between the role of the "mega university" as conceptualized by Daniel (1998) and the role of the research university and also drawing on Schramm's (1977) distinction between "big media" and "little media," argued that, whereas mega universities might rely on big media to respond to a mass audience, research universities might rely on little media to offer a seemingly postindustrial form of education, or "little distance education" (LDE).

COMPARATIVE STUDIES OF EDUCATIONAL TELEVISION AND CLASSROOM INSTRUCTION

In the early days of research on educational television, mediated education was often compared with classroom instruction. In 1967, Chu and Schramm, researchers at Stanford University, examined 207 studies involving 421 separate comparisons of educational television and conventional classroom instruction. These studies and a follow-up study done in 1975 showed that there were no statistically significant differences between classroom instruction and educational television, a finding confirmed by subsequent studies (Johnson, Aragon, Shaik, & Palma-Rivas, 2000; Machtmes & Asher, 2000; Moore & Thompson, 1990; Saba, 2000; Wetzel, Radtke, & Stern, 1994).

MEDIA RESEARCH AND "CONFOUNDING VARIABLES"

Kumata (1960) summarized the results of research conducted on educational television in the late 1950s. This comprehensive review of data-based research literature clearly indicated the importance of learner traits in learning from television. Salomon and Snow (1970); Snow and Salomon (1968); Salomon (1969, 1971); Cronbach and Snow (1977); and Snow, Federico, and Montague (1980), among other researchers, conducted a series of studies based on the idea that if learner traits are paired with the right treatment attributes (mediated or otherwise), learning outcomes could be predicted and controlled. Aptitude-treatment interaction (ATI) clarified several issues related to cognition and mediated instruction. It also revealed that the combinations of cognitive states and media variables are potentially unlimited, preventing a simple or final analysis of the impact of media on learning. In 1985, Clark and Salomon presented a comprehensive review of research on media and teaching and referred to the problem as one of "confounding variables." (Clark, 2001)

Snow summarized the strengths and weaknesses of ATI research as follows (quoted in Kearsley, 1994):

1. Aptitude treatment interactions are very common in education.
2. Many ATI combinations are complex and difficult to demonstrate clearly, and
3. No particular ATI effect is sufficiently understood to be the basis of instructional practice. http://www.gwu.edu/~tip/cronbach.html

Commenting on research conducted in the late 1970s and 1980s, Jonassen and Grabowski (1993) likewise acknowledged the complexity generated by ATI matching: "ATIs also interact with processing requirements of the learning task to produce complex performance differences" (p. 30).

GLOBAL CHANGE AND TRANSITION

In recent years, a confluence of dramatic changes in the U.S. economy, technological inno-vations, and historic international developments, such as the end of the Cold War, propelled distance education from its usual peripheral position to the center of attention in various institu-tions. Distance education, or e-learning (the name that corporate America has ascribed to it), is now estimated to be a multibillion-dollar industry. The impact of these historic elements on the expansion of distance education illustrates that distance education is a complex phenomenon affected by myriad interrelated factors.

This was not the first time that social events had influenced distance education and its wide acceptance and popularity in the United States. The success of the Public Broadcasting Service in the 1960s and the increased availability of telecommunication satellites prompted experi-mental use of satellite-based instructional television in Alaska, American Samoa, Colorado, the Appalachian Mountain region, the heartland (University of Mid-America), and the eastern United States in the 1970s and 1980s.

NEW TECHNOLOGIES AND IDEAS

Another source of complexity was the introduction of the Internet and the rapid increase in its use. Various forms of Internet communication led to new ideas with implications for the theory of distance education. For example, Harasim (1990) presented a formal view of the practice of computer-mediated communication that highlighted its social nature, collaborative environment, and capability to amplify intellectual discourse and foster the social construction of knowledge.

With a long history of data-based research on mediated education from a cognitive perspec-tive, Salomon (1997) presented a balanced view of individual as well as group contributions to the process of socially constructing knowledge in computer-mediated communication. Thus, "distributed cognition" in computer-mediated communication became the source of another dichotomy in learning—the role of the individual versus the role of the group.

RELATED DISCIPLINES

Other sources of complexity in distance education include disciplines that are closely related to the field, such as adult education and the principles of adult learning as defined and elabo-rated by Malcolm Knowles (1975) and extension cooperatives and their pioneering efforts in establishing mobile libraries (in early 1900s), educational radio (in the 1920s), and educational television (in the 1940s).

In summary, distance education is a complex phenomenon consisting of many interrelated factors. These factors change over time and are not static. The nature of the complexity of distance education is explored further in the next section.

COMPLEXITY

As noted, many factors are involved in the formation, adoption, and application of distance education, including these:

- Global social, and economic developments.
- Industrial and postindustrial organizational structures.

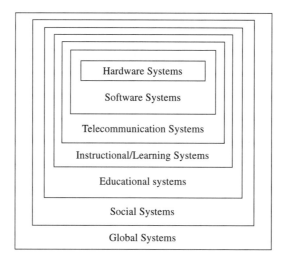

FIG. 1.1. The hierarchy of interacting subsystems that affect distance education.

- Media attributes involved in the production and presentation of instructional materials.
- Learner traits of various kinds and their interaction with media attributes.
- Myriad factors related to teaching and tutoring as well as the formation of learning communities.
- Individual differences in perception, information processing, cognition, motor behavior, and affective states.
- Increasing variety of attributes in emerging digital media, such as virtual reality-based tele-immersion and tele-presence.

These factors exist in a set of nested and hierarchical subsystems that have their own internal behavior, but each subsystem also affects and is affected by all of the others no matter at what level (see Fig. 1.1).

Apparent dichotomies in the way distance education has been conceptualized and defined by its theorists have emerged. In discussing recent social changes and the emergence of postmodern culture, Peters (1988) stated,

> There has in fact been a deep structural change in values that allows the modern self to be distinguished from the post-modern self. It might be better to refer to a *shift* of values, which took place in the following dimensions: from rationality to irrationality, from unemotional action to emotional expression, from institutional roles and standards to individual roles and standards, from duties to society to orientation towards personal gratification . . .

> As he noted, "The consequence of this change is that the post-modern self is disposed to behaviour that no longer corresponds to distance education in its industrial character" (p. 124).

Additional dichotomies occur in the following cases:

- The principles of industrial distance education as articulated by Peters (1998) contrast with the principles presented by Garrison and Anderson (1999), which describe a postindustrial view of the field.
- The practice of distance education encompasses disparate methods. For example, some practitioners are involved in "asynchronous" distance education whereas others provide "synchronous" distance education.

- Disciplines that have had a heavy influence on distance education contain contrary theories and schools of thought. As a prime example, in the field of psychology, objectivist teaching contrasts with the more recent but very popular constructivist learning.
- Distance education is often held up for comparison with so-called face-to-face, campus-based, or traditional education. Although research has indicated that there is no significant difference between distance education and classroom instruction, issues of parity of esteem have lingered on for years.

Teacher-centered versus learner-centered education, content-centered versus case-based instruction, decontextualized versus contextualized instruction, and elitist versus democratic educational systems are other examples of contrasting theories and practices.

RESOLVING THEORETICAL DICHOTOMIES

American pragmatism is a school of thought that focuses on action and on the ideas of "practice," and the "practical." According to William James (1907), one of its pioneering thinkers, pragmatism is based on a familiar philosophical view, empiricism, but the empiricism propounded by the pragmatists is of a radical kind and introduces a new temperament into philosophy. Indeed, the pragmatists hold that theories are instruments rather than "answers to enigmas, in which we can rest" (James, 1907, p. 26).

This attitude toward theories opens the door to reconciling seemingly contrasting ideas. As James (1907) explained,

> Pragmatism unstiffens all our theories, limbers them up and sets each one at work. Being nothing essentially new, it harmonizes with many ancient philosophic tendencies. It agrees with nominalism for instance, in always appealing to particulars; with utilitarianism in emphasizing practical aspects; with positivism in its disdain for verbal solutions, useless questions, and metaphysical abstractions. (p. 26)

Another radical aspect of the American pragmatists is their disdain for intellectual tendencies. Having no dogma or doctrines, pragmatism is a "method" that might lead into various schools of thought and ideas. To make this point, James used imagery attributed to the Italian pragmatist Papini, who visualized pragmatism as a hotel corridor leading into various rooms.

> Innumerable chambers open out of it. In one you may find a man writing an atheistic volume; in the next some one on his knees praying for faith and strength; in a third a chemist investigating a body's properties. In a fourth a system of idealistic metaphysics is being shown. But they all own the corridor, and all must pass through it if they want a practicable way of getting into or out of their respective rooms. (p. 27)

Ultimately, the pragmatist's quest is not a search for the relative, despite the fact that it came into being at the turn of the 20th century, when the idea of relativity was formed and adopted by physics. James is very clear in stating that pragmatism is not a negation of the concept of absolute truth, although as humans we might only arrive at an approximation of the truth.

Cornel West (1989), in his analysis of James' position, saw pragmatism as a "happy harmonizer" and a "mediator and reconciler." According to West, James liked to juxtapose polar opposites in a rhetorical list:

The tender-minded versus the tough-minded.
Rationalistic (going by principles) versus empiricist (going by facts).

Intellectualistic versus sensationalistic.
Idealistic versus materialistic.
Optimistic versus pessimistic.
Religious versus irreligious.
Free willist versus fatalistic.
Monistic versus pluralistic.
Dogmatical versus skeptical.

This list is analogous to the set of distance education-related dichotomies mentioned in the preceding section.

PRAGMATISM APPLIED

According to several accounts, we live in a period of transition—from the industrial to the postindustrial (Bell, 1973), from the modern to the postmodern (Lyotard, 1989), and from the analog to the digital (Negroponte, 1995). As early as 1970, Toffler warned of a "future shock." The epochal changes that are occurring have created situations of great contrast and confusion. We have one foot in the old and another in the new, and they are leading us in seemingly opposite directions and toward paradoxical destinations. For example, those who generate theories for or conduct research in distance education have speculated that the concept of "distance" in education would eventually evaporate, if it has not done so already!

A robust paradigm is therefore needed to reconcile these contradictions and paradoxes and support the field in the foreseeable future. If distance education theory is to be paradigmatic, it has to explain education when instructor and learner are under the same roof as well as when they are not. Reconciliation does not mean compromising, homogenizing, or standardizing. Nor does it mean simply calling for the "equivalency" of distance education and on-campus education, as Simonson, Schlosser, and Hanson (2000) have done.

Quite the contrary, the kind of reconciliation needed would, at least in the foreseeable future, promote and accommodate pluralism. Pragmatism, then, is proposed as an appropriate reconciler and mediator. But a paradigm, in addition to being a "worldview," includes methods, and these either confirm the status quo or point to anomalies leading to the next revolution (Kuhn, 1970).

SYSTEMS AS PHILOSOPHICAL RECONCILERS

West (1989) dated the dawn of the postmodern era back to 1945, when Europe was decimated, the colonial powers were leaving Asia and Africa, and the United States had clearly emerged as a world power. The idea of systems initially flourished just as the world was beginning to realize the paradoxes of modernity and the scientific culture that created it. Lyotard (1989) defined the contours of a new postmodern paradigm as follows:

> Postmodern science—by concerning itself with such things as undecidables, the limits of precise control, conflicts characterized by incomplete information, "*fracta*" catastrophes, and pragmatic paradoxes—is theorizing its own evolution as discontinuous, catastrophic, nonrectifiable, and paradoxical. It is changing the meaning of the word *knowledge*, while expressing how such a change can take place. It is producing not the known, but the unknown. And it suggests a model of legitimation that has nothing to do with maximized performance, but has as its basis difference understood as paralogy. (p. 60)

Systems science is the quintessential Jamesian tool for understanding relationships between things and not looking for a single answer to a problem within the confines of a dogma. In postmodern science, understanding the whole involves understanding the parts, but also examining the interrelations between the parts. The origins of the postmodern science are clearly visible in the following quotation from James, *Pragmatism*, (1907), which encapsulates systems, hierarchy, complexity, and chaos theories:

> Human efforts are daily unifying the world more and more in definite systematic ways.... The result is innumerable little hangings-together of the world's parts within the larger hangings-together, little worlds, not only of discourse but of operation, within the wider universe. Each system exemplifies one type or grade of union, its parts being strung on that peculiar kind of relation, and the same part may figure in many different systems, as a man may hold various offices and belong to several clubs. (p. 61)

Ludwig von Bertalanffy, who was born in Austria in 1901 and died in the United States in 1972, formalized the idea of systems in his seminal book *General System Theory*, first published in 1968:

> Similar general conceptions and viewpoints have evolved in various disciplines of modern science. While in the past, science tried to explain observable phenomena by reducing them to an interplay of elementary units investigatable independently of each other, conceptions appear in contemporary science that are concerned with what is sometime vaguely termed "wholeness," i.e. problems of organizations, phenomena not resolvable into local events, dynamic interactions manifest in difference of behavior of parts when isolated or in a higher configuration, etc.; in short, "systems" of various orders not understandable by investigation of their respective parts in isolation. Conceptions of and problems of this nature have appeared in all branches of science, irrespective of whether inanimate things, living organisms, or social phenomena are the subject of study. (von Bertalanffy, 1988, pp. 36–37)

In clarifying von Bertalanffy's concept of system, Davidson (1983) said, "The common denominator of the various definitions of *system* is the idea of interaction. On various occasions, Bertalanffy defined a system as 'a set of elements standing in interaction,' 'a complex of interacting elements,' and 'a dynamic order of parts and processes standing in mutual interaction'" (p. 26).

Accountability for interaction is one of the main features of a general system. Interaction is of crucial importance in understanding distance education as a group of actors (e.g., learners, instructors, and instructional designers) who participate in interactive communication. Furthermore, von Bertalanffy was careful to give due credit for some of his ideas to the British mathematician and philosopher Alfred North Whitehead. Whitehead (1938) challenged the Cartesian duality of body and mind and devised a philosophy in which an *actual occasion* was a complex weaving of *prehensions* in the *process of becoming*. Whitehead revealed the temporal and dynamic nature of systems and the role of time in interactions in general systems—an element that is rarely considered in education theory and research.

Built upon the principles of general systems theory, the new discipline of chaos theory has opened the way for understanding the seemingly irreconcilable behavior of certain subsystems in their interaction with larger system components (Briggs & Peat, 1989; Hall, 1993; Kiel & Elliott, 1997; Williams, 1997). Distance education in various organizational structures—from large global enterprises made possible by telecommunication satellites and the Internet to local self-organized study groups and learning communities—manifests certain system characteristics, including the following:

Complexity. Human organizations, including those involved in distance education, are complex. In the words of Briggs and Peat (1989), "Every complex system is a changing part of a greater whole, a nesting of larger and larger wholes leading eventually to the most complex dynamical system of them of all, the system that ultimately encompasses whatever we mean by order and chaos—the universe itself " (p. 148).

Hierarchical. Living complex systems are hierarchical. Ahl and Allen (1996) stated, "We defined a complex system as one in which fine details are linked to large outcomes" (pp. 29–30). James (1907) conceptualized the idea of hierarchy as "innumerable little hangings-together of the world's parts within the larger hangings-together, little worlds" (p. 61), and Briggs and Peat (1989) referred to "a nesting of larger and larger wholes" (p. 148).

Dynamic. Live, complex systems are dynamic; they change in time and evolve. In contrast, static systems remain unchanged (Roberts, Andersen, Deal, Garet, & Shaffer, 1983).

Nonlinearity. Living organisms manifest nonlinear behavior, which is "qualitatively different from that of the sum of individual parts" (Thelen & Smith, 1994, p. 45).

Self-organizing. Complex, dynamic, and nonlinear systems manifest adaptive behavior, "an emergent property which spontaneously arises through the interaction of components (Thelen & Smith, 1994, p. 45).

Chaotic and ordered. "The basic idea is that nothing novel can emerge from systems with high degree of order and stability, such as crystals. On the other hand, completely chaotic systems, such as turbulent fluids or heated gases, are TOO formless. Truly complex things— amoebae, bond traders, and the like—appear at the border between rigid order and randomness" (*Horgan*, 1995).

DISTANCE EDUCATION AS A COMPLEX SYSTEM

Peters (1967), applying the principles of industrialization, defined distance education as follows:

Distance study is a rationalized method—involving the division of labor—of providing knowledge which, as a result of applying the principles of industrial organization as well as the extensive use of technology, thus facilitating the reproduction of objective teaching activity in any numbers, allows a large number of students to participate in university study simultaneously, regardless of their place of residence and occupation. (p. 125)

Later he acknowledged the emergence of a postmodern era in distance education. Extending his definition to the postindustrial and the postmodern era, *distance education can be defined as a complex, hierarchical, nonlinear, dynamic, self-organized, and purposeful system of learning and teaching* (see Fig. 1.1).

SYSTEMS METHODOLOGY

Systems methodology has been used for understating many phenomena, including organic life (von Bertalanffy, 1988), industrial manufacturing (Forrester, 1961), developmental learning (Smith and Thelen, 1993), cognition and action (Thelen & Smith, 1994), learning (Kelso, 1995), management (Ackoff and Emery, 1981), education (Banathy, 1992; Salisbury, 1990), and a host of others (Meadows et al., 1974; Meadows & Robinson, 1985). Coldeway (1990),

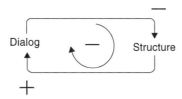

FIG. 1.2.   Feedback loop between dialog and structure.

Vazquez-Abad and Mitchell (1983), and Moore and Kearsley (1996) called for approaching distance education from a systems point of view and using systems methods to understand its complexity.

More specifically, Moore (1983) embedded the concept of distance in education in a social science framework. He defined *transactional distance* in terms of the relationship between dialog (autonomy) and structure, thus opening the way for a postmodern interpretation of distance in education. Saba (1989) used a system dynamics modeling approach to computer simulation (Roberts et al., 1983) to demonstrate Moore's concept of transactional distance in a causal loop between structure and dialog. Applying a system dynamics method accomplished two theoretical aims: (a) It introduced the concept of *virtual contiguity* (in contrast to *separation of instructor and learner*) and (b) it demonstrated the dynamic (time-based) relationship between dialog (autonomy) and structure. Achievement of these goals was made possible by presenting a feedback loop that showed the cybernetic relationship between instructor and learner (Fig. 1.2).

Constructing such feedback loops provides a method for reconciling seemingly opposite concepts. In the situation illustrated in Fig. 1.2, for example, there is a negative feedback loop between structure and dialog. A negative feedback loop provides a mechanism for determining how much transactional distance is desired and required at each point in time. If the learner needs more direct instruction, structure and transactional distance both increase. If the learner requires more autonomy, transactional distance decreases as dialog increase and structure decreases.

The inverse relationship between structure and autonomy (dialog) is at the highest hierarchical level in the instructional/learning subsystem depicted in Fig. 1.3. Structure and autonomy can be further represented in relationships that define learner control and instructor control. These feedback loops were in fact used in Saba and Shearer (1994) to test the validity of the system model presented in Fig. 1.3.

Additional feedback loops could be developed to reconcile and test the validity of other dichotomous constructs in specific subsystems, such as the objectivist-constructivist construct (Fig. 1.4). The primary hypothesis here is that novice learners require more structure, leading to objectivist instruction at the beginning of a course or instructional session. As the learner acquires expertise, the need for structure decreases and autonomy increases, which leads to learning patterns of behavior that are more constructivist.

As additional theoretical constructs are clarified and become available, systems methodology has the capacity for adding them to the model. For example, in recent years, there has been discussion of emotional intelligence in the learning processes as well as in performance (Gardner, 1993a, 1993b). The emotive factor could be added as a system variable or as a filter or controller for cognitive and behavior processes (Fig. 1.5).

These theoretical speculations concern the instructional/learning level. Similar constructs could be developed at other system levels. For example, at the hardware level, synchronous-asynchronous affordance of a particular communication medium could be added, which would have ramifications for variables at the instructional/learning level. Such dichotomous

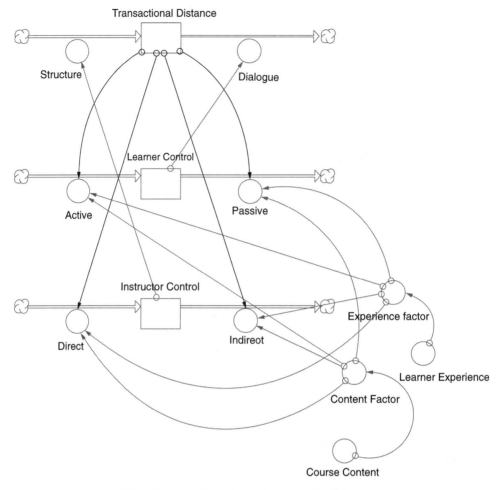

FIG. 1.3.   Causal loop diagram of transactional distance.

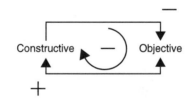

FIG. 1.4.   Objectivist-constructivist feedback loop.

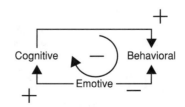

FIG. 1.5.   Cognitive-behavioral feedback loop.

constructs are, therefore, a matter of degree of variability as determined by the tolerance of the learner for autonomy and the requisite structure imposed by the instructor or the instructional organization.

As shown in Saba and Shearer (1994), an important feature of system dynamics is that data of various types can be used to represent such variables. In this 1994 data-based study, for example, discourse analysis was used to measure the rate of instructor control and learner control. Data generated through analyzing the conversation between 30 learners and one instructor in 30 individual sessions was used to discover whether there was an inverse relation between dialog and structure.

In recent years, researchers in the field have used a variety of data collection methods and data types. For example, Fulford and Zhang (1993) and Gunawardena (1995) used student self-reporting in a survey study, McDonald and Gibson (1998) conducted extensive interviews of students, and Chen and Willits (1999) and Tsui and Ki (1996) used conversation and discourse analysis to collect their data. Systems methods are resilient enough to encompass these and other data types. Model refinements may result from incorporating such variables in subsystem elements. Hopefully, consilience with the nature and reality of the distance education environment will emerge as a result.

LEARNERS AT THE CUSP OF CHAOS

Learners interact with their environments. They receive information, nourishment, and affection to maintain a steady state (i.e., a system status necessary for living and thriving). Learners are also self-organizing and adapt themselves to their environment in creative and nonlinear ways (Donahoe & Palmer, 1994; Mainzer, 1994; Singer, 1995). Learners as entities differ from dissipative systems, whose behavior moves toward a point of equilibrium, inactivity, and stability.

As Kelso (1995) stated in more technical terms,

> A dynamical system lives in a *phase state* that contains all the possible states of the system and how these evolve in time. A dissipative dynamical system is one whose phase space volume decreases (dissipates) in time. This means that some places (subsets in the phase space) are more preferred than others. These are called *attractors*: no matter what the initial value of *x* is, the system converges to the attractor as time flows to infinity. For example, if you stretch a spring or displace a damped pendulum, they will eventually wind down and stop at their equilibrium positions. The attractor in each case is a fixed point or simply *point attractor*. (p. 53)

In contrast, learners, by definition, learn, and they also create and contribute to society. Their learning behavior does not point to a state of equilibrium. Working at the level of the brain subsystem, Kelso (1995) demonstrated that the human brain itself is a nonlinear, self-adaptive organ of the body. His experiments and those of his colleagues showed that learning is a "specific modification of already existing behavioral patterns in the direction of the task to be learned." This principle is congruent with earlier studies by Gagné and Glaser (1987), which confirmed that prior learning is the most important predictor of future learning. In Kelso's terms, "The nature of the attractor layout prior to learning must be established to know *what* has been modified and *what* has been learned" (p. 162).

Kelso's experiments also confirmed another earlier finding by Gagné (Gagné and Glaser 1987)—that feedback to the learner on the results of learning is another crucial factor in learning. Kelso (1995) emphatically states that "without such feedback, learning does not typically occur" (p. 171).

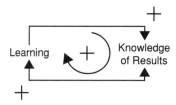

FIG. 1.6.   Knowledge of results—learning feedback loop.

Providing knowledge of results, however, is a positive feedback loop, which does not stabilize the system. It actually increases system instability and moves it towards "phase transition" and ultimately "chaos" if not tempered by negative feedback loops in the system (Fig. 1.6).

For learners to learn, their brains must hover at the cusp of chaos, and, while learning, their "entire attractor layout changes" (Kelso, 1995). Learning is in fact a process of successive approximations in which new attractors are strengthened and some of the prior attractors are weakened. The result, however, is not more of the same behavior that existed prior to learning. In learning, the learner's general patterns of behavior undergo changes, often unpredictable ones. Learning, thus, is an emergent behavior of the learner, a concept that is best understood in the context of systems technology.

SYSTEMS TECHNOLOGY

Systems technology has become possible with the advent of the computer and its ability to process data at a high rate of speed. In the 1960s and the early 1970s, mainframe computers were used to run simulation programs modeling various systems, such as business organizations, industrial works, and natural habitats. Using a mainframe, for example, Saba and Root (1977) developed a system dynamics model to study the behavior of organizational subsystems in educational television. Mainframes, however, were expensive to run, and although their number-crunching had speeded up to previously unimaginable rates, it was still time consuming to program them, examine the code for errors, and rerun the experiment.

Microcomputers made systems simulation relatively inexpensive and even faster than previous generations of mainframes. Off-the-shelf software that dramatically facilitated simulation of various systems also became available. For example, Saba and Twitchell (1988) used Dynamo, a version of system dynamics ported to the Apple II computer, for studying governance of distance education systems. Later, a system dynamics program was ported to the Macintosh. Called STELLA, it was used for a data-driven study by Saba and Shearer (1994) intended to verify the relationship between dialog and structure in transactional distance based on Moore's (1983) theoretical constructs.

Modeling distance education as a complex adaptive and nonlinear behavior of various "agents" (e.g., instructors, learners, instructional designers, administrators, instructional television program traders, investors in e-learning dot-com companies, and government decision makers) requires system technologies capable of handling parallel computation architectures. Singer (1995) and Holland (1996, 1999) have described the make-up of complex adaptive systems and their emergent behavior. Their description can be summarized as follows:

- A complex adaptive system encompasses numerous interacting agents whose aggregate behavior is to be understood.

- The aggregate behavior of such agents is nonlinear and cannot be derived from a summation of individual component behavior.
- The nonlinear aggregate behavior of individual agents results in emergent behavior.
- Such emergent behavior, although unpredictable, is lawful.
- The agents are morphologically diverse (e.g., students, faculty, instructional designers, and administrators).
- The removal of one agent type leads the system to reorganize itself to make up for the gap in the system.
- The structure of the system continuously evolves, leading to the emergence of new agents and new relationships.
- The agents are characterized by internal models, which are built-in rule-governed procedures that allow for the anticipation of consequences.

A current study aimed at modeling dynamic, complex distance education systems has adopted StarLogoT 2001 as one of its software programs. Developed by Uri Wilensky, StarLogoT 2001 is a derivative of LOGO, developed by Seymour Papert at MIT, and is based on StarLogo, developed by Michael Resnick—all under the auspices of the National Science Foundation (Young, 2000). StarLogo allows the modeling of many agents as well as types of agents, the inclusion of agents that can "sense" other agents and agent types, the use of "primitives" built into the agents to "follow" what they "sense," and the defining and reifying of the agents' worlds by specifying their environment and the context of their behavior (Resnick, 2000).

In this study, whereas StarLogoT 2001 is being used for modeling individual agents and agent types, STELLA will be used to model the output of StarLogoT 2001 simulations for observing the behavior of aggregate meta-agents and thus the behavior of the systems at increasingly complex hierarchical levels (Resnick, 2000).

CONCLUSION

The American approach to distance education requires a paradigm congruent with the pragmatic temperament in order to absorb the rapid changes in the field that are being fueled by global developments, technological innovations, and a shift to a postindustrial era in economics. Pragmatism, as defined by James, can be used to bring more conceptual clarity to current theories and models of distance education. More specifically, it can set the stage for a systems view of distance education and provides the foundation for employing systems philosophy, methodology, and technology to establish an epistemology capable of serving the field in the foreseeable future.

If distance education is to be the educational paradigm, distance education theory must explain the whole of education and not only when teacher and learner are separated in space and time. Such separation can be bridged by communication technology, a fact demonstrated by teachers and students everywhere. But if students and teachers are separated by the total absence of dialog, as occurs in many classrooms across the country and around the world, bringing them together until they stand nose to nose will not offer a solution.

Approached from a systems view, distance education subsumes other forms of education, including what is generally known as face-to-face or traditional education. The pragmatic paradigm goes even further than that and posits that distance education is a product of the postindustrial information culture. While schools traditionally tried to standardize instruction to make people on the factory floor capable of performing routine jobs the challenge of distance education is to respond to individual differences and make instruction as diversified as possible.

In other words, the goal is to fuel the engine of postindustrial culture, the survival of which depends on innovation, not uniformity.

It is of paramount importance to realize that a systems research methodology for distance education must involve tracing data for each individual learner, including his or her prior knowledge (phase state), achievement of learning objectives, and, perhaps most important, construction of new knowledge. As indicated in Saba (1999) and Saba (2000), data from hundreds of comparative studies show "no significant difference" between mediated education and classroom instruction. However, the experimental methods used in these studies are ill-equipped to shed light on dissimilarities between distance and face-to-face education that might exist. They cannot, for example, detect the *emergent* properties of constructivist learning, where significant differences in learning usually manifest themselves. Treating the learner as an individual and expecting but not determining emergent learning affirms the learner as an autonomous, independent, responsible agent.

A test of a new paradigm is its ability to accommodate the older ones while explaining hitherto unexplained phenomena. Systems philosophy, methodology, and technology afford a pragmatic paradigm for distance education that treats "distance" as a social construct in a postindustrial context while subsuming industrial constructs developed in a physical science paradigm. The analysis presented here is hopefully sufficient for demonstrating that this new paradigm has the methodological potential to explain what has transpired in distance education already and to suggest future developments. Among other things, the new paradigm should be able to explain the contextual crafting of the *moment* of teaching and learning experience as the instructional-learning process unfolds in time and produces both expected, determinate behavior and general patterns of emergent behavior the nature of which is anticipated but not determined in advance.

REFERENCES

Ackoff, R., & Emery, F. (1981). *On purposeful systems*. Chicago: Aldine, Atherton.

Ahl, V., & Allen, T. F. H. (1996). *Hierarchy theory*. New York: Columbia University Press.

Banathy, B. H. (1992). *A systems view of education: Concepts and principles for effective practice*. Englewood Cliffs, NJ: Educational Technology Publications.

Bell, D. (1973). The coming of post-industrial society. New York: Basic Books.

Briggs, J., & Peat, F. D. (1989). *Turbulent mirror: An illustrated guide to chaos theory and the science of wholeness*. New York: Harper & Row.

Chen, Y-J., & Willits. F. K. (1999). Dimensions of educational transactions in a videoconferencing learning environment. *American Journal of Distance Education, 13*(1), 45–59.

Chu, G. C., & Schramm, W. (1967). Learning from television: What the Research Says. (ERIC Document Reproduction Service No. ED914900)

Clark, R. E. (2001). (Ed.). *Learning from media: Arguments, Analysis, and evidence*. Greenwich, CT: Information Age Publishing.

Coldeway, D. O. (1990). Methodological issues in distance educational research. In M. G. Moore (Ed.), *Contemporary issues in American distance education* (pp. 386–406). Oxford: Pergamon Press.

Cronbach, L., & Snow, R. (1977). *Aptitudes and instructional methods: A handbook for research on interactions*. New York: Irvington.

Daniel, S. J. (1998). *Mega-universities and knowledge media: Technology strategies for higher education*. London: Kogan Page.

Davidson, M. (1983). *Uncommon sense: The life and thought of Ludwig von Bertalanffy, father of the general systems theory*. Los Angeles: J. B. Tarcher.

Donahoe, J. W., & Palmer, D. C. (1994). *Learning and complex behavior*. Boston: Allyn & Bacon.

Dubin, R. (1978). *Theory building* (2nd ed.). New York: The Free Press.

Forrester, J. W. (1961). *Industrial dynamics*. Cambridge, MA: MIT Press.

Fulford, C. P., & Zhang, S. (1993). Perception of interaction: The critical predictor in distance education. *American Journal of Distance Education, 7*(3), 8–21.

Gagné, R. M., & Glaser, R. (1987). Foundations in learning research. In R. M. Gagne, (Ed.). *Instructional technology: Foundations*. Hillsdale, NJ: Lawrence Erlbaum Associates.

Gardner, H. (1993a). *Frames of mind: The theory of multiple intelligences*. New York: Basic Books.

Gardner, H. (1993b). *Multiple intelligences: The theory in practice*. New York: Simon & Schuster.

Garrison, R. D., & Anderson, T. D. (1999). Avoiding the industrialization of research universities: Big and little distance education. *American Journal of Distance Education, 13*(2), 48–63.

Gunawardena, C. (1995). Social presence theory and implications for interaction and collaborative learning in computer conferencing. *International Journal of Educational Telecommunications, 1*(2-3), 147–166.

Hall, N. (Ed.). (1993). *Exploring chaos: A guide to the new science of disorder*. New York: W. W. Norton.

Harasim, L. M. (1990). Online education: An environment for collaboration and intellectual amplification. In L. M. Harasim, (Ed.), *Online education: Perspective on a new environment* (pp. 39–64). New York: Praeger.

Holland, J. H. (1996). *Hidden order: How adaptation builds complexity*. Cambridge, MA: Perseus.

Holland, J. H. (1999). *Emergence: From chaos to order*. Cambridge, MA: Perseus.

Holmberg, B. (1995). *Theory and practice of distance education*. London: Routledge.

Horgan, J. (1995). From complexity to preplexity. *Scientific American*. Vol. 279. #12. 106–109.

James, W. (1907). *Pragmatism*. Buffalo, NY: Prometheus.

Johnson, S. D., Aragon, S. R., Shaik, N., & Palma-Rivas, N. (2000). Comparative analysis of learner satisfaction and learning outcomes in online and face-to-face learning environments. *Journal of Interactive Learning Research, 11*(1), 29–49.

Jonassen, D. H., & Grabowski, B. L. (1993). *Handbook of individual differences, learning and instruction*. Hillsdale, NJ: Lawrence Erlbaum Associates.

Kearsley, G. (1994). Aptitude-treatment interaction. In L. Cronbach and R. Snow, *Explorations in learning and instruction: Theory into practice database* [On-line]. Available: http://www.gwu.edu/~tip/cronbach.html

Keegan. D. (1993). A typology of distance teaching systems. In K. Harry, M. John, and D. Keegan, (Eds.), *Distance education: New perspectives* (pp. 62–76). London: Routledge.

Kelso, S. (1995). *Dynamic patterns: The self-organization of brain and behavior*. Cambridge, MA: MIT Press.

Kiel, L. D., & Elliott, E. (Eds.). (1997). *Chaos theory in the social sciences: Foundations and applications*. Ann Arbor, MI: University of Michigan Press.

Knowles, M. (1975). *Self-directed learning: A guide for learners and teachers*. New York: Cambridge University Press.

Kuhn, T. S. (1970). *The structure of scientific revolutions* (2nd ed.). Chicago: University of Chicago Press.

Kumata, H. (1960). A decade of teaching by television. In W. Schramm, (Ed.). *The impact of television: Selected studies from the research sponsored by the National Educational Television and Radio Center*. Urbana, IL: University of Illinois Press.

Lyotard, J. F. (1989). *The postmodern condition: A report on knowledge*. Minneapolis, MN: University of Minnesota Press.

Machtmes, K., & Asher, J. W. (2000). A meta-analysis of the effectiveness of telecourses in distance education. *American Journal of Distance Education, 14*(1), 27–46.

Mainzer, K. (1994). *Thinking in complexity: The complex dynamics of matter, mind, and mankind*. Berlin: Springer-Verlag.

McDonald, J., & Gibson, C. C. (1998). Interpersonal dynamics and group development in computer conferencing. *American Journal of Distance Education, 12*(1), 7–25.

Meadows, D. H., & J. M. Robinson. (1985). *The Electronic Oracle*. Chichester, England: Wiley.

Meadows, D. L., Behrens, W. W., III, Meadows, D. H., Naill, R. F., Randers, J., & Zahn, E. K. O. (1974). *Dynamics of growth in a finite world*. Cambridge, MA: Wright-Allen Press.

Moore, M. G. (1983). The individual adult learner. In M. Tight, (Ed.), *Adult learning and education* (pp. 153–168). London: Croom Helm.

Moore, M. G. (1989). Three types of transaction. In M. G. Moore & G. C. Clark (Eds.), *Readings in principles of distance education* (pp. 100–105). University Park, PA: The Pennsylvania State University.

Moore, M. G., & Kearsley, G. (1996). *Distance education: A systems view*. Belmont, CA: Wadsworth.

Moore, M. G., & Thompson, M. M. (1990). *The effects of distance learning: A summary of literature* (Monograph 2). University Park, PA: The American Center for the Study of Distance Education.

Negroponte, N. P. (1995). *Being digital*. New York: Knopf.

Peters, O. (1998). *Learning and Teaching in Distance Education : Analysis and Interpretation from an International perspective*. London, UK., Kogan Page.

Peters, O. (1994). Distance education and industrial production: A comparative interpretation in outline (1967). In D. Keegan, (Ed.), *The industrialization of teaching and learning* (pp. 107–127). London: Routledge.

Resnick, M. (2000). *Turtles, termites and traffic jams: Exploration in massively parallel microworlds*. Cambridge, MA: MIT Press.

Roberts, N., Andersen, D. F., Deal, R. M., Garet, M. S., & Shaffer, W. A. (1983). *Introduction to computer simulation.* Reading, MA: Addison-Wesley.

Saba, F. (1989). Integrated telecommunications systems and instructional transaction. *American Journal of Distance Education, 2*(3), 17–24.

Saba, F. (2000). *Research in distance education: A status report.* Available: http://www.irrodl.org/content/v1.1/farhad.pdf

Saba, F., & Root, G. (1977). Educational television: A new frontier. *Proceedings of the International Conference on Cybernetics and Society, IEEE* (pp. 111–114). Washington, DC: IEEE Press.

Saba, F., & Shearer, R. L. (1994). Verifying key theoretical concepts in a dynamic model of distance education. *American Journal of Distance Education, 8*(1), 36–59.

Saba, F., & Twitchell, D. (1988). Research in distance education: A system modeling approach. *American Journal of Distance Education, 2*(1), 9–24.

Salisbury, D. F. (1990). General systems theory and instructional systems design. *Performance and Instruction, 29*(2), 1–11.

Salomon, G. (1969). What does it do to Johnny?: A cognitive-functionalistic view of research on media. (ERIC Document Reproduction Service No. ED 034 734)

Salomon, G. (1971). Heuristic models for the generation of aptitude-treatment interaction hypotheses. Jerusalem: Hebrew University of Jerusalem. (ERIC Document Reproduction Service No. ED 059 589)

Salomon, G., (1997). Interaction of media, cognition, and learning. Jossey-Bass.

Salomon, G., & Snow, R. E. (1970). Commentaries on research in instructional media: An examination of conceptual schemes. Bloomington, IN: Indiana University. (ERIC Reference No.: ED 044 900).

Schramm, W. (1977). *Big Media, Little Media.* Beverly Hills, CA: Sage.

Simonson, M., Schlosser, C., & Hanson, D. (2000). Theory and distance education: A new dimension. *American Journal of Distance Education, 13*(1), 60–75.

Singer, J. L. (1995). Mental processes and brain architecture: Confronting the complex adaptive systems of human thought In H. J., Morowitz, and J. L., Singer, (Eds.), *The mind, the brain and complex adaptive systems* (pp. 1–9). Reading, MA: Addison-Wesley.

Smith, L. B., & Thelen, E. (1993). *A dynamic systems approach to development: Applications.* Cambridge, MA: MIT Press.

Snow, R. E., & Salomon, G., (1968). Aptitudes and instructional media. *Audio Visual Communications Review, 16,* 341–357.

Snow, R., Federico, P., & Montague, W. (1980). *Aptitude, learning, and instruction* (Vols. 1 & 2). Hillsdale, NJ: Lawrence Erlbaum Associates.

Thelen, E., & Smith, L. B. (1994). *A dynamic systems approach to the development of cognition and action.* Cambridge, MA: MIT Press.

Toffler, A. (1970). *The future shock.* New York: Random House.

Tsui, A. B. M., & Ki, W. W. (1996). An analysis of conference interactions on TeleNex: A computer network for ESL teachers. *Educational Technology Research and Development, 44*(4), 23–44.

Vazquez-Abad, J., & Mitchell, P. D. (1983). A systems approach to planning a tele-education system. *Programmed Instruction and Educational Technology, 20*(3), 202–209.

von Bertalanffy, L. (1988). *General system theory: Foundations, development, applications* (Rev. ed.). New York: George Braziller.

Wedemeyer, C. A. (1981). *Learning at the back door: Reflections on the non-traditional learning in the lifespan.* Madison, WI: University of Wisconsin Press.

West, C. (1989). *The American evasion of philosophy: A genealogy of pragmatism.* Madison, WI: University of Wisconsin Press.

Wetzel. D. D., Radtke, P. H., & Stern, H. W. (1994). Instructional effectiveness of video media. Hillsdale, NJ: Lawrence Erlbaum Associates.

Whitehead, A. N. (1938). *Modes of thought.* New York: Macmillan.

Williams, G. P. (1997). *Chaos theory tamed.* Washington, DC: Joseph Henry Press.

Young, P. (2000). *A dynamic model: Simulating the distance education environment.* Unpublished manuscript.

2

Correspondence Study in the American University: A Second Historiographic Perspective

Von V. Pittman
University of Missouri-Columbia
pittmanv@missouri.edu

Distance education is developing in a hurry at the postsecondary level. As its pace of innovation and adoption accelerates, many practitioners and advocates seem anxious to leave its past behind. The faculty, administrators, and instructional developers and designers promoting it are definitely results oriented. To the extent that they have a guiding philosophy, it is pragmatism. This orientation toward the future is both obvious and unremarkable. These educators tend to have little inclination to reflect on the achievements, failures, and meaning of their predecessors' work.

Yet, correspondence study was indeed the first distance learning format employed by postsecondary American institutions, and for generations it was the only one. It has had a limited but significant impact on college teaching. It provided not only an impetus for electronically assisted distance education formats but also an administrative home. At least as important is the fact that correspondence study often provided the funds and expertise that universities tapped in order to attempt to develop innovative—and frequently foolish or ill-conceived—telecommunications schemes.

The historians of education, scholars whose task it is to analyze and illuminate, have devoted little attention to distance education, even though hundreds of thousands of college students have used one or more correspondence courses to further their progress toward graduation. Given its low profile, the still relatively small number of students who have used it, and the extremely small share of university resources expended on it, this lack of interest is understandable, albeit regrettable.

In 1990, an anthology edited by Michael Moore, entitled *Contemporary Issues in American Distance Education*, surveyed the state of scholarship and practice in distance education. It included an essay I wrote on the historiography of correspondence study (Pittman, 1990). That piece, hereinafter cited as the "*CIADE* essay," demonstrated the lack of reflective historical treatments of collegiate-level correspondence courses by enumerating the extant secondary works and pointing to obvious gaps. It provides a starting point for this chapter, which will consider the current state of historiography for the first century of distance education in the American university. In addition, this chapter reviews a body of literature—mainly doctoral dissertations and anthology chapters—that received only scant mention in the 1990 *CIADE* essay. Finally, it suggests several areas for new research, most virtually untouched by historians of education.

RECENT DEVELOPMENTS IN THE HISTORIOGRAPHY OF CORRESPONDENCE STUDY

Social and Intellectual Context

The *CIADE* essay noted a lack of "systematic analysis" in the historiography of correspondence study. It cited as important a number of books that were not actual histories. Such works as Bittner and Mallory's *University Teaching by Mail* (1933) and Wedemeyer and Childs's *New Perspectives in University Correspondence Study* (1961) are arguably still among the best books ever written on the subject. For all their merit, however, they are descriptive rather than reflective. Although they are invaluable to the historian as resources, they are not works of history. They present snapshots of the practice of collegiate correspondence study and provide some narrative background in order to set a context but offer little in the way of analysis. No book-length interpretive history of the field has been written since the *CIADE* essay appeared. However, scholars have begun to take a more serious look at correspondence study (also known as independent study).[1]

The best interpretation of independent study's place in American higher education appears in Joseph Kett's *The Pursuit of Knowledge Under Difficulties: From Self-Improvement to Adult Education in America, 1750–1990*, which appeared in 1994. Kett took his title from that of an 1830 book by George L. Craik. While first published in Britain, Craik's collection of inspirational biographical sketches of worthy and persevering autodidacts became extremely popular in the United States, complementing the widespread belief in self-help as well as the ideology of Jacksonian democracy. Kett's book, a social and intellectual history of adult and continuing education in the United States, placed university extension and continuing education programs—including correspondence study—squarely in the American tradition of voluntary self-improvement. Universities became one of many providers of education meant to promote self-improvement, along with proprietary correspondence schools, community evening classes, lyceums, traveling chautauquas, and other agencies.

Kett described how extension efforts, including correspondence courses, developed in universities while never really becoming part of them. It was always a poor fit, he maintained. Like many other extension and continuing education programs, correspondence study departments became, in reality, self-supporting small businesses operating within tax-supported public institutions. Kett explored the association of correspondence courses and lecture-based extension classes with an alleged lowering of standards that caused professional academics to regard them skeptically. Yet, by 1960, university adult education programs, like those of other providers, came to hold "a secure but marginal niche in American education" (p. xviii). While it deals with much more than independent study, *The Pursuit of Knowledge Under Difficulties* is essential to any serious study of this form of instruction.

---

[1]Early collegiate-level correspondence study was often called "home study" to distinguish it from the product of proprietary schools. For much the same reason, colleges and universities began to call it "independent study" beginning in the late 1960s. The three terms will here be used interchangeably.

The publisher's blurb on the back cover of Kett's book proclaims it the "first history of nontraditional education in America." This is not precisely the case. Charles A. Wedemeyer's *Learning at the Back Door: Reflections on Non-traditional Learning in the Lifespan* (1981) has a better claim to that distinction. Like Kett, Wedemeyer stressed the voluntary nature of nontraditional education and placed correspondence study and other forms of distance education in the context of a larger self-improvement movement. Whereas Kett took the position that the institutions of higher education absorbed and accommodated some of the adult education programs and methods, however grudgingly, Wedemeyer saw nontraditional education as a revolt against the elitism of the established education system. Although neither Wedemeyer nor Kett dealt extensively with distance education, both books provide a valuable historical and intellectual context.

History by Anthology

Since the publication of *CIADE*, a number of anthologies on the general subject of distance education have appeared. A fair number have included one or more chapters with an historical orientation. Indeed, the *CIADE* essay itself is an example of this type of chapter.

In regard to the early history of distance education, the most important of these books is *The Foundations of American Distance Education: A Century of Collegiate Correspondence Study*, edited by Barbara Watkins and Steve Wright (1991). The Independent Study Division of the National University Continuing Education Association (now known as the University Continuing Education Association)[2] produced this anthology to celebrate the first 100 years of collegiate distance education (dated from the founding of the University of Chicago and its correspondence program in 1892). It represents the single most important contribution to the history of collegiate correspondence study published since the *CIADE* essay.

The first two chapters, one each by editors Watkins and Wright, survey the history of correspondence study in the American university. Chapters on two specialized areas of collegiate programming—high school (Young & McMahon, 1991) and courses offered without college credit (Rose, 1991)—follow, then one on the unending controversy over the academic quality of correspondence study within a university setting (Pittman, 1991). Finally, Van Kekerix and Andrews (1991) contribute a particularly useful piece on early attempts by university independent study departments to incorporate electronic technology into their instructional formats.

Other anthologies have included chapters on the history of correspondence study, either as background for discussions of more modern programs and events or as token offerings representing one of the smaller areas of scholarship within the larger field of distance education. J. Peter Rothe's (1986) chapter in *Distance Education in Canada* (Mugridge & Kaufman, 1986), published prior to *CIADE*, is an example of the former type of writing. Rothe notes the earliest Canadian correspondence programs, describes the development of institutions based in whole or in large part on distance education, and ends with a discussion of early electronic formats. A chapter entitled "Origins of Distance Education in the United States," by Sherow and Wedemeyer (1990), serves the same purpose in *Education at a Distance: From Issues to Practice*, edited by Garrison and Shale (1990). This piece is almost certainly the last signed work of Charles Wedemeyer's distinguished career.

"Harper's Headaches" (Pittman, 1995) meets the latter purpose—that of including the history of correspondence study in a more general research monograph, in this case a monograph

---

[2]The University Continuing Education Association was founded in 1915 as the National University Extension Association (NUEA). It changed its name to the National University Continuing Education Association (NUCEA) in 1979, and then in 1996 it dropped "National" from its title.

on the subjects of policy and administration published by the American Center for the Study of Distance Education (Duning & Pittman, 1995). The author used this chapter to compare and point to parallels between today's administrative problems and those faced by William Rainey Harper, widely regarded as the founder of collegiate correspondence study.

Institutional Histories

Institutional histories of major American universities rarely mention correspondence or independent study. The *CIADE* essay noted that only the excellent (but dated) history of the University of Wisconsin (Curti & Carstensen, 1949) gives it substantive treatment. Histories of extension and continuing education divisions—often written and published in-house—frequently are useful, but they, too, tend to be old and outdated. On the other hand, scholars researching the history of distance education will find several books on other postsecondary institutions quite helpful.

Gene Getz's *MBI: The Story of Moody Bible Institute* (1986) recounts the history of an institution that is, among other things, a two-year college. Moody initiated its correspondence program in 1901, placing it among the pioneers of this teaching method. Moody then built a program with huge enrollments and developed a worldwide reach.

Regents College: The Early Years (Nolan, 1998) is the story of an innovative external degree institution. Recently renamed Excelsior College, Regents College of the University of the State of New York (not the same thing as the State University of New York, confusingly enough) grew out of the practice of granting college credit by examination. In 1972, it began awarding external degrees, the first granted in the United States since the 19th century. One of the several means Regents students could use to acquire credit was—and still is—independent study. Until recently, Regents offered no distance education courses of its own, but its students enrolled in other independent study courses in such great numbers as to have an impact on virtually every university program in the United States. Because it is so unconventional, Regents' story is as confusing as it is interesting. Donald Nolan, who served as a member of its founding board of directors, recounts it deftly.

The Province of Alberta founded Athabasca University in 1970. Originally intended to be a conventional institution, Athabasca later developed along lines influenced by the British Open University. It began using teams of content specialists, instructional designers, and editors to develop "home study" courses in 1975. It is now a mature and innovative university, committed entirely to distance education. T. C. Byrne's *Athabasca University: The Evolution of Distance Education* (1989) offers a thorough history.

New Critics

In the *CIADE* essay, books by Thorstein Veblen (1918) and Abraham Flexner (1930) were presented as the major examples of early criticism of correspondence study from within academia. While dismissive and scornful remarks have always been common on campus, thoughtful, detailed criticism has been rare. But this is not necessarily good news. It could be argued that, despite evidence to the contrary, a preponderance of academics consider independent study inferior by definition, even beneath contempt. However, a few thoughtful critics have weighed in. Some have been not opponents of distance education but rather proponents of other formats.

Reflecting on major university independent study divisions, Becky Duning (1987) worries not so much about the format itself as about the state of its leadership. The prevailing generation of independent study directors has failed to appreciate the potential of electronically enhanced formats, she argues. By not embracing electronic delivery enthusiastically—and the prophecy of its advocates—independent study directors risk becoming irrelevant to the future of distance education. In an unpublished but widely disseminated paper, Carla Montgomery (1993), associate dean of the Graduate College at Northern Illinois University, uses negative assumptions about correspondence study to damn electronic formats. After all, they might be "the electronic equivalent of the correspondence-course-by-mail" (p. 2). Thus, she says, graduate schools would be justified in refusing to accept them for transfer credit due to "questions" about academic integrity and quality.

By far the most flamboyant academic critic of distance education in the past decade has been David Noble, a history professor who has worked at UCLA and Toronto's York University. Noble has been particularly critical of online education, which he recently warned is "leading to a dangerous relaxation of sound financial-management practices and legal safeguards of the public interest, a bending of the rules of established procedure, and quite possibly a breaking of the law" (Young, 2000).

Professor Noble has developed an essentially Marxist critique in which he sees an unholy alliance of "dot-com" companies and university administrations combining forces to teach more students at a lower cost, thus oppressing the faculty by eliminating positions and constraining their autonomy (Noble, 1997, 1998a, 1998b). Indeed, his critique is reminiscent of that of Veblen (1918), who, though not a Marxist, railed against William Rainey Harper and other university presidents, sarcastically calling them "captains of erudition" for their proclivity for fund-raising among captains of industry.

In the fourth of a series of copyrighted papers posted on the Web page of the Communications Department at the University of California at San Diego, Noble looks back at distance education's early history. Entitled "Rehearsal for the Revolution" (1999), his paper, based mainly on a jaundiced reading of some of the major secondary works cited in the *CIADE* essay, damns the origins and history of university-level correspondence study and describes the work of correspondence study programs as essentially the same as that of the crasser commercial schools. Concentrating on the programs of major universities, he characterizes their advertising as "shameless," their quality as "shoddy" (p. 5), and their purpose as simply raising cash. He labels University of Wisconsin president Charles Van Hise and Louis Reber, among the founding fathers of the university extension movement, as "two engineers attuned especially to the training needs of industry" (p. 9) and thus presumably in cahoots with the tycoons of the day.

Noble wrote his piece as a cautionary tale, preceding it with one hackneyed warning about the lessons of the past from Santayana and ending it with Marx's equally trite quotation on the same subject. He contends that the history of correspondence study provides an ominous warning of the consequences of online education. Noble's essays have subsequently been published in book form (2001).

Jack Simmons (2000), of Savannah State University, echoes Noble by characterizing distance education as "a means by which universities may reduce their costs while increasing their enrollments" (p. 4). Ironically, Simmons, like Noble, disseminates this message on the Internet. He makes the case that the standardization involved in asynchronous learning presents a significant threat to academic freedom. However, Simmons's argument also exhibits a strong concern about how changing modes of teaching could affect the teaching roles of professors. Thus, his apprehension of an altered faculty lifestyle matches his loftier appeal to academic freedom.

The Attrition of Resources

Perhaps the greatest area of concern for present and future research into distance education's past should be the rapid—and accelerating—loss of primary records and in-house publications. This problem is not new, of course. Charles Wedemeyer, who had an acute appreciation of the need to preserve the history of independent study, told a colleague about a collection he had developed in the extension library at the University of Wisconsin: "I requested all NUEA institutions to send three representative correspondence courses to our library of materials on correspondence study, along with any materials developed by each institution on course development, teaching, revision, production, and other aspects of the field" (Letter to B. Holmberg, June 25, 1984). Wedemeyer said that the University gave him no resources for expanding this collection and that its development ceased with his retirement in 1976. In the early 1990s, the University of Wisconsin-Extension closed its library. Some of the materials were transferred to the university's archives, but others, particularly those gathered from other institutions, were discarded.

Many of the materials in the extension library were products of the day-to-day operations of individual independent study departments. Others originated with professional associations. Such items as course writer guides, statistical compilations, director handbooks, and the like formed a minor but important body of unpublished, uncatalogued writings, often called "fugitive literature." Recent trends in the reorganization of independent study, other forms of distance education, and continuing education divisions in general have aggravated the loss of this kind of resource. (A later section describes some extant examples of useful fugitive literature.) Many of the offices that once housed such artifacts have been merged with larger departments or dispersed, their staffs reassigned to several units.

Another source of useful research materials has stalled. The *CIADE* essay described an oral history project that the Independent Study Division of the National University Continuing Education Association had just begun. This project collected the structured reminiscences of 27 persons active in the field, mainly in the 1950s, 1960s, and 1970s. Gayle Childs, the retired director of the University of Nebraska's program and a preeminent figure in the field, began work on a monograph based on the typescripts of these oral histories. However, ill health ended this effort; Dr. Childs died in 1997.

Originally, the Independent Study Division had intended to collect oral histories from all retiring professionals, but the project languished. The division made no effort to gather further surveys to add to the collection, now housed in its archives at Penn State University. Because of a reorganization of the parent association, the division no longer exists. Therefore, it is unlikely that this project will ever be revived. However, the documents that were collected represent a rich source of data for scholars. In addition, Loyola University (Chicago) independently collected the oral history of its long-time director, Mary Lou McPartland, who served during the same time as the project's interviewees.

Fortunately, the *American Journal of Distance Education (AJDE)* continues to be a source of first-person data. Since 1987, it has recorded the experiences, perspectives, and insights of working professionals in distance education through its "Speaking Personally" interviews. The American Center for the Study of Distance Education, headquartered at Penn State, recently issued a collection of all the interviews published from 1987 through 1999 (Moore & Shin, 2000). Anyone interested in independent study will find the interviews with Charles Wedemeyer, Gayle Childs, Michael Lambert, and Betsy Powell particularly informative. Scholars and professionals in all areas of distance education owe the *American Journal of Distance Education* and the American Center thanks for collecting and publishing these pieces.

At the time of the *CIADE* essay, the ISD initiated another project for the purpose of preserving the historical record of independent study. It had opened negotiations with the Penn State libraries to establish an archival collection. The parties signed a contract for the deposit of materials shortly thereafter. In the years immediately following, many university independent study offices sent large collections of records, handbooks, study guides, annual reports, and other artifacts to Penn State. The shelf list quickly grew to more than 60 pages. The collection is an invaluable resource, but this project also has languished in recent years. Indeed, because one of the parties to the contract, the Independent Study Division, no longer exists, further development of this collection seems unlikely.

Another organization of independent study professionals, the American Association for Collegiate Independent Study (AACIS), has begun negotiations with Thomas Edison State College for the deposit of AACIS papers. However, it is extremely unlikely that this collection will ever rival the Independent Study Division's archives. Unlike the University Continuing Education Association, AACIS has no institutional members. Its members join as individuals, not as representatives of colleges or departments. Therefore, they do not control the documentary records of their offices to the extent that the Independent Study Division's members once did.

UNDERUSED AND UNDERAPPRECIATED: UNPUBLISHED AND OBSCURE SOURCES

The Dissertation Literature

The 1990 *CIADE* essay gave cursory attention to doctoral dissertations, but it suggested that these documents could be useful to researchers, especially when they dealt with individual university programs. Further, it called Thomas Gerrity's Columbia University Teachers College dissertation, *College-Sponsored Correspondence Instruction in the United States* (1976), "arguably the best single historical work on collegiate correspondence education" (Pittman, 1990, p. 70). Even so, the *CIADE* essay greatly underestimated the value of doctoral research. Further digging has turned up a sizable number of pertinent dissertations that make up a valuable body of unpublished secondary literature.

Dissertations give us the best picture of three very early correspondence programs. Illinois Wesleyan University offered courses and degrees—from the bachelor's to the Ph.D.—on an *in absentia* (nonresident) basis using correspondence study well before the University of Chicago's program opened in 1892. Henry Allan did a masterful job telling this story in his 1984 dissertation, written for his doctorate from the University of Chicago. Richard Bonnell's dissertation, *The Chautauqua University* (1988), is the only secondary work on the Chautauqua Institute that gives detailed attention to its academic credit-granting arm. Like Illinois Wesleyan, the Chautauqua University depended largely on correspondence study. Sheila Sherow (1989) tells the story of a 19th-century correspondence program created by a major university. In 1892, the Pennsylvania State College (now Penn State) designed the "Chautauqua Home Reading Course in Agriculture." Initially modeled after the courses of Chautauqua Literary and Scientific Circle (but totally unrelated to it), this program evolved into a group of rigorous credit-bearing correspondence courses.

The *CIADE* essay noted the strange fact that no full biography of William Rainey Harper, one of the seminal figures in the history of American higher education, then existed. None has been written subsequently. However, it turns out that there is a rich vein of dissertation literature on Harper, his American Institute of Sacred Literature, and his vision for the University of Chicago. Although none of these works is primarily a biography, and only one is specifically devoted to extension, all contribute to understanding Harper, his commitments as an educator, and his vision of higher education.

Lars Hoffman (1978) deals primarily with Harper's association with other Baptists. In a more ambitious work, James Wind (1983) provides a thorough exposition of Harper's theological position and demonstrates its relationship to his commitment to the diffusion of knowledge. Wind makes a persuasive case for the close relationship between Harper's religious beliefs and his development of the Extension Division at the University of Chicago. Reed (1980) also depicts Harper's commitment to both Baptist theology and educational innovation.

Engle's 1954 dissertation is less analytical and minus the religious dimension. Engle is particularly informative when describing Harper's role as a promoter of the university. Plath (1989) also details Harper's promotional skills as part of a study of leadership style, including his ability to compromise and frequently to prevail despite entrenched opposition. Two dissertations describe more peripheral aspects of Harper's presidency at Chicago. Blake (1966) recounts the development of the science curriculum, and Cook (1993) describes the Extension Division in her thesis on the development of evening classes in the city of Chicago.

Beginning in 1880, at the Baptist Union Theological Seminary in Morgan Park, Illinois, Harper developed his famous correspondence courses in Hebrew, which he took along to Yale, then brought back to Chicago as the core of the University's Home Study Department. Kenneth Beck (1968) tells this story in his dissertation on the American Institute of Sacred Literature, an often overlooked institution in the history of adult education.

Two early dissertations describe the integration of the Extension Division into the organizational structure of the University of Chicago. Clem Thompson wrote his dissertation on the operation of the Extension Division in 1932, using data generated in the first large-scale review of the university. A decade later, William Haggerty (1943) described Harper's original vision, then the changes in the university's organization and purpose since his death. For the most part, Storr's *Harper's University* (1966) supersedes these works. However, Fay's more recent dissertation (1976) provides additional analysis, particularly with respect to the success or failure of each University Extension department. She says that Correspondence-Study was the only successful unit among them in Chicago's first two decades. All of these dissertations place Harper in a much larger context than his involvement in correspondence study. Still, scholars of correspondence study will find them useful.

Several other unpublished treatises merit mention because they deal with subjects rarely encountered in the existing body of published secondary works. Lorenzo Timmons's (1930) master's thesis includes an early examination of the controversial problem of transfer credit for correspondence courses. Collegiate correspondence study programs have long suffered from comparison with proprietary schools, and Andrew Hadji (1931) describes the rapid rise—and the shortcomings—of some of these schools in his University of Chicago dissertation.

Almost all of the secondary works cited in the *CIADE* essay describe the independent study programs of state flagship and land grant institutions. Thus, Thomas Jenkins's 1953 study of the correspondence programs offered by teachers colleges stands alone. Indeed, absolutely nothing else about this sector of correspondence study seems to exist. A number of universities have long operated high school correspondence courses and programs, but they have received little scholarly attention. James Van Arsdall (1977) wrote an excellent history of the prototype of this kind of program, which was founded and operated by the University of Nebraska-Lincoln.

Two more doctoral dissertations deserve a look. In 1974, Roger Young, already a veteran practitioner in the field, took the pulse of university administrators with respect to correspondence study programs. Like Gerrity (cited previously), Young concluded that the 1970s presented great opportunities for expansion and innovation. Marv Van Kekerix's 1986 dissertation on the State University of Nebraska, an early telecourse program, seems particularly noteworthy. Scholars and especially practitioners of distance education have traditionally written success stories. The State University of Nebraska, however, was the prototype and immediate predecessor of the mightily hyped University of Mid-America (UMA), which turned out to be one of the most notorious flops in the history of distance education. Van Kekerix adroitly chronicles its rise and fall.

Anyone who has ever written a dissertation knows the odds of publishing it as a book, at least without extensive revision, are long. As time passes, the prospect becomes extremely unlikely. Housed in only one library and catalogued by University Microfilms, they generally pass into obscurity. This is unfortunate. In the field of correspondence study, much of the best work available can be found in them.

Some "Classics" of Fugitive Literature

The previous section makes reference to fugitive literature: unpublished, uncatalogued, and for the most part uncollected documents. Such materials as reports, in-house organs, manuals for course authors, and study guides tell us a great deal about the craft of correspondence study. Historians would consider some of these works primary sources, others secondary. The Independent Study archives at Penn State contain numerous such documents; others reside in various independent study departments and continuing education divisions. A very few university archivists have shown some interest in maintaining a sample of materials from the programs at their schools. Earl Rogers, a now retired special collections librarian and archivist at the University of Iowa, stood out in this respect. For the most part, however, the ephemera of independent study are drifting away.

A sample of the fugitive literature of independent study should illustrate its value. These examples are not intended to be exhaustive but simply to provide insights into the value of such artifacts in examining distance education's past.

Unlike doctoral dissertations, master's theses are generally not catalogued—except perhaps in the library of the schools at which they were written—making it impossible to sort and search for them by title or subject matter. Yet, some of them can be helpful for examining particular departments or universities at specific points in time, such as Grace Donehower's master's thesis (1968), which examines the relationship between operational policies and their effects on correspondence study enrollments at the University of Nevada between 1963 and 1965. Some theses are available in archival collections; a few others may be found in the continuing education offices at the universities where they were produced.

Documentation of the success or failure of innovative programs or approaches, for the most part, can be found only in the offices where they originated. In the early 1950s, the University of Wisconsin conducted its Rhinelander Center Project (University of Wisconsin, 1955). The report on this project is important because it documents a major university's early experiment with an external degree. Yet, documents such as this one are often either consigned to obscurity or discarded, disappearing without a trace.

Almost all independent study departments regularly produce and update handbooks for course authors and instructors. Collectively, these documents can illustrate changes in the design, mechanics, style, and instructional philosophy of the independent study format and the administration of courses. Individually, they can shed light on the programs they represent.

Two examples should suffice. The design and content of a manual from the University of California (Lawson, 1994) reflects its Center for Media and Independent Study's dependence on a scattered adjunct faculty, none of whose members are full-time university employees. Therefore, it reads quite differently from handbooks designed by departments that employ mainly the faculty and graduate students of their own institutions. The University of Iowa's manuals for its course authors have always reflected its Guided Correspondence Study program's commitment to clear and engaging prose and to capturing the individual voices of its faculty. A recent issue said, "We believe it is important for you [course authors] to find a voice in your written materials that is informal, engaging, and clearly interested in helping students master the course content. The material you are preparing is, after all, a *guide*, not merely a workbook" (University of Iowa, 1994, p. 17).

Manuals from other institutions may exhibit a greater concern for standardization or overall course design, and these preferences and values can change over time. Therefore, this subgenre of fugitive literature can be of considerable value to the researcher.

Perhaps the most detailed instructional material for authors of correspondence courses can be found in a study guide on developing and teaching courses written by Joseph Kleiner (1966) at the University of Wisconsin-Extension. Kleiner wrote it to walk faculty through the course development process, offering feedback as they finished the course's eight units. He also wanted to help faculty understand how students experienced the correspondence format. This study guide contains such lessons as "Correspondence Study Learning Theory" and "Designing the Correspondence Lesson." This unusual study guide was once filed in the University of Wisconsin-Extension library. Whether it survived the dismantling of that facility is unknown.

The University Continuing Education Association's Independent Study Division, which operated from the late 1960s through the late 1990s, produced some useful but now generally forgotten documents of potential historical interest. This division was an unusual entity, for unlike the other divisions of the association, it also functioned as an autonomous organization. Throughout its life, it promoted professional development and the creation of standards of practice. In April 1972, the division held a workshop in Columbia, South Carolina, for the purpose of discussing and selecting materials that would help new directors adopt the best practices of their craft. After further refinement and editing, the ISD produced the *Handbook for Independent Study Directors* (Division of Independent Study, 1975). Although the handbook once was shelved in every independent study department, by now most copies have probably disappeared.

The growing variety of distance education media and formats caused concern within the Independent Study Division, as did ambiguities and occasional conflicts resulting from its de facto status as an autonomous organization within a larger organization. In 1989, in response to these issues, the division appointed a Task Force on the Status of the Division of Independent Study. After grappling with its members' concerns, the task force issued a report (1990) that provided a number of recommendations about needed organizational responses. The significance of this report has increased with the opportunities and problems that have subsequently emerged in the broader field of distance education. Because the report was distributed to all members of the Independent Study Division, an indeterminate number of copies are scattered around the country.

These six examples represent many noncatalogued artifacts capable of providing information and some valuable insights about the practice of independent study in American universities. They are prime examples of the sort of documents now disappearing as a result of major organizational changes in college-level distance education. The loss of this fugitive literature will detract from larger studies of distance education in the future.

TOPICS MERITING FURTHER RESEARCH

Anyone with an interest in the history of distance education, especially independent study, will find a wide choice of significant questions that merit serious consideration. The role of the various professional organizations that involved themselves with independent study is an obvious example. Two articles on the early years of the National University Extension Association (the original forerunner of the University Continuing Education Association) provide a start. Edelson (1991) described the organization's determination to earn respect for the correspondence and extension lecture programs of their universities. As an organization, it set and articulated standards of quality, carefully separating itself from less prestigious types of institutions, such as teachers colleges. It advanced the principle of "campus equivalence" in hopes of having the courses of its members' schools achieve a stature comparable to that of on-campus classes. Pittman (1998) also looked at the association's efforts at setting standards for correspondence study but concluded that its ambitions, though noble, were flawed from the beginning. Additional studies of this group's impact on the growth of distance education would be useful, along with studies of competing or complementary organizations.

Considering the current enthusiasm for electronic distance education formats, the early attempts to combine correspondence study with telecommunications constitute another obvious research topic. Yet little work has been done in this area. The best treatment of attempts to use broadcast radio for instruction is more than 60 years old, Carroll Atkinson's *Radio Extension Courses Broadcast for Credit* (1941). E. B. Kurtz (1959), a professor of engineering at the University of Iowa, compiled a book on the first experiments with instructional television that took place almost 70 years ago. While still useful, in spite of being very old, both of these books are entirely descriptive, offering nothing in the way of insight or analysis.

The 1950s and 1960s saw serious new attempts to develop television as a distance education format. Purdy (1980) contributed a brief overview of these early efforts. Van Kekerix and Andrews's (1991) anthology chapter on the same subject is more detailed and thoughtful and more firmly linked to independent study. Some areas lack even short descriptive treatments. For example, the use of the telephone in teaching, especially in Wisconsin, has not been described adequately.

Broadcast telecourses, with their huge budgets, splendid video productions, and large enrollments, generated a lot of ink in the 1960s and 1970s. Despite claims to the contrary, they were a variant of traditional independent study. Their history has not yet been subjected to scholarly scrutiny. It is particularly disappointing that the Annenberg/Corporation for Public Broadcasting telecourse project receives no mention (although the film series for a single course does) in two recent studies of public television (Day, 1995; Jarvik, 1997).

The graduate programs of some of the nation's finest engineering colleges provide a twist on the usual manner in which technology has been combined with independent study. In the late 1960s, Stanford University began transmitting some of its courses to industrial sites via Instructional Television Fixed Service (ITFS). With the advent of videocassette recorders, and at the request of students, the faculty began to allow students to view their lectures on tape rather than in real time. Schools of the caliber of the Massachusetts Institute of Technology, the University of Illinois, and many other first-rank engineering colleges adopted this format. Its popularity led to the creation of the National Technological University.

Over the years, students and their employers pressed for less and less structure and synchronicity. For example, students initially had to gather to view the tapes in groups in the presence of a "tutor" and follow a strict week-by-week schedule. Few schools now insist on either of these formalities. The usual trend in distance education has been to use new technologies to make independent study more closely resemble the conventional classroom. The engineering programs, on the other hand, dispensed with structure and thus increasingly came to resemble traditional independent study. The story of this teaching format is as obscure as it is successful. To the extent that its story has been recorded at all, it has been primarily in contemporaneous publications and promotional materials. It deserves better.

University-sponsored high school programs also merit more attention than they have received to this point. The University of Nebraska-Lincoln program originated in 1929 as a means of serving small, isolated schools. It pioneered in offering a full high school diploma via correspondence and in securing regional accreditation. Van Arsdall's 1977 dissertation capably conveys most of its long history; however, this dissertation stands alone. An article or monograph that deals with all of the high school independent study programs would prove useful, especially in light of today's sudden interest in virtual secondary schools.

An examination of the often unsavory association of independent study and intercollegiate athletics is long overdue. Just as big-time college sports have corrupted numerous other aspects of university life, they have occasionally had a pernicious effect on independent study. Athletic department staffs have sometimes used independent study's unique administrative practices—such as off-cycle registration and completion—as loopholes when trying to maintain the eligibility of their "scholar-athletes." There has been no scholarly work on this problem. For anyone who might be interested, however, Wolff and Yaeger's 1995 story in *Sports Illustrated* provides an excellent starting point.

Finally, there are the big questions—those that will require systematic study. First, why did such an innovative and useful means of instruction not have a larger impact on postsecondary education? Then, what are the implications of the history of independent study for the long-term future of all distance education? Both the large questions and the smaller ones provide ample opportunities for historians of education.

CONCLUSION

There is no shortage of topics for historical narrative and analysis in the history of independent study, and the resources for such work are rich and varied. When dissertations are considered, the body of secondary sources increases dramatically. And at the moment several excellent collections of primary sources are available for study. However, the best two are stagnant. The acquisition of primary source materials has come to a halt for the National University Extension Association papers filed in the adult education archives at Syracuse University as well as for the Independent Study Division's collection at Penn State. Further, the closure of the University of Wisconsin-Extension library resulted in the dispersal of an excellent body of research materials.

An even greater loss of resources is ongoing. The closures, reorganizations, and mergers within the continuing education and other units that manage distance education are having a devastating effect. The resources for the study of distance education's past are being scattered, discarded, or destroyed. For example, only one complete set of the National University Extension Association's *Proceedings* is known to exist. The fugitive literature that illuminates the day-to-day work of professionals in the field can be found only in a few university libraries and one or two private collections. Veterans of the field, many of whom made significant contributions, are retiring and passing away without having left any memoirs, while the collection of oral histories has been abandoned.

The loss of primary resources represents the greatest barrier to future scholarship in the history of distance education. This is significant not only for historians of higher education but for future administrators and practitioners in the field. Many of them will continue to find it easy to believe that distance education was invented yesterday.

REFERENCES

Allen, H. C., Jr. (1984). *History of the non-residential degree program at Illinois Wesleyan University, 1873–1910: A study of a pioneer external degree program in the United States.* Unpublished doctoral dissertation, University of Chicago.

Atkinson, C. (1941). *Radio extension courses broadcast for credit.* Boston: Meador.

Beck, K. N. (1968). *The American Institute of Sacred Literature: A historical analysis of an adult education institution.* Unpublished doctoral dissertation, University of Chicago.

Bittner, W. S., & Mallory, H. F. (1933). *University teaching by mail: A survey of correspondence instruction conducted by American universities.* New York: Macmillan.

Blake, L. C. (1966). *The concept and development of science at the University of Chicago, 1890–1905.* Unpublished doctoral dissertation, University of Chicago.

Bonnell, R. K. (1988). *The Chautauqua University: Pioneer university without walls, 1883–1898.* Unpublished doctoral dissertation, Kent State University, Kent, OH.

Byrne, T. C. (1989). *Athabasca University: The evolution of distance education.* Calgary, Canada: University of Calgary Press.

Cook, S. A. (1993). *The origins and development of evening undergraduate education in Chicago.* Unpublished doctoral dissertation, Loyola University of Chicago.

Craik, G. L. (1830). *The pursuit of knowledge under difficulties.* London: Knight.

Curti, M., & Carstensen, V. (1949). *The University of Wisconsin: A history* (Vols. 1 & 2). Madison, WI: University of Wisconsin Press.

Day, J. (1995). *The vanishing vision: The inside story of public television.* Berkeley, CA: University of California Press.

Division of Independent Study. (1975). *Handbook for independent study directors.* Madison, WI: University of Wisconsin-Extension.

Donehower, G. M. (1968). *Variables associated with correspondence study enrollments at the University of Nevada, 1963–1965.* Unpublished master's thesis, University of Nevada-Reno.

Duning, B. S. (1987). Independent study in higher education: A captive of legendary resilience? *American Journal of Distance Education, 1*(1), 37–46.

Duning, B. S., & Pittman, V. V. (Eds.). (1995). *Distance education symposium 3: Policy and administration.* University Park, PA: The American Center for the Study of Distance Education.

Edelson, P. J. (1991). Codification and exclusion: An analysis of the early years of the National University Extension Association (NUEA), 1915–1923. *Continuing Higher Education Review, 55*(3), 176–188.

Engle, G. W. (1954). *William Rainey Harper's conceptions of the structuring of the functions performed by educational institutions.* Unpublished doctoral dissertation, Stanford University, Stanford, CA.

Fay, M. A. (1976). *Origins and early developments of the University of Chicago Extension Division, 1892–1911.* Unpublished doctoral dissertation, University of Chicago.

Flexner, A. (1930). *Universities: American, English, German.* New York: Oxford University Press.

Garrison, D. R., & Shale, D. (Eds.). (1990). *Education at a distance: From issues to practice.* Malabar, FL: R. E. Kreiger.

Gerrity, T. W. (1976). *College-sponsored correspondence instruction in the United States: A comparative history of its origins (1873–1915) and its recent developments (1960–1975).* Unpublished doctoral dissertation, Columbia University Teachers College, New York.

Getz, G. A. (1986). *MBI: The story of Moody Bible Institute.* Chicago: Moody Press.

Hadji, A. G. (1931). *Private correspondence school: Their growth and marketing methods.* Unpublished doctoral dissertation, University of Chicago.

Haggerty, W. J. (1943). *The purposes of the University of Chicago.* Unpublished doctoral dissertation, University of Chicago.

Hoffman, L. (1978). *William Rainey Harper and the Chicago Fellowship.* Unpublished doctoral dissertation, University of Iowa, Iowa City.

Jarvik, L. (1997). *PBS, behind the screen.* Rocklin, CA: Prima.

Jenkins, T. S. (1953). *Correspondence course instruction: An investigation of practices, regulations, and course syllabi as developed in state teachers colleges.* Unpublished doctoral dissertation, University of Oregon, Eugene.

Kett, J. F. (1994). *The pursuit of knowledge under difficulties: From self-improvement to adult education in America, 1750–1990.* Stanford, CA: Stanford University Press.

Kleiner, J. L. (1966). *An introduction to the method of correspondence study.* Unpublished study guide, University of Wisconsin-Madison.

Kurtz, E. B. (1959). *Pioneering in educational television, 1932–1939.* Iowa City, IA: State University of Iowa.

Lawson, J. (1994). *Handbook for instructors.* Berkeley, CA: University of California Extension Center for Media and Independent Learning.

Montgomery, C. W. (1993). *Some issues in the remote delivery of graduate course work and programs.* Paper delivered at the Illinois Association of Graduate Schools, Rock Island, Illinois.

Moore, M. G. (Ed.). (1990). *Contemporary issues in American distance education.* New York: Pergamon Press.

Moore, M. G., & Shin, N. (Eds.). (2000). *Speaking personally about distance education: Foundations of contemporary practice.* University Park, PA: American Center for the Study of Distance Education.

Mugridge, I., & Kaufman, D. (Eds.). (1986). *Distance education in Canada.* London: Croom Helm.

Noble, D. F. (1997). *Digital diploma mills: Part I. The automation of higher education.* University of California, San Diego. Department of Communication. Available: http://communication.ucsd.edu/dl/ddm1.html

Noble, D. F. (1998a). *Digital diploma mills: Part II. The coming battle over online instruction.* University of California, San Diego. Department of Communication. Available: http://communication.ucsd.edu/dl/ddm2.html

Noble, D. F. (1998b). *Digital diploma mills: Part III. The bloom is off the rose.* University of California, San Diego. Department of Communication. Available: http://communication.ucsd.edu/dl/ddm3.html

Noble, D. F. (1999). *Digital diploma mills: Part IV. Rehearsal for the revolution.* University of California, San Diego. Department of Communication. Available: http://communication.ucsd.edu/dl/ddm4.html

Noble, D. F. (2001). Digital diploma mills: *The automation of Higher Education.* New York: Monthly Review Press.

Nolan, D. J. (1998). *Regents College: The early years.* Virginia Beach, VA: Donning.

Pittman, V. V. (1990). Correspondence study in the American university: A historiographic perspective. In M. G. Moore (Ed.), *Contemporary issues in American distance education* (pp. 67–80). New York: Pergamon Press.

Pittman, V. V. (1991). Academic credibility and the "image problem": The quality issue in collegiate independent study. In B. L. Watkins & S. J. Wright (Eds.), *The foundations of American distance education: A century of collegiate correspondence study* (pp. 109–134). Dubuque, IA: Kendall/Hunt.

Pittman, V. V. (1995). Harper's headaches: Early policy issues in collegiate correspondence study. In B. S. Dunning, & V. V. Pittman (Eds.), *Distance education symposium 3: Policy and administration* (pp. 19–31). University Park, PA: American Center for the Study of Distance Education.

Pittman, V. V. (1998). Low-key leadership: Collegiate correspondence study and campus equivalence. *American Journal of Distance Education, 12*(2), 36–45.

Plath, P. J. (1989). *The fox and the hedgehog: Liberal education at the University of Chicago.* Unpublished doctoral dissertation, University of Illinois at Urbana-Champaign.

Purdy, L. N. (1980). The history of television and radio in continuing education. In M. N. Chamberlain (Ed.), *New directions for continuing education: Number 5. Providing continuing education by media and technology.* San Francisco: Jossey-Bass.

Reed, J. E. (1980). *A study of William Rainey Harper's educational principles: Modifications and innovations in an era of change.* Unpublished doctoral dissertation, New Orleans Baptist Theological Seminary.

Rose, S. L. (1991). Collegiate-based noncredit courses. In B. L. Watkins & S. J. Wright (Eds.), *The foundations of American distance education: A century of collegiate correspondence study* (pp. 67–92). Dubuque, IA: Kendall/Hunt.

Rothe, J. P. (1986). An historical perspective. In I. Mugridge & D. Kaufman (Eds.), *Distance education in Canada* (pp. 4–24). London: Croom Helm.

Sherow, S. (1989). *The Pennsylvania State College: A pioneer in nontraditional agricultural education.* Unpublished doctoral dissertation, The Pennsylvania State University.

Sherow, S., & Wedemeyer, C. A. (1990). Origins of distance education in the United States. In D. R. Garrison & D. Shale (Eds.), *Education at a distance: From issues to practice* (pp. 7–22). Malabar, FL: R. E. Krieger.

Simmons, J. (2000). The future of academic freedom: Educational technology and academic freedom. *DEONEWS, 10*(3). Available: http://www.ed.psu.edu/acsde/deos/deosnews/deosarchives.asp.

Storr, R. J. (1966). *Harper's university: A history of the University of Chicago.* Chicago: University of Chicago Press.

Task Force on the Status of the Division of Independent Study. (1990). *The status of independent study: 1990 and beyond.* Washington, DC: National University Continuing Education Association.

Thompson, C. O. (1932). *The extension program of the University of Chicago.* Unpublished doctoral dissertation, University of Chicago.

Timmons, L. Z. (1930). *A study of correspondence study, for college credit, in Texas colleges and universities.* Unpublished master's thesis, Lubbock Texas Technological College.

University of Iowa. (1994). *Faculty guide for developing and instructing guided correspondence study courses.* Iowa City, IA: University of Iowa.

University of Wisconsin. (1955). *Experiments in correspondence study.* Unpublished report, University of Wisconsin Extension Division.

Van Arsdall, J. E. (1977). *The stated and operative objectives of the University of Nebraska extension high school program, 1929–1975.* Unpublished doctoral dissertation, University of Nebraska-Lincoln.

Van Kekerix, M. J. (1986). *The SUN experience: A historical analysis of the State University of Nebraska program utilizing the organizational life cycle perspective.* Unpublished doctoral dissertation, University of Nebraska-Lincoln.

Van Kekerix, M. J., & Andrews, J. (1991). Electronic media and independent study. In B. L. Watkins & S. J. Wright (Eds.), *The foundations of American distance education: A century of collegiate correspondence study* (pp. 135–157). Dubuque, IA: Kendall/Hunt.

Veblen, T. (1918). *The higher learning in America: A memorandum on the conduct of universities by business men.* New York: B. W. Huebsch.

Watkins, B. L. (1991). A quite radical idea: The invention and elaboration of collegiate correspondence study. In B. L. Watkins & S. J. Wright (Eds.), *The foundations of American distance education: A century of collegiate correspondence study* (pp. 1–35). Dubuque, IA: Kendall/Hunt.

Watkins, B. L., & Wright, S. J. (Eds.). (1991). *The foundations of American distance education: A century of collegiate correspondence study.* Dubuque, IA: Kendall/Hunt.

Wedemeyer, C. A. (1981). *Learning at the back door: Reflections on nontraditional learning in the lifespan.* Madison, WI: University of Wisconsin Press.

Wedemeyer, C. A., & Childs, G. B. (1961). *New perspectives in university correspondence study.* Chicago: Center for the Study of Liberal Education for Adults.

Wind, J. P. (1983). *The Bible and the university: The messianic vision of William Rainey Harper.* Unpublished doctoral dissertation, University of Chicago.

Wolff, A., & Yaeger, D. (1995, August 7). Credit risk. *Sports Illustrated, 83*(6), 46–55.

Wright, S. J. (1991). Opportunity lost, opportunity regained: University independent study in the modern era. In B. L. Watkins & S. J. Wright (Eds.), *The foundations of American distance education: A century of collegiate correspondence study* (pp. 37–66). Dubuque, IA: Kendall/Hunt.

Young, J. R. (2000, March 31). David Noble's battle to defend the 'sacred space' of the classroom. *Chronicle of Higher Education.* Online edition. Available: http://chronicle.com.

Young, R. G. (1974). *A critical analysis of the views and opinions of university administrators toward university correspondence study.* Unpublished doctoral dissertation, University of Nebraska-Lincoln.

Young, R. G., & McMahon, M. (1991). University-sponsored high school independent study. In B. L. Watkins & S. J. Wright (Eds.), *The foundations of American distance education: A century of collegiate correspondence study* (pp. 93–108). Dubuque, IA: Kendall/Hunt.

3

Evolution of National and Regional Organizations

Charles E. Feasley
Oklahoma State University
cfeasle@okstate.edu

DIMINISHING DECENTRALIZATION

Although the United States continues to have a substantially decentralized system of higher education, emerging information technologies are shifting quality control processes toward increased voluntary centralization. In contrast to many countries, the United States has had no national curriculum in postsecondary education (or lower levels). This situation stems from the facts that (a) most postsecondary funding is not from the national government and (b) most funds from the national government are connected to a voluntary system of institutional and professional accrediting groups. But the large front-end expenditures that are required to develop and deliver many distance education offerings have stimulated individual colleges and universities to form consortia within metropolitan areas, states, regions, and nations as well as internationally (Feasley, 1995). In addition, partnerships have emerged between postsecondary institutions and business corporations, especially those that have development and/or instructional delivery capabilities.

For the purpose of examining the evolution of American distance education organizations, these organizations are divided into four groups: pioneering national organizations, curriculum specializing organizations, technology networking organizations, and regional consortia and virtual universities. Examples of each type are discussed.

Pioneering national organizations are so named in recognition of the historically broad geographic representation of their membership as well as the diverse media coverage and complex scope of their distance education goals.

Curriculum specializing organizations focus on small segments of the total postsecondary education spectrum. The first example discussed is the American Distance Education Consortium (ADEC), whose curricular focus is on the agricultural sciences. The other two examples, the Association for Media-Based Continuing Education for Engineers (AMCEE) and the National Technology University (NTU), are directed toward engineering, the industrial sciences, and the management of technology. Curriculum specializing organizations usually have a national membership.

The three examples of technology networking organizations are the National University Teleconference Network (NUTN), the Instructional Telecommunications Council (ITC), and the Public Broadcasting Services Adult Learning Services (ALS). These three were begun with a national membership that shared a common interest in a particular type of delivery system (satellite conferencing, telecourses, and broadcast television, respectively).

As for the fourth and last type of distance education organization, regional consortia and virtual universities have geographic distributions of memberships and goals that are reflective of preexisting regional parent organizations.

CASE STUDIES, BENEFITS, AND A CAUTION

Lewis (1983) provided a broadly representative yet richly detailed early picture of the overlapping activities of postsecondary education and the telecommunications industry. His introductory section alerts readers to the stimuli for such activities, which include changing student demographics and the economic constraints of postsecondary institutions as well as the availability of newer modes of communication and shifting sources of funding for public television and radio. In his discussion of the impact of technology on postsecondary education, Lewis mentioned ALS, NUTN, and AMCEE, three organizations that are examined in more detail in this chapter.

All 70 case studies presented by Lewis (1983) are helpful because they include descriptions in which the organizations are compared with regard to 16 topics:

1. Organization.
2. Telecommunications program.
3. Educational mission.
4. Telecommunications technology.
5. Curriculum.
6. Faculty roles.
7. Delivery system.
8. Enrollment.
9. Administrative structure.
10. Finances.
11. Noteworthy features.
12. Problems encountered.
13. Observations about distance learning.
14. Future plans.
15. Resources available.
16. Contact person. (p. 17)

In addition to noting that one of the most striking trends associated with the use of telecommunications technologies by educators is the extent of formal and informal collaboration between educational institutions, Lewis (1983) also listed various functions performed by surveyed consortia that benefit individual member institutions:

- Leasing or purchasing electronic and print instructional materials.
- Producing electronic and print instructional materials.
- Using telecommunications facilities and air time.
- Promoting and marketing educational programming.
- Raising funds and sharing resources.

- Providing reciprocal registration arrangements for consortium members.
- Conducting faculty and staff development activities. (p. 22)

A more current, internationally-oriented review of cooperative approaches to distance education can be found in Feasley (1995).

Although there are more choices for program descriptions today, caution is needed. Just as enthusiasm for new delivery technologies prompted the formation of the technology networking organizations discussed in this chapter, current zealousness about online education can prompt neutral observers such as the respected college reference guide publisher Peterson's to conclude that distance learning consortia are associations or partnerships that cooperate in providing online education and have a minimum agreement to list program information and the online courses of member institutions on a common Web site (*Peterson's Guide*, 2000). It is hoped that both publishers and readers consider the word *online* as an umbrella term meaning "readily available" so that many off-line offerings using videotape, audiotape, computer disk, CD-ROM, and print delivery systems are not overlooked.

PIONEERING NATIONAL ORGANIZATIONS

Increasing numbers of writers have noted that the history of correspondence instruction within U.S. higher education offers many insights for distance learning policy today. For example, Berg (1999) stated that correspondence courses (a) did not try to replace traditional higher education; (b) were aimed at nontraditional student populations who did not have access to higher education; and (c) grew out of the university extension movement, not the university proper. As supporting evidence, Berg provided a useful chronology of many historical events, especially the 1926 Carnegie Corporation study of private correspondence schools, which found that more students were enrolled in correspondence schools than in all traditional higher education institutions combined but that standards to protect the public from poor quality or fraud were lacking (Berg, 1999). For a comprehensive historical and philosophical examination of nontraditional education, readers are directed to Wedemeyer (1981).

Soon after the 1926 Carnegie study, a trade association known as the National Home Study Council (NHSC) was founded to promote sound educational and business practices among the home study schools (Fowler, 1981). The author of the Carnegie Study, John Noffsinger, served as the first executive director of the NHSC and initiated reform efforts, including the promulgation of a list of minimum standards for proprietary schools (Knowles as cited in Pittman, 1990, p. 68).

As noted elsewhere in this chapter, in 1959 NHSC was approved by the U.S. Office of Education as a nationally recognized accrediting agency, which enabled students in NHSC member schools to be eligible for federal aid without the schools being accredited by the seven regional associations that accredit most schools, colleges, and universities in the United States. In 1994, with 56 institutions serving three million students, NHSC was renamed the Distance Education and Training Council (DETC), while continuing to be a national accrediting agency to both the U.S. secretary of education and to the Commission on Recognition of Postsecondary Accreditation ("NHSC Gets New Name," 1994).

In a more recent development, DETC has joined with six other agencies to form the Council of Recognized National Accrediting Agencies, which represents over 300 institutions serving more than four million students. One fourth of those nationally accredited institutions offer degrees (Lambert, 1999).

A large oversight in Berg's (1999) history of correspondence instruction is his failure to mention the National University Extension Association (NUEA) while stating that traditional higher education correspondence courses were held to the standards of regionally accredited institutions and did not have a separate group of standards. In the preface to a compendium of original historical documents to commemorate the 75th anniversary of the association, its president acknowledged that few conversations in continuing higher education today or national conference programs reflect the rich heritage of either the adult education movement in America or the association's place in that movement (Shannon, 1990). That compendium details the important role that U.S. nonprofit correspondence study professionals played in the establishment of NUEA in 1915, the adoption in 1922 of Standards for Extension Credit Courses (applicable to both class and correspondence courses), and the recommendation in 1931 of a set of correspondence study standards to supplement the 1922 standards (Rohfeld, 1990).

Watkins (1991), Wright (1991), and Pittman (1991) were able individually to utilize a wide range of primary and secondary historical resources to document the same conclusion—that U.S. university-based correspondence study practitioners played a key role in the establishment of NUEA and its early creation of standards for correspondence courses. Regardless of variations in the materials used, the common conclusion drawn by the authors was that the existence of both types of correspondence study programs (nonprofit and proprietary) appeared to spur each other into more vigorous attention to issues of quality, especially as documented through research.

Although Pittman has published a remarkable range of evidence to examine how the notoriety of some proprietary home-study schools has had a negative impact on collegiate correspondence programs, he noted Noffsinger's assertion that proprietary schools could never have succeeded if collegiate programs had not popularized the correspondence method (Pittman, 1990). In 1915, more surprising praise was offered by Charles R. Van Hise, president of the University of Wisconsin and presiding officer of NUEA during its initial year. He said that proprietary schools, not the university, first found the opportunity of instruction by correspondence, exactly as education in medicine and law were first developed not in connection with the university but in the proprietary school (Van Hise, 1990). Although such remarks were made near the start of the 20th century, almost half a century later the two most renowned practitioner-scholars in American correspondence study, Charles Wedemeyer and Gayle Childs (1961), conceded that progress in the field was still hampered by its association in the popular mind with the sleazy promotional and financial operations of some of the proprietaries (cited in Pittman, 1992). Despite such disappointments, both Wedemeyer and Childs provided leadership within NUEA in both research on the effectiveness of different methods of instruction and in establishing good standards of practice. Duning (1987) and Pittman (1987) point to the roles played by research and flexibility in explaining the resilience of the American collegiate correspondence study.

Although the leadership of NUEA by individual correspondence study professionals was described in various ways by Watkins (1991), Wright (1991), and Pittman (1991), in 1955, when NUEA adopted a division structure and correspondence study was among the five charter units, division members gained a new sense of group coherence and common purpose. Nonetheless, after the U.S. Office of Education designated the NHSC's Accrediting Commission as a nationally recognized accrediting agency in 1959, the new Correspondence Study Division feared its member institutions would be directly affected. As a result, the division offered a special workshop for over half its members in order to create a Criteria and Standards document, approved by the division in 1962 and by the NUEA board a year later (Pittman 1991).

In 1980, the Correspondence Study Division was renamed the Independent Study Division (ISD) to reflect the fact that many types of technologies were being used in addition to print. In the same year, the parent organization was renamed the National University Continuing

Education Association [NUCEA], and then in 1999 it dropped the word "National" from its name to attract international member schools, thereby becoming UCEA. In addition to revising the Criteria and Standards document, which can be found on the UCEA Web site (UCEA, 2001), ISD members have operated almost two dozen different committees. These committees have, among other accomplishments, conducted an annual research survey; established an archives at Penn State University; conducted an oral history project; and given awards for excellence in catalogs, courses, publications, and professional service.

At the same time as it changed its name to UCEA, the association, while retaining a board of directors and keeping regions, reengineered itself significantly by eliminating all 20 division specializations, which had been popular with the preponderance of individual members. Instead three broader units were created: The Commission of Futures and Markets, the Commission on Leadership and Management, and the Commission on Learning and Instructional Technologies. Within each commission with adequate numbers of interested members, communities of practice may be established. In some cases, such as the Distance Learning Community of Practice, there has been substantial reestablishment of the activities of former divisions—in this instance, the Division of Educational Telecommunications and the Division of Independent Study (Duning, Van Kekerix, & Zaborowski, 1993, pp. 220, 222). However, even before the reengineering was under serious discussion, substantial reallocation (50–75%) of annual conference programming sessions away from the divisions toward use by the national conference committee and staff prompted the creation of a separate organization (American Association for Collegiate Independent Study [AACIS]) for professionals who serve individual learners rather than students who learn in groups. AACIS has been in existence just long enough to have held its ninth annual national conference in the fall of 2001 (AACIS, 2002). About twice as many independent study professionals are members of AACIS as were members of the Independent Study Division of UCEA because the AACIS annual conference costs half as much to attend as UCEA and the AACIS annual dues are half as much as those of UCEA.

Although the United States Distance Learning Association (USDLA) has only been in existence since 1987, it has been classified as a pioneering national organization for two reasons. First, on the national level, it has successfully involved U.S. senators and representatives in its regular conferences and in national policy forums (in 1991, 1997, 1999 and 2001), to develop and publish national policy recommendations for legislative and administrative proposals. Second, with its 3,000 members, USDLA has stimulated broad participation across the United States by beginning in 1993 to establish local chapters in many states and one for the employees of the federal government. Pescatore (2000) provided a good description of one of the largest chapters of USDLA, the Oklahoma Distance Learning Association, which includes members in all the sectors that use distance learning, including schools, telemedicine, business, and the military. McAuliffe (2000) and Flores (2000) described how the Federal Government Distance Learning Association works on the integration of existing infrastructure with emerging technologies that can reach the populations of military and civilians directly at their job sites. USDLA also holds annual meetings with leaders of distance learning programs in Europe and Asia (USDLA, 2001).

CURRICULUM SPECIALIZING ORGANIZATIONS

The Association for Media-Based Continuing Education of Engineers (AMCEE) is a private, nonprofit association formed in 1976 by representatives of 12 engineering schools (Lewis, 1983). Currently there are 29 engineering universities who are members, and these jointly offer over 1,000 different courses covering 15 technical and engineering-related disciplines (AMCEE, 2001).

AMCEE features noncredit short courses that are videotaped in high-quality studio environments and offered with specially designed study guides and regular textbooks as support material. AMCEE chose this blend to take advantage of the logistical and financial benefits of videotaped classes and the pedagogical and marketing advantages of studio-produced noncredit courses ("NUCEA's Distance Education Through Telecommunications," as cited by Duning, Van Kekerix, & Zaborowski, 1993).

The National Technological University (NTU) was established in 1984 as a private, nonprofit, accreditation-seeking institution that broadcast, via satellite, carefully chosen courses from 24 top engineering schools in the United States. It earned full accreditation status from the North Central Association of Schools and Colleges in 1986 and is now on the maximum length 10-year review cycle (Bagley, 2000). NTU has shared a satellite network with AMCEE and has been said to have evolved out of discussions by the AMCEE board of directors (May & Lumsden, 1988, as cited in Verduin & Clark, 1991). In 1999, NTU created a for-profit learning service organization called the National Technological University Corporation (NTUC) to perform certain functions it feels are essential for securing clients ("NTU Changes to Keep up With Corporate Markets," 1999). This corporation was acquired by Sylvan Learning Systems in 2002 (Arnone, 2002).

At present more than 50 universities contribute over 1,400 courses to fulfill all requirements of the 18 NTU Master of Science degrees that are offered for highly mobile engineers, scientists, and technical managers. Most students are employees of the more than 250 corporations and other universities that receive the courses via satellite, videotape, or the Internet. Noncredit professional development programs are produced by one third of the NTU academic course–producing universities and another seven professional associations or companies. NTU courses are also available on six statewide networks, on five multi-campus networks, and via three international distributors. NTU has granted more than 1,400 master's degrees to individuals who have completed their study while being employed full-time (out of the total 1,550 degrees it has awarded). NTU has a board of trustees, an executive advisory board, an administrative contact steering committee, and a site coordination steering committee (NTU, 2001).

AG*SAT was formed by 23 land grant institutions in 1989. During the spring of 1992, seven credit courses were offered nationwide via satellite and other distance learning technologies. The courses originated from 7 different land grant institutions and were used by 18 of 35 affiliated AG*SAT institutions (Levine, 1992). It has been said that its academic, extension, and research programs are offered intra- and interstate, regionally, nationally, and internationally, depending on need and efficiency of distribution by its 46 land grant universities (NUCEA, 1993).

In a recent interview by Bill Anderson of Janet K. Poley, American Distance Education Consortium (ADEC) president of the renamed successor to AG*SAT, there is a description of the 60-member consortium's extensive activities in grant management, professional development, public education (through its extensive Web site, with many links that can be used by anyone), technology research (most recently wireless Internet via satellite), and international outreach (Anderson, 2000). ADEC's structure includes a board of directors, principal contact officers, a program panel, and staff (ADEC, 2001).

An article by Jackson (1994) described how the similar interests of the consortium members facilitated his research on incentives through Delphi surveying of 20 agricultural science faculty and extension educators from 42 universities who had delivered a credit course or noncredit program via the AG*SAT network. The most important incentive was the network offered an efficient way to reach larger audiences. In addition to identifying four other incentives that had been important to them personally, the respondents agreed on six more incentives that may be attractive to other instructors.

TECHNOLOGY NETWORKING ORGANIZATIONS

Oberle (1990) provided a helpful case study of the early years of the National University Teleconference Network (NUTN), from its founding in 1982, when it encompassed fewer than 70 universities, to its development into an organization whose membership at the time was four times greater in size and included a much more diverse mixture of postsecondary educational institutions than at its start. A bandwagon effect was notable from the very beginning, when only 5% of the charter members had access to satellite receive capability. Subsequently the heavy financial burden on the longtime host institution, Oklahoma State University, prompted the transfer of NUTN headquarters to Old Dominion University.

Oberle (1990) also explained how nonmember institutions such as high schools, companies, associations, and government agencies could receive NUTN programs and services. Training and globalization were additional benefits identified, and these have expanded since then through partnerships with many of the organizations mentioned in this chapter. A key reason for the ongoing success of NUTN is the sustained broad participation of its leaders in its overall advisory board and in specialized resource or planning groups. Duning, Van Kekerix, and Zaborowski (1993) noted that NUTN adopted in 1991 an experimental set of standards for live videoconferencing. Moore and Kearsley (1996) offered a brief case study of NUTN as one of the more successful satellite television consortia.

The Instructional Technology Council (ITC) is an affiliated council of the American Association of Community Colleges. Prior to assuming its present name (in 1981), the group, much smaller in membership, was known as the Task Force on Uses of Mass Media in Learning. The name change was partly to reflect the fact that its interests had broadened beyond producing and marketing (Zigerell, 1982). ITC's location in Washington, D.C., enables it to serve as a legislative liaison. The results of an early ITC policy meeting on adult learners was summarized by Brock (1990). ITC has also influenced local institutional policies and practices on telecommunications by writing for presidents and trustees (RDR Associates, 1998) and for academic administrators and faculty (Tulloch & Sneed, 2000).

ITC's current mission is to provide leadership, information, and resources to expand and enhance distance learning through the effective use of technology. Although it represents nearly 600 institutions in the United States and Canada and includes single institutions, regional and statewide systems, for-profit organizations, and nonprofit organizations, two-year colleges make up the core of its membership. Current benefits of membership include a newsletter and listserv, grants information, awards, publications, and research (ITC, 2001). The respect that ITC has garnered in those areas can be noted in the Kellogg Foundation's recent selection of ITC as the coordinating home for the National Alliance of Virtual Colleges (ITC, 2001; Young, 2000).

As described by Brock (1990) and Lewis (1983), in 1981, its initial year of operation, PBS's Adult Learning Services (ALS) enabled 555 colleges and universities to enroll 53,000 students in television-assisted courses (telecourses). A later innovation, ALS's Adult Learning Satellite Service (ALSS), established in 1988, was identified by Welch (1992) as a more direct way to deliver programming to users, and according to a progress report 250,000 students were enrolling annually in at least one of over 50 telecourses resulting from partnerships between U.S. colleges and universities (over half of the total number involved in some way) and the nation's public television stations (96% of them involved). Mention was also made of the business programming strand of ALSS, known as The Business Channel (TBC). This latter programming effort has subsequently been the focus of partnerships with Williams Telecommunications (initially) and then, very recently, the National Technological University Corporation ("PBS' Business Channel Merges with NTUC," 1999).

Another more recent picture of ALS is contained in an interview of its former director of learning innovations, Shirley M. Davis, by Darcy Hardy in the American Journal of Distance Education (Hardy, 2000). Davis stated that ALS serves 500,000 students per year in partnership with 1,000 colleges and universities and public television stations in every state. A major factor in the growth of ALS has been its expansion of offerings to include 85 telecourses (enough to enable students to pursue an associate degree at the more than 200 institutions that are part of ALS's Going the Distance Project) and 30–40 live satellite events each year for the professional development of faculty and administrators (Hardy, 2000).

While PBS has worked with elementary and secondary schools for a much longer time than higher education, it has broadened the types of programs offered and media used. In regard to the new audiences of higher education, Davis described how ALS has expanded the range of services for faculty, staff, and students (Hardy, 2000). For example Project Access has created a neutral Web site for learner-directed decision-making and for blending of learning and working elements in users' lives. Regular visits to the ALS Web site (www.pbs.org/ALS) will alert readers to new delivery options, such as streaming courses and web courses.

REGIONAL CONSORTIA AND VIRTUAL UNIVERSITIES

In addition to starting their own individual virtual universities, as California, Kentucky, and Minnesota have done, many states have formal interstate compacts, such as 16 states in the Southern Regional Education Board (founded in 1948) and the 14 states in the Western Interstate Commission for Higher Education (founded in 1956), which have fostered two of the larger virtual universities in the country, the Southern Regional Electronic Campus (SREC) and Western Governors University (WGU), respectively. In both cases there was an ongoing internal technology resource group—the SREB Educational Technology Cooperative and the Western Cooperative for Educational Telecommunications—to draft extensive plans and then remain available for further assistance. Because of its effective leadership and some national government funding, the Western Cooperative was able to develop a document, Principles of Good Practice for Electrically Offered Academic Degree and Certificate Programs (Western Cooperative for Educational Telecommunications, 1995), that has become a de facto national quality standard used in whole or substantial part for many of the U.S. regional accrediting associations and virtual universities. In fact, by 2000, all eight U.S. regionally accrediting associations had obtained help from the Western Cooperative in preparing a common document.

Within the published literature can be found some useful comparisons of the three U.S. virtual universities that have been given the greatest publicity: WGU, SREC, and the California Virtual University (CVU). That sequence reflects a descending order of geographical scope with regard to the location of provider institutions. When this chapter was written, WGU continued to be the only state-funded virtual institution that was seeking a full regional accrediting status in order to offer its own degrees. Because WGU was using program provider institutions from multiple regional accrediting areas, it stimulated the formation of a new Inter-Regional Accreditation Committee, which in November 2000 declared that WGU had been awarded candidate status, which is the second of the three steps toward full regional accreditation (Carnevale, 2000). Another national objective achieved by WGU is designation as a federal aid demonstration program, which allows certain calendar and tracking conditions to be waived.

Because most virtual universities do not seek to offer direct degrees or attain accreditation, each is primarily a marketing Web site (with a searchable database for offerings) and a source for services (student support, faculty training, etc.). Most virtual universities have used pilot and expanding phases of offerings, subsequently including private colleges and private sector programs (Winer, 1998). Although WGU and SREC are said to have the ability to achieve economies of scale not normally available at the state level, state systems are seen as the only place to handle many policy matters while responding to satisfy local needs more rapidly ("States Are Now Setting up Their Own Virtual Universities," 1998).

Despite the economies of scale achievable by institutional providers in a large state like California (economies of scale equal to those of WGU or SREC), the scope of other ambitions may produce unexpected difficulties. Unlike other state virtual institutions, CVU has focused on the global export of education in direct challenge to other institutions, especially WGU. However, if diversity of funding, even including corporate support, is confined to just the one state's environment, local economic downturns can be more devastating than at WGU, which has secured support from international corporations and distance learning providers. In addition to the discrepancy between its goals and funding, CVU also probably suffered from being too dependent on three systems of facultycentered providing institutions (Berg, 1998; Blumenstyk, 1999a), especially as the influence of faculty members in regard to CVU may have been strengthened by their recent success in derailing the establishment of a for-profit limited liability corporation to be set up by the California State University system in conjunction with four technology companies.

In contrast to CVU, WGU is seen as having a more learner-centered agenda that can attract the support of many nonproviders but that might take much longer to achieve because of the university's looser connection with traditional provider institutions (Berg, 1998).

FUTURE CHALLENGE AND PROMISE

Although Jones International University, the first university to offer all its courses and services via the Internet, is a subsidiary of a for-profit company, the greatest concern of the evaluation team that agreed to give it regional accreditation is whether the university will be able to support itself in the future (Blumenstyk, 1999b). Since the derailment of CVU is said to be from a lack of financial support from existing institutions (Blumenstyk, 1999a), the challenge of maintaining necessary support is here now. The existence of similar situations for nonprofit and profit-making providers is reminiscent of the early years of correspondence study in the United States. Yet today's marvels of technological support and the promise of human capital investment offer more encouragement than in the past. As Wedemeyer (1985) observed,

"Today however, programs of distance study, independent study external study, and open learning are provided from the viewpoint that physical distance between learner and teacher is a situation to be exploited for its benefits to the learner, rather than as a disadvantage" (p. 1026).

REFERENCES

American Association for Collegiate Independent Study [Online]. (2002). Available: http://www.aacis.org

American Distance Education Consortium [Online]. (2001). Available: http://www.adec.edu

Arnone, M. Sylvan Learning Systems to Acquire National Technological [Online]. (2002). Available: http://chroni-cle.com/free/2002/03/2002032001u.htm

Anderson, B. (2000). Speaking personally with Janet K. Poley. *American Journal of Distance Education, 14*(3), 75–81

Association for Media-based Continuing Education for Engineers, Inc. [Online]. (2001). Available: http://www.amcee.org

Bagley, J. (2000, July 18). Interview with Gearold Johnson, academic vice president, National Technological University. *Information Technology in Postsecondary Education, 3*, 4–5.

Berg, G. A. (1998). Public policy on distance learning in higher education: California State and Western Governors Association initiatives. *Ed Journal, 12*(7), 1–8.

Berg, G. A. (1999). Contemporary implications of the history of correspondence instruction in American higher education. *Education at a Distance, 13*(3), 11–17.

Blumenstyk, G. (1999a). California Virtual University will end most of its operations. *Chronicle of Higher Education, 45*(30), A30.

Blumenstyk, G. (1999b). In a first, the North Central Association accredits an on-line university. *Chronicle of Higher Education, 45*(28), A27.

Brock, D. (1990). Research needs for adult learners via television. In M. G. Moore (Ed.), *Contemporary issues in American distance education* (pp. 172–181). Oxford: Pergamon Press.

Carnevale, D. (2000, November 28). Accrediting committee grants candidate status to Western Governors University. *Chronicle of Higher Education Daily News*, p. 1–3. Available: http://chronicle.com/free/2000/11/2000112801U.htm

Duning, B. S. (1987). Independent study in higher education: A captive of legendary resilience. *American Journal of Distance Education 1*(1), 37–46.

Duning, B. S., Van Kekerix, M. J. & Zaborowski, L. M. (1993). *Reaching learners through telecommunications.* San Francisco: Jossey-Bass.

Feasley, C. E. (1995). International perspectives on cooperative approaches to distance education. In D. Sewart (Ed.), *One world, many voices: Quality in open and distance learning* (pp. 77–80). Birmingham, England: International Council for Distance Education and the Open University.

Flores, J. (2000). Distance learning booms in government market. *Government Video, 11*(9), 86.

Fowler, W. A. (1981). The national home study council: Distance education leadership for five decades. *Distance Education, 2*(2), 234–239.

Hardy, D. W. (2000). Speaking personally with Shirley M. Davis. *American Journal of Distance Education, 14*(2), 71–74.

Instructional Technology Council [Online]. (2001). Available: http://www.itcnetwork.org

Jackson, G. (1994, February). Incentives for planning and delivering agricultural distance education. *Agricultural Education Magazine*, pp. 15–16.

Lambert, M. P. (1999, Fall). The national associations: A valuable resource for academe. *DETC News*, pp. 14–17.

Levine, T. K. (1992). *Going the distance: A handbook for developing distance degree programs.* Washington, DC: Annenberg/CPB.

Lewis, R. (1983). *Meeting learners' needs through telecommunications: A directory and guide to programs.* Washington, DC: American Association for Higher Education.

McAuliffe, T. (2000). Education connection. *Government Video, 11*(9), 6.

Moore, M. G., & Kearsley, G. (1996). *Distance education: A systems view.* Belmont, CA: Wadsworth Publishing.

National University Continuing Education Association. (1993). *The electronic university: A guide to distance learning.* Princeton, NJ: Peterson's Guides.

NHSC gets new name after 68 years: Distance Education and Training Council. (1994, Spring). *DETC News*, p. 1.

NTU changes to keep up with corporate market. (1999, May 11). *Information Technology in Postsecondary Education, 2*, 7.

National Technological University [Online]. (2001). Available: http://www.ntu.edu

Oberle, E. M. (1990). The national university teleconference network : A living laboratory for distance learning research. In M. G. Moore (Ed.), *Contemporary issues in American distance education* (pp. 81–95). Oxford: Pergamon Press.

PBS' business channel merges with NTUC. (1999, October 15). *Distance Education Report, 3*, 6.

Pescatore, M. J. (2000). Oklahoma professionals convey importance of distance learning. *Government Video, 11*(9), 68–69.

Peterson's guide to distance learning programs 2001. (2000). Lawrenceville, NJ: Peterson's Guides.

Pittman, V. V. (1987). The persistence of print: Correspondence study and the new media. *American Journal of Distance Education, 1*(1), 31–36.

Pittman, V. V. (1990). Correspondence study in the American university: A historiographic perspective. In M. G. Moore (Ed.), *Contemporary issues in American distance education* (pp. 67–80). Oxford: Pergamon Press.

Pittman, V. V. (1991). Academic credibility and the "image problem": The quality issue in collegiate independent study. In B. L. Watkins & S. J. Wright (Eds.), *The foundations of American distance education: A century of collegiate correspondence study* (pp. 109–134). Dubuque, IA: Kendall/Hunt.

Pittman, V. V. (1992). Amateurs, tough guys and a dubious pursuit: Crime and correspondence study in popular culture. *American Journal of Distance Education, 6*(1), 40–50.

RDR Associates, Inc. (1998). *New connections: A guide to distance education.* Washington, DC: Instructional Telecommunications Council.

Rohfeld, R. W. (Ed.). (1990). *Expanding access to knowledge: Continuing higher education.* Washington, DC: National University Continuing Education Association.

Shannon, D. W. (1990). Preface. In R. W. Rohfeld (Ed.), *Expanding access to knowledge: Continuing higher education* (pp. i–iii). Washington, DC: National University Continuing Education Association.

States are now setting up their own virtual universities. (1998). *Virtual University News, 1*(16), 1, 3.

Tulloch, J., & Sneed, J. (Eds.). (2000). *Quality enhancing practices in distance education: Teaching and learning.* Washington, DC: Instructional Telecommunications Council.

United States Distance Learning Association [Online]. (2001). Available: http://www.usdla.org

University Continuing Education Association [Online]. (2001). Available: http://www.nucea.edu

Van Hise, C. (1990). The university extension function in the modern university. In R. W. Rohfeld (Ed.), *Expanding access to knowledge: Continuing higher education* (pp. 20–35). Washington, DC: National University Continuing Education Association. (Original work published in 1915).

Verduin, J. R., Jr., & Clark, T. A. (1991). *Distance education: The foundations of practice.* San Francisco: Jossey-Bass.

Watkins, B. L. (1991). A quite radical idea: The invention and elaboration of collegiate correspondence study. In B. L. Watkins & S. J. Wright (Eds.), *The foundations of American distance education: A century of collegiate correspondence study* (pp. 1–25). Dubuque, IA: Kendall/Hunt.

Wedemeyer, C. A., & Childs, G. B. (1961). *New perspectives in university correspondence study.* Chicago: Center for the Study of Liberal Education for Adults.

Wedemeyer, C. A. (1981). *Learning at the back door: Reflections on nontraditional learning in the lifespan.* Madison, WI: University of Wisconsin Press.

Wedemeyer, C. A. (1985). Correspondence study. In T. Husen & T. N. Postlethwaite (Eds.), *International encyclopedia of education* (pp. 1026–1030). London: Pergamon.

Welch, S. (1992). PBS Adult Learning Service. In P. Portway & C. Lane (Eds.), *Technical guide to teleconferencing and distance learning* (pp. 277–278). San Ramon, CA: Applied Business Telecommunications.

Western Cooperative for Educational Telecommunications. (1995). *Principles of good practice for electronically offered academic degree and certificate programs.* Boulder, CO: Western Interstate Commission for Higher Education.

Winer, R. M. (1998). Three virtual universities gear up for fall openings. *Education at a Distance, 12*(11), 12–14.

Wright, S. J. (1991). Opportunity lost, opportunity regained: University independent study in the modern era. In B. L. Watkins & S. J. Wright (Eds.), *The foundations of American distance education: A century of collegiate correspondence study* (pp. 37–66). Dubuque, IA: Kendall/Hunt.

Young, J. R. (2000). Virtual universities pledge to ease transfer and encourage other kinds of collaboration. *Chronicle of Higher Education, 46*(35), A45.

Zigerell, J. (1982). Video vitality: Consortium has it. *Community and Junior College Journal, 45*(2), 16–18.

4

The History of Distance Education Through the Eyes of the International Council for Distance Education

Ellen L. Bunker
Instructional Systems Research and Development, Inc.
ebunker@starpower.net

The International Council for Open and Distance Learning (ICDE), perhaps the largest and best known of distance education associations, had its beginnings in the second quarter of the 20th century, inspired by visionary educators using correspondence education. ICDE began as a one-time conference in 1938, but conveners and participants, cheered by the success of this first conference, voted to hold a second and possibly a third conference. At the second conference, the delegates voted to form a permanent association and selected the International Council on Correspondence Education (ICCE) as the name. The association retained this name until the 1982 conference, at which the delegates voted to change the name to the International Council for Distance Education.

The idea for holding an international conference came from J. W. Gibson, a visitor from Canada, who attended the National Conference on Supervised Correspondence Study in New York in 1936. Gibson, the director of high school correspondence instruction for the province of British Columbia, shared with other delegates knowledge he had about correspondence education in several countries and then suggested that an international conference be held. Delegates at the New York conference were enthusiastic about the idea (Broady, 1938). Rex Haight, chair of the New York conference, supported the idea and later served as president for the first conference. Gibson served as chairman of the program committee, assisted by Earl T. Platt from Nebraska and Haight from Montana (Broady, 1948b). The work of planning the conference fell to Gibson and the Department of Education of British Columbia, and it was, in Knute O. Broady's words, "bravely conceived and magnificently carried out" (Broady, 1948b, p. 89). William R. Young, president for the fourth conference, proposed for Gibson the title of "Father of the International Conference on Correspondence Education," earned through his "perseverance, industriousness, and ability" (Young, 1953, p. 15).

At the second conference, held in 1948, the delegates voted unanimously to establish a more permanent international council (Broady, 1948a). At the third conference, held in 1953 in Christchurch, New Zealand, a committee presented a proposed "Constitution and Rules" for the council that was adopted by the delegates. As these rules helped the council became more established, conferences began to follow a more regular schedule (Table 4.1).

REVIEW OF RESEARCH ON ICDE HISTORY

If we are to look at the history of distance education through the eyes of ICDE, we must have some understanding of previous research in this area. "Doing history," which is a "process of selecting and arranging evidence in order to interpret and explain human actions" (Johnson, n.d.), is a way of understanding the past, of taking a series of events and human actions and bringing them into a focus that helps us to appreciate and understand where we are now and to guide us as we plan where we will go in the future.

In looking at the history of ICDE, we find the evidence of "events" and "actions" recorded in conference proceedings, reports, and official statements of policy. However, since many of the conference proceedings, like much of the foundational literature in distance education, are difficult for most distance educators to find, it is also difficult for current educators to "do history," to understand the ideas, practices, and efforts of early distance educators. In addition, many distance education practitioners and researchers today are new to distance education, having come to this area of education from various backgrounds. They may bring a "professional self-knowledge" from these backgrounds (Johnson, n.d.), but have little knowledge of the longer historical presence of correspondence and distance education and of the work and ideas of the many distance educators throughout the world. Therefore, research is needed to bring together some of the foundational work of these educators and to organize the findings in a way that will help the distance educators of today gain guidance from the work of those of the past.

Previous historical studies on correspondence and distance education have made some information available (see, e.g., Bittner and Mallory, 1933; Bunker, 1998b; MacKenzie, Christensen, and Rigby, 1968; Marriott, 1981; Moore, 1991; Moore and Kearsley, 1996; Noffsinger, 1926; Perry, 1977; Pittman, 1996 and 1998; Sherow and Wedemeyer, 1990; Watkins and Wright, 1991). The amount that has been done, however, is small in relation to the size of the field of study, as Pittman aptly points out in Chapter 2 of this volume. Likewise, very little work has been done on preserving the history of ICDE (see, e.g., Bunker, 1998a and Young, 1953). Also, few studies have focused on professional conferences, even in other fields. Such research, notes Amy Rose (1992, p. 10) is "amazingly sparse" (see, e.g., Drolet, 1982; Elton, 1983; Garvey, Lin, Nelson, and Tomita, 1979; Griffith and Garvey, 1966; Petry, 1981; Rosenfeld, Stacks and Hickson, 1990; Thrush, 1996; Tootelian, Bush, and Stern, 1992; Tritsch, 1991).

Bunker (1998a), analyzing the ICDE conferences from 1938 to 1995 and using an analysis tool from rhetoric (Porter, 1986, 1992), studied ICDE as a group of individuals and institutions "bound by a common interest"—correspondence or distance education—in order to find shared assumptions, practices, and aims that characterize that community as well as to document changes over time. Since such groups change frequently and are, therefore, hard to study, the analysis tool looks at data collected from official publications ("forums" of the group) and assesses "approved communication" to identify rules, standards, beliefs, and practices of the group. Within this framework, the Bunker study searches for themes and patterns that are recorded in the forum of conference proceedings.

As shown in Table 4.1 above, ICDE has held 20 conferences. The first section below contains a brief general description of each conference. Following the general description is a discussion of trends and patterns revealed in Bunker's analysis of the ICDE conference proceedings.

TABLE 4.1

ICDE Conferences

No.	Year	Location	Leadership
1	1938	Victoria, British Columbia, Canada	Rex Haight, president; J. W. Gibson, organizing secretary; Earl Platt, program committee chair; Frank Cyr, program committee member; Knute Broady, conference executive
2	1948	Lincoln, Nebraska, USA	Knute Broady, president; J. W. Gibson, vice-president; H. C. Etter, secretary; N. F. Thorpe, organizing secretary; G. J. Buck, program committee chair
3	1950	Christchurch, New Zealand	A. G. Butchers, president; G. J Buck, vice-president; K. O. Broady, past president; N. F. Thorpe, secretary
4	1953	State College, Pennsylvania, USA	W. R. Young, president; Eric N. LePetit, G. J. Buck, Edith Lucas, Sylvia Haight, Nancy Fitch, R. W. Cumberworth, and N. F. Thorpe, vice-presidents
5	1958	Banff, Alberta, Canada	G. J. Buck, president and organizing secretary-treasurer; Eric LePetit, Edith E. Lucas, Sylvia Haight, A. J. Betheras, Elizabeth Powell, Norman Braden, and Homer Kempfer, vice-presidents; William Young, past president; G. F. Bruce, arrangements and entertainment committee chair
6	1961	Gearhart, Oregon, USA	G. J. Buck, past president; Knute Broady, honorary president; Donald Cameron, Norinne Tempest, Sven Hartman, Lloyd Jamieson, John Villaume, and G. J. Buck, vice-presidents; Chas Dean, program committee chair
7	1965	Stockholm, Sweden	Donald Cameron, president; Sven Hartman, first vice-president and program committee chair; Renée Erdos, F. Lloyd Hansen, Mitoji Nishimoto, and John Villaume, vice-presidents
8	1969	Paris, France	Renée Erdos, president; Donald Cameron, past president; Knute Broady, honorary president; Börje Holmberg, Mitoji Nishimoto, I. J. Sloos, Charles Wedemeyer, and Solomon Inquai, vice-presidents
9	1972	Warrenton, Virginia, USA	Charles Wedemeyer, president; Börje Holmberg, Edward Estabrooke, Einar Rørstad, Elias Pereira, and M. Kaunda, vice-presidents; Renée Erdos, past president; Robert Allen and Ripley Sims, program committee co-chairs
10	1975	Brighton, United Kingdom	Börje Holmberg, president; William Fowler, Peter Kinyanjui, Tadashi Koretsuné, Horst Mohle, Ripley Sims, and Charles Wedemeyer, assistants; Gunnar Granholm, program committee chair; Erling Ljoså, proceedings editor
11	1978	New Delhi, India	David Young, president; Mary L. McPartlin, Otto Peters, Bakhshish Singh, Kevin Smith, and Hafiz Wali, vice-presidents; Robert Wentworth, program chair
12	1982	Vancouver, British Columbia, Canada	Bakhshish Singh, president; Audrey Campbell, Michael Carbery, Erling Ljoså, Otto Peters, and Kevin Smith, vice-presidents; Audrey Campbell, conference host; John Daniel, program committee chair
13	1985	Melbourne, Queensland, Australia	John Daniel, president; Bakhshish Singh, past president; Joseph Ansere, John A. Bååth, Janet Jenkins, David Sewart, and Kevin Smith, vice-presidents; Barry Snowden, treasurer; Jerry Grimwade, conference manager; David Sewart, editor; John Thompson, publications secretary
14	1988	Oslo, Norway	Kevin Smith, president; John Daniel, past president; Liz Burge, Ben Gitau, Gisela Pravda, David Sewart, and Maureen Smith, vice-presidents; Barry Snowden, secretary/treasurer; Reidar Roll, conference manager; David Sewart, program committee chair
15	1990	Caracas, Venezuela	David Sewart, president; Kevin Smith, past president; Reidar Roll, secretary general; Marian Croft, Michael Moore, Ronnie Carr, Barbara Matiru, Bruce Scriven, and Raj Dhanarajan, vice-presidents; Armando Villarroel, conference manager; Marian Croft, program chair
16	1992	Bangkok, Thailand	Executive committee same as 1990 conference; Bruce Scriven, program chair and editor; Roy Lundin and Yoni Ryan, editors
17	1995	Birmingham, United Kingdom	Marian Croft, president; David Sewart, past president; Reidar Roll, secretary general; David Sewart, program chair

(Continued)

TABLE 4.1 (Continued)

No.	Year	Location	Leadership
18	1997	State College, Pennsylvania, USA	Armando Rocha Trindade, president; Reidar Roll, secretary general; Bernard Loing, Ross H. Paul, Armando Villarroel, John Samuel, James C. Taylor, Marmar Mukhopadhyay, and Gary Miller; vice-presidents; Marian Croft, past president
19	1999	Vienna, Austria	Armando Rocha Trindade, president (until June 24, 1999); Molly Corbett Broad, president (from June 25, 1999); Reidar Roll, secretary general; Hugh Africa, Gary Miller, Bernard Loing, David Hardy, Marta Mena, Marmar Mukhopadhyay, Abdul Khan, Jim Taylor, Alexander Ivannikov, Anne Auban, Helmut Hoyer, Arief Sukadi Sadiman, and Tam Sheung Wai, vice- presidents; Marian Croft, past president
20	2001	Düsseldorf, Germany	Molly Corbett Broad, president; Reidar Roll, secretary general; Hugh Africa, Gary Miller, David Hardy, Marta Mena, Abdul Khan, Jim Taylor, Alexander Ivannikov, Anne Auban, Helmut Hoyer, Arief Sukadi Sadiman, and Tam Sheung Wai, vice-presidents; Helmut Hoyer, program chair

Source: Department of Education, Victoria, British Columbia.

ICDE WORLD CONFERENCES 1938–2001

Conference 1: Victoria, British Columbia

As noted above, the first conference was held in August 1938 in Canada, hosted by the Department of Education for British Columbia. No clearly stated theme was given for this first conference, although the purposes of the conference were listed in the pre-conference literature and quoted by Haight in his foreword to the proceedings. These purposes included the exchange of experience, the examination of different points of view, the evaluation of results, the consideration of unsolved and difficult problems, the examination of different techniques, the standardization of procedures, and the planning for further critical study of technical research problems involved in correspondence education (Haight, 1938).

In addition, conference sessions were organized around three different section meetings:

Section I: The Organization, Promotion and Accreditation of Correspondence Instruction.

Section II: The Preparation of Correspondence Courses.

Section III: The Work of the Correspondence Instructor—Teaching, Evaluating and Recording of Results.

These section meetings were the "peak" of the conference and focused on "numerous and . . . practical" matters (Gibson, 1938, p. 43). Delegates interested in correspondence study at the elementary level asked for an addition to the program schedule to allow them to meet together, and so another section was formed during the conference.

Conference 2: Lincoln, Nebraska

The second conference was held at the University of Nebraska, October 11–15, 1948. Knute O. Broady had been elected at the first conference in 1938 to serve as president of the second conference. The second conference, originally planned for 1940, was delayed until 1948 by the onset of World War II. The members of the conference planning committee collected documents about correspondence education from different institutions and prepared a pre-conference bulletin featuring these reports. These descriptive reports regarding correspondence education included 26 reports from the United States, 7 each from Australia and Canada, and 1 each from Denmark, New Zealand, Norway, South Africa, and the Union of Soviet Socialist Republics (Merwin & Lowdon, 1948).

As in the case of the first conference, no explicit theme was stated. However, the conference was planned in "compliance with the wishes of the delegates from the 1938 Conference"—that is, that another conference be held and that "an organized group . . . study the question as to whether or not present correspondence services are adequately meeting the need for this form of education" (Buck, 1948, p. 97). Further, one of the purposes of the conference was to examine "ways and means of improving services given by correspondence educational organizations" (p. 97).

The conference committee selected nine topics for consideration, assigning delegates to do advance work on these topics and come prepared for discussions with other conference delegates. The topics included the following:

The instructional staff of correspondence schools.
The preparation of correspondence courses.
Instruction.
Methods of study and their effectiveness.
Armed services courses: implications for adult education.
Methods of evaluating students' work.
Libraries, traveling laboratories, and other mobile units; school bulletins and magazines; auxiliary organizations; and publicity.
Guidance in relation to correspondence instruction.
Organization and administration of correspondence schools.

Nearly all the addresses in this conference focused on experiences from different countries— Australia, New Zealand, Canada, Sweden, and the United States—although one dealt with basic concepts in correspondence instruction, one focused on correspondence education in the military, and one discussed correspondence education's relationship to overall curriculum planning.

Conference 3: Christchurch, New Zealand

The third conference was held in New Zealand, in April 1950. The preface pages, titles, and program listings in the proceedings make no mention of specific objectives, themes, or purposes for this conference. However, the delegates at this conference prepared the first draft of the constitution and the general objectives of the council. It can be assumed that the objectives written for the constitution also served as the objectives for this conference.

The primary objectives of the council, as given in the first constitution, included the promotion of knowledge and improvement of correspondence education throughout the world, the fostering of good fellowship among correspondence educators, the exchange of materials and information, the convening of conferences, and the publishing the conference proceedings.

The conference was organized primarily by sections, with only a few addresses and papers. The subject matter for these sections included 1) primary education by correspondence; 2) correspondence methods for handicapped pupils; 3) post-primary education by correspondence (focusing on language, libraries, and social sciences); 4) post-primary education by correspondence (focusing on math, science, and commercial subjects); 5 and 6) technical education by correspondence (comprising two sections); 7) organization and administration; 8) associated services; 9) course production; 10) radio in correspondence education; 11) education in special fields (with reports focusing on teacher training, religious education, leadership training for the blind, and staff training); and 12) developments and future research.

Conference 4: State College, Pennsylvania

The fourth conference was held in August 1953, with The Pennsylvania State College serving as host. Again no specific conference theme was chosen by the conference program planning committee or by the executive committee. However, in his opening address relating the history of the council's conferences, Young (1953) noted that the delegates had come to this conference to "promote the knowledge of correspondence education throughout the world" (p. 17), the first of the objectives of the constitution drafted at the third conference. The addresses and papers were not categorized into subsections and covered a variety of topics and levels of correspondence education. Of the 31 papers, 6 were country reports, 9 related to specific methods of correspondence education (e.g., administration or teaching in supervised correspondence study or the use of television in courses), and 5 discussed course or curriculum development. The remaining addresses and papers discussed a wide variety of administrative issues—learner characteristics, specific subject areas, and correspondence education's relationships with other educational areas. This conference did contain several reports based on research, including a report on completion rates from the United States Armed Forces Institute (USAFI) and one on factors influencing the examination performance of external students at the University of Queensland in Australia.

Conference 5: Banff, Alberta

The fifth conference returned to Canada, hosted by the Banff School of Fine Arts in June 1957. This conference was the first to have an explicitly announced theme. Although neither the title of the conference proceedings nor the conference program gave the theme, Buck (1957) stated in his president's report, "In coming to a decision with regard to a central idea about which the Conference could be organized, it soon became apparent that the title 'What the Correspondence Method Can, and Does, Contribute Towards Meeting the Modern Demands Made on Education' was appropriate" (p. 31). Buck also listed six objectives for the conference:

1. Obtain the participation of delegates.
2. Develop a broad understanding of the uses of correspondence education.
3. Learn about the work of contemporary correspondence education institutions.
4. Suggest and discover improved methods for correlating correspondence instruction with resident instruction.
5. Give information for those establishing correspondence education services.
6. Enhance the educational status of correspondence education students.

The conference was divided between general sessions and sectional meetings. Ten categories were established for the sectional meetings: elementary, use of television, university, development of uniform statistics, technical education by correspondence, use of supplementary materials for children studying by correspondence, high school, a question box, effective psychological motivation, and useful criteria for text selection. Buck (1975) noted that the conference was planned from the suggestions of the participants and was based on a series of five letters sent to members soliciting their help in developing the conference.

Conference 6: Gearhart-by-the-Sea, Oregon

The sixth conference convened at Gearhart-by-the-Sea, in Oregon, October 22–27, 1961. This conference did not have an announced theme; however, the ideas for the conference were collected from the membership by the planning committee and, as Viron Moore (1961) states in his report as the president, the conference was planned "in accordance with the majority of suggestions that were made." Moore noted that the assistance from the members reflected a "cooperative professional spirit" and the common good as expressed in the constitution: "to promote knowledge of correspondence education throughout the world and to foster good fellowship and better understanding among correspondence educators of all nations" (Moore, 1961, p. 29). The conference sessions focused on reports of correspondence education from around the world (e.g., in sessions such as "Japan Tells Her Story") and sectional meetings dealing with elementary-, secondary-, technical-, and university-level issues. Three specialized sectional meetings were held to discuss publicity and promotion, learning machines, and supervised correspondence study.

Conference 7: Stockholm

The seventh conference marked a change in the number of delegates attending and the number of countries represented by the delegates. The conference, the first to be held in Europe, convened in Stockholm, June 13–17, 1965. Donald Cameron was president for this conference. His selection also represented a change; in previous conferences, the president was from an institution at or near the host site of the conference. During the elections for officers at the sixth conference, this situation was discussed, and a delegate recommended that a member from Europe, Sven Hartman, be chosen as the president for the next conference. Hartman, however, declined the nomination, and Cameron was elected. Hartman served as first vice-president and program and arrangements committee chair.

The themes for this conference, although not clearly stated in the title or introductory pages, emerged from a survey conducted by Charles Wedemeyer that he reported on during his keynote address at the conference. His survey (Wedemeyer, 1965) looked at trends in correspondence education around the world, and the results formed the six themes for the conference:

1. New methods, and technologies and their uses in correspondence education, the integration of mass media into correspondence education, and the improvement of instruction by correspondence.
2. The linking of correspondence education with formal school instruction.
3. The use of correspondence education in the continuing education of adults.
4. Research and experimentation in correspondence education.
5. Correspondence education in developing countries.
6. Improving the qualifications and acceptance of correspondence education.

The conference primarily consisted of presentations and discussion in panels designed to focus on the themes, although four addresses were given on ideas and trends in various parts of the world (Australia, India, Japan, and Europe).

Conference 8: Paris

The eighth conference was again held in Europe, this time at UNESCO House to commemorate the council's affiliation with UNESCO. The conference extended from May 10 to May 23, 1969. To assist with the planning of the conference, Renée Erdos, president, sent letters two years before the conference soliciting suggestions for subjects and speakers from the council's members. Over 40 members responded, and subjects for the conference were chosen in accordance with the number of people interested in them (Erdos, 1969).

In order to place no restriction on member suggestions, a theme was chosen after the suggestions had been made. Erdos (1969) notes that as "the programme took shape, however, it so clearly expressed the interest of members in future developments, both in education and administration, that a theme emerged: 'Correspondence Education Looks to the Future.'"(p. 16).

Balbir (1969), in his welcoming address, listed subthemes of the conference as "1) educational technology in correspondence education; 2) external studies at the university level; 3) the place of correspondence instruction in technical education and training; 4) the training of manpower by correspondence education in African countries; and 5) correspondence education in UNESCO activities" (p. 4).

Conference 9: Warrenton, Virginia

Charles Wedemeyer served as president for the ninth conference, held in May 1972. This conference featured the following theme: "Between Evolution and Revolution . . . Correspondence Study Lost or Found?" In discussing the conference theme, Bakhshish Singh (1972) noted that the theme is "relevant not only to the development of correspondence study but also to the formulation of future educational policies the world over" (p. 2). Singh also listed theme-related subjects that were discussed at different sessions in the conference and that functioned as the topics for the summary analysis chapters in the proceedings:

1. Correspondence study in the perspective of rapidly expanding alternative learning opportunities.
2. The role of education technology in correspondence education.
3. Educational policy development and innovation at the national level.
4. "Education: Year 2000"—theoretical, technical, legal, or cultural problems.
5. Implication of three research studies on the improvement and spread of correspondence education.
6. Developmental trends by geographical areas—Europe; North, Central and South America; Asia; and Africa.

Conference 10: Brighton, England

The 10th conference, held in 1975, had been scheduled for Japan, but because the members from Japan were not able to garner sufficient support from institutions and the government to host the conference, the location was changed to Brighton. In their introduction to the conference papers, Gunnar W. Granholm, chair of the program committee, and Erling Ljoså, editor for the conference papers and the proceedings, described the variety in distance education (or correspondence or home study) programs worldwide as background for introducing the theme of the conference. The planning committee choose the theme to help identify the components of the "man-materials system with which we are working" in distance education (Granholm & Ljoså, 1975, p. 6). The wording of the theme appears as follows in Granholm and Ljoså's introduction:

The System of Distance Education an analysis of educational and administrative sub-systems and components, with reference to their

- purposes
- significance
- characteristics
- interrelationship
- cost effectiveness

and the implications of these functions for the evaluation of distance education programmes with respect to

—information
—counselling

—student activities
—two-way communication

and, on the other hand,

—marketing
—management (p. 6)

The conference papers were grouped into four main sections:

1. The system of distance education.
2. Modes of teaching in distance education.
3. Distance education and the open learning trend.
4. Student service, student activity, and two-way communication.

Conference 11: New Delhi

The 11th conference convened in India, the first conference in Asia. Held November 8–15, 1978, it again had an explicitly stated theme: "Correspondence Education: Dynamic and Diversified." In addition, it focused on four specific areas: administrative practices, teaching methods, student counseling, and applied research. David Young (1978), in writing the preface to volume 1 of the conference papers, quotes from the pre-conference literature for the first conference in 1938 and states that the aims are "still valid for ICCE's Eleventh World Conference" (p. 7). Although there have been changes in the world, he claims that the "need for correspondence educators to consult with one another, to aid one another's research, and to prove that they are an increasingly vital part of worldwide education, remains" (p. 7).

Conference proceedings published after 1978 are much more uniform in appearance. They contain mainly papers and addresses and no longer include minutes from meetings, committee reports, or descriptions of social activities or field trips. Consequently, they reveal less about the process of developing conference programs and more about the content of individual presentations.

Conference 12: Vancouver

In 1982, the conference "revisited its birthplace" (Daniel, Stroud, & Thompson, 1982a, p. 4), returning to British Colombia. This conference, as noted above, marked the "rebirth" of ICCE as ICDE, the International Council for Distance Education. A new form of publication emerged from the 1982 conference. The program committee decided to produce a "book" from the conference, entitled *Learning at a Distance: A World Perspective*. In addition, a report and handbook were published. No theme is mentioned in the book produced from the conference. The program committee used a version of the Delphi technique to collect topics of interest from members and to choose contributors to write about them.

The editors noted that the papers reflect a common theme: "distance education becoming a major shaping force in societies all over the world" (Daniel, Stroud, & Thompson, 1982b, p.5). The book is divided into seven sections, which together suggest a set of subthemes:

1. International trends.
2. Learning at a distance and national development.
3. The process of learning at a distance—recent research and development.

4. Student support and regional services.
5. Policymaking and management.
6. Diverse subjects, diverse approaches.
7. The contribution of media and technology to learning at a distance.

Conference 13: Melbourne

The conference in 1985 went to the southern hemisphere for the second time. As one innovation, the conference papers were not published on paper but were prepared on microforms. This allowed delegates to send papers of any length, and all were included in the collection of conference papers without editing by the conference planning committee. As a result, the collection totaled nearly 3,000 pages (48 microfiche cards). The microfiche cards included no information about the conference (e.g., table of contents, program schedule, list of delegates or officers, etc.).

However, a report was published for this conference (ICDE, 1985). In this publication, the conference theme is given as "Flexible Designs for Learning," and the following sub-themes were listed: the learners, the social context, the disciplines, learning resources, and organisation. Writing for the conference committee, Kevin Smith (1985a) noted that the main theme "reflected . . . many imaginative presentations for which the Program Committee had appealed in an attempt to add variety to more traditional forms of delivery" (p. 1). Because of the number of responses to the call for conference participation, the focus was on parallel rather than plenary sessions. In addition, this conference featured 19 special interest group sessions—libraries in distance education, new institutions, new technologies, instructional design, distance education and developing societies, research, schools, technical education, women's international network, disabled students, private proprietary colleges, counselling, study centers, continuing education, professional development, teaching history, teaching English as a second language, teaching business studies, and teaching mathematics (Smith, 1985b).

Conference 14: Oslo

The 1988 conference, held from August 9 to 16, took "Developing Distance Education" as its theme. Twelve subthemes were also listed: national development, specific target groups, economics of distance education, course design and creation, media and communications technology, collaboration and credit transfer, student support and counselling, continuing education, research, women in distance education, management and organisation, and distance education—a developing concept (ICDE, 1988).

Conference 15: Caracas

The 15th conference, held in November 4–10, 1990, was the first situated in Latin America. Its theme was "Distance Education: Development and Access." Subthemes included distance education and development; strategies for developing distance education; distance education and developing countries; literacy—the challenge of the '90s; research and development; producing materials for distance education; the students of the '90s—new client, new needs; technology applications; and planning the future. Sewart (1990) identifies the theme of the conference book as "that of scholarship directly addressing and supporting practical needs and aiding the training of professionals" (p. 8).

The Caracas conference was bilingual, an innovation for ICDE. Each morning and afternoon session featured a keynote address followed by parallel sessions. Delegates could choose from parallel sessions given either in Spanish or English. Two proceedings volumes were published, one with papers in English and one with papers in Spanish.

Conference 16: Bangkok

In 1992, the conference returned to Asia, hosted by the Sukhothai Thammathirat Open University. At this time, the conferences changed from being held every three or four years to convening every other year. The editors note that the overall theme of the conference, "Distance Education for the Twenty-First Century," was "purposely chosen to be forward-looking, thereby encouraging presenters to concentrate on issues perceived to be of particular relevance to future developments" (Scriven, Lundin, & Ryan, 1993a, p. xi). The presentations from this conference were originally categorized under nine subthemes, but because not all presentations provided papers suitable for including in the book, the original subthemes were renamed and the papers reclassified to form seven chapters: distance education and development; development of materials; students in distance education; applications of technology; distance education—theory and research; case studies; and so, back to the future.

Conference 17: Birmingham, England

The theme of the 1995 conference was "One World, Many Voices: Quality in Open and Distance Learning." The subthemes included developing human potential, developing the professional community, primary and secondary education, quality, student support, technology, and women's issues. Because of the quantity of presentations, the proceedings were published in two volumes.

Conference 18: State College, Pennsylvania

In 1997, The Pennsylvania State University hosted the 18th conference, whose theme was "The New Learning Environment: A Global Perspective." The conference focused on several daily themes, including the changing technological environment; the new education paradigm; technology, education, and sustainable development; and opportunities for international cooperation. The conference program also noted a rather long list of interest areas: primary through secondary school applications; technology applications and emerging technologies; research and evaluation in distance and open learning; distance education in developing countries; organizational issues (faculty, infrastructure, institutional, and regulatory policies); pedagogical issues; promotion and marketing strategies; partnerships and alliances; workplace training and education; and student/learner support. For the first time, the conference proceedings were published on CD-ROM rather than in print.

Conference 19: Vienna

The 19th conference, held in 1999, was titled "The New Educational Frontier: Teaching and Learning in a Networked World." It featured university, school, and training strands, and within each strand a set of six tracks helped to focus the discussion and presentation. These tracks included open learning and distance education as a strategic tool for development; the new learning environments; globalization of education—benefits and constraints; policy and strategy development; breaking down barriers through education and training; and markets and marketing. Again, the proceedings were published on CD-ROM.

Conference 20: Düsseldorf

The ICDE scheduled the 20th conference for April 1–5, 2001. The main conference theme, "The Future of Learning—Learning for the Future: Shaping the Transition," was designed to help conference participants "explore how open learning and distance education, virtual training and e-learning will find their positions in a perpetually changing world in the coming years" (ICDE, 2000, p. 4). Core events include plenary, parallel, and poster sessions.

TRENDS AND PATTERNS

Bunker (1998a) searched for themes and patterns recorded in the ICDE conference proceedings that could provide insight about alternatives facing distance educators today. Not only did shared assumptions, practices, and aims appear in the proceedings, but several trends were discovered, including the importance of access as a key value for distance educators, the commitment of distance educators to quality, the need for research to inform practices, the high value placed on international participation and representation in the membership of the council, and the role of educational technology in distance education and its place in the discourse of the conferences.

First, the discourse of the ICDE conferences reveals an unremitting allegiance to the belief in the value of providing *access* to education for all learners, no matter how dispersed or disadvantaged by economic, personal, or political situations. For example, in opening the conference in 1938, Knute Broady, chair of the first meeting, made a clear statement of the motivations and ideals that had brought the delegates together, claiming these values for all of the delegates:

> Now, we are gathered here to-day to enlarge our ideas and to take stock. We are deciding on new steps, perhaps even upon a new direction, and in all of this, ladies and gentlemen, we are motivated by what we consider a very practical ideal which I believe is accepted in all parts of the world . . .

> By equality of educational opportunity we mean extending education of equal quality to every one, no matter how humble his birth, no matter where he may live, and no matter what his reasonable aspirations may be. We think that is a very practical ideal—an ideal to which we can all subscribe, and I trust that everything that we do in this conference will be evaluated in terms of it. (Broady, 1938, p. 10)

Over the years, this general commitment to access remains undiminished. Wedemeyer (1965) reaffirmed it in a major keynote address in the 1965 conference in Stockholm, reminding delegates that although all types of education are directed toward the hopes and aspirations of learners, none do so "so openly, so nakedly, as correspondence education. The correspondence student is generally one who has not been able to satisfy hopes and aspirations in the ordinary, regular, easier way" (p. 9).

The proceedings also reveal a recognition of the need for interaction and communication with learners. Since the separation of learners from instructors necessitates the use of media to allow interaction, the discourse data show continual efforts by conference participants to enhance the development and promotion of interaction. Although the necessity of using some form of mediation was clearly acknowledged in the very first conferences, the media never became the principal theme of any of conference. In addition, data show that the need for flexibility and variation in meeting needs of the learners was a common discourse theme.

Second, the commitment to access was followed closely by a commitment to providing education *equal in value* to traditional education. In order to ensure this equality, distance educators constantly sought academic credibility for their educational offerings. Because distance education was an alternative to conventional education, distance educators were required to prove the efficacy of their efforts. The discourse in the proceedings contains continual references to quality, standards, accreditation, status, and credibility in both the teaching-learning and in management domains of distance education. The issue of credibility lead participants in the conferences to discuss means of improving instruction, interaction with learners, applications of communications technologies, and support for learners.

Concern for access and equity is present in many different forms in the data from the early years of the conference. However, because of the change in format of the conference proceedings in 1982, fewer data are available for use in analyzing the motives and values of the conference planners and officers from that year to the present. Do council members still hold to these primary values of access and quality? Further research is needed to determine whether the ICDE has moved away from a commitment to the values of access and quality and, if so, what values have replaced them. Knowing the answer could provide better guidance for all of us as we plan future programs across the nation and throughout the world.

Third, concerns for academic credibility lead ICDE practitioners to persistently call for more *research* into the methods and practices of distance education. References to the need for more research appear in the data from all conferences. At the first conference, the need for research was recognized and a research committee established. This committee became an ongoing part of the council's early organizational structure. In an effort to spur delegates on to more research, the proceedings of the first conference in 1938 included a list of needed research (Table 4.2) (Butchers, 1938). The delegates to the conference were encouraged to work on these research topics before the next conference.

TABLE 4.2
Summary of Topics Suitable for Research (From 1938 Conference)

What becomes of graduates of CI schools? How do they fare?
What classes of students, what specific needs should be served by CI?
Is CI more effective carried on in the home or in or through the nearest school?
How much supervision should be given?
What roles should be played by the supervisors?
What is the cost of CI? How does it compare with other types of education?
What should be the organization of the centre?
How can library facilities be organized for correspondence students?
How can one personalize CI?
Should there be co-ordination of various phases of CI?
What should be the length of a unit?
How far should we go in the use of itinerant teachers and mobile materials versus bringing students to the CI center?
What effect does each of these plans have on community life?
What use can be made of intelligence tests in CI?
What is the role of guidance and counsel?
What value has radio in experimental CI?
What is the place of vocational training and placement for CI students?
How can one teach sciences and technical subjects by correspondence?
How should health education, physical examinations be handled?
How will peculiar problems be met in teaching incapacitated students?
Can anything be done to provide parent education by correspondence?

Note: CI = Correspondence Instruction.

The discourse on research also shows a consistent acknowledgment that the amount of research and the dissemination of the results are inadequate. Statements to this effect are usually accompanied, however, by the concession that improvement has "recently" been made. For example, Buck stated in 1948 that a small amount of "objective research in this field has been done, but not nearly enough" (p. 99), and Wedemeyer made the same point in 1965, asserting that there has "never been sufficient scholarship poured into this field" (p. 16). In reporting as chair of the research committee in the 1969 conference, Childs wrote that there is a "substantial and growing worldwide body of literature relating to correspondence instruction. . . . It must be noted, however, that even though the volume of literature may be increasing this does not indicate any great upsurge in research activity. Evidences of carefully done research are still hard to come by" (p. 40). In the 1982 conference proceedings, the editors stated that research on distance learning had been characterized until recently by a wide gap between reality and rhetoric, but they expressed the hope "that future writing will give increasing importance to rigourous studies with properly defined variables and boundaries" (Daniel, Stroud, & Thompson, 1982c, p. 86). Again in 1992, research concerns merited a chapter in the proceedings. The editors noted that a historical analysis showed that research was a fairly recent phenomenon, but, in contrast to the past, reports at that conference contained research from around the world (Scriven, Lundin, & Ryan, 1993b).

Although research reports appear in most of the conferences, including reports from research committees, these reports never seemed to carry enough weight to convince the majority of conference speakers that sufficient research was being conducted. As complaints about lack of research still occur in meetings of distance educators, perhaps some effort needs to be made to analyze the findings and results from previous studies, such as those contained in the 60 years of ICDE conference proceedings.

Fourth, *international representation* is a distinctive feature of ICDE and emerges as a theme in the analysis. All discourse related to origin, policies and philosophies, conference planning, and conference themes exhibit a commitment to foster broad representation. The sense expressed in the discourse of "mutual esteem" for all distance educators from all countries providing all types of education is consistent and powerful.

Bunker's (1998a) analysis shows that the early leaders viewed the conference as an international professional gathering and made a sustained effort to choose themes and topics consistent with its international character. In fact, support for wide international representation became even more pronounced in the 1960s and 1970s, when the number of countries represented at the conference jumped from the earlier core of four countries (Australia, Canada, New Zealand, and the United States) to a much larger and more widely distributed group of countries. Topics directly related to international issues and concerns are part of nearly all conferences in the 1980s and 1990s.

This pattern is especially important for distance educators today, who face a nearly overwhelming growth in the possibilities for international distance education. Issues of collaboration and cooperation between countries confront distance educators working in many different sectors. The fact that ICDE has always been committed to international distance education suggests that its conference proceedings over the past 60 years could provide valuable guidance to those working today to establish distance education internationally.

Fifth, the amount of discourse devoted to *educational technology* in the ICDE conference proceedings is relatively small given that the emergence of new communications technologies is always cause for excitement and that distance education must rely on some form of media to provide interaction. Discourse about technology was present in every conference in some form, even when technology was not designated a conference subtheme. However, through all the conferences, educational technology remained only one topic in the total discourse about distance education. In most of the conferences, it was the focus of only one of 5 to 12 subsections.

This pattern has changed little over the years, even though more and more papers began appearing in the sections devoted to educational technology. The emphasis remained on distance education as a whole, with technology relegated to the role of mediator for that education. Overall, the ICDE conference has never become an "education technology" or "communications technology" conference but has stayed committed to the larger goal of providing access to education for nontraditional learners education. Learning from ICDE distance educators of the past, distance educators today would do well to keep the focus of their work on the educational elements of teaching and learning at a distance rather than letting the massive and rapid increase of new technologies drive the development, design, and purposes of their programs and courses.

CONCLUSION

Because the communications technologies that have helped to fuel the expansion of distance education in the last few years have been developed relatively recently, distance education is often viewed as a new field of study. Even the term *distance education* has not been popularly and widely used until lately (Moore, 1990). When distance educators believe they are using new media in a new field, important theories, research, and practices from the past are overlooked (Moore, personal conversation, February 2, 1997). As Pittman states in Chapter 2 of this volume, some current "practitioners and advocates seem anxious to leave the past behind," with the result that the implementation of distance education programs reflects little professional self-knowledge. In addition much that was learned in the past becomes lost as the new replaces rather than joins the old.

Distance education has been a means of educating those who could not or would not make use of traditional forms of education for more than a century. To neglect "where we have been" hinders our understanding of "where we want to go" (Johnson, n.d.). For example, disregarding the decades of experience and knowledge represented in this handbook by the chapters contributed by Holmberg, Peters, and others will cause unnecessary missteps on our way to providing quality distance education.

Looking historically at global distance education will give us an appreciation of the present and a perspective on the future (Hinckley, 1984). In other words, it will help us construct, understand, and evaluate the choices that we make in planning new programs, adapting new technologies, and serving new learners as well as in evaluating and improving service to current learners.

If we, as distance educators today, are to have a rich knowledge base on which to construct, understand, and evaluate future choices, we must consider the important work done by distance educators from the last century. The fact that the literature may easily become fugitive does not excuse us from making an effort to learn from those in the past. Members and leaders of ICDE have, throughout its history, been committed to strong educational values and to the sharing of good practices in distance education. As stated by Thomas Mann (1965), the best response to the question of what to do in situations presenting many new choices is to "'assist the new without sacrificing the old.' The best servitors of the new . . . may be those who know and love the old and carry it over into the new."

REFERENCES

ICDE Conference Proceedings
Report of the First International Conference on Correspondence Education. (1938). Victoria, BC: Department of
  Education, Victoria, BC.

Proceedings of the Second International Conference on Correspondence Education. (1948). Lincoln, NE: The University of Nebraska University Extension Division.

Proceedings of the Third International Conference of Correspondence Education. (1950). Wellington: New Zealand Education Department's Correspondence School for Third International Conference of Correspondence Education.

Proceedings: Fourth International Conference on Correspondence Education. (1953). State College, PA: Pennsylvania State College General Extension Services.

Record of proceedings: The Fifth International Conference of the International Council on Correspondence Education. A manual on correspondence education, G. J. Buck (Ed.). (1957). Banff, BC: Banff School of Fine Arts.

Proceedings of the Sixth International Conference on Correspondence Education. (1961). Gearhart, Oregon: General Extension Division, Oregon State System of Higher Education.

Proceedings of the Seventh International Conference of the International Council on Correspondence Education. (1965). Stockholm, Internation Council on correspondence Education.

Proceedings of the Eighth International Conference of the International Council on Correspondence Education. (1969). Paris: International Council on Correspondence Education.

Current issues and approaches in distance education. The proceedings of the Ninth World Conference of the International Council on Correspondence Education. (1972). Warrenton, Virginia: International Council on Correspondence Education.

The system of distance education: Vol. 2. Papers to the 10th ICCE International Conference. (1975). Brighton, England: International Council on Correspondence Education.

Correspondence education: Dynamic and diversified: Vol. 2, The proceedings with the additional papers. (1978). New Delhi: International Council on Correspondence Education.

Learning at a distance: A world perspective. (1982). Edmonton, AB: Athabasca University/International Council on Correspondence Education.

ICDE conference file: 13th World Conference [Microfiche]. (1985). Melbourne: International Council of Distance Education.

Developing distance education: Papers submitted to the 14th World Conference. (1988). Oslo: International Council for Distance Education.

Distance education: Development and access. (1990). Caracas: International Council for Distance Education.

La educacion a distancia: Desarrollo y apertura. (1990). Caracas: International Council for Distance Education.

Distance education for the twenty-first century: Selected papers from the 16th World Conference of the International Council for Distance Education. (1993). Bangkok: International Council for Distance Education.

One world many voices: Quality in open and distance learning. Selected papers from the 17th World Conference of the International Council for Distance Education. (1995). Birmingham, England: International Council for Distance Education.

The new learning environment: A global perspective [CD-ROM]. (1997). State College, PA: International Council for Distance Education.

The new educational frontier: Teaching and learning in a networked world [CD-ROM]. (1999). Vienna: International Council for Distance Education.

The future of learning—Learning for the future: Shaping the transition. [CD-ROM]. (2001). Düsseldorf, Germany: International Council for Distance Education.

Other Sources

Balbir, J. (1969). Welcoming address. In *Proceedings of the Eighth International Conference of the International Council on Correspondence Education* (pp. 1–4). Paris: International Council for Correspondence Education.

Bittner, W. S., & Mallory, H. F. (1933). *University teaching by mail: A survey of correspondence instruction conducted by American universities.* New York: Macmillan.

Broady, K. O. (1938). Minutes of first general meeting. In *Report of the First International Conference on Correspondence Education* (p. 10). Victoria, BC: Department of Education, Victoria, BC.

Broady, K. O. (1948a). Foreword. In *Proceedings of the Second International Conference on Correspondence Education* (pp. 1–2). Lincoln, NE: The University of Nebraska University Extension Division.

Broady, K. O. (1948b). The unfinished business of the First International Conference. In *Proceedings of the Second International Conference on Correspondence Education* (pp. 89–96). Lincoln, NE: The University of Nebraska University Extension Division.

Buck, G. J. (1948). The plan of the second conference. In *Proceedings of the Second International Conference on Correspondence Education* (pp. 97–101). Lincoln, NE: The University of Nebraska University Extension Division.

Buck, G. J. (1957). President's report. In G. J. Buck (Ed.), *Record of proceedings: The Fifth International Conference of the International Council on Correspondence Education: A manual on correspondence education* (pp. 30–34). Banff, AB: Banff School of Fine Arts.

Bunker, E. L. (1998a). *An historical analysis of a distance education forum: The International Council for Distance Education world conference proceedings, 1938 to 1995.* Unpublished doctoral dissertation, The Pennsylvania State University, State College.

Bunker, E. L. (1998b). Gaining perspective for the future of distance education from early leaders. *American Journal of Distance Education, 12*(2), 46–53.

Butchers, A. G. (1938). Report of research committee. In *Report of the First International Conference on Correspondence Education* (pp. 221–226). Victoria, BC: Department of Education, Victoria, BC.

Childs, G. (1969). Committee on research. Reports from chairmen of standing committees. In *Proceedings of the Eighth International Conference of the International Council on Correspondence Education* (pp. 40–49). Paris: International Council for Correspondence Education.

Daniel, J. S., Stroud, M. A., & Thompson, J. R. (1982a). Preface. In *International Council for Distance Education 1982 Conference Report and Hand book* (p. 4). Edmonton, AB: Athabasca University/International Council for Distance Education.

Daniel, J. S., Stroud, M. A., & Thompson, J. R. (1982b). Preface. In *Learning at a distance: A world perspective* (pp. 5–6). Edmonton, AB: Athabasca University/International Council for Correspondence Education.

Daniel, J. S., Stroud, M. A., & Thompson, J. R. (1982c). The process of learning at a distance: Recent research and developments. In *Learning at a distance: A world perspective* (pp. 86–87). Edmonton, AB: Athabasca University/International Council for Correspondence Education.

Drolet, J. C. (1982). *Evaluation of the Seaside Health Education Conferences and Nutrition Education Training Programs in the Oregon School Systems.* Unpublished doctoral dissertation, University of Oregon, Eugene.

Elton, L. (1983). Conferences: Making a good thing rather better? *British Journal of Educational Technology, 3*(14) 200–215.

Erdos, R. (1969). President's report. In *Proceedings of the Eighth International Conference of the International Council on Correspondence Education* (pp. 13–16). Paris: International Council on Correspondence Education.

Garvey, W., Lin, N., Nelson, C. E., & Tomita, K. (1979). Research studies in patterns of scientific communication: II. The role of the national meeting in scientific and technical communication. *Communication: The essence of science* (184–224). Oxford: Pergamon Press.

Gibson, J. W. (1938). Announcement to delegates. In *Report of the First International Conference on Correspondence Education* (pp. 43–44). Victoria, BC: Department of Education, Victoria, BC.

Griffith, B. C., & Garvey, W. D. (1966). The national scientific meeting in psychology as a changing social system. *American Behavioral Scientist, 9*(6), 3–8.

Granholm, G. W., & Ljoså, E. (Eds.). (1975). Introduction. In *The system of distance education: Vol. 1. Papers to the 10th ICCE International Conference* (p. 6). Brighton, England: International Council on Correspondence Education.

Haight, R. C. (1938). Foreword. In *Report of the First International Conference on Correspondence Education* (pp. 8–9). Victoria, BC: Department of Education, Victoria, BC.

Hinckley, G. B. (1984, July). The faith of the pioneers. *Ensign.* [Church of Jesus Christ of Latter-day Saints].

International Council for Distance Education (1985). *Flexible designs for learning: Report of the Thirteenth World Conference of ICDE.* Melbourne: International Council for Distance Education.

International Council for Distance Education. (2000). *The future of learning—Learning for the future: Shaping the transition.* Pre-conference publicity for the Twentieth World Conference on Open Learning and Distance Education. Düsseldorf, Germany: International Council for Distance Education.

Johnson, H. C. (n.d.). *Every student his own historian: A brief guide to inquiring historically.* Unpublished manuscript, Pennsylvania State University, State College.

MacKenzie, O., Christensen, E. L., & Rigby, P. H. (1968). *Correspondence instruction in the United States.* New York: McGraw-Hill.

Mann, T. (1965). Introduction. In H. Hesse, *Demian.* New York: Harper & Row.

Marriott, S. (1981). *A backstairs to a degree: Demands for an open university in late Victorian England.* Leeds, England: Leeds Studies in Adult and Continuing Education.

Merwin, E. R., & Lowdon, J. (Eds.). (1948). *Pre-conference bulletin: International Conference on Correspondence Education.* Lincoln, NE: Extension Division of the University of Nebraska.

Moore, M. G. (1990). Introduction: Background and overview of contemporary American distance education. In Moore, M. G. (Ed.) *Contemporary issues in American distance education* (p. xiv). Oxford: Pergamon Press.

Moore, M. G. (1991). International aspects of independent study. In *The foundations of American distance education: A century of collegiate correspondence study.* Dubuque, IA: Kendall/Hunt.

Moore, M. G., & Kearsley, G. (1996). *Distance education: A systems view.* Belmont, CA: Wadsworth.

Moore, V. A. (1961). President's report. In *Proceedings of the Sixth International Conference on Correspondence Education* (pp. 27–29). Gearhart, Oregon: General Extension Division, Oregon State System of Higher Education.

Noffsinger, J. S. (1926). *Correspondence schools, lyceums, chautauquas.* New York: Macmillan.

Perry, W. (1977). *The open university.* San Francisco: Jossey-Bass.

Petry, G. H. (1981). A history and analysis of scholarly papers presented at the seven Academic Finance Associations from 1939 through 1980. *Financial Management 19*(2), 93–104.

Pittman, V. V. (1996). Harper's headaches: Early policy issues in collegiate correspondence study. In B. S. Duning, & V. V. Pittman, (Eds.), *Distance education symposium 3: Policy and administration.* (ACSDE Research Monograph No. 11). University Park, PA: American Center for the Study of Distance Education.

Pittman, V. V. (1998). Low-key leadership: Collegiate correspondence study and "campus equivalence." *American Journal of Distance Education, 12*(2), 36–45.

Porter, J. E. (1986). Intertextuality and the discourse community. *Rhetoric Review*, 5(1), 34–47.

Porter, J. E. (1992). *Audience and rhetoric: An archaeological composition of the discourse community.* Englewood Cliffs, NJ: Prentice Hall.

International Council for Distance Education. (1988). *Programme: Developing distance education: 14th World Conference on Distance Education* (p. 33). Oslo, Norway, 9–16 August, 1988.

Rose, A. (1992, September/October). Conferences in the 1990s: How far have we really come? *Adult Learning* p. 10.

Rosenfeld, L. B., Stacks, D. W., & Hickson, M. (1990). Perceptions of professional associations: Part 2. Role and impact of professional outlets on faculty development. *Communication Education, 38*(3), 171–180.

Scriven, B., Lundin, R., & Ryan, Y. (1993a). Preface. In *Distance education for the twenty-first century: Selected papers from the 16th World Conference of the International Council for Distance Education* (pp. xi–xii). Bangkok: International Council for Distance Education.

Scriven, B., Lundin, R., & Yoni Ryan, Y. (1993b). Commentary: Chapter 5—distance education—theory and research. In *Distance education for the twenty-first century: Selected papers from the 16th World Conference of the International Council for Distance Education* (pp. 322–323). Bangkok: International Council for Distance Education.

Sewart, D. (1990). Preface. In *Distance education: Development and access* (pp. 7–8). Caracas: International Council for Distance Education.

Sherow. S., & Wedemeyer, C. A. (1990). Origins of distance education in the United States. In D. R. Garrison, & D. Shale, (Eds.), *Education at a distance: From issues to practice* (pp. 7–22). Malabar, FL: Robert E. Krieger Publishing Co.

Singh, B. (1972). The 9th ICCE World Conference. In *Current issues and approaches in distance education. The proceedings of the Ninth World Conference of the International Council on Correspondence Education* (pp. 1–3). Warrenton, Virginia: International Council on Correspondence Education.

Smith, K. C. (1985a). Preface. In *A flexible design for learning: Report of the Thirteenth World Conference of ICDE* (p. 1). Melbourne: International Council for Distance Education.

Smith, K. C. (1985b). Program report. In *A flexible design for learning: Report of the Thirteenth World Conference of ICDE* (p. 42). Melbourne: International Council for Distance Education.

Thrush, J. P. (1996). *A model for assessing professional development: An empirical evaluation of a regional foreign language conference* (p. 59). Unpublished doctoral dissertation, University of Wisconsin, Madison.

Tootelian, D. H., Bush, R. F., & Stern, B. L. (1992). Business educators' use of conferences, journals, and textbooks. *Journal of Education for Business, 67*(6), 366–370.

Tritsch, L. (1991). A look back on the Seaside Conference. *Journal of Health Education, 22*(2), 70–84.

Watkins, B. L., & Wright, S. J. (1991). *The foundations of American distance education: A century of collegiate correspondence study.* Dubuque, IA: Kendall/Hunt.

Wedemeyer, C. A. (1965). Correspondence education in the world of today. A general survey of the field: Ideas, principles, trends, new developments. In *Proceedings of the Seventh International Conference of the International Council on Correspondence Education* (pp. 8–18). Stockholm: International Council on Correspondence Education.

Young, D. (1978). The ICCE president's preface. In *Correspondence education: Dynamic and diversified: Vol. 1. The advance papers* (pp. 7–8). New Delhi: International Council for Correspondence Education.

Young, W. (1953). History of the International Conference on Correspondence Education pp.15–18. In *Proceedings: Fourth International Conference on Correspondence Education.* State College, PA: Pennsylvania State College General Extension Services.

5

Organizational Models in Higher Education, Past and Future

Donald E. Hanna
University of Wisconsin-Extension
dehanna@facstaff.wisc.edu

DISTANCE EDUCATION, EMERGING ORGANIZATIONAL MODELS, AND CHANGE

Distance education in the current educational environment is inevitably about changing existing organizational practices through the development of new structural, pedagogical, and technological models. This has always been true, as distance education programs and processes departed from those used in more traditional instructional settings; however, until recently the changes that distance education brought were not transformational changes in universities but rather procedural and process changes designed to deliver existing programs, courses, and services.

Schlecty (1997) describes three basic forms of organizational change:

1. Procedural change, which has to do with altering how organizational tasks are accomplished.
2. Technological change, which consists of changing the means by which the job is done.
3. Structural and cultural (systemic) change, which consists of changing the nature of the work itself and reorienting its purpose.

This chapter addresses emerging distance education organizational models in relation to each of these forms in ways that elucidate future directions in the field.

There are many reasons why the move toward distance education is inextricably linked with changing organization processes and procedures as well as developing new organizational models. Demand for learning across the globe is increasing as national economies become increasingly based on knowledge and the pace of technological change continues to accelerate. Rapidly growing and increasingly youthful populations in many areas of the world are also fueling pressures on higher education institutions to respond in new and creative ways. In all countries, continuous learning for adults is becoming essential as jobs change and entire career tracks are eliminated and new ones develop. Access to education from any location, at any time, for any age, and in many ways is critical for individual and collective well-being. Democratization also requires an educated populace, providing further pressure upon governments to increase educational opportunity for all. Clearly, educational access at all levels and in all contexts globally is more important than ever before, and it is no exaggeration to suggest that it is an element of strategic global positioning within societies and economies.

Along with this elevated importance has come increasing pressure on traditional universities to be creative and innovative in providing the maximum access possible and to provide this access as efficiently as possible. Reductions in public subsidies for higher education are forcing even traditional universities to search for new ways of organizing and paying for instructional programs that depend on new organizational assumptions, models, and strategies for providing not only distance learning but also campus-based learning.

CHANGING ORGANIZATIONAL CONTEXTS AND STRATEGIES

The distinction between on-campus learning and distance learning is blurring at warp speed as campus residence halls are wired, wireless access to the Internet is created, classes with both on-campus and off-campus students are organized through computer conferencing, and multiple formats for learning are provided as options to more and more students. Although the value of campus-based classroom learning and socialization, especially for young people preparing for their lives as adults, will be important long into the future, even a cursory look at how universities are organizing to provide this learning shows a dramatic departure from past educational practices.

The Extended Traditional University

Recent trends and studies in the United States indicate that learners, especially adults, expect institutions of higher education to be responsive to their individual needs, which increasingly means providing course schedules and formats that are convenient, easily accessed, and independent of fixed times and locations (Dillman, Christenson, Salant, & Warner, 1995; Mayadas, 2001; Primary Research Group, 1997, 1998, 1999). Where distance learning programs previously were operated largely at the margins of traditional universities and were focused almost exclusively on meeting the needs of adult students, the changing context for learning has forced a rethinking of institutional strategies even among traditional universities (Dolence, Norris, & Society for College and University Planning, 1995; Graves, 1997; Hall, 1995; Hanna, 1998, 2000c; Rowley, Lujan, & Dolence, 1997, 1998; Van Dusen, 1997). Universities have developed increasingly sophisticated units charged with leading change in order to address new needs and new markets. Such change for the most part has not been transformational but rather concerned largely with changing procedures and processes to better serve new audiences. The changes have been highly entrepreneurial, market oriented, and responsive to these growing clienteles. A variety of programming strategies have been tested, including duplication, replication, diversification, niche programming and technologies, and aggregation (see Hanna, 2000b).

Distance Education/Technology-Based Universities

The environment for higher education across the globe is increasingly competitive, turbulent, and unsettled, and, as Hannan and Freeman (1989) note, uncertain, volatile environments support diverse organizational forms. Kaufman (1991) indicates that the increase in diversity of organizational forms is, in and of itself, a critical factor adding further to the complexity of the environment over time. Indeed, over the past 30 years, new institutional forms of higher education have emerged. These range from smaller national universities formed in many countries around independent or distance education teaching strategies to mega-universities[1] with enrollments of more than 100,000 students learning at a distance (Daniel, 1996). In many countries around the world, these large-scale mega-universities organized around distance learning are a fundamental component of national economic development and educational strategies.

Smaller institutions of this type in the United States include Empire State University, Thomas Edison State University in New Jersey, and the College of Lifelong Learning in New Hampshire. Hanna (2000c) describes these new universities as falling within the category of distance education/technology-based universities, and these are but one of the organizational forms that have emerged in response to new and expanded needs and new opportunities. In this context, Kaufman (1991) suggests that, just as nature abhors a vacuum, organizations abhor uncertainty. The new programming opportunities of this volatile environment result in ever-increasing forms of competition, at the same time producing responses from existing universities that attempt to minimize the uncertainty created by new and emerging models. In this way, the door has opened to an entirely new form of university, one that operates in the business world, including representation on Wall Street.

For-Profit Universities

During the past several decades, a small number of for-profit universities[2] have been established in order to take advantage of lucrative 'high-end' learning "markets" created by the accelerating pace of change and the changing structure of the global economy (Hanna, 2000d). These relatively new universities are generally founded by entrepreneurial leaders (see Sperling, 2000), often frustrated by a lack of responsiveness and change in traditional universities and motivated in part by the opportunity to generate revenue. Some of these new universities are less than three years old.

Although the for-profit financial model might appear to be technologically or culturally transformational, the actual instructional models and strategies utilized by these for-profit institutions are often quite conventional, relying upon face-to-face instruction and relatively traditional pedagogical processes and strategies. Most of the for-profit universities are now adding online programs, but enrollments in these programs are generally quite small, in contrast to their face-to-face classroom enrollments. In addition, only a few for-profit universities (Jones International University, Concord University, and Cardean University) have been organized exclusively around making programs available only on the Internet, and to date the degree-seeking student enrollment in all of these "online universities" combined may not approach five figures, a relatively small blip on the radar screen of higher education.

Strategic Alliances

Collaborations or strategic partnerships that bring together two or more universities are also being formed to increase the competitive positions of existing universities. In a growing number of cases, university-business strategic alliances are being formed to build organizational

---

[1]Examples of mega-universities are the United Kingdom Open University, the China TV University System, the Indira Ghandhi Open University (India), the Universitas Terbuka (Indonesia), the Payame Noor University (Iran), the Korea National Open University, the University of South Africa, the Centre National d'Ensiegnement a Distance (France), the Universidad Nacional de Educacion (Spain), the Sukhothai Thammathirat Open University (Thailand), and Anadolu University (Turkey).

[2]Examples of these for profit universities include the University of Phoenix, DeVry University, Strayer University, Capella University, Argosy University, and Walden University.

capacity to deliver new services and programs and to reach new audiences. These new collaborations and alliances have many different forms and involve blending organizational missions, goals, programs, capabilities, and personnel to create new learning strategies and opportunities. Kaufman (1991) suggests that alliances are effective in times of complexity and competition in at least three ways: first, they spread risk; second, they enable the organization to incorporate new ideas; and third, they help the organization to bypass cultural prohibitions against previously heretical ideas or practices.

The first major examples of formal strategic alliances in distance learning are relatively recent and were generally formed between organizations (university to university or university to business) in a single country. National Technological University (NTU) in the United States, founded in 1982 as a separate degree-granting institution working in partnership with other major institutions to offer degrees in engineering, is an excellent early example of this type of alliance. NTU was preceded in organization by American Association for Multimedia Continuing Education for Engineers (AAMCEE), a group of engineering schools that collaboratively marketed noncredit engineering courses.

Such alliances are now becoming global in nature. One example is Universitas 21 (http://www.universitas.edu.au/), an alliance of leading universities from Asia, Australia, the United Kingdom, and North America. Universitas 21 has begun to form its own strategic alliances, entering into agreements first with Murdoch Corporation and more recently with Thomson Learning. Although these types of international alliances appear impressive on the surface, they have yet to actually organize programs, courses, or services beyond those provided by their members, and whether or not they add value in the long-run is very much open to question. For one thing, they face a major challenge: overcoming the significant differences in culture, operational understandings, and educational practices among their members and arriving at a common vision, mission, and direction.

Western Governors University is another example of a strategic alliance designed to gain market advantage and serve students more effectively. Originally formed by the governers of the western states in 1996 as a clearinghouse and marketing vehicle for distance learning courses for universities throughout the West, WGU quickly learned that something more was needed to attract both partners and students. The formation of WGU was in one sense a call to arms for traditional universities in the West to expand their own distance learning programs aggressively, which is what in fact happened. Western Governors University has more recently selected as a core programmatic feature the concept of competency-based degrees, enabling it to occupy a relatively unfilled programming niche in distance learning. Once a competency-based degree was designed and developed, WGU and its partners set about the task of matching the course offerings of partner institutions to each required degree program competency so that students could progress toward the WGU degree.

Also becoming prevalent are business-university alliances, such as UNext.com, a business that has developed its own university, Cardean University, and established partnerships with a number of universities to offer online courses to adult students. In another type of alliance, a university and company might develop an agreement according to which the university provides online course content and the company provides the online web-based platforms for computer conferencing, course management, and content delivery (First Class, TopClass, WebCT, Blackboard, e-Education, and e-College are examples of such alliances). These platforms have been developed with many different features, and they relieve universities of significant development and implementation costs.

In this competitive environment, with the pace of change accelerating, with learners becoming more knowledgeable and sophisticated, with greater diversity and numbers of organizations coming into existence, and with the high cost of investing in new technologies, strategic planning and careful organizational development in distance education are increasingly critical.

Further, an understanding of learning models and pedagogical choices and the academic, financial, and marketing implications of these choices is essential.

EVOLVING LEARNING MODELS AND CONCEPTS
OF DISTANCE EDUCATION

Until just a few years ago, distance education was conceptualized as involving a teacher (T) interacting asynchronously (A) with a single student (S). Separated by distance, the teacher and student engaged in a structured two-way exchange (Keegan, 1988, 1993; Moore, 1973; Moore & Kearsley, 1996; Peters & Keegan, 1994) mediated by print and electronic technologies (T:A:S:1>1). Wedemeyer (1981) emphasized the independence of learner action within this model, and Keegan (1990) specifically excluded the learning group as a primary context for distance education learning and teaching, although he acknowledged the possibility of "occasional meetings for didactic and social purposes" (p. 44). This model of learning was adopted in university correspondence or independent learning courses in the United States at the turn of the 20th century and was expanded dramatically with the development of open universities in the latter half of the century. In the United Kingdom, Europe, Australia, New Zealand, and many other countries, print-based materials, audiocassettes, and other learning resources were used to create a common framework for learners to access university courses and degree programs at times and schedules convenient to leamens.

Over the past two decades, a large number of countries, especially those with higher education systems unable to meet the burgeoning demand created by rapidly growing populations and economic circumstances, have responded to the demand by creating open universities based on the independent learner model. As already noted, many of these universities have very large enrollments, in the hundreds of thousands (Daniel, 1996). This development led Peters to suggest that distance education could be described as an industrial form of education, where mass distribution, standardization, division of labor, and assembly-line procedures were defining characteristics (Peters & Keegan, 1994). Referring to the development of national open universities, Evans (1999) called these focused efforts "single-mode" distance teaching universities, in contrast to single-mode campus-based universities or the mixed-mode universities described by Rumble (1986).

In the United States, Thomas Edison (New Jersey) and Empire State (New York) were created based on the concept of offering degrees using the T:A:S:1>1 model. Until the past decade or two, other more established universities in the United States offered courses but usually not full degrees using this model. In Australia and New Zealand, on the other hand, many campus-based universities long ago started offering full degree programs at a distance using the T:A:S:1>1 model; these universities were known as dual-mode institutions, reflecting the fact that they offered degrees both on-campus and at a distance. The term *dual-mode* has gradually been supplanted in Australia by *flexible learning*,[3] but the structures of the universities have remained largely unchanged (Evans, 1999). From a policy perspective, this model fit well within traditional universities in that it involved little change in curriculum, placed minimal demands on faculty, and could be budgeted in such a way as to be self-sufficient. The model relies upon intrinsic independent learner motivation for success (Holmberg, 1989, p. 189; Sewart, Keegan, & Holmberg, 1983, p. 168). Course completion rates for this model

---

[3]For example, the University of Wollengong defines flexible learning as allowing the duration and intensity, place, method, and delivery medium of the instruction to reflect the learning objectives, the needs of the student, the subject and course requirements, and the judgement of the teacher (http://cedir.uow.edu.au/NCODE/info/definitions.html#flexdef).

have consistently been quite low, and for the individual learner, this represents a serious disadvantage. Some scholars have argued that low completion rates occur because adults have targeted learning goals other than course and degree completion (Wedemeyer, 1981, p. 556). However, it is also the case that, from a program financial perspective, low course completion rates have resulted in greater institutional profit per student served, and such financial reinforcement of negative outcomes acts as an unfortunate disincentive to rectify this weakness of the model.

In a more recent type of distance education program, a teacher (T) is connected synchronously (S) with students S^2 in remote locations (T:S:S^2:1>S^2). The most common form, prevalent in the United States, involves connecting a teacher with off-campus learners via audio-conferencing, video-conferencing, or computer-conferencing at scheduled times. Very often, especially when video connections are used, students still travel to a central location, such as a community site or an educational center, to access the technology and to meet with other students. Yet this requirement is rapidly changing as systems become more robust in their connective capabilities and technology access in homes and businesses improves.

Both of these traditionally structured types of distance education and the associated pedagogical strategies are heavily dependent on teacher-directed instructional goals and activities and have become quite limiting as the Internet and the World Wide Web have developed. Indeed, they still largely represent Schlecty's first dimension of change, that of the adoption of procedural changes that alter how the task of teaching is accomplished. Although the T:S:S^2:1>S^2 model has been effective in addressing the issues of completion rates and course comparability, its requirement that students meet together in real time presents a serious impediment for many busy adult students.

A third set of distance education models are currently being developed. In these models, students are dynamically connected through the Internet and other advanced technologies with each other, with faculty mentors, and with institutional academic support structures in ways not imagined just a few years ago, and the available choices regarding pedagogy, technology, culture, and strategy are becoming increasingly complex and blurred. Students are provided with continuous and regular opportunities to interact with each other and with the teacher but to do so asynchronously. The teacher (T) is connected asynchronously (A) with students (S^2) who are able to interact with both the teacher and with other students around collaborative discussions, assignments, and team projects (T:A:S^2:1>S^2). The Sloan Foundation has provided millions of dollars of financing of web-based online instruction to almost 50 universities and colleges throughout the 1990s. It is worth noting, however, that the foundation funds only those institutions whose online programs do not require synchronous interaction among students.

In these emerging models, what is on-campus and what is off-campus in most traditional institutions is growing more difficult to discern, and independent learning is increasingly mixed with collaborative learning (Hanna, 2000c). Technologies are also rapidly converging, so that video, audio, and print are all coming together through the Web in support of learning, and access to these advanced technologies is growing (Dede, 2000; Graves, 1997). Even today, however, whether learners in online Web-based courses are required to interact only with their instructors or also with other learners is a point of distinction between instructors and between organizational models that are in place or under development at many universities (Hanna, Glowacki-Dudka, & Conceição-Runlee, 2000). In fact, this may emerge as a singular point of distinction between degree programs and courses offered at a distance, which otherwise will likely become more and more similar from one institution to another in the areas of technology employed, modes of access, services provided, and content delivered.

These new pedagogical frameworks and organizational models have come into prominence in concert with the development and application of constructivist learning theory in higher education (Hanna, 2000a; Winn, 1997). What constructivist principles (Lambert et al., 1995, pp. 17–18.) suggest is that, to create effective learning environments, the main focus, rather than being on the knowledge, teaching performance, and competence of the teacher, should be on fostering the engagement of the student with both the instructional content and with other students, creating opportunities inside and outside of the "classroom" to learn and to demonstrate or model what has been learned, and using assessment strategies that enable the growth and development of the learner in more personally meaningful and measurable ways. In a sense, learning changes from being the product of an "industrial process of mass distribution of knowledge" to becoming a process whereby each learner's need for knowledge is addressed through customized and highly personal strategies initiated by the learner with assistance from and in consultation with the teacher.

TECHNOLOGICAL MODELS

Schlecty's (1997) second major process for change involves changing the means by which work is accomplished. In this context, the changes in distance education practice have been dramatic if not profound. For most of the 20th century, distance education involved pen and paper, the typewriter, and the postal service, which provided the sole link between the individual instructor and the individual student. Electronic technologies have increasingly changed the interaction between instructor and student. With the development of radio and then television, it became possible to transmit educational courses, programs, and content widely using these mass media distribution channels. More recently, satellite distribution enabled even broader access to university courses, and the emergence of teleconferencing software, which allows many people to be connected together simultaneously, added to the power of these technologies by enabling interaction between and among students and teachers. Some universities developed an electronic technological framework for their distance education programs, investing heavily in expensive satellite equipment (e.g., University of Alaska, Chico State University, and Old Dominion University), audioconferencing equipment (University of Wisconsin), electronic blackboards (University of Illinois), and computers (New Jersey Institute of Technology).

However, none of these technologies has fundamentally challenged the basic learning models of universities. Generally, they have been used to enable universities to do what they were already doing but more expansively and more efficiently rather than to change radically either the content or the instructional processes employed. Even when two-way interactive video was developed, the first models, such as those employed at Ohio University and at Washington State University in the mid-1980s, were organized around the principle of not requiring faculty members to adjust their teaching in any way. Instead, the model was intended simply to extend what the faculty member was already doing to new sites and to more students. More recent video systems enable or sometimes require the faculty member to manage the technology but still rely on the faculty member to act as content distributor in the same way as the traditional lecture does.

However, the development and deployment of the Internet has radically altered the technological environment for distance learning, opening up many new possibilities for connecting learners and teachers, as noted in the previous section. The Internet has made possible not only the World Wide Web, a powerful new way of distributing and sharing knowledge globally, but also new ways of creating virtual interactions among people. These interactions began with simple e-mail, added power with the growth of listservs, and have since evolved into numerous strategies for creating powerful new opportunities for online interaction. While there is considerable debate about whether the Internet is a "disruptive" or sustaining technology in regard to higher education,[4] there is little disagreement that its arrival has opened up many new possibilities for delivering education.

New universities have been established and existing universities have made adaptations to take advantage of new computer-mediated conferencing systems and the emergence of the Web to enable asynchronous and synchronous interaction among students and the teacher. The goal of these technology-based approaches to learning is to minimize the physical and psychological separation of the learner from the instructor. The verdict is still out, however, about how much teaching and learning using online Web-based platforms will change either the process or the strategies for learning at a distance.

Early adopters are attempting to document or demonstrate the financial advantages of online instruction. The Sloan Foundation has funded numerous venues for discussing the challenge of "scaling up" or serving more students at less cost (than through face-to-face courses) and has funded a number of universities with the goal of demonstrating the greater efficiency of online instruction. In a recent online forum hosted by the *Chronicle of Higher Education*, entitled "Is Anyone Making Money on Distance Education?" Frank Mayadas (2001), Sloan's program officer, indicates that Sloan expects "online education to definitely become less expensive than campus education, though not by a very large amount (maybe 20% less)." Karelis (1999), formerly director of the Fund for the Improvement of Postsecondary Education, argues that capital-intensive technology-mediated instruction will be more expensive unless enrollments become very large and that in order for enrollments to become large, certain changes in accepted practice must be made, such as employing lower-paid teaching assistants, graduate assistants, and "people whose academic preparation does not qualify them for faculty positions" to handle classroom interaction and content delivery while relying on faculty members for content development and overall guidance and coordination. Unfortunately, such shifts in focus are directly counter to some of the emerging pedagogical models designed to link faculty with students more interactively in the construction of knowledge. Today, being connected is within the realm of possibility for learners separated by distance, and connection with others and to increasingly sophisticated sources of content is becoming central to the learning process.

However, technology is interjected into the learning process even as it makes the connection between the student and the teacher possible across distance. Whether audio, video, text, or a combination of all three basic means of communication, the technology chosen influences to a great extent what can and cannot be done in the learning environment. Its presence is always a "fourth force" in the classroom, the other three forces being the content to be learned, the teacher, and the student. For many reasons, this fourth force has until recently been employed primarily to extend the teacher's reach rather than to empower the student, a concept that is transformational and involves radically changing assumptions about learning and teaching.

---

[4]See L. Armstrong (2000) for an interesting argument that distance learning is a "disruptive" technology for higher education. Drawing from *The Innovator's Dilemma* by Clayton Christensen, Armstrong describes new technologies as either sustaining or disruptive to an industry group. "A sustaining technology enables an industry to improve existing products. A disruptive technology plays a more dramatic role. Disruptive technologies initially lead to "inferior" products by the usual standards of the industry, but offer a markedly different set of benefits and a lower cost structure. Initially, customers and producers in the established market reject the new technology as inadequate. However, new companies pick up this technology and apply it to emerging markets viewed as unimportant by the mainstream. Soon demand for the new disruptive technology in these emerging markets drives and enables improvements to it until it reaches a quality level that meets the expectations of the mainstream market. At this point, mainstream customers perceive the disruptive technology as providing a superior product, because it brings additional benefits compared to the established technology. Given its lower cost structure, the disruptive technology then rapidly displaces the established products, and leads to revolutionary change in the industry."

TRANSFORMATIONAL CHANGE AND ORGANIZATIONAL MODELS

Understanding the complex dynamics of cultural values, conflict, and organizational change in universities is critical to building a framework for analyzing issues in distance education. Bergquist (1992), writing about traditional campus-based universities, characterizes most as involving a mix of four primary internal cultures interacting with each other in different ways depending on the mission, programs, and historical framework of the specific institution. The four internal cultures described by Bergquist are as follows:

1. *The managerial culture* finds meaning in the organization of work and conceives of the institution's enterprise as the inculcation of specific knowledge, skills, and attitudes in students to help them become successful and responsible citizens.
2. *The developmental culture* finds meaning in furthering the personal and professional growth of all members of the collegiate community, defined as the people are part of the campus environment.
3. *The negotiating culture* is concerned with and responsible for establishing and executing equitable and egalitarian policies and procedures for the distribution of resources and benefits in the institution.
4. *The collegial culture*, which in most cases is the core of the institution, is sustained primarily by faculty members. It finds meaning in the academic disciplines. It values faculty research, scholarship, teaching, and governance and wants to hold sway over the institution's most important assets—its curriculum and its faculty.

In adapting Bergquist's work to be more applicable to emerging organizational models and university cultures, Hanna (2000c) introduces a fifth important culture that is emerging as a powerful force in universities worldwide—the *entrepreneurial culture*. The entrepreneurial culture values the ability to change and to change quickly; respond to market forces; connect with and generate support from external audiences and constituencies; and introduce new ideas, programs, delivery mechanisms, and goals and purposes into the other four cultures described by Bergquist.

McNay (1995) frames organizational options differently, suggesting that four dominant cultures within universities have been in major transition over the past decade. These four cultures—the collegium, bureaucracy, corporation, and enterprise—are all present in most universities, but McNay notes that in many universities there has been a general evolution toward the enterprise model.

As this chapter illustrates, dramatic changes in higher education are underway, and distance education programs and technologies are very often major drivers of this change. These changes are more than simple procedural changes or ways of conducting business; they represent fundamental shifts in values, assumptions, and missions and will result in new cultural assumptions and understandings over time.

Table 5-1 presents some of the ways that changing values and mission may change decision-making and leadership in the future. Of particular note is the culture's orientation to change. Musselwhite (2000) has developed an instrument called the Change Style Indicator, which measures individual preferences toward change (see also the Discovery Learning Web site, http://www.discoverylearning.net). The Change Style Indicator provides feedback to individuals using a continuum from Conserver to Pragmatist to Originator. Although no clear assignment to organizational models or culture can be established yet, the data collected thus far suggest that individuals in enterprises (businesses, manufacturing, and for-profit organizations) tend to be stronger originators that those in government, education, and non-profit organizations. As universities develop enterprise orientations, their comfort in originating new institutional directions, programs, and innovations should grow.

TABLE 5.1
The Changing Cultures of Higher Education

	Collegial	Managerial	Entrepreneurial
Orientation to change	Conservers	Pragmatists	Originators
Leadership	Stewardship	Preservation	Visionary
Values	Faculty, program	Administrative efficiency	Client-oriented
Decision-making	Restricted, shared internal	Vertical, top-down	Horizontal, shared with stakeholders
Support structures	Program-driven	Rule-focused	Learner-focused
Key messages	Quality	Efficiency	Market-driven
Communication strategies	Internal	Vertical, formal	External/internal, horizontal, informal
Systems and resources	Duplicated according to need	Stable, efficient, and pre-organized	Evolving "as needed"
Key messages	Stick together	Don't rock the boat	Seize the day
Alliances	Value not easily recognized	Unnecessary	Sought out and implemented
Organizational features	Specialized	Segmented and vertical	Integrated and cross-functional
Budgets	Stable, priority programs	Tightly controlled	Fluid, opportunity seeking
Actions	Evolutionary	Targeted	Revolutionary
New Programs	Complement existing programs	Fit existing structures	Make new markets or force new structures
Competition	Avoid competition	Minimize competition through regulation	Exploit competitive advantage
Strategies	Improve quality	Improve efficiency	Establish new market "niches"
Faculty and staff values	Independence	Authority and predictability	Collaboration
Rewards	Individual	Functional	Organizational

CONCLUSION

Higher education in general has been primarily concerned with the education of young adults in residential settings rather than with distance learning programs primarily organized through stable correspondence programs. In both of these contexts, however, educational life has been relatively predictable. Change was viewed, as Schwahn and Spady (1998) suggest, as a destination, an event, that, although episodic in nature, was quite predictable. Major change has been viewed within the academy as either unnecessary or risky, but this orientation is likely to change as the environment for education becomes more volatile.

Schlecty (1997) stated:

> Until recently, structural and cultural change has been viewed by many as largely beyond the direct control of leaders and planners. Therefore, rather than asking, How can organizations be reoriented so that they do new things and serve new ends? leaders and planners have asked, How can organizations be made to serve the ends they now serve more efficiently? and, How can organizations do the jobs they now do better? Given these latter questions, culture and structure are likely to be viewed as impediments to change, rather than as the content that must be changed.

And from another perspective more critical to change in the current culture and structure of higher education, emerging organizational, pedagogical, and technological models of distance education will continue to be threatening to the core of higher education.

Universities with active distance learning programs are now operating in a more competitive and business-like environment than ever before. In many cases, distance learning programs are charged with providing leadership for new ideas, approaches, and models and with leading organizational change. The leaders of these programs are much more likely to view change as a journey and to plan processes into the institution that assist in assessing options and implementing new program directions. According to Schwahn and Spady (1998), change is a continuous process, highly chaotic in nature, but necessary for organizational renewal and even survival. Even when change is viewed as "disruptive to the existing order," as David Noble and others have argued (Armstrong, 2000; Noble, 1998; Winner, 1998), there is no question that distance learning has the potential to radically transform educational practice in higher education.

This chapter is intended to provide the reader with an understanding of the fundamental issues and concepts concerning the historical development of distance learning within higher education organizations and with a glimpse of organization models for the future. The reader may find its contents useful in interpreting the other chapters from the perspectives of teaching, learning, policy, administration, strategy, economics, and marketing.

REFERENCES

Armstrong, L. (2000). Distance learning: An academic leader's perspective on a disruptive product. *Change, 32*(6), 20–27.

Bergquist, W. H. (1992). *The four cultures of the academy: Insights and strategies for improving leadership in collegiate organizations.* San Francisco: Jossey-Bass.

Daniel, S. J. (1996). *Mega-universities and knowledge media: Technology strategies for higher education.* London: Biddles Ltd.

Dede, C. (2000). Advanced technologies and distributed learning in higher education. In D. E. Hanna (Ed.), *Higher education in an era of digital competition: Choices and challenges* (pp. 71–91). Madison, WI: Atwood Publishing.

Dillman, D. A., Christenson, J. C., Salant, P., & Warner, P. D. (1995). *What the public wants from higher education: Workforce implications from a 1995 national survey* (Technical Report 95-52). Pullman, WA: Washington State University.

Dolence, M. G., Norris, D. M., & Society for College and University Planning. (1995). *Transforming higher education: A vision for learning in the 21st century.* Ann Arbor, MI: Society for College and University Planning.

Evans, T. (1999). From dual-mode to flexible delivery: Paradoxical transitions in Australian open and distance education. *Performance-Improvement Quarterly, 12*(2), 84–95.

Graves, W. H. (1997). Adapting to the emergence of educational micro-markets. *Educom Review, 32*(5).

Hall, J. W. (1995). The revolution in electronic technology and the modern university: The convergence of means. *Educom Review, 30*(4).

Hanna, D. E. (1998). Higher education in an era of digital competition : Emerging organizational models. *Journal of Asynchronous Learning, 2*(1).

Hanna, D. E. (2000a). Approaches to learning in collegiate classrooms. In D. E. Hanna (Ed.), *Higher education in an era of digital competition: Choices and challenges* (pp. 45–70). Madison, WI: Atwood Publishing.

Hanna, D. E. (2000b). Emerging organizational models : The extended traditional university. In D. E. Hanna (Ed.), *Higher education in an era of digital competition: Choices and challenges* (pp. 92–113). Madison, WI: Atwood Publishing.

Hanna, D. E. (Ed.). (2000c). *Higher education in an era of digital competition: Choices and challenges.* Madison, WI: Atwood Publishing.

Hanna, D. E. (2000d). New players on the block: For-profit, corporate, and competency-based learning universities. In D. E. Hanna (Ed.), *Higher education in an era of digital competition: Choices and challenges* (pp. 139–164). Madison, WI: Atwood Publishing.

Hanna, D. E., Glowacki-Dudka, M., & Conceição-Runlee, S. (2000). *147 practical tips for teaching online groups: Essentials of Web-based education.* Madison, WI: Atwood Publishing.

Hannan, M. T., & Freeman, J. (1988). *Organizational ecology.* Cambridge, MA: Harvard University Press.

Holmberg, B. (1989). *Theory and practice of distance education.* New York: Routledge.

Karelis, C. (1999). *Education technology and cost control: Four models* [Online]. Available: http://www.ed.gov/offices/OPE/FIPSE/LAAP/reading.html

Kaufman, H. (1991). *Time, chance, and organizations: Natural selection in a perilous environment* (2nd ed.). Chatham, NJ: Chatham House Publishers.

Keegan, D. (1988). On defining distance education. In D. Sewart, D. Keegan, and B. Holmberg, (Eds.), *Distance education: International perspectives.* New York: Routledge, Chapman & Hall.

Keegan, D. (1990). *Foundations of distance education.* (2nd ed.). New York: Routledge.

Keegan, D. (1993). *Theoretical principles of distance education.* New York: Routledge.

Lambert, L., Walker, D., Zimmerman, D. P., Cooper, J. E., Lambert, M. D., Gardner, M. E., & Slack, P. J. F. (Eds.). (1995). *The constructivist leader.* New York: Teachers College Press.

Mayadas, F. (2001). *Is anyone making money on distance education.* [online]. Available: http//chronicle.com/

McNay, I. (1995). From the collegial academy to corporate enterprise: The changing cultures of universities. In T. Schuller (Ed.), *The changing university?* (pp. 105–115). Buckingham, England, Bristol, PA: Open University Press; Society for Research into Higher Education.

Moore, M. G. (1973). Toward a theory of independent learning and teaching. *Journal of Higher Education, 44,* 661–679.

Moore, M. G., & Kearsley, G. (1996). *Distance education: A systems view. Belmont,* CA: Wadsworth.

Musselwhite, W. C. (2000). *Change style indicator: Research and development report.* Greensboro, NC: Discovery Learning Press.

Noble, D. (1998). *Digital diploma mills* [Online]. Available: http://www.firstmonday.dk/issues/issue3_1/noble/index.html

Peters, O., & Keegan, D. (1994). *Otto Peters on distance education: The industrialization of teaching and learning.* New York: Routledge.

Primary Research Group. (1997, 1998, 1999). *The survey of distance learning programs in higher education.* New York: Primary Research Group.

Rowley, D. J., Lujan, H. D., & Dolence, M. G. (1997). *Strategic change in colleges and universities: Planning to survive and prosper.* San Francisco: Jossey-Bass.

Rowley, D. J., Lujan, H. D., & Dolence, M. G. (1998). *Strategic choices for the academy: How demand for lifelong learning will re-create higher education.* San Francisco: Jossey-Bass.

Rumble, G. (1986). *The planning and management of distance education.* London: Croom Helm.

Schlechty, P. C. (1997). *Inventing Better schools: An action plan for educational reform.* San Francisco: Jossey-Bass.

Schwahn, C. J., & Spady, W. G. (1998). *Total leaders: Applying the best future-focused change strategies to education.* Arlington, VA: American Association of School Administrators.

Sewart, D., Keegan, D., & Holmberg, B. (1983). *Distance education: International perspectives.* London; New York: Croom Helm; St. Martin's Press.

Sperling, J. G. (2000). Rebel with a cause: The entrepreneur who created the University of Phoenix and the for-profit revolution in higher education. New York: Wiley.

Van Dusen, G. C. (1997). *The virtual campus: Technology and reform in higher education.* Washington, DC: Graduate School of Education and Human Development, George Washington University.

Wedemeyer, C. A. (1981). *Learning at the back door: Reflections on non-traditional learning in the lifespan.* Madison, WI: University of Wisconsin Press.

Winn, W. (1997). *Learning in hyperspace* [Online]. Available: http://www.umuc.edu/ide/potentialweb97/winn.html

Winner, L. (1998). *Report from the digital diploma mills conference* [Online]. Available: http://www.oreilly.com/people/staff/stevet/netfuture/1998/Jun0298_72.ht ml#3

6

A Theory of Distance Education Based on Empathy

Börje Holmberg
FernUniversität, Germany
boerje.holmberg@strandhusen.se

It is work aiming at a theory of distance education carried out during the last four decades that constitutes the background of this chapter. Before the term *distance education* became established (when the terms used for this concept were *correspondence education, home study,* and *independent learning*), I argued in favor of a conversational approach to course development (Holmberg, 1960, pp. 15–16) and later attempted to formulate a theory of distance education in which empathy between the learner and the teaching organization was assumed to favor learning and to be a decisive desideratum in teaching (Holmberg 1983; 1985; 1991; 1995b; 1997; 2001; Holmberg, Schuemer, & Obermeier 1982; and elsewhere). My attempts paid scant attention to the technological developments that occurred the last few decades of the 20th century. Further, I used a somewhat unfortunate terminology. I referred to the conversational character of distance education as "didactic," an adjective in many cases taken to indicate an authoritarian approach (the opposite of what was meant). Instead of *guided didactic conversation*, I now prefer the term *teaching-learning conversation* (Holmberg, 1999; Lentell, 1997). In spite of the deficiencies indicated, the gist of the theory remains valid.

WHAT KIND OF THEORY IS POSSIBLE?

If by *theory* we mean a systematic ordering of ideas about the phenomena of a field of inquiry, as Gage (1963 p. 102) defines it, a theory of distance education is obviously possible. If, on the other hand, the intent is to explain all social, educational, and organizational conditions of distance education, the possibility of identifying and wording such a theory appears remote. It is not much easier to develop a theory that meets Keegan's (1983) criterion—that it should be able to "provide the touchstone against which decisions—political, financial, educational, social— . . . can be taken with confidence" (p. 3).

What should be possible, however, and what I believe I have developed, is a deductive theory applying to specified aspects of distance education (e.g., a teaching theory of distance education is within reach). Such a theory represents a structure of reasoned explanations open to intersubjective testability. This means that it has internal consistency as a logical system and generates a set of hypotheses logically related to one another in explaining and predicting occurrences. It is important that it should be expressed in such a way that research data capable of possibly falsifying (refuting) the theory can be collected. The hypotheses to be tested should be of the "If A . . . then B" or "The more (less) A, the more (less) B" character. Theory building of this type represents the rationalist approach of Karl Popper (1980), to which I adhere.

THE CONCEPT OF DISTANCE EDUCATION

Conceptual clarity must be the basis of any theory attempt. My attempt is based on the following understanding of distance education, which will be presented rather comprehensively, as it is immediately related to the theory.

There seems to be general agreement that, as I put it as early as 1977, distance education covers forms of study that are not under the continuous, immediate supervision of tutors present in classrooms or on the same premises as their students but that nevertheless benefit from the planning, guidance and teaching of a tutorial organization (p. 9). The most lucid and detailed description of the characteristics of distance education seems to be one given by Keegan (1990, p. 44), who lists the following criteria:

- The quasi-permanent separation of teacher and learner throughout the length of the learning process (this distinguishes it from conventional face-to-face education).
- The influence of an educational organization both in the planning and preparation of learning materials and in the provision of student-support services (this distinguishes it from private study and teach-yourself programs).
- The use of technical media—print, audio, video, or computer—to unite teacher and learner and carry the content of the course.
- The provision of two-way communication so that the student may benefit from or even initiate dialogue (this distinguishes it from other uses of technology in education).
- The quasi-permanent absence of the learning group throughout the length of the learning process so that people are usually taught as individuals and not in groups, with the possibility of occasional meetings for both didactic and socialization purposes.

The last-mentioned characteristic need no longer apply. Groups of learners can cooperate although being geographically separated. Teleconferencing (audio and video) is possible, even if not very practical in many cases, as it requires students to keep to a timetable that cannot possibly suit all students. Most distance students are adults with jobs, families, and various social commitments, and these often prevent them from taking part in classes, whether face to face or in any other synchronous form. Computer conferencing offers a practical solution, as it can be arranged asynchronously and be adapted to self-paced study. The teaching organization can then regularly invite students who have finished certain specified parts of a course to a computer seminar lasting one or more weeks, during which students can take part at any time, early in the morning, late in the evening, at night, or whenever it suits them.

Group work is usually highly appreciated, at least by universities and schools, and, particularly in the American educational tradition, classes are regarded with considerable respect. The fact that a distance course may have hundreds or thousands of students at the same time, that in most distance education there are no classes, and that any group work will have to be dependent on individual timetables and choices is still something new to many Americans in the traditional educational sector. The group work arranged in asynchronous computer seminars for students following their own timetables differs from but can well replace conventional classes.

With this reservation about the possibility of group work, Keegan's (1990) definition is accurate. It is important to realize that distance education encompasses both the presentation of subject matter (i.e., one-way traffic) and interaction, between students and tutors and between individual students (peer-group interaction). While the one-way traffic, according to my conversational approach, simulates communication, the interaction represents real communication.

Computer technology is useful for both. Despite the fact that it seldom makes sense to present subject matter in the form of long texts on the Net and that printed texts thus dominate as sources of information, the one-way traffic can avail itself of the advantages of computer technology. When tutors find that certain parts of a course cause particular difficulties, supplementary explanations can be given on the Net. In the same way, additional information, suggestions for consideration, and so forth can supplement preproduced learning material. Naturally, the search for sources and information, a useful academic exercise, also belongs here.

For the second constituent element, interaction, modern technology is of decisive importance. Although it has always been possible for students and tutors to interact by correspondence and for a long time on the telephone, modern technology also makes student-student interaction possible. Students can interact freely on the Net and do so to a great extent in several degree courses and other types of education and training (see, e.g., Bernath & Rubin, 1999). Student-tutor interaction benefits from computer technology as well. Sending assignment solutions, comments, and questions and answers by e-mail can eliminate the delay caused by postal delivery. Spontaneous contact between students and tutors can even be inspired by the use of electronic mail.

THE THEORY

The description given of the concept of distance education and the characteristics illuminated in connection with it can be seen as part of the theory of distance education and are inevitably a basis for theorizing. Some of my later theory presentations, although paying special attention to the empathy approach, are not limited to this aspect of teaching and learning but are considerably wider (see Holmberg, 1997).

My basic theory, which concerns learning, teaching, and organization (or administration), can be summarized as follows:

1. Distance education mainly serves individual learners who cannot or do not want to make use of face-to-face teaching (i.e., usually working adults who wish to learn for career purposes or for personal development).

2. Distance learning is guided and supported by noncontiguous means, primarily preproduced course materials and mediated communication between students and a supporting organization (school, university, etc.) responsible for course development, instructional student-tutor interaction, counseling, and administration of the teaching-learning process inclusive of arrangements for student-student interaction. Distance education is open to behaviorist, cognitive, constructivist, and other modes of learning. It may inspire metacognitive approaches.

3. Central to learning and teaching in distance education are personal relations between the parties concerned, study pleasure, and empathy between students and those representing

the supporting organization. Feelings of empathy and belonging promote the students' motivation to learn and influence the learning favorably. Such feelings are fostered by lucid, problem-oriented, conversation-like presentations of learning matter expounding and supplementing the course literature; by friendly mediated interaction between students, tutors, counselors, and other staff in the supporting organization; and by liberal organizational-administrative structures and processes. Factors that advance the learning process include short turnaround times for assignments and other communications between students and the supporting organization, suitable frequency of assignment submissions, and the constant availability of tutors and advisers.

For a fruitful further development of this thinking, see Juler (1990), who is concerned with discourse rather than conversation. As for conversation-like presentations of demanding texts, see Peters's (1998, pp. 20–23) criticism and my reply (Holmberg 1999). It should be noted that a conversation-like presentation of subject matter usually results in modest density of information and some redundancy.

TESTABLE HYPOTHESES GENERATED BY THE THEORY

Hypotheses can be and have been generated by the thinking behind this theory formulation. They are testable and have to some extent been tested. Consideration of the three parts of the theory above illuminates this.

The basic hypothesis here can be worded as follows: If (when) distance education is provided, then learners can study anywhere and at any time and can follow their own individual timetables. This hypothesis has been tested in practice all over the world since the end of the 19th century (Holmberg 1995b). Large numbers of students do study without face-to-face support and without being bound by timetables or classes. They can freely choose what, where, and when to study and can also in many, if not most, cases begin, interrupt, and finish their study whenever it suits them. A great number of reports testifies to this (e. g., Holmberg 1995a).

The second part of the theory is largely descriptive. The hypothesis about the applicability of the modes of teaching referred to has been carefully studied and shown to be nonrefutable by Bååth (1979), Weingartz (1981, 1990), Jegede (1992), Garland (1995), and others. The hypothesis that metacognitive processes can be inspired by and promote distance education was tested and supported by Thorpe (1995) and Evans (1991).

The role of empathy inherent in my theory of teaching-learning conversations generated four hypotheses: (a) The stronger the conversational characteristics, the stronger the students' feelings of personal relationship to the supporting organization; (b) the stronger the students' feelings that the supporting organization is interested in making the learning matter personally relevant to them, the greater their personal involvement; (c) the stronger the students' feelings of personal relationship to the supporting organization and of being personally involved with the learning matter, the stronger the motivation and the more effective the learning; (d) the more independent and academically experienced the students, the less relevant the conversational characteristics.

Three empirical investigations (Holmberg, Schuemer, & Obermeier, 1982) subjected these four hypotheses, as one unified theory, to rigorous falsification attempts (questionnaires and comparisons between experimental group and control group). The testing was, in Popper's spirit, carried out under circumstances as unfavorable as possible to the theory (advanced university-stage courses and experienced academics as students). No consistent statistically significant corroboration emerged, but the tendency in all the three studies favored the theory. The students who took part in the investigations stated that they felt personally involved by the conversational presentations, their attitudes to them were favorable, and those belonging to the experimental group did marginally better in their performance on assignments than the control group.

We are thus entitled to state that the third part of the theory has not been falsified, although the empirical support is far from overwhelming. As far as I know, only the validity of the fourth hypothesis has been seriously queried by critics. Mitchell (1992) insisted that the principles of the conversational approach "are relevant in all aspects of education" (p. 130).

A study by Rekkedal (1985) indirectly supports the empathy approach by showing statistically significant favorable influences of a personal tutor-counselor system. The importance of short turnaround times for assignments has also been empirically tested by Rekkedal (1983), who demonstrated that these are correlated with course completion. Some reservations as to the general validity of Rekkedal's findings have been expressed following the completion of intercultural studies in Australia and the United States. In some cases, however, the students in these studies regularly also took part in face-to-face sessions, which may have made the quick return of assignments with tutors' comments less important than in pure distance education (Barker et al., 1986), or comparisons were made between immediate feedback (via so-called field scoring) and reasonably short turnaround times—under two weeks (Diehl, 1989). On Diehl's study, see Rekkedal (1989).

A further hypothesis related to the third part of the above theory is that frequent communication opportunities, (also called "high submission density") favor learning. This hypothesis was studied with great acumen by Bååth (1980), who found no consistent difference with regard to course completion or test results between students given a great number of communication opportunities (assignment submissions) and those given fewer opportunities of this kind. A replicating study (Holmberg & Schuemer, 1989) proved no more conclusive. It is probably correct to interpret this as an indication that it is the quality rather than the quantity of communication that is decisive. On this conclusion, see Bååth (1989, p. 85).

THE RELEVANCE OF THE THEORY

It would seem to be a truism that empathy between student and teacher promotes learning, but what is definitely no truism is that feelings of empathy, belonging, and even friendship can be fostered by noncontiguous means and that a conversational style is instrumental in this endeavor. The fact—and regrettably it is a fact—that hundreds of distance education courses all over the world are more like handbooks than conversational presentations of instructional content testifies to this. So does the frequent occurrence of ticking off and mere marking of students' assignments. The development of empathy requires not only the speedy return of assignments, but helpful conversational comments and suggestions on each assignment submitted. Both in preproduced course materials and in the personal interaction between students and tutors, students should be addressed directly, as in comments like "I suggest you should now ... " The use of modern information and communication technology makes the conversational approach particularly important.

THE INFLUENCE OF SOCIAL AND TECHNOLOGICAL
DEVELOPMENTS ON THE THEORY

As indicated at the beginning of this chapter, modern developments have not changed the content of the theory. What has changed are the uses made of distance education and the technology serving it. The availability of the World Wide Web has directed the attention of many educators and students to distance education, which has caused considerable proliferation of distance education programs outside the established providers (e.g., the British Open University and the other specialized distance-teaching universities and the so-called dual-mode universities in various parts of the world) (Holmberg, 1995a, pp. 9–12). It has also led to the use of computer technology, which provides the basis for improvements of teaching-learning effectiveness.

Communication on the Net, with its opportunities for spontaneous interaction, underlines the importance of the empathy approach and the conversational style. It is tempting in computer communication to limit messages to very short statements. Distance education tutors can keep messages short in conversational contexts in which it is quite clear that the recipient—that is, the student—understands what is being said and regards such messages as natural replies or supplementary statements. However, full explanatory comments expressed in a personal way are often needed. A tutor working to create empathy will realize this. In fact, the relevance of the theory is now greater than when it was first developed.

However, it should be stressed that the theory as formulated here is limited to the methodological considerations of learning, teaching, and organization-administration. Among the considerations not included are "exogenous" factors, such as "economic, . . . demographic, cultural, political and social contexts" (Campion & Guiton, 1991, p. 2).

STUDIES CLOSELY RELATED TO THE THEORY AND NEW REQUIREMENTS

My identification of a conversational style as conducive to learning (Holmberg, 1960) evidently represents an insight shared by other educators. Entirely independently of my early suggestions, much important work has been centered on conversation in education. Of particular interest are Pask's cybernetic conversation theory which concerns the learning of complex subject matter (Entwistle, 1978; Pask, 1976a, 1976b), and Forsythe's "learning system as a new paradigm for the information age" (Forsythe, 1985), in which the learner, the learning partner (teacher), and "the knowledge that may be the substance of their conversation" (p. 10) are the basic components. Her identification of the evocative, provocative, and convocative types of interaction (Forsythe, 1986, pp. 22–23) can be seen as something of a guideline for a conversational approach.

Among the studies closely related to my theory evidently belong Rekkedal's and Bååth's (discussed above) and the replication of Bååth's investigation of the impact of high submission density carried out by me and Schuemer (mentioned above).

Here, as in all scholarly research areas, much remains to be done. There has been little distance education research based on rationalist deductive theory building and testing, at least as far as the basic character of distance education is concerned. The studies that qualify include Graff (1970), Boyd (1993), and Lehner (2000). I should welcome replications of the Holmberg, Schuemer, and Obermeier (1982) study and would recommend that Web-based courses should be made the objects of study. Maybe then the explanatory and predictive power of the theory would be strengthened to the point that the theory could provide a consistent view of effective learning and teaching in distance education.

EPISTEMOLOGICAL RESERVATIONS

I stated at the outset that I adhere to Popper's epistemological principles. It should be added that my theory is not nomological in Popper's sense; that is, it does not apply everywhere and under all circumstances, the reason being that it is "impossible to determine an absolute set of instructional procedures that will be "best," for different learners, or for different learnings by one learner" (Hosford, 1973, p. 114). In education we must, *nolens volens*, limit our claims to predicting what will usually apply, to tendencies rather than to inevitable consequences of conditions and actions.

A further reservation is that my theory may appear to stress prediction more than a truly Popperian theory would do. As Popper (1980) stated,

> I . . . wish to make it clear that I consider the theorist's interest in explanation—that is, in discovering explanatory theories—as irreducible to the practical technological interest in the deduction of predictions. The theorist's interest in predictions, on the other hand, is explicable as due to his interest in the problem whether his theories are true; or in other words, as due to his interest in testing his theories—in trying to find out whether they cannot be shown to be false. (p. 61)

Whether predictive power is regarded as the aim of the theory, which is usually the practitioner's view, or whether prediction is just seen as the criterion of a true theory, I claim that my theory has not only predictive value but also some explanatory power, as it implies a consistent view of effective learning and teaching in distance education and identifies a general approach favorable to learning and to teaching efforts conducive to learning.

REFERENCES

Bååth, J. A. (1979). *Correspondence education in the light of a number of contemporary treaching models.* Malmö, Sweden: LiberHermods.

Bååth, J. A. (1980). *Postal two-way communication in correspondence education.* Lund, Sweden: Gleerup.

Bååth, J. A. (1989). Submission density, amount of submission questions, and quality of student-tutor dialogue: A comment on Holmberg and Schuemer. In B. Holmberg (Ed.), *Mediated communication as a component of distance education* (pp. 81–89). Hagen, Germany: FernUniversität, ZIFF.

Barker, L. J., Taylor, J. C., White, V. J., Gillard, G., Khan, A. N., Kaufman, D., & Mezger, (1986). Student persistence in distance education: A cross-cultural multi-institutional perspective. *ICDE Bulletin, 12*: 17–36.

Bernath, U., & Rubin, E. (Eds.). (1999). *Final report and documentation of the virtual seminar for professional development in distance education.* Oldenburg, Germany: Carl von Ossietzky Universität.

Boyd, G. (1993). A theory of distance education for the cyberspace era. In D. Keegan (Ed.), *Theoretical principles of distance education* (pp. 234–253). London: Routledge.

Campion, M., & Guiton, P. (1991). Economic instrumentalism and integration in Australian external studies. *Open Learning, 6* (2), 12–20.

Diehl, G. E. (1989). Some thoughts on delayed and immediate feedback: The effect of field scoring on time to completion in career development courses: Comparison of two pretest modalities on end of course test performance. In B. Holmberg (Ed.), *Mediated communication as a component of distance education.* Hagen, Germany FernUniversität, ZIFF.

Entwistle, N. J. (1978). Knowledge structures and styles of learning: A summary of Pask's recent research. *British Journal of Educational Psychology, 48*, 255–265.

Evans, T. (1991). An epistemological orientation to critical reflection in distance education. In T. Evans & B. King (Eds.), *Beyond the text: Contemporary writing on distance education* (pp. 7–18). Geelong, Australia: Deakin University Press.

Forsythe, K. (1985). *A web of diamonds: The learning system as a new paradigm for the information age.* Paper presented at the 32nd Annual World Assembly of the International Council on Education for Teachers, Vancouver, BC.

Forsythe, K. (1986, May). *Understandisng the effectiveness of media in the learning process.* Paper presented at the World Congress of Education and Technology, Vancouver, BC.

Gage, N. L. (1963). *Handbook of research on teaching.* Chicago: Rand McNally.

Garland, M. R. (1995). Helping students achieve epistemological autonomy. In D. Sewart (Ed.) *One world, many voices: Quality in open and distance learning* (2nd ed.; pp. 77–80). Milton Keynes, UK: ICDE/The Open University.

Graff, K. (1970). *Voraussetzungen erfolgreichen Fernstudiums: Dargestellt am Beispiel des schwedischen Fernstudiensystems.* Hamburg, Germany: Lüdke.

Holmberg, B. (1960). *On the methods of teaching by correspondence.* Lund, Sweden: Gleerup.

Holmberg, B. (1977). *Distance education: A survey and bibliography.* London: Kogan Page.

Holmberg, B. (1983). Guided didactic conversation in distance education. In D. Sewart, D. Keegan & B. Holmberg (Eds.), *Distance education: International perspectives* (pp. 114–122). London: Croom Helm.

Holmberg, B. (1985). The feasibility of a theory of teaching for distance education and a proposed theory [ZIFF Papiere 60]. Hagen, Germany: FernUniversität.

Holmberg, B. (1991). Testable theory based on discourse and empathy. *Open Learning, 6*(2), 44–46.

Holmberg, B. (1995a). *Theory and practice of distance education.* London: Routledge.

Holmberg, B. (1995b). The evolution of the character and practice of distance education. *Open Learning, 10*(2), 47–53.

Holmberg, B. (1997). Distance-education theory again. *Open Learning, 12*(1), 31–39.

Holmberg, B. (1999). The conversational approach to distance education. *Open Learning, 14*(3), 58–60.

Holmberg, B. (2001) *Distance education in essence.* Oldenburg, (Germany): Bibliotheks-und Informations system der Universität Oldenburg.

Holmberg, B., & Schuemer, R. (1988). *Tutoring frequency in distance education: An empirical study of the impact of various frequencies of assignment submission.* [Research Monograph No. 1]. University Park: American Center for the Study of Distance Education.

Holmberg, B., Schuemer, R., & Obermeier, A. (1982). *Zur Effizienz des gelenkten didaktischen Gespräches* [with a summary in English]. Hagen, Germany: FernUniversität, ZIFF.

Hosford, P. L. (1973). *An instructional theory: A beginning.* Englewood Cliffs, NJ: Prentice Hall.

Jegede, O. (1992). Constructivist epistemology and its implications for research in distance learning. In T. Evans & P. Juler (Eds.), *Research in distance education* (2nd ed.; pp. 21–29). Geelong, Australia: Deakin University.

Juler, P. (1990). Promoting interaction: Maintaining independence: Swallowing the mixture. *Open Learning, 5*(2), 24–33.

Keegan, D. (1983). *Six distance education theorists.* Hagen, Germany: FernUniversität, ZIFF.

Keegan, D. (1990). *Foundations of distance education.* London: Routledge.

Lehner, H. (2000). Success and failure of distance education in the "Age of Knowledge" [in German and English; ZIFF Papiere 115]. Hagen, Germany: FernUniversität, ZIFF.

Lentell, H. (1997). Professional development, distance education, correspondence tuition, and dialogue. *Open Praxis, 1*, 44–45.

Mitchell, J. (1992). Guided didactic conversation: The use of Holmberg's concept in higher education. In G. E. Ortner, K. Graff & H. Wilmesdoerfer (Eds.), *Distance education as two-way commuication: Essays in honour of Börje Holmberg* (pp. 123–132). Framkfurt am Main: Peter Lang.

Pask, G. (1976a). Conversational techniques in the study and practice of education. *British Journal of Educational Psychology, 46*, 12–25.

Pask, G. (1976b). Styles and strategies of learning. *British Journal of Educational Psychology, 46*, 126–148.

Peters, O. (1998). *Learning and teaching in distance education.* London: Kogan Page.

Popper, K. (1980). *The logic of scientific discovery.* London: Hutchinson.

Rekkedal, T. (1983). The written assignments in correspondence education: Effects of reducing turn-around time. *Distance Education, 4*, 321–252.

Rekkedal, T. (1985). *Introducing the personal tutor/counsellor in the system of distance education.* Oslo: NKI.

Rekkedal. T. (1989). Assignments for submission and turn-around time in distance education: A comment on Diehl, G.E. In B. Holmberg (Ed.), *Mediated communication as a component of distance education* (pp. 33–43.) Hagen, Germany: FernUnversität, ZIFF.

Thorpe, M. (1995). Bringing learner experience into distance education. In D. Sewart (Ed.), *One world many voices: Quality in open and distance learning* (pp. 364–367). Milton Keynes, England: International Council for Distance Education and The Open University.

Weingartz, M. (1981). *Lernen mit Texten.* Bochum, Germany: Kamp.

Weingartz, M. (1990). *Selbständigkeit im Fernstudium.* Hagen, Germany: FernUniversität, ZIFF.

7

Learning With New Media in Distance Education

Otto Peters

FernUniversität-Gesamthochschule in Hagen
Otto.Peters@FernUni-hagen.de

INTRODUCTION

Digitalization, which is penetrating many areas of our daily working and private lives with increasing speed, is also having an effect on university teaching, especially since the introduction of the Internet. Traditional universities and distance universities are being confronted with new tasks. Both teachers and students must acquire new attitudes to these digital media because they considerably alter the pedagogical structure of studying at university. They have to find their way in the new situation, recognize the specific teaching and learning potentials of modern information and communication media, devise and test new forms of learning and teaching, and integrate them into their daily work. Here, traditional and distance universities start from different pedagogical preconditions. This chapter discusses the changes that new information and communication media will bring about in distance education. This topic is not only current, it is also becoming more and more significant.

Before the term is dealt with, it must be made clear what "new media" means in the context of this chapter.

Old and New Media

From the start, media play a different role in distance education than in studying in a traditional university. They enable distance education in the first place; it cannot take place without them. They act as "carrier media," performing a function that is missing in teaching and learning on site. However, because each medium influences and changes the pedagogical structure, the question as to which carrier media to use for distance education is not only a practical or technical issue but also a pedagogical issue. This fact by itself indicates that distance education presents us with a fundamentally different starting situation. If we envisage the corresponding teaching and learning situation in a university (where university teachers themselves function as "carrier media"), the pedagogically relevant difference becomes clear immediately.

The term "new media" is now on everyone's lips. Since the audiovisual movement, this has meant above all the so-called mass media—film, radio, and TV. Later, other media were added, such as audio- and videocassettes. These older media will not be discussed here. The chapter will concentrate instead on the "newer" media—the electronic media, including the digitized media and media systems (note that the required software must not be forgotten [Baumgartner & Payr, 1994], for it may have its own didactic influences). These have led to fundamental changes in ideas about teaching and learning media in the recent past. Today, we understand teaching and learning media to be first of all the personal computer (PC) and the digital learning environment, networks, offline and online CD-ROMs and databases, and the hardware and software necessary, for example, for arranging video conferences, virtual seminars, and computer-supported co-operative learning and working. These are "new media" in the real sense of the term, and they enable us to gain access to a new world of teaching and learning.

To measure the radical change caused by using these new media in distance education, the role of the old media will first be sketched.

When organized distance education began about 150 years ago, the written and the printed word, the railway, and the post were the foundations of this form of learning. With the book as the main medium, the interplay of these technical media was typical for distance education of the first generation, which extends into our own times. They are extremely important, because they characterized this type of distance education and enable us to define distance education in all cases as *studying enabled by media*. Since its founding years, teaching and learning behavior in distance education has been determined above all by technical media, whereas these media were hardly used at all for over a hundred years for teaching and learning at European universities. In fact, they were often rejected there, in part vehemently. Books may be regarded as the exception.

A new era began with the use of the radio and television as carrier and presentation media in addition to books. The distance universities and open universities that were founded in many parts of the world from about 1970 accordingly offered distance education using multiple media. Quite naturally, these media required different teaching and learning behaviors, and these in turn altered the pedagogical structure, making it reasonable to speak of a second generation of distance education.

At present we are experiencing the beginning of the third generation as a result of the unheard-of advances in information and communications technologies and their increasing use. The third generation is characterized, not by the combination or "interlinking" of several media, but by their "integration" on the basis of multimedia technology and the PC. Wurster (1999) therefore speaks of the "integrating learning environments" (p. 53) now available to distance students. With regard to the pedagogical use of the integrated new media, it has created a fundamentally new situation, and once again teaching and learning behaviors are changing in response.

Pedagogical Dimensions of Networked Computers

The central medium is now the PC. However, because of the enormous advances in computer, multimedia, and network technologies, especially in the areas of display, transmission, and storage, the PC is by no means a single medium but rather a complex, multifunctional aggregate of several media. In spite of its name, the personal computer is no longer just a "computer" but rather an extraordinarily versatile communications medium that unites and bundles functions previously carried out separately by several different media or media systems. The PC serves at the same time as a carrier, distribution, display, instruction, and interactive medium. In addition, it provides pedagogically useful services that traditional media are completely unable to do. It also exercises specific teaching functions as a memory, transmission, and distribution tool and, not least, as a word processor and animation appliance. Finally, it outperforms all other media because of its capacity for rapid and ubiquitous data access and data exchange and because it can generate virtual rooms and virtual realities in a unique manner.

Those who plan and design teaching are now, as it were, in a media Seventh Heaven. At the same time, the technologies under discussion can only develop their effects when they have been programmed to do so with appropriate operating and application software. In a certain sense, therefore, it is the software programs that are the real new media, in particular because preliminary pedagogical decisions are often made regarding their development.

The PC differs as follows from all the technical media that have ever been used in the history of teaching and learning. Teachers and students are fascinated by the power they exude. Why is it so much more attractive than classical teaching and learning media? According to Turkle (1998), people find it fascinating because of the possibility of "talking" with it, being led by it into virtual worlds, or using it to extend their own intellectual capabilities. If, for example, our memories (our internal data storage units) fuse symbiotically with the computer's external memory, we experience a growth in strength and an extension of the self. This is experienced as something pleasant and even enjoyed unconsciously or in a restrained manner. Here, the important question for distance students is whether this particular effect of the PC influences learning motivation. There are indications of this in teaching practice.

The PC, with its hardware and software, is then at the center of the integrated digital learning environment, but standard technical equipment, such as loudspeakers, a modem, a printer, and a fax machine, also has to be available. Even with these additions, the PC does not attain its full importance until networks are added, with their servers, search engines, and expert systems. This configuration integrates the new media, allowing the digital learning environment not only to determine the structure of the learning process but to reconstitute it.

Pedagogical Variety.   Even uninitiated observers are able to appreciate the pedagogical multifunctionality of the digital learning environment after their first experience with it. Yet they have difficulty comprehending it fully (as do experts), not only can learning texts be presented to students, but so can two- or three-dimensional graphics, color illustrations, audio and video sequences, and even two- or three-dimensional animation and simulations. Their integration alone would be an invaluable pedagogical advance, but there are additional and much deeper pedagogical possibilities, namely increased *interactivity* and *individualization* and greater opportunity for *independent learning.*

Virtual Learning Spaces.   PCs can generate virtual learning spaces, and these offer pedagogical design dimensions that no one has yet thought of in real learning spaces. Ten of these new learning spaces (Peters 2000a) are pedagogically interesting and usable in an innovative manner, namely, the spaces for instruction, information, communication, collaboration, exploration, documentation, multimedia, text processing, illustration, simulation and the spaces in virtual reality.

We are dealing here with distinct virtual spaces (i.e., independent of each other) in which specific pedagogical actions can be carried out. The majority of them are not derived from traditional forms of teaching and learning but from the specific technological situation of the PC. Naturally, not one of these spaces actually exists. For students, what is "real" is only the digital learning environment, with the monitor's screen as the interface. In contrast, virtual spaces are only created if the imagined empty space behind the screen is made into the "stage" for actions (in our case, for pedagogical actions).

Favoring Autonomous Learning.   If we examine these virtual learning spaces, we come to realize that learning in distance education does not have to consist merely of the reception of intensified presentations of course contents. It can, in fact, be brought about easily, and perhaps above all, by means of independent pedagogical actions by the students themselves. Typical examples include interacting with adaptive teaching programs, searching for information in databases all over the world, communicating and collaborating with other participants in the teaching and learning process, exploring areas of knowledge (e.g., in hypertexts), becoming immersed in virtual worlds, storing and requesting material that has been learnt, handling knowledge that has already been acquired and documented (knowledge management), and portraying problems and their solutions using word processing and multimedia and publishing the results on the Web. The new media possess an absolutely amazing potential for innovation, and we cannot fail to be impressed from the start by the enormous opportunities for the pedagogical reform of distance education offered by them.

It is a fact that actions in these virtual learning spaces do encourage far-reaching, even radical changes. Higher levels of *activity* and of *interactivity* are achieved relatively easily. And there are many other obvious and promising possibilities for developing autonomous and self-regulating learning behavior. Even more, the digital learning environment actually promotes the development of autonomous learning. Self-direction, which always has to be presupposed for learning by distance students, can be raised with the help of a PC to a qualitatively higher level. For important pedagogical reasons, it would be irresponsible not to make use of these new chances for pedagogical optimization.

FAVORABLE PRECONDITIONS IN DISTANCE TEACHING UNIVERSITIES

When a traditional university decides to increase the amount of teaching done using PCs and the Internet, this is not the same thing as when a distance teaching university decides to increase the use of these tools. In contrast to traditional universities, distance universities are already prepared in many ways for the necessary tasks, a fact usually overlooked, above all by those who see the difference between the two types of university disappearing with the introduction of Internet-based learning and speak of their convergence (Tait & Mills, 1999). Teachers and students at distance universities already have the attitudes, strategies, and experience needed to facilitate the use of electronic media. In addition, at distance universities, not only the whole teaching body but the whole administration (a costly, complex organizational-technical "operating system") is geared exclusively to the learning requirements of distance students. On the whole, learning in distance education is structurally close to learning in virtual spaces. This is obvious in the following:

- Distance universities have long experience in looking after students who live away from the university location. *Distributed learning*, now being propagated, is nothing new for them. They have already developed techniques for bridging the distances between teachers and students—not just geographic distances but also of mental, social, and cultural "distances".
- The teachers and students in a distance university have a different attitude toward *technical media* because, as noted, these media enable teaching and learning over a distance in the first place. The importance of technical media can be seen in the use of language as well: Distance universities are often referred to as "media universities."

- The teachers are used to using teaching texts that have been compiled carefully with the help of *instructional design* experts and tested and evaluated empirically. Pedagogically, therefore, their teaching is on a professional level.
- *Asynchronous learning* has been practiced at distance universities from the very start. It is structurally necessary and not an innovation first achieved through digitization.
- The teachers have developed techniques for *supporting* students working in isolation to make studying easier for them and to motivate them to study. They make efforts to keep up the links with the students. These efforts find an expression in the study centers, in which tutors, mentors, and counselors are integrated into the provision of support.
- The students have already gained experience in *autonomous, self-directed learning*, at least in so far as they themselves plan and fix the location, time, and circumstances for learning.
- Teaching is particularly close to the *world of employment*, as the students are usually employed themselves, and the tutors and mentors often are as well.
- Distance universities have already opened up to *new, unconventional groups of students.* The teachers are already used to working together with older students, many of whom have jobs. They have established *adult university education* as a regular and freely accessible offer.
- Since their foundation, distance universities have practiced *lifetime learning*, which international educational organizations have continuously demanded for decades.
- Distance universities have already made a noteworthy contribution to the establishment of *mass higher education*, which has become necessary globally. They have developed suitable strategies and techniques for teaching and learning for large, in fact very large, groups of students.
- Distance universities contributed at an early stage to *reducing the costs of studying*, as Daniel (1998a, p. 1) has pointed out. In his judgement, a place in the Open University in the United Kingdom is only half as expensive as in comparable traditional British universities.
- Distance universities have always been *extraordinarily flexible* institutions. For example, they have adapted to advances in media technologies, as indicated by the three generations of distance education referred to above. In addition, distance education is able to react quickly to new learning requirements and to adjust to groups of people who are neglected by traditional universities or by the educational system as a whole.

If we remember what is to be achieved with learning on the Internet and in virtual universities, we come quickly to the following conclusion: distance universities have already gone far toward achieving many of the goals that advocates of online learning and the virtual university wanted to achieve. We can point to pedagogical approaches that have already been consolidated by and are characteristic of distance universities but are usually totally lacking in traditional universities. This fact explains why a virtual distance university will have a different pedagogical profile than a virtual university sprung from a traditional university.

STAGES ON THE ROAD TO THE "LEARNING SPACE VIRTUAL UNIVERSITY"

What is the role played by the new media in distance universities in view of the favorable conditions referred to above? To what extent and in what way are they used and what are the effects on learning behavior? We can see that all distance universities are experimenting with the new media, often with the declared aim of establishing a "virtual university" in which the complete process of teaching and learning will be determined by an integrated system of new media. Distance teaching universities in which degree courses can be taken online are already approaching this goal.

The transition from the media used during the first and second generations of distance education to the new media and the development of virtual universities is a complex process. We now will examine a practical example to impart an overview of the various initiatives and experiments that are necessary for using the new media in distance education and that in the end can lead to the creation of a virtual university. By looking at the establishment of the "learning space virtual university" of the FernUniversität in Hagen, we can see how this institution faced up the challenges of the new media step by step and how this forced students to alter their learning behavior. Reviewing the actual practice of learning in a distance teaching university can act as a supplement to the theoretical discussion of virtual learning environments (Peters, 2000b).

Besides possessing the pedagogically relevant features of distance teaching universities that structurally favor their transformation into virtual universities, the FernUniversität has for decades realized certain elements of the teaching and learning process with the help of electronic media. Employment of these media originally occurred in small experiments, then in individual learning modules and training sequences. These modules and sequences were part of the normal operating system, but from today's point of view they could be considered modules for the establishment of a virtual university. Finally, in the last few years, efforts have been concentrated on online learning. First, there were experiments with digitized courses, which were offered parallel to traditional printed distance education courses. These experimental courses culminated in the provision of two fully digitized degree courses. Of course, these digitized courses are mere islands in the great sea of courses provided by the FernUniversität. On the whole, however, the experience gained from these courses gives the FernUniversität a head start in this field (see Kaderali, 1999).

A total of 34 approaches to digitizing learning have been developed and tested in stages by the FernUniversität and have since proved their worth in everyday work (see Appendix). Twelve of these are sketched below.

Electronic Administration of Distance Students' Files

In distance education, administering student files electronically is important not only for organizational reasons (because of the large number of students) but also for pedagogical reasons. Because teachers do not normally meet their students or meet them just for short periods in study centers, they have to gain a general picture of them through the available data. Only with the help of the computer are they able to gain an overview of the age, sex, occupation, address and so on, of large populations of students. The files also contain the students' achievements, and they can be requested by both teachers and students to enable them to discuss the students' study career. Often, the students open written examinations they have already taken to inform themselves or others of earlier learning steps and learning results. Looking at prior examinations helps orientation, can strengthen motivation, and provides data for pedagogical research.

Electronic Evaluation of Course Development

With the help of computers, the effects of the carefully developed teaching texts were already being examined in the founding years of the FernUniversität. Course units were evaluated by external experts who stated that they would do this as representatives of the students. Their opinions and impressions were polled using a standardized questionnaire with a marking record. In this way, the computer was able to provide initial results (formative evaluations). Finished courses were also checked in this way. Some students were given a questionnaire with their course units, which they marked and returned. The findings were then interpreted by experts from the center for the development of distance education and passed to the teachers. In this way error rates and degrees of difficulty were ascertained. Because of the usually large number of students at a distance university (sometimes thousands of students enroll in an individual course), it was only possible with the help of electronic data processing to gain a reliable overview of the effects of course syllabuses on students. The findings contributed to the optimization of the prepared courses, which in turn led to changes in teaching behavior.

Electronic Advisory Service for Potential Students

From 1979 to 1983, those who were interested in studying at the FernUniversität and who wanted to know whether they were suited for it were offered detailed computer-supported advice (Fritsch, 1982). The goal was to supply them with information that would facilitate their decision. This was done through a preliminary course, "Studying at the FernUniversität," that prompted potential applicants to think about their study wishes in combination with their learning and life situations. Following this course, they were given a questionnaire designed to further advance the process of self-enlightenment. The questionnaire was evaluated by the central computer. Advice was then provided, not by means of a standard letter, but by a detailed computer letter that reflected the individual situation of each applicant. The advice in this letter was not intended to replace a personal discussion with a student counselor but only to take the pressure off of such discussions. This was necessary, because about 5,000 advice letters were sent each semester. In this way, potential students were provided with much more information tailored to their needs than they could possibly obtain in an interview with a personal counselor.

Electronic Correction of Written Assignments

To motivate students and accustom them to interactive learning behavior in a distance course, the teaching texts contain numerous practical self-test assignments. With the help of machine-readable marking sheets, students can find out through the computer whether they have solved the problems and how their work is to be graded. They receive a computer letter with this information (Raiser, 1991). This system contains approaches to promoting self-directed learning.

Written assignments are either corrected by the FernUniversität's correctors or also with the help of computers, particularly in the subjects of accounting, cost accounting, and commercial balance sheets. The computer center uses the support of the mechanical correction systems LOTSE and operational accounting (bRw), both of which were developed by the FernUniversität and have been in use since 1977.

The electronic correction system affects the learning process by including information on the overall grade and the student's achievements in each grade notification.

Electronic Drill Exercises

Since 1984, in addition to the printed teaching materials, some departments have offered computer-supported practical exercises and training on disk. These are "assignment and examination trainers," first of all for extending and strengthening the specialist vocabulary for *English for Mathematicians* and *English for Economists* and for solving the problems in the course *Mathematics for Economists*. The drill and practice exercises are oriented toward the corresponding behaviorist instruction models and are therefore interactive throughout. At the same time, however, self-controlled branches could be integrated. For example, in the program *Macro-Toolbox*, economics students can experiment independently with models so that they can learn to handle larger econometric simulation models in their working lives.

Electronic Teaching in Continuing Education

Since 1990, computer-supported teaching programs have been developed on central topics of printed distance education courses in order to strengthen, extend, supplement, and simplify understanding. These teaching programs can also be worked through independently of the courses. At present, for example, teaching disks are offered in the Department of Computer Science on the following subjects: knowledge-based systems, neural networks, programming language C, UNIX-SOL, relational database language, object-oriented database systems, and fuzzy logic.

These continuing education programs are based on models that treat learning as active information processing. They therefore are directed toward the "active construction of individual knowledge, experience and behavior potentials" (Heuel & Postel, 1993, p. 267). "Self-direction" and "interaction" are the most important pedagogical goals.

Online Seminars

In 1995, the university started experimenting with virtual seminars (Wiendieck & Üstünsöz, 1995), particularly in the social sciences and the humanities. These seminars were titled Labor and Information Psychology, Methods of Psychology, Political Science, Therapeutic Pedagogy, Special Pedagogy, and Economic Informatics. Fourteen virtual seminars have since been held at the Institute for Psychology alone. Seemingly, in social science and humanities departments there is a greater demand for discussion than in scientific-technical departments, at least in distance education. Computer-supported seminars enable a group of students to communicate and collaborate with or without the guidance of teachers. Whether or not teachers are involved, there is usually a lively exchange of e-mail messages and attached text (which are read and answered with a time lag) and also a free exchange of knowledge and opinions via newsgroups. The experiments show that there is no way in which the teaching and learning behavior of traditional seminars can be imitated. Online seminars instead have proved to be teaching of a special kind located roughly between instruction with printed material and oral seminars.

Experiments were also carried out with videoconferencing (Ewert, Hauff, Mielke, & Prümmer, 1998). This is a new medium for teaching and learning in distance education and has definite advantages and disadvantages. It will certainly improve the communicative structure of distance education, but it cannot serve as a substitute for personal communication.

Online Drill

Since the beginning of the 1990s, a general software infrastructure for Internet-supported exercises has been developed and tested in four departments. The research relevant to this is carried out by the chair of Practical Informatics III and the chair of Ecological Psychology in the framework of the *WebAssign project* (Six, Ströhlein, & Voss 2001; Voss, Ströhlein, Brunsmann, & Six, 2000). The infrastructure supports all activities involved with drill, in particular solving problems and correcting and evaluating solutions. Preliminary tests enable students to work several times through a problem they have solved incorrectly. Only the final solution, which is either in manual or mechanical form, is evaluated. The system regulates the coordination of the activities of students, correctors, and counselors. It is so advanced that it can be integrated into the coming learning space virtual university.

Online Practical Training

The opportunities that are opening up here can be seen in an example from the robot laboratory of the Department of Electrical Engineering. Students can carry out engineering experiments with a robot without being physically present themselves. They control the robot through the Internet, follow its movements using video, and then evaluate the measured values (Hoyer, 1998). This type of remote control can be transferred to other laboratory situations.

Online Tutorials

In traditional distance education, support for distance students is provided above all by mentors in study centers. Since the introduction of the Internet, advice and help are no longer requested by telephone alone but also by e-mail (Kleinschmidt, 1999). An example of this is the support provided for students of the course Introduction to the Methodology of Political Science. Mentors provide students with their e-mail addresses and answer their questions. They also give students minor problems to solve or solve them together with the students. Support can then take on the character of preparation for the next written examination.

Using The University Library Online

The current online library services have been documented by Pieper and Schmauss (1999) and by Schmauss (2000). These services were provided in the 1980s via Datex-P, but since the early 1990s they have been provided via the Internet. In addition, since 1995 the university library has had its own home page on the Web. The whole stock of 660,000 books and 3,100 journals is documented in an online catalog (OPAC) that can be researched via the Internet. The Internet can also be used by students to access national and international library catalogs, specialized electronic information, specialized databases, full texts, and the document delivery system JASON-WWW for North Rhine Westphalia. A journal contents service is being developed. Students can also reserve books via the Internet or extend loan periods. A virtual semester apparatus is planned.

Learning Space Virtual University

If we take all the activities just described, we see a mosaic of experience with digital teaching and learning that can be integrated into an overall system. However, their harmonization will require a differentiated process of development, testing, and evaluation such as the one under construction at the FernUniversität since 1995. In the Departments of Practical Informatics and Communications Systems, work has been carried out intensively and at great expense on developing, testing, and optimizing a model for operating virtual universities. The findings and experiences gained through the use of multimedia and communications technology form the basis of this project. The ambition of the project groups is to optimize the technical installations for operating a virtual university but at the same time to develop an overall *concept* of a virtual university. They want to bundle data courses, interactive multimedia modules, and teleconferencing with other services in the university in order to be in a position to exercise all the functions of a university. Not only are teaching and research optimized, but so are access to the administration and the library, access to current information, and opportunities for informal discussions, counseling, and learning support (Hoyer, 1999).

An example can illustrate these efforts. On the PC screen, the learning portal that shows students how to use these services includes the following elements:

Teaching (where access to virtual teaching is shown).
Research (where teachers and students can obtain information on the status of research in individual teaching fields).
"News" (where current information on the system, the department, or the course can be obtained, as on a blackboard).
Shop (where above all additional teaching and learning programs can be bought).
Cafeteria (for informal contacts with other students, including private contacts).
Office (where all administrative processes are carried out).
Library (where books can be reserved, digital books or journals read, and bibliographic research carried out).
Information (where all questions about the FernUniversität are answered, potential students can "tour" the FernUniversität, and talks with mentors take place). (Schlageter, 2000, p. 135)

Because of this portal, students no longer need to leave their digital learning environment but can access all of the university's services and those of the study centers. An initial result is the fully digitized degree course ET Online, which is provided in German and English and for which the degree of Bachelor of Science can be awarded (Kaderali, 1999). Development started in 1995, and since then it has been tested by 5,000 students. Students can check their registered particulars here, access electronic teaching materials, and communicate with mentors and other students. Second, the virtual Bachelor's Degree Course in Computer Science has just been completed. Third, a virtual mathematics degree course is being prepared. These are the first steps in transforming a distance teaching university into a virtual university (Hoyer, 2000).

CHANGES IN LEARNING BEHAVIOR

Digitized degree courses presuppose new learning behaviors. It is not just a matter of students' finding their way around in the abstract world of a virtual university and accustoming themselves to a completely different way of working. Experience alone will probably be sufficient for this. What is more important is for students to acquire the skills needed to think and act independently, be clear about their own learning requirements, take the initiative, develop the ability to recognize quality differences quickly, evaluate the advantages and disadvantages of defined learning paths, make a well-founded choice between several course syllabuses, reflect on their own learning, and contribute to the creation of a culture of digital communication. In other words, predominantly externally directed students have to change into predominantly internally directed students. The pedagogical goal here is the development of autonomously acting students who initiate, control, and evaluate their work themselves.

CONSEQUENCES

At the FernUniversität, the transition from distance education to online learning was not sudden but has already lasted many years. The process of transformation will probably continue for some time to come and may even remain open-ended because of rapid technical and social changes. Many people took part in the process and performed many functions, including professors of practical informatics and communications. The entrenchment of the transformation process in research has an extremely beneficial effect, as it contributes concepts and processes to the project. At the same time, research makes the FernUniversität relatively independent of commercial ties, dependencies, and restrictions, which is even more significant because in some countries more and more universities that want to teach online are outsourcing important academic functions. Frequently, not only software and technical monitoring but even the digitized teaching programs and the pedagogical support for students are bought from outside companies. This is only mentioned to show the problems with which distance education institutions can be faced if they use the new media without being adequately prepared and equipped.

SUMMARY AND EVALUATION

We discussed the structural affinity between distance education and Web-supported learning, sketched preliminary approaches to learning with the new media, and described the pedagogical structure of the learning space virtual university. This chapter considers two concluding issues: What are the pedagogical gains that make the described use of the new media appear advisable if not absolutely essential? And how is the prescribed use of the new media to be evaluated from the perspective of cultural history?

Pedagogical Gains

If we look at the large number of new media as they are now used in the organization and operation of the digital learning environment, we are able to detect the following positive effects.

Improvements in External Working Conditions.   Two factors that have never played any role in traditional pedagogy, *time savings* and *comfort*, are important for employed distance students, as they suffer from a chronic lack of time and have difficulty attending regular teaching events, counseling, and tutorials in study centers or other institutional centers. With the new media, the sequence of learning and teaching acts is rapid and the return times for corrections are short.

As far as comfort is concerned, this appears at first glance to be an external characteristic. However, its special importance becomes clear on a second glance. The rapid access to desired information, instruction, and course syllabuses of various origins, as well as the much easier access to joint discussions and collaborative activities, goes beyond the "user-friendliness" of technical media stressed by Bates (1995). What is in fact being created is a radically new situation in which everything is available at the click of a mouse—everything, that is, required for reading, looking up, studying, training, repeating, constructing, organizing, informing, storing, remembering, and browsing and navigating. Because of the savings in time and effort, the word *comfortable*, in the sense of imparting comfort, may be used here as a working term, though *convenience* might be a more fitting term.

Special Distance Education Pedagogical Benefits.   The next set of benefits concern the pedagogical structure of distance education. The new media can provide partial and sometimes surprisingly effective compensation for the pedagogical deficiencies of distance education of the first and second generation. The most significant of these deficiencies are as follows:

- The widespread reduction of representation modes to the single medium of print.
- The dependence on one-way communication when using mass media (print, TV, radio).

- The drastic reduction of formal and informal social contacts between students and between students and teachers.
- The considerable spatial and social isolation of students.
- The inadequate participation of students in the scientific process.

With the help of the new media, it is possible to use and combine several modes of representation, facilitate and strengthen two-way communications, initiate social contacts virtually, reduce the isolation of students, and enable participation in virtual collaborative research projects. Above all, physical distance can be changed into *virtual proximity* for distance students, enabling "telepresence," or "mental presence with physical absence" (Kleinschroth, 1996, p. 237). Each distance education theoretician and practitioner should value these third-generation advantages and see the virtual university as the culmination of all efforts to improve learning conditions for distance students.

Inherent Advantages of the Digital Learning Environment.   In addition to the pedagogical advantages referred to above are the advantages characteristic of digital working methods. Below are listed the six most important:

- The ability to strengthen and bundle several presentation modes using multimedia.
- Easy access to a broad range of information.
- The ability to communicate and cooperate independent of the location (simultaneously or with a time lag).
- The ability to increase activity and interactivity with the help of adaptive learning programs.
- The availability of technical means for storing and presenting knowledge.
- The possibility of developing autonomous learning.

These potential advantages change the learning process—its organization, contents, methods, and social forms—and generally make it more flexible. The pedagogical consequences of such changes are still not entirely foreseeable. It is important, first of all, to recognize the specific possibilities of the digital learning environment and then to use them in a new way on the basis of pedagogical reflection. Not what is technically feasible, not hardware advertised and sold commercially, but what is pedagogically desirable should be in the foreground. The basic principle can be stated thus: "The use of new media . . . may not be linked with an additive approach but must be linked with a systematic approach" (Reinmann-Rothmeier & Mandl, 1999, p. 6). Only in this way can the new media become an "impulse for a change of forms of teaching and learning which have become ineffective." This change has to be comprehensive, because "transformation is paramount for success" (Eisenstadt & Vincent, 1998, p. 13).

Misgivings.   The enthusiasm for the wonderful instruments of the new media, especially in a virtual university, is not unmixed. Educationists are bothered by the question of how they will be used in practice. Will many teachers be tempted to use these expensive and extraordinarily versatile technological tools in a one-dimensional manner, to imitate and perpetuate and aggravate traditional teaching and learning down to the very last detail? Will many restrict themselves to recording their lectures on video, transfering them to a CD-ROM, and then feeding them into the virtual university? Will others simply have their teaching texts digitized and placed on the Internet, wrongly viewing the Internet as mainly an instrument for distribution? Will universities use the new media just ot extend conventional instruction to remote groups through satellite and video conferencing? This is the system of teacher-centered remote group learning that was so fiercely attacked by Daniel (1998b, p. 25).

If the new media are only used in these ways, great opportunities will have been lost, including the opportunity to reform the curricula and work out methods of teaching and learning that are appropriate for the virtual university. The virtual university must develop its own pedagogical profile and not simply imitate the methods of campus or distance teaching universities.

Second, the cheerful confidence of those protagonists of online learning who believe that the interactivity and communication lacking in distance education could be provided and compensated by the new media is a self-delusion. Communication mediated through technical media remains mediated communication and cannot replace an actual discussion, an actual argument, discourse among people gathered at a single location. Mediated communication and real communication are related in the same way as a pencil sketch and an oil painting of the same subject. What happens in a discussion between two or more people is only partly mediated electronically. What is missing is the consciously perceived presence of the others, their aura, the feeling of being together, which arises in a different manner in every meeting. All this makes communication genuine and lively. A virtual university that does without face-to-face events and restricts interaction to exchanging e-mails and videoconferencing will always remain a surrogate university.

In light of these problems, is it advisable to imagine a virtual university as an independent and enclosed institution? Should we not rather consider how it might be integrated into "the university of the future" (Peters, 1998, p. 219; see also Peters, 2000c)? The answer is that, yes, the virtual university, rather than providing the prevailing pattern, should add its extraordinary efficacy, flexibility, adaptability, and variability to the university of the future—a university in which face-to-face academic discourse and "academic social life" (Casper 1997, p. 25) occur just as naturally as the proven forms of distance education. The pedagogical contributions enabled by the new media should be extremely welcome in a mixed mode university of this nature.

Evaluation.   The use of the new media in distance education cannot be compared with the use of the early technical media. We are not dealing here with pedagogical progress along traditional paths and in a traditional setting but are entering new territory and are experiencing an unequalled breach of tradition. Learning and teaching in the digital age have to be redefined. We need only think about the fundamentally new requirements that autonomous learning places on the evaluation of the "learning success" (Baumgartner, 2000) to accept this truth. The pedagogical paradigm change puts students and teachers in distance education in a difficult new situation, and it will take some time before they are accustomed to it. Indeed, the question must be asked whether they ever will be. It is probably best to regard the new media and their continuing development as constant determinants of future learning—as both a challenge and a chance.

Consider, for instance, the radical "mediatizing" (Haefner, 1987, p. 33) of teaching and learning that is seen as a serious consequence of the use of PCs and computer networks. This mediatizing comes in both moderate and radical forms. In moderate mediatizing, computer networks serve only to supplement and enrich conventional forms of teaching and learning. Here they are an additive that can be left out where required. Radical mediatizing, on the other hand, is "disruptive" (Garrison & Anderson, 2000, p. 27) and leads to the dissolution of conventional forms of teaching and learning, although it can cause their restructuring into completely new learning scenarios. In distance education, the link between teachers and students was mediatized from the start. The printed material and the written letter mainly came between the two. The new media strengthen and radicalize this process. In addition, they extend it by mediatizing existing islands of direct interaction (e.g., study centers).

The use of the new media in distance education confronts us with issues that did not arise with the old media. Not only does it change the attitudes, the behavior, and the learning action of students, as well as the structure of the institution, but it is also part of those structural changes that the postindustrial information and knowledge society imposes on us.

NEW MEDIA RESEARCH

Overview

The following kinds of reports and other publications pertain to the use of the new media in distance education.

Empirical Reports on Actual Practice.   Although such reports are more numerous than any other kind, their findings can often only be generalized conditionally because of the uniqueness of the situation in each case. In addition, many are "works in progress." Even in the early 1990s, reports of this nature were read at NATO Advanced Research Workshops and published in the proceedings. The volumes that are relevant to our subject include *Computer-Based Learning Environments and Problem Solving* (De Corte, Linn, Mandl, & Verschaffel, 1992), *Collaborative Learning Through Computer Conferencing* (Kaye, 1992), and *Collaborative Dialogue Technologies in Distance Learning* (Verdejo & Cerri, 1994). More recent examples are Nestor and Mandl's (1997) *Experiences With a Virtual Seminar* and reports on the same subject by Heidbrink (1996), Bernath and Rubin (1999), Bernath (2000), Wenning (2000) and Schulmeister (2001, p. 256) are available from the FernUniversität.

Analyses Grounded in Learning Psychology.   These are of particular importance for practice because they provide criteria with whose help the new phenomena of online learning can be interpreted correctly. In this terrain, which is strange for most university teachers but also for educationists and pedagogical experts, many try to experiment with traditional forms of teaching and learning. The analyses described here help them to reorient themselves in the transformation of pedagogical action that has now become necessary. Examples include the chapter "Learning and Teaching with the Computer" by Mandl, Gruber, and Renkl (1997); the article "Problem-Oriented Learning With Multimedia" by Reinmann-Rothmeier and Mandl (1997); the article "The Virtual University from a Pedagogical Point of View" by Schulmeister (1999); and the article "Fernunterricht und neue Informationstechnologien" by Astleitner and Leutner (1998).

Institutional Research Reports.   Because most distance universities have been dealing for years with the new opportunities provided by online learning, for obvious reasons they have already done research on problems that would seem to be resolvable by professional instruction designers and instruction technicians. In the Open University, the Knowledge Media Institute was established expressly for the purpose of doing research on online learning in distance education. This institute has published a report on its work (Eisenstadt & Vincent, 1998) containing several chapters—"Knowledge Media," "Collaboration and Presence," and "Knowledge Systems on the Net"—that provide information on important aspects of learning with the new media. Examples from the institutional research at the FernUniversität are listed in the annual reports of the Zentrum für Fernstudienentwicklung (Center for the Development of Distance Education) (1999, 2000). One section of this center is concerned specifically with interactive media, develops Web-based teaching methods and new integrating software, and supervises the mechanical correction systems. Relevant articles have been submitted by Wurster (1997, 1999), Prümmer (2000), Helms (1999), Ewert, Hauff, Mielke, and Prümmer (1998), Bartels (1997), Geiersbach, Prümmer, and Rossie (1997), and Laaser (1990).

Reports on Applied Cognition Research.   Aspects of online learning have been researched for some years by the Department of Applied Cognition Research of the German Institute for Distance Education Research at the University of Tübingen. Its main areas of work in the field of virtual learning environments are, among others, visualizing, navigation, cooperation, participation and communication, and structuring the supply of information in virtual seminars. Examples of such reports include two contributed chapters, "Vergleichende Bewertung von Methoden zur Beurteilung von Lern- und Informationssystemen: Fazit eines Methodenvergleichs" by Tergan (2000) and "Partizipation im virtuellen Seminar in Abhängigkeit von der Moderationsmethode: Eine empirische Untersuchung" by Friedrich, Hesse, Ferber, and Heins (2000b).

Because of the rapid development of new technologies and new applications in distance education, empirical projects face considerable problems. To begin with, such projects naturally require a great deal of time. Then, when their findings are finally presented, they are often outdated in part, especially if overriding pedagogical issues have not been adequately considered.

Contributions From Other Disciplines.   Because the digitalization of learning environments is but one part of the global move toward a "virtual society," it is also important to research economic, political, and cultural dimensions of this transformation. For this reason, we must also take into account philosophical contributions (e.g., on the phenomenon of virtuality; Baudrillard, 1989; Friesen, Berr, Karsten, Lenk, & Sanders, 2000), sociological studies (e.g., on the characteristics of the information or knowledge society; Bühl, 1997), cultural history studies (e.g., on the historical and present-day metamorphoses of perceptions of space and time; Burckhardt, 1997; Virilio, 1999), and communication science studies (e.g., on the consequences of computer-mediated communication; Beck, 1998).

Desiderata

For pedagogical reasons, it is essential that research is carried out on the following aspects of using the new media in distance education:

- Learning situations in a virtual seminar.
- Stages and forms of autonomous, self-directed learning in the virtual learning environment.
- New forms of evaluation, in particular, with autonomous learning, where the evaluation criteria of expository teaching and receptive learning cannot apply.
- Web-based support and counseling for self-learners, which are of increasing importance and will have to be fully reconceived.
- The pedagogical relevance of different forms of virtual collaborative learning as well as opportunities for and constraints on experimenting in the virtual learning space.

Selected Findings

Following are brief descriptions of studies that can deepen our understanding of learning with new media in distance education.

Adaptivity.   On the basis of instruction psychology theories, Leutner (1997) analyzed the extent of the support that learners in a learning environment can obtain and reports on empirically tested possibilities of adaptive teaching functions. As adaptive teaching functions, he named learning time, instruction sequence, task difficulty, help for learning by discovering, and link to existing knowledge.

Artificial Intelligence Tools.   In the research project Virtual Learning Spaces of the National Polytechnic Institute in Mexico City, Guzman and Nunez-Esquer (1998) developed the prototype of an M.Sc. degree syllabus in which work is carried out with the help of artificial intelligence tools. With the help of these tools, the students' prior knowledge is diagnosed, individual learning paths are stipulated, and suitable learning materials are put together. The Internet is also searched for suitable work by means of a tool (Claritex) that analyses articles by their main topic, organizes synchronous learning activities, and coordinates partnership work for students with the same or similar learning paths.

Automated Tutoring.   Albert and Thomas (2000) examined the pedagogical functions of an interactive software tool that leads distance students through specific tasks and problem solutions at the Open University Business School.

Change, Technological.   When new media are to be integrated into conventional university structures for purpose of establishing online learning a complex change must be initiated. Bates (2000) analyzed this process and developed strategies for college and university leaders.

Collaboration.   Dave and Danahy (2000) described a project to develop a "shared virtual design studio" (p. 57) in which architecture students in Switzerland, Canada, and Australia work together. The students do not jointly design the same building project, but in each case students in one city design a building project in another city with the help of the local students. This approach to collaboration contributes to the achievement of several educational goals because design knowledge for architects, landscape architects, and urban planners is mediated at the same time and in a combined form.

Computer-Mediated Conferencing.   Salmon (1999) traced the history of computer-mediated conferencing, which started at the Open University as early as 1988, and described the role it plays at present in the Open University Business School. Participation in computer-mediated conferences is motivated by the need to establish closer links to the teaching-learning system, to communicate with others, and to obtain and provide information. The author showed how these conferences can also take place with larger numbers of participants.

Constructivist Learning.   Schank (1997) described a virtual learning concept aimed at encouraging active and self-directed learning at higher learning goal levels and aiding in the solution of complex and knowledge-intensive tasks. Important criteria are goal-directedness and learning from mistakes (cf. Astleitner & Schinagl, 2000, p. 97).

Disabled Learners Online.   Ommerborn and Schuemer (2000) researched the "opinions of disabled students on PC use in distance education." (p. I) Computers prove in various and specific ways to be "aids to compensate for problems and deficits resulting from the disability." (p. VIII).

Drill.   Voss et al. (2000) reported on the WebAssign project, which is being developed by Hans-Werner Six and his team to make an infrastructure for academic drill available as a component of a virtual university. The WebAssign system, which provides Web-based and flexible support for all those taking part in drills, has now been tested in eight teaching areas.

Emotions.   Astleitner (n.d.) and Astleitner and Schinagl (2000) researched strategies for making online learning more "atmospheric." Twenty recommendations for achieving this goal were offered. Five types of emotion are differentiated: fear, envy, anger, sympathy and pleasure.

Human-Computer Interface.   Robson (2000) examined the role played in online learning by the attitude of the students to the computer, a factor usually ignored. Human interface theories have to be taken into account when planning, implementing, and evaluating learning because they have an effect on the cognition, behavior, interactions, and individualization of learners. In particular, an accurate evaluation is not possible until this has been done.

Interactivity.   Haack (1997) reported in detail on forms of interaction in hypermedia learning environments and discusses relevant influencing factors. According to Haack, appropriate intervention and control opportunities allow for all "consideration of the individual needs of learners" (p. 162). They prove their value "when interested and experienced learners actively work out a branch of knowledge" (p. 163).

Isolation.   In a pilot study, Lake (1999) attempted to reduce the number of distance student dropouts by means of an online counseling course that supports the social and academic integration of distance students. The campus and the buildings are used here as metaphors, work with partners is arranged, and the formal character of academic teaching is reduced through informal contacts and discussions (virtual cafeteria). By these means, distance students are successfully brought out of their physical and mental isolation.

Knowledge Management.   Online learning is a matter of handling networked and therefore complex information and knowledge stores intelligently and responsibly. Mandl and Reinmann-Rothmeier (1998) diagnosed the demand for knowledge management. They regarded this activity as an interdisciplinary research topic because it has to be processed not only from the aspect of the individual but also from societal areas and knowledge domains. The central criteria are self-responsibility, self-direction, and cooperation.

Learning Support.   The study by Friedrich and Ballstaedt (1995), which is based on the findings of cognition psychology, investigated learning processes in a digital learning environment. The authors differentiated between direct, indirect, and interactive learning support and illustrated these types of support from technological, constructivist, and ecological perspectives. Indirect learning support through the design of the learning environments is particularly important for learning with the new media in distance education, but at the same time interactive learning support is important for all virtual support measures. Direct learning support takes place through strategy training and should also be researched. It would be interesting to find out the relationship between the three types of support in a system of "combined learning support."

Motivation.   Cornell and Martin (1997) highlighted the importance of motivation for online learning by diagnosing seven "key principles" (Astleitner & Schinagl, 2000, p. 58), namely, variation and curiosity, relevance, challenge, positive results, positive impression of the teaching materials, readability, and generating interest.

Mummy Research.   At the Institute for Mathematics and Data Processing in Medicine at the University of Hamburg, a virtual mummy can be unwound and given non destructive examinations (see http://www.uke.unihamburg.de/institute/imdm/idv/forschung/mumie/).

Quality Criteria.   On the basis of evaluation studies, Behrens (1999) established that "technology centrism" dominates in online learning and that pedagogical aspects are not considered sufficiently. He offered a theoretically and empirically developed criteria grid with which online learning can be described, evaluated, designed, and prospectively developed.

Ranking.   In the United Kingdom, the quality of teaching in all universities is measured systematically every year by the Quality Assurance Agency. In the agency's first report, the Open University was ranked 10th out of 98 tested universities, which makes it, with Oxford and Cambridge, one of the country's top 10 universities. This finding and other research led Keegan (2000) to state, "'Both from research and practical evidence it seems clear that academic excellence can be achieved by distance systems, whether they teach the traditional distance education or on the web" (p. 78).

Test Method.   Jeger (2000) classified the online test methods developed up to now in the literature and described a flexible application of such tests in the framework of the OLAT (Online Learning and Testing) project at the Institute for Informatics at the University of Zurich.

Virtual Blackboard.   In the Fraunhofer Institut für Arbeitswirtschaft und Organisation work has been carried out since the beginning of April 2000 on the EU project Virtual Blackboard. The aim is to develop a virtual lecture room in which students from all over the world can hear lectures and participate interactively (see: www.virtual-blackboard.iao.fhg.de).

Virtuality.   The research group of Friesen et al. (2000) attempted "to contrast constructively two pointed positions which are apparently indissolubly at variance with one another: the 'phenomenology of displacement and the ontology of detachment' "(p. 5). They discussed the possibility of displacing space, time, and sensory perception and noted that the detachment of the mind from the body is often held to be impossible. In contrast, they claimed that in fact the mind can detach itself from the body and gain ontological independence of virtual reality.

Virtual Seminar.   Friedrich, Hesse, Ferber, and Heins (2000a) checked the hypothesis that a problem-oriented presentation has a more positive effect on the number of active participants than a neutral presentation without a contextual reference. This hypothesis could not be confirmed. One presenter was in fact clearly more successful than three other moderators taking part in the experiment. It is obvious that he offered much shorter contributions with less contextual input.

Friedrich, Heins, and Hesse (1998) examined the influence that institutional support has on the willingness of participants in a virtual seminar to continue their online interaction and cooperation. In a virtual seminar, the teacher stopped his assistance after 3 weeks and invited the participants to continue discussing independently in the remaining week (low institutional support). At the end of another virtual seminar, the participants were invited to continue working in small groups for four more weeks in accordance with the exact job orders and schedule and with the goal of recording the findings in a text published on the Internet (high institutional support). This type of intensified institutional support successfully motivated students to continue their self-directed learning.

Friedrich and Hron (2001) developed a framework model for designing and evaluating virtual seminars based on the input-output models of empirical teaching research. Their model designates and describes critical variables and constraints of online learning.

In a field experiment, Friedrich, Hron, Tergan, and Jechle (2001) studied the effects of a weak and a strong variant of the procedural support of cooperative text production in virtual learning groups. There are no unambiguous findings. However, the internal climate of the groups had an effect. If it was regarded as positive, more people took part, and the cognitive stimulus content of the written assignments was assessed more positively.

Virtual Society. Bühl (1997) developed a theory of the virtual society, examined the technology, and analyzed its role in science fiction literature and its actual applications in economics, politics and culture. For the field of education and training, he arrived at the following conclusion: "The profound changes to the technological basis, micro-electronics, networking, virtualising and the accompanying changes to socialization also modify the reproduction mechanisms of the knowledge and information basis of society from the ground up" (p. 358).

CONCLUSION

The research mentioned in the preceding section makes up a kaleidoscope of many selective approaches. What is missing are significant large-scale studies that identify and verify the integral pedagogical effects of the new media on a theoretical, empirical, and interdisciplinary basis. So far, only the outline of this area of research has become clear, and there are currently no relevant research capacities and no funding for large-scale research projects. In sum, research into learning with new media is still an unchartered territory.

REFERENCES

Albert, S., & Thomas, C. (2000). A new approach to computer-aided distance learning: The "automated tutor." *Open Learning, 15*(2), 141–150.

Astleitner, H. (n.d.). *Emotionen und web-basierte Erziehung: Strategien für eine emotionalisierte Aus- und Weiterbildung.* Working paper, Institute of Educational Sciences, University of Salzburg, Austria.

Astleitner, H., & Leutner, D. (1998). Fernunterricht und neue Informationstechnologien: Aktuelle Entwicklungen. *Zeitschrift für Pädagogik, 44*(1), 106–123.

Astleitner, H., & Schinagl, W. (2000). *High-level Telelernen und Wissensmanagement: Grundpfeiler virtueller Ausbildung.* Frankfurt: Peter Lang.

Bates, A. (1995). *Technology, open learning and distance education.* London: Routledge.

Bates, A. W. (2000) Managing Technological Change. San Francisco: Jossey-Bass.

Bartels, J. (1997). Der multimediale Dateikurs als Lehrelement im Fernstudium. In J. Wurster (Ed.) *Virtuelles Kolloquium: Medienentwicklung im Fernstudium.* Hagen, Germany: FernUniversität.

Baudrillard, J. (1989). *Philosophien der neuen Technologien.* Berlin: Merve.

Baumgartner, P. (2000). *Evaluation vernetzten Lernens.* In: Hartmut Simon (ed.): Virtueller Campus. Münster, Germany: Wachsmann.

Baumgartner, P., & Payr, S. (1994). *Lernen mit Software.* Innsbruck, Austria: Österreichischer Studien-Verlag.

Beck, K. (1998). Lehren und Lernen in der "Informationsgesellschaft": Prognosen über den Einsatz und die Folgen computervermittelter Kommunikation im Bildungswesen. In E. Prommer & G. Vowe (Eds.), *Computervermittelte Kommunikation: Öffentlichkeit im Wandel.* Munich: UVK-Medien.

Behrens, U. (1999). *Teleteaching is easy!? Pädagogisch-psychologische Qualitätskriterien und Möglichkeiten der Qualitätskontrolle für Teleteaching Projekte.* Landau, Germany: Verlag Empirische Pädagogik.

Bernath, U. (2000). Erfahrungen mit einem virtuellen Seminar. *Einblicke, 31,* 17–19.

Bernath, U., & Rubin, E. (Eds.). (1999). *Final report and documentation of the Virtual Seminar for Professional Development in Distance Education.* Oldenburg, Germany: Bibliotheks- und Informationssystem der Universität Oldenburg.

Bühl, A. (1997). *Die virtuelle Gesellschaft. Ökonomie, Kultur und Politik im Zeichen des Cyberspace.* Opladen, Germany: Westdeutscher Verlag.

Burckhardt, M. (1997). *Metamorphosen von Raum und Zeit: Eine Geschichte der Wahrnehmung.* Frankfurt: Campus.

Casper, G. (1997). Eine Welt ohne Universitäten? (Werner Heisenberg Lecture). München: Bayerische Akademie der Wissenschaften und Carl Friedrich von Siemens Stiftung, July 3, 1996. (Quoted from a broadcast manuscript of the Tele-Akademie des Südwestfunk, January 26, 1997)

Cornell, R., & Martin, B. L. (1997). The role of motivation in Web-based instruction. In B. H. Khan (Ed.), *Web-based instruction* (pp. 93–100). Englewood Cliffs, NJ: Educational Technology Publications.

Daniel, J. (1998a, April 15). *Knowledge media for mega-universities: Scaling up new technology at the open university.* Paper presented at the Shanghai Open and Distance Education Symposium Shanghai Radio and Television University.

Daniel, J. (1998b). Can you get my hard nose in focus? Universities, mass education and appropriate technology. In M. Eisenstadt & T. Vincent (Eds.), *The knowledge web: Learning and collaborating on the Net* (pp. 21–30). London: Kogan Page.

Dave, B., & Danahy, J. (2000). Virtual study abroad and exchange studio. *Automation in Construction, 9,* 57–71.

De Corte, E., Linn, M.C., Mandl, H., & Verschaffel, L. (Eds.). (1992). *Computer-based learning environments and problem solving.* New York: Springer.

Eisenstadt, M., & Vincent, T. (1998). *The knowledge web: Learning and collaboration on the Net.* London: Kogan Page.

Ewert, J., Hauff, M., Mielke, W. H., & Prümmer, C. von (1998). Multipointvideokonferenzen in der Lehre der Fernuniversität: Erste Erfahrungen mit einem innovativen Lehrkonzept. In Gesellschaft der Freunde der FernUniversität, *Jahrbuch* (pp. 25–38). Hagen, Germany: FernUniversität-Gesamthochschule.

Friedrich, H. F., & Ballstaedt, S. P. (1995). Förderung von Lernprozessen und Lernstrategien. *Grundlagen der Weiterbildung, 4,* 207–211.

Friedrich, H. F., Heins, J., & Hesse, F. W. (1998). Learning tasks and participation in self-organised learning activities in virtual seminars. In P. Marquet, S. Manthey, A. Jaillet, & E. Nissen (Eds.), *Internet-based teaching and learning* (pp. 95–100). Proceedings of IN-TELE '98. Frankfurt, Germany: Peter Lang 1999.

Friedrich, H. F., Hesse, F. W., Ferber, S., & Heins, J. (2000a). Evaluation einer Strategie zur Moderation virtueller Seminare. In H. Krahn & J. Wedekind (Eds.), *Virtueller Campus '99: Heute Experiment–morgen Alltag?* (pp. 127–137). Munich: Wachsmann.

Friedrich, H. F., Hesse, F. W., Ferber, S., & Heins, J. (2000b). Partizipation im virtuellen Seminar in Abhängigkeit von der Moderationsmethode: Eine empirische Untersuchung. In M. Fechter & C. Bremer (Eds.), *Die virtuelle Konferenz: Neue Möglichkeiten für die politische Kommunikation.* Essen, Germany: Klartext-Verlag.

Friedrich, H. F., & Hron, A. (2001). Überlegungen zur Gestaltung und Evaluation virtueller Seminare. In H. M. Niegemann & K. Treumann (Eds.), *Lehren und Lernen mit neuen Medien.* Munich: Wachsmann.

Friedrich, H. F., Hron, A., Tergan, O., & Jechle, T. (2001). Unterstützung kooperativen Schreibens in virtuellen Lernumgebungen. In P. Handler (Ed.), *Textproduzieren in elektronischen Medien: Strategien und Kompetenzen* [Proceedings of the 4th PROWITEC-Colloquium, Vienna, 2000]. Frankfurt: Peter Lang.

Friesen, H., Berr. K., Gerdes, K., Lenk, A., & Sanders, G. (2000). *Philosophische Dimensionen des Problems der Virtualität in einer globalen Mediengesellschaft.* Oldenburg, Germany: Bibliotheks- und Informationssystem der Carl von Ossietzky Universität Oldenburg.

Fritsch, H. (1982). Industrialized counselling: Developing a system that takes care of all: Pre-unknown information gives more time for person-to-person contacts. In J. S. Daniel et al. (Eds.) *Learning at a distance: A world perspective* (pp. 140–141). Edmonton, AB: Athabasca University.

Garrison, R., & Anderson, T. (2000). Transforming and enhancing university teaching: Stronger and weaker technological influences. In T. Evans & D. Nation (Eds.), *Changing university teaching. Reflections on creating educational technologies* (pp. 24–33). London: Kogan Page.

Geiersbach, F.-W., Prümmer, C. von, & Rossie, U. (1997). *Evaluation der CD-ROM zum Kurs "Psychologie der sozialen Beeinflussung."* Hagen, Germany: Fernuniversität-Gesamthochschule, Zentrum für Fernstudienentwicklung. Institutional report.

Guzman, A., & Nunez-Esquer, G. (1998). Virtual learning spaces in distance education: Tools for the EVA project. *Expert Systems with Applications 15,* 205–210.

Haack, J. (1997). Interaktivität als Kennzeichen von Multimedia und Hypermedia. In L. J. Issing & P. Klimsa (Eds.), *Information und Lernen mit Multimedia* (pp. 151–166). Weinheim, Germany: Beltz.

Haefner, K. (1987). Medienpädagogik im Computerzeitalter. In L. J Issing (Ed.), *Medienpädagogik im Informationszeitalter* (pp. 33–52). Weinheim, Germany: Deutscher Studienverlag.

Heidbrink, H. (1996). Ein virtuelles Methodenseminar an der Fernuniversität. In B. Batinic (Ed.), *Internet für Psychologen.* Göttingen, Germany: Hogrefe.

Helms, F. P. (1999). *Evaluation des CD-ROM-Kurses Grundzüge der Betriebswirtschaftslehrer II.* Hagen, Germany: FernUniversität-Gesamthochschule, Zentrum für Fernstudienentwicklung. Institutional report.

Heuel, E., & Postel, M. (1993). Lernen und Üben mit dem Computer: Beispiele aus der Praxis der Fernuniversität. In Gesellschaft der Freunde der Fernuniversität, *Jahrbuch* (pp. 265–279). Hagen, Germany: FernUniversität.

Hoyer, H. (1998). *Reale Systeme im Virtuellen Labor.* Working Paper, Chair of Process Control, FernUniversität-Gesamthochschule, Department of Electrical Engineering.

Hoyer, H. (1999) "Lernraum Virtuelle Universität": Challenge and Opportunity for the FernUniversität. In G. E. Ortner & F. Nickolmann (eds.) Socio-Economics of Virtual Universities. Weinheim, Germany: Beltz, pp. 213–222.

Hoyer, H. (2000). Die FernUniversität auf dem Wege zur Virtuellen Universität. Gesellschaft der Freunde der Fern-Universität, *Jahrbuch* (pp. 43–56) Hagen, Germany: FernUniversität.

Jeger, S. P. (2000). *Online-Testmethoden: Klassifikation, Implementierung und konzeptionelle Weiterentwicklung.* Submitted dissertation, Institute for Computer Science, University of Zurich.

Kaderali, F. (1999). *Virtuelle Universität: ET-Online.* Hagen, Germany: FernUniversität-Gesamthochschule, Fachbereich Elektrotechnik, Fachgebiet Kommunikationssysteme.

Kaye, A. R. (Ed.). (1992). *Collaborative learning through computer conferencing.* New York: Springer.

Keegan, D. (2000). *Distance training. Taking stock at a time of change.* London: Routledge-Palmer.

Kleinschmidt, A. (1999). Virtual tutoring in distance education. In European Association of Distance Teaching Universities, *ESC 98 conference proceedings* (pp. 29–32). *Heerlen, The Netherlands: Open Universiteit.*

Kleinschroth, R. (1996). *Neues Lernen mit dem Computer.* Reinbek, Germany: Rowohlt.

Laaser, W. (1990). Interaktive Lehrprogramme für den PC: Standortbestimmung. In Gesellschaft der Freunde der Fernuniversität, *Jahrbuch* (pp. 211–225). Hagen, Germany: FernUniversität.

Lake, D. (1999). Reducing isolation for distance students: An on-line initiative. *Open Learning, 14,* (3), 14–23.

Leutner, D. (1997). Adaptivität und Adaptierbarkeit multimedialer Lehr- und Informationssysteme. In L. J. Issing & P. Klimsa (Eds.), *Information and Lernen mit Multimedia* (pp. 139–149). Weinheim, Germany: Beltz.

Mandl, H., Gruber, H., & Renkl, A. (1997). Lernen und Lehren mit dem Computer. In F. E. Weinert & H. Mandl (Eds.), *Psychologie der Erwachsenenbildung* (pp. 437–467). Göttingen, Germany: Hogrefe.

Mandl, H., & Reinmann-Rothmeier, G. (1998). Wissensmanagement im Internet: Herausforderung für das Lernen in der Zukunft. In U. Beck & W. Sommer (Eds.), *Proceedings of LERNTEC 98.* Karlsruhe, Germany: Karlsruher Kongress- und Ausstellungs-GmbH.

Nestor, N., & Mandl, H. (1997). Lernen in Computernetzwerken: Erfahrungen mit einem virtuellen Seminar. *Unterrichtswissenschaft, 25,* (1), 19–33.

Ommerborn, R., & Schuemer, R. (2000). Meinungen behinderter Studierender zur PC-Nutzung im Fernstudium [ZIFF-Papiere 114]. Hagen, Germany: FernUniversität-Gesamthochschule, Zentrum für Fernstudienforschung.

Peters, O. (1998). *Learning and teaching in distance education.* London: Kogan Page.

Peters, O. (2000a). Ein didaktisches Modell für den virtuellen Lernraum. In W. Marotzk, D. M. Meister, & U. Sander (Eds.), *Zum Bildungswert des Internet.* Opladen, Germany: Leske und Budrich

Peters, O. (2000b). Digital learning environments: New possibilities and opportunities. *International Review of Research in Open and Distance Learning, 1*(1), 1–19.

Peters, O. (2000c). The transformation of the university into an institution of independent learning. In T. Evans & D. Nation (Eds.), *Changing university teaching* (pp. 10–23). London: Kogan Page.

Pieper, D., & Schmauss, D. (1999). Die Universitätsbibliothek Hagen: Auf dem Weg zur Digitalen Bibliothek. In Gesellschaft der Freunde der FernUniversität, *Jahrbuch* (pp. 71–82). Hagen, Germany: FernUniversität.

Prümmer, C. von (2000). *Verfügbarkeit und Nutzung von Computern und Informations- und Kommunikationsmedien (IuK) im Fernstudium.* Hagen, Germany: FernUniversität-Gesamthochschule, Zentrum für Fernstudienentwicklung. Instituional report.

Raiser, H. (1991). Die Nutzung von Personalcomputern in den maschinellen Korrektursystemen LOTSE und Betriebliches Rechnungswesen (bRw). In Gesellschaft der Freunde der FernUniversität *Jahrbuch* (pp. 194–201). Hagen, Germany: FernUniversität.

Reinmann-Rothmeier, G., & Mandl, H. (1997). Problemorientiertes Lernen mit Multimedia. In K. A. Geissler, G. v. Landsbert, & M. Reinartz (Eds.), *Handbuch Personalentwicklung und Training* (pp. 1–22). Cologne; Germany Verlagsgruppe Deutscher Wirtschaftsdienst.

Reinmann-Rothmeier, G., & Mandl, H. (1999). *Lernen mit neuen Medien: Eine Chance für neue Konzepte und innovative Ziele.* Munich: Ludwig Maximilian University, Chair for Empirical Educational Science and Psychology of Education. Working paper.

Robson, J. (2000). Evaluating on-line teaching. *Open Learning, 15*(2), 151–172.

Salmon, G. (1999). Computer mediated conferencing in large scale management education. *Open Learning, 14*(2), 34–43.

Schank, R. (1997). *Virtual learning: A revolutionary apporoach to building a highly skilled workforce.* New York: McGraw-Hill.

Schlageter, G. (2000). Die neue Welt des e-learning: Quo vadis, Fernuniversität? In H. Hoyer (Ed.), *Ralf Bartz: 25 Jahre Kanzler an der Fernuniversität* (pp. 126–139). Hagen, Germany: Zentrale Vervielfältigungsstelle der FernUniversität.

Schmauss, D. (2000, September). *Library and information support for distance learners at the FernUniversität: An experience and a project: Digital library and virtual library.* Paper presented at the Millennium Conference of the European Association of Distance Teaching Universities (EADTU), Paris.

Schulmeister, R. (1999). Virtuelle Universitäten aus didaktischer Sicht. *Hochschulwesen, 6,* 166–174.

Schulmeister, R. (2001) Virtuelle Universität. Virtuelles Lernen. Munich, Germany: Oldenbourg.

Six, H-W., Ströhlein, G., & Voss, I. (2001, April). Evaluation of WebAssign. Paper presented at the 20th World Conference of the International Council on Distance Education (ICDE), Düsseldorf, Germany.

Tait, A., & Mills, R. (1999). *The convergence of distance and conventional education: Patterns of flexibility for the individual learner.* London: Routledge.

Tergan, S.-O. (2000). Vergleichende Bewertung von Methoden zur Beurteilung der Qualität von Lern- und Informationssystemen. In P. Schenkel, S.-O. Tergan, & A. Lottmann (Eds.), *Qualitätsbeurteilung multimedialer Lern- und Informationssysteme: Evaluationsmethoden auf dem Prüfstand.* Nuremberg, Germany: Bildung und Wissen Verlag und Software GmbH.

Turkle, S. (1998). *Leben im Netz: Identität in Zeiten des Internet* (*Life on the Screen* [1995]). Reinbek, Germany: Rowohlt.

Verdejo, M. F., & Cerri, S. A. (Eds.). (1994). *Collaborative dialogue technologies in distance education.* New York: Springer.

Virilio, P. (1999). *Fluchtgeschwindigkeit* (*La vitesse deliberation*, Paris [1995]) Frankfurt: Fischer Taschenbuch.

Voss, J., Ströhlein, G., Brunsmann, J., & Six, H.-W. (2000). Universitärer Übungsbetrieb über das WWW. Hagen, Germany: FernUniversität-Gesamthochschule. Working paper.

Wenning, N. (2000). *Onlineseminar: Seminar online? Erfahrungen und Anregungen zu einem internetbasierten Lehrangebot.* Hagen, Germany: FernUniversität: Institute of Educational Science and Research. Working paper.

Wiendieck, G., & Üstünsöz, D. (1995) Einsatz neuer Medien an der Fernuniversität: NetNews. In Gesellschaft der Freunde der Fernuniversität, *Jahrbuch* (pp. 35–45). Hagen, Germany: FernUniversität.

Woodley, A. (1999). Doing institutional research: The role of the partisan guerrilla. *Open Learning, 14*(2), 52–57.

Wurster, J. (1997). Virtuelles Colloquium: Medienentwicklung im Fernstudium. Hagen, Germany: FernUniversität-Gesamthochschule, Zentrum für Fernstudienentwicklung. Berichte und Materialien.

Wurster, J. (1999). Integrierende Lernumgebungen der virtuellen Universität: Modularisierung und Differenzierung. In Gesellschaft der Freunde der Fernuniversität, *Jahrbuch* (pp. 35–45). Hagen, Germany: FernUniversität.

Zentrum für Fernstudienentwicklung. (1999). *Jahresbericht.* Hagen, Germany: FernUniversität-Gesamthochschule.

Zentrum für Fernstudienentwicklung. (2000). *Jahresbericht.* Hagen, Germany: FernUniversität-Gesamthochschule.

APPENDIX: LEARNING WITH NEW MEDIA
IN DISTANCE EDUCATION

Stages on the way to the "learning space virtual university" of the FernUniversität in Hagen

Year	Type of Digitizing	Changes in Learning Behavior	Changes in Teaching Behavior
1975	Use of a central computer to control distance education operations.	Inspection of own files, including earlier written examinations and the grades for them. Greater transparency.	Wide-ranging documentation of performance data. Comparative overview of the performances of various population segments are possible. Where necessary, course syllabuses are optimized accordingly.
1976	Empirical evaluation of course materials with standard questionnaires as marking vouchers.	Teaching text criticism by students. They enter their opinions and assessment in a coded questionnaire.	Formative and summative evaluation. Teachers check the teaching text criticisms from students and external experts and amend the teaching texts where necessary.
1977	Computer-aided correction systems LOTSE and bRw (operational accounting).	Students code their learning results on the basis of selective or numerical answers and enter them in a machine-readable marking code.	Teachers work in accordance with pedagogical aspects not only with tutor-marked assignments but also with computer-marked assignments.
1979	Digital study start advice STEB.	Detailed advice for potential students on the basis of their individual interests, inclinations, and learning situations in the form of individually compiled computer letters.	Teachers, study counselors, and instruction technicians collaborate to provide relief for personal study counseling through this computer-aided advisory system. Where necessary, this computer-aided advisory system should also dissuade potential students if misguided conceptions of distance studying become apparent.
1980	Introduction of interactive access to study centers on central computers.	Interactive process of programming training.	
1980	Teletext as information medium.	Low-cost request of study information.	Flexible provision of information relevant for studying.
1982	Teletext-computer network for computer communication from home.	Low-cost dialogue access for students to information, to advice, and in some cases to assignments and practical training.	Compilation and provision of digitized information and assignments
1984	First PC in a study center.	Decentralized and close-to-home use of IT resources.	Training in word processing and presentation and teletext communication.
1984	Computer access for distance students via EARN/BITNET (Internet predecessors).		Scientists begin exchange of information.

(Continued)

Year	Type of Digitizing	Changes in Learning Behavior	Changes in Teaching Behavior
1985	First digital teaching modules and disks.	Students learn on the screen: they are activated through the interactivity and profit from the elucidation through multimedia, in particular, animation and simulation. They alter, store, and manage the acquired knowledge.	Collaboration with instructional technologists is necessary. Study letters can be sent easily in the form of teaching disks. The development of digital courses begins.
1986	Institutional access to the Internet.	Students can request data and information and training tasks and send in assignment solutions.	The Internet takes up a place alongside the network of postal links. Information and teaching texts distributed via the Internet.
1987	Step-by-step introduction of electronic word processing.	Reading is made easier through better printing quality and greater variety of the graphics.	New forms of presenting texts on-screen are developed. Teaching texts can now be stored and easily updated and corrected. Teachers develop semi-professional skills for designing teaching texts.
1987	DFN Deutsches Forschungsnetz (German Research Net). Training disks are offered to supplement and deepen the work with the printed study material.	Students use the training disks above all to prepare for examinations.	Use of the Web in the framework of research projects. Development of teaching and training disks.
1992	Introduction for teachers and their assistants to professional use of the relevant software.		Teachers increasingly use the help of experts in instruction technology to become more competent in designing online teaching texts.
1993	Using links with Gopher and WWW services.	Important precondition for online learning.	Important precondition for the distribution of teaching texts.
1993	Network infrastructure throughout the university. All workplaces connected to the Internet.	Introduction of WWW and news services for students.	When developing teaching texts, teachers and their assistants can make use of the varied information available on the Internet and communicate and collaborate with one another virtually.
1994	First course materials on CD-ROM.	Students learn with more extensive on-screen learning texts: they are activated through the interactivity and profit from the elucidation through multimedia, in particular, animation and simulation. They alter, store, and manage the acquired knowledge.	Collaboration with instructional technologists is necessary. Study letters can be sent easily in the form of teaching CDs. The development of digital courses begins.

(Continued)

Year	Type of Digitizing	Changes in Learning Behavior	Changes in Teaching Behavior
1995	Start of the development work for the degree course ETOnline (electric engineering).	The first students test the digitized teaching materials by working through them parallel to working with the printed material. They have constant access to the teaching materials placed on the Web, to their personal files, and to the stored grades given for written examinations.	Developing and testing online courses and permanent optimization of the technical infrastructure for online learning.
1995	Step-by-step introduction of ISDN videoconferences for teaching and oral examinations.	Students take part in synchronous virtual seminars. Students abroad are examined in virtual oral examinations.	Teachers plan, organize, and lead video seminars and gather experience with online oral examinations.
1996	Broadband connection to the Internet/DFN.	Students can work online and offline. They become accustomed to the use of links in the framework of presentations similar to hypertext. Various forms of literature research and information acquisition.	First attempts at improving the pedagogical design of the presentation of learning contents on the screen through multimedia and interactivity. Opening up the services of the university library in Hagen and other libraries via the Internet.
1996	First courses and teaching material on the Internet.	Learning on-screen. Downloading of required learning units. Virtual computer conferences.	Teachers conceive and develop specific online modules, course units, or course packages.
1996	First pilot system for the development of an all-round software infrastructure for Web-based practical training on the basis of WebAssign.	Learners can enter their solutions up to 10 times, and these are returned before the final evaluation with the points already received so that they can be worked on again.	Teachers have to formulate the written assignments with regard to a highly differentiated evaluation system.
1997	Conversion of the IT systems for distance education organization and administration to client-server processes.		Intensified integration of teaching staff into the control systems of distance education organization.
1997	Digitizing distance education courses.	Several accesses and learning paths available. Links enable various extensions and deepening of the learning texts.	Structurally changed presentation. Along with linear forms, teachers use complex forms of presentation of knowledge. Solutions similar to hypertext are created
1997	Production of learning software on disks.	Learning facilitated through new modes of presentation. Improved graphics standard, learning with window-driven menus, more learner autonomy, interactivity, drill and practice.	Teaching through particularly carefully and expensively developed presentation of complicated facts or those which are difficult for other reasons.

(Continued)

Year	Type of Digitizing	Changes in Learning Behavior	Changes in Teaching Behavior
1998	Production of learning software on CD-ROMs.	As with disks, additional learning with multisensory and simulated presentations.	Teaching with video sequences, animation, simulations and virtual practical training.
1999	Start of virtual bachelor's degree in informatics.	Students in informatics degree course can carry out their studies completely on the Web and have to train in Web-based learning as the standard form of acquiring knowledge and developing it further. They have to internalize this new and completely different form of learning and teaching.	The main task consists of planning a didactically practical and productive combination of multimedia and interactive teaching texts, virtual seminars, virtual discussions and co-operation and in this way to create a digital learning environment which provides sufficient space for autonomous learning as well.
2000	Central technical platform for Web-based studying. Start of bachelor's degree ET Online in German and English.	Broad use of learning space virtual university. Students in ET Online degree course can carry out their studies completely on the Web and have to train in web-based learning as the standard form of acquiring knowledge and developing it further. They have to internalize this new and completely different form of learning and teaching.	Aligning course syllabuses and practical training to Web functions. The main task consists of planning a didactically practical and productive combination of multimedia and interactive teaching texts, virtual seminars, virtual discussions and co-operation and in this way to create a digital learning environment which provides sufficient space for autonomous learning as well.

8

A Theory of Critical Inquiry in Online Distance Education

D. Randy Garrison
University of Calgary
garrison@ucalgary.ca

Terry Anderson
Athabasca University
terrya@athabascau.ca

Walter Archer
University of Saskatchauan
walter.archer@usask.ca

Online learning represents a new paradigm for distance and distributed learning. Furthermore, this new paradigm is affecting education in general: the previously marginal subfield of distance education has become a central focus of the field of education because of the flexibility and general attractiveness of its new paradigm.

What distinguishes online learning from previous paradigms of distance education is its ability to create critical communities of inquiry. That is, as distance educators we are now able to do what was previously impossible—conduct collaborative learning regardless of time and place. This ability to provide interactive learning experiences characterized by critical discourse is what has attracted the attention of traditional educators and institutions. Ironically, it has also seriously challenged the subfield of distance education to hold its place as a leader in its own area of expertise, since many other educators and trainers from the public and private sectors are now becoming involved with online learning (Tait & Mills, 1999).

The question here is whether the subfield of distance education has the vision and theoretical foundation to distinguish itself as a leader in shaping new initiatives related to developments in online learning. It is not enough for distance educators to be good practitioners. To be leaders, scholars working in the field of distance education must demonstrate theoretical insight as well as retain their position as innovative practitioners. One challenge they face is to provide a theoretical framework with the potential to explain and shape distance education practice in the area of interactive online education. The theory outlined in this chapter is intended to be a practical tool that will help educators think through their needs and understand the pedagogical, technological, and organizational options open to them.

BACKGROUND

Theoretical interests and developments in the field of distance education have progressed from a preoccupation with organizational (structural) concerns to transactional (teaching and learning) issues (Garrison, 2000). Motivating this transformational shift are recent advances in communications technology and developments in social learning theory. The emergence of new asynchronous and synchronous communications technology has made possible collaborative distance education experiences based on adaptive teaching and learning transactions. This new transactional era of distance education has been largely shaped by the ability of computer-mediated communication (CMC) to create a community of learners at a distance. The theoretical challenge faced by distance education is to construct transactional frameworks and models that will explain, interpret, and shape practice made possible by highly interactive communications technologies, especially CMC in general and computer conferencing in particular.

CMC encompasses a wide range of online applications. The CMC application that best represents the new era of distance education is computer conferencing. Computer conferencing often integrates other CMC applications such as e-mail, and, recently, synchronous audio- and videoconferencing. Computer conferencing has aroused widespread interest as the Internet had developed and matured. In particular, World Wide Web standards have transformed "computer conferencing from a single-media (text) to a multi-media environment" (Garrison, 1997, p. 4). Despite the ever-increasing popularity of computer conferencing, our understanding of this communications technology has lagged behind adoption rates.

Computer conferencing has been utilized extensively to enhance classroom learning as well as to increase access to educational experiences at a distance. Articles on the educational uses of CMC and computer conferencing began appearing in the 1980s. One of the first articles to cause distance educators to take note was by Roxanne Hiltz (1986). She argued that CMC could be used to build a "virtual classroom." Paulsen and Rekkedal (1988) discussed the potential of CMC and stated that "the most exciting challenge in the long run will be to apply the new technology to create new and more efficient learning situations, rather than replicate the traditional classroom or distance learning environment" (p. 363).

This same message was carried forward by Kaye (1987, 1992; Mason & Kaye, 1989), another early researcher in CMC and computer conferencing. Kaye (1987) rightly noted that CMC is "qualitatively different from other interpersonal and group communication media" (p. 157). Kaye (1992) recognized that computer conferencing represented a new form of collaborative learning that goes beyond information exchange and necessitates moderated critical discourse to realize new and worthwhile understanding. Lauzon and Moore (1989) were the first to recognize that the potential of computer conferencing represented a new generation of distance education characterized by networked, asynchronous group communication. Like her contemporaries, Harasim (1987, 1989, 1990) argued strongly "that online education (by which I mean, predominantly, computer conferencing) represents a unique domain of educational interaction" (1987, p. 50). She argued for a collaborative instructional design to accompany computer conferencing, thus integrating many of the emerging social learning theories being developed by constructivist learning theorists. Henri (1992) advocated and provided a framework to systematically study computer conferencing. This may have been the first coherent theoretical approach to studying this new communications technology. She identified both cognitive and social dimensions of computer conferencing that enhance learning outcomes.

While research into CMC has continued and intuitive principles have proliferated, few studies "are grounded in systematic, rigorous inquiry . . . [and] few attempts to present theories or research models of any aspect of CMC study have emerged" (Romiszowski & Mason, 1996, p. 443). This general lack of systematic and theoretically coherent approaches to research in CMC has continued to the present. The next section is an attempt to remedy this lacuna in distance education research.

A FRAMEWORK AND MODEL

Much of the research and practice in computer conferencing during the 1990s focused on and took advantage of the social and democratic features of the technology (Gunawadena, 1991, 1995; Harasim, 1990). One study that focused on the ability of this medium to support higher-order learning was Garrison (1997). The essential role of the moderator as facilitator of the learning process was also emphasized by several researchers (Fabro & Garrison, 1998; Feenberg, 1989; Gunawardena, 1991; Kaye, 1992). These three essential elements (social, cognitive, and teaching) form the core of the framework outlined below.

Garrison, Anderson, and Archer (2000) constructed a conceptual framework for a multi-faceted study of computer conferencing effectiveness in supporting critical thinking in higher education. The first assumption of that study was that an educational experience intended to achieve higher-order learning outcomes is best embedded in a community of inquiry composed of students and teachers (Lipman, 1991). This assumption is also consistent with the educational philosophy of Dewey (1959), who described education as the collaborative reconstruction of experience. The distance education context for this study is not independent learning but rather a context of collaborative, constructivist learning within a community of learners. This is a sharp departure from models and theories of distance education that maximize the independence of individual learners.

However, before describing the core elements of the framework, it is necessary to digress to a very brief discussion of the importance of the communication mode within which this online community of inquiry is created. Currently and for the immediately foreseeable future, CMC is predominantly a text-based, asynchronous form of interaction in which communication occurs through written language and without the paralinguistic and nonverbal communication characteristic of classroom-based learning. Although the absence of paralinguistic and nonverbal communication may create an initial barrier for at least some learners, there are compensating advantages. The use of the written word may encourage discipline and rigor, and the asynchronous nature of the communication may encourage reflection, resulting in contributions to the discussion that are more complex and demonstrate more advanced stages of critical thinking (Archer, Garrison, & Anderson, 2000; Feenberg, 1989). However, this is far from being established, and much more basic research in this area is required if we are to understand and apply this knowledge.

To define the functioning of this community of inquiry, Garrison et al. (2000) proposed three overlapping elements—social presence, cognitive presence, and teaching presence (see Fig. 8.1). As noted previously, a number of scholars have devoted considerable attention to understanding the necessity and creation of climate or social presence in an educational computer conferencing environment. Within our model, we define social presence as the ability of learners to project themselves (i.e., their personal characteristics) socially and emotionally, thereby representing themselves as "real" people in a community of inquiry. From a review of the literature, three broad categories of social presence, along with indicators of these categories, were identified (Garrison et al., 2000). Through an iterative process of analysis of transcripts of educational computer conferences, adjustment, and re-application, these categories and their associated indicators were refined (Rourke, Anderson, Garrison, & Archer, 2000). The resulting instrument was used to detect and quantify levels of social presence in different computer conferences.

The second element in the framework is cognitive presence. We define cognitive presence "as the extent to which learners are able to construct and confirm meaning through sustained reflection and discourse in a critical community of inquiry" (Garrison, Anderson, & Archer, 2001). The concept of cognitive presence is grounded in the critical thinking literature and more specifically operationalized by the practical inquiry model derived to a large extent from the work of Dewey (1933). This model consists of four phases of critical inquiry that are

Community of Inquiry

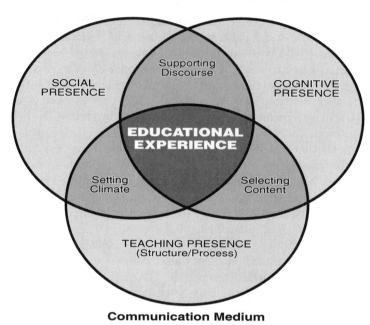

Communication Medium

FIG. 8.1. Elements of an educational experience. Reprinted from The *Internet and Higher Education*
2 (2–3), 1–19 Garrison, D. R., Anderson, T., & Archer, W., Critical inquiry in a text-based environment:
Computer conferencing in higher education, 2000, with permission from Elsevier Science.

idealized and, as a result, are not sequential or immutable. The four phases are the triggering
event, exploration, integration, and resolution (Fig. 8.2). Categories corresponding to each of
these phases were developed and tested, along with descriptors and indicators of each category
(Garrison et al., 2001).

The finding of most interest was that most of the discussion analyzed was coded in the
exploration category (42%). Only 13% of the responses were coded in the integration or
meaning construction category, and fewer yet (4%) in the resolution or application category.
Several explanations are possible, but the most likely is that the course objectives and/or
the facilitation of the conference were not congruent with achieving higher-order learning
outcomes characteristic of the later phases of critical thinking.

We now turn to the third element of the framework, teaching presence, so crucial to realizing
intended learning outcomes. Teaching presence is defined "as the design, facilitation and
direction of cognitive and social processes for the purpose of realizing personally meaningful
and educationally worthwhile learning outcomes" (Anderson, Rourke, Garrison, & Archer,
2001). Based on this definition and the results of our validation work we identified three
categories, design and organization, facilitating discourse, and direct instruction, each with a
set of indicators. The preliminary analysis of teaching presence revealed important differences
between the transcripts of the courses studied. The frequency of the teacher responses in each
category was largely attributable to instructional approaches as well as subject differences.
The conclusion is that teaching presence is a very complex process that must be studied in the
context of a wide range of factors such as intended learning outcomes, instructional strategies,
student characteristics, and practical factors such as class size and the familiarity of participants
with the technology.

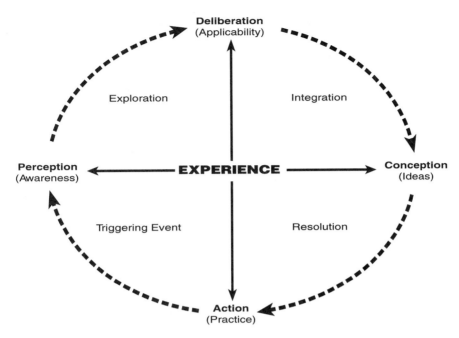

FIG. 8.2. Practical inquiry. Reprinted from The *Internet and Higher Education* 2 (2–3), 1–19 Garrison, D. R., Anderson, T., & Archer, W., Critical inquiry in a text-based environment: Computer conferencing in higher education, 2000, with permission from Elsevier Science.

The previous description indicates the nature of the theoretical framework and initial findings associated with a major research project to study higher-order learning in a text-based computer conferencing environment. Much work remains to be done, but we believe that this work may provide a scaffold for systematically and coherently studying the complexities of CMC and computer conferencing in an online educational environment. We now turn our attention to these communications technologies and offer suggestions as to how they might best be used in current and future distance education contexts.

TECHNOLOGICAL ISSUES

It is rather surprising that in spite of the tremendous increase in interest in CMC and its use to support campus and distance education, the basic structure and tools of computer conferencing have not changed significantly in the past decade. Early conferencing users will recall systems such as Confer, Parti, Cosy, and Forum that offered the same threaded discussion, quoting, and notification systems found in modern systems such as WebCt, Lotus Learning Space, and Blackboard. Beyond compatibility with the Web, few design or functional improvements are apparent. The reasons for this slow progress are many, but probably a main cause is the inability of educators to clearly articulate, based on pedagogical theory or practical experience, their need for more specialized tools.

This section focuses on the value and potential application of some newer tools, particularly multimedia and real-time applications, whose effect is to diversify and improve the capacity of CMC systems. Our goal is to assist developers and users in creating and using next-generation conferencing tools that function within powerful collaborative and constructivist pedagogical theory to support high-quality learning in distance and campus learning contexts.

One of the most important features of the Web as originally envisioned by its creator, Tim Berners-Lee (1999), is its ability to be used as a tool for creation as well as distribution. Creation and construction, in both collaborative and individual contexts, are critical to the development of higher-order learning and communication skills (Bruner, 1990). Given their pedagogical value, it is no surprise to find that CMC tools constitute the most important component of most online courses currently being developed and delivered in formal education contexts (Salmon, 2000). Thus, enhancing the capacity, ease of use, and affordability of these tools is critically important for both research and practice.

Bruce and Levin (1997) suggest that educational technology uses can be classified according to a taxonomy based on a four-part division suggested years ago by John Dewey: inquiry, communication, construction, and expression. We use this taxonomy to illustrate ways in which CMC systems can be made more functional and multi-purposed so as to better serve the needs of networked teachers and learners.

Inquiry

In distance education, individual inquiry is largely facilitated by the provision of access to information databases and other resources in libraries and on the Web. As networked learning becomes more pervasive, the capacity to use CMC for inquiry and research purposes, including interviews, focus groups, and surveys, will expand. Further, the move to network-based application service providers and the "webification" of tools for many tasks, including data analysis and presentation, will make it possible to easily incorporate learning activities using these tools into course and program designs. Finally, the inquiry function now popularized in notions of "knowledge management" calls for ever more sophisticated systems to retrieve, manipulate, and re-purpose content created by other teachers and learners as a component of the formal education process.

Communication

Asynchronous communication in text-based format has been a defining feature of current CMC systems. Next-generation CMC systems will expand the modes of communication available to include video, audio, and virtual reality systems accessible synchronously and asynchronously. This expansion of modes should bring with it an expansion of our research agenda. Most CMC research to date has focused on asynchronous text-based communication, as that mode of CMC has proved to be the most practical and hence the most used in educational contexts. Full implementation of new modes of CMC for educational purposes should be preceded and accompanied by research focused on these new modes.

Although text-based synchronous meetings and lectures (chats) have been used for over a decade by education organizations such as Diversity University (see http://www.du.org/), we find these tools to be clumsy, confusing, and not an efficient use of learner time. Problems related to turn-taking, organization and navigation, required skill sets of participants, and differences in typing speed plague many of these educational chat-based or MOO (Mud Object Oriented)–based systems. More successful and popular has been the use of synchronous audio teleconferencing (Anderson & Garrison, 1995) and videoconferencing to deliver and support education at a distance.

However, audio- and videoconferencing have not generally been integrated into CMC systems. Concerns about the cost and availability of the necessary bandwidth, combined with distance education's traditional imperative to extend and not restrict access, have resulted in a "lowest common denominator" approach in which distance educators avoid applications that require higher bandwidth. However, every year access becomes a less significant barrier to institutions, teachers, and users, as tools become more efficient and less costly and bandwidth becomes cheaper and more widely available. In particular, a product like Centra Symposium (www.centra.com) provides a suite of Internet-based software tools, including Net-based audioconferencing, whiteboard, text chat, application sharing, presentation annotation tools, Web safari, learner response systems, and automatic recording of class sessions. Others (e.g., CuSeeMe, Mbone) go further and support primitive forms of multipoint videoconferencing.

Within distance education, two opposing teaching ideologies have affected educators' choice of communication tools. Advocates of synchronous communication argue that real-time learning environments are critical for coalescing the class experience, providing high levels of socialization, and supporting crucial feedback between teachers and students and that they can be used very effectively for increasing social integration of students into the distance education experience (Roberts, 1998). It has also been argued that synchronous learning provides an easier, less threatening transition from classroom-based instruction for both students and instructors. Advocates of asynchronous communication point to the greater independence from temporal and geographical barriers and the opportunity for more reflective participation provided in asynchronous learning environments (Feenberg, 1989). Next-generation CMC environments will allow instructors and students to mix and match synchronous and asynchronous tools based on curricular goals, individual teaching and learning preferences, and lifestyle and access constraints.

Next-generation CMC tools will also support integration of video and audio clips that can be accessed asynchronously. Kirschner (1991) found that the provision of audio clips containing comments on student assignments in distance education was perceived by the students as being of higher quality than text-based feedback. Provision of feedback also took less teacher time. Most new desktop machines come equipped with microphones and recording software, and video recording systems can be purchased and installed on newer computers for under $200. Thus, we see considerable value in adding such multimedia systems to CMC systems. However, inserting, indexing, and retrieving video or audio clips is awkward and only marginally supported in current CMC systems.

Pedagogical improvements to CMC systems are also needed. A number of educational and workplace CMC systems have incorporated classification systems that require formalization of the user's response, forcing participants to actively place their responses into predefined categories. For example, students may be forced to classify their posting into a category such as question, response, rebuttal, or clarification. The classification systems used have been based on speech act theory, argumentation theory, and workflow or can be user-defined by the teacher or a researcher. Such formalization systems have been criticized (Shipman & Marshall, 1999) as unnecessarily constraining to users by forcing them to structure their activity in unexpected ways. They may also be understood differently by different people, may cause loss of information that is outside of the prescribed structure, and may require making explicit what is difficult or undesirable to articulate. Dourish, Holmes, Marqvardsen, and Zbyslaw (1996) have even gone so far as to characterize such systems as "naziware" due to the compulsory labeling component. We find such criticisms to be overstated, as one of the primary functions of a teacher is to prescribe and evaluate student input and develop metacognitive awareness, thus encouraging deeper levels of engagement and deeper understanding. Like Duffey, Dueber, and Hawley (1998), we believe such systems may have pedagogical value and, assuming they can be customized and their use made optional by individual teachers, can become useful tools for educational CMC.

Construction

The value of collaboration has been a consistent theme in theories (Harasim, Hiltz, Teles, & Turoff, 1995) and research (Bonk & King, 1998) related to CMC use in education. Collaboration takes place in asynchronous contexts in a less structured way through participation in computer conferencing and in a more structured manner in the creation of projects and the joint authorship of papers and presentations.

Collaboration in the computer conferencing environment takes place through amplification or rebuttal of previous postings in the conference or through queries in response to earlier postings. Although most computer conferencing systems allow for automatic quoting of previous comments, Feenberg (2000) argues that authors should be able to browse, sort, review, and cut and paste between separate "reading windows" and "creation windows" both visible simultaneously. Feenberg also suggests there be a capacity for file management through support for active keywords creation and hierarchical filing of comments for later retrieval by any participant.

More sophisticated tools are required for the joint authorship of documents by distributed groups or individuals. Most collaborating authors have experienced the frustration of editing an "older than latest" version of a collaborative document or struggled with creating a single document from one that has been simultaneously edited by two or more persons. The Basic Support for Cooperative Work (BSCW) (Horstmann & Bentley, 1997) tool set contains sophisticated tools for document management that support version control, signing out of documents for editing, annotation and commenting of changes, and archiving of earlier versions of documents. These are important enhancements that go beyond the "presentation workplaces" provided in many of today's conferencing systems.

The capacity to share and collaborate using graphic creation tools is becoming more useful as individual drawing, drafting, and presentation tools become more widely available and easier to use. Next generation CMC systems will need to incorporate document and application sharing tools that allow users to manipulate a common screen even if the application is installed on only one of the users' machines. Such capacity is already available in tools such as Timbucktoo, Symposium, and Netmeeting but is uncommon in CMC packages intended specifically for education.

Expression

The final category of education technology use is "expression." Music, art, multimedia, and video production are areas where archiving, collaboration, and time-shifting tools provided by network-based conferencing systems can support individual and collaborative construction. We see increased emphasis on collaborative production of projects, presentations, and artifacts relevant to the world of work. CMC systems for educational use will need to incorporate or at least provide simple interface connections to tools needed to create such products.

Many of the tools designed and tested by researchers in computer-supported collaborative work and human computer interface studies during the last decade can be incorporated into educational applications of CMC (Twidale & Nichols, 1998). We recommend that developers and users continue to develop educational CMC systems to provide an increasing diverse and powerful set of CMC tools for inquiry, communication, construction, and expression.

PEDAGOGICAL ISSUES

Present practice in the use of computer conferencing has been largely driven by technology. That is, the ubiquity and inexpensiveness of computer conferencing and the Internet has allowed many educators to adopt this technology. Further, although its employment may be based on a variety of reasons, these do not often include pedagogical ones. Computer conferences are commonly used simply to allow students to visit or chat or as an optional discussion forum (not used by many students) in addition to the main mode of delivery, which is usually a course package or lecture.

The focus and challenge here is to understand pedagogically the use of computer conferencing to support purposeful higher-order learning. This means going beyond enhancing course packages, using e-mail to contact tutors, or putting computer-generated and enhanced lectures online. Educators must first understand that computer conferencing represents a new era of distance education in that it makes possible the creation of a critical community of learners not constrained by time or place. Second, educators must develop pedagogical principles and guidelines that will directly facilitate deep and meaningful approaches to teaching and learning. In other words, they must ensure that they encourage critical thinking online and have as the outcome of the educational experience critical thinkers who have learned to learn.

Although there is a plethora of guidelines and suggestions on how to conduct a computer conference (Berge, 1995; Paulsen, 1995; Salmon, 2000), these are generally surface types of suggestions (e.g., "be responsive"). However, the Web and computer conferencing must be used for more than merely accessing information more efficiently. As Fraser (1999) suggests, the extent to which you have not taken advantage of the "expanded horizons for communicating ideas . . . is the extent to which you have done nothing of pedagogical value by using the Web" (p. B8). In Fraser's words, doing anything with these new media that does not expand our horizons is "pedagogically pointless." (p. B8) This is ever more true with regard to CMC and computer conferencing.

The challenge facing researchers and teachers in distance education is to develop a more sophisticated understanding of the characteristics of the new technology and of how we might harness this potential to enhance critical thinking and higher-order learning. As important as critical thinking is as an educational process and goal, we educators often fall far short of achieving it. The reasons include an inability to define critical thinking and a lack of systematic empirical research into how to facilitate it (Kuhn, 1999). In terms of fostering critical thinking skills, Kuhn states that "teachers have been offered remarkably little in the way of concrete examples of what these skills are—what forms they take, how they will know when they see them, how they might be measured" (p. 17).

This is certainly the case in distance education, but here the problem is compounded by a technology and communication medium whose characteristics have not been well researched. McLoughlin and Luca (2000) state that computer conferencing "has become mainstream pedagogic practice. . . . However, there is limited empirical evidence that online learning and asynchronous text based communications support the higher order forms of learning" (p. 1). Distance educators have much work to do to investigate the nature of those online interactions that can be shown to support critical thinking and higher-order learning outcomes. The question that remains is how this task of improving our understanding of such online interactions can be framed.

Certainly the literature suggests that a stronger teaching presence is required in computer conferencing—a presence, we might add, that shapes cognitive and metacognitive processing. Teachers must be able to understand and design learning activities that facilitate higher-order learning outcomes. A good start is the practical inquiry model discussed briefly here and more extensively elsewhere (Garrison et al., 2000). This may provide a coherent model for systematically identifying the phases of critical thinking and associated skills and activities as well as communicating to the students in a metacognitive manner the process that they must ultimately take responsibility to monitor. For example, activities should be designed and moderated so as to focus on the appropriate phase of critical thinking and ensure that the learners progress to the next phase and gain a metacognitive understanding of the process they are engaged in. Kuhn (1999) reinforces this point when she argues that "the development of metacognitive understanding is essential to critical thinking because critical thinking by definition involves reflecting on what is known and how that knowledge is justified" (p. 23).

Unfortunately, the simple adoption of technology does not resolve issues related to the teaching of critical thinking and metacognitive understanding. Moreover, it does not fundamentally change approaches to teaching and learning for the better. It has been argued elsewhere that technology can have both a strong and weak influence on the educational transaction (Garrison & Anderson, 2000). The weak approach is to enhance and thereby reinforce existing teaching practices. On the other hand, the

> stronger influence of technology on teaching would fundamentally change our outcome expectations, and thereby, how we approach the teaching and learning transaction. . . . Here the focus is on the quality of learning outcomes (ie, developing critical thinkers) and adopting approaches to teaching and learning that are congruent with such outcomes. (Garrison & Anderson, 2000, p. 25)

Teaching presence unifies and focuses the teaching and learning transaction. However, as noted, the first challenge in this regard is to develop a comprehensive understanding of the characteristics of this new medium of communication and the implications for supporting an educational community of inquiry using this medium. Although we have begun the process of providing a coherent framework, much work remains to be done before we fully understand the pedagogical implications of using this technology in a variety of contexts and for a variety of purposes. The power and potential of the technology may be enormous, but realizing this potential will depend on conceptual models and principles as well as well-founded guidelines and techniques. We must use the flurry of research activity now surrounding this technology to understand how we might do things differently to enhance the quality of learning outcomes, not just add glitz to existing practice.

It is important that learning technologies be used in the service of worthwhile educational goals. Learning technologies can be a catalyst to shape and change our educational practices for the better. However, this shaping and changing will not be without pain and can result in considerable disruption to current structures.

ORGANIZATIONAL ISSUES

> The current structure and organization of most universities and colleges is largely historical and . . . largely unsuited to new forms of technological delivery. (Bates, 2000, p. 36)

As Postman (1992) argued, not only do new technologies compete with old ones, but surrounding "every technology are institutions whose organization—not to mention their reason for being—reflects the world-view promoted by the technology" (p. 18). This section concentrates on the great majority of educational institutions whose current organization reflects the worldview promoted by the technology of face-to-face classroom instruction and that are having this worldview challenged by the rapidly expanding technology of online learning (Tait & Mills, 1999). We leave to other scholars the discussion of the impact of online learning on "autonomous distance teaching institutions" (Keegan, 1993) whose organization already reflects the worldview promoted by technologies of distance education (though in most cases technologies older than online learning). The best known set of institutions falling into this category are the "mega-universities" described by Daniel (1996).

We also leave to other scholars (e.g., those cited in Keegan, 1993, p. 73) the discussion of what Keegan (1993) refers to as the "Australian integrated model," sometimes called the "New England model" (with reference to the University of New England in New South Wales). This model may be seen as a possible future for today's conventional, campus-based institutions. However, the latter are far from achieving this balanced approach to on- and off-campus delivery. Therefore our discussion will centre on the state of a typical institution of higher education today, in which a few small ventures into online learning represent the institution's current progress in any mode of distance delivery.

For educational institutions built around face-to-face classroom instruction, the advent of online learning presents a crisis situation, in the classic sense of being both an opportunity and a threat. These institutions have before them the opportunity to use this new mode of instruction to improve the instruction offered to on-campus students and to reach out to other learners who are not able or willing to enroll in face-to-face, on-campus programs. The threat is at least twofold: that other providers will serve these potential off-campus students and begin to attract the students who currently attend on campus (Kirkpatrick & Jakupec, 1999; Marchese, 1998) and that a move to embrace online learning will seriously compromise the academic values held by the institution (Katz & Associates, 1999; Noble, 1997, 1998).

We have argued elsewhere (Archer, Garrison, & Anderson, 1999) that distance education, for conventional institutions of higher education, is what Harvard business professor Clayton M. Christensen (1997) refers to as a "disruptive technology"—that is, a new technology that requires an organization to do things in a fundamentally different way. This contrasts with what Christensen (1997) refers to as a "sustaining technology," a new technology that represents simply an improvement on current practices. Archer et al. (1999) suggested that educational institutions can benefit by paying attention to the insights derived by Christensen and others (e.g., Day & Schoemaker, 2000) regarding ways in which established business firms (analogous to established educational institutions) can cope successfully with disruptive technologies. Although start-up firms, unhampered by large size (and need for large profits), inertia, and entrenched organizational culture, have an inherent advantage when dealing with disruptive technologies. Christensen (1997, p. 99) describes four ways in which established firms have successfully adopted such technologies:

1. They embedded projects to develop and commercialize disruptive technologies within a section of their organization whose customers needed them, even if the mainstream, most profitable customers of the parent organization did not.
2. They placed such projects within autonomous sections of their organizations that were small enough to get excited about small opportunities and small wins.
3. Since the ultimate uses or applications of disruptive technologies are unknowable in advance, they planned to fail early and inexpensively in the trial-and-error search for a market for each disruptive technology.
4. When commercializing disruptive technologies, they found or developed new markets that particularly valued the attributes of the disruptive products rather than trying to force the disruptive products into their established, mainstream markets.

Archer et al. (1999) suggested that established educational institutions can protect their core academic values while at the same time adopting the disruptive technology of distance education (particularly online education) through judicious adaptations of the four strategies sketched below:

1. The main responsibility for online learning should be assigned to the continuing studies unit (sometimes referred to as extension or continuing education department), as the "customers" of this unit are part-time learners, often midcareer professionals or other knowledge workers, who are unable or unwilling to enroll in on-campus programs. For such learners, by far the largest part of the cost of attending a full-time on-campus program is the opportunity cost of foregone income. They need a technology, such as online learning, that spares them this cost. In contrast, recent graduates from high school,

who make up the mainstream market for conventional institutions, are not particularly interested in online delivery since they do not face such high opportunity costs for on-campus attendance.

2. Continuing studies units are typically rather small, at least as compared with conventional institutions. Therefore, they are much more likely to give online learning a high priority and invest the time and energy necessary to make it succeed.

3. Continuing studies units typically use sessional instructors, whose contract terminates with the end of the course they are hired to teach. In contrast to mainstream departments, which have long-term commitments to tenured instructional staff, these units can afford to probe the market with program offerings that may very well fail, since they can easily shift focus to a different type of program and try again.

4. As noted under the previous point, continuing studies units can probe for new, emerging markets for online programs through an iterative process of program development, offering, redevelopment, and reoffering in a much more agile fashion than the mainstream departments.

We are not alone in our contention that the continuing studies unit is the place in which universities can incubate programs that make use of the disruptive technology of online learning. Katz (1999) states that, for introducing, technology-enriched instruction "a much more likely structural and behavioral model is found in the context of university extension operations. Many university extension operations and other academic institutions that cater to the needs of the working adult student have developed values, business systems, and capabilities that will be required in this new context" (p. 38).

Moving online learning beyond continuing studies and making it a significant part of the operation of the rest of the institution remains a significant challenge. The Australian integrated model, in which on-campus and distance delivery is coordinated throughout the institution, is a possible model for the evolution of our conventional campus-based institutions (Johnson, 1999). However, getting there from here will present problems to which solutions are only beginning to emerge.

CONCLUSION

Online learning facilitated by computer-mediated communication is radically changing education. Discussions of the effects of CMC technology on education are not mere speculations about what the future might bring: The changes are rapidly becoming part of modern educational practice at all levels. A number of commentators have suggested, in fact, that the impact of these changes might be so great that our current educational institutions might not survive (e.g., Duderstadt, 1999; Perelman, 1992).

Whatever its impact on the educational system as a whole, the adoption of CMC to support asynchronous collaborative learning has opened a new era in distance and distributed education. The problem for the field of distance education is that we do not have the theoretical models and research to guide its practical application and to fully imagine its potential and impact.

Of paramount importance is to understand how we can use CMC technology to support and facilitate critical thinking and higher-order learning outcomes. Much research and development remains to be done in order to create the dynamic patterns of pedagogical practice that will facilitate productive educational transactions.

The strategic approach to research advocated here begins with a coherent model that focuses on the critical thinking process and not on an unordered listing of cognitive skills. The model described above could be used to provide metacognitive awareness for researchers and students.

Without metacognitive awareness, there are serious questions as to whether researchers will have a coherent framework for studying this complex process systematically and whether students will have an adequate cognitive map for learning how to learn and become self-directed, cognitively autonomous learners.

There seems to be little question that our present understanding of the use of CMC and computer conferencing for purposes of online learning is seriously limited. Progress will necessitate a concerted and multipronged approach to studying the technology, pedagogy, and organization of online learning. Moreover, scholars in the field of distance education must take a leading role in this work or risk being marginalized in an area where we have previously provided innovative leadership. The importance to the field of distance education of further research on the use of CMC for purposes of online learning should not be underestimated. Perhaps no other area of study will have a greater impact on the future of distance education.

REFERENCES

Anderson, T., & Garrison, D. R. (1995). Transactional issues in distance education: The impact of design in audio-teleconferencing. *American Journal of Distance Education, 9*(2), 27–45.

Anderson, T., Rourke, L., Garrison, D. R., & Archer, W. (2001). *Assessing teaching presence in a computer conference context.* Journal of Asynchconous hearning Networks, 5(2) Available: http://www.aln.org/alnweb/journal/jaln-vol5issue2v2.htm

Archer, W., Garrison, D. R., & Anderson, T. (1999). Adopting disruptive technologies in traditional universities: Continuing education as an incubator for innovation. *Canadian Journal of University Continuing Education, 25*(1), 13–30.

Archer, W., Garrison, D. R., & Anderson, T. (2000). *The textuality of computer mediated communication: Consequences for the use of CMC in education.* Unpublished manuscript.

Bates, A. W. (2000). *Managing technological change: Strategies for college and university leaders.* San Francisco: Jossey-Bass.

Berners-Lee, T. (1999). *Weaving the Web.* London: Orion.

Berge, Z. L. (1995). Facilitating Computer Conferencing: Recommendations From the Field. Educational Technology. 35(1) 22–30.

Bonk, C., & King, G. (1998). *Electonic collaborators: Learner-centered technologies for literacy, apprenticeship, and discourse.* Hillsdale, NJ: Lawrence Erlbaum Associates.

Bruce, B. C., & Levin, J. A. (1997). Educational technology: Media for inquiry, communication, construction, and expression. *Journal of Educational Computing Research, 17*(1), 79–102. Available: http://www.lis.uiuc.edu/chip/pubs/taxonomy/index.html>http://www.lis.uiuc.edu/chip/pubs/taxonomy/index.html

Bruner, J. (1990). *Acts of meaning.* Cambridge, MA: Harvard University Press.

Christensen, C. M. (1997). *The innovator's dilemma: When new technologies cause great firms to fail.* Boston: Harvard Business School Press.

Daniel, J. S. (1996). *Mega-universities and knowledge media: Technology strategies for higher education.* London: Kogan Page.

Day, G., & Schoemaker, P. (2000). Avoiding the pitfalls of emerging technologies. *California Management Review, 42*(2), 8–33.

Dewey, J. (1933). *How we think* (Rev. ed.). Boston: D. C. Heath.

Dewey, J. (1959). My pedagogic creed. In J. Dewey, *Dewey on education* (pp. 19–32). New York: Teachers College, Columbia University. (Original work published 1897)

Dourish, P., Holmes, J. M. A., Marqvardsen, P., & Zbyslaw, A. (1996). Freeflow: Mediating between representation and action in workflow systems. In *Proceedings of Computer Supported Cooperative Work.* (Conference Boston) NY: ACM.

Duderstadt, J. J. (1999). Can colleges and universities survive in the information age? In R. N. Katz & Associates, *Dancing with the devil: Information technology and the new competition in higher education* (pp. 1–25). San Francisco: Jossey-Bass.

Duffy, T., Dueber, B., & Hawley, C. (1998). Critical thinking in a distributed environment: A pedagogical base for the design of conferencing systems. In C. Bonk & G. King (Eds.), *Electonic collaborators: Learner-centered technologies for literacy, apprenticeship, and discourse* (pp. 51–78). Hillsdale, NJ: Lawrence Erlbaum Associates.

Fabro, K. R., & Garrison, D. R. (1998). Computer conferencing and higher-order learning. *Indian Journal of Open Learning, 7*(1), 41–54.

Feenberg, A. (1989). The written word: On the theory and practice of computer conferencing. In R. Mason & A. R. Kaye (Eds.), *Mindweave: Communication, computers and distance education* (pp. 22–39). Oxford: Pergamon Press.

Feenberg, A. (2000). *A new software genre: Discussion management* [Online]. Available: http://www.rohan.sdsu.edu/faculty/feenberg/textweaver/indexhyp.htm

Fraser, A. B. (1999). Colleges should tap the pedagogical potential of the World Wide Web. *Chronicle of Higher Education, 48,* B8.

Garrison, D. R. (1997). Computer conferencing: The post-industrial age of distance education. *Open Learning, 12*(2), 3–11.

Garrison, D. R. (2000). Theoretical challenges for distance education in the 21st century: A shift from structural to transactional issues. *International Review of Research in Open and Distance Learning, 1*(1), 1–17.

Garrison, D. R., & Anderson, T. (2000). Transforming and enhancing university teaching: Stronger and weaker technological influences. In T. Evans & D. Nation (Eds.), *Changing university teaching: Reflections on creating educational technologies.* London: Kogan Page.

Garrison, D. R., Anderson, T., & Archer, W. (2000). Critical inquiry in a text-based environment: Computer conferencing in higher education. *The Internet and Higher Education 2*(2-3), 87–105. Available: http://sciserv.ub.unibielefeld.de/elsevier/10967516/

Garrison, D. R., Anderson, T., & Archer, W. (2001). Critical thinking, *cognitive presence*, and computer conferencing in distance education. *American Journal of Distance Education, 15*(1), 7–23.

Gunawardena, C. N. (1991). *Collaborative learning and group dynamics in computer-mediated communication networks.* (Research Monograph of the American Center for the Study of Distance Education No. 9). University Park, PA: Pennsylvania State University.

Gunawardena, C. N. (1995). *Social presence theory and implications for interaction and collaborative learning in computer conferencing.* Paper presented at the Fourth International Conference on Computer Assisted Instruction, Hsinchu, Taiwan. March

Harasim, L. M. (1987). Teaching and learning on-line: Issues in computer mediated graduate courses. *Canadian Journal of Educational Communication, 16,* 117–135.

Harasim, L. M. (1989). Online education: A new domain. In R. Mason & A. R. Kaye, (Eds.), *Mindweave: Communication, computers, and distance education* (pp. 50–62). New York: Pergamon.

Harasim, L. M. (Ed.). (1990). Online education: Perspectives on a new environment. New York: Praeger.

Harasim, L., Hiltz, S., Teles, L., & Turoff, M. (1995). *Learning networks: A field guide to teaching and learning online.* London: MIT Press.

Henri, F. (1992). Computer conferencing and content analysis. In A. R. Kaye, (Ed.), *Collaborative learning through computer conferencing* (pp. 117–136). New York: Springer-Verlag.

Hiltz, S. R. (1986). The "virtual classroom": Using computer mediated communication for university teaching. *Journal of Communication, 36*(2), 95–104.

Horstmann T., & Bentley, R. (1997). Distributed authoring on the Web with the BSCW shared workspace system. *Standard View, 5*(1), 9–16.

Johnson, S. (1999) Introducing and supporting change towards more flexible teaching models. In A. Tait & R. Mills (Eds.), *The convergence of distance and conventional education* (pp. 39–50). New York: Routledge.

Katz, R. N. (1999). *Competitive strategies for higher education in the information age.* In R. N. Katz & Associates, *Dancing with the devil: Information technology and the new competition in higher education* (pp. 27–49). San Francisco: Jossey-Bass.

Katz, R. N., & Associates (1999). *Dancing with the devil: Information technology and the new competition in higher education.* San Francisco: Jossey-Bass.

Kaye, T. (1987). Introducing computer-mediated communication into a distance education system. *Canadian Journal of Educational Communication, 16,* 153–166.

Kaye, T. (1992). Learning together apart. In T. Kaye (Ed.), *Collaborative learning through computer conferencing* (pp. 1–24). New York: Springer-Verlag.

Keegan, D. (1993). A typology of distance teaching systems. In K. Harry, M. John, & D. Keegan (Eds.), *Distance education: New perspectives* (pp. 62–76). London: Routledge.

Kirkpatrick, D., & Jakupec, V. (1999). Becoming flexible: What does it mean? In A. Tait & R. Mills (Eds.), *The convergence of distance and conventional education* (pp. 51–70). New York: Routledge.

Kirschner, P. (1991). Audiotape feedback for essays in distance education. *Innovative Higher Education, 15*(2), 185–195.

Kuhn, D. (1999). A developmental model of critical thinking. *Educational Researcher, 28*(2), 16–25.

Lauzon, A., & Moore, G. (1989). A fourth generation distance education system: Integrating computer-assisted learning and computer conferencing. *American Journal of Distance Education, 3*(1), 38–49.

Lipman, M. (1991). *Thinking in education.* Cambridge: Cambridge University Press.

Marchese, T. (1998, May). Not-so-distant competitors: How new providers are remaking the postsecondary marketplace. *AAHE Bulletin.* Available: http://www.aahe.org/bulletin/bull_1may98.htm

Mason, R., & Kaye, A. R. (1989). *Mindweave: Communication, computers, and distance education.* New York: Pergamon.

McLoughlin, C., & Luca, J. (2000). Cognitive engagement and higher order thinking through computer conferencing: We know why but do we know how? *Teaching and Learning Forum 2000.* Available: http://cleo.murdoch.edu.au/confs/tlf/tlf2000/mcloughlin.html

Noble, D. F. (1997, October). Digital diploma mills: The automation of higher education. *Bulletin of the Canadian Association of University Teachers.* Available: http://www.caut.ca/english/bulletin/98%5Fsept/digital%5F1.htm

Noble, D.F. (1998, March). Digital diploma mills: Part II. *Bulletin of the Canadian Association of University Teachers.* Available: http://www.caut.ca/english/bulletin/98%5Fsept/digital%5F2.htm

Paulsen, M. (1995). Moderating educational computer conferences. In Z. Berge & M. Collins (Eds.), *Computer mediated communication and the online classroom* (pp. 81–90). Cresskill, NJ: Hampton Press.

Paulson, M. F., & Rekkedal, T. (1988, August). Computer conferencing: A breakthrough in distance learning or just another technological gadget? In D. Stewart & J. S. Daniel (Eds.), *Developing distance education* (pp. 362–364). Papers submitted to the 14th ICDE World Conference, Oslo.

Perelman, L. J. (1992). *School's out: Hyperlearning, the new technology, and the end of education.* New York: Morrow.

Postman, N. (1992). *Technopoly: The surrender of culture to technology.* New York: Knopf.

Roberts, J. (1998) *Compressed video learning.* Montreal: Cheneliere/McGraw-Hill

Romiszowski, A. J., & Mason, R. (1996). Computer-mediated communication. In D. H. Jonassen (Ed.), *Handbook of research for educational communications and technology* (pp. 438–455). New York: Macmillan.

Rourke, L., Anderson, T., Garrison, D. R., & Archer, W. (2001). Methodological issues in the content analysis of computer conference transcripts. *International Journal of Artificial Intelligence in Education, 12*(1), 8–22.

Salmon, G. (2000). *E-moderating the key to teaching and learning online.* London: Kogan Page.

Shipman, F., & Marshall, C. (1999). Formality considered harmful: Experiences, emerging themes, and directions on the use of formal representations in interactive systems. *Computer Supported Cooperative Work, 8,* 333–352.

Tait, A., & Mills, R. (Eds.). (1999). *The convergence of distance and conventional education.* New York; Routledge.

Twidale M., & Nichols D. (1998). A Survey of applications of CSCW for digital libraries. (Technical Report CSEG/4/98). Lancaster, England: University of Lancaster, Computing Department. Available: http://tina.lancs.ac.uk/computing/research/cseg/projects/ariadne/docs/survey.html

9

Modes of Interaction in Distance Education: Recent Developments and Research Questions

Terry Anderson
Athabasca University
terrya@athabascau.ca

This chapter focuses on the social, pedagogical, and economic impact of interaction in distance education. It reviews six types of interaction by extending an earlier discussion (Moore, 1989) of forms of interaction to include teacher-teacher, teacher-content, and content-content interaction. It also suggests new areas and approaches to research that will expand our understanding and competence when using the tools and approaches related to these six forms of interaction.

DEFINING INTERACTION IN DISTANCE EDUCATION

Interaction is a complex and multifaceted concept in all forms of education. Traditionally interaction focused on classroom-based dialogue between students and teachers. The concept has been expanded to include mediated synchronous discussion at a distance (audio- and video-conferencing); asynchronous forms of simulated dialogue, such as Holmberg's (1989) "guided didactic conversation" and mediated asynchronous dialogue (computer conferencing and voice mail); and responses and feedback from inanimate objects and devices, such as "interactive computer programs" and "interactive television."

Wagner (1994) addressed the problem of definition and defined interaction (in a distance education context) as "reciprocal events that require at least two objects and two actions. Interactions occur when these objects and events mutually influence one another"(p. 8). This definition seems satisfactory in its simplicity, having captured the major components of reciprocity and multiple actors and avoiding further restrictions on meaning or application. Simpson and Galbo (1986), however, argued that the essential characteristic of interaction "is reciprocity in actions and responses in an infinite variety of relationships" (p. 38). This definition, while attempting to be widely inclusive, seems to exclude many important educational interactions.

No teacher or student is capable of an "infinite variety" of relationships, and certainly we do not see the full gamut of human relationships in formal educational courses. I argue later that the range of interactions with so-called intelligent machines is also large (but not infinite) and that relationships between humans and machines can and do evolve through adaptation, although the possible set of interactions is currently more restrictive when nonhuman actors are involved.

The exclusion of nonhumans from the definition of interaction was also adopted by Daniel and Marquis (1988), who use the term *interaction* "in a restrictive manner to cover only those activities where the student is in two-way contact with another person (or persons)" (p. 339). Although I sympathize with the theological rationale for placing human communication in a distinct context from that inhabited by machines, the discussion that follows illustrates that there are many types of learning and teaching. Formal education is usually accomplished both with and without exclusively human interaction, and it is becoming increasingly difficult to qualitatively differentiate between the two. Further, I believe that it is impossible to determine with certainty which exact combination of human and nonhuman interaction is necessary for effective instruction with any group of learners or for the teaching of any subject domain, and thus forcing the term *interaction* to refer to only activity between certain types of actors seems counterproductive in an educational setting.

Wagner (1994) attempted to resolve the issue of whether interaction encompasses communication with nonhumans by drawing a sharp and qualitative distinction between the term *interaction*, which she retains for communicative relationships between human beings, and *interactivity*, which she uses to refer to the currently more limited communication between humans and machines. This distinction is not apparent in the writings of many distance education authors, nor among computer and cognitive scientists who have developed whole subdisciplines, including cybernetics and a field named human computer interaction (HCI) (see http://www.hcibib.org/). Thus, it seems futile to try to propagate the use of different words for communication involving the two major types of actors (human and nonhuman) in modern distance education.

Wagner also takes a narrow view of interaction by focusing exclusively on "instructional interaction"—those events that are designed to change the behavior of students. I take a wider view of interaction and consider it to occur throughout the whole education system. Instruction, teaching, learning, and administration each have a place within education systems, and interactions between them affect every other component in mutually dependent relationships. Thus, this chapter deals with interactions between, for example, teachers and teachers that, although not strictly instructional, are integral to the distance education context.

In summary, despite concerns about the application of Wagner's simple and broad definition of interaction, her definition does seem to include the essential components and nature of interaction without compromising or restricting the wide range of possible types of interaction. I next turn to a discussion of the value of interaction in education settings and then to a description of the different types of interaction encountered in a distance education context.

THE VALUE OF INTERACTION IN DISTANCE EDUCATION

John Dewey's (1938) "transactional" conception of activity-based education views an educational experience as a "transaction taking place between an individual and what, at the time, constitutes his environment" (p. 43). Dewey's description not only fits neatly with the complex shifting of time and place that defines distance education but also emphasizes the importance of interaction with the various human and nonhuman actors that constitute the environment. For Dewey (1916), interaction is the defining component of the educational process that occurs when the student transforms the inert information passed to him or her from another and constructs it into knowledge with personal application and value.

Dewey's stress on interaction is reinforced by Laurillard (2000), who argued that a university education must go far beyond access to information or content and include "engagement with others in the gradual development of their personal understanding" (p. 137). This engagement is developed through interaction between teachers and students and forms the basis of Laurillard's conversational approach to teaching and learning. However, interaction with teachers or student peers, without access to content, is likely to result in interaction more typical of a pub chat than a high-quality educational experience. Garrison and Shale (1990) defined all forms of education (including that at a distance) as interactions among teachers, students, and content. Thus, both human and nonhuman interactions are integral and reciprocal components of a quality educational experience, whether delivered at a distance or on campus.

Most classroom teachers and researchers have stressed the value of interaction within the educational process. Chickering and Gamson (1987) found that interaction between students, among students, and between teachers and students (in a campus context) are three of the seven indictors of quality that have emerged in the research on university-level education. Distance education theorists (Garrison, 1991, 2000; Holmberg, 1991; Moore & Kearsley, 1996) and researchers (Anderson & Garrison, 1995; Harasim, 1990; Henri & Rigault, 1996; Katz, 2000; Saba & Shearer, 1994; Soo & Bonk, 1998; Winn, 1999) have each focused on the pedagogical, motivational, and economic costs and benefits of interaction and generally ascribe critical importance to it.

Michael Hannifin (1989) itemized the functions that interaction purports to support in an educational context:

- *Pacing.* Interactive pacing of the educational experience operates in a distance context from both a social perspective, as in keeping an educational group together, and an individual perspective, as in prescribing the speed with which content is presented and acted on.
- *Elaboration.* Interaction serves to develop links between new content and existing schema, allowing learners to build more complex, memorable, and retrievable connections between existing and new information and skills.
- *Confirmation.* This most behavioral function of interaction serves to reinforce and shape the acquisition of new skills. Confirmational interaction traditionally takes place between student and teacher but is also provided by feedback from the environment through experience and interaction with content in laboratories and while working through content formatted in computer-assisted tutorials and from peers in collaborative and problem-based learning
- *Navigation.* This function prescribes and guides the way in which learners interact with each other and with content.
- *Inquiry.* Hannafin's conception of inquiry focused on inquiry related to a computer system that was displaying content and monitoring student response. The interconnected and more widely accessible context for inquiry now provided by the Internet opens the door to a much greater quantity and quality of inquiry.

To these I would add the "study pleasure and motivation" that Holmberg (1989, p. 43) describes as developing from interaction and the relationship between the teaching and learning parties.

It can be seen that interaction fulfills many critical functions in the educational process. However, it is also becoming more apparent that there are many types of interaction and indeed many actors (both human and inanimate) involved. As a result of this complexity, a number of distance education theorists have broken the concept of interaction down into component types based largely on the roles of the human and inanimate actors involved.

FORMS OF INTERACTION IN DISTANCE EDUCATION

Moore (1989) described three forms of interaction in distance education: interaction between students and teachers, interaction between students, and the interaction of students with content. I discuss each of these in turn and provide three additional forms later in this chapter. However, first I discuss and set aside two additional forms of interaction described by distance education theorists.

Hillman, Willis, and Gunawardena (1994) described a type of interaction that they called "learner/interface interaction," which they defined as the "process of manipulating tools to accomplish a task" (p. 34). Learner/interface interaction focuses on the access, skills, and attitudes necessary for successful mediated interaction. All forms of interaction in a distance education context are, by definition, mediated forms of interaction. Thus, learner/interface interaction is not a unique form of interaction but rather a component of each of the other forms of interaction whenever they occur in a distance education context. I choose not to discuss learner/interface interaction as a separate form of interaction but do not deny that acquisition of communication and technical skills is an integral component of the hidden curriculum of distance education (Anderson, 2002).

Sutton (2000), building on insights from Fulford and Zhang (1993) and Kruh and Murphy (1990), postulated yet another form of interaction known as "vicarious interaction." In distance education, as in classroom-based interaction, not all students interact during individual classes or even during the course of a complete course. However, they may "interact" vicariously. Sutton defined vicarious interaction as what "takes place when a student actively processes both sides of a direct interaction between two other students or between another student and the instructor" (p. 4). Sutton found that those who interacted vicariously had read, appreciated, and learned from the interactions of others, but they felt no desire to interact themselves and perceived that such interaction would have added little to the course of study. Thus, one cannot discount vicarious interaction as a useful learning modality. However, vicarious interaction is a variation on all forms of interaction and is not really a distinct form in that it necessarily occurs in combination with other forms and requires the active interaction of other players to be realized.

Anderson and Garrison (1998) have expanded the discussion on interaction to include three other forms of interaction: teacher-teacher, teacher-content, and content-content (see Fig. 9.1). Harkening back to Dewey's reminder that education takes place within an existing social and environmental context, it should be noted that Fig. 9.1 simplifies real life by omitting the larger sphere of interaction that exists outside of formal education. Interactions between students and teachers on the one hand and their families, workplaces, and communities on the other dramatically influence the context in which formal education takes place. Burnham and Walden (1997) refer to interactions of this kind as "learner-environment interactions." These interactions are conditioned by broader societal norms and expectations related to gender, race, and a variety of other sources of social status. They are very complex, often idiosyncratic, and generally lie beyond the scope of this chapter. However, they cannot be ignored when situating this interaction model in any real situation.

Student-Teacher Interaction

Beginning with Plato and continuing with later educators, notably John Dewey, much has been written about the importance of interaction between students and instructors. Many of the pedagogical benefits of teacher-student interaction, especially those related to motivation (Wlodkowski, 1985) and feedback (Laurillard, 1997, 2000), are equally relevant in

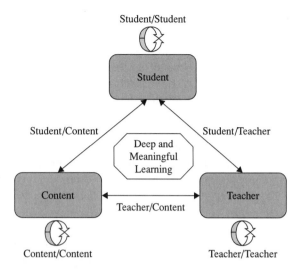

FIG. 9.1. Modes of interaction in distance education. From "Learning in a Networked World: New Rules and Responsibilities, T. Anderson and D. R. Garrison, 1998, in C. Gibson (Ed.), *Distance Learners in Higher Education* Madison, WI: Atwood Publishing, 1998. Reprinted with permission.

classroom-based and distance education. Studies of audioconferencing (Parker & Olgren, 1980) and videoconferencing (Hearnshaw, 2000; Katz, 2000) show that effective student-teacher interaction can and does take place but that these synchronous media (in themselves) seem to have little direct impact on educational outcomes (Russell, 2000). As with much research on media, the instructional design or the application of the technology seems to be a far greater determinant of the educational results than the use of the media per se (Clark, 1994). Recent work has extended the study of student-teacher interaction into the area of text-based distance education. (Garrison, Anderson, & Archer, 2000; Harasim, Hiltz, Teles, & Turoff, 1995), and the findings indicate that quality student-teacher interaction does take place, even in the "lean" context of a text-based medium.

Of major concern to both teachers and administrators are the high workloads and attendant costs that seem to be associated with student-teacher interaction. From an administration perspective, Daniel and Marquis (1988) noted that the costs of human interaction "tend to increase in direct proportion to the number of students" (p. 342). Berge and Muilenburg (2000) report survey results that identify teacher concern about time requirements as the largest barrier to adopting networked forms of distance teaching. Schifter (2000) found that the related issue of lack of technical support provided by the institution and concern about faculty overload were top inhibiting factors for faculty members, whether they participated in distance education or not.

Is this perception of excessive workload a function of unfamiliarity with the media and appropriate instructional design or is based on an accurate assessment of a form of education that can take place "anywhere, anytime"? Early evidence from small-scale research involving actual logging of teacher time in fact indicates that faculty perceptions of increased overload for online courses may be exaggerated or at least premature. Lesh (2000) and Hislop (2000) found that once teachers become experienced with both the course content and the delivery media, the time requirements of Web-based courses and courses delivered face to face do not differ significantly.

Interaction must provide "relative advantage" (Rogers, 1995) to teachers who have become accustomed to a system that supports temporal restriction on teacher-student interaction. It is difficult to imagine a distance education teacher telling students he or she will respond to e-mail only during regular office hours, on Tuesdays, between 2:00 and 4:00 PM! Thus, there is a need for logging and analyzing the actual tasks engaged in by distance teachers using both synchronous and asynchronous forms of teacher-student interaction. The quality and quantity of student-teacher interaction is dependent on the instructional design and selection of learning activities developed for the instructional program. Teachers must learn to plan activities that maximize the impact of interactions with students and provide alternative forms of interaction when time constraints become excessive. We can expect that more sophisticated forms of student-content and student-student interaction, coupled with instructional designs that make more efficient use of faculty time, will over the long run reduce the perception that teacher-student interaction requires an excessive amount of time.

Student-Student Interaction

The rich educational value of collaborative and cooperative learning was not available to students involved in first-generation distance education (i.e., correspondence study). Work on the social construction of knowledge (Brown & Duguid, 2000; Rogoff, 1990), situated learning (Lave, 1988), and the applications of these theories to education have resulted in a rich and growing body of knowledge related to student-student interaction and collaborative learning (Johnson, Johnson, & Smith, 1991; Slavin, 1995). Most of this research has focused on classroom-based delivery, largely with school-age children. However, adult and especially professional learners have also been shown to benefit from interaction with others about common professional concerns and aspirations (Brookfield, 1987; Schön, 1991). Damon (1984) noted that "intellectual accomplishments flourish best under conditions of highly motivated discovery, the free exchange of ideas and the reciprocal feedback between mutually respected individuals" (p. 340).

The act of engaging in learner-learner interaction forces learners to construct or formulate an idea in a deeper sense. John Dewey predated modern constructivist theorists when he described this formulating process as "getting outside of it, seeing it as another would see it, considering what points of contact it has with the life of another so that it may be got into such form that [the learner] can appreciate its meaning" (Dewey, 1916, p. 5). This most social component of the distance education process is what allows distance education to move beyond independent study and be reconceptualized as "education at a distance" (Shale, 1990).

The communication of an idea to other students also raises the interest and motivation of the interactors—in large part because of the associated psychological commitment and risk taking involved in publicly espousing one's views. The communicator's motivation and interest rises as he or she eagerly awaits responses from peers. This state of heightened psychological attention is related to the increased "mindfulness" that Langer (1989) identified as critically important to the development of a mindful approach to learning. Langer (1997) described mindfulness (opposite of mindlessness) as having three important characteristics: the continuous creation of new categories, openness to new information, and an implicit awareness of more than one perspective. Each of these characteristics enters a hyper state when the student interacts with peers, stimulating their capacity and motivation to learn.

Interaction with peers is also a critical component of the formal curriculum in many disciplines. The capacity to participate effectively in teams, communicate with colleagues and other professionals, liaise with clients, and generally demonstrate highly developed communication skills is critical to both vocational and personal success. The necessary communication skills are both taught and practiced as major objectives of most higher education programming and are integral to the training process in many professional programs. Programs offered both on campus and at a distance must be able to provide means for this type of communication to take place.

Despite the pedagogical benefits of learner-learner interaction, it is also known that some students purposely select distance education formats that allow for study that is independent of contact and the temporal restraints associated with paced and interactive forms of campus-based or distance education (Daniel & Marquis, 1988; Pagney, 1988). Distance education's rich tradition of independent study has been expanded to include many types of learning opportunities through the use of a variety of synchronous and asynchronous group-based learning activities. This expansion, however, has not been uniformly appreciated by all distance educators. Arnold (1999), for example, argued that by focusing on individual learning designs, distance education can be more customized and "be closer to the content of the learning process and closer to the comprehension and grasp of the problems by individual learners" (p. 5).

Despite the contentions of those who value independent forms of distance education over collaborative forms or vice versa, we can no longer assume that distance education is, by definition, either an individual or a collaborative process. If we do build forms of student-student interaction into our distance education programming, we should ensure that our instructional designs promote student-student interactions that are pedagogically grounded and produce enough learning and motivational gains to justify the restrictions on the students' temporal independence. Further, the diversity of types of distance education compels us to be explicit in our promotion of distance education programming so that students can make informed choices that meet their individual needs and desires for student-student interaction.

Research related to student-student interaction needs to focus on assessing the type of student and the type of content for which increased levels of student-student interaction produce the highest and most satisfactory levels of learning. Further, we need to know how student-student interaction impacts the students' lifelong attitudes and approaches to learning (Entwhistle & Ramsden, 1983). We need instruments and techniques that allow students to reliably assess their own preference and capacity to engage in both independent and collaborative study. Likewise, we need tools and practical theories that allow distance education teachers to determine the appropriate mix of independent and collaborative learning activities based on a complex set of factors, including teaching style, approaches to learning and teaching, student needs, educational goals, and cost implications.

Student-Content Interaction

The majority of student time, in all forms of adult education, is consumed by interactions with a variety of educational content. In classroom-based education, this has meant study using texts and other library resources. In traditional distance education, this has meant study with texts and electronic resources, often supplemented by faculty-created study guides.

Current technologies provide a wide variety of media alternatives for creating content for student interaction. Tuovinen (2000) classified these media into five basic categories: sound, text, graphics, video, and virtual reality. He paid particular attention to combinations that include sound with any of the other media, arguing that sound and visual images are processed by different parts of the brain and that combinations of sound and other media are less likely to produce cognitive overload then other combinations.

Learner-content interactivity in educational contexts can take many forms and serve a variety of functions. Sims (1997) reviewed taxonomical classification systems of student-media interactions and proposed a "developers classification" that included object, linear, support, update, construct, reflective, simulation, hyperlinked, and immersive and nonimmersive virtual forms of interactivity. Tuovinen (2000) added multimedia creation as a separate, more constructive form of student-content interactivity. The creation of content is alleged to benefit learning through the development of the structure, strategies, and skills needed for effective content creation (Dunlop, 1999).

It is beyond the scope of this chapter to review the 30 years of experimental study related to student-content interaction (see Moore & Thompson, 1997). It is, however, probably safe to say that the research results have not been as conclusive as desired by either the proponents or opponents of the use of mediated learner-content interaction. The classic debate between Clark (1994) and Kozma (1994) on the extent to which media influence learning served to inform but hardly resolve this issue. All would agree that conducting research in situ that meaningfully isolates the confounding variables of design, media, content, context, learners, and measurement is an extremely challenging task. In a recent article, Clark (2000) suggested that any evaluation of student-content interaction must recognize that every distance education context consists of two distinct levels of student-content interaction, the first dealing with attributes of the media that support the interaction and the second with the "technology" of the learning or instructional design. The conflation of these two separate types of student-content interaction, according to Clark, is at the root of many of the terminological and research problems debated in the literature. Although it is conceptually useful to differentiate and even measure these interactions as distinct events, Marshall McLuhan's (1964) famous quip that the "the medium is the message" reminds us that simple reductionism often fails to identify sympathetic reactions between variables. For example, Diaz (2000) made a convincing argument that research designs informed from an "instructivist worldview" are not likely to inform learner-centered and constructivist forms of learning, in which relationship and communication far outweigh the effect of the media that support the educational transaction. Research methodologies that illuminate differences within the applications of particular sets of learners or instructional designs are likely to be more productive than methodologies designed to compare the effects of interactions across different media and instructional designs.

The capacity of the Internet to store, catalog, and deliver such content, supplemented by the capacity of computers to support a rich variety of computer-assisted instruction, simulations, and presentation creation tools, is significantly altering the context of student-content interaction. In particular, work with the development, cataloging, and distribution of such content, broadly referred to as learning objects (Downes, 2000) promises to provide teachers, developers, and students a vastly expanded set of student-content interaction resources. The pioneering work of the MERLOT consortium (http://www.merlot.org) and CAREO (www.careo.org) in augmenting learning objects with metatags, peer reviews, learning activities, and user comments and in providing these value-added resources freely to all is an excellent example of the way in which educators need to collaboratively build, evaluate, and distribute materials for student-content interaction.

A variety of new network services allow students to direct and automate their interaction with content. For example, students may now request customized versions of newspapers, excerpts from mailing lists and newsgroups, and information about new products or new research (usually delivered by personal e-mail). Further development of autonomous agents will provide students with increasingly powerful tools to search, evaluate, select, and "interact" with networked-based learning content. The interactions are not restricted to text-based media. For example, Compaq's "speechbot technology" (http://speechbot.research.compaq.com/) currently allows for searching and selecting thousands of hours of radio and other audio content, and Ditto (www.ditto.com) contains a searchable index that covers over 6 million images and sketches.

Content may also be programmed to interact with the learner at a variety of levels of sophistication and support. The goal of these "adaptive" systems is to customize interaction for individual student needs, including the "ability to set the level of the lesson closely to the student's current and changing level of understanding, to alter instructional strategies and provide remedial tutoring as required, to respond to student input at various levels from keystroke to the overall plan of the solution to the problem, and finally to detect and analyze mistakes in terms of conceptual errors" p. 10 (Eklund, 1995 p. 10). Research determining how content can best be programmed to interact with the unique cognitive attributes of individual learners is the subject of much human computer interaction study (Hedberg & Perry, 1985). Content can also be programmed to act as an independent agent, undertaking tasks such as notification, note taking, summarizing, and other clerical and administrative tasks for learning groups or individuals (Negatu & Franklin, 1999; Whatley, Beer, Staniford, & Scown, 1999). Early research has shown that this form of automated and always available assistance "holds promise for improving completion rates, learner satisfaction, and motivation" (Thaiupathump, Bourne, & Campbell, 1999). However, programming such "intelligent software" is expensive and research related to cost-effectiveness and actual use and performance is necessary to guide ongoing development of student-content interaction.

There is no doubt that student-content interaction can perform some functions of the educational transaction formerly accomplished exclusively through teacher-learner interaction. The appropriate amount, efficiency, and efficacy of this substitution of machine for human labor will dominate learner-content research for the foreseeable future. It is interesting to speculate if and when intelligent content agents will be able to routinely pass the equivalent of an "educational Turing test" (i.e., be sophisticated enough to keep students guessing as to whether they are interacting with human or nonhuman teachers).

Research issues related to student-content interaction will focus on the development and evaluation of new forms and tools of student-content interaction. Methodologies that focus on the analysis of the actual use of such objects gathered through interviews, talk-alouds, surveys, and student logs will be most useful. The results will be used to assist developers and tutors in both creating and modifying existing objects and in selecting and assigning the most appropriate sets of learning activities based on student-content interaction. An added benefit of the rich resources available will be the growing capacity to design multiple paths through content based on a variety of learning needs and preferences. Finally, the shared environment of network-based distance education allows for rapid inclusion of student-created content and its incorporation into current and subsequent versions of distance education courses.

Teacher-Content Interaction

The first of three forms of interaction initially highlighted by Anderson and Garrison (1998) is interaction between teachers and content. As noted above, the development and application of content objects will become an increasingly important component of the teacher's role in both distance and classroom-based education. The intelligent network provides opportunities for teachers to create learning objects that are automatically updated by publications, data, and other research-based artifacts. For example, objects can be created that display and then calculate trends from real-time data sources such as economic indicators, climate monitors, or other sensory data. Teachers will interact with content through use of adaptable search engines that will learn from previous teacher behavior to effectively and periodically search the networks for relevant information and data.

Teachers will play a critical role in the creation of learning objects that then become autonomous agents able to support student-content interaction. For example, the Northern Light search engine (http://www.northernlight.com) employs humans to train computers to identify Web resources, subject matter, and other data using a predefined thesaurus to add metatags or identification categories to the resource's data record. Thus, teacher-content interaction, by becoming automated, turns into a form of content-content interaction.

The role of teacher-content interaction is focused on the instructional design process. Teachers and developers create and re-purpose research results and other discipline-related information in the process of creating content. Easier tools for the creation of content, from simple presentation and illustration packages to complex, authoring environments, allow teachers to more directly create content than in earlier eras, when graphics designers and programmers performed much of this work. Although many have argued for the pedagogical and administrative superiority of content produced by teams of experts as opposed to "Lone Rangers" (Bates, 1995), the recent explosion of largely instructor-created content fabricated with the aide of authoring and delivery systems such as WebCT and Blackboard illustrates that teachers can (either alone or with minimal consultative assistance) turn out effective and acceptable content. One often overlooked advantage of such "homegrown" content is that it permits the instructor to continually update and annotate content throughout the course. In other words, the instructional design process can continue throughout the learning sequence rather than end before learner-content interaction takes place, as is necessitated in the various forms of "canned" instruction (Tuovinen, 2000).

Finally, we can expect these authoring and distribution systems to become more comprehensive, functional, and user-friendly as they evolve in both commercial and "open source" production models. Forms of teacher-content interaction will become more automated as "intelligent agents" and "wizards" are incorporated into course creation packages, making maintenance, additions, and updating of content easier and less time consuming. Where greater work is needed is in the development of more sophisticated pedagogical tools for teacher-content interaction. Tools are needed that assist teachers in designing and administrating courses based on a wide variety of pedagogical theories and diverse learning activities. Current tools too often limit our perception of and capacity to manage online learning to threaded discussion and content exposition. I find it somewhat depressing to note the lack of pedagogical innovation incorporated into many of the sophisticated content development and delivery tools currently on the market. For example, the threaded discussion conference tools I use to deliver courses today (including WebCt and First Class) show very little pedagogical enhancement relative to the conferencing tools (such as Confer, Parti, and Cosy) used on mainframe systems 20 years ago. My hope is that the combination of object repositories and pedagogically driven development and delivery tools will create opportunities for much more significant teacher-content interaction, leading in turn to the development of more sophisticated and powerful teacher-created learning environments and teacher-student interaction.

In summary, teacher-content interaction tools support the production of increasingly sophisticated teacher-produced content and courses, thus keeping alive the tradition and practice of instructor-produced forms of "little distance education" (Garrison & Anderson, 1999). It is doubtful that these tools will ever be powerful enough to allow instructors to produce programming of "Disney" quality (even assuming they could acquire the necessary skills). However, teachers, by using these tools, are becoming increasingly able to create powerful distance learning programming that supports high levels of critical teacher-learner interaction.

Despite these optimistic projections for teacher-content interaction, it is clear that administration and management concerns must be addressed before the costs and benefits of teacher creation and interaction with content can be fully measured. Thus, the major research issues related to teacher-content interaction revolve around workload, changing skill sets, copyright, and the contentious relationship between teaching and research, especially in the university context (Brand, 2000). Research on these issues should make heavy use of interviewing, analysis of teacher work, and focus groups with practicing distance education teachers and developers.

Teacher-Teacher Interaction

The pervasiveness of low-cost multimedia networks is providing unprecedented opportunities for teacher-teacher interaction. It is crucial that such networking be exploited if teachers are to take maximum advantage of developments in both their own discipline and developments in distance teaching and pedagogy. This interaction between and among teachers forms the basis of the learning community within formal education institutions. Anderson, Varnhagen, and Campbell (1998) found that the first and most important source of assistance and insight into both technical and pedagogical challenges comes not from technical or pedgagogical experts but from colleagues close at hand to the individual teacher. This presents challenges to distributed education organizations in which the faculty may not meet face to face on a daily basis. One solution to this problem is to take advantage of the networks to create extensive communications and knowledge management systems. Experience with network-based professional development (Anderson & Mason, 1993; Williams, 1997) illustrates that this form of teacher-teacher interaction can deliver tremendous cost savings and is the basis for emerging virtual communities of distance educators.

We are currently seeing the emergence of first-generation distance teaching "portals" in which resources, experiences, tools and forums for teacher-teacher exchange are gathered at a single Web location. These portals provide a form of collaborative knowledge management and thereby support distance education teachers and researchers. These portals are supported by commercial software vendors (e.g., http://www/webct.com, www.blackboard.com), postsecondary institutions (e.g., http://www.uwex.edu/disted/home.html, http://www.umuc.edu/ide/), and nonprofit professional organizations (e.g., http://node.on.ca/, http://www.digitallearning. org/about.htm, and http://eduport.com/). These sources will likely consolidate as the distance education industry matures, leaving a limited number of high-quality, full-service distance education portals in support of teacher-teacher interaction.

Research in this area should focus on the perceived value of teacher-teacher interaction, the extent and costs of this interaction, and barriers to cross-disciplinary collaboration, among other issues.

Content-Content Interaction

Computer scientists and educators are creating intellegent programs or agents that "differ from conventional software in that they are long-lived, semi-autonomous, proactive, and adaptive" (Massachusetts Institute of Technology, 2000). We are seeing early examples of programs written to retrieve information, operate other programs, make decisions, and monitor resources on the networks. As an example, such an agent could be designed by an agricultural economics instructor teaching a lesson on futures marketing. The agent could regularly update the lesson examples by retrieving information from online future quotations and alerting the instructor or learners if any unusual activity is taking place. The lesson thus becomes "ever green" and gains in relevance by displaying real information from today's marketplace. As another example, a program being developed at the University of Saskatchewan (see http://www.cs.usask.ca/i-help/) allows students to create and maintain "user agents" that offer and negotiate for help on various course-related topics. In the process of finding and soliciting this help, the individual user agent negotiates with the agents of other students to determine a cost and projected value of the service.

Internet search engines are other examples where intellegent agents are interacting with each other as they continuously scour the networks, sending their discoveries back to central databases. Next-generation systems will use intelligent agents to search multiple Web indices and support selective winnowing of results (Kapur & Zhang, 2000). In the near future, teachers will create and use learning resources that continuously improve themselves through their interaction with other intelligent agents. Segal (2000) has projected that "the Web will slowly disappear into devices and into the enviornment around us. This means the browser is not a pointer, but an active collector, retriever, connoisseur, extractor and store of all our information" (p. 12). Research in this mode will focus on both development and testing of agents designed to undertake a variety of educational tasks. This research is by definition multidisciplinary, calling on the resources of computer scientests, linguists, educators, and others. The methodologies employed will include machine analysis of agent use and interviews with and surveys of creators and consumers of agent services.

INTERACTION CHOICES

Interaction of any of the six types described above may take place in either synchronous or asynchronous time and be delivered through text, audio, video, virtual reality, or combinations of these communication genres. Unfortunately, too many distance educators and institutions in the past have tended to define themselves and defensively argue for the superiority of the particular technology and instructional design most in harmony with their current delivery model and practice. Such "technocentrism" is becoming less justifiable as the convergence of media on the Internet allows teachers and institutions to create or select any combination of mediated interaction possible in synchronous or asynchronous time.

The vast range of choices creates challenges, however, as educators and administrators are forced to make numerous decisions related to media use and interaction applications, often with limited or biased knowledge bases. For example, despite years of study, it is still unclear which students studying what types of content under what conditions and using which instructional design benefit most from synchronous as opposed to asynchronous interaction. It appears that students report positive experiences and achieve measurable learning outcomes using both forms of interaction, and confounding variables in real-life situations may make such questions unanswerable, in which case individual preferences, costs (from student, teacher, and institutional perspectives), and other issues related to the marketplace and convenience will be the largest determinants of media choice.

Allowing the marketplace to determine distance education format and offerings does carry an implicit danger, namely, that the critical service function of distance education—to enhance access to programming—may be placed at risk. Certainly there are large differences in the access that various groups possess to the different forms of technology needed to participate in distance education. See Damarin (2000) for a very useful set of five "principles" for decision making that are designed to reduce rather than exacerbate the "digital divide."

Distance educators have traditionally chosen the most accessible medium for delivery and excluded mediated alternatives that limit access by requiring student ownership of equipment, high bandwidth connectivity, or the payment of high fees by students. In general, this approach has been successful in that communications theorists have consistently underestimated the extent to which mediated, interactive relationships and communities flourish despite the restrictions of limited bandwidth, asynchronicity, and other constraints of "lean" media (O'Sullivan & Hoffner, 1998). However, because the cost of voice and video connectivity (in both synchronous and asynchronous formats) continues to fall as availability continues to rise, we can expect to see increased use of richer media to support interaction in distance education. For example, the use of audio feedback on assignments (provided through mailed audiotapes) has been shown to provide a significantly greater amount of feedback, to be perceived by students as more personable, and not to require an increase in the time commitments of instructors (Kirschner, Brink, & Meester, 1991). Yet asynchronous audio feedback has been little used in distance education. The ubiquity of computers with low-cost microphones and video cameras as well as the availability of sophisticated Java-based voice and video messaging and conferencing systems (e.g., http://www.wimba.com) will usher in an era of richer student-teacher and student-student interaction in distance education.

CONCLUSION

To summarize, each of the six modes of interaction in distance education needs systematic and rigorous theoretical and empirical research using a variety of research tools and methodologies. Greg Kearsley (1995) provided a list of eight questions related to interaction, the answers to which are critical to our development of effective distance education programming. These questions relate to the effect of frequency of interaction; the type of learners, subject matter, and learning objectives for which interaction is most critical; and the effect of interaction on learner satisfaction. These questions need to be answered with reference to all six forms of interaction. Additional questions related to cost, time requirements, and other workload implications are critical in an expanding era of distance education programming. Unfortunately, the answers to these questions remain largely unanswered seven years after Kearsley posed them to the community of distance education researchers.

The search for single-faceted solutions that generalize to the many diverse contexts of distance education is likely a quixotic quest. We are developing a growing mosaic of distance education technologies and practices, with no single "best way" to use interaction. Each institution, discipline, region, and user group will develop unique cultural practices and expectations related to their need for and use of interaction. This is not to say that all applications are equally effective or efficient. Too much of our practice in distance education is not "evidence based," and our actions and instructional designs are often grounded on untested assumptions about the value of modes of interaction (or lack thereof). Thus, the research opportunities that focus on interaction in all its forms are boundless, yet critically important.

Daniel and Marquis's (1988) seminal challenge to distance educators in the late 1980s was to "get the mixture right" between independence (student-content interaction) and interaction (mainly student-teacher interaction). In the 21st century we are still challenged to get the mixture right, only now we must consider combinations of all six modes of interaction. Appropriate mixtures will result in increased learning and exciting new educational opportunities; inappropriate mixes will be expensive, exclusive, and exigent. Our responsibility as professional distance educators remains—to insure that the modes of interaction that we practice and prescribe maximize the attainment of all legitimate educational objectives and support and increase motivation for deep and meaningful learning. Further, we are challenged to do all of this at expenditure rates that are affordable to both providers and consumers.

I conclude with the words of John Dewey, who noted in 1916 that "every expansive era in the history of mankind has coincided with the operation of factors which have tended to eliminate distance between peoples and classes previously hemmed off from one another" (p. 100). As distance educators, we follow in this noble tradition of using our most technologically "expansive" of eras to reduce the social, technical, economic, and geographic distances that hem us off from one another.

REFERENCES

Anderson, T. (2002). The hidden curriculum of distance education. *Change Magazine, 33*(6), 28–35.

Anderson, T., & Garrison, D. R. (1995). Critical thinking in distance education: Developing critical communities in an audio teleconference context. *Higher Education, 28*, 183–199.

Anderson, T., & Garrison, D. R. (1998). Learning in a networked world: New roles and responsibilities. In C. Gibson (Ed.), *Distance learners in higher education.* Madison, WI.: Atwood Publishing.

Anderson, T., & Mason, R. (1993). The Bangkok Project: New tool for professional development. *American Journal of Distance Education, 7*(2), 5–18.

Anderson, T., Varnhagen, S., & Campbell, K. (1998). Faculty adoption of teaching and learning technologies: Contrasting earlier adopters and mainstream faculty. *Canadian Journal of Higher Education, 28*(2-3), 71–98.

Arnold, R. (1999). Will distance disappear in distance education? *Journal of Distance Education, 14*(2), 1–9.

Bates, T. (1995). *Technology, open learning and distance education.* London: Routledge.

Berge, Z., & Muilenburg, L. (2000). Barriers to distance education as perceived by managers and administrators: Results of a survey. In M. Grey (Ed.), *Distance Learning Administration Annual 2000.*

Brand, M. (2000). Changing faculty roles in research universities: Using the Pathways Strategy. *Change, 32*(6), 42–45.

Brookfield, S. (1987). Recognizing critical thinking. In S. Brookfield (Ed.), *Developing critical thinkers* (pp. 15–34). Oxford: Jossey-Bass.

Brown, J. S., & Duguid, P. (2000). *Social life of information.* Cambridge, MA: Harvard Business School Press.

Burnham, B., & Walden, B. (1997). Interactions in distance education: A report from the other side. In *Proceedings of the Adult Education Research Conference, Oklahoma State University.* Available: http://www.edst.educ.ubc.ca/aerc/1997/97burnham.html

Chickering, A. W., & Gamson, Z. F. (1987, March). Seven principles of good practice in undergraduate education. *AAHE Bulletin,* 3–6. Available: www.byu.edu/fc/pages/tchlrnpages/7princip.html

Clark, R. (1994). Media will never influence learning. *Educational Technology Research and Development, 42*(3), 21–29.

Clark, R. (2000). Evaluating distance education: Strategies and cautions. *Quarterly Review of Distance Education, 1*(1), 3–16.

Damarin, S. (2000, July-August). The "digital divide" versus digital differences: Principles for equitable use of technology in education. *Educational Technology,* 17–22.

Damon, W. (1984). Peer Interaction: The untapped potential. *Journal of Applied Developmental Psychology, 5,* 331–343.

Daniel, J., & Marquis, C. (1988). Interaction and independence: Getting the mix right. In D. Sewart, D. Keegan, & B. Holmberg (Eds.), *Distance education: International perspectives.* (pp. 339–359). London: Routledge.

Dewey, J. (1916). *Democracy and education.* New York: Macmillan.

Dewey, J. (1938). *Experience and education.* New York: Collier Macmillan.

Diaz, D. (2000, March-April). Carving a new path for distance education research. *Commentary.* Available: http://horizon.unc.edu/TS/commentary/2000-03a.asp

Downes, S. (2000). *Learning objects.* Available: http://www.atl.ualberta.ca/downes/naweb/column000523.htm

Dunlop, J. (1999). Developing web-based performance support systems to encourage lifelong learning in the workplace. *WebNet Journal, 1*(2), 40–44.

Eklund, J. (1995). Adaptive learning environments: The future for tutorial software. *Australian Educational Computing, 10*(1), 10–14.

Entwhistle, N., & Ramsden, P. (1983). *Understanding student learning.* London: Croom Helm.

Fulford, C. P., & Zhang, S. (1993). Perceptions of interaction: The critical predictor in distance education. *American Journal of Distance Education, 7*(3), 8–21.

Garrison, D. R. (1991). Critical thinking and adult education: A conceptual model for developing critical thinking in adult learners. *International Journal of Lifelong Education, 10*(4), 287–303.

Garrison, D. R. (1999). Will distance disappear in distance education? A reaction. *Journal of Distance Education, 14*(2), 10–13.

Garrison, D. R. (2000). Theoretical challenges for distance education in the 21st century: A shift from structural to transactional issues. *International Review of Research in Open and Distance Learning, 1*(1). Available: http://www.irrodl.org/content/v1.1/randy.pdf

Garrison, R., & Anderson, T. (1999). Avoiding the industrialization of research universities: Big and little distance education. *American Journal of Distance Education, 13*(2), 48–63.

Garrison, R., Anderson, T., & Archer, W. (2000). Critical inquiry in text-based environment: Computer conferencing in higher education. *The Internet and Higher Education, 2*(2-3), 87–105.

Garrison, D. R., & Shale, D. (1990). A new framework and perspective. In D. R. Garrison & D. Shale (Eds.), *Education at a distance: From issues to practice* (pp. 123–133). Malabar, FL: Kreiger.

Hannafin, M. J. (1989). Inter-action strategies and emerging instructional technologies: Psychological perspectives. *Canadian Journal of Educational Communication, 18,* 167–179.

Harasim, L (1990). *On-line education: Perspectives on a new environment.* New York: Praeger.

Harasim, L., Hiltz, S., Teles, L., & Turoff, M. (1995). *Learning networks: A field guide to teaching and learning online.* London: MIT Press.

Hearnshaw, D. (2000). Effective desktop videoconferencing with minimal network demands. *British Journal of Educational Technology, 31*(3), 221–227.

Hedberg, J., & Perry, N. (1985). Human-computer interaction and CAI: A review and research prospectus. *Australian Journal of Educational Technology, 1*(1), 12–20. Available: http://cleo.murdoch.edu.au/gen/aset/ajet/ajet1/win85p12.html

Henri, F., & Rigault, R. (1996). Collaborative distance learning and computer conferencing. In T. Liao (Ed.), *Advanced educational technology: Research issues and future potential* (pp. 45–76). New York: Springer.

Hillman, D., Willis, D. J., & Gunawardena, C. (1994). Learner-interface interaction in distance education: An extension of contemporary models and strategies for practitioners. *American Journal of Distance Education, 8*(2), 30–42.

Hislop, G. (2000, November). Instructor time for online learning. In *Proceedings of the Sixth Asynchronous Learning Conference.*

Holmberg, B. (1989). *Theory and practice of distance education.* London: Routledge.

Holmberg, B. (1991). The feasibility of a predictive theory of distance education: What are we allowed to expect? In B. Holmberg & G. Ortner (Eds.), *Research into distance education.* Frankfurt: Peter Lang.

Johnson, D., Johnson, R., and Smith, K. (1991). *Active learning cooperation in the college classroom.* Edina, MN: Interaction Book Co.

Kapur, K., & Zhang, J. (2000). Searching the Web using synonyms and sense. *WebNet Journal, 2*(3), 604–609.

Katz, Y. (2000). The comparative suitability of three ICT distance learning methodologies for college level instruction. *Education Media International, 37*(1), 25–30.

Kearsley, G. (1995). The nature and values of interaction in distance education. In *Third Distance Education Research Symposium.* University Park, PA: American Center for the Study of Distance Education.

Kirschner, P., Brink, B., & Meester, M. (1991). Audiotape feedback for essays in distance education. *Innovative Higher Education, 15*(2), 185–95.

Kozma, R. (1994). Will media influence learning? Reframing the debate. *Educational Technology Research and Development, 42*(2), 7–19.

Kruh, J., & Murphy, K. (1990, October). Interaction and teleconferencing: The key to quality instruction. *Annual Rural and Small Schools Conference.* Manhatten, KS. Kansas Static University. (ERIC Document Reproduction Service No. ED 329 418)

Langer, E. (1989). *Mindfulness.* Reading, MA: Addison-Wesley.

Langer, E. (1997). *The power of mindful learning.* Reading, MA: Addison-Wesley.

Laurillard, D. (1997). *Rethinking university teaching: A framework for the effective use of educational technology.* London: Routledge.

Laurillard, D. (2000). New technologies and the curriculum. In P. Scott. (Ed.), *Higher education re-formed* (pp. 133–153). London: Falmer Press.

Lave, J. (1988). *Cognition in practice: Mind, mathematics, and culture in everyday life.* Cambridge: Cambridge University Press.

Lesh, S. (2000, November). Asynchronous versus synchronous learning: A comparative investigation of the effectiveness of learner achievement and faculty time demands. In *Proceedings of the Sixth Asynchronous Learning Network.*

Lipman, M. *Thinking in education.* (1991). Cambridge: Cambridge University Press.

McLuhan, M. (1964). *Understanding media: The extensions of man.* Toronto: McGraw-Hill. Massachusetts Institute of Technology. (2000). *Software Agents Group.* Available: http://mevard.www.media.mit.edu/groups/agents/

Moore, M. (1989). Three types of interaction. *American Journal of Distance Education, 3*(2), 1–6.

Moore, M., & Kearsley, G. (1996). *Distance education: A systems view.* Toronto: Wadsworth.

Moore, M., & Thompson, M. (1997). *The effects of distance learning.* University Park, PA: American Center for the Study of Distance Education.

Negatu, A., & Franklin, S. (1999). Behavioral learning for adaptive software agents. In *the ISCA Fifth International Conference.* Raleigh, NC: International Society for Computers and Their Applications. Available: http://www.msci.memphis.edu/~ franklin/behaviorLearning.html

O'Sullivan, P., & Hoffner, C. (1998, November). Across the great divide: Melding mass and interpersonal theory through mediated relationships. Paper presented at the National Communication Association Annual Conference, Available: http://www.ilstu.edu/~posull/OS&H1998.htm

Pagney, B. (1988). What advantages can conventional education derive from correspondence education? In D. Sewart, D. Keegan, & B. Holmberg (Eds.), *Distance education: International perspectives* (pp. 157–164). London: Routledge.

Parker, L., & Olgren, C. (1980). *Teleconferencing and interactive media.* Madison, WI: University of Wisconsin-Extension Press.

Rogers, E. (1995). *Diffusion of innovations* (4th ed.). New York: Free Press.

Rogoff, B. (1990). *Apprenticeship in thinking: Cognitive development in social context.* New York: Oxford University Press.

Russell, T. (2000). *The no significant difference phenomenon.* Available: http://cuda.teleeducation.nb.ca/nosignificantdifference

Saba, F., & Shearer, R. (1994). Verifying key theoretical concepts in a dynamic model of distance education. *American Journal of Distance Education, 8*(1), 36–59.

Schifter, C. (2000, March-April). Faculty motivators and inhibitors for participation in distance education. *Educational Technology,* 43–46.

Schön, D. (1991). *The reflective practitioner: How professionals think in action.* Avebury, England: Ashgate Publishing.

Segal, B. (2000). Who said what: Quotable quotes from Information Highway 2000. *Information Highway, 7,* 12.

Shale, D. (1990). Toward a reconceptualization of distance education. In M. Moore. (Ed.), *Contemporary issues in american distance education.* (pp. 333–343). Oxford: Pergamon Press.

Simpson, R., & Galbo, J. (1986). Interaction and learning: Theorizing on the art of teaching. *Interchange, 17*(4), 37–51.

Sims, R. (1997). *Interactivity: A forgotten art?* Available: http://www.gsu.edu/~ wwwitr/docs/interact

Slavin, R. (1995). *Cooperative learning theory, research, and practice.* Boston: Allyn & Bacon.

Soo, K., & Bonk, C. (1998). Interaction: What does it mean in online distance education? Paper presented at World Conference on Educational Telecommunications, Freeburg Germany. (ERIC Document Reproduction Service No. ED 428 724)

Sutton, L. (2000). *Vicarious interaction in a course enhanced through the use of computer- mediated communication.* Unpublished doctoral dissertation, Arizona State University, Tempe.

Thaiupathump, C., Bourne, J., & Campbell, O. (1999). Intelligent agents for online learning. *Journal of the Asynchronous Learning Network, 3*(2). Available: http://www.aln.org/alnweb/journal/Vol3_issue2/Choon2.htm

Tuovinen, J. (2000). Multimedia distance education interactions. *Education Media International, 37*(1), 16–24.

Wagner, E. D. (1994). In support of a functional definition of interaction. *American Journal of Distance Education, 8*(2), 6–26.

Whatley, J., Beer, M., Staniford, G., & Scown, P. (1999, September-October). Group project support agents for helping students work online. *Education Technology.* Available: http://www.isi.salford.ac.uk/staff/jw/HCII99.htm

Williams, M. (1997). Connecting teachers: A professional development model in a distance education context. In T. Muldner & T. Reeves (Eds.), *Educational multimedia, hypertext and telecommunications* (vol. 2; pp.). Association for the Advancement of Computing in Education. Available: http://www.home.gil.com.au/~ shellyw/mid_calgery.htm

Winn, W. (1999). Learning in virtual environments: A theoretical framework and considerations for design. *Education Media International, 36*(4), 271–279.

Wlodkowski, R. (1985). *Enhancing adult motivation to learn.* San Francisco: Jossey-Bass.

II

Learning and Learners

10

Learners and Learning: The Need for Theory

Chère C. Gibson
University of Wisconsin-Madison
ccgibson@facstaff.wisc.edu

LEARNERS: A FOCUS WORTHY OF ATTENTION!

It goes without saying that learners and learning are at the heart of the distance education enterprise. Thus, it comes as a bit of a surprise that Koble and Bunker (1997) determined that only 17% of the 117 articles published in the *American Journal of Distance Education* in its first 8 years of publication had a focus on learners, learning, and learner support. Further, almost half of these articles focused on the application of media for learning. Scriven's (1991) analysis of the articles in the first 10 years of *Distance Education* (Australia) found 21% of articles focused on learners and learner support. Coldeway's (1995) examination of Canada's *Journal of Distance Education* found only 19.5% of the articles focused on learners and learning.

The analyses of research foci in three of the major distance education journals illustrate several concerns. One relates to the limited focus on learners and learning in the research of distance education. If we are concerned with providing both access to education and training AND success in this endeavor, it would appear that increased research in the areas of learners and learning is warranted.

A second concern, and the major focus of this chapter, relates to the nature of the research on learners and learning. Many of the articles on learners and learning appear to be without theoretical or conceptual foundation raising an interesting set of issues and questions. A related issue concerns theory in general. Should the field of distance education generate new theories related to learners and learning or should the field build on existing theories in the literature of elementary, secondary and adult education? And, if researchers borrow theory from other educational disciplines, should these theories be used 'as is' or modified in any way? If they are to be modified, how should they be modified? And if we are to generate theory in distance education, which areas are in greatest need?

Borrowing a framework from adult education, this chapter examines the current state of research related to learners and learning in distance education with emphasis on usage and testing of theories from other fields and theory development in distance education.

Boyd and Apps (1980) attempted to define adult education through a three-dimensional model that focuses on what they called the transactional mode; the client focus; and the personal, social, and cultural systems. Three transactional modes are described: the individual, group, and community modes. An example of the individual mode is an adult working independently pursuing a correspondence course with little, if any, interaction with others. In the group mode, the learner is a member of a group such as an online class. In the community transactional mode, the individual participates with others in trying to resolve a community problem (e.g., a video-satellite program aimed at decreasing youth violence). Although, at first blush, the community mode appears to parallel the group mode, the focus of the community mode is intergroup communications with groups in the community, whereas the group mode focuses on intragroup communications.

The three learning situations are coupled with three client foci. Parallel to adult education, distance education serves three potential clients: individuals, groups, and communities. Coupling transactional mode and client focus provides us with a deeper look at the distance education enterprise. Consider an individual who is registered for a correspondence course on fundraising. It might appear that she is trying to enhance her individual understanding of the concept, but, on closer examination, she is part of a larger community group raising money for a nonprofit organization. A group gathers to participate in a videoconference on management skills, but who is the client? The individual who wants to move ahead in the organization? Perhaps, but it could also be the group itself striving to be more effective as a group by learning how to enhance their processes and procedures. Or the client could be a community-focused group consisting of members of several branch offices coming together to learn about management in order to return to deal with management problems in their own offices (Moore, 1980).

Lastly, Boyd and Apps suggested that all human enterprises participate in three types of systems—personal, social, and cultural systems. The personal system is "defined by the set of distinguishing qualities or characteristics that affect his (her) activity" (p. 9). For our distance learner, we might think of the person's goals, motivation, learning history, and abilities as part of his or her personal system. A social systems consist of interacting roles, relationships, norms, and rules of that unique group (e.g., the family group as contrasted with one or more work groups). Lastly, a cultural system consists of values, beliefs, customs, laws, and so on, that have an impact on individuals. The appropriateness of learning in adulthood and at a distance as well as laws about financial aid for adult part-time distance learners serve as examples.

What emerges is a cube, with each dimension (transactional mode, client focus, and type of system) having three aspects or facets. For example, we can focus on individual women learning via correspondence within a culture that believes women should be excluded from higher education given the definition of traditional women's roles in the home. Or we could turn our attention to the individual learning online in a group with very prescribed group member roles and responsibilities. Or to the community member participating in a community downlink focusing on teen sexual behavior in a society that bans premarital relations.

Although challenging, linking the three interrelated systems together provides an organizing structure to explore and categorize existing research on learners and learning. For the most part, the research reviewed here includes only studies with theoretical frameworks or constructs or those that purport to engage in theory development. A variety of research paradigms are reflected in the research in the field, and all are included in the discussion. Studies mentioned are simply examples of the research in the particular category. Reflecting on existing research, including the modification of existing theory and the generation of theory, allows us to begin to identify theoretical gaps and overlaps.

THE INDIVIDUAL—OUR MOST COMMON CLIENT

Given the purported learner-centered focus of distance education, it seems logical, in reviewing distance education research, to use the client as the major organizing principle, then to tie in the transactional mode and the system perspective. It is noteworthy that most research on learners and learning conducted over the last 10 years has focused on the individual, whether learning alone or in a group.

Individual Client, Individual Mode, Personal System

The greatest amount of research to date has focused on the individual client and the individual transaction mode (i.e., situations in which the individual is learning alone). Correspondence education best exemplifies this mode. Early research emphasized personal systems, with an emphasis on learner characteristics, specifically demographics. The Wallace (1996) study revisited the demographics and motivation of distance learners and documented for one particular Canadian population that distance learners are changing over time, suggesting that assumptions made about the distance learners of yesterday may not be valid for today or tomorrow. Both Paul (1998) and Sherry (1996) echoed Wallace's findings and showed additionally that a growing number of younger learners are combining face-to-face and distance education in order to gain flexibility in scheduling their academic pursuits.

Demographics have increasingly been coupled with psychographics—for example, motivation, learning strategies, learning styles, locus of control, and academic self-concept. One long-standing focus of research has been persistence. Models of persistence in face-to-face higher education, such as the work of Tinto (1975), have served as the foundation for researchers such as Kember, Murphy, Siaw, and Yuen (1991), Fjortoft (1996), and others. Modifications of existing theories have also resulted. These modifications include the introduction of additional variables, such as those related to both personal and social systems, and the broadening of variable definitions. The incorporation of social systems into the definition of social integration provides an example. One personal variable added as a result of this line of research is motivation.

Motivation reappears in a line of research focusing on learning strategies that builds on the early work of Marton and Saljo (1976). As an example, Olgren's (1992) research on learning outcomes in an independent study course highlighted the relationships among and between learning outcomes and goals, motivation, and learning strategies employed by the individual learners. Research on learning styles (a type of research that is somewhat related and builds on a conceptual framework that suggests that matching teaching style and learning style will yield enhanced academic gains and persistence) has been less productive in terms of enhancing our theoretical understanding of individuals learning alone and at a distance (Gibson & Graf, 1992).

Academic self-concept, another learner psychographic, has been shown to be predictive of academic success in both face-to-face and distance education. Recent research on distance learning has expanded existing models from K-12 education to include variables related to learning in adulthood, at a distance, and with technology as part of an adult distance learner's academic self-concept (Gibson, 1996).

In one of the few studies to focus on race, class, or gender as critical personal variables, May (1994) studied women pursuing distance education through both home study and audio teleconferencing. Among her conclusions, she stated that the distance education experience was "a significantly different experience for female learners than for male learners. Distance education was 'easier for a man' " (p. 94). For May's learners, family responsibilities remained the same, and study schedules revolved around the needs of others. This finding was echoed by Gillis, Jackson, Braid, MacDonald, and MacQuarrie (2000) in another study focusing on women learners, which leads us to consider the impact of social systems on learners and learning.

Individual Client, Individual Mode, Social System

What emerged from a focus on individuals learning in an individual transactional mode is the realization that these learners aren't really alone; that is, their academic success is somewhat dependent on the social systems in which they exist. Support from family members, friends, employers, and others for a learner's studies has emerged as a key variable in persistence studies by Kember et al. (1991), Powell, Conway, and Ross (1990), and Gibson and Graf (1992) as well as studies of academic outcome studies (Cragg, 1991; Gibson, 1998; Gillis et al., 2000).

Tallman's (1994) study highlighted the importance of student satisfaction for course completion. Positive interactions with program staff had a major influence on that satisfaction, with a key persistence variable being a mandatory orientation seminar. Overall, research seems to indicate the importance of social systems in the provision of educational, emotional, economic, and logistical support to distance learners.

Individual Client, Individual Mode, Cultural System

In studies whose dominant focus is the learner in a independent study mode, cultural variables have not played a dominant role. Garland (1994) explored the situational, institutional, and dispositional factors that constitute barriers to completion, paralleling the work of adult educator K. Patricia Cross (1981). Her findings highlight epistemological problems and uncover an underlying cultural theme: the social contradiction between the role of an adult and the role of a student and the related need for personal control to maintain psychological power.

Recognizing that context both informs learners' identity and provides barriers and enhancers necessitating an ongoing process of negotiation, neglecting context seems fraught with perils. However, in studies on learners learning as members of groups, culture emerges more often as a focus of research.

Questions Remain for Individual Learners in Individual Modes of Learning

It's obvious that there are very few studies that explore the social and cultural systems and their impact on the learner and learning, perhaps because of our preoccupation with psychological variables in educational research in North America. We ignore the fact that the learner exists within a larger system of interrelating roles and responsibilities, mores and laws, all of which impact progress toward learning.

With few exceptions, research focusing on the lone learner isolated from other learners is a phenomenon of the early 1990s and is becoming less prevalent as researchers and educators move toward technologies that enable group contexts for learning. One might ask questions such as the following: Are we ignoring a mode of distance education that remains prominent and viable as we shift our attention to the newer technologies? Are there still unanswered questions? To what extent are the answers of old applicable to instances where computer-based, on-desk/on-demand job aides and training occur within a work setting? Although the learner is not part of a learning group, he or she is in a rich environment for learning. What do we know about learning in this increasingly common mode of building competence in business and industry?

Individual Client, Group Mode, Personal System

As we increasingly incorporate audio-, video-, and computer conferencing into the education and training of learners at a distance, our research focus has turned to the individual learning in a group transactional mode. This has been by far the most common focus of our research on learners and learning in the last 10 years. Once again, the major client focus of the research has been the individual rather than a group or the community. And as in earlier research on correspondence education, the system under examination has most often been the personal system. Two chapters in this volume highlight the research on individuals learning in a group mode: Wisher and Curnow (Chapter 22) provide an excellent review of the impact of increasingly prevalent video-based instruction on learning and Winiecki's chapter (14) reviews online discussion.

Returning to our analysis of the nature of research on learners and learning in a group, we note that an emphasis on persistence emerges once again. Pugliese's (1994, 1996) research in the mid-1990s focused on a number of psychological variables, including the theoretical constructs of loneliness, communications apprehension, and locus of control and their impact on social integration and persistence of learners in telecourses. Pugliese (1994) essentially found no significant impact on social integration and persistence. Reflecting on the variables commonly used in theoretical models of persistence in traditional education, he concluded, "However important the factors of social integration may be in traditional education, they cannot be said to account for the withdrawal and withdrawal/failure problem of telecourses. Telecourses apparently minimize both the assets and liabilities of social skills" (p. 34).

Dille and Mezack (1991) might be quick to disagree. Exploring the personal variables of locus of control and learning style on successful completion of telecourses, they determined both variables had an impact.

These studies by Pugliese and by Dille and Mezack show why it is important to replicate research studies to understand what additional intervening variables might influence personal variables such as persistence and to ensure that our studies build on each other toward a greater comprehension of the subject as a whole.

Biner, Bink, Huffman, and Dean's (1995) research was designed specifically "to improve upon the Dille and Mezack (1991) research by providing a more comprehensive exploratory study of distance learner personality and achievement" (p. 47). Sixteen personality factors were explored, and many were determined to impact both participation and performance in telecourses. The variability in research findings raises the issue of generalizability of findings on learners and learning, a key consideration for those who are making programmatic decisions based on the published research of the day.

Other lines of research that have focused on the individual client in a group transactional mode include work by Wilkes and Burnham (1991) on motivation and learner satisfaction. Building on motivation theory and existing instrumentation from adult education, they found no relationship between motivation and satisfaction, "suggesting that the sources of variation in satisfaction lie elsewhere" (p. 49). They noted that their finding parallels the finding of research on traditional education and proposed that "this finding may be true across different learning environments and settings."

In contrast, Bruning, Lanids, Hoffman, and Grosskopf (1993) and Bruning (1996), building on the long history of research on self-efficacy in traditional education and generating findings that were somewhat inconsistent with theoretical predictions, reminded us of the domain-specific nature of efficacy judgements. Context and content emerged as possible intervening variables. Dillon's thoughtful and provocative chapter in Chapter 16 provides a detailed review of the constructs that impact the learner's approach to learning and lists suggestions for future research.

A growing number of studies have begun to focus on learning in computer conferencing contexts. Burge's (1994) study of learner perspectives on learning online built on theoretical frameworks within cognitive psychology, specifically learning strategies. Control, inclusion, loss of affective clues, and a number of stressors emerged as key variables. Further, Burge determined that the Tessmer and Jonassen (1988) taxonomy of learning strategies closely paralleled the strategies used in the online environment. Suggested modifications include the incorporation of "... an addition of a new group of strategies named Meta-Context Management" (p. 38). Burge noted that "meta-context is the set of interpersonal dynamics, and the individual student's sense of purpose and presence in those dynamics" (p. 38). Thus the social context of learning in the group mode emerges as a significant variable.

Individual Client, Group Mode, Social System

The social system variable that has attracted the most attention by far is interaction, specifically learner-learner and learner-instructor interaction. Based on the recent meta-analysis of research focusing on the effectiveness of telecourses conducted by Machtmes and Asher (2000), and their finding that interaction significantly influences learner achievement, the attention is well founded.

Interaction has been explored in a variety of ways. In addition, there is a growing focus on interaction in the online environment. Several studies have explored determinants of interaction in the online environment, including Bullen (1998), Kanuka and Anderson (1998), and McLean and Morrison (2000). Bullen also explored the link between learner characteristics and critical thinking, tying his findings back to cognitive development and the *Reflective Judgement* model of King and Kitchener (1994).

Critical thinking, interaction, and the generation of a "community of inquiry" (Lipman, 1991) in audio teleconferencing was a focus of an Anderson and Garrison (1995) study. Anderson and Garrison concluded, "The instructional design upon which the interactive sessions were planned and orchestrated significantly influenced student's perception of this learning. Merely acquiring and using the technology without regard for the development of opportunity for regular and sustained interaction between and among teacher and learners provided no guarantee that a critical community of learners would result" (p. 42). Hilgenberg and Tolone (2000) echoed Anderson and Garrison's conclusions and suggested a relationship not only between instructional design and critical thinking but also between instructional design and student satisfaction in the context of video-based teaching and learning.

May's (1993) study on collaboration and learner interaction, including the use of audioconferences, suggests that caution is necessary, as she uncovered "women's reservations about, and in some cases resistance to, the value and desirability of increased collaboration" (p. 47). Multiple life roles and the impact of context need to be considered in the design of learning environments with high levels of interaction. Fraser and Haughey (1999), in their exploration of the issues facing administrators of nursing programs offered at a distance, noted that "learners did not seem to have the same concerns about interaction [as the faculty]" (p. 54). They also suggested that learners' lack of participation could be attributed to a number of factors, from inappropriate time schedules to long distance cost factors to contextual factors, including instructional design.

Individual Client, Group Mode, Cultural System

Although the news media has focused its attention on the increased diversity of the U.S. population documented by the 2000 census, research in distance education has failed to embrace culture as a variable to any great extent. One exception has been the writings of Sanchez (1996) and Sanchez and Gunawardena (1998), which focus on Hispanic learners, their learning style, and designing for learning in group contexts that are culturally diverse.

Consideration of race, class, and gender continues to be missing in research conducted on individuals learning in a group transactional mode. As Burge (1998) noted in her review of literature on gender in distance education, "Gender-related differences in how adults learn cannot be dismissed as indulgences of privileged academics. They require sustained attention, knowing that 'distance' raises psychological barriers to programs and course completions as well as geographical and fiscal barriers" (p. 40). The impact of social and cultural variables is also worthy of attention but seems to get little. We talk about the possibility of a digit divide yet fail to explore how technologies and instructional design impact learners across contexts and cultures.

A GROWING EMPHASIS ON LEARNING COMMUNITIES

Boyd and Apps (1980) argued eloquently for the group as a distinct phenomenon, more than simply a collection of individuals. A group is an integrated whole with forces and systems of its own. In reviewing the research focused on the group as a client, it appears that this is an area ripe for investigation.

Group Client, Individual Mode, Personal, Social, or Cultural System

One of the benefits of distance education often touted is its ability to deliver a consistent message. For example, teams of engineers can benefit from Web-based training. The message is constant and consistent, available at a time and place convenient to the learner, and this way all team members will get the same information and be able to operate in similar ways within the team context. No research was found that focused on groups or teams learning individually via any of the available technologies.

Group Client, Group Mode, Personal, Social, or Cultural System

Occasionally researchers look at the group transactional mode while maintaining a group client focus and considering the impact of social systems. The recent and growing emphasis on the dynamics of online groups is a case in point. Focusing on the dynamics of instructional groups, McDonald and Gibson (1998) utilized the earlier work of Schutz to explore online group dynamics, discovering strong parallels to face-to-face group development. Murphy and Collins' (1997) research focuses on another aspect of group dynamics, that of the development of communication conventions in instructional electronic chats.

The growing emphasis on the creation of learning communities, particularly in the online environment, has led to a variety of other lines of research on group development. The topics of investigation include group climate, group interaction, group involvement, and social presence. Research on social presence builds on the concept of social presence in traditional education and focuses on the contribution of social presence to group cohesion and group satisfaction. The studies of Gunawardena (1995) and Gunawardena and Zittle (1997), as well as that of Rourke, Anderson, Garrison, and Archer (1999), have led to a greater understanding of the construct and its impact on learning.

Wilson, Gunawardena, and Nolla (2000) remind us of the cultural influences on group development. Individual group members vary in their tolerance for ambiguity, in their value systems (e.g., individualism versus collectivism), and in their responses to high- or low-context communications, and thus each group has its own unique set of values, mores, and roles, and its own unique culture. For a more detailed discussion of the research on group development in online learning communities, see Chapter 51.

Distance education research will need to increase its emphasis on the group as a client working in a group transactional mode as we increasingly engage in online learning and other interactive modes of teaching and learning that enable groups to develop virtually. The research of the 1950s through the 1970s might provide a rich repository of possible theoretical frameworks to borrow and modify given the focus on groups and group development in traditional education and work group environments.

THE COMMUNITY AS CLIENT

The Boyd and Apps model posits the community as a client focus as well as a transactional mode. It's not hard to imagine a community as a client for those in continuing education. A representative of the roads department joins a video-satellite program on potholes and their repair (a major expenditure in a county's budget) with the intention of sharing the new information with colleagues for immediate application. The learning appears individual, but actually our learner is but an emissary, ready to share his or her understanding with the community members he or she represents. Faculty and administrators from all over the country join a program on intellectual property and copyright for the purpose of helping the "academic community" they represent to better understand the appropriate laws and encouraging more lawful behavior among both faculty and administrators. Examples abound; research does not.

If we are to continue to offer education and training designed with a community client in mind and delivered in a community mode, it would seem essential to engage in research that begins to address related questions. These might include the following: To what extent does the information shared with a member of a community get delivered within that community? What models of instructional design facilitate the transfer of knowledge to community members? What social or cultural factors influence the impact of community-focused distance education? If organizations continue to refer to themselves as learning communities and provide specialized training to members within the community for the community, we need to ensure that research is available to ensure maximum impact.

THEORY GENERATION: A GROWING TREND

Although the majority of research in the field of distance education could be described as theory testing, theory generation is growing. In 1993, Desmond Keegan edited *Theoretical Principles of Distance Education*. The book assembled authors from around the world to share their thinking on one of five different perspectives on distance education: didactic, academic, analytical, philosophical, and technological. Two of the authors in the didactic underpinnings section of the book are North American leaders in theory development in the field, Michael Moore and Randy Garrison. Their thinking has driven much of the generation, modification, and testing of theories specifically addressing the unique nature and structure of distance education.

Moore's Theory of Transactional Distance

Emerging in 1983 out of research and writing done in the 1970s and 1980s, Moore's theory of transactional distance has generated considerable interest and been extensively tested in the past 20 years. A number of researchers have tested one or more of the key variables and/or their relationships to determine how they affect learning at a distance. Studies include Gayol's (1996) exploration of the model in the context of computer-mediated conferencing and Chen and Willits' (1998, 1999) analysis of the theory's concepts in a videoconferencing learning environment. Chen and Willits' work has highlighted the possible multifaceted dimensions of the variables in the theory. Vrasidas and McIssac (1999) noted in their findings that "Elements of structure such as required activities led to more interactions and increased dialogue among the participants" (p. 32), contradicting the earlier findings of Saba and Shearer (1984) and hypotheses stated by Moore (1973). Perhaps the online environment is sufficiently different in communication pattern to suggest a modification for this instructional context. Hillman, Willis, and Gunawardena (1994) would posit that we need to broaden our look at interaction to include learner-interface interaction (i.e., manipulation of the tools needed to accomplish a task).

In 1988, Saba proposed a systems dynamics model to represent the relationship among the variables of dialogue and structure and the resultant transactional distance. Saba and Shearer (1994) continued this line of work by doing a study to verify key theoretical concepts in the emerging dynamic model of transactional distance. Their work refined the theory of transactional distance, adding elements related to teacher and learner control.

Learner Control

The concept of learner control, based on Moore's (1976) "second dimension" of independent learning, which is learner autonomy, has generated considerable interest and, through the work of Randy Garrison and Myra Baynton, gained theoretical clarity. For instance, Garrison and Baynton (1987) demonstrated that control is a multifaceted construct consisting of three essential dimensions: competence, independence, and support. Testing this model, Baynton (1992) determined that "some congruence with the original model was apparent . . . [the three original factors] accounted for 39.6% [of the variance] . . . and three minor factors . . . appeared complementary to the dominant categories" (p. 24). These factors were value orientation, access to resources, and flexibility. Further, Baynton noted that "the environment in which the learner operates was also identified as an important factor" (p. 26).

For a discussion of support, specifically academic advising, see Chapter 13.

Self-Directed Learning

A related line of thinking that links many of the above variables together occurs in Chapter 11 of this volume, on self-directed learning.

Additional Theoretical Considerations

Three additional chapters in Keegan's (1993) book focus on the academic underpinnings of distance education, all contributed by North Americans. Amundsen (1993) provided a succinct overview of theory development to date, then posited a model that places learning at the center, includes teachers, learners, and content as principal components, and represents distance as having a significant impact on all components of the teaching and learning process. Sauvé (1993) noted that "distance" is the defining characteristic of distance education and that it makes this kind of education different from all other modes of teaching and learning—an issue hotly debated in the fall 1999 issue of the *Journal of Distance Education*. It is also distance that necessitates the incorporation of one or more technologies to establish a relationship between teachers and learners.

The attributes of these technologies, the psychographics of the learner, and the resultant learning outcomes are the foci of theory development by Smith and Dillon (1999). Saba (1996) wrote a reaction to this particular theoretical framework, criticizing it for lacking a dynamic system perspective on distance education and recommending the theory of transactional distance as a better framework. Gibson (1993), the third author in the academic underpinnings section of the Keegan (1993) book, suggested that the models posited to date remained narrow in focus. She argued that human development is the result of many overlapping spheres of influence, and until those spheres are recognized and explored systematically, the jigsaw puzzle will remain incomplete.

A Recent Noteworthy Development

In spite of the pervasiveness of the psychological view of distance learning, a new model has emerged. Put forward by Garrison, Anderson, and Archer (2000), it is entitled the community of inquiry model (see Garrison, Anderson, & Archer, 2001; Rourke et al., 1999). In this model, educational experience is at the center of the three intersecting circles of social presence, cognitive presence, and teaching presence—three of the main elements of educational experience. Additional elements identified include setting climate, supporting discourse, and selecting content. The model begins to expand beyond a preoccupation with the psychological to include the social. Contextual variables are still missing, but it is early in the model's development. The model is closely tied to theoretical models that have been shown to have utility in distance education and also to measurement tools.

Tools to Enhance Theory in Distance Education

In order to reach the goal of theoretical understanding, a number of researchers have engaged in the development of tools for data collection and data analyses, including instruments to measure students' attitudes toward televised courses (Biner, 1993; Biner, Dean, & Mellinger, 1994).

Researchers have also devised tools to assess and categorize interactions within group modes of learning. Cookson and Chang (1995), for instance, developed the Multidimensional Audioconferencing Classification System (MACS) "to generate new knowledge about the categories and patterns of instructional interactions not manifest when using models based on conventional face-to-face instruction" (p. 31).

Sherry, Fulford, and Zhang (1998) focused on interaction as well in their development of a tool to assess learners' perceptions of interactions between learner and instructor and between learner and learner in video-based instruction. The learner's view of the overall level of interaction and the extent to which the environment supports interaction is also sought. As another example, Gunawardena, Lowe, and Anderson (1997) developed a constructivist interaction analysis model for computer conferencing.

Assessing social presence has also been the focus of recent research, including that of Rourke et al. (1999), which complements the development of the new model noted above. And the identification of at-risk students in videoconferencing and Web-based distance education has emerged as yet another focus of instrument development (Osborn, 2001).

What's interesting to note is that, although distance education researchers have embraced the borrowing of theory, they have borrowed few instruments from related disciplines, such as educational psychology. Using a common set of tools has its pluses and minuses, but it does allow for the aggregation of data!

CONCLUSION

A selective review of the research literature on learners and learning highlights several key points. First, there is a paucity of research on learners and learning at a distance. Further, what research exists is often descriptive and/or atheoretical, uninformed by theoretical or conceptual frameworks emerging from the field of distance education or borrowed from related disciplines. On a more positive note, when a theory is borrowed, there seems to be a growing awareness of the need to look critically at its applicability, to be explicit about its value and shortcomings, and to suggest modifications based on testing in a distance education environment.

The growth in theories about learners and learning at a distance is promising, and this trend must continue if the field is to advance. The concomitant development of tools and methods will also aid the field by enabling researchers to aggregate data that share common definitions and data-collection techniques. Relating studies to each other—that is, building on the knowledge gained through earlier quality research—will be a vital part of constructing a knowledge base for researchers and practitioners alike. We do need to beware of overgeneralization, however, and be forthcoming about the rate of attrition suffered by our studies (Machtmes & Asher, 2000).

Our research continues to place an emphasis on the individual and on personal systems. This emphasis is not entirely unexpected given that most distance educators would suggest that individual learning outcomes make up our primary mission. However, as May (1994) eloquently noted, "Despite high participation rates [in distance education], there is little attention towards gender issues in distance education (Coulter, 1989) nor to women's preferred ways of knowing and preferred ways of learning (Clinchy, Belenky, Goldberger, & Tarule, 1985)." Research with a focus on race, class, and gender as critical variables is sorely missing. Learners with disabilities, either physical or psychological, are essentially invisible in the research, although their participation in distance education has been enhanced through the variety of technologies that distinguish our field of practice.

There is a growing recognition of the importance of context. Our focus on social context has been confined, for the most part, to dynamics within the learning group. To quote Anderson and Garrison (1995), "Unlike the typically unfruitful search for the general learning effect of any particular medium, studies that focus on the influence of instructional design on learning outcomes will be a productive focus for future research in distance education" (p. 42). The design of the instruction and its implementation create a social environment in which learning may occur. To ignore the importance of this context is to neglect a powerful influence on the learner and on learning, as we have come to understand through cognitive psychology. The following chapters in this volume provide a solid point of departure for future research in this area: "Constructing Knowledge Learner by Learner" (Chapter 12), "Cognitive and Learning Factors in Web-based Environments" (Chapter 17), and "Exploring the New Conception of Teaching and Learning in Distance Education" (Chapter 27).

Distance education researchers, through their continued focus on the individual learner, are seemingly ignoring important issues related to team training and the learning organization that go beyond individual growth and development. We have the tools and we have the demand. What we don't have is research to inform our practice.

As Thomas Henry Huxley once noted, "Those who refuse to go beyond fact rarely get beyond fact ... almost every step [towards progress] has been made by the invention of an hypothesis which, through verification, often had little foundation to start with" (quoted in Wedemeyer, 1981, p. 10). Although those who gravitate toward naturalistic and critical research paradigms might shudder at this expression of the logical-positivist quantitative research paradigm, they would surely agree that we need to go beyond fact in order to better understand learners and learning at a distance *if* we are to move beyond providing access to education and ensuring success in learning. Systematic research is a beginning to that ideal end. In other words, we need to head Moore's (1990) call to fill in the theoretical spaces, especially through empirical study. And we need to do it now!

REFERENCES

Amundsen, C. (1993). The evolution of theory in distance education. In D. Keegan, (Ed.), *Theoretical principles of distance education* (pp. 61–79). London: Routledge.

Anderson, T., & Garrison, R. (1995). Transactional issues in distance education: The impact of design in audiotele-conferencing. *American Journal of Distance Education, 9*(2), 27–42.

Baynton, M. (1992). Dimensions of "control" in distance education: A factor analysis. *American Journal of Distance Education, 6*(2), 17–31.

Biner, P. (1993). The development of an instrument to measure student attitudes toward televised courses. *American Journal of Distance Education, 7*(1), 62–73.

Biner, P., Bink, M., Huffman, M., & Dean, R. (1995). Personality characteristics differentiating and predicting the achievement of televised-course students and traditional-course students. *American Journal of Distance Education, 9*(2), 46–59.

Biner, P., Dean, R., & Mellinger, A. (1994). Factors underlying distance learner satisfaction with televised college-level courses. *American Journal of Distance Education, 8*(1), 60–71.

Boyd, R., Apps, J., & Associates. (1980). *Redefining the discipline of adult education.* San Francisco: Jossey-Bass.

Bruning, R. (1996). Examining the utility of efficacy measures in distance education research. In C. Gibson, (Ed.), *Distance education symposium 3: Learners and learning* (Research Monograph No. 13; pp. 17–29). University Park, PA: American Center for the Study of Distance Education.

Bruning, R., Lanids, M., Hoffman, E., & Grosskopf, K. (1993). Perspectives on an interactive satellite-based Japanese language course. *American Journal of Distance Education, 7*(3), 22–38.

Bullen, M. (1998). Participation and critical thinking in online university distance education. *Journal of Distance Education, 13*(2), 1–32.

Burge, E. (1994). Learning in computer conferencing contexts: The learners' perspective. *Journal of Distance Education, 9*(1), 19–43.

Burge, E. (1998). Gender in distance education. In C. Gibson, (Ed.), *Distance learners in higher education: Institutional responses for quality outcomes.* (pp. 25–45). Madison, WI: Atwood Publishers.

Chen, Y., & Willits, F. (1998). A path analysis of the concepts in Moore's theory of transactional distance in a videoconferencing learning environment. *Journal of Distance Education, 13*(2), 51–65.

Chen, Y., & Willits, F. (1999). Dimensions of educational transactions in a videoconferencing learning environment. *American Journal of Distance Education, 13*(1), 45–59.

Clinchy, B. M., Belenky, M. F., Goldberger, N. R., & Tarule, J. M. (1985). Connected education for women. *Journal of Education, 167*(3), 28–45.

Coldeway, D. (1995, May). *A research agenda for distance education: Setting targets for learners and learning.* Paper presented at the Third Research Symposium in Distance Education, University Park, PA.

Cookson, P., & Chang, Y. (1995). The multidimensional audioconferencing classification system (MACS). *American Journal of Distance Education, 9*(3), 18–36.

Coulter, R. (1989). Women in distance education: Towards a feminist perspective. In R. Sweet (Ed.), *Post-secondary distance education in Canada: Policies, practices and priorities* (pp. 11–22). Athabasca, AB: Athabasca University and the Canadian Society for Studies in Education.

Cragg, B. (1991). Nurses' experience in a distance course by correspondence and audioteleconference. *Journal of Distance Education, 6*(2), 39–57.

Cross, K. P. (1981). *Adults as learners.* San Francisco: Jossey-Bass.

Dille, B., & Mezack, M. (1991). Identifying predictors of high risk among community college telecourse students. *American Journal of Distance Education, 5*(1), 24–35.

Fjortoft, N. (1996). Persistence in a distance learning program: A case in pharmaceutical education. *American Journal of Distance Education, 10*(3), 49–59.

Fraser, J., & Haughey, M. (1999). Administering student-related concerns in nursing distance education programs. *Journal of Distance Education, 14*(1), 34–57.

Garland, M. (1994). The adult need for "personal control" provides a cogent guiding concept for distance education. *Journal of Distance Education, 9*(1), 45–59.

Garrison, D., Anderson, T., & Archer, R. (2000). *Critical inquiry in a text-based environment: Computer conferencing in higher education.* Unpublished manuscript.

Garrison, D., Anderson, T., & Archer, W. (2001). Critical thinking, cognitive presence, and computer conferencing in distance education. *American Journal of Distance Education, 15*(1), 7–23.

Garrison, D., & Baynton, M. (1987). Beyond independence in distance education: The concept of control. *American Journal of Distance Education, 1*(3), 3–15.

Gayol, Y. (1996). The use of computer networks in distance education: An analysis of the patterns of electronic interaction in a multi-national course. In C. Gibson (Ed.), *Distance education symposium 3: Learners and learning* (Research Monograph No. 13; pp. 61–69). University Park, PA: American Center for the Study of Distance Education.

Gibson, C. (1993). Toward a broader conceptualization of distance education. In D. Keegan (Ed.), *Theoretical principles of distance education* (pp. 80–82). London: Routledge.

Gibson, C. (1996). Toward an understanding of academic self-concept in distance education. *American Journal of Distance Education, 10*(1), 23–36.

Gibson, C. (Ed.). (1996). *Distance education symposium 3: Learners and learning* (Research Monograph No. 13). University Park, PA: American Center for the Study of Distance Education.

Gibson, C. (1998). Social context and the collegiate distance learner. In C. Gibson, (Ed.), *Distance learners in higher education: Institutional responses for quality outcomes* (pp. 113–126). Madison, WI: Atwood Publishers.

Gibson, C., & Graf, A. (1992). Impact of adults' learning styles and perceptions of barriers on completion of external baccalaureate degree programs. *Journal of Distance Education, 7*(1), 39–51.

Gillis, A., Jackson, W., Braid, A., MacDonald P., & MacQuarrie, M. (2000). The learning needs and experiences of women using print-based and CD-ROM technology in nursing distance education. *Journal of Distance Education, 15,*(1), 1–20.

Gunawardena, C. (1995). Social presence theory and implications for interaction and collaborative learning in computer conferences. *International Journal of Educational Telecommunications, 1*(2-3), 147–166.

Gunawardena, C., Lowe, C., & Anderson, T. (1997). Interactional analysis of a global online debate and the development of a constructivist interaction analysis model for computer conferencing. *Journal of Educational Computing Research, 17*(4), 395–429.

Gunawardena, C., & Zittle, F. (1997). Social presence as a predictor of satisfaction within a computer-mediated conferencing environment. *American Journal of Distance Education, 11*(3), 8-26.

Hilgenberg, C., & Tolone, W. (2000). Student perceptions of satisfaction and opportunities for critical thinking in distance education by interactive video. *American Journal of Distance Education, 14*(3), 59–73.

Hillman, D., Willis, D., & Gunawardena, C. (1994). Learner-interface interaction in distance education: An extension of contemporary models and strategies for practitioners. *American Journal of Distance Education, 8*(2), p. 30–41.

Kanuka, H., & Anderson, T. (1998). Online social interchange, discord and knowledge construction. *Journal of Distance Education, 13*(1), 57–74.

Keegan, D. (Ed.). 1993. *Theoretical principles of distance education.* New York: Routledge.

Kember, D., Murphy, D., Siaw, I., & Yuen, K. (1991). Toward a casual model of student progress in distance education: Research in Hong Kong. *American Journal of Distance Education, 5,* 3–15.

King, P., & Kitchener, K. (1994). *Developing reflective judgement: Understanding and promoting intellectual growth and critical thinking in adolescents and adults.* San Francisco: Jossey-Bass.

Koble, M., & Bunker, E. (1997). Trends in research and practice: An examination of the *American Journal of Distance Education* 1987–1995. *American Journal of Distance Education, 11*(2), 19–38,

Lipman, M. (1991). *Thinking in education.* Cambridge: Cambridge University Press.

Machtmes, K., & Asher, J. (2000). A meta-analysis of the effectiveness of telecourses in distance education. *American Journal of Distance Education, 14*(1), 20–46.

Marton, F., & Saljo, R. (1976). On qualitative differences in learning: I-outcomes and processes. *British Journal of Educational Psychology, 46,* 4–11.

May, S. (1993). Collaborative learning: More is not necessarily better. *American Journal of Distance Education, 7*(3), 39–50.

May, S. (1994). Women's experience as distance learners: Access and technology. *Journal of Distance Education, 9*(1), 81–98.

McDonald, J., & Gibson, C. (1998). Interpersonal aspects of group dynamics and group development in computer conferencing. *American Journal of Distance Education, 12*(1), 7–25.

McLean, S., & Morrison, D. (2000). Sociodemographic characteristics of learners and participation in computer conferencing. *Journal of Distance Education, 15*(2), 17–36.

Moore, M. (1973). Toward a theory of independent learning and teaching. *Journal of Higher Education, 44,* 661–679.

Moore, M. (1976). A model of independent study. In *Investigation of the interaction between cognitive style of field independence and attitude to independent study among adult learners who use correspondence independent study and self-directed independent study* (Chap. 2). Unpublished doctoral dissertation, University of Wisconsin-Madison.

Moore, M. (1980). Independent study. In R. Boyd, J. Apps, and Associates (Eds.), *Redefining the discipline of adult education* (pp. 16–31). San Francisco: Jossey-Bass.

Moore, M. (1990). Recent contributions to the theory of distance education. *Open Learning, 5*(3), 10–15.

Moore, M. (1993). Theory of transactional distance: The evolution of theory in distance education. In D. Keegan, (Ed.), *Theoretical principles of distance education* (pp. 22–38). London: Routledge.

Murphy, L., & Collins, M. (1997). Development of communications conventions in instructional electronic chats. *Journal of Distance Education, 12*(1-2), 177–200.

Olgren, C. (1992). Adults' learning strategies and outcomes in an independent study course. Unpublished doctoral dissertation, University of Wisconsin-Madison.

Osborn, V. (2001). Identifying at-risk students in videoconferencing and Web-based distance education. *American Journal of Distance Education, 15*(1), 41–54.

Paul, R. (1998). Learning from international partnerships in distance education. In *14th Annual Canadian Association for Distance Education Conference Proceedings* (pp. 280–282). Banff, AB: Athabasca University Press.

Powell, R., Conway, C., & Ross, L. (1990). Effects of students' predisposing characteristics on students' success. *Journal of Distance Education, 5*(1), 5–19.

Pugliese, R. (1994). Telecourse persistence and psychological variables. *American Journal of Distance Education, 8*(3), 22–39.

Pugliese, R. (1996). The loneliness of the long distance learner. In C. Gibson (Ed.), *Distance education symposium 3: Learners and learning.* (Research Monograph No. 13; pp. 30–41). University Park, PA: American Center for the Study of Distance Education.

Rourke, L., Anderson, T., Garrison, D., & Archer, W. (1999). Assessing social presence in asynchronous text-based computer conferencing. *Journal of Distance Education, 14*(2), 50–71.

Saba, F. (1996). Dede's distributed learning: A systematic perspective. *American Journal of Distance Education, 10*(2), 60–64.

Saba, F., & Shearer, R. (1994). Verifying key theoretical concepts in a dynamic model of distance education. *American Journal of Distance Education, 8*(1), 36–59.

Sanchez, I. (1996). An analysis of learning style constructs and the development of a profile of Hispanic adult learners. Unpublished doctoral dissertation, University of New Mexico, Albuquerque.

Sanchez, I., & Gunawardena, L. (1998). Understanding and supporting the culturally diverse distance learner. In C. Gibson (Ed.), *Distance learners in higher education: Institutional responses for quality outcomes* (pp. 47–64). Madison, WI: Atwood Publishers.

Sauvé, L. (1993). What's behind the development of a course on the concept of distance education. In D. Keegan (Ed.), *Theoretical principles of distance education* (pp. 93–112). London: Routledge

Scriven, B. (1991). Ten years of "Distance Education." *Distance Education, 12*(1), 137–153.

Sherry, L. (1996). Issues in distance learning. *International Journal of Educational Telecommunications, 1*(4), 337–365.

Sherry, L., Fulford, C., & Zhang, S. (1998). Assessing distance learners' satisfaction with instruction: A qualitative and quantitative measure. *American Journal of Distance Education, 12*(3), 4–28.

Smith, P., & Dillon, C. (1999). Comparing distance learning and classroom learning: Conceptual considerations. *American Journal of Distance Education, 13*(2), 6–23.

Tallman, F. (1994). Satisfaction and completion in correspondence study: The influence of instructional and student support. *American Journal of Distance Education 8,*(2), 43–57.

Tessmer, M., & Jonassen, D. (1988). Learning strategies: A new instructional technology. In *World yearbook of education, 1988* (pp. 29–47). London: Kogan Page.

Tinto, V. (1975). Drop-out from higher education: A theoretical synthesis of recent research. *Review of Educational Research, 45,* 89–125.

Vrasidas, C., & McIssac, M. (1999). Factors influencing interaction in an online course. *American Journal of Distance Education, 13*(3), 22–36.

Wallace, L. (1996). Changes in demographics and motivations of distance education students. *Journal of Distance Education, 11*(1), 1–31.

Wedemeyer, C. (1981). *Learning at the back door: Reflections on non-traditional learning in the lifespan.* Madison, WI: University of Wisconsin Press.

Wilkes, C., & Burnham, B. (1991). Adult learner motivations and electronic distance education. *American Journal of Distance Education, 5*(1), 43–50.

Wilson, P., Gunawardena, C., & Nolla, A. (2000). Cultural factors influencing online interaction and group dynamics. In *Proceedings of the 16th Annual Conference on Distance Teaching and Learning* (pp. 449–456). Madison, WI: University of Wisconsin-Madison.

11

Self-Directed Learning and Distance Education

D. Randy Garrison
University of Calgary
garrison@ucalgary.ca

Self-directed learning (SDL) is an intuitively appealing concept. Perhaps because of this, the concept has attracted interest from fields of practice such as education, nursing, medical education, and business. Its adoption and impact, however, has generally been limited by its less-than-coherent and comprehensive conceptual development. Much of the confusion can be attributed to the fact that it emerged largely from an informal context where learner freedom was a sine qua non (Rogers, 1969; Tough, 1971). When applied to formal educational contexts, it was often seen as a means to shift from a teacher-centered to a learner-centered approach to education. Notwithstanding the need for such a shift, it became as much a slogan as a defensible approach to teaching and learning. One explanation for the marginal status of SDL in distance education is the lack of conceptual development.

The position of this chapter is that we require a conceptual understanding of SDL that might practically shape the design and delivery of education in a variety of settings as well as guide further research into the concept. Despite the apparent compatibility of distance education and the concept of SDL, there has been little theoretical development since the seminal work in the early 1980s linking SDL with distance education. Perhaps the ultimate question is whether SDL is worthy of consideration as a means of understanding or facilitating distance education. In fact, the goal here is to explore this question. To this end, the chapter updates our understanding of SDL, identifies the core themes and issues surrounding the concept, and explores implications for the study and practice of distance education.

REVIEW OF SELF-DIRECTED LEARNING

As with many concepts in education, the genesis of SDL may well be attributed to John Dewey, with his focus on the experience of the learner. However, in the latter half of this century, the concept more directly emerged from the humanist philosophy of Carl Rogers and was developed and popularized within adult education by individuals such as Allan Tough (1971) and Malcolm Knowles (1975). Rogers (1969) was largely responsible for outlining the concept of self-direction. He was a psychotherapist who strongly believed in personal responsibility and freedom to choose. This translated into a "nondirective" approach accompanied by extreme trust in the individual to learn and learn how to learn. Although the primary means of learning was "intensive group experience," there was little room for lessons or criticism from the group facilitator.

In the early 1970s, SDL emerged full force in the field of adult education and remains today its most researched topic and reflective of the practice of adult education and learning at its best. The person most responsible for this is Malcolm Knowles. Knowles (1970) made Rogers' concept of self-direction the core of his approach to facilitating learning in an adult education context (i.e., andragogy). This nondirective approach, which was central to adult education for the next 20 years, was reinforced through the pioneering research of Allan Tough (1971), who studied individual informal learning projects in the natural societal setting. Clearly, the foundation of the interest and movement in SDL was a focus on the freedom and responsibility of the individual learners to construct their own learning experiences. It was also a rejection of an excessively teacher-centered traditional educational experience, which too often demonstrated little trust and respect for the competency of individuals to take responsibility for learning.

With distance education preoccupied with issues and concepts of independence and autonomy, SDL was perhaps inevitably attractive to researchers in the field. Charles Wedemeyer in the 1960s was perhaps the first to break from the term *correspondence study*, and he replaced it with *independent study* or *learning* to reflect a particular philosophy of teaching and learning. He noted the conceptual consistency of the terms *independent study, learning at a distance*, and *self-directed learning*. Wedemeyer (1971) advocated freedom and choice (i.e., control) for the learner but pointed out that independent study in distance education unsatisfactorily offers "less freedom in goal determination and activity selection" (p. 551).

Michael Moore also associated the terms *independence, autonomy*, and *self-directed learning*. Similar to Wedemeyer, Moore's early focus was on pedagogical issues, and he offered a theory of transactional distance framed by two dimensions: distance teaching and learner autonomy. According to Moore (1972), distance and autonomy are the "twin foundations of independent learning" (p. 84). Distance teaching, consisting of individualization (later labeled *structure*) and dialogue, would seem to reflect institutional and educational variables. Autonomy appears to view the transaction from the learner's perspective. It is through the autonomy dimension that Moore addresses the concept of SDL, which builds upon Rogers' concept of an educated person as one who has learned how to learn. Autonomy concerns the degree of control the learner has over preparation, execution, and evaluation of his or her learning. In subsequent publications (Moore, 1993; Moore & Kearsley, 1996), Moore treated autonomy as a personality characteristic associated with self-directedness and personal responsibility.

Moore (1982, 1986) was the first to publish a paper specifically exploring the implications of SDL for distance education. For Moore, a self-directed learner is an autonomous learner. In analyzing the elements and values of SDL, Moore attempted to redress the balance of control in distance education. His object was to defend the learner and the values of freedom and control against the encroachment of the industrialized distance education organization. As a result of this passionate defense of SDL and the distance learner, issues of balance were raised. In reaction to Moore's paper, Willen (1984) commented that his arguments are "too diffuse and too general" and called for a deeper analysis of SDL in an educational context. The central question remained, how might SDL shape the development of distance education?

Following Moore's and Willen's lead, Bagnall (1988) attempted to provide a deeper analysis of the meaning of SDL in a distance education context. He suggested adopting SDL as an appropriate educational standard to provide a "radically different conception and valuation of distance education . . . the ideal of the fully autonomous individual learner" (p. 93). In adopting this standard, Bagnall concluded that self-direction could reduce structural differences between face-to-face and distance education—differences that have frequently been taken as grounds for devaluing distance education.

Considering the period in which Bagnall's article was written (i.e., when the industrial model was dominant), his interpretation and adoption of SDL appears more a rationalization of what seemed at the time to be the insurmountable structural constraint of distance. At the core of SDL during this period was learner control of both internal and external aspects of the learning experience. Morgan (1985) addressed the apparent total learner control of the learning experience in a critique of independent learning. He argued that for students to be totally independent "they would need to be self-educating" (p. 39). However, a "whole-hearted commitment to self-directed learning" would mean giving up any attempt to direct students' learning, the implication being that SDL misses a crucial dimension of an educational experience — "the extent to which control is shared between student and institution with regard to teaching and learning" (p. 39).

Next, in exploring the meaning and role of SDL in a distance education context, Garrison (1987) identified two key issues: the role of the facilitator and the context for learning. First, Garrison emphasized that there is very much a need for guidance by way of a facilitator. Second, he claimed that SDL is relevant to the formal educational context and that the means "exist to mediate the transactional dialogue between learner and facilitator to make self-directed learning worthwhile and efficient" (pp. 311–312). The goal of Garrison's article was to move the concept and application of SDL from the informal and independent approach to learning inherent in its early manifestation. The core argument was that the complementary issues of control and responsibility for students and teachers must be considered in any conceptualization of SDL if it is to have relevance for distance education or any educational experience.

THEMES AND ISSUES

As noted previously, for distance educators, interest in SDL emerged from the structural constraints of distance education and the independence of distance learners. Naturally, during this period a dominant theme in the theory and practice of distance education was autonomy. Autonomy was also integral to the concept of SDL, which is why theorists attempted to adopt the concept of SDL to explain and shape distance education practice. A second and related theme to be explored here is that of control. This theme more directly emerged from SDL theory but was also seen as relevant to the theory and practice of distance education. We next explore these two themes and the issues of SDL in the context of distance education.

Autonomy

Independence and autonomy have been associated with the industrial model of distance education. The industrial model brought with it considerable efficiencies by providing access to learning through mass-produced independent study packages. The result was increased access but at the cost of institutionalized isolation of learners and a reduced role for teachers during the learning process.

Moore (1993) was one of the first to gently challenge this view of autonomy by integrating it with distance teaching (i.e., structure and dialogue). His theory of transactional distance (see previous section) recognizes the importance of dialogue between and among teacher and learners in an educational experience. Also, through the autonomy dimension and SDL, transactional distance goes beyond control by raising important cognitive issues. He also raised the issue of responsibility associated with self-directedness. However, as is discussed in the next section, the implications of cognitive responsibility in distance education remain to be fully explored.

Another key individual associated with the theme of autonomy is Otto Peters, who conceptualized the industrial organizational model of distance education. Interestingly, it is Peters (1998) who now believes that the industrial approach to distance education needs to be seriously examined, especially the externally prescribed, heavily structured courses, expository teaching, and receptive learning lacking in spontaneous dialogue that are characteristic of it. What he asks for is greater "pedagogical imagination" and treatment of students not as the "objects but the subjects of the teaching process" (p. 98). He recommends that division of labor be limited or abolished and that learning be organized in "smaller working groups" and around study objects.

What Peters (1998) is advocating is "informal, self-determined learning" (p. 107). In essence, this type of learning is very closely associated with the view of Rogers (1969) and Tough (1971), as it transfers considerable trust and responsibility to the learner. Peters classifies it as a potential new form of distance education, with the dominant pedagogic pattern being "autonomous, self-guided learning." According to Peters, for students to be autonomous is for them to be "meta-cognitively, motivationally and behaviorally active participants in their own learning" (p. 48). This description has parallels core to a SDL model put forward by Garrison (1997), in which monitoring, motivation, and management are core components (this model is discussed in the next section).

Although the nature of autonomous learning is complex and beyond the scope of this chapter, it is, as Peters (1998) suggested, a topic that distance educators cannot avoid discussing. The main reason is the growing importance of informal, lifelong learning and developments in electronic telecommunications. Traditional education, including distance education, must be consistent with the less formal aspects of lifelong learning. Because of this fact, the influence of distance education as a field of study and practice could easily expand. However, as relevant as Peters' concept of autonomous learning might be for informal learning and society at large, it does not address distance education's role and responsibility in the area of facilitating or supporting effective formal learning. The challenge is to conceptually construct a continuum of learning at a distance that ranges from the informal to the formal. Certainly SDL could be the core concept spanning such a perspective.

As appealing as autonomous and self-determined learning is in an era where continuous learning is highly valued, we remain challenged by the concept. Candy (1991) states emphatically that the "ideology of autonomy" associated with SDL has created educational imbalances. The challenge for all educators is to critically examine SDL in terms of the roles and responsibilities of educators and educational institutions. An educational transaction should not diminish the appropriate roles and responsibilities of teachers and learners whether the communication (dialogue) is mediated or not.

Although it is appropriate to encourage autonomy and independence of thought through the process of constructing personal meaning, even the innermost learning activities occur in a social context mediated by communicative action. Difficult educational and learning decisions must be made with regard to goals, curricula, and approaches. In this sense, *autonomy* may be the wrong term or concept to employ, as its connotation tends to reflect a false ideal.

Control and Responsibility

Throughout the 1980s, SDL in a distance education context was invariably associated with the theme of control. The tendency was to give as much control as possible to the learner without serious consideration of the appropriateness of such an approach for purposes of learning and education. As a result, serious questions were raised about the nature of an educational experience when the role of the educator is virtually nonexistent. These questions were compounded by a conceptual ambiguity. SDL could refer to an independent pursuit of learning, a way of organizing instruction, or a personal attribute (Candy, 1987). Possibly as a result of this ambiguity and the attendant confusion, interest in using SDL to guide or rationalize the practice of distance education appeared to diminish in the 1990s—as it did to an extent in adult education.

In an attempt to provide some coherence and order to the concept of SDL, Garrison (1997) provided a comprehensive model from an educational "collaborative constructivist" perspective. This model was an attempt to broaden the application of SDL by identifying three core components: self-management, self-monitoring, and motivation. The keys to describing and understanding these components are the themes of control and responsibility. Self-management reflects concerns about external control issues and what learners do in achieving intended educational outcomes. It was argued that through a collaborative process of sharing and balancing control between teacher and student, the appropriate balance between educational norms and personal choice would be ensured. Self-monitoring introduced the theme of cognitive responsibility for constructing meaningful and educationally valid knowledge. Self-monitoring includes both internal and external critique and confirmation and therefore gives rise to both student and teacher responsibilities.

Both control and responsibility are essential for the third component of SDL: motivation. Without some sense of control, it is very difficult for students to assume responsibility for their learning and to achieve deep and meaningful outcomes. Motivation in the form of commitment to a learning goal and the tendency to persist is most essential for self-directed learning. Control and choice strengthen motivation, which in turn builds a sense of responsibility. However, as necessary as a sense of control is, without appropriate support and guidance learners may not persist or achieve the desired educational outcomes.

From an educational perspective, quality of learning outcomes is not simply a question of student control and responsibility. The teacher also plays an integral role in education as a transactional process and has his or her own legitimate and often necessary control and responsibility concerns. It is the teacher who is charged with the responsibility of clarifying goals, shaping learning activities, and assessing learning outcomes. Furthermore, in collaboration with students, teachers are responsible for establishing the balance of control that will ensure worthwhile outcomes and continuing efforts to learn (Garrison, 1993). As regards "education" at a distance in particular, many teaching and learning factors must converge in balancing control and responsibility for an efficient and effective educational experience to occur.

Control and responsibility are issues for both student and teacher in any educational experience. The themes of control and responsibility have been introduced as a means of understanding transactional issues associated with an educational experience. That is, it expands the concept of SDL to include personal and shared perspectives inherent in any educational experience. This focus reflects developments in the theory and practice of distance education from structural (organizational) concerns to transactional (communication) concerns (Garrison, 2000).

IMPLICATIONS FOR DISTANCE EDUCATION

The concept of SDL in distance education has focused on the freedom of the learner to control the goals and activities of the learning process. Although cognitive autonomy and the predisposition to take control and responsibility for one's learning are important assets, so are opportunities to test personal meaning and reconstruct social knowledge. This is where the idea of an educational transaction is important. The challenge for distance educators is to integrate opportunities for dialogue and collaboration into any concept of SDL.

John Dewey (1959) made it clear that the educational process is a collaborative reconstruction of experience. He stated "that the educational process has two sides—one psychological [cognitive] and one sociological; and that neither can be subordinated to the other or neglected without evil results following" (p. 20).

It is argued here that the psychological or cognitive side of the educational process has been largely neglected in the conceptualization and adoption of SDL in a distance education context. Yet SDL implicitly is founded upon the acquisition by the student of a disposition and an ability to learn (i.e., the student has learned to learn). Paradoxically, the omission of cognitive attributes is due to an excessive reliance on individual cognitive autonomy and the reduction in importance of the transactional element of an educational learning experience. The fact is that all critical reflection has its origins in the transactional shared world. Up to now, SDL has been largely associated with individual external control issues. However, education is a transactional experience between the personal world of the learner (meaning focused) and the shared world of society (knowledge focused). Education is a purposeful and collaborative experience that is inherently normative and community based.

Communities of inquiry are generally integral components of an adult higher education experience. In these educational contexts, community is considered essential for higher-order learning and deep understanding (Garrison & Archer, 2000). What is core to communities of inquiry is the opportunity to question, challenge, diagnose misconceptions, and achieve mutual understanding. Although Peters and others include reflection in autonomous, self-determined (directed) learning, the question is how to ensure that critical reflection occurs as part of fortuitous informal learning events. The possibility of creating legitimate educational communities of inquiry at a distance is transforming the theory and practice of the field (Garrison, Anderson, & Archer, 2000).

In this regard, O'Donnell (1999) attempted to incorporate the concept of critical communities of learning into a concept of SDL. In addition, he rejected "individualistic and nomothetic theories" (p. 256) in arguing for "selves-directed" and dialogic learning. Dialogic learning in an educational context must consider social and cultural values and knowledge when "interpreting consensual norms" and understanding one's situation. As O'Donnell (1999) stated, "Learning is seen as a process of mutual interaction, but without a critical component this form of learning corresponds only to a form of normative instrumental action" (p. 257).

Clearly the individual has a responsibility to make sense of educational content and perhaps resolve personal issues. Although making sense of content does require some degree of critical reflection, it does not provide the climate, external perspective, and modeling necessary to encourage the development of intersubjective understanding and renewal of societal knowledge. Transactional elements within a critical community of inquiry will have to be articulated for distance education to be relevant and flourish in this communication age. A good starting point might be the integration of the theory and practice of SDL and critical thinking (cognitive and metacognitive abilities) in a distance education context.

The creation of communities of learners both synchronously and asynchronously has become a reality in distance education through developments in online learning and computer referencing (Garrison et al., 2000). It is no longer a structural imperative to advocate and design autonomous SDL, where external control is the overriding issue. The transactional era of distance education has arrived (Garrison, 2000). For this reason, SDL must evolve if it is to have any meaning for the field of distance education.

Conceptually, much work remains to be done to understand SDL in a transactional era of distance education. Autonomy and control are insufficient in themselves to fully utilize the concept of SDL. Consistent with Peters (1998), thought should be given to metacognitive and motivational factors if SDL is to be a viable and relevant concept in distance education in the 21st century. It would seem that, for any student, SDL is predicated on the student's having learned how to learn and having acquired the necessary epistemic and metacognitive awareness. If SDL is about controlling one's learning and achieving meaningful and worthwhile outcomes, then epistemic cognition (i.e., cognitive development), metacognitive awareness, and motivational factors are preconditions. Garrison's (1997) model of SDL has considerable potential to integrate issues related to motivational disposition (entering task), strategic planning (self-management), and metacognitive awareness (self-monitoring). It is strongly suggested that consideration be given to these higher-order cognitive dispositions and perspectives so that SDL can truly reflect autonomous learning as discussed by Moore (1993) and Peters (1998).

From an applied perspective, another challenge is to develop guidelines to facilitate reflective thinking and metacognitive processes associated with learning to learn. For SDL to have real pragmatic value in an educational context, the focus must shift to cognitive responsibility issues and transactional support for critical reflection. The ability of distance education to provide control of the external learning tasks through well-designed learning packages must be balanced against concerns associated with modeling and diagnosing the internal cognitive (i.e., critically reflective) processes leading to higher-order outcomes (learning to learn).

In this context, distance educators must consider what it means to be an autonomous and self-directed learner. Is SLD a process and goal we should be identifying ourselves with? What are the conceptualization challenges? Is the current conceptualization of SDL, with its exclusive focus on external control issues, a viable framework for distance education? What is the legitimate role of the teacher in SDL? What reflective value is there in a transactional community of inquiry? What are the limits of self-direction within an educational context? What technological and societal changes argue for SDL?

Other worthwhile tasks might include articulating the comprehensive model of SDL offered by Garrison using Moore's theory of transactional distance. How might the concepts of monitoring and management inform issues of dialogue and structure? Can the themes of responsibility and control be mapped onto the dimensions of distance teaching and learner autonomy? Starting from perspective of a self-determined and cognitively autonomous learner (Peters, 1998), how might we incorporate the legitimate control and responsibility concerns of the teacher to construct a continuum of informal, nonformal, and formal learning?

This line of research could also lead to a reassessment of the nature of distance education and an identification of the characteristics of the field that are changing as a result of technological and social transformations. The field of distance education must be capable of transforming itself if it is to remain viable, relevant, and a leader in accessible continuous learning.

CONCLUSION

The concept of self-directed learning has considerable potential to help distance educators understand student learning. To be a viable concept, however, it must also inform the teaching and learning transaction. In addition, if it is to have meaning and relevance for distance educators, it must be framed within a transactional perspective that considers both the private and shared worlds of the learner. As distance education enters the transactional era, the concept of self-directed learning must reflect both constructivist and collaborative perspectives. In this way, it could become a powerful concept, capable of illuminating and shaping the field.

REFERENCES

Bagnall, R. G. (1988). Reconceptualising and revaluing distance education from the perspective of self-direction. In D. Sewart & J. Daniel (Eds.), *Developing distance education* (Papers submitted to the ICDE 14th World Conference, Oslo).

Candy, P. C. (1987). *Reframing research into "self-direction" in adult education: A constructivist perspective.* Unpublished doctoral dissertation, University of British Columbia, Vancouver.

Candy, P. C. (1991). *Self-direction for lifelong learning.* San Francisco: Jossey-Bass.

Dewey, J. (1959). My pedagogic creed. In J. Dewey, *Dewey on education* (pp. 19–32). New York: Teachers College, Columbia University. (Original work published 1897).

Garrison, D. R. (1987). Self-directed and distance learning: Facilitating self-directed learning beyond the institutional setting. *International Journal of Lifelong Education, 6*(4), 309–318.

Garrison, D. R. (1993). An analysis of the control construct in self-directed learning. In H. B. Long (Ed.), *Emerging perspectives of self-directed learning* (pp. 27–43). Norman, OK: University of Oklahoma Research Center for Continuing Professional and Higher Education.

Garrison, D. R. (1997). Self-directed learning: Toward a comprehensive model. *Adult Education Quarterly, 48*(1), 15–31.

Garrison, D. R. (2000). Theoretical challenges for distance education in the 21st century: A shift from structural to transactional issues. *International Review of Research in Open and Distance Learning, 1*(1), 1–17.

Garrison, D. R., & Archer, W. (2000). *A transactional perspective on teaching-learning transaction: A framework for adult and higher education.* Oxford: Pergamon.

Garrison, D. R., Anderson, T., & Archer, W. (2000). Critical inquiry in a text-based environment: Computer conferencing in higher education. *The Internet and Higher Education, 2*(2–3), 1–19.

Knowles, M. (1970). *The modern practice of adult education: Andragogy versus pedagogy.* New York: Association Press.

Knowles, M. (1975). *Self-directed learning.* New York: Association Press.

Moore, M. G. (1972). Learner autonomy: The second dimension of independent learning. *Convergence, 5*(2), 76–88.

Moore, M. (1982). *Self directed learning and distance education* (Ziff Papiere 48). Hagen, Germany: FernUniversität.

Moore, M. (1986). Self-directed learning and distance education. *Journal of Distance Education, 1*(1), 7–24.

Moore, M. (1993). Theory of transactional distance. In D. Keegan (Ed.), *Theoretical principles of distance education* (pp. 22–38). London: Routledge.

Moore, M. G., & Kearsley, G. (1996). *Distance education: A systems view.* New York: Wadsworth.

Morgan, A. (1985). What shall we do about independent learning? *Teaching at a Distance, 26,* 38–45.

O'Donnell, D. (1999). Habermas, critical theory and selves-directed learning. *Journal of European Industrial Training, 23*(4-5), 251–261.

Peters, O. (1998). *Learning and teaching in distance education: Analyses and interpretations from an international perspective.* London: Kogan Page.

Rogers, C. R. (1969). *Freedom to learn.* Columbus, OH: Charles E. Merrill.

Tough, A. (1971). *The adult's learning projects.* Toronto: Ontario Institute for Studies in Education.

Wedemeyer, C. A. (1971). Independent study. In R. Deighton (Ed.), *Encyclopedia of education* (Vol. 4; pp. 548–557). New York: Macmillan.

Willen, B. (1984). *Self-directed learning and distance education: Can distance education be a good alternative for self-directed learners?* (Uppsala Reports on Education 21). (ERIC Document Reproduction Service No. 257 430). Uppsala University, Uppsala, Sweden.

12

Constructing Knowledge at a Distance: The Learner in Context

Daniel Granger
California State University, Monterey Bay
Dan_Granger@csumb.edu

Maureen Bowman
Naval Postgraduate School
msbowman@nps.navy.mil

In his 1977 account of the first 5 years of the Open University, Walter Perry, its first vice-chancellor, lamented,

> It is very depressing to go on offering a course knowing that a great many of your students are not going to succeed; and moreover that the failure is going to be much more frequent amongst those very deprived adults whom one is especially trying to help. We have not yet succeeded in solving this dilemma. (p. 188)

The solution of this dilemma is not the Open University's challenge alone. Perry's recognition of the dilemma was an early indicator that, for much of the uneducated portion of a population, simple access to a centrally prepared program is not sufficient. Distance education worldwide has been driven by the need to provide access to learning for those most in need of education. Implicitly and explicitly, distance educators have struggled to make the leap from providing access to educational programs to facilitating successful learning. Even as (now Lord) Perry's work was being penned, educators at the Open University and elsewhere were reflecting on and critiquing existing practice. Their goal was to make successful learning accessible to and possible for each individual who desires it, whatever the background and context. But where in the educational process are the learner and the learner's context considered?

ARE ALL LEARNERS THE SAME?

As early as 1974, the Open University's own journal, *Teaching at a Distance*, was publishing critical inquiries about the rigidity of its curriculum (Harrison, 1974, p. 2). Sharpening the point a few issues later, Farnes (1974) noted,

A student with the OU must find time for study and select courses but has very little responsibility for anything else in his studies: "all decisions are made for him: what is to be learnt, the sequence in which it is to be learnt, the materials he is to study: when in relation to other materials he should read page thirty-eight . . . there is little opportunity for the student to adapt a course to his own particular interests or to relate it to his past experience." Tutors are in the same position and cannot set or modify assignments. (p. 2)

Two years later, David Sewart (1976) of the Open University bluntly described the issue: "In the past we have looked to the central production of a somewhat inflexible package . . . in crude terms we must begin to concentrate on the learner rather than the teacher" (p. 1).

Course developers in the early years of the Open University had spoken of "tutor-proofing" their courses so they could not be easily modified. Tutors were not to be extensively engaged with the course materials or with the students. As Daniel and Marquis noted in 1977,

> Official documents tell tutors that "in this essentially home-based teaching system, where attendance at the occasional tutorial is voluntary, your relationship with students is formed mainly through the exchange of assignments." In a revealing phrase Kirk, herself a tutor, after quoting this directive states, "Thus, the part-timer's teaching duties are regarded *merely* [italic added] as the assessment of, and support for, a centrally designed programme" (p. 351).

In the words of one long-time observer, the "BOU posited an ideal curriculum for all students then planned how to deliver it" (Hall, 1991, p. 140). Overlooked was that too often students themselves are not "ideal."

In the same year, 1977, Moore's *On a Theory of Independent Study* explicitly noted the shift that the Open University articles had suggested:

> The change to a learner centred educational universe has been due to a growing acceptance by learners and teachers of three basic principles long discussed by educators but not widely acted upon. The first of these is the recognition that each individual learns each content area or skill in different ways, and probably at different times from other learners; if learning has any one characteristic it is idiosyncrasy, and the concept of a "class" of learners is therefore a foolish paradox. The second principle is that effective learning is experiential; whether interpreted in a phenomenological or behaviourist's framework, the principle is that one can best learn by experiencing. The third principle is that learning in the new world of rapid change must be lifelong. (p. 69)

Focusing specifically on a population akin to those Perry seemed most concerned about, Freire's *Pedagogy of the Oppressed* was first published in England in 1972. Although Freire's primary concern was for those subject to hegemonic control through the control of information and education, his theories presaged the emergence of constructivism in higher education. In critiquing the centrally controlled curriculum, he noted, "The students are not called up to know, but to memorize the contents narrated by the teacher" (Freire, 1972, p. 53). Freire is a clear supporter of learner-centered education, not just in the sense that the learner is the object of the educator's attention but also in the sense that the learner and the learner's context are considered components of the educational process. The social construction of knowledge necessarily involves the learner's context as a critical component. As Freire (1972) points out, "Many political and educational plans have failed because their authors designed them according to their own personal view of reality, never once taking into account (except as mere objects of their action), the *men-in-a-situation* toward whom their programme was ostensibly directed" (p. 66). Freire offers, as a counter to what he calls the "banking" model of passive deposits of education into the student, "problem-posing education, [in which] men develop their power to perceive critically *the way they exist* in the world *with which* and *in which* they find themselves; they come to see the world not as a static reality, but as reality in process, in transformation" (p. 56).

Again, Freire seems to presage the concern with critical thinking and problem solving in contemporary educational literature. Throughout this period, from the 1960s to the present, we have witnessed a social, educational, epistemological, and technological ferment that has shaken established assumptions about our place in the world and how we can function within it. Much of this change has challenged uniformity, a single order, in favor of diversity. We now speak of paradigm shifts, and nonlinear chaos theory prevails where once stood the hierarchical linearity of the Great Chain of Being.

Moore's article on independent study reflects more than the world of distance education, which in many ways was still in its infancy in the early 1970s. Since World War II, recognition of the importance of education (e.g., the G.I. Bill in the United States) and the increasing diversity of those who pursue it have posed a serious challenge to the "one size fits all" notion, even for a single institution (see Lehmann, 1988). The 1950s and 1960s saw the rise of the community colleges and the integration of state normal schools into statewide university systems. The intent consistently was to provide the appropriate education to an increasing and increasingly diverse student body.

Distance education did not take hold as quickly in the United States as in the commonwealth nations, however, both because education in the United States is the province of states, not the federal government, and because it was assumed that existing institutions met the vast majority of needs. Furthermore, many early applications of distance education in the 1980s utilized one-way distribution technologies such as satellite transmission or slow-scan TV to provide basic access to highly motivated students. The pedagogical weaknesses of these models were implicitly conceded, and efforts to improve their effectiveness focused on ancillary supports, not learner contexts, which were difficult to engage with and alter. Even the next-generation interactive compressed video courses required considerable planning and effort on the part of instructors to achieve some of the effectiveness of small lecture classes. Learner-centeredness, especially individual learner–centeredness, was not a hallmark of distance education during this era.

By the late 1960s, amidst the ferment over the Vietnam War, there was considerable concern about the mechanization of education, symbolized by emerging computer technology. "Do not bend, fold, spindle, or mutilate," the legend on computer keypunch cards, was taken by students as a battle cry for themselves. New institutions were conceived and created during the last years of the Vietnam War, along with new communications technologies. The explicit intent of these institutions was to be more responsive to student (and would-be student) needs. The Open University, originally to be called the University of the Air, was the brainchild of the British Labor Party, and it opened its doors in 1971, the same year Regents College in New York and its New Jersey counterpart, Thomas Edison State College, were founded. State University of New York Chancellor Ernest Boyer created Empire State College to enable students to develop individualized degree programs using new media. Similar institutional experiments included Governors State University in Illinois, Evergreen State College in Washington State, and New College in Sarasota Florida.

Some of these experiments have survived and become institutionalized, others have migrated back toward traditional educational models. But the national educational atmosphere was charged, and the period from the late 1960s to the present saw profound changes, including movement toward the "learner centred educational universe" noted by Moore. The significant changes in ideas about teaching and learning were probably best summarized by Arthur Chickering and Zelda Gamson (assisted by, among others, A. Astin, C. M. Boyer, K. P. Cross,

R. Edgerton, and J. Gaff) in their 1987 article:

> We offer seven principles based on research on good teaching and learning in colleges and universities.... Good practice in undergraduate education:
>
> 1. Encourages contact between students and faculty.
> 2. Develops reciprocity and cooperation among students.
> 3. Uses active learning techniques.
> 4. Gives prompt feedback.
> 5. Emphasizes time on task.
> 6. Communicates high expectations.
> 7. Respects diverse talents and ways of learning. (p. 3)

Chickering and Gamson pointed out that "the ways different institutions implement good practice depends very much on their students and their circumstances" (p. 4). That researchers and practitioners to this day continue working to elaborate and refine the implications of these principles is testimony to their robustness. In the original conceptualization of these principles, however, there was little thought given to nonclassroom learning. In fact, a number of the principles seem to imply that good teaching and learning require the close proximity of teacher and learners (if not face-to-face contact).

Applications of technology to teaching and learning increased considerably in the late 1980s and early 1990s with the rising popularity of the Internet, then catapulted forward following the introduction of the World Wide Web. In 1994, Stephen Ehrmann collaborated with Arthur Chickering to review the application of these principles to teaching and learning following the advent and spread of the new technologies. Their application to distance learning is readily apparent. Ehrmann provided specific technology-related examples of how the principles applied, frequently noting the benefits of asynchronous learning in which students and teacher are separated from each other physically yet in close communication (Chickering & Ehrmann, 1994).

Enthusiasm for the potential of teaching and learning with the new technologies escalated dramatically with the commercialization of the World Wide Web in 1994. Education was coming to be seen less as a loss leader for a democratic society than as a profit center for the providers of educational technologies and a "business" for educators themselves (see, e.g., unext.com). Productivity, long a concern of the business and for-profit sector, was introduced to education as a reasonable goal. In 1995, Educom, an organization encompassing over 600 U.S. colleges and universities concerned with information technology (IT), convened a roundtable of higher education administrators, policy analysts, faculty members, and independent IT consultants. In a conversation led by William Massy, director of the Stanford Institute of Higher Educational Research, and Robert Zemsky, director of the Institute for Research on Higher Education at the University of Pennsylvania, the talk focused on "how the infusion of information technology into the educational process can reverse the declining productivity of American higher education" (Massy & Zemsky, 1995, p. 1). From that conversation and their additional research, Zemsky and Massy produced a monograph on academic productivity, *Using Information Technology to Enhance Academic Productivity.*

In speaking of IT's potential, Massy and Zemsky noted two major benefits: economies of scale and mass customization. Although the authors provided some detail about mass customization, their interest was clearly in economies of scale. The monograph extensively uses commercial and marketplace imagery, off-putting to many academics, who seek refuge from that in the academy. Perhaps more noticeable, though, is the emergence here and elsewhere of a tendency to talk about academic uses of technology using business terms like *productivity.* As Massy and Zemsky noted, the investment in technology by colleges and universities will increase dramatically. It only makes sense to ask about the "return on investment."

Inevitably, colleges and universities (and a growing number of commercial providers) see a need to think strategically about their productivity. Zemsky and Massy made the critical point that academic productivity must be viewed as *learning* productivity, not as financial return or even the traditional measures of faculty productivity—research studies and class preparations. Learning productivity was not customarily measured, at least partly because measuring it is notoriously difficult to do. In any case, the concern for productivity has led to, on the one hand, some faculty resistance to new ways of thinking about their work and thus caution about the use of technology, and, on the other hand, an efflorescence of commercial and semi-commercial "learning" companies offering products or services to students, faculty, and institutions (e.g., Web CT, e-College, Blackboard, and Prometheus). The dominant faculty and institutional purpose in using IT is often to serve those students who can readily demonstrate "productivity," that is, well-prepared students who can progress even more rapidly using learning technologies. These same technologies are capable of opening doors to learners otherwise unable to participate in the educational experience, such as working adults, individuals with disabilities, and those not in proximity to a university, to name a few. They are also capable of aiding learners not previously successful in traditional educational settings by providing holistic, knowledge-based frameworks that interact across subject areas.

Mass customization, unlike *productivity*, is an awkward phrase that actually suggests something beneficial to humans—that through technology the learning needs of each person can be met (see also Farmer, 1997, p. 489; Gardner, 2000, pp. 43–44). However, with the quasi-commercial push for productivity and its public policy counterpart, accountability, it has for the most part come to mean flexibility within a fairly limited range, such as adding a synchronous chat to a lecture course or putting classroom lectures on video or even streaming video. What it might mean instead is education that is designed to meet the needs of individual learners (e.g., education that includes diagnostic assessments, curricula tailored to learning styles and personal contexts, and heuristic performance evaluations).

In 1995, the focus on "learning productivity" was given a different spin in Barr and Tagg's important article on the new learning paradigm. Although Barr and Tagg did not shrink from discussing the *business* of education, their discussion was not narrowly targeted at technology-mediated learning activities. Instead, they explored the paradigm shift that occurs when the goal is no longer to provide instruction but "to produce learning" (p. 13). In fact, they delineated the implications of this shift in considerable detail, admitting that learning technologies will play a significant role but maintaining the focus on student learning: "Under the Learning Paradigm, producing more with less becomes possible because the more that is being produced is learning and not hours of instruction" (p. 23).

Fundamental to this paradigm shift, according to Barr and Tagg, is the learning theory that undergirds it, one antithetical to the priesthood paradigm that has prevailed since the Middle Ages, in which many are called but few are chosen. As they stated, "Under the Learning Paradigm, faculty—and everyone else in the Institution—are unambiguously committed to each student's success. The faculty and the institution take an R. Buckminster Fuller view of students: human beings are born geniuses and designed for success" (p. 23). This conviction, in fact, seems to inform the thinking of all those who espouse a learner-centered approach to education. Creating an educational approach, much less a system, that embodies this conviction, however, is a Herculean task, as was acknowledged by Lord Perry in 1977.

Alongside the concern with productivity and the growth of accountability, we have seen efforts to create more learner-centered environments. Teaching and learning have been given featured roles, and the use of technology has been "institutionalized" in the formation of Teaching and Learning with Technology Roundtables at over 400 institutions across the United States (see http://www.tltgroup.org). Distance learning as well has assumed a more prominent role, but often within the framework of institutional productivity (i.e., as a way to serve more students more cost effectively). Distance learning has become an alternative delivery mode taken up by many on-campus learners (and faculty) for a variety of reasons, including scheduling convenience, perceived course quality, and the use of technology (see the March 27, 1998, issue of the *Chronicle of Higher Education*). A Pew-funded Center for Academic Transformation was even established in 1999 because of the initial Educom emphasis on productivity in 1995. The Pew project focuses specifically on large-enrollment courses making innovative use of technology in order to achieve substantial savings of money and time with the same or better learning accomplishments (http://www.centerRPI.edu/PewHome.html). Most Pew projects are not targeted at distance learners, although all use technology. Access, especially access to successful learning experiences for underserved populations, has not been a high priority. Yet the components for success do exist.

RECOGNIZING AND RESPONDING TO LEARNER DIFFERENCES

Many institutions across the United States have created teaching and learning centers focused on incorporating innovative pedagogies into their teaching practices. For the most part, distance learning activities have been kept separate, often owing to their primary association with technology or their peripheral relationship to main campus activities. Rarely is distance education accorded first consideration for improvements in program design or pedagogical development. Even the leaders of the national Teaching and Learning with Technology Roundtable, Steve Gilbert and K. C. Green, are only marginally supportive of the pedagogical effectiveness of distance learning (comments made at the Teaching with Technology conference, Phoenix, July 2000), not even mentioning it on their extensive TLT Web site, (http//:www.tltgroup.org).

In fact, distance education and its close cousin distributed learning are in a number of ways considerably closer to the learning paradigm than are most campus programs, and the solution to Walter Perry's concern is most likely to be found there. Ironically, as developments in distance education are found to be successful, they are incorporated into mainstream educational practices, with little memory of their origin (See Granger, 2000).

The term *distributed learning* appeared in the educational technology literature in the mid-1990s, signaling recognition of a concept important for realizing a strategy to construct knowledge from the learner's perspective. Saltzberg and Polyson (1995) define *distributed learning* as

> not just a new term to replace the other "DL," distance learning. Distributed learning is an instructional model that allows instructor, students, and content to be located in different, noncentralized locations so that instruction and learning occur independent of time and place. The distributed model can be used in combination with traditional classroom-based courses, with traditional distance learning courses, or it can be used to create wholly virtual classrooms. (p. 1)

This concept of distributed learning, embedded in the theory though often not in the practice of distance learning, goes beyond delivery of instruction and embraces the context of the learner. Within this expanded conception of the learning environment, learners have access to content, experts (the teacher and beyond), peers, and services that can be used to fit the learning styles and needs of individuals.

A framework for revising the design of teaching and learning structures resides in a distributed resources environment. In this setting, teaching and learning are no longer within the purview of autonomous teachers designing instructional environments to which passive learners arrive. Instead, learning resources are jointly identified by learners and teachers and assembled in a variety of formats; the teachers become the facilitators of knowledge construction. Learners gain a greater degree of control over how, what, when and, where their learning occurs. Faculty gain greater flexibility and a wider range of resources with which to organize environments that maximize learning opportunities. Institutions benefit from effective, coordinated, and accessible resources for learning opportunities across the organization. Barr and Tagg (1995) identified the potential for moving from "educational atomism" to a structure where learning environments and experiences are organized by "methods that work better for student learning and success" and noted that they expected "even these to be redesigned continually and to evolve over time" (p. 20).

Technology, as an enabler of distributed resources, furthers the practice of a systems approach requiring integration across the organization to maximize new capabilities. For example, learning management systems integrate functions and services students need to achieve success (e.g., access to courses, learning materials, and instructors; advising and tutorial assistance; library resources; and interactions with other learners).

Yet universities have been slow to recognize the advantages of rethinking their mission in light of the learning paradigm, as pointed out by Barr and Tagg (1995, p. 14), and have been even slower to embrace a systems approach to all their endeavors. Rather than starting at the institutional level with holistic restructuring, most institutions have instead continued the "craft" approach to teaching and learning:

> They think that by moving cameras, computers, and microphones into the classrooms, schools, universities, and training departments, they can increase enrollments, provide new curricula, and save money without doing anything else. According to this view, once the technology is in place, there is little else to be done except let teachers get on with practicing their craft as they have always done. (Moore & Kearsley, 1996, p. 6)

At the broadest level, an institution must undertake the redesign of basic access. Every aspect of communication must be seen as part of an integrated web, from a learner's first inquiry through each process designed to help the learner achieve her or his learning goals and from the design and delivery of a single course through the interdependence of all courses within the curriculum. Technology facilitates multidirectional communication, and the hypermedia environment of simultaneous information resources brings benefits of interconnectivity and versatility to the institution all the way through to each individual learner (Verduin & Clark, 1991, p. 205).

More fundamental to the success of these systems, though, are the underlying philosophies, policies, and practices of the institution. Recognition and acceptance that anything that happens in one part of the system affects the other parts is a necessary first step. Also needed is to form mechanisms to network management functions so that development and operation of each "unit" requires a connection with every other unit (Moore & Kearsley, 1996, p. 6). In practice, functional teams of department managers approach consensus-driven decision making, leaving behind the individual unit autonomy model currently in place in most institutions. For this to occur, commitment to the recruitment and continuous development of personnel possessing the attitude and skills required for collaborative management must be clearly visible in the mission and vision of the institution. The development of policy and the procedure-building process is not easily accomplished, and dedication, persistence, and practice are required. Some of the necessary changes at the institutional level include revised admission and registration procedures, orientation programs for students and personnel, and special support services for learners and instructors utilizing distributed resources. Technology can be seen as a catalyst for this fundamental philosophical shift because electronic networking requires human networking. Emerging technologies, including distributed learning management systems, portals that connect a variety of resources (admissions, library access, advising, and technical support) under one user-friendly gateway, and electronic databases that store and merge information resources, are capable of providing the infrastructure for the redesign and integration necessary.

BEGINNING WITH THE LEARNER

A systems approach to instructional design enables the building of a learning environment consistent with the new learning paradigm adumbrated by Freire, Moore, Chickering, Gamson, and many others. This type of environment offers the following:

- Learner-centeredness within a context familiar to the learner.
- Individual construction of knowledge directed toward goals important to the learner.
- Contextual or experiential learning characterized by authentic interactions within the learning context (or community).

These qualities, which are necessarily interrelated, provide an integrated and supportive learning environment that begins by validating what the learner knows and enables her or him progressively to broaden the reach of the known to encompass goals identified (and perhaps modified) in the course of the learning journey. None of the strategies discussed here are particularly new, and several have been employed by existing institutions for many years. However, the systems approach, facilitated by educational technologies, permits the practice of these approaches in ways that are effective for nontraditional as well as traditional learners and their institutions. Components may include these:

- Recognition of the learner's familiar community, perhaps established through study of self, context, and learning.
- A senior mentor, guide, or learning companion to provide consistency and support (personal and academic) throughout a student's program.
- Orientation programs that bridge past and future learning by identifying strengths and skill needs for future learning success. These programs can provide opportunities for building virtual learning communities, engaging in metacognitive activities, and establishing a learning identity.
- Assessment of prior learning, validating past learning and linking it to future goals. This is particularly valuable for adult learners.
- Constructivist course designs within a dynamic curriculum that uses experiential activities within the learners' real-life context when possible. Examples include community-based learning such as service learning activities.
- A web of support components navigated with a mentor's help. The web might include advisors, instructors, supplemental instruction and online tutorial resources, community resources, peer tutors, and special interest groups.

A systems-grounded learning design approach holds the promise of not only integrating previously disconnected structures but also mass customizing learning environments, giving every student the opportunity to achieve success and adding to the institution's ability to increase learning productivity. Learning design strategies, when aggregated and approached from a holistic perspective, can accomplish the goal of constructing knowledge learner by learner regardless of whether the learners are served at a distance or through a campus-based curriculum. Combining and approaching design strategies holitically is critical for many nontraditional learners:

If nontraditional students are to be adequately prepared for academic success, then there must be substantial transformations in their very conceptions of education and in their sense of themselves as learners. Settings must be constructed to help nontraditional students experience education as something more than simply memorization and recitation. Put another way, they must be initiated into the intellectual community and enticed to participate in its practices. (McGrath & Spear, 1987, p. 20)

The ability of "intellectual communities" or "learning communities" to provide a supportive environment for learning has been documented and celebrated widely (see, e.g., Mathews et al., 1997). Yet the terms used to describe the students of whom we speak—*marginal, underserved,* or *at risk*—convey the sense that they lack full membership in the academic community. Insofar as a feeling of membership is critical to full and effective engagement in the learning enterprise, programs and institutions can provide orientation and entry programs incorporating metacognitive activities that benefit all students, not simply those for whom college is an alien environment. Learning autobiographies, for instance, have proven an effective means for exploring identity, learning styles, and one's relationship to the learning environment. When these are shared in online peer learning groups, learners reflect on their own and other learning approaches in ways that encourage experimentation and a more assured sense of self (see, e.g., http://classes.CSUMB.edu/HCOM/HCOM350-02/world/index.html).

Done at a distance in asynchronous discussions, sharing learning autobiographies can provide opportunities for inquiry that is often awkward in face-to-face settings. These explorations of self and context enable learners to "place" themselves in relation to learning and to find a distinctive "voice" in the learning community, explaining to themselves how they have come to higher learning—through what struggles and toward what goals (McGrath & Spear, 1987, p. 18; Sleeter, 1996, p. 179). Their goals frequently are powerfully personal rather than predominantly academic and often provide learners with the motivation they need to continue their studies.

Instructional design for distributed learning starts from the perspective of the learner's needs. This does not mean that individual needs assessments are conducted for every student but that the design is based on principles grounded in learning theory and is directed toward creating settings where learners with varying abilities, experiences, and levels of motivation and self-directedness can each achieve success. Active learning strategies and cooperative, situational, social, and problem-based learning models are integrated to form a learning process that allows learners to gather and analyze information, reflect on previous understandings, and interact with others to synthesize new constructions of meaning and knowledge.

Because the distributed learning model supports multiple approaches, it allows teachers to develop courses that match teaching strategies with an individual student's readiness for learning. The less self-directed learner has the organizational structure, subject matter focus, performance objectives, materials, activities, and opportunity for feedback he or she needs to be successful. The more self-directed learner has the resources to pursue learning goals more independently while still having the ability to interact with the instructor and the other learners (Grow, 1991).

An individual's learning identity provides the foundation for the construction of knowledge accomplished within a context familiar to and directed toward goals identified by the learner. Subsequent studies can take best advantage of this foundation by employing a constructivist approach, enabling each learner progressively to build toward his or her goals as they align with those of the educational program. As Jonassen et al. (1995) reminded us, "Learning environments are constructivist only if they allow individuals or groups of individuals to make their own meaning for what they experience rather than requiring them to 'learn' the teacher's interpretation of that experience or content" (p. 13).

The curriculum in this system, then, rather than a set of disciplinary givens, is dynamic, recognized as the ongoing pursuit of truth. Truth itself is a moving target, subject to the changing membership and perspectives of the knowing community. For example, culture, gender, and socioeconomic status each act as a prism through which truth is refracted. In the diverse populations served by distributed and distance learning, it becomes appropriate to "teach at the boundaries," to draw out and study perspectival differences. Confronting these borders and their possible permeability enables learners to engage subject, self, and other in a powerful heuristic.

> The mediating role of the curriculum, and thus its effectiveness with diverse students, can itself be enhanced by rendering it more explicitly dynamic; that is, by recognizing and beginning with the contingencies of the individual student as well as the ultimate indeterminacy of the field of study. By conceptualizing curriculum as process, rather than as a predetermined course of study, one can successfully acknowledge the contingencies and idiosyncrasies of the student, the field of study and their intersections. (Granger, 1993, p. 173)

The role of faculty in the distributed learning setting is central, as suggested by Barr and Tagg (1995). They act as "designers of learning methods and environments" and facilitators of interaction to "develop every student's competencies and talents" (p. 17). Barr and Tagg's paradigm, deeply rooted in constructivist pedagogy, emphasizes the active engagement of learners in ways respectful of their individual needs and contexts. Much in alignment with this, Jonassen et al. (1995) noted that this constructivist approach "engages learners in knowledge construction through collaborative activities that embed learning in a meaningful context and through reflection on what has been learned through conversation with other learners" (p. 13). They also stated that "knowledge is a function of how the individual creates meaning from his or her experiences . . . . Constructivists engage the learners so that the knowledge they construct is not inert, but rather usable in new and different situations" (p. 11). Therefore, an important emphasis of constructivist beliefs about learning is the need for embedding learning in real-world situations in which learners function as part of a community of practitioners helping to solve real-world problems. The distributed framework supports this by focusing away from the classroom toward a larger context incorporating the personal and professional setting of the learner. An important implication is that the role of the designer shifts from creating prescriptive learning situations to developing environments that engage learners and require them to construct the knowledge that is most meaningful to them.

A systems perspective on instructional design for distributed learning also gives emphasis to a need to restructure the role of faculty in the development of courses and programs. It is not realistic for a single teacher to design, develop, and teach effective distributed learning courses, and conventional structures in colleges and universities have not supported the advancement of collaborative distributed learning development. Individual innovators have taken on the task of experimenting with the use of distributed resources in their courses, usually without the assistance of instructional designers and multimedia specialists and without an institutional commitment to support their efforts. Examples abound of faculty frustration and burnout from attempts to move forward without the institutional support required (e.g., compensation, training, and equipment). Yet, these independent efforts have achieved considerable success in providing settings where learners gain greater control and responsibility for constructing knowledge. Institutional strategies that treat learning and curriculum design as a holistic process, involving functional teams that pair faculty with other professionals knowledgeable and skilled in learning theory, instructional design methodology, and communication and delivery technologies, hold far greater promise than the traditional "craft" approach, in which independent courses are designed and taught by individual instructors.

Beyond the creation of course "learning environments," another role emerging for faculty and for advanced students as well is that of mentor to individual students. Typically a mentor "converses" with a student throughout her or his studies to provide continuity of advice and information based on knowledge of the student's learning background and goals. The mentor may first connect with the student when acting as the student's guide during orientation or degree-planning work, being sensitive both to the requirements of the academic program and to the student's needs in negotiating that program. Later, the mentor can provide counsel and assist the student in accessing resources, whether personal or academic, and even occasionally act as an advocate. The mentor, for example, might recognize the need for additional work in writing, math, or critical thinking and direct the student to appropriate resources. Many off-campus and distance students are unaware of virtual writing labs or the wealth of online tutorials and supplemental instruction opportunities in a range of skill areas (Kulik, 1994, p. 27; Shaya, Petty, & Petty, 1993, p. 711). Because they are online, they provide a comforting anonymity and can be used repeatedly with no negative consequence. An attentive mentor, then, can often make the critical difference to a student's learning success.

CONCLUSION

Distance and distributed learning emerged in response to a convergence of need and possibility. Its modern origins can readily be traced to the social, intellectual, and technological changes wrought by the Industrial Revolution. Its subsequent evolution encompasses changes not only in learning needs and (mostly communication) technologies but in processes and applications as well. The "business" of technology, the product life cycles of Moore's law, and the attendant systems processes extend inevitably to the fields that employ them. Thus we have seen the introduction of concerns about productivity and return on investment. There is now a real "business" of education.

For the most part, new pedagogical approaches have revitalized interest in teaching and learning, but the need to demonstrate short-term results (the business world measures success in terms of quarterly profits) has blunted the initial driving purpose of distance learning—to provide access. In spite of this, the systems thinking of the business world can be and is being merged with the results of a large body of research that tells us how people learn and how they can best be supported—a marriage that can serve those hitherto effectively excluded from mainstream society. Distance and distributed learning programs, learner and learning centered by definition, are in a particularly strong position to employ the new pedagogical approaches) effectively. Undoubtedly, distance learning is liable to the distractions attendant on its technological tools and business affiliations. But well used, these are resources that will enable us to increase access to learning in ways that will allow all students, especially those formerly excluded, to be truly successful.

REFERENCES

Barr, R. B., & Tagg, J. (1995). From teaching to learning: A new paradigm for undergraduate education. *Change, 27*(6), 13–25.

Chickering, A., & Gamson, Z. (1987). Seven principles for good practice in undergraduate education. *AAHE Bulletin, 39*(7), 3–7.

Chickering, A., & Ehrmann, S. (1994). Implementing the seven principles: Technology as lever. Available: http://www.tltgroup.org/programs/seven.html

Daniel, J., & Marquis, C. (1977). Interaction and independence: Getting the mixture right. *Teaching at a Distance, 14,* 29–44.

Farmer, J. (1997). Using technology. In J. Gaff, J. Ratcliff, & Associates (Eds.), *Handbook of the undergraduate curriculum.* San Francisco: Jossey Bass. 476–492.

Farnes, N. (1974). Student-centred learning. *Teaching at a Distance, 3*(2). (From A. Gaskell & R. Mills (Eds.), *Quality and control in learning and teaching at a distance: Summaries of articles selected from Teaching at a Distance and Open Learning,* 1989, Milton Keynes, England: International Council for Distance Education and the Open University) p. 8.

Freire, P. (1972). *Pedagogy of the oppressed.* Harmondsworth, England: Penguin.

Gardner, H. (2000). *The disciplined mind.* New York: Penguin.

Granger, D. (1993). Reflections on curriculum as process. In T. Evans & D. Nation (Eds.), *Reforming open and distance education* (pp. 169–181). London: Kogan Page. 169–181.

Granger, D. (2000). Review of Otto Peters, *Learning and Teaching in Distance Education. The American Journal of Distance Education 14(1).:*

Grow, G. O. (1991). Teaching learners to be self-directed. *Adult Education Quarterly, 41*(3), 125–149.

Hall, J. W. (1991). *Access through innovation: New colleges for new students.* New York: NUCEA and Macmillan.

Harrison, B. (1974). The Teaching-learning relationship in correspondence tuition. *Teaching at a Distance, 1*(2). (From A. Gaskell & R. Mills (Eds.), *Quality and control in learning and teaching at a distance: Summaries of articles selected from Teaching at a Distance and Open Learning,* 1989, Milton Keynes, England: International Council for Distance Education and the Open University). p. 6.

Jonassen, D., Davidson, M., Collins, M., Campbell, J., Itang, B. B. et al. (1995). Constructivism and computer mediated communication in distance education. *American Journal of Distance Education, 9*(2) 7–26.

Kulik, J. (1994). Meta-analytic studies of findings on computer based instruction. In E. Baker & H. Oneil, Jr. (Eds.), *Technology assessment in education and training* (pp. 9–33). Lawrence Erlbaum Associates.

Lehmann, T. (1988). Fulfilling democracy's promise through education. *Golden Hill* (SUNY Empire State College), 4, 5–43.

Massy, W. F., & R. Zemsky. (1995). *Using information technology to enhance academic productivity.* Washington, DC: Educom.

Matthews, R. S., Smith, B. L., MacGregor, J & Gabelnick. F. (1997). Creating learning communities. In J. Gaff, J. Ratcliff, and Associates (Eds.), *Handbook of the undergraduate curriculum* (pp. 457–475). San Francisco: Jossey-Bass.

McGrath, D., & M. B. Spear. (1987). The politics of remediation. In K. M. Ahrendt (Ed.), *Teaching the developmental education student* (pp. 11–21). San Francisco: Jossey Bass.

Moore, M. G. (1977). *On a theory of independent study* (ZIFF Papiere 16). Hagen, Germany, FernUniversität.

Moore, M. G., & G. Kearsley. (1996). *Distance education: A systems view.* New York: Wadsworth.

Perry, W. (1977). *The Open University.* San Francisco: Jossey-Bass.

Saltzberg, S., & Polyson, S. (1995, September). Distributed learning on the World Wide Web. *Syllabus,* pp. 10–14.

Sewart, D. (1976). Introduction: Learning from a distance. *Teaching at a Distance, 5*(1). (From A. Gaskell & R. Mills (Eds.), *Quality and control in learning and teaching at a distance: Summaries of articles selected from Teaching at a Distance and Open Learning,* 1989, Milton Keynes, England: International Council for Distance Education and the Open University). p. 9.

Shaya, S., Petty, H., & Petty, L. (1993). A case study of supplemental instruction in biology focused on at-risk students. *BioScience, 43,* 709–711.

Sleeter, C. E. (1996). Multicultural education and empowerment. In E. Steltenpohl, J. Shipton, & S. Villines (Eds.), *Orientation to college: On becoming an educated person* (pp. 178–180). Belmont, CA: Wadsworth.

Verduin, J. R. Jr., & Clark, T. A. (1991). *Distance education: The foundations of effective practice.* San Francisco: Jossey-Bass.

13

Academic Advising in Distance Education Degree Programs

Robert F. Curry
Old Dominion University
rcurry@odu.edu

Good academic advising contributes to a caring environment, students' academic and career development, and a positive public image through satisfied students (Greenwood, 1984). Academic advising is the one function that covers both academic and student services; it deals with students from their first day at the institution to graduation (Gordon, 1992).

A student's success in distance learning is often determined by the quality of academic advising and other student services (Miller, 1993; Wagner, 1993). Distance learners are usually returning students, at least 25 years old, and employed (Peterson's, 1998). As reported by Sloan and Wilmes (1989), meetings with an academic advisor may be the first and only institutional contact adult students have outside the classroom. This is probably even more true for distant students, who may not have a classroom; if they do, it is away from the main campus.

CURRENT STATUS

Academic advisors currently face challenges in advising distance education students. This section discusses the role and practice of academic advising in distance education and presents summaries of articles about specific practices at individual institutions.

Challenges of Academic Advising in Distance Education

Despite advising's importance, it is often an activity that is not adequately staffed or rewarded (Habley, 1998). With large caseloads and multiple responsibilities, advisors may not have adequate time for advising students. Advisors face these difficulties regardless of the student population served, but advising students at a distance presents additional challenges.

Because of the physical separation of advisor and student, communication may be infrequent and impersonal. If the advisor never meets the student individually, the student may not be comfortable sharing personal information that may affect academic choices and outcomes. Without such disclosure, the advisor may have difficulty understanding the educational planning needs of the student (Reed & Sork, 1990).

The Role and Practice of Academic Advising in Distance Education

Fornshell (1993) described academic advising in the graduate computer and information sciences program at Nova University. Administrators had been concerned that distance education students were feeling frustrated and isolated. A plan was developed and implemented to provide distance students with the same level of advising services as students on campus had access to.

Students have initial advising when they visit the campus for orientation and course instruction. After training on using the technology, they receive instruction and academic advising through electronic classroom sessions. Approximately six students participate in each real-time advising session by teleconferencing, allowing students to exchange ideas with each other and the advisor. To protect privacy, students are identified by user code rather than name. If issues of a personal or sensitive nature are mentioned, advisors suggest the student call the next day. At two institute meetings a year, students have the opportunity to consult with faculty advisors in a more traditional face-to-face meeting (Fornshell, 1993).

The University of Arizona offers a Master of Arts program in Library Science through the Web and using other computer-based instruction. Changes in the program's policies and procedures are announced electronically on a general school distribution list. Students are responsible for the information posted in this manner (Wilka & Fitzner, 1998).

To help students feel connected to the institutions, students have a "virtual happy hour." Since students cannot talk face to face with each other after class or gather for coffee, these periods allow discussion of curricular issues, internship opportunities, and other topics related to the discipline (Wilka & Fitzner, 1998).

Advisors also set virtual office hours or schedule appointments with students. In addition to these live electronic interactions, advisors also use e-mail and list communication (Wilka & Fitzner, 1998).

At Old Dominion University, a digital satellite system with one-way video and two-way audio is the primary means of delivering distance education courses. The University offers bachelor's completion and graduate degrees through this program, named TELETECHNET. At sites throughout Virginia and some additional locations, site directors and staff operate a "mini campus" for the University. Staff members are available to assist students with admissions, registration, financial aid, advising, military student issues, disability accommodations, career information, and other support services. Sites are open 7 days a week for approximately 82 hours. The personal interest that site directors take in their students leads to a positive university experience, demonstrated on a student survey conducted each year by the director of assessment. In addition, the site staff's support is a factor in the student retention rate of approximately 86% (Barnett & Kline, 1999).

These three institutions have advising practices that are delivered in different ways: in person, through electronic classrooms, and by electronic distribution list. The advisor role, however, is consistent with the description given by Gordon (1992), as the advisors provide a wide range of services throughout the students' time with the institution.

REVIEW OF RESEARCH

Research on academic advising in distance education is not extensive. Because few studies have been published, international programs are included for review, and the U.S. research that is available is described in considerable detail. The review begins with the international research, followed by the U.S. research (separated by type of distance education program: associate, baccalaureate, and other certificate or degree programs).

International Programs

Several international studies have relevance for distance advising in the United States. Potter (1998) surveyed students who had taken credit courses through distance education at one of three Canadian universities. The majority of these students were enrolled in undergraduate degree programs. Students rated the following support services as important or very important: information about specific programs, general information about distance education opportunities, advice about course selection, orientation to media or course delivery format, and help with the application process. When students were asked to rate the accessibility of the services, a lower percentage of students rated each service accessible than rated it important.

In an open-ended question, students were asked to identify factors that caused difficulties in their academic progress. The most frequently mentioned issues were insufficient time because of multiple responsibilities and difficulty in financing their education (Potter, 1998).

Lalande (1995) reported on psychoeducational workshops provided through audio teleconferencing; the audience consisted of registered nurses enrolled in a bachelor's program at the University of Calgary. Workshop topics included "Preparation for the Student Role," "Developing Independent Learning Skills: Information Selection and Evaluation," "Stress Management for the Multiple-Role Adult," and "Strategies for Career Planning for Nurses." According to student evaluations, the majority of students believed objectives of the workshop were somewhat or completely met. A qualitative analysis of the written comments indicated that participants found the workshops helpful and informative. Attendance was lower than desired, so a questionnaire was mailed to all students in the program. As their reasons for not attending the workshops, students most frequently mentioned having other commitments or being too busy. The author concluded that effective student services can be provided by teleconferencing technology.

In a study of students at the Open University in Scotland, Carr and Ledwith (1980) found that 63% of respondents considered valuable the advice that they received from an introductory advising session, an open house, and mailed written material before enrollment. Students indicated that information on courses, advice on time needed for study and preparatory work, and reassurance by institutional representatives were the most helpful types of assistance. Nevertheless, 66% of respondents stated that they would have benefited from more advice, in particular on the level and pace of coursework.

Bowser and Race (1991) evaluated the orientation program for new students in distance education programs at an institution in Australia. Students attended orientation sessions the week before the academic year began in 14 centers. Students ranked the opportunity to meet other students as the most important function of the session. Clarification of academic, administrative, and enrollment information was also rated high in importance.

Associate Degree Programs

From questionnaires sent to 59 two-year higher education institutions with distance education programs, Paneitz (1997) identified 10 institutions for her research. This sample of 10 was chosen based on the means of delivering student services. In addition to the requirement of having an associate degree program available at a distance, Paneitz sought a wide range of technology used in providing advising, counseling, and library/media services. Forty cover letters and questionnaires were sent to the contact person for each of the institutions. The contact persons distributed the questionnaires randomly to students enrolled in distance education degree programs. A total of 183 out of the 400 questionnaires were returned, for a response rate of 46%.

For the study, Paneitz distinguished three levels of technology:

- No technology. Students must come to the main campus for advising.
- Low technology. Advising is done with the assistance of a toll-free telephone number and/or a fax machine.
- High technology. Students have access to a toll-free number and a fax machine for advising. In addition, advising is done using at least one other means, such as voice mail, e-mail, computer bulletin, or videotapes.

Paneitz surveyed distance students on their use of academic advising. In high-technology institutions, the following percentages of students reported using academic advising for scheduling of classes (83%), initial degree planning (80%), referral to remedial or study skill assistance (76%), and guidance on transfer to 4-year schools (48%). These high percentages of use were also reported at no-technology and low-technology institutions. Paneitz concluded that the means of providing the advising service may not be important in getting students to use it, but that advising should be provided in some manner.

Students were also asked to rate their satisfaction with advising services. The majority of students were satisfied or very satisfied with the assistance in identifying remedial and study skills classes, assistance with initial degree planning, and assistance with transferring to 4-year institutions. There were no significant differences in satisfaction based on level of technology in providing the services.

Students at low-technology institutions were less satisfied with the advising provided for class scheduling than those at institutions with either no or high technology. This no-tech face-to-face advising was considered as desirable as high-tech e-mail or voice mail. Paneitz suggested that low-tech schools should upgrade technology to increase student satisfaction. She added, however, that face-to-face contact may also be helpful when feasible.

Academic advising was considered the most essential student service by distance students. Thirty-nine percent ranked it first, while 31% ranked it second in importance behind library/media services, career counseling, tutorial services, or personal counseling.

Paneitz concluded that academic advising is the most essential student service for distance students in 2-year institutions. She also concluded that technology will play a larger role in future years in providing student services to distance students. She indicated, however, that having an efficient and consistent process for providing advising services is more important than spending resources on high-technology delivery systems.

The questionnaire sent by Paneitz to distance students provided valuable data on the use of advising services and student satisfaction with the services. A strength is that the survey was completed by students at multiple institutions with varied delivery models for academic advising. Although the response rate was not very high, the randomness of the selection offsets this fact as regards the study's validity. The comparisons based on level of technology, however, should be considered with caution. Other variables were not controlled and may have been factors in the differences in satisfaction noted.

Tallman (1994) studied students who had taken correspondence courses from Southeastern College, a private, religiously affiliated institution. He developed the Student Satisfaction Questionnaire (SSQ) for the study. The SSQ was mailed to a proportionately stratified sample of students ($N = 505$) who had completed correspondence courses. The sample was stratified so that there would be a proportional representation of all students by month of course completion. Three hundred and eleven students returned the study, for a response rate of 61%. In addition, the demographic characteristics of the nonrespondents were analyzed, and these did not differ significantly from those of students who did respond. Sixty-eight percent of the respondents were enrolled in an external degree program at Southeastern, with an additional 11.3% seeking a degree from another institution. It was not stated which degree the respondents were pursuing, although *Peterson's Guide to Distance Learning Programs* (1998) indicated the institution offered both associate and baccalaureate degree programs.

The admission process was the most influential factor in student satisfaction. Important components were helpfulness of admissions personnel, "user-friendliness" of admissions materials, and the orientation session (telephone or face to face). Although admissions dealt with the preenrollment process, other variables involved satisfaction while attending. Of the variables during enrollment, assistance provided by the continuing education staff was the most significant factor in student satisfaction. In order of significance, this variable was followed by contact with advisors, feeling a part of the institution, promptly returned phone calls, and motivation inspired by advisors.

Although this is a solid study, the college is a very specialized institution, with a limited number of majors. The results can be generalized to other similar institutions but may not be applicable to other kinds of institutions.

Baccalaureate Degree Programs

Trent (1993) studied the academic advising services associated with the Statewide Nursing Program of California State University, in which faculty travel to distance sites to teach accelerated classes. Although instruction is face to face, advising is done at a distance because students attend classes away from the main campus. Academic advising occurs through telephone conversations with faculty advisors. A survey sent to students in the program brought 172 responses, for a 53% response rate. Students indicated they were generally not satisfied with academic advising; 51% disagreed or strongly disagreed with the statement that they had received satisfactory advising.

From a list of advising functions on the survey, students identified the following as important:

- Assistance in completing a program of study.
- Analyzing past academic experiences when planning a program of study.
- Identifying experiential learning and testing options when planning a program of study.
- Signing and sending a program of study form to an administrative office for the initial step in a graduation audit.

Results indicated that the functions of identifying experiential testing options and signing a program of study were being provided. Students reported that they were not given assistance in completing a program of study and analyzing past experiences as part of this program.

In a list of statements related to advisor style, students identified the following as important:

- Conveyed a genuine desire to assist.
- Exhibited a patient manner.
- Treated me as an individual.
- Maintained confidentiality of discussions.
- Made me feel my concerns were important.
- Provided accurate information.
- Helped find alternative sources of assistance when needed.
- Provided clear explanations.
- Allowed me to make up my own mind.

- Provided sufficient opportunities to schedule advising sessions.
- Provided adequate time during appointment.

The majority of students in the study responded that these statements were true of their advisor.

The survey included an open-ended question about services that had not been provided. Some students expressed views different from the majority opinion concerning advisor style as reported from the multiple-choice portion of the survey. With statements such as "don't think she [advisor] knows who I am," 13% of students responded that they wanted more "individual- ized" attention from their advisor. Twenty-five percent of the students said advisors were "not available" as often as desired and that advisors had given them "vague or incorrect" information.

In response to an open-ended question asking which are the three most important functions of advising, the students most commonly named these (listed in order of frequency):

1. Provide accurate information.
2. Explain assessment options.
3. Be available when needed.

The Statewide Nursing Program did not meet all definitions of distance education, since students have face-to-face instruction. Because advising was done at a distance, however, the study is relevant. Trent (1993) showed the necessity of advising for RN to BSN students and provided descriptive data related to advising functions and styles considered important. It was a sound study with a good response rate. Although the sample was not random, students were representative of the population, as students in the beginning, in the middle, and at the end of the program were included.

For a doctoral dissertation, Curry (1997) conducted a national survey of academic advising in distance education. Institutions selected for the sample had a least one baccalaureate degree program available at a distance, using primarily electronic means of instruction. While only 89 institutions met the study's sample criteria, 73 surveys were returned, for a response rate of 82%. Results from the Academic Advising in Distance Education Survey were compared to data from American College Testing's Fourth National Survey of Academic Advising (Habley, 1993). Using these data, Curry compared and contrasted current goals and practices of distance education programs with those of institutions as a whole.

Academic practices were found to be similar for distance education and institutions as a whole in that faculty advisors were the most frequent delivers of advising services. There were differences in other practices, with less utilization of group advising, institutional reference materials, and advising evaluation in distance education.

The advising goals of the National Academic Advising Association (NACADA) were listed on Curry's survey. His results indicate that distance education programs have greater achieve- ment of NACADA's advising goals than do institutions as a whole. The mean of means for the advising goals in distance education was 3.97, compared with 3.31 for institutional advis- ing programs. With a rating of 4 indicating satisfactorily achieving a goal, distance education programs were closer to that aggregate achievement level than institutions as a whole. In addi- tion, mean achievement was higher for each of the eight advising goals in distance education programs (see Table 13.1). Results pertaining to goal achievement were subjective, reported by one survey respondent for institutional advising programs and distance education advising programs.

Although some respondents disagreed, the goals of distance education advising programs are largely consistent with NACADA's goals. The goal cited as not relevant most often was assisting students in developing decision-making skills. Still, 82% of institutions reported it was relevant for distance education students.

TABLE 13.1

Mean Achievement of Advising Goals by Survey Category

NACADA Advising Goal	Distance Education	ACT
Assisting students in self-understanding and self-assistance	3.63	2.82
Assisting students in their consideration of life goals	3.87	3.12
Assisting students in developing an educational plan	4.23	3.48
Assisting students in developing decision-making skills	3.82	2.71
Providing accurate information about institutional policies	4.42	3.99
Making referrals to other support services	3.74	3.43
Assisting students in evaluation of progress toward established goals and educational plans	4.16	3.49
Providing information about students to the institution	3.94	3.47
Mean of means	3.97	3.31

Note. The data in column 2 are from *Academic Advising in Distance Education*, by R. F. Curry, 1997, doctoral dissertation, College of William and Mary, *Dissertation Abstracts International, 58-02 A*, 396. Copyright 1997 by Robert F. Curry. Adapted with permission.

Note. The data in column 3 are from *Fulfilling the Promise? Final Report: ACT Fourth National Survey of Academic Advising*, by W. R. Habley, 1993, Iowa City, IA: American College Testing Program. Copyright 1993 by American College Testing. Adapted with permission.

Most respondents indicated it was likely that advisors and distance education students would develop personal relationships. (In Fielstein's study [1989], 83% of students indicated it was important that advisors be personally acquainted with those they advise.) A respondent who reported that a personal relationship was likely added this qualification: "If indicating a satisfactory comfort level in their interactions as opposed to a social type relationship" (Curry, 1997).

Using Curry's (1997) dissertation results, Curry, Baldwin, and Sharpe (1998) wrote an article on academic advising practices specifically for distance education students. The focus included means of communication and types of advisors for distance students. When asked the top three means of communication between advisors and distance education students, institutions reported telephone conversations in real time most often (94%), followed by in-person conversations (61%), written correspondence by mail (55%), telephone conversations through voice mail (33%), and non-real-time computer conferencing using technologies such as e-mail (33%).

Faculty advisors, academic department heads, full-time advisors, part-time advisors, para-professional advisors, and peer advisors were listed as possible advisor types on the survey. All were reported as used by some institutions in distance education. Although the academic advisor was most often reported as being based on the main campus, some institutions also reported the use of each advisor type based closer to distant students. In addition to the listed choices, respondents indicated other types of advisors. Most often mentioned was an individual connected to the distance education office, such as a central administrator or site director.

A discriminant analysis statistical procedure was undertaken to determine the practices most consistent with achieving NACADA's advising goals. The two practices identified were providing advisors with an academic advising handbook and having advising-oriented courses for students on the main campus. Although the statistical results were not conclusive, an advising handbook is certainly a helpful tool for those advising distance education students. Requiring students to come on campus may not be feasible or consistent with the goals of some distance education programs (Curry, 1997).

In addition to noting the importance of an advising handbook, Curry, Baldwin, and Sharpe (1998) gave several recommendations. These recommendations are encouraging advisors to develop personal relationships with students, providing a campus referral directory for advisors, and evaluating advisors and advising programs.

Curry's (1997) dissertation and article based on it (Curry, Baldwin, & Sharpe, 1998) contain the most comprehensive national data on academic advising in distance education currently available. The high response rate resulted in a valid study despite the small population at the time. Institutional representatives may have been overly favorable when reporting goal achievement, but the respondents did seem to have knowledge of advising practices. Given the fast-changing environment of distance education, however, the results can no longer be considered current. The percentage of institutions with advisors using e-mail, for example, is likely much higher than reported through this research.

Workman and Stenard (1996) conducted interviews with 60 students enrolled in distance education programs at Eastern Oregon State College. The institution offers distance learning programs through external degrees, weekend college, independent study, and telecommunications. Results of interviews with students at the main campus and six regional centers were consistent in identifying five needs of students.

1. Clarity of programs, policies, and procedures for consistency and assistance in student planning.
2. Increasing self-esteem.
3. Identification with institution.
4. Developing interpersonal relationships with peers, faculty, and staff.
5. Accessibility of student support services.

All students interviewed reported that the center directors were their most important resource. Many students indicated they would have dropped out without the support and assistance of these center directors.

The institution developed several programs to help meet the needs identified by students. One program provided a "Back to School Night," broadcast to the off-campus audience. This interactive televised presentation was held for prospective students. Before the televised presentation, information packets were made available at regional centers. Each of the 50 students attending the session completed an evaluation form; 90% rated the student services presentations as "good" to "excellent."

The study by Workman and Stenard (1996) is valuable because of the interviews with students. One weakness is that the authors did not identify how students were selected for the interviews. In addition, it was not reported in which type of distance education program the students were participating. Students taking classes through independent study, weekend colleges, and telecommunications may have different needs. These omissions in the sample information make in difficult to generalize the results to other institutions.

Other Degree and Certificate Programs

Beitz (1987) studied academic advising in distance graduate library science programs in the United States. She conducted a telephone survey of library administrators at all schools that offered off-campus courses. Most institutions were not using telecommunications to deliver courses and did not offer entire degree programs at a distance. The majority of programs had academic advising by telephone (61%), but students were encouraged to come to the main campus for advising sessions when possible.

Some schools had faculty members provide in-person advising services to students when faculty traveled to sites for teaching. Beitz reported that most of the library schools did not require advising. For students who took the time to seek advising, however, it was available and effective. Beitz concluded that a planned program of advising services was essential for the success of distance education programs offered by professional schools.

Because the study included few programs that used telecommunications to deliver distance education (only 20% did), very technical means of academic advising were not reported. All 18 programs offering off-campus courses were surveyed, and the survey was valid for this specialization (library science) during this time period.

Wang (1997) did a case study to assess Maine's statewide distance education network. This network offers distance education courses to homes, high schools, businesses, and other sites. Classes are televised using one- or two-way video. Through the distance education network, off-campus students can pursue associate's, bachelor's and master's degrees, and certificates of graduate studies.

The methodology included interviews, survey questionnaires, and analysis of documents. The findings relevant to academic advising were obtained from a survey questionnaire sent to students.

A total of 1,400 survey questionnaires were distributed to students; only 248 questionnaires were returned, for an 18% response rate. For a question on quality of academic advising, the study reported the following responses: excellent (22%), good (22%), acceptable (24%), not acceptable (10%), poor (2%), not applicable (15%) and left this section blank (7%). The researcher was concerned that 15% of the respondents indicated academic advising was not relevant for them. She speculated that lack of time for academic advising and the independence of the adult students could be factors in their avoidance of the services. She said academic advising should be considered useful given the length of time away from school for many adult learners, lack of choice in course selection, and probable need to take courses from multiple distance education centers.

Open-ended questions gave students opportunities to express comments related to their distance education experiences. The researcher indicated that students in rural and remote areas appreciate convenient access to distance education but would prefer classes that are more traditional if given the choice. Distance students have often been out of school for some time and need "hand-holding" in the beginning to learn the use of electronic technologies. Once they learn the technology, however, they like it and want more.

The questionnaire results cannot be considered valid for the population because of the very low return rate. The researcher acknowledged that summer was not the best time to reach students. The questionnaire did not include what degree, if any, the student was pursuing. Perhaps the students who said academic advising did not apply were taking a distance education course only out of personal or professional interest. Categories based on degree level would have been valuable to distinguish differences among students who were pursuing associate, baccalaureate, or graduate degrees.

An online survey was included with the final exam for four Web-based courses at the University of Central Florida. There were 48 students who voluntarily responded, but the authors of the study (Greer, Hudson, & Paugh, 1998) did not indicate the size of the population. These students were obtaining teacher certification in vocational education. In rating the student support services, the respondents indicated never used (10%), poor (0%), average (42%), or above average (48%). In rating the student services in the College of Education for majors, the respondents indicated never used (58%), poor (0%), average (20%), or above average (23%). The institution's student academic resource center has an online site with self-help information in such areas as learner attitudes, reading and comprehension, skills, note taking, and math study skills.

This study indicates that students who use student services may find them helpful but that many students may never access them. This was a specialized study of students obtaining teacher certification. The fact that the volunteer response rate was not stated further limits the study's geneneralizability.

RECOMMENDATIONS FOR FURTHER RESEARCH

While some knowledge of academic advising in distance education has been gained, the review of research demonstrates that voids in the literature exist. A study similar to Curry's (1997) should be done approximately every three years. Trends and new developments can be identified by periodically surveying administrators. Future national studies of academic advising in distance education should include associate and baccalaureate programs for consistency with NACADA's national surveys. This research will provide the knowledge needed for comparing and contrasting the advising goals and practices in distance education and those of institutions as a whole.

Workman and Stenard's (1996) study identified student needs at one institution, but a national survey of distance education students should be conducted. This study of academic advising needs would provide quantitative data from the student perspective. Associate, baccalaureate, and graduate students should be surveyed. Information based on solid research will help advisors develop appropriate advising services for distance students.

These national surveys would provide quantitative data. For gathering rich qualitative data to gain additional insights, several case studies are recommended.

One case study should compare advising for students in a professional degree program and a nonprofessional degree program. An institution with distance learning options for varied degree programs may need to provide very different services for the different student populations. An RN student, for example, will likely have very different advising needs than a liberal arts major.

A case study of academic advising at institutions with Web-based instruction should be done. It should include interviews of advisors and students. Among the topics of investigation would be the relationship between advising methods and instruction mode, the use of Web discussion groups, and possible means of establishing rapport when face-to-face contact is not involved in advising.

A case study focusing on students' perceptions of advising throughout their academic careers is needed. A longitudinal study would be ideal, but researchers can also study separate groups of students concurrently as long as some are beginning a program, others are taking courses about midway through the program, and still others are nearing completion of the program. Graduates of the distance education program should also be included in this study. In-depth interviews of students and graduates would be the primary method of data collection.

Masters and doctoral students are often neglected in advising research. Although Wang (1997) included graduate students in her study, the data were not distinguished from the data for the undergraduate students. A case study should focus specifically on advising issues of graduate students in distance education. Although a graduate student's academic needs are very different from an undergraduate's, the more advanced students will still have issues related to pursuing a degree at a distance.

Trent (1993) evaluated academic advising at one institution, and Wang (1997) included academic advising in a statewide study. Curry (1997) found that only 33% of distance education programs regularly evaluated the overall effectiveness of advising services. These evaluations are needed at individual institutions. Institutions should publish the results of studies possessing a sound research design, providing models for other institutions to adapt and use.

CONCLUSION

This chapter describes practices in academic advising in distance education degree programs. Research is not extensive and does not provide definitive answers on best practices. As additional research is undertaken, the information gained can be used to improve advising services.

It is important that attention be devoted to the issue of academic advising in distance education. Research by Paneitz (1997) found that academic advising was the most essential student service in associate degree programs available at a distance. Studies by Beitz (1987), Curry (1997), and Trent (1993) also demonstrated the importance of academic advising for distance education students pursuing baccalaureate or graduate degrees.

One important research topic is the advisor-student relationship. Some students in Trent's study (1993) expressed a need for a more individual approach. Curry's (1997) survey indicated that advisors were developing personal relationships with their distance education students. One way to help personalize the advising process is for advisors to have Web pages with pictures and biographical information. Another way is through friendliness and the personalization of telephone and e-mail contacts. Concern with confidentiality can make this personalization difficult in group electronic discussions. Fornshell (1993) described the use of codes rather than names for identifying participants in an electronic advising session. If this type of session was a student's only advising contact, use of a code could be seen as making a reality of the student's worst nightmare: being treated "like a number." In the program Fornshell described, students visited the campus twice a year for in-person advising. Although Workman and Stenard (1996) and Barnett and Kline (1999) reported the importance of in-person assistance, face-to-face contact may cease to be possible as students become more geographically dispersed. No matter what the means of communications used, academic advisors should make every effort to treat each student as an individual.

Additional national and institutional studies will continue to advance our knowledge about academic advising in distance education degree programs. Although distance education programs and student services are diverse, some issues are relevant for academic advising of any student at a distance. As advisors examine knowledge in the field and practices that have been successful, they can choose the strategies that will make advising most accessible and helpful to their own distance education students.

REFERENCES

Barnett, E. M., & Kline, J. P. (1999). The role of site directors in faculty and student success. In *Distance learning '99* (Annual Conference on Distance Teaching and Learning proceedings). (ERIC Document Service Reproduction No. ED 440 287)

Beitz, N. C. (1987). Academic advisement for distance education students. *Journal of Education for Library and Information Science, 27,* 279–287.

Bowser, D., & Race, K. (1991). Orientation for distance education students: What is it worth? *Distance Education, 12*(2), 109–122.

Carr, R., & Ledwith, F. (1980). Helping disadvantaged students. *Teaching at a Distance, 18,* 77–85.

Curry, R. F. (1997). Academic advising in distance education. (Doctoral dissertation, College of William and Mary, 1997). *Dissertation Abstracts International, 58-02 A,* 396.

Curry, R. F., Baldwin, R. G., & Sharpe, M. S. (1998). Academic advising in baccalaureate distance education programs. *American Journal of Distance Education, 12*(3), 42–52.

Fielstein, L. L. (1989). Student priorities for academic advising: Do they want a personal relationship? *NACADA Journal, 9*(1), 33–38.

Fornshell, G. K. (1993). Academic advisement for distance learners. *Journal of Instruction Delivery Systems, 7*(3), 17–19.

Gordon, V. N. (1992). *Handbook of academic advising.* Westport, CT: Greenwood.

Greenwood, J. D. (1984). Academic advising and institutional goals: A president's perspective. In R. B. Winston, Jr., T. K. Miller, S. C. Ender, T. J. Grites & Associates (Eds.), *Developmental academic advising* (pp. 64–88). San Francisco: Jossey-Bass.

Greer, L. B., Hudson, L., & Paugh, R. (1998). Student support services and success factors for adult on-line learners. (ERIC Document Service Reproduction No. ED 441 155) Paper presented at the Annual Conference of the International Society for the Exploration of Teaching Alternatives (28*th,* Cocoa Beach, FL).

Habley, W. R. (1993). *Fulfilling the promise? Final report: ACT fourth national survey of academic advising.* Iowa City, IA: American College Testing Program.

Habley, W. R. (1998). A personal epilogue. In W. R. Habley, & R. H. Morales (Eds.), *Current practices in academic advising: Final report on ACT's fifth national survey of academic advising* (pp. 65–66). Manhattan, KS: National Academic Advising Association.

Lalande, V. (1995). Student support via audio teleconferencing: Psycho-educational workshops for post-bachelor nursing students. *American Journal of Distance Education, 9*(3) 62–73.

Miller, G. E. (1993). Comparing distance education programs. In *The electronic university: A guide to distance learning*. Princeton, NJ: Peterson's Guides. pp. xiii–xiv.

Paneitz, B. (1997). Community college students' perceptions of student services provided when enrolled in telecourses. (Doctoral dissertation, Colorado State University 1997) Dissertation Abstracts International, 58-09A, 3394.

Peterson's guide to distance learning programs. (1998). Princeton, NJ: Peterson's Guides.

Potter, J. (1998). Beyond access: Student perspectives on support service needs in distance learning. *Canadian Journal of University Continuing Education, 24*(1), 59–82.

Reed, D., & Sork, T. J. (1990). Ethical considerations in distance education. *American Journal of Distance Education, 4*(2), 30–43.

Sloan, D., & Wilmes, M. B. (1989). Advising adults from the commuter perspective. *NACADA Journal, 9*(2), 67–75.

Tallman, Frank D. (1994) Satisfaction and completion in correspondence study: The influence of instructional and student-support services. *American Journal of Distance Education, 8*(2), 43–57.

Trent, B. A. (1993). An evaluation of student perceptions of academic advising in a RN/BSN distance educational nursing program (Doctoral dissertation, University of San Diego, 1993) *Dissertation Abstracts International, 54*, 780.

Wagner, E. D. (1993, April). Variables affecting distance educational program success. *Educational Technology*, 28–32.

Wang, J. (1997). Statewide collaboration in adult continuing education: A case study of distance education in Maine. (Doctoral dissertation, Northern Illinois University 1997) Dissertation Abstracts International, 58-06A, 2044.

Wilka, K., & Fitzner, S. (1998). Distance education "lifeguards": Saving students from traditional waters. (Eric Document Reproduction Service No. ED 422 884) Proceedings of the Annual Conference on Distance Teaching and Learning (14th, Madison, WI)

Workman, J. J., & Stenard, R. A. (1996). Student support services for distance learners. *DEOSNEWS, 6*(3), pp. 1–11.

14

Instructional Discussions in Online Education: Practical and Research-Oriented Perspectives

Donald J. Winiecki
Boise State University
dwiniecki@boisestate.edu

INTRODUCTION

It can be argued that discussion is one of the oldest forms of instruction (Gall & Gall, 1990; Larson, 2000). Online education through asynchronous learning networks (ALNs) provides the opportunity for the development of innovations in educational practice. Although instructional discussion is not an innovation, it is an essential component of social learning, community-based learning, and other practices that are considered valuable features of online education (Harasim, Hiltz, Teles, & Turoff, 1996; McIsaac & Gunawardena, 1996; Romiszowski & Mason, 1996). Thus, it makes sense to research this blend of the old (classroom discussion) and the new (ALNs) with the aim of understanding and improving practice.

FACE-TO-FACE CONVERSATION

What Do We Know About the Way People Talk When They Have a Conversation?

Conversation analysis (CA) is a sociological research perspective that focuses on the construction and acknowledgement of societal practices through conversation (Couper-Kuhlen & Selting, 1996; Hutchby & Wooffitt, 1998; Sacks, 1963; Sacks, Schegloff, & Jefferson, 1978; ten Have, 1999). CA has found that conversation is structured in regular ways (Ford, 1999; Heritage, 1997; Hopper, 1992; Hutchby & Wooffitt, 1998; Sacks, 1963; Sacks et al., 1978; Schegloff, 1972, 1986, 1991; ten Have, 1999; Winiecki, 1999, in press). In other words, a de facto "technology of conversation" appears to exist. Four fundamental components of this putative technology of conversation are turn-taking, overlap, repair, and formulations. Each of these components is described below.

```
[SN-4:3]

Sharon:    You didn' come tuh talk tuh Karen?

Mark:         No, Karen- Karen' I 're having a fight,

        (0.4)

Mark:         after she went out with Keith an' not

    with (me).

Ruthie:    hah hah hah hah

Karen:    Wul Mark, you never asked me out.
```

FIG. 14.1. Prototypical conversational turn-taking. *Note.* From "A Simplest Systematics for the Ogranization of Turn Taking for Conversation," by H. Sacks, E. Schegloff, and G. Jefferson, 1978, in J. Schenkein (Ed.), *Studies in the Organization of Conversational Interaction* (p. 29), New York: Academic Press, 1978. Reprinted with permission.

Turn-taking.   Speakers normally take turns at speaking in a conversation (Sacks et al., 1978). (It is not uncommon for there to be short periods during which more than one person is speaking at once, known as overlap [Jefferson, 1986; Sacks et al., 1978].) Conversational behavior is often classified by variations in turn-taking and speaker-change "rules" (Heritage, 1997).

Interactants exhibit turn-taking patterns related to the context and topic under discussion (Sacks et al., 1978). Orientation to a particular turn-taking scheme is reflexive evidence that interactants are acknowledging the extant scheme (if only tacitly). Turn-taking reflects not only the type of conversation being conducted but also the interactants' orientation toward maintaining or changing that type of conversation (Heritage, 1997; Sacks et al., 1978). Fig. 14.1 displays a turn-taking sequence typical of a social conversation (see Appendix for a glossary of terms and symbols).

It has been shown that classroom interaction is typically characterized by a turn-taking system in which the teacher controls the sequence and pace of turns. For example, while observing a classroom, one would expect to hear the following: (a) teacher states information, (b) teacher asks a question, (c) teacher prompts for response, (d) student responds, (e) teacher evaluate responses (teacher talk) (McHoul, 1978; Mehan, 1978). This pattern is recognizable as a "lesson" in a conventional classroom.

Overlap.   Through turn-taking, interactants orient to a phenomenon known as the *turn-construction unit* (TCU) (Heritage, 1997; Hutchby & Wooffitt, 1998; Jefferson, 1986; Schegloff, 2000; ten Have, 1999). A TCU is ended at the point where a turn is "hearably" complete. In conversation, a TCU is instantiated at the point where other parties typically attempt to begin a new turn (Jefferson, 1986; Sacks et al., 1978).

Because it is common for interactants to misjudge the precise timing of turn completion, among other things, it is common to find violations of the turn-taking rule near a TCU. If this happens, conversational overlap occurs (Hutchby & Wooffitt, 1998; Jefferson, 1986; Sacks et al., 1978; Schegloff, 1991, 2000; Schegloff, Jefferson, & Sacks, 1977; ten Have, 1999). Overlaps are usually very short because one of the overlapping parties typically terminates his or her turn, allowing the other to continue. Fig. 14.2 displays conversational overlap typical

```
[Labov:Battersea:A:7]

        Parky:      Oo what they call them dogs that pull

           sleighs.

                    (0.5)

        Parky:      S-sledge dogs.

                    (0.7)

 →      Man:        Oh uh :: uh

                        [

 →      Tourist:    Uh-Huskies.
```

FIG. 14.2. Prototypical conversational overlap. *Note.* From "A Simplest Systematics for the Ogranization of Turn Taking for Conversation," by H. Sacks, E. Schegloff, and G. Jefferson, 1978, in J. Schenkein (Ed.), *Studies in the Organization of Conversational Interaction* (pp. 15–16), New York: Academic Press, 1978. Reprinted with permission.

of a social conversation. Arrows indicate the utterances and location of conversational overlap (see Appendix).

Repair.   The need for repair occurs when a speaker must clarify a statement, reintroduce information that is necessary to understand the current comment, apologize for a problematic event, and so on. Different repair strategies and tactics have been defined by conversation analytic research (Ford, 1999; Hutchby & Wooffitt, 1998; Jefferson, 1986; Sacks et al., 1978; Schegloff, 1991, 2000; Schegloff et al., 1977).

Although tactics and strategies differ, repair has one common purpose: to realign the perspectives of participants in the conversation with the viewpoint that is being presented by the current speaker. Fig. 14.3 displays a conversational repair used to remedy a misunderstanding in a social conversation.

In noninstructional conversation, the individual who commits an error is usually the one who accomplishes a repair (Jefferson, 1986; Schegloff et al., 1977). However, in instructional interactions it is common for the teacher to initiate repair of a student's (mis)statement (i.e., correct it) (Ford, 1999; McHoul, 1990).

Formulations.   Formulations contain "the gist of an informant's earlier statements" (Heritage, 1985). Heritage (1985) indicates that formulations are relatively rare in casual conversation but more common in institutionalized talk. Instruction is one such form of institutionalized talk where formulations are common (McHoul, 1978, 1990; Winiecki, in press).

Formulations are commonly used in conversations to clarify implicit meanings, for the speaker to offer an understanding of the emerging dialog in order to have it authenticated or repaired by the other speaker(s), or to orient other conversationalists to "what is really going on here" (Garfinkel & Sacks, 1970; Heritage & Watson, 1979; Schegloff, 1972). Fig. 14.4 displays a simple example of conversational formulation. The arrow indicates where formulating is taking place (see Appendix).

```
CDHQ:152

      A:    Which one::s are closed, an' which ones are

            open.

      Z:    Most  of  'em.  This,  this,  this,  this

            ((pointing to map))

                          [

→     A:                  I 'on't  mean  on  the

            shelters, I mean on

            the roads.

      Z:    Oh!
```

FIG. 14.3. Prototypical conversational repair of misunderstanding. *Note.* From "Conversation Analysis and Socially Shared Cognition," by E. Schegloff, 1991, in L. B. Resnick, J. M. Levine, and S. D. Teaslly (Eds.), *Perspectives on Socially Shared Cognition* (p. 159), Washington, DC: American Psychological Association, 1991. Reprinted with permission.

Although conversation varies significantly in topic, context, membership, and so on, it is nonetheless structured in regular ways (Ford, 1999; Heritage, 1997; Hopper, 1992; Hutchby & Wooffitt, 1998; Sacks, 1963; Sacks et al., 1978; Schegloff, 1972, 1986, 1991; ten Have, 1999; Winiecki, 1999, in press). The communicative effectiveness of conversations is arguably affected by an orientation to these regularities. Research shows that conversations reflect reliable patterns of turn-taking, overlap, repair, and formulation. These four factors could be considered fundamental to the structural composition of conversational interaction (Sacks, 1963). Consequently, studies of instructional discussions could make use of these fundamental elements in order to construct an understanding of the "technology of *instructional* talk" (Sacks, 1963).

What Do We Know About the Use of Discussion in Education?

The Status of Research.   Literature on instructional discussion as a teaching method tends toward introspection based on anecdotal experiences of successful instructors (Brookfield, 1998; Gall & Gall, 1990; Larson, 2000; Wilen, 1990). Most empirical studies on classroom talk restrict their attention to face-to-face classrooms (Ford, 1999; Heyman, 1986; McHoul, 1978, 1990). Of these, few focus on the factors described above and how these factors are manipulated to (a) deliver new instructional content and (b) facilitate social negotiation of understanding (Black, Levin, Mehan, & Quinn, 1983; Cerratto & Waern, 2000; Ford, 1999; McHoul, 1978, 1990; Quinn, Mehan, Levin, & Black, 1983; Winiecki, 1999, in press).

What Is Instructional Discussion Used For?   Instructional discussion is recommended when instructional goals require analysis, synthesis, and evaluation (Brookfield, 1998; Gall & Gall, 1990) or when the process of peer-to-peer activity is an instructional goal (Brookfield, 1998; Gall & Gall, 1990; Larson, 2000; Phillips & Santoro, 1989). Discussion is appropriate for accomplishing these goals because discussants collaborate in both divergent activities

[TVN:Tea]

```
    C:    What in fact happened was that in the course

          of last year, .hh the price when up really

          very sharply, .hhh and ugh the blenders did

          take advantage of this: uh to obviously to

          raise their prices to retailers. 0.7) .hhh

          They haven't been so quick in reducing their

          prices when the world market prices come

          down. (0.3) .hh And so this means that price

          in the sh- the prices in the shops have

          stayed up .hh really rather higher than we'd

          like to see them.

          (0.7)

→   Int: So you you're really accusing them of

profiteering.
```

FIG. 14.4. Conversational formulation. *Note.* From *Conversation Analysis: Principles, Practices, and Applications* (p. 152), by I. Hutchby and R. Wooffitt, 1998, Cambridge: Cambridge University Press, 1998. Reprinted with permission.

(contributions of data from class members) and convergent activities (analyzing, synthesizing, and evaluating information) to negotiate an understanding of specific and general principles related to instructional content. Instructional discussion is facilitated when the leader acts as a "more capable peer" (Vygotsky, 1978) rather than an autocrat (Brookfield, 1998; Gall & Gall, 1990; Larson, 2000). The same process facilitates the learning practices of group discussion and group decision-making (Gall & Gall, 1990; Larson, 2000; Phillips & Santoro, 1989).

Phases of Instructional Discussion.   Wilen (1990) identifies four phases of instructional discussion: (a) entry, (b) clarification of subject matter, (c) collaborative investigation, and (d) closure or synthesis. These four phases are elements of several practitioner models for classroom instruction (Gagné, Briggs, & Wager, 1992; Laurillard, 1993). In the *entry* phase, prior knowledge is reviewed and linked to the new topic area. During *clarification*, the discussion leader models an analysis of the topic under discussion. The discussion leader also prompts others to perform analyses of the topic. The *collaborative investigation* phase involves classifying and sorting information—perhaps constructing temporary classification structures to aid learners. During *closure*, the discussion leader guides other discussants to synthesize the discussion. Wilen's phases (1990) describe a set of divergent and convergent steps alternating between (a) analysis of the topic area and (b) synthesizing topical information into new or accommodated categories.

What's Missing From Research on Instructional Discussion?   Beyond the identification of general methods and explication through examples (Wilen, 1990), the literature leaves it up to the savvy of the discussants to decide when to advance the discussion to another phase, continue in a phase, or reinitiate a phase. This highlights a gap in the literature and a need for empirical research on instructional discussion.

Based on the literature, instructional discussion contains several general phases and loosely organized segments of divergent and convergent activity. However, these segments and the means for using them to facilitate instructional activity are not well-defined. Although conversation analysis implicates a technology of conversation, research has not established a similar technology of instructional conversation.

ONLINE COMMUNICATION

What Do We Know About Online Communication in General?

The Status of Research on Computer-Mediated Communication.   There appears to be a common notion that there is a paucity of research on computer-mediated communication (CMC). It has been observed that this is in fact not the case. There is a substantial amount of literature on the topic of CMC, although it is scattered through the literature of a great many fields, including the social sciences, organizational and business research (Baron, 1998; Baym, 1996; Cherny, 1999; Duranti, 1986; Ferrara, Brunner, & Whittemore, 1991; Fulk, Schmitz, & Schwarz, 1992; Gains, 1999; Hermann, 1995; Herring, 1996; Kiesler, Siegel, & McGuire, 1984; McCarthy, Wright, & Monk, 1992; Murray, 1989, 1991; Reed, 2000; Reed & Ashmore, 2000; Rintel & Pittam, 1997; Spears & Lea, 1994; Stanton & Weiss, 2000; Wallace, 2000; Walther, 1996; Wilkens, 1991), and education (Black et al., 1983; Bresler, 1990; Cerratto & Waern, 2000; Garcia & Jacobs, 1998, 1999; Harasim et al., 1996; Muscella & DiMauro, 1995; Owen, 2000; Phillips & Santoro, 1989; Quinn et al., 1983; Romiszowski & Mason, 1996; Salmon, 2000; Wasson & Morch, 2000; Winiecki, 1999, in press). It is also perhaps appropriately described as lacking in paradigmatic, conceptual, or scientific unity (Rice, 1992).

Social Effects of Online Communication.   Unlike conventional talk that always occurs in real time between interactants (e.g., face to face or over the telephone), online communication can be classified into two general categories, synchronous and asynchronous. Synchronous communication (frequently called "chat") involves real-time or near real-time interaction between persons at a distance from each other. During synchronous communication, interactants type messages to each other when their conversation partners are currently online and available to read and respond. In asynchronous communication, the interactants are not online at the same time. E-mail, listservs, newsgroups, and threaded discussion systems are common asynchronous communication media.

Initially, the obvious features of synchronous and asynchronous CMC led communication researchers to predict that chat would reflect linguistic behaviors similar to talk and that e-mail would reflect linguistic behaviors similar to formal, written communication (Baron, 1998; Black et al., 1983; Bringham & Corbett, 1997; Ferrara et al., 1991; Fulk et al., 1992; Kiesler et al., 1984; McCarthy et al., 1992; Murray, 1989; Walther, 1996). Subsequently, empirical research has identified that the speech patterns and linguistic registers common in CMC are an amalgam of face-to-face and written communication (Duranti, 1986; Ferrara et al., 1991) and that the selective appropriation of face-to-face and written communication is dependent on the context of the message, the characteristics of the interactants, and the functionality of the tool being used (Rintel & Pittam, 1997).

Subsequent research began to discover that the text-only nature of most CMC reduced the possibility that social cues could be expressed easily (e.g., prosodic features of the speaker's voice, body posture, and facial expressions). This led to a hypothesis that the technological limits of text-only CMC (or the "reduced social cues" permitted in it) lead to a decrease in the availability and thus importance of traditional forms of status and power, supposedly reducing problems associated with those factors that normally emerge in face-to-face meetings (Baron, 1998; Kiesler et al., 1984; Walther, 1996).

More recent research indicates that, although novices and short-lived CMC interactions tend to exhibit the "reduced social cues" phenomenon, online communication behaviors between experienced users or those that span a longer duration are affected by the degree of knowledge that interactants have about the status of their fellow interactants. Specifically, messages from a low-status to a high-status person or to a person of unknown status will usually exhibit a more formal communication style than messages from a high-status person to a low-status person or between persons of equivalent status (Baron, 1998; Fulk et al., 1992; Gains, 1999; Rintel & Pittam, 1997; Spears & Lea, 1994; Wallace, 2000; Walther, 1996). This may be traceable to the observation that, due to the text-only nature of most CMC, traditionally visual social cues (office accommodations, clothing style, age, etc.) are not easily communicated, but these and other social or status attributes will eventually be alluded to in their statements over time (Rintel & Pittam, 1997). In other words, as people become more experienced in CMC, their interactions gradually reveal things that can affect social communication patterns.

The Nature of Synchronous CMC.   Synchronous CMC is commonly known as *chat*, presumably after the popularity of Internet Relay Chat (IRC), a commonly available network of synchronous CMC resources and topic areas. Software tools for hosting chat have improved in reliability and features but retain the text-based nature of IRC (Fig. 14.5). Chat software typically displays interaction in one "window pane" and posts each new turn at the bottom of this pane. As new comments are posted, older ones scroll up and off the visible screen area. Depending on the software used, these older comments can be reviewed by scrolling up and down through the software. New comments are typed in the "composition pane" before sending.

Most chat can be defined as *half-duplex*, meaning that a message is composed and then sent in two separate steps (unlike face-to-face conversation, where participants hear the utterance as it is being spoken). Once the message is composed and sent, the computer system posts it so that every participant can see it. The result is a series of messages appearing in the chat software in close enough sequence to seem to be accomplished in real time (Baym, 1996; Bresler, 1990; Cerratto & Waern, 2000; Cherny, 1999; Herring, 1996; McCarthy et al., 1992; Murray, 1989, 1991; Muscella & DiMauro, 1995; Owen, 2000; Reed, 2000; Reed & Ashmore, 2000; Rice, 1992; Rintel & Pittam, 1997; Schriner & Rice, 1989; Wasson & Morch, 2000). Half-duplex synchronous chat has been compared to CB radio talk or walkie-talkie talk (Murray, 1989, 1991) because of the limitation that only one party can post a message at a time. Even if two messages are sent at the same time, the host computer system does not permit two messages to "overlap" and will display them in a serial order, removing the appearance of overlap (Murray, 1989, 1991). Other chat tools permit communication in a *full-duplex* manner. In full-duplex chat, all parties can see each message as the message is being composed (Garcia & Jacobs, 1998, 1999).

Like conventional talk, chat exhibits turn-taking, overlap, repair, and formulations. However, these features in chat differ depending on whether the media system supports half-duplex or full-duplex communication (Black et al., 1983; Cherny, 1999; Garcia & Jacobs, 1998, 1999; Murray, 1989, 1991).

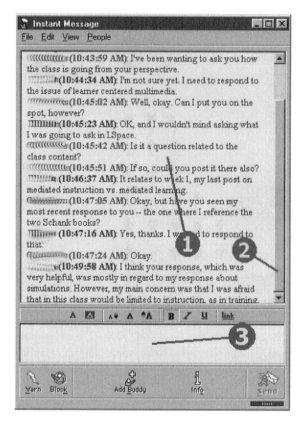

FIG. 14.5. Synchronous chat window (American Online "Instant Messenger").

The Nature of Asynchronous CMC.   Unlike chat, which requires participants to all be online at the same time, asynchronous CMC (ACMC) permits participants to receive and send messages at times of their own choosing—"time shifting" the interaction, as it is called. As with half-duplex synchronous chat, asynchronous CMC messages are composed and sent in two separate steps, and the host computer posts them to be viewed by other participants.

However, unlike synchronous chat software tools that display the messages in a single stream of messages, software tools used to conduct ACMC typically contain features that organize and present messages in a way that reifies different conversational topics and turn-taking structure (Winiecki, in press). Fig. 14.6 displays a typical ACMC software system. Most ACMC software tools contain a "threaded" view, where message titles are listed according to topics and turn-like sequences. Indented message titles in the threaded view indicate that the indented message is a response to the one immediately above it. For example, the message A in Fig. 14.6 is a response to message B. Messages in the threaded view that are at the same level of indentation are not responses to each other rather are both responses to the message they are indented from. For example, message C in Fig. 14.6 is also a response to message B.

In addition to depicting threads, the contents of a message selected in the threaded view (no. 1, Fig. 14.6) is displayed in another window in some ACMC software (no. 2). In the software displayed, a person responds to the message visible in the bottom window by clicking on the button labeled "New Response" (no. 3). Unlike the software tools available for chat communication, these features in ACMC software enhance the participant's ability to perceive the general flow of topics and messages by simple inspection.

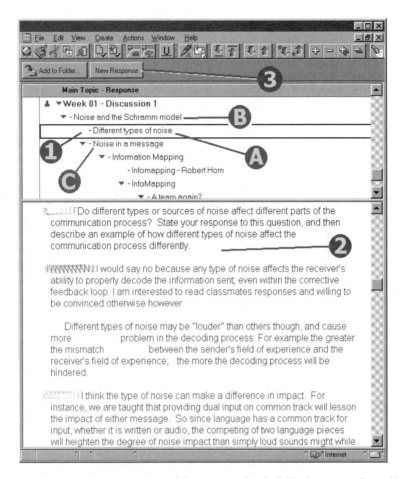

FIG. 14.6.   View of message threads and the contents of an individual message. (Lotus Notes)

Research on ACMC has not typically addressed conversation analytic topics. Rather it has been typified by the research described above in "The Status of Research on CMC." Researchers who have looked at the potential for studying text-mediated interaction from a conversation analytic angle have questioned the efficacy of researching "context-dependent" and "context-shaping" linguistic behavior when the context is not "there" in any one place or time (Mulkay, 1985; Nelson, 1994; Reed & Ashmore, 2000). Consequently, there is a gap in the research literature, and filling it could add to our understanding of how ACMC is actually accomplished and allow us to use such knowledge to make ACMC a more effective tool for achieving particular goals (similar to what has been done in the literature on computer-mediated decision-making systems, as described above).

Reed (2000) and Winiecki (1999, in press) observe that, far from being machine or software controlled, online discussion is the ordered product of human activity. Reed (2000) refers to the reflexive relation between social and technological factors (with imminence of the social) as a "foregrounding" of human over mechanical factors. Fulk et al. (1992) echo this reflexive relation and suggest structuration-like effects between technological features of the mediation system and the human interactants undertaking to accomplish discussion asynchronously. Empirical research on the structure of online discussions is discussed below.

Research on Online Discussions

The Instrumental Use of Computer-Mediated Communication. From its inception, online communication has been used in business as a medium for delivering information, accomplishing meetings, and hosting decision-making sessions (Kiesler et al., 1984). The latter purpose has been the focus of a substantial amount of research (Kiesler et al., 1984; Rice, 1992; Walther, 1996). The Delphi method of research and problem-solving was heavily influenced by the capabilities of CMC (Baron, 1998), and a great many studies have concluded that e-mail's relative paucity of social information (e.g., the "reduced social cues" phenomenon noted above) leads to a decrease in the importance of the status and power of the interactants (Kiesler et al., 1984; Walther, 1996).

Research on business applications of online communication has typically focused on two things: first, the use of it and other "information technologies" to improve access to data and the distribution of data (Rice, 1992), and, second, its use and effectiveness in facilitating business and bureaucratic processes (Kiesler et al., 1984; Rice, 1992; Walther, 1996). Research on the use of online discussion for the latter purpose shows consistently that there are specific practical factors that accompany the successful and economic use of computer-mediated discussion techniques for information delivery, problem solving, and decision making (Kiesler et al., 1984; Walther, 1996).

Use of CMC for Business-Oriented Decision Making. Similar to models of educational discussion, decision making involves a series of divergent and convergent phases. Different reviews of the literature consistently support the idea that divergent phases benefit when discussants are not aware of the power or status of other discussants—the so-called "reduced social cues" benefit of CMC (Kiesler et al., 1984; Rice, 1992; Walther, 1996). This benefit was verified by experimental research that showed differences in the quantity of divergent comments made by persons who were aware of the status and power of other discussants as compared with those made by persons who were anonymous to each other. (Although no claim is being made here that students in an instructional discussion should be anonymous to each other, the establishment of an instructional environment where differences in status and power do not exist is consistent with advice on the use of discussion in educational applications [Brookfield, 1998; Gall & Gall, 1990; Larson, 2000; Wilen, 1990]).

In contrast, the convergent phase of decision making is facilitated by the existence of a known leader whose job it is to guide the group through evaluation of the information generated during the divergent phase (Walther, 1996). To Walther (1996), the divergent phase of decision making is facilitated by reduced social and status information (what he calls *impersonal discussion*), and the convergent phase is facilitated by the existence of a central, higher-status individual who facilitates decision making (referred to as an *interpersonal discussion*). (This too, is consistent with advice from Gall and Gall [1990] and Larson [2000], namely, that in the convergent phase of instructional discussion the instructor should guide and coach students through the process of synthesizing and evaluating information generated during the divergent phase.)

Research on the attributes of CMC postulate that different factors affect the performance of conversational interaction. One strand of research focuses on the "reduced social cues" inherent in text-only CMC and concludes that CMC is naturally more egalitarian. The other strand proposes that social and contextual factors surrounding CMC do emerge over time, and these factors will impact interaction in CMC. However, it has been observed that because contextual and social cues emerge gradually in CMC, they would affect only computer-mediated conversations that last for a fairly long time or in cases where interactants have interactive histories that predate the use of CMC (Baron, 1998; Kiesler et al., 1984; Spears & Lea, 1994; Walther, 1996).

Thus, an initial state where reduced social cues exist, followed by the emergence of social and contextual factors, facilitate different phases of computer-supported decision making.

In addition to the social and instrumental effects of mediated communication, research on the use of synchronous and asynchronous media in discussion-type interaction has identified conversation patterns that resemble the conversation analytic factors of discussion described at the beginning of this chapter. However, accomplishment of these practices varies (apparently) according to social context and the constraints presented by the media. In order to clarify these practices and suggest their utility in developing an understanding of the technology of online conversation, the following sections of this chapter explore a conversation analytic view of online discussion and online educational discussion.

CONVERSATION ANALYTIC RESEARCH ON CMC

Toward a Provisional "Technology of Chat"

As described above for conventional talk, recent research on CMC that takes a conversation analytic perspective has exposed conversation patterns that are common in face-to-face conversation (Reed, 2000; Winiecki, 1999, in press). However, these features are manifested differently depending (apparently) on the social context and constraints imposed by the media (Cherny, 1999; Murray, 1989, 1991; Reed & Ashmore, 2000). In other words, turn-taking, overlap, repair, and formulations occur in chat but have different outward appearances and also different social effects on the accomplishment of conversation from those described in conversation analytic literature on face-to-face talk (Sacks et al., 1978).

Turn-Taking in Chat.   Fig. 14.5 shows that turns in a chat are independent chunks of data analogous to a turn-construction unit (TCU). Research has shown, however, that while turns in a chat appear to be sequential, they may not be (Garcia & Jacobs, 1998, 1999; Murray, 1989, 1991).

Depending on the context of interaction, the sequential turn-taking system may be disrupted in several ways (Murray, 1989). Each of these results in disruptions of the ability to read and decode a sequence of messages as a serial transcript of comments. First, two comments can be sent in rapid succession, each of which address different topics, before anyone responds to the first comment. Second, a comment may not be responded to, effectively "orphaning" that topic. Third, during a series of turns on a single topic, another interactant may post a comment unrelated to the surrounding messages (Murray, 1989, 1991). Finally, an interactant may comment on a turn posted much earlier in the chat. Murray (1989, 1991) indicated that these disruptions occur because there is no way for interactants to know that another person wants to make a comment (normally, prosody, posture, and other audible or visual factors are used by interactants to sense when other persons are vying for a turn). Thus, comments are simply posted as the composer chooses, without consistent orientation to the sequence of turns.

Face-to-face talk normally complies with the principles of turns and minimal occurrence of overlap (Sacks et al., 1978). However, interactants in a synchronous chat are not so constrained and can begin composing a message at any time and send it at any time, leading to what has been classified as a "competition" for the next turn (Cherny, 1999; Murray, 1989). The frequency of these disruptions in serialized turn-taking has been observed to increase with the number of interactants in a chat—more interactants lead to more such disruptions (Bresler, 1990; Cerratto & Waern, 2000; Cherny, 1999). The lack of an explicitly sequential turn-taking order leads to the possibility that more than one topic can be introduced and discussed at once. Because all messages appear serially in the chat window, there is also a possibility that contiguous messages in the chat window will not address the same topic. In some cases, the readers will be able to decode messages and determine which topic they belong to. In other cases, because messages are posted by the system as they are submitted by their authors, contiguous messages may appear to be related but may not have been so intended by their authors. This results in a so-called phantom turn (Garcia & Jacobs, 1998, 1999) and a high probability that the interactants will become disoriented.

Although the potential for a breakdown in turn-taking within a multi-person, multi-topic chat exists, it is important to note that disruptions to serial turn-taking are not necessarily fatal to the purposes of a discussion. Murray (1989, 1991) observed that experienced users of synchronous online communication systems do not orient to a sequential turn-taking system as they appear to in a face-to-face conversation (Sacks et al., 1978). Instead, they orient to the overarching purpose of the chat—the action being addressed rather than each individual turn in the conversation (Murray, 1989, 1991). The implication is that the use of media that imposes unique constraints on participants in a discussion results in the development of unique alternative orientations to conversational practice (Ferrara et al., 1991; Winiecki, 1999, in press).

In another study, McCarthy et al. (1992) found that interactants in synchronous CMC developed conversational techniques for improving the coherence of chat that might otherwise suffer from the breakdown described above—what amounts to constructing their messages to restore some of the continuity lost when sequential messages are not related conversational turns. Initially, McCarthy et al. (1992) identified that when interactants collaborate on the construction of a conversation in chat, they are more aware of what is meant in the messages contained in that chat. However, this collaboration implies that the interactants are actively reading, decoding, composing, and so on, and are not passive observers of the messages. Thus, the degree of participation in constructing a chat affects the degree to which interactants understand the context and implications of the contents of that chat. In other words, passive observers (readers) do not understand the chat to the same extent as do active participants (contributors).

Additionally, in their controlled study, McCarthy et al. found that participants used the name of the author or prefaced their message with a topical gloss to signify the intended referent of a message when that referent was not in the immediately preceding message in the chat window. That is, when the composer of a message knew that participants in a chat could not assume that the previous turn in the chat window was relevant to his or her message, the message would be composed to include information that would help others attach the new message to one that was previously sent. It is important to note that this has not been observed to occur with the same frequency in qualitative or uncontrolled research of "naturally occurring" chat. This is presumably due to the highly competitive nature of message-posting observed in synchronous CMC (Cherny, 1999)—a tactical reduction of content in messages to accelerate message production and delivery.

Overlap in Chat.   As described above, publicly visible conversational overlap does not occur in chat simply because of the half-duplex nature of chat software and the technological mediation of the host computer system—messages are posted by the host computer as they are sent by their authors (Garcia & Jacobs, 1998, 1999; Murray, 1991). Research has shown that interactants do modify messages being composed to account for the contents of messages that beat them to posting (Garcia & Jacobs, 1998, 1999), but this behavior is hidden from other interactants. In other words, although overlap and its effects on other interactants exist, overlap does not occur socially and so does not contribute to the social construction of context, as it does in face-to-face talk.

Repair in Chat.   Conversational repair occurs in chat in ways similar to conventional conversation. For example, subsequent to an error in action or technology (e.g., if the network connection is abruptly terminated, then reestablished) or during the writing process, a chat participant can correct something that was contributed in an earlier message (Rintel & Pittam, 1997).

When overlap occurs in synchronous chat, conversational repair in a chat can also be covert. This has been observed when another participant beats the writer to a response (Garcia & Jacobs, 1999). In this case, the writer may edit (or repair) the message currently being composed to accommodate the contents of the new posting. However, nobody but the writer sees or even knows of this self-repair (Garcia & Jacobs, 1998, 1999). Due to its covert nature, this form of repair does not affect the ongoing chat in the same way that a publicly visible repair would (Jefferson, 1986; Sacks et al., 1978; Schegloff, 2000; Schegloff et al., 1977).

Formulations in Chat.   A review of the literature did not find empirical research evidence for formulations in synchronous chat. In fact, the opposite was found. Multiperson chat interactions reflect a highly competitive system requiring interactants to read and compose text very quickly in order to post comments that add to the ongoing dialog (Cerratto & Waern, 2000; Cherny, 1999). The suspected reason is that taking the time to carefully formulate prior turns in a comment would have the side effect of making the writer fall behind in the rapidly advancing, multivoiced, multitopic chat system (Cerratto & Waern, 2000; Cherny, 1999; McCarthy et al., 1992).

Research Toward a Provisional Technology of ACMC

Like chat, ACMC has been found to share structural similarities with face-to-face conversation (Reed, 2000; Winiecki, 1999, in press). However, also like chat, these features are manifested differently depending (apparently) on the social context and constraints imposed by the media employed (Winiecki, in press). Research has shown that turn-taking, overlap, repair, and formulations exist and are important features in the social construction of discussion and of helping others keep up with the discussion while reducing problems associated with phantom turns (Garcia & Jacobs, 1998, 1999) and multiplication of topics (Black et al., 1983) and cognitive difficulties associated with forgetting what has transpired previously in the asynchronous discussion (Winiecki, 1999). The following sections of this chapter describe findings of recent research on ACMC that details how interactants use resources and features of ACMC software to accomplish turn-taking, overlap, repair, and formulations (Winiecki, in press).

All of the transcripts used here are taken from a semester-long graduate course delivered via ACMC by a mid-sized university in the northwestern United States. Names in the text of these transcripts have been altered to protect the identity of participants. The class from which these data were taken contained 19 students. The students were distributed throughout the United States and Canada during the semester in which these data were collected. The average age of the students at the time of this class was 43 years old.

Turn-Taking in ACMC.   Conversation analytic research on conventional talk demonstrates that most conversational behaviors are facilitated or made possible by the sequencing structure of turn-taking (Heritage, 1997; Sacks et al., 1978). Although some research on synchronous CMC concludes that sequential turns are less critical in synchronous CMC (e.g., chat) than in conventional talk (Murray, 1989, 1991), experienced students engaged in ACMC consistently reflect an orientation toward conversational turns by "reconstructing" it in their messages (Winiecki, in press). These reconstructed turns are accomplished through tactical use of the quoting feature common to ACMC software.

The quoting feature enables the user of an ACMC software application to initiate a reply to someone else's message and copy contents of that message into the message being composed

(Reed, 2000). (Not all ACMC software has this feature, however. The software used in the class from which the following transcripts were taken does not have automatic quoting capability. Instead, students use rudimentary copy and paste functions in the computer's operating system to place a quotation from one message into a message being composed [Winiecki, in press].)

I have indicated elsewhere that there are two ways in which conversational turn-taking can be instantiated in ACMC (Winiecki, in press). First, indented threading (Fig. 14.6) may depict a sequence of conversational turns. Because a thread indicates the relatedness of entire messages, this may be called "inter-message turn-taking" (Winiecki, in press). Second, it is common for the creator of a message to copy parts of the message being responded to into the body of the message being composed. By writing replies to the quoted text, the author creates a new message that can be read as a series of turns, like a transcript of spoken interaction. When this occurs, the message author is reconstructing a turn-taking sequence out of prior and new statements. This second phenomenon may be called "intra-message turn-taking" (Winiecki, in press). The following sections address the use of intra-message turn-taking only.

A prototypical case of reconstructed turn-taking is exhibited in Fig. 14.7. This message, created by Gus, is the second in a thread following a question from the instructor. Gus has copied lines 2–11 from the previous message (in which Crystal replied to a message posted by Dave) and then added his new content at the end of the copied material.

In addition to quoting and adding a new message, Gus has also added a salutation on line 1 and a self-identifier at the beginning of his new message, on line 13 ("Gus then bugs poor Crystal:"). (Similar attributions on lines 2 and 6 were added by Crystal in the previous message.) These attributions signify who is saying what in this reconstructed turn-taking

Txt Color	Line #	Comment:
Blue	1.	Hi Crystal,
Black	2.	Dave posted:
|	3.	1. Are there certain types of instructional objectives to
|	4.	which text, graphics, or a
|	5.	composite or text and graphics, are **well-suited**? <snip>
|	6.	
Purple	7.	Crystal replies: I think text and graphics can be
|	8.	effectively used for all of the above instructional
|	9.	objectives. For example:
|	10.	<snip>
|	11.	In all of the above examples, the graphics and text serve
|	12.	aid retention. The learners are given more than just the
|	13.	content. The graphics provide clarity, guide their
|	14.	understanding and act as a memorable event or anchor for
|	15.	long-term memory.
|	16.	
Blue	17.	Gus then bugs poor Crystal: I think most of us would agree
|	18.	that text and graphics can be effectively used for any of
|	19.	Gagne's five learned capabilities. I am curious to see what
|	20.	you think (and more importantly perhaps what Dr. Dave
|	21.	thinks) about which of the five learned capabilities text
|	22.	and graphics are **well-suited** for, and which they are not
|	23.	particularly well-suited for. I believe there must be a
|	24.	difference in the suitability of text and graphics otherwise
|	25.	Dr. Dave wouldn't have asked it (or would he?).

FIG. 14.7. Prototypical case of reconstructed turn-taking. *Note.* From "Reconstructing Talk: Conversational Patterns in the Asynchronous Classroom," by D. J. Winiecki, in press, in D. Penrod (Ed.), *WebTalk: Writing as Conversation*, Hillsdale, NJ: Lawrence Erlbaum Associates.

message. The creators of these various messages have also changed the colors of their respective contributions, as indicated in the left-hand column of Fig. 14.7. Color change also signifies that different speakers are engaged in this reconstructed turn-taking message.

It is important to note that, although the example is a prototypical instance of reconstructed turn-taking, it is not the only way that such reconstruction may be manifested (Winiecki, in press). Regardless of the specific formatting, the important features of reconstructed turn-taking appear to be (a) copying or quoting from prior messages and pasting them into the message and (b) adding new comments to the message in a way that makes it possible to read the sequence of turns as if it were a transcript of turns in a spoken interaction (Winiecki, forthcoming). Reconstructed turn-taking is also utilized in similar reconstruction of conversational overlap, as described below.

Overlap in ACMC. As indicated above, conversational overlap occurs when a new speaker begins a speaking turn before the prior speaker has finished a turn. Although they are frequently associated, overlaps are not necessarily interruptions. This is the case because overlaps usually occur at turn-construction units, or TCUs (Hutchby & Wooffitt, 1998). According to Hutchby and Wooffitt (1998), TCUs usually correspond to sentences, clauses, or other linguistic categories. Formally, however, a TCU occurs whenever a turn is hearably complete. Thus, fellow interactants are in the position of using their judgment to determine when they may safely begin speaking.

The ACMC message in Fig. 14.7 exhibits attributes of overlap as described above. On lines 4 and 8, Gus has included the marker "<snip>" to indicate that he has snipped (removed) portions of Dave's and Crystal's comments at a TCU, leaving only the segments that are relevant to the new message contents added in lines 1–18. This has the effect of overlapping other statements made by those authors in their original messages. Upon reading the completed message, the fragments taken from other messages can be read as complete statements, thus, similar to TCUs. Gus has used reconstructed turn-taking to simulate or reconstruct overlap of the full statements made by Dave and Crystal.

The critical features of reconstructed overlap appear to be (a) use of reconstructed turn-taking and (b) snipping of prior messages in such a way that (c) only portions of the messages are retained, (Winiecki, in press). It is obviously possible for a message's author to accidentally or intentionally use reconstructed turn-taking and reconstructed overlap to take prior comments out of context. Where this has been observed to occur, the original message's author or others frequently intervene to repair the intended meaning.

Repair in ACMC. Repair occurs when utterances are altered by subsequent turns (McHoul, 1990). Thus, conversational repairs correct or call prior statements into question. Repairs can be self-initiated when a speaker applies them on himself or herself, or other initiated, when another speaker prompts the need for a repair. In other-initiated repairs, the original speaker or others may actually accomplish the repairing statement. Both of these kinds of repairs have been observed to occur in ACMC (Winiecki, in press).

Fig. 14.8 displays a message containing segments from two messages (lines 1–20), plus new text added by this message's author (lines 22–27). In her comment (lines 23–27), Stella seeks a repair based on the other messages included in this reconstructed turn-taking (e.g., "But in my understanding . . . "). Fig. 14.8 is an example of other-initiated other-repair (Schegloff et al., 1977).

The critical features of conversational repair in ACMC appear to be (a) use of reconstructed turn-taking and perhaps snipping of prior messages in such a way as to (b) highlight the need for repair and/or (c) introduce a correction or other form of repair applied to the messages included in the reconstructed turn-taking (Winiecki, in press).

Txt Color	Line #	Comment:
Blue	1.	Dave nudged:
Black	2.	Remember some of the advice that was given on the use of
|	3.	video materials? It was stated that the
|	4.	instructor/guide/more-capable-peer/etc. should (a) introduce
|	5.	the video before it is shown, (b) play the video, (c)
|	6.	interrupt the video where there is a poignant event
|	7.	{"teachable moment"}, and then (c) facilitate a discussion
|	8.	after playing the video. At a minimum, the facilitated
|	9.	discussion should play the part of Gagne's event #9 --
|	10.	enhance retention and transfer. In other words, the
|	11.	discussion should provide a conceptual framework to attach
|	12.	what was seen and heard in the video to the goals of the
|	13.	instruction.
|	14.	Could a similar thing be done with role plays? I agree that
|	15.	the instructor would have to be much more resourceful to
|	16.	work things together ad hoc.
|	17.	
Blue	18.	Charlie responds,
Black	19.	Using Gagne's objectivist approach, I think it would be
|	20.	*necessary* to establish expectancies (event 2) so that the
|	21.	learner would be oriented to the import of the role-play.
|	22.	The role-play itself would inform events 4, 5, and 6. An
|	23.	after action review would inform events 7, 8, and 9. (I
|	24.	think.)
|	25.	But, if I'm approaching this as a constructivist, doesn't
|	26.	the mere act of "framing" expectancies taint the the learner
|	27.	with my "construction" of the right outcome? So, shouldn't
|	28.	the role playing leave the learner free to construct or
|	29.	derive meaning from the experience without prejudice?
|	30.	
Blue	31.	Stella counters:
Black	32.	Dave's explanation of framing role plays shows that they are
|	33.	suited to more than just constructivist approaches. But in
|	34.	my understanding, a constructivist approach doesn't mean you
|	35.	don't have objectives or goals of learning. The instructor
|	36.	introduces the role play and desired outcomes. The learner
|	37.	interacts in the role play, constructing his own
|	38.	interpretation or meaning in relation to the outcome. <...>

FIG. 14.8. Other-initiated repair in the context of reconstructed turn-taking. *Note.* From "Reconstucting Talk: Conversational Patterns in the Asynchronous Classroom," by D. J. Winiecki, in press, in D. Penrod (Ed.), *WebTalk: Writing as Conversation*, Hillsdale, NJ: Lawrence Erlbaum Associates.

Formulations in ACMC. As has been shown, asynchronous discussions can contain many comments from many persons. The result is seen as a prolonged series of messages in a thread (A in Fig. 14.9). In a situation where multiple snips representing reconstructed turns and overlaps are included in each subsequence of a long thread, the size of the resulting message will eventually grow to the point where the economizing potential of reconstructed turns and overlaps is lost. In a situation like this, experienced students in an online course have been observed to formulate, or (synopsize) components of prior messages so that the gist of what has been said is reduced to one or two sentences (B in Fig. 14.9). Thus, formulations can be used to reduce a large amount of information into a short statement.

Formulations have also been used to clarify the purpose, or illocution (Austin, 1962), of a message, disambiguate a comment, and signal a topic shift (Winiecki, in press). In all cases, the formulation is a mechanism for including meta-information in a comment. In other words, a formulation provides information about the information in a message.

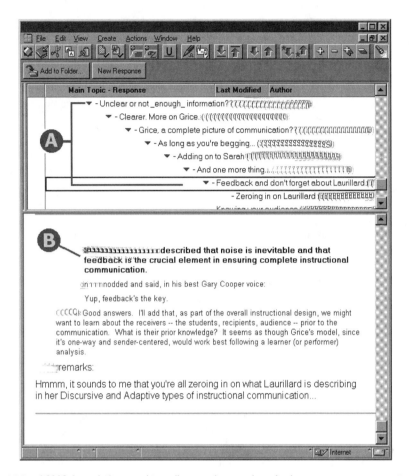

FIG. 14.9. ACMC formulation used to collapse a long series of prior messages or reconstructed terms. (Lotus Notes)

The literature on synchronous and asynchronous CMC indicates that features of the media used to conduct synchronous CMC affect how conversational practice is accomplished. Research has also found that interactants actively adapt conversation patterns and develop new techniques that accommodate for media features and constraints in ways that resemble conversational patterns commonly found in face-to-face conversation.

PROPOSING A TECHNOLOGY FOR ASYNCHRONOUS INSTRUCTIONAL DISCUSSIONS

Applying Research on the Structure of Online Instructional Discussion

The original research reported above takes a conversation analytic approach (Sacks, 1963) and adopts one of its principles—that scientific research on human action must begin through a close description of the object of analysis. In this research, the object of analysis is asynchronous instructional discussion in distance education. In particular, this research addresses the discursive "talk-in-interaction" patterns that constitute asynchronous discussion. This research has identified four principal patterns of asynchronous discussion: reconstruction of turn-taking, overlap, repair, and formulations.

Following Sacks' (1963) research, once the constituent components of asynchronous discussion are adequately described, we may begin to work toward a scientific understanding of how students learn from discussion in asynchronous classroom environments. The findings of this research can be considered as an early step in the development of an authentic technology (Clark & Estes, 1999a, 1999b) for conducting online instructional discussion. For now, however, the following research-based techniques are proposed as a starting point for improving the practice of asynchronous instructional discussion.

Reconstructing Turns to Clarify the Sender's Intended Reading of Prior Comments. As indicated by Black et al. (1983) and Quinn et al. (1983), it is common for interactants in ACMC to include multiple topics in their messages. A writer responding to any message will insert an appropriately threaded message in the threaded display (Fig. 14.6). However, when replying to a message containing more than one topic, the writer can increase the clarity of his or her message by including a strategic snip of the previous message to let readers know what part of that message is being replied to (Winiecki, in press). This has the effect of reconstructing turn-taking so that the subsequent message can be read and understood as a conventional conversation.

In addition to being an adaptation of the common turn-taking system, this reconstruction of turns also reflects an effort to initiate the convergent phase in the conversation. In an instructional discussion, for example, by signifying that a convergent phase is being initiated, the instructor (or another student) can clarify that the goal is shifting and that the others in the discussion are expected to direct their energies at the new goal being posed in that message.

Reconstructing Overlap to Clarify How Multiple Topics Are Being Answered. If a reply to a multitopic message will actually address more than one of the topics, the message creator can use strategic snips of the desired topics and reconstruct turns in such a way as to overlap each topical TCU. Although retaining the potential clarifying effects of reconstructed turns, this technique also signals that the message is not attempting to enter a convergent phase simply because it continues to address more than one topic.

Reconstructing Repairs. As shown by McHoul (1978, 1990), repairs in instructional conversation (or recitation) are valuable from an instructional standpoint to improve the probability that all students are aware of correct information. By using the reconstruction of turns and/or overlaps to introduce instructional repairs, the instructor (or other students) can reorient the discussion so that misunderstandings are repaired and correct information is always available.

Formulating Important Information. The technique of reconstructing turns acts to economize the cognitive effort of readers in ACMC by specifying the history of a particular comment. However, continued replies to messages containing reconstructed turns can grow to a large size, destroying the otherwise economizing effect. Formulating prior messages and reconstructed turns into a succinct comment before entering a reply can restore the economy.

These four techniques for improving online instructional discussions are based on the qualitative observation of conversational behavior in instructional ACMC. Students in instructional ACMC have shown, through their use of these techniques and their reactions to messages that don't include these techniques, that they improve the instructional efficacy of instructional discussion. The precise effect of these techniques is not yet known, however, nor is the point at which they become relevant in an instructional discussion.

CONCLUSION

Although many instructional methods are effective in online education, discussion is particularly appropriate for the social analysis, synthesis, and evaluation of instructional content. As shown above, business-oriented decision-making scenarios and instructional discussions follow a similar topography—a series of divergent and convergent phases in which the group first identifies information of potential relevance to the group's goal (divergent), followed by guided analysis, synthesis, and evaluation of this information on the way to reaching conclusions or decisions.

The original research included in this chapter is used to present descriptions of computer-mediated conversation that are based on sociologically oriented conversation analytic research. The advice presented is offered as a prototype technology for identifying divergent or convergent behavior of students in an online instructional discussion. Online instructors can use this information to guide their decisions to prompt students toward divergent activity or convergent activity. Additionally, online instructors and students can use this information to explicitly model divergent and convergent activity to classmates or perhaps signal a switch from one phase to another. Finally, it is hoped that the research reported here can be used as the foundation for further research to create an "authentic technology" (Clark & Estes, 1999a, 1999b) for facilitating online instructional discussion.

REFERENCES

Austin, J. (1962). *How to do things with words*. Oxford: Oxford University Press.

Baron, N. (1998). Letters by phone or speech by other means: The linguistics of email. *Language & Communication, 18*, 133–170.

Baym, N. (1996). Agreements and disagreements in a computer-mediated discussion. *Research on Language and Social Interaction, 29*, 315–345.

Black, S., Levin, J., Mehan, H., & Quinn, C. (1983). Real and non-real time interaction: Unraveling multiple threads of discourse. *Discourse Processes, 6*, 59–75.

Bresler, L. (1990). Computer-mediated communication in a high school: The users shape the medium (Part 1). *Journal of Mathematical Behavior, 9*, 131–149.

Bringham, M., & Corbett, J. M. (1997). E-mail, power and the constitution of organizational reality. *New Technology, Work and Employment, 12*(1), 25–35.

Brookfield, S. J. (1998). Discussion. In M. W. Galbraith (Ed.), *Adult learning methods: A guide for effective instruction* (Vol. 2; pp. 169–186). Malabar, FL: Krieger.

Cerratto, T., & Waern, Y. (2000). Chatting to learn and learning to chat in collaborative virtual environments. *M/C: A Journal of Media and Culture, 3*(4). Available <http://www.api-network.com/mc/0008/learning.html>

Cherny, L. (1999). *Conversation and community: Chat in a virtual world*. Stanford, CA: Center for the Study of Language and Information.

Clark, R. E., & Estes, F. (1999a, March-April). The development of authentic educational technologies. *Educational Technology*, 5–15.

Clark, R. E., & Estes, F. (1999b, November-December). Authentic educational technology: The lynchpin between theory and practice. *Educational Technology*, 5–13.

Couper-Kuhlen, E., & Selting, M. (1996). *Prosody in conversation: Interactional studies*. Cambridge: Cambridge University Press.

Duranti, A. (1986). Framing discourse in a new medium: Openings in electronic mail. *Quarterly Newsletter of the Laboratory of Comparative Human Cognition, 8*(2), 64–71.

Ferrara, K., Brunner, H., & Whittemore, G. (1991). Interactive written discourse as an emergent register. *Written communication, 8*(1), 8–34.

Ford, C. E. (1999). Collaborative construction of task activity: Coordinating multiple resources in a high school physics lab. *Research on Language and Social Interaction, 32*, 369–408.

Fulk, J., Schmitz, J. A., & Schwarz, D. (1992). The dynamics of context-behavior interactions in computer-mediated communication. In M. Lea (Ed.), *Contexts of computer-mediated communication* (pp. 7–29). Hertfordshire, England: Harvester Wheatsheaf.

Gagné, R., Briggs, L., & Wager, W. (1992). *Principles of instructional design* (6th ed.). Fort Worth, TX.: Harcourt Brace Jovanovich.

Gains, J. (1999). Electronic mail: A new style of communication or just a new medium? An investigation into the text features of e-mail. *English for Special Purposes, 18*(1), 81–101.

Gall, J. P., & Gall, M. D. (1990). Outcomes of the discussion method. In W. W. Wilen (Ed.), *Teaching and learning through discussion: The theory, research, and practice of the discussion method.* (pp. 25–44). Springfield, IL: Charles C Thomas.

Garcia, A. C., & Jacobs, J. B. (1998). The interactional organization of computer-mediated communication in the college classroom. *Qualitative Sociology, 21*, 299–317.

Garcia, A. C., & Jacobs, J. B. (1999). The eyes of the beholder: Understanding the turn-taking system in quasi-synchronous computer-mediated communication. *Research on Language and Social Interaction, 32*, 337–367.

Garfinkel, H., & Sacks, H. (1970). On formal structures of practical action. In J. C. McKinney & E. A. Tiryakian (Eds.), *Theoretical sociology: Perspectives and developments* (pp. 337–366). New York: Appleton-Century-Crofts.

Harasim, L., Hiltz, S. R., Teles, L., & Turoff, M. (1996). *Learning networks: A field guide to teaching and learning online.* Cambridge, MA: MIT Press.

Heritage, J. C. (1985). Analyzing news interviews: Aspects of the production of talk for an overhearing audience. In T. v. Dijk (Ed.), *Handbook of discourse analysis* (Vol. 3; 95–119). London: Academic Press.

Heritage, J. C. (1997). Conversation analysis and institutional talk. In D. Silverman (Ed.), *Qualitative research: Theory, method and practice* (pp. 161–182). Thousand Oaks, CA: Sage.

Heritage, J. C., & Watson, D. R. (1979). Formulations as conversational objects. In G. Psathas (Ed.), *Everyday language: Studies in ethnomethodology* (pp. 123–162). New York: Irvington.

Hermann, F. (October 1995). *Listserver communication: The discourse of community building.* Paper presented at CSCL 95, Computer Support for Cooperative Learning, Bloomington, IN.

Herring, S. C. (1996). *Computer-mediated communication: Linguistic, social and cross-cultural perspectives.* Philadelphia: John Benjamins Publishing Co.

Heyman, R. D. (1986). Formulating topic in the classroom. *Discourse Processes, 9*(1), 37–55.

Hopper, R. (1992). *Telephone conversation.* Bloomington, IN: Indiana University Press.

Hutchby, I., & Wooffitt, R. (1998). *Conversation analysis: Principles, practices, and applications.* Cambridge: Polity Press.

Jefferson, G. (1986). Notes on latency in overlap onset. *Human Studies, 9*, 153–183.

Kiesler, S., Siegel, J., & McGuire, T. W. (1984). Social psychological aspects of computer-mediated communication. *American Psychologist, 39*, 1123–1134.

Larson, B. E. (2000). Classroom discussion: A method of instruction and a curriculum outcome. *Teaching and Teacher Education, 16*, 661–677.

Laurillard, D. (1993). *Rethinking university teaching: A framework for the effective use of educational technology.* London: Routledge.

McCarthy, J., Wright, P., & Monk, A. (1992). Coherence in text-based electronic conferencing: Coupling text and context. *Journal of Language and Social Psychology, 11*, 267–277.

McHoul, A. (1978). The organization of turns at formal talk in the classroom. *Language in Society, 7*, 183–213.

McHoul, A. (1990). The organization of repair in classroom talk. *Language in Society, 19*, 349–377.

McIsaac, M. S., & Gunawardena, C. N. (1996). Distance education. In D. J. Jonassen (Ed.), *Handbook of research for educational communications and technology* (pp. 403–437). New York: Macmillan.

Mehan, H. (1978). The competent student. *Anthropology & Education Quarterly, 11*(3), 131–152.

Mulkay, M. (1985). Conversations and texts: Structural sources of dialogic failure. In M. Mulkay (Ed.), *The word and the world: Explorations in the form of sociological analysis* (pp. 79–102). London: Allen & Unwin.

Murray, D. E. (1989). When the medium determines turns: Turn-taking in computer conversation. In H. Coleman (Ed.), *Working with language: A multidisciplinary consideration of language use in work contexts* (pp. 319–337). New York: Mouton de Gruyter.

Murray, D. E. (1991). The composing process for computer conversation. *Written Communication, 8*(1), 35–55.

Muscella, D., & DiMauro, V. (1995). *Talking about science: The case of an electronic conversation* (ERIC Document Reproduction Service No. ED 395765)

Nelson, C. K. (1994). Ethnomethodological positions on the use of ethnographic data in conversation analytic research. *Journal of Contemporary Ethnography, 23*, 307–329.

Owen, M. (2000). Structure and discourse in a telematic learning environment. *Educational Technology & Society, 3*(3), 179–189.

Phillips, G. M., & Santoro, G. M. (1989). Teaching group discussion via computer-mediated communication. *Communication Education, 38*, 151–161.

Quinn, C., Mehan, H., Levin, J., & Black, S. (1983). Real education in non-real time: The use of electronic message systems for instruction. *Instructional Science, 11*, 313–327.

Reed, D. (2000). *Making conversation: Sequential integrity and the local management of interaction on Internet newsgroups.* Unpublished Manuscript.

Reed, D., & Ashmore, M. (2000). The naturally occurring chat machine. *M/C: A Journal of Media and Culture,*3(4) Available: [http://www.api-network.com/mc/0008/machine.html]

Rice, R. E. (1992). Contexts of research on organizational computer-mediated communication: A recursive review. In M. Lea (Ed.), *Contexts of computer-mediated communication* (pp. 113–144). London: Harvester Wheatsheaf.

Rintel, E. S., & Pittam, J. (1997). Strangers in a strange land: Interaction management on Internet Relay Chat. *Human Communication Research, 23,* 507–534.

Romiszowski, A. J., & Mason, R. (1996). Computer-mediated communication. In D. J. Jonassen (Ed.), *Handbook of research for educational communications and technology* (pp. 438–456). New York: Macmillan.

Sacks, H. (1963). Sociological description. *Berkeley Journal of Sociology, 8,* 1–16.

Sacks, H., Schegloff, E., & Jefferson, G. (1978). A simplest systematics for the organization of turn taking for conversation. In J. Schenkein (Ed.), *Studies in the organization of conversational interaction* (pp. 7–55). New York: Academic Press.

Salmon, G. (2000). *E-moderating: The key to teaching and learning online.* London: Kogan Page.

Schegloff, E. A. (1972). Notes on a conversational practice: Formulating place. In D. Sudnow (Ed.), *Studies in social interaction* (pp. 75–119). New York: The Free Press.

Schegloff, E. A. (1986). The routine as achievement. *Human Studies, 9,* 111–152.

Schegloff, E. A. (1991). Conversation analysis and socially shared cognition. In L. B. Resnick, J. M. Levine, & S. D. Teasly (Eds.), *Perspectives on socially shared cognition* (pp. 150–171). Washington, DC: American Psychological Association.

Schegloff, E. A. (2000). Overlapping talk and the organization of turn-taking in conversation. *Language in Society, 29*(1), 1–63.

Schegloff, E. A., Jefferson, G., & Sacks, H. (1977). The preference for self-correction in the organization of repair in conversation. *Language, 53,* 361–382.

Schriner, D. K., & Rice, W. C. (1989). Computer conferencing and collaborative learning: A discourse community at work. *College Composition and Communication, 40,* 472–478.

Spears, R., & Lea, M. (1994). Panacea or panopticon? The hidden power in computer-mediated communication. *Communication Research, 21,* 427–459.

Stanton, J. M., & Weiss, E. M. (2000). Electronic monitoring in their own words: An exploratory study of employees' experiences with new types of surveillance. *Computers in Human Behavior, 16,* 423–440.

ten Have, P. (1999). *Doing conversation analysis: A practical guide.* Thousand Oaks, CA: Sage Publications.

Vygotsky, L. S. (1978). *Mind in society.* Cambridge, MA: Harvard University Press.

Wallace, D. (2000). E-mail and the problems of communication. *M/C: A Journal of Media and Culture, 3*(4) Available <http://www.api-network.com/mc/0008/email.html>

Walther, J. B. (1996). Computer-mediated communication: Impersonal, interpersonal, and hyperpersonal interaction. *Communication Research, 23,* 3–43.

Wasson, B., & Morch, A. I. (2000). Identifying collaboration patterns in collaborative telelearning scenarios. *Educational Technology & Society, 3,* 237–248.

Wilen, W. W. (1990). Forms and phases of discussion. In W. W. Wilen (Ed.), *Teaching and learning through discussion: The theory, research, and practice of the discussion method* (pp. 3–24). Springfield, IL: Charles C Thomas.

Wilkens, H. (1991). Computer talk: Long-distance conversations by computer. *Written Communication, 8*(1), 56–78.

Winiecki, D. J. (1999). Keeping the thread: Adapting conversational practice to help distance students and instructors manage discussions in an asynchronous learning network. *DEOSNEWS* [Online], *9*(2).

Winiecki, D. J. (forthcoming). Reconstructing talk: Conversational patterns in the asynchronous classroom. In D. Penrod (Ed.), *WebTalk: Writing as conversation.* Hillsdale, NJ: Lawrence Erlbaum Associates.

APPENDIX
TRANSCRIPTION GLOSSARY

(0.5)	The number in brackets indicates a time gap in tenths of a second.
(.)	A dot enclosed in a bracket indicates a pause in the talk of less than two-tenths of a second.
=	The 'equals' sign indicates 'latching' between utterances. For examples:

```
S1: yeah September seventy six=
                 [
S2:              September
S1: =it would be
S2: yeah that's right
```

[ ]	Square brackets between adjacent lines of concurrent speech indicate the onset and end of a spate of overlapping talk.
.hh	A dot before an 'h' indicates speaker in-breath. The more h's the longer the breath.
hh	An 'h' indicates an out-breath. The more h's the longer the breath.
(( ))	A description enclosed in a double bracket indicates a non-verbal activity. For example ((banging sound)). Alternatively, double brackets may enclose the transcriber's comments on contextual or other features.
-	A dash indicates the sharp cut-off of the prior word or sound.
:	Colons indicate that the speaker has stretched the preceding sound or letter. The more colons the greater the extent of the stretching.
!	Exclamation marks are used to indicate an animated or emphatic tone.
( )	Empty parentheses indicate the presence of an unclear fragment on the tape.
(guess)	The words within a single bracket indicate the transcriber's best guess at an unclear utterance.
.	A full stop indicates a stopping fall in tone. It does not necessarily indicate the end of a sentence.
,	A comma indicates a 'continuing' intonation.
?	A question mark indicates a rising inflection. It does not necessarily indicate a question.
*	An asterisk indicates a 'croaky' pronunciation of the immediately following section.
↓↑	Pointed arrows indicate a marked falling or rising intonational shift. They are placed immediately before the onset of the shift.
a:	Less marked falls in pitch can be indicated by using underlining immediately preceding a colon:

```
S: we(.) really didn't have a lot'v cha:nge
```

a:	Less marked rises in pitch can be indicated using a colon which itself is underlined:

```
J:  I have a red shi:rt,
```

Under	Underlined fragments indicate speaker emphasis.

CAPITALS	Words in capitals mark a section of speech noticeably louder than that surrounding it.
o o	Degree signs are used to indicate that the talk they encompass is spoken noticeably quieter than the surrounding talk.
Thaght	A 'gh' indicates that the word in which it is placed had a guttural pronunciation.
> <	'More than' and 'less than' signs indicate that the talk they encompass was produced noticeably quicker than the surrounding talk.
→	Arrows in the left margin point to specific parts of an extract discussed in the text.
[H:21.3.89:2]	Extract headings refer to the transcript library source of the researcher who originally collected the data.

Note. From Conversation Analysis: Principles, Practices, and Applications (pp. vi–vii), by I. Hutch by and R. Wooffitt, 1998, Cambridge: Polity Press, 1998. Reprinted with permission.

15

Group Development in Online Learning Communities

Kayleigh Carabajal
The University of New Mexico
kcarabajal@tvi.cc.nm.us

Deborah LaPointe
The University of New Mexico
debla@unm.edu

Charlotte N. Gunawardena
The University of New Mexico
lani@unm.edu

INTRODUCTION

Early proponents of online education presented a compelling vision of computer-mediated communication (CMC) as a medium uniquely capable of supporting the creation of communities of learners actively engaging in time- and place-independent group interaction. Mason and Kaye (1989, p. 3) envisioned this potential as, "a means for the weaving together of ideas and information from many people's minds, regardless of when and from where they contribute." This vision of networked minds presupposes the formation and development of a cohesive group of individuals united in pursuit of a common learning goal. In order to facilitate effective group learning in this medium, it is critically important for educators to understand how online learning groups form, develop, accomplish tasks, and change over time.

The literature of psychology, sociology, and management is rich with group development theory and models developed and validated within a face-to-face environment. Computer-mediated communication (CMC), however, produces social environments markedly different from those commonly observed in face-to-face settings. Research suggests that communication and the very nature of the group itself changes when interactions are computer-mediated (Burt, Grady, & McMann, 1994). While a growing body of research contributes to our understanding of the effects of CMC within learning environments, a dearth of research on group development provides little evidence, other than anecdotal, that effective learning groups can and do develop online (Siegel, Dubrovsky, Kiesler, & McGuire, 1986; McDonald & Gibson, 1998; Sudweeks & Allbritton, 1996).

The challenge faced by online educators is to unite the empirical evidence of the effects of CMC on online learning communities with the literature on group development in order to construct a comprehensive conceptual framework that will guide practice in the design of effective online learning environments. The purpose of this chapter is to discuss group development models, identify variables related to group development within online learning communities (OLCs), and suggest future directions for research on online group development.

THE SOCIAL DIMENSION AND TASK DIMENSION
OF GROUP DEVELOPMENT

Groups are an integral part of society. Group researchers posit that adults voluntarily join groups in an effort to satisfy needs, using them as a powerful tool to promote emotional sustenance and aid in accomplishing tasks. In the ideal form two basic types of small groups exist: primary groups that specialize in the emotional relationships of members, and task groups, which are organized solely to accomplish specific instrumental goals or tasks (Ridgeway, 1983). In reality, all groups have some primary (social)- and some task-group dimensions, and the two types are best viewed as polar extremes of a continuum, not a clear-cut dichotomy (Acock, Dowd, & Roberts, 1974). What differs among groups is the relative importance placed on one pole over the other.

As group members organize themselves in pursuit of their group goals, their attention and the content of their communication progress from one of these dimensions to the other (Ridgeway, 1983). Conflicts develop between high-performance, task-oriented learning goals and the social-emotional needs of the members. When one aspect of this conflict is resolved, the topic of group communication shifts to the next. The more cohesive a group, at any point in time, the greater its ability to resolve the problem of its current stage and move forward into the next. Achieving a balance in this interplay between the social-emotional and task-oriented needs of the individual group members forms the basis for most group development theories explored in the following section.

Group development is a characteristic ascribed to groups as they change over time, a function of both group structure and group process (Hare, Blumberg, Davies, & Kent, 1994; Ridgeway, 1983; Mennecke, Hoffer, & Wynn, 1992). The formation of group structure, i.e., the emergence of statuses, roles, and norms, occurs during the process of group development. Group processes are composed of the constantly changing patterned behaviors or interactions through which the group progresses toward a goal. Group development represents "the degree of maturity and cohesion that a group achieves over time as members interact, learn about one another, and structure relationships and roles within the group" (Mennecke et al., 1992, p. 526).

THEORIES OF GROUP DEVELOPMENT APPLIED TO CMC

The notion that groups progress through a natural series of stages over their life cycle has long been shared by researchers. While some interest in the stages of group development can be seen in the writings of behavioral scientists in the 1920s and 1930s, Bales conducted the first empirical studies in the early 1950s (Hare, 1976). Since then, studies relying on observer reflections (Bennis & Shepard, 1956; Bion, 1961) and empirical studies employing observation systems (Bales & Strodbeck, 1951; Schutz, 1958; Wheelan & McKeage, 1993) support the conclusion that as groups move through stages associated with successive turning points in the cycle of group activities, these stages can be identified and described (Wheelan & Kaeser, 1997).

Several widely accepted models have been proposed in an attempt to define how groups develop over time. Mennecke et al. (1992) posit that group development models may generally be classified into one of three categories: progressive, cyclical, and nonsequential models. Early progressive and cyclical models focus on the sequential stages of group development. More recently, nonsequential models shift this focus and recognize contingent factors that may impact and alter the stages observed. A reconciliation or convergence in these models is, however, possible. In this section, two prominent examples of each category are presented, illustrated by studies within the context of CMC. Strikingly, few such studies exist, leaving the development of online groups largely uninvestigated (McDonald & Gibson, 1998).

Progressive Models

Progressive models imply that groups exhibit an increasing degree of maturity and performance over time (Mennecke et al., 1992). Bales' (1950) equilibrium model assumed that a group is continually dividing its efforts between instrumental (task-related) needs and expressive (social-emotional) needs. Bales proposed a systematic classification system to study the occurrence of instrumental and expressive acts as the group seeks to maintain this balance through three distinct progressive phases: (i) orientation (exploration), (ii) evaluation (seeking opinions), and (iii) control (norms that guide action). Successful group outcomes are dependent on two factors, how well it can solve the tasks facing it (task function) and how well the group can maintain member satisfaction (socioemotional function).

In perhaps the most widely known group development model, Tuckman (1965; Tuckman & Jensen, 1977) synthesized the results from 50 earlier studies and presented a linear "Team Development Model" that assumes groups develop in a definite order of progression from one phase to the next. This model defines five stages of group development: (i) forming (dependence and testing), (ii) storming (conflict), (iii) norming (structure and cohesion), (iv) performing (goal attainment), and (v) mourning (adjournment). Each of the stages contains two aspects: interpersonal relationships (group structure) and task behaviors. This distinction is similar to that of Bales' task-oriented and socioemotional behaviors (Bales & Strodbeck, 1951).

Gunawardena et al. (2001) used Tuckman's progressive model to examine if there are differences in perception of online group process and development between participants in Mexico and in the United States. Survey data indicated significant differences in perception for the norming and performing stages of group development. The groups also differed in their perception of collectivism, low power distance, femininity, and high-context communication. Country differences, rather than age and gender differences, accounted for the differences observed. Focus group participants identified several factors that influence online group process and development: (i) language, (ii) power distance, (iii) gender difference, (iv) collectivist versus individualist tendencies, (v) conflict, (vi) social presence, and (vii) time frame and technical skills.

Cyclical Models

Cyclical models may be categorized as either linear or recurring. A linear life cycle model assumes a sequence of events that are similar to other life cycle models—a cycle of birth, growth, maturation, and, finally, death. These models differ from the progressive models by the emphasis placed on the terminal phase prior to group dissolution or regeneration (Mennecke et al., 1992). Mann, Gibbard, and Hartmann (1967) presented a life cycle model used to describe the group's behavior toward leaders. It specified the character and behavior of subgroups and how these subgroups influenced the group's "center of gravity" (Hare, 1976).

Recurring cyclical models have in common the assumption that groups continually absorb themselves with the same issues, oscillating between various issues that can never be resolved in more than a partial or temporary way (Mann et al., 1967). Phases emerge, recede, and reemerge to be confronted in greater depth (Sudweeks & Allbritton, 1996). The "fundamental interpersonal relationships orientation" (FIRO) (Schutz, 1958) model attempts to explain group development in response to three interpersonal needs: (i) inclusion of members in the group, (ii) control of members' activities, and (iii) affection between members. Schutz' theory maintains that interpersonal areas of need do not occur in mutually exclusive phases. All three areas are always present, each emphasized at different times. Every interpersonal relation is based upon a principle of group integration and group resolution. Group members will back out of the group using a sequence of behaviors opposite the sequence used as they entered the group.

McDonald and Gibson (1998) applied Schutz' (1958) model to investigate the characteristics and patterns of social interactions in asynchronous (not real-time) CMC groups to determine patterns of group development based on interpersonal needs. They investigated whether predictable patterns of communication could be discovered within the complex text-based corpora of asynchronous interactions. Through qualitative analysis of the content of messages, predictable patterns emerged and were detected, with interpersonal issues constituting 40%–75% of communication interaction. The researchers concluded that online groups could, in fact, deal with the interpersonal needs of members and form into cohesive, functioning groups; further, factors inherent within the technology, i.e., text-based, time-independent, computer-mediated interaction, require adjustments in teaching techniques and learning strategies.

Nonsequential Models

In contrast, nonsequential models do not imply any specific sequence of events; rather, the events that occur are assumed to result from contingent factors that change the focus of the group's activities. From this perspective, groups may follow different developmental paths based on the interplay of variables that impact group structure and group process.

According to McGrath's (1990, 1991) "Time, Interaction, and Performance" (TIP) model, groups interact with and contribute to systems at three levels and perform three distinct functions: production, well-being, and member-support functions. These functions are similar to the task-related and socioemotional needs that Bales (1950) and others (Tuckman, 1965) have suggested groups must attend to during group interaction. Groups realize these functions through several modes of group activity and group process: inception, problem solving, conflict resolution, and execution (performance). The TIP model represents a multidimensional view of group process incorporating the interaction of the group function and the projects or tasks undertaken by the group. The TIP model also suggests that group process and development must be investigated both in terms of task-related behaviors and their socioemotional behaviors. According to McGrath (1990, 1991) viewing groups on one dimension alone is insufficient for understanding how a group develops over time.

Gersick (1988, 1989) proposed a punctuated equilibrium model that posits group development and change occur in a somewhat discontinuous, stepwise manner. Stable periods of "habitual routines" are altered by abrupt transitional periods. Groups hold to current practices (an equilibrium position) until forced to alter those practices because of crises or temporal constraints (a state of disequilibrium). This model is built on the premise that the patterns of behavior observed through group development will vary in a dependent manner according to the cues encountered by the group as they process a task.

Sudweeks and Allbritton (1996) explored the concepts of collaborative communication patterns and group development processes by applying a combinational model based upon Tuckman's (1965) progressive model and influenced by the theoretical perspective of Gersick (1988, 1989) in a "natural" electronic group setting. In comparing the results of their analysis with results predicted within a face-to-face group, they concluded that collaborative groups within a CMC environment exhibit delayed developmental stages, taking longer to develop norms and social relationships, and plan and assign tasks. They concluded that any model of group development must understand and account for the interplay of task-related and socioemotional processes. This research represents a pioneering attempt to apply a convergent perspective to group development by exploring progressive, sequential stages in group development in combination with contingent factors.

From the many views outlined in this brief overview, it is evident that group development is a complex process, yet some consistent themes run through the apparently divergent perspectives. Because most models were developed in highly dissimilar settings, ranging from therapy groups to ad hoc experimental groups, it is hardly surprising that different observers see varying numbers of stages, that different events are emphasized, and that different labels are attached to basically similar processes. However, all models, other than the punctuated equilibrium model (Gersick, 1988, 1989), possess similar stages. This suggests that each of the models likely represent one example of many different possible development paths that groups potentially pass through as a consequence of variations in number of variables (Mennecke et al., 1992). More recent models acknowledge that the precise nature or sequence of development varies with the group structure, group composition, situation or behavioral setting in which the group must function, goals of the group, physical and technological environment, task type, and other contingencies (McGrath, 1990, 1991; Poole & Roth, 1989; Mennecke et al., 1992).

Second, it is also likely that certain stages found consistently throughout the models are crucial for a group to achieve success as it develops, but that the order in which they occur may be less important than was proposed by earlier sequential models (Poole, 1983). This suggests that if the contingent factors warrant, at least some of the traditional phases will be observed as a group develops over time (McGrath, 1990, 1991). Further, the health and success of a group may be in jeopardy if the member-support (social dimension) functions of the group are neglected (McGrath, 1991; Mennecke et al., 1992).

Finally, over time, newer models of group development assume a less deterministic and far more dynamic view of group development. According to Mennecke et al. (1992), the nonsequential models share the following concepts: (i) groups are composed of individuals who not only contribute resources but also diminish resources within the group, and (ii) groups are components of a larger system responding to inputs from the environment and generating outputs for that environment. This dynamic and adaptive approach is in direct contrast to the earlier progressive and cyclical models that inherently assume groups to be closed systems possessing a static developmental pattern unresponsive to environmental demands.

THE GROUP AS A SYSTEM AND THE TECHNOLOGICAL DIMENSION

Increasingly, researchers are viewing groups as social systems. From this perspective, every component in the system affects and is subsequently affected by every other component. A change in one component affects changes in all other components as the process evolves over time, and focusing on one part to the exclusion of another distorts our understanding of the whole. Groups are open systems that have free interchange and communication with the external environment, which also means that a group will be influenced by the environment.

Arrow, McGrath, and Berdahl (2000) argue for a systems perspective in the study of groups by positing that not only are groups complex, adaptive, and dynamic, but also that any definition of a group must also include the tools used by the members. This sets the stage for the addition of a technological dimension to the investigation of online group development. OLCs interact, form, and develop using networked telecommunication systems as tools to facilitate encoding, transmitting, and decoding messages. Members of OLCs create, exchange, perceive information, and engage in group activities via synchronous (real-time) or asynchronous (delayed-time) formats. Computer-mediated (CM) groups promote different communicative behaviors because CM environments are subjected to the influence of three attributes of the medium that impact the nature of the communication interaction: time independence, text-based communication, and computer-mediated interaction (Harasim, 1989, 1990). These attributes have a profound effect upon group structure, process, and development within OLCs.

Time-Independent Communication

Most OLCs are based on asynchronous communication enabling learners ample time to reflect before contributing to the group discussion. Such critical reflection should serve as a contributing factor to the overall achievement of learning goals; however, communication anxiety (the feeling of speaking into a vacuum) can result when a group member receives no immediate reaction or response to comments posted online (Feenberg, 1989). The technology that affords rapid exchange also makes unusual delay in acknowledgment a sign of rejection by the group. This unpredictable time lag between sending and receiving messages also makes the achievement of social cohesiveness, so necessary for effective performance of a group task, problematic (Davies, 1989).

Text-Based Communication

Initial phases of group development in this text-based medium may evidence a social equality unlike that found in face-to-face groups. Status development and differentiation is likely based upon influential messages rather than hierarchical status based on physical and social cues such as gender, race, socioeconomic status, and physical features (Harasim, 1989). Freeing people from the bonds of physical appearance may serve to enable communication at the level of ideas (Harasim, 1993) and increase active participation by otherwise normally reticent members of the group. Gunawardena et al. (2001) noted in a recent cross-cultural study that in countries where power-distance is greater, CMC is perceived as an equalizing medium. The absence of nonverbal cues such as voice intonations, facial expressions, and gestures may lead to misunderstanding of the intent of the communication, making it difficult to resolve conflicts of ideology or interest (Harasim, 1990, 1993). The simultaneous submission of messages to all members of the group facilitates the free exchange of ideas, the sharing of multiple perspectives, and the creation of an interpersonal distance resulting in an equalizing effect on participation (Olaniran, 1994). However, participants who do not perceive themselves to be good writers may be less likely to post messages that will be viewed universally. This may prove particularly constraining to non-native speakers of the language (Gunawardena et al., 2001).

Computer-Mediated Interaction

CMC is an interactive medium that encourages active participation from participants. While OLCs are particularly appropriate for collaborative learning approaches because they support the shared space essential for sustained group interactivity, participants who do not desire to interact or who have poor computer skills are less likely to participate. Discussions, featuring evenly distributed participation, are what this medium fosters best. CMC does not lend itself to patterns of leadership and the assumption of group roles that involve one person dominating the shared space for a long period of time.

ORGANIZATIONAL FRAMEWORK FOR UNDERSTANDING CURRENT RESEARCH IN CMC

During the past fifteen years researchers have investigated the causes for the process and performance differences found between face-to-face and CM groups with varying success. Researchers have debated the underlying mechanisms for the differences found with explanations ranging from information-restrictive to social process–driven perspectives (Hiltz, Johnson, & Turoff, 1987). According to Walther and Burgoon (1992), most of the research in this area has been conducted without much guidance from preexisting theory, or even from a common framework. In addition, only a few studies have examined the process differences that may occur within different CM conditions. Understanding how different groups form and develop within variant CMC environments may help illuminate the differences between groups.

By definition, all groups consist of two or more members who must be aware of their membership within the group, have a common goal, and have some degree of interdependence (McGrath, 1984). Since all groups function within a dynamic environment, their development is tempered by many different elements. One model for analyzing the elements that impact group behaviors and performance has been presented by Hackman and Morris (1975). This model suggests that groups are bounded by three phases of group patterns that include entry (E), process (P), and outcome (O) variables. Entry elements consist of all contingency factors present at the outset of the group formation: member characteristics, culture, group size, access to resources, task type, behavioral setting, and externally imposed time constraints. Process elements are the influences on the group that stem from the actual activities in which the group engages: communication interaction, cohesion, work and participation norms, process procedures (i.e., decision making and problem solving), and leadership. Group communication interaction consists of the frequency, distribution, direction, and influence of communication within the group. Outcomes are what the group produces and achieves and may include tangible deliverables such as reports, projects, and documents, but also less tangible outputs such as the quality of the outcomes, member satisfaction, and changes in the nature of the group. A group's outcome is shaped by certain entry variables that are mediated by the communication interactions occurring between the group members (Lorsch, 1987). This model suggests that the differences between particular entry elements and outcomes may be traced in time to specific changes in the functioning or process of the group. Figure 15.1 presents an organizational framework for investigating the group process variables as they are embedded within the dimensions impacting group development in OLCs.

The hexagons in the framework represent the dimensions of online group development. The task and social dimensions are recognized as forces underlying the process of group development in face-to-face environments. The addition of the technological dimension acknowledges the third consideration in online environments (Harasim, 1993). The three diamonds represent the group system variables or contingency factors that may impact differential developmental paths in OLCs. The arrows in the diagram represent the dynamic process through which entry elements influence group processes and these, in turn, influence outcomes and group history. The majority of research on the effects of CMC has targeted outcomes, leaving the impact of entry elements such as task type and behavioral setting largely unexplored. This organizational

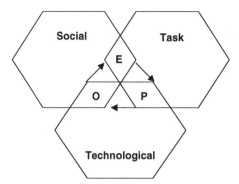

FIG. 15.1. Organizational framework including group process variables and the dimensions that impact group development in OLCs.

framework provides a comprehensive model for uniting the empirical evidence of the effects of CMC on online learning communities, the unique attributes of CMC, and the dimensions of traditional group development theory. The following section presents research relating to each dimension and group process variable utilizing this organizational scheme.

ONLINE GROUP DIMENSIONS

Technological Dimension

Research relating to the technological dimension indicates the choice of the CMC technology has important consequences for the successful accomplishment of group tasks and the successful maintenance of the group (Ahern & El-Hindi, 2000). The technology provides a gathering place that reinforces the group's purpose and meets its needs (Kim, 2000). The technological dimension has both a technical and a social component. The effectiveness of the communication medium is largely dependent upon the tools that facilitate a shared dialogue (Gallini & Zhang, 1997), and, for a given task, depends on the degree to which there is a fit between the richness of information that can be transmitted and the information richness requirements of the task (Hollingshead, McGrath, & O'Connor, 1993). The technology must allow group members to contribute private knowledge, provide scaffolded assistance and the interaction tools needed to adequately relate concepts, experience, and knowledge, and provide a space for the group's working memory, long-term memory, and archives for the group's extended memory (Smith, 1994).

From the social perspective, a critical factor in the technology is its social presence, defined as the degree of salience of the other person in the interaction and the consequent salience of the interpersonal relationship. Social presence is both a factor of the medium as well as of the communicators and their presence (Gunawardena & Zittle, 1997). Social presence determines the degree to which collaborative partners perceive each other, moderates the communication that focuses on the socioemotional communication, and maintains the group's well being.

Task Dimension

A predominant finding is that CMC and face-to-face groups differ in the frequency and content of interactions with face-to-face groups generating more communication units than CMC. While CMC groups may generate fewer messages, they compensate by exchanging more task-oriented messages as a proportion of their total messages (Hillman, 1999; Kahai & Cooper,

1999) and outperform face-to-face groups on brainstorming tasks (Hollingshead, McGrath and O'Connor, 1993). The diversity of opinions generated may be responsible for the fact that CMC groups experience more difficulty reaching consensus and exhibit more choice shift (defined as the degree in which team decisions differ from the initial opinions of the members). This productivity loss in CMC groups is overcome as more group members contributing to the group discussion maximize the group's potential (Olanrian, 1994; Hedlund, Ilgen & Hollenbeck, 1998).

Social Dimension

The purpose of every group discussion is twofold: (i) to ensure group goal achievement and (ii) to provide some member satisfaction and keep the group together (Pavitt & Johnson, 1999). The group task interactions involve interaction among multiple participants, who need to maintain some degree of mutual caring and understanding (Baker, Hansen, Joiner, & Traum, 1999). The group task may require group members to question and clarify their underlying assumptions. Group members will have to feel a certain level of caring and trust to disclose those assumptions. Therefore, the social aspect of CMC is an important element that contributes to the overall satisfaction of a task-oriented or academic computer conference (Gunawardena and Zittle, 1997). Research implies only 40% of a face-to-face group process is spent on task-focused interactions, suggesting more than half of a group's communication is off task (Huang & Wei, 2000). The amount of time computer-mediated groups interact humanizing or socializing in their environment is less (Hillman, 1999). This low amount of off-task communication may hinder the computer-mediated group's ability to maintain group well being and provide member support necessary for gaining and maintaining consensus and supporting the group decision or problem solution (McDonald & Gibson, 1998; Kahai & Cooper, 1999). Yet, positive interpersonal relationships can develop in online groups (Brandon & Hollingshead, 1999). In fact, Walther found several instances wherein CMC groups surpassed the level of affection and emotion found in traditional face-to-face groups (Walther, 1996).

GROUP SYSTEM VARIABLES THAT IMPACT ONLINE GROUP DEVELOPMENT

Entry Elements

Member Characteristics/Attitudes/Skills

Each online group member brings his or her existing explicit and tacit knowledge, belief systems, cognitive abilities, and individual ways of constructing new knowledge to the group. The influence of individual members can be quite significant. When one member is particularly adept at the skills required by the group task, that individual's skill shades and shapes the group's success (Pavitt & Johnson, 1999; Alexander & Murphy, 1999). One member's individual sense of authority in a particular knowledge domain or skill area and a sense of how to use resources to upgrade knowledge or skills impact the group's functions (Gallini & Zhang, 1997). As long as teams have one member who is very open to using and learning with technology, teams have the potential to take advantage of process gains offered by computer-assisted communication technologies (Colquitt, LePine, Hollenbeck, Ilgen, & Sheppard, 2002). Other studies have found the effects of gender differences maintain themselves in online communication with men focusing on task-oriented activities and women on group maintenance activities (Dennis, Kinney, & Hung, 1999).

Group Size

Group size has been found to affect idea generation (Mennecke & Valacich, 1998). CMC is interactive, and its success in accomplishing tasks requires worthwhile contributions from all group members. Critical group size seems to be approximately seven members (Mennecke & Valacich, 1998). As online group size increases, the proportion of messages contributed by the most active members remains constant at approximately 44 percent. Other members, however, contribute proportionately fewer messages (Bonito & Hollingshead, 1997). This decreased participation results as group members feel the group becomes less efficacious with increased membership.

Task Types

Tasks vary in terms of their scale, complexity, duration, solution, multiplicity, intellectual activities, and required style of interaction (Smith, 1994; Benbasat & Lim, 1993). Much of the variation found in group process and outcomes between face-to-face groups and CMC groups is the result of task type (Baltes, Dickson, Sherman, Bauer, & LaGanke, 2002). The differences among types of tasks require different styles of group communication and technology support, which accordingly influences and moderates group processes (Huang & Wei, 2000; Wheelan & Kaeser, 1997).

Problem-solving tasks are of two types—judgmental and intellective. Judgmental tasks have no demonstrably correct solutions, focus the interaction on discussing members' opinions, and reach for consensus. Intellective tasks have a correct solution, focus the interaction on the exchange of information, and reach for decision-making. Intellective tasks require technology such as databases and expert performance support systems to help group members find the correct answer and deal with the rationale for choices (Benbasat & Lim, 1993).

The decision-making involved in intellective tasks requires convergent thinking, which is more difficult to achieve in CMC's text-based environment (Harasim, 1993; Jehng, 1997). Members must reconcile divergent information, attitudes, opinions, and mixed motives. Certain types of CMC formats such as debate formats may further hinder online groups from coming to group synthesis (Gunawardena, Lowe, & Anderson, 1997).

Hidden-profile tasks distribute unique, yet complementary information to each group member. Although all the information from all group members is needed to effectively complete the tasks, group members frequently fail to disclose their unique information as they feel they are in a minority position, holding a piece of information inconsistent with the information held by others (Mennecke & Valacich, 1998). Consequently as tasks grow in size and complexity, maintaining consistency and coherence in group products and process becomes increasingly important and difficult, requiring more organization, more of the group's resources, and more support technology to ensure full and equal participation (Smith, 1994).

Behavioral Setting

The group's behavioral setting mediates online group development. The communication and learning processes embedded within institutions create social structures. These social structures determine (i) what gets said and by whom, (ii) standard ways of communicating called communicative genres, and (iii) the template that helps identify the group as a distinct community (Ahern & El-Hindi, 2000). Online courses take on the values, expectations, genre, and template of face-to-face class communication patterns, roles, and expectations. Group participants share a schema for how interactions within an educational setting are conducted. Online group members select a role suited to those expectations and behave accordingly in online courses. Such adoption of a shared understanding of roles, events, and expected educational tasks affects group communication, thereby creating less need for explicit communication (Mennecke & Valacich, 1998).

Culture

Culture impacts online group development and process as cultural groups apply their rules for interacting and using artifacts to the online environment. Major cultural differences expressed through different ways of communicating and interacting and differences in communication styles reveal themselves in CMC (Gunawardena et al., 2001). In Gunawardena et al.'s (2001) study, Mexico and USA groups differed in their perception of collectivism, power distance, femininity, and high context communication. The Mexico group felt CMC equalized status differences while the USA group felt CMC's lack of nonverbal cues led to misunderstandings.

Process Elements

Participation

Differences in participation are a function of group composition entry variables (Bonito & Hollingshead, 1997) but wield a large impact on group process. Individual group member's tasks orientations, goal orientations, strategy orientations, and motivations for participating in CMC, such as the desire to achieve good grades or to be regarded as a good group member, impact participation and interaction in the group (Vrasidas & McIsaac, 1999). An individual group member's commitment to the online group, engagement with its tasks, and individual accountability reflect a complex relationship between personal and situational factors that lead to differing approaches to learning and to the quality of the collaborative setting (Brandon & Hollingshead, 1999; Garrison & Archer, 2000). Factors that influence individual participation in online groups are preference or need for social interaction (Vrasidas & McIsaac, 1999; Gunawardena & Zittle, 1997; Gallini & Zhang, 1997), technical skills and equipment, and ability to effectively use language, netiquette, and emoticons (Davis & Brewer, 1997). Online group members' influences and responsibilities outside the online community also impact member participation (Kember, 1995).

Several studies have found that members of CMC groups participate more equally than members of face-to-face groups and produce more independent opinions. This greater equality of participation may be partly due to the absence or lack of social context cues in CMC, its ability to equalize status (Kiesler, Siegel, & McGuire, 1984) and less risk of embarrassment (Baltes, et al., 2002). Interestingly, however, the uninhabited interaction and more equal participation of CMC group members do not necessarily render enhanced decisionmaking or group effectiveness (Baltes, et al., 2002).

Roles, Status, and Leadership

Status and its implied expectations are less obvious in CMC due to reduced social cues. However, roles, status, and their implied expectations are still mirrored through messages posted and influence group behavior. Those members who participate most frequently become leaders. Generally, a group leader and the quality of leadership have tremendous impacts on group development in several ways. Group leaders share and model their assumptions, which other members internalize. Evolving formal leadership begins to inhibit CMC members from suggesting further unorthodox, alternative solutions and reduce member satisfaction

(Benbasat & Lim, 1993). Group members mimic and orient their writing to the message styles of leaders and other members who post first (Murphy et al., 1996; Bonito & Hollingshead, 1997; Davis & Brewer, 1997).

Communication Patterns

CMC facilitates communication, thinking, and working patterns as group participants freely generate ideas without turntaking interruptions and with reduced evaluation anxiety (Siegel, et al., 1986; Jheng, 1997). The online group's critical thinking process as it works on a task over time is revealed as its members first explore divergent views, converge toward a plan, and subsequently test its plan and product (Garrison, Anderson, & Archer, 2001).

Participants in computer-mediated groups post more divergent views as they may be less likely to defer to authority and often support their written statements more rigidly than their spoken words (Hillman, 1999; Olaniran, 1994). Individual accountability is easily established in the online environment through permanent written postings. The anticipation of future interaction, monitoring by other group members, and possibly meeting group members face to face later may propel group members to generate large numbers of ideas to later avoid criticisms of free-riding or social loafing (Olaniran, 1994; Kollock & Smith, 1999).

Strauss (1996) has found that CMC groups may generally suffer from attention-blocking. Attention blocking occurs when group members focus on preparing their own postings and are unable to attend to other members' comments.

As mentioned earlier, one of the group's purposes is to ensure member satisfaction and hold the group together. Using ground rules, emoticons, direct address, humor, praise, and self-disclosure are communication strategies that serve to create and maintain the group's well being. However, CMC groups must be socially connected enough to be fault tolerant and able to survive instances when an individual or team fails to accomplish an assigned task. CMC groups can survive such slipups by initially devising the means to recognize such failures through monitoring work, checking milestones, and having the means to correct problems (Smith, 1994; Brandon & Hollingshead, 1999).

The work patterns of online groups vary. One group may engage in brainstorming, planning, drafting, or editing as a single coherent group that periodically delegates tasks for individuals. A second group may spend a majority of its time individually examining resource material, building a plan, drafting, revising, and reviewing and occasionally joining other group members for a meeting (Smith, 1994). A third group may produce a number of instrumental, intermediate products that help the group produce the final product. A fourth group may produce one product that goes through several versions. Each group requires supporting technology.

Group History

Whether the group is a full-fledged, experimental, or bona fide group with the expectation of continued interaction impacts group communication, process, and outcomes (Pavitt & Johnson, 1999; Olaniran, 1994; Kollock & Smith, 1999). Online groups in early stages send messages that focus on learning about each other and coming to trust each other (Olson & Olson, 1997). They later send a greater proportion of fight statements as they work through the early stages of group development to learn how to collaborate on a task. Frequently interacting online groups tend to make more supportive and critical remarks and arguments, ask more questions about problems and solutions, make more comments about the group, and ask more questions overall than do individuals or infrequently interacting groups (Jessup, Edbert, & Connolly, 1995–1996; Olson & Olson, 1997). More mature work groups send a higher percentage of work statements (Wheelan & Kaeser, 1997). However, Mennecke and Valacich (1998) found that some established groups that share history and a similar frame of reference make assumptions about the task before them, overlook important information, and engage in less explicit communication.

Outcomes

A predominant number of research studies explore the impact of the medium on group outcomes (Huang & Wei, 2000) by comparing computer-mediated groups with face-to-face groups. The comparative research has generally explored a number of factors on which face-to-face groups and online groups differ, including volume (or frequency) of communication across team members, message content, distribution of communication among team members, time needed to make decisions, decision quality, and member satisfaction (Hedlend et al., 1998; Davis & Brewer, 1997; Baltes, et al., 2002; Mennecke & Valacich, 1998).

Decision Quality

Generally, CMC groups take four to ten times longer to make a decision and may be somewhat more risktaking (Kiesler & Sproull, 1992). Without guidance from an effective moderator, some online group members do not strive for group coherence but focus on formulating their own thoughts out loud (Pavitt & Johnson, 1999). Generally, over time, however, no difference in decision quality exists between face-to-face and CMC groups (Olaniran, 1994; Dennis et al., 1999; Hollingshead et al., 1993).

Production

Methods of evaluation and rewards have been found to be an important mediating variable. When group members know how the group will be evaluated or rewarded, the group members act accordingly. When speed of task execution is rewarded, CMC groups gain time by reducing social communication and increasing task-oriented interaction to maintain output quality (Kahai & Cooper, 1999).

Satisfaction

Membership satisfaction is an important group-outcome variable. When participants are more satisfied with the group process and support, they are more likely to continue participating (Kahai & Cooper, 1999). Baltes et al. (2002) in their meta-analysis of CMC and group decision making found anonymous CMC groups have significantly lower satisfaction with decision making than face-to-face groups. Nonanonymous CMC groups perform more poorly than face-to-face groups yet are equally satisfied with the decision-making process.

CRITICAL ANALYSIS OF THE EXISTING RESEARCH

The research presented in this chapter has examined the application of traditional face-to-face group development models to CMC environments and the effects of CMC on key group process variables. This compilation provides empirical evidence that online groups can form, interact, and accomplish tasks through the online technology, yet the addition of the technological dimension distinguishes the online groups from the face-to-face groups in several ways. Online groups generate fewer messages, write at length, and take longer to complete their tasks in both synchronous and asynchronous environments. There are many things we still as yet do not know concerning CMC's impact on online group structure, process, and development. While some of the gaps in the literature may be attributed to a lack of research on group development, critical concerns emerge surrounding the assumptions upon which past research has been conducted, methodological issues in the research process, and the lack of a systems perspective. Following are suggestions for future research into group development in OLC.

First, existing research appears founded on the underlying assumptions that group development in the traditional face-to-face environment represents the ideal situation; and, therefore, group development in the online environment occurs within a less-than-ideal or a deficiency perspective. Researchers differ in the descriptors they apply to the online environment—a reduced social cues environment, an anonymous and impersonal environment of weak ties, a pseudo community, or a middle landscape—yet the underlying assumptions are similar. Such unexamined assumptions shape our thoughts, research designs, tools, and inquiry process; such assumptions limit our studies and restrict the results we see to those familiar and comfortable (Senge, 1990). More seriously, these unexamined assumptions overlook the strengths of on-line group development—equalization of participation, greater diversity, and more thoughtful elaboration of ideas, and more time for reflection and inquiry. These strengths are actually the basic components of critical thinking and cognitive presence and are considered indicators of high levels of thinking, of deep and meaningful learning, ostensibly the reason for inclusion of online conferencing within a distance learning environment. As the current call for research about distance learning in general appeals to researchers to end the comparative studies, now, too, is the time to end comparative studies of traditional group and online group development. It is time to examine the patterns, cycles, and interrelationships of online groups in order to derive models, laws, and theories of online group development.

Second, much of the past CMC research has been conducted on ad hoc groups composed of two to five members under experimental conditions (Bordia, 1997; Warkentin, Sayeed, & Hightower, 1997). Disallowing the time needed for participants to become accustomed to the technology and to each other may reflect examining a group in only one stage of development. Little is known about group development in asynchronous text-based settings. Primarily, the models that have been applied in investigating group development in OLCs represent progressive or cyclical models. Little available research has addressed contingent factors or utilized nonsequential models. The available literature points to a very real need to develop theory and research to understand the process of group development in natural electronic learning communities.

Third, current online group research reports many of the group elements have been studied as isolated, independent variables when actually the online group exists as a system of variables with relationships and interrelationships that create a dynamic complexity. Systems thinking is, therefore, useful for studying online group complexity from multiple perspectives (Garrison & Archer, 2000). We need to creatively conduct group development research within the CMC environment from a systems perspective linking the social, task, and technological dimensions to the entry, process, and outcome variables.

Fourth, the preceding discussions have been primarily concerned with processes leading to uniformity and cohesiveness in groups. Nearly all the group research has been based on judgment tasks that have no demonstrably correct solution with group consensus as the goal (Hedlund et al., 1998). But the processes of group development often involve divisive forces as well. A number of group development models highlight the importance of conflict to group development. We need research and proven strategies not only for guiding community building or group cohesion but also for managing conflict among the diverse learners in the online environment.

Finally, how does the process of group development relate to the quality of the learning outcomes for online communities? To take full advantage of the potential of the medium for group learning, designers need to understand the technology and how it relates to the social interaction and learning tasks at hand. What the models and the research fail to tell us is how variations in group structure, process, and development relate to differences in learning outcomes, and fail to address those aspects of group life and collaborative learning that make each group unique.

RECOMMENDATIONS FOR FUTURE RESEARCH

CMC is a unique educational medium, a domain that challenges distance educators to explore group development theory and research from a new perspective. What hasn't changed in this environment is that learners continue to join online groups in an effort to satisfy a myriad of needs from both the social and task dimension. What has changed is that the technological mediation alters the very nature of the communication patterns that occur. Regional, national, and global networking possibilities facilitate an increasingly diverse group composition, changing patterns of standardization and differentiation in group structure, and alternative sequencing of group process events. Researchers must acknowledge these differences and strive to develop a research methodology for online group development that reflects the advantages of the medium. Multiple methods of data collection including inductive analyses are warranted in an effort to discover variability in group development within an environment impacted by an additional dimension. The major thrust of the research has addressed outcome variables. While scholars devote much attention to the importance of community building in OLCs (Palloff & Pratt, 1999), large gaps exist in our understanding of the impact of the social dimension, input variables, and the impact of these contingency factors on learning outcomes.

This analysis introduces more questions than it answers. First, how variable is group development online? What does and does not change as groups develop a history over time? Which variables serve to facilitate the process of group development and under what conditions? Which stages are crucial for successful learning outcomes? What are the most effective practices that foster group development? How influential are the characteristics of the group's moderator? What is the relationship between communication patterns and group development in an online learning community? Perhaps most importantly, does group development drive communication or do certain communication patterns drive group development? These questions promote an exciting and fertile field of research for distance educators in the future. Nearly 15 years have passed since early writers presented a vision of online groups sufficiently well developed as to produce a "weaving together" of "many minds add." Fifteen years have passed since scholars noted the dearth of research on group development in CMCs. As this analysis has shown, a surprising gap in the literature still exists—leaving this area one of the largest challenges in the field of online education.

REFERENCES

Acock, A. C., Dowd, J. J., & Roberts, W. L. (1974). *The primary group: Its rediscovery in contemporary society.* Morristown, N.J.: General Learning Press.

Ahern, T. C., & El-Hindi, A. E. (2000). Improving the instructional congruency of a computer-mediated small-group discussion: A case study in design and delivery. *Journal of Research on Computing in Education, 32*(3), 385–400.

Alexander, P. A., & Murphy, P. K. (1999). Learner profiles: Valuing individual differences within classroom communities. In P. L. Ackerman, P. C. Kyllonen, & R. D. Roberts (Eds.), *Learning and individual differences* (pp. 414–436). Washington, DC: American Psychological Association.

Arrow, H., McGrath, J. E., & Berdahl, J. L. (2000). *Small groups as complex systems: Formation, coordination, development, and adaptation.* Thousand Oaks: Sage Publications, Inc.

Baker, M., Hansen, T., Joiner, R., & Traum, D. (1999). The role of grounding in collaborative learning tasks. In P. Dillenbourg (Ed.), *Collaborative learning: Cognitive and computational approaches* (pp. 31–63). New York: Pergamon.

Bales, R. F. (1950). *Interaction process analysis*. Cambridge, MA: Addison-Wesley.

Bales, R. F., & Strodbeck, F. L. (1951). Phases in group problem solving. *Journal of Abnormal and Social Psychology, 46*, 485–495.

Baltes, B. B., Dickson, M. W., Sherman, M. P., Bauer, C. C., & LaGanke, J. S. (2002). Computer-mediated Communication and group decision making. A meta-analysis. *Organizational Behavior and Human Decision Processes, 87*(1), 156–179.

Benbasat, I., & Lim, L. (1993). The effects of group, task, context, and technology variables on the usefulness of group support systems: A meta-analysis of experimental studies. *Small Group Research, 24*(4), 430–462.

Bennis, W. G., & Shepard, H. A. (1956). A theory of group development. *Human Relations, 9*, 415–437.

Bion, W. R. (1961). *Experiences in groups* (2nd ed.). New York: Basic Books.

Bonito, J. A., & Hollingshead, A. B. (1997). Participation in small groups. In Burleson, Brait, R. (Ed.), *Communication yearbook 20* (pp. 227–261). Beverly Hills, CA: Sage Publications.

Bordia, P. (1997). Face-to-face versus computer-mediated communication: A synthesis of the experimental literature. *The Journal of Business Communication, 34*(1), 99–120.

Brandon, D. P., & Hollingshead, A. B. (1999). Collaborative learning and computer-supported groups. *Communication Education, 48*(2), 109–126.

Burt, M. T., Grady, M., & McMann, G. (1994). *Interaction analysis of an inter-university computer conference*. Paper presented at the Distance Learning Research Conference, College Station, Texas.

Colquitt, J. A., LePine, J. A., Hollenbeck, J. R., Ilgen, D. R., and Sheppard, L. (2002). Computer-assisted communication and team decision-making performance the moderating effect of openness to experience. *Journal of Applied Psychology, 87*(2), 402–410.

Davies, D. (1989). Computer-supported cooperative learning: Interactive group technologies and distance learning systems. In R. Mason & A. Kaye (Eds.), *Mindweave* (pp. 228–231). Oxford: Pergamon.

Davis, B. H., & Brewer, J. P. (1997). *Linguistic individuals in virtual space*. Albany, NY: State University of New York Press.

Dennis, A., Kinney, S., & Hung, Y. (1999). Gender differences in the effects of media richness. *Small Group Research, 30*(4), 405–437.

Feenberg, A. (1989). The written world: On the theory and practice of computer conferencing. In R. Mason & A. Kaye (Eds.), *Mindweave* (pp. 228–231). Oxford: Pergamon.

Gallini, J. K., & Zhang, Y. (1997). Socio-cognitive constructs and characteristics of classroom communities: An exploration of relationships. *Journal of Educational Computing Research, 17*(4), 321–339.

Garrison, D. R., Anderson, T., & Archer, W. (2001). Critical thinking, cognitive presence and computer conferencing in distance education. *The American Journal of Distance Education, 15*(1), 7–23.

Garrison, D. R. & Archer, W. (2000). *A transactional perspective on teaching and learning: A framework for adult and higher education*. Kidlington, Oxford: Elsevier Science Ltd.

Gersick, C. J. G. (1988). Time and transition in work teams: Toward a new model of group development. *Academy of Management Journal, 31*, 941.

Gersick, C. J. G. (1989). Marking time: Predictable transitions in task groups. *Academy of Management Journal, 32*, 274–309.

Gunawardena, C. N., Lowe, C. A., & Anderson, T. (1997). *Interaction analysis of a global on-line debate and the development of a constructivist interaction model for computer conferencing*. Paper presented at the Annual Convention of the American Educational Research Association. New York, New York.

Gunawardena, C. N., Nolla, A. C., Wilson, P. L., Lopez-Islas, J. R., Ramirez-Angel, N., & Megchun-Alpizar, R. M. (2001). A cross-cultural study of group process and development in online conferences. *Distance Education 22*(1). 85–121.

Gunawardena, C. N., & Zittle, F. J. (1997). Social presence as a predictor within a computer-moderated conferencing environment. *The American Journal of Distance Education, 11*(3), 8–26.

Hackman, J. R., & Morris, C. G. (1975). Group tasks, group interaction process, and group performance effectiveness: A review and proposed integration. In L. Berkowitz (Ed.), *Advances in experimental social psychology* (Vol. 8). New York: Academic Press.

Harasim, L. (1989). Online education: A new domain. In R. Mason & A. Kaye (Eds.), *Mindweave* (pp. 50–62). Oxford: Pergamon.

Harasim, L. M. (1990). Online education: An environment for collaboration and intellectual amplification. In L. Harasim (Ed.), *Online Education: Perspectives on a new environment* (pp. 39–64). Westport, CT: Praeger.

Harasim, L. M. (1993). Networlds: networks as social space. In L. Harasim (Ed.), *Global networks: An introduction* (pp. 15–34). London, England: The MIT Press.

Hare, A. P. (1976). *Handbook of small group research*. New York: The Free Press.

Hare, A. P., Blumberg, H. H., Davies, M. F., & Kent, M. V. (1994). Small group research: A handbook. Norwood, NJ: Ablex Publishing Company.

Hedlund, J., Ilgen, D. R., & Hollenbeck, J. R. (1998). Decision accuracy in computer-mediated versus face-to-face decision-making teams. *Organizational Behavior and Human Decision Processes, 76*(2), 30–47.

Hillman, D. C. A. (1999). A new method for analyzing patterns of interaction. *The American Journal of Distance Education, 13*(2), 37–47.

Hiltz, S. R., Johnson, K., & Turoff, M. (1987). Experiments in group decision making, 1: Communications process and outcome in face-to-face vs. computerized conferences. *Human Communication Research, 13*(2), 225–252.

Hollingshead, A., McGrath J., & O'Connor, K. (1993). Group task performance and communication technology: A longitudinal study of computer-mediated versus face-to-face work groups. *Small Group Research, 24*(3), 307–333.

Huang, W. H., & Wei, K. K. (2000). An empirical investigation of the effects of group support systems (gss) and task type on group interactions from an influence perspective. *Journal of Management Information Systems, 17*(2), 181–206.

Jehng, J. J. (1997). The psycho-social processes and cognitive effects of peer-based collaborative interactions with computers. *Journal of Educational Computing Research, 17*(1), 19–46.

Jessup, L. M., Edbert, J. L., & Connolly, T. (1995–1996). Understanding computer-supported group work: the effects of interaction frequency on group process and outcome. *Journal of Research on Computing in Education, 28,* 190–208.

Kahai, S. S., & Cooper, R. B. (1999). The effect of computer-mediated communication on agreement and acceptance. *Journal of Management Information Systems, 16*(1), 165–189.

Kember, D. (1995). *Open learning for adults: A model of student progress.* Englewood Cliffs, NJ: Educational Technology Publications.

Kiesler, S., Siegel, J., & McGuire, T. (1984). Social psychological aspects of computer-mediated communication. *America Psychologist, 39,* 1123–1134.

Kiesler, S. & Sproull, L. (1992). Group decision making and communication technology. *Organizational Behavior and Human Decision Processes, 52,* 96–123.

Kim, A. J. (2000). *Community building on the web.* Berkeley, CA: Peachpit Press.

Kollock, P., & Smith, M. (1999). Communities in cyberspace. In M. Smith & P. Pollock (Eds.), *Communities in cyberspace* (pp. 3–25). Berkeley, CA: Routledge.

Lorsch, J. W. (1987). *Handbook of organizational behavior.* Englewood Cliffs, NJ: Prentice-Hall.

Mann, R. D., Gibbard, G. S., & Hartmann, J. J. (1967). *Interpersonal styles and group development.* New York: Wiley.

McDonald, J., & Gibson, C. C. (1998). Interpersonal dynamics and group development in computer conferencing. *The American Journal of Distance Education, 12*(1), 7–47.

McGrath, J. E. (1984). *Groups: Interaction and performance.* Englewood Cliffs, NJ: Prentice-Hall.

McGrath, J. E. (1990). Time matters in groups. In J. Galegher, R. E. Kraut, & C. Egido (Eds.), *Intellectual teamwork, social and technlogical foundations of cooperative work.* Hillsdale, NJ: Lawrence Erlbaum.

McGrath, J. E. (1991). Time, interaction, and performance (TIP): A theory of groups. *Small Group Research, 22*(2), 147–174.

Mennecke, B. E., Hoffer, J. A., & Wynn, B. E. (1992). The implications of group development and history for group support system theory and practice. *Small Group Research, 23*(4), 524–573.

Mennecke, B. E., & Valacich, J. S. (1998). Information is what you make of it: the influence of group history and computer support on information sharing decision quality and member perceptions. *Journal of Management Information Systems, 15*(2), 173–197.

Murphy, K. L., Cifuentes, L., Yakimovica, A. D., Segur, R., Mahoney, S. E., & Kodali, S. (1996). Students assume the mantle of moderating computer conferences: a case study. *The American Journal of Distance Education, 10*(3), 20–37.

Olaniran, B. A. (1994). Group performance in computer mediation and face-to-face. *Management Communication Quarterly, 7*(3), 256–284.

Olson, G. M., & Olson, J. S. (1997). Research on computer-supported cooperative work. In M. G. Helander, T. K. Landauer, & P. V. Prabha (Eds.), *Handbook of human-computer interaction* (2nd ed.) pp. 1433–1456. New York, NY: Elsevier Science B. V.

Palloff, R. M., & Pratt, K. (1999). *Building learning communities in cyberspace.* San Francisco, CA: Jossey-Bass Publishers.

Pavitt, C., & Johnson, K. (1999). An examination of the coherence of group discussions. *Communication Research 26*(3), 303–321.

Poole, M. S. (1983). Decision development in small groups: A multiple sequence model of group decision making. *Communication Monographs, 50,* 321–344.

Poole, M. S., & Roth, M. S. (1989). Decision Development in small groups: V. Test of a contingency model. *Human Communications Research, 15,* 549–589.

Ridgeway, C. L. (1983). *The dynamics of small groups.* New York: St. Martin's Press.

Schutz, W. C. (1958). *FIRO: A three-dimensional theory of interpersonal behavior.* New York: Holt, Rinehart.

Senge, P. M. (1990). *The fifth discipline*. New York, NY: Doubleday.

Siegel, J., Dubrovsky, V., Kiesler, S., & McGuire, T. W. (1986). Group processes in computer-mediated communication, *Organizational Behavior and Human Decision Processes, 37*, 157–187.

Smith, J. B. (1994). *Collective intelligence in computer-based collaboration*. Hillsdale, NJ: Lawrence Erlbaum Associates.

Stranss, S. G. (1996). Getting a clue: The effects of communication media and information distribution on participation and performance in computer-mediated and face-to-face groups. *Small Group Research, 27*(1) (1996), 115–142.

Sudweeks, F., & Allbritton, M. (1996). Working together, working apart. In C. D. Keen, C. Urquhart, & J. Lamp (Eds.), *Proceedings of the 7th Australasian conference of information systems (ACIS96), 2*, Department of Computer Science, University of Tasmania, 701–712.

Tuckman, B. W. (1965). Developmental sequence in small groups. *Psychological Bulletin*, 63, 384–399.

Tuckman, B. W., & Jensen, M. A. C. (1977). Stages in small group development revisited. *Group and Organizational Studies, 2*, 419–427.

Vrasidas, C., & McIsaac, M. S. (1999). *The American Journal of Distance Education, 13*(3), 22–36.

Walther, J. B. (1996). Computer-mediated communication: Impersonal, interpersonal and hyperpersonal interaction. *Communication Research, 23*(1), 3–43.

Walther, J. B., & Burgoon, J. K. (1992). Relational communication in computer-mediated interaction. *Human Communication Research, 19*(1), 50–88.

Warkentin, M. E., Sayeed, L., & Hightower, R. (1997). Virtual teams versus face-to-face teams: An exploratory study of a web-based conference system. *Decision Sciences, 28*(4), 975–997.

Wheelan, S. A., & Kaeser, R. M. (1997). The influence of task type and designated leaders in developmental patterns in groups. *Small Group Research, 28*(1), 94–128.

Wheelan, S. A., & McKeage, R. (1993). Developmental patterns in small and large groups. *Small Group Research, 24*(1), 60–83.

16

Learner Differences in Distance Learning: Finding Differences that Matter

Connie Dillon
The University of Oklahoma
cdillon@ou.edu

Barbara Greene
The University of Oklahoma
bgreene@ou.edu

One important difference between distance and traditional learners is the fact that distance learners typically learn in more independent environments. As a result, the concept of independence has been an important construct in the evolution of distance education theory. To establish a context for this chapter, it is important to make a distinction between "distance" learning and "distributed" learning. The growth in the capacity of telecommunications technologies is blurring the boundaries between distance and traditional instruction. Online and web-based instruction is becoming increasingly common in traditional as well as distance courses. As a result, our resident learners are being required to learn in much more independent environments than they have in the past. This is a positive trend if we believe that experience as an independent learner will ultimately foster independent learning. But this trend may pose new challenges in our quest to accommodate the unique needs of each individual learner. So within the context of this chapter, "distributed" learning is used to reflect the fact that many of our "distance" technologies are being applied in traditional resident learning environments. If this is true, any discussion of the issues surrounding learners who learn at a distance will also inform the wider spectrum of online learning, irrespective of physical distance.

Moore and Kearsley (1996) argued that the concept of distance should not refer to physical separation of teachers and learners alone, but rather to the "pedagogical" distance between different understandings and perceptions. Thus, transactional distance refers to a psychological separation or gap in understanding and meaning. But as Moore and Kearsley suggest, transactional distance is a factor on the campus or even in a classroom. Certainly physical distance increases the "transactional" distance a learner experiences because some form of technical media must be used to mediate the communication between teacher and learner. The field of distance education emerged years ago within the context of serving learners who cannot otherwise come to campus due to time or geographic constraints. But the use of distance technologies in traditional classroom settings is growing at a phenomenal rate. We may have "outdistanced" the geographic distance, but we still have much work to do with respect to the transactional distance. So within the context of this chapter, "distributive" learning is used to reflect the fact that many of our distance technologies are being applied in traditional resident learning environments. Thus the concept of transactional distance encompasses distributive learning.

One striking feature of our schools is the fact that unlike so many other sectors of our society, schools have changed very little over the past century. Other aspects of our lives are full of variety and in some cases individuals seem overrun with choice. If Bellamy (2000), who wrote *Looking Backward* (first published in 1898), had suddenly emerged from the 19th century into a factory, an office, or a library of today, he would surely feel out of place. However, today's classroom would be quite familiar. While the marketplace is ripe with choice, the classroom is still a product of the "mass production" mentality of the industrial age. That is why the whole the Aptitude Treatment Interaction (ATI) movement was so exciting in its day with its promise to help us design instruction that matched the learning needs of individuals (Snow & Lahman, 1984). Unfortunately, the promise of ATI has largely been unrealized.

Researchers in the field of distance education still believe technology can help educators individualize the learning experience. This is evident in the literature and its captivation with the concept of learning styles.

Providing teachers and course designers with information that can improve the cognitive efficiency of each learner's experience is still clearly an important goal (Cobb, 1997). However, this is a goal that still eludes us. This chapter poses the argument that continuing our current approach to researching learner differences in distance education will prove unproductive. Following a brief review of the research on learner variables in distance education, the chapter addresses the need for "reconceptualizing" our questions about learner differences and uses this argument as a basis for conceptualizing the construct of learner-instructor interaction. Finally, the chapter concludes with some recommendations for future research.

LEARNER VARIABLES IN DISTANCE EDUCATION RESEARCH

Many researchers have attempted to identify learner factors that impact learning in distance education settings. Much of this research examines either learner style variables or learner psychological variables. Some of the studies examine the cognitive style constructs, most often the construct of field dependence/field independence. These studies examine the relationship between learner variables and participation, attitudes, and achievement. This review here narrows the focus to research on learner differences specifically related to achievement.

Oxford, Young, Ito, and Sumrall (1993) explored motivation, language learning strategy, and learning style as predictors of language learning achievement of 107 high school students enrolled in a Japanese language class. Findings showed that motivation (related to career and academic factors) was a moderate predictor of language learning achievement. Learning styles were not predictors of performance, although the findings showed a relationship between learning style and motivation. Students with a preference for auditory modalities demonstrated higher levels of motivation than students with preferences for visual and kinesthetic learning.

Dille and Mezack (1991) examined learning styles and locus of control as predictors of success in a course delivered to both college telecourse students and on-campus students. The study consisted of 151 students who were enrolled in 4 telecourses. The average age was 27.5. Kolb's Learning Style Inventory (LSI) was used to measure cognitive style preference and Rotter's Internal Locus of Control Scale was used to measure the construct locus of control. Students with an internal locus of control received higher letter grades in the course than students with an external locus of control. In addition, successful students scored higher than the unsuccessful students on the concrete experience scale of the LSI. However, when looking at the abstract conceptualization minus concrete experience, the successful students scored higher than the unsuccessful students did. Multiple regression indicated that the only predictor of success was locus of control, with the more successful students reporting scores in the "internal" range.

Expanding upon the work of Dille and Mezack (1991), Biner, Bink, Huffman, and Dean (1995) used the Personality Assessment Instrument to identify differences in personality factors between students enrolled in interactive television (ITV) and traditional courses. In addition, they sought to determine whether any personality types predicted successful performance in a telecourse. The sample of the study was 164 students in the ITV treatment and 200 traditional students taking the same course on campus in the broadcast classroom. They reported that telecourse students differed from their traditional counterparts on four factors: a) intelligence (abstract thinking); b) emotional stability; c) trust; and d) compulsivity. An analysis of second-order factor scores suggested that telecourse students had higher scores on two factors: dependence and control. Correlations between personality factors and final course grade identified some differences between telecourse and traditional students. For the traditional student, higher grades were associated with greater emotional stability, seriousness, shyness, imaginativeness, and liberalism. Telecourse students with higher grades showed greater self-sufficiency and less compulsivity. In addition, they found a significant relationship between grades and the expedient-conscientious factor. Telecourse students with high grades scored higher on the expedience dimension while traditional students scored higher on the conscientiousness dimension. While it is important to note that the telecourse population differed in terms of age and gender (telecourse students were more likely to be older and female), analyses using age and gender as independent variables did not yield effects for the variables.

The relationship between telecourse persistence and psychological variables was examined by Pugliese (1994). The constructs studied were loneliness, communication apprehension, communication competence, and locus of control. A researcher used a telephone survey with 306 students participating. The sample included both traditional and nontraditional students. None of the factors predicted persistence.

Using Canfield's Learning Styles Inventory, Coggins (1988) surveyed a sample of 164 students (all 26 years of age or older) enrolled in a correspondence-based external degree program. She found that positive expectancy of performance (confidence) favorably affects the completion rate of students enrolled in correspondence study. However, conditions of learning and preferred learning modality appear to have no impact upon completion. While not statistically significant, noncompleters showed a higher preference for peer and instructor affiliation than did completers.

CONCEPTUALIZING THE PROBLEM

Clearly, it is difficult to draw any conclusions from this line of research. While the research provides some evidence that learner differences should be considered, clearly our best guidance to teachers is to tell them to use a variety of strategies and media so that surely we can effectively teach most of the people some of the time.

Perhaps our assumptions about learner differences are wrong. What if there is no such thing as learning "type" or "style"? Or if such a construct does exist, what if it has nothing to do with helping individuals learn? Learning styles actually mean many different things, depending upon the instrument used.

Sometimes learner styles are viewed as "preferences," as many of the instruments used measure learner preferences (including modality preferences). Most of these studies fail to show a relationship between a learner's preference, instructional treatment, and performance, and there is little, if any, evidence that supports the assumption that learner preferences impact learning. In fact, some research suggests that when given the opportunity to do what they "prefer" learners may not make the best choices. Belland, Taylor, Canelos, Dwyer, and Baker (1985) found that first-year college students (N=100) who chose the pace of learning using computer- assisted instruction did not perform as well on both amount learned and performance competency as subjects whose pace was controlled externally. In addition the high achievers opted for more feedback than the low achievers. Using a sample of 65 sixth-grade students enrolled at a private school, Carrier, Davidson, and Williams (1985) found that high-ability students selected more elaboration options than did low-ability students. These researchers suggest that the assumption that allowing students to exercise their own judgment will improve performance may be faulty.

Second, finding reliable and valid measures of types, such as the popular learning style constructs, has been difficult despite sustained efforts by researchers. Three commonly used instruments in distance education research are the Myers-Briggs Type Indicator (MBTI), the Canfield Learning Style Inventory, and Kolb's Learning Style Inventory. The MBTI is based upon Jungian theory and assesses perception and judgment. The Canfield Learning Styles Inventory examines academic, structural, and achievement conditions, expectancy of performance, and mode of learning. Finally, based upon experiential learning theory, the Kolb Learning Style Inventory examines concrete experience, reflective observation, abstract conceptualization, and active experimentation (Sewall, 1986).

Analyses of the validity and reliability of these instruments is far from conclusive (Sewall, 1986; Pittenger, 1993; Geiger, Boyle, & Pinto, 1992; Koob & Funk, 2002). The nature of populations used to establish the norms is one concern. The subjects used were selected from populations that were above average in terms of intellectual ability, educational level, and income levels (Sewall, 1986). A second concern is that all the instruments use nominal rather than interval data. Analyses suggest that the factors examined are not dichotomous, as presumed, but rather interval (Sewall, 1986; Pittenger, 1993). In addition, some of the instruments use ipsative scores. An ipsative score is one that varies based upon an individual's response on the other elements of the instrument. Therefore, an individual's score on one element is dependent upon his of her responses to the others. Thus, individual scores cannot be compared to others because they may differ in terms of degree. In addition, the interdependent nature of the data provided by these instruments may be unsuited to measures of reliability used (Sewall, 1986; Pittenger, 1993). Likewise, with the exception of the MBTI, the studies that have been conducted to establish reliability and validity are inconclusive. Finally, little evidence exists to suggest these instruments predict achievement or achievement-related behaviors, such as effort (Sewall, 1986; Pittenger, 1993; Geiger et al., 1992; Koob & Funk, 2002). While the MBTI may be an effective instrument for assessing "personality" characteristics, little evidence exists to support its ability to help us "predict" how learners will perform under given conditions.

At issue is the fact that learner styles, cognitive styles (such as field dependence/field independence), and personality constructs are described in the literature as relatively "constant," that is, these are factors in us that are not subject to change. Therefore, the only way to approach the design of instruction when trying to accommodate learner differences is to change the instruction rather than to change the learner. But the most important goal of all education, including distance education, is to help learners learn how to learn. Even if the concept of learner styles were a valid construct, our ultimate goal should be to help learners learn in a variety of situations and under a variety of conditions, because that is the nature of the learning society in which we live.

Our most important task as educators is indeed to help learners build a repertoire of approaches to learning so that they can learn to learn under the variety of circumstances that life will surely bring. This goal seems particularly critical in an environment of rapid technological change. If we focus upon how we can modify the instruction to accommodate the individual, are we not preparing dependent rather than independent learners? If we focus, instead, upon how learners approach a particular learning situation, we can help them learn to modify their approaches to accommodate a variety of learning situations. Studies by Gibson (1996) support this conclusion by offering evidence that learners do in fact change their view of learning over time in ways that impact how well they learn, even throughout the experience of a single course.

A more powerful and expedient method of addressing individual learner needs may be to identify effective approaches to learning and then help students acquire the metacognitive skills needed to adopt those approaches in settings where they have been found to lead to success. Perhaps we should turn our attention from what learners "are" and instead focus upon what learners "do." A more productive line of inquiry then focuses upon how learners "approach" learning, rather than upon learner styles or psychological traits.

The construct "approaches to learning" refers to the characteristics that learners bring to achievement settings. Unlike traits, these can vary from setting to setting, and they define the stance learners take toward learning in particular settings. For the purposes of this analysis, approaches to learning include the goals, self-efficacy, and strategy use that students report in different achievement settings.

There are two main reasons for choosing this line of inquiry. First, there is a large body of empirical research showing that differences in approaches to learning are powerful predictors of both effort and achievement (e.g., Ames, 1992; Greene & Miller, 1996; Greene, DeBacker, Ravindran, & Krows, 1999; Miller, Behrens, Greene, & Newman, 1993; Miller, Greene, Montalvo, Ravindran, & Nicholls, 1996; Nicholls, 1989; Pintrich & Garcia, 1991). So, while there has been scant evidence for the importance of learning styles, there is an abundance of evidence supporting the importance of approaches. Second, and perhaps more important, is the "ethics" of continuing to focus upon how to modify instruction to accommodate learning preferences when we suspect that learners will be better served, in the long run, by instruction that encourages them to be more flexible in their approaches across the variety of learning settings they are sure to face. Instruction could then focus upon fostering goals and enhancing self-efficacy as well as upon teaching students what strategies will help them across different achievement settings

THE APPROACHES TO LEARNING CONSTRUCTS

Approaches to learning is operationalized in terms of achievement goals, self-efficacy, and reported strategy use following what has been a fruitful trend in motivation research since the mid-1980s. Each of these constructs is described below.

First, achievement goals are the reasons students report for trying to learn in a particular achievement setting (Miller et al., 1996). There is considerable research that supports the importance of the distinction between learning goals (also called mastery or task-oriented goals) and performance goals. Learning goals are goals that are related to the desire to increase one's understanding or skill level. In contrast, performance goals (also called ego-oriented goals) are related to the desire to perform better than others and protect one's ego (e.g., Miller et al., 1996; Pintrich & Garcia, 1991). This research has consistently found a positive relationship between learning goals and self-regulation, strategy use, and effort (e.g., Greene and Miller, 1996; Miller et al., 1993; Pintrich & Garcia, 1991), and has sometimes found a negative relationship between performance goals and productive achievement behaviors (Greene & Miller, 1996; Zimmerman and Martinez-Pons, 1990). Additionally, there is evidence that future goals show similar positive relationships with productive achievement behaviors as do learning goals (e.g., Miller et al., 1996). Future goals refer to distant goals (e.g., eligibility for extra-curricular activities, college admission, and career opportunities) that to some extent are contingent on current task performance but not inherent in the performance itself.

Self-efficacy refers to the confidence learners have in their ability to successfully perform the achievement task currently confronting them (Bandura, 1986). According to self-efficacy theory, when we doubt our ability to respond effectively in a given situation, we often try to avoid the situation or diminish its importance to us. Tasks that we believe to be within our range of competence (i.e., our self-efficacy is high) are more likely to be approached eagerly and with considerable effort than are tasks that we believe are outside our range of competence (i.e., our self-efficacy is low). Thus our efforts to learn in a particular situation are partially determined by our confidence in our ability to successfully perform a particular task. There is a great deal of correlational research that supports these theoretical assumptions (Ames & Archer, 1988; Greene & Miller, 1996; Greene et al., 1999; Miller et al., 1996; Pintrich & Garcia, 1991; Zimmerman and Martinez-Pons, 1990). Importantly, this research strongly supports the domain specific nature of self-efficacy (c.f., Marsh, 1992). In other words, self-efficacy is not the same as global self-esteem nor is it a type that remains constant across achievement settings involving different content. However, it has been found to function nearly identically to expectancy motivation as examined by Coggins (1988).

While achievement goals and self-efficacy are the abstract manifestations of approaches, strategy use is the concrete manifestation, in that strategies are the behaviors a learner employs during the learning process. In fact, strategy use is generally depicted in motivation research as influenced by goals and self-efficacy (e.g., Greene & Miller, 1996; Miller et al., 1996; Pintrich & Garcia, 1991). Researchers often evaluate strategies based on a distinction between deep and shallow processing. Deep strategies involve processing new information in terms of how it relates to existing knowledge. The to-be-learned information is elaborated on and integrated with knowledge already residing in memory. Shallow strategies involve processing new information separate from existing knowledge and in the form in which it was originally encountered. The strategy of rote memorization, along with other types of superficial engagement with new information (e.g., simply reading a chapter twice), captures the notion of shallow processing.

There is evidence that deep strategy use is important for learning and achievement (e.g., Greene & Miller, 1996; Pintrich & De Groot, 1990). There is also some evidence that shallow processing strategies may hinder learning (Greene & Miller, 1996; Ravindran & Greene, 1999). This construct has been studied in the distance education literature. For example, Kember and Harper (1987) found a relationship between surface approach to study and nonpersisters in a correspondence study program.

However, some research suggests that the two types of strategies are often related to one another (e.g., Greene & Miller, 1996; Miller et al., 1996) and what is shallow in one achievement setting might be deep in another. For instance, Joughlin, Lai, & Cottman (1992) examined the constructs of deep and surface learning with a sample of 1,843 distance students. In contrast to expectations, they found that the item related to memorizing loaded with the deep approach and the item related to questioning loaded with the surface approach. They, too, suggested that the teaching context might impact which approaches to learning are successful.

A series of studies is currently examining the constructs of self-efficacy, motivation, and study strategies in a chemical engineering course that used primarily CD-ROM and web-based strategies. Successful and less successful students were compared using an Approaches to Study Instrument designed to assess motivation, goals, and strategies. Students with a final grade of B or better were classified as successful; students with a final grade of D or F were classified as unsuccessful. The findings from the first phase of the study were somewhat surprising because the successful and less successful students showed little differences in level of motivation, effort, and goal orientation (Dillon, Greene, & Crynes, 2000). To learn more about the factors contributing to success, selected students from the two groups were interviewed (Greene, Dillon, & Crynes, 2001). Analysis of the interviews identified some important differences between the successful and less successful students. The less successful students focused upon memorizing and applying what they had memorized. The successful students focused upon understanding the concepts. The less successful students skipped the easier parts of the work and in doing so may have failed to take advantage of the opportunity to activate prior learning. While the successful students reported skimming the easier parts, they were also looking for areas that they failed to understand. The successful students talked about "how they learned" and the less successful students did not. Both groups used surface strategies, but the successful students also used deep strategies and appeared to be aware of the difference between these approaches. They seemed to be able to use this awareness to make decisions about how to approach learning whereas the less successful students continued to rely upon strategies that were not working.

Perhaps there is some value in knowing that a learner is a visual learner or has a high internal locus of control. Perhaps there is also some danger in this approach as well. For while it might be of benefit to understand that a learner is a "field dependent" learner, it may impact the teacher's or that learner's confidence in his or her ability to learn the material, particularly if those involved know that research suggests that field-dependent learners do not perform as well as field-independent learners. With literature supporting a relationship between positive self-efficacy and performance, "typing" a learner may indeed be self-defeating. Likewise, there may be some strategies teachers can use to help field-dependent learners improve their performance, but since this construct is a "trait," those strategies may not be robust to changing conditions. However, teachers can certainly help learners change their approach to study.

LEARNER DIFFERENCES AND
LEARNER-INSTRUCTOR INTERACTION

Improving our understanding of how learners "approach their study" may improve our understanding of the construct of learner-instructor interaction. Those of us in distance education often talk about the importance of interaction in distance education. Moore (1989) has defined three types of interaction: learner-learner, learner-instructor, and learner-content and argues that learner-instructor interaction is a crucial component that facilitates the other two and creates an effective learning environment. While true, it seems equally true that learner-instructor interaction can also interfere with learning. Online communication can be easily misinterpreted, due in part to the lack of visual and facial cues. Online teachers are encouraged to provide timely and detailed feedback. However, online teachers often do not have any information about how the student responds to this feedback. In fact, students may interpret a high level of feedback as negative feedback when in reality a teacher is merely posing questions to stimulate student thinking. So obviously, learner-instructor interaction is more than just something that should be present, it is something that should be characterized in terms of its quality.

Independent learners exercise greater autonomy in their learning decisions than dependent learners. This is a positive feature of independent learning environments only if the learners have the ability to make effective learning decisions. Using Moore's theory of transactional distance (Moore & Kearsley, 1996), we might hypothesize that learners who have not learned to make effective decisions about their approaches to learning will benefit from more structure and more dialogue. Likewise, learners who are autonomous learners will require less structure and less dialogue. Some form of learner-instructor interaction is required to assess which learners will thrive in an independent environment and which will struggle.

What constitutes effective learner-instructor interaction? Perhaps a focus on student "approaches" to learning can help us develop the construct of learner-instructor interaction by providing a basis for making judgments about the appropriate relationship between structure and dialogue for a given learner. While technologies provide us with the ability to tailor our interactions in many forms, the "independent" environment prevents us from receiving the immediate feedback we can readily see in the classroom. Are students nodding their heads ... or are they nodding to sleep? Do the students seem confused or do they show nods of understanding? Right now, our technologies do not communicate these nuances to us. We have to make judgments about these using other means. Perhaps greater understanding about each learner's approach to learning will help us improve our interactions with him or her. All too often, students use approaches that have been successful in the past, even though the problem has changed. Should a teacher assume that this is a "style" issue and therefore modify the instruction? Or should a teacher recognize this as a "surface" approach to learning and help the student change his or her behavior? While a teacher might give good, detailed feedback on the specific problem, that teacher may have served the student better by providing feedback that can be generalized to other very different settings. Our learner-instructor interactions should include strategies that will help students engage in metacognitive processing. Teachers should provide learners with prompts to help them reflect upon what they understand and what they do not understand, what part of the problem is easy and what is hard. In other words, effective learner-instructor interaction should be designed not only to help learners understand the content, but also to help them understand themselves as learners.

FUTURE RESEARCH

Not every learner will succeed in every learning setting. However, many learners have the potential to succeed but lack skills and understanding about how they approached learning. These are skills that can be learned. Future research should test these ideas. First, we should turn our focus from learner traits to learner approaches and develop instruments that we can use to help us learn more about the relationship between approaches to study and performance. Second, we should place more emphasis upon research that examines within-group differences than between-group differences. In other words, we should turn our focus to how learners in distributed settings differ and how these differences relate to performance rather than continuing to compare the effectiveness of distributed versus traditional learning. Finally, we should implement different instructional treatments within a "distributed" setting to see if we can indeed narrow the gap between the successful and less successful learners.

The growth of distributed learning throughout higher education will continue to place more responsibility for learning upon the learner. However, we may find it more difficult to diagnose learning needs as learners work in more independent learning environments. As Garrison and Baynton argue (1987), independent learning is not desirable if learners lack the support they need to succeed. We must strive to ensure that all learners who have the potential to be successful are ultimately successful. When designing distributed learning environments, we must focus upon strategies that help students learn how to learn, whether our learners are learning at a "distance" or learning in more independent learning on campus. Bellamy may no longer recognize the classroom as distributed technologies continue to pervade our schools. The recognition that learners have different needs was indeed a revolutionary theory, one that promised to move us from mass education to individualized learning. However, the step from recognition to reality has proven formidable. Rather than focusing upon how to modify the instruction to accommodate the preferences of the learner, we should instead focus upon modifying the learning approaches to meet the demands of the instruction.

REFERENCES

Ames, C. (1992). Classrooms: Goals, structures, and student motivation. *Journal of Educational Psychology, 84,* 261–271.

Ames, C., & Archer, J. (1988). Achievement goals in the classroom: Students' learning strategies and motivation strategies. *Journal of Educational Psychology, 80,* 260–267.

Bandura, A. (1986). *Social foundations of thought and action: A social cognitive theory.* Englewood Cliffs, NJ: Prentice Hall.

Bellamy, Edward. (2000). *Looking Backward: From 2000 to 1887.* Bedford, MA: Applewood Books.

Belland, J. C., Taylor, W. D., Canelos, J., Dwyer, F., & Baker, P. (1995). Is the self-paced instructional program, via microcomputer-based instruction, the most effective method of addressing individual learning differences? *Educational Communication and Technology Journal, 33*(3), 185–198.

Biner, P. M., Bink, M. L., Huffman, M. L., & Dean, R. S. (1995). Personality characteristics differentiating and predicting the achievement of televised-course students and traditional-course students. *The American Journal of Distance Education, 9*(2), 46–60.

Carrier, C., Davidson, G., & Williams, M. (1985). The selection of instructional options in a computer-based coordinate concept lesson. *Educational Communication and Technology Journal, 33*(3), 199–212.

Cobb, T. (1997). Cognitive efficiency: Toward a revised theory of media. *Educational Technology, Research and Development, 45*(4), 21–35.

Coggins, C. C. (1988). Preferred learning styles and their impact on completion of external degree programs. *The American Journal of Distance Education, 2*(1), 25–37.

Dille, B., & Mezack, M. (1991). Identifying predictors of high risk among community college telecourse students. *The American Journal of Distance Education, 5*(1), 24–35.

Dillon, C., Greene, B., & Crynes, B. (2000). The Impact of learner differences on student performance in distributed learning environments. *Proceedings of The Research Workshop of the European Distance Education Network* (1st, Prague, Czechoslavakia, March 16–17), 113–115.

Garrison, D. R., & Baynton, M. (1987). Beyond independence in distance education. *The American Journal of Distance Education, 1*(3), 3–15.

Geiger, M. A., Boyle, E. J., & Pinto, J. (1992). A Factor analysis of Kolb's Revised Learning Style Inventory. *Educational and Psychological Measurement, 52*(3), 753–759.

Gibson, C. G. (1996). Toward an understanding of academic self-concept in distance education. *American Journal of Distance Education, 10*(1), 23–36.

Greene, B. A., DeBacker, T.K., Ravindran, B., & Krows, A. J. (1999). Goals, values, and beliefs as predictors of achievement and effort in high school mathematics classes. *Sex Roles, 40*(5), 421–458.

Greene, B. A., Dillon, C. L., & Crynes, B. (2001). *Technology-based distributed learning in post secondary education: Learner differences in strategy use and achievement.* Paper presented at the 2001 American Educational Research Association, Seattle, WA, April 10–14.

Greene, B. A., & Miller, R. B. (1996). Influences on course performance: Goals, perceived ability, and self-regulation. *Contemporary Educational Psychology, 21,* 181–192.

Joughlin, G., Lai, T., & Cottman, C. (1992). *Distance learners' approaches to studying: The Nature of "deep" and "surface" approaches reconsidered.* Paper presented at the World 16th Conference of the International Council for Distance Education, Bangkok, Thailand, November 8–13. ERIC Document 357226.

Kember, D., & Harper, G. (1987). Implications for instruction arising from the relationship between approaches to studying and academic outcomes. *Instructional Science, 16,* 35–46.

Koob, J. J., & Funk, J. (2002). Kolb's Learning Style Inventory: Issues of Reliability and Validity. *Research on Social Work Practice, 12*(2), 293–308.

Marsh, H. W. (1992). *SDQIII.* Campbelltown, Australia: University of Western Sydney, Publication Unit.

Miller, R. B., Behrens, J. T., Greene, B. A., & Newman, D. (1993). Goals and perceived ability: Impact on student valuing, self-regulation and persistence. *Contemporary Educational Psychology, 18,* 2–14.

Miller, R. B., Greene, B. A., Montalvo, G. P., Ravindran, B., & Nicholls, J. D. (1996). Engagement in academic work: The role of learning goals, future consequences, pleasing others, and perceived ability. *Contemporary Educational Psychology, 21,* 388–442.

Moore, M. (1989). Three types of interaction. *The American Journal of Distance Education, 3*(2), 1–7.

Moore, M., & Kearsley, G. (1996). *Distance Education: A Systems view.* Belmont, WA: Wodsworth Pub Co.

Nicholls, J. G. (1989). *The Competitive Ethos and Democratic Education.* Cambridge, MA: Harvard University Press.

Oxford, R., Young, P., Ito, S., & Sumrall, M. (1993). Factors affecting achievement in a satellite delivered Japanese language program. *The American Journal of Distance Education, 7*(1), 11–25.

Pintrich, P. R., & De Groot, E. V. (1990). Motivational and self-regulated learning components of classroom academic performance. *Journal of Educational Psychology, 82,* 33–40.

Pintrich, P. R., & Garcia, T. (1991). Student goal orientation and self-regulation in the college classroom. In M. Maehr & P. R. Pintrich (Eds.), *Advances in motivation and achievement: Goals and self-regulatory processes* (Vol. 7, pp. 271–402). Greenwich, CT: JAI Press.

Pittenger, D. J. (1993). The Utility of the Myers-Briggs Type Indicator, *Review of Educational Research, 63*(4), 467–488.

Pugliese, R. R. (1994). Telecourse persistence and psychological variables. *The American Journal of Distance Education, 8*(3), 22–39.

Ravindran, B., & Greene, B. A. (1999). *The role of goals, beliefs and cognitive engagement in the prediction of preservice teachers' knowledge integration.* Paper presented at the 2000 annual meeting of the American Educational Research.

Sewall, T. J. (1986). *The measurement of learning style: A critique of four assessment tools.* Green Bay, WI: Assessment Center, University of Wisconsin. ERIC Document Reproduction Service No. ED 267-247.

Snow, R. E., & Lahman, D. F. (1984). Toward a theory of cognitive aptitude for learning from instruction. *Journal of Educational Psychology, 76*(3), 347–376.

Zimmerman, B. J., & Martinez-Pons, M. (1990). Student differences in self-regulated learning: Relating grade, sex, and giftedness to self-efficacy and strategy use. *Journal of Educational Psychology, 82*, 51–59.

17

Cognitive and Learning Factors in Web-Based Distance Learning Environments

Michael Hannafin
The University of Georgia
hannafin@coe.uga.edu

Janette R. Hill
The University of Georgia
janette@coe.uga.edu

Kevin Oliver
*Virginia Polytechnic Institute
and State University*
kmoliver@vt.edu

Evan Glazer
The University of Georgia
eglazer@coe.uga.edu

Priya Sharma
The Pennsylvania State University
psharma@psu.edu

LEARNING IN WEB-BASED ENVIRONMENTS

Research on Web-based learning can prove difficult to benchmark since the field is highly fluid and changes rapidly. Costigan (1999) noted, "We are still at the point where we have to gain a better understanding of the trees [individual characteristics of the Internet/Web] before the forest makes any sense" (p. xxiv). According to Windschitl (1998), "the volume of diverse information, the currency of information, the availability of data sets for inspection or down-loading, and the wealth of visual information—*should* promote a richer inquiry experience for learners, especially in the typical classroom where stale resource materials do little to stimulate students' interest" (p. 29).

While the possibilities appear limitless, the reality often has proven disappointing. There is a great deal of activity in and information about Web-based learning (e.g., Boettcher & Conrad, 1999; Leflore, 2000), but only limited empirical research has emerged (Hill & Hannafin, 1997; Roschelle & Pea, 1999; Windschitl, 1998). To further complicate matters, many researchers report equivocal, nonsignificant, or even contradictory findings (see, for example, Russell, 1999). As a result, both researchers and practitioners are left more confused than enlightened.

It is important to establish a broader framework for understanding Web-based learning. In the following sections, we examine the relevance and significance of existing research in both Web-based learning as well as computer-mediated learning. We examine two factors: cognitive and learning. Cognitive and learning factors share both similarities with and distinctions from one another. Cognitive factors initiate an individual's mental processing or stimulate individual cognitive processes, while learning factors cause students to engage specific to-be-learned concepts, content, or skills in particular ways. In effect, cognitive factors optimize the unique ways individuals process knowledge to optimize personal relevance and meaning, while learning factors amplify the ways individuals are expected to know or understand content, concepts, and skills.

COGNITIVE FACTORS

For Web-based learning environment (WBLE) practices to advance, we need a principled view of the processes that underlie learning generally as well as those specifically applicable to Web-based learning. We focus our cognitive factor discussion on the following primary areas: prior knowledge, metacognition, system knowledge and prior experiences, self-efficacy, learning styles, and motivation.

Prior Knowledge

Prior knowledge reflects existing cognitive structures that are "the principal factor influencing the learning and retention of meaningful new material" (Ausubel, 1963, p. 217). Prior knowledge has played a significant role in learning and retention across a wide range of technology-based learning environments (see, for example, Hill & Hannafin, 1997; Land & Hannafin, 1996). In two open-learning studies with 24 and 139 university students respectively, Portier and van Buuren (1995) found that students with high prior knowledge of statistics utilized more embedded support devices than students with limited prior knowledge. The interaction between prior knowledge and use of embedded support was most pronounced for processing (i.e., figures, examples) and testing devices (i.e., exercises, self-checks). Consistent with learner control research in computer-based instruction, the researchers suggested that since high prior knowledge students generally make better learning choices, they might benefit from unrestricted access to and use of available tools and relevant information. Further, students with limited prior knowledge might require structure and guidance, restricted initial access, and directed scaffolding over extended periods of time.

Metacognition

Awareness of cognition is the essence of metacognitive skills that play an important role during learning (Hill & Hannafin, 1997). In typical learning environments, students must process considerable information represented using visual (video, live action, pictures), textual (words, paragraphs), aural (spoken word, song, music), and tactile (touch, resistance) symbol systems. In computer-based learning, including WBLEs, much of this activity is done independently and without the benefit of a teacher or peer collaborator. Students must utilize their metacognitive knowledge and skill extensively to assess their ongoing understanding, evaluate alternative approaches, select one or more approaches, and reassess their understanding (Linn, Shear, Bell, & Slotta, 1999). In some cases, they perform well, while in others they do not. In one study, distance students reported a greater need to engage in metacognitive thinking to compensate for limitations in their learning environments (e.g., not having instant access to peer/instructor feedback). White (1995), in a comparative analysis of 37 classroom and distance learning students, found that distance students were more likely than traditional students to monitor their comprehension and identify problems impeding task completion, as well as more likely to manage their own learning. The absence of a "live" instructor in the distance environment may engender greater self-reliance; distance students cited it as a contributing factor to increased metacognitive activity.

Another study illustrates that while metacognitive thinking is necessary and important in distance environments, many students fail to monitor or regulate their own learning. Marland, Patching, and Putt (1992) investigated undergraduate college students while they interacted with distance learning materials. While students exhibited metacognitive planning, their strategies were "simplistic." For example, students would reread passages and underline important points, but rarely translated ideas into their own words or illustrate concepts. Students' metacognitive thinking was superficial and descriptive rather than reflective and prescriptive, and responses to metacognitive awareness were simplistic (e.g., reread a passage). The researchers suggested the inclusion of embedded activities that "make explicit the study strategies they could or should use" (Marland, Patching, & Putt, 1992, p. 215). Such activities include asking students to convert concepts into everyday forms and structures, anticipate possible outcomes of such application, and generate evaluation criteria.

System Knowledge and Prior Experiences

The importance of prior experience and success in the use of computer-based applications is well documented. For example, Hill and Hannafin (1997) found that system knowledge impacted the learners' ability to successfully locate resources in an information system. This finding was consistent in other computer environments as well. In a survey of online nursing students, inadequate Web knowledge and computer illiteracy were the most frequently identified barriers to Web use (Thiele, Allen, & Stucky, 1999). In another survey of 48 graduate students dispersed across seven remote sites, Bielema (1997) found 28% of all e-mail posts were related to technical difficulties, including problems with connectivity, student accounts, and use of software tools.

Yet' despite the lack of technical experience, a significant number of students unfamiliar with such tools continue to enroll in distance courses (Roblyer, 1999). Given that limited system knowledge seemingly does not deter enrollment, alternative means to support learners must be considered. Researchers have demonstrated that scaffolding can minimize problems associated with a lack of system knowledge or prior technical experience. In DeBourgh's (1999) study of a distance course with 44 adult learners, techniques were embedded within the Web-based course to minimize limitations in system knowledge, including protocols for accessing the instructor and prompt responses from the instructor to both student questions and submitted assignments.

Other researchers have indicated that early intervention to compensate for limited technical skills is important. Winfield, Mealy, and Scheibel (1998) suggested strategies to "build up user confidence with technology" (p. 446) as part of their instructional design model for Web-based courses. A series of learning activities were recommended for the early stages of distance courses to demonstrate competence in such basic skills as posting discussion comments, replying to others' comments, and submitting assignments.

While it seems intuitively reasonable that limited system knowledge and technical difficulties would impact motivation and learning, the available research does not generally support this claim. Learning appears to continue to the extent support systems are provided to help students manage the inevitable technical problems.

Self-Efficacy

Self-efficacy reflects the confidence learners report in approaching and handling new tasks (Bandura, 1993). Prior research indicates that self-efficacy influences the likelihood of engaging a task or instruction, the confidence reported in learning, and the likelihood that such knowledge or skill will be applied (Hill & Hannafin, 1997; Pajares, 1996). In a study of print versus televised instruction, for example, Salomon (1984) found that individual perceptions influenced both the effort invested and the resulting learning. To the extent individuals perceived the task and their self-efficacy as high, they invested more mental effort toward learning. When perceived task demands were high but self-efficacy was low, students tended to give up easily or failed to engage the learning materials.

Generally, students who view their ability to learn as unrestricted have higher self-efficacy than students who view their abilities as innate and unchangeable. Some evidence suggests that older students tend to view ability as relatively stable and unchanging (Dweck & Leggett, 1988). If so, they may perceive a limited ability to profit from Web-based instruction. Additionally, students who perceive themselves as being in control of their environment tend to report higher self-efficacy than do those who have failed to persevere on prior tasks (Bandura, 1993). This construct seems particularly applicable to system knowledge and prior experiences with Web technology, suggesting distance learners should be adequately trained and prepared to manage these potentially confusing and uncontrollable new environments.

Little research has been conducted specifically on the impact of self-efficacy on learning in Web-based learning environments, although some evidence suggests the presence of a relationship. In a pilot study involving 19 nursing students, a negative relationship was reported between fear of making mistakes and test scores (Papa, Perugini, & Spedaletti, 1998). Students who believed they were able to master a distance challenge tended to achieve more. The converse of these findings suggests the possibility of learning decrements when students lack self-efficacy. To help students with low self-efficacy, distance learning environments may need to reify perceptions of cognitive ability, comparisons with peers, and controllability of the environment (Bandura, 1993).

Cognitive and Learning Styles and Preferences

The roots of cognitive and learning style research are strongest in Aptitude-Treatment Interaction (ATI) research, where learning was hypothesized as greatest where instructional media and activities matched various learner attributes and styles. Indeed, a significant body of learning style and preference research based on Kolb's (1985) *Learning Style Inventory* continues to thrive. Cognitive styles are defined as "characteristic self-consistencies in information processing that develop in congenial ways around underlying personality trends" (Messick, 1984, p. 61). Thus, cognitive style refers to the way in which learners process information to make sense of their world (Jonassen & Grabowski, 1993).

Learning styles, on the other hand, refer to learner preferences for different types of learning activities. Though intuitively appealing, learning styles and preferences often are not significantly related to student achievement or course comprehension. To the contrary, nearly two decades ago Richard Clark (1982) described "antagonism" between how students reportedly prefer to learn versus the approaches found most effective: Students may learn best from the instruction they like least, and vice versa. The quest to differentiate instruction to accommodate learner styles and preferences may prove far more costly than warranted with regard to learning effects.

Terrell and Dringkus (1999–2000) found the majority of their 98 distance learning students preferred working alone and were "more interested in abstract concepts and ideas than people" (p. 233). These classifications were consistent with Kolb's (1985) "converger" and "accommodator" classifications. In research conducted with 189 Hong Kong nursing students, Weety (1998) found that study packages with limited communication encouraged students to become more independent (i.e., self-directed, analytical) after their course. Still, many field-dependent students desired more social interaction in the course and complained about the lack of communication with instructors and peers.

Despite the preference for concrete versus abstract environments, or for self-study versus social environments, few distance studies have actually proved students learn less or interact differently because they prefer one mode to another. Learning style characteristics do not typically predict whether the student will succeed or fail in a distance environment. In a research study with 58 undergraduate students, learning styles did not affect student attitudes toward a traditional course with Web components, nor did they influence student achievement (Day, Raven, & Newman, 1998). Likewise, Kranc (1997) found learning style factors neither impacted cognitive outcomes nor predicted the performance of 55 adult students in a North Carolina distance course.

Terrell and Dringus (1999–2000) found the effect of learning style on dropout status was not significant. Although students classified as accommodators had a 20–24% higher dropout rate than any other learning style, this finding was presumably related to preferences for active experimentation and communication with peers—variables limited in the online environment.

Motivation

Motivation is often examined according to four dimensions: choice of tasks, effort, persistence, and achievement (Pintrich & Schunk, 1996). Choice of tasks refers to one's willingness to engage an activity without external pressure. Effort refers to the level with which one engages a task (e.g., using strategies, elaborating documents). Persistence refers to the time one is willing to spend on a task. Achievement is viewed as an indirect indicator of motivation since it is based upon the prior three indices—choice of tasks, effort, and persistence.

Several researchers and theorists have examined motivation and learning from computer-based instruction. Mark Lepper and his colleagues proposed empirically-based strategies, rooted in psychological research and theory, to motivate learners during computer-based learning (see, for example, Lepper, 1985; Lepper & Chabay, 1985; Lepper & Gurtner, 1989; Lepper & Malone, 1987). Keller (1988) adapted his Attention, Relevance, Confidence, Satisfaction (ARCS) motivational model of instruction to computer courseware design, suggesting that students will learn better if environments can get their *attention*, help them to *see relevance* in learning tasks, help them to feel *confident* they can succeed on tasks, and *satisfy* their learning with both internal and external rewards.

Fjortoft (1996) surveyed 198 adults in a distance learning pharmacy course and found "intrinsic benefits" related to persistence. If adults perceived that the course contained job-related information to help them advance their careers, it increased their willingness to complete distance courses.

Bullen (1998) noted that some students were not intrinsically motivated by mandatory participation in online conferencing. Students stated that some of their required discussion simply restated others' work and lacked insight. Mandatory posting requirements appear to motivate students extrinsically to receive grades rather than intrinsically to engage one another and develop better understanding.

Researchers have found several techniques to be effective for increasing motivation. In a pilot and follow-up research study with distance students in a University of London extension program, Visser, Plomp, and Kuiper (1999) found that motivational messages that included confidence-building statements promoted greater retention rates than distance courses that did not utilize motivational messages. Some classes received generic prewritten messages, while other classes received similar messages personalized by the instructor to address specific student needs or concerns. Both formats improved motivation and retention.

LEARNING FACTORS

Research in emerging learning environments has focused on a wide range of research-based design factors (Hannafin, 1992). Of the various design factors that influence student learning in a Web-based learning environment, we focus on five: learning context, opportunities for active learning, resources, tools, and scaffolds.

Learning Context

Given the right environment and conditions, learning can be enhanced and transfer strengthened. This may prove more complex than typically assumed. The ability to support both *knowing that* and *knowing how* is important within Web-based learning environments, with their varied informational resources and tools and largely virtual learning context. Oliver and Herrington's (2000) research indicates that the use of authentic contexts and problem-based activities is successful for creating engaging WBLEs. Further, these elements provide the necessary framework and structure for mediating and supporting student learning within a Web-based environment.

Authentic, context-rich Web-based learning contexts can also facilitate learning. The Little Planet Literacy project (peabody.vanderbilt.edu/ctrs/lsi/morelp.htm) serves as one example of a context-rich Web-based activity. The goal of the activity is to use problem-solving strategies to drive an automobile to a final destination using a nonlinear path. The learner is provided a variety of tools (e.g., ruler, protractor, and calculator) and manages a variety of variables (e.g., money, road obstacles, gasoline, pit stops, different forms of currency) in order to accomplish a task—real situations, tools, and problems. Given that prior research has demonstrated the effectiveness of situated or authentic learning in classrooms (Brown, Collins, & Duguid, 1989) and in computer-based learning environments (Herrington & Oliver, 1998), contextualized Web-based activities such as Mapamatic Desert Challenge may provide authentic alternatives.

In addition to providing authentic learning contexts and tasks, Web-based environments must also frame the learning activity and relationships with respect to prior knowledge. Bills' (1997) study investigates the effects of structure and interactivity on the achievement of undergraduate students receiving Internet-based instruction. Structure is defined as an instructional strategy that frames the learning activity; interactivity is defined as the instructional strategy that provides opportunities for the student to participate actively in the learning activity. Students who were provided both structure and interactivity performed significantly better than did students who were provided interactivity but no structure.

Bills' (1997) research indicates the primacy of structure over interactivity in learning, especially in the context of open environments such as the Web. This research also reinforces the relationship between structure and the richness of cognitive association and representation (Gifford, 1997), indicating that structure may promote meaningful learning by facilitating the application of prior knowledge to the current learning context and to newer real-life contexts.

Opportunities for Active Learning

Silberman (1996) defined an active learning environment as one where students' needs, expectations, and concerns influence the teacher's instructional strategies. Active learning environments stimulate student motivation, encourage student participation, and contain both personal and humanistic elements (Powers & Guan, 2000). For example, the JASON project (http://www.jason.org/) is a learning community comprising students and researchers who explore student questions through online interactions in the context of a science journey in remote locations. McGonigle and Mastrain (1998) established active participation goals within a nursing course and provided a variety of interactive activities that increased student enthusiasm for learning as well as increased achievement beyond course expectations. Likewise, in a study involving 142 college students and their preferences for interaction within a Web-based environment, Donaldson and Thomson (1999) found differences between attitudes toward open student-to-student communication and didactic instructor-to-student communication. Interpersonal communication played a key role in learner satisfaction.

The importance of active student-peer interaction is also illustrated in Cooney's (2000) research with 10th graders in a collaborative, online English course. The interaction patterns in the online class varied considerably from traditional teacher-led classes. The online environment gave students the opportunity to expand their understanding and reach higher levels of analysis by collaborative sharing of perspectives. The ability to construct shared understanding resulted in both greater participation as well as in-depth, consistent performance. Cooney further indicated that students felt intellectually challenged by the close involvement with peer work, resulting in higher levels of individual analysis and group understanding. Given the students' positive response to student-to-student communication, online course developers may need to create more learner-centered approaches to Web-based education.

Other aspects of active learning include the personal and humanistic elements of an environment, such as faculty-student contact and "perceived caring." Research indicates that students' perceptions are correlated with perceived problems and importance attributed by the course instructor (Daugherty & Funke, 1998). The instructor's perceived caring improves both student attitudes toward class and their perception of their learning. Bohlken's (1998) research indicates that an environment that supports reciprocal listening and caring between student and instructor—especially through dynamic personal interaction—increases both perceived caring and perceived learning. Incorporating personal and dynamic modes of interaction within a Web-based learning environment may enhance student perceptions of and attitudes toward both the class and their learning.

Resources

Perkins (1991) identified resources as important constituents of any learning environment. Resources may be broadly classified as static or dynamic (Hill & Hannafin, 2001) depending on the stability of their content. For example, static resources such as print-based books and materials contain stable content that cannot be easily modified or updated. Many Web-based dynamic resources, such as weather databases and online news services, are continuously updated and modified. Human experts and collaborators may similarly be considered as dynamic resources.

Haycock (1991) noted that intellectual and physical access to a variety of such resources is important. Haycock underscored the importance of ensuring appropriate correspondence between student ability and available resources, i.e., students' content knowledge and reading ability play an important role in determining the appropriateness and usefulness of resources. Very complex and sophisticated content that may be appropriate for graduate students may not be as effective or useful for high school students. Although a resource may be both appropriate and useful, students may require some guidance or scaffolding in the procedures and uses of the resource.

Research reports substantiate this need. Oliver's (1999) research indicates that students need guidance and orientation on the use of specific resources and tools. The absence of guidance or scaffolding—both procedural and metacognitive—may result in ineffective resource use (or lack of use altogether). Slotta and Linn's (2000) research on eighth graders' use of Web resources indicated that when provided orientation and ongoing scaffolding on the use of resources and tools, students performed effectively during a learning task. Thus, effective Web-based learning environments often feature a variety of resources—static and dynamic— as well as procedural and metacognitive guidance on the use of the resources.

WebQuests (http://edweb.sdsu.edu/webquest/webquest.html) are examples of how resource use can be scaffolded in WBLEs. Access to resources coupled with a motivating question in a WebQuest may help students develop higher-order thinking skills (March, 1998). Each WebQuest follows a recommended structure: an introduction, a task, the process used to accomplish the task, Web resources, how the task will be evaluated, and a conclusion. This design enables scaffolding and structure without restricting creativity in the appearance or content of the activity—characteristics inherent in many Web-based activities.

Tools

Web-based learning environments may also contain a variety of communication and exploration tools. Communication tools include e-mail, electronic discussion boards, listservs, teleconferencing, and other similar modes of e-communication. Communication tools influence learning in a variety of ways. First, communication tools play a mediating role in influencing new patterns of thought and cognitive functioning (Wertsch, 1991). These mediating tools—including symbols, diagrams, software visualizations, electronic messages, and WWW homepages—can be either static or dynamic. They promote cognitive change by altering cultural meanings and institutional settings.

Communication tools can also assist in internalizing cognitive functions by acting as partners in the zone of proximal development (Vygotsky, 1978). Research indicates that communication tools may give rise to shared intellectual benefits during the course of learning collaborations and collective knowledge-building experiences (Scardamalia & Bereiter, 1996). Schrage (1990), for example, indicated that the most efficient collaborative tools were those that created a "mental shared space"—electronic whiteboards, conferencing tools, and group brainstorming tools—all of which promote social interaction and productivity.

Web-based learning environments may also include tools that support learning and exploration. Laffey, Tupper, Musser, and Wedman (1998) developed a tool that both guided student work and enabled students to represent, share, and socially construct knowledge during project-based learning. Their system guides students in the use of the myriad of available resources, and in assessing their planning, reflection, and collaboration during learning. Through the use of the tool, students significantly deepened their understanding of the content due to tool-stimulated reflection and articulation. In addition, students found the tool useful in representing their work.

Several exemplary sites demonstrating tool use are viewable on the Web. Artemis (hice.eecs.umich.edu/sciencelaboratory/artemis/index.html) is a Web-based environment created by the Center for Highly Interactive Computing in Education that uses a variety of tools to help middle-grade students inquire about and research issues in science. Tools and resources such as a filtered search engine, shared folders, driving question folders, note cards, a search history database, a thesaurus, and a dictionary allow students to access, organize, and communicate information from magazines, journals, and Web pages located in the Middle Years Digital Library. Such tools and resources allow users to experiment with basic concepts and construct complex models that build on existing knowledge (Morrison & Collins, 1995). Providing a variety of tools that support different types of cognitive exploration and experimentation results in a rich learning environment capable of meeting a variety of both learner and learning community goals.

Scaffolding

A scaffold may be defined as assistance that is initially provided to support the learner in executing a learning task; it is gradually faded as the learner becomes more independent and competent in achieving the learning task. Scaffolds may be classified as conceptual, metacognitive, procedural, and strategic (Hannafin, Land, & Oliver, 1999). Scaffolds are provided within Web-based environments to improve student learning, task certainty and execution, and enthusiasm.

A variety of scaffolding techniques has been examined in WBLEs. Slotta and Linn (2000) focused on the scaffolding of learning within the Web-based Knowledge Integration Environment (KIE). Eighth graders were asked to survey six Web sites related to passive solar energy. With the help of KIE's scaffolding tools—procedural and metacognitive—students were asked to evaluate the Web sites and ask and address critical questions that would help to relate the content to a specific project. Empirical evidence from the study's results indicates that scaffolding tools positively influenced students' critiques and their ability to ask critical questions (Slotta & Linn, 2000).

Other scaffolding evidence has been reported for Computer Supported Intentional Learning Environments (CSILE) (Scardamalia et al., 1992). The built-in communication and collaborative tools provided within the environment allow students to scaffold each other's learning, resulting in increased metacognitive skills, learning, and interest as well as participation (Scardamalia & Bereiter, 1996). These results indicate that scaffolding is an effective strategy for supporting and guiding learning both in Web-based and non-Web-based learning environments.

Another example of a scaffolded WBLE is the Deformed Frog Mystery (http://wise.berkeley. edu/WISE/demos/frog-activity/). Created using the Web Integrated Science Environment (WISE), the Deformed Frog Mystery scaffolds grades 5–12 students in developing a rationale about why frog mutations occur (Linn et al., 1999). The activity is structured around possible questions that the students might ask: "What's the problem?" "Where are the deformed frogs?" "What's in the water?" and "Why study frogs?" Within each question, structure is provided to help students organize their thinking and evaluate information. The researchers found that students were able to successfully analyze complex scientific content with this system. In particular, students with a history of low academic performance exemplified strong gains in cognitive engagement.

PROBLEMS & ISSUES: TOWARD A WBLE RESEARCH AGENDA

The research reviewed thus far enables us to optimize practice based on existing evidence, as well as to identify the unknowns and speculate on areas of need. In the final section, we propose a framework for a research agenda centered around six areas: 1) learners and learning factors; 2) instructors and teaching factors; 3) domain and task factors; 4) organization and sequence factors; 5) community and communication factors; and 6) assessment.

Learners and Learning

Fundamentally, learning is idiosyncratic in nature. Learning is a highly personalized process involving complex interactions among personal traits, experience, prior knowledge, values, and a host of related factors. Researchers focus on things like how individuals come to know, believe, understand, or do things—all as a matter of broad principle rather than individual precision. Researchers—Web-based and other—necessarily constrain the variables they account for, the measures they study, and methods of communicating findings. Independent of method, experimental-quantitative through observational-qualitative, the study of learners and learning is largely a process of managed imprecision.

Still, some factors have surfaced related to the success of Web-based learning environments. Motivation to learn plays a key role, but not all learners are motivated intrinsically to learn. In many cases, initial motivation may be high but difficult to sustain; in others, initial motivation may be lacking. And, while some strategies have proven helpful in motivating reluctant learners, questions exist as to their applicability across learners of different ages, developmental readiness, and experience. It is important to define the role of individual motivation to learn via WBLEs, and the manner in which learning strategies influence extrinsic versus intrinsic motivation to learn.

It is also important to understand learners' decision making as they seek and evaluate resources. To the extent WBLEs limit resources to those provided and constrain access to other resources, it may be less important how (or if) learners seek and use information on their own. On the other hand, many WBLEs—especially those that are open in nature—rely on learners to initiate and pursue ideas using the full resource potential of the Web. Hill (1999), for example, reported several information-seeking approaches, each influenced by factors such as prior knowledge, expectations (or lack of) for a query or search, and the extent to which comprehension is actively monitored and managed. We understand comparatively little of the dynamics of the identifying-seeking-evaluating processes vital to effective Web-based learning. We need to identify learning strategies that guide the formulation of particular interpretations and cognitive strategies that assist in sense-making for individual purposes.

Instructors and Teaching

Web-based teaching involves perspectives, models, and methods that differ from traditional, "live and in-person" approaches. Many instructors, including some currently immersed in Web-based approaches, lack familiarity with successful, proven strategies (Brandon & Hollingshead, 1999). Others lack technological competencies needed for even basic course implementation (Carr, 2000; Lowther, Jones, & Plants, 2000). In some cases, the needs can be remedied by targeted professional development; in others, the needs reflect deeply held concerns related to dubious quality, workload, and intellectual property. It is important to differentiate the barriers that can be identified and remedied directly from those that reflect more fundamental concerns and values. Skills can often be changed far more readily than underlying conceptual beliefs; we need to better understand the interplay between effective strategies and the beliefs that influence how (or if) they will be deployed.

It is also important to study the developmental transition of instructors from providers to facilitators (Jones & Wright, 1999). Epistemological and pedagogical habits of both mind and action are tacitly reified, complicating the transition to Web-based approaches. Most of our teachers' pedagogical apprenticeships involved didactic approaches, which were strengthened through their own teaching practices. Becoming facile as a learning facilitator is a developmental undertaking, involving shifts in both beliefs and methods. It may involve the rehosting of traditional materials and methods as an initial step, but transformation is needed to optimize Web-based teaching and learning. These transformational processes must be better defined and understood.

Domains and Tasks

For-credit WBLEs typically involve accountability for specific domain knowledge and skills. Whereas basic knowledge and verbal information are generally communicated adequately via specific course resources, skills—especially complex skills—often are not. Many performance-oriented tasks, traditionally mentored or demonstrated in live situations, are difficult to convey effectively in virtual environments. Methods and techniques associated with complex performance via WBLEs need to be identified and validated across domains and tasks.

A second concern focuses on problems associated with domain requirements; significantly more Web-based courses are offered in domains whose knowledge base can be readily decomposed. WBLEs involving structured disciplines, characteristic of business, scientific, mathematical, and engineering domains, tend to be more widespread; the relationships between and among concepts and skills are easier to articulate by consensus, specify, and operationalize. The same cannot be said for many domains in the humanities and the arts. The capacity to experience a culture, to express and perceive an emotion, and to sense tactile stimulation or olfactory sensation has not been manifested well in WBLEs. While some Web-based applications have emerged in areas such as ethics and philosophy, we need to explore research where domain content and concepts are more interpretive and less absolute in nature.

A final issue relates to the extent to which Web-based learning is more a harnessing or emancipating enterprise. To be certain, a good deal of appropriate Web use involves harnessing technology's potential to provide learning opportunities independent of spatial and temporal barriers; indeed, the explosion of Web course activity is testimony to such applications. On the other hand, far less effort has been focused on the broader but potentially more significant utility of the Web as a means to identify and address unique, individual learning interests. Truly user-centered, open learning systems emancipate learners from conventional models of personal or professional growth. They aid the individual in establishing and refining learning interests and needs, not simply supporting those prescribed by colleges, universities, and businesses. Web-based systems that support truly open, user-centered learning require a much more extensive understanding of the relationship among learner, domain, and structure variables than is presently available (Hannafin & Land, 2000).

Organizing and Sequencing

The organizing and sequencing of Web-based resources, tools, and activities varies as a function of the control exercised by external agents and the manner in which resources are provided. To the extent a WBLE is essentially a closed system, a great deal of control is exercised as to which and when resources and tools are provided, as well as the flow and sequence of activities; research on computer-based and multimedia learning already provides sufficient guidance for such applications. To the extent a WBLE is open, in terms of access to resources as well as the pedagogical framework, organization and structure are complicated. Research is needed to clarify how learners organize and link candidate resources into coherent conceptual wholes, as well as generate dynamic learning sequences using such resources (Gall & Hannafin, 1994).

Navigation can prove especially problematic in Web learning environments. Navigating open Web systems can disorient and overload the cognitive resources of many users (Barab, Bowdish, & Lawless, 1997). Disorientation is less a problem of sequence and structure than a state of cognitive disarray; it is less a failure of knowing what is possible than understanding how to exorcise those possibilities. The task is not simply to make clear what choices are available and where they lead, but to help learners to reflect on current understanding, anticipate learning needs, and select options accordingly.

Another issue relates to the quality and quantity of time spent learning with Web-based resources. Online learning generally requires more time, especially in open learning systems as the responsibility for organizing and sequencing resources shifts to the individual (Marjanovic, 1999). In many cases, this is both satisfactory and desired such as where learning involves the progressive refining of understanding, considering multiple points of view, or comparing and contrasting competing perspectives. In others, however, this is considered inefficient, such as where specific knowledge and skill must be mastered under explicit time limits. To-be-learned knowledge and skills can be organized and sequenced to optimize efficiency, but this may well come at the expense of deeper, more reflective learning; reflection can be increased as well, but typically with less efficiency. While it may be possible to support both mastery and reflection (see, for example, Bonk, Cummings, Hara, Fizchler, & Lee, 2000; Zhao, 1998), it is important to understand the tradeoffs associated with organization and sequence decisions.

Community and Communication

A great deal of research effort has been devoted to the role of communication technologies in online learning communities (see, for example, Moller, 1998). Several factors have been associated with the sense (or lack there of) of community, ranging from completion, perceived self-efficacy, satisfaction, and achievement. Community building involves establishing both technical affordances needed to communicate at a distance as well as social dimensions of communication itself.

Few dispute the importance of establishing and strengthening community, but it is not always easy to do so. Threaded discussions, emphasizing topics designed to elicit dialog and idea sharing, have been used as a democratic means to engage a community of participants in substantive dialog. Yet reports of frustration with stream-of-consciousness threads, a tendency of individuals to dominate discussions, and a lack of clarity as to the purposes of the discussions have surfaced. Concerns have been voiced over unequal contributions and inequitable workload among individual participants in group projects and assignments—assignments designed to promote collaboration and community. It is clear that community is not the product of simple technological or procedural measures, but involves developing and cultivating a shared sense of purpose and commitment (Hill, in press). The anonymity afforded many Web-based learning participants may simplify the bonding process for some but paradoxically make it possible for others to isolate or alienate themselves from their community.

Assessment

Perhaps no factor influences the nature and effectiveness of a learning environment as much as assessment. Assessment practices define importance, from the teacher to the student, in explicit ways. They also define what is not important insofar as performance and grading are concerned. While it may not be the teacher's intent to signal or otherwise limit what a student should learn, some aspects of a student's work "count" while others do not.

In WBLEs, this can be especially problematic since formal assessments often provide the sole gauge of student progress. As with many approaches, a tendency to value product quantity over quality of activity has emerged (Gunawardena, Lowe, & Anderson, 1997). Despite the myriad of multimedia tools available, practices have focused heavily on written work (O'Reilly & Patterson, 1998). Assessment practices have largely been mapped over from traditional teaching-learning approaches, but may not provide either suitable evidence of student learning or may simply emphasize those aspects of learning that are easy to assess (Hannafin, Reeves, & Hayden, 2001).

How do we assess the different kinds of learning embodied in Web-based approaches? Portfolios have been advocated for some time, but little guidance has emerged as to how such evidence should be assessed. Collaboration is valued highly in many WBLEs, but we tend to assess the products rather than collaboration processes per se. Many Web-based activities purport to promote problem solving or critical thinking, but the assessment practices reflect lower-level verbal information and simple skills. The distant nature of Web-based approaches renders difficult many observational and participatory assessments, but it is important to determine how best to implement them.

CONCLUSIONS

We have attempted to cite, describe, and interpret a good deal of research related to and/or implemented via Web-based learning. We speculated that considerable wisdom might be gleaned from research that predated the Web; we also anticipated that research on Web-based learning might shed light on several important issues related to the continued enhancement and extension of WBLEs. Indeed, both have proven true.

Yet we are intrigued by what is not yet known, the inconsistencies between and among researchers and their studies, and the seemingly endless number of unresolved research problems and issues. The publication base related to Web-based teaching and learning is considerable, yet the knowledge base remains relatively primitive and disorganized. The intellectual credibility of Web-based learning rests with those who engage in principled research and theory building—the grounded study of difficult problems and issues and the science of implementation over intuitive practices and popularization of craft.

REFERENCES

Ausubel, D. P. (1963). Cognitive structure and the facilitation of meaningful verbal learning. *Journal of Teacher Education, 14*, 217–221.

Bandura, A. (1993). Perceived self-efficacy in cognitive development and functioning. *Educational Psychologist, 28*(2), 117–148.

Barab, S., Bowdish, B., & Lawless, K. (1997). Hypermedia navigation: Profiles of hypermedia users. *Educational Technology Research and Development, 45*(3), 23–41.

Bielema, C. L. (1997). How computer-mediated communication (CMC) can work to enhance distance delivery of courses. *Journal of Applied Communications, 81*(4), 3–17.

Bills, C. G. (1997). *Effects of Structure and Interactivity on Internet-Based Instruction.* Paper presented at the Interservice/Industry Training, Simulation, and Education Conference, Orlando, FL, December 1–4. (ERIC Document ED 416317).

Boettcher, J. V., & Conrad, R. M. (1999). *Faculty guide for moving teaching and learning to the Web.* Mission Viejo, CA: Leagues for Innovation in the Community College.

Bohlken, B. (1998). Reciprocal listening with and from the heart in the electronic classroom. (ERIC Document Reproduction Service. No. ED 416 554).

Bonk, C. J., Cummings, J. A., Hara, N., Fischler, R. B., & Lee, S. M. (2000). A ten-level Web integration continuum for higher education. In B. Abbey (Ed.), *Instructional and Cognitive Impacts of Web-Based Education* 37–51. Hershey, PA: Idea Group Publishing.

Brandon, D. P., & Hollingshead, A. B. (1999). Collaborative learning and computer-supported groups. *Communication Education, 48*(2), 109–129.

Brown, J. S., Collins, A., & Duguid, P. (1989). Situated cognition and the culture of learning. *Educational Researcher, 18*(1), 32–42.

Bullen, M. (1998). Participation and critical thinking in online university distance education. *Journal of Distance Education, 13*(2), 1–32.

Carr, S. (2000, July). After half a course, a professor concedes distance education is not for him. *The Chronicle of Higher Education.* Available online: http://www.chronicle.com/free/2000/03/2000032801u.htm.

Clark, R. (1982). Antagonism between achievement and enjoyment in ATI studies. *Educational Psychologist, 17*, 92–101.

Cooney, D. H. (2000). Sharing aspects within Aspects: Real-time collaboration in the high school English clasroom. In B. Abbey (Ed.), *Instructional and cognitive impacts of Web-based education* (pp. 263–287). Hershey, PA: Idea Publishing Group.

Costigan, J. T. (1999). Forests, trees, and Internet research. S. Jones (Ed.), *Doing Internet research: Critical issues and methods for examining the net* (pp. xvii–xxiv). Thousand Oaks, CA: Sage.

Daugherty, M., & Funke, B. (1998). University faculty and student perceptions of Web-based instruction. *Journal of Distance Education, 13*(1), 21–39.

Day, T. M., Raven, M. R., & Newman, M. E. (1998). The effects of World Wide Web instruction and traditional instruction and learning styles on achievement and changes in student attitudes in a technical writing in an Agri-communication course. *Journal of Agricultural Education, 39*(4), 65–75.

DeBourgh, G. A. (1999, February). *Technology is the tool, teaching is the task: Student satisfaction in distance learning.* Paper presented at the annual meeting of the Society for Information Technology and Teacher Education, San Antonio, TX. (ERIC Document Reproduction Service No. ED 432 226).

Donaldson, J. L., & Thomson, J. S. (1999). Interpersonal communication strengthens Web-based instruction. *Journal of Applied Communications, 83*(3), 22–32.

Dweck, C. S., & Leggett, E. L. (1988). A social-cognitive approach to motivation and personality. *Psychological Review, 95*(2), 256–273.

Fjortoft, N. F. (1996). Persistence in a distance learning program: A case in pharmaceutical education. *American Journal of Distance Education, 10*(3), 49–59.

Gall, J. E., & Hannafin, M. J. (1994). A framework for the study of hypertext. *Instructional Science, 22*, 207–232.

Gifford, L. J. (1997). *Graduate students' perceptions of time spent in taking a course by Internet versus taking a Course in a regular classroom.* Paper presented at the Annual Mid-South Educational Research Association Conference, New Orleans, LA, November 4–6, 1998. (ERIC Document ED 427767).

Gunawardena, C. N., Lowe, C. A., & Anderson, T. (1997). Analysis of a global online debate and the development of an interaction analysis model for examining social construction of knowledge in computer conferencing. *Journal of Educational Computing Research, 17*(4), 397–431.

Hannafin, M. J. (1992). Emerging technologies, ISD, and learning environments: Critical perspectives. *Educational Technology Research and Development, 40*(1), 49–63.

Hannafin, M. J., & Land, S. M. (2000). Technology and student-centered learning in higher education: Issues and practices. *Journal of Computing in Higher Education, 12*(1), 3–30.

Hannafin, M. J., Land, S., & Oliver, K. (1999). Open learning environments: Foundations and models. In C. Reigeluth (Ed.), *Instructional design theories and models: A new paradigm of instructional theory* (pp. 115–140). Mahwah, NJ: Erlbaum.

Hannafin, M. J., Reeves, T. C., & Hayden, J. J. (2001). Understanding and addressing multiple stakeholder needs: Evaluation and the world of policymakers. In W. Heineke & J. Willis (Eds.), *Research Methods for Educational Technology* (pp. 251–267). Greenwich, CT: Information Age Publishing.

Haycock, C.-A. (1991). Resource-based learning: A shift in the roles of teacher, learner. *NASSP Bulletin, 75*(535), 15–22.

Herrington, J., & Oliver, R. (1998). *Using situated learning and multimedia to promote higher order thinking.* Paper presented at the EdMedia and EdTelecom, Charlottesville, VA.

Hill, J. R. (1999). A conceptual framework for understanding information-seeking in open-ended information systems. *Educational Technology Research and Development, 47*(1), 5–28.

Hill, J. R. (in press). Strategies and techniques for community building in Web-based learning environments. *Journal of Computing in Higher Education.*

Hill, J. R., & Hannafin, M. J. (1997). Cognitive strategies and learning from the World-Wide Web. *Educational Technology Research and Development, 45*(4), 37–64.

Hill, J. R., & Hannafin, M. J. (2001). Teaching and learning in digital environments: The resurgence of resource-based learning. *Educational Technology Research & Development, 49*(3), 37–52.

Jonassen, D. H., & Grabowski, B. L. (1993). *Handbook of individual differences, learning, and instruction.* Hillsdale, NJ: Lawrence Erlbaum.

Jones, R., & Wright, C. (1999). Online guided learning. *Educational Technology & Society, 2*(3) 115–118.

Keller, J. M. (1988). Use of the ARCS motivational model in courseware design. In D. Jonassen (Ed.), *Instructional designs for microcomputer courseware* (pp. 401–434). Hillsdale, NJ: Erlbaum.

Kolb, D. (1985). *Learning style inventory.* Boston: Hay/McBer Training Resources Group.

Kranc, B. M. (1997). *The impact of individual characteristics on telecommunication.* Unpublished doctoral dissertation, North Carolina State University.

Laffey, J., Tupper, T., Musser, D., & Wedman, J. (1998). A computer-mediated support system for project-based learning. *Educational Technology Research and Development, 46*(1), 73–86.

Land, S., & Hannafin, M. J. (1996). A conceptual framework for the development of theories-in-action with open learning environments. *Educational Technology Research and Development, 44*(3), 37–53.

Leflore, D. (2000). Theory supporting design guidelines for Web-based instruction. In B. Abbey (Ed.), *Instructional and cognitive impacts of Web-based education* (pp. 102–117). Hershey, PA: Ideas Group.

Lepper, M. R. (1985). Microcomputers in education: Motivational and social issues. *American Psychologist, 40*(1), 1–18.

Lepper, M. R., & Chabay, R. W. (1985). Intrinsic motivation and instruction: Conflicting views on the role of motivational processes in computer-based education. *Educational Psychologist, 20*(4), 217–230.

Lepper, M. R., & Gurtner, J. (1989). Children and computers: Approaching the twenty-first century. *American Psychologist, 44*(2), 170–178.

Lepper, M. R., & Malone, T. W. (1987). Intrinsic motivation and instructional effectiveness in computer-based education. In R. E. Snow & M. J. Farr (Eds.), *Aptitude, learning, and instruction, III: Conative and affective process analysis* (pp. 255–286). Hillsdale, NJ: Lawrence Erlbaum Associates.

Linn, M., Shear, L., Bell, P., & Slotta, J. (1999). Organizing principles for science education partnerships: Case studies of students learning about rats in space and deformed frogs. *Educational Technology Research and Development, 47*(2), 61–84.

Lowther, D. L., Jones, M. G., & Plants, R. T. (2000). Preparing tomorrow's teachers to use Web-based education. In B. Abbey (Ed.), *Instructional and Cognitive Impacts of Web-Based Education.* Hershey, PA: Idea Group Publishing.

March, T. (1998). The WebQuest Design Process. Available online at http://www.ozline.com/learning/theory.html.

Marjanovic, O. (1999). Learning and teaching in a synchronous collaborative environment. *Journal of Computer Assisted Learning, 15*, 129–138.

Marland, P., Patching, W., & Putt, I. (1992). Thinking while studying: A process tracing study of distance learners. *Distance Education, 13*(2), 193–217.

McGonigle, D., & Mastrain, K. (1998). Learning along the way: Cyberspacial quests. *Nursing Outlook, 46*(2), 81–86.

Messick, S. (1984). The matter of style: Manifestations of personality in cognition, learning, and teaching. *Educational Psychologist, 29*(3), 121–136.

Moller, L. (1998). Designing communities of learners for asynchronous distance education. *Educational Technology Research and Development, 46*(4), 115–122.

Morrison, D., & Collins, A. (1995). Epistemic fluency and constructivist learning environments. *Educational Technology, 35*(5), 39–45.

Oliver, K. (1999). *Student use of computer tools designed to scaffold scientific problem solving with hypermedia resources: A case study.* Unpublished doctoral dissertation, University of Georgia, Athens, GA.

Oliver, R., & Herrington, J. (2000). Using situated learning as a design strategy for Web-based learning. In B. Abbey (Ed.), *Instructional and cognitive impacts of Web-based education* (pp. 178–191). Hershey, PA: Idea Group Publishing.

O'Reilly, M., & Patterson, K. (1998). *Assessing learning through the WWW.* Paper presented at the 7th International World Wide Web Conference, Brisbane, Australia.

Pajares, F. (1996). Self-efficacy beliefs in academic settings. *Review of Educational Research, 66*(4), 543–578.

Papa, F., Perugini, M., & Spedaletti, S. (1998). Psychological factors in virtual classroom situations: A pilot study for a model of learning through technological devices. *Behaviour & Information Technology, 17*(4), 187–194.

Perkins, D. N. (1991). Technology meets constructivism: Do they make a marriage? *Educational Technology, 31*(5), 18–23.

Pintrich, P. R., & Schunk, D. H. (1996). *Motivation in education: Theory, research, and applications.* Englewood Cliffs, NJ: Prentice-Hall.

Portier, S. J., & van Buuren, H. A. (1995). An interactive learning environment (ILE) to study statistics: Effects of prior knowledge on the use of embedded support devices. *European Journal of Psychology of Education, 10*(2), 197–207.

Powers, S. M., & Guan, S. (2000). Examining student needs. In B. Abbey (Ed.), *Instructional and cognitive impacts of Web-based education* (pp. 200–216). Hershey, PA: Idea Publishing Group.

Roblyer, M. D. (1999). Is choice important in distance learning? A study of student motives for taking Internet-based courses at the high school and community college levels. *Journal of Research in Computing in Education, 32*(1), 157–171.

Roschelle, J., & Pea, R. (1999). Trajectories from today's WWW to a powerful educational infrastructure. *Educational Researcher*, 22–25.

Russell, T. (1999). *The "no significant difference" phenomenon.* Chapel Hill, NC: Office of Instructional Telecommunications.

Salomon, G. (1984). Television is "easy" and print is "tough": The differential investment of mental effort in learning as a function of perceptions and attributions. *Journal of Educational Psychology, 76*(4), 647–658.

Scardamalia, M., & Bereiter, C. (1996). Adaptation and understanding: A case for new cultures of schooling. In S. Vosniadou, E. D. Corte, R. Glaser, & H. Mandl (Eds.), *International perspectives on the design of technology-supported learning environments* (pp. 149–163). Mahwah, NJ: Lawrence Erlbaum.

Scardamalia, M., Bereiter, C., Brett, C., Burtis, P. J., Calhoun, C., & Smith, L. N. (1992). Educational applications of a networked communal database. *Interactive Learning Environments, 2*(1), 45–71.

Schrage, M. (1990). *Shared minds: The technologies of collaboration.* New York: Random House.

Silberman, M. (1996). *Active learning: 101 strategies to teach any subject.* Boston: Allyn & Bacon.

Slotta, J. D., & Linn, M. C. (2000). The Knowledge Integration Environment: Helping students use the internet effectively. In M. J. Jacobson & R. B. Kozma (Eds.), *Innovations in science and mathematics education: Advanced designs for technologies of learning* (pp. 193–226). Mahwah, NJ: Lawrence Erlbaum Associates, Inc.

Terrell, S. R., & Drinkgus, L. (1999–2000). An investigation of the effect of learning styles on student success in an online learning environment. *Journal of Educational Technology Systems, 28*(3), 231–238.

Thiele, J. E., Allen, C., & Stucky, M. (1999). Effects of Web-based instruction on learning behaviors of undergraduate and graduate students. *Nursing and Health Care Perspectives, 20*(4), 199–203.

Visser, L., Plomp, T., & Kuiper, W. (1999, February). *Development research applied to improve motivation in distance education.* Paper presented at the annual meeting of the Association for Educational Communications and Technology, Houston, TX. (ERIC Document Reproduction Service No. ED 436 169).

Vygotsky, L. S. (1978). *Mind in society: The development of higher psychological processes.* Cambridge, MA: Harvard University Press.

Weety, L. S. C. (1998). The influence of a distance-learning environment on students' field dependence/independence. *The Journal of Experimental Education, 66*(2), 149–160.

Wertsch, J. V. (1991). A sociocultural approach to socially shared cognition. In L. B. Resnick, J. M. Levine, & S. D. Teasley (Eds.), *Perspectives on socially shared cognition* (pp. 85–100). Washington, DC: American Psychological Association.

White, C. (1995). Autonomy and strategy use in distance foreign language learning: Research findings. *System, 23*(2), 207–221.

Windschitl, M. (1998). The WWW and classroom research: What path should we take? *Educational Researcher, 27*(1), 28–33.

Winfield, W., Mealy, M., & Scheibel, P. (1998). Design considerations for enhancing confidence and participation in Web based courses. *Proceedings of the Annual Conference on Distance Teaching & Learning*, 445–450. (ERIC Document Reproduction Service No. ED 422 885).

Zhao, Y. (1998). Design for adoption: The development of an integrated Web-based education environment. *Journal of Research on Computing in Education, 30*(3), 307–328.

18

Gender Equity Online, When There Is No Door to Knock On*

Cheris Kramarae
Center for the Study of Women in Society, University of Oregon
cheris@oregon.uoregon.edu

The majority of U.S. undergraduate college students are women. The majority of U.S. students taking online courses are women. And for the first time, because of the new types of computer-based classes, online women students seemingly do not need to worry about being identified and stereotyped by their gender—or their race or age or appearance. Online, it would seem, the focus can be on both women's and men's academic discussions, on their minds.

So online there are no, or at least few, gender equity problems? Unfortunately, there *are* problems experienced primarily by women that call for attention from all distance education administrators, teachers, and students. We have a special opportunity and responsibility right now to make sure that past sexist practices, which have been a problem on most campases, are not perpetuated online.

This chapter draws heavily on research conducted for a report for the American Association of University Women (AAUW), including interviews with more than 100 women and men, and more than 400 survey questionnaires completed by university teachers and students (online and on campus) and potential students from a great variety of backgrounds (Kramarae, 2001). In addition, I have benefited from discussions with graduate students and teachers from a dozen countries working together in a "Future of Higher Education" course at the International Women's University in Germany in 2000.

WOMEN RE-ENTERING FORMAL EDUCATION

For more than a century, adult women, differing widely in age, interests, economic and marital status, and amount of formal education, have used distance education to try to complete courses and degrees after having interrupted their education, often for family reasons. Many women

---

*Title adapted from David Sadker, "Gender Equity: Still Knocking at the Classroom Door," *Educational Leadership* (April 1999), pp. 22–26, http://www.sadker.org/eq-leader.htm.

who once attended university classes had to drop out of universities to take care of children or other family members. That "drop out" terminology, disliked by many women, will probably change if lifetime learning becomes the norm in the United States for both women and men.

Sometimes these students are called second-chance students (Guri-Rosenblit, 1999, p. 227). Their numbers have increased in the past years and, with the expanded opportunities offered by online courses, are expected to increase even more in the coming years. In fact, returning to college has become such a usual pattern that some people argue that we no longer need special names such as "re-entry women," "second-chance students," or "nontraditional students" for those who do it (Ross-Gordon & Brown-Haywood, 2000, p. 14). Yet while they may no longer be accurately called nontraditional students, many of them still are experiencing some of the same factors that caused the interruption (e.g., financial stresses, heavy family responsibilities, concern about academic abilities, and/or very limited time for additional responsibilities). The existence of online courses and programs does not, by itself, respond to many of the needs of women who are attempting to reenter.

AT A DISTANCE, FOR A LONG TIME

Given the exclusion of women from many traditional institutions of education in earlier centuries, the foundation of distance learning in the United States and the United Kingdom is especially interesting. In Scotland, between 1877 and 1931, St. Andrews University offered an external, higher education degree designed specifically for women. In the United States, the State of New York allowed the Chautauqua Institute (a summer training program for Sunday school teachers) to award degrees through mail instruction. In 1891 the University of Chicago offered the first university-sponsored correspondence course (Guri-Rosenblit, 1999, pp. 3–4). Others followed, and for more than a century women have been heavy users of distance education courses—in fact, they have been the majority of students in correspondence courses.

However, even though their numbers have been large, they have been considered to be individuals working on the sidelines of higher education to fulfill individual goals, rather than as thousands of women responding to social constraints, taking a common action to change their social and educational situation. Considering these women *only* as individuals does not help us recognize the particular difficulties that women as a social group have had or their political and ideological struggles and successes in higher education.

Now, as distance education programs have evolved by means of technology and, under various social and financial pressures, have become important factors in the long-term planning of universities, the search is on not only for successful, cost-efficient online courses and programs, but also for additional students to take the courses. Adult women, who in general have more restrictions on their mobility than adult men, are still considered one of the prime constituencies of an increasing online student pool.

TIME—AND TIME AGAIN

"Distance learning is a good option—or compromise—for women with children and without much free time" was a refrain that ran through the interviews. A few of the men also mentioned the value of distance learning for men with family responsibilities. But both women and men posited distance learning as a remedy for the problems that women with children, in particular, have with time.

In one sense the reasons for this refrain are simple. Most women enrolled in online courses have even less time to call their own than do most traditional students in face-to-face environments; in addition to taking their courses, many of them serve as primary caretakers of family members and also work at jobs outside the home. Women, especially those with children, have less "free" time away from their family responsibilities and other work. Distance education allows them to both stay at home *and* study, at least in the evenings or when off work, while still taking care of home duties, being available to others when needed. Men are more likely to have time that they can use more or less as they wish, in or out of the home. (See Greenstein, 2000; and Hersch & Stratton, 1997 for discussions of research on housework, employment, and time.)

However, in another sense this thinking about time ignores many characteristics of time as it is experienced today by women and men in the United States (as well as in many other countries). If we see types of time as primarily "linear/masculine" time or as "process/feminine" time, we can visualize the one as a straight line—easily broken into component units and single use—and the other as cyclical—continuous, and relational. We are most familiar with the linear time as describing men's careers and public histories. The cyclical time is known as private time, as women in the home often carry out several tasks at once such as caring for children while cooking meals and cleaning. The linear formal work is usually given more importance (even though it is interwoven with the informal process work, and, indeed, is impossible without the informal process work). (See the discussions of time in Woodward & Lyon, 2000.)

Institutions have historically been more concerned with separating the public linear formal work world from the feminine process world, and in treating the linear work world as more legitimate and important, than in relating them. If it were otherwise, we would likely long ago have set up educational systems with schedules, costs, and provisions that served more equally all workers with all kinds of responsibilities. While this view of time is too dichotomized (most public leaders must also be available for many tasks at the same time), those men and women who want to advance in their careers usually need to demonstrate autonomy from their private/home responsibilities and thereby their commitment to their jobs.

A need to hide the private responsibilities is often particularly important for women who want to advance themselves in their careers by taking advanced courses and degrees, while still maintaining familial relationships. Distance learning courses can, in this way, be particularly valuable for women who can thus more easily pass the "availability tests" at job and at home. Also, interviews indicate that since women are often considered responsible for "extra" babysitting costs that occur if they had to spend "extra" time out of the home attending off-line courses, they can often "save" some expenses by taking online courses.

Most of the women interviewed who were going (in many cases returning) to college have multiple responsibilities. Many single parents are caring for young children, many are the sole provider or co-contributor to their family's income, and some others are taking care of aging or ill parents. On the one hand they talk about their "right" to continue their education, or about the importance to their own careers and to their family income of continuing their education. But many of them also talk about the tension between their wish to take courses and their need to fulfill family responsibilities. While most of those with young families indicate that they are well-organized and that they prioritize activities, their scheduling is mostly a matter of determining the order in which they could get all their activities done most efficiently.

Many of the women respondents talked and wrote, with satisfaction, about distance education allowing them the possibilities of doing several tasks at once, as they discuss tradeoffs they make in their carrying out (while often enjoying and sometimes resenting) many family responsibilities and in their pursuit of their career goals. Many of them also recognized that, as women, they had more time-crunch problems than men tend to have.

If we want distance learning to work for people with many time demands, we will call for pragmatic measures to encourage more research about how women and men actually try to fulfill their family and career wishes, and create programs the aim of which is to better structure distance learning to help women work toward these goals. This would be more meaningful than just saying that distance learning (in whatever form) is a good (or only) option for women with children.

Most of the student mothers talking about their times for studying mentioned late evening or very early morning hours. Given that most of the women also had part- or full-time jobs, their preference for setting their own times for study does not seem surprising. However, late evening hours are not necessarily the only "natural" time for adults to study; researchers evaluating a graduate online course in the United Kingdom found that men were most likely to mention studying from 4 to 8 P.M. while the majority of the women studied later, fitting in their study times after fulfilling other commitments (Richardson & French, 2000, p. 305).

In sum, management of time has many special aspects. A review of previous studies indicates that students often find electronic discussions in courses very time-consuming, especially for those students who also meet face to face on campus during regularly scheduled times. One study found that students who performed poorly on a final exam blamed their performance on their reduced incentive to attend classes since class notes and lecture materials were available electronically. Another study found students appreciative of their e-mail communication when it was with an instructor who promised to return all messages within a 24-hour time frame. (See Chapman, 1998, for a review of literature including ways that type of course and educational status are related to student attitudes and participation.)

Faculty Time

Faculty time issues can quickly become student concerns. In interviews, online faculty have noted that developing and teaching online courses are remarkably time-consuming activities, even when the technology processes work well. Estimates of time vary since teachers' involvement and course requirements vary. But suggestions to double or triple the amount of time needed for face-to-face classes are not uncommon (see Palloff & Pratt, 1999, p. 49). Many of the online faculty interviewed enjoyed teaching their courses—if their heavy preparation load were acknowledged by the administration and compensated for by a reduced number of classes.

Most faculty members are accustomed to working long work weeks. However, under the current higher education system—which imposes ever-heavier teaching loads, larger classes, and increased pressure to bring in external grant funding and to publish—adequate preparation time for online courses might not be possible unless the teachers make some adjustments (Kirkpatrick & Jakupec, 1999, p. 65). The difficulty of dealing with too much e-mail was a recurring theme in the interviews with many university professors.

Coordinating collaborative Web-based courses takes a great deal of time for faculty members, particularly if they are trying to stay aware of the online discussions in the small group discussions that are a part of many Web-based courses. Their continual involvement seems important in order to discourage any harassment (especially in undergraduate courses) and to help guide and to support discussions. These factors suggest that Web-based courses need to be much smaller than many of the large lecture courses now offered in traditional programs in classrooms and auditoriums. One study of the value of collaborative learning online for an MBA program concludes with the suggestion that unless a college is prepared to commit substantial new resources to online programs, developing Web-based courses and programs is not a good idea (Arbaugh, 2000, p. 508).

CURRICULUM AND COOPERATIVE LEARNING: WHAT'S AVAILABLE?

Many students interviewed about their online experiences or plans report that they cannot get the subject matter they want online. Not being able to find a particular topic they want or need is not an unusual complaint; some students have always had difficulties getting the specific courses they want at the time they want them. But of course one of the supposed benefits of online education is that it can be what is needed, when it is needed. In the past, "geographical place" has often functioned as a prime barrier to access to higher education. It continues to be a factor in the online courses and programs that require some on-campus time.

Many of the women interviewed talked about the types of courses and programs that they cannot find at any time. Most of the women taking online courses have done a lot of thinking about the kinds of careers they want for themselves. For example, they talked about art education programs for handicapped children and adults in institutions, starting independent businesses that cater to handicapped children, and writing narrative computer programs for children and adults. We need to know more about women's lives and career plans to know what online programs are most useful for women.

Further, students may find that the material and the assignments in the available courses have little to do with their lives. Using the problems, interests, and experiences of the students (e.g., connecting the learning with the everyday life of the students) is a generally acknowledged way of actively engaging students (Palloff & Pratt, 1999, pp. 116–118). Yet many teachers may know very little about their students' lives, interests, knowledge, and experiences.

Proponents of shared learning suggest that if learning, particularly adult learning, is to be successful and long-lasting, students must be able to deal with the world as they experience it, very actively and continually involved in the creation of knowledge. (See the discussions in, for example, Merriam & Brockett 1997, pp. 250–252.) Yet for all the efforts to get students to work together on projects, most of the students find that their online learning experiences are still based primarily on didactic methods of instruction, with competitive, individual grading.

Many online students mention enjoying online discussions but are fervent in their wish to do their assignments independently. A social worker, married and with children at home, reported,

> I'm enrolled in a statistics course [online] and it does require quite a bit of group work. I am not finding it particularly helpful because.... I don't like waiting for other members to get around to doing the assignments. I like group work that requires discussion without involving the entire group in turning in a written paper. I am pretty busy just like my classmates and I really want to do the work and not keep track of my group members.

Almost all of the students interviewed who have taken courses online and on campus indicate that they feel that the online work is much more difficult. Part of this problem appears linked to the way the material and the students' lives are not well connected. One Ph.D. student, a married university instructor without children, said about an education course,

> She [the professor] put six readings online just for one of the four assignments during the week! And this is just one course. I think I am crazy to be taking two online courses while teaching an online course at the same time. Maybe the university is too concerned about the quality issue, so they overdo it. Much of the material seems almost useless. I pray to survive.

This student is fortunate in that she has ready access to a computer, her online courses are considered a legitimate part of the teaching work she is doing, she is not trying to take courses on top of a full-time job, and she is not taking care of children or an aged parent. She is more likely to survive than many other women who, however able to go without much sleep and however willing to study seemingly irrelevant material, do have physical limits.

Brookfield (1995) writes: "Knowing something of how students experience learning helps us build convincing connections between what we want them to do and their own concerns and expectations" (p. 93). Yet, in mixed-sex classes, unless the teacher is sincerely interested in and has information about women's experiences in the courses and in their full lives, getting to know something important about the individual women students' learning and life experiences will not happen for teacher or students.

Students report that online courses are often less flexible than on-campus courses. Responsible online teachers are understandably interested in providing a set, "full disclosure," syllabus for online students who often are enormously busy and who often need to carefully plan their work schedule for the entire course time. Given this situation, teachers concerned about gender and race equity have a special responsibility to plan their syllabi with a good knowledge of the feminist scholarship in the area. The "curriculum" includes not only the topic but also the ways that women and men's work and interests are involved in the agenda and research of any field of study. As women's studies research during the last 30 years makes very clear, every study area is influenced by gender (itself a complex concept), including the questions and methods of investigation and the standards of "merit," "rigor," and "impartiality." (See, for example, *Feminist Periodicals*; Hartcourt, 1999; Hayes & Flannery, 2000; Kramarae & Spender, 2000; *New Books on Women and Feminism*; Paul, 2000.)

THE COST OF IT ALL

Many people remain convinced that eventually, at least, distance learning will be a relatively inexpensive method of education. However, certainly for new programs, the costs for universities and students (in faculty development, implementation, delivery, and equipment) may be substantially higher. Currently, many institutions are charging the same for distance learning and equivalent on-campus courses. Many women with difficult economic situations are expressing keen interest in taking courses; however, at the moment distance learning opportunities are disproportionately taken by those who already have access to needed resources.

Students using online resources may find that tuition and access to computer equipment are not the only possible expenses. For example, several companies are offering, for a fee, online access to searchable books and journals, to help students write their papers more quickly without trips to the library. It is, of course, highly likely that much of the material most useful for research papers (including book texts) will not be available through such services. This consideration raises other, pedagogical, issues. Some faculty are especially concerned that this situation will perpetuate the separation of the haves and the have-nots (Blumenstyk, 2000, p. A41).

The cost of education was the single most frequently discussed topic by the students or potential students who responded to questions about online education. Understanding the varying meaning of the costs of education also requires understanding of the structural inequalities of power in families. For example, my interviews indicate that the cost of child care is most often added to the women's list of expenses, but not to the men's cost of education. Successful students report that they have obtained the support of other family members. But many report heavy demands put upon them at home, which often makes it difficult for them to take and complete distance education courses.

MASTERING COMPUTER-MEDIATED COMMUNICATION

Many online educators have written about the value of computer-mediated communication (CMC), particularly about the importance of creating "community" through discussion groups. For example, Guri-Rosenblit (1999) writes of the importance of "extensive group interaction and the creation of collective intelligence by an on-line community" (p. 163).

Increasingly, online teachers and students connect to the Internet to post and receive assignments, share feedback, and discuss topics. Students can respond to questions and discussions seemingly as fully as they want, which would seem a great improvement from the ways women are often silenced or cut off in on-campus courses. However, in actuality, students usually learn how long their responses "should" be, dependent in part upon their online "status." For example, many women report that they are criticized for posting responses that are "too long." Offline stereotypes, including the one about women talking too much, follow women online.

We need much more research on the conduct of discussions specifically in online courses. Recent research indicates the following: Students indicate that they know, or try to know, the gender of the other students in discussions. In mixed-sexed discussions, men use more turns and more words online than do women, who are less likely to continue posting when their messages receive no response (Herring, forthcoming). Women's topics tend to receive fewer responses from others, both females and males. Women are unlikely to control the topics of discussion except in groups when they are a clear majority (Hert, 1997).

While many teachers consider CMC as being at the heart of learning online and many students enjoy the online conversations, many of the women interviewed report finding the conversations threatening, time-consuming, and frustrating. Some of the women in classes with many male students organized women-only groups, without the knowledge of the teachers. Setting clear regulations regarding acceptable participation, along with the monitoring of the discussions, are ways teachers can help make the conversations equitable (Korenman & Wyatt, 1996). If the teacher is sensitive to gender communication issues and encourages discussions on topics introduced by women, communication is not as likely to be dominated by males (King, 2000).

Relatively few women have been instrumental in creating the software and hardware of the Internet. Men have established most of the programming, as well as the interactional norms on the Internet and, later, on the World Wide Web. Looking, even briefly, at the specific norms of interaction online helps us see that what is increasingly seen as "just normal" online interaction has been created by individuals, out of their own experiences.

One of the relatively few women who works as a computer programmer has pointed out that the early computer engineers have required us to use online some rather particular ideas about interaction. In fact, in making requests or replies online, we don't even have to talk to or involve anyone else. Many interactive services are delivered on demand, free from the restrictions of scheduled time. Ellen Ullman writes that this kind of interactivity requires, for all users, the asynchrony of the (very male) engineering culture, in which engineers leave messages rather than interrupt any other engineer's thinking or sleeping time: "Engineers seem to prefer the asynchronous life, or at least be used to it. But what about the rest of us ... Soon we may all be living the programming life" (1995, p. 143).

In brief, the point is that the design of information technology has not been determined on the basis of what works well for educational purposes or what works equally well for women and men.

Research in the United States throughout the 1970s, 1980s, and 1990s has illustrated some of the distinctive expectations and interactional patterns that women and men often employ, especially to foster connections with and support of others. For example, many women use talk to build connections with others, sharing personal feelings, experiences, fear, and problems. Generalizations about gender difference are difficult and dangerous, given individual differences as well as important cultural differences. However, we can say that talk between women friends tends to be personal, expressive, and supportive, disclosing intimate information and showing caring. Men also value friendships, of course, but they are more likely to seek companions than confidants, and some of the research suggests that they, unlike many women, are more likely to perceive talking as a limited way to be close. (See Wood, 1999, for a review of gender and communication research on this matter.)

There are critical implications for all our new educational practices, indeed for our lives, as we increasingly use, for our maintenance of friendships, and work and education interactions, communication systems that were developed by engineers, many of whom, according to Ellen Ullman, are predisposed or trained to avoid much talk with other humans (1995, p. 141).

As with all new technologies, designers have made decisions about what the processes will do and how they should be used. As with all new technologies, users will make some alterations based on their own needs and cultural ideas and values. In interviews, many of the online women students talked about how, cut off from using and interpreting nonverbal expressions, they have had to learn new ways of explaining themselves and "reading" others. A flight instructor taking online courses reported that by actively participating in online forums over the period of a term, she learned how to read the reactions of others. A cashier taking online courses explained that when she was in an online discussion with other students, she learned how to make the others aware that she was listening by adding her opinions often.

However, those women who are accustomed to a close reading of nonverbal cues as an integral part of their communication are finding online communication limiting. For example, the women interviewed about emoticons (the likenesses of human faces, made from typing symbols to indicate a variety of emotions and reactions, often used to soften the tone) did not find them of much value. The most common emoticon is the on-its-side smiley, constructed from keyboard symbols :-) that, combined, connote a smile or happiness. Emoticons may give indications about how a message is to be read, but, in general, they cannot be read as accurately as actual smiles and other nonverbal actions. Further, emoticons are not the same cross-culturally. For example, the basic smiley is :-) in the United States but it is (^_^) or (^^) in Japan where people perceive the shape of the eyes as part of smiles. Perhaps more importantly, the most frequently used Japanese emoticon is (^_^;) or (^^;), a representation of a face with cold sweat, used when the Japanese writers are afraid they are saying something too strongly (Sugimoto & Levin 2000, p. 144). While many students find online courses particularly stimulating when students come from several cultures, they also find that cross-cultural communication principles are seldom explicitly discussed or honored.

The design/decision processes and the regular ways of talking online have not been constructed in negotiation among the people who are taking online courses in the United States or abroad. Listening closely to the perceptions of the students, both women and men—those online now and those who are not—may help with future, more equitable design systems. As one online student said, "Emoticons, caps and exclamation points are pathetic online emotional displays. You can tell women weren't involved in designing computer keyboard symbols."

OVERALL CRITICAL CONSIDERATIONS

Most of the women in the AAUW study indicated that they did not feel guilt when studying, in their homes, for online courses. However, most of them then wrote about how they try to make certain that the needs of their families are met before they do their own studying, in most cases late at night or early in the morning. The single women or the single parents were more likely to say that they did not feel guilty, because they have to, or can, make their own decisions.

The family is, of course, shaped by cultural influences. The women in so-called traditional families constantly alluded to their understandings of their responsibilities to their spouses and children. That is, as the mother, their primary responsibility is to meet many of the home, educational, emotional, and medical needs of the others in the home. A few pointed out that while this is a socially constructed situation, women are having to deal with the resulting heavy work loads not through social programs that would provide childcare and financial support but through individual solutions.

Several wrote explicitly about how they are not being supported in their interest in and need for continued learning. One woman, a 40-year-old online graduate student, stated,

> We are made to feel guilty if we go to school when we "should" be taking care of children. Our government is not really interested in children or in education. If there was real interest, then the officials will begin by asking what is best for all human beings? What systems do we need to make things work the best? We would not start by saying, "Oh online education is great for women who have to take care of children." Listen to the assumptions behind that statement.

Because there is no general societal support for women taking courses once they have home and child-care responsibilities, the women may actually place higher demands on themselves to compensate for perceived selfishness when they pursue educational goals (Campbell, 2000, p. 32).

Women taking online courses often indicate that if it were not for distance learning opportunities they would not be able to return to university or certificate programs. However, most of those women with families also say that taking courses online is often very difficult. Many find that they receive little support from their families. In addition, the lack of institutional support comes by way of inflexible schedules and deadlines for assignments and exams, requirements of too many credit hour loads per term for obtaining loans, requirements for technological equipment that may be out of the women's economic control, and requirements for travel, extra fees, and special arrangements such as videoconferencing (Campbell, 2000, p. 32).

Teachers and institutions could help in a number of ways. Recognizing some of the pressures that women, especially, might be experiencing, institutions could consider building more flexibility into their schedules when students need that, and setting up "rent-to-own" leasing, or interest-free loan programs for required equipment. Institutions could put special attention on interviewing students who "drop out" to see if more flexible opinions would have made a difference to students' abilities to finish courses.

FUTURE RESEARCH NEEDED

Women and men do not necessarily have different needs from and experiences with online education. People are not necessarily naturally sharply divided into two categories, and, in fact, trying to sort all behavior into binary categories may make researchers overlook many similarities. Distance education is, however, yet another institution where gender and power differences are constructed, and to ignore the ways that gender is under construction online is to ignore many difficult experiences of real people.

Needed now is more information about the students' lives, i.e., the context of their studies:

1. We need to know not only what kinds of equipment are available at home and at work, but also when the equipment is available for online courses. Research about experiences, access, and opportunities needs to be much more nuanced.
2. We need to discover the type and extent of women's access to information via informal channels. One study of women in business and political leadership positions in 27 countries, including the United States, found a higher level of access to informal information channels and more satisfaction with their degree of access to informal channels than the men reported. More qualitative information about women's existing information

networks is needed, along with analyses of how distance learning programs can recognize and utilize the various types of knowledge held by current and potential students.

3. We know that time is a critical issue for almost everyone involved in online learning, but we now need to study time as a gendered concept. The earlier assumption was that working online would allow teachers and students to save time, or at least rearrange their work time to better fit individual schedules. However, women with spouses and children often must accommodate themselves to extra home-time responsibilities, a fact that has an impact on when and where they can study. The particularities of their time crunches offer an excellent rich focus for additional research.

4. We know that distance education courses are used by many people who are unable to attend on-campus courses, but we will need more research about how women and men actually try to fulfil their often competing family needs and their career needs, and how distance learning can be best structured to work with their goals.

5. We also need more information about *online conversations*. Given the importance that teachers put on computer-mediated conversations in online courses, we need to know more about these conversations. For example, does participation in online discussion change depending upon whether the teacher (woman or man) includes a lot of information on women's contributions to the course topic, and depending upon the ratio of women and men in the class? Given that women and men often enroll in online courses with different experiences and goals, and that online conversations are often not equitable, we need more research on the specifics of the conversations and the student satisfaction levels. We need research on whether gender-related differences in CMC conversations in online courses are generalizable across computer program formats, assignments, and course topics.

6. We need more information about the teachers' assumptions about learning needs. Interviews with teachers, administrators, and students indicate that there is still tension in many programs over which takes priority—the technology or the (often differing) learning needs of students. Adult students know how they best study and learn. Many women, and men of minority groups, have their own learning systems, based on out-of-classroom cultural learning processes. Many U.S. women report that they do not learn primarily through challenge and debate—a method currently favored by teachers of many graduate courses. Further, students whose native language is not English may have to distort their interests and experiences in order to participate in online conversations. For just one example, Indian people in several Arizona tribes tend to be silent in social situations when the role expectations of the participants are unclear. Asking them to participate in online conversations with those they do not know may be the same as asking them to commit social wrongs (Baldwin, 1995, p. 119). Further, some students will have individual differences such as learning primarily by auditory means. In any class, teachers and students all need information about differing ways of learning and conversing, so that there is reciprocal understanding and respect.

7. Finally, we need to *use* a lot of the research that has been done by the many academics doing studies related to gender equity issues, including the extensive research coming from Women's Studies programs.

Some of the reasons for the lack of research about women in distance education can be located in the ways "adult education historians continue to write women out of historical research and not questioned their absence" (Hugo, 1990, p. 6). Leaving out the women is so prevalent that it comes to be accepted as natural and in need of no explanation (Merriam & Brockett, 1997, p. 241). Women in online education have the paradoxical experience of being simultaneously invisible—even while they are the core constituency of distance learning.

While online education utilizing the new technologies would seem to offer important new opportunities for women and men interested in higher education courses and degrees, many of the equity issues present in campus courses are also, if in somewhat differing forms, still present online.

REFERENCES

In order to give some information about gender perspectives and about the types of work that women and men have published on this topic, when available first names are included in this reference list.

Arbaugh, J. B. (2000). An exploratory study of the effects of gender on student learning and class participation in an Internet-based MBA course. *Management Learning, (31)*4, 503–519.

Baldwin, George D. (1995). Computer-mediated communnication and American Indian education. In Zane L. Berge and Mauri P. Collins (Eds.), *Computer-mediated communication and the online classroom* (pp. 113–136). Cresskill, N.J.: Hampton Press.

Blumenstyk, G. (2000, Dec. 1). Digital library company plans to charge students a fee for access. *The Chronicle of Higher Education*, p. A41.

Brookfield, Stephen (1995). *Becoming a critically reflective teacher.* San Francisco: Jossey-Bass.

Campbell, Katy (2000). The promise of computer-based learning: Designing for inclusivity. *IEEE Technology and Society Magazine*, Winter 1999/2000, 28–34.

Chapman, Gerianne (1998). Factors affecting student attitudes and use of computer-mediated communication in traditional college courses. *Journal of Instruction Delivery Systems, (12)*4, 21–25.

Feminist Periodicals. A current listing of contents, 1981-present. [Table of contents from more than 80 feminist periodicals, both popular and scholarly.]

Greenstein, Theodore N. (2000). Economic dependence, gender, and the division of labor in the home: A replication and extension. *Journal of Marriage and the Family, 62*, 322–335.

Guri-Rosenblit, Sarah (1999). *Distance and campus universities: Tensions and interactions: A comparative study of five countries.* Oxford and New York: Elsevier Science Inc.

Hartcourt, Wendy (1999). *Women @Internet: Creating new cultures in cyberspace.* London and New York: Zed Books.

Hayes, Elsabeth, & Flannery, Daniele D., with Ann K. Brooks, Elizabeth J. Tisdell, & Jane M. Hugo (2000). *Women as learners: The significance of gender in adult learning.* San Francisco: Jossey-Bass.

Herring, Susan C. (forthcoming). Getting and holding the floor in listserv discussions. In Susan C. Herring (Ed.), *Computer-Mediated Conversation.*

Hersch, Joni, & Stratton, Leslie S. (1997). Housework, fixed effects, and wages of married workers. *The Journal of Human Resources, 32*(2), 285–307.

Hert, Philippe (1997). Social dynamics of an on-line scholarly debate. *The Information Society, 13*, 329–360.

Hugo, Jane (1990). Adult education history and the issue of gender: Toward a different history of adult education in America. *Adult Education Quarterly, 41*(1), 1–16.

King, Lisa J. 2000. Gender issues in online communities. *CPSR Newsletter, 18*(1), *http://www.cpsr.org/publications/newsletters/issues/2000/Winter2000/king.html.*

Kirkpatrick, Denise, & Jakupec, Victor (1999). Becoming flexible: What does it mean? In Alan Tait and Roger Mills (Eds), *The convergence of distance and conventional education: Patterns of flexibility for the individual learner* (pp. 51–70). London and New York: Routledge.

Korenman, Joan, & Wyatt, Nancy (1996). Group dynamics in an E-mail forum. In Susan Herring (Ed.), *Computer-mediated communication: Linguistic, social and cross-cultural perspectives* (pp. 225–242). Amsterdam: John Benjamins.

Kramarae, Cheris (2001). *The third shift: Women learning online.* Washington, DC.: American Association of University Women.

Kramarae, Cheris, & Spender, Dale (Eds.) (2000). *Routledge international encyclopedia of women: Global women's issues and knowledge* (4 volumes). New York: Routledge.

Merriam, Sharan B., & Brockett, Ralph G. (1997). *The profession and practice of adult education: An introduction.* San Francisco, CA: Jossey-Bass.

New Books on Women and Feminism. Madison: University of Wisconsin, 1979- . Semiannual. [Entries grouped by discipline.]

Palloff, Rena M., & Pratt, Keith (1999). *Building learning communities in cyberspace: Effectives strategies for the online classroom.* San Francisco: Jossey-Bass.

Paul, Elizabeth (2000). *Taking sides: Clashing views on controversial issues in sex and gender.* Guilford, CT: Dushkin/McGraw-Hill.

Richardson, Helen J., & French, Sheila (2000). Education on-line: What's in it for women? In Ellen Balka & Richard Smith (Eds.), *Women, work and computerization: Charting a course to the future* (pp. 300–307). Boston: Kluwer Academic Publishers.

Ross-Gordon, Jovita, & Brown-Haywood, Delicia (2000). Keys to college success as seen through the eyes of African American adult students. *The Journal of Continuing Higher Education, 48*(3), 14–23.

Sugimoto, Taku, & Levin, James A. (2000). Multiple literacies and multimedia: A comparison of Japanese and American uses of the Internet. In Gail E. Hawisher & Cynthia L. Selfe (Eds.), *Global literacies and the World-Wide Web* (pp. 133–153). London and New York: Routledge.

Ullman, Ellen (1995). Out of time: Reflections on the programming life. In James Brook & Iain A. Boal (Eds.), *Resisting the virtual life: The culture and politics of information* (pp. 131–143). San Francisco: City Lights.

Wood, Julia. (1999). *Gendered lives: Communication, gender, and culture (3rd ed.)*. Belmont, CA: Wadsworth Publishing Company.

Woodward, Alison, & Lyon, Dawn (2000). Gendered time and women's access to power. In Mino Vianello & Gwen Moore (Eds.), *Gendering elites: Economic and political leadership in 27 industrialized societies* (pp. 91–103). London: Macmillan Press, and New York: St. Martin's Press.

III

Design and Instruction

19

Instructional Design in Distance Education: An Overview

Rick Shearer
The Pennsylvania State University
sail57@earthlink.net

When one thinks about how to discuss instructional design in distance education several alternatives can come to mind. One could discuss the subject in terms of the traditional ISD (Instructional Systems Design) systems approach or ADDIE model, or it could be discussed in terms of technologies, in terms of types of interactions, in terms of learner autonomy and learner control, or in a multitude of other ways including an emphasis on costs. In truth all of these elements are part of the formula that defines the design and development of a course to be offered at a distance. However, in all these approaches there is an underlying acknowledgment or understanding that a particular technology is being utilized to bridge the distance between the student, the instructor, and the learning organization. Key to anyone of the technologies chosen is how it allows or does not allow the other elements of the course to behave in a systems environment where all the elements or variables interact.

In distance education we have, in many ways, several critical factors that need to be reviewed prior to even considering how the course will be presented and function. These include the audience characteristics, geographic dispersion of the audience, the technologies available to the audience, the goals of the learners, the goals and missions of the learning organization, the costs that must be recovered, the costs of delivery, the political environment at the time for the learning organization, the faculty compensation, and the market competition. All of these factors come into play in designing a course at a distance before we even look at the learning goals and objectives of the actual course. In many instances these factors will often dictate the technologies we use to deliver a course at a distance even before one conducts content analysis or instructional analysis. While discussing technology at the beginning of the design process can appear backward to classic instructional design it tends to surface early in discussions in distance education.

Single-mode and dual-mode institutions of distance education have striven for years to integrate the latest technologies into their courses in an effort to provide the student at a distance a richer learning experience and a feeling of connectedness to the education enterprise

and instructors. The field has used and experimented with education radio, educational television, audio graphics, two-way interactive teleconferencing, computer-based education, the
telephone, the fax, learning centers, and now the Internet. Each of these technologies has had
their pluses and minuses in terms of impact on factors that go into designing and delivering
a course at a distance. Some have added immediacy of presentation and instructor feedback,
others have provided cost economy of scale for the education institutions, while other technologies have simply provided needed access for the learners. Over the past five to ten years
much has been published about online learning and has in some ways been presented as a
panacea, however, there is no single best solution for designing a course at a distance.

In any field of study it is often important to take a step back and look at how the field
has conducted its business in the past. With regard to distance education, a reflective look
back at older technologies may help us examine how we are trying to use the Internet in
today's distance education courses. It is important to look at how these earlier technologies
not only provided access, but also provided learner autonomy, learner control, teacher-student
interaction, structure in the learning experiences, and a multitude of other factors.

DISTANCE EDUCATION DESIGN FACTORS

Prior to looking at a few of the older technologies it would be good to review the constructs
surrounding several of the design variables that go into the making of a course for distance
delivery. Those that will be reviewed here are: leaner autonomy/learner control, interaction,
access, and costs/economies of scale.

Learner Autonomy/Learner Control

One often sees the terms *learner autonomy, learner control, self-directed learning*, and
independence used in an interchangeable way or in conjunction with one another. To a large
degree what authors are referring to is the amount of control the learner has over his or her
learning situation. At one level we can look at the amount of control a learner has over his or
her interaction with the course content at the course level. At another level we can look at the
amount of control the learner has in establishing learning objectives and assessment strategies.
And yet at a level of greater abstraction we can look at the amount of control the learner has
over his or her entire learning experience (i.e., finances, registration, credit transfer, and so
on). However, as Brookfield (1985) states "It is simplistic for us to conceive of self-direction
solely in terms of command of self instructional techniques." Learning is not done completely
in a vacuum, but is conducted within a particular social context. As Moore (1973) stated "The
autonomous learner is not to be thought of as an intellectual Robinson Crusoe, castaway and
shut-off in self-sufficiency."

Therefore, to quote Mezirow (1985), "There is probably no such thing as a self-directed
learner." in that no learner is completely shut off from the influences of society and the learning organization. Nor do students want to be. At times they will portray characteristics of
being extremely independent, as described by Knowles (1975) where he defines self-directed
learning as "a process where the students will take the initiative without the help of others in
diagnosing their learning needs, formulating goals, identifying human and material resources,
and evaluating learning outcomes." At other times students will look for the learning organization to intervene when the content to be studied is not clear or the learning outcomes are not
well conceptualized in the learners' mind.

What is clear, however, is that learner autonomy and learner control are very important in a
distance education learning environment. Here students are often isolated geographically from
the instructor and institution and must behave in a more autonomous manner in order to meet

their learning goals and those of the institution. The amount of control that the design of a distance education course provides these learners is critical to the their successful completion of the course. If we provide too much structure within pacing, sequencing, and timing of assessment, then the learner, with competing life demands, may be forced to drop out. If we provide too little structure then the learner may feel cut off and flounder through the course. Also, the type of control referred to here is not simply the control over how one interacts with the course and the instructor, but as Garrison and Baynton (1989) argue control is a dynamic balance between independence, power, and support, where power can be viewed as a psychological dimension of the learner and involves the learner's motivation, cognitive style, emotional maturity, and attitude. And support refers to the support of family, financial, the administrative processes of the institution, and so on.

Therefore, the course design, in consideration of the institution's policies and goals, must build in, whenever possible, time for students to catch up on work and assignments and provide alternative periods of assessment. The course design should also provide, where possible, adequate levels of self-assessment and alternative representation of concepts to account for different cognitive styles. Thus these types of control variables for the autonomous/self-directed learner are essential to providing a positive learning experience.

Interaction

When one thinks of interaction we often think in terms of verbal communications between two individuals or a group. However, there are several forms of interaction, some verbal and some nonverbal. Moore (1989) has discussed interaction for distance education in terms of learner-instructor, learner-learner, and learner-content interactions. Hillman, Willis & Gunawardena et al. (1994) have discussed interaction in terms of learner-interface, while Moore (1980) and Saba and Shearer (1994) have discussed interaction in terms of dialog. Further, Holmberg (1981) discussed interaction in terms of a guided didactic conversation that occurs in the printed study guide between the author and the learner. In essence all of these forms of interaction often come into play during a distance education course including interaction with the learning organization. How we accommodate and provide for these different forms of interaction is often a function of the technology chosen to deliver the course to the distant student. The amount of interaction we provide in a distance learning environment also contributes to the degree of isolation a student may feel, or as Moore (1980) described, the amount of transactional distance that exists between the learner and the instructor.

Over the years much has been written in the fields of computer-aided instruction (CAI) and computer-based education (CBE) in terms of interface design and the need for a user-friendly and intuitive interface. This body of literature has primarily dealt with the navigational aspects of self-contained courses and the ease with which an end user can navigate through the program and understand what is to be accomplished to meet the learning objectives. There is also a new body of literature being written concerning the interface design for Web-based courses. While this aspect of course design is extremely important for assisting the student in navigating through the course and the course requirements, the three levels of interaction described by Moore (1989) are perhaps more central to what we view as interaction in a distance education course.

The interaction between the learner and the content goes beyond pure navigational and directional concerns and implies what Holmberg (1981) discusses as the guided didactic conversation. This type of conversation or interaction between the student and the content can occur whether the content is in print or in an electronic form of text. It refers to the way the author writes to the student when describing the intricacies of the subject matter. It is in the way that examples are presented and discussed and how the author may write to the student in the first person. For students in a traditional print-based correspondence course this type of interaction is essential, as it is through the printed word that they hear the author's/instructor's voice. Not unlike a well-written novel where the author speaks to you through the characters and not simply at you, it is this conversational form in the distance education course where the author brings himself or herself into the course and goes beyond the simple presentation of content. For many distance education students, who are studying in an asynchronous mode, the learner-content interaction is the primary voice they hear through their studies. Even when coupled with other forms of interaction this guided didactic conversation is the course element that they often rely on to get them through the course.

Learner-content interaction can also be seen in video and audio lectures where well-written scripts have the presenter/instructor having a conversation with the learner about the content. Here the content is not simply presented and discussed as if giving a lecture to someone, but the program script has the presenter pose questions and provide insights. As one can imagine, writing in this style, whether for print, educational television, or radio, is not something that comes easily to many, and it is in the development of these guided didactic discussions that the design team's editorial staff and production staff can contribute greatly to the effort.

Moore's other categories, learner-learner interaction and learner-instructor interaction, may be more familiar, especially in today's world as much has been written about the use of e-mail and bulletin boards/listserves in providing the opportunity for discussion between learners and the instructor. However, these categories have existed in many forms prior to the Internet. Interaction between the learners and the learner-instructor has occurred through the postal service, by means of the telephone, by means of learning centers, and synchronously for students enrolled in two-way interactive video courses or audio graphics courses. What has become key to the idea of interaction between learners and the instructor is timely interaction.

This idea of timely interaction ties into Moore's (1980) concept of transactional distance. Here the concept of distance is discussed as one of a psychological separation rather than a geographic separation. Moore discusses the idea of transactional distance as an interaction between levels of dialog and levels of structure or learner control within a course. The greater the level of dialog the lower the psychological feeling of separation. As Saba (1989) illustrated in his systems dynamic model, these two variables feed back onto each other, thus causing a natural ebb and flow of the level of transactional distance. However, what is yet to be answered is what one means by dialog in different delivery systems. Saba and Shearer (1994) conducted a study using a prototype desktop computer video system to explore this idea further. They proposed a typology of interaction categories in order to examine speech acts that occurred during a 30-minute lesson. Categories such as classroom management, passive, active, direct, and indirect, emerged. What is important here is the attempt to separate nonmeaningful dialog from meaningful instructional dialog. This is an area that needs to be examined further in other delivery environments, especially the Internet where all forms of interaction may not be for meaningful instructional purposes.

Thus learner-learner interaction and learner-instructor interaction needs to be examined not only for how it occurs, but also for the frequency of occurrence, timeliness of interactions, and in terms of type of interaction (conversation, questions, elaboration, and so on). We also need to examine how we account for passive observation of dialog and interaction. This type of analysis will help in answering the current question posed by instructors of online courses. What is the appropriate level of interaction one should have in his or her course?

Access

Access has been one of the cornerstones of distance education since the first correspondence course. Making learning opportunities available to the disenfranchised has been a primary goal of distance educators and adult educators for over a century. However, access has many attributes. In today's literature, there is no shortage of articles and news stories on the emerging digital divide. But this is just one way of looking at the concept of access. Access issues in education can be viewed in terms of gender, culture, financial, geographic, supply and demand, disabilities, preparedness (entrance exam qualifications), motivational (self-esteem), language, and a number of other ways. To view access as strictly a concern of geographic separation or simply as a concern of technology access when we design courses is too limiting a view. To design distance education courses and curriculums of study without acknowledging the variety of access issues that the intended audience may face can lead to the exclusion of many who may otherwise be interested in or need the course of study.

Traditionally in distance education we have thought of access primarily as an issue of geographic separation of the learner and the instructor. And in many ways the technologies we have employed in the delivery of courses have been used to address this concern. However, technologies such as print, radio, and TV (with closed captioning) have also addressed a range of disabilities, cultural, and financial issues of access. These are technologies that can reach broad audiences, are relatively inexpensive to receive, are often readily available in most countries, and can address the needs of those who have special visual or auditory needs.

As discussed by Kaziboni (2000), access to higher education in postindependent Zimbabwe is as much a factor of culture as it is geography and finances. Here women still face many pressures from husbands and the husband's family about attending school. The husbands feel that the women should not neglect their family duties, and they fear losing control of their wives. Ding (1999) discusses, in his article on distance education in China, technologies such as radio, television, and print that not only address the geographic separation of a vast population, but also address the supply-demand equation. China has more adults who want to attend institutions of higher education than they have space or facilities to accommodate. Therefore, distance education is helping address the supply side of access to education for China. Financial concerns are also an important aspect of access. Here many of the single-mode and mega-distance education institutions have used educational radio, television, and other technologies to produce and distribute education with great economies of scale. In this way they can keep the cost of higher education at a level that the general public can afford.

Issues of access are extremely important for the field to be aware of as we witness how the Internet and the World Wide Web are being integrated into distance education courses. In a recent report, *Who's Not Online*, from the Pew Internet and American Life Project (Lenhart, 2000), extrapolation from the surveys indicate that roughly half of the adults (18+) in America still do not have Internet access. While this number is changing dramatically every year, as is evident from the UCLA Internet Report: Surveying the Digital Divide (cited in Bartlett, 2000), which states that Internet usage went from 19 million in 1997 to 100 million in 1999, it is still a staggering number to contemplate when we think about access to online courses. Internationally, a report by WRI Research (Wired Digital Inc., 2000) indicates that 80% of the world population is being left out of the global communications system. William Ruckelshaus, the chairman of WRI, points out that 4 billion people in the world make $5 a day or less and another 1.5 billion have incomes between $1,500 and $20,000 annually. These statistics are critical to consider when we design and develop courses to be offered at a distance. When we integrate various technologies into distance education courses we are knowingly disenfranchising a large portion of the population. It can also be argued that the integration of these technologies increases the cost of education to the student not only through the need for information technology access, but also due to the fact that the cost of developing technology-rich courses will be much greater. It is also important to consider issues of access related to disabilities and supply and demand for education when we integrate the Internet and other computer technologies.

Costs/Economies of Scale

The phrase *economy of scale* is a benchmark in the literature of distance education. It is one of the main cornerstones that many of the mega distance education universities have relied upon in order to fulfill their mission of making education opportunities more broadly available to the general public. Costs for designing and developing courses for distance education have normally been associated with high fixed costs of development and low delivery (variable) costs to the students. In this way, as the number of students taking any one course increased the development costs were spread across a large student body, thus making the development cost per student low. This has essentially been the rationale behind the high costs that distance education providers have put into the production of education television and radio broadcasts and traditional print correspondence courses. However, each technology used in delivering a distance education courses has its own unique cost structure.

When designing courses for a distance education audience it is important to understand the unique cost implications for each technology. For as we add technology to a course we not only drive up the costs of development, but can also drive up the costs to the students for delivery. If we look at some of the cost analysis that has been conducted at the Open University of the United Kingdom and other distance education institutions (Hülsmann, 1999), we see that the benchmark media that all other distance education courses are measured against is print. This is not surprising as print can have a relatively low cost for production, and duplication and distribution of print-based courses tend to be low. Also courses developed in this medium tend to have a long shelf life before they need to be revised. Once we move up the technology continuum we add development costs as we are now changing the printed narrative of the course authors into audio, video, or a host of other interactive technologies. In looking at the studies presented by Hülsmann (1999) where they have used a measure of "Development cost per student learning hour by medium" other technology costs are measured in terms of a ratio to print. Here we see that educational television is roughly 180 times that of print, CD-ROM 40 times that of print, and audio (cassette tapes) is 34 times that of print. What is important to note here is all these technology forms are canned productions meant to have long shelf lives and be accessible by a large student population.

The concepts of long shelf life and large student audience is what allows for economies of scale. What is unclear since the adoption of the Internet technologies and World Wide Web is whether one can design a course that will have a long shelf life and be available to a large number of students. Many distance education institutions have incorporated the Internet into their courses in order to provide a greater sense of connectedness between the learners and the instructor and institution. It is hoped that this provides a greater sense of community and timeliness of feedback. However, what is not clear is to what extent this limits the number of student who can enroll in a single section of a course. For once we as designers add greater interactivity between the student and the instructor we may be limiting the number of students that a faculty member can effectively interact with. For some institutions that are experimenting with cohort or semester-based distance education courses, this aspect of connectedness can be quite limiting in terms of the number of students who can take an individual section of a course. And obviously the more individual course sections an institution needs the greater the variable costs in terms of instructor salaries. The addition of the Internet technologies into open enrollment courses will also add some limitations in terms of level of instructor-learner interaction that a single instructor/tutor can handle.

The shelf life of a course must also be looked at when we as designers integrate the World Wide Web into distance education courses. Learning management tools like WebCT, Blackboard, Angel, and others allow faculty and authors a greater degree of flexibility in terms of updating and revising courses. With this flexibility we may, however, lose a degree of shelf life that will dramatically impact the economies of scale. If we are constantly revising courses, then additional development costs are incurred that will reduce the impact of even a large student audience. Thus, as designers we need to strive for content presentation that can be stable for three to five years to ensure a degree of shelf life. However, this is a tough compromise between the desire for continuous improvement of academic quality and the need for the course to have economies of scale. Therefore, a decision needs to be made between what content can exist in a fixed form for three to five years and what aspects of the course can be updated each semester or year through means of electronic postings to bulletin boards.

The analysis of costs associated with delivering courses at a distance is complex. As demonstrated by Keegan (1996) where he examines several formula-based approaches to the topic. There are several factors in the cost equation, and these must be viewed in a systemic manner as there is no simple cause-effect relationship. For designers it is important to be congnicent of how decisions we make in the design of a distance education course not only impact the development costs, but also the delivery costs to the students.

TECHNOLOGY IN DISTANCE EDUCATION

How, then, have we used technologies in the design of distance education courses to address the four factors outlined above? To some extent we have already talked about print and the Internet as we discussed learner autonomy, interaction, access, and costs. However, to further examine the question of how we as a field have used technologies in distance education let us take a brief look at how print, educational television, two-way interactive video teleconferencing, and the Internet and the World Wide Web provide for or diminish these four design factors.

Print

For many designers and distance education institutions, print (nonelectronic text) is still the most versatile medium for the delivery of course content. It is user-friendly, is easily transported, can be marked up readily, and most everyone knows how to use the medium. In terms of learner autonomy and learner control print provides each learner the opportunity to move through the content in a linear fashion, or in a self-designated pattern where they may browse, jump ahead, or read the conclusions for each section first. Of course print provides no more control over pace than many other media, as much of the pace and structured sequence is often determined by the instructor or learning institution. Of course print has its drawbacks in that we are limited in our expression of ideas. Print alone cannot provide alternative forms for expressing concepts. It is not a visual or auditory medium and limits us in this regard. Also, as a stand-alone medium it must be coupled with other technologies (postal service, fax, telephone, or Internet) to provide for interactions with the instructor/tutor and institution. The type of technology, coupled with the printed learning material, also determines the timeliness of interactions between the learners and the instructor and institution.

While print has its limitations, it does generally provide the greatest degree of access and cost-efficiencies in terms of:

- individuals who know how to use the medium.
- ease of distribution nationally through the postal systems.
- adaptability to address several disabilities.
- being fairly inexpensive to duplicate.
- tendency to have a long shelf life.
- low production costs (excludes aspect of author payment, which can be the same for any course independent of media).
- no additional equipment needed by the learners.

These aspects of access and costs can change for print when the distance education institution begins to consider access by students beyond the geographic bounds of one's country. Once distance education providers start to think of access as a global issue they are faced with language decisions, cost of distribution to and within other countries, and changes in forms of interaction. In cases where institutions are addressing the learning needs of an international audience they may end up with a course product that is similar, but different, and has its own cost structure in terms of the fixed and variable costs associated with course development and delivery.

Today print continues to be a part of almost every distance education course regardless of the primary delivery technology. For almost every course there tends to be a print package that accompanies other course materials. It may be in the form of reading packets, case studies, or most commonly a study guide or student handbook that describes how to get started, how to interact with the instructor and educational institution, and how to use the other media. Therefore, as Bates (1995) states, "Print is, and will remain, a most important technology for open and distance teaching."

Educational Television

Educational television has been researched and debated from numerous viewpoints since the early 1950s. Many have looked at the effects of children's programming such as Sesame Street, others have examined the impact of television production attributes like color (Chu & Schramm, 1975), and still others have explored why the technology failed to meet the goals that higher education hoped the medium would help them reach (Oshins, 1981). As an instructional technology, educational television is a wonderful study in terms of potential and failure to deliver. Why this is so, is not the focus of this chapter; however, we do want to examine the media for how it allowed or did not allow for learner autonomy and interaction, and how it contributed to greater access.

When one looks at the literature on educational television we see that it is discussed not only in terms of broadcast television, but also in terms of satellite broadcasts, ITFS, closed circuit, and in some cases as programming, which was captured and replayed on video tape. For the purpose of this discussion we focus primarily on the terrestrial broadcast and satellite modes of delivery.

Probably the greatest advantage of educational television whether a terrestrial broadcast or satellite feed is the vast population that each of these delivery modes can reach. In the 1950s and 1960s as television became widely adopted in the United States and other countries its vast reach was viewed as a means of addressing the educational needs for many disenfranchised citizens. Legislation was passed in many countries that set aside a portion of the broadcast spectrum for public access programming. This type of legislation allowed educational networks to utilize a portion of the broadcast bandwidth to beam educational programming to individual homes or to rural schools. While television as a technology for distance education greatly enhanced access, it was not without its drawbacks. The production of educational programming was very expensive and increased as the viewing audience became more sophisticated in what they expected from television. As television production values improved, the costs increased. To produce programming that was more than just a talking head became expensive, and the costs had to be absorbed through higher tuition or greater economies of scale.

For distance education there also seemed to be an inverse correlation between educational television's ability to increase access and learner autonomy/learner control and interaction. Broadcast television or satellite feeds are in general push type technologies in that they are only one way. They do not allow for any real immediacy of interaction nor do they allow for a great deal of learner control. Educational programs in general were often prerecorded and scheduled to air at a set time. Until the adoption of the VCR, learners had to tune into broadcasts at given times each day and then complete follow-up lessons, which were generally delivered through print in a study guide or resource notebook. Thus, the learning experience was highly structured and allowed very little control over how the learner interacted with the media. Also, interaction with the instructor or institution was generally by the postal service or telephone. In terms of Moore's (1980) model of transactional distance learners who were participating in educational television courses were at a great psychological distance from the instructors.

This is not to say that these limitations to educational television inhibited its value. For even today, through initiatives like PBS's Going the Distance, educational television programming when coupled with the Internet or other communications technologies, and video recording technologies, can be quite successful not only in increasing access, but also in providing greater connectedness between the learners and the instructors. Television and video provide us with a visual medium that has the ability to portray concepts and emotions in a way few other media can. How we use television and/or video in the design of courses to assist learners in visualizing concepts can have a dramatic impact on learning. However, as designers we must always be cognizant of the costs of production, the shelf life of the programming, and how we couple this technology with others to provide for interaction, and to some degree aspects of learner control.

Two-way Interactive Video Teleconferencing

In the late 1980s and early 1990s two-way interactive video teleconferencing over land lines was being marketed and discussed as the next panacea for distance education. It was viewed as a means of providing real-time interactive learning environments for students at a distance. The technology was rapidly being adopted by corporations for training and administrative purposes, and institutions of higher education were adapting the technology to meet the learning needs of students at satellite campuses and regional learning centers. While there is no doubt that the technology provided a means of real-time interaction between the instructor and the learners, and between the learners, it in essence was an extension of the boundaries of the traditional classroom. The technology as implemented provided narrow access, had high equipment and setup costs, and allowed for very limited learner control. This is not to say that the technology does not have its place in the field of distance education, just that it is limited in terms of audience.

As two-way interactive video, in the early 1990s, relied on high speed telephone lines and sophisticated bridging technologies it was not only expensive to set up but also expensive to deliver. In the early 1990s institutions were spending from $50,000 and up to purchase and set up two-way interactive video systems and rooms. It was also costing roughly $.50 per minute per ISDN line or switched 56 circuit to carry the live video signals. As the technology basically provided an extension of the traditional classroom the numbers of sites that received the broadcast was usually limited to 5 with no more than 75–100 students total. Any more than this number and the level of interaction would drop dramatically to the point where the advantages of the technology were diminished. It was also the case that learners had to travel to the locations that had the equipment installed.

Therefore, the cost structure, limited audience, and need for sophisticated telephony technologies greatly limited the impact the technology had on increasing access to educational opportunities. Nor did the technology provide for a great deal of learner autonomy or control any different than we witness in a traditional classroom. The pace and sequence were set and the time of day for participation was set with no way of recording the class for later. Therefore, as a distance education technology, two-way interactive video quickly receded from the spotlight as the Internet and World Wide Web became more prevalent in society. Today, as is evident in Schreiber and Berge's (1998) book, we find two-way interactive video teleconferencing used primarily by corporations for training where they have the means for groups of employees to gather at corporate locations to participate in short courses and just-in-time learning modules.

As designers of distance education courses it is important to understand the strengths and weaknesses of this technology. Internet technologies have now advanced to the point where we are starting to see video teleconferencing conducted over high speed IP backbones along with some experimentation in two-way video over 56 kb modems. As the technology and bandwidth improve it is only a matter of time until designers are faced with deciding how or how not to integrate aspects of two-way interactive video into distance education courses.

The Internet and World Wide Web

The introduction of the Internet and World Wide Web into distance education courses has elevated the public awareness of the field in a way that we have not seen previously. This increased awareness has led to a reexamination of the field and, to the chagrin of many, a public mind-set that views distance education only in terms of the Internet and the World Wide Web. Unfortunately, this view of distance education has tended to ignore the vast amount of existing research that has been conducted in the field and in the other related fields such as CAI (computer-aided instruction) and CBE (computer-based education). Also, in the rush to use the new Internet technologies, issues of access, cost to students, and learner autonomy have not been widely addressed in the literature.

Institutions and in many regards designers were so caught up in the ability to present information online and build elaborate communication environments that little thought was going into how the technologies were impacting the students and the instructors. While there is no doubt that the Internet has improved the capability for more immediacy of feedback and synchronous chats, it has at the same time limited access.

As discussed in the sections on Access and Costs, the Internet can have a tremendous negative impact on the accessibility by individuals to distance education courses. Even within the United States, where approximately half of the households are still not connected to the Internet, an institution can significantly narrow its reach by adding computer and Internet technologies. Distance education institutions that deliver their courses over the Internet are requiring that individuals not only have access to the necessary infrastructure, but also that they must pay for some sort of access to these technologies. If the reach of the institution is to be global in scope, then the Internet and computer technologies can poise an even greater barrier. One also needs to consider the issues of comfort with technology and the ability to use the technology that come into play when we incorporate computers and the Internet into distance education courses.

The aspects of learner autonomy and learner control also need to be examined as we design courses that use the Internet and the World Wide Web. Many institutions have attempted to model their distance education offerings after the traditional campus-based semester system. While this fits well within existing policies and within the normal faculty contract timeframes, it may not work well for the independent learner. The question remains of whether this structure assists students in completing their course work or adds to drop-out rate. The inability of some adult students to work in such a structured environment that competes for their time with work, family, and other social commitments needs to be considered. In many ways we may be establishing pace, sequence, interaction requirements, and technology requirements that eliminate the ideas of anytime and anyplace. These aspects of the courses may resemble the traditional classroom model so closely that we have in fact negated, to a large degree, any feelings of independence and learner control. A key question to be answered by many distance education providers is what audience they are attempting to address when they develop courses to be delivered online. Some may argue that in many cases we are designing distance education courses to fit within the policies and procedures of the traditional university structure and not to address the unique needs of learners at a distance.

CONCLUSION

As instructional designers of distance education courses and programs we make a series of conscious choices each time we design and develop a course to be delivered to distant students. In some cases the decisions we make are for pedagogical reasons, in others they are for access reasons, and yet at other times the design decisions we make are based on costs. Each time we decide to use a particular technology or combination of technologies we need to be very clear on why we are using the chosen technology and for what purpose. Knowing and understanding the strengths of each technology at our disposal, whether the latest Internet tool or an old faithful like print, are critical to defending and implementing our design decisions.

All too often we witness those who latch onto the latest technology tool in the hope that the technology will finally solve all the problems encountered in delivering a course at a distance. However, this is often done without a careful consideration or understanding of how the new technology will impact learner autonomy, access, or end-user costs. To develop a better mousetrap should not always be the goal for distance education. Understanding the specific attributes that each technology, whether old or new, brings to the design table is essential in helping the learner meet his or her educational goals. It is critical that we take a systems view of how the technologies we choose impact all the components of a distance education delivery system. While a new technology may sometimes appear to address a particular problem, like animated demonstrations of a difficult topic, the cost of supporting the student in the use of the new tool may outweigh the benefits.

In the development of distance education courses, there is no one best technology, and it is usually a combination of technologies that produces the best course in terms of meeting the learners' educational objectives. In many ways print is still the most dependable means for the delivery of content. This media, when combined with others like the Internet or CD-ROM, can produce a powerful learner experience. Delivery and production costs must also be in the forefront of our decisions. For if as designers the design decisions are driven by the goal of reduced delivery costs to an international audience, then one may decide to provide the study guide/content by means of a downloadable PDF (Portable Document Format) file. Here we are passing on the printing and delivery costs to the students but may in the long run save the student very expensive postal costs.

It is essential, therefore, that designers of instructional material for distance education courses understand the strengths and weaknesses of a vast array of technologies and how the older technologies have been deployed in the past to address the multitude of design factors.

REFERENCES

Bartlett, M. (2000). *Internet to be bigger than TV—UCLA report:* [Online] http://www.newsbytes.com/pubNews/00/157162.html.

Bates, A. W. (1995). *Technology, open learning, and distance education.* London: Routledge.

Brookfield, S. (1985). Self-directed learning: A critical review of research. In S. Brookfield (Ed.), *Self-directed learning: From theory to practice.* New Directions For Continuing Education. No. 25 (pp. 5–16). San Francisco, CA: Jossey-Bass.

Chu, G., & Schramm, W. (1975). *Learning from television: What the research says.* (ERIC Document Reproduction Services No. ED 109985).

Ding, X. (1999). Distance education in China. In K. Harry (Ed.), *Higher education through open and distance learning* (pp. 176–189). New York: Routledge.

Garrison, D. R., & Baynton, M. (1989). Beyond independence in distance education: The concept of control. In M. G. Moore & G. C. Clark (Eds.), *Readings in principles of distance education* (pp. 16–28). University Park, PA: American Center for the Study of Distance Education.

Hillman, D. C. A., Willis, D. J. and Gunawardena, C. N. 1994. Learner-interface interaction in distance education: An extension of contemporary models and strategies for practitioners. *American Journal of Distance Education, 8*(2), 30–42.

Holmberg, B. (1981). *Status and trends of distance education.* London: Kogan Page.

Hülsmann, T. (1999). The costs of distance education. In K. Harry (Ed.), *Higher education through open and distance learning* (pp. 72–84). New York: Routledge.

Kaziboni, T. (2000). Picking up threads—women pursuing further studies at the University of Zimbabwe. *Studies in the Education of Adults, 32*(2), 229–240.

Keegan, D. 1996. *Foundations of distance education* (3rd ed.) London: Routledge.

Knowles, M. (1975). *Self directed learning: A guide for learners and teachers.* New York: Cambridge Book.

Lenhart, A. (2000). September 21, 2000. *Who's not online.* Pew Internet and American Life Project. Washington, DC. http://www.pewinternet.org/reports

Mezirow, J. (1985). A critical theory of self-directed learning. In S. Brookfield (Ed.), *Self-directed learning: From theory to practice.* New Directions For Continuing Education. No. 25 (pp. 17–30). San Francisco, CA: Jossey-Bass.

Moore, M. G. (1973). Towards a theory of independent learning. *Journal of Higher Education, 44*(12), 661–679.

Moore, M. G. (1980). Independent study. In R. Boyd, J. Apps, and associates (Eds.), *Refining the discipline of adult education* (pp. 16–31). San Francisco: Jossey-Bass.

Moore, M. G. (1989). Three types of interaction. In M. C. Moore & G. C. Clark (Eds.) *Readings in Principles of Distance Education* (pp. 100–105). The American Center for the Study of Distance Education. The Pennsylvania State University. University Park, PA.

Oshins, J. H. (1981). "Snap, crackle, and pop": Learning from television. *Change, 13*(7), 8–10.

Saba, F. (1989). Integrated telecommunications systems and instructional transaction. In M. G. Moore & G. C. Clark (Eds.), *Readings in Principles of Distance Education* (pp. 29–36). University Park, PA: American Center for the Study of Distance Education.

Saba, F., & Shearer, R. L. (1994). Verifying key theoretical concepts in a dynamic model of distance education. *American Journal of Distance Education, 8*(1), 6–59.

Schreiber, D. A., & Berge, Z. L. (1998). *Distance training: How innovative organizations are using technology to maximize learning and meet business objectives.* San Francisco, CA: Jossey-Bass.

Wired Digital Inc. (2000). *On creating digital dividends.* [Online] http://www.wired.com/news/technology/

20

Developing Text for Web-Based Instruction

Diane J. Davis
University of Pittsburgh
djdavis@pitt.edu

One of the major issues that faculty encounter as they design Web-based courses is how to incorporate the vast amounts of textual materials common in college-level courses. There is ample evidence to suggest that the use of text, at least in any substantive quantity, is problematic for online instruction. Faculty are told that learners seem to prefer to read textual materials in hard-copy form and will print to read any lengthy online instructional text. In these cases, the Web becomes a text file dissemination device for online or Web-enhanced courses.

Most instruction in higher education, regardless of pedagogical approach, requires use of text. Whether an instructor is providing course enhancement through the Web or a complete online course, text will be an integral part of the instruction. This chapter examines literature related to the use of online text. Specifically, it focuses on how research and practice can inform our use of electronic text for instruction.

DEFINITIONS

Electronic text comes in a variety of forms. Some authors differentiate between *hypertext*, which is characterized by embedded links and nodes (see Unz & Hesse, 1999, for example), and *serial text*, which is designed to be read in a linear, sequential manner. Thuring, Hannemann, and Haake (1995) further distinguish between *hyperbases*, browsable databases that can be freely explored by the reader, and *hyperdocuments* "that intentionally guide readers through an information space, controlling their exploration along the lines of a predetermined structure" (p. 57). The term *hypermedia* typically refers to hypertext that incorporates other media such as audio, video, and graphics. For the purpose of this chapter, the term *continuous hypertext* is used to refer to the kinds of text we are most likely to encounter in Web-based courses. This term is adapted from Muter (1996) to refer to hypertext that is intended to be used in a manner predetermined by the designer, and that may or may not include graphics, audio, or video.

In examining research and practice in the area of online text, this chapter does not focus on technical elements of web page design, such as typeface, spacing, and use of color. Nor does it look at the design of navigation systems per se, except as that design relates to the specific concept under discussion. These important topics are addressed in other literature on the design of electronic text (e.g., Moter, 1996). Parlangeli, Marchigiani, and Bagnara (1999), for example, show how obscurity in navigational systems can negatively affect learning. Muter (1996) provides a comprehensive review of research on interface design techniques to optimize the reading of continuous text.

TEXT AND THE WEB

A great deal of information is available on the design of good Web sites and it includes guidelines on the use of text (Morkes & Nielsen, 1997, for example). We are told to "keep it short," "use bullets," "highlight important information," and so on. Most of us—perhaps especially those of us who teach in colleges and universities—find these guidelines to be antithetical to academic writing styles and to the way we communicate to students about our disciplines. Nevertheless, if we ignore that advice and upload our best lectures and commentary, we know that students are likely to print them and we're merely providing a different delivery mechanism for our print materials. If we assume that our students will print to read and therefore provide our textual materials in print or in printable files, we lose the opportunity to use embedded links, illustrations, and activities—some of the key instructional utilities of the Web that led us to it in the first place. All these options fail to exploit the Web's potential to encourage the learner's active engagement and interactivity with the content of our courses (see, for example, Reinking, 1994). Research on the use of online text for instruction, although limited, does offer some insight that can assist the developers of continuous hypertext for instruction.

READING ONLINE

One message that has a fair amount of research support is that learners do not read lengthy text online. Ward and Newlands (1998), for example, in a study on use of Web-based lectures, found that two-thirds of their students immediately printed the online lectures and most of the others read first at the computer, then printed the lectures. Only 2 of 48 reported that they read and studied the documents on the computer. Other studies support this observation of learner behavior (Oliver, Omari, & Herrington, 1998, for example).

There also is evidence to suggest that online reading is problematic for students. Studies comparing online with print reading have indicated that people read electronic text more slowly (Gould et al., 1987; Gray & Shasha, 1989) and that it is more tiring than reading from print (Cushman, 1986; Wilkinson & Robinshaw, 1987).

Web course designers should interpret this research with caution, keeping in mind that the Web is a relatively new instructional medium—as Shneiderman (1997) points out, "still in the Model T stage of development" (p. 27). More recently, LaCroix (1999) suggests that modern technology has eliminated many of the problems that contributed to slower and more tiring reading of computer screens and indicates that screen reading now can be as fast as reading from printed text. Similarly, Hartley (1987) cites research showing that:

> screen size, the number of characters per line, whether the image is positive (dark characters on a light background) or negative (light characters on a dark background), and screen resolution are important issues here. (p. 13)

Hartley also points to studies suggesting that, when looking for specific information, people search electronic text more carefully than printed text and therefore take extra time. So, while reading online may be no more efficient than reading in print, newer evidence suggests that it is not so technically problematic that faculty should sacrifice its potential benefits by abandoning its use.

What about students' apparent preference for hard copy printed materials? As early as 1987, James Hartley cautioned that:

> It may take years for people to become as familiar with electronic text as they are with printed text, and during this time electronic text may develop beyond our wildest dreams. (p.14)

Many of our current and potential online students regularly use the Web for recreation and commerce. They've come to expect sites that are easy to browse, pages that are easy to scan, and concise messages that enable them to reach their goals as quickly as possible. With time and experience, it is reasonable to assume that students' expectations—and thus their effective Web-learning strategies—can evolve to accommodate different kinds of electronic text designed for different purposes. Just as students have learned to approach the reading of a textbook differently than they approach reading a magazine, we can expect that they will learn to read their online course materials differently than they read a dot com Website. Experience and expectations are important determinants of behavior.

The fact that students are most accustomed to reading academic text in its printed form may in part explain their tendency to print electronic course materials in order to read them. Ward and Newlands (1998) observed in their study of online lectures that students "seem to have been trying to replicate the conditions of a traditional lecture system" and failed to adapt their study methods to the new system (p.182). Lemke (1998) elaborates on this theme and describes new forms of multimedia and metamedia literacies required for the 21st century.

Just as students are not yet accustomed to learning from online text, faculty are not yet experienced in its development. There were so many examples of early faculty attempts to duplicate their printed materials online that the term "shovelware" evolved to describe the phenomenon. These early materials failed to take advantage of the interactivity of the Web and it is not surprising that students merely printed them to read offline. As faculty become more experienced in the design and use of continuous hypertext, they are developing course materials that optimize use of the Web as an instructional tool—materials that therefore include embedded incentives for use online.

INTERPRETATIONS OF RESEARCH: FURTHER CAUTIONS

A fair amount of the inquiry and observation supporting today's "common knowledge" about authoring online text is focused not on use of the Web for instruction, but rather on its use for commercial and recreational purposes. Many of the best guides for writing on the Web, both online and in print, are intended for the design of attractive and effective commercial Web sites. The oft-cited works of Morkes and Nielsen (1997) and Nielson (2000) are examples. Even the highly referenced Yale Style Guide (Lynch & Horton, 1997) refers readers to Sun Microsystems *Guide to Web Style* and the *Ameritech Web Page User Interface and Design Guidelines.* Information about the design of good Web *sites* is useful and important, but its ability to be generalized to the design of good Web *courses* is limited, not in the least because of the difference in purpose. Purpose, or the task at hand—and most notably the complexity of that task—has proven to be a critical factor in research on the efficacy of hypertext. Chen and Rada (1996) address task complexity in their meta-analysis of experimental studies on interacting with hypertext. The fact that so much more is known about creating good Web *sites* than is known about creating good Web *courses* probably reflects the reality that there are more good sites than good courses to study. That this reality is changing, however, is evidenced by Campbell (2000) in her review of theory-based architectures and frameworks for Web design, and in the examples of good practice she provides.

Another problem of overgeneralization is the failure to distinguish between research and observation about different types of computer-based text. Some of the best articles on the use of electronic text (Gillingham, 1993; van Nimwegen, Pouw & van Oostendorp, 1999; and Unz and Hesse, 1999, for example) are based on hypertext systems designed for searching. These are collections (or nodes) of searchable information distinguished by frequent use of links and referred to by Thuring et al. (1995) as *hyperbases*. Some of the findings from research on hyperbases seems easily generalizable to the more *linear* structure of the continuous hypertext of interest in this chapter. However, hyperbase research typically focuses on the system's "searchability," and, when used for instruction, on students' ability to locate answers to specific questions using the system, while continuous hypertext is used for overall comprehension. Just as caution is warranted in generalizing results of research on printed text to electronic text (Hartley, 1987; Muter, 1996), so should we be cautious in applying the conclusions of research on one form of hypertext to the design and use of a form created for an entirely different purpose. Unz and Hesse (1999) call for the development of a classification scheme for hypertext systems for just this reason—the difficulty of comparing and generalizing results from hypertext research.

Limitations in our ability to learn from research point out that the inquiry, observation, and experience that will form the foundation for the design and development of continuous instructional hypertext is yet in its infancy. Overgeneralization should not discourage us from trying to develop, evaluate, and improve instructional text for Web-based courses. To this end, the remainder of this chapter focuses on three broad, fundamental text design concepts: purpose, structure, and interactivity.

Purpose

People seem to learn more effectively and efficiently when they approach the learning activity with specific purposes in mind. They need to understand why they are reading a particular text, for example, and what kind of information they should be looking for as they read it. Given the greater potential for distraction, via links or scrolling for example, this principle is particularly important for online text.

Well-designed instructional text should include, early on, a rationale explaining the function of the text and should convey what the instructor expects the student to learn from it. This is not to suggest that students will fail to learn other things from a text, but rather that they are more likely to learn what the instructor intends them to learn from it if those expectations are known. Some text authors communicate reader purpose by including specific objectives at the beginning of text. Bernard and Lungren (1994) remind us, however, that learning objectives are more effective—and more likely to be read—if linguistically interesting and embedded in the natural flow of the text. Unz and Hesse (1999) point to the lack of identified purpose as a shortcoming in many studies on the use of hypertext for learning.

Structure

One of the most pervasive themes in literature on text comprehension is the importance of structure. Piolat, Roussey, and Thunin (1997) point to research suggesting that structure may be even more important in electronic text because of the lack of physical cues regarding the length of the document and its parts. Gillingham (1993) observed that links to multiple texts with differing structures adds to the naturally ill-structured nature of some hypertext. In their discussion of text design for distance education, Bernard and Lundgren (1994) emphasize the importance of clear, concise writing for text comprehension, regardless of medium. To explain the importance of structure in electronic text, Thuring et al. (1995) point to research that shows that a readers' ability to understand and remember a text, to construct a "mental model of it, depends upon its degree of coherence which has been shown to be facilitated by a well-defined structure and rhetorical cues that reflect its structural properties" (p. 58). Both Bernard and Lungren (1994) and Parlangeli and his colleagues (1999) point to the value of structure in reducing cognitive load—clear, consistent structure enables the reader to focus more mental effort on reading and comprehending text content. LaCroix's (1999) series of experiments supports the notion that text comprehension involves global as well as local levels of processing and uses whole text structure as input.

Strategies for providing structure in electronic documents include use of tables of contents, overviews, headings and subheadings, graphical maps, and stable screen layout. LaCroix (1999), for example, found that readers respond to global structure indicators, such as headings, menu order, and underlining, when they are reading complex expository text to synthesize information. Bernard and Lundgren (1994) encourage the use of continuity overviews in text designed for distance learning. Continuity overviews show the relationship between previous reading and the new reading assignment. Chen and Rada (1996) review research on the potential value of graphical maps for overcoming lower ability in spatial relations, an ability that seems to have more influence on one's efficiency in using hypertext than do variables such as cognitive style and learning style. It is important to note here that use of a Web browser to display structure may be inadequate. The research of Wenger and Payne (1994) found that use of a graphical browser to show text structure did not increase recall or comprehension of the material, nor did it increase recall of the text structure. It did, however, increase the actual amount of text that was read.

While this chapter does not specifically include a discussion of navigation and screen design, these factors have particular importance for the structure and coherence of electronic text, and the amount of cognitive load required for its use. For example, use of the page format, as opposed to scrolling, has been shown to enable users to develop a better "sense of text" (Piolat et al. 1997). Stable screen layout, visualization of structure, and descriptive links increase document coherence and reduce cognitive load (Thuring et. al., 1995). Use of embedded "closed" screens (information nodes that open and close within a document, but do not exit the document) helps prevent reader disorientation and retains the text's structural coherence.

Carefully selected metaphors, such as file cabinets, bookshelves, or shopping malls, also have been used successfully for structuring and navigating hyperbases (Trumbull, Gay, & Mazur, 1992; Shneiderman, 1997; Streitz, 1988). Metaphors may also have application for more linear instructional text, particularly for organizing multiple readings in a section or across the entire course. One could easily imagine how content-relevant metaphors could be used to add structure to academic readings, such as a museum display for a history or an anthropology course, or a street scene for a course in social psychology. Metaphors have the added advantage of providing opportunities for students to activate prior knowledge and relate it to current learning as they consider how the metaphor relates to the new information.

Both Bernard and Lundgren (1994) and Unz and Hesse (1999) suggest that having students create their own structure for information is a valuable learning aid. However, this technique is used as a synthesizing task after the student already has read (or browsed) the content materials, so would be useful as an end-of-reading activity.

Regardless of the strategies selected, clarity in document structure is of paramount importance in the design of continuous instructional hypertext. Great care should be taken to explicate and reinforce that structure in order to reduce cognitive load and facilitate learner comprehension.

Interactivity

Probably the single greatest advantage of electronic text over printed materials is its capacity for interactivity. With online text, students can access related information through links, visualize through dynamic applets, and answer questions and receive immediate feedback. Instructors can enhance student motivation and learning through use of application exercises, feedback, and a variety of media in their online texts. In short, the interactive nature of electronic text offers instructors the opportunity to increase the powerful educational effects of active learning (Reinking, 1994; Campbell, 2000). Moore (1989) describes three types of interaction in distance education: learner-content interaction, learner-instructor interaction, and learner-learner interaction. Each is relevant to the discussion of Web-based course design, but the emphasis here is on learner-content interaction as affected by the design of continuous instructional hypertext. It is interesting, although perhaps not surprising, to note that Soo and Bonk (1998) found that experienced distance education instructors rated asynchronous "learner-material interaction" more important for learning than either synchronous teacher-learner or synchronous learner-learner interaction in distance education courses.

As Bernard and Lungren (1994) conclude, good learners don't just read; they also organize, reiterate, rehearse, and practice. Procedures shown to encourage elaboration, such as planning, attending, encoding, reviewing, and evaluating, can be intentionally facilitated within online text through use of:

- Explicit text structure
- Learning objectives
- Text-embedded questions
- Pretests
- Directions for reading
- Metacognitive prompts
- Graphs, diagrams, illustrations
- End of reading activities and posttests: questions, problems
- Feedback

The first of these examples, *explicit text structure* and *learning objectives*, were addressed above. *Text-embedded questions* can be used to reinforce students' perception of structure, as well as to enable them to assess their own comprehension of the content. Questions and other embedded activities can be used to break larger sections of text into smaller, more manageable pieces, thus potentially alleviating concerns related to extensive scrolling and reading online. Course management systems, with their built-in quiz functions, facilitate the use of embedded questions and feedback. Instructors can use surveys and quiz tools for *pretesting* to prompt relevant prior learning as students enter a new topic or content area. Bernard and Lungren (1994) remind us that text-embedded questions should elicit higher level as well as lower level learning. The research of Oliver et al. (1998) highlights the importance of providing specific space to answer Web-text embedded questions. Students in that study who worked without a printed guidebook rarely took notes while reading, even though they were directed to do so, and answered only those questions for which space was provided.

Explicit *directions for reading* may help to overcome any natural reluctance or preconceived idea the learner may have about reading online. Because students may expect to scan Web-based materials, or to print them for closer reading—and because the instruction may intend for different textual materials to be used in different ways—instructors should include specific directions about how students are expected to use the electronic text. Specific directions for use of online materials can be combined with *metacognitive prompts* (suggestions for learning strategies, questions about perceived comprehension, or reminders of prior learning) to improve reading comprehension and performance (Bernard & Lundgren, 1994; Topping, 2001).

Graphs, diagrams, and multimedia illustrations, again with appropriate directions about their intended use, can facilitate comprehension of ideas presented in text. Hartley (1987) identified some of the emerging capabilities and limitations of electronic graphics and animations. More recently, Scaife and Rogers (1996) offer a thorough and thoughtful explanation of the need to develop theoretical propositions to explain how and why graphical presentations are effective for learning. Possible explanations include aiding comprehension through visualization, reducing cognitive load, and better simulation of the real world. Multimedia materials will increase interactivity to the degree that we design them to do so and should be accompanied by specific assignments that require students to interact with the materials. In designing continuous text for Web-based courses, great care should be taken to avoid the need for learners to install files and perform lengthy downloads unless these activities are warranted by the instructional value of the material. Graphics, animations, audio, and video should be used judiciously in Web-based courses, and with the recognition that students may be accessing the course through a modem.

End-of-reading problems and activities provide further opportunities to encourage learner-content interaction through application, synthesis, and evaluation of the content. A major advantage of the Web is that instructors can design these activities to be completed individually or collaboratively, with the latter providing opportunities for interaction with other students as well as with the content of the course. Problems and exercises are more effective when they are graded and *feedback* is provided (Bernard & Lungren, 1994).

Interactivity is a primary pedagogical benefit of online text. Unless interactivity is a major goal, there is little reason to use continuous instructional hypertext rather than print for teaching/learning materials. These strategies can be used to effectively increase learner-content interaction in Web-based distance and distributed learning courses.

SUMMARY

This chapter argues that continuous hypertext can be used effectively in online and Web-enhanced courses. Evidence is emerging to counter earlier warnings that students are unable to read anything but the briefest, most condensed text in an online format. Online course text can be carefully designed to incorporate what we have learned from research on electronic text, although that research still is limited. The slowly emerging popularity and availability of e-textbooks and readers will provide opportunities to create and evaluate new versions of instructional hypertext. Distance education faculty should be encouraged to add to the current body of knowledge in this important area of study.

REFERENCES

Bailey, L. (Compiled by). (1999 March). *Introduction to web page evaluation and design*. Available online: http://www.chelt.ac.uk/lis/lbailey/quilt.htr.

Bernard, R. M., & Lundgren, K. M. (1994). Learner assessment and text design strategies for distance education. *Canadian Journal of Educational Communication, 23*(2), 133–152.

Campbell, K. (2000). The web: Design for active learning. University of Alberta: Academic Technologies for Learning. Available online: http://www.atl.ualberta.ca/articles/idesign/activel.cfm.

Chen, C., & Rada, R. (1996). Interacting with hypertext: A meta-analysis of experimental studies. *Human Computer Interaction, 11*(2), 125–156.

Cushman, W. H. (1986). Reading from microfiche, VDT and the printed page: Subjective fatigue and performance. *Human Factors, 28*(1), 63–73.

Gibson, D. L. (1994). The effects of screen layout and feedback type on productivity and satisfaction of occasional users. *Journal of Information Systems, 8*(2), 105.

Gillingham, M. G. (1993). Effects of question complexity and reader strategies on adults' hypertext comprehension. *Journal of Research on Computing in Education, 26*(1), 1–15.

Gould, J. D., Alfaro, L., Barnes, V., Finn, R., Grischkowsky, N., & Minuto, A. (1987). Reading is slower from CRT displays than from paper: Attempts to isolate a single variable explanation. *Human Factors, 29*(3), 269–299.

Gray, S. H., & Shasha, D. (1989). To link or not to link? Empirical guidance for the design of nonlinear text systems. *Behavior Research Methods, Instruments, & Computers, 21*(2), 326–333.

Hartley, J. (1987). Designing electronic text: The role of print-based research. *Educational Communication and Technology, 35*(1), 3–17.

Jin, Z., & Fine, S. (1996). The effect of human behavior on the design of an information retrieval system interface. *International Information & Library Review, 28,* 249–260.

LaCroix, N. (1999). Macrostructure construction and organization in the processing of multiple text passages. *Instructional Science, 27,* 221–233.

Lemke, J. L. (1998). Metamedia literacy: Transforming meanings and media. In D. Reinking, M. C. McKenna, L. L. Labbo, & D. Kieffer. (Eds.), *Handbook of literacy and technology* (pp. 283–301). Hillsdale, NJ: Lawrence Erlbaum Associates, Inc.

Lynch, P. J., & Horton, S. (1997). Yale C/AIM Web Style Guide, 2nd ed. Available online: http://www.info.med.yale.edu/caim/manual/.

Moore, M. G. (1989). Three types of interaction. In M. G. Moore (Ed.), *The American Journal of Distance Education, 3*(2), 1–7.

Morkes, J., & Nielsen, J. (1997). *Concise, scannable, and objective: How to write for the web.* Available online: http://www.useit.com/ papers/webwriting/writing.htm.

Muter, P. (1996). Interface design and optimization of reading of continuous text. In H. van Oostendorp & S. de Mul (Eds.), *Cognitive aspects of electronic text processing* (pp. 161–180). Norwood, NJ: Ablex Publishing Corporation.

Muter, P., & Marutto, P. (1991). Reading and skimming from computer screens and books: The paperless office revisited. *Behavior & Information Technology, 10,* 257–266.

Nielson, J. (2000). *Designing web usability: The practice of simplicity.* Indianapolis, IN: New Riders Publishing.

Nielson, J., & Tahir, M. (2001). *Homepage usability: 50 websites deconstructed.* Indianapolis, IN: New Riders Publishing.

Oliver, R., Omari, A., & Herrington, J. (1998). Investigating implementation strategies for WWW-based learning environments. *International Journal of Instructional Media, 25*(1), 121.

Parlangeli, O., Marchigiani, E., & Bagnara, S. (1999). Multimedia systems in distance education: Effects of usability on learning. *Interacting with Computers, 12*(1), 37–49.

Piolat, A., Roussey, J., & Thunin, O. (1997). Effects of screen presentation on text reading and revising. *International Journal of Human—Computer Studies, 47,* 565–589.

Reinking, D. (1994). *Electronic literacy* (Perspective Series No. 1-PS-N-07). Athens, GA, and College Park, MD: The National Reading Research Center.

Scaife, M., & Rogers, Y. (1996). External cognition: How do graphical representations work? *International Journal of Human—Computer Studies, 45,* 185–213.

Shneiderman, B. (1997). Designing information-abundant web sites: Issues and recommendations. *International Journal of Human—Computer Studies, 47,* 5–29.

Streitz, N. A. (1988). Mental models and metaphors: Implications for the design of adaptive user-system interfaces. In H. Mandl & A. Lesgold (Eds.), *Learning issues for intelligent tutoring systems* (pp. 164–186). New York: Springer.

Thuring, M., Hannemann, J., & Haake, J. M. (1995). Hypermedia and cognition: Designing for comprehension. *Communications of the ACM, 38*(8), 57–66.

Topping, K. J. (2001). Electronic literacy in school and home: A look into the future. Available online: http://www.readingonline.org/international/future.

Trumbull, D., Gay, G., & Mazur, J. (1992). Students' actual and perceived use of navigational and guidance tools in a hypermedia program. *Journal of Research on Computing in Education, 24*(3), 315–328.

Uncle Netword's. (1999). *Writing Webtext.* Available online: http://www.uncle-netword.com/articles/writeweb1.htm.

Unz, D. C., & Hesse, F. W. (1999). The use of hypertext for learning. *Journal of Educational Computing Research, 20*(3), 279–295.

van Nimwegen, C., Pouw, M., & van Oostendorp, H. (1999). The influence of structure and reading-manipulation on usability of hypertexts. *Interacting with Computers, 12,* 7–21.

Wagner, M. J., & Payne, D. G. (1994). Effects of a graphical browser on readers' efficiency in reading hypertext. *Technical Communication, 41*(2), 224–233.

Ward, M., & Newlands, D. (1998). Use of the web in undergraduate teaching. *Computers & Education, 31*, 171–184.

Weller, M. J. (2000). The use of narrative to provide a cohesive structure for a web based computing course. *Journal of Interactive Media in Education, 2000* (1), 1–20.

Wilkinson, R. T., & Robinshaw, H. M. (1987). Proof-reading: VDU and paper text compared for speed, accuracy and fatigue. *Behaviour and Information Technology, 6*(2), 125–133.

21

From Teletraining to e-Learning and Knowledge Management

Alan G. Chute
Avaya Inc.
achute@avaya.com

INTRODUCTION

In today's Information Age, learning in the corporate environment is no longer confined within the four walls of a corporate classroom. The instructor, armed with a textbook, is no longer the sole resource in the learning experience. Information resources are everywhere, and people need access to these resources at anytime and from anywhere. The emerging corporate learning environment is envisioned as a system for connecting learners with these distributed learning resources.

Because of the exponential growth of the importance of information and continuous learning in our society, corporations are creating new and more powerful ways to manage knowledge resources and provide distance learning experiences. Corporations are migrating from stand-alone teletraining, distance learning, and knowledge management initiatives to integrated e-learning solutions. In my opinion the integration of distance learning (DL) and knowledge management (KM) is e-learning (see Fig. 21.1). The Webster dictionary defines "e-" as a prefix that can mean among other things "thoroughly" as in <evaporize>. I define e-learning as "a strategy for connecting learners with distributed knowledge resources."

It is widely recognized that the acceleration in the development and deployment of innovative e-learning systems will be astonishing in the next few years. In fact, John Chambers, CEO of Cisco Systems, a recognized leader in the expansion of the Internet, told the *New York Times* in November 1999 that learning will be the next "killer application" for computer technology. He went on to say that e-learning "will make email look like rounding error." In other words, the impact and scope of e-learning will be huge.

BACKGROUND

Our legacy educational systems were designed to meet the impact of the needs of the Industrial Age and are now attempting to meet the needs of the Information Age. Learning resources are no longer tightly controlled, rather they are readily accessible from knowledge resources

DL + KM = e-Learning

Figure 1. e-Learning

FIG. 21.1.

worldwide. Information is everywhere, and the challenges for educational and training institutions are to develop the tools for managing the knowledge resources and provide appropriate access to this information.

Distance learning and knowledge management are the building blocks for the 21st century e-learning environment. Business like AT&T, Lucent Technologies, and Avaya Inc. have begun to address the needs of their employees through the establishment of next generation e-learning systems and e-learning methodologies. The challenge is to make e-learning programs and knowledge resources available anytime, anywhere, and in a form that is relevant to the specific needs of the students.

This chapter presents a retrospective look at 20 years of corporate distance learning experiences at AT&T, Lucent Technologies, and Avaya Inc. The review starts with early findings from the teletraining and then our experience with knowledge management and e-learning projects we have designed and implemented. I have reported what our distance learning innovators have learned regarding the design and management of technology-supported learning systems. I have summarized the work of over a hundred of my colleagues who have conducted research and development projects over the years at the AT&T National Teletraining Center (NTC), the Lucent Technologies Center for Excellence in Distance Learning (CEDL), and the Avaya Inc. Customer Relationship Management (CRM) Institute. The overarching missions of these organizations have been to leverage communications systems to enable employees to have access to the knowledge, skills, and tools necessary for them to perform their jobs in increasingly complex and sophisticated work environments. We have a passion for providing the most up-to-date learning resources to students at a time and place convenient to them. To that end we have continued to investigate, develop, and demonstrate innovative applications for state-of-the-art communication technologies within our organizations.

Distance learning is both a technology system and a process that connects learners with distributed learning resources. A complete distance learning system must integrate the planning, delivery, and management of learning by using a combination of information technology and telecommunication services. The delivery media most commonly used over the past 20 years have been audio, audiographics, video, and Internet.

Audio teleconferencing uses conventional telephone lines that are networked together to provide an interactive, shared-audio space between instructor and students. Audiographics teleconferencing provides users with the capability to interact with one another through two-way voice and graphic communication and to share images simultaneously on high-resolution, color monitors. The screen images can be annotated with the aid of graphics tablets, which further enhance the participants' capability to interact spontaneously with one another.

Video teleconferencing provides several modes of delivery. Broadband communication channels enable all locations to see live, full-motion video from the originating site. Newer technologies enable two-way visual and two-way audio communication between all locations connected by high-speed, high-capacity digital lines, including Internet protocol. Video, together with audio and audiographic technology, and Internet make up a continuum of delivery options that can provide either very basic (audio only) or very sophisticated (full-motion video) levels of presentation.

The Internet has enabled learners to access knowledge resources anytime, anywhere, and in anyway that is meaningful to the learner. The challenge with the Internet is to create discipline around how to manage the knowledge resources, foster collaboration, and share knowledge. Knowledge management (KM) is a multifaceted business discipline that treats knowledge like a form of capital. That is, it uses it to make more knowledge and protect it, and cause others within the organization to do the same so that the organization is profitable. Typically, cultural transformation is necessary in people, impacting attitudes and behaviors toward knowledge, its use and obligations toward it. Business processes, practices, and technology tools aid in the use of leveraging knowledge as a capital asset. KM systems can serve as learning resources in the fast-paced change of the current business environments.

DISTANCE LEARNING PROJECTS

The research and development initiatives at AT&T, Lucent Technologies, and Avaya Inc. have been focused on increasing our understanding of the various psychological, sociological, ergonomic, and environmental factors involved in distance learning, and toward improving our ability to effectively manage the distance learning environment. The major projects described in this chapter represent part of an overall programmatic research effort to optimize and proliferate specific distance learning technologies within the broader context of distance education. Many of the findings and recommendations discussed have been implemented in the design, delivery, and management of AT&T, Lucent Technologies, and Avaya Inc. distance learning courses. Those that are nonproprietary are shared with clients interested in the deployment of effective distance learning systems.

National Teletraining Network (NTN)

In 1984, the instructional effectiveness studies at the AT&T National Teletraining Network demonstrated that teletraining was an effective and efficient alternative to face-to-face instruction. In one study, several modes of delivery and their respective student achievement outcomes were compared (Chute, Bruning, & Hulick, 1984). Two intact groups of students were presented with either traditional face-to-face classroom instruction or remote teletraining instruction. The teletraining mode utilized an electronic conference board, two-way voice communication, and interactive graphics capability. Transmissions over standard telephone lines linked instructors with their distant students. The course content and the amount of instruction were identical for both groups. The results showed that while pretest scores between the two groups were not found to be significantly different ($t = 1.73$, df $= 20$), the posttest scores of the teletrained group were significantly higher than those of the traditional classroom group ($t = 6.24$, df $= 20$). Students appeared to learn from the teletraining mode as well, if not better, than they did from the face-to-face mode.

How well students learn in a teletraining mode is directly proportionate to how well they accept the experience. Internal students at AT&T were asked to compare the effectiveness of teletraining with the effectiveness of face-to-face instruction. Surveys were obtained in 1984 over a 6-month period from 329 students enrolled in 45 face-to-face classes and 590 students enrolled in 32 teletraining classes. Students from each group were asked to respond to questions that pertained to course relevance and design and to the overall quality of instruction. No significant differences were found between the responses of the two groups in any of the response categories. This suggested that students perceived courses delivered via teletraining and traditional, face-to-face modes as being equally effective.

Client Teletraining Network (CTN)

In 1985, studies at the Client Teletraining Network assessed how clients responded to newly developed courses and to teletraining in general. The researchers reported a high level of acceptance and student satisfaction with the teletraining mode of delivery (90 percent) and a high level of satisfaction with the content of each course.

In addition, they reported that student satisfaction was related to: (1) whether the content was relevant to their jobs and challenging enough for their level of expertise, (2) whether the cost for teletrained courses was less than the cost for face-to-face courses, (3) whether the transmitted visuals were of broadcast quality, and (4) whether the courses were interaction oriented. They also found that clients thought short teletraining sessions (one-half to a full day), conducted in full-motion video at a site near their office, were very appealing.

Related to instructional effectiveness and learner acceptance is the concept of instructional appeal. Traditional attempts to improve training tend to focus on effectiveness, efficiency, and affordability as the critical areas of high-quality training. According to the 1985 study, those areas were not sufficient to ensure that the training would be well received or that the trainees would return in the future. In other words, "better—faster—cheaper" is not good enough. A fourth factor—"appeal"—should also be considered, especially in a business environment where training success is due, in part, to how much satisfaction the client anticipates from the experience. While there seems to be little doubt that teletraining can provide effective, efficient, and affordable alternatives to face-to-face training, the dimension of appeal needs to be addressed in teletrained instruction.

The researchers argue that the factors related to the appeal and delivery of training should be identified and addressed so the receptability of teletraining can be increased. In order to identify these factors, the appeal of the three modes of instruction was examined. Results based on observational, questionnaire, and interview data suggested that teletraining can be made more appealing by focusing attention on the instructional elements, the social needs, and the innovation-adoption aspects of teletraining. By implementing these strategies into the design and delivery of teletrained instruction, you can increase the level of satisfaction that learners experience in teletraining.

Video Teletraining Network (VTN)

In 1988, studies examined students' video teletraining network concerns, experiences, expectations, and feelings in a day-and-a-half long teletrained course using naturalistic inquiry. Results show: (1) what students experience in teletraining is influenced by their prior needs and expectations, (2) among students' major concerns is the feasibility of teletraining applications within their organizations and the cost of both equipment and services, (3) students believe the on-site coordinator is critical to the success of a course, and (4) proper instruction and guided practice are essential to removing the "myth and magic" from teletraining. Instructors should maintain an awareness and sensitivity to the concerns of students so as to better meet their needs.

Along similar lines, a study was conducted to determine to what extent learners in teletraining attribute their success or failure to the learning environment. The results showed that students attributed more impact to factors such as: mood, effort, ability, attitude, a need to do well, the quality of materials, and the design of instruction as critical success factors more important than the medium of the teletraining itself.

Knowledge Net Project

Lucent Technologies in the 1990s implemented a number of knowledge management initiatives including: the Call Center Institute, the Lucent Knowledge Universe, and the Knowledge NET project. The purpose of these projects was to enhance the impact of the KM discipline on instructional effectiveness, business results, customer relationships, and quality of work-life for their associates. The projects were internally focused and sought to apply theoretical principles into real-world settings. Although associates reported that the resources developed from these projects were essential, they could not easily point to precise quantifiable business return on investments (ROI) impacts. However, it became clear that KM and e-learning were rapidly converging as both appeared to be geared toward providing highly relevent, just-in-time knowledge.

In 1998, Lucent Technologies expanded its KM with additional initiatives and was ranked among the top two dozen companies practicing KM. One of these projects, the Knowledge Net, was implemented in 1999 by the Professional Services Organization, an externally focused consultancy in the call-center market. The Knowledge Net Project tested assumptions about the use of communities of practice and communities of interest as a means for focusing consultants on the use of core knowledge that they needed to do their jobs, smarter, better, faster. The Knowledge Net Project was built upon some underlying principles of knowledge management. The communities had specific roles and responsibilities like: mentor, subject matter expert (SME), and community leader. Researchers tested the value of those roles and found them useful in dividing the labor of a knowledge community. They also found that to fully exploit the capabilities of KM they needed certain types of infrastructure enhancements to the technology systems that needed to be funded and supported at the chief information officer (CIO) and chief executive officer (CEO) organization levels. Without that executive support KM would only have a "ripple" effect at a departmental level and not realize a "tsunami" impact that is possible with an enterprise-wide commitment to knowledge management and knowledge sharing.

CRM Portal

In 1999, based on promise in the potential of Knowledge Net and other KM initiatives, senior management created the CRM Portal to address the KM needs of a strategic solution group for Lucent's CRM (Customer Relationship Management) business. This was a unit responsible for changing the focus of the call-center business from one of hardware, software, and services to one that focuses on the impact on our customer's customers. The technology support system developed in house was a vertical portal rich in contextual metadata, associating knowledge assets with different job groups, each with unique job tasks (see Fig. 21. 2).

Anyone could nominate a knowledge asset to the CRM Portal. The CRM Portal was able to track usage by user, by asset, and by nominator. This capability gave Lucent Technologies the potential of identifying key contributors to the company's body of knowledge, key users of that knowledge, and the ability to learn about the use of knowledge within the company. In addition, it gave the company a basis for drawing peer attention to those who contributed to the body of knowledge and to those who most used it. This made possible the ability to contact users to get at other measures of quality of assets. For example, the company could determine whether the use of the asset had a positive impact on business results. If a positive result was achieved, they could then determine to what extent and in what area of the business it impacted (i.e., grew or protected revenue, reduced expenses, improved customer and/or employee satisfaction). This tracking enabled the company to reward such behavior accordingly, further driving the cultural transformation toward awareness of knowledge as capital.

FIG. 21.2.   CRM Portal.

A managing editor function was assigned to a single person in each strategic solution group who ensured consistency in the application of the metadata and added some as well. Finally an indexing tool was used to make some of the last metadata decisions. Key reinforcement practices were undertaken to maintain the visibility of the CRM Portal and its assets to the user community. This was accomplished through monthly calls with key audience groups and specific familiarization sessions done with those responsible for making content decisions for their solution. These were called "First Friday's" conferences.

ASK Center

The CRM Portal's success was such that with the spinoff of certain of Lucent's lines of business into a new company named Avaya, the decision was made to integrate, for the most part, the marketing funding and decision making. The CRM Portal was designated to be broadened to all of the five strategic solutions groups within the company. In 2001, the CRM Portal was renamed the Avaya Solutions Knowledge (ASK) Center. The expanded knowledge base of the ASK Center created a level of complexity for the knowledge management schema, necessitating the development of a conceptual model to help describe the way knowledge was segmented and differentiated. A solution was to manage knowledge in a knowledge cube (see Fig. 21.3). One axis was the strategic solutions disciplines, another was the product information, and the last was the market distribution channels. Users could find information by following an information map along a linear axis or employ a very powerful search engine, which utilized the rich contextual metadata that described every knowledge object in the database.

The ASK Center (see Fig. 21.4) is the single most powerful and dynamic resource for Avaya sales and marketing expertise. It provides a wealth of knowledge, ranging from information and news to marketing materials, sales collateral, training, and various support services. And the ASK Center enables employees to share their knowledge and experience with other employees worldwide.

The ASK Center gives employees access to all of Avaya's channel marketing knowledge and expertise in a way that makes most sense to them. There are several ways to find what

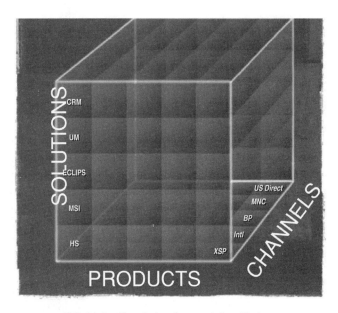

FIG. 21.3. Knowledge Segmentation Strategy.

they need. The Map function provides a menu of case studies, presentations, white papers, competitive information, and so on.

The Search function can focus a search on a solution, an author, a topic, or a date and delimit the results to slides, documents, applications, and video media types. The Guide function tunes into what people are working on at the time. The Guide asks questions and then retrieves items most relevant to the task at hand.

The Web site provides shortcuts to get quick access to background on Avaya solutions, collateral, customer references, performance support tools, and the like. Spotlights are included for each of the Avaya Solutions groups to call attention to unique strategic events, learning, and updates on Avaya alliances. Each selection includes a brief abstract that helps users decide

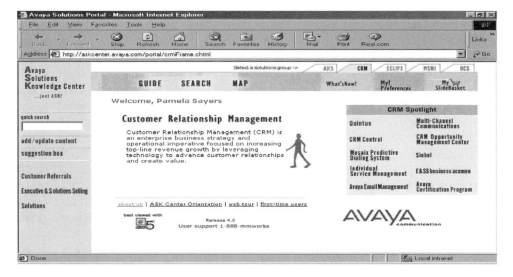

FIG. 21.4. ASK Center.

whether to dig deeper or to continue a search. Some items provide a list of related training courses that have been recommended by education experts at Avaya. There are affinity links that allow users to check out related content that colleagues are using. The ASK Center includes powerful tools like the Presentation Chunker, an innovative feature that makes it easy to access and share PowerPoint content. At a glance, users can view all the slides from any PowerPoint presentation, can add slides to their SlideBasket from different presentations, and download slides to their PC with a single click. The Presentation Chunker can also be employed during live sessions to conduct online meetings and presentations to large groups. But more on collaboration in a just moment.

Ask Center supports knowledge sharing and self-nomination of content for the Web site. Users can easily share their own files and web links with other users—by clicking the add/update content. Users receive valuable feedback and information on how their content is being accessed, and rated, by other Avaya associates. The ASK Center facilitates collaboration with a growing number of communities of practice. These groups share a dynamic library of information, threaded discussions, and downloadable materials, securely, for members only. Local program administrators can update content, manage who has access, and send courtesy messages to group members informing them of what's new.

Users can further personalize the ASK Center to fit the way they work. When users identify their organizational function, the interface adjusts to their job context. From here, they set personal preferences to customize their own ASK Center home page. If users are new to the ASK Center, they are invited to visit us and get acquainted. A quick start for first-time users and an online tour are always available from the home page. The ASK Center is dynamic, growing, and improving all the time, making Avaya expertise and knowledge accessible, usable, and useful to employees worldwide.

COST-AVOIDANCE AND ROI ANALYSES

Distance learning and KM initiatives have produced significant cost-benefits for AT&T, Lucent Technologies, and Avaya over the many years. Historically, the benefits have been computed as cost-avoidance benefits and/or ROI benefits.

For distance learning programs the costs previously incurred from travel expenses and lost productivity were avoided by using the teletraining medium. The research conducted in this area provided evidence that teletraining is a cost-effective alternative to face-to-face information delivery.

Courses and Seminars

Teletraining produced significant travel cost-avoidance for AT&T. Major savings were realized for the courses, and update programs were delivered via teletraining. The savings resulted from travel costs and productivity-related costs that were avoided by using the teletraining medium. The information presented here substantiates the fact that teletraining was a cost-efficient alternative to face-to-face delivery of training (Chute, 1990). In computing the cost-avoidance figures for the 1989 courses delivered via audiographic teletraining, the assumption was made that students would have had to travel to Cincinnati, Ohio, to receive this training if teletraining were not an alternative. During 1989, 3,650 students attended teletrained sessions of courses in the training curriculum. The average course length in 1989 was seven hours. An average round-trip air fare of $400 and a per diem cost of $100 for lodging and daily expenses resulted in a total cost-avoidance per student of $500 per course. The cost-avoidance savings for 3,650 students was $1,825,000.

The cost-avoidance for not traveling is offset somewhat by the line and bridging expenses associated with teletraining. A typical teletrained course at the University of Sales Excellence had one host site and four remote sites. This configuration incurred expenses for five lines and five ports on the bridge. Bridging expenses were based on AT&T Alliance Teleconferencing Services. Equipment capital investments were not considered in these calculations since existing equipment was used; only operating expenses were included. Using these figures, the total network expenses for the 170 teletrained sessions were $217,600. Subtracting the network expenses from the cost-avoidance figure produced a net cost-avoidance of $1,607,400, or $440 per student. Travel cost-avoidance was only part of the actual savings realized from teletraining. Substantial employee productivity savings also occurred through the reemployment of nonproductive time spent traveling, time spent waiting in airports, and time spent catching up on work once back at the home location. Assuming the average nonproductive time was six hours per student, the total expense was $525,600, or $144 per student, adding this savings to the earlier travel cost figure produced a total cost avoidance of $2,133,000, or $584 per student.

These data support the assertion that audiographic teletraining is clearly a cost-efficient way to deliver courses. The benefits included both direct travel cost-avoidance and increased productivity resulting from reduced nonproductive time. Similar calculations were performed to determine the cost-avoidance for the audio update programs via the National Teletraining Network. The following two assumptions were made in doing these calculations. First, students from the 350 field locations would not travel to Cincinnati to participate in a 60-minute training session; therefore, each presenter would have to travel to 70 major cities across the country to reach the students. Second, students would utilize ground transportation from local or remote locations to attend a training session in one of the 70 locations. If each presenter had traveled to 70 locations, costs incurred would have been $100 for local expenses and $400 for air fare; the travel cost for each presenter would have been $35,000. For the 254 update programs presented in 1989, the cost avoided was $8,890.00.

The cost analysis for the update programs also accounts for the expenses associated with the operation of the network. The cost of the long distance calls made to Cincinnati by each of the remote locations was $278,000. A dedicated bridge located in Cincinnati was used for the programs. The 1989 expenses incurred for leasing and operating the dedicated bridge was $311,000. The expenses incurred for facsimile, mailing of visuals, and xeroxing of handout materials used for the programs during 1989 was $61,000. The net cost-avoidance for the 1989 audio update programs was $8,250,000, or $32,480 per program.

Cost-Efficiency Model

Since the cost of delivering instruction is an important consideration in many training programs, the AT&T staff developed a spreadsheet model on cost-efficiency that can assist clients in selecting a medium or media suited to their budgets and needs. The model was later incorporated into an AT&T Electronic Performance Support Tool (EPST) titled the Training Delivery Consultant. The tool provided charts, figures, and formulae based on industry-accepted value or values determined by experts in the field of instructional technology. Figures provided by the client were evaluated on two levels of detail—macro and micro. The macro level compares the basic costs of implementing delivery options including: face-to-face, programmed instruction, computer-based education, audio teleconferencing, audiographic teleconferencing, and video teleconferencing. Included were the annual cost figures for equipment, maintenance/updating, trainees, instructors, support staff, and delivery of instruction. The micro level reveals each individual cost factor, the formulae used to derive the cost figures, and the actual dollar amounts used in the computations.

To demonstrate the effectiveness of the model, a hypothetical situation was developed in which 2,000 people were expected to receive 8 hours of training within a 1-year period. By incorporating various details and figures of the particular training situation, a total cost figure was computed and the most cost-efficient method of instruction was identified. The results indicated that all technologies listed above were more cost-efficient than face-to-face delivery. It was concluded that, if an analysis proceeds only to the point where the initial costs of equipment and course development are determined, then any form of instruction delivered by advanced technologies would naturally appear to cost more. However, by factoring in cost-savings figures, it can be shown that the actual cost of instruction utilizing advanced-delivery technologies is lower than the face-to-face mode. This and other cost-benefit studies conducted by the AT&T National Teletraining Center provide evidence that teletraining is an economical alternative to face-to-face information delivery.

ROI Analysis of CRM Portal

In 2000, the cost-benefit analysis for the CRM Portal KM initiative was conducted by employing a return on investment methodology. ROI analysis seems more appropriate for KM initiatives since it is difficult to quantify any cost-avoidance related to travel expense. The ROI analysis involved at a high level three things: Project benefit versus cost, a time and sales tracking mechanism, and actual ROI based upon outputs of tracking mechanisms over a certain period of time. The first phase of the analysis involved focus groups of users who documented their specific sales, accounts protected, or expenses reduced as a result of the CRM Portal. Later, their middle managers who operate in both the tactical and the strategic spheres provided estimates in the areas of derived value, enabling the team to estimate an ROI of $140M annually for the entire Avaya sales population.

The ROI need not be stated always in terms of money coming in versus money expended. The outcomes realized versus resources expended can be of any nature relevant to the organization. The ROI analysis answered key questions executives had, when faced with funding and other resource allocation decisions. The ROI provides answers to the basic question, "Why are we doing this?"

The question forced strategic alignment with corporate goals and included ROI against some kind of hurdle rate (a fixed level of benefit beneath which investments of resources are usually not made). ROI also enables a comparative analysis. For example, there's just so much resource to go around, programs competing for resources are ranked by ROI, and resources are dedicated to programs according to order in the ranking until resources run out. Decisions were made regarding those in the lowest rankings as to whether funding is to be reduced or eliminated.

ROI Anaysis of ESSba

Avaya's goal is to be an e-business solutions company, the goal requires a sales force to employ a multilevel selling skills model that addresses executive selling, technology-oriented selling, and operational management selling. The executive selling model emphasizes the value of Avaya's business solutions rather than its products. This selling model also requires an "executive conversation" with a C-club member (i.e., CEO, CFO) in the client organization. Training to support the new business model is provided to executive sales managers via the Executive and Solution Selling business acumen (ESSba) course that was built following an e-learning model. The 200-hour course includes three 2-hour teleconferences, many online learning modules, and 2 weeks of intensive role-play instruction delivered over a 2 1/2-month period of time. The ESSba focuses on the skills and knowledge needed to have an executive conversation. The focus is on "*how* to sell to an executive, not *what* to sell." Over 200 people have gone through the course, including senior sales leaders. The impact of the ESSba was to increase close rate, increase return on sales (ROS), broaden product mix of each sale, reduce sales cycle by 90 days, and generate over 36.3M in incremental revenue reported with a 46.1 percent program ROI.

INSTRUCTOR COMPETENCIES

AT&T, Lucent Technologies, and Avaya have had a strong interest in maintaining a high level of instructor effectiveness in their training programs. However, as can be expected, instructors can differ widely in the way they approach similar instructional tasks. To identify the common attributes that expert teachers share, an analysis of top AT&T instructors was conducted in 1984 and researchers were able to develop a competency-based model that provided a basis for instructor selection, evaluation, career management, assignment, and training. Expert instructors were found to possess skills or knowledge in these areas: basic learning theory, organizing/managing materials and learning environment, managing course structure and organization, administration/evaluation, verbal and nonverbal presentation methods, responding to trainees, questioning of trainees, coordinating group activities, subject matter expertise, teaming, and teletraining skills.

The model was validated with responses obtained from fifty-seven managers, instructors, and instructional technologists. Based on their work, AT&T implemented a six- to nine-month instructor certification program that taught people how to perform more effectively as instructors. The program was geared to refining instructors' skills periodically over a 36-month period.

THE PHYSICAL LEARNING ENVIRONMENT

Emerging video and Internet technologies have enabled educators and trainers to create more personalized distance learning solutions that are delivered at the learner's workstation rather than in a dedicated distance learning classroom. Emerging technologies have made possible more seamless integration of voice, video, and data connections among learners, instructors, subject matter experts, the Internet, virtual libraries, and educational content providers. Future broadband technology applications will make high-bandwidth education and training easily accessible, convenient, and more cost-efficient for the learners and for the education provider.

Group video teleconferencing systems in many ways resemble the traditional classroom environment. However, it is important that educators see group video teleconferencing as more than just a way to extend classes to off-campus locations. Special emphasis should be given to ways to gain attention, maintain attention, encourage participation, and structure the learning context for the remote learners.

The use of desktop video conferencing and Internet video collaboration is becoming increasingly important. Desktop video systems offer video teleconferencing capabilities as well as multipoint-shared software telecollaboration. Students at multiple sites can not only see and hear each other, but they can simultaneously collaborate on the same software application. The International Telecommunications Union (ITU) standards for data telecollaboration and interoperability among switched digital networks H.320, LAN/WAN environments H.323, and analog voice networks H.324 have dramatically accelerated the deployment of innovative distance learning solutions.

As networks migrate to even higher bandwidth capacity, educators will experience superior audio and video quality and multimedia capabilities that are desirable for many distance learning solutions. Fiber optic backbone networks are often designed in private network for increased throughput, reliability, and overall quality. With the deployment of public asynchronous transfer mode (ATM) networks and education service provider (ESP) networks, many of today's distance learning systems will migrate to broadband ATM networks.

The enhanced technological potential of group or desktop video teleconferencing and Internet video collaboration requires educators and trainers to reconceptualize the pedagogical techniques they use for face-to-face instruction and leverage the unique capabilities of these powerful communications media. Two-way video conferencing is one distance learning technology that allows for heightened interaction and activity usually confined to the classroom.

When creating the physical environment, we learned that we needed to consider both the facilitator site and the learner sites. Generally, increased attention should be given to the location, appearance, and comfort of video conferencing rooms. Ideally, rooms will be created for video conferencing only. When this is not possible, steps can be taken to create the best learning environment available.

With desktop video conferencing and Internet video collaboration the instructor's desktop computer and the participants' desktop computers become learning tools. As with group video conferencing, there are some specific guidelines for the workspace that will enhance the effectiveness of the technology to facilitate learning programs. We learned to provide enough workspace around the computer and display, avoid strong back lighting such as facing the camera toward a window or other strong light source, avoid aiming the camera at ceiling lights, and if possible, use only cool white (3200 degree Kelvin) fluorescent or white incandescent lights. Clear incandescent or older fluorescent lights tend to cause yellowish video images.

The number of participants sharing a desktop video PC should be no more than two or three at each location. Beyond that number, it is too hard for individuals to see or be seen on the computer monitor. A larger monitor can be attached to the computers, but generally that reduces the quality of the live video image. One of the most important item of Internet video collaboration is the Share Application. The Share Application enables the instructor and the participants to share a software program and work in the same documents. What is critical is the shared application can create real-time interactive learning activities from brainstorming to software programming applications. The learners can participate together to design reports, graphs, or charts, or collaborate on research projects all at a distance. If used effectively, Internet video collaboration–shared applications can dramatically enhance collaborative learning goals in a distance learning environment.

The physical learning environment and the pedagogical skills employed by the instructor are both critically important in the planning of distance learning programs. Having the right video teleconferencing technology in place is only half the story; skillfully presenting a relevant learning experience that is well organized, appropriate to the learning context, and very interactive is essential to enable the learners to achieve their goals and expected outcomes.

MEDIA ATTRIBUTES

Applied research is generally geared toward finding cost-effective solutions to practical problems. NTC researchers investigate ways that clients can get maximum use out of their investments in highly sophisticated teletraining technologies. One of NTC's objectives was to generate information that will get technology up and running as quickly and as smoothly as possible. In 1988, audiographics was the state-of-the-art technology that lies at the heart of AT&T's teletraining system. To identify what features users of audiographic systems want in an ideal system, a number of instructors and technologists were surveyed. From their responses ten critical features emerged including a desire for high-quality audio, high-resolution imagery, an annotation capability, and a key-pad response capability. Future design should incorporate these features to make the devices easier to operate and to improve the system's overall effectiveness.

Along similar lines, researchers were also interested in identifying which audiographic control functions teletrainers considered critical to their online teaching success. In a study with twelve expert teletrainers, fourteen such functions were identified from a list of twenty-four and then ranked in order of importance. These findings were further supported by written responses to the instruction, "List five of the most critical features you would require as keys on an audiographic peripheral device." The nominations for various functions were tallied, then ranked in order of magnitude. A correlation coefficient was computed between these and the fourteen function items. The results indicated a strong, positive relationship between the two rankings ($r = .86$).

In terms of psychological characteristics, the respondents' collective views about audio-graphic interfaces suggested guidelines for future audiographic designs. For example, respondents indicated that only a handful of functions was necessary in order to make them comfortable with instructing online but that this handful was critical to respondents' teletraining success. In addition, respondents said they preferred functions that facilitated quick and simple screen control over functions that were more elaborate but cumbersome to use. In general, when online instructors wanted an interface that helped reduce the already complex nature of teletraining rather than contribute to it.

INTERNET CAPABILITIES

At Avaya, the Internet is the primary vehicle for providing learning experiences, reference materials and up-to-date information. The Internet is now the preferred method for content browsing and e-mail communication between learners and instructors. Learners like the ability to get their questions answered at a time and place convenient to their needs. Invariably, when learners who use e-mail regularly are asked if they found an Internet-based course to be interactive, they respond that the Internet course provided them more access to their instructors and other learners than their face-to-face courses. While the Internet can be the method for providing learners the information they need, at a place and at the time they need it, there are a variety of considerations like access, multimedia content, and testing that instructors and educational service providers need to consider when placing multimedia course information and reference materials on the Internet.

Inexpensive dial-up access to the Internet is readily available today in many areas of the world. LAN, WAN, and wireless access are provided by many educational and training organizations to support a full range of multimedia learning experiences. Future broadband networks will substantially remove restrictions on the amount and types of multimedia resources that can be accessed quickly by the learners.

The type of content placed on the Web should be interactive and relevant to the learners. An entire course need not be hosted as in the case of the ESSba curriculum; some content may be delivered best in other modes of instruction. It is important to incorporate some multimedia technology into the learning experience because it will contribute to the appeal of the learning and provide the learner with a variety of methods to assimilate the information. Incorporating technology such as streaming audio, video, interactive graphics, text chats, and e-mail exchanges will provide a stimulating interactive experience for the learner; however, multimedia should be an enhancement to the course design, not a distraction. Where appropriate, educational designers should consider utilizing high-quality SCORM multimedia knowledge objects that are provided by education service providers.

Educational providers will often need to validate the learning experience, and testing on the Internet is becoming a reality. Testing on the Internet can be accomplished using traditional methods such as true or false, multiple-choice, and essay questions. Instructors can go online and create test questions that can be immediately available for the learners' use. Learners can take the test at their leisure. Because learners have the ability to collaborate with others, some instructors use online testing only for quizzes and not for exams. However, this collaboration can be a very positive learning activity. When two or more learners get together to take a quiz, they are actually collaborating in a manner that would not have taken place in the traditional method. By collaborating, learners can get other viewpoints regarding a particular subject, thus enhancing the study group's learning.

FUTURE RESEARCH DIRECTIONS

Today, educators and corporate trainers are faced with the challenge of providing quality educational programs for an ever-increasing number of students who are globally dispersed. The Information Age and the high rate of technological change have opened new job opportunities for millions. There is a need for more training and retraining to prepare people for the workplace.

One potential solution is to develop student-centered, technology-based, knowledge management systems that will provide users with the ability to access the information and training they need anywhere, anytime. The ASK Center is a first step toward a solution that is easy to use, easy to support, and easy to manage. The information is available in online databases, backed by support and documentation, and can be accessed through personal computers or personal digital assistants (PDAs). In addition, the system is able to tell what formal training programs are available and provide links to lists of course schedules, instructors, and training locations when necessary. Such a system has the capability to assist users in narrowing or broadening the search for information and has the capability to monitor user patterns (e.g., number of times help was needed during a session). Knowing how users interact with the system is very helpful in the development of future courses, expert systems, and other pertinent knowledge management resources.

Over the years our close working relationships with the training organizations at AT&T, Lucent Technologies, and Avaya and the Bell Labs organization have afforded us a unique opportunity to engage in programmatic research to improve the effectiveness and efficiency of technology-based learning systems. Our case-based research studies are programmatic in the sense that, over a period of years, the individual studies have served to weave a fabric of sound instructional research on which the development of sophisticated learning systems can be based. The findings of each study are to be tied to the development of an integrated, networked e-learning environment model.

Research projects still need to be conducted that will answer critical questions for the development of the future e-learning and knowledge management strategies. The following research projects have been identified as important topics for successful development and implementation of e-learning and knowledge management: natural language, artificial intelligence, adaptive learning strategies, adaptive testing strategies, message design attributes for emerging technologies, student motivation enhancement, and learning management systems.

The overall requirement for further research calls for the findings to be disseminated through a variety of technology-based systems. Initially the Web will be used to share ideas and information among faculty from academic institutions and a variety of knowledge management organizations. Later, information modules should be developed for the Web-based synchronous seminars (webinars) for interested parties to access.

More research is required in a number of other areas to further refine the e-learning and knowledge management applications in order to keep pace with technological developments that enhance the capabilities of interaction in these instructional systems. New research disciplines will include: communities of practice, communities of interest, divergent knowledge bases, brain exchange networks, return on investment from knowledge management programs, and value-derived measures. The promise of a "systemic" approach to instructional design, delivery, and evaluation offers an interesting direction when contrasted with the more traditional "systematic" models currently being used in corporate training environments. The CRM Institute will continue to expand its effort in a variety of research and development areas in an attempt to understand more clearly the types of problems and benefits that are involved in e-learning and e-business applications areas.

CONCLUSION

Our vision for e-learning is a seamless networked learning environment that integrates voice, video, and data connections among learners, instructors, experts, virtual libraries, the Internet, and support services. At the center is the distance learner, connected with both real-time and nonreal-time links to these resources (see Fig. 21.5). Networked e-learning environments can make education and training more accessible, convenient, focused, effective, and cost-efficient for the learners and education service providers.

Distance learning networks make training and advanced education possible in cases where time and budgetary constraints make it difficult to organize face-to-face training. However, to make e-learning work, instructors and providers must harness the potential of synchronous and asynchronous Internet communication technologies to create powerful, learner-centered networks.

Synchronous communication technologies, such as desktop video teleconferencing and interactive group video teleconferencing, enable live, real-time interaction between instructors and learners. Instructors, subject matter experts, and learners see and hear one another at all

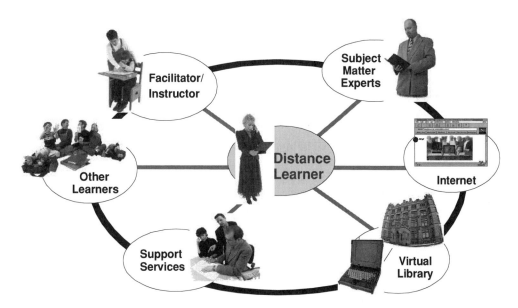

FIG. 21.5. The Networked e-Learning Environment.

sites and engage in interaction similar to face-to-face classroom interactions. Asynchronous communication technologies, such as e-mail, multimedia databases, virtual libraries, and the Internet, support non real-time interactions and access to vast information resources at a time and place convenient to the learners.

The challenge is to implement the right combination of synchronous and asynchronous technologies to create a rich mosaic of networked learning environments consistent with the mission of the educational service provider, learner expectations, and/or the delivery style of the instructor. For example, a desktop video teleconferencing network can link instructor and learners for presentation and discussion of key course concepts. The data collaboration capabilities of such a system enable the instructor and the learners to share software for simultaneously editing documents, completing spreadsheet exercises, or creating graphic presentations. Learners can continue the discussion through an e-mail network with other learners and subject matter experts. Additional multimedia resources like reference articles, journals, magazines, and multimedia news clips can be accessed from a virtual library or the Internet to supplement and enrich the course content. The e-learning networks can be used for all forms of education to improve the reach of programs, stretch education and training dollars, manage knowledge resources of an enterprise, and deliver just-in-time educational content to learners anywhere, anytime.

The challenge of creating an effective e-learning environment is to determine what learners truly need and how to reasonably accommodate their needs. At some point in the near future, all of the broadband technological capabilities described here and more will be supported. Learners, instructors, and educational service providers will then have rich options in determining how to create, navigate, and experience learning. Our early experiences with distance learning networks, the Internet, and virtual libraries foreshadow the future networked e-learning environments. Simple functions such as the "bookmark" feature of the Internet browsers of today will be enhanced significantly to provide us with the ability to bookmark our journeys in an electronic world. Intelligent electronic agents that understand learner interest and requirements will assist learners in locating and navigating virtual libraries. They will be able to store learning experiences in a virtual space for learners and for others to re-experience and interact with knowledge resources again and again.

Networked e-learning environments will run the gamut from a single educational organization's private network to very large complex ESP "knowledge utilities" built on years of collaboration and partnering. These ESPs will adhere to knowledge object publishing standards like SCORM so that very-high quality knowledge objects can be created once and then reused many times and in many customized ways. There exist many challenges, both technological and pedagogical, that must be addressed on the road ahead. We will need new tools to store voice, video, and data files, facilitate finding them, and present them in forms usable with multiple systems. Tools needed include information indexing agents, search engines, expert systems, scenario builders, massive multimedia storage, and broadband multimedia networks. The networked e-learning environment will need to be flexible enough to accommodate rapid change. We need to start now to begin our journey on this revolutionary and evolutionary path toward this future e-learning environment.

REFERENCES

Most of the reference information for this chapter is derived from the work of over a hundred of my colleagues who have helped design and implement distance learning systems and Web portals for AT&T, Lucent Technologies, and Avaya. In particular, I want to acknowledge the work and contributions to this summary of the following innovators: Dr. Barbara Garvin-Kester, Mrs. Mary Hulick, Dr. Burton Hancock, Dr. Lee Balthazar, Mrs. Eleanor Goldstein,

Dr. John Wedman, Mr. Herbert Bivens, Dr. Marc Rosenberg, Dr. Carol Poston, Mrs. Pamela Sayers, Mr. David Williams, Mr. Walter Beier, Mr. John McNeely, and Mr. Steve Foreman.

Chute, A. G. August (1990). Strategies for implementing teletraining systems. *Educational and Training Technology International, 27*, 4.

Chute, Alan G., Bruning, K. K., & Hulick, M. K. (1984). AT&T communications national teletraining network: Applications, benefits, and costs. Cincinnati, OH: AT&T Communications Sales and Marketing Education.

DISCLAIMER

This chapter presents ideas and opinions that are held by the author and are not necessarily the official position of Avaya Inc.

22

Video-Based Instruction in Distance Learning: From Motion Pictures to the Internet

Robert A. Wisher
U.S. Army Research Institute
wisher@ari.army.mil

Christina K. Curnow
Caliber Associates
curnowc@calib.com

Video-based instruction is a common denominator in many forms of distance learning. Although correspondence courses have played a larger overall role, instruction delivered through video has been a mainstay in distance learning since the early days of the black and white educational film (Freeman, 1923). The Internet is revitalizing the use of video for instructional purposes. The race is on to create streaming technologies using Internet protocol packets for delivering high-fidelity, full motion video to the desktop. Throughout the past century, an underlying assumption has been that video can be a vital ingredient to learning.

There is little doubt that a well-designed video component stimulates the interest level of students. Plainly, though, video is not essential for all distance learning. Successful examples of learning from phonographic recordings (Rulon, 1943), educational radio (Woelfel & Tyler, 1945), tape-recorded lectures (Popham, 1961), and audio teletraining (Wisher & Priest, 1998) have demonstrated the efficacy of voice alone or voice with printed materials, to name just a few alternatives to video. How necessary the inclusion of video, particularly high-quality video, is to the process of learning from a distance is debatable. As with many issues, the answer depends. It depends on the types of tasks being taught, the individual characteristics of the students, the role of the instructor, and the instructional alternatives available.

This chapter reviews the important findings on the impact of video-based instruction on learning. The main focus is on distance learning, but there are many forms of learning. These include the psychological, persuasive, and vicarious aspects of video communication. Considered to a lesser extent in this chapter, then, is the impact on learning from exposure to mass video communications, such as learning during casual television viewing. Although such environments might lack the formal structure and design of distance learning, they can sway opinion, influence behavior, and alter mannerisms and attitudes. These also are examples of learning from video.

The acquisition and modification of knowledge must be enduring, and learners must become capable of performing actions they could not perform beforehand. Distance learning refers to learning without the physical presence of an instructor. A more precise description includes the use of specialized course development techniques, specialized instructional techniques, and the application of a communicative technology as defining attributes of distance learning (Moore & Kearsley, 1996).

Our interest is to offer an historical perspective on the empirical evidence of learning from video-based instruction. This review spans nearly a century, from empirical investigations of learning during instructional silent films to prescriptions for its use in on-demand learning portals on the Internet. Our review concentrates on motion video and animations rather than still pictures or graphics. One interpretation of video-based instruction regards it generally as "the branch of educational theory and practice concerned primarily with the design and use of messages which control the learning process" (AVCR, 1963, p.18). Within the framework of our review, video shapes an instructional message that is conveyed through a communicative technology. Communicative technologies are the physical means by which instructional messages are transmitted to the learner. Examples relevant to motion video include educational films, instructional television, videodiscs, CD-ROMs, and digital video over the Internet.

VIDEO AND LEARNING: A COGNITIVE PERSPECTIVE

Instructional messages are those patterns of signs and symbols that modify behavior in any one of the three instructional domains: cognitive, affective, and psychomotor (Fleming & Levie, 1978). Video-based instruction is a form of an instructional message that has, with few exceptions, two components: a video component and a verbal component. The verbal component may take the form of captioned text or, as is typically the case, the spoken word carried through an auditory channel. The inception of silent educational films at the start of the 20th century had a curious theoretical rationale for reliance on the visual approach to instruction: Experts believed that visual materials served as an antidote for the verbal component of the classroom (Saettler, 1990). Other pioneering approaches had the instructor explain the visual content while a silent film played or offer an explanation immediately afterward. When sound was introduced in the late 1920s, the verbal component became predominantly auditory.

In terms of an instructional message, video-based instruction is really a form of multimedia. For example, in video teletraining, an auditory narration serves as the verbal component while video images are displayed. The importance of quality audio has been recognized in the distance learning research literature (Garrison, 1990; Hardy & Olcott, 1995). Indeed, educational programs available through cable television rely on audio as much as video to deliver the instructional message. Instructional CD-ROMs often include an audio accompaniment to motion video. In contemporary distance learning applications, then, instruction from a video component is mediated by an audio component. Figure 22.1 depicts a notional pathway from a video-based instructional message to a learning outcome. Because the components are interdependent, it is appropriate to take account of audio in a review of the efficacy of video-based instruction. Unfortunately, the contribution of the audio component is poorly documented in most studies of "video-based" instruction. Before our review of the literature, a cognitive perspective on the linking of video content with an audio component and their collateral influence on learning is suggested.

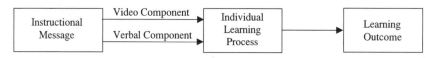

FIG. 22.1.   Generic Model of Learning From Video.

Video and Audio Integration

A practical framework for understanding the mental integration of video and audio as a mediator of learning is the research reported by Professor Richard Mayer and colleagues at the University of California, Santa Barbara. Mayer developed a generative model of multimedia learning (Mayer, 1997; Mayer & Moreno, 1998). The model stems from laboratory experiments that investigated learning outcomes while a student viewed computer-generated animations. The independent variable was the verbal component, which was conveyed by either auditory narration or on-screen text. The central issue was how best to bundle for learning the instructional message (the video and verbal components) in light of the limitations of a student's working memory. A larger implication is that the effect of this memory limitation ranges well beyond the laboratory, extending to any video-based learning environment.

The psychological theory underlying Mayer's research is a dual-processing theory of working memory. This theory stems from Paivio's (1986) research on a dual-coding approach to mental representations. Working memory, a construct from an information-processing framework of cognition, refers to the early, fragile, and temporary storage of perceptual images. It is an initial step of the learning process. It holds both visual and auditory images independently, but has a limited capacity for each. While the images briefly persist in working memory, learners attempt to promptly organize them into coherent representations before they quickly disappear (see Fig. 22.2). It is essential for learners to establish referential connections between the visual and auditory stores and to do so within a few seconds. These steps are comparable to Gagne's selective perception of stimulus features and semantic encoding phases of learning (Gagne, 1985).

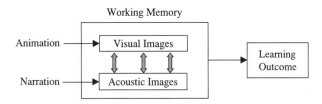

FIG. 22.2.   Mayer's Depiction of Working Memory.

Mayer's investigations were conducted in controlled laboratory conditions. The subject areas included the understanding of natural phenomena (lightning formation) or the understanding of the mechanics of everyday things (the operation of a car's braking system). In one condition, students viewed the video (computer animation) with on-screen text as the verbal component. In another condition, the same video was viewed with an auditory narration as the verbal component. Learning outcomes were assessed through a retention test, a matching test, and a transfer test. In each content area, learners exposed to the auditory narration condition outperformed their counterparts on all three tests. Mayer interpreted this as the "split-attention" effect in which multimedia learners can more readily integrate video with auditory narration while they are maintained separately in working memory. In contrast, as depicted in Fig. 22.3,

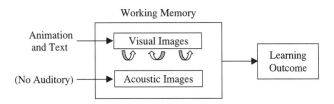

FIG. 22.3.   Interference Effect in Visual Working Memory.

the "on-screen text" visual competes with the image of the animation in the visual area of working memory. This competition results in less efficient encoding and, subsequently, a potential decrease in the learning outcome.

The importance of Mayer's research is that one cannot exclude the contribution of the audio component when assessing the impact of video on learning. Unfortunately, the research in distance learning usually neglects the properties of the audio component. In some circumstances, it might be possible that the audio component contributes more to learning than the video component does. The video, however, often receives much of the credit.

VIDEO AND LEARNING: HISTORICAL ANTECEDENTS

The Silent Film Era

The use of pictorial sequences for instructional purposes dates to 1902, when Charles Urban of London presented educational films illustrating slow and time-lapse motion of natural phenomena, microscopic examinations of objects, and undersea views of marine life (Saettler, 1990). The use of silent films for education was regarded as an aid to teaching rather than a self-contained instructional package. Thomas Edison was an early pioneer in producing films for classroom showing. Regrettably, much of the Edison Library's collection of natural and physical science films were destroyed by fire in 1914. By the early 1920s, with thousands of educational titles, a distinction was forming between the educational and entertainment motion picture. The sound-on-picture advancement in filmmaking would not yet be available until the late 1920s.

During the silent film era, several large-scale empirical studies on learning effectiveness were conducted in public schools. Notably, Weber (1928, cited in Saettler, 1990) conducted a pioneering study that used a pictorial medium rather than verbal tests to measure learning outcomes. The Eastman Kodak Company sponsored this large-scale evaluation of the effectiveness of silent instructional films. In this study, more than 10,000 students and 200 teachers in 12 cities viewed 20 instructional films in geography and general science. Control groups were encouraged to use any appropriate classroom media for teaching the same subjects. The results, as measured by objective tests, demonstrated the group viewing instructional films scored higher by a substantial and significant margin (Wood and Freeman, 1929, cited in Saettler, 1990).

The Introduction of Sound

Despite the introduction of the sound-on-film option in the late 1920s, educational film companies were beginning to fail, due largely to the economic depression. Commercial vendors could not survive without external support. The federal government, one of the first large producers and consumers of motion pictures for instructional purposes, continued its support of the young industry during the 1930s, particularly in the areas of agriculture and soil conservation. Mass communication films for eradicating contagious diseases among farm animals were apparently successful. In the military, the use of educational films had become established as an acceptable method to inform the public on matters of civil defense and as a method to train service personnel on occupational tasks. As the country mobilized for World War II, the widespread use of educational films for training purposes was adopted. More than four hundred instructional films were produced for the military during the war effort.

Mass Communications. The most thoroughly documented study on the effectiveness of these training films was the evaluation of the *Why We Fight* series of orientation films. The four films were shown to recruits during their first two months in the military. As reported in

Hovland, Lumsdaine, and Sheffield (1949), the *Why We Fight* series represents a classic study on educational films, rigorously conducted and fully reported in a 345-page volume.

The series of 50-minute orientation films were developed on the basis of a belief that a large segment of the draftee population lacked knowledge about the events that led to America's entrance into the war. It was also thought that knowledge of these events would lead men to more willingly accept the transition from civilian life to soldier life. Hovland et al. (1949) investigated the effects of one orientation film, *The Battle of Britain*, on the knowledge, opinions, and general attitudes of new recruits going through basic training. This film recounted the role that the British had played in World War II. Of all of the orientation films, this was the most thoroughly studied.

Units of soldiers were randomly selected for the study ($n = 2,100$) with half viewing the film and later completing the questionnaire, and half completing the questionnaire without viewing the film. Results indicate that the film was effective for improving soldiers' knowledge of the events concerning the air war over Britain in 1940. The film was also effective in changing opinions about events specifically covered in the film. Overall, the film was considered a successful training tool and an effective instructional device for mass communications.

Audiovisual Communications Emerge

The early period of research on instructional media informed educators and the public on its legitimacy for transmitting educational content while documenting its instructional effectiveness (Allen, 1971). Comprehensive reviews of the first fifty years of educational films indicated distinct advantages for this form of video-based instruction over classroom instruction. In the 1950s, television materialized as the new video medium. It promised to reach farther than films with an aim of a television, *ergo* a classroom, in every home someday. During the 25-year period between 1952 and 1977, there were 533 major articles, 935 research abstracts, and 762 doctoral dissertations in audiovisual education along with an additional 293 research studies sponsored by the National Defense Education Act (Torkelson, 1977).

The period from the mid-1950s to the mid-1960s can be labeled "the decade of educational television." From hundreds of evaluative studies of instructional television, equal effectiveness in comparison to the face-to-face classroom emerged as the dominant finding (Allen, 1971). Most studies, however, ignored an examination of the specific features of television that contributed most to this equivalency such as individual differences between students or to the learning conditions under which television operates most effectively. The research literature on educational television has been extensively reviewed elsewhere, such as the comprehensive review by Chu and Schramm (1967) and a more recent, exhaustive review by Seels, Berry, Fullerton, and Horn (1996). A review on the effectiveness of various video media in instruction is offered by Wetzel, Radtke, and Stern (1994).

In the years following World War II, the military services were leaders in experimentation on the video medium as an instructional tool. Studies on the use of video for learning perceptual and motor skills, for representing three-dimensional space, and for training complex sequential tasks were conducted by prominent experimental psychologists (Allen, 1971). A selection of findings relevant to contemporary applications of distance learning are presented here.

Color.   Color is an example of pictorial detail where a learning benefit may or may not be achieved. Although viewers commonly prefer color, it has not generally been found to be an effective learning variable. For example, a study by Kanner and Rosenstein (1960) investigated the effectiveness of color television versus black-and-white (monochrome) television on training performance. A sample of 368 soldiers undergoing training in the signal corps was matched on aptitude and divided into two groups. Each group observed the same eleven lessons of training, one through monochrome television and the other through color television. The televised courses were taught in the same manner as they were in the conventional classroom. However, when the color of an instructional element was relevant (e.g., different colors of wire) the instructor stated aloud the color for the benefit of the students in the monochrome group. Tests were administered at the end of each lesson.

Ten out of 11 comparisons between the color or monochrome groups showed no significant differences in learning. However, when divided by aptitude, high-aptitude groups learned significantly more from monochrome television instruction and low-aptitude soldiers learned significantly more from color television. The test items were also analyzed based on items that referred to color and those that did not. No differences were found between the color and monochrome groups for test items that referenced color. The authors suggested that since color is sufficiently familiar, the names of the colors can verbally substitute for the visual cue during instruction and transfer to a performance test.

In another study that examined preferences for color versus black-and-white films, Vander-Meer (1954) divided college students into two groups, half of whom viewed two instructional films in color and two in monochrome while the other half viewed the opposite version of the same films. Although students preferred the color films, there was no relationship between preference and learning. This lack of a learning effect has generally been found when color is used simply to add realism (Wetzel et al., 1994). On the other hand, color may aid learning to the extent that it serves as an attention-gaining, organizational, or discrimination-cuing function (Chute, 1980; Moore & Nawrocki, 1978).

Sound Effects.   Although sound effects that accompany video have an ability to arouse and sustain interest in a presentation, its effect on learning has been inconsistent. Viewer interest can be increased through the introduction of different voices, laughter, music, and background noise. Sound effects appear to be effective markers for highlighting important points in a video presentation, thus increasing the opportunity for learning (Bryant, Zillman, & Brown, 1983). However, when used merely as diversion (Travers, 1967), or as background noise to add realism to narrative (Barrington, 1972), they have no effect on learning.

One classic study that examined the effect of auditory diversion on video-based instruction was reported by Neu (1950). This study investigated the effect on learning of viewing a film that included attention-gaining sound and visual cues that were either relevant or irrelevant to the instruction. Five versions of a film on the use of machine-shop measuring instruments were prepared: (1) a basic film with no attention-getting devices, (2) a version with visual cues relevant to the content, (3) a version with irrelevant visual cues, (4) a version with relevant sound cues, and (5) a version with irrelevant sound cues. For each version with attention-gaining devices, 26 relevant or irrelevant cues appeared at the same point of the film. The learners were $n = 2,631$ military recruits randomly assigned to 1 of the 5 film versions. They were tested for learning and recall of the attention-gaining devices.

Results indicate no significant differences in learning between the basic film and the films with visual cues, whether relevant or irrelevant, and relevant sound cues. However, the irrelevant sound condition resulted in significantly lower scores. There was no relationship between the recall of attention-gaining devices and learning. The authors conclude that the use of intricate film techniques such as spotlighting, magnification, zooms, and stop motion that are employed to gain the learner's attention may not affect learning. However, irrelevant information (particularly sound) may have a negative effect on learning.

Motion Video.   A study by Allen, Cooney, and Weintraub (1968) indicates the addition of spoken verbal information eliminates the superiority of motion over conditions of still presentation. In the study, differences in learning between motion pictures and still slides are not found with students over several different types of audio narration. The pattern of results over a number of other comparison conditions indicate that the effect of motion on learning is minimal when accompanied by verbal narration. The effect of adding sound to either motion or still presentations was more powerful than that of adding motion to either silent or sound presentations.

Motor Skills.   Some learning can be achieved through careful observation of the key features of a demonstration of the skill to be performed. Feedback of one's actual performance plays a central role in learning motor skills (Adams, 1987). Even mental practice (the symbolic rehearsal of a physical activity) undertaken by individuals has been shown to improve performance across many types of motor tasks when compared to control groups (Feltz & Landers, 1983). As cited in Wetzel et al. (1994), Rothstein and Arnold (1976) reviewed more than fifty studies that used videotape replays for learning sports skills. Overall, they found positive effects of videotape feedback on skill learning in 37 percent of the studies. A more detailed analysis suggests that video replays are more effective for advanced performers, for longer periods of training, and when directed viewing procedures that focus attention on relevant aspects of the skill are employed.

Instructional Video Examples in Higher Education

The large majority of research on video-based instruction has been conducted in educational settings. An analysis of the hundreds of "no-significant-difference" studies reported by Russell (1998) determined that 87 percent were conducted in an educational, rather than training, environment (Wisher & Champagne, 2000). Three examples that deal with educational concerns, namely instruction in abstract topics, the retention of knowledge, and student attitudes toward video-based instruction, are offered.

Abstract Topics.   A study by Ketcham and Heath (1963) investigated the effectiveness of college-level educational films that did not utilize direct visual presentation of content. The purpose of the investigation was to create a film to teach an abstract topic, whereby the images in the video in no way reproduced the soundtrack. For the experiment, a 26-minute, black-and-white film about the life and work of William Wordsworth was produced. The film included frequent quotations from Wordsworth's poetry and was filmed in England and France. The audio portion of the film recounted events from Wordsworth's life and summarized poems that he had written. The video portion showed scenes that complemented the audio portion but did not add additional information. For example, when recounting Wordsworth's childhood, a picture of his boyhood home was shown.

Subjects were $n = 152$ undergraduates randomly selected and placed into 1 of 6 groups: audio and video, single viewing; audio only, single viewing; audio and video, viewed three times; audio only, viewed three times; audio and video, viewed three times, with note taking and study time; and conventional classroom methods. A verbal aptitude test served as a covariate in the analyses. A knowledge test that asked questions pertaining only to the audio portion of the film was administered following the film.

Results indicate that sound with visual images, which do not directly depict the content matter of a film, resulted in greater learning than sound alone. Multiple presentations of the film (with or without pictures) produced greater learning than a single presentation. Three presentations with audio and video produced the highest achievement, but the scores were not significantly different from the three sound-only groups, or the three audio-and-video-plus-notes group. The study also found that the type of presentation that is used matters less for high-aptitude students than for low-aptitude students. The authors conclude that films can work well under both normal and optimum viewing conditions for abstract material.

Knowledge Retention.   A study by Jacobs and Bollenbacher (1960) examined whether there were differences in the amount of subject matter retained by students in a biology class taught through television versus students attending a traditional classroom course. Participants were $n = 360$ students, half of whom attended the traditional course. The other half was given television instruction or traditional classroom instruction on alternating days. Results of the final test demonstrated that the learning outcomes for the two delivery methods were not significantly different for students of below average and average ability. However, for above average students the television group scored significantly higher than the traditional group. Twenty-two months after the course ended, students were given an alternate form of the final test. There were no significant differences in retention between the groups.

Student Attitudes.   A study by Bobren and Siegel (1960) compared an engineering course taught in a regular classroom to the same course taught through television. The course required students to meet in small laboratory sections, rather than as a large group, to allow them to clearly observe the equipment being demonstrated. A sample of $n = 112$ subjects participated in the experiment, assigned to either a closed-circuit television or regular classroom group. At the end of the course, students completed attitude surveys about the course and the manner in which it was taught. Midterm grades and final grades were also obtained.

There were no significant differences found between the television and regular classroom groups on the midterm or final exam. However, students in the television groups rated the course significantly lower on 10 out of 11 scales. The television group found the course less pleasant, clear, fair, good, successful, meaningful, wise, understandable, interesting, and simple than the conventional class group. For 8 of 11 scales, the television group rated the instructors significantly lower than the conventional group. This is an early example of lower satisfaction with a distance learning alternative. However, the study showed no significant difference in performance between groups.

Video Teletraining

Video teletraining is a modern use of instructional television, often using compressed video signals transmitted directly over telephone lines or over analog or digital satellite transmissions to classrooms equipped with a downlink capability. A two-way audio connection is nearly always available and two-way video between instructors and student sites is becoming increasingly common.

Air Traffic Quality Assurance Training.   Lennon and Payne (1997) examined the differences in student reaction and learning outcomes between distance learning (one-way video/two-way audio) and comparison traditional classroom groups of quality assurance specialists of the Federal Aviation Administration. The 7-day course was delivered on two occasions by 4 instructors to a total of 31 employees in the classroom group and to 18 employees at 4 distance learning sites. There were no significant differences on any of the 12 reaction measures, which were rated on a 5-point scale and included pace of training, relevance to job, effectiveness of instructors, and overall quality between the 2 groups. In addition, there were no differences between the groups on either the pretest or posttest knowledge measures.

Engineering Training Off Campus.   In a study on engineering training at the graduate level, Stone (1988) examined the characteristics of students enrolled in off-campus degree and continuing education programs compared to characteristics of on-campus students. Data were collected over a five-year period. The distance learning group received either a one-way video/two-way audio satellite transmission or a videotaped version of the lectures; the comparison group received the same lectures in the classroom.

The distance learning sample contained off-campus students ($n = 726$) and the comparison group was composed of students ($n = 302$) attending the lectures face-to-face with the instructors. The dependent variable was grade point average (GPA). An analysis of variance indicated that the distance learning group for the degree program had achieved a significantly higher GPA than the on-campus comparison group while the continuing education students had a GPA comparable to the on-campus group. This did not have a direct comparison to an on-campus program but, in view of the sample, would likely equate to the on-campus degree group. These data clearly support the supposition that video teletraining and videotape, in combination with the printed text, were equally effective in training technical knowledge and skills.

VIDEO AND LEARNING: THE COMPUTER ERA

The introduction of the computer to mediate learning was a turning point in video-based instruction. Video programs had been limited to a linear continuity, with few possibilities for rapid access to specific sequences. The computer ushered in the era of interactive video, in which rapid access to video images became a factor in the design of instruction. This also represented a shift in the use of video from classroom instruction to individualized learning.

The earliest examples parallel developments in programmed instruction in the late 1950s and early 1960s. The uses of motion video, however, tended to be dynamic graphic displays illustrating X-Y relationships, such as the relationship between temperature and relative humidity. The development of the videodisc, an analog form of video, in the late 1970s, initiated the widespread use of full-motion video under computer control. In the late 1980s, the development of digital video made the manipulation, editing, storage, distribution, and archiving of video images easier and more convenient. Its most common delivery form is the CD-ROM. The compression and transmission of digital video over the Internet is the next anticipated step in the evolution of video-based instruction. The instructional effect of each of these video technologies is reviewed.

Learning from Videodisc

Videodisc technology offers rapid, random access to a large database of video quality images and sequences. Its introduction coincided with the wider availability of the personal computer, to which it became interfaced, creating the interactive videodisc as an educational technology. The videodisc uses metallic-plastic discs to code information as tiny pits in a transparent substrate with a reflective coating. During play, the pits modulate a laser signal that is decoded into auditory and video signals. A 12-inch videodisc stores up to 30 minutes of full-motion video, or 54,000 frames, on each side along with 2 tracks of audio.

Fletcher (1990) conducted a quantitative analysis of the education and training effectiveness of interactive videodisc instruction. In that analysis, empirical studies comparing interactive videodisc instruction to conventional instruction were segmented into three groups: higher education, industrial training, and military training. The various learning outcomes investigated included (1) knowledge outcomes, which assessed a student's knowledge of facts or concepts presented in the instructional program; (2) performance outcomes, which assessed a student's skill in performing a task or procedure; (3) retention, which measured the durability of learning after an interval of no instruction; and (4) the time to complete the instruction. The effect sizes, or the difference between the mean scores of the treatment and comparison groups divided by the standard deviation of the control group, were computed for each of the 28 studies identified.

TABLE 22.1

Average Effect Sizes for Four Types of Knowledge Outcomes (Fletcher, 1990)

Learning Outcome	Effect Size
Knowledge	.361
Performance	.334
Retention	.650
Time to Complete	1.185

The results of Fletcher (1990) meta-analysis are presented in Table 22.1 for the breakout by learning outcome and in Table 22.2 for the breakout by instructional group.

The conclusion of the Fletcher (1990) analysis is that interactive video instruction is both effective and less costly than conventional instruction and should be routinely considered and used in military education and training.

Learning from CD-ROM

In comparison to the videodisc, the CD-ROM (Compact Disc–Read Only Memory) offers a more convenient package for distribution. The nearly universal availability of a CD drive in most personal computers broadens its acceptance. CD-ROMs can store up to 650 megabytes of any combination of text, graphics, sound, video, and animation in digital form. Thus, it is an excellent choice for multimedia-based instructional approaches (Barron & Orwig, 1995). Other useful applications are the storage of reference material, encyclopedias, databases, and educational games. CD-ROMs are often used in lieu of correspondence manuals. We were not able to identify an appropriate meta-analysis of the instructional effectiveness of CD-ROMs; however, we would expect the effects on learning outcomes to be comparable to videodisc effects.

Learning from Internet-delivered Video

The Internet, a nonproprietary delivery system, has captivated the interest of educators and trainers as a means to deliver instructional messages whenever and wherever needed. The proliferation of Web-based courseware technologies multiply the opportunities and challenges facing higher education as well as training environments (Gray, 1999). Creative software developers are persistently introducing techniques for the content of web pages to become more dynamic. As streaming video and audio technologies become widely available, more distance learning Web sites will attempt to capitalize on these dynamic forms of instructional messages. As students' access to broadband connectivity increases, video will increasingly become an integral component of Web-based distance learning programs.

Video over the Internet is, of course, a form of digital video. Its implementation has several options and trade-offs. As specified by Sykes and Swinscoe (1994), these include: (1) image size

TABLE 22.2

Average Effect Sizes for Three Instructional Groups (Fletcher, 1990)

Instructional Group	Effect Size
Higher Education	.660
Industrial Training	.174
Military Training	.385

and resolution; (2) update rate; (3) color resolution; (4) qualitative aspects; (5) accompanying audio; and (6) cost. For example, a developer must choose between three basic image sizes (640 by 480, 320 by 240, or 160 by 120 pixels). Since the resolution in pixels per inch is the same in the three cases, the demand for bandwidth increases with the size of the image, if one desires a seamless flow of video images. As another example using update rates, 30 frames per second (fps) is considered the norm and 24 fps is perceptually indistinguishable. Halving the update rate to 12 to 15 fps reduces bandwidth demand by a factor of 2, but at a cost of reduced video quality. There are similar trade-offs for the other options. How these choices affect learning is considered shortly.

In order to reduce the size of video files without reducing quality, a variety of video compression techniques can be used (Barron & Varnadoe, 1994). The compression scheme chosen depends on the desired resolution of the image as well as the memory available for video storage. The JPEG and MPEG compression programs are two of the more popular formats. A related option for Internet learning providers is to stream the video/audio to a buffer on a client computer.

Video streaming refers to a compressed video file being sent by a streaming server to a client (i.e., student). The streaming procedure is in response to a student request for a web page containing embedded videos. The client begins to play the incoming multimedia stream from a buffer shortly after the video file data are received and temporarily stored. The video begins to play before the entire download is complete, while pieces that have already played are removed. Video streaming thus allows students to view large files without having to collect and store them. There are currently no standards for video streaming. The Real Time Streaming Protocol is an example of a proposed open standard for delivery of real-time media over the Internet.

Early Examples.   How is this technology best employed? Distance learning providers can exploit streaming video and audio to deliver lectures over the Internet to students' computers at school, work, or home at any time. This technology will clearly widen the access of asynchronous instructional programs. There are currently few examples in the research and evaluation literature on the effective use of streaming technologies in Web-based learning environments. One example is documented by Ingebritsen and Flickinger (1998) in which biology courses were offered through streaming audio of an instructor's voice accompanied by a series of slides, presented through a Web browser, containing diagrams, photographs, and other visual aids. Another example is a case study on synchronous Web-based training for Coast Guard personnel reported by Arnold and Palmore (2000). Student performance in the Web environment was comparable to that of the resident classroom comparison group. The use of video, however, was apparently limited to electronic whiteboarding and two-way document sharing.

Early Advice.   Empirical evaluations of video over the Internet will undoubtedly grow over time. One distance learning provider has observed "Although streaming video is too new to have been subjected to formal studies of its effectiveness, I suggest that key attributes are its ability to promote learner convenience, learner flexibility, and learner control" (Greenberg, 2000, p. 196). A cautionary note was suggested by Fisher (2000), who pointed out "If very high-resolution, detailed graphics or video are needed to support your learning objectives, then the Web may not be the best environment. A true Internet environment should be limited to lower-resolution graphics and brief audio and video segments. At this point in time, multimedia over the Internet is still evolving" (Fisher, 2000, p. 67). Bonk and Cummings (1998) offer recommendations for student-centric approaches to Web-based learning.

VIDEO AND LEARNING: BRIDGING "CLASSIC" FINDINGS
TO INTERNET PLATFORMS

Why should considerations for video-based instruction on the Internet be any different from video-based instruction in general? This section addresses this question. The findings reported earlier from educational motion pictures, instructional television, and interactive videodiscs will be recast with the Internet as the delivery medium. The relevance of Mayer's generative model of multimedia learning is considered in view of the emerging practices of using video on the Internet.

Reapplication of Findings

The seminal 213-page report on "Learning from Television: What the Research Says" by Chu and Schramm (1967) cataloged 59 conclusions from the research and evaluation literature on instructional television. Our review of those conclusions identified at least 20 that could apply directly to the use of video on the Internet, and possibly to future video delivery technologies. We have selected four conclusions as illustrations of bridges between "classic" findings and contemporary issues in video-based instruction. Each conclusion is listed in italics with a page reference from the Chu and Schramm (1967) report followed by a brief consideration of its relevance to Internet delivery.

- *Attention-gaining cues that are irrelevant to the subject matter will most probably have a negative effect on learning from instructional television. (p. 50)*
  Web-based developers can become captivated with novel functions made possible by evolving technologies rather than a consideration of what really impacts learning. Information that seems catchy, but is really irrelevant, can diminish a learning outcome. As detailed earlier, Neu (1950) demonstrates that attention-gaining cues in an educational film do not enhance learning, and sounds irrelevant to the content actually decrease learning. Caution should be taken in applying the "bells and whistles" made easily available through point-and-click design templates without a pedagogical basis for their application.
- *Repeated showings of a television program will result in more learning, up to a point. But teacher-directed follow-up, where available, is more effective than a second showing of the same program. (p. 60)*
  Early lessons from online learning indicate that it is an entirely new type of educational experience requiring a redesign of instructor roles, responsibilities, and commitments (Bonk & Wisher, 2000; Besser & Bonn, 1997). A mere repetition of video clips for instruction cannot replace the importance of student-instructor interaction to improve learning outcomes. As detailed earlier, Hayman and Johnson (1963) found that repeated viewing of a video produces minor improvements of learning while teacher-directed intervention resulted in far greater improvements. Virtual access to instructor assistance should be an option after multiple replays of an instructional video have not produced the desired learning outcome.
- *Where accurate perception of images is an important part of learning, wide viewing angle and long distance will interfere with learning from instructional television. (p. 68)*
  The proliferation of digital cameras connected to the Internet, the appeal of live web casts, and the fingertip availability of archival video clips offer the learner a spectrum of images with various zooming and panning features, shot lengths, motion-generated depth cues, and camera angles. At a sensory level, cinematic displays are a clear demonstration of the fact that the information in the light to the eye is ambiguous (Hochberg, 1986). Based on historical findings, these crafty techniques can ultimately interfere with the learning process. As illustrated earlier in the review of Hayman (1963), learning from

video is influenced by the relative location of the viewer and moderated by the type of task being taught. Consideration should be given, then, to the nature of the task and the visual properties of the instructional message.

- *Liking instructional television is not always correlated with learning from it. (p. 123)*

Empirical evaluations are often restricted to a student's satisfaction with a video-based course. In a study by Walsh, Gibson, Miller, & Hsieh (1996) the most common area of inquiry on instructional effectiveness was categorized as student opinion questionnaire (59 percent), instructor opinion questionnaire (39 percent), and comparative test results (36 percent). Similarly, informal observations by administrators and other stakeholders are based on first impressions influenced more by their extensive exposure to professional-quality television programming (approximating 20,000 hours of individual viewing experience for American adults, on average) rather than a cognitive perspective on the learning process. As detailed by Payne (1999), there is not evidence of a relationship between learner satisfaction and performance in the video teletraining literature. As commercial broadband technology grows to offer high-quality video to any learning site, the use of video with "instructional enhancements" will likely proliferate. Students and administrators might react positively to a certain video program delivered on the Internet, but that same program might actually prove to be instructionally ineffective. Caution should be taken in interpreting the affective reactions by students and administrators. More importantly, steps should be taken to obtain objective learning outcomes as the legitimate measure of effectiveness.

Video Realism and Learning

An inexorable pursuit by providers of distance learning is to provide learners with the highest quality video achievable. Although this can bring advantages from a student satisfaction perspective, its learning benefit is less certain. Visual realism may be characterized as the extent to which a visual depicts the real thing or cannot be differentiated from it (Wetzel et al., 1994). Detail can facilitate learning to the extent that certain details are relevant to the learning outcome. The extension of this qualification is that instructional effectiveness may be limited if too much information is given as a consequence of realism with high degrees of detail. Dwyer (1978) indicates that excessive detail in realistic pictures or models of the heart may be less effective than appropriately detailed line drawings.

This observation parallels many of the findings from research on the training effectiveness of simulators, which demonstrates that higher fidelity aviation simulations (e.g., graphics) do not necessarily improve learning or transfer to actual equipment (Hays and Singer, 1989). Similarly, in research on virtual environments, Johnson and Stewart (1999) report data that indicated no improvement in visual-spatial learning when the more immersive, and costly, visual display environments are used. In a study by Wisher and Curnow (1999), the visual presence of an instructor in a distance learning program was manipulated as being either on or off. Although students perceived that not being able to view the instructor decreased their ability to learn, two measures of learning outcomes indicated no difference in learning performance between the two conditions of visual presence.

As with instructional television, training simulators, and virtual reality environments, it is not always necessary to increase the video capability of a distance learning program in order to increase training effectiveness. Too often, developers and designers become captivated with technical capabilities rather than an examination of the influence of media on the underlying learning process (Sherry, 1996). As depicted earlier in Mayer's generative model of multimedia learning (Figures 22.2 and 22.3), the video component must be thoughtfully integrated with the verbal component for learning, retention, and transfer to occur.

VIDEO AND LEARNING: WHAT ARE THE LESSONS?

The research findings on video-based instruction are voluminous. The underlying theme of the findings are really quite simple: If the classroom environment is replicated, the learning outcomes are replicated, i.e. the "no significant difference" phenomenon (Russell, 2002). When the conditions of learning are appropriately modified, notably informative individualized feedback is offered, a learning effect size on the order of one-half standard deviation emerges (Fletcher, 1990). When the feedback approximates that of a human tutor, as can be the case with intelligent tutoring systems, the effect size can be one full standard deviation or more (Woolf & Regian, 2000).

Video-based instruction has progressed from the audiovisual stage (1940s and 1950s) to the educational media stage (1960s and 1970s) to the instructional technology stage (1980s to mid-1990s) to what might be called the Internet stage (circa 1994). The antiquated terminology of the audiovisual heydays—fluorescent chalk, lantern slides, anamphoric lenses, lenticual screens, pantographs, and telemation devices—has been replaced by a new nomenclature: instant messaging, bandwidth, browsers, video streaming, and graphical user interfaces to name a few. Undoubtedly, the future will offer new video avenues for the learner. Virtual reality (Dede, 1996), the handheld, wireless Web (Shotsberger & Vetter, 2000), and spatially immersive visual displays that project stereo images on three walls and the floor are examples of the changing medium of instructional video.

What hasn't changed is the nature of the human capacity to learn and remember, to acquire and modify knowledge, skills, and beliefs. Clark (1983) has argued for the tremendous influence that instructional design plays in any medium. The video medium can have a facilitative effect on learning, as nearly a century of research has demonstrated, but the conditions of learning will always be important. Whether through video-based instruction or other media, researchers and developers in the Internet and future eras must acknowledge that the medium is only as good as the design of the instructional message it conveys.

REFERENCES

Adams, J. A. (1987). Historical review and appraisal of research on the learning, retention, and transfer of human motor skills. *Psychological Bulletin, 101*, 41–74.

Allen, W. H. (1971). Instructional media research: Past, present, and future. *AV Communications Review, 19*(1), 5–18.

Allen, W. H., Cooney, S. M., & Weintraub, R. (1968). *Audio implementation of still and motion pictures.* Final report (USOE Final Report, Project No 5-0741). Los Angeles: University of Southern California, Research Division, Department of Cinema. (ERIC Document Reproduction Service No. ED 021 462).

Arnold, R., & Palmore, R. (2000). Shifting from resident to asynchronous web-based training: A U.S. Coast Guard case study. *Proceedings of the 16th Annual Conference on Distance Teaching and Learning*, Madison, WI.

AVCR. (1963). The changing role of the audiovisual process in education: A definition and glossary of related terms. *AV Communications Review, 11*(1), Monograph No. 1.

Barrington, H. (1972). Instruction by television—two presentations compared. *Educational Research, 14*, 187–190.

Barron, A. E., & Varnadoe, S. (1994). Digital video in training. *Proceedings of the 16th Interservice/Industry Training Systems and Education Conference*, Orlando, FL.

Barron, A. E., & Orwig, G. W. (1995). *Mutimedia technologies for training: An introduction.* Englewood, CO: Libraries Unlimited.

Besser, H., & Bonn, M. (1997). Interactive distance-independent education. *Journal of Education for Library and Information Science, 38*(1), 35–43.

N. B. The authors would like to thank Dr. Richard Mayer and Dr. Michael Molenda for earlier comments. Portions of this chapter were prepared while the first author was a visiting scholar at the Center for Research on Learning and Technology at Indiana University, Bloomington. The views expressed are those of the authors and do not necessarily reflect the views of the U.S. Army or the U.S. Army Research Institute for the Behavioral and Social Sciences.

Bobren, H., & Siegel, S. (1960). Student attitudes toward closed-circuit instructional television. *AV Communication Review, 8*(3), 124–128.

Bonk, C. J., & Cummings, J. A. (1998). A dozen recommendation for placing the student at the center of Web-based learning. *Educational Media International, 35*(2), 82–89.

Bonk, C. J., & Wisher, R. A. (2000). *Applying collaborative and e-learning tools to military distance learning: A research framework* (Technical Report 1107). Alexandria, VA: U.S. Army Research Institute for the Behavioral and Social Sciences.

Bryant, J., Zillman, D., & Brown, D. (1983). Entertainment features in childrens' educational television: Effects on attention and information acquisition. In J. Bryant & D. R. Anderson (Eds.), *Children's understanding of television: Research on attention and comprehension* (pp. 221–240). San Diego: Academic Press.

Chu, G. C., & Schramm, W. (1967). *Learning from television: What the research says*. Stanford, CA: Institute for Communication Research (ERIC, ED 014900).

Chute, A. G. (1980). Effect of color and monochrome versions of a film on incidental and task-relevant learning. *Educational Communication and Technology Journal, 28*, 10–18.

Clark, R. E. (1983). Reconsidering research on learning from media. *Review of Educational Research, 53*(4), 445–459.

Dede, C. (1996). The evolution of distance education: Emerging technologies and distributed learning. *The American Journal of Distance Education, 10*(2), 4–36.

Dwyer, F. M. (1978). *Strategies for improving visual learning*. State College, PA: Learning Services.

Feltz, D. L., & Landers, D. M. (1983). The effects of mental practice on motor skill learning and performance: A meta-analysis. *Journal of Sports Psychology, 5*, 25–57.

Fisher, S. G. (2000). Web-based training. One size does not fit all. In K. Mantyla (Ed.), *The ASTD 2000 distance learning yearbook: The newest trends and technologies* (pp. 63–75). New York: McGraw-Hill.

Fleming, M., & Levie, H. (1978). *Instructional message design*. Englewood Cliffs, NJ: Educational Technology Publications.

Fletcher, J. D. (1990). Effectiveness and cost of interactive videodisc instruction in defense training and education (IDA Paper P-2372). Alexandria, VA: Institute for Defense Analyses.

Freeman, F. N. (1923). Requirements of education with references to motion pictures. *The School Review, 31*, 340–350.

Gagne, R. M. (1985). *The conditions of learning* (4th ed.). New York: Holt, Rinehart & Winston.

Garrison, D. R. (1990). An analysis and evaluation of audio teleconferencing to facilitate education at a distance. *American Journal of Distance Education, 4*(3), 13–24.

Gray, S. (1999). Collaboration Tools. *Syllabus, 12*(5), 48–52.

Greenberg, G. (2000). Designing a world wide web project using streaming video. *Proceedings of the 16th Annual Conference on Distance Teaching and Learning*, Madison, WI.

Hardy, D. W., & Olcott, D. (1995). Audioteleconferencing and the adult learner: Strategies for Effective Practice. *American Journal of Distance Education, 9*(1), 44–59.

Hayman, J. (1963). Viewer location and learning in instructional television. *AV Communication Review, 11*(4), 27–31.

Hayman, J., & Johnson, J. (1963). Exact vs. varied repetition in education television. *AV Communication Review, 11*(4), 96–103.

Hays, R. T., & Singer, M. J. (1989). *Simulation fidelity in training system design: Bridging the gap between reality and training*. New York: Springer-Verlag.

Hochberg, J. (1986). Representation of motion and space in video and cinematic displays. In K. Brophy, L. Kaufman, & J. Thomas (Eds.), *Handbook of perception and human performance. Volume 1: Sensory processes and perception* (Chapter 22, pp. 1–64). New York: John Wiley and Sons.

Hovland, C., Lumsdaine, A., & Sheffield, F. (1949). *Experiments on mass communication*. Princeton, NJ: Princeton University Press.

Ingebritsen, T. S., & Flickinger, K. (1998). Development and assessment of web courses that use streaming audio and video technologies. *Proceedings of the 14th Annual Conference on Distance Teaching and Learning*, Madison, WI.

Jacobs, J., & Bollenbacher, J. (1960). Retention of subject matter in televised biology. *AV Communication Review, 8*(6), 275–280.

Johnson, D. M., & Stewart, J. E. (1999). Use of virtual environments for the acquisition of spatial knowledge: comparison among different visual displays. *Military Psychology, 11*(2), 129–148.

Kanner, J., & Rosenstein, A. (1960). Television in army training: Color vs. black and white. *AV Communication Review, 8*, 243–252.

Ketcham, C., & Heath, R. (1963). The effectiveness of and educational film without direct visual presentation of content. *AV Communication Review, 11*(4), 114–123.

Lennon, C., & Payne, H. (1997). A comparison between IVT and resident versions of FAA's quality assurance course. *Proceedings of the 13th annual conference on Distance Teaching and Learning, 13*, 181–186.

Mayer, R. (1997). Multimedia learning: Are we asking the right questions? *Educational Psychologist, 32*(1), 1–19.

Mayer, R., & Moreno, R. (1998). A split-attention effect in multimedia learning: Evidence for dual processing systems in working memory. *Journal of Educational Psychology, 90*(2), 312–320.

Moore, M. G., & Kearsley, G. (1996). *Distance education: A systems view*. Belmont, NY: Wadsworth.

Moore, M. V., & Nawrocki, L. H. (1978). The educational effectiveness of graphic displays for computer assisted instruction (Technical Paper No. 332). Arlington, VA: U.S. Army Research Institute for the Behavioral and Social Sciences.

Neu, M. (1950). The effect of attention gaining devices of film-mediated learning, Vol. 1 (Technical Report #SDC 269-7-9). The Pennsylvania State College Instructional Film Research Program.

Paivio, A. (1986). *Mental representation: A dual coding approach*. Oxford, England: Oxford University Press.

Payne, H. (1999). A review of the literature: Interactive video teletraining in distance learning courses (2nd ed.). Atlanta, GA: Spacenet, Inc. and the United States Distance Learning Association.

Popham, W. J. (1961). Tape recorded lectures in the college classroom. *AV Communications Review, 9*(2), 109–118.

Rothstein, A. L., & Arnold, R. K. (1976). Bridging the gap: Application of research on video-tape feedback and bowling. *Motor Skills: Theory into Practice, 1*, 35–62.

Rulon, P. J. (1943). A comparison of phonographic recordings with printed materials in terms of knowledge gained through their use alone. *Harvard Educational Review, 13*, 63–76.

Russell, T. L. (2002). The "no significant difference phenomenon. [Available online]: http://teleeducation.nb.ca/nosignificantdifference.

Saettler, P. (1990). *The evolution of American educational technology*. Englewood, CO: Libraries Unlimited.

Seels, B., Berry, L. H., Fullerton, K., & Horn, L. J. (1996). Research on learning from television. In D. Jonassen (Ed.), *Handbook of research for educational communications and technology* (pp. 299–377). New York: Macmillan.

Sherry, L. (1996). Issues in distance learning. *International Journal of Educational Telecommunications, 1*(4), 337–365.

Shotsberger, P. G., & Vetter, P. (2000) The handheld web: How mobile wireless technologies will change web-based instruction and training. *Educational Technology, 40*(3), 49–52.

Stone, H. R. (1988). Variations in characteristics and performance between on-campus and video-based off-campus engineering graduate students. *Continuing Higher Education, 36*, 18–23.

Sykes, D. J., & Swinscoe, P. C. (1994). Digital video for multimedia, what are the alternatives? *Proceedings of the 16th Interservice/Industry Training Systems and Education Conference*, Orlando, FL.

Torkelson, G. M. (1977). AVCR—One quarter century: Evolution of theory and research. *AV Communications Review, 25*, 317–358.

Travers, R. M. (1967). Research and theory related to audiovisual information transmission (U.S. Office of Education contract No OES-16-006). Kalamazoo: Western Michigan University. (ERIC Document Reproduction Service No. ED 081 245).

VanderMeer, A. W. (1954). Color vs. black-and-white in instructional films. *Audio-Visual Communication Review, 2*, 121–134.

Walsh, W. J., Gibson, E. G., Miller, T. M., & Hsieh, P. Y. (1996). *Characteristics of distance learning in academia, business, and government*. (AL/HR-TR-1996-0012). Brooks Air Force Base, TX: Human Resources Directorate.

Weber, J. (1928). Comparative effectiveness of some visual aids in seventh grade instruction. In J. J. Weber (Ed.), *Picture values in education*. (pp. 37–52) Chicago: Educational Screen.

Wetzel, C. D., Radtke, P. H., & Stern, H. W. (1994). *Instructional effectiveness of video media*. Mahwah, NJ: Lawrence Erlbaum Assoicates.

Wisher, R. A., & Champagne, M. V. (2000). Distance learning and training: An evaluation perspective. In S. Tobias and J. D. Fletcher (Eds.), *Training & retraining A handbook for business, industry, government, and the military*. New York, NY: Macmillan Reference USA.

Wisher, R. A., & Curnow, C. K. (1999). Perceptions and effects of image transmissions during internet-based training. *The American Journal of Distance Education, 13*(3), 37–51.

Wisher, R. A., & Priest, A. N. (1998). Cost-effectiveness of audio teletraining for the U.S. Army National Guard. *The American Journal of Distance Education, 12*(1), 38–51.

Woelfel, N., & Tyler, I. K. (1945). *Radio and the school*. Tarrytown-on-Hudson, NY: World Book Company.

Wood, B. D., & Freeman, F. N. (1929). *Motion pictures in the classroom*. Boston: Houghton-Mifflin.

Woolf, B. P., & Regian, J. W. (2000). Knowledge-based training systems and the engineering of instruction. In S. Tobias and J. Fletcher (Eds.), *Training & retraining: A handbook for business, industry, government, and the military* (pp. 339–356). New York: Macmillan Reference USA.

23

Frameworks for Research, Design, Benchmarks, Training, and Pedagogy in Web-Based Distance Education

Curtis J. Bonk
Indiana University
cjbonk@indiana.edu

Vanessa Dennen
San Diego State University
vdennen@mail.sdsu.edu

INTRODUCTION

Administrators in higher education face decisions about what resources, activities, tools, partners, and markets are important to Web-based courses. Decisions in these areas can dramatically impact the effectiveness of Web-based instruction.

It is our premise here that, before forging ahead with new partnerships and marketing initiatives, an overall plan or perspective as well as many subplans or ideas for Web-based learning[1] are needed. Consequently, in this chapter, we provide a set of frameworks from which to reflect e-learning practices and opportunities. Additionally, we detail a number of pedagogical practices intended to make the frameworks come alive.

COLLEGE INSTRUCTOR ONLINE LEARNING SURVEY

A recent survey of college faculty cosponsored by JonesKnowledge.com and CourseShare.com found that the barriers to e-learning in most college settings included time to learn the technology, shortages of instructional development grants and stipends, limited recognition by departments and institutions in promotion and tenure decisions, and minimal instructional design support (Bonk, 2001). According to this study, recognition, collaboration, technical support, online sharing of pedagogical practices, and instructional design assistance are all ways to increase the adoption of Web-based technologies in college teaching. Such findings

---

[1] In this chapter, we interchangeably use the terms *online learning, Web-based learning*, and *e-learning*. Such terms refer to online instruction and distance learning made possible by the World Wide Web.

are important to administrators struggling with how to jump-start faculty technology integration within their universities and departments.

This study also determined that respondents—who, for the most part, were early adopters of the Web and had posted course syllabi, personal profiles, or Web resource reviews to either MERLOT.org or the World Lecture Hall on the Web—are finding a myriad of ways to incorporate the Web in their teaching. In fact, more than half of the faculty in this study had posted online syllabi and lecture notes, used online cases or problems, established asynchronous discussion forums in their classes, tried out different search engines, utilized articles and journal links, and found online glossaries for their classes. What they still wanted, however, were more pedagogical tools, advice, and communities for their online teaching and learning efforts. Not only did they request additional instructional development advice, technical support, release time, and course development stipends, they also wanted pedagogical ideas on how to use the Web in their teaching. In particular, they asked for tools that would foster greater student critical and creative thinking in their Web-based teaching efforts. Finally, there was a felt need for online teaching guidance, mentoring, and expert answers to problems.

PEDAGOGICAL VOID

Despite these findings of the need for pedagogical tools for the Web, most online courseware is pedagogically negligent (Bonk & Dennen, 1999). Most e-learning tools available at the time of this writing provide templates and guidelines for warehousing students and providing static course material. However, assistance in developing rich situations for collaborative knowledge construction, information seeking and sharing, reflection, debate, and problem-based learning is generally overlooked in the design of standard courseware tools.

As Oliver and McLoughlin (1999) note, there is too much focus on providing repositories of information over engineering innovative and dynamic Web-based learning experiences. They advocate guidelines for designing constructivist learning environments rich in knowledge construction experiences, social interaction, learner ownership and reflection, and opportunities to appreciate multiple perspectives. To support such guidelines, they offer frameworks for reflecting on constructivist learning principles and associated online tasks (e.g., metacognition and online journals, collaboration and various group discussion techniques, articulation and electronically sharing examples of work in progress, and active learning and the creation of Web reports or reviews of electronic resources). They also link these tasks and principles to specific tools and resources that can be designed for the Web such as URL posting, concept mapping, online surveys, note taking, and electronic debates (see also Oliver, Omari, & Herrington, 1998).

ONLINE LEARNING SUMMARY REPORTS

As online teaching and learning takes center stage in college teaching environments around the globe, there are a number of reports and initiatives to help administrators, instructors, politicians, and funding agencies make sense of the opportunities that the Web presents. For example, a recent report by the Institute for Higher Education Policy (2000) identified 24 key benchmarks for online learning quality related to course development, material reviews, student interaction and feedback, access to resources, technical support, student advisement, and the evaluation of learning outcomes. Similarly, a report from Pennsylvania State University and the AT&T Foundation detailed a set of guiding principles and practices for the design and development of distance education (Innovations in Distance Education, 2000). Other papers and Web sites document the Web courseware technologies and collaborative tools confronting institutions for decisions and directions. Such technologies multiply the opportunities and challenges facing higher education (Gray, 1998, 1999; Looms, 2000).

Some clarity is emerging. A report from a year-long faculty seminar on online teaching and learning at the University of Illinois reviewed the types of students and instructional methodologies typically found in online environments (The Report of the University of Illinois Teaching at an Internet Distance Seminar, 1999). Their review pointed to aspects of high-quality teaching in online environments and led to various recommendations for faculty related to facilitating online learning and guiding student interactions. A report from the TeleLearning Network Centers of Excellence (TeleLearning NCE) of Canada compared eight key postsecondary institutions offering e-learning in a competitive analysis of course/programs, pedagogy, and learner support (Massey & Curry, 1999). In this report, Massey and Curry provided a preliminary analysis of universities emerging in this field such as Stanford University, Nova Southeastern, Western Governors University, Indiana University, the University of Illinois, Open University UK, University of Phoenix Online, and California Virtual University. In addition, they addressed expansion plans, marketing, faculty, learners/clients, and course production and delivery. Such reports provide useful insights into the direction of online technologies and course delivery.

Other distance learning reports look at the existing research. For example, Bonk and Wisher (2000) extensively documented the online learning research literature and then detailed a set of experiments that address the gaps in the current research. In contrast, Russell (1999) summarized the nonsignificant results of distance learning research since 1928 as well as a scant few studies that actually indicate some positive and negative differences. Still other reports note that distance learning research too often lacks reliable and valid testing instruments and neglects theoretically grounding (National Center for Education Statistics, 1999; Phipps & Merisotis, 1999; Wisher, et al., 1999). Many such reports also point out that distance learning fails to account for the higher drop-out rates experienced in Web-based instruction.

ONLINE LEARNING FRAMEWORKS

The documentation of online learning quality benchmarks, tools, market trends, competitive analyses, and research gaps within these reports simply touches the surface of the types of studies needed for enhancing Web-based teaching and learning in higher education settings. Moreover, actual studies of faculty teaching via distance learning marginally address the pedagogical aspects of this new teaching and learning environment, opting instead to focus on issues of satisfaction, compensation, ownership, course load, and job security (e.g., National Educational Association, 2000). Consequently, there is a growing need for pedagogical frameworks for considering the Web in one's teaching.

Higher education faculty and administrators need useful frameworks for utilizing the Web in instruction. A series of research studies (Bonk & King, 1998) and online course experiments (Bonk, 1998; Bonk, Fischler, & Graham, 2000; Bonk, Hara, Dennen, Malikowski, & Supplee, 2000) at Indiana University spurred the development of various online learning frameworks.[2] Some of these studies explored the forms of learning assistance and mentoring found in online learning environments (Bonk & Sugar, 1998; Kirkley, Savery, & Grabner-Hagen, 1998) and the structure of online tasks (Dennen, 2000). Others have investigated online case creation and mentoring with preservice teachers (Bonk, Daytner, Daytner, Dennen, & Malikowski, in press; Bonk, Hara et al., 2000; Bonk, Malikowski, Angeli, & East, 1998; Bonk, Malikowski, Angeli, & Supplee, 1998).

---

[2]Many of these frameworks have been more fully reported elsewhere; see articles cited for more details.

TABLE 23.1

Framework of the Effects of Instructional Frameworks for the Web on Practical Online
Learning Initiatives

Instructional Frameworks for the Web	Online Learning Initiatives				
	1. Research Agendas	2. Tool Development Initiatives	3. Instructional Design Benchmarks	4. Instructor Training Programs	5. Pedagogical Guidelines, Reports, Resources, and Materials
1. Psychological Justification	Guides research	Justifies tool design	Provides benchmark criteria	Use as theoretical basis in training	Guides pedagogy
2. Participant Interaction	Variable as well as outcome of research	Influences tool design	Embedded in benchmarks	Provides training content	Generates activity ideas
3. Level of Web Integration	Provides classification system				
4. Student and Instructor Roles	Variable as well as outcome of research	Influences tool design	Embedded in benchmarks	Provides training content	Generates activity ideas
5. Pedagogical Strategies	Variable as well as outcome of research; focuses research funding	Establishes goals for tool design and funding sponsorship	Provides benchmark criteria	Provides training content	Generates activity ideas

Using much of this research as a base, Bonk and his colleagues have outlined five Web-based instruction frameworks relating to (1) psychological justification of online learning; (2) participant interaction; (3) levels of Web or technology integration; (4) instructor and student roles; and (5) pedagogical strategies. When combined, these five factors address issues pertaining to the overall learning environment and sense of community present in online courses. They can be used to plan, design, teach, and evaluate online courses. These general frameworks also lead to five practical initiatives: (1) focused programs of research in e-learning; (2) tool development efforts; (3) instructional design benchmarks for e-learning; (4) instructor training programs; and (5) teaching tips and guidelines. Table 23.1 demonstrates how each framework impacts and influences each practical initiative.

Framework #1: Psychological Justification for Online Learning

The first area of the model considers how use of the Web relates to current psychology theory. For instance, Bonk and Cummings (1998) linked 14 learner-centered psychological principles (LCPs) from the American Psychological Association (1993, 1997) to a dozen guidelines for using the Web in instruction. The LCPs, which are based on a meta-analysis of hundreds of psychological studies (Alexander & Murphy, 1994), highlight the importance of helping learners construct meaning, represent knowledge, link new information to old, monitor their own critical and creative thinking, and achieve complex learning goals. These principles also focus on how to foster student curiosity and intrinsic motivation, challenge students with appropriately high and challenging standards, recognize individual differences in learning, and nurture social interaction and interpersonal reasoning. As such, the LCPs are especially relevant to adult distance education settings since they tend to attract adult learners who want personally meaningful activities (Wagner & McCombs, 1995) as well as instructors who are willing to experiment with and employ a variety of instructional techniques to accommodate individual student needs (Bonk, 2001). Bonk and Cummings (1998) specifically linked each of their 12 practical guidelines to one or more of the APA principles:

1. Establish a safe environment and a sense of community;
2. Exploit the potential of the medium for deeper student engagement;
3. Let there be choice;
4. Facilitate, don't dictate;
5. Use public and private forms of feedback;
6. Vary the forms of electronic mentoring and apprenticeship;
7. Explore recursive assignments that build from personal knowledge;
8. Vary the forms of electronic writing, reflection, and other pedagogical activities;
9. Use student Web explorations to enhance course content;
10. Provide clear expectations and prompt task structuring;
11. Embed thinking skill and portfolio assessment as an integral part of Web assignments;
12. Look for ways to enhance the Web experience.

Each of the above 12 guidelines were linked to more than 1 of the 14 LCPs. For instance, the third recommendation on allowing students choice online related to fostering student intrinsic motivation to learn, natural curiosity, and creativity (LCP #8). It also related to the effects of motivation and guided learning on effort (LCP #9) and addressed individual differences in learning (LCP #12).

An additional psychological framework offered by Bonk and Cunningham (1998) documented collaborative learning tools from three theoretical perspectives. More specifically, Bonk and Cunningham explicated the learner-centered, constructivist, and sociocultural beliefs, principles, and approaches that inform the use of electronic conferencing and collaborative media. While detailing this framework, they point out that as educators have responded to passive, compartmentalized learning of the past century, new ways for thinking about teaching and learning have emerged. Most importantly, they explain and define key constructivist and sociocultural terminology and principles in relation to collaborative tools. For instance, new tools for online learning were linked to cognitive apprenticeship opportunities. Intersubjectivity was related to tools for building shared meaning or a temporarily shared space such as electronic whiteboards, conferencing, group brainstorming tools, and interactive debate forums (for additional explanation of such relationships, the reader is advised to read that chapter at: http://php.indiana.edu/~cjbonk/chap2.doc).

Similarly, Bonk (1998) linked tools and activities in an online undergraduate educational psychology course to specific sociocultural principles and techniques. Such linkages were provided for the survey course, lab experiences, and field reflection components of that course. Across these efforts, the overall intent was to clarify the psychological principles underlying different online courses and activities.

Framework #2: Participant Interaction

This second framework offers a means to reflect on the types of interaction structures that the Web affords as well as the possible players or participants in typical online learning situations (Cummings, Bonk, & Jacobs, 2002). As noted in Table 23.2, Bonk and his colleagues document how online interactions among three key participants—instructors, students, and practitioners—should be investigated and made more explicit through the use of different media.

TABLE 23.2
E-Learning Communication Flow among Instructors, Students, and Practitioners/Experts

	To Students	To Instructors	To Practitioners/Experts
From Instructors	Syllabus, schedule, profiles, tasks and tests, lecture notes and slides, feedback and email, resources, course changes	Course resources, syllabi, lecture notes and activities, electronic forums, teaching stories and ideas, commentary	Tutorials, online articles, listservs, electronic conferences, learning communities, news from discipline/field, products to apply in field
From Students	Models or samples of prior work, course discussions and virtual debate information, introductions and profiles, link sharing, personal portfolios, peer commenting or evaluation	Class voting and polling, completed online quizzes and tests, minute papers, course evaluations and session feedback, reflection logs, sample student work	Resumes and professional links, Web page links, field reflections and commentary
From Practitioners/Experts	Web teleapprenticeships, online commentary and feedback, e-fieldtrips, internship and job announcements	Survey opinion information, course feedback, online mentoring, listservs	Discussion forums, listservs, virtual professional development team explorations and communities

To evaluate the types of interactions found in higher education courses, Cummings et al. (2002) evaluated a number of education syllabi posted to the World Lecture Hall (see http://www.utexas.edu/world/lecture/) for indicators of learning interaction. This framework opens up discussion on the types of interactions and information exchanges that are important and perhaps absent in learning. For instance, in this particular study, there was minimal practitioner involvement in one's courses.

This matrix provides an opportunity to examine how online learning tools can be used to engage different participants. As such, it widens one's views on the range of online participants, the forms of online instruction, the degree and type of interactions online, and the online environments that may soon be common. This is just one view of online interaction. For instance, Bonk, Medury, and Reynolds (1994) developed a similar framework to understand the levels of interaction fostered by synchronous and asynchronous computer conferencing and collaborative writing tools.[3] Collectively, such frameworks are powerful aides in tool selection and instructional design processes as well as reflection on instructional options and challenges where minimal guidelines exist.

Framework #3: Level of Web or Technology Integration

A third model highlights ten distinctive levels of Web integration (Bonk, Cummings, Hara, Fischler, & Lee, 2000). These levels range from syllabus sharing to posting course materials on the Web, to having online discussions, to placing an entire course on the Web, to coordinating an entire program on the Web. In effect, such levels afford a useful way of examining how fully a particular course uses the Web and demonstrate a future path of integration that an instructor might work toward. Rather than simply referring to a course as a Web course or acknowledging that it has a Web presence, these levels, which, are summarized in Table 23.3, provide a way of being more specific in categorizing a Web-based course.

---

[3]Note that more than 30 synchronous and asynchronous tools were reviewed in that particular study.

TABLE 23.3
A Continuum of Web Integration in College Courses (Bonk, Cummings et al., 2000; Bonk &
Dennen, 1999; Rowley, Lujan, & Dolence, 1998)

Levels of Web Integration	*Description*
1. Marketing/Syllabi via the Web	Instructors use the Web to promote course and teaching ideas via electronic fliers and syllabi.
2. Student Exploration of Web Resources	Students use the Web to explore preexisting resources, both in and outside of class.
3. Student-Generated Resources Published on the Web	Students use the Web to generate resources and exemplary products for the class.
4. Course Resources on Web	Instructors use the Web to create and present class resources such as handouts, prior student work, class notes, and PowerPoint presentations.
5. Repurpose Web Resources	Instructors take Web resources and course activities from one course and, making some adjustments, use them in another.
6. Substantive and Graded Web Activities	Students participate with classmates in Web-based activities such as weekly article reactions or debates as a graded part of their course requirements.
7. Course Activities Extending Beyond Class	Students are required to work or communicate with peers, practitioners, teachers, and/or experts outside of their course, typically via computer conferencing.
8. Web as Alternate Delivery System for Resident Students	Local students with scheduling or other conflicts use the Web as a primary means of course participation, with the possibility of a few live course meetings.
9. Entire Course on the Web for Students Located Anywhere	Students from any location around the world may participate in a course offered entirely on the Web.
10. Course Fits within Larger Programmatic Web Initiative	Instructors and administrators embed Web-based course development within larger programmatic initiatives of their institution.

The first five levels largely represent informational or resource repository uses of the Web, whereas the later five levels require a significantly greater time commitment on the part of students and instructors. Once at Level 6, where graded activities typically begin, there is more reliance on student interaction and instructor facilitation for online learning success. In fact, at the top three levels of Web integration, the Web becomes the primary delivery platform for the course. In Bonk, Cummings et al. (2000), not only are each of the 10 levels described with examples and key issues, but student issues and instructional design guidelines are detailed at each level (for an earlier draft, see: *http://php.indiana.edu/~cjbonk/paper/edmdia99.html*).

This framework was designed to help educators think more deeply about the level of Web integration. Each decision about course design has long-term implications for student attitudes, social interaction, and overall learning. Reflecting on the levels of Web integration or technology use is yet another way for instructors as well as instructional designers to grasp the range of options for their online course and tool development efforts. Once a decision has been made regarding the level of Web integration, an instructor might investigate and select instructional strategies that make the Web effective at that level.

Framework #4: Instructor and Student Roles

The fourth framework concerns the roles of instructors and students in online learning environments. Web-based tools such as asynchronous discussion forums can be used to alter traditional instructor-led discussion formats and promote student interaction, critique, and collaboration activities based on constructivist learning theories. Students may be broken into small discussion groups, each simultaneously monitored but not necessarily run by the instructor, in which they might assume roles such as coordinator/leader, starter or resource investigator, summarizer, secretary or scribe, advocate or encourager, specialist, implementer, and reviewer or editor of results (Bonk, Wisher, & Lee, in press). Role play is sometimes difficult for students at first, but they tend to learn more from taking responsibility for their own learning (Dennen & Bonk, in review).

While student roles may be assigned at the activity level, the online instructor must constantly shift between instructional, facilitator, and consultant roles. Mason (1991) advocated three key roles of the online instructor: (1) organizational, (2) social, and (3) intellectual. The organizational role entails setting the agenda, objectives, timetable, and procedural rules for posting and interaction. In contrast, the social role involves sending welcoming messages, thank-you notices, prompt feedback on student inputs, and a generally friendly, positive, and responsive tone. Of the three roles Mason describes, the intellectual role is the most crucial since it includes probing responses, asking questions, and refocusing discussion. It also entails setting goals, explaining tasks and overlooked information, weaving disparate comments, synthesizing key points raised and identifying unifying themes, directing discussion, and generally setting and raising the intellectual climate of the course or seminar. In effect, Mason's framework allows teachers an opportunity to reflect on the multiple roles or hats of the instructor in online courses.

In expanding on Mason's framework, Ashton, Roberts, and Teles (1999) and Berge (1995) provide a slightly different framework to document the social, pedagogical, managerial, and technological actions that instructors can use to enhance their online courses. Berge (1995) elaborates on these four instructional roles or actions to make suggestions for instructors. For instance, his pedagogical recommendations include presenting conflicting opinions and finding unifying threads, whereas the social recommendations talk about using introductions and accepting lurkers. While his managerial recommendations talk about being clear and avoiding overloads, his technical recommendations include using technical support and providing time to learn new software features. These frameworks have since been used to describe the various components of online courses (Bonk, Kirkley, Hara, and Dennen, 2002).

As is clear from Table 23.4, there are many ways to teach online courses. In Bonk, Kirkley et al. (2001), the framework is elaborated upon and more ideas are provided via stories from four different instructors who are teaching courses online. By understanding how instructors can use the Web to design and enhance student social interaction, knowledge building, higher order thinking, and reflection, we can improve learning in all types of educational environments.

Framework #5: Pedagogical Strategies

As the growth in this area of teaching explodes, it becomes important to understand various pedagogical strategies that can be used for online teaching, such as problem-based learning (Koschmann, 1996; Dennen, 2000). However, as alluded to earlier, there is a dearth of knowledge about pedagogical tools and strategies for the Web.

Ron Oliver from Edith Cowan University in Australia is one of the few leaders in online pedagogy (Oliver & Herrington, 2000; Oliver & McLoughlin, 1999). Morton Paulsen from NKI College of Computer Science in Oslo, Norway, is one of the others (Paulsen, 1995). Oliver and his colleagues offer frameworks for thinking about instructional strategies that one might use for online teaching and learning. Their experimentation bridges technology and psychological theory by providing thinking-related templates for online tool development. For instance, they focus on how Web tools can foster student articulation, collaboration, intentional learning, and goal setting. They also connect these constructivist principles to Web-based resources such as bulletin boards, asynchronous conferencing, concept mapping, and survey tools that might be employed for student debates, reflection, cooperative group situations, and

TABLE 23.4
Summary of the Pedagogical, Social, Managerial, and Technological Roles of the
Online Instructor (Ashton et al., 1999; Berge, 1995; Bonk, Kirkley, et al., in press; Mason, 1991)

	General Components and Questions	*Examples*
1. Pedagogical Role	Assume facilitator or moderator role and ask questions, encourage student knowledge building, design a variety of instructional activities, elicit reflection, weave or summarize discussions, identify themes in discussions, offer constructive criticism, push to articulate ideas and explore resources, and provide explanations and elaboration where necessary	problem-based learning tasks, peer feedback tools, electronic cases, team activities, discussion forums, role play, constructive controversy, field reflections, Web site and resource evaluations, and online debates
2. Social Role	Create a friendly and nurturing environment or community feel, exhibit a generally positive tone, foster some humor, personalize in messages, display empathy and interpersonal outreach, and create community feel	cafes, digitized class pictures, online guests and visitors, jokes, and online stories or anecdotes
3. Managerial Role	Coordinate assignments with set due dates and extensions, assign groups and partners, present clear expectations, set office hours, clarity grading and feedback policies, and overall course structuring	online chats, detailed syllabus, course FAQs, online gradebook and portfolios, track login data, and calendar of events
4. Technological Role	Assist participants with technology issues, clarify problems encountered, and notify when the server is down	orientation tasks, help systems, tutorials, and vote on preferred technologies

online discussions. Few scholars or tool designers understand these linkages between tools, theories, and techniques. Consequently, Oliver's leadership role is vital in promoting the Web as a learning environment based on socioconstructivist instructional design principles and practices.

Bonk and Reynolds (1997) designed a similar framework in detailing a set of instructional strategies for the Web and linking them to relevant creativity, critical thinking, and cooperative learning literature. For instance, role play, what if activities, online journals, and brainstorming tasks were linked to creative thinking; idea ranking, flowcharting, comparison and contrast, critiques and rebuttals, summary writing, and case analysis were linked to critical thinking; and group investigations, round-robins, project-based learning, Web buddy, asynchronous conferencing, and panel discussions and symposia were examples of cooperative learning tasks for the Web. In addition, the overall instructional approach was linked to cognitive apprenticeship ideas and activities.

The initial pedagogical framework from Bonk and Reynolds has been extended in Table 23.5 to include motivational techniques and principles. As is shown by this table, there are many pedagogically and instructionally interesting activities available for online learning environments. For example, the Web offers a unique forum for classroom discussion, role-play, case-based discussion, brainstorming, special guest appearances, and collaborative learning.

As noted in Table 23.6, some of these pedagogical strategies heavily employ reading and writing. One popular and effective reading and writing strategy is the starter-wrapper technique (for examples, see Hara, Bonk, & Angeli, 2000). In this method, the starter summarizes the chapter ideas and issues for a particular week. The starter also provides questions meant to jump-start discussion. In the wrapper role, students reflect on issues and themes discussed during the week or unit as well as the issues that remain open. In effect, students are the teachers here. The instructor might respond within this discussion as a second wrapper by

TABLE 23.5

Online Learning Pedagogical Activities by Thinking and Learning Model

(Bonk & Reynolds, 1997)

Motivational and Ice-Breaking Activities	Creative-Thinking Activities
1. 8 Noun Introductions	1. Brainstorming
2. Coffee House Expectations	2. Role-Play
3. Scavenger Hunts	3. Topical Discussions
4. Two Truths, One Lie	4. Web-Based Explorations and Readings
5. Public Commitments	5. Recursive Tasks
6. Share-A-Link	6. Electronic Séances
Critical-Thinking Activities	Collaborative Learning Activities
1. Electronic Voting and Polling	1. Starter-Wrapper Discussions
2. Delphi Technique	2. Structured Controversy
3. Reading Reactions	3. Symposia or Expert Panels
4. Summary Writing and Minute Papers	4. Electronic Mentors and Guests
5. Field Reflections	5. Round-robin Activities
6. Online Case Analyses	6. Jigsaw and Group Problem Solving
7. Evaluating Web Resources	7. Gallery Tours and Publishing Work
8. Instructor- as well as Student-Generated Virtual Debates	8. E-mail Pals/Web Buddies and Critical/ Constructive Friends

pointing out what topics and issues were accurately portrayed and what issues still need further discussion and clarification. He or she weaves discussion fragments while directly teaching content only when necessary. Those who are not starters or wrappers might take on various roles such as devil's advocate, pessimist, or optimist.

Of course, there are many other reading and writing techniques for online environments. For instance, students might respond to articles online in small groups or individually. They might also comment on the confusing as well as clear aspects of a class in a weekly minute or muddiest point paper. Such formative feedback will help the instructor make weekly shifts in class.

What about motivation? The permanency of this electronic text, however brief, and ability to comment on or revisit it are motivating aspects of online learning. Also motivating are cooperative learning techniques such as jigsaw, wherein students might divide or subdivide their learning quests and responsibilities. Students also might be sorted in pro and con groups on controversial topics for online debates. They might vote on or nominate topics or articles for these discussions. Similarly, they might post cases or topics of importance based on fieldwork or internship experiences. Student posting of cases, instead of instructor or prepackaged problems, adds to the authenticity and currency of the online classroom. As these examples indicate, no matter what the online course, there are likely many opportunities to embed reading and writing activities.

Whereas Table 23.6 focuses on reading and writing activities, Table 23.7 lists online instructional activities concerned with student interaction, publication, and community building. Activities mentioned in that table include ice breakers and closing activities, scavenger hunts, polling or voting, symposia, and online publication of student work. In terms of ice breakers, we have found that having students post eight nouns that best represent their personality or interests is usually engaging and highly informative since the first few nouns or descriptors may come easy but requiring eight nouns forces students to self-reflect and open up. Along these same lines, the critical friend, Web buddy, or e-mail pal methods, also listed in the table, are ways to encourage student interaction and direction. As such, they also extend the feedback possibilities beyond the instructor. A critical friend might provide candid feedback on one's work or weekly statements of encouragement or assignment reminders. Having the ability to contact someone beyond the teacher reduces attrition rates while raising student satisfaction.

TABLE 23.6

Online Reading and Writing Techniques (Bonk, 1998; Bonk & Reynolds, 1997; Oliver, Omari, &
Herrington, 1999; Paulsen, 1995)

---

1. Starter-Wrapper (Hara, Bonk, & Angeli, 2000)
   a. Starter-Wrapper Conventional: Starter reads ahead and starts discussion and wrapper (and perhaps the teacher) summarizes what was discussed; others participate.
   b. Starter-Wrapper with Roles: Same as #1 but include roles for other participants (optimist, pessimist, devil's advocate, coach, questioner, mediator, connector, commentator, bloodletter, etc.).
   c. International Starter-Wrapper: Such discussion occurs with students from other countries and classrooms. Each site alternates starting and wrapping the weekly discussion. Perhaps pair students at remote sites for starter and wrapper roles.
2. Article Discussions
   a. Reading Reactions with No Choice: Students post critiques of or reactions to a small set of preassigned articles and react to posts of a certain number of peers.
   b. Reading Reactions with Extensive Choice: List all the articles in their reading packet within an online discussion tool. Next, assign students to reply to a set number of those articles. They decide which articles they want to discuss and reply to, however.
   c. Students Article Free Choice: Have students select a set number of articles to read for the semester and have them post summaries of some of them to Web as well as respond to the summaries of their peers.
   d. Assigned Reading Reactions in Teams: Assign students to read and react to a particular set of articles that they are responsible for, and, near the end of that discussion, summarize and comment on the discussions of another group.
3. Jigsaw
   a. Research Article Jigsaw: Assign students to groups and then segment an article or set of articles within groups (e.g., member #1 reads introduction and literature review; #2 reads the methods section, #3 reads the findings, #4 reads the conclusions and implications, etc.). In each group, students summarize the research flaws and confounds in an electronic discussion and share what was learned.
   b. Book Jigsaw: Divide students into groups and then divide chapters within groups (e.g., member #1 reads chapters 1 & 2; #2 reads 3 & 4, etc.). Students discuss ideas and findings in an electronic conference and share what learned. Perhaps summarize and present the key book ideas to other groups.
4. Web Explorations and Readings
   a. Evaluate Existing Articles: Students search for electronic articles on a topic and summarize, categorize, and/or react to them.
   b. Generate Reading Packet: Students find a set of similar articles on a topic and create an electronic reading packet.
5. Field Observations Reactions
   a. Individual Observations: Students observe situations in their field or discipline during internship or job experiences and reflect on how these experiences relate to current course material. Instructors post issues or questions for student reaction.
   b. Private Online Diaries: Students reflect on field or internship observations in a private online journal (with or without instructor feedback).
   c. Team Observations: Teams reflect on different aspects of field or internship experiences and summarize them for other teams.
6. Structured Controversy
   a. Assigned Roles: Assign two students a pro side and two students a con side and debate an issue electronically and then switch roles and come to compromise; perhaps later post a reflection on the compromise positions of 1–2 other groups.
   b. Chosen Roles: Same as in "a" above, but students select their own roles.
7. Topical Discussions
   a. List possible topics for discussion and have students vote on them and sign up to take the lead on one or more weeks.
   b. Have students brainstorm list of possible conferencing topics and then take responsibility to lead a week of discussion.
8. Cases
   a. Instructor-Generated Cases: Place set number of cases on the Web and link to a bulletin board system or conferencing tool for students to discuss. These cases can be used as collaborative quizzes that instructors and students from other universities or institutions can use.
   b. Student-Generated Cases: Have students generate a set number of cases during the semester based on field experiences or job-related experiences and respond to a set number of peer cases.

(Continued)

TABLE 23.6 (Continued)

    c. Exam Preparation Cases: Post a set number of cases for each small group to discuss and answer (these might
       be on their exam) and all groups must respond to the solutions of one other group.
    d. Team Cases: Post case situations and have students respond in small groups.
  9. Debates
    a. Reading Reactions as Debates with Free Choice: Assign a set number of articles to read, but student reactions
       on one or more of these must be in the form of a debate.
    b. Reading Reactions in Teams: Assign students to read a particular article or set of articles and also assign pro
       and con sides of a debate on such reading(s).
 10. Minute Or Muddiest Point Papers
    a. Individual Minute Papers: Have students send the instructor 1–2 minute reflections via e-mail perhaps to
       recap a class or to summarize things that remain unclear.
    b. Team Minute Papers: Have students share their minute papers in a group and summarize their key points for
       the instructor and/or for other groups.

Naturally, there are other ways to engage and involve students in one's online class. Students might get involved in an online scavenger hunt intended to familiarize them with the resources and tools available on the Web or with a certain content area. Some tools enable students to vote on issues or post their work to the Web. Chat tools foster opportunities for synchronous guest experts or speakers. The structure of such interactions and overall outcomes varies widely. Guests might simply come in to comment on the quality student postings. At the same time, students might chat with peers in their class who form panels of experts. They also might brainstorm in small groups. Other tools allow students to comment on or rate the work of their peers. If students know that there is an authentic audience beyond the teacher who might read, review, and question their work, then they might get more selective and reflective on their work. Having a gallery of student work is not only motivational for current students, but it also can become a model or standard for future students and instructors.

Online discussion is a vital part of e-learning courses. Instructors can assume many roles here. Typically a conversational or informal role allows for more student participation and dialogue. Formal or directive statements indicate an authoritative model of instruction. Weedman (1999) showed that online environments can foster informal and exploratory conversation that allows students and instructors to take risks and share knowledge. Similarly, in a study of 80 college undergraduates, Ahern, Peck, and Laycock (1992) found that a conversational style of interaction from the instructor produced higher and more complex levels of student participation. When online instructors were more informal and spontaneous in their commenting, students became more interactive with each other, compared to conditions wherein the instructor simply posed formal topic-centered statements or questions. In effect, responding to teacher questions or statements online is simply an extension of the recitation method; the more teacher-centered the environment, the less student exploration, engagement, and interaction. As Tharp and Gallimore (1988) demonstrated with their highly acclaimed "instructional conversation" method, students need to be invited into the discourse through complex interactions of instructor and peer assistance.

GOALS OF ONLINE LEARNING FRAMEWORKS

Hopefully, the five frameworks presented in this chapter can be integrated to offer practical outcomes and enhanced e-learning opportunities for students. As noted earlier in Table 23.1, the five instructional frameworks for the Web lead to e-learning initiatives related to: (1) research agendas; (2) tool development initiatives; (3) instructional design benchmarks;

TABLE 23.7

Other Online Learning Pedagogical Ideas (Bonk, 1998; Bonk & Reynolds, 1997; Herrington & Oliver, 1999; Paulsen, 1995)

1. Ice Breakers and Closing Activities (Thiagarajan, 1998)
   a. Eight Nouns Activity: Have students introduce themselves using eight nouns and then explain why they chose each noun.
   b. Coffee House Expectations: Have everyone post 2–3 of their expectations for the course in the online coffeehouse.
   c. Treasure Hunts: Have everyone list interests, where born, hobbies, favorite places to visit, job, major, etc., and then have them find one thing in common and one thing different about each member of the class.
   d. Brainteasers: Post a crossword puzzle, scrambled saying, competition, riddle, dilemma, or "IQ test" and see who can solve it.
   e. Psychic Massage and Positive Strokes: At the end of the semester or unit, have students nominate a student for whom they must all compliment for his or her contributions to the online class ("the best thing I like about (name) is").
2. Scavenger Hunt
   a. Instructor Generated: Send students on an online scavenger hunt. Such a technique is a useful way to acclimate them to using Web technologies or to a particular content area.
   b. Student Generated: Have students generate a scavenger hunt for the class as an optional or a bonus assignment.
3. Voting and Polling
   a. Minority Views: Have students vote on issues before class and then pull out the minority views at the start of class before the majority opinion dominates (tools like SiteScape Forum and eGroups have a polling and/or voting tool).
   b. Class Decisions: Use voting and polling tools to make important or interesting class decisions. This provides students with a voice or choice within the class.
4. Interactive Peer and Guest Commenting
   a. Link Ratings: Have students not just suggest Web links for the class but also require them to rate or rank those suggested by their peers.
   b. Profile Commenting: Have students comment on what they have in common with their peers directly in any peer profile and perhaps rate the degree of commonality.
5. Peer Feedback Roles
   a. E-mail Pal or Web Buddies: Assign everyone a partner to comment on his or her work (privately or publicly) and generally help each other out during the semester such as with providing peer feedback on self-tests and assignments.
   b. Critical or Constructive Friends: Assign students a critical or constructive friend who analyzes and critiques one's work as well as points out positive aspects of it while providing additional support where deemed necessary.
6. Round-robin Activities
   a. Storytelling: Have students create a story or scenario by having one person in the group start the story and send to the next group member who adds to it and forwards it on and so forth. The story circulates to everyone in the group. When done, students share their stories with either their entire group or the class.
   b. Problem Solving: Have students start answering a question or topic and forward their partial answers to someone in their group who adds comments or ideas to it and passes it on till it circulates to everyone in the group. The goal here is to solve the problem originally posed. When done, students share their solutions, case analyses, etc., with either the entire group or class.
7. Gallery Tours and Publishing of Student Work
   a. Individual Work: Post student work to the Web as a classroom legacy or archival record to display course expectations to future students.
   b. Work with Feedback: Post student individual or group projects to the Web and have expert panel, practitioners, or community members evaluate them.
8. Symposia
   a. Inside Experts: Have an online panel(s) or symposium(s) of student experts at the end of the semester after students have gone deep into a topic.
   b. Outside Experts: Have students vote on a set of outside experts they would like to invite for a panel discussion or online symposia and then invite these individuals. Hold symposia and then debrief.
9. Brainstorming
   a. Brainstorming without Evaluation: Have students brainstorm ideas on the Web and then post these to the Web. Perhaps create a top ten list.
   b. Nominal Group Process: Have students brainstorm ideas on the Web and then rank and rate the ideas generated. Calculate average ratings and distribute or create a top ten list.
10. Guest Experts
    a. Real-Time Chat: Bring in a guest expert to discuss issues in a real-time chat with preset questions or spontaneous discussion.
    b. Asynchronous Discussion: Bring in an outside expert for a week or month to discuss some topic of significance to the class in an asynchronous online discussion.

(4) instructor training programs; and (5) pedagogical guidelines and materials. The ultimate goal is to enhance and transform research, tool design and development, and teaching practices related to online teaching and learning.

Research Agendas

First of all, given the quality problems with existing e-learning research (Wisher et al., 1999), a focus on future e-learning research is important. For instance, after reviewing the e-learning literature, Bonk and Wisher (2000) detail ten key experiments to address the gaps in the research as well as a set of 17 secondary experiments (for a free download of this paper, see http://php.indiana.edu/~cjbonk/Dist.Learn%20(Wisher).pdf). Many of these experiments relate to both higher education and military settings. Of course, those researching the questions posed in this and other reports need a forum in which to share their findings.

Tool Development Initiatives

Second, these frameworks can help tool designers grasp aspects of their tools that are noticeably absent or not working effectively, thereby seeding future generations of online Web-based teaching tools. In Bonk and Dennen (1999), for instance, we designed creative thinking, critical thinking, and cooperative learning activity templates intended to spur courseware development efforts. Instead of summarizing existing tools, we noted the types of online learning tool templates that could be developed in the near future for critical and creative thinking as well as cooperative learning. Such tool templates were designed to foster or jump-start the development of pedagogical tools for the Web, thereby extending the instructional options for teachers and students online. In Bonk, Hara et al., (2000), we similarly noted features of more effective case-based learning tools (e.g., case commentary features, options for shrinking or expanding case views, opportunities to hyperlink different cases, etc.) as well as ideas for creating online communities and textbook support tools.

Instructional Design Benchmarks

Third, as the Institute for Higher Education Policy (2000) report noted, work in e-learning can lead to benchmarks and advice for designing instruction. Better instructional design within online courses and standards of success will increase acceptance for e-learning both within higher education as well as the surrounding community. Not surprisingly, Bonk's (2001) recent survey indicates that most college faculty need more instructional design support in their e-learning course development efforts.

Instructor Training Programs

Fourth, having online learning frameworks can help administrators reflect on the training programs needed for more effective and extensive faculty use of these tools in their teaching. There is a preponderance of internal and external support for faculty online teaching efforts. In terms of outside support, there are several recent online training programs and Web sites (e.g., FacultyTraining.net, WebBasedTrainers.com, the Learning Resources Network, TelesTraining.com, and CourseShare.com). There are also new courses and certificate programs for those desiring online teaching and management credentials (e.g., JonesKnowledge.com, Walden Institute, the University of Wisconsin [see http://www.wisc.edu/depd/index.html], and the Center for Research on Learning and Technology at Indiana University). Some aggregators of college teaching resources and information (e.g., MERLOT.org, HungryMinds.com, UniversalClass.com, and CourseShare.com) also provide valuable information for instructors and students. Additionally, online university consortia and communities are portals to resources meant to enhance college teaching and learning.

In addition to external resources, there are a myriad of internal instructor training resources and supports. For instance, campuses such as Indiana University fund media centers and instructional support services, centers for teaching and learning, instructional consulting offices, distributed or distance learning offices, and online access to best practices. More specifically, some faculty training programs offer on-site technical support, mentoring programs, brown bag lunch talks, instructional development grants and stipends, awards and recognitions, summer institutes, online discussions, and so on. Such training programs are extremely varied.

Pedagogical Guidelines, Reports, Resources, and Materials

Finally, in addition to instructor training programs, Web instruction frameworks should encourage online teaching guidelines as well as useful instructional reports, resources, and materials. Most large universities have reports, newsletters, and other publications to understand the e-learning trend (e.g., Cronin & Duffy, 1997). In addition, a myriad of books and special journal issues are beginning to offer e-learning clarity and guidance for those making key technological or instructional decisions.

Bonk, Wisher, and Lee (in review), for instance, document 10 key benefits and associated implications of e-learning. For example, since students are excited to publish work online, the instructor, with proper permissions, might create a classroom legacy and archive of best class products. These authors also discuss 10 key problems and solutions related to online learning that can help new as well as experienced instructors avoid common pitfalls of the online teaching experience. Consequently, they recommend providing explicit expectations and guidelines related to when and how much to post as well as samples of prior student work and other forms of structuring online tasks. Despite many e-learning inroads, there remains a need for additional guidelines related to instructor course development, course facilitation, student interaction and participation, feedback and grading practices, and so on.

LINKING FRAMEWORKS TO LEARNING COMMUNITIES

Hopefully the above frameworks and overall structure for online frameworks will assist administrators creating e-learning policies, instructors attempting to foster online collaboration and interaction, and policymakers funding e-learning research, design, and training initiatives. Of course, it is important to not only better understand e-learning psychological principles, interaction patterns, tools, roles, and strategies, but also there is a pressing need to link these frameworks into an investigation of how online communities are formed and sustained. Such an ultimate framework must address issues related to psychological safety or tone, shared online histories or knowledge, instructional flexibility, student autonomy and individualization, project collaboration and product development, idea sharing, social support, respect and empathy, online rituals, and team building, camaraderie, and identity development (Barab & Duffy, 2000; Schwier, 1999). Many open issues exist here today.

FINAL THOUGHTS

As higher education instruction is stretched into new electronic environments, e-learning frameworks will play a vital role in helping instructors, administrators, and policymakers reflect on their decisions concerning the theoretical perspectives, tools, activities, interaction patterns, roles, and instructional strategies pertinent to online learning. Frameworks can also lead to more focused research agendas, enhanced tool and courseware designs, prominent course and program comparison benchmarks, well-planned instructor training programs, accessible pedagogical materials and reports, and better overall online teaching and learning environments. As courses and programs for online learning mount, there will be additional (and perhaps better) frameworks, perspectives, and models that can assist in improving Web-based teaching and learning. Let's make it so.

ACKNOWLEDGMENTS

Portions of this chapter can be found in the proceedings of the 16th Annual Conference on Distance Teaching and Learning; see Bonk, C. J., & Dennen, V. P. (2000, August). More advances in Web pedagogy: Fostering interaction and the online learning community (pp. 475–481). *Proceedings of the 16th Annual Conference on Distance Teaching and Learning*, Madison, WI.

REFERENCES

Ahern, T. C., Peck, K., & Laycock, M. (1992). The effects of teacher discourse in computer-mediated discussion. *Journal of Educational Computing Research, 8*(3), 291–309.

Alexander, P. A., & Murphy, P. K. (1994). *The research base for APA's learner-centered psychological principles.* Paper presented at the American Educational Research Association annual meeting, New Orleans, LA.

American Psychological Association. (1993). *Learner-centered psychological principles: Guidelines for school reform and restructuring.* Washington, DC: American Psychological Association and the Mid-continent Regional Educational Laboratory.

American Psychological Association. (1997). *Learner-centered psychological principles: A framework for school redesign and reform.* Washington, DC: American Psychological Association, http://apa.org/ed/lcp/html.

Ashton, S., Roberts, T., & Teles, L. (1999). *Investigation the role of the instructor in collaborative online environments.* Poster session presented at the CSCL '99 Conference, Stanford University, CA.

Barab, S. A., & Duffy, T. (2000). From practice fields to communities of practice. In D. Jonassen & S. M. Land (Eds.), *Theoretical foundations of learning environments* (pp. 25–56). Mahwah, NJ: Lawrence Erlbaum Associates.

Berge, Z. L. (1995). Facilitating computer conferencing: Recommendations from the field. *Educational Technology, 35*(1), 22–30.

Bonk, C. J. (1998, April). *Pedagogical activities on the "Smartweb": Electronically mentoring undergraduate educational psychology students.* Paper presented at the American Educational Research Association annual convention, San Diego, CA. (See http://php.indiana.edu/~cjbonk/paper/smart_paper.html.)

Bonk, C. J. (2001). *Online teaching in an online world.* Bloomington, IN: CourseShare.com. [see http://PublicationShare.com].

Bonk, C. J., & Cummings, J. A. (1998). A dozen recommendations for placing the student at the centre of Web-based learning. *Educational Media International, 35*(2), 82–89.

Bonk, C. J., Cummings, J. A., Hara, N., Fischler, R., & Lee, S. M. (2000). A ten level Web integration continuum for higher education. In B. Abbey (Ed.), *Instructional and cognitive impacts of Web-based education* (pp. 56–77). Hershey, PA: Idea Group Publishing.

Bonk, C. J., & Cunningham, D. J. (1998). Searching for learner-centered, constructivist, and sociocultural components of collaborative educational learning tools. In C. J. Bonk & K. S. King (Eds.), *Electronic collaborators: Learner-centered technologies for literacy, apprenticeship, and discourse* (pp. 25–50). Mahwah, NJ: Erlbaum.

Bonk, C. J., Daytner, K., Daytner, G., Dennen, V., & Malikowski, S. (2001). Using Web-based cases to enhance, extend, and transform preservice teacher training: Two years in review. *Computers in the Schools, 18*(1), 189–211. NY: Haworth Press.

Bonk, C. J., & Dennen, V. P. (1999). Teaching on the Web: With a little help from my pedagogical friends. *Journal of Computing in Higher Education, 11*(1), 3–28.

Bonk, C. J., Fischler, R. B., & Graham, C. R. (2000). Getting smarter on the Smartweb. In D. G. Brown (Ed.), *Teaching with technology: Seventy-five professors from eight universities tell their stories* (pp. 200–205). Boston, MA; Anker Publishing.

Bonk, C. J., Hara, H., Dennen, V., Malikowski, S., & Supplee, L. (2000). We're in TITLE to dream: Envisioning a community of practice, "The Intraplanetary Teacher Learning Exchange." *CyberPsychology and Behavior, 3*(1), 25–39.

Bonk, C. J., & King, K. S. (Eds.). (1998). *Electronic collaborators: Learner-centered technologies for literacy, apprenticeship, and discourse.* Mahwah, NJ: Lawrence Erlbaum.

Bonk, C. J., Kirkley, J. R., Hara, N., & Dennen, N. (2001). Finding the instructor in post-secondary online learning: Pedagogical, social, managerial, and technological locations. In J. Stephenson (Ed.). *Teaching and learning online: Pedagogies for new technologies* (pp. 76–97). London: Kogan Page.

Bonk, C. J., Malikowski, S., Angeli, C., & East, J. (1998). Case-based conferencing for preservice teacher education: Electronic discourse from the field. *Journal of Educational Computing Research, 19*(3), 269–306.

Bonk, C. J., Malikowski, S., Angeli, C., & Supplee, L. (1998, April). *Holy COW: Scaffolding case-based "Conferencing on the Web" with preservice teachers.* Paper presented at the American Educational Research Association (AERA) annual convention, San Diego, CA.

Bonk, C. J., Medury, P. V., & Reynolds, T. H. (1994). Cooperative hypermedia: The marriage of collaborative writing and mediated environments. *Computers in the Schools, 10*(1/2); 79–124.

Bonk, C. J., & Reynolds, T. H. (1997). Learner-centered web instruction for higher-order thinking, teamwork, and apprenticeship. In B. H. Khan (Ed.), *Web-based instruction* (pp. 167–178). Englewood Cliffs: Educational Technology Publications.

Bonk, C. J., & Sugar, W. A. (1998). Student role play in the World Forum: Analyses of an Arctic learning apprenticeship. *Interactive Learning Environments, 6*(1–2), 1–29.

Bonk, C. J., & Wisher, R. A. (2000). *Applying collaborative and e-learning tools to military distance learning: A research framework* (Technical Report #1107). Alexandria, VA: U.S. Army Research Institute for the Behavioral and Social Sciences. (Note: This report has unlimited distribution. See: http://php.indiana.edu/~cjbonk/Dist.Learn%20(Wisher).pdf.)

Bonk, C. J., Wisher, R. A., & Lee, J. (in press). Moderating learner-centered e-learning: Problems and solutions, benefits and implications. In T. S. Roberts (Ed.). *Online Collaborative Learning: Theory and Practice.*

Cronin, B., & Duffy, T. M. (1997). *Distributed education and Indiana University: Context, trends, and assumptions.* Bloomington: Indiana University.

Cummings, J. A., Bonk, C. J., & Jacobs, F. R. (2002). Twenty-first century college syllabi: Options for online communication and interactivity. *Internet and Higher Education, 5*(1), 1–19.

Dennen, V. (2000). Task structuring for on-line problem based learning: A case study. *Educational Technology and Society, 3*(3), 329–336.

Dennen, V., & Bonk, C. J. (in review). *Cases, conferencing, and communities of practice: A qualitative study of online mentoring for preservice teachers.*

Gray, S. (1998). Web-based instructional tools. *Syllabus, 12*(2), see http://www.syllabus.com/syllabusmagazine/sep98_magfea2.html.

Gray, S. (1999). Collaboration tools. *Syllabus, 12*(5), 48–52.

Hara, N., Bonk, C. J., & Angeli, C., (2000). Content analyses of on-line discussion in an applied educational psychology course. *Instructional Science, 28*(2), 115–152.

Herrington, J., & Oliver, R. (1999). Using situated learning and multimedia to investigate higher-order thinking. *Journal of Educational Multimedia and Hypermedia, 8*(4), 401–421.

Innovations in Distance Education. (2000). *An emerging set of guiding principles and practices for the design and development of distance education.* Pennsylvania State University, www.outreach.psu.edu/de/ide/.

Institute for Higher Education Policy. (2000). *Quality on the line: Benchmarks for success in Internet-based distance education.* Washington, DC: The Institute for Higher Education Policy.

Kirkley, S. E., Savery, J. R., & Grabner-Hagen, M. M. (1998). Electronic teaching: Extending classroom dialogue and assistance through email communication. In C. J. Bonk, & K. S. King (Eds.), *Electronic collaborators: Learner-centered technologies for literacy, apprenticeship, and discourse* (pp. 209–232). Mahwah, NJ: Erlbaum.

Koschmann, T. D. (Ed.). (1996). *CSCL: Theory and practice of an emerging paradigm.* Mahwah, NJ: Lawrence Erlbaum Associates.

Looms, T. (2000, November 17). *Survey of course and test delivery/management systems for distance learning.* http://www.seas.gwu.edu/%7Etlooms/assess.html.

Mason, R. (1991). Moderating educational computer conferencing. *DEOSNEWS, 1*(19), 1–11.

Mason, R. (1998). Models of online courses. *Asynchronous Learning Networks Magazine, 2*(2), 1–11.

Massey, C., & Curry, J. (1999). *Online post-secondary education: A competitive analysis.* Burnaby, BC, Canada: TeleLearning Network Centers of Excellence (NCE).

National Center for Education Statistics (NCES), (1999). (Lewis, L., Snow, K., Farris, E., Levin, D., & Greene, B.). (1999). *Distance education at postsecondary education institutions: 1997–98* (National Center for Education Statistics, NCES 2000-013). Washington, DC: U.S. Department of Education.

National Educational Association. (2000, June). *A survey of traditional and distance learning higher education members.* Washington, DC: The National Education Association.

Oliver, R., & Herrington, J. (2000). Using situated learning as a design strategy for Web-based learning. In B. Abbey (Ed.), *Instructional and cognitive impacts of Web-based education* (pp. 178–191). Hershey, PA: Idea Group Publishing.

Oliver, R., & McLoughlin, C. (1999). Curriculum and learning-resources issues arising from the use of web-based course support systems. *International Journal of Educational Telecommunications, 5*(4), 419–436.

Oliver, R., Omari, A., & Herrington, J. (1998). Exploring student interactions in collaborative World Wide Web computer-based learning environments. *Journal of Educational Multimedia and Hypermedia, 7*(2/3), 263–287.

Paulsen, M. F. (1995). Moderating educational computer conferences. In Z. L. Berge and M. P. Collins (Eds.), Computer mediated communication and the online classroom, Volume 3: Distance learning (pp. 31–57). Creskill, NJ: Hampton Press.

Phipps, R., & Merisotis, J. (1999). *What's the difference?: A review of contemporary research on the effectiveness of distance learning in higher education.* Washington, DC: The Institute for Higher Education Policy.

Rowley, D. J., Lujan, H. D., & Dolence, M. G. (1998). *Strategic choices for the academy: How demand for lifelong learning will re-create higher education.* San Francisco: Jossey Bass.

Russell, T. L. (1999). *The "no significant difference phenomenon."* Chapel Hill, NC: Office of Instructional Telecommunications, North Carolina University. http://cuda.teleeducation.nb.ca/nosignificantdifference/.

Schwier, R. A. (1999). *Turning learning environments into learning communities: Expanding the notion of interaction in multimedia.* In B. Collis & R. Oliver (Eds.), Proceedings of Ed-Media 99: World Conference on Educational Multimedia, Hypermedia and Telecommunications, Seattle, Washington, Norfolk, VA: Association for the Advancement of Computers in Education, 282–286.

Tharp, R., & Gallimore, R. (1988). *Rousing minds to life: Teaching, learning, and schooling in a social context.* Cambridge, MA: Cambridge University Press.

The Report of the University of Illinois Teaching at an Internet Distance Seminar. (1999). *Teaching at an Internet distance: The pedagogy of online teaching and learning.* University of Illinois Faculty Seminar, Urbana-Champaign, IL: The University of Illinois.

Thiagarajan, S. (1998, March). What can an icebreaker do? *Thiagi GameLetter: Seriously fun activities for trainers, facilitators, and managers, 1*(1), p. 2, San Francisco, CA: Jossey-Bass/Pfeiffer.

Wagner, E. D., & McCombs, B. L. (1995). Learner centered psychological principles in practice: Designs for distance education. *Educational Technology, 35*(2), 32–35.

Weedman, J. (1999). Conversation and community: The potential of electronic conferences for creating intellectual proximity in distributed learning environments. *Journal of the American Society for Information Science, 50*(10), 907–928.

Wisher, R. A., Champagne, M. V., Pawluk, J. L., Eaton, A., Thornton, D. M., & Curnow, C. K. (1999). *Training through distance learning: An assessment of research findings* (U.S. Army Research Institute for the Behavioral Sciences Technical Report 1095). Alexandria, VA: U.S. Army Research Institute for the Behavioral Sciences.

24

Designing Instruction for e-Learning Environments

Som Naidu

The University of Melbourne, Australia
s.naidu@unimelb.edu.au

INSTRUCTIONAL DESIGN IN CONTEMPORARY OPEN AND DISTANCE LEARNING (ODL)

Contemporary open and distance learning (ODL) is widely known for spearheading and refocusing our attention on several aspects of teaching and learning. The most pervasive of them all, perhaps, is the recognition of the important role and function of instructional design. Others include the role and function of electronic publishing and distribution of study materials, use of alternative and noncontiguous delivery technologies in teaching and learning (i.e., alternative to face-to-face instruction), asynchronous communication among participants in learning and teaching, and ownership of intellectual property and copyright.

In much of traditional face-to-face education, what passes for instructional design was and still is, rightly or wrongly, the sole responsibility of the teacher in charge. This situation changed with the advent of nontraditional distance teaching and learning practices. Teachers in charge, largely as subject matter experts, could no longer be seen to be responsible for the entire teaching and learning transaction. The development of printed and other types of study materials for independent study by distance learners required a team effort with significant input in the educational process from instructional designers and media producers. This brought into the educational process specialized skills in various types of media production, subject matter representation, and in supporting student learning in technology mediated educational environments.

Despite this growing recognition of the important role and function of instructional design in ODL, educators have, on the whole, failed to make the best use of the opportunities that alternative delivery technologies can provide. Evidence of this is all around us in the form of innumerable university course Web sites that contain little more than the schedule, a brief outline of the course content, PowerPoint slides of the lecturer's notes, and sometimes, sample examination papers. Instead of exploiting the unique attributes of information and communications technologies, such practices replicate the "education is equal to the transmission of information" model of teaching that is so common in conventional classroom practice. Regardless of the capabilities of the delivery medium, the nature of the subject matter content, and learner needs, much of educational practice continues to be teacher directed and delivery centered. Rarely have we paused to think about why we are teaching the way we do teach and support learning and whether our instructional approaches are based on sound educational principles of cognition and learning.

This kind of instructional practice has led to a great deal of frustration for learners and teachers, many of whom have grown increasingly skeptical about the educational benefits of the newer delivery technologies (see Kirkwood, 2000; Rumble, 2000; Schellens & Valcke, 2000). The source of much of this frustration has to do with the failure of instructional designers and subject matter experts to come up with instructional and learning designs that best match the type of the subject matter and the needs of learners within the parameters of their learning environments.

CONTEMPORARY DEVELOPMENTS IN OPEN AND DISTANCE LEARNING

Surveys by the U.S. Department of Education's National Center for Education Statistics (2000, March) show that the number of "distance education-like" programs in the United States has been increasing exponentially, and many more institutions plan to establish distance education programs in the next few years. The U.S. National Survey of Information Technology in Higher Education (1999), as part of its Campus Computing Project, carries out surveys annually on the use of information and communications technology in higher education. One of its recent surveys (1999, February) reveals that:

- An increasing number of college courses are incorporating information and communications technology, including use of e-mail as part of their teaching and learning transactions, Internet resources as part of the syllabus, and the World Wide Web for presenting course materials.
- Students and faculty alike are spending an increasing amount of their study time on the Internet and both student and faculty percentages in this regard are highest in research universities.
- Across all sectors of higher education, a growing number of institutions are using the World Wide Web to provide students access to admission forms, financial aid applications, course catalogs, and other related material.

The proliferation of information and communications technology (ICT) in conventional, campus-based educational settings is clearly blurring the traditional boundaries between distance education and campus-based, face-to-face educational practices. However, it is not an objective of this chapter to trace in great detail contemporary developments in distance education, nor is its goal to define the various forms of educational activity that incorporate open and distance learning practices.

The focus of attention in this chapter is on designing learning and instruction for educational settings that incorporate use of information and communications technologies. The preferred terminology for such educational settings is e-learning. One of the most comprehensive descriptions of e-learning describes it "as the systematic use of networked multimedia computer technologies to empower learners, improve learning, connect learners to people and resources supportive of their needs, and to integrate learning with performance and individual with organisational goals" (Goodyear, 2000). This definition has two main parts—a reference to information and communications technology (and in particular to the systematic use of this technology) and a reference to purposes or goals. While e-learning embraces distance education practices, distance education's broader scope also incorporates print-based correspondence education. Hence it is meaningful to equate e-learning with distance education, but distance education is not necessarily e-learning (Rosenberg, 2001).

The use of the term *e-learning* is growing rapidly all around the world and frequently being used interchangeably with terms such as *online learning, virtual learning, distributed learning, networked learning,* and *web-based learning.* Despite their unique attributes, each of these terms fundamentally refers to educational processes that utilize information and communications technology to mediate asynchronous as well as synchronous learning and teaching activities. Indeed, with the exception of conventional open and distance learning, it can be argued that the emergence of *e-learning, online learning, virtual learning, distributed learning, networked learning, and web-based learning,* is directly linked to the development of and access to a reliable and robust information and communications technology infrastructure. Without access to this kind of infrastructure support, the viability of such educational activities is undermined and those without access to such support are increasingly disadvantaged from accessing the educational opportunities they afford.

E-learning appears to be growing out of three distinct directions:

1. From within educational providers, which have historically offered open and distance learning opportunities either in a single, dual, or mixed mode.
2. From conventional campus-based educational institutions that have never been involved in open and/or distance learning. Such institutions are applying information and communications technology to support and enrich their campus-based, face-to-face learning and teaching experience. Their goal, in most cases, is to increase flexibility and efficiency in the belief that doing so will enable them to tap into niche markets and student populations, which were previously out of their reach.
3. From the corporate sector, where many organizations are favoring e-learning to conventional residential workshop-based approaches to staff training. The corporate world is increasingly finding e-learning to be an attractive model as it offers flexible and "just-in-time" learning opportunities.

Forces driving the growth and development of e-learning include:

1. The increasing accessibility of information and communications technologies and also their decreasing cost.
2. The capacity of information and communications technology to support and enrich conventional educational practices through resource-based learning and synchronous and asynchronous communication.
3. The need for flexible access to learning opportunities from distributed venues such as the home, workplace, the community learning center, as well as the conventional educational institution.
4. The demand from isolated and independent learners for more equitable access to educational opportunities and services.
5. The belief among many educational institutions that the application of information and communications technology will enable them to increase their share in an increasingly competitive educational market.
6. The need, among educational institutions, to be seen to be "keeping up with the times" in order to attract the attention of parents, students, and other donors.

7. The belief and the expectation that e-learning will reduce costs and increase productivity and institutional efficiency.

There are also forces working against the growth of e-learning and these include:

1. The lack of access to reliable communications networks with sufficient bandwidth capacity in most parts of the world. Even in relatively developed and affluent societies such as North America, Western Europe, and Australia, major disparities along geographical and socioeconomic lines exist in access to this infrastructure. This kind of disparity is arguably the most critical issue that is impeding the proliferation of e-learning.
2. The lack of basic necessary ICT appliances such as computers and modems, including know-how, which is increasing the "digital divide" and widening the gap between the "have" and the "have-nots."
3. Intellectual property and copyright laws that restrict the sharing of information and collaborative arrangements.
4. The up-front costs of establishing an e-learning program, even if savings can be achieved over time and economies of scale. The costs of hardware, software, and ongoing electronic communication for both the institution and the learners are a major deterrent.
5. Absence of suitable and effective models of learner support that are designed for supporting learners in e-learning environments.
6. Reticence and a lack of enthusiasm on the part of faculty to embrace information and communications technology in their teaching and in supporting learning. A large number of faculty still lack the necessary skills to effectively use these technologies and are unsure about the merits of incorporating them in their teaching. Some of this fear is driven by student demands and expectations for lecturers to be lecturing and also by the incentives and rewards for promotion and tenure that are currently in place in many educational institutions. The latter tend not to reward excellence in teaching as much as they do reward excellence in research. The educational philosophy that faculty hold, and what is likely to work in their own discipline areas, is also a major contributing factor in the adoption of these technologies.

ATTRIBUTES AND CAPABILITIES OF e-LEARNING EDUCATIONAL TECHNOLOGIES

E-learning educational technologies are information and communications technologies that enable the delivery and use of information in electronic formats. This chapter does not attempt to describe the form and functions of these technologies as there is an abundance of literature in print as well as in electronic form on these technologies (see Rapaport, 1991; Collis, 1996). Instead, by way of an introduction, it briefly recounts the critical and unique attributes of these technologies. These attributes are a) the flexibility that e-learning educational technologies afford; b) electronic access to a variety of multimedia-based material that these technologies enable; and c) opportunities for learning and teaching that they afford.

The Flexibility That E-Learning Educational Technology Affords

Flexible access to information is the most identifiable attribute of e-learning educational technologies. Learner choice is at the heart of the concept of flexible access, which incorporates the facility to access subject matter content and support at a time, place, and pace that is suitable and convenient for the individual learner, rather than the teacher and/or the educational organization. Flexible access to subject matter content and learning activities orchestrated via e-learning technologies across classrooms, workplaces, homes, and community settings is the defining characteristic of what has come to be known as flexible and distributed learning (see Dede, 2000; 1996). E-learning educational technologies such as various forms of "groupware" and computer conferencing technologies can support collaborative inquiry among students who are in different locations and often not online at the same time (e.g., Edelson, Gordin, & Pea, 1999; Edelson & O'Neill, 1994). Through a mixture of emerging e-learning technologies, learners and teachers can engage in synchronous and asynchronous interaction across space, time, and multiple interactive media (see Gomez, Gordin, & Carlson, 1995). With the help of these technologies and telementors, students from different locations can create, share, and master knowledge about authentic real-world problems (see Edelson, Pea, & Gomez, 1996; Gordin, Polman, & Pea, 1994).

Electronic Access to Hyper-Media and Multimedia-Based Resources

E-learning educational technologies also enable the delivery of subject matter content in a variety of media formats that is not possible within the spatial and temporal constraints of conventional educational settings such as the classroom or the printed study materials commonly used in open and distance education (Dede, 2000). This means that learners in distributed settings can have access to a wide variety of educational resources all via their desktops, in a form that is adaptable and amenable to individual approaches to learning (Spiro, Feltovich, Jacobson, & Coulson, 1991). These educational resources are, moreover, accessible to learners at a time, place, and pace that is convenient to them (Pea, 1994; Pea & Gomez, 1992). Typically they may include any combination of components like:

- Hyperlinked textual material, incorporating pictures, graphics, and animation.
- Videotaped elaboration of subject matter, including interviews, and panel discussions.
- Hyperlinked multimedia elements such as QTVs, simulations, graphics, and animations.
- Just-in-time access to a range of electronic databases, search engines, and online libraries.
- Just-in-time access to coaching and assistance via telementors, e-communities, and peers.

The one limitation to this for many at the moment is the capability of their networks and bandwidth to deliver this information (Dede, 1991). But this situation is sure to change and for some, very rapidly indeed.

OPPORTUNITIES FOR LEARNING AND TEACHING THAT E-LEARNING AFFORDS

Research in learning and instruction suggests that people learn most effectively by pursuing realistic goals that are also intrinsically motivating (Schank, Fano, Jona, & Bell, 1994). Learning is also greatly enhanced when it is anchored or situated in meaningful and authentic problem-solving contexts (Barron et al., 1998; Brown, Collins, & Duguid, 1989; The Cognition and Technology Group at Vanderbilt, 1990). While "goal-based learning" is not constrained by any particular media type, certain delivery technologies can impede anchored instruction or situated learning. Conventional classroom-based instruction, for instance, while it may be cost-effective, is constrained to a large extent by its fixed time and space in being able to situate learning in realistic contexts. Printed text as well, while it affords transportability, is limited by its inability to incorporate anything other than text, pictures, and illustrations.

Contemporary e-learning educational technologies, with their temporal and spatial flexibility and ability to support resource-rich multimedia content, afford us the opportunity to develop educational opportunities that are known as "generative learning environments" (The Cognition and Technology Group at Vanderbilt, 1991). These are learning environments that are based on a theoretical framework that emphasizes the importance of anchoring or situating instruction in meaningful, problem-solving contexts. A major goal of this approach is to create shared learning environments that permit sustained exploration by students and teachers to enable them to understand the kinds of problems and opportunities that experts in various areas encounter and the knowledge that these experts use as tools. Experts are known to be very familiar with the endemic nature of their disciplines or domains of practice. In order for novices to approximate this level of familiarity with the discipline, they need to become immersed in the culture of that discipline. This necessitates access to a range of resources and experiences, including multimedia-based simulation of components that are not readily accessible in real time, such as certain aspects of biological and medical science, engineering, and educational practice.

Quality of E-Learning Practices

In the midst of all this interest in and proliferation of e-learning, there is a great deal of variability in the quality of e-learning and teaching. However, this shouldn't be any surprise as there are just as many instances of poor and reckless face-to-face teaching as there are instances of excellence in that regard as well. In 1997, a group of adult educators from the University of British Columbia in Canada carried out an investigation of Web-based courses (Boshier, Mohapi, Moulton, Qayyaum, Sadownik and Wilson, 1997). This is a somewhat dated study, and this snapshot of Web-based courses will be undoubtedly replaced by the fast pace of change in this area, but it does shed some interesting light on e-learning and teaching practices, which are probably, on the whole, not very different at the moment. The focus of this investigation is on the attractiveness and face validity of "stand-alone" Web-based courses. These researchers defined a stand-alone course as one that "might include supplemental material but can be completed entirely without face-to-face interaction with an instructor" (Boshier et al., 1997, p. 327).

Of the 127 subjects they reviewed, the investigators classed 19 of them as "not enjoyable" to walk through, 42 were considered as "mildly enjoyable," 43 as "moderately enjoyable," 19 as "very enjoyable," and 4 as a "complete blast." They also found that very few of the courses surveyed offered much interactive capability for the learner or opportunity for collaborative learning. They found that many of the courses seemed to have been overly driven by an obsession with statement of objectives, assessment outcomes, and a hierarchical ordering of subject matter content, as opposed to a focus on building rich resource-based learning environments around enduring themes. The researchers concluded from this study that the biggest challenge for Web-based course developers seemed to be conceptual, not technological. They suggest that course developers ought to be focussing more on how to make their courses "attractive, accessible and interactive" (p. 348).

RECOGNIZING THE NEED TO RECONSIDER CONTEMPORARY APPROACHES TO E-LEARNING

It should be no longer necessary to reiterate that media in itself can have little impact on the quality of teaching and learning (see Clark, 1983; Kozma, 1991). There is no doubt that information and communications technologies offer tremendous opportunities for building rich and resource-based learning environments. However, these technologies are mere vehicles of the educational transaction and on their own cannot substantially enhance learning and teaching. Despite this, in the rush to embrace e-learning, many educators are able to do little more than post the course syllabus and Powerpoint slides of their lectures on a course Web site. This is little different from making photocopies of such material and distributing them in class. However, while posting the course syllabus and one's lecture notes on the Web is a very worthwhile use of this technology, there is a whole lot more that information and communications technology can enable by way of supporting learning and teaching. To make the most of the opportunities that these technologies offer, careful attention needs to be paid foremost to the *pedagogy* of the learning and teaching transaction. This refers to the "design architecture" of the learning and teaching environment and it incorporates, *inter alia*, consideration of how subject matter content will be presented, what the learners would do, how learning will be supported, what would comprise formative and summative assessment, and how feedback will be provided.

There is no shortage of advice on how to design rich and resourceful e-learning environments and reconsider our approaches to teaching and learning to ensure that we are making the most of the delivery technologies we are employing (see Burgess & Robertson, 1999; French, Hale, Johnson, & Farr, 1999). In fact, we do not have a choice in this regard. The changing needs of education and training in both business and higher education are forcing a reconsideration of our conventional approaches to teaching and learning. This incorporates, among other things, the changing role of the classroom teacher from one of being a "sage on the stage" to a "guide on the side." It also includes the changing nature of student learning from one of being "teacher-directed" to being "student-directed" or "student-centered." Information and communications technology has a significant role to play in supporting these foreshadowed changes in the nature of teaching and learning.

French et al. (1999) suggest three ways in which information and communications technology can be used to effectively support a self-directed and student-centered learning environment. These are (1) augmenting teaching; (2) virtual learning; and (3) progressive application. *Augmenting teaching* is based on the premise that educators can enrich their current teaching practices by supporting their classes with one or more aspects of ICT-based activities. Augmented classes may use anything from making use of the Web for distributing information about the course to e-mail communication for discussion between students and teachers and among students, and collaborative computer conferencing among students for group work. *Virtual learning* refers to the process of learning and teaching on the Internet without any face-to-face contact between or among the participants. In this mode, the Internet replaces conventional lecture formats, creating new opportunities for self-directed and flexible learning. Finally, *progressive application* refers to the process of applying ICT-based technologies to teaching and learning progressively as one develops his/her confidence in the use of the technology and its imperatives. The concept of progressive application of the technology is based on the notion of just-in-time learning, which is the process of having educational access at the time when one needs to learn something.

PEDAGOGICAL APPROACHES FOR OPTIMIZING E-LEARNING

This section of the chapter discusses a selection of pedagogical approaches that reflect the foregoing approaches to student-centered learning and that also attempt to make the most of the opportunities afforded by information and communications technology. The focus in this chapter is on the design architecture of these approaches and not on the outcomes of their implementation for learning and teaching. Evidence of these can be found in their specific applications (see associated references cited in text).

Distributed Problem-Based Learning

Problem-based learning (PBL) is a widely used approach to learning and teaching that uses an instructional problem as the principal vehicle for learning and teaching. The analysis and study of this problem comprises several phases that are spread over periods of group work and individual study (Barrows & Tamblyn, 1980; Evensen & Hmelo, 2000; Schmidt, 1983). *Distributed problem-based learning* refers to the use of this strategy in a networked computer-supported collaborative learning environment (CSCLE) where face-to-face communication among participants is not essential (see Fig. 24.1). The process starts with the presentation of a problem via a case or vignette that could be presented to learners via the network (cf. Fig. 24.1: Presenting the problem). Next, learners work individually to engage in problem analysis. During this phase they generate explanations for the occurrence of the problem in this case (cf. Fig. 24.1: Expressing first perceptions of the problem). Based on this exercise they identify what they know and do not know about the problem at hand and make decisions about individual research (cf. Fig. 24.1: Exploring the problem and first perceptions). As the next step, this individual study is carried out and its results are reported to the group via the collaborative learning network. Following this, a reevaluation of the problem takes place and the first perceptions are probably revised (cf. Fig. 24.1: Revising first perceptions of the problem). All of this is followed up with the preparation and presentation of a critical reflection, which is a personal synthesis of the discussion that has ensued via the network (cf. Fig. 24.1: Preparing and posting a critical reflection record).

The bulk of the learning task in this model takes place in an electronic environment that is supported by computer-mediated communications technology (see Naidu & Oliver, 1996). For each one of the topics addressed in the course, the learning experience in this electronic environment may unfold in stages over a defined period such as four weeks. In the first week students are required to articulate their first perceptions of the problem as presented to them. They develop some hypotheses, which are their conjectures regarding the problem including its causes, effects, and possible solutions; outline how they were going to go about searching for evidence to support their hypotheses; and then collect that evidence. They "post" these comments on the electronic environment so that everyone can read others' approach to the understanding and resolution of the same problem. In the second week, after reading the initial reactions and comments of others on their own thoughts, students reexamine their first perceptions of the problem. They expand and refocus their conjectures regarding the problem and, if necessary, revise their hypotheses and data-gathering strategies and post these on the electronic environment. In the third week, as a result of the online discussions students would be able to identify new or related issues, revise their conjectures regarding the problem, and perhaps make modifications to their problem-resolution strategies. In the fourth week they prepare and present their own "critical reflection record" on the electronic environment. This comprises their final comment on the problem situation and how they sought to resolve it.

Critical Incident-Based Computer-Supported Collaborative Learning

There is growing interest in building learning environments that focus on supporting groups of learners engaged in reflection on critical incidents from their workplace (Wilson, 1996). A model of learning and instruction that embodies the essence of this focus is the "Critical incident-based computer supported collaborative learning" (see Fig. 24.2). It is so called because the model integrates reflection on and in action, collaborative learning, and computer-mediated communication into a holistic model of learning and instruction. This model of learning and instruction is inspired, *inter alia*, by knowledge of the fact that practitioners regularly encounter in the workplace critical incidences that present them with learning opportunities

Distributed Problem-Based Learning			
Presenting the problem on the CSCLE			
• Outline the problem situation and its attributes. • Describe the learning process, and define the learning task.			
Participants post their first perceptions of the problem on the CSCLE			
Issues	Hypotheses	Method	Data
Learners articulate their first perceptions of the problem	Learners state their conjectures about the problem	Learners identify and choose data collection strategy	Learners gather data and share this with their peers
Participants explore the problem and their first perceptions on the CSCLE			
Issues	Hypotheses	Method	Data
Learners explain and justify their first perceptions	Learners expand and focus their conjectures	Learners agree to revise their action plan if necessary	Learners gather additional data and share with peers
Participants may revise their first perceptions of the problem on the CSCLE			
Issues	Hypotheses	Method	Data
Learners identify any new or related issues to problem	Learners revise their conjectures re: the problems	Learners make adjustments to their action plan	Learners gather additional data and share with peers
Participants prepare and post a critical reflection record on the CSCLE			
In this last phase learners present a "critical reflection record" that synthesizes the discussion that has taken place on the computer-supported collaborative learning environment. This is more than a record of what transpired and reflects each person's understandings of the problem.			

FIG. 24.1.   Distributed Problem-Based Learning.

(see Naidu & Oliver, 1999). It serves to teach learners to recognize these critical incidences as learning opportunities, reflect on them critically while in action, and then finally share these reflections in a computer-supported-collaborative learning environment.

A critical incident (from the workplace) presents a learner with a learning opportunity to reflect *in* and *on* action. A learner can do this by keeping a *learning log*, which is a record of learning opportunities presented. The log records how one approaches the incident, successes and failures with it, and any issues that need to be resolved (e.g., things not fully understood or concepts that "didn't make sense"). The critical attribute of the learning log is that it concentrates on the process of learning. It is not a diary of events nor is it a record of work undertaken, rather it is a personal record of the occasions when learning occurred or could have occurred. The learning log also relates prior learning to current practice and is retrospective and reactive in action.

Learners engage in this process of critical incident-based learning in a phased manner. Phase one in the process comprises identifying a critical incident. Learners do this by identifying an incident from their workplace, which they consider as being significant to their roles. They describe the *what, when, where*, and *how* of this critical incident including its special attributes and more importantly the learning gain they derived from this incident. Phase two comprises

Critical Incident-Based Computer-Supported Collaborative Learning

Phase I: Identifying Critical Incident on CSCLE

Identify	Describe	Attributes	Learning
Learners identify an incident from their workplace, which they consider as being significant.	Learners describe this incident in terms of what happened, when, where, and how without revealing names and identities.	Learners identify the special attributes or aspects of this incident that sets it apart from all others in their experience.	Learners reflect on what happened to them in terms of the learning gain for them.

Phase II: Presenting Your Learning Log on CSCLE

Learners post their reflections (i.e., "learning logs") on the computer-supported learning environment. It should:

- help them remember what happened as part of that critical incident;
- explain to themselves and others reading it why they did what they did;
- evaluate their action and that of others who were involved in the incident;
- outline what they should or shouldn't have done, in retrospect;
- how they would behave given a similar incident in the future;
- describe what they believe they learned from that critical incident.

Phase III: Discussing the Learning Logs on CSCLE

Presenting their learning log, in the manner described, is the first task as part of this exercise. After learners have done that, they study carefully all the learning logs presented on the system by the other students.

Learners attempt to make insightful comments and observations on other's learning logs directly and by offering empathy, encouragement and helpful suggestions, both from their own knowledge base and their personal experiences.

Phase IV: Theory and Practice

This last phase has to do with learners making the connection between theory and practice.

This process should lead to a summary **Critical Reflection,** which should focus on the:

- extent to which learners feel that the theory helped them cope with the critical incident they encountered at work.
- adequacies and inadequacies of their theoretical knowledge with regard to their performance during that critical incident.
- enlightenment they may have gained from reflecting on the learning logs of their peers and the reflections of peers on their own learning logs.

FIG. 24.2. Critical Incident-Based Computer-Supported Collaborative learning.

the presentation of the learning log via the computer-mediated communication system. This log outlines to the group the critical nature of the incident and the reasons for the actions taken by the practitioner during the encounter with the incident. It includes reference to what should or shouldn't have been done and the learning gain derived from the incident. Phase three comprises the discussion of the learning logs posted on the systems by all students. Learners attempt to make insightful comments and observations about other's learning logs with the explicit intention of learning from the pool of experience that lies there in front of them in this shared electronic space.

Finally, phase four is about the coalescence of theory and practice, that is, bringing theory to bear upon practice and practice to inform theory. This last phase in the process has to do with learners making the connection between what they are being presented as part of their formal education and what they are being confronted with as a part of their daily work. This process leads to a summary reflection, which seeks to identify the extent to which learners feel that the theory enabled them to cope with the critical incident they encountered at their workplace. It also reflects the adequacies and inadequacies of their theoretical knowledge and any enlightenment learners may have gained from reflecting on the learning logs of their peers and from the reflections of others on their own learning logs.

Goal-Based Learning

A goal-based scenario (GBS) is essentially a simulation in which learners assume a main role in the pursuit of a mission or task associated with their main role in the scenario (Schank, 1990, 1997). In order to achieve this goal, the learner needs to acquire particular skills and knowledge. This is where the learning is taking place. Goals in this context refer to the successful completion of the task at hand, not the achievement of grades. A GBS serves both to motivate learners and also to give them the opportunity to "learn by doing." As long as a goal is of inherent interest to learners, and the skills needed to accomplish those goals are the targeted learning outcomes, we have a match and a workable GBS. The important idea here is that a GBS is organized around "performance" skills, and the result is a student who can perform the specified task (Schank & Cleary, 1995).

The intent of goal-based scenarios, such as the one presented in Fig. 24.3, is to present students with a contrived but an authentic scenario, which offers them an opportunity to learn by making mistakes in a safe environment (see Naidu, Oliver, & Koronios, 1999). Mistakes offer real opportunities for learning when these are accompanied by timely and potent feedback.

Clinical Decision Making in Nursing:		
A Goal-Based Scenario		
• **Goal**: The "goal" for the learner in this simulation is to deal with a crisis situation and develop an action plan for managing the patient's situation.		
Phase I: Case Encounter		
• Learners encounter the case at *handover* where they are explained its history and pathology.		
Phase II: Understanding Problem		
Precipitating event	**Identifying its causes**	**Managing the crisis**
Learner encounters the precipitating event.	Learner seeks to locate the causes of the precipitating event.	Learner attempts to deal with the crisis and contain it.
Phase III: Seeking Solutions		
Making decisions	**Listening to stories**	**Case-based reasoning**
Learners are required to make decisions about patient care.	They listen to experts and ask questions about their experiences.	Learners attempt to reason on the basis of the experts' stories.
Phase IV: At the Case Conference		
Raising issues	**Listening to stories**	**Developing care plan**
Learners explore new and related issues to the problem by reviewing sources of information.	They ask experts additional questions about their experiences.	Learners develop their final care plan based on experts' stories.
Phase V: Developing a Care Plan		
• Learners submit their care plan to the supervisor and receive feedback on their decision making.		

FIG. 24.3. Clinical Decision Making in Nursing Practice: A Goal-Based Scenario.

As learners enter the particular learning environment illustrated in Fig. 24.3, the learning context is explained, as is their "goal" within it, which is not the same as a learning outcome but a means to achieving one or more learning outcomes. Following this, users proceed to the *handover* (cf. Phase I: Case Encounter). This is a routine event in nursing practice, where nurses coming on for duty are brought up to date by their outgoing colleagues on the condition of patients who are in their care. After handover nurses move on to attend to routine nursing care activities and meeting patients' needs by administering medications and ensuring patients' comfort. Following the administration of antibiotics to one of their patients, users are met with a precipitating event. A precipitating event in this instance is an emergency situation that causes a chain of events. It requires nurses to make complex decisions under the pressure of time. In the first instance, the nurse must do everything that is necessary to manage the crisis situation before recommending a care plan. In order to do this, it is necessary to first understand the crisis situation, including its causes (cf. Phase II: Understanding the Problem). In order to arrive at a correct diagnosis, the nurse can access a whole range of information including documentation on hospital procedures/protocols and stories by expert practitioners (experienced nurses), which also comprise advice on appropriate procedures to follow or not to follow under such circumstances (cf. Phase III: Seeking Solutions).

Following this diagnosis nurses must take appropriate action to manage the crisis situation. A number of resources are available to users at this point for them to be able to make informed decisions about what are the appropriate actions to take in situations like this. These comprise electronic resources on anaphylaxis including intervention strategies and case studies of anaphylaxis. However, the most important resource that users have access to in this learning environment is the stories of experienced nurse practitioners. Users are able to make informed decisions after having listened to the experiences of expert practitioners. This kind of knowledge comes only with experience over many years and is not normally available in textbooks. Most e-learning environments fail to bring good stories to the learning context. Finally, when a draft care plan has been developed, users proceed to a case conference (cf. Phase IV–V: Case Conference–Developing Care Plan). This is a place where users have the opportunity to reflect upon their own care plans and those of others. There is the opportunity here to engage in questioning, critiquing, negotiating meanings, and commenting on alternative approaches of care that are deemed appropriate to the case.

Learning by Designing

Designing as a means for acquiring content knowledge is commonly used in practice-based disciplines such as engineering and architecture (Hmelo, Holton, & Kolodner, 2000; Newstetter, 2000). The obvious benefit of a design task is its inherent situatedness or authenticity. In design-based learning activities, students' understanding is "enacted" through the physical process of conceptualizing and producing something. The structures created, functions sought, and behaviors exhibited by the design solution also offer a means to assess knowledge of the subject matter. As such a student's conceptual understanding or misunderstanding of domain knowledge can be ascertained from that artifact. The failure of that artifact, for example, may suggest an incomplete understanding of the subject matter.

A big advantage of setting a design task as the basis for the study of the subject matter (such as *Designing the "Virtual Print Exhibition,"* see the next section) is the variety of cognitive tasks required to move from a conceptual idea to a product. These include *information gathering, problem identification, constraint setting, idea generation, modeling and prototyping,* and *evaluating.* These tasks represent complex learning activities in their own right, and when they become the environment in which knowledge of the subject matter is constructed, students have the opportunities to explore that content in the different phases and through different representations (see Naidu, Anderson, & Riddle, 2000).

> *Designing a "Virtual Print Exhibition" Activity.* The *National Gallery* is planning a major exhibition to celebrate the re-opening of its print room in 2003, for which they have received a grant of $100, 000. You and your colleagues have been asked to put together a *virtual exhibition* from the newly developed electronic database of old master print collection in the library. To accomplish this task, you will need to prepare a proposal in which you design, install, and curate an exhibition online, focusing on an appropriate theme of your choice. The director of the Gallery would like to see you put together a detailed plan with time lines and a budget with a detailed rationale before he or she can release the funds for you to begin work. The group with which you will work will have access to an asynchronous computer conference facility, to which you and your colleagues will be automatically subscribed. You must conduct all your planning activity using this medium. You should complete the concept of the proposal in five weeks and submit it for discussion and feedback from other curators in the gallery as well as the exhibition committee. You will also be required to present your team's proposal in a seminar to the director of the museum.

The complexity of design activities such as these makes them excellent vehicles for knowledge acquisition. Moreover, design complexity requires iterative activity toward better solutions that can support refinement of concepts. Design complexity also dictates the need for collaboration. A workable team possessing different kinds of knowledge and skills can tackle complexity more successfully than an individual. On student teams, one student might have good research skills, another domain knowledge, another drawing and representation skills, and another construction skills.

Web-Based Role-Play Simulation

Role-play simulations are situations in which learners take on the role profiles of specific characters in a contrived educational game. As a result of playing out these roles, learners are expected to acquire the intended learning outcomes as well as make learning enjoyable. While role-play is a commonly used strategy in conventional educational settings, it is less widely used in distributed Web-based learning environments. The technology is available now to support the conduct of role-play simulations on the Web (see Naidu, Ip, & Linser, 2000). The essential ingredients of a Web-based role-play simulation are a) goal-based learning; b) role-play simulation; and c) online Web-based communication and collaboration. Let us consider each one of these in turn.

First, goal-based learning is acknowledged as a strong motivator of learning. Typically, goal-based learning comprises a scenario or context that includes a trigger or a precipitating event. This event may be presented as a critical event and usually requires an immediate response from students. The second critical ingredient of this learning architecture is role-play, both in the sense of playing a role, playing with possibilities and alternative worlds, and playing to "have fun." Students are organized into teams to play out particular roles within the context of the given crises or situation. In order to play out their roles effectively they need to do research. The third critical ingredient of this learning architecture is the Web. The Web houses the virtual space for the role-play; it enables communication and collaboration among students and between the students and the facilitators. A role-play simulation generator enables the creator of the simulation to specify the roles that are central to the operation and the success of the role-play simulation (see Naidu, Ip, & Linser, 2000). This generator also enables the simulation creator to define tasks, create conferences, assign rights to participants in these conferences, as well as provide specific information and scaffolds to support the simulation.

CHALLENGES POSED BY E-LEARNING AND DIRECTIONS
FOR FURTHER RESEARCH

A great deal of work has been done in supporting students' learning with various types of technologies in open and flexible educational settings (see for example, Bates, 1990; Collis, 1996; and Khan, 1997). These authors survey several technologies including: print; radio; audio-cassettes; telephone; computer-based applications such as electronic databases and CD-ROMs; and computer-mediated communication technologies including e-mail, computer conferencing, bulletin boards, electronic document exchange and transfer, audio and video conferencing, broadcast television, and the Internet. Many of these technologies are ideal vehicles for content delivery and supporting communication, but in themselves, they are lacking in the capability to support or "scaffold" student learning activity in e-learning environments.

A *learning scaffold* is best described as a "transitional support strategy or mechanism" that is put in place to guide student learning in desirable directions or to enable the development of desirable cognitive skills in students. The expectation is that when the scaffold is removed from the learning context, the targeted skills become part of a learner's repertoire of learning skills. Parents or human teachers are excellent examples of learning scaffolds. Among other things, of course, they are there to provide advisement and support when these are most needed. At some point in the development of the child these types of supports are progressively removed and as such are no longer accessible or accessible to them only in limited ways. Children go on to live and function in society independently of the supports and advisement previously provided by their parents and teachers.

Similarly, learners in e-learning and open, distance, and flexible learning environments who often work independently with self-instructional study materials need help with the organization and management of resources as well as the skills to critically reflect on information they may have gathered. A considerable amount of work has gone on in supporting student learning with various types of cognitive tools and strategies in conventional technology-enhanced learning environments (see, for example, Gordin, Edelson, & Gomez, 1996; Scardamalia & Bereiter, 1994). Very little exists in the area of "cognitive support tools" for supporting student learning in e-learning and open, distance, and flexible technology-enhanced learning environments. Existing software-based cognitive tools provide support to students for learning in *face-to-face educational settings* where other forms of advisement and support are also available (see Scardamalia & Bereiter, 1991; Schauble, Raghaven, & Glaser, 1993). These support tools help learners organize their arguments for presentation and also guide them in their cognitive processes. They are, however, less effective in *e-learning* and *open, distance, and flexible educational settings* where learners do not have access to additional advisement and support.

Work on developing scaffolds for student learning activity in e-learning and open and flexible learning environments is sorely lacking. Existing work on supporting student learning with various types of learning and study strategies (see for instance the works of Weinstein & Mayer, 1986; Schon, 1987, Candy, 1991; Schmeck, 1988) suggest that the development of learning strategies (for example *learning how to learn*) can influence learner characteristics. These authors argue that employing these strategies and methods can help with the cognitive process, which in turn affects learning outcomes. They have identified several categories of learning strategies, namely *rehearsal, elaboration, organizational, self-monitoring*, and *motivational*. These strategies provide a pedagogically sound framework for supporting learning how to learn, and it is suggested here that they can also be used to guide work on scaffolding student learning in the contexts of e-learning, open, distance, and flexible learning environments.

REFERENCES

Barron, B. L., Schwartz, D. L., Vye, N. J., Moore, A., Petrosino, A., Zech, L., Bransford, J. D., & The Cognition and Technology Group at Vanderbuilt. (1998). Doing with understanding: Lessons from research on problem and project-based learning. *Journal of the Learning Sciences, 3/4,* 271–312.

Barrows, H. S., & Tamblyn, R. (1980). *Problem-based learning: An approach to medical education.* New York: Springer.

Bates, A. W. (1990). Media and technology in European distance education. In T. Bates (Ed.), *The EADTU Workshop on Media, Methods and Technology.* Heerlen, The Netherlands: European Association of Distance Teaching Universities.

Boshier, R., Mohapi, M., Moulton, G., Qayyaum, A., Sadownik, L., & Wilson, M. (1997). Best and worst dressed web courses: Strutting into the 21st century in comfort and style. *Distance Education, 18*(2), 327–349.

Brown, J. S., Collins, A., & Duguid, P. (1989). Situated cognition and the culture of learning. *Educational Researcher, 18*(1), 32–42.

Burgess. B., & Robertson, P. (1999). *Collaboration: How to find, design and implement collaborative internet projects.* http://www.bonuspoint.com/learnres.html#Anchor-Learning-49575. Saratoga, CA: BonusPoint, Inc.

Candy. P. C. (1991). *Self-direction for life-long learning.* San Francisco: Jossey-Bass.

Clark, R. E. (1983). Reconsidering research on learning from media. *Review of Educational Research, 53*(4), 445–460.

Collis, B. (1996). *Tele-learning in digital world: The future of distance learning.* London: International Thompson Computer Press.

Dede, C. (1991). The evolution of constructivist learning environments: Immersion in distributed, virtual worlds. In B. G. Wilson (Ed.), *Constructivist learning environments: Case studies in instructional design,* (pp. 165–175). Englewood Cliffs: NJ: Educational Technology Publications.

Dede, C. (1996). Emerging technologies and distributed learning. *American Journal of Distance Education, 10*(2), 4–36.

Dede, C. (2000). Emerging technologies and distributed learning in higher education. In D. Hanna (Ed.), *Higher education in an era of digital competition: Choices and challenges.* New York: Atwood.

Edelson, D. C., Gordin, D. N., & Pea, R. D. (1999). Addressing the challenges of inquiry-based learning through technology and curriculum design. *The Journal of the Learning Sciences, 8*(3&4), 391–450.

Edelson, D. C., & O'Neill, D. K. (1994). The CoVis collaboratory notebook: Supporting collaborative scientific inquiry. In *Recreating the revolution: Proceedings of the National Educational Computing Conference* (pp. 146–152). Eugene, OR: International Society of Technology in Education.

Edelson, D. C., Pea, R. D., & Gomez, L. (1996). The collaboratory notebook: Support for collaborative inquiry. *Communications of the ACM, 39,* 32–33.

Evensen, D. H., & Hmelo, C. E. (Eds.). (2000). *Problem-based learning: A research perspective on learning interactions.* Mahwah, NJ: Lawrence Erlbaum Associates, Inc.

French, D., Hale, C, Johnson, C., & Farr, G. (1999). *Internet based learning: An introduction and framework for higher education and business.* London, UK: Kogan Page.

Gomez, L. M., Gordin, D. N., & Carlson, P. (1995). A case study of open-ended scientific inquiry in a technology supported classroom. In J. Greer (Ed.), *Proceedings of AI-Ed '95, Seventh World Conference on Artificial Intelligence in Education* (pp. 17–24). Charlottesville, VA: Association for the Advancement of Computing in Education.

Goodyear, P. (2000 November 17th). What is e-learning? Unpublished Working paper, Center for Studies in Advanced Learning Technology. Lancaster University, Lancaster, England.

Gordin, D. N., Edelson, D. C., & Gomez, L. M. (1996). Scientific visualization as an interpretive and expressive medium. In D. C. Edelson & E. A. Domeshek (Eds.), *Proceedings of the International Conference on the Learning Sciences, July 1996, Evanston, IL* (pp. 409–414). Charlottesville, VA: Association for the Advancement of Computing in Education.

Gordin, D. N., Polman, J. L., & Pea, R. D. (1994). The climate visualizer: Sense-making through scientific visualization. *Journal of Science Education and Technology, 3,* 203–226.

Hmelo, C. E., Holton, D. L., & Kolodner, J. L. (2000). Designing to learn about complex tasks. *The Journal of the Learning Sciences, 9*(3), 243–246.

Khan, B. (1997). *Web-based instruction.* Englewood Cliffs, NJ: Educational Technology Publications, Inc.

Kirkwood, A. (2000). Learning at home with information and communications technologies. *Distance Education, 21*(2), 248–259.

Kozma, R. B. (1991). Learning with media. *Review of Educational Research, 61*(2), 179–211.

Naidu, S., Anderson, J., & Riddle, M. (2000). The virtual print exhibition: A case of learning by designing. In R. Sims, M. O'Reilly, & S. Sawkins, (Eds.), *Learning to choose: choosing to learn (Short papers and works in progress)* (pp. 109–114). Lismore, NSW: Southern Cross University Press.

Naidu, S., Ip, A., & Linser, R. (2000). Dynamic goal-based role-play simulation on the Web: A case study. *Educational Technology & Society, (3)*3, Available: http://ifets.ill.org/periodical/vol_3_2000/b05.html

Naidu, S., & Oliver, M. (1996). Computer supported collaborative problem-based learning (CSC-PBL): An instructional design architecture for virtual learning in nursing education. *Journal of Distance Education, XI*(2), 1–22.

Naidu, S., & Oliver, M. (1999). Critical incident-based computer supported collaborative learning. *Instructional Science: An International Journal of Learning and Cognition, 27*(5), 329–354.

Naidu, S., Oliver, M., & Koronios, A. (1999). Approaching clinical decision-making in nursing practice with interactive multimedia and case-based reasoning. *The Interactive Multimedia Electronic Journal of Computer Enhanced Learning* [Available online]: http://imej.wfu.edu/.

National Survey of Information Technology in Higher Education (1999). *Distance Learning in Higher Education*. Produced by the Institute for Higher Education Policy for the Council for Higher Education Accreditation. Encino, CA: The Campus Computing Project.

Newstetter, W. C. (2000). Guest editor's introduction. *The Journal of the Learning Sciences, 9*(3), 247–298.

Pea, R. D. (1994). Seeing what we build together: Distributed multimedia learning environments for transformative communications. *The Journal of the Learning Sciences, 3*(3), 285–299.

Pea, R. D., & Gomez, L. (1992). Distributed multimedia learning environments: Why and how? *Interactive Learning Environments, 2*(2), 73–109.

Rapaport, M. (1991). *Computer mediated communication*. New York: John Wiley & Sons, Inc.

Rosenberg, M. J. (2001). *E-learning: Strategies for delivering knowledge in the digital age*. New York: McGraw-Hill.

Rumble, G. (2000). Student support in distance education in the 21st Century: Learning from service management. *Distance Education, 21*(2), 216–235.

Scardamalia, M., & Bereiter, C. (1991). Higher levels of agency for children in knowledge building: A challenge for the design of new knowledge media. *The Journal of the Learning Sciences, 1,* 37–68.

Scardamalia, M., & Bereiter, C. (1994). Computer support for knowledge-building communities. *The Journal of the Learning Sciences, 3,* 265–283.

Schank, R. C. (1990). *Tell me a story*. Evanston, IL: Northwestern University Press.

Schank, R. (1997). *Virtual Learning: A revolutionary approach to building a highly skilled workforce*. New York: McGraw-Hill.

Schank, R. C., & Cleary, C. (1995). *Engines for Education*. Hillsdale, NJ: Lawrence Erlbaum Associates. http://www.ils.nwu.edu/~e_for_e/, Engines for Education ("hyper-book").

Schank, R., Fano, A., Jona, M., & Bell, B. (1994). The design of goal-based scenarios. *The Journal of the Learning Sciences, 3*(4), 305–345.

Schauble, L., Raghaven, K., & Glaser, R. (1993). The discovery and reflection notation: A graphical trace for supporting self-regulation in computer-based laboratories. In S. P. Lajoie & S. J. Derry (Eds.), *Computers as cognitive tools* (pp. 319–337). Hillsdale, NJ: Lawrence Erlbaum Associates.

Schellens, T., & Valcke, M. (2000). Re-engineering conventional university education: Implications for students' learning styles. *Distance Education, 21*(2), 361–384.

Schmeck, R. R. (Ed.). (1988). *Learning strategies and learning styles*. New York: Plenum Press.

Schmidt, H. G. (1983). Foundations of problem-based learning. Some explanatory notes. *Medical Education, 27,* 11–16.

Schon, D. A. (1983). *The reflective practitioner*. New York: Basic Books.

Schon, D. A. (1987). *Educating the reflective practitioner*. San Francisco: Josey-Bass.

Spiro, R. J., Feltovich, P. J., Jacobson, M. J., & Coulson, R. L. (1991). Cognitive flexibility, constructivism, and hypertext: Random access instruction for advanced knowledge acquisition in ill-structured domains. *Educational Technology, 31*(5), 24–33.

The Cognition and Technology Group at Vanderbilt. (1990). Anchored instruction and its relationship to situated cognition. *Educational Researcher, 19*(6), 2–10.

The Cognition and Technology Group at Vanderbilt. (1991). Technology and the design of generative learning environments. *Educational Technology, 31*(5), 34–40.

The United States Department of Education's National Center for Education Statistics. Washington, DC. (2000). *Quality on the line: Benchmarks for success in internet-based distance education*. Prepared by the Institute for Higher Education Policy. Washington, DC.

Weinstein, C. E., & Mayer, R. E. (1986). The teaching of learning strategies. In M. Wittrock (Ed.), *Handbook of research on teaching* (pp. 315–327). New York: Macmillan.

Wilson, B. G. (Ed.). (1996). *Constructivist learning environments: Case studies in instructional design*. Englewood Cliffs, NJ: Educational Technology Publications.

ACKNOWLEDGMENTS

The pedagogical approaches for optimizing e-learning that are presented in this chapter are being applied in several courses with the collaboration and enthusiastic support of the following colleagues: Mary Oliver <Mary.Oliver@unisa.edu.au> (Distributed problem-based learning; Critical incident- based computer-supported collaborative learning); Jaynie Anderson <j.anderson@finearts.unimelb.edu.au> (Learning by designing), Albert Ip <albert@DLS.au.com> and Roni Linser <ronilins@ariel.ucs.unimelb.edu.au> (Web-based role-play).

25

A Model of Web-Based Design
for Learning

Richard H. Hall
University of Missouri-Rolla
rhall@umr.edu

Steve E. Watkins
University of Missouri-Rolla
watkins@umr.edu

Vicky M. Eller
University of Missouri-Rolla
veller@umr.edu

In this chapter, we review a model that serves as a framework for the design of Web-based learning environments. The model consists of seven basic components: directionality, usability, consistency, interactivity, multimodality, adaptability, and accountability.

Figure 25.1 presents our framework for design of Web-based learning environments. Three themes guide this model. First, an overriding direction, taking into account learners, context, and goals, should be carefully and thoughtfully identified as a first step in design, and this should serve as a guide for all further development. This difficult but crucial first step is often left out, or is forgotten once further design and development proceed. The direction of all design, development, and assessment should flow directly from the theme delineated. Second, proper design is largely a matter of striking the proper balance between elements of simplicity and complexity. New designers have the tendency to overdo "bells and whistles," including superfluous multimedia components that don't contribute to the learning goals. On the other hand, seasoned designers often focus strictly on elements of simplicity, usability, and consistency, sacrificing dynamic and interactive components that could potentially enhance learning within the context of the objectives. We argue that effective design is a delicate balance between these two contrasting positions. Third, evaluation and assessment are basic parts of any design process, both formative and summative. Without this accountability component a designer never really knows how effective a given Web-based learning environment is, and there is no mechanism for improvement in future design. This framework, which can serve as a guide for the design and development of Web-based learning environments, will also serve as the framework for further discussion in this chapter.

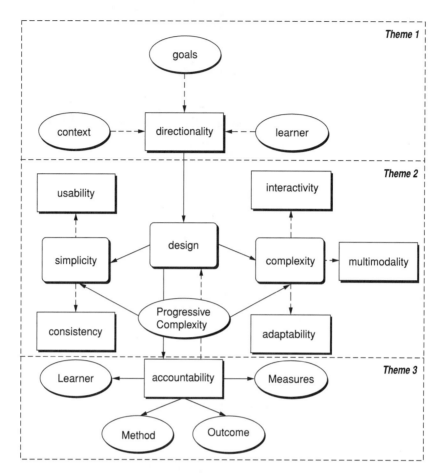

FIG. 25.1. Web Design for Learning Model. (Squares represent the seven basic components of the model.)

DIRECTIONALITY

A fundamental principle of instructional design for computer-based and Web-based instruction is that thoughtful planning should proceed development. There is no question that this first step of developing an overriding direction, and developing a model for how to best translate this to the learner using Web-based multimedia as a tool, is the most important step in the design and development process. Unfortunately, the process of analyzing the audience (i.e., the learners), of defining the usage context, and of defining the learning goals is often overlooked.

The developer must take into account the intended audience for the learning environment to be developed effectively. With respect to learners, research indicates that the most important factor in hypermedia performance is knowledge and experience (Lanza & Roselli, 1991; Dillon & Weston, 1996; Dillon & Gabbard, 1998). Of course, one advantage of Web-based instruction is that the software can be adapted to the learner in various ways and this is discussed in the following adaptation section. However, as a general rule of the thumb, a straightforward and consistent navigational structure will aid users who are less knowledgeable and experienced. Hypermedia research has consistently shown that low-ability novice users can become easily disoriented without clear guidance and consistency, while more advanced learners can benefit from the flexibility of a more complex navigational design (Shin, Schallert, & Savenye, 1994; Dillon & Gabbard, 1998). However, this is not to say that all complex design elements, discussed later, will most strongly benefit the expert user. On the contrary, some elements of complexity such as the use of multimedia simulation and interactivity may be particularly effective for novices. Another popular set of learning variables that can be taken into account are learning styles (Gardner, 1993, 1994; Sternberg, 1997). However, it's important to note that there is little experimental evidence that tailoring instruction to learning styles is effective (Pittenger, 1993; Brooks, 1997).

Web-based learning should be designed differently depending on the learning context or environment. One of the most fundamental context factors in Web-based instruction is the setting (i.e., distance versus face to face). Although the purpose of this book is to provide guidance for distance educators, it is important to note that at this time there are still many more students learning in traditional face-to-face settings, and the Web is also often used as an adjunct for these classes. Further, hybrid approaches that involve a mixture of face-to-face and distance approaches can also be effective (Horton, 2000). The important point, for the Web-based instructional designer, is that the design of the class materials should differ signficantly for these different approaches. It is generally not a good practice to simply use materials designed for an entirely distance class as support for a face-to-face class, or vice versa. For example, materials for a class to be taught completely at a distance should contain more specific content and should be more self-contained. Further, those who are designing for a purely distance class should use download of intensive media more sparingly, since the chances are students will be relying more on slower Internet connections.

Although a designer must consider the audience and the context in which Web-based learning will take place, the most important factors in guiding the whole process of design and development are the learning goals. The goals of learning should be clear to the designer, and these should then be communicated to the learner. Of course real learning is more than simply memorizing facts, hence the learning goals should involve some sort of application and/or integration of foundational knowledge. The "problem-based scenario" method, developed by Roger Schank (Schank & Cleary, 1995), is an example of a starting point that will lead to the development of effective modules. The first task for a designer, within the problem-based scenario approach, is to identify target skills to be learned and the rest of the scenario develops from there.

DESIGN FACTORS

Once the overriding pedagogical plan for a given module or set of modules has been identified, a more detailed plan for the Web-based learning environment is formulated. This process is basically one of balancing design components of simplicity and complexity. On one hand it is important that the designer create a module that is easy to navigate, downloads quickly, and includes only the most fundamental information. On the other hand, it is equally important that the designer create a rich and meaningful learning experience, which often requires dynamic and interactive media components that interfere with the usability of a module. In terms of the learner, the objective is to provide an experience that is novel, rich, and creative enough to keep the learner engaged and interested, while at the same time creating an environment that is user-friendly enough to keep the learner from becoming overwhelmed and frustrated in such a way that it interferes with learning.

Simplicity

Usability.   Within the context of our model, usability simply refers to all those factors in the software design that make the experience for the learner simpler and stress free. Technical problems and download time can prove to be particularly important in a Web-based environment. In fact, much of the literature that currently exists on Web design focuses on the importance of usability and simplicity of design. This is perhaps most dramatically represented by "Usability Guru" Jacob Nielsen, who advocates Web design devoid of bells and whistles, including graphics unless they are absolutely essential (Nielsen, 2000). For example, in his list of top ten mistakes in Web design, number two is "Gratuitous Use of Bleeding Edge Technology" (Nielsen, 1996). The focus of Nielsen's advice is for corporate sites when the goal is for the user to get information simply and quickly or to transact some business, so his views are not completely germane with respect to Web-based learning.

Other common advice from those with experience in instructional Web design focus on the need for simplicity in design. For example:

- Text presented on a given page should be limited (Cotrell & Eisenberg, 1997; Jones & Farquhar, 1997);
- Scrolling should be avoided (Shotsberger, 1996);
- Graphics and multimedia should be used only when they directly support the materials and serve a clear instructional purpose (DeBra, 1996; Cotrell & Eisenberg, 1997; Everhart, 1997); and
- Design components that increase download time should be limited as much as possible (Cotrell & Eisenberg, 1997).

Consistency.   Within our design model, the term *consistency* refers to the simplicity of the higher order design elements of site organization. One of the fundamental advantages of hypertext is the potential for representing complex knowledge via multiple associative links (Frick, Corry, & Bray, 1997; Reeves & Reeves, 1997). Unfortunately, the large amount of freedom and control that this allows the learner may be detrimental for the novice learner (Large, 1996; Niemiec, Sikorski, & Walberg, 1996). In fact, there is a surprising amount of research with hypertext systems that indicates that including too much learner freedom can, contrary to expectations, decrease learning effectiveness (Large, 1996; Niemiec et al., 1996). This is not so surprising when one considers how complex, and novel, is the hyperspace for the average learner. This phenomenon has led to the phrase "lost in hyperspace" (Nielsen & Lyngbaek, 1990; Burbules & Callister, 1996). For this reason, one of the most important design principles, which is supported both by Web-designer–published experiences and by research on hypertext learning environments, is that the learner should be provided with guidance (Jacobson, Maouri, Punyashloke, & Christopher, 1995; Smith, Newman, & Parks, 1997).

There are a number of ways that the Web-based-training designer can combat the "lost in hyperspace" problem and provide the learner with some guidance. The first method is to create a clear and systematic organization scheme for the learning site (Schneiderman & Kearsley, 1987; DeBra, 1996). The usual/prototypical path through the pages should be obvious (Goldberg, 1997), and the information should be in a modular fashion within a well-structured hierarchy (Smith et al., 1997; Young & Watkins, 1997). In this same vein the main points should be obvious to the learner (Shotsberger, 1996). A clear organization also includes consistency in design across all the pages of a site (Shotsberger, 1996; Cotrell & Eisenberg, 1997; Everhart, 1997; Young & Watkins, 1997). The pages within a given site should not greatly differ in appearance within the same site and certainly within the same-level sections. The learner should be immediately aware if a hyperlink takes him or her outside the designer's site.

Complexity

Interactivity.   Interactivity is probably one of the most commonly used terms in discussions of computer-based instruction of all sorts. This is not surprising given that there is a large body of educational research indicating that learners learn most effectively when they are activity engaged in learning, as opposed to passively reading or listening (Brooks, 1997). Most of us recognize this intuitively, based on our own learning experience, despite the fact that so much of education involves passive techniques such as lecture. One of the great promises of computer-based and Web-based instruction is that it can potentially facilitate the process of integrating activity into education. Interactive components of Web-based software are those that require that the learner carry out some activity besides simply reading or listening. Hypertext, such as the World Wide Web, is well suited for increasing activity in that just requiring that the learner click through pages of hypertext in a nonlinear fashion demands a level of activity greater than traditional textbook/linear reading. More complex and rich activity can be added by requiring that the learners answer questions, locate specific information, research topics, and even create their own stories and scenarios.

Multimodality.   Another fundamental potential advantage of Web-based instructional tools in comparison to traditional text formats is that the Web offers the possibility of presenting materials in multiple (i.e., audio, visual, textual) modalities. A basic premise of cognitive flexibility theory, a popular theory of complex learning, is that students learn complex information most effectively if they are allowed to experience the information in various formats (Jacobson & Spiro, 1995). Further, basic cognitive research in multimedia learning indicates that dynamic simulations in combination with audio can be particularly effective for increasing student learning, so long as the audio is directly related to the information to be learned (Moreno & Mayer, 2000). It is also true that integrating rich and dynamic multimedia into the learning experience can increase student interest and motivation (Smith & Jones, 1989).

Dynamic multimedia on the Web should not be simply a matter of transferring the classroom lecture to a computer screen (Horton, 2000). This is important, since video distance education is now being transferred to the Web in many cases, and the easy strategy is simply to use the necessary video compression and transfer the videos to the Web. Despite the compression techniques, this approach is download intensive and often requires additional plug-ins. Further, this does not capture the personal nature of face-to-face lectures anyway. In short, it does not take advantage of the unique properties of the Web. Instead, the presentation can be redesigned to take advantage of the strengths of the Web format for enhancing learning. First, the lectures can be broken down into small segments and a front, back, and pause button can be added to provide the leaner with control and flexibility. Second, instead of just showing the learner the lecture simply as a "talking head," relevant dynamic graphics can be interspersed throughout the lecture that provide the learner with multiple representations and a framework for the lecture.

Adaptability.   Besides the term interactivity, the term *adaptability* is probably the most commonly heard word when educational Web designers are describing the learning environments they have created. One reason for the popularity of the term is that, within the educational community at large, the notion of tailoring learning to a student's preferred learning style has become a popular goal. Moreover, one of the great potential strengths of instructional hypermedia is that the instruction can be tailored to the learner in a number of ways. First, the learner can select a preferred format. For example, auditory learners could select audio instruction. Second, the Web module itself could collect information based on the learner's response to learning styles questionnaires, navigation patterns, or assessment performance. Unfortunately, although the idea of tailoring instruction to multiple learning styles has a lot of intuitive appeal, the efficacy of such an approach has very little support in the research (Pittenger, 1993; Brooks, 1997). Further, there is the fact that the creation of many versions of the same module is certainly going to require additional time and resources. Rather than creating learning environments that adapt to students' learning styles or preferences, a more promising approach is to adapt learning to students' skills and abilities, in that there is evidence that student ability is the single most important individual factor in determining students' performance with instructional hypermedia (Lanza & Roselli, 1991; Dillon & Weston, 1996; Dillon & Gabbard, 1998).

Progressive Complexity

The instructional Web designer is often faced with a dilemma due to the conflicting need to introduce simplicity and complexity into the Web-based learning environment. On one hand the designer can create a site that is primarily text, simple to navigate, and straightforward in content presentation. On the other hand, the designer can create a site rich in interactive multimedia, with elaborate demonstrations and simulations. The former is user-friendly in that the site is highly usable and consistent, while the latter may very likely result in more effective learning, particularly for the novice who might require more elaborate content representation. One potentially effective method of addressing this dilemma is to present the user with multiple versions of the content in a progressively complex manner, from the simplest and most usable to the most complex and interactive (a method we refer to as "progressive complexity"). The more complex versions are displayed only if the more simple displays do not result in effective learning. The criteria for effective learning can be based on the learner's own perception or based on some embedded assessment and system feedback. In this case, the more complex versions would be presented if the learner did not pass some base-line assessment criterion. Thus, the additional download and usability cost associated with more elaborate displays come into play only if truly necessary. (Figure 25.2 depicts a progressive complexity design with three levels of complexity.)

Accountability

The ideal assessment model consists of multiple methodological and measurement methodologies. In this section we introduce four important characteristics of a thorough assessment model—learner variables, experimental methodology, outcomes, and measures.

Learner Variables.   Assessment studies should take into account learner variables in order to control for learner differences and in order to examine the interaction of individual differences with Web-based modules in student performance. For example, as mentioned earlier, students who are more experienced and knowledgeable may benefit more from modules where there is an emphasis on complexity in design. As we pointed out in the adaptability section, there

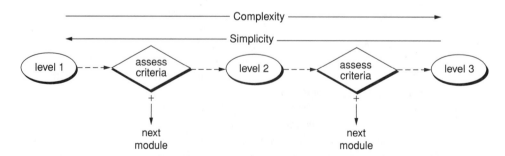

FIG. 25.2. Progressive Complexity Design with 3 Levels of Complexity.

is evidence that student expertise is the most important factor in accounting for differences in performance with educational hypermedia (Lanza & Roselli, 1991; Dillon & Weston, 1996; Dillon & Gabbard, 1998). Although learning styles appear to play a less important role in determining performance with instructional hypermedia, it is our view that inventories based on Sternberg's thinking styles (Sternberg, 1997) and Gardner's multiple intelligences (Gardner, 1993, 1994) theories have the most theoretical and empirical support. There is evidence that the dimensions measured by inventories based on these theories can be important factors in how a given student learns most effectively (Gardner, 1994; Sternberg, 1997).

Experimental Methodology. An ideal assessment program will employ four basic experimental methodologies, applied in a progressive fashion from formative to summative, as the program moves from design to development to application. In stage 1, software and instructional design evaluation, design is evaluated before the development of any software begins. Basic research constitutes the second stage. During this stage, research on basic components of the educational innovations is carried out with relatively small samples of students. In these experiments a researcher/designer is freer to employ systematic and controlled experiments that focus on specific components of software design and also to solicit more detailed qualitative protocol from study participants. During the applied levels of research it is often difficult to use control groups for pragmatic and ethical reasons. In addition, it is difficult to do controlled comparison studies in applied studies due to methodological complications (Hall, Watkins, & Ercal, 2000). The third stage, applied research, consists of research conducted within the context of actual learning environments. Initially, this can be carried out using prototype modules or series of modules. This will allow for assessment of specific modules and design factors within the context of classes and allows summative assessment to begin before all development is completed. Finally, applied summative evaluation can be carried out on the "final product" within the context of the learning environment for which it was intended.

Outcomes. Important outcomes to be considered across experiments are learners' attitudes, problem solving, and conceptual knowledge. Attitudes to be considered are variables such as course satisfaction, motivation, and perception of knowledge gained. Problem solving is assessed, both in terms of traditional computation problems and more advanced application problems. Finally, conceptual knowledge is assessed. Conceptual knowledge can be viewed as the recognition of structural relationships among course concepts and the ability to apply this integrative knowledge to novel problems. This type of structural knowledge is a defining characteristic of expertise across science and technology domains (Glaser & Bassok, 1989; Royer, Cisero, & Carlo, 1993).

Measures. Outcomes are assessed using subjective (qualitative and quantitative) problem solving (basic and higher level) and pathfinder associative networks measures. The subjective measures are used to assess students' attitudes, motivation, and perception of knowledge gained. The qualitative measures consist of open-ended narrative questions, and the subjective-quantitative items consist of Likert-scale (agree-disagree) statements. Questions and items are developed as appropriate depending on the goals of a given experiment. Problem-solving measures can range from fairly simple computation problems with clear right and wrong answers to advanced/higher level problem-solving items that require students to integrate multiple concepts and to apply these concepts to novel "real-life" problems. One of the most effective and well-researched ways to measure knowledge interconnectivity is via Schvaneveldt's Pathfinder associative networks approach (Schvaneveldt, 1990; Johnson, Goldsmith, & Teague, 1995), in which students rate the similarity of concepts, and a knowledge space is created using graphing techniques, which is subsequently compared to a prototype expert knowledge space.

REFERENCES

Brooks, D. W. (1997). *Web-teaching: A guide to designing interactive teaching for the World Wide Web*. New York: Plenum Press.

Burbules, N. C., & Callister, T. A. (1996). Knowledge at the crossroads: Some alternative futures of hypertext learning environments. *Educational Theory, 46*, 23–50.

Cotrell, J., & Eisenberg, M. B. (1997). Web design for information problem-solving: Maximizing value for users. *Computers in Libraries, 17*(5), 52–57.

DeBra, P. M. (1996). *Hypermedia structures and systems*. Retrieved from the World Wide Web: http://wwwis.win.tue.nl:8001/2L690.

Dillon, A., & Gabbard, R. (1998). Hypermedia as an educational technology: A review of the quantitative research literature on learner comprehension, control, and style. *Review of Educational Research, 68*, 322–349.

Dillon, A., & Weston, C. (1996). User analysis HCI—The historical lessons from individual differences research. *International Journal of Human-Computing Studies, 45*, 619–638.

Everhart, N. (1997). Web page evaluation: Views from the field. *Technology Connection, 4*, 24–26.

Frick, T. W., Corry, M., & Bray, M. (1997). Preparing and managing a course web site: Understanding systematic change in education. In B. H. Khan (Ed.), *Web-based instruction*. Englewood Cliffs, NJ: B. H. Khan. 431–436.

Gardner, H. (1993). *Frames of mind: The theory of multiple intelligences*. (10th anniv. ed.). Basic Books. New York, New York.

Gardner, H. (1994). *Multiple intelligences: The theory in practice*. Basic Books.

Glaser, R., & Bassok, M. (1989). Learning theory and the study of instruction. *Annual Review of Psychology, 40*, 631–666.

Goldberg, M. W. (1997). CALOS: First results from an experiment in computer-aided learning. *Proceedings of the ACM's 28th SIGCSE Technical Symposium on Computer Science Education*. 48–52.

Hall, R. H., Watkins, S. E., & Ercal, F. (2000, April). *The horse and the cart in web-based instruction: Prevalence and efficacy*. Paper presented at the annual meeting of the American Educational Research Association, New Orleans, LA.

Horton, W. (2000). *Designing Web-based training*. New York: Wiley & Sons, Inc.

Jacobson, M. J., Maouri, C., Punyashloke, M., & Christopher, K. (1995). Learning with hypertext learning environments: Theory, design, and research. *Journal of Educational Multimedia and Hypermedia, 4*, 321–364.

Jacobson, M. J., & Spiro, R. J. (1995). Hypertext learning environments, cognitive flexibility, and the transfer of complex knowledge: An empirical investigation. *Journal of Educational Computing Research, 12*, 301–333.

Johnson, P. J., Goldsmith, T. E., & Teague, K. W. (1995). Similarity, structure, and knowledge: A representational approach to assessment. In P. E. Nichols & S. F. Chipman (Ed.), *Cognitively diagnostic assessment* (pp. 221–249). Hillsdale, NJ: P. E. Nichols and S. F. Chipman.

Jones, M. G., & Farquhar, J. D. (1997). User interface design for Web-based instruction. In B. H. Khan (Ed.), *Web-based instruction*. Englewood Cliffs, NJ: B. H. Khan.

Lanza, A., & Roselli, T. (1991). Effects of the hypertextual approach versus the structured approach on active and passive learners. *Journal of Computer-Based Instruction, 18*, 48–50.

Large, A. (1996). Hypertext instructional programs and learner control: A research review. *Education and Information, 14*, 96–106.

Moreno, R., & Mayer, R. E. (2000). A coherence effect in multimedia learning: The case for minimizing irrelevant sounds in the design of multimedia instructional messages. *Journal of Educational Psychology, 92*, 117–125.

Nielsen, J. (1996). *Top ten mistakes in web design. Alertbox, 5*. Retrieved May 23, 2000, from the World Wide Web: http://www.useit.com/alertbox/9605.html.

Nielsen, J. (2000). *Designing web usability: The practice of simplicity*. Indianapolis, IN: New Riders Publishing.

Nielsen, J. & Lyngbaek, U. (1990). Two field studies of hypermedia usability. In C. Green & R. McAleese (Ed.), *Hypertext: Theory into practice II*. Intellect Press, Oxford, 64–72.

Niemiec, R. P., Sikorski, C., & Walberg, H. J. (1996). Learner-control effects: A review of reviews and a meta-analysis. *Journal of Educational Computing Research, 15*, 157–174.

Pittenger, D. J. (1993). The utility of the Myers-Briggs type indicator. *Review of Educational Research, 63*, 467–488.

Reeves, T. C., & Reeves, P. M. (1997). Effective dimensions of interactive learning on the world wide web. In B. H. Khan (Ed.), *Web-based instruction*. Englewood Cliffs, NJ: B. H. Khan.

Royer, J., Cisero, C., & Carlo, M. (1993). Techniques and procedures for assessing cognitive skills. *Review of Educational Research, 63*, 201–243.

Schank, R. C., & Cleary, C. (1995). *Engines for education*. Mahwah, NJ: Lawrence Erlbaum.

Schneiderman, B., & Kearsley, G. (1987). User interface design for the hyperties electronic encyclopedia. *Proceedings 1st ACM Conference on Hypertext*, 184–194.

Schvaneveldt, R. W. (1990). *Pathfinder associative networks: Studies in knowledge organization*. Norwood, NJ: Ablex Publishing Corp.

Shin, E., Schallert, D., & Savenye, C. (1994). Effects of learner control, advisement, and prior knowledge on young students' learning in a hypertext environment. *Educational Technology Research and Development, 42*, 33–46.

Shotsberger, P. G. (1996). Instructional uses of the world wide web: Exemplars and precautions. *Educational Technology, 36*(2), 47–50.

Smith, P. A., Newman, I. A., & Parks, L. M. (1997). Virtual hierarchies and virtual networks: Some lessons from hypermedia usability research applied to the World Wide Web. *Journal of Human-Computer Studies, 47*, 67–95.

Smith, S. G., & Jones, L. L. (1989). Images, imagination, and chemical reality. *Journal of Chemical Education, 66*, 8–11.

Sternberg, R. (1997). *Thinking styles*. Cambridge, MA: Cambridge University Press.

Young, F. L., & Watkins, S. E. (1997, April). *Electronic communication for educational and student organizations using the world wide web*. Paper presented at the annual Midwest Section Conference of the American Society for Engineering Education, Columbia, MO.

26

Distance Education and the Role of Academic Libraries

Susan McKnight

Deakin University, Australia

suemck@deakin.edu.au

The role of the academic library in support of distance education has been long-standing and pivotal in assisting students to succeed in their learning endeavours. Over the past 100 years, however, the role has changed radically and the future will see even more significant change as increased emphasis is placed on providing online learning and teaching environments.

This chapter does not seek to provide a history of library services for distance education students. Historical and comparative information on the development of library services for distance education students may be found in Slade and Kascus (1996), Small (1997), and Brophy and Craven (1998). Rather it focuses on the library's direct link with learning and teaching at a distance and how this link is becoming more and more explicit. The research focuses, primarily, on the changing and expanding role of the academic library in Australian higher education and especially at Deakin University, which has been involved in distance education since its inception in 1974. However, references are drawn from experiences and trends elsewhere.

The basic philosophy behind library services for distance education students is that off-campus students have the right to expect the same level of service and access to resources as on-campus students to help them succeed in their university endeavours. Libraries are in existence, not just to be the custodians of bibliographic material but to "help people teach and learn," which is the purpose statement of the Deakin University Library (see http://www.deakin.edu.au/library/). This philosophy has seen the development of library services, from the rudimentary provision of books to distance education students attending lectures in regional and rural venues away from the home university campus, to the full partnership between librarian and academic to ensure that students can gain information literacy skills and access information resources pertinent to their discipline in the course of their learning.

THE PAST

Few institutions of higher education would argue against the notion that the library plays a key role in the academic mission of the university. It is part of the fabric of higher education and maintains a high profile on the university campus. However, when discussing the role of the library in distance education, its pivotal place has not always been assumed by the library or recognized by university management, either in the traditional delivery of information resources to students or in the benefit of a closer liaison between librarian and academic staff in developing courses for distance education delivery and planning learning support.

The primary role of the distance education library has been to provide bibliographic and resource materials, principally books, to students who were studying off campus. In the early days of distance education in Australia (from 1911 to the 1940s), books were carried in sturdy suitcases and delivered to students at study centers by academic staff who were visiting to provide a lecture (Crocker, 1987). As external studies departments developed curricula that could be studied without attendance at regular lectures, and more and more students studied in this mode, many library services moved to postal delivery directly to students or placed selected textbooks at regional public libraries for the use of distance education students. Over time, courier services, replacing or supplementing postal services, were used to guarantee a faster delivery of library materials.

The number of students studying via distance education was relatively small. However, by 1949, The University of Queensland, a pioneer in distance education since 1911, established the Thatcher Memorial Library, with a library collection to support students studying in the University's External Studies Unit. Often the resources available for students were confined to the specialist collections of such external studies libraries, but over time, distance education students have been able to avail themselves of the full range of library services and collections in their particular university library system. Before the full range of services to distance education students were mainstreamed, requests for interlibrary loans and online literature searches were often referred from the specialist external studies library to the central library, thus creating a "second-class" status for the library staff involved in the distance education facility (Crocker, 1987). This had a detrimental impact on the relationship between external studies libraries and the faculty staff that they served, as well as with the distance education students. Over time, Australian universities incorporated their external studies collections into the mainstream library service and this problem of perception was overcome and distance education students benefited from the broader collection and increasing range of services available to them.

The first survey on Australian and overseas library services for distance education students was conducted by Store (1981). A second Australian survey was conducted in 1986 (Bundy, 1988). Together with the results of these surveys, discussions in the library literature of the 1980s focused on the need to provide a basic level of library service to distance education students by the home institution, highlighting the special needs of these students and the deficiencies in the existing level of service provision. Institutions of higher education were beginning to take seriously their responsibilities for supporting distance education students, including the necessary library support, rather than focusing solely on the academic program. At Deakin University, for instance, it has been a guiding philosophy that "students have rights." "Translated into the library's services, all students, regardless of mode of study, have the right to expect a similar level of library service and support. Therefore, the off-campus library service aims to ensure remote students have similar opportunities to make reference inquiries, borrow books, obtain journal articles, and undertake independent research as do on-campus students." (McKnight, 1998, p. 54).

Despite this, many distance education students, at least in Australia, used the resources of other libraries or used their home library in person. Visiting the library in person is often the preferred method of gaining access to library services for those students who, although enrolled in distance education mode, are in fact not geographically remote to their university. For the truly remote student, visiting a library in their local community can be a viable option. Indeed, it was found that many part-time distance education research-level students at Deakin

University are staff members of other higher education institutions and, therefore, had access to library collections and services where they were employed (Macauley & McKnight, 1998). This situation would not be unique to Deakin University.

Up until the late 1990s, there appeared to be no explicit link between learning and teaching and library services, whether for on-campus or off-campus students. The library was a separate organizational unit on the campus, often linked to a specific discipline or range of disciplines and not seen as part of the traditional teaching process. The only library activities related to the learning and teaching process were liaison with academic staff about the items cited on reading lists for off-campus students and for negotiating opportunities, usually at residential schools, for information literacy training to be provided by the library for distance education students. In 1978, the role of External Studies Librarian of Townsville's College of Advanced Education in North Queensland stressed the following functions:

1. To act as an identifiable person to whom students can confidently write or phone concerning bibliographical and resource materials problems;
2. To liaise with external studies lecturers on all matters of resource provision for external students;
3. To meet with students to discuss problems, provide reader education programs;
4. To prepare guides for external students;
5. To develop and review policies of resource provision. (Crocker, 1987)

These functional statements represented the norm, but the situation is changing.

THE PRESENT

Distance education has gained in respectability over the years. Curran states, "It can be said that distance teaching at university level is now a substantive and well established component of higher education in a wide range of countries and continues to expand at a significant rate" (Curran, 1995). In Australia, the environment has moved dramatically from when only a few institutions were charged with the responsibility of providing tertiary education opportunities to students who were remote from the (predominately) metropolitan universities. Today, most if not all universities engage in some form of distance education, particularly using information technology to deliver online curriculum and support. Based on sound pedagogy and learning theory, distance education is now accepted as a viable and sound alternative to face-to-face tuition. It also offers learning opportunities to students who, for whatever reason, choose not to study on campus.

As the reputation of distance learning has improved over time, so too has the profile of students changed. In the 1980s, distance education students were older, and mostly part-time, and used libraries for reference services as well as for the delivery of books (Winter & Cameron, 1983). Today, using Deakin University as an example, approximately 55 percent (15,000 people) of the total enrolments are off-campus students or mixed mode students who are studying a combination of on- and off-campus subjects (Deakin University. Planning Unit, 2000). The profile is of younger students, especially in mixed mode studies, who combine full-time study, part-time work to pay for their studies, and their social life. These students demand more flexible learning packages, increasingly online, that are supportive of their learning needs. The library has had to address the new demands of these students. It has done so by becoming a partner in the learning and teaching process.

Today, the library is breaking away from its physical boundaries and supporting students wherever they are, whether on or off campus. With the increasing use of technology, the traditional communication and delivery mechanisms used by libraries of telephone, facsimile, post, and courier are supplemented by electronic mail, computer conferencing, and instructional management system and World Wide Web (WWW) interfaces. The distinction between on- and off-campus students is irrelevant as access to an ever-increasing range of library resources and services is delivered via the Web. On-campus students, using either library or general computing laboratory workstations, access the myriad of library services and information resources available online, which were aimed, initially, at supporting distance learners. At Deakin University Library, it was found that all users, whether off-campus students nationally or internationally, academic staff, or on-campus students, benefit from improving access and delivery for off-campus students and mainstreaming these services (McKnight, 1998).

In recognition that students could live anywhere in Australia, the Council of Australian University Librarians introduced a national reciprocal borrowing scheme in July 2001. Under this scheme, students and academic staff from all universities that are members of the Australian Vice-Chancellors Committee can borrow books in person from any university library. Prior to this, most states had local reciprocal borrowing schemes, but only for staff and students from universities in that state. Therefore, students studying at a university in another state could not automatically gain borrowing privileges from local university libraries. This level of cooperation took a long time to achieve as an Australian university library national reciprocal borrowing scheme was first mooted in 1980.

As universities move more subjects online, from the student's perspective, the distinction is blurred as to where the curriculum ends and the information support services of a library begin. Today, the library is beginning to work in partnership with teams of curriculum designers, educational developers, graphic designers, and academic staff to ensure that online learning environments take into consideration both the explicit curriculum content and the supporting information resources at the design stage. This is a significant shift in the role of the librarian in the academic library. To make learning in the online environment as rich and as seamless as possible, it is no longer best practice to simply link to the library's home page from a subject home page. Rather, the specific information resources, regardless of where these are physically or virtually located, need to be built into the learning environment from the outset.

In addition, information literacy skills, such as the ability to discover, evaluate, and manage information resources, need to be included in the curriculum. Libraries have, for a long time, been involved in the delivery of reader education or information literacy classes to students (and academic staff). Students would come to the library on a voluntary basis to attend reader education classes. Increasingly, these forms of instruction have been, or are being considered, for inclusion in the formal part of the curriculum. The level of inclusion varies from institution to institution and ranges from librarians delivering information literacy instruction as part of a formal class or tutorial with or without an assessment of what has been learnt to information literacy becoming an assessable part of the subject being studied.

Libraries became involved in online training in the 1990s, often in response to the need to provide information literacy training for distance education students. It was of concern to librarians and academic staff that these students were not benefiting from the on-campus reader education classes that help equip on-campus students with the skills required for independent research and study. With today's emphasis on lifelong learning and the attainment of generic skills that equip a student for the workforce and continued self-paced study, information literacy skills are a must.

An example of a WWW-based library catalog tutorial can be found at http://www.deakin.edu. au/library/tutorials/smartsearcher/. This tutorial was designed with the assistance of educational developers and academic staff and was tested on a group of students before finalization. In this way, librarians were demonstrating the same professional characteristics of traditional educators in the design of curriculum material and learning environments.

One of the implications that result from the changing role of the librarian, from being a custodian of books to being a true partner in learning and teaching, is the need for librarians to have more formal skills in educational and learning theories. Currently, formal professional librarianship training pays little or no heed to this development. In the future, professional training and also ongoing professional staff development will need to incorporate elements of learning theory and educational theory. Without such skills, librarians may be reluctant to take the expanded role and may not be accepted by academic staff if they do. Of course, not many academic staff have formal training in education either.

During the 1990s, universities across the world began to expand into markets offshore. This has had a profound impact on libraries supporting cohorts of international students. The vagaries of sending parcels of books and photocopies to rural parts of a vast continent such as Australia has nothing on the high costs and problems associated with the physical delivery of information resources to individuals living in Asia and Africa, for instance, but studying at an Australian university. Some countries pose few obstacles for the safe delivery and return of books to the home library. However, in the experience of Deakin University, the customs services of some Asian countries have impounded books on arrival or the postal service has simply not delivered the parcels. The use of courier services, which have experience in dealing with local customs services, has improved delivery rates but at a significant cost to the library service. Clearly, the introduction of the Internet and the ability to provide access to a myriad of electronic information resources has gone a long way toward overcoming access and delivery problems.

The Internet, alone, is not the sole answer though. Many countries that are being targeted for international distance education programs do not enjoy the access or reliability to the Internet, as do their western colleagues. Therefore, librarians and educators need to deliver resources and training in a variety of formats that make it easy for these distance students to learn. CD-ROM, such as the Deakin Learning Toolkit (McKnight, 2000), provide an extremely useful medium to deliver instruction and information about library services and resources without the need to be online. These CDs can also provide links to Internet resources should the student have a WWW connection. Of course, these CDs are not used solely to deliver library services. The design and development of such aids to support and enhance distance learning usually involve a partnership between all parts of the university, from the IT division, student enrolment and support areas, faculties, and the library. In this way, librarians can often bring insights and enhancements to the final product given their long-standing involvement in distant learner support.

The offshore market also includes cohorts of students studying at partner (host) institutions in their home country but studying degrees from international universities. Depending on the contracts for such twinning partnerships, the library service may be provided by the host institution or the home university. Either way, negotiations and liaison between library services is required to ensure the availability of appropriate information resources and services. Librarians need to be actively involved in the negotiation process or have established clear and precise guidelines on the appropriate level of library services and resources required to support undergraduate and postgraduate degree programs so that twinning partner contracts reflect these needs. This requires liaison with both academic staff offering offshore programs as well as international office negotiators.

Unfortunately, this has not always been the case, and some contracted library services have not been adequate for the level of study undertaken. Others have been outstanding. A key driver for library services to be provided by the offshore host institution is cost. International universities are often fearful that the market will not bear the real cost of appropriate library services to support learning and teaching. This is indeed unfortunate as it casts doubt on the value of library services in any academic setting. Concern on the variable quality of library services to offshore students has prompted the formation of the CAVAL (Cooperative Action by Victorian Academic Libraries) Offshore Group that is developing guidelines for library services to offshore students. This Victorian initiative may inform the development of national (Australian) guidelines for these services.

A further dilemma for library services involved in offshore support is that of cultural differences. Of course, this is not just an issue for the library, but for the academic program as well. There is a need to understand different learning styles and tailor training and support to be effective in the particular context with which the students are familiar. Whether or not to provide interfaces to library services in a variety of languages is another issue in the international marketplace.

Other categories of distance education students pose interesting challenges for librarians. Providing resources and information literacy training to students who are in prison sometimes poses similar problems as the customs barriers in some foreign countries. CDs, such as the Deakin Learning Toolkit, have been a success in delivering services to these students. Students with disabilities also pose service challenges, and librarians need to be aware of WWW disability guidelines to make sure that services delivered via the Internet are accessible to these students.

FORMAL LINKS TO LEARNING, TEACHING, AND RESEARCH

Burge, Snow, and Howard (1989), Heery (1996), Jagannathan (1996), McManus (1998), and Shklanka (1990) advocated a role for librarians in partnership with educators in the design of learning environments. According to Middleton and Peacock (2000, p. 208), these writers and others emphasize: (a) the importance of reliable and equitable access to the resources of host institution libraries; (b) the need for the development of course materials with reference to incorporation of resource materials; (c) the need for joint development by academics and librarians of course materials; (d) the need for promotion of library services; (e) the need for dialog between learners and instructors to be supported by organized mechanisms for information access; (f) the need to carry out evaluation of library resource provision as part of course evaluation; and (g) the need for evaluation of library system utilization.

In 2001 this is becoming a reality. An informal survey of Australia's 39 publicly funded universities was conducted to ascertain the library's formal role in learning and teaching. University librarians were asked:

> if you have included in your strategic plans (or equivalents) the aim to work more closely with academic staff/faculty staff to "transform teaching and learning," to "participate more actively in teaching and learning" or activities that would lead to this result e.g. library staff participating in curriculum (re) developments, information literacy training included in the curriculum, library staff participation in teaching and learning committees or curriculum committees or similar activities). (McKnight, S., e-mail questionnaire to Council of Australian University Librarians, February 21, 2001)

The purpose of this survey was to gauge the validity of the assertion put earlier in this chapter that libraries were involved in a changing and expanding role in higher education. An overwhelming 20 of the 21 respondents gave a positive answer. The degree of involvement varied but the future direction was clearly evident by the responses.

By far the major thrust of the libraries surveyed was the inclusion of information literacy skills into the curriculum, either imbedded into the discipline-specific information or as assessable tests within foundation or first-year subjects. These initiatives are a far cry from voluntary information literacy or reader education classes offered by university libraries during orientation week. It reflects a growing trend in Australian higher education to embody generic attributes, such as information and IT literacy, into the curriculum, with responses such as:

Queensland University of Technology library has taken a leading role in the development of information literacy and has collaborated closely with faculties to integrate information skills and concepts into the curriculum of a number of foundation units. (Callan, P., Poirier, J., Tweedale, R. & Peacock, J., 2001)

RMIT University Library will contribute directly to learning outcomes by being at the forefront in the development of integrated information literacy programs for lifelong learning, creativity, practicality, a global imagination and ongoing professional development. (RMIT University, 2001)

Respondents also indicated an increasing involvement in the development or redevelopment of education programs, especially as these were adapted for flexible, online delivery:

Improve the integration of Library services and resource identification into course planning" (University of Wollongong Library's 2001 Strategic Plan)

The Library's scholarly information resources, services and products will be integrated with the courses as far as possible and access will be seamless to the user. (University of New South Wales Library Strategic Plan, 2001)

In the Customer Perspective, the aim is for "significantly improved learning experiences." (Deakin University Strategic Plan 2001–2003)

The recent EDUCAUSE in Australasia 2001 conference also demonstrated the evolving role of libraries and the underpinning of information technology in the higher education sector. For the first time this conference invited practitioners from university teaching and learning centers to join with library and IT professionals in exploring the conference theme of "The Power of 3: Bringing together Teaching & Learning, Library, and Information Technology." (Available online: http://www.gu.edu.au/educause2001.)

Papers presented at this conference included a number that highlighted the collaboration and co-operation between course developers and the librarian, for example: "Horses for Courses: Teamwork in Delivering Integrated Information Resources to Students" (Young, 2001), "Strategic Collaboration for Online Delivery" (Reid, 2001), and "May the Course Be with You ... Development of a Single Access Point for Course Information and Learning Materials" (Koppi & Terry, 2001).

Universities, as well as focusing on learning and teaching, also concentrate on research. The library's link to the research agenda of a university has normally been confined to collection development, interlibrary loan services, and on-campus research support. However, a pilot project at Deakin University aims to enhance graduate outcomes by providing tailored information literacy tuition to the candidate (and supervisor) at the crucial literature review stage of a thesis. Research by Macauley (2001) highlights the need to ensure that researchers, both doctoral candidates and their supervisors, have effective information literacy skills. The aim of the pilot project is to enhance research completions and involve linking a liaison librarian to the supervisory team for a number of PhD students to ensure the development of information literacy skills. The model was developed in recognition of the special support needs of off-campus higher degree research students (Macauley & McKnight, 1998). While, in practice, the librarian's role is not quite of cosupervisor (as originally envisaged), it is a significant recognition of the importance of the librarian to the research process. The project is only in its third year, so results are not yet available to test whether candidates completed with less angst and in a shorter time frame. Caspers (1999) also identified the need for distance education research students to become effective literature reviewers and has developed a WWW-based tutorial that presents the literature review process as a linked series of problems to solve.

ECONOMIC, POLITICAL, AND SOCIAL ISSUES

There have been a number of key drivers in explaining the increasing role of the library in learning, teaching, and research. On the economic side, students are demanding value for the fees paid toward their higher education. With the increasing focus on the student as customer/client, all parts of the university, including libraries, are striving to ensure value for money and to provide services to achieve the university's strategic mission. Another driver is that distance education students have as much right to expect effective library services as traditional on-campus students. Therefore, services have been enhanced to ensure easy access and equitable delivery of resources and services. The delivery of library services to offshore students has highlighted the tension between the true cost of delivering an appropriate level of service and the price that the market will bear. Library services are in danger of being relegated to the category of services seen as "add-on extras" and paid in addition to basic fees rather than being seen as integral and non-negotiable in the delivery of high-quality education.

An interesting recent development in Australia and internationally has been the concept of national site licenses for electronic information resources. Such decisions made for the national interest place library collections and services in a precompetitive environment although all the participating universities are competing for students. These political (and economic) decisions mean greatly enhanced access to information resources for all students and are of enormous benefit to distance education students.

The demands of students who need to juggle full-time study with part-time or casual work, and full-time workers studying part-time, necessitates easy access to library services and resources as well as academic programs. All libraries, regardless of whether they serve distance education or on-campus students, need to provide a wide range of online resources and services that are tightly integrated with the curriculum to facilitate this. In this way, learning experiences for all students will be enhanced.

THE FUTURE

According to Slade (2000, p. 6),

> Almost as much has been written about library services for open and distance learning in the past five years as in the previous 65 years. The phenomenal growth of the literature reflects to a large degree the changing role of the library at the end of the twentieth century and the convergence of on- and off-campus library services as the electronic era blurs the boundaries between conventional and distance education and between remote and in-person users of libraries.

Students do not care nor need to understand the difference between curriculum materials and the supporting information resources of libraries. Therefore, it will be the norm for librarians to be part of the multidisciplinary team responsible for creating new learning resources and environments and for the seamless delivery of the curriculum and support materials to students. They will actively participate in computer conferences and electronic reference desks that students will use to enhance their learning experiences. Creth (1996) identified this in her Follett lecture when she said librarians need to see themselves as part of the teaching and research endeavor and participate as active and integral members of the education team.

Libraries will continue to provide a hybrid of print and electronic services, ensuring that distance education students as well as on-campus students gain the benefit of the new technologies and services delivered via the WWW as well as maintaining access to the myriad of information resources that will remain in print format. The high cost of maintaining multiple formats will ensure that university libraries cooperate in the acquisition, delivery, and storage of information resources. National and regional electronic site licenses, buying consortia, and cooperative stores for little used material will be the norm.

The data management skills of librarians will also come to the fore as universities grapple with the complexities of managing digital environments of WWW pages and curriculum materials, as well as the traditional library resources purchased and leased from publishers. Management of copyright licenses, permissions, and university intellectual property will become even more important as the learning space moves online and will, most likely, be managed by librarians. The influence of the academic librarian will extend well beyond the physical and virtual walls of the university library.

REFERENCES

Brophy, P., & Craven, J. (1998). Lifelong learning and higher education libraries: Models for the 21st century. In P. Thomas & M. Jones (Eds.), *The eighth off-campus library services conference proceedings, Providence, Rhode Island 1998.* Mount Pleasant, MI: Central Michigan University.

Bundy, A. (1988). Home institutions' library service to external students, survey, December 1986. In. C. Crocker (Ed.), *Coordination of library services to external students* (appendix). Sydney, Australia: Library Association of Australia.

Burge, E. J., Snow, J. E., & Howard, J. L. (1989). Distance education: Concept and practice. *Canadian Library Journal, 46*(5), 329–335.

Callan, P., Poirier, J., Tweedale, R., & Peacock, J. (2001). Practice makes information literacy perfect: Models of educational collaboration at QUT. In J. Frylinck (Ed.), *Partners in learning and research: Changing roles for Australian technology network libraries.* Adelaide, South Australia: University of South Australia Library.

Caspers, J. S. (1999). Hands-on instruction across the miles: Using a web tutorial to teach the literature research process. *Research Strategies, 16*(3), 187–197.

Creth, S. (1996). *The electronic library: Slouching toward the future or creating the new information environment* (Follett Lecture Series). http://www.ukoln.ac.uk/follett/creth/paper/html.

Crocker, C. (1987). Getting it right down under: Off-campus library services in Australia. In B. M. Lessin (Ed.), *Off-campus library services conference proceedings, Nevada, 1986.* Mount Pleasant, MI: Michigan University Press.

Curran, C. (1995). University distance teaching: Library support and the new technologies. In A. Irving & G. Butters (Eds.), *Proceedings of the first libraries without walls conference,* Mytilene, Greece, 9-10 September 1995.

Deakin University. Library. *Strategic Objectives and Performance Indicators 2001–2003* (http://www.deakin.edu.au/library/stratplan/uniframework.htm)

Deakin University. Planning Unit. (2000). Course Enrolment Statistics. http://www.deakin.edu.au/planning_unit/2000/stats/enrols.html.

Heery, M. (1996). Academic library services to non-traditional students. *Library Management, 17*(5), 3–13.

Jagannathan, N. (1996). Library and information services for distance learners. *Resource Sharing & Information Networks, 11*(1–2), 159–170.

Koppi, T., & Terry, C. (2001). May the course be with you...development of a single access point for course information and learning materials. In EDUCAUSE in Australasia 2001 http://www.gu.edu.au/ins/its/educause2001/content2a.html.

Macauley, P. (March 2001). *Doctoral research and scholarly communication: Candidates, supervisors and information literacy.* Unpublished PhD Thesis, Faculty of Education, Deakin University, Geelong.

Macauley, P., & McKnight, S. (1998). A new model of library support for off-campus postgraduate research students. In M. Kiley & G. Mullins (Eds.), *Quality in postgraduate research: Managing the new agenda: Proceedings of the 1998 quality in postgraduate research conference.* Adelaide, Australia: The Advisory Centre for University Education.

Macauley, P., & McKnight, S. (2001). Representation on supervisory panels: a model of collaboration, in A. Bartlett & G. Mercer *Postgraduate research supervision, transforming (r)elations*, NewYork, Peter Lang, 113–122.

McKnight, S. (1998). Library services to off-campus students: An Australian perspective. In P. Brophy et al. (Eds.), *Libraries without walls 2: The delivery of library services to distant users.* London: Library Association Publishing pp. 53–62.

McKnight, S. (2000). Delivering Library Services to Remote Users: The Deakin Learning Toolkit. In P. Brophy et al. (Eds.), *Libraries without walls 3: The delivery of library services to distant users* 175–182. London: Library Association Publishing.

McManus, M. (1998). The way I see it: Neither Pandora nor Cassandra: Library services and distance education in the next decade. *College & Research Libraries News, 59*(6), 432–435.

Middleton, M., & Peacock, J. (2000). Library services to external students from Australian universities: the influence of flexible delivery upon traditional service provision. *Reference Librarian*, 69/70, 205–217.

Reid, I. (2001). Strategic collaboration for online delivery. In EDUCAUSE in Australasia 2001. http://www.gu.edu.au/ins/its/educause2001/content2a.html.

RMIT University. (2001). Library vision. Available at http://www.lib.rmit.edu.au/overview/vision.html.

Shklanka, O. (1990) Off-campus library services—A literature review. *Research in Distance Education, 2*(4), 2–11.

Slade, A. L. (2000). International trends and issues in library services for distance learning: Present and future. In P. Brophy et al. (Eds.), *Libraries without walls 3: The delivery of library services to distant users.* London: Library Association Publishing. 6–48.

Slade, A., & Kascus, M. (1996). *Library services for off-campus and distance education: The second annotated bibliography*, Englewood, CO: Libraries Unlimited.

Small, M. (1997). Virtual universities and their libraries: A comparison of Australian and North American experiences. In I. Godden (Ed.), *Advances in Librarianship*, 21 (25–46). San Diego: Academic Press.

Store, R. (1981). *Looking out from down under: A preliminary report of a survey of library services to external students in Australia and overseas.* Townsville, Australia: Townsville College of Advanced Education.

University of New South Wales. Library (2001). *Strategic plan* (http://www.library.unsw.edu.au/~libadmin/policy/stratplan2001.html)

Winter, A., & Cameron, M. (1983). *External students and their libraries: An investigation into student needs for reference material, the sources they use, and the effects of the external system within which they study.* Geelong, Australia: Deakin University.

University of Wollongong. Library, (2001). *Strategic plan* (http://www.library.uow.edu.au/about/planning/pdfs/stratsum.pdf)

Young, C. (2001). Horses for courses: Teamwork in delivering integrated information resources to students. In EDUCAUSE in Australasia 2001. http://www.gu.edu.au/ins/its/educause2001/content2a.html.

27

Exploring the New Conception of Teaching and Learning in Distance Education

Morris Sammons
University of Kentucky
msamm2@uky.edu

The traditional conception of teaching and learning activities was used with what Nipper (1989) refers to as the "first and second generation systems" in distance education (p. 63), the first generation being that of printed materials and the second that of print combined with some form of broadcast media. He adds, "The main objectives of the first and second generation systems have been the production and distribution of teaching/learning material to the learners" (p. 63). In this conception, adjustments made because of distance were handled "by implementing effective presentation and distribution methods" (Nipper, 1989, p. 64).

Authority and control over how material is presented and especially what material is presented rests with the teacher as the scholar/expert of the material. In the case of materials designed by a team, scholars and experts of the subject content decide what is to be presented. The content consists of facts and ideas drawn from an established body of "codified knowledge" (Twigg, 2000, p. 42), i.e., a discipline or professional field. In this conception, the teacher assumes the role of directing, guiding, and assisting learners. Learners' attention is focused on the teacher and the content because they determine what happens in the learning environment.

In this teacher-centered conception, teaching and learning are characterized by formalized activities. As much as possible of what the teacher says and does in a traditional, face-to-face classroom is designed into the printed materials. Ideally this includes the nuances and implicit factors of a face-to-face environment. As far as interactive communication is concerned, Nipper points out that in the first and second generations of distance education, "Communication with the learners has been marginal, and communication amongst the learners has been more or less non-existent" (p. 63). The communication that does occur is usually teacher-to-learner and typically in the form of comments and questions (Nipper, 1989, p. 64).

In the traditional conception of teaching and learning activities, success is measured primarily by how well each individual student understands, retains, and repeats the content presented. Assigned learning tasks are to be accomplished individually, and each individual's mastery of the subject matter is measured separately. Learning activities are "highly structured and organized... for the student to later follow, with participation by the student often being pre-specified by the instructor and designed to ensure mastery of particular content" (Bannon-Ritland & Milheim, 1999, p. 2). The context for teaching and learning in this conception is well defined and bounded.

The content presented to learners is also well defined and bounded. It is believed that everyone acquires knowledge of a particular subject matter in the same way. This is true whether the learner intends to become an expert in that field or not. Fundamental ideas, information, and vocabulary must be understood and retained first, then more complex ideas are mastered incrementally (Twigg, 2000). Bannon-Ritland and Milheim (1999) say that according to this view, "information of the external world is mind-independent and can be characterized in objective, concrete terms which are transmitted or communicated from the instructor to the student" (p. 2). According to Brown, Collins, and Duguid (1989):

> Many methods of didactic education assume a separation between knowing and doing, treating knowledge as an integral, self-sufficient substance, theoretically independent of the situations in which it is learned and used. The primary concern of schools often seems to be the transfer of this substance, which comprises abstract, decontextualized formal concepts. The activity and context in which learning takes place are thus regarded as merely ancillary to learning—pedagogically useful, of course, but fundamentally distinct and even neutral with respect to what is learned. (p. 32)

In contrast to the traditional conception of teaching learning activities for distance education, advocates of the new, learner-centered conception contend that Web-based technologies can and should be used in distance education to generate a teaching and learning environment substantially different from that of the traditional one. For example, Ruhleder and Twidale (2000) state, "The availability of increasingly robust Web-based networked technologies offers opportunities for creating and sustaining collaborative, reflective learning experiences" (p. 1). In a learner-centered environment, again in contrast to the traditional conception of distance learning, learners are actively engaged in dynamic teaching and learning activities. Brown, Collins, and Duguid (1989) argue that, "approaches that embed learning in activity and make deliberate use of the social and physical context are more in line with the understanding of learning and cognition that is emerging from research" (p. 32). The activities, that is, are designed to prompt and promote the cognitive processes learners use naturally as they work toward understanding of their experiences. In the context of the activities, cognitive processes are, then, the "result of active engagement in and with the world coupled with reflections upon the relationship between ideas, actions, and outcomes" (Ruhleder & Twidale, 2000, p. 1).

In this conception, teaching and learning activities are based on constructivist principles of learning that are rooted in cognitive psychology and elaborated by Jerome Bruner (Kearsley, 1996a). Kearsley (1996a) states that, according to Bruner, the fundamental principle of learning is that "learners construct new ideas or concepts based upon their current/past knowledge. The learner selects and transforms information, constructs hypotheses, and makes a cognitive structure to do so. Cognitive structure (i.e. schema, mental models) provide meaning and organization to experiences and allows the individual to go beyond the information given" (p. 1).

Following constructivist learning theory, learning environments that prompt cognitive engagement are ones in which learners discover or work out for themselves an understanding of a new experience through careful reflection and critical analysis. As Harasim (1989) states, "Knowledge according to this view is something that emerges through active dialogue, by formulating ideas into words and building ideas and concepts through the reactions and responses of others to these formulations" (p. 50). These environments include problem situations in circumstances learners have not experienced before. As Briner (1999) points out:

The student is pursuing a problem or activity by applying approaches he or she already knows and integrating those approaches with alternatives presented by other team members, research sources, or current experience. Through trial and error, the student then balances pre-existing views and approaches with new experiences to construct a new level of understanding. (p. 1)

It is critical to understanding the new conception to note that the difference between it and the traditional conception is not simply that learners are presented with problem-based activities that guide learning toward comprehension of specific concepts, facts, and theories. The new conception is not merely a way to use Web-based technologies to deliver established, bound content in new forms. It is not a method for getting individual learners to formulate the same solutions, i.e., the same answer, or to independently acquire the same knowledge as other learners. Two fundamental features of the new conception make deeper level differences clear. One, learners collaborate with other learners and with the teacher about the problem situation, and two, meaningful ideas are constructed collaboratively about real experiences.

These two features can be explained by describing how Web-based technologies are used in a distance education setting. If there were no Web-based technologies, it would be extremely difficult, if not impossible, to apply the new, learner-centered conception in distance education. Once problem situations have been presented, Web-based technologies are used for obtaining, processing, and storing information and for communicating. As Harasim (1989) notes:

The on-line environment is particularly appropriate for collaborative learning approaches which emphasise group interaction. Much more than a technical device for exchanging information, computer conferencing facilitates the sharing of knowledge and understanding among members of a group who are not working together at the same time or place. Computer conferencing was developed expressly to facilitate the interactivity of group communication, maintaining an ongoing common transcript of the interactions among the many people discussing a topic. (p. 52)

Each of the several ways Web-based technologies get used in the learner- centered conception need to be delineated. First, learners are encouraged to use the vast amount of information accessible via the Web as primary resources in work on the problem situation. Bonk and Reynolds (1997) point out that, "Web browsing tools now exist to explore and search for information, dynamically view the results of one's choices, and send these findings to instructors and peers" (p. 168). By using the Web in this way, "The predominant source of content shifts from the textbook and the teacher to a more varied source of information. Further, the nature of content becomes dynamic, versus the static texts published on a certain date" (Relan & Gillani, 1997, p. 44).

Web-based technologies also get used for communication. In most cases, communication is in the form of text or writing, but it may include material in other media, e.g., audio or video files. Where larger amounts of bandwidth are available, communication may include synchronous audio and video among multiple locations, but at this time, larger amounts of bandwidth are not prevalent. Communication is synchronous or asynchronous, and it may occur between two or more individuals. A variety of forms can be used altogether, and while individuals in a teaching and learning setting do have to adjust to this form of communication, it is also true that "Computer bulletin boards, electronic mail, computer conferencing, videotex and synchronous dialogue programs are now employed by millions of people all over the world" (Feenberg, 1989, p. 22). As Feenberg (1989) further notes, an interesting feature of computer mediated communication "is not its purported inhumanity, but rather its lively, rapid iterations, almost rapid enough to recall spoken conversation" (p. 23). It is because learners and the teacher can communicate among themselves that collaboration occurs, and this is a necessary condition for having learner-centered teaching and learning activities.

Another feature of Web-based technology vital to a learner-centered approach in distance education is the capability of information and communication to be recorded for later use and for sharing with others. This capability enables learners to reflect on information encountered at an earlier time. Each learner needs to reflect on information encountered whether it is found on the Web, provided by the teacher, presented as a part of a problem situation, or results from collaboration. Only through reflection can an individual begin to generate the meaning that the information has for him or her. Ruhleder and Twidale (2000), for example, point out, "Reproducibility makes it much easier to discuss what has been done in the past, allowing students to re-read and refer to earlier discussions. This reification provides one avenue for discovering relevant and authentic examples of an abstract concept under discussion" (p. 11).

Having threaded e-mail discussions or archived synchronous chat sessions along with access to the information others have encountered on the Web establishes a shared context for the learners. As learners and the teacher communicate among themselves in this shared context, a social dimension is added, and according to the learner-centered conception, this sets up the conditions for learning. In describing this type of learning activity, Ruhleder and Twidale (2000) state, "Collaborative activity presents an opportunity for reflection and interpretation of events by providing a shared context for the interpretation of individual experience" (p. 1). Harasim (1989) adds, "Collaborative learning activities use cooperative task structures based upon active learner participation and peer interaction in achieving a common good" (p. 51). Briner (1999) further points out:

> The student is pursuing a problem or activity by applying approaches he or she already knows and integrating those approaches with alternatives presented by other team members, research sources, or current experience. Through trial and error, the student then balances pre-existing views and approaches with new experiences to construct a new level of understanding. (p. 1)

Because instances of the group's interactive processing are archived for later consideration, what happens among different members of the group is accessible. The record is public, in a sense, and this is important because:

> By making the process public, students realize that their very provisional rough ideas are entirely normal, and that the iterative, *collaborative* development process can work for them. Concepts such as the inevitability of trade-offs, and multiple conflicting goals become much clearer when put into practice. (Ruhleder & Twidale, 2000, p. 8)

According to the learner-centered conception, having learners involved with real situations or simulations of them is critical to effectively engaging them and to making their experience most meaningful. Learners' activities are to be situated in the context of real circumstances. Brown et al. (1989) explain that "Authentic activities then, are most simply defined as the ordinary practices of the culture" (p. 34). This idea is based on elaborations of the learning theories of Vygotsky made by Lave and Wenger and later by Brown, Collins, and Duguid (Kearsley, 1996b). According to Kearsley (1996b), "Lave argues that learning as it normally occurs is a function of the activity, context and culture in which it occurs (i.e., it is situated)" (p. 1). Herrington and Oliver (1998) cite research by Brown, Collins, and Duguid when they say that a situated learning environment "provides an authentic context that reflects the way knowledge will be used in real-life, that preserves the full context of the situation without fragmentation and decomposition, that invites exploration and allows for the natural complexity of the real world" (p. 2). Examples, or "context-based exemplars" (Ruhleder & Twidale, 2000, p. 4), are provided of what individuals do who are regularly involved in these kinds of situations. Examples are presented of the way "knowledge will be used in real life" (Herrington & Oliver,

1998, p. 4). Putting this idea in more concrete terms, Freberg (2000) points out, "While a student may balk at having to memorize the features of clinical psychological evaluation, the principles come alive when the student reads and evaluates Mike Tyson's clinical assessment from the Nevada Gaming Commission" (p. 48).

The above explanations of the learner-centered conception indicate that what learners do in a distance education setting is qualitatively different from their activities in the traditional conception. The contrast is amplified as learners progress through a course. In the learner-centered conception, collaborative activities proceed as new and different interpretations are needed. The activities for a given course are related to experiences that concern a domain of information, knowledge, and practice. As learners work through authentic situations from a domain, their activity is described as a "cognitive apprenticeship" (Brown et al. 1989, p. 37). Explaining this idea, Brown and Collegues (1989) state:

> Collaboration also leads to articulation of strategies which can then be discussed and reflected on. This, in turn, fosters generalizing grounded in the students' situated understanding. From here, students can use their fledging conceptual knowledge in activity, seeing that activity in a new light, which in turn leads to further development of conceptual knowledge. (p. 39)

They explain that what is learned becomes a tool for further learning (Brown et al., 1989). They state that the notion of cognitive apprenticeship "helps to emphasize the centrality of activity in learning and knowledge and highlights the inherently context-dependent, situated, and enculturating nature of learning" (1989, p. 39).

Looking back at the description of the traditional conception of teaching and learning activities in distance education presented earlier, the differences between the fundamental ideas of that conception and those of the new, learner-centered conception are significant. A description of the roles the teacher is to play in the learner-centered conception puts these differences in the context of practice, i.e., what the teacher actually does. Further, an examination of these roles discloses some important implications for distance education practice. Describing and examining all the roles or even most of them in any meaningful detail is beyond the scope of this chapter. For purposes of this discussion, the description of most of the roles will be general and brief, and as a result, these roles will be grossly oversimplified. Since learning is a collaborative activity in this conception, the examination focuses on the set of roles concerned with facilitating collaboration. To complete this chapter, some implications these roles suggest for distance education practice are mentioned.

In general, the teacher's roles in a learner-centered setting encompass a wide assortment of activities. Prior to the beginning of the course, the teacher must formulate problem situations to present to the students and organize details of the presentation. This will involve gathering information and resources pertinent to the situations presented, organizing it, and making it accessible to learners, e.g., listing Web sites, setting up links to the collected resource material, and arranging for access to library databases. The teacher also sets up and organizes the communication mechanisms that will be used, e.g., bulletin boards and synchronous chat sessions. After the situations are presented, the teacher works with the students to facilitate their learning. Finally, the teacher must evaluate the students' learning.

In this setting, students work collaboratively with the teacher and with each other on some type of situation that has been presented. What the teacher does to facilitate learning will vary with the particular circumstances of a specific event that occurs. Describing what teachers do in a learner-centered environment, Sherry and Wilson (1997) state:

> Thus, a whole range of activities may be appropriate, depending on the needs of the situation, prior knowledge and repertoire of skills of the audience, and the learning support available to

students. A committed instructor will explore different activities, adding bit by bit to his or her own storehouse of strategies, as different opportunities present themselves. (p. 71)

Various scholars and researchers have categorized teachers' learner- centered activities in different ways. See, for example, the work of Feenberg (1989), Davie (1989), Bonk (2000), Milliron and Miles (2000), and Harasim, Hiltz, Teles, and Turoff (as cited in University of Illinois, 1999). Four categories of activities for facilitating collaboration are briefly described here. These categories are a synthesis and adaptation of those already formulated. Except for one of them, the categories loosely follow those presented by Bonk (2000). The categories are 1) technological activities, 2) pedagogical activities, 3) social activities, and 4) psychological activities. It should be noted that these categories represent an artificial formulation. In reality, there is much overlap among them. Indeed, a given facilitating act by a teacher may involve more than one or perhaps even all of the activities.

Technological activities that facilitate collaboration "frame the use of the Web for students" (Girod & Cavanaugh, 2001, p. 42). As with any distance education course, there are practical matters to be handled. The special features of Web-based technologies that will be used in a course should be explained to students in the beginning, and information about these features should be readily available either from the teacher or online. Examples of such features are threaded discussions and archives of material developed by groups of students. Another aspect is providing examples of how Web-based technologies can be used to present and express ideas with different media (Girod & Cavanaugh, 2001). This enables students to expand their thinking of how interpretations of ideas can be communicated beyond what are, in most cases, text-based expressions. These can be provided while participating in collaborations.

Students are encouraged to seek and use resources accessible through Web-based technologies. What is available through the Web increases every day, so there is an abundance of resources. In the context of a course, however, the teacher has to be aware that this abundance can be a problem. Citing his earlier research, Duchastel (1997) points out, "the danger of getting lost in the vastness of the Web and not properly fulfilling learning expectations can be a very real one and will require proper instructional support" (p. 180).

It is also important for the teacher to demonstrate and emphasize how to critically evaluate the quality of what is found and why this is important. As Freberg (2000) states, "We need to assist students in learning how to evaluate the credibility and appropriateness of information" (p. 50). In other words, it is important that students see how to be good "consumers of information" (Milliron & Miles, 2000, p. 59). Girod and Cavanaugh (2001) explain:

Teachers must model methods for judging the trustworthiness of information by checking it against other sources, executing mental experiments to investigate the logic of purported claims, and asking critical questions about the origins of claims. Students should be taught to scrutinize knowledge carefully and hold all information as suspect until a reasonable level of certainty can be established. (p. 42)

Another important technological activity for the teacher is providing support for working with the Web-based technologies whenever it is needed by students (Bonk, 2000). In a learner-centered setting, the teacher participates with the students in the learning activities. One aspect of this participation is being alert to problems that arise and being prepared to manage them. If the problems are technical, either for an individual or for the whole group, then the teacher should respond quickly and be able to provide assistance, to suggest solutions, and to direct students to system support services. "Group emails about sudden technological problems are another way to smooth out problems and lessen their impact" (Bonk, 2000, p. 12).

The teacher also should look for individual differences in students' abilities using the Web-based technologies employed in the course. Except in unusual cases, there are likely to be differences in prior experience and ability with the Web-based technologies in any group of students. The degrees of differences could be extremely large. These differences also may vary among the types of technology that get used. In these cases, the teacher has to be prepared to judge the effects of the differences on individuals and the group and to present appropriate interventions so that participation in collaborative activities is not inhibited. In short, the teacher has to manage the diversity of experience and ability among the students.

The second category of ways the teacher facilitates learning consists of pedagogical activities. With these activities, the teacher assists learners with their interpretations and constructions of meaning, but does so as a participant with the students in the learning activities. Bonk (2000) enumerates some of these activities when he states, "Here, an instructor links ideas across assignments, gives feedback, sets goals, provides instructions, offers advice, summarizes or weaves disparate student comments, and refers to outside resources or experts in the field" (p. 12). Davie (1989) puts the point this way: "The tutor must be able to set and communicate the intellectual climate of the course or seminar; model the qualities of a scholar; support, mould, and direct the discussion; design a variety of educational experiences; and comment helpfully on students' work" (p. 76).

As a participant with the group, the teacher guides and coaches the students' learning. Feenberg (1989) explains that the teacher makes "meta-comments" which are comments that "summarize the state of the discussion, identifying its unifying themes and points of disagreement" (p. 34). He states, "Such weaving comments supply a unifying overview, interpreting the discussion by drawing its various strands together in a momentary synthesis" (1989, p. 35). When the teacher makes these comments to particular students, "it encourages these participants and implicitly prompts them to pursue their ideas" (Feenberg, 1989, p. 35). Bonk and Reynolds (1997) explain:

> As assisters of learning, instructors manage and structure tasks, model and demonstrate ideas, provide questions and feedback, coach or scaffold learning, encourage students to articulate beliefs and ideas, foster student reflection and self-awareness, push student explorations and application of skills, and directly instruct when appropriate. (p. 168)

When these pedagogical activities are performed, the role of the teacher shifts from that of "dispensing knowledge" (Girod & Cavanaugh, 2001, p. 44) in the traditional conception to facilitating collaborative learning.

To promote collaboration among learners in a distance education setting, the teacher also has to engage in social activities, and this is the third category. After individual learners begin to interpret elements of the problem or project situation presented to them, they then begin to work with each other. Collaboration, however, does not happen spontaneously, and it does not necessarily proceed smoothly. This is especially true when the collaborators are in different locations, most often communicating asynchronously in writing. Discussing collaboration in this type of setting, Feenberg (1989) says:

> It would be a mistake to treat this as essentially a technical issue. Although technology is important for any mediated activity, it cannot "automate" what is in reality a social encounter based on specific social practices. These social practices are unusually complex because of the difficulty of mediating organised group activity in a written environment. (p. 28)

Hedegaard (1996) adds that interaction among learners "establishes a more intense and tedious environment" (p. J-2).

Communication among members of a group is always complicated, and it is even more complicated when it is not verbal and face to face, when it is in writing, and when it is asynchronous. The social activities of the teacher are ways of managing these conditions. In a collaborative learning setting, the teacher performs the roles of a coordinator and a moderator (Bonk, 2000; Feenberg, 1989; Brown & Johnson-Shull, 2000). The teacher coordinates collaboration with such activities as "explaining assignments, assigning partners, and establishing due dates and extensions" (Bonk, 2000, p. 12). If small groups are used, then the teacher "needs to organize meeting times, . . . offer ways to contact the instructor for questioning, update the students on the course accomplishments, and point out changes or revisions in the course plan" (Bonk, 2000, p. 12).

Performing the role of a moderator, on the one hand, involves establishing the conditions for communication. On the other hand, the role involves maintaining communications. In a distance education setting with individuals at different locations, there is no common "tacit dimension" (Feenberg, 1989, p. 33) of the communication that is to take place. These factors must be added, and this is a moderating activity. As Feenberg (1989) explains:

> Human relationships (the "pragmatics" of communication) differ for example, in meetings, courses, informal conversations, parties, doctor's visits and so on. As soon as we enter a room, we orient ourselves according to the tacit cues of the conversation we are about to join. These contextual cues establish a mood from which flow norms, roles and expectations. In the absence of visible cues, on-line moderators must make an explicit choice for the group they lead, reducing the strangeness of the medium by selecting a familiar system of roles and rules derived from everyday life. (pp. 33–34)

Bonk (2000) enlarges on this notion when he explains that, "A good moderator is aware of the flexible nature of teaching online. He or she can effectively shift between instructor, facilitator, and consultant roles while recognizing that the course is no longer based simply on instructor lecture and student memorization" (p. 10).

In the role of a moderator, the teacher also maintains collaborative communication among students. The aim of maintaining collaborative communication is to promote a shared awareness and identity among the students, the sense of a learner community. To perform this role, the teacher must be acutely sensitive to what is needed (Brown & Johnson-Shull, 2000). Brown and Johnson-Shull (2000) explain that, in some cases, the teacher might perform the role of moderator by managing students who contribute so often or at such length that other students limit their contributions. The dominating contributions may be about the learning task, or they may be simply informal, socializing comments. As a general rule, socializing online as a part of course activities needs to be managed, particularly when it throws students' thinking off-track. Bonk (2000), however, adds, "I have found that social comments of students often motivates other students to come online and read what each other had to say. In some cases, therefore, instead of limiting social talk, you might try encouraging it" (p. 12).

The key to performing the role of moderator, according to Brown and Johnson-Shull (2000), is for the teacher to be responsive. This may mean, as Bonk pointed out, not managing students' interactions. Other situations may call for direct intervention, as in the case of dominating contributors. By being responsive in the role of moderator, the teacher can maintain a balance of contributions among the students, and this will facilitate collaborative communication.

The last category is that of psychological activities. These concern the affective dimensions of the leaner-centered setting. Cornell and Martin (1997) state that the teacher can facilitate interaction among students by humanizing and personalizing the setting. By assuming this role, the teacher motivates students to take part in learning activities. Bonk (2000) gives examples of this role when he says that the teacher can provide "welcoming statements, thank you notices, invitations, apologies, discussion of one's own online experiences and humor" (p. 12). He further elaborates this idea when he states that teachers "should try to be responsive to student needs and set a generally positive and friendly tone that invites them to be candid about the way the course is proceeding" (p. 12). Implicit in this role is the idea that the teacher relates to students as individuals who are working toward a common goal. By demonstrating this behavior to each student, the teacher facilitates students' collaborative interactions with him or her and with each other by establishing a supportive and humane context.

Distance education teachers who accept the learner-centered conception of teaching and learning activities will incorporate the principles of this conception in their practice. These teachers will promote collaborative learning by striving to effectively perform the roles associated with the four categories of activities that facilitate collaboration. To accomplish this, however, teachers must adapt to the implications of these activities for their practice. To conclude this chapter, several important ones are explained.

In a learner-centered environment, what the teacher does is more important than how much information the teacher knows about a given subject area. By virtue of this, the teacher is in a different position relative to the students than has traditionally been the case. The teacher is not "the sole authority or repository of answers" (Sherry & Wilson, 1997, p. 68). The teacher works to generate "an infrastructure for constructive discourse and negotiation of meaning among the students—an environment that supports not only transmission of information and management of roles and activities, but also social support for the efforts of the members of the learning community" (Sherry & Wilson, 1997, p. 68).

Once such an infrastructure is set up, the teacher must maintain it. Sherry and Wilson (1997) allude to this maintenance in the above quote by stating that the teacher also manages roles and activities. Management of the social dynamics of a collaborative learning environment requires continuous judgments by the teacher, and this is another implication for practice of the learner-centered conception. Bonk, Cummings, Hara, Fischler, and Lee (1999) and several associates describe it this way:

> Instructors have daily and moment-to-moment decisions about how best to teach students. Should they rely on questioning techniques and playing devil's advocate or should they try to give extensive praise and encourage student participation? Should they rely on previous canned lecture material or should they push students to explore the Web for similar resources? Should they encourage dialogue among the entire class or small group learning or partner activities? (p. 10)

Describing the management skills the teacher needs, Bonk (2000) explains in another publication, "It takes one part common sense, two parts patience and three parts instructional savvy to know when to point students to other messages, when to create a useful summary, when to point out conflicting opinions, and when to request additional information and comments" (p. 12).

The teachers' judgments on how to intervene are particularly critical to maintaining a collaborative learning environment. If a teacher's interventions are too direct and add too much control over the situation, learners can interpret this as the teacher assuming an authoritative role. If this happens, learners will tend to give way to the authority and wait for more instructions. If a teacher's interventions are too casual and informal, then they will be ineffective. In either case, collaborative interaction can break down (Harasim as cited in University of Illinois, 1999).

Being able to make good judgments comes with experience and practice. Brown and Johnson-Shull (2000) explain:

> There are no fool-proof formulae, recipes, or shrink-wrapped packages for teaching, online or otherwise. Human interactions are fickle and capricious. It may be that, despite the very clean and

orderly machines that we use to engage each other, the machinations of the human psyche will always manufacture a cluttered mess that can only be sorted out and understood by humans in the midst of the mess. (p. 4)

There is, however, one other implication for practice, and a teacher can more readily adapt to it. To accomplish the four categories of activities that facilitate collaborative learning, a teacher has to be attentive to all the elements involved. In their final report, sixteen University of Illinois faculty who participated in a year-long seminar about using technology in distance teaching concluded that, "high quality online instruction can occur. . . . if professors take the time and effort to maintain the human touch of attentiveness" (University of Illinois, 1999, p. 29).

To conclude, the foregoing explanation and analysis does indicate that adopting the learner-centered conception of teaching and learning activities in distance education practice requires major changes in the thought and action of teachers who are accustomed to the traditional, teacher-centered conception. When actualized in practice as a method for teaching in distance education, there are weaknesses in this conception, though none of them are explored here. Extensive critical analyses of the learner-centered conception and of its actualization in practice should be continued. Becoming an effective teacher in a learner-centered environment will require effort to develop the needed skills. Most of all, it will require time to gain the experience needed to master the learner-centered activities and to acquire the powers of judgment needed to effectively facilitate and maintain a collaborative learning environment. Adopting the learner-centered conception in distance education practice does present a way to utilize the power of Web-based technology for communicating at a distance and a way for actively engaging students in learning. It does provide one way, that is, to make adjustments in teaching and learning when time and distance separate the teacher and the students.

REFERENCES

Bonk, C. J. (2000, Fall). My hats on to the online instructor. *E-Education Advisor,* 10–13.

Bonk, C. J., Cummings, J. A., Hara, N., Fischler, R. B., & Lee, S. M. (1999). A ten level web integration continuum for higher education: New resources, partners, courses, and markets. Retrieved October 30, 2000, from the World Wide Web: http://php.indiana.edu/~cjbonk/paper/edmdia99.html.

Bonk, C. J., & Reynolds, T. H. (1997). Learner-centered web instruction for higher order thinking, teamwork, and apprenticeship. In B. H. Khan (Ed.), *Web-based instruction* (pp. 167–178). Englewood Cliffs, NJ: Educaional Technology Publications.

Bannon-Ritland, B., & Milheim, W. D. (1999). Existing WBI courses and their design. Available at: http://www.virtual.gmu.edu/EDIT611/b-rchapter.htm.

Briner, M. (1999). Constructivism. Retrieved July 1, 2000, from the World Wide Web: http://curriculum.calstatela.edu/faculty/psparks/theorists/501const.htm.

Brown, J. S., Collins, A., & Duguid, P. (1989). Situated cognition and the culture of learning. *Educational Researcher,* 18, 32–42. Retrieved July 29, 2000, from the World Wide Web: http://www.ilt.columbia.edu/ilt/papers/JohnBrown.html.

Brown, G., & Johnson-Shull, L. (2000, May–June). Critical reading: Teaching online: Now we're talking. *The Technology Source,* May-June. Retrieved June 15, 2000, from the World Wide Web: http://horizon.unc.edu/TS/reading/2000-01.asp.

Cornell, R., & Martin, B. L. (1997). The role of motivation in web-based instruction. In B. H. Khan (Ed.), *Web-based instruction* (pp. 93–100). Englewood Cliffs, NJ: Educational Technology Publications.

Davie, L. (1989). Facilitation techniques for the on-line tutor. In R. Mason, & A. Kaye (Eds.), *Mindweave: Communication, computers, and distance education* (pp. 74–85). Oxford: Pergamon Press.

Duchastel, P. (1997). A motivational framework for web-based instruction. In B. H. Khan (Ed.), *Web-based instruction* (pp. 178–184). Englewood Cliffs, NJ: Educational Technology Publications.

Feenberg, A. (1989). The written word. In R. Mason & A. Kaye (Eds.), *Mindweave: Communication, computers, and distance education* (pp. 22–39). Oxford: Pergamon Press.

Freberg, L. (2000, March). Integrating Internet resources into the higher education classroom. *Syllabus,* 13, 7, 48–50.

Girod, M., & Cavanaugh, S. (2001, April). Technology as an agent of change in teacher practice. *Technological Horizons in Education Journal*, pp. 40, 42, 44, 46–47.

Harasim, L. (1989). On-line education: A new domain. In R. Mason & A. Kaye (Eds.), *Mindweave: Communication, computers, and distance education* (pp. 50–62). Oxford: Pergamon Press.

Hedegaard, T. (1996). Computer-mediated online education: Lessons learned by the university of phoenix. *Ed Journal*, 10, 1–3.

Herrington, J., & Oliver, R. (1998). Critical characteristics of situated learning: Implications for the instructional design of multimedia. Retrieved July 1, 2000, from the World Wide Web: http://www.cowan.edu.au/lrn_sys/educres/article1.html.

Kearsley, G. (1996a). Constructivist theory. Learning with software: pedagogies and practices. Retrieved July 1, 2000, from the World Wide Web: http://www.educationau.edu.au/archives/cp/04c.htm.

Kearsley, G. (1996b). Situated learning. Learning with software: pedagogies and practices. Retrieved July 1, 2000, from the World Wide Web: http://www.educationau.edu.au/archives/cp/04k.htm.

Milliron M. D., & Miles, C. L. (2000, November-December). Education in a digital democracy: Leading the charge for learning about, with, and beyond technology. *Educause Review*, 50–62.

Nipper, S. (1989). Third generation distance learning and computer conferencing. In R. Mason & A. Kaye (Eds.), *Mindweave: Communication, computers, and distance education* (pp. 63–73). Oxford: Pergamon Press.

Relan, A., & Gillani, B. B. (1997). Web-based information and the traditional classroom: Similarities and differences. In B. H. Khan (Ed.), *Web-based instruction* (pp. 41–46). Englewood Cliffs, NJ: Educational Technology Publications.

Ruhleder, K., & Twidale, M. (2000). Reflective collaborative learning on the web: Drawing on the master class. *First Monday*, 5 (5). Retrieved June 2, 2000, from the World Wide Web: http://www.firstmonday.dk/issues/issue5_5/ruhleder/index.html.

Sherry, L., & Wilson, B. (1997). Transformative communication as a stimulus to web innovations. In B. H. Khan. (Ed.), *Web-based instruction* (pp. 67–74). Englewood Cliffs, NJ: Educational Technology Publications.

Twigg, C. A. (2000, May–June). Course readiness criteria: Identifying targets of opportunity for large-scale redesign. *Educause Review*, 41–49.

University of Illinois. (1999). Teaching at an Internet distance: The pedagogy of online teaching and learning. The report of a 1998–1999 University of Illinois faculty seminar. Retrieved March 4, 2000, from the World Wide Web: http://www.vpaa.uillinois.edu/tid/report/tid_report.html.

IV

Policies, Administration, and Management

28

Public Policy, Institutional Structures, and Strategic Implementation

Lucille Pacey
The Pacey Group
lucillep@insinc.ca

Erin Keough
Open Learning and Information Network
ekeough@mun.ca

The core business of educational institutions is to create, preserve, transmit and apply knowledge. (Duderstad, 1997, p. 2)

INTRODUCTION

There are a number of jurisdictional overlaps that influence distance learning. For the sake of simplicity, this chapter assumes that distance learning is substantially affected by two policy areas, education and telecommunications, and that these are in turn influenced by an increasing emphasis on innovation and partnership. The chapter argues that distance learning practitioners need to be alert to the complexity of the environment in which the field of distance learning exists and the avenues of influence available to them to achieve desired policy design.

POLICY MODEL

There are many models that help elucidate the public policy process. Some are more linear and describe the process as a series of steps, including

- Agenda setting and problem definition.
- Design, which encompasses setting goals and objectives as well as selecting appropriate implementation instruments.
- Implementation.
- Evaluation.

Some argue that the linear or staged systems outlined above are too simplistic and take into account neither the normative influence (value equations) nor the pluralist nature (multiple avenues of influence) of many modern states. Institutionalists, for instance, hold that state institutions (e.g., legislatures, the U.S. Constitution, the Charter of Rights) are the primary determinants of how policy is formulated and implemented. Yet others hold that "interests" are the primary determinants. The United States is well known for its pluralistic form of governance, with multiple levels of input from a variety of government and nongovernmental agencies and powerful advocacy groups. Although pluralism is not quite as inculcated in the culture, Canadians too have a variety of ways to influence both what goes on the policy agenda and, to a lesser extent, how policy is implemented.

Some theorists describe the various players involved in shaping public policy more inclusively, as follows:

> Policy community: All the groups and agencies that have an active interest in a policy area. The policy community includes civil servants in the relevant government departments, institutions such as universities, interest groups, and individuals who have a public presence through making representation to government commissions or hearings or through providing information to the media.
>
> Policy network: A group within the policy community that adheres to a specific opinion or approach or wishes to influence the implementation of policy in a specific direction. Typically, there are several policy networks within a policy community. A simple version of a policy network might be an advocacy group, but a network usually implies a more complex collection of agencies and individuals working towards a similar end.

As with many complex environments, each model mentioned above illuminates a different facet of the process. (For a basic overview of public policy theory, see Pal, 1992, and Wiarda, 1991.)[1]

We have taken an adaptive approach and combined elements of more than one model to explain the influence of public policy on the development of distance learning. We use variations on a systems model (see Fig. 28.1) that was a popular tool in the 1970s but still has relevance today. Included is a discussion of the possible role of distance educators in the policy community. The systems model places a linear analysis model within a general environment of many coexisting and interrelated systems.

Figure 28.1 depicts inputs from the environment that pass through the various public agencies (in the case of distance learning, those agencies associated with education and telecommunications). The policy system takes a number of decisions and actions that result in the definition of a set of goals, objectives, and related implementation instruments or programs intended to shape a certain set of outcomes. A policy typically speaks to context, resources, activities, and desired outcomes. However, the environment often dictates that the observed outcomes, both in general trends and at the institutional level, differ from those intended. The evaluation process looks at the inputs (and the intended and observed outcomes) to determine what, if any, changes in the implementation programs are necessary. Often in North America the evaluation phase is not a broadly based formal evaluation but rather an iterative process in which feedback is gathered from a variety of knowledgeable groups and key stakeholders (policy community). Using an iterative feedback process allows incremental change to be made in response to a changing general environment.

---

[1]As can be appreciated there is an extensive body of literature in the area of public policy and policy analysis from which the previous paragraphs have been drawn. Given the anticipated audience of this book, rather than citing the key authors in any one of the fields, the following two citations are general texts that provide a high level view of the various schools of thought, which in turn provide citations to the relevant authors. Pal, Leslie, A. (1992) *Public Policy Analysis: An Introduction.* 2nd Edition. Nelson Canada, Scarborough, Ontario.Wiarda, Howard J. (Ed.). (1991). *New Directions in Comparative Politics.* Westview Press Inc. Boulder Colorado.

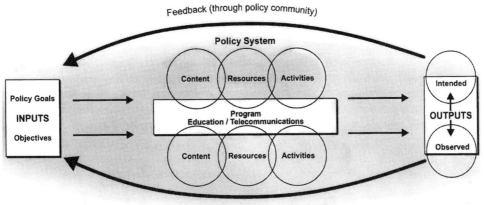

FIG. 28.1.   The public policy process.

THE CONTEXT

Policy Goals: Objectives and Programs

It appears that during the final years of this millennium an opener and broader concept of learning that endeavours to mobilize and link all learning options and formats within a more open learning–networked society to ensure a greater development of skills is gaining acceptance within the international discussion as a premise for an educational reform that is based on life long learning. (Dohmen, 1996, p. 35)

Goals and Objectives

The demands of a knowledge-based economy have exponentially increased the expectations and pressures placed on formal education systems to deliver relevant, current, and industry-related education and training. It is commonly held that 21st-century workers will experience several career changes. There is a demographic shift in industrialized countries toward an older population. At the same time, globalization is making national workforces more diverse due to immigration and general workforce mobility. In response to these national and international trends, there has been an increased emphasis in government policy on providing avenues for lifelong learning to maintain currency of workforce skills and on holding all public agencies more accountable not only for their expenditures but for the quality of their outputs (Advisory Council on Science and Technology, 1999; Duderstat, 1997; Information Highway Advisory Council [IHAC], 1995b; Mathews, 1998).

Ensuring access to information-communications technologies (ICTs) for the purposes of learning, creating knowledge industries, and promoting wider access to information is also a priority objective for many countries. The U.S. government (*National Information Infrastructure*, 2000) is considering a new definition of universal service that reflects the need to access data. In just the last 2–3 years, as more media rich information has become the norm and more essential government services are moving to online formats, the ICT focus has changed from basic Internet access to broadband access (Kennard, 2000b; *Future-Proof IT Infrastructure*, 1999; Manitoba Innovation Network, 2000). As information becomes more easily available through ICTs, a more informed citizenry is gradually shifting the locus of power away from centralized agencies to communities and individuals. Governments are striving to ensure equity of access to the tools and services of the knowledge economy. For educators, the outcome, desired or not, is that learners have become increasingly discerning and qualified consumers and have a growing expectation that educational opportunities will be available at their convenience, not where and when the institutions find convenient.

In the early 1990s, content creation was the goal of many policy programs. Producing high-quality content that is accessible and relevant and that can be manipulated to create new content and new forms of knowledge continues to be a priority in both the public and private sectors. However, the close of the decade saw a subtle but significant change in language and program objectives. Now governments are pointing to innovation as the key to economic health. Policy programs currently look to support innovation, of which advanced content (individualized, interactive, and media rich) is only one outcome. Although creators of advanced content are major contributors to the knowledge economy, they now take their place among many other knowledge creators, such as basic scientists, writers, and health researchers (Martin, 2000). Content's time in the limelight is over, having become just another output of the innovation that can serve to build a better society. This new focus has significant implications for education providers.

Through encouraging public-private partnerships, governments hope to ensure that the knowledge created in research and higher education institutions gets to market as knowledge products. In education, these partnerships often include software developers, distribution and telecommunications providers, governments, and educational institutions. New forms of partnership and different kinds of partners are evolving regularly and rapidly.

In linking the outputs of educational systems to a strong, prosperous economy, policymakers seek to change services for learners, access points for education and training delivery, and models of organizations. A major challenge facing any nation in this complex environment is to ensure that its education system acts as an anchor to maintain its economic health, develops informed citizens who are innovative and creative, and delivers educational opportunities close to the clients through the ubiquitous availability of "smart" telecommunications and information systems. These are not inconsequential tasks, especially when it must also capitalize on the knowledge creation abilities possessed by all its citizens.

Programs

Policy programs define and shape the intended outcomes. Many different instruments are used to facilitate the common objectives woven through various jurisdictions to ensure equitable and ubiquitous services to citizens. This section describes a selection of policy programs in education and telecommunications.

Education.   The rapid pace of technological change entails that the education system must not only prepare citizens for employment but also train them for the several careers they will expect to have throughout their lives. It must also provide learning opportunities in a variety of convenient locations.

Governments traditionally have supported the education system through direct funding and in some instances through research grants. Increasingly, however, to encourage more rapid response time, nations have been using more specific vehicles such as following:

- Direct funding for the introduction of information communications technologies (ICTs) into the classroom and for connecting schools and institutions to the Internet (SchoolNet, Computers in Schools, and e-Rate).
- Funding continuing professional education for teachers to ensure desired learner outcomes.

- Creating public agencies such as the Office of Learning Technologies, Human Resources Development Canada, to raise awareness of technology-based learning and act as catalysts for innovation in technology-enabled lifelong learning. In the United States, the Office of Secondary Education's FIPSE program was created to encourage similar goals. These agencies in turn use a variety of mechanisms, including funding programs, to achieve their ends (Office of Learning Technologies, 1999; U.S. Department of Education, 2001a).
- Creating advisory councils that inform ministers and ensure broad-based representation in the formulation of public policy regarding issues such as standards for products and materials, the development of national content, and appropriate copyright and intellectual property regulations. Examples include the Information Highway Advisory Council in Canada and the Advisory Council for the National Information Infrastructure in the United States.
- Establishing funding programs to support learning through the Internet and the development of advanced content. Examples include CANARIE's Learning and Learnware Programs in Canada and the Learning Anywhere Anytime Program in the United States.
- Promoting direct international marketing of educational product services and associated knowledge-based assets by various agents of government, which underscores education's role as an economic driver.

Telecommunications.   As distance educators, we are aware that there have been numerous policy instruments to achieve a more responsive, modern, and accessible information and telecommunications infrastructure.

Some argue that the decision to deregulate and depend upon competition to achieve the goal of universal and equitable access, while enhancing the position of large business, has disadvantaged small businesses, low socioeconomic groups, and those living in sparsely populated rural areas (Parker & Hudson, 1995; U.S. Congress, 1991). In Canada, literally hundreds of representations were made to the Canadian Radio/Television and Telecommunications Commission (CRTC, 1995), Canada's regulator, during its Information Highway Hearings, by various policy networks (small businesses, residents of rural areas, schools, libraries, and volunteer organizations), each sending this same message regarding universality and cost-effective access to the highway of the future. These types of inputs have influenced a number of programs intended to mitigate the possible negative impacts of telecommunications policies.

In the telecommunications domain, in addition to directed programs and broad-based consultations, as in education, instruments also include regulation, despite a trend away from regulation and toward competition:

In Canada there are special tariffs or customer categories for education, health, and public libraries (CRTC, 1996).

The Connecting Canadians Agenda implemented programs to join all schools, 5,000 volunteer groups, and 10,000 communities to the Internet. In the year 2000, programs to create 12 Smart Communities (or regions) to explore ways of bringing advanced networks and applications to the community level, establish a government online initiative, and develop advanced content have marked a transition from providing basic Internet access to providing broadband access. The e-Rate speaks to many of these same objectives in the United States. Also supporting this shift from basic to broadband access are programs such as CA*Net 4 in Canada and Internet 2 in the United States. Both networks increase bandwidth significantly among their educational and research institutions. It will only be a matter of "web-time" before advanced content will be the only content available to citizens, including rural or low-income families. As advanced content products become the norm, and with them a need for high-speed access, agencies and governments are increasingly looking for ways to provide the essential infrastructure in a more effective, efficient, and equitable manner than has been characteristic of commercial avenues. Already we are seeing public responses to this situation. High-speed, wide-area networks are being created by municipalities and school boards. Governments worldwide are seriously looking at the role of government in the provision of the essential infrastructure (e.g., the Manitoba Innovation Network, the Swedish Government), and most of them have established very short time lines for decision making.

INNOVATION AND PARTNERSHIPS

Economic growth is much more about changes in technology that allow us to produce new goods and services and to produce them in new and innovative ways. It is about invention and innovation, scientific experimentation and new management techniques.... Knowledge products are relatively new, today's innovation must similarly support a rapidly emerging information age. There is a legitimate role for government in producing an educated workforce, investing in human capital, and in the creation and diffusion of scientific knowledge wherever the market cannot do so. (Bevilacqua, 1998, pp. 25–26)

Although not addressed as discrete policy areas, innovation and partnership development are significant drivers in all policy domains, including education and telecommunications. Recent government budgets have announced programs with hundreds of millions of dollars attached to them to encourage innovation and the creation of new partnerships.

To grow their economies, governments seek not only to fuel innovation but also to nurture the relationships that turn innovative ideas and intellectual property into marketable products. The development of partnerships, more specifically public-private partnerships, continues to be a stated goal in these programs. Examples include these:

In 1998, the Canadian Fund for Innovation (CFI) was established as a means to upgrade Canada's educational research infrastructure, including laboratories and necessary equipment but excluding telecommunications. Evidence of matching funding from the private sector was required if a university was to obtain funding, thus addressing the national research agenda while promoting productivity. Two years later this program was enhanced with a commitment of $900 million in funding for 2,000 research chairs in the 2000 budget (Martin, 2000).

Five years ago, a program to support national network centres of excellence (NCEs) was announced. The NCEs covered a wide range of strategic knowledge areas. The TeleLearning Network of Centres of Excellence dealt directly with the design, creation, and delivery of "advanced content." Like other programs it promotes shared research initiatives between public institutions and the private sector (*TeleLearning Network of Centres of Excellence*, 1999). More recently, Canarie and Heritage Canada co-founded a joint program to promote research and content for the advanced internet (Canarie, 2002).

The emphasis on innovation provides tremendous challenges and opportunities for one of the primary creators of content and knowledge—the education system.

INTENDED OUTCOMES

In an era of decreased direct funding, governments are implementing policies through using their treasuries, public awareness campaigns, government departments, and arms-length agencies to do the following:

- Address the continual learning needs of 21st-century citizens and workers.
- Encourage innovation in the creation of knowledge products.
- Develop media rich content that will serve the needs of learners and the economy.
- Compel educational institutions to form partnerships in order to access research funds for their distance or distributed learning endeavors and use these research funds to innovate, not maintain the status quo.
- Encourage all players, including educational agencies, to look at linkages between education and economic opportunities.
- Encourage broader community participation in and control over the community aspects that can benefit from ICT applications, including choice in learning opportunities and delivery approaches.
- Decentralize the locus of information access, including access to educational opportunities.
- Provide broadband highways that give all citizens the opportunity to participate in the knowledge economy.
- Use "public" sector delivery to drive the creation of that infrastructure—by the public or private sector.

What impact do the enhanced position of education in a knowledge society, the influence of so many policy areas, and the rapid pace of change have on distance educators and their institutions? Are distance educators still change agents or just struggling to keep up?

INSTITUTIONAL PLANNING

During any public policy formulation and implementation cycle, the very institutions and agencies that the government seeks to influence are going through parallel planning and implementation phases. The pace of change in this new environment, coupled with decreases in the direct funding given to public institutions, is shortening the available cycle. At the same time, it is compelling educational institutions to leverage core strengths and develop partnerships to enhance and/or develop new education services.

As in the case of public policy, there are several schools of thought as to how best to manage and plan for institutional change. Kotter (1996) argues that powerful macro-economic forces such as those described earlier will continue to grow stronger, resulting in more pressure on institutions to enhance quality of services and products, reduce costs, and increase productivity. Most institutions have established some process that allows them to chart a course for change and to evaluate their success. The results have been neutral at best and in some instances disruptive and disappointing to the institutional leaders. Mintzberg (1994) suggested that the weakest link in any planning initiative is the creation and implementation of strategies and tactics. Most models will help an institution to take into account that it is a subsystem of a larger system whose actions or reactions shape the institution's environment and therefore its opportunities for success. In an era when consumers have many choices, public institutions need mechanisms to continually assess the environment so that they can identify and implement the programs and services that meet their clients' needs while at the same time attending to their mandates and their internal institutional culture.

A variety of influences impact the institutional planning process. Public policy does so through its direct and indirect programs. These influences may come in the form of targeted funding programs, which emphasize partnerships or even suggest the learner profile. Other factors that influence institutional planning include the mandate of the institution (regional, national, or international), the targeted student population (pre- or postbaccalaureate), the faculty, the financial resources, and institutional values. In institutions in which distance education is separated from the mainstream and housed in a separate operating unit, tensions between the campus-based services and distance education services can influence how distance education is conceived and how effectively it can adjust to external environmental factors.

Can institutions preserve academic integrity while attending to the external policy influences that are wide reaching and major in their intent? Will governments be able to hold institutions with a greater private component as accountable as public institutions when it comes to the quality of distance learning? Can distance educators lead this change in the same way they led the movement toward increased access in the first half of the 20th century?

The greatest challenge for any distance learning department or institution is not the planning itself but the implementation of the plans and the evaluation of the outcomes. When the external policy process is changing rapidly, the available institutional response time is shortened. This can create extreme pressure for an institution to react and allows seemingly little opportunity to determine that the direction taken is appropriate to the institution's mandate and values. Establishing responsive feedback loops, either formally or through the institutional equivalent of a policy network, is essential to ensuring that the institution can effectively respond to and shape change.

The challenges are particularly acute in education because of the influences of ICTs. The ICT revolution is being driven by every national government as a cornerstone to a healthy economy. Education and innovation are key in the creation of knowledge, and institutions have had significant expectations placed on them through the public policy process. Concomitant with the push to "wire" all educational institutions is an assumption that these same institutions will be able to generate revenues that until today were not available to them. This presumes that the values of the institution are consistent with this agenda. What a disappointment when the institution does not generate these additional revenues and decides to scale back its distance education offerings or to charge the distance learner special assessment fees for the use of telecommunications and the other value-added services that are necessary to a good distance education model.

There is no easy answer to the planning dilemma. Some may argue that planning is a waste of time: Others will commit to building a plan but ultimately do not match resources and finances to the plan to make sure it is achievable. Others will become slaves to the plan and risk missing new opportunities. If distance educators are to remain leaders of change, they must plan and they must pay particular attention to the responsive implementation component of their plan. The plan is only a framework for action. In order for the plan to be acceptable to the institutional community, it must be understandable, reflect the values of the institution, speak to the learner as the core of the enterprise, and communicate the "wins" to the institutional community. Above all, however, the plan itself must not be static; it must be flexible enough to reach its overall objective while responding to a fluid environment.

OBSERVED OUTCOMES

... "view the relevance of higher education in the 21st century that begins from the changes that are taking place in the production of knowledge.... The major change is the emergence of a distributed knowledge production system and within this system knowledge is characterised by a set of attributes.... The main change, as far as the universities are concerned, is that knowledge production and dissemination—research and teaching—are no longer self contained activities, carried out in relative institutional isolation. They now involve interaction with a variety of other

knowledge producers. In this situation, connections will increasingly involve the use of the poten-
tialities of the new information and communications technologies. (Gibbons, 1998, p. i)

The policy programs are supporting change and have intended outcomes. These programs, combined with the planning cycle of institutions, do produce change in the environment. If, however, traditional institutions can or will not change, something will evolve to fill the gap. In the case of education today, the educational delivery systems described below are a few of the new forms providing services where traditional agencies did not.

Institutional Structures

Because of advances in digital networks and, arguably, policy initiatives such as those mentioned above, institutes of learning have become part of a global networked society. Further, as loci of learning opportunities, they share the stage with libraries, community access sites, workplaces, and the home. So what are the education arrangements of the late 21st century that link the institutions to the community?

Historical Distance Learning Structures

Distance education has existed through various correspondence programs since the end of the 19th century. Three decades ago it began to achieve more acceptance in the university sector as a delivery mode. In the contemporary secondary environment, all Canadian universities and colleges now offer one or more distance programs. Many dual-mode universities are making full programs available and are seeking niche markets for students who are willing to pay the full costs of education and its delivery. In the United States, four out of every five institutions of higher education offer one or more courses at a distance, and one-third offer one or more complete degree programs at a distance.

A little over two decades ago, the second institutional arrangement for distance learning emerged: the single-mode institution, catering only to distance students. The first such institution was Britain's Open University. Today, many countries have open universities or open colleges, but their numbers are relatively small compared to their dual-mode counterparts.

Although there has been growth in the numbers of providers of distance education, client groups, and points of access, one program per university can hardly be interpreted as an appropriate response to the increased need and the rapid change in policy direction discussed in previous sections. Although it could be argued that access has been enhanced over a 20-year period through increased institutional activity and increased access locations, there is less evidence that diversification of program offerings has occurred. In particular, in the postsecondary environment many institutions are collapsing their range of offerings in general arts, education, and business programs to meet high enrollment demands. New curricula to meet the demands of a knowledge-based economy are less prevalent and still need to be developed.

Strategic Alliances and Private Provision

As indicated, public policy programs have encouraged partnerships and collaborative models. A number of organizational forms that display these characteristics have evolved.

For-Profit Agencies.   Perhaps the best known for-profit educational structure is the corporate university, which addresses the entire human resource development spectrum of a single corporation, from skill training through to formal management programs. Although in early iterations these universities tended to be contained within a corporation or a subsidiary, more recently they encompass public and private alliances. For example, a corporate university may buy seats in the programs of public institutions or contract public institutions to provide just-in-time learning opportunities and/or develop curriculum related to the corporation's needs.

Public-Private Partnerships.   These take two forms. In one, public or not-for-profit agencies outsource services such as registration, database construction, student tracking, record-keeping, and financial management to a private agency. In the second, not-for-profit institutions provide intellectual property and knowledge, while software development or multimedia companies package this into an educational product and distribute it. In this latter type of partnership, the public institutions maintain their knowledge creation and teaching roles, while the private firms provide the distribution mechanism. It would not be unreasonable to speculate that these two types of public-private alliances might combine into a single model encompassing knowledge creation (public), content development (private), and distribution of student services (private).

Public-Public Collaboration.   A wide variety of public-public partnerships have evolved to meet learner demands, address the requirements of the economy, and rationalize the costs of creating and transmitting relevant distributed learning opportunities. Many secondary institutions are joining forces to share curriculum and the production of mediated courses in order to offset the initial high investment costs of technology-based courses. Equally important, these partnerships broaden the options available to learners and provide greater flexibility in delivery and greater access to a more diverse program menu.

Lifelong Learning and Cost

National programs to provide a competitive educational environment have increased the access to education to some degree, particularly for adult learners. Creating a broad diversity of program offerings remains a challenge (duplication exists despite new technology), as do issues of equity between distance and face-to-face students. As an example on equity issues, licenses for distributed online library databases are much more expensive than licenses for the same electronic databases used within the confines of a campus library. In the public-private alliance publishing model outlined above, students will likely pay each time they access a resource. Traditionally, libraries have purchased resources that are used many times by many students. Will on-demand resources be offered on a "one-time, each-time payment" basis? Will there be a possibility of reuse by the same student within a time frame without an additional fee? For students who must access online resources through low-bandwidth channels, the download times will be longer than for those on higher speeds links, causing variations in student costs. In addition, there is a tendency for institutions to off-load access charges to students (e.g., ISPs and e-mail accounts), and students are frequently charged more for electronically mediated courses even though they cost less.

Telecommunications: Information Highway

There is a rapidly evolving telecommunications environment, including the increasing requirement for broadband access driven by the creation and use of advanced content. To a certain extent, this trend has been facilitated by deregulation, which works in locations where there is sufficient competition to protect users. Both Canada and the United States, however, have discovered how difficult it is to ensure effective competition. New policy programs are being explored in many countries to deal with what could be categorized as market failure in rural areas related to this now essential infrastructure.

Proximity to Customers

Together, the pervasiveness of networks and the ever-increasing emphasis on open competition and a free market model have resulted in the delivery of services closer to the consumer. Once we went to a teller in a bank; now we get our weekly cash from a machine in the mall. Health care is becoming community based, and in England people will soon be able to have X-rays taken in Boots (a large chain of pharmacies). Post offices, once independent locations, are now found in drug and corner stores, and you can even purchase your stamps on the Internet. Other forms of e-commerce abound. The delivery of services closer to the consumer is a fact of life, and those in education and training must follow this trend.

FEEDBACK

According to a systems view of policy, the formulation, implementation, and evaluation of policy is organic in nature. In other words as programs are initiated and evolve, they directly and indirectly cause incremental refinements and adjustments to public policy.

As indicated earlier, governments will often create task forces, commissions, or special review bodies through which they seek formal input on policy implementation on a time-sensitive task. Arms-length government agencies have advisory boards and/or steering committees that guide adjustments and change. Institutions look to internal and external constituents to adjust structures, educational services, and delivery models. In a market economy, members of the policy community can also influence public policy through letters to the editor, petitions, representations at public hearings, and participation in community based reviews, or alternatively individuals can join a group of people committed to achieving specific types of outputs (policy networks).

These are legitimate and effective means of providing policy feedback, and distance learning practitioners should make every effort to participate in this part of the cycle if they wish to see their needs and values reflected in the system as a whole.

THE MODEL APPLIED

This section presents two examples of the policy process described in previous sections. There is no cause and effect relationship implied.

Education

Public education policy in the United States is mandated through the U.S. Department of Education. In November 2000, the department released the agenda report *Learning Without Limits* (U.S. Department of Education, 2000). This report was the outcome of an extensive set of meetings throughout the country with 75 special groups as well as several regional meetings with stakeholders. This consultation process was intended to identify the key challenges facing the postsecondary system and the department's roles and appropriate actions. Overall, the report included five major themes that reflected the input from the various stakeholder groups. These themes represent a national agenda for postsecondary education for the next 5 years.

A theme that is pertinent to distance educators is that of "integrating technology and distance education into the curriculum." The report outlined a variety of challenges regarding this theme and set action steps or programs to move the policy agenda forward. Goals included the evolution of new organizational structures, the development of partnerships, increased quality and access, and the creation of new financial models for postsecondary institutions. One targeted program put in place to help achieve these intended outcomes is the Distance Education Demonstration Program. This program encourages institutions to experiment with potential alternatives for student aid that are less restrictive and prohibitive to the distance learner, thereby mitigating any unfavorable bias experienced by these learners. A second targeted program is the Learning Anywhere Anytime Program (LAAP), a funding program administered under the auspices of the Fund for the Improvement of Postsecondary Education (FIPSE). LAAP is a grant program established to broaden access to technology-enabled distance learning. LAAP promotes public-private partnerships and facilitates experimentation with new models of service and course delivery. Many interesting projects have been initiated under this program, all of which embrace multiple partnerships. They are long-term projects with deliverables that are intended to add to the knowledge base of the distance educators in the country. Examples include Standards for Accessible Learning Technologies (SALT) and BATE: Borderless Access to Training and Education. Each of these involves public-private partnerships, has intrastate sectoral representation, and targets high-need learners (U.S. Department of Education, 2001a, 2001b).

The outcomes of these and other LAPP-funded projects will provide information that government and stakeholder groups can use to assess the effectiveness of the policy program and determine whether to adjust distance education policy for the future. It is possible that the projects implemented under the auspices of LAAP will achieve different levels of success and that some will be sustainable whereas others will not be. In any case, each of the lessons learned will inform future developments in the public policy arena.

The systems approach to policy development and evaluation is predicated on the cultural values of a pluralist society where policy communities and policy networks have the opportunity to influence the changing landscape.

Telecommunications

In the early 1990s, in Canada literally hundreds of groups made unsolicited representations to the information highway hearings held by CRTC (1995). These groups stressed to the regulator the importance of quality and ubiquitous digital networking for the delivery of social programs, including distance learning and telehealth. This, among many other factors, influenced the Canadian government's decision to form the Information Highway Advisory Council (IHAC, 1995a). Five working groups consisting of knowledgeable stakeholders from across the country conducted studies, held roundtables, and used other formal and informal means to gather input. One working group was assigned to learning and training. Soon after the IHAC report was tabled, the government, in the 1997 Speech from the Throne, announced its Connecting Canadians Agenda (Industry Canada, 1998). In line with this policy government funds were used to help deploy the information highway to 10,000 communities in Canada through such programs as SchoolNet, the Community Access Program (CAP), and VolNet (which connected 5,500 voluntary agencies). As a CAP site was equipped with four to six computers, many small schools found it advantageous to house a site, and thus they often applied to do so. In order to be chosen, schools had to change their policies to allow public access to buildings during hours when they would normally be closed (e.g., during summer).

In the final years of the connectedness agenda, the Smart Communities program provided up to $5 million to 12 communities to encourage the deployment and application of broadband networking. The government also provided funding to CANARIE (a public-private initiative) in three phases to deploy a T-1, an ATM, and finally a gigabit network connecting all universities and other research agencies in Canada so that they could continue to innovate with advanced products to be used in this broadband environment.

Informal feedback from the university and college community to the government through CANARIE and SchoolNet committees indicated that, although connectivity was important, the ability to create content of various types to move on these networks was equally important. In CANARIE's Phase 3 funding, Industry Canada provided substantial funds to be used by educational institutions in partnership with private firms to create e-learning, e-health, and e-business applications.

Throughout the early implementation of the connectedness agenda, groups realized that when government funding was withdrawn, connectivity costs were still too high to allow them to fulfill their mandate to increase access to learning opportunities. Once again, many made representations to a CRTC hearing, and a decision was consequently reached that hospitals, public libraries, and public education facilities were new customer groups and therefore could negotiate a different fee (CRTC, 1996).

As high-speed networks became more important for the health and wealth of the country, the government created two additional task forces. The Online Task Force invited many university and college presidents to consult on the challenges of and mechanisms for transforming more postsecondary programs into online programs. The task force's report, published in February 2001, addressed policy changes at both the government and institutional levels that were needed if this initiative was to be successful. The National Broadband Task Force, composed of representatives of carriers and vendors and of user stakeholders, is investigating the barriers, social and economic issues, and models of implementation associated with the government's commitment to make broadband networking available to every Canadian community by 2004. Through these two task forces and their consultations with stakeholders and the policy community, the government is continuing to evolve its policies on distance learning and telecommunications.

These two high-level examples, one in education and one in telecommunications, serve to indicate some contact points in the interactive and incremental approach to policy formulation and implementation at the public and institutional levels. They do not exemplify a neat cause-and-effect relationship.

FURTHER RESEARCH

Research is the basis for the creation of knowledge. In the field of distance learning, there are ample opportunities at present to investigate effective mechanisms to create advanced (individual, interactive, and media rich) content and to incorporate it into learning environments facilitated by high-speed networks. Many of these research opportunities are covered in other chapters. This section, therefore, concentrates on research that relates to institutional and public policy and planning.

The provision of lifelong learning opportunities is both a market need and an intended outcome of public policy programs. New educational institutional forms have evolved, but there is a trend for both these and traditional institutions, through their distance learning programs, to off-load a higher portion of the cost of education to distance learners than to those students participating in traditional learning settings. Most documentation indicates that, over time, distance learning is more cost-effective than face-to-face learning. If students are studying for their first postsecondary credential, why are they being penalized? If public policy is encouraging lifelong learning as a key to productivity and economic prosperity, what additional policy instruments do governments need to consider in addition to those dealing with access?

Although facilitating lifelong learning in support of a knowledge-based society and delivering services closer to the citizen are objectives of public policy, a number of outstanding issues need to be investigated to realize these goals. What types of new institutional models best suit the learners' needs? What steps can be taken by traditional institutions to be more responsive to the new environment? Until self-regulation becomes a reality, should a government require transitional insurance to protect students against the failure of institutions, have mandatory guidelines for operation within the country, require licenses or other accrediting procedures, or, less intrusively, require evidence of a quality assurance process such as ISO certification? Governments need to address fair use guidelines, appropriate licensing structures, and possibly educational access tariffs. At the same time, institutions should set reasonable use policies, look at their purchasing policies, and review the roles of their libraries in light of the current student needs. Distance educators, given their long history of providing educational opportunity outside the traditional classroom, should investigate the best models for this new environment. Their investigations can inform the management of the process of change that current initiatives have begun.

A telecommunications policy, environment Koenig and Sione (1997) argued that the information highway as a technology is relatively immature. They hold that the information highway has arrived at the third stage of technological diffusion without having passed through stage 2. Other industries, such as the railway, telephones, broadcasting, and electrification, went through all of these stages:

Phase 1. Research and early innovation are carried out by only a few groups.
Phase 2. Regulated diffusion of the technology permits the normative values of the country, such as types of acceptable content and access (social, financial, and geographic), to be addressed through the development and implementation of relevant public policies.
Phase 3. Competition is allowed because adequate infrastructure and knowledge exist and costs are sufficiently low.

The authors claimed that in 5 to 10 years, the information highway has proceeded from phase 1 to 3 with no pause in phase 2. Some already have recognized that, although competition may have been a necessary first step, new policy must now be implemented to ensure the same normative outcomes that regulation did. What are the parameters of that policy?

Are competition laws adequate to ensure fair and effective competitiveness when no company wants to compete? Some authors argue governments must refrain from over intervention and instead concentrate on genuine problem areas (e.g., nondiscriminatory access to bottleneck facilities and consumer protection in residual pockets of monopoly), implementing some form of subsidy where competition will not be viable (Globerman, 1996; Janish, 1994). Concern over rates and quality of service (important in days of monopoly) decreases compared with worries about access, interconnectivity, price caps, and greater efficiency. New regulatory issues, such as privacy, conflict with law enforcement, and freedom of speech, have become more pressing. From a research perspective, technical, legal, financial, and social issues abound.

There is an assumption that bandwidth will become irrelevant within the next few years. This may be a laudable position but to date we are a long way from making unlimited bandwidth universally available at a reasonable cost. Government and institutional policymakers must accept that if "the big pipe" is the classroom of the 21st century, then communications cost must become equivalent to "bricks and morter" costs and should be accepted as a state and institutional responsibility. The current trend to off-load all these infrastructure costs onto the student returns us to the days when education was the privilege of the financial elite. We would argue, therefore, for renewed and enhanced programs on the policy agendas. Distance educators must play a role in the formulation of these programs through research and participation in the public policy process.

Applied research and evaluation are necessary to inform the policy cycle both at the public and the institutional level. New ideas can help shape policy goals, and evaluation can help fine-tune programs. However, carrying out research is not the only role for distance educators. Research achieves little if the results stay in academic journals. Distance educators must become active policy networkers on institutional committees and advisory councils participating in round tables and other activities to ensure that they can provide input on behalf of their learners.

CONCLUSION

The rate of change in the world at large and in public policy requires that institutions first plan and second adopt models for planning that are less linear and are more responsive to rapid adjustments in the marketplace. A myriad of new learning institutions, corporate universities, virtual universities, and public-private partnerships have evolved to fill the void left by traditional institutions. Traditional institutions have also been complacent about the provision of more flexible learning environments. One distance education course per university does not speak to the current need to reach learners in the home and workplace. The linear planning model is proving to be ineffective, for the environment is demanding that we implement "on the go"—that is, "plan" and "do" in concert.

Distance educators can shape the environment instead of only reacting to it, but to do so they must have input into public policy process. They could have the necessary input by becoming involved in the education policy community and helping determine public policy objectives at the formulation stage. Their increased involvement, combined with a more responsive planning process at the institutional level, will help distance educators retain their reputation as innovators and leaders in education. Distance educators can provide balance to the public policy process because they have the ability to cross over a multitude of different structures and bring cohesion where appropriate.

REFERENCES

Advisory Council on Science and Technology. (1999). *Stepping up: Skills and opportunities in the knowledge economy* (Catalogue No. C2-467/2000). Ottawa: Industry Canada.

Bevilacqua, M. (1998). *Report of the standing committee on finance: Facing the future's challenges and choices for a new era.* Ottawa: Public Works and Services Canada.

Canadian Radio/Television and Telecommunication Commission. (1995). *Competition and culture on Canada's information highway: Managing the realities of transition* (Catalogue No. BC92-531/1995). Ottawa: Public Works and Government Services Canada.

Canadian Radio/Television and Telecommunication Commission. (1996). *Tariff for educational and health services entities* (Telecom Decision CRTC 96–9).

Canarie (2002). http://www.canarie.ca

Dohmen, G. (1996). *Life long learning: Guidelines for a modern education policy.* Bonn: Federal Ministry of Education, Science, Research and Technology.

Duderstadt, J. J. (1997). The future of the university in an age of knowledge. *Journal of Asynchronous Learning Networks* [Online serial], *1*(2). Available: http://www.aln.org/alnweb/journal/jaln.htm

A future-proof IT infrastructure for Sweden (Report). (1999). Stockholm: IT Commission Stockholm.

Gibbons, M. (1998). *Higher education relevance in the 21st Century.* Washington, DC: The World Bank.

Globerman, S. (1996). Competition and regulatory policies for the I-way. *Policy Options, 17*(8), 11–15.

Industry Canada. (1998). *Education and training services: Part 1. Overview and prospects.* Ottawa: Author. Ministry of Supply and Services.

Industry Canada. (2001). *The e-learning e-volution in colleges and universities,* A Pan-Canadian Challenges The Advisory Committee for Online Learning. Ottawa: Ministry of Supply and Services.

Industry Canada. (2001). *The New National Dream: Networking the Nation for Broadband Access.* Report of the National Broadband Task Force. Ottawa: Ministry of Supply and Services.

Information Highway Advisory Council. (1995a). *Connection, community content: The challenge of the information highway.* Ottawa: Ministry of Supply and Services.

Information Highway Advisory Council. (1995b). *Making it Happen: Final report of the learning and training working group*. Ottawa: Ministry of Supply and Services.

Janish, H. (1994). Recasting regulation for a new telecommunications era. *Policy Options, 15*(1), 20–27.

Kennard, W. (2000). *Telecommunications @ the millennium: The telecom act turns four*. [Online]. Federal Communications Commission, Office of Plans and Policy. Available: Washington, DC. http://www.fcc.gov/speeches/kennard/2000/telecomatthemillenniumbw.pdf

Koenig, M. & Sione, P. (1997). World at stage III, but the net at stage II. *Journal of the American Society for Information Science, 49*, 853–859.

Kotter, J. (1996). *Leading change*. Boston: Harvard Business School Press.

Manitoba Innovation Network. (2000, June). *Accelerating the deployment of Manitoba's broadband network infrastructure* (White paper prepared by Broadband Project Office). Winnipeg MB: Author.

Martin, P. (2000). *The budget speech*. Available: http://www.canoe.ca/FedBudget2000/speeche/speech1e.htm

Matthews, D. (1998). *The transformation of higher education through information technology: Implications for state higher education finance policy* [Online]. Western Interstate Commission for Higher Education. Boulder, CO Available: http://www.wiche.edu/IT&Finance.htm

Mintzberg, H. (1994). *The rise and fall of strategic planning*. New York: The Free Press.

The national information infrastructure: Agenda for action [Online]. (2000). Available: http://www.ibiblio.org/nii/NII-Executive-Summary.html

Office of Learning Technologies. (1999). *Your partner in lifelong learning* [Online]. Available: http://olt-bta.hrdc-drhc.gc.ca/about/backgrnd.html

Pal, L. A. (1992). *Public policy analysis: An introduction* (2nd ed.). Scarborough, ON: Nelson Canada.

Parker, E. B., & Hudson, H. E. (1995). *Electronic byways: State policies for rural development through telecommunications*. Washington, DC: Aspen Institute.

TeleLearning Network of Centres of Excellence [Online]. Vancouver, BC Available: http://www.nce.gc.ca/blurbs/teleleng.htm

U.S. Congress, Office of Technology Assessment. (1991). *Rural America at the crossroads: Networking for the future* (OTA-TCT-471). Washington, DC: U.S. Government Printing Office.

U.S. Department of Education. (2000). *Learning without limits: An agenda for the Office of Postsecondary Education* [Online]. Available: http://www.ed.gov/offices/OPE/AgenProj/report/toc.html

U.S. Department of Education. (2001a). *Fund for the Improvement of Postsecondary Education (FIPSE)* [Online]. Available: www.ed.gov/offices/OPE/FIPSE/welcome.html

U.S. Department of Education. (2001b). *Learning Anytime Anywhere Partnerships (LAPP)* [Online]. Available: http://www.ed.gov/offices/OPE/FIPSE/LAAP/index.html

Wiarda, H. J. (Ed.). (1991). *New directions in comparative politics*. Boulder, CO: Westview Press.

29

Distance Education Policy Issues: Statewide Perspectives

Michael Simonson
Nova Southeastern University
simsmich@nova.edu

Tamara Bauck
Department of Education and Cultural Affairs
State of South Dakota
tammy.bauck@state.sd.us

THE IMPORTANCE OF POLICIES

A policy is defined as a written course of action, such as a statute, procedure, rule, or regulation, that is adopted to facilitate program development (King, Nugent, Eich, Mlinek, & Russell, 2000). A distance education policy is a written course of action adopted by an institution to facilitate the development of distance education programs.

Policies provide a framework for the operation of distance education. They form a set of agreed rules that explain roles and responsibilities. Policies can be compared to laws of navigation, rules of the road, or language syntax. They define a standard method of operation, such as "no wake zone," "keep to the right," or "subject and verb must match." Policies give structure to unstructured events and are a natural step in the adoption of an innovation, such as distance education. The institutionalization of a new idea includes the development of rules and regulations (policies) for the use of the innovation (Rogers, 1995). One key indicator that distance education is moving into the mainstream is the increased emphasis on the need for policies to guide its effective growth.

Berge (1998) and Gellman-Danley and Fetzner (1998) have proposed models for distance education policy. These models have been reported and evaluated a number of times in the literature (King, Lacy, McMillian, Bartels, & Fredilino, 1998; King, Nugent, Eich, et al., 2000; King, Nugent, Russell, Eich, & Lacy, 2000) and seem to provide a useful framework for an investigation of distance education policy.

POLICY CATEGORIES

For this discussion, policies for distance education will be divided into seven categories (Gellman-Danley & Fetzner, 1998; King, Nugent, Eich, et al., 2000). The categories are as follows (see also Table 29.1):

Policy area 1: Academic. The key issues in this area concern academic calendars, accreditation of programs, course quality, course and program evaluation, Carnegie units, grading, admissions, and curriculum review and approval processes.

Policy area 2: Fiscal, geographic, and governance. The key issues concern tuition rates, special fees, full time equivalencies, state mandated regulations related to funding, service area limitations, out-of-district versus in-district relationships, consortia agreements, contracts with collaborating organizations, board oversight, administration cost, and tuition disbursement.

Policy area 3: Faculty. The key issues concern compensation and workloads, design and development incentives, staff development, faculty support, faculty evaluation, intellectual freedom, and union contracts.

TABLE 29.1

List of Policies

I. Academic policies
  A. Students
    1. Admission policies
    2. Grading policies
    3. Academic records
  B. Faculty
    1. Evaluation
    2. Credentials
  C. Curriculum
    1. Accreditation
    2. Course/program approval
    3. Course/program evaluation
    4. Carnegie unit determination
II. Fiscal, geographic, and governance policies
  A. Fiscal
    1. Tuition collection and disbursement
    2. Special fees
    3. State funding
    4. Administrative costs
    5. Telecommunications costs
  B. Geographic
    1. In-district vs. out-of-district
    2. Consortia agreements
  C. Governance
    1. Board oversight
    2. Consortia contracts
    3. Provider contracts
III. Faculty policies
  A. Compensation
    1. Design and development incentives
    2. Overload compensation
  B. Evaluation
    1. Course evaluation
    2. Promotion and contract
    3. Intellectual freedom
  C. Support
    1. Staff development/training
    2. Course/program support
    3. Local facilitators
IV. Legal policies
  A. Intellectual property
  B. Copyright
  C. Liability
    1. Student
    2. Faculty
    3. School
V. Student policies
  A. Academic
    1. Advising
    2. Resources and laboratories
    3. Training
    4. Testing and assessment
  B. Nonacademic
    1. Equipment and software
    2. Financial aid
    3. Privacy
    4. Access and equity
VI. Technical policies
  A. System
  B. Contractual agreements
VII. Philosophical policies
  A. Vision
  B. Mission
  C. Activities

Policy area 4: Legal. The key issues concern intellectual property agreements, copyright, and faculty, student, and institutional liability.

Policy area 5: Student. The key issues concern student support, academic advising, counseling, library services, student training, financial aid, testing and assessment, access to resources, equipment requirements, and privacy.

Policy area 6: Technical. The key issues concern system reliability, connectivity, technical support, hardware and software, and access.

Policy area 7: Philosophical. The key issues concern the institution's approach to and acceptance of distance education and how its values, mission, and vision relate to distance education.

These seven policy areas are discussed below and the importance of each explained. It is essential that distance education courses be considered of high quality and comparable to traditionally offered courses. Often the term *equivalent* (or *equivalency*) is used when distance education courses are described. Simonson, Schlosser, and Hanson (1999), in discussing the equivalence of distance and traditional education, emphasized that distant and local learners have fundamentally different environments in which to learn. Yet, just as a triangle and a square are considered equivalent if they have the same area even though they are quite different, distant and local learners should be provided equivalent learning experiences that may be quite different but that "cover the same area." Learning experiences are anything that happens to the student to promote learning, including what is observed, felt, heard, or done (Simonson et al., 1999).

Equivalent is not the same as equal. Rather, equivalent experiences can be similar or they can be considerably different. The key to equivalency is that the totality of learning experiences for each learner should cover the same area, even if the individual experiences might be unique. The attempt to make learning equal for distant and local learners is an exercise in futility. Instead, instructional designers should create multiple learning experiences that can be assigned to or selected by students to permit the attainment of course objectives. Watkins and Schlosser (2000) have proposed a model for course design that applies the concept of equivalent learning experiences. Also, policies for distance education should support the provision of equivalent rather than equal learning experiences.

Academic Policies

Academic issues are in many respects at the heart of why policies are critical. Academic issues concern the overall integrity of the course. They concern students, instruction, curriculum, and program. They probably have the longest and most widespread impact as students take courses, earn diplomas, and move to other schools or on to higher education. Academic policies help ensure that institutional integrity is maintained.

A increasingly common approach to distance education policy development is the so-called integrated approach. In this approach, the same procedures are used for distance education as for other kinds of education. Instead of developing new structures and policies for distance education, the intent is to modify existing structures, regulations, rules, and policies to integrate distance education into the entire educational system. Flexibility is a necessary ingredient of the integrated approach. Teachers, administrators, and policymakers should recognize that changes do not reflect a weakening or that modification is not a threat to integrity. Rather, the policy changes necessitated by the development of a distance education program are merely part of the natural evolution of a school, district, or state to accommodate technology-based instruction. Watkins and Schlosser (2000) discussed Carnegie units and described processes for demonstrating how distance education courses can be compared to traditional face-to-face classes where "seat time" is measured.

Once an institutional commitment to distance education is made, academic policies should be reviewed and distance education requirements should be integrated into regulations. The following are examples of academic issues that need to be considered:

Course schedules and academic calendars, especially for synchronous learning experiences.
Event, course, and program approval and evaluation.
Student admission.
Grading and assessment of students.
Grade recordkeeping and reporting.
Accreditation.

Fiscal, Geographic, and Governance Policies

The central issue behind most fiscal, geographic, and governance policies is ownership—ownership of the course, the student, and the curriculum. The institution with ownership is the one that has ultimate responsibility and whose decisions are final.

Most of the time, the school offering the unit, course, or program has ownership, but if a student is taking only one course as part of a locally offered diploma, then in most respects the diploma-granting school is the responsible institution. Most often several policies statements need to be in place that relate to various situations in which courses are delivered or received.

With ownership comes the question of costs. Certainly the school offering a unit, course, or program has considerable expenses, but so does the receiving school and even the student. In a sharing relationship between units or schools, the hope is that costs will average out over a period of time. In other words, if three schools enter into a relationship to share courses and do so uniformly, the costs of offering and receiving courses will be fairly equal for the three schools. Conversely, if one school does most of the offering of units, courses, or programs, then that school will have disproportionate expenses. Policies are needed to clarify how situations such as this are to be dealt with.

Other fiscal policies for schools offering instruction include those related to tuition, network fees, room and equipment expenses, administration of student files and records, and troubleshooting. Schools receiving courses have costs for room maintenance, library and media support, reception equipment, and student support. Technology fees are often levied to support distance education costs. If fees are implemented, policies need to be in place to determine who collects and distributes this money and how expenditures are monitored.

Finally, agreements to regularly review costs and to share revenues are important. Often it is difficult to anticipate costs, so if an agreement can be made in good faith to review expenses and income yearly or quarterly, it is easier to establish working consortia.

Determining geographic service areas is also a difficult administrative task. Traditionally, schools clearly identified areas they served, such as districts, counties, or regions. With electronic distribution of instruction, these boundaries are invisible. Regulations that set particular geographic limits for schools may need to be clarified or altered when distance education programs are started.

Governance is closely related to finances and geography. What school board is responsible for courses delivered at a distance, the receiving or the sending board? Policies need to clarify this issue before problems emerge.

Faculty Issues

Faculty (or labor-management) issues can easily be the most difficult for policy developers, especially if teachers are unionized. Increasingly, existing labor-management policies are being extended to cover distance education. Clearly, faculty need to be recognized for their efforts and expertise in working with distant learners, and until distance education becomes mainstream and expected of all teachers, policies need to be in place that clarify distance teaching responsibilities.

Key issues include class size, compensation, design and development incentives, recognition of intellectual property of faculty, office hours, staff development for teachers, and other workload issues. Many recommend that labor-management policies be kept flexible, since many issues in this area are difficult to anticipate (Gellman-Danley & Fetzner, 1998). However, faculty issues should be resolved early on in order to avoid critical problems later. Once again, the concept of integration is important. Integrating distance education faculty policy with traditional labor-management policy seems to be the best strategy in most cases.

Legal Issues

Many faculty and administrators are ignorant of the legal issues involved in distance education. Policies regarding copyright and fair use, liability for inappropriate use of telecommunications networks, and intellectual property are important to establish. When units, courses, and programs are offered at a distance, they are easily scrutinized, and violations are very apparent. In addition to setting clear policies related to these issues, many institutions are developing comprehensive staff development or training programs that deal with copyright and liability.

Ownership of intellectual property is an important issue for distance education. When courses or portions of courses are packaged for delivery to the distant learner, the question of who owns the "package" becomes an obvious issue, more obvious than when students enter a classroom in a traditional school. On one side of the issue are those who emphasize the property side of the intellectual property equation. This group often argues that the school is the owner of any work produced by faculty during working hours and using school resources. At the other extreme are those who feel the contribution of knowledgeable faculty (the intellectual component of intellectual property) is most important. This camp advocates course ownership by faculty.

Most would agree that both elements are necessary and that neither extreme best serves the school (Simonson, Smaldino, Albright, & Zvacek, 2000). Often, policies that mandate sharing any profits after expenses with faculty who develop instruction for distant learners are best. The exact split for this sharing should be negotiated, and the policies should be developed before the courses are offered.

Student Policies

Student services should be integrated. In other words, policies related to students learning at a distance should be reflected in the general student policies. However, the general policies may need to be modified to accommodate the distant learners. Specifically, if asynchronous instruction is being offered, then support services will need to be available when students need them. For example, if a school offers courses such as advanced placement calculus to students in other schools, then distant students may need to be able to access support services outside of regular school hours. Homework hotlines may need to be established and be available to all students, not just distant learners. Library and media center resources should be available to everyone, and computer laboratories should be of equal quality. Policies related to students and their needs are often overlooked but become more critical in a distance education environment.

Student support policies should be clear, flexible, and widely understood, not only by students but also by faculty. Policies related to feedback from instructors should be monitored, and special requirements of distance learners, such as mailing of assignments, use of e-mail, access to Web sites, and proctoring of exams, should be clear and designed to help the student be a successful distant learner.

Technical Policies

Usually, some organization owns the network used for distance education or is responsible for its reliability. If a private-sector business is the provider, then clear expectations must be in place, and all members of a consortium should be part of the relationship. If a public agency, such as a state education department or public television station, is the telecommunications service provider, then very clear chain-of-command responsibilities should be in place. Often, telecommunications policies are not the same as other policies related to the distance education enterprise since they are not related to the educational mission of the organizations involved and often they are mandated by the private or public provider of services. However, telecommunications procedures should be understood by all involved with managing distance education.

Policies related to student and faculty technical issues, such as the quality of personal computers needed by students who learn at home, should be established. Hardware, software, and connectivity minimum requirements should be clearly explained.

Philosophical Issues

Often overlooked when policies are developed are those that relate to the vision, mission, and understanding of distance education. Many recommend that, when an educational organization decides to become involved in offering or receiving distance education, its vision and mission statements should reflect its commitment to distance education.

Of more direct importance to the success of distance education is the recognition that this type of education is credible, of high quality, and appropriate. Distance education is new to most and misunderstood by many (Rogers, 1995), and thus training, administrator support, publicity, and attention to quality are important components of a successful and accepted distance education program (Simonson et al., 2000). Organizational policies related to these issues should include distance education.

SAMPLE POLICIES

Sample policy statements in each of the seven areas are listed below. These samples, taken from Title 92, Nebraska Department of Education, Chapter 10, are intended to illustrate the kinds of issues that state and district distance education policies typically address.

Academic

- To be an accredited high school in Nebraska, the school must provide access to 400 instructional units for each student each school year.
- Schools provide required instructional units on site or through a combination of local and distance learning programs.
- Up to 100 instructional units of the 400 unit instructional program requirements of the high school may be met through the use of courses presented primarily through one or more forms of distance learning technologies, such as satellite, regional course sharing, or other audio-video distance learning.
- Each course is shown on the high school class schedule.
- At least one student is enrolled and participating in each course to be counted.

- Each student enrolled in a course is assigned to a local certificated teacher who monitors student progress and general appropriateness of the course.
- Off-site courses are made available to all students at the school's expense.
- At least one student enrolled in each course used towards compliance with the instructional program requirement.
- Class is scheduled . . . each day that school is in session with a certificated teacher present (one teacher may supervise several courses within a single class period).
- The distance education class must be shown on the high school class schedule.
- Carnegie class time equivalents will be the same for television courses as for any course.

Fiscal

- Students pay the same fees for distance education classes as for classes delivered on-site.

Faculty

- Instructors hired to teach distant students must meet the standards and procedures used by the institutions for regular instructors.
- Instructors teaching on interactive distance education will be compensated at the rate of $500 per remote site.
- Instructor training, including system use and suggested teaching procedures, shall be a requisite prior to teaching a course via the distance learning system.
- The school will provide 12 clock hours of formal training, including at least 8 hours using the network.

Legal

- Course materials will be reviewed by appropriate school officials to insure copyright regulations are strictly adhered to.
- Course materials developed locally will be the property of the originating school, unless special arrangements are made in writing.

Student

- Students . . . must have the same services, the same options for continuing education, and the same choices of delivery methods as the traditional on-site students.

Technical

- Students must remain in sight of the video camera.
- Students must respect the equipment.
- Three violations and students are dismissed from the distance education class.
- Classes missed because of technical problems will be rescheduled and required.

Philosophical

- [It] is the mission of . . . school district . . . using electronic or other technologies to provide high quality educational experiences.
- Courses delivered to distant learners are consider equivalent to those offered traditionally.
- Each student, prior to graduation, will enroll and complete at least one course delivered using distance education technologies.

CONCLUSION

Integrated policies for distance education are preferred (King et. al., 1998). In other words, policies that provide guidance and direction to educational systems should seamlessly incorporate the concept of distant delivery of instruction. Students should be defined by their enrollment in a course or program, not by whether they are distant or local learners (Simonson et. al., 2000). Initially, distance education policies will probably need to coexist for a time with policies regarding face-to-face education. Ultimately, they should be integrated to indicate that distance education is a routine and regularly occurring component of the educational enterprise. Policies are merely tools to facilitate program integrity.

In order to plow straight rows, the farmer does not look down at the ground, but at the end of the field.

REFERENCES

Berge, Z. (1998). Barriers to online teaching in post-secondary institutions: Can policy changes fix it? *Online Journal of Distance Learning Administration* [Online serial], *1*(2). Available: http://www.westga.edu/~distance/Berge12.html

Gellman-Danley, B., & Fetzner, M. (1998). Asking the really tough questions: Policy issues for distance learning. *Online Journal of Distance Learning Administration* [Online serial], *1*(1). Available: http://www.westga.edu/~distance/danley11.html

King, J., Lacy, D., McMillian, J., Bartels, K., & Fredilino, M. (1998). The policy perspective in distance education: A futures landscape/panorama. Paper presented at the 1998 Nebraska Distance Education Conference, Lincoln, NE. Available: http://www.unl.edu/NN21/jking.html

King, J., Nugent, G. Eich, J. Mlinek, D., & Russell, E. (2000). A policy framework for distance education: A case study and model. *DEOSNEWS* [Online serial], *10*(10). Available: http://ed.psu.edu/acsde/deos/deosnews.html

King, J., Nugent, G., Russell, E., Eich, J., & Lacy. D. (2000). Policy frameworks for distance education: Implications for decision makers. *Online Journal of Distance Learning Administration* [Online serial], *3*(2). Available: http://www.westga.edu/~distance/king32.html

Rogers, E. (1995). *Diffusion of innovations* (4th ed.). New York: The Free Press.

Simonson, M., Schlosser, C., & Hanson, D. (1999). Theory and distance education: A new discussion. *American Journal of Distance Education*, *13*(1), 60–75.

Simonson, M., Smaldino, S., Albright, M., & Zvacek, S. (2000). *Teaching and learning at a distance: Foundations of distance education*. Upper Saddle, NJ: Prentice-Hall.

Watkins, R., & Schlosser, C. (2000). Capabilities-based educational equivalency units: Beginning a professional dialogue. *American Journal of Distance Education*, *14*(3), 34–47.

30

Accreditation: Quality Control in Higher Distance Education

Amy Kirle Lezberg
University of Qatar
alezberg@aol.com

HISTORICAL BACKGROUND

Unlike most other countries in the world, the United States has never had a ministry of higher education directly regulating the quality of its postsecondary institutions of learning; such control is not among the powers granted to the federal government by the U.S. Constitution. Instead, in order to operate legally, institutions must, like other business, be licensed, with each of the 50 individual states setting rules governing the institutions incorporated within its borders. Rooted in the differing political philosophies of each state, the rules they have established range from the almost nonexistent to others that are quite stringent (Bear & Bear, 1998). For the most part, such rules describe the minima necessary for initiating an institution of higher education rather than set effectiveness criteria for the instruction offered. Because of the variety of requirements, private accreditation associations, devoted to both the evaluation of current performance and the encouragement of continuing improvement, have for more than a hundred years provided the primary mechanism for assuring employers, governments, and, most importantly, students and their families that degree-granting institutions were offering acceptable levels of education (Young, Chambers, & Kells, 1983).

INVOLVEMENT OF THE REGIONAL ACCREDITING ASSOCIATIONS

The most widely accepted and respected of these bodies in the United States are the following six regional associations: the Middle States Association of Colleges and Schools, the New England Association of Schools and Colleges, the North Central Association of Colleges and Schools, The Northwest Association of Schools and Colleges, The Southern Association of Schools and Colleges, and the Western Association of Schools and Colleges (see www.chea.org for information about these associations). These currently accredit about 3,500 institutions of higher education (i.e., those offering academic degrees from the associate to the doctorate level). The range of institutions encompasses public and private institutions, research universities and community technical colleges, secular and religious schools, and such independent members as Harvard, Stanford, Wellesley, and Duke, as well as their state-supported members, including the public institutions of virtually every state in the nation.

The specific regional accrediting association by which an institution is recognized is determined by the geographic location in which it is chartered. The 50 states having been divided up for historical reasons into regions that in some instances correspond with common usage (e.g., the New England Association accredits institutions in the six New England states) but in others do not (e.g., the North Central Association accredits institutions in 19 states, ranging from West Virginia to Arizona and North Dakota). By common agreement, a satellite campus of an institution accredited by a region other than that in which the satellite is located conform to the standards of the home region, and a representative of the home region is included on any committee that visits the satellite for accreditation review.

Of course, not all instruction takes place in geographically distinct locations. In response to an increase in distance education offerings, criteria and standards for the acceptability of such programs have been established by two major groups: since 1955 by the Distance and Education Council, an accrediting body devoted solely to non-site-based education (see www.detc.org) and throughout the 1990s by various educational bodies whose members are regionally accredited institutions, such as the American Council on Education and the Western Interstate Commission for Higher Education. By the end of the century, however, the regional accrediting associations and their commissions on higher education realized that there was a need for them to at least provide guidelines in this area, and they acted, first individually and then, more recently, as a unified group, to establish regulations that would allow their members to include distance education offerings within their overall institutional accreditation.

As early as 1986, indeed, the North Central Association of Schools and Colleges, the largest of these associations, had evaluated and bestowed membership upon National Technological University, which offers graduate degrees in engineering to working professionals through courses designed and delivered by faculty with full-time appointments at institutions that are themselves accredited both institutionally by the appropriate regional association and programmatically through the American Board of Engineering Technology (ABET). In so acting, the North Central Association established the importance of focusing on the effectiveness with which an entity delivers education rather than on the physical location where credits are earned. Consequently, when the number and variety of courses, programs, and complete degrees offered through electronically mediated technology began to proliferate in the last decade of the 20th century, the regional accrediting associations had experience and precedent to draw on as they considered the way in which such offerings could demonstrate that they conformed to the overriding set of four requirements as well as to the standards of the relevant association. That is, even without the impetus provided by expressions of concern by the federal government, the six regional accrediting bodies had begun to meet in order to determine whether they could include distance education offerings within the existing accreditation of site-based institutions as well as accredit newly developing entities, both for-profit and non-profit, by expanding and explicating their standards.

What was being confronted reflected changes in the academy brought about by distance education, which has transformed the way in which professors teach, students learn, and researchers collaborate. Amidst such changes, it is not at all surprising that the regional accrediting associations faced the question of whether regionalism, though it had served the country and its educational institutions so well for so long, was now, in fact, obsolete, as Perley and Tanguay (1999) and the letters responding to their article in *the Chronicle of Higher Education* argued.

Further, in addition to formulating rules for quality control, the regionals were aware that they also had to consider carefully the identification and training of those who would enforce such regulations, both as on-site visitors and members of their central decision-making bodies, and to identify credible methodologies for evaluating such programs and for establishing new entities offering higher education. By the end of the decade, in fact, each of the regional accrediting bodies had added at least one member to its commissions of higher education with expertise in the implementation of distance education programs.

The associations were further aware that questions would arise about the meaning of regional boundaries when dealing with education in which the instructor might be in one state while the learner was in another. It was quickly becoming evident that, because new entities might be in a position to seek a charter and therefore accreditation from more than one association, it would be necessary to ensure that accreditation standards made accreditation shopping—that is, looking for the easiest association by which to be accredited—impossible or at least difficult.

Among the issues that had to be addressed by the regional accrediting associations was the fact that, although they do pay some attention to graduate studies and research, they tradition-ally have taken as their model residential liberal arts colleges and therefore focus primarily on undergraduate education. Consequently, the standards set by institutional accreditation asso-ciations not only address the qualifications of faculty and general expectations for curricular offerings but also attend to library and information services and such noncurricular matters as student services (including athletics, residence halls, and counseling) and the organizational or administrative format of the institution. The general, if sometimes unspoken, assumption seems to be that education is more than the transfer of cognitive knowledge and also involves the behavioral and affective domains of human activity. An associated assumption is the suc-cess of education depends upon its taking place at certain times and in certain places where both a faculty member and his or her students are present in a locale appropriate for learning and with immediate access to a properly staffed library in which information resources can be located. Indeed, so pervasive was this belief that for many years most traditional colleges and universities did not assign correspondence courses—the first form of distance education and usually delivered by pen, paper, and the U.S. Postal Service—the same academic credit as site-based courses. Often, such offerings were, at best, granted continuing education credit. The vast majority of these institutions, whether publicly supported or in the independent sec-tor, were accredited by one of the six regional accrediting bodies, and they offered credentials that were generally accepted in transfer by other regionally accredited institutions as well as accepted as establishing eligibility for certain forms of financial aid and employment (Council on Postsecondary Accreditation, n.d.).

THE DISTANCE EDUCATION AND TRAINING COUNCIL

Furthermore, even though off-campus learning was, technically, covered by an institution's accreditation, for the first three quarters of the 20th century, the regional accrediting associ-ations concentrated almost exclusively on quality control of the site-based education offered by their members. There were, however, other, nontraditional institutions that did grant de-grees through correspondence, including some that granted credits but had no campus at all at which instruction could take place. That is, during the period when the regional accrediting bodies were focusing on the quality control of education delivered at sites where students, faculty, and resources could all be found in the same place at the same time, organizations were arising that offered instruction and credentials to those who could or would not attend such institutions. As with site-based education, the growth of such programs was followed by recognition of the need to distinguish those that actually delivered education from those that merely supplied credentials. In 1926, owing to the proliferation of various entities that were offering credentials to students who completed a course of study not at the institution offering it but through the mail, the Home Study Council was formed. Its stated purpose was "to promote sound educational standards and ethical business practices within the correspondence school field" (Distance Education and Training Council, 1998, p. 7). Having established standards for membership, the council, in 1955, was recognized by the U.S. Department of Education as an accrediting association, membership in which was a reliable guarantee of quality. Four years later, in response to the growing variety of modes for delivering education, the council changed its name to the Distance Education and Training Council (DETC), promoting itself as the only accrediting association devoted entirely to institutions offering distance education.

Recognition of DETC as an accrediting body, made it possible for consumers to have some assurance as to the legitimacy of certain correspondence schools, even when unaware of what such recognition entailed. In fact, in order for an accreditation association to be listed by the U.S. Government as a reliable judge of institutional quality, it must undergo a review by the U.S. Department of Education every 5 years. Although the exact tone and wording of the standards of each accrediting body, whether DETC or any other of the national or regional accreditors, are quite distinctive and reflect its individual character, each applies its standards to ensure that every member institution

Has a mission and purposes appropriate to higher education.
Has the resources available to accomplish its mission and purposes.
Is currently meeting its mission and purposes.
Seems likely to continue meeting its mission and purposes for the foreseeable future.

However, despite recognition by the U.S. Department of Education and membership in the Council for Postsecondary Education (COPA) and its successors (CORPA and CHEA), the umbrella organizations for institutional and specialized accrediting associations, DETC has still not been able to assure students enrolled in its members' programs that they will be able to automatically transfer their credits to regionally accredited institutions, the majority of mainstream institutions of higher education currently operating in the United States. To some extent, this reflects the fact that, although certain DETC programs may offer advanced degrees, others are postsecondary but not necessarily appropriate to higher education. Indeed, although the council currently accredits more than 60 distance education institutions, some offer programs lasting only four weeks. In addition, since accreditation is voluntary and membership-based, the refusal of many regionally accredited institutions to automatically accept credits earned from DETC-accredited entities seems to reflect the attitude of those institutions that the membership, which establishes and applies the specific standards of an accrediting body, interprets the four criteria required by the government through standards which are not as stringent as those set by the regionals.

QUALITY ASSURANCE IN DISTANCE EDUCATION—THE NINETIES

By 1995, a U.S. Department of Education survey had revealed that distance education courses and in some case whole programs were being offered by more than 90% of the institutions that enroll more than 10,000 students and by 85% of institutions that enroll between 3,000 and 10,000 students. By 1997–1998, according to the National Center for Education Statistics, the number of offerings using electronically mediated instruction rather than traditional correspondence course methodologies had more than doubled, with 44% of 2- and 4-year higher education institutions offering distance education, up from 33% in 1995 (American Council of Education, 2000). That is, although some offerings were still using the old-fashioned pen, pencil, and post office approach to learning, increasingly institutions were delivering education through communication technologies—fax machines (for the delivery of exams and journal articles from on-site libraries), e-mail (for conversation, consultation, and constant communication), telephone (for language lab assignments), chat rooms and threaded conversations (for student-to-student discussions), CD-ROMS, one-way video, and interactive TV (which allows geographically distant students to interact with the instructor and each other). And of course many programs combined two or more of these technologies to begin to give reality to the idea of instruction on an any time, any place basis.

Wanting the assurance of external quality control mechanisms for distance education, institutions sought guidance throughout the last decade of the 20th century from their regional institutional accrediting associations about quality control of such offerings that they were beginning to institute, understandably loath to add yet another specialized accrediting association to those already on campus. As electronically mediated instruction became more prevalent and requests for guidance from member institutions became more pervasive, a number of organizations to which these institutions also belonged and which were interested in preserving the quality of higher education offerings came up with sets of rules and guidelines to assist members in their activities. Some, like the Western Interstate Commission on Higher Education (WICHE), established a separate body the Western Cooperative for Educational Telecommunication (1996), devoted to the development of guiding principles and consultation on mediated instruction. Others, however, such as the American Council on Education, developed suggested procedures as just one among the many things they did for their members.

THE MOVEMENT FROM STRICT REGIONALISM TO NATIONAL COOPERATION

Meanwhile, however, the regionals were slowly coming to understand that even within the constraints of regionalism certain national standards had to be agreed upon. In discussing the standards they adopted to meet the need of measuring quality in distance education programs in ways that would ensure they were comparable to site-based programs, it is worthwhile to consider how they were adopted, for never before had these accrediting associations considered yielding their sovereignty over members to achieve a nationwide consensus. As a group, the regional associations had already ascribed to the WICHE guidelines as they then were, and several of the associations had adopted rules and regulations governing their own membership. Others were well along in adopting such standards before 1993, when it became clear that what was needed was a joint statement of expectations with which any institution, in order to be regionally accredited, would have to conform. A task force composed of representatives of the six regional accreditation associations was from (with an observer from their umbrella organization, CHEA), and its first job was to review the various documents from each region as well as from other organizations. Looking for any standards that might make the inclusion of distance education offerings within a region's accreditation either impossible or difficult, it discovered that the qualitative nature of the great majority of standards already allowed the accreditation of such disparate entities as Harvard University and Quinsigamond Community College. Reviewing documents from outside organizations, the task force further concluded that, although suitable as a starting point in their work, the existing guidelines were too broad for their eventual purpose, as they could be applied equally to degree-granting and non-degree-granting programs. The task force eventually suggested a set of expanded criteria, which, after consideration by the members of each association, were accepted with minor linguistic changes by all eight commissions accrediting higher education institutions (the six commissions on higher education of the regional accreditors and the Commission on Technical and Vocational

Schools of the New England Association of Schools and Colleges and the Commission on Community and Technical Colleges of the Western Association of Schools and Colleges). In adopting such policies, they were, of course, following the long tradition of adapting to changing social needs that had allowed them to include within their membership community colleges, teachers colleges, and single-purpose graduate programs (see, e.g., the New England Association's Policy on the Accreditation of Academic Degrees and Certificate Programs Offered Through Distance Education, at www.neasc/cihe/disted2.htm).

INSTITUTIONAL CONCERNS

Prior to their meeting, the accrediting bodies had surveyed their members to discover what specific problems they were concerned with (New England Association of Schools and Colleges, 1994). Most frequently mentioned were the following concerns:

> First and foremost was the need to be assured of the integrity of the degree, by which respondents meant not only that the person receiving the degree was the one who had done the work toward it but also that the requirements for online credit were similar to those for on-site instruction, as both would grant similar credit.
>
> Additionally, institutions were concerned about cost and accessibility for both students and institutions.
>
> There was a concern about student-faculty and student-student interaction absent face-to-face involvement and shared classrooms.
>
> Many administrators were concerned about faculty development, which is so much a part of higher education in the United States, in cases where the faculty members were part-time and never on (the possibly virtual) campus. Faculty, on the other hand, wanted clarification on how posting their syllabi and notes on the Internet might impact their compensation, workloads, and intellectual property rights.
>
> All respondents were concerned about students' having guaranteed access to academic support services, including comprehensive information resources.
>
> All respondents wanted to be assured that both students and faculty members would be provided the guidance and training needed to gain appropriate technological expertise.

ADAPTING REGIONAL STANDARDS TO INCORPORATE DISTANCE EDUCATION

With these concerns in mind, the task force decided that the associations could expand their already existing standards to include distance education within institutional accreditation for two major reasons. First, the standards already existing within the various regional accrediting associations emphasized educational outcomes and required that institutions command resources (both human and other) for their effective achievement. That is, the assessment of educational outcomes was already established as an indicator of institutional quality. Next, the standards of the various associations made it clear that they were more interested in the academic control and expertise of those who designed and delivered the courses than they were the in full-time, part-time, or adjunct status of those persons.

Nevertheless, looking at the standards that were already applied to site-based institutions, the accreditors recognized that they would have to adapt some of them to the particular necessities of distance education. For example, although the accreditors require that institutions admit only those students who can benefit from the program offered, they do allow an institution to have open admissions if it supplies appropriate remediation for those who need help in order to work at the collegiate level. For distance education, this rule had to be extended to include technological expertise needed by the undergraduate in order to complete the program. The requirement for library and information resource personnel likewise had to be expanded to include student access to a help desk.

In addition to specific issues to be dealt with within individual institutions, there were also questions about the meaning of regional boundaries when dealing with education in which the instructor might be in one state while the learner was in another.

Although the individual accrediting associations ascribed to the general principles contained in the joint guidelines, the actual wording adopted by each reflected the language and approach characteristic of the individual association. The issue of institutions without a regional base became prominent with the establishment and eventual accreditation (in 2000) of Western Governors University, which catered to students in three (eventually five) of the six accrediting regions. In response to its founding, a separate commission, the Interregional Accrediting Commission, was set up, but the rules promulgated for that one institution are now in place to serve as precedents for others.

THE CURRENT REGULATIONS

As the number and complexity of distance educations programs continued to increase, the regional commissions realized that they had to rewrite their policy yet again to develop one document to which all could ascribe without modification. In August 2000, a draft of the "Statement of Regional Accrediting Commissions on the Evaluation of Electronically Offered Degree and Certificate Programs" was published. This statement, which places technologically mediated instruction squarely within the context of regional accreditation, was prepared under a contract from GRAC (the regional accrediting association group within CHEA) by WICHE, and it marks the first time the regional commissions have jointly issued a set of rules rather than developing guidelines to be restated in terms suitable for each region. Recognizing that they have to strike a balance between accountability and imaginative experimentation, the accrediting associations see this very much as a work in progress, that is, as a set of regulations that may be further developed as new methodologies evolve that allow for the delivery of education of the same quality as has been traditional in site-based education. (The quotations below are taken from the draft version. The revised statement can be found on the Web site of each regional accrediting association.)

As a preamble to listing the regulations, the statement sets forth several values and principles that will guide this and future documents:

- that education is best experienced within a community of learning where competent professionals are actively and cooperatively involved with creating, providing, and improving the instructional programs;
- that learning should be dynamic and interactive, regardless of the setting in which it occurs;
- that instructional programs leading to degrees having integrity are organized around substantive and coherent curricula which define expected learning outcomes;
- that institutions accept the obligation to address student needs related to, and to provide the resources necessary for, their academic success;
- that institutions are responsible for the education provided in their name;
- that institutions undertake the assessment and improvement of their quality, giving particular emphasis to student learning; and
- that institutions voluntarily subject themselves to voluntary oversight. (p.)

Although the regional commissions limit their scope to degree-granting institutions, they are aware that "their field of view increasingly includes educational entities and configurations which test conventional ideas as to what constitutes an institution of higher learning." They understand that the new technologies allow for numerous forms of collaboration between accredited institutions and entities outside the academy, but they consider it essential "that accountability be clearly fixed within the accredited entity and that reasonable guarantees are provided to assure the continued availability of necessary resources outside the institution's control."

The regional accrediting commissions, aware that technologically mediated instruction may call into question the whole notion of regional accountability, note that, at least for the present, most online programming leading to degrees "originates from within traditional institutions which have a substantial academic infrastructure within a single region." Where this is not the case (e.g., Western Governors University), cooperative arrangements between the several regions involved will be established.

The guidelines are separated into five components, each introduced by a general statement of principle, which is followed by explications.

1. *Institutional Context and Commitment. Electronically offered programs both support and extend the roles of educational institutions. Increasingly they are integral to academic organization with growing implications for institutional infrastructure.* All distributed education supports the stated mission of the institution, whose budget and policy statements reflect its commitment to the students for whom the program is designed. The institution assures adequate physical plant and technical facilities with appropriate training provided for instructors and students and maintains appropriate academic oversight; as a result, all transfer and articulation policies can judge courses on their outcomes rather than their mode of delivery. The selection of technologies for a program is based on their appropriateness for the students and curriculum and all aspects of the program comply with any legal or regulatory requirements of the jurisdictions in which the institution operates (i.e., regarding disabilities, copyright law, etc).

2. *Curriculum and Instruction. Methods change, but standards of quality endure. The important issues are not technical but curriculum-driven and pedagogical. The big decisions are made by qualified faculty and focus on learning outcomes for an increasingly diverse student population.* Through appropriate processes of curriculum development and review, the institution ensures that each program results in collegiate-level learning outcomes appropriate to the degree awarded. Academically qualified persons participate fully in decisions involving curricula. Programs include all courses necessary for their completion and institutions include a coherent plan for students to access these courses. No matter who supplies part of a program—whether it is another institution or even a non-accredited entity—the institution awarding the degree is wholly responsible for the performance of every segment of the program. Consequently, outcome expectations should be carefully specified in any contracts or agreements into which the institution enters. The program design must allow for appropriate interaction between student and faculty and student and student, and the success of that interactive component should be documented.

3. *Faculty Support. As indicated above, faculty roles are becoming increasingly diverse and reorganized. For example, the same person may not perform both the tasks of course development and direct instruction to students. Regardless of who performs which of these tasks, important issues are involved.* In developing electronically offered programs, institutions must provide clear guidelines for faculty workloads, compensation, intellectual property rights, and the implications of participation on a faculty member's professional evaluation. Both those who design and those who deliver courses are provided with ongoing orientation and training to help them become proficient in the use of the program's technologies and to develop strategies for student interactions.

4. *Student Support. Colleges and universities have learned that the twenty-first century student is different, both demographically and geographically, from students of previous generations. These differences affect everything from admissions policy to library services. Reaching these*

students, and serving them appropriately, are major challenges to today's institutions. The institution must have a commitment to the continuation of the program for a sufficient period of time for all admitted students to complete the degree or certificate in a publicized time frame. Prior to admitting the student, the institution ascertains that the student is qualified to benefit from the program, informs the student of the technological requirements of the program, and informs the student about prospective costs, curriculum design and time frame information resource availability, and informs the student about arrangements for interaction with faculty and other students. The institution ensures the availability of such student services as career counseling, academic advising, tutoring, training in the use of library resources that are available, bookstore services and referrals for student learning differences, physical challenges, and personal counseling. A sense of community among students is encouraged by the distribution of student directories, encouragement of study groups, and including distance education students in such on-campus events as graduations and representation in student government.

5. *Evaluation and Assessment. Both the assessment of student achievement and the evaluation of overall programs take on an added importance as new techniques evolve. For example, in asynchronous programs, the element of seat time is essentially removed from the equation. For these reasons, the institution conducts sustained, evidence-based and participatory inquiry as to whether distance learning programs are achieving objectives. The results of such inquiry are used to guide curriculum design and delivery, pedagogy, and educational processes, and may affect future policy and budgets perhaps having implications for the institution's role and mission.* Documented assessment of student achievement is conducted for each course and for the program as a whole, in which student achievement is compared to the intended learning outcome. Examinations take place in circumstances that include firm student identification; appropriate procedures assure the security of personal information in the conduct of assessments and the dissemination of results. Overall program effectiveness is determined by such measures as the extent to which student learning matches program objectives and student intent, the degree of student and faculty satisfaction with the program, and the effectiveness of the program in comparison with campus-based alternatives. (pp.)

As the members of the regional accrediting associations review this draft, they may suggest changes, which, in order to be adopted, will have to be agreed upon by all of the commissions. As mentioned, however, any regulations adopted must be seen as part of an organic process of adjustment as new entities and modes of delivery arise to challenge their relevance. Even before the adoption of this policy, one distance education institution, the University of Phoenix, a campus-free and profit-making entity (unlike the great majority of institutions of higher education), not only was enrolling more than 55,000 students in its various programs (including 17,000 in programs that are offered only online) but had achieved accreditation through the North Central Association. Other institutions, enrolling fewer students, had also achieved such accreditation. Thus, today students interested in enrolling in distance education should be warned to distrust any institution that claims that it cannot be regionally accredited because it lacks a campus, a full-time faculty, or a bricks- and-mortar library and set of classrooms.

The regional accrediting associations feel confident that, as new forms of distributed education arise, they will have both the expertise and adaptability to continue ensuring that higher education, no matter how it is delivered, meets the same standards of quality control that traditional site-based institutions have already achieved.

REFERENCES

American Council of Education. (2000). Higher education and national affairs. Available: www.acenet.edu/hena/facts_in_brief/2000/00_01_31_tib.html

Bear, J. B., & Bear, M. P. (1998). *Bear's guide to earning degrees nontraditionally.* El Cerrito, CA: Ten Speed Press.

Council on Postsecondary Accreditation. (n.d.). *The role and value of accreditation.* Available: www.nearsc.org/cihe/diherole.htm

Distance Education and Training Council. (1998). *Accreditation handbook.* Washington, DC: Author.

New England Association of School and Colleges. (1994). *Survey on distance education activities.* Bedford, MA: Author.

Perley, J. & Tanguay, D. M. (1999, October 29). Accrediting on-line institutions diminishes higher education. *Chronicle of Higher Education.* (See also ensuing colloquy.)

Western Cooperative for Educational Communications. (1996). *Distance education: A planner's handbook.* San Fancisco: Author.

Young, K. E., Chambers, C. M., & Kells, H. R. (1983). *Understanding accreditation.* San Francisco: Jossey-Bass.

31

Quality and Its Measurement
in Distance Education

Annette C. Sherry
University of Hawaii at Manoa
asherry@hawaii.edu

Translating ideals of academic excellence into applicable terms for providers and users of distance education is not an easy task. Providing exemplary pedagogical experiences within rapidly changing technological environments requires the combined efforts of everyone engaged in the distance learning enterprise. In this new century, with distance education expanding worldwide, the urgency of quality assurance is apparent.

The organization of this chapter's exploration of quality measurement in distance learning is depicted in Fig. 31.1.

As suggested by the dashed frame, the chapter begins by "framing" the overall condition of distance learning today through an introduction that recognizes the variety of large and small providers (represented by the thick and thin dashed lines of the frame) who engage in designing and delivering distance education. The lighting bolt primarily represents Internet-based delivery but also symbolizes by its repetition other electronic means for delivering instruction. Fittingly, the learners are at the core of the distance learning picture, whose dynamic and fluctuating nature is indicated by the jagged dashed lines. Factors encompassing the evaluation of the learners' four main types of responses to their experiences are presented next, as the learners are the main focus. To engender a better understanding of the framework in which learning occurs, the chapter then explores issues surrounding quality at the institutional and faculty levels. Although institutional and faculty issues are somewhat distinct, as indicated by the dashed line used to separate the institution and the faculty, they are interrelated, indicated by the use of similar shades of gray. The policies and procedures that institutions choose to implement directly impact faculty responses, as do faculty initiatives within the institution. For these reasons, institutional and faculty issues are commingled to some extent during the discussion of sample guidelines and projects intended to illuminate exemplary distance learning. Descriptions of representative global, national, and institutional initiatives and projects are also used to illustrate relevant points.

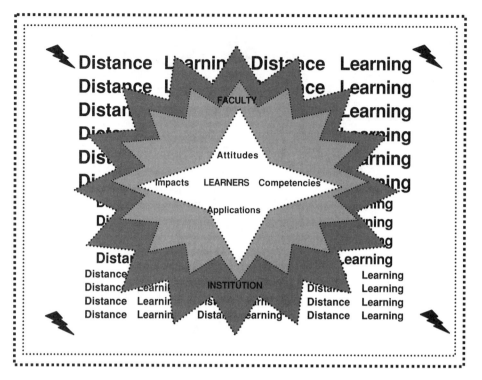

FIG. 31.1.   Relationship of quality responses by the institution and faculty to core student outcomes (attitudes, competencies, applications, and impacts) in a dynamic distance learning environment.

Because of the increasing selection of the Internet as the delivery mode and the strong growth of distance learning in higher education, that delivery mode and that level of education are emphasized throughout this chapter. The emphasis on higher education is represented in Fig. 31.1 by the larger size of the words *Distance Learning* at the top of the figure. Recognizing that in this type of learning, rigid standardization is difficult and often not warranted, the chapter concludes with a condensed compilation of critical factors that appear to be related to quality in distance learning. The wording is intended to achieve a balance between depth and breadth and make the compilation useful within diverse institutional cultures. The goal is to allow all engaged in distance learning—institutions, faculty, and students—to preserve the cultural values of their institutions as they translate the concepts into formats that assist them in determining their unique expressions of academically grounded, quality-based distance learning.

DEMAND AND STANDARDS

Concerns are raised that it is demand rather than sound pedagogy that is shaping expansion. Quality-based issues are not always at the forefront of decisions about distance education. Finding and promulgating answers to questions about appropriate usage, integration, and teacher training may begin to address this situation (Gladieux & Swail, 1999).

Demand

Projected increases in college enrollment (Lewis, Farris, Snow, & Levin, 1999) and real and anticipated budget constraints in higher education appear to be shaping decisions to deliver more courses and programs by means of the predominantly asynchronous Internet. The perceived ease and cost-effectiveness of this delivery mode contributes to the increasing frequency with which it is selected to deliver distance learning. For example, 557 U.S. colleges and universities indicated that 47% offer one or more courses entirely on the Internet, and 39% integrate the Internet into course syllabi (K. Greene, 2000).

Standards

Besides this rapid growth, another development at the start of the 21st century is the proliferation of educational consortia and for-profit corporations that initiate or expand programs and courses in response to potential students' demands for anytime, anywhere education. Many of these recently formed alliances cut across geographic lines and public-private institutional divisions. As the "business" of education expands, it is critical to ensure that the credits earned from electronically delivered programs and courses first and foremost reflect the academic standards of the Academy rather than credits on a balance sheet.

EVALUATION SCHEMES

Evaluation schemes that are useful, feasible, and accurate and adhere to legal and ethical procedures can offer information to assist learners in selecting appropriate learning environments (American Evaluation Association, 2000). Enhanced models for systematically designing instruction can be based on this type of data to readily guide instructional teams and individual faculty members in designing and delivering exemplary learning experiences for distance learners. Adopting a continuous process for rigorous improvement (Deming, 1992) based on findings from evaluations could lead institutions and consortia that deliver distance learning to become recognized for their excellence.

GUIDELINES

Existing guidelines and initiatives offer structure for investigators who seek answers to the question of how quality-based distance learning might look. In the latter part of the 20th century, quality measures for distance education reflected the fairly widespread view that this nontraditional type of education differed from traditional education *primarily* in the special or temporal separation between the student and instructor. When conducting evaluations at postsecondary institutions in the United States, the eight regional accreditation commissions follow *Guidelines for Distance Education: Principles of Good Practice* (Western Association of Schools and Colleges, 1997). The similarities of these guidelines to indicators of effective teaching and learning in traditional education, such as the ones contained in *Seven Principles for Good Practice in Undergraduate Education* (Chickering & Gamson, 1987) and Brookfield's (1990) insights into adult learning, are highlighted in Table 31.1. Similar concepts from all three guides are aligned horizontally within the boundaries of a single page to allow quality-based constructs to be visually conceptualized.

In this table, effective teaching is described in a similar manner but from different perspectives. The institution's perspective is reflected in *Guidelines for Distance Education*, the instructor's in *Seven Principles*, and the learner's in Brookfield's adult learning insights. The individual components of each of the three main constructs appear to be expressed with sufficient breadth to avoid rigid standardization and homogeneity, yet they also appear sufficiently specific to offer guidance in understanding the distance learning experience. A potential

TABLE 31.1
Viewpoints on Quality

Institutional Viewpoint	Instructor's Viewpoint	Learner's Viewpoint
C/I—Provides (at program level) for timely and appropriate faculty to student and student to student interactions	Encourages student and faculty contact	Connects to learning activity and own life
	Encourages reciprocity/cooperation among students	Participates in peer learning community
L/L—Ensures student access to and effective use of library resources L/L—Provides appropriate labs/facilities/equipment	Uses active learning techniques	Balances active and reflective modes of learning
E/A—Ensures comparability to campus-based programs by evaluating DE programs (including measuring student satisfaction, learning outcomes and retention) SS—Represents programs, requirements, and services accurately SS—Monitors whether students make appropriate use of learning resources	Gives prompt feedback	Anticipates emotional ambivalence toward learning
SS—Provides for informed student use of support for technology and equipment SS—Provides means to resolve student complaints	Emphasizes time on task	Anticipates fluctuating pattern of learning
C/I—Ensures currency of materials, programs, and courses C/I—Assumes (at faculty level) oversight/responsibility for rigor of programs and quality of instruction in DE E/A—Ensures integrity of student work, credits, and degrees F/F—Makes DE a viable part in all long-range planning, budgeting, and policy development C/I—Provides clear DE policies on materials ownership, copyright, compensation packages, and revenue distribution E/A—Establishes criteria for recruitment and admission	Communicates high expectations	Has peak learning experiences
C/I—Provides appropriate faculty support services for distance delivery SS—Provides adequate access to a range of academic and student support services C/I—Provides appropriate training for DE faculty F/F—Possesses appropriate equipment, technologies, and technical expertise for distance learning C/I—Ensures technology used is appropriate to nature and objectives of programs	Respects diverse talents and ways of learning	Perceives instructor as credible and authentic

Note. C/I = curriculum and instruction; E/A = evaluation and assessment; F/F = facilities and finances; L/L = library and library resources; SS = student services

Note. Items in column 1 are from *Guidelines for Distance Education: Principles of Good Practice,* Western Association of Schools and Colleges. Copyright 1997 by the American Association for Higher Education. Adapted with permission.

Note. Items in column 2 are from "Development and Adaptations of the Seven Principles for Good Practice in Undergraduate Education," by A. W. Chickering and Z. F. Gamson, 1996. *New Directions for Teaching and Learning, 4,* pp. 75–80. Copyright 1996 by the American Society for Training and Development. Adapted with permission.

Note. Items in column 3 are from *The Skillful Teacher: On Teaching, Trust, and Responsiveness in the Classroom,* by S. D. Brookfield, 1990, San Francisco: Jossey-Bass. Copyright by John Wiley & Sons, Inc. Adapted with permission.

strength of this triadic prototype is that each of the three main components rests on a firm foundation.

Guidelines for Distance Education, created from an earlier version developed by the Western Interstate Commission on Higher Education, has been in use since 1997. *Seven Principles* is based on years of research on undergraduates' college experiences, has been widely distributed throughout the United States, and has been revisited (Chickering & Ehrmann, 1996) for its applicability to technology. Like the seven principles presented in Chickering and Gamson (1987), Brookfield's (1990) insights emerged from extensive studies (in this case, studies of adults in higher education). Unlike the other two guides, Brookfield's main points appear in narrative form and are not referred to by him as guidelines. Rather, he conveys his findings about adults and effective learning by describing what must occur for a learner to have a full, rich, honest adventure. His main points, however, are clearly captured by the distinct concepts that appear in Table 31.1.

This table may be read horizontally to obtain an understanding of one construct of quality in distance learning from three perspectives. The first row, for example, suggests that (a) when the institution at the programmatic level of curriculum and instruction sets policies and expectations and provides equipment (e.g., hardware and software) for faculty to use to interact with students; (b) when faculty members themselves establish an instructional climate that welcomes openness between their students and themselves; and (c) when their students have access to the means for communicating, it is likely that they will ask the instructors questions about learning materials and apply metacognitive strategies to construct meaningful connections between the content and their personal lives. In like manner, the table can be read vertically for a holistic view of a quality-based learning experience from the perspective of one of the three types of stakeholders. For example, adult learners who (a) seek connections to learning and to their lives; (b) interact with peers in their learning community; (c) have periods of active learning balanced with periods reflection about their learning; (d) question their positions in the learning community; (e) recognize that their learning may be a pattern of advances followed by small retreats before advancing again; (f) challenge themselves to reach difficult learning goals; and (g) view the instructor as knowledgeable and trustworthy are possibly more likely to have a successful learning adventure.

Although the concepts appearing in Table 31.1 are broad enough to encompass additional issues that might arise, their lack of specificity does not take into account a perspective that began to appear toward the start of the 21st century. Although effective traditional education is still seen as the core of quality-based distance learning, the distinctiveness of the distance learning experience is increasingly recognized.

As a result, the eight regional accreditation commissions for postsecondary education have proposed revisions to distance learning accreditation standards (Regional Accrediting Commissions, 2000). Although two of the five major categories of *Guidelines for Distance Education*, Curriculum and Instruction and Evaluation and Assessment, were retained, two others, Libraries and Learning Resources and Student Services, were subsumed into the new categories of Faculty Support and Student Support. By their presence, these two new categories indicate the perceived importance of support for successful distance learning. Specific items appearing in the Faculty Support section relating to course design, delivery and oversight, workload, and professional evaluation suggest that distance learning faculty members may play somewhat different roles than their counterparts in traditional environments.

Additionally, technical support issues are emphasized not only for faculty but also for "those responsible for program development . . . working directly with students" and for students (Regional Accrediting Commissions, 2000, p. 9). Components within the Student Services category are quite specific about technology. For example, components related to admissions include information about expected access to technology; technological literacy level; range of library, learning, and support services; arrangements for faculty and peer interaction; and the nature and challenges of the technology-based learning environment.

A new Institution Context and Commitment category includes components of the Facilities and Finances category found in the *Guidelines for Distance Education*. This new category represents an attempt to address unique institutional issues in the evolving distance learning arena, including the creation of flexible, varied organizational structures; the targeting of financial resources; study that leads to degrees or certificates obtained through distance learning or a combination of delivery modes; provision of and support for technologies that best help students achieve learning objectives; and adherence to legal requirements, such as copyright law, intellectual property issues, and export restrictions on sensitive information and technologies.

ACADEMIC VALUES

Despite international concern about the notable challenge to basic academic values posed by distance learning (Eaton, 2000) and about the possible jeopardy to core institutional values as accreditation standards are modified, these values may very well be affirmed by and even benefit from distance learning. For example, a community of learning—a recognized value in site-based education—may be viewed as impossible to establish in distance education, where there is no site. The purpose of such a community, however, might be honored by establishing an alternative beyond physical space (Eaton, 2000). As in the world of fashion, the "fit" may very well improve as "one-size-fits-all" distance learning evolves into more sophisticated "tailor-made" institutional responses that result in better matches between learning objectives and outcomes for distance learners.

EVALUATION IN DISTANCE LEARNING

Although in traditional education the emphasis on comprehensive evaluation decreased during the last decade (Kezar, 1999), pressures for accountability from sources external to postsecondary institutions engendered an increased institutional focus on improving teaching and learning (Lazerson, Wagener, & Shumanis, 1999). Not surprisingly, evaluation studies prevailed where new and innovative programs occurred (Kezar, 1999). Researchers studying evaluation in traditional higher education settings have found it is feasible to gather attitudinal data from students about global and multidimensional instructional factors as part of program and course evaluations (Abrami, d'Apollonia, & Cohen, 1990; Cashin & Downey, 1992; Centra, 1993; Cohen, 1981; Feldman, 1989a, 1989b; Marsh, 1984).

Data-Gathering Scheme

Framing any discussion of the quality of distance education should be a consideration of the attitudes, competencies, and achievements of distance learners. Kirkpatrick's (1994) Four Levels of Evaluation offers an appropriate structure for examining these important learner aspects (Belanger & Jordan, 2000).

At Level 1, learners' attitudes about the learning environment or their learning may be gathered by administering surveys before, during, and after their learning experience. Capturing their perceptions at Level 1 is a critical part of an evaluation process because of the effect that students' perceptions can have on their approaches to learning. At Level 2, students' knowledge transfer (i.e., what they learned) can be assessed using skill- and knowledge-based tests or projects. At the next level, the transfer of learned behaviors (applications) can be assessed by administering surveys on how learning is being applied in comprehensive and complex authentic projects, through observations made at the work site, through control group testing, or through certification processes at the end of programs. At the final level, measuring organizational impact is especially challenging because it typically entails follow-up with employers to determine how the former students' learning contributes to their current performance (e.g., ways in which it has improved their ability to provide services). The first two levels can be a part of the formative evaluation. All four levels can contribute to a summative evaluation.

Views about learning through distance education and overall student satisfaction toward distance education, as well as more specific attitudes, are typical Level 1 attitudinal items. The relationship between the students' views and their success in a course (Pascarella et al., 1996) can provide useful insights about student learning. Student outcomes, such as grades and test scores, are typical behavioral elements collected to continue composing a picture of the Level 2 learning of these students (Kirkpatrick, 1994; Phipps & Merisotis, 1999).

End-of-Course Evaluations

In marked contrast to the mid-1990s when there were few models for systematically assessing distance education (Biner, Bink, Huffman, & Dean 1995; Thorpe, 1993; Zvacek, 1994), institutions are now apt to support an evaluation scheme designed to measure the first two tiers, attitudes and competencies, using centrally administered, computerized databases. Faculty from traditional and virtual settings tend to access these databases of closed- and open-ended items when developing end-of-course evaluations. Evaluation of distance learning for improving distance learning is becoming a priority (Bers, 1999).

Review of a typical computerized end-of-course databank evaluation system, CAFÉ (Course and Faculty Evaluation), in place at a Pacific region Research I university, indicates that most of the 300-plus items in the database have general utility for traditional and distance education offerings. Only six of the items, however, approach specific aspects of distance education. For example, the item "Audiovisual materials (or computers) used in this course were well chosen," although somewhat dated in its terminology, could have a profound impact on subsequent hardware and software decisions for courses offered to remote learners (University of Hawaii, 2000).

Results from Meta-analyses

Meta-analyses of existing evaluation data about distance learning do offer Level 1 findings. Such analyses indicate that distance learners generally like learning at a distance although they tend to prefer face-to-face contact. As for Level 2, the data indicate that distance learners generally do as well as their traditional counterparts in terms of grades and test scores (Phipps & Merisotis, 1999). A considerable void, though, occurs in the evaluation literature in regard to Level 3 and Level 4, even in the case of traditional education. Given reports that Internet-delivered instruction, by its very nature, tends to support authentic project-based learning, the Level 3 gap may begin to be addressed. Determining work site impact, however, is an ongoing challenge in regard to all types of learners.

IMPORTANCE OF COMMUNICATION PATTERNS TO EVALUATION

A growing body of research on distance learning stresses the importance of interactive communication patterns (Morrison & Adcock, 1999).

Need for Effective Interaction

Consequences may be severe when socialization, a basic human need, is minimal. Barriers to interaction may impact instruction negatively and to a significant degree. A review of more than two million learners over 25 years of age who studied at the Open University in the United Kingdom suggests that communication that is only one way leads to failure and massive dropout problems (Gladieux & Swail, 1999).

Perceptions of isolation may also suggest "transactional distance" (Moore, 1989), with students indicating diminished satisfaction with their distance learning experience if they perceive little opportunity for interaction (Fulford & Zhang, 1993). When face-to-face instruction does not occur, tone of voice, facial expression, and body language often cannot be transmitted in Web-based, audio-based, print-based, or combined delivery modes, thus compromising communication. Interaction can even be impaired in interactive video when microphones, camera angles, or compression factors are inadequate (Herring & Smaldino, 1997).

Measuring Types of Interaction

Evaluating three key types of communication patterns in a distance learning situation can highlight occurrences and the quality of three key components for success in distance learning: learner-to-instructor, learner-to-learner, and learner-to-content interaction (Moore, 1989). In *Seven Principles of Good Practice* (Chickering & Ehrmann, 1996), two of these constructs appear to be captured by the terms "student-faculty contact" and "cooperation among students" (Table 31.1).

Level 1 data-gathering tools, surveys, such as one developed by Fulford and Zhang (1993), can be employed to capture students' perceptions about their interactions with their instructors and peers and their attitudes toward interaction overall. The short administration time for most surveys, such as Fulford and Zhang's 14-item survey, contributes to their usefulness for both formative and summative evaluations.

Factors related to interacting with content are also key predictors of quality (Inman, Kerwin, & Mayes, 1999). Such factors include three that appear in *Seven Principles of Good Practice* (Chickering & Gamson, 1987), that is, engaging in active learning, spending time on task, and receiving prompt feedback.

Another critical communication factor is interactivity with the technology or technologies employed to deliver instruction. This fourth factor, learner-to-technology interactivity (Wagner, 1994), depends on the types of technologies—the asynchronous tools of e-mail, fax machines, surface mail, and threaded discussions and the synchronous ones of telephones, teleconferences, and chat rooms—and how they are used.

Naturalistic Approaches

Uncovering the effectiveness of print-based independent study courses, Web-based courses, threaded online discussions, audioconferencing, videotapes, and live two-way interactive television separately or in some combination can be difficult (Sherry, 1996). Adapting a more time-intensive, naturalistic, or qualitative-based evaluation technique, such as having an objective facilitator collect data from students on all aspects of the instructional environment (Clark & Bekey, 1979), is an avenue worth exploring.

In Small Group Instructional Diagnosis (SGID), students' initial responses about what helps or hinders learning or needs changing are subsequently ranked by the entire class for consideration by their instructor in time for changes *before* the course ends. A 1998 study indicated the potential for using SGID to assess learning at a deeper level in a distance educational setting that employed interactive video (Sherry, Fulford, & Zhang, 1998). Whether a Web-based threaded discussion format could readily incorporate a third-party facilitator and provide anonymity remains to be studied.

Developing theoretically grounded analysis schemes for massive amounts of data challenges ethnographers who enter distance education "cybercourses." Extensive records of real-time chat sessions and delayed-time threaded discussions, e-mail, course content, and uploaded student projects provide text-based data to add to the student tracking information (e.g., number of "hits" at the site and numbers of postings to discussions).

These numerous artifacts from the virtual world demand exploratory research, particularly for neophyte investigators, on the research process itself. Guided experiences for studying learner interactions in computer conferencing systems, such as the directed studies offered to selected doctoral students at one southwestern university, show promise for developing research skills for future study of the virtual world. Results from these investigations could indicate the shape of designs for future online communications (McIsaac, Blocher, Mahes, & Vrasidas, 1999).

Human Observation

For any researcher who enters cyberspace, respect for the privacy and integrity of the learners is a critical consideration. This dictum is suggested in one of the *Seven Principles for Good Practice* (Chickering & Gamson, 1987)—respect for diverse talents and ways of learning— and specifically addressed in the Association for Educational Communications and Technology (AECT) Professional Code of Ethics (AECT, 2001). The availability of data does not imply open access. Researchers who want to use online data for a study need to follow ethical and institutional procedures designed to protect participants by informing them of the intent of the study, securing their written permission to observe their virtual transactions, and providing confidentiality.

Studies of distance learners may focus on videotapes. Analyzing these tapes often reveals hidden concerns whose resolution can improve the learning environment. It is, however, difficult and time consuming to assess the transmissions between instructor and students (Herring & Smaldino, 1997) and determine the actual versus perceived communication patterns among learners in two-way video and audio classes (Fulford & Zhang, 1993).

Computer-based Analyses

Computer-based data gathering and analyses can dramatically decrease the amount of time a researcher spends working with data as well as offer potentially reliable data. Beyond basic worldware (software developed and used for tasks typically undertaken by the general population, such as word processing, database, and spreadsheet, programs, as opposed to educational software) are dedicated software programs for performing specific tasks for data-rich studies. The programs are designed to readily capture and analyze qualitative and quantitative data gathered in actual or virtual settings.

Self-Reports

Self-reports of interactions and other incidents tend to play a prominent role in the distance education literature, particularly in effectiveness studies. The most frequently occurring studies in a review conducted by Phipps and Merisotis (1999) deal with operational and administrative aspects of course and program design. Notably they report that, despite the many advocates of empirical studies and the investigation of student services issues, many studies have an anecdotal basis and few address support services issues.

Comprehensive Evaluations

Combined "in-house" and commercial evaluation approaches are becoming more common now that assessing the relatively intangible and complex construct of "learning" has the added challenge of measuring somewhat intangible learners—that is, virtual students. Commercially available, valid, reliable evaluation instruments and systematic evaluation schemes are being tailored for distance learning, obviating the need to adapt tools and processes that at best were simply awkward for distance learners. One such program (Ehrmann, 2000) is guided by *Seven Principles for Good Practice* (Chickering & Gamson, 1987). The Flashlight™ Program of the Technology Learning Group (Flashlight, n.d.), an affiliate of the American Association of Higher Education and sponsored by twelve major publishing and technology companies, offers a comprehensive package of evaluation services, including a database of close to 500 validated survey items designed to capture student attitudes toward all types of teaching and learning practices and the use of identified technologies.

The technologies include audioconferences, software applications, courseware, electronic communications, graphing and scientific calculators, Web page and multimedia creation and use, television, videotapes, and voice mail. The survey items measure students' satisfaction with training and their overall satisfaction as well their assessment of their achievement of learning objectives, their skill levels, and the time they spent with technology. Open-ended questions are available to gather unanticipated data. Other critical factors related to student success can be evaluated using demographic and academic items that address, for example, academic goals and retention. This survey also includes codes for 14 educational strategies, such as "rich and rapid feedback," and "positive addition to technology." More importantly, training for distance practitioners in designing and conducting individualized, relevant evaluations at their own institutions is available.

An analysis of research on technology use in higher education suggests three important points. First, *how*, not *what*, technology is used is what matters. Second, the changes that occur in the learning environment throughout a student's entire educational process appear to have a more significant impact on learning than what occurs through using technology at discrete times or in separate courses. Third, applying findings that relate to technology integration at a specific institution can provide insights about learning at that institution and can ultimately impact that institution (Ehrmann, 1997).

As more comprehensive evaluation processes evolve, with new measurement instruments, processes, dedicated software, and technologies, and as more researchers receive both evaluation training and cyber-based training, consistent evaluation plans can be anticipated that will contribute to quality-based improvement for distance learners.

EMERGING GUIDELINES AND PROJECTS

Whereas evaluation processes encompass specific criteria related to quality, actual and emerging distance education projects provide holistic views that indicate directions for improvement. The projects that follow are typical in this regard, offering glimpses into aspects they exemplify. Although the structure of distance learning, which was developed on principles of instructional design, has a sound foundation, the ground this foundation rests on in this Information Age often resembles quicksand more than bedrock. Policymakers attempting to brace this edifice continue to engage in the delicate process of balancing breadth and depth.

Global Initiatives

The expanding globalization of distance education, particularly at the college level, has heightened awareness in academic communities of the importance of ensuring quality. With the

Internet-based learning market estimated to reach $46 billion by 2006 (Morton, 2001), it is not surprising that for-profit corporations are developing Internet-based distance learning offerings. For example, smarthinking.com, established by Sylvan Learning Systems in partnership with nine other companies, secured a $450 million contract with the U.S. Army to deliver virtual tutoring (Morton, 2001).

Consortia

Given the complexity of combinations that can exist, consortia face special challenges in addressing quality, particularly during their formative stages.

Governance.   As multinational educational consortia form, new governance issues include determining responsibility for awarding degrees and certificates and defining credits earned from distributed course offerings. The magnitude of the problems that can arise is indicated by the failure in the 1980s of a proposed educational alliance for telecommunications. The alliance disbanded after higher education officers in the United States were unable to reach agreement on accreditation. Furthermore, in this instance there were no international partners, only concern expressed by individual states about identification at a national level (Web-based Education Commission, 2000).

A response to institutional responsibility for degrees that typifies the responses of many is reflected in an Internet-based venture begun in 2000 to meet Asian marketplace needs. The Global Alliance for Transnational Education (GATE) (2000), which is based in Hong Kong and has programs at institutions in Canada, the United Kingdom, the Netherlands, Taiwan, Australia, New Zealand, and the United States, will award degrees to graduates from the nine member institutions.

A more unusual plan is evolving for the nascent Universitas 21, a multiple university and corporate venture initiated in 2000 by Auckland University and 18 worldwide university partners and a corporate one, Thomson Learning. Plans call for graduates to receive their degrees and certificates in the name of Universitas 21. Course design, testing and assessment, and student database management are to be the responsibility of Thomson. Reconsideration of membership by two universities over governance issues related to regulations, however, points up the challenges such multinational ventures face.

Criteria for Global Entities.   When quality appears questionable, a drastic response may occur. In the mid-1990s legislators in Hong Kong reacted to subpar offerings by unscrupulous global educational providers with legislation designed to regulate "non-local higher education providers" (French, 1996). More commonly, global efforts to provide quality-based distance learning revolve around quality standards that can simultaneously guide systematic evaluations of student-centered distributed learning while supporting unique initiatives for students and local practice across nations.

Established to deal with issues of quality in higher education and corporate training delivered nation to nation, GATE is one organization that offers this type of written guidance for "best practices." Its *Principles for Transnational Education* contains guidelines intended to provide structure for practice and certification purposes. The guidelines are grouped into 10 categories:

1. Goals and objectives.
2. Standards.
3. Legal and ethical matters.
4. Student admissions and enrollment.
5. Human resources.
6. Physical and financial resources.

7. Teaching and learning.
8. Student support.
9. Evaluation.
10. Third Parties.

Each principle is written to assist international experts in determining quality. For example, according to a guideline in the standards category, the educational provider (home institution) is expected to offer programs and experiences to students in the host country comparable to programs at its home base, with any needed modifications made to accommodate unique features of the delivery mode. A guideline in the last category states that third parties are expected to have explicit written agreements delineating each partner's role and commitment. Although no guarantees regarding reciprocal accreditation, professional licensing or employment recommendations are offered, full disclosure to students is expected.

Similarly, the Committee for Quality Assurance in Higher Education in Australia and the Quality Assurance Agency for Higher Education (QAAHE) in the United Kingdom provide written guidance for distance learning. Although QAAHE (2001) frames its criteria within the six major categories of system design, academic standards and quality in design, approval and review processes, quality assurance and standards in management aspects, student development and support, communication and representation, and assessment, the concepts are elaborated with 23 aspects related to the main categories. Like the principles promulgated by GATE, QAAHE's guidelines recognize the laws and regulations of the countries served, but not as prominently. One needs to read through the categories to locate that concept within the system design category. Planners who use the QAAHE guidelines receive additional help in the form of "expectations." Disseminating the results from analyses that employ such guidelines so that all constituencies can make fully informed decisions for institutional planning, enrollment, and ongoing pedagogical improvements is yet another challenge.

Considering the fast-growing, predominantly time- and geographic-independent distance delivery world of the Internet and the proliferation of written quality assurance guidelines, initiatives are now under way to reexamine many of these guidelines to ensure that quality is maintained. Additionally, calls are heard about which quality-based issues can be communicated in what ways to all countries and to present and future students by all types of providers (Council for Higher Education Accreditation, 2000).

National Initiatives

At the beginning of the 21st century, accreditation associations in the United States, like many organizations throughout the globe, continued their efforts in monitoring the quality of institutions of higher education.

Revised Distance Education Guidelines.   Institutions offering distance education that volunteer to participate in an accreditation study are judged using quality standards for distance education that were developed during the previous decade. Broadly stated, these standards were based on the then prevailing idea that "good teaching is good teaching" (Ragan, 2000). In other words, they were based on principles set forth by Chickering and Gamson (1987) for face-to-face classroom teaching. In an evaluation study of four online courses offered at a major midwestern university (Graham, Cagiltay, Lim, Craner, & Duffy, 2001), the standards appeared to offer specific guidance that connected the seven principles to specific strategies for distance education instructors (e.g., offer students clear guidelines for student-faculty interaction).

Again, similar to the guidelines of international accrediting bodies, these formal guidelines for distance learning are being reconceptualized to emphasize more overtly (a) the unique aspects of Internet-based or combined Internet-based and face-to-face meetings that make up the learning process, (b) faculty and learner support, and (c) the role of the institution. Future examination of the use of the newer version that is formally adopted should provide answers about its utility (Regional Accrediting Commissions, 2000).

Government Study.   Despite a philosophy of inclusion and review, questions about quality for distance learners remain. During a recent year-long U.S. congressional study of Internet-based education, federal regulations were identified as hindering Internet-based distance education (Web-based Education Commission, 2000). Three regulations caused particular concern. First, the "12-hour rule" specifies a certain amount of "seat time" to meet eligibility requirements for maximum amounts of Title IV financial aid. Second, the "50% rule" calls for institutions participating in the Title IV funding programs to deliver at least 50% of their instruction in a "classroom-based environment" (p. 91). Third, payment by a postsecondary institution of third-party providers for "hits" of Web portals by potential students can endanger the institution's eligibility for federal student financial aid. Originally, all three regulations were instituted to protect learners from engaging in inferior or fraudulent educational ventures, but with the growth of the Internet, questions are now being raised about the current usefulness of the regulations. Studies are currently under way at selected U.S. universities to study the possibility of exemptions to the 50% rule. The results may ultimately warrant changes to this rule.

It is noteworthy that administrators in the United States at the pre-K through 12 level also face struggles with state and local regulations. Their particular challenges in this area include impediments to transferring academic credit, licenses, and professional credentials across district or state lines; getting funding on a per student basis and for Web-based initiatives; changing the traditional 10-month pay periods; and accommodating variations in teacher-student ratios (Web-based Education Commission, 2000). On the positive side, federal implementation of the e-rate established for low-cost Internet entry at U.S. schools appears to be supporting a school-wide Internet connectivity rate of 98% (Cattagni & Westat, 2001). Although connectivity rates are higher in instructional rooms at the most affluent schools (82%) than in instructional rooms at the poorest schools (60%), continued growth seems likely.

Regulatory concerns are but one part of the quality assurance picture. To implement Deming's continuous program of improvement (Richie, 1994), evaluation and improvement need to be ongoing.

Specifically Focused Projects

The preceding projects and initiatives are intended to lead to a "stamp of approval" for all aspects of distance learning for all the partners they reach. The following processes target specific aspects of the distance learning milieu.

Internet-Specific Distance Learning Guidance.   The repertoire of existing models and criteria for measuring quality in distance education also reflects the trend toward providing Internet-based education using resources specific to that type of education.

In an attempt to specify quality, the National Education Association and its corporate partner, Blackboard Inc., recently presented 24 benchmarks for such distance learning (Institute for Higher Education Policy, 2000). These benchmarks, which cover course development, course structure, teaching and learning, student and faculty support, and evaluation and assessment, emerged after a review of 45 benchmarks developed by others. Three that are unique to this list offer insights into emergent issues deemed essential by distance education faculty and administrators: (a) a reliable technology system, as fail-safe as possible; (b) an agreement between faculty and students on completion times for student assignments and faculty responses; and (c) accurate, quick answers to questions for student services (Institute for Higher Education Policy, 2000).

Determining criteria for accepting distance education courses in a publicized database can also be a critical quality-based issue. Qualifications for membership in the Sloan Asynchronous Learning Network (ALN), a consortium established to provide a quality-based database for online degree and certificate programs, gives insights into the process of including online courses in a database. Their criteria for listing such courses in their database emphasize the similarity between these and face-to-face courses in terms of faculty, class size, and regional accreditation. They also state that no special equipment other than computer connectivity to the Internet be required and that, when delivery is primarily asynchronous, interaction occurs in learning cohorts. Additionally, all courses in the database must be offered and lead to degree or certificate completion. Finally, membership in their network is open only to postsecondary institutions who received grants from the Sloan Foundation for online education or who were accepted through a peer review process. In the 1999-2000 academic year, approximately 2,000 distinct courses and 200 degree or certificate programs served over 115,000 students (Sloan ALN Consortium, n.d.).

Faculty Senate Role.   Strong sentiments favoring traditional faculty governance appear in recommendations for faculty oversight, documentation of guidelines by local academic senates, and in faculty bargaining issues. These sentiments are exemplified in *Guidelines for Good Practices: Effective Instructor-Student Contact in Distance Learning* (Academic Senate for California Community Colleges, 2000). This document, published by the faculty senate of the California Community Colleges, addresses the importance of faculty governance.

Professional Development.   Given the general agreement that typical "one-shot" workshops are far from effective, long-term and ongoing faculty design and development workshops are supporting faculty as they examine newer, more complex technologies and try to apply them to their teaching. For example, in a 3-year Innovations in Distance Education Project conducted for faculty members and staff from three Pennsylvania universities, participants identified principles directed primarily toward guiding the design and development of distance education (Ragan, 2000). The participants acknowledged that their findings are applicable to on-site instruction, too. Many specific references to distance teaching and learning appear in a structured, five-category listing of principles and practices for distance education, such as creating and maintaining a learning community through electronic communication; selecting accessible, appropriate technologies for distance learners; and preparing and supporting their use on a continual basis. The similarity of the principles the participants developed to those of other distance educators and models supports the constructivist approach they followed throughout their learning. The design of this project suggests the merits of doing a follow-up study to determine the relationship between the participants' ownership of these principles and their application of them as they design and deliver instruction for their students.

Support Services Project.   In this mix of consortia, specifics for student services for geographically dispersed learners tend to receive limited attention. Grants, however, can give such focus. For example, The Learning Anytime Anywhere Partnership (LAAP), offers federal funding for partners who develop distance learning models that, among other things, provide campus-based students services such as job placement, academic counseling, and library services to their distance learners in unique ways (U.S. Government. Office of Postsecondary Education, 2001).

ANALYSIS OF THE APPLICATION OF DISTANCE STUDENT EVALUATION DATA TO INSTRUCTIONAL DESIGN

Current indicators continue to suggest that, at the instructor and student levels, quality-based experiences for distance learners spring from systematic instructional design. During the design process, however, determining real rather than perceived needs for multiple constituencies can be a complex task. Analyzing distance learners, who tend to be more diverse than traditional students, poses additional challenges. For example, gender issues need to be considered, (i.e., it may be useful to acknowledge the diverse life experiences of female students) (Burge, 1998). In addition, taking into account psychosocial characteristics may allow shy and second-language students to flourish, as asynchronous communications gives them the chance to compose measured responses (Maloney, 1999). The physical and cognitive challenges experienced by some learners may be met by representing content in ways consistent with the use of adaptive devices (Thompson, 1998).

The unique opportunities offered by available technologies, even if they are time consuming, combined with instructors' finite capability to implement various media and devices, the accessibility and usability of diverse and newer technologies for students, and dispersed student support services and library resources make contextual analyses particularly critical when assessing quality. Collaborating with colleagues, which may be perceived as a luxury by some, can be a challenge for others in terms of shared vision, time, and materials. Students' attraction to innovative teaching environments and their view of the various "mindware" technologies deserve consideration during materials selection (Salomon, Perkins, & Globerson, 1991; Thompson, 1998), as do multiple representations of the same content to address different learner needs (Gibson, 1998). Incorporating chat rooms, electronic bulletin boards, private mail, or combinations of these appears to enhance students' course interactions (Parke & Tracy-Mumford, 2000).

Studying Software Applications

Answers are needed for questions about how to best guide teachers to become effective designers of online learning. An example of an effort to improve course design is an integrated software shell at the Learning Technology Center at Vanderbilt University. STAR.Legacy (Software Technology for Action and Reflection) is software that teachers can adapt to integrate six main areas—generating ideas, examining multiple perspectives, researching and revising, testing, disseminating results, and reflecting—into instruction they develop. Software like this application has the potential to help teachers adapt challenging course material for online instruction incorporating an inquiry-based approach (Schwartz, Brophy, Lin, & Bransford, 1999).

Readily available e-mail and commercial Web-based courseware applications also deserve study and attention at the design stage. Over the course of two years, Wegner, Holloway, and Wegner (1999) found that significantly more interaction occurred between the instructor and distance learners and between the learners themselves when e-mail was used. Furthermore, Internet-based research sites were accessed more frequently when these were embedded within the course itself, as opposed to sites that were external to the online course structure. Offering further support for the value of using combined courseware was the finding that no significant differences appeared between the experimental and the control groups' use of communication tools that were external to the courseware application—fax machines and telephones.

Studying the factors surrounding course management software will become increasingly important when assessing quality in the coming years if plans for adopting this type of program continues on the path reported by over 469 two- and four-year public and private colleges and universities in the United States. Although only slightly over 14% of the technology administrators who responded to the annual Campus Computing Survey report using course management software, close to 58% have established standards for this type of application (K. Greene, 2000).

There are indications that features integrated into commercial course application software, such as Blackboard CourseInfo, Learning Tree, Virtual-U, and WebCT, can support organized course content; include multiple perspectives on issues; archive data automatically; incorporate the instructional strategies of modeling and scaffolding, and encourage participation, dynamic engagement, and peer feedback *when* faculty members incorporate these features into instructional design and delivery. Unwary novices, however, may follow the somewhat linear structure of the course content features of these courseware tools (Dabbagh, 2000).

Studying Emerging Technologies

Studying applications of emerging technologies is critical for effective distance learning given their integral role in this type of education. One such example is the Center for Innovative Learning Technologies (CILT). It was formed as a national, institution-independent resource to stimulate research on and development of technology that could potentially contribute to online learning for K-14 levels of education. Its focus on examining the use of visualization and modeling for complex learning, technology and assessment models, advanced communication tools, and inexpensive computing innovations offers the promise of better informed use of newer technologies for learning. For example, electronic solutions are being examined to determine their potential for virtual collaboration, such as tools for remote learning team interactions using multi-formatted materials; innovative presentations of virtual environments; enhanced searches of metafiles, such as might occur with XML applications for Web browsers; and cognitive scaffolding using tools that guide reflection about and identification of critical relationships (Pea et al., 1999).

RESEARCH FINDINGS AND BEST PRACTICES FOR INSTRUCTIONAL DESIGNERS AND INSTRUCTORS

In the midst of a scholarly discourse that raises questions about the dynamic, developing nature of distance education studies; that requests deeper explorations of values and concepts held by external and internal constituencies; that queries the wisdom of dissolving geographic and academic boundaries (Eaton, 2000); and that offers cultural interpretations for initiatives seen by some as liberating and by others as oppressive (Agre, 1999), the global warming for distance learning continues.

It may be that the gap between scholarly discourse on distance learning concerns and distance learning practitioners may be narrowed through global initiatives, such as revised guidelines for quality assurance, or through innovative research collaboratives, such as the Center for Innovative Learning Technologies. Distance learning stretches across a wide band of the educational spectrum, including an increasing number of business enterprises and consortia encompassing educational organizations and corporations. Translating quality factors that are themselves undergoing scholarly scrutiny in order to reach results that in turn can be used to improve practice can be intimidating and open to interpretation.

GUIDING DISTANCE LEARNING PRACTICE

Given the expanding active distance learning engagement worldwide, suggestions for maximizing quality can be formed into a list, or even a checklist, that suggests a job aid in order to encourage application by practitioners (Tilaro & Rossett, 1993).

Using the broad headings in Table 31.1—Institution, Faculty, and Student—the following list attempts to summarize pertinent scholarly recommendations and research-based findings that have implications for pedagogical practice. In the interests of brevity, issues that could very well appear in slightly different versions in several categories are listed only once. For example, although the student category may appear brief, numerous recommendations that, if implemented, might improve student experiences are more directly the responsibility of the institution and faculty and consequently only appear in those categories. It should be noted, too, that many concepts in the list are encompassed in many of the guidelines developed by the professional associations cited in this chapter. For ease of reading, references to those sources were purposely limited.

Institutional Guidelines

1. A philosophical shift to conceptualizing the traditional and virtual learning offerings of a single governing institution as a borderless, melded entity (i.e., a "hub of learning" that has a clear mission statement and clearly designated institutional responsibilities) may impact planning and implementation (Parker, 1997; Regional Accrediting Commissions, 2000).
2. A flexible governance and organizational structure that takes into account institutional culture and values, encompasses academic oversight of programs and courses, and extends decision making regarding technology beyond the chief information officer may lead to more creative responses and quicker implementation (Parker, 1997; Regional Accrediting Commissions, 2000).
3. Financial resources should be allocated for distance education, including the following (B. Greene, 2000; Institute for Higher Education Policy, 2000; Johnstone, 2000; Parker, 1997; Regional Accrediting Commissions, 2000; Stein, 2001; Web-based Education Commission, 2000):
   - Ongoing commitment of fiscal resources for the purpose of selecting, implementing, testing, and maintaining technologies and upgrading or replacing technologies with newer, more powerful, appropriate iterations to support teaching may enhance learning.
   - Funds for initial and ongoing training and adequate support services for faculty, staff, students, and all responsible for providing services directly to students may improve quality.
   - Compensation for faculty engaged in distance learning design and implementation that recognizes workload, and intellectual property right issues (possibly through tiered ownership agreements or royalty distributions) may address reward issues for those providers.
   - Budgeting for instructional resources, such as virtual libraries, copyright clearances, and site licenses for instructional materials, as well as for timely, adequate, accurate cyber-based support services, such as online registration, university bookstore services, testing, tutoring, and academic counseling, may provide equitable resources for distance learners.
   - Financial resources devoted to supporting research and evaluation studies and investigating consortia options related to sustaining programs may contribute to improved distance learning.
4. Strategic plans may direct decision making about critical distance learning issues, such as problems associated with traditional revenue sources when a physical institution and a virtual institution are blended. For example, in-state and out-of-state tuition plans may become impediments when student enrollment is used as the basis for funding

(K. Greene, 2000; Inman et al., 1999; Institute for Higher Education Policy, 2000; Johnstone, 2000).

5. Development, implementation, dissemination, and review of policies and technological solutions in accordance with laws and requirements to meet specific aspects of distance learning suggest a commitment to quality. Such policies would include an acceptable use policy to address privacy, personal identification, and safe usage issues as well as policies on censorship, plagiarism, and standardization of technology (Institute for Higher Education Policy, 2000; Kearsley, 2000; Parker, 1997; Regional Accrediting Commissions, 2000; Web-based Education Commission, 2000).

6. Testing the system prior to program initiation may support the development of contingency plans (Quality Assurance Agency for Higher Education, 2001).

7. Strategies to address institutional factors identified as leading to success in higher education—availability of financial aid, access to resources, and contact with faculty—may lead to equitable access for all potential constituencies (Pascarella et al., 1996; Tinto, 1993):

   • Changes in federal regulations that preclude limits on funds for distance learners, reconsideration of tuition policies based on traditional geographic service area, and financial aid packaged to encompass costs of necessary hardware and software may address the first factor.

   • A process for selecting technologies that includes criteria for adopting universally available, affordable communication tools with technological adaptations for students' visual, auditory, or motor impairments may promote the second factor by improving access for all potential and current students, especially when selection occurs continually to take advantage of newer technologies that can be implemented with minimal disruption to teaching and learning.

   • Coupling plans for newer technology adoption with physical resources (e.g., ergonomic, regularly upgraded computer workstations for faculty and Web-based course application packages with their embedded communication tools) and with human resources (e.g., experts in newer technologies and support staff to provide ongoing technical assistance to faculty and students) may promote the third factor, active communication among faculty and students.

8. Conducting regularly planned analyses and evaluation studies of components, or of the entire distance education system, may uncover seemingly conflicting situations and areas for improvement:

   • Systems analysis of the particular distance learning situation to identify learners who are educationally underprepared or overworked, culturally distanced or lacking confidence, potential dropouts or nonenrolling students may lead to improved support and retention strategies (Dabbagh, 2000; Institute for Higher Education Policy, 2000; Morrison & Adcock, 1999; Parke & Tracy-Mumford, 2000; Phipps & Merisotis, 1999; Regional Accrediting Commissions, 2000; Thompson, 1998).

   • Assessing and documenting overall program objectives in relation to learning outcomes, student satisfaction, and resource and technology use through the employment of multiple methods may provide information that meets standards for utility (focused information needed by intended users), feasibility (realistic, careful, cost-effective data gathering and tactful reporting), accuracy (valid and reliable data), and propriety (adherence to legal and ethical procedures that respect the welfare of all affected) (American Evaluation Association, 2000; Institute for Higher Education Policy, 2000; Regional Accrediting Commissions, 2000).

9. Initiatives to help distance learners become a part of the larger academic community, such as strategies for broad-based study groups and on-site special events, hold promise

for connecting these learners to intangible benefits that this community traditionally offers its students (Institute for Higher Education Policy, 2000).

10. Disseminating institutional standards for distance learning (e.g., accreditation), publicizing program and course availability, and providing online and on-site access to the general public have the potential to lead to informed educational program selections (Institute for Higher Education Policy, 2000).

11. Explaining academic policies and practices to constituencies as people driven, not technology driven, may send a message that the institution respects the goal of helping everyone in the community to lead a balanced life more than utilitarian solutions (Yeaman, 2000).

Faculty Guidelines

1. Reconceptualized curricula decisions may lead to team efforts in the design and/or delivery of instruction, to interdisciplinary offerings, and to creative approaches to bridging face-to-face and virtual space (Institute for Higher Education Policy, 2000; Parker, 1997).

2. Effectively designed instruction has the potential to enhance distance learning (Dabbagh, 2000; Kearsley, 2000; Parker, 1997; Ragan, 2000):

   - Courses that employ constructivist principles that move students along a continuum to self-direction and have valid and credible content have a likelihood of conveying to the learners that expectations for their success are high.

   - Instruction that is problem based, flexible, and uses course tools that incorporate Web page features and offer multiple perspectives may lead to higher levels of achievement.

3. Clear learning goals that connect to learning outcomes, not simply available technologies, may support active and reflective learning. The goals can be conveyed to learners "in whatever manner suits the design model—in print, face to face, or via a Web site" (Ragan, 2000, p. 22; see also Inman et al., 1999; Regional Accrediting Commissions, 2000).

4. Orientation sessions with specific technologies and processes show support for student learning (Institute for Higher Education Policy, 2000; Kearsley, 2000; Regional Accrediting Commissions, 2000):

   - Introductions that direct students to resources for questions about aspects of the course may contribute to student-instructor communications and lead to provision of timely feedback.

   - Instruction in conducting research, locating online resources, evaluating online resources, and uploading assignments can convince learners that they can work with those technologies, moving them toward more seamless use during the course.

5. Advice about factors related to successful distance learning may help students acquire realistic expectations, and tangible aides, such as guides and clear due dates, may help students avoid procrastination (Institute for Higher Education Policy, 2000; Kearsley, 2000; Parker, 1997; Regional Accrediting Commissions, 2000).

6. Instruction on specific attributes of the technologies employed for student-faculty exchanges, such as techniques for engaging in online threaded discussions and subsequent moderation of them, may assist learners in weaving discussion concepts. During the modeling, identifying social, procedural, expository, explanatory, and cognitive types of interaction, as well as instruction about functioning on a virtual team, may also serve to encourage anticipated types of communication (Bailey & Luetkehans, 1998; Burge, 1998; Dabbagh, 2000; Lesniak & Hodes, 2000; Offir & Lev, 2000; Winograd, 2000).

7. Communication from faculty that directly engages students and offers timely feedback may contribute to interchanges and the students' subsequent success in the course. In some instances, required participation may be warranted to overcome avoidance behaviors evidenced by some students (Burge, 1998; Dabbagh, 2000; Inman et al., 1999; McIsaac et al., 1999).

8. Criteria for authentic project-based learning and adapted Web-based materials; discussion formats that have "text.alt" descriptors added to describe images; links; captioned video; and other design aspects and adaptive devices to engage visually, hearing, and mobility impaired students may contribute to developing the students' expertise (Kraft, 2000; Lowe & Roberts, 2000; Sherry, Billig, Jesse, & Watson-Acosta, 2001).

9. Providing metacognitive models for developing concepts or models and having learners develop their own has the potential to support deep thinking by the students (Marland, 1997; Olgren, 1998).

10. Worldware, with its shared editing features, may draw multiple students into considering content during editing (Anderson & Garrison, 1988).

11. Using multiple evaluation methods (in both short- and long-term studies) that are designed to measure and document students' learning and their use of technology (and that may employ technology for data collection, analysis, interpretation, and dissemination of results) may improve teaching and learning as well as the use of technology itself (Institute for Higher Education Policy, 2000; Regional Accrediting Commissions, 2000; Sherry et al., 2001; Wade, 1999).

12. Active participation in ongoing professional development may lead to the identification and application of research findings, "best practices," and technological advancements in a timely manner (Barone, 2001; Ehrmann, 1997).

13. Authentic reassessments of the teaching and learning climate may lead to clarity and appropriate learning outcomes (Institute for Higher Education Policy, 2000).

Student Guidelines

1. Prior to enrollment, realistic assessments by potential students of their personal attitudes toward their academic commitment, self-directed and collaborative learning, support from significant others, financial resources, available time, academic readiness, and access to and literacy in the technologies and resources to be employed may set the stage for their successful distance learning experiences (Dabbagh, 2000; Institute for Higher Education Policy, 2000; Kearsley, 2000; Regional Accrediting Commissions, 2000).

2. Students from diverse cultural backgrounds who engage in explicitly communicating their expectations for online behavior early in the course to all involved may avoid inadvertent future cultural gaffes (Kearsley, 2000).

3. Learners who use computer-based "agents" or "bots" to link to guides for processes and software and to online materials or who create their own intelligent agents to seek out and update content automatically may be drawn into the content of the learning materials more readily, thus supporting their cognitive strategies (Anderson & Garrison, 1988; Inman et al., 1999).

CONCLUDING QUESTIONS

Guidelines from professional associations and job aids like the preceding list suggest questions that might be developed about quality when determining directions for collegial and scholarly planning, implementing, and measuring of distance learning programs and courses. Multiple questions related to excellence, however, remain. They are posed here for their implicit relationship to improving quality for distance learners.

What factors will contribute to dynamic partnerships and collaborative ventures at international, national, state, institutional, corporate, and programmatic levels to enrich the distance learning experience for all and yet will maintain the values respected in academia and in unique institutional cultures? For example, the trend in developed nations toward Internet-based delivery for distance education remains to be scrutinized to determine the suitability of this form of delivery for all global entities, particularly in emerging nations (Marchessou, 2000). How can current and new configurations of educational institutions sustain themselves within new paradigms for financial structuring? For example, defining the roles that federal and state governments should, or do, play in shaping and funding to advance distance learning is a fundamental issue (Lips, 2000; Marchessou, 2000; Web-based Education Commission, 2000). With much of what is currently known about effective pedagogy for distance learning based on data from successful, committed adult learners, what quality-based designs and strategies might be employed to uplift and sustain people of all ages who face perceptual and actual barriers to learning? For example, research designed to reveal underlying factors affecting persistence in school for all age groups of these learners needs to be carried out (Sherry & Sherry, 1996; Simpson & Head, 2000).

How might the process of teaching and learning with its embedded social and cultural values be recognized by each member of any partnership and yet manage to have the individual partners maintain their unique characteristics (Mauriello, 1995; Newson, 1999)?

Additionally, what processes might support the institutional distance learning community's search for authentic, relevant information in diverse forms while facing ambiguity and fluctuations in laws regulating intellectual property rights (U.S. Copyright Office, 1998)? For example, the concept of intellectual property rights may very well undergo change as vast amounts of course materials are made available in the public domain, such as the planned release and dissemination of nearly all of MIT's teaching materials over the Internet as part of their OpenCourseWare initiative (Richards, 2001).

Finally, given the prevalence of 24 times 7 time frames and the technology intensiveness of many environments, it is essential that institutions consider ways to nurture balanced lives for their administrators, faculty, staff, and learners. If, as Saba (1999) posits, distance education is at the Model T stage, it would appear that research on quality in distance education (research based primarily on learners' attitudes and knowledge rather than on learning outcomes or impact) is at the "SUV towing a little red wagon" stage. Yet the recent emphasis on continuous quality assurance has fueled greater interest in conducting more comprehensive research and evaluation studies. This growing interest, coupled with yet unknown technological advances, may very well propel distance learning into a quality-based "warp drive."

REFERENCES

Abrami, P., d'Apollonia, S., & Cohen, P. (1990). Validity of student ratings of instruction: What we know and what we do not. *Journal of Educational Psychology, 82*(2), 219–231.

Academic Senate for California Community Colleges. (2000). *Technology in Education: A summary of practical policy and workload language* [Online]. Available: http://www.academicsenate.cc.ca.us/Academic%20Senate%20Web/Publications/Papers/Technology_educationpolicysummary.htm#intro

Agre, P. E. (1999). The distances of education. *Academe, 85*(5), 37–41.

American Evaluation Association. (2000). *The program evaluation standards: Summary of the standards* [Online]. Available: http://www.eval.org/EvaluationDocuments/progeval.html

Anderson, T. D., & Garrison, D. R. (1988). Learning in a networked world: New roles and responsibilities. In C. C. Gibson (Ed.), *Distance learners in higher education: Institutional responses for quality outcomes* (pp. 97–125). Madison, WI: Atwood.

Association for Educational Communications and Technology. (2001). *Code of professional ethics* [Online]. Available: http://www.aect.org/AboutAECT/Ethics.html

Bailey, M. L., & Luetkehans, L. (1998, August). *Ten great tips for facilitating virtual learning teams.* Paper presented at the 14th Annual Conference on Distance Teaching and Learning, Madison, WI.

Barone, C. (2001). Conditions for transformation: Infrastructure is not the issue. *Educause* [Online], *36*(3). Available: http://www.educause.edu/pub/er/erm01/erm013w.html

Belanger, F., & Jordan, D. H. (2000). *Evaluation and implementation of distance learning: Technologies, tools and techniques.* Hershey, PA: Idea Group.

Bers, T. (1999). The impact of distance education on institutional research. *New Directions for Institutional Research, 103*, 61–78.

Biner, P. M., Bink, M. L., Huffman, M. L., & Dean, R. S. (1995). Personality characteristics differentiating and predicting the achievement of television-course students and traditional-course students. *American Journal of Distance Education, 9*(2), 46–60.

Brookfield, S. D. (1990). *The skillful teacher: On technique, trust, and responsiveness in the classroom.* San Francisco: Jossey-Bass.

Burge, E. (1998). Gender in distance education. In C. C. Gibson (Ed.), *Distance learners in higher education: Institutional responses for quality outcomes* (pp. 25–45). Madison, WI: Atwood.

Cashin, W. E., & Downey, G. (1992). Using global student rating items for summative evaluation. *Journal of Educational Psychology, 84*, 563–572.

Cattagni, A., & Westat, E. F. (2001). *Internet access in U.S. public schools and classrooms: 1994–2000* [Online]. Washington, DC: U.S. Department of Education, National Center for Education Statistics. Available: http://nces.ed.gov/pubsearch/pubsinfo.asp?pubid=2001071

Centra, J. A. (1993). *Reflective faculty evaluation: Enhancing teaching and determining faculty effectiveness.* San Francisco: Jossey-Bass.

Chickering, A. W., & Gamson, Z. F. (1987). Development and adaptations of the seven principles for good practice in undergraduate education. *New Directions for Teaching and Learning, 4*, 75–81.

Chickering, A. W., & Ehrmann, S. C. (1996). Implementing the seven principles: Technology as lever. *AAHE Bulletin* [Online]. Available: http://www.aahe.org/technology/ehrmann.htm

Clark, J. A., & Bekey, J. (1979). Use of small groups in instructional evaluation. *Insight to Teaching Excellence, 1*(1), 2–5.

Cohen, P. A. (1981). Student ratings of instruction and student achievement: A meta-analysis of multisection validity studies. *Review of Educational Research, 51*, 281–390.

Council for Higher Education Accreditation. (2000, January 27). *Summary report internationalizing quality assurance invitational seminar* [Online].Washington: DC. Available: http://www.chea.org/Commentary/international-quality.html

Dabbagh, N. H. (2000). The challenges of interfacing between face-to-face and online instruction. *TechTrends, 44*(6), 37–42.

Deming, W. E. (1992). *The world of W. Edwards Deming.* Knoxville, TN: SPC.

Eaton, J. S. (2000, June 15). *Core academic values, quality, and regional accreditation: The challenge of distance learning* [Online]. Washington, DC: Council for Higher Education Accreditation. Available: http://www.chea.org/commentary/core-values.cfm

Ehrmann, S. C. (2000). *The Flashlight program: Spotting an elephant in the dark* [Online]. Washington, DC: The TLT Group. Available: http://tltgroup.org/programs/elephant.html

Ehrmann, S. C. (1997). Asking the right questions: What the research tells us about technology and higher learning [Online]. *CPB Annenberg Learner.org.* Available: http://www.learner.org/edtech/rscheval/rightquestion.html

Feldman, K. A. (1989a). The association between student ratings of specific instructional dimensions and student achievement: Refining and extending the synthesis of data from multisection validity studies. *Research in Higher Education, 30*, 583–645.

Feldman, K. A. (1989b). Instructional effectiveness of teachers as judged by teachers themselves, current and former students, colleagues, administrators and external (neutral) observers. *Research in Higher Education, 30*, 137–194.

Flashlight^{TM}: Helping you analyze and improve educational uses of technology [Online]. Washington, DC: The TLT Group. Available: http://www.tltgroup.org/programs/flashlight.html

French, N. (1996). *Some thoughts on the implications of the IT revolution on higher education in Hong Kong* [Online]. Hong Kong: University Grants Committee. Available: http://www.ugc.edu.hk/english/documents/speeches/it_he.html#TOP

Fulford, C. P., & Zhang, S. (1993). Perceptions of interaction: A critical predictor in distance education. *American Journal of Distance Education, 7*(3), 8–21.

Gibson, C. C. (1998). The distance learner's academic self-concept. In C. C. Gibson (Ed.), *Distance learners in higher education: Institutional responses for quality outcomes* (pp. 65–76). Madison, WI: Atwood.

Gladieux, L. E., & Swail, W. S. (1999). *The virtual university and educational opportunity: Issues of equity and access for the next generation: Policy perspectives.* New York: College Board Publications. (ERIC Document Reproduction Service No. ED 428 637)

Global Alliance for Transnational Education. (2000). *History and secondary enrollment* [Online]. Available: http://www.edugate.org/history.html

Graham, C., Cagiltay, K., Lim, B-R., Craner, J., & Duffy, T. M. (2001, March-April). Seven principles of effective teaching: A practical lens for evaluating online courses. *The Technology Source* [Online]. Available: http://horizon.unc.edu/TS/default.asp?show=article&id=839

Greene, B. (2000). *Teachers' tools for the 21st century: A report on teachers' use of technology* (NCES 2000-102) [Online]. Washington, DC: U.S. Department of Education, National Center for Education Statistics. Available: http:nces.ed.gov/pubs2000/2000102A.pdf

Greene, K. (2000). The 2000 national survey of information technology in U.S. higher education: Summary report [Online]. *The Campus Computing Project.* Available: http://www.campuscomputing.net/

Herring, M., & Smaldino, S. (1997). *Planning for interactive distance education: A handbook.* Washington, DC: AECT Publications.

Inman, E., Kerwin, M., & Mayes, L. (1999). Instructor and student attitudes toward distance learning. *Community College Journal of Research and Practice, 23,* 581–591.

Institute for Higher Education Policy. (2000, April). *Quality on the line: Benchmarks for success in Internet-based distance education* [Online]. Washington, DC: Author. Available: http://www.ihep.com

Johnstone, S. M. (2000). Online consortia may fall short. *Syllabus, 14*(4), 30.

Kearsley, G. (2000). *Online education: Learning and teaching in cyberspace.* Belmont, CA: Wadsworth.

Kezar, A. U. (1999). *Higher education trends (1997–1999): Program evaluation.* Washington, DC. George Washington University, Washington, DC, Graduate School of Education and Human Development. (ERIC Document Reproduction Service No. ED 435 352)

Kirkpatrick, D. L. (1994). *Evaluation training programs: The four levels.* San Francisco: Berrett-Koehler.

Kraft, N. (2000, January 11). Criteria for authentic project based learning [Online]. Denver, CO: RMC Research Corporation. Available: http://www.rmcdenver.com/useguide/pbl.htm

Lazerson, M., Wagener, U., & Shumanis, N. (1999). *What makes a revolution: Teaching and learning in higher education, 1989–2000.* Stanford, CA: National Center for Postsecondary Improvement. Stanford University, School of Education. (ERIC Document Reproduction Service No. ED 440 579)

Lesniak, R. J., & Hodes, C. L. (2000). Social relationships: Learner perceptions of interactions in distance learning. *Journal of General Education, 49*(2), 34–43.

Lewis, L., Farris, E., Snow, K., & Levin, D. (1999). *Distance education at postsecondary education institutions 1997–1998* [Online]. Washington, DC: U.S. Department of Education. National Center for Education Statistics. Available: http://nces.ed.gov/pubsearch/pubsinfo.asp?pubid=2000013

Lips, C. (2000). *"Edupreneurs": A survey of for-profit education.* Executive summary (Policy Analysis No. 386) [Online]. Cato Institute. Available: http://www.cato.org

Lowe, N., & Roberts, S. (2000, October). *Web sites for the blind.* Paper presented at the Annual Meeting for the Association for Educational Communications and Technology, Denver, CO.

Maloney, W. A. (1999). Brick and mortar campuses go online. *Academe, 85*(5), 19–24.

Marchessou, F. (2000). Some ethical concerns in ed-tech consultancies across borders. *Educational Technology Research and Development, 48*(4), 111–115.

Marland, P. (1997). Towards more effective open and distance teaching. London: Kogan Page.

Marsh, H. E. (1984). Students' evaluations of university teaching: Dimensionally, reliability, validity, potential biases, and utility. *Journal of Educational Psychology 76*:707–754.

Mauriello, C. E. (1995). The policy of national standards. *Thought and Action, 11*(2), 121–130.

McIsaac, M. S., Blocher, J. M., Mahes, V., & Vrasidas, C. (1999). Student and teacher perceptions of interaction in online computer-mediated communication. *Educational Media International, 36*(2), 121–131.

Moore, M. G. (1989). Editorial: Three types of interaction. *American Journal of Distance Education, 4*(2), 1–6.

Morrison, G. R., & Adcock, A. B. (1999). Distance education research: Messages to the field. *TechTrends, 43*(5), 14–18.

Morton, F. (2001, May 14). The new e-learning thing. *Washtech.com* [Online]. Available: http://www.washtech.com/news/morton/9740-1.html

Newson, J. (1999). Techno-pedagogy and disappearing context. *Academe, 85*(5), 52–55.

Offir, B., & Lev, J. (2000). Constructing an aid for evaluating teacher-learner interaction in distance learning. *Educational Media International, 37*(2), 91–97.

Olgren, C. H. (1998). Improving learning outcomes: The effects of learning strategies and motivation. In C. C. Gibson (Ed.), *Distance learners in higher education: Institutional responses for quality outcomes* (pp. 77–95). Madison, WI: Atwood.

Parke, M., & Tracy-Mumford, F. (2000). *How states are implementing distance education for adult learners* (State policy update). Washington, DC: National Institute for Literacy. (ERIC Document Reproduction Service No. ED 438 398)

Parker, A. (1997, Fall-Winter). How-to manual: Research from the field. *Educational Technology Review*, 7–10.

Pascarella, E. T., Whitt, E. J., Nora, A., Edison, M., Hagedorn, L. S., & Terenzini, P. T. (1996). What have we learned from the first year of the National Study of Student Learning? *Journal of College Student Development, 37*(2), 182–192.

Pea, R. D., Tinker, R., Linn, M., Means, B., Bransford, J., Roschelle, J., His, S., Brophy, S., & Songer, N. (1999). Toward a learning technologies knowledge network. *Educational Technology Research and Development, 47*(2), 19–38.

Phipps, R., & Merisotis, J. (1999). *What's the difference? A review of contemporary research on the effectiveness of distance learning in higher education.* Washington, DC: Institute for Higher Education Policy. (ERIC Document Reproduction Service No. ED 429 524)

Quality Assurance Agency for Higher Education. (2001, November 27). Distance learning guidelines [Online]. Gloucester, England. Author. http://www.qaa.ac.uk/public/dlg/guidelin.htm

Ragan, L. C. (2000). Good teaching is good teaching: The relationship between guiding principles for distance and general education. *Journal of General Education, 49*(2), 10–22.

Regional Accrediting Commissions. (2000, Feb. 25). *Statement of the Regional Accrediting Commissions on the evaluation of electronically offered degree and certificate programs and guidelines for the evaluation of electronically offered degree and certificate programs* (Draft) [Online]. Boulder, CO: Western Interstate Commission for Higher Education. Available: http:wiche.edu/Telecom/Guidelines.htm

Richards, P. (2001, April 4). MIT to make nearly all course materials available free on the World Wide Web. *MIT News* [Online]. Available: http://web.mit.edu/newsoffice/nr/2001/ocw-facts.html

Richie, M. L. (1994). *Management for educational technology services: A guide to application of the Deming management method for district, university and regional media and technology centers.* Washington, DC: Association for Educational Communications and Technology.

Saba, F. (1999). Distance education: An introduction. *Distance-Educator* [Online]. Available: http://www.distance-educator.com/portals/research_deintrolhtml

Salomon, G., Perkins, D. N., & Globerson, T. (1991). Partners in cognition: Extending human intelligence with intelligent technologies. *Educational Researcher, 20*(3), 2–9.

Schwartz, D. L., Brophy, S., Lin, X., & Bransford, J. D. (1999). Software for managing complex learning: Examples from an educational psychology course. *Educational Technology Research and Development, 47*(2), 39–59.

Sherry, A. C., Fulford, C. P., & Zhang, S. (1998). Assessing distance learners' satisfaction with instruction: A quantitative and a qualitative method. *American Journal of Distance Education*, 12(3), 4–28.

Sherry, A., & Sherry, F. (1996). The influence of computer confidence on retention in college. *Journal of Research on Computing in Education, 29*, 298–314.

Sherry, L. (1996). Issues in distance learning. *International Journal of Educational Telecommunications, 1*(4), 337–365.

Sherry, L., Billig, S., Jesse, D., & Watson-Acosta, D. (2001). Assessing the impact of instructional technology on student achievement. *T.H.E. Journal, 28*(7), 40–43.

Simpson, J., & Head, L. (2000, October). *Red hot tips: Improve retention in your distance education courses.* Paper presented at the League for Innovation International Conference, Chicago. (ERIC Document Reproduction Service No. ED 444 617)

Sloan ALN Consortium. (n.d.). *Criteria of an asynchronous learning network program* [Online]. Needham, MA: Alfred P. Sloan Foundation. Available: http://www.sloan-c.org/catalog/alncriteria.htm

Stein, S. (2001). The media production model: An alternative approach to intellectual property rights in distance education. *Educause Review* [Online], *36*(1). Available: http://www.educause.edu/ir/library/pdf/erm0111.pdf

Thompson, M. M. (1998). Distance learners in higher education. In C. C. Gibson (Ed.), *Distance learners in higher education: Institutional responses for quality outcomes* (pp. 9–24). Madison, WI: Atwood.

Thorpe, M. (1993). *Evaluating open and distance learning* (2nd ed.). Essex, England: Longman.

Tilaro, A., & Rossett, A. (1993). Creating motivating job aids. *Performance and Instruction, 32*(9), 13–20.

Tinto, V. (1993). *Leaving college: Rethinking the causes and cures of student attrition.* Chicago: University of Chicago Press.

U. S. Copyright Office. (1998, October 28). *Copyright Office study on distance education* [Online]. Available: http://www.loc.gov/copyright/disted/

U. S. Government, Office of Postsecondary Education. (2001, January 16). *The Learning Anytime Anywhere Partnerships [LAAP]* [Online]. Available: http://www.ed.gov/offices/OPE/FIPSE/LAAP

University of Hawaii. (2000). *CAFÉ: A course and faculty evaluation for UH Manoa* [Online]. Available: http:/www.café.hawaii.edu/café_catalog.asp

Wade, W. (1999). Assessment in distance learning: What do students know and how do we know they know it? *T.H.E. Journal, 27*(3), 94–96.

Wagner, E. D. (1994). In support of a functional definition of interaction. *American Journal of Distance Education, 8*(2), 6–29.

Web-Based Education Commission (2000). *The power of the Internet for learning: Moving from promise to practice* [Online]. Washington, DC: Author. Available: http://interact.hpcnet.org/webcommission/text.htm

Wegner, S. B., Holloway, K. C., & Wegner, S. K. (1999). The effects of a computer-based instructional management system on student communications in a distance learning environment. *Journal of International Forum of Educational Technology and Society* [Online], *2*(4). Available: http://ifets.ieee.org/periodical/vol_4_99/wegner.html

Western Association of Schools and Colleges (1997). *Guidelines for distance education: Principles of good practice* [Online]. Available: http://www.wascweb.org/senior/guide/pgpa1.htm

Winograd, D. M. (2000). *The effects of trained moderation in online asynchronous distance learning.* Unpublished doctoral dissertation, Arizona State University, Tempe, AZ. (Digital Dissertations No. AAT 9976354)

Yeaman, A. (2000). Coming of age in cyberspace. *Educational Technology Research and Development, 48*(4), 103–107.

Zvacek, S. M. (1994). *Evaluating distance education programs using a system approach.* Paper presented at the Annual Meeting of the Association for Educational Communications and Technology. Nashville, TN.

32

Distance Education Policy Issues: Towards 2010

Peter J. Dirr

President, Public Service Telecommunications Corporation
Director, Professional Development Institute
for Cable in the Classroom
pdirr@cox.net

INTRODUCTION

This chapter traces its roots to 1990, when the author, then deputy director of the Annenberg/CPB Project, wrote a chapter entitled "Distance Education: Policy Considerations for the Year 2000," which appeared in *Contemporary Issues in Distance Education* (Moore, 1990). At that time, the author suggested six questions that researchers might address to develop baseline information on the newly emerging field of distance education. Those questions were as follows:

How needed is distance education in the United States?
Who are the clients for distance education? What are their needs?
Who should pay for distance education and how much?
Can newer technologies help distance education overcome some of the barriers to traditional education opportunities?
Where will our next generation of distance educators come from? What types of training will they need?
What are the research needs of distance education as we approach the year 2000?

Some of those questions are as valid today as they were in 1990, especially given the growing number of persons participating in distance education in the United States.

In writing his 1990 chapter, the author relied entirely on issues from his own experiences in reviewing hundreds of proposals for funding and then in overseeing several of the leading distance education projects of the time. In preparing the current chapter, he has relied on a review of articles on distance education that have appeared in *The Chronicle of Higher Education*, the *American Journal of Distance Education*, and various other sources of distance education literature. The variety of articles almost defy classification, but certain issues emerge from their midst as being more central than others. Some issues were identified in composite lists developed by national or regional organizations such as accrediting bodies or governing boards. Others emerged as single issues but were cited by many sources.

COMPOSITE LISTS OF ISSUES

Some groups, especially national and regional planning organizations, have compiled composite lists of issues facing distance education. For example, the American Council on Education (ACE) issued a publication in March 2000, *Developing a Distance Education Policy for 21st Century Learning*. In it, ACE identified the following seven areas in which policies must be reviewed or developed:

Intellectual property policies.
Ownership of distance education courses.
Faculty issues (e.g., teaching load, preparation time, and class size).
Student issues (e.g., increased access, privacy issues, and disabled students).
Limiting liability.
Commercialization (e.g., direct agreements, consortia, and royalties or licenses).
Teaching beyond state and international borders.

The Council for Higher Education Accreditation (CHEA) has contracted with the Institute for Higher Education Policy (IHEP) to conduct a series of literature reviews and original research called *Distance Learning in Higher Education* (Institute for Higher Education Policy [IHEP], 1999; Council for Higher Education Accreditation [CHEA], 1999; n.d.). Those reports document the expanding universe of distance learning and the growth of statewide virtual universities. Among the issues identified are the following:

Equity gap.
Digital divide.
Lack of teacher training.
Battle over encryption.
Works made for hire.
Contractual transfers (as faculty members switch institutions).
Security and privacy.

Student Aid for Distance Learners: Charting a New Course, a separate report from the Institute for Higher Education Policy (1998), enumerates several student aid policy issues that are unique to students pursuing distance education. They suggest that student aid should be

Learner-centered, following the student through his or her academic program.
Available without regard to the mode of instructional delivery.
Awarded only to students in accredited programs of study.
Tied to standards of academic progress and not arbitrary measures of time.

They also suggest that regulations should allow flexibility on the part of institutions and that aid amounts and limits should focus on lifetime standards rather than annual or institutional maximums.

Working for a consortium of the six regional accrediting associations, the Council of Regional Accrediting Commissions (2000) prepared a draft of *Guidelines for the Evaluation of*

Electronically Offered Degree and Certificate Programs. Those guidelines focus on the following areas, indicating policy issues for institutions of higher education to consider in developing distance education programs:

Institutional context and commitment.
Curriculum and instruction.
Faculty support.
Student support.
Evaluation and assessment.

Reviewing contemporary research on the effectiveness of distance learning in higher education, Phipps and Merisotis (1999) cite the following gaps in research:

Student outcomes for programs rather than courses.
Differences among students.
Investigation of reasons for dropout rates.
Differences in learning styles related to particular technologies.
The interaction of multiple technologies.
The effectiveness of digital "libraries."
A theoretical or conceptual framework.

The review identifies three broad implications of the current research: (a) the notion that distance education provides "access" but computer-mediated learning requires special skills and technical support that might not exist; (b) technology cannot replace the human factor; and (c) technology is not nearly as important as other factors, such as learner tasks, learner characteristics, student motivation, and the instructor.

That same pair also wrote *Quality on the Line: Benchmarks for Success in Internet-Based Education* (Phipps & Merisotis, 2000), in which they identified 24 benchmarks considered essential to ensuring excellence in Internet-based distance education. The benchmarks fall into seven categories:

Institutional support (3).
Course development (3).
Teaching/learning (3).
Course structure (4).
Student support (4).
Faculty support (4).
Evaluation and assessment (3).

This author, in a review of the status of distance and virtual education in the United States in 1999 (Dirr, 1999a), identified the following as important trends in the profession:

The pervasiveness of change.
Growing commercial interests in education.
The importance of partnerships and alliances.
The unbundling of the educational process.

An Internet search for policies on distance education reveals a robust body of literature on the policies of individual institutions. In one instance, a group of researchers (King, JW; Nugent, GC; Eich, JJ; Mlinek, DL; & Russell, EB, 2000) studied the written distance education policies of all the tertiary institutions in the state of Nebraska. They found that most existing policies dealt with

> Academic areas (62 policies).
> Faculty issues (49).
> Students (39).
> Technical issues (29).

Academic issues emphasized course integrity, especially ensuring the "equivalency" of distance education programs with regular on-campus instruction. Measures of equivalency included class time, course content, student services, prerequisite skills, and instructor qualifications. The University of Nebraska system had the most policies (103), followed by community colleges (48), state colleges (32), and independent colleges (32). The researchers found that legal and cultural issues were not addressed in any sector. They also found that written policies were more structured where collaborative efforts exist. They attributed this to the need to develop and communicate "rules of participation" for the collaborative efforts. They concluded that "multi-institutional arrangements might be an excellent opening to cultivate and generate fundamental policy actions."

Looking across these composite lists of policy issues facing distance education, one sees that faculty and student issues appear on almost all the lists, as do academic and curriculum issues. Beyond those categories, the lists present a quite disparate grouping of additional issues.

SINGULAR CITATIONS OF POLICY ISSUES

In addition to composite lists of policy issues, more than 100 articles over the past 2 years in *The Chronicle of Higher Education* alone have dealt with policy issues that affect distance education in the United States. The articles might not have been labeled as policy issues, but they certainly have policy implications for the future of distance education and, in some cases, of higher education in general. In most cases, the issues addressed in those articles are also found in the composite lists of policy issues cited above.

For convenience, the singular citations have been classified by the author in the following categories: quality issues, equity and access, collaboration and commercialization, globalization, intellectual property rights, the role(s) of technology in distance education, faculty issues, student issues, and research and evaluation. Because many of the citations in this section are drawn from *The Chronicle of Higher Education*, reporters Blumenstyk, Carnavale, Carr, and Young will be referenced often.

Quality Issues

Several articles have addressed the issue of how to maintain quality in distance education courses and programs. At a September 2000 meeting of education officials from 30 nations, participants recognized distance education as a means for learners to become "exchange students" without passports or costly plane tickets. They sought to identify ways to foster coordination among institutions. High on their list was the development of ways to measure the quality of distance education courses and programs (Young, 2000d)

Sometimes, the issue of quality is dealt with subtly. In an editorial in the *American Journal of Distance Education*, Michael Moore (2000) notes that two articles in that issue addressed the question of whether distance teaching requires more or less work from the faculty than traditional teaching. Just below the surface of that question, however, lie the issues of "quality" of instruction and the amount of interaction between the instructor and student.

Following up on an announcement of the development of new guidelines for distance education developed by the Council of Regional Accrediting Commissions for the six regional accrediting agencies, *Office.com* interviewed Charles M. Cook, of the New England Association of Schools and Colleges, who observed that, although the guidelines sought to ensure quality distance education experiences, they also anticipated a new pedagogy, one that shifts toward the learner and away from the teacher (Shorr, 2000). This carries an important message for researchers who, in the future, will be studying the quality of distance education courses. Cook points out that because the assumptions of what happens in a traditional classroom cannot be made about an online course, "distance education will be held to a more explicit and possibly more detailed set of criteria than would be applied in a traditional classroom" (p. 2). If explicit criteria are developed for distance education courses, might those same criteria be used to challenge the assumptions that underlie traditional classroom experiences? Is it not possible that holding distance education to higher standards might have a ripple effect, raising the standards for all of higher education?

There is also an emerging body of evidence that distance education might be having qualitative impact on *how* students learn. For example, Lang (2000) asks skeptically whether an asynchronous environment can foster substantive critical thinking given the lack of gestures and subtle nonverbal clues that students have in face-to-face instruction. In the end, he argues that online discussions can develop high-level thinking skills, citing the experiences of faculty and students involved in online Writing Across the Curriculum courses. Because words do not disappear and can be read, reread, and revised, all online participants have an equal opportunity to organize their thoughts clearly. Furthermore, since the conversation is not confined to an artificial time limit, all participants have an equal opportunity to speak.

The Pew Charitable Trusts have been influential in encouraging new ways to evaluate the quality of learning experiences. With $3.3 million in funding, the trusts have supported the development of the National Survey of Student Engagement. (Reisberg, 2000) The survey measures the extent to which colleges encourage actual learning by scoring students' responses to 40 questions. More than 63,000 undergraduates filled out a questionnaire in Spring 2000. The questionnaire addresses five benchmarks: the level of academic challenge, the amount of active collaborative learning, student interaction with faculty members, access to enriching educational experiences (e.g., internships and study abroad programs), and the level of campus support (e.g., social life and help in coping with nonacademic responsibilities).

Not all of the efforts to improve the quality of distance education have come from within the traditional higher education sector. Blumenstyk and McMurtrie (2000) reported on the tension being caused in higher education circles by a fairly new accrediting agency, Global Alliance for Transnational Education (GATE). Created by Glenn Jones, founder of Jones International University, the first fully online university accredited in the United States, GATE is an international accrediting agency for technology-based education programs and institutions. Originally run by a nonprofit group, GATE has now become one of Jones' several for-profit businesses related to distance education. Critics charged that, as a for-profit company tied to Jones' other businesses, GATE is riddled with conflicts of interest resulting from the marriage between the corporate and academic worlds. In a letter to the editor responding to critics, Jones (2000) noted that for-profit corporations are increasingly playing a leading role in distributed education and that "traditional nonprofit institutions are no longer the sole gatekeepers of quality education."

Other solutions of the quality issue might also emerge from the private sector. Recognizing the "vacuum in cyberspace" when it comes to reliable information with which to evaluate online courses, some Web sites such as NewPromise.com, eCollege.com, and HungryMinds have begun to allow students who have taken online courses to post evaluations of those courses, similar to the way Amazon.com posts evaluations of the books it sells or eBay allows buyers to rate sellers of auctioned items (Carnavale, 2000a).

Equity and Access

At the turn of the century, the professional literature and the public press were full of references to the "digital divide"—the gulf between the affluent and the poor in terms of access to telecommunications services and computer technologies. There was general concern that the digital divide would have a major impact on access to distance education opportunities. Phipps and Merisotis (1999) pointed out that, even though most studies of distance education courses concluded that these courses compare favorably with classroom-based instruction and that students in these courses enjoy higher satisfaction than students in traditional classes, the notion that distance education provides "access" to higher education opportunities might be mistaken. Many distance education courses require computer-mediated technologies and skills and technical support that certain students might not have.

Increasingly, colleges and universities are attending to the need to make online courses accessible for all students, including the handicapped. In "Colleges Strive to Give Disabled Students Access to On-Line Courses," Carnavale (1999a) reported that colleges are finding that they must include the virtual equivalents of wheelchair ramps when building online courses. To understand the requirements, colleges are urged to consider the guidelines developed by the California Community Colleges system.

Collaboration and Commercialization

An overriding theme of much of today's literature is the extent to which alliances among colleges and between colleges and commercial interests are playing leading roles in the development and delivery of distance education at the higher education level. More has been written on this topic than any other. However, since this theme is covered in depth elsewhere in this handbook (see Chapter 5) this theme is only noted briefly here.

Many collaborations are driven by the need of the partners to provide their offerings to more students each year, thereby increasing their revenues each year. This is as true for colleges and universities as it is for the commercial firms with whom they partner. For, although enrollments in U.S. colleges and universities are growing steadily and tuition costs are growing along with them, the increased enrollments by themselves cannot provide sufficient fuel for expansion.

The scope of the collaborations and the factors that motivate them are quite varied. Some are regionwide alliances, such as Kentucky Virtual University (Young, 2000e), Western Governors University, and the Southern Regional Educational Board's Electronic Campus (Carnavale, 2000c). Others bring together groups of institutions that share interests, such as Jesuit-NET, a collaborative effort of 24 of the 28 Jesuit universities in the United States (McMurtie, 2000), and Universitas 21, a network of 17 or 18 prestigious universities in 10 countries (Maslen, 2000; Shecter, 2000; *Chronicle of Higher Education*, 2000b). The collaborators often struggle to devise relationships that draw on the strengths of each to create and deliver new products to meet the perceived needs of vast populations of adult learners.

Sometimes, the collaborations involve a commercial partner (most notably a publisher) along with institutions of higher education. Other times, institutions of higher education have established their own commercial distance education programs to extend their academic programs to new groups of learners. Cornell University, for example, formed a for-profit distance education entity named e-Cornell (Manjoo, 2000), Temple University created Virtual Temple (Carr, 1999), and the University of Maryland formed UMUC OnLine.com, a for-profit arm to market its online courses to new groups of students (Carnavale, 1999b). (Author's Note: Temple University quietly shut down Virtual Temple early in 2001, less than 18 months after its inauguration, because it was not economically viable.)

One rather recent distance education collaborator is the U.S. federal government, especially the military. Educational opportunities are seen as a key incentive for attracting and retaining recruits to voluntary service. In the final days of 2000, the U.S. Army funded a six-year $453 million project to deliver distance education courses to soldiers all over the world. The project, Army University Access Online, involves a commercial company (Pricewaterhouse-Coopers), 10 companies, and 29 colleges. By the middle of 2001, it had already enrolled more than 4,000 persons in distance education courses. The U.S. Navy initiated a similar program around the same time.

Globalization

Interwoven into many of the collaborations is the theme of globalization. The very technologies used for distance education today make it possible for an institution to think beyond its traditional borders. The technologies also make it possible for a potential student to seek education opportunities from tertiary institutions throughout the world. This trend holds the potential of having a major impact on traditional institutions.

Because this theme is dealt with in depth elsewhere in this Handbook (see Mason, Foley, and Visser), only a few examples will be mentioned here as evidence of its importance. Many U.S. universities have already begun to extend their distance education programs into other countries as a way to expand their student populations. Currently enrolling about 75,000 students in the United States, the University of Phoenix plans to add another 75,000 students in such diverse countries as China, India, Mexico, and Brazil (Blumenstyk, 2000a). Carnegie Mellon University plans to offer online programming courses to 15,000 students in India (Overland, 2000). The University of Bar-Ilan in Israel is developing Virtual Jewish University to deliver Jewish studies courses to learners throughout the world (Watzman, 2000). And on a more global level, the World Bank is setting up distance learning centers in countries that lack good telecommunications infrastructures so that learners in those countries might have access to educational opportunities offered in other parts of the world (Carnavale, 2000e).

One challenge that will face all institutions offering distance education over the next decade will be to develop new guidelines and policies that allow the expansion of educational opportunities through distance education while at the same time providing learners with appropriate courses of instruction and student support services.

Ownership and Intellectual Property Rights

The issue of ownership and intellectual property rights is one of importance in all sectors of education today. For a more detailed discussion than occurs here, see Chapter 33.

This issue shows up on many of the composite lists of issues facing distance education. *Developing a Distance Education Policy for 21st Century Learning* (American Council on Education, 2000) lists intellectual property rights first on its list of issues that must be reviewed and addressed. *Distance Learning in Higher Education* (CHEA, 1999) cites "works made for hire" and "joint works" as two of the policies that must be addressed. Written policies of many tertiary institutions that offer distance education programs address the issue of the intellectual property rights of the institution and of individual faculty members.

Policy at San Diego State University requires that faculty and the university must agree on who owns an online course before the course begins (Carnavale, 2000b). A faculty committee at the University of Illinois has recommended that professors retain ownership and control of online courses (Young, 2000a).

Aside from the issue of ownership of online courses, the issue of copyright raises many questions for which there is no clear answer. In fact, the congressional Web-based Commission

(Carr, 2001) referred to the copyright law as a "horse and buggy on the Information Super-highway." The "Napster" case in the United States and the "iCrave.com" case in Canada have provided vivid examples of how the law and policies lag behind practices supported by new technologies. It is safe to say that it is not currently clear just how the copyright laws will apply to digitized content.

The Role of Technology in Distance Education

Colleges and universities in the United States have been increasing their spending on informa-tion technologies, including those used in distance education. A study of liberal arts colleges by David L. Smallen of Hamilton College and Karen L. Leach of Colgate University shows that in the decade of the 1990s the typical liberal arts college doubled its spending on information-technology services (Olsen, 2000). Information technology spending at liberal arts colleges at the end of the 1990s was typically 3.5% to 5.2% of total institutional spending. PC replacement costs accounted for 14% to 24% of the total.

A broader annual study of technology use by tertiary institutions, the Campus Computing Project, by Kenneth C. Green, showed that, in spite of increased expenditures on information technology, institutions of higher education still have a long way to go (Carlson, 2000). The 2000 study found that 60% of all college courses use e-mail as a tool for instruction, and 30% of all courses have Web sites. In spite of that high level of use of the technology by faculty members, administrators remain skeptical about its value. Only 14% of administra-tors agree with the statement "Technology has improved instruction on my campus." Green believes that, in the absence of empirical evidence of impact, the increase in technology use might begin to slow. He noted that "some technology trends in society at large have yet to catch on in academe," citing the absence of any meaningful use of personal digital assistants (PDAs) by colleges. He further noted that "academe is far behind the private sector when it comes to e-commerce." Only 19% of colleges have e-commerce services such as tuition payment.

Perhaps educators have reason to be at least slightly timid about jumping on the technology bandwagon. Noguchi (2000) noted that many businesses are suffering because they bet on Web-based growth rates that are well beyond what could be delivered. That has led to the downfall of several dot-com companies. Rather than banking completely on the Internet, Noguchi encourages businesses to think of the Internet as enhancing what they already do, an extension of the business rather than a revamping of it. That is not bad advice for colleges and universities with distance education programs.

Distance education has existed through correspondence courses for more than a century. Access to distance education was accelerated in the 1970s with the introduction of television-based lessons that were broadcast throughout the United States on public television stations. The advanced capabilities of Internet-based courses have greatly expanded the reach of distance education courses, opening new opportunities for learners to continue their education. But the sad fact is that we know little about the impact that these technologies have on access or the quality of education being provided.

One question that has been raised regularly for at least three decades is, How effective is the use of technology in education? This question has been raised specifically about distance education. Some studies in recent years have addressed the issue of the roles and effectiveness of technology in distance education. Unfortunately, many of those studies have been unidi-mensional; that is, they have focused on a single technology in isolation from the many other variables that impact the effectiveness of teaching and learning. Many of the studies also suf-fered from the "horse race" syndrome; that is, they attempted to compare a technology-based course with a traditional course to see which came out ahead in terms of student learning. This approach suffers from two flaws: First, it holds up the traditional course as the standard to be emulated rather than asking whether things might be done differently (and maybe better) by using the power of the technologies. Second, it overlooks the "sample bias" that is inherent in the research methodology when potential students cannot be randomly assigned to traditional or distance education courses.

Faculty Issues

Many faculty issues emerge from the literature. Faculty concerns and needs are referenced in most of the composite lists of issues cited at the beginning of this chapter.

A study of 402 college faculty members drawn from the 85,000 members of the National Education Association found that faculty members who have taken part in developing and/or offering distance education courses are generally enthusiastic about the experience and benefits of teaching distance education courses (Carr, 2000b). They might feel that they put in more work on distance education courses than on traditional courses, but they also believe the benefits outweighed the extra work involved.

Some faculty members have used students as a shield to question the appropriateness of distance education courses. When Fairleigh Dickenson University decided to require that *all* its undergraduates take at least one distance education course annually, in part to help students become "global scholars" who are able to use the Internet for a variety of purposes, the American Federation of Teachers (AFT) questioned whether that was an appropriate requirement for students who do not do well in distance education courses.

Nevertheless, some faculty members express fears about distance education. Some fear that they might be replaced by the very distance education courses they help develop (Carnavale & Young, 1999). Others fear that distance education might take jobs away from Ph.D.s and put them in the hands of business executives and poorly paid part-timers (Carr, 1999). Still others resist distance education because they fear it will increase competition from foreign institutions (Young, 2000d).

One thing that seems to increase faculty opposition to distance education is when administrators commit to distance education programs without adequate consultation with the faculty. This became a major issue when Cornell University established e-Cornell to deliver distance education courses (Manjoo, 2000) and when Temple University established Virtual Temple (Carr, 1999).

The San Diego State University policy on distance education (Carnavale, 2000b), developed by the faculty senate, contains several requirements that reflect the concerns of faculty:

Professors must oversee online courses in their fields.
Students must have "substantial, personal, and timely" interaction with faculty members and other students.
Faculty and the university must agree on who owns the course before it begins.
Students must be assured of access to appropriate resources and services.
Full-time professors must not be replaced by part-time instructors.

Another concern of faculty members is that distance education might be leading to a new learning paradigm and changed roles for the faculty. That concern seems to be supported by some of the literature. The draft guidelines from the Council of Regional Accrediting Commissions to help colleges and universities review the quality of electronically offered online degree and certificate programs anticipate a new pedagogy, one that shifts toward the learner and away from the teacher (Shorr, 2000). Some see the emergence of multi-university portals and statewide virtual universities as evidence of a new learning paradigm in which the faculty role changes from teacher to designer of interactive materials and guide for students (Von Holzen, 2000).

Perhaps the most interesting trend in terms of potential impact on the roles of the faculty member in distance education is the "unbundling" of the parts of the educational process. This phenomenon was identified by this author in 1999 as one of the leading trends in distance and virtual learning in the United States (Dirr, 1999a). Since then, the theme has appeared several times. In September 2000, Johnstone noted that the tasks of teaching and supporting students' learning are becoming "unbundled." One way of breaking out the components is as follows: curriculum development, content development, information delivery, mediation and tutoring, student support services, administration, and assessment. As these functions, most of which have traditionally been done by individual faculty members, are unbundled, it becomes possible to ask who might best perform each function and which of the functions might be contracted out. Distance education has provided a fertile testing ground for exploring such arrangements. A growing number of statewide institutions and consortia provide administrative services for online students. Follet, Amazon.com, and others offer electronic bookstore and library services. Others offer testing services. The most recent addition to the field is smarthinking.com, an online tutoring service with coverage 24 hours a day, 7 days a week.

The theme of contracting out unbundled services appeared again in December 2000. A new digital-library company announced plans to offer students online access to searchable books and journals (Blumenstyk, 2000b). For a fee of about $20 to $30 per month, students would have access to 50,000 scholarly books and journals (150,000 by the year 2003). The resources would be searchable by keywords, leading some faculty to fear a "cut-and-paste" approach to research and report writing, an approach that could lower the effort that students put into their studies. About the same time, the faculty union at New York University was expressing its concerns that new roles for faculty hired by the university's online subsidiary would begin to break down the teaching function into a series of discrete tasks performed by different people, which could lead to the "disassembling and de-skilling of the profession" (Carr, 2000c).

A counterbalance to such faculty fears can be found in a monograph issued by the League for Innovation (Young, 2000b). The "Faculty Guide for Moving Teaching and Learning to the Web," by Judith Boettcher and Rita-Marie Conrad of the Corporation for Research and Educational Networking, is intended to encourage faculty members to break a course down into component functions and explore how they can fulfill each component without meeting in a physical classroom.

Student Issues

Distance education programs and courses have become known for being more "student centered" than many other university programs, in part because many distance education programs are developed in response to specific perceived needs of the students. But how well are distance education programs doing in responding to student needs? Few empirical data exist.

Young (2000c) interviewed seven adult students who were taking online courses. For several, the courses provided a chance to be back in college, an opportunity they would not have had absent distance education. Many reported a "nagging guilt—that they should be logging on to their courses' Web pages more often." Those who were most successful had developed a regular schedule for working on their courses.

The oft-reported isolation of the distance learner was supported to some extent by these interviews. The students stated that they missed instant feedback from their professors. They also found taking exams a logistical challenge, especially if they had to travel to the campus to take the exams. Although generally satisfied with their distance education experiences, these students recognized that distance education is probably not appropriate for everyone.

Hara and Kling (1999) also studied a small group of students (six) enrolled in a Web-based distance education course. They identified several "frustrations" that inhibited student performance in the course. These included a felt need to compete among each other on the volume of e-mail messages submitted, a perceived lack of feedback because of the lack of physical presence of the instructor and other students, technical problems and the absence of personnel to provide technical support, and ambiguous instructions from the instructor. The students dealt with these frustrations by venting them with each other over the Internet. The authors do not end up condemning distance education but rather caution institutions against advertising only the virtues of computer-mediated distance education when promoting courses.

These studies possibly reflect the way that many distance education courses have been developed. They have evolved out of campus-based courses, and faculty members focus almost all their attention on getting the "content" of the course transferred to a new medium, the Internet. However, a new emphasis began to emerge in the late 1990s, spurred in part by a funding program of the Fund for the Improvement of Post Secondary Education (FIPSE). The fund encouraged institutions, in submitting proposals for funding, to think about the entire student experience when designing distance education courses. As much emphasis was placed on making quality student support services accessible at a distance as was devoted to quality presentation of course content.

One of the recipients of a FIPSE grant was the Western Cooperative for Educational Telecommunications (WCET), an organization that has played a leading role in looking at how support services are provided to students studying at a distance. The goal of the WCET-FIPSE project was to identify colleges and universities that had developed quality "suites" of student support services that were delivered to students at a distance. From a survey of 1,028 institutions, the project learned that most institutions that offered distance education courses had concentrated on "delivery" of existing courses without developing new support services for students studying electronically. Most held firm to traditional structures and policies for student support services (Dirr, 1999b).

The findings of that study led WCET to create its *Guide to Developing Online Student Services* (Krauth & Carbajal, 1999). This guide offers a series of "good practices" for delivering student services via the Internet. It ends with a section called "Outstanding Web-Based Student Services Systems," which highlights some institutions that have shifted from a "provider" perspective to a "customer-centered" orientation for providing student support services. The most advanced institutions have created decision support systems that offer students a variety of opportunities for self-help and customized services. The guide notes that within the past couple of years a number of software companies have begun to develop products that assist institutions in making the transition to a customer-centered orientation.

For-profit and non-profit companies are also developing resources that help students sort through the thousands of online courses that are available and to choose a course that best fits each student's needs and interests. Rose (2000) evaluated 21 online course databases designed to help students locate the right course or program. Criteria for evaluating the databases included user-friendliness, search capabilities, reliability, course offerings, course information, and connectivity. Usability ratings for each service are posted on the Web at http://teleeducation.nb.ca/media/reports.shtml.

Another student issue that continues to lurk in the background of distance education is the number of dropouts from distance education courses. It is generally recognized that enrollments in distance education courses are increasing, but so is the number of dropouts (Carr, 2000a). National figures do not exist, but anecdotal information suggests to some that dropout rates are higher in distance education courses than in traditional courses. Direct comparisons across institutions are difficult because institutions do not report completion and dropout rates in any consistent way. Some speculate that distance education dropout rates are higher because distance education students are older than traditional students and have busier schedules. Others argue that the nature of distance education courses is at fault in that they cannot supply the personal interaction that some students crave. This is certainly an area that deserves further research.

Some colleges have entered the world of distance education without fully considering implications for disabled students. They were surprised, for example, that they must include the virtual equivalents of wheelchair ramps on their Web sites when building online courses (Carnavale, 1999a). This can raise the cost of developing online courses. Provisions of the Americans With Disabilities Act and the Vocational Rehabilitation Act are generally interpreted to apply to online education programs even though the U.S. Office of Civil Rights has not yet issued rules for online courses. In the meantime, colleges are being urged to use guidelines developed by the California Community Colleges system.

The report of the congressional Web-Based Education Commission has already been referenced above (Carnavale, 2001). That report recognized that students in distance education courses and programs are penalized by existing laws and regulations. One regulation that is specifically targeted is a requirement that to be eligible for full student aid a student must take at least 12 hours of classes each semester. The whole question of student aid for students enrolled in distance education courses was studied by IHEP (1998). In its report, *Student Aid for Distance Learners: Charting a New Course*, IHEP suggests several principles for future policies regarding student aid for distance education:

Student aid should be available without regard to mode of instructional delivery.

Delivery of student aid should be learner centered, with aid following the student through the academic program.

Aid should be awarded only to those in accredited programs of study.

Awarding of aid should be tied to standards of academic progress and not arbitrary measures of time.

Regulations should allow flexibility on the part of institutions.

Aid amounts and limits should focus on lifetime standards rather than annual or institutional maximums.

Research and Evaluation

The need for research and evaluation in distance education is generally recognized. However, that need is rarely given shape. Consequently, although many studies can be found, there is little organization among them, and cumulatively they do not add up to a significant body of research on topics that are critical for guiding the future of distance education. As in 1990, this author will encourage the research community to concentrate their energies on a limited number of questions so that the sum total of their research efforts might have far more impact on the future of distance education than if they were without a focus.

Certainly some quality research and evaluation is being done in distance education. Phipps and Merisotis (1999), of IHEP, with backing from the American Federation of Teachers and the National Education Association, analyzed what current research tells us and does not tell us about the effectiveness of distance education. They found that many of the questions educators have about distance education are unanswered by existing research. In their opinion, although there is a "not insignificant body of original research" (p. 1), little of it is dedicated to explaining or predicting distance education phenomena. From their perspective, three broad measures of effectiveness dominate the research: student outcomes, student attitudes, and overall student satisfaction.

According to Phipps and Merisotis, most of the studies of distance education conclude that distance education compares favorably with classroom-based instruction and that students enjoy higher satisfaction with distance education courses than with classroom-based courses. However, their review of research suggests that many of the research studies are of questionable value, rendering the findings inconclusive in the opinion of the reviewers. The current research suffers from key shortcomings: It does not control for extraneous variables and cannot show cause and effect, it does not use random selection of subjects, and the validity and reliability of the instruments are often questionable.

In looking at gaps in current research, Phipps and Merisotis identify the following needs:

Studies of student outcomes for complete programs of study rather than single courses.
Careful attention to the differences among students.
Investigation of reasons for dropout rates.
Research on how differences in learning style relate to different technologies.
Research on the interaction of multiple technologies.
Research on the effectiveness of digital "libraries."
Development of a theoretical or conceptual framework.

Using a modified Delphi technique, Rockwell, Furgason, and Marx (2000) surveyed educators in Nebraska to identify needs for distance education research and evaluation. They identified four topic areas:

Cooperation and collaboration among institutions, including postsecondary and secondary schools.
Designing the educational experience to meet the unique needs of distance learners.
Teacher preparation, especially in competencies that are unique to distance education.
Educational outcomes, especially participation and completion rates.

Smith and Dillon (1999) tackled the difficult problem of how to conduct comparative studies that will withstand critical review. They note that most comparative studies have suffered from "confounding factors" in their methodologies, making the findings suspect. They propose a schema to address the issue of confounding factors, the Media Attribute Theory, a framework based on identifying the defining categories of attributes that are embedded within each delivery system and media used in a distance education course. The categories of attributes they suggest include realism/bandwidth, feedback/interactivity, and branching/interface.

Writing in *The Chronicle of Higher Education*, Dan Carnavale (2000d) reported on a study, "Criteria for an Excellent Online Course," by Lee Alley, chief executive officer of World Class Strategies, Inc. Alley stated that some aspects of distance education that were considered novelties a few years ago are now considered "essentials" for quality distance education. He specifically cited regular interaction between students and faculty and among students, a student-centered approach, and built-in opportunities for students to learn on their own. He concluded that distance education is changing the theoretical underpinnings of tertiary education by forcing an understanding that "you don't transmit knowledge; knowledge is constructed." This will inevitably lead to a change from faculty-centered to student-centered instruction.

Ongoing tracking of developments and issues in distance education has been a characteristic of the work of CHEA and IHEP. Since at least 1998, these two organizations have worked together to issue an annual report, *Distance Learning in Higher Education*. The report looks at the status of distance education at the tertiary level in the United States, tracking growth, identifying trends, and raising issues. The organizations have also undertaken focused studies of distance education, such as IHEP's *What's the Difference? A Review of Contemporary Research on the Effectiveness of Distance Learning in Higher Education* (Phipps & Merisotis, 1999) and *Quality on the Line: Benchmarks for Success in Internet-Based Education* (Phipps & Merisotis, 2000).

One issue that has gotten sporadic attention from researchers is the cost of distance education. Brian M. Morgan, a professor at Marshall University, has developed an interactive spreadsheet that will help an institution compute the likely costs it will incur in offering distance education courses (*Chronicle of Higher Education*, 2000a). The worksheet is available online at http://webpages.marshall.edu/~morgan16/ onlinecosts. Morgan (2000) also wrote an extensive background paper, "Is Distance Learning Worth It? Helping to Determine the Costs of Online Courses," in which he identified the research he did (several original surveys) to obtain the data on which he based the algorithms used in the interactive worksheet. The paper contains many helpful references and insights.

Businesses might be even more concerned about the cost of providing learning opportunities than some colleges and universities. Writing in the *Washington Post*, Evans (2000) noted that Internet-based lessons are rapidly overshadowing traditional manuals and face-to-face classes in many corporations. According to International Data Corporation, which follows more than 200 e-learning companies, the e-learning market will grow from $550 million in 1998 to $11.4 billion in 2003, especially in view of the need of companies to deliver up-to-the-minute training to workers all over the globe without having them leave their places of work. Not all e-learning is online because not every place on earth has the bandwidth needed to accommodate interactive learning over the Internet.

Whalen and Wright (1999) used a case study approach to analyze the cost-benefit of Web-based telelearning at the Bell Online Institute. They examined the relative importance of several design elements and presented a detailed cost-benefit analysis model of courses that Bell uses to train employees and customers. Three courses (each equivalent to a 2-day classroom course) were developed and offered on four learning platforms (WebCT, Mentys, Pebblesoft, and Symposium). Fixed and variable costs were computed for each, including the cost of the delivery platforms and transmission costs, salaries, hardware, and license fees. The authors concluded that "Web-based training has higher fixed costs than classroom-based training but those costs are offset by lower variable costs in course delivery" given a large enough number of students over time.

CONCLUSION

There are many policy issues concerning distance education that must be addressed over the next decade. There is little evidence in the literature to indicate that they will be addressed in any systematic way. That, along with the fact that distance education holds the potential to have a greater impact on higher education than any other single phenomenon for several decades, leads this author to suggest that the education community consider adopting a framework, a focus, and funding that will permit systematic development of policies that can advance quality distance education. A systematic approach will also facilitate the documentation and validation of the impact distance education has on the lives of learners.

As a starting point, the author suggests that the policy issue areas identified above serve as the framework for policy development. The focus might be created by carefully crafting a few questions in each policy area. One possible schema is as follows.

Quality Issues

1. How can the quality of distance education be measured reliably and validly? What criteria are appropriate for assessing the quality of distance education? Are those same criteria appropriate for assessing the quality of classroom-based education?
2. Do tertiary institutions have clear policies about distance education course and program quality? Are procedures for monitoring quality in place? Is responsibility for monitoring quality clearly identified?

3. Do distance education courses provide adequate opportunity for interaction between students and instructors and among students?

4. Can distance education take advantage of some of the new approaches to evaluating the long-term impact of classroom-based education programs?

5. Is the evaluation of the quality of distance education having an impact on the quality of classroom-based education?

6. What support do tertiary institutions provide faculty to help them make most effective use of available technologies to create quality courses and programs?

7. What impacts are for-profit companies having on the quality of distance education programs at traditional tertiary institutions?

8. How are student evaluations of online courses and programs impacting the quality of those courses and programs?

9. What revisions have accrediting organizations and licensing agencies made to their criteria to assess the quality of distance education programs and courses?

Equity and Access Issues

1. How accessible are distance education programs for disabled students? What are tertiary institutions doing to make their distance education programs more accessible?

2. What are tertiary institutions doing to ensure that distance learners have access to the technologies needed to take their distance education courses?

3. What are tertiary institutions doing to provide distance learners with the technical support and training they might need to use their distance education courses?

Collaboration and Commercialization Issues

1. What overall impact are collaborative agreements having on the development and delivery of distance education courses and programs?

2. How are tertiary institutions coping with the "competition" from for-profit companies that provide distance education courses and programs? Who are the new players in the field?

3. How does the quality of distance education programs and courses developed by alliances differ from the quality of programs and courses developed by a single institution?

4. How does the quality of distance education programs and courses developed by for-profit companies compare with the quality of programs and courses developed by traditional tertiary institutions?

5. Has collaboration with for-profit partners been a boon or a bust for distance education programs at U.S. tertiary institutions?

6. What has happened to some of the distance education partnership arrangements that were heralded as groundbreaking in 1997 and 1998?

7. How have accrediting organizations and licensing agencies dealt with new programs and organizations created through collaborative agreements?

8. How has the "unbundling" of the components of the traditional educational program affected the roles and responsibilities of persons and organizations involved in distance education programs?

9. What new institutions are evolving to develop and offer distance education courses and programs and services as a result of collaborative arrangements and globalization?

10. What impacts are collaborative arrangements having on pedagogical practices?

11. What are the long-term political, pedagogical, and institutional implications of programs that teach across state and national borders?

12. What impact are collaborative agreements and/or commercialization having on work-force preparation?

13. What impact does a tertiary institution experience when it sets up a for-profit subsidiary for distance education?

14. What impact has the government had as a new player in developing and offering distance education programs?

Globalization Issues

1. How has the trend toward globalization changed over the years and what impact has that trend had on the distance education and classroom education programs of tertiary institutions in the United States?

2. How have government agencies tagged with the responsibility for tertiary education dealt with increased globalization?

3. What impact have distance education practices, policies, and/or programs in other countries had on the distance education programs of U.S. tertiary institutions?

4. Have foreign markets meant greater opportunities for U.S. tertiary institutions or greater competition? In other words, are U.S. institutions finding that they can attract large numbers of students from foreign countries to their distance education courses or are they losing students to foreign institutions through the Web?

Ownership and Intellectual Property Rights

1. How have institutional policies that allow faculty members to own online courses or share in revenues from those courses changed the relationship between faculty and the institution?

2. How well are institutions dealing with the very complex questions of ownership and intellectual property rights of the university and the faculty members?

3. How is the federal government responding to the issues raised by the congressional Web-Based Education Commission, especially its recommendations for changes in the "fair use" provisions of the copyright law and in the federal 12-hour and 50% rules?

4. How have developments outside the education sector, such as the Napster and iCrave.com cases, affected institutional policies on ownership and intellectual property rights?

The Role of Technology in Distance Education

1. How have institutions adjusted their budgets to ensure the availability and reliability of the technologies needed for many of today's distance education courses?

2. How well is tertiary education doing in keeping up with technology trends in society? Are universities making effective use of available technologies to support distance education?

Faculty Issues

1. What is being done at tertiary institutions to prepare faculty to adapt to new roles and to understand the new pedagogy required for distance education?

2. What is being done at tertiary institutions to prepare faculty to use the technologies needed for distance education? Are they provided with creative and technical support when developing and offering distance education courses?

3. What empirical evidence exists on the impact of distance education on the roles and responsibilities of faculty members? On the impact that distance education has had on

the number and rank of faculty employed? Is there any evidence that the unbundling of education components is resulting in new classes of faculty and staff?

Student Issues

1. What evidence exists that distance education students have access to all necessary aspects of their programs at a distance? Can they enroll at a distance, get textbooks and library resources, have access to faculty and other students, get reliable administrative information, and take exams?
2. What training and assistance is available for students who must use technology in their distance education courses?
3. What support or services exist to help students choose appropriate distance education programs and courses?
4. Do students believe that their distance education courses are equivalent to or better than on-campus courses they have taken?
5. If students have experience with distance education courses from tertiary institutions and from for-profit companies, what do they have to say about each?
6. What is being done to lower the number of students who drop out of distance education courses?
7. How are students with disabilities being accommodated in distance education courses?
8. How have federal regulations changed to make distance education an attractive alternative for students?
9. What changes have been made in student aid policies toward putting distance education on an equal footing with on-campus education?

Research and Evaluation

1. How can the research community mobilize to improve the quality of research on distance education? Might the community agree to focus on a few topics for 2 years at a time on a rotating basis? Might the community develop specialized "virtual research centers" that pull together several researchers with similar interests and support their research on topics related to their interests?
2. How can the research community be encouraged to develop new research models, alternatives to the "horse race" model?
3. What can be done to encourage the research community to examine the effectiveness of complete programs of study rather than single courses?
4. How can differences in student learning style be factored in to studies of distance education programs?
5. What conceptual framework might help the cumulative work of the research community be more effective than their individual efforts?
6. How can the emerging breed of online professional journals speed the dissemination of research on distance education and increase its impact?

REFERENCES

American Council on Education. (2000). *Developing a distance education policy for 21st century learning.* Washington, DC: American Council on Education.

Blumenstyk, G. (2000a, August 11). Company that owns the U. of Phoenix plans for a major foreign expansion. *Chronicle of Higher Education*, p. A44.

Blumenstyk, G. (2000b, December 1). Digital-library company plans to charge students a fee for access. *Chronicle of Higher Education*, p. A41.

Blumenstyk, G., & McMurtrie, B. (2000, October 27). Educators lament a corporate takeover of international accreditor. *Chronicle of Higher Education*, p. A55.

Carlson, S. (2000, October 27). Campus survey finds that adding technology to teaching is a top issue. *Chronicle of Higher Education*, p. A46.

Carnavale, D. (1999a, October 29). Colleges strive to give disabled students access to on-line courses. *Chronicle of Higher Education*, p. A69.

Carnavale, D. (1999b, December 17). U. of Maryland University College creates for-profit arm to market its on-line courses. *Chronicle of Higher Education*, p. A49.

Carnavale, D. (2000a, February 18). Assessing the quality of online courses remains a challenge, educators agree. *Chronicle of Higher Education*, p. A59.

Carnavale, D. (2000b, May 12). A college's detailed policy on distance education. *Chronicle of Higher Education*, p. A49.

Carnavale, D. (2000c, May 19). Two models for collaboration in distance education. *Chronicle of Higher Education*, p. A53.

Carnavale, D. (2000d, October 27). Study assesses what participants look for in high quality online courses. *Chronicle of Higher Education*, p. A46.

Carnavale, D. (2000e, December 8). World Bank becomes a player in distance education. *Chronicle of Higher Education*, p. A35.

Carnavale, D. (2001, January 5). Army picks consulting group to run distance-education effort. *Chronicle of Higher Education*, p. A46.

Carnavale, D., & Young, J. R. (1999, December 17). Who owns on-line courses? Colleges and professors start to sort it out. *Chronicle of Higher Education*, p. A45.

Carr, S. (1999, December 17). For-profit venture to market distance-education courses stirs concerns at Temple. *Chronicle of Higher Education*, p. A46.

Carr, S. (2000a, February 11). As distance education comes of age, the challenge is keeping the students. *Chronicle of Higher Education*, p. A39.

Carr, S. (2000b, July 7). Many professors are optimistic on distance learning, study finds. *Chronicle of Higher Education*, p. A35.

Carr, S. (2000c, December 15). A day in the life of a new type of professor. *Chronicle of Higher Education*, p. A47.

Carr, S. (2001, January 5). Commission says federal rules on distance education must be updated. *Chronicle of Higher Education*, p. A46.

Chronicle of Higher Education. (2000a, July 28). Online. *Chronicle of Higher Education*, p. A53.

Chronicle of Higher Education. (2000b, December 15) Online. *Chronicle of Higher Education*, p. A47.

Council for Higher Education Accreditation. (1999). *Distance learning in higher education: Update number two.* Washington, DC: Author.

Council for Higher Education Accreditation. (n.d.). *Distance learning in higher education: Update number three.* Washington, DC: Author.

Council of Regional Accrediting Commissions. (2000). *Guidelines for the evaluation of electronically offered degree and certificate programs* (Draft). Denver: Author.

Dirr, P. J. (1999a). Distance and virtual learning in the United States. In G. Farrell (Ed.), *The development of virtual education: A global perspective* (pp. 23–48). Vancouver: Commonwealth of Learning. Available: http://www.col.org/virtualed

Dirr, P. J. (1999b). *Putting principles into practice: promoting effective support services for students in distance learning programs* (A report on the findings of a survey). Denver: Western Cooperative for Educational Telecommunications. Available: http://www.wiche.edu/telecom/projects/studentservices/Survey/Report.pdf

Evans, S. (2000, May 15). Net-based training goes the distance: Employers find e-learning saves costs, time. *Washington Post*, p. 20, Washington Business section.

Hara, N., & Kling, R. (1999). Students' frustration with a Web-based distance education course. *First Monday* [Online serial], 4(12). Available: http://www.firstmonday.dk/issues/issue4_12/hara

Institute for Higher Education Policy. (1998). *Student aid for distance learners: Charting a new course.* Washington, DC: Author.

Institute for Higher Education Policy. (1999). *Distance learning in higher education.* Washington, DC: Author.

Johnstone, S. M. (2000, September). Distance learning: Unbundling faculty roles. *Syllabus*, Vol. 14, No. (2), 26.

Jones, G. R. (2000, December 1). The Future of international accreditation [Letter to the editor]. *Chronicle of Higher Education*, p. B20.

King, J. W., Nugent, G. C., Eich, J. J., Mlinek, D. L., and Russell, E. B. (2000). A policy framework for distance education: A case study model. *DEOSNEWS, 10*(10), pp. 1–7.

Krauth, B., & Carbajal, J. (1999). *Guide to developing online student services.* Denver: Western Cooperative for Educational Telecommunications.

Lang, D. (2000, September). Critical thinking in Web courses: An oxymoron? *Syllabus, 14,* 20.

Manjoo, F. (2000). Virtual U. *Cornell Magazine On/Line, 103*(1). Available: http://Cornell-magazine.cornell.edu/Archive/July2000/JulyVirtualU.html

Maslen, G. (2000, June 2). Rupert Murdoch's company joins with 18 universities in distance-education venture. *Chronicle of Higher Education,* p. A47.

McMurtie, B. (2000, May 12). Jesuit colleges try to bring their values to online education. *Chronicle of Higher Education,* p. A45.

Moore, M. (1990). *Contemporary issues in distance education.* State College, PA: Pennsylvania State University.

Moore, M. (2000). Is distance teaching more work or less? *American Journal of Distance Education, 14*(3), 1.

Morgan, B. M. (2000). *Is distance learning worth it? Helping to determine the costs of online courses.* Huntington, WV. Marshall University.

Noguchi, Y. (2000, December 4). A tough time for consultants. *Washington Post,* p. E1.

Olsen, F. (2000, October 27). New data on technology spending offer benchmarks for college administrators. *Chronicle of Higher Education,* p. A46.

Overland, M. A. (2000, October 27). Carnegie Mellon U. will offer online programming classes in india. *Chronicle of Higher Education,* p. A47.

Phipps, R., & Merisotis, J. (1999). *What's the difference? A review of contemporary research on the effectiveness of distance learning in higher education.* Washington, DC: Institute for Higher Education Policy.

Phipps, R., & Merisotis, J. (2000). *Quality on the line: Benchmarks for success in Internet-based education.* Washington, DC: Institute for Higher Education Policy.

Reisberg, L. (2000, November 17). Are students actually learning? *Chronicle of Higher Education,* p. A67.

Rockwell, K., Furgason, J., & Marx, D. (2000). Research and evaluation needs for distance education: A Delphi study. *Online Journal of Distance Learning Administration, 3*(3). Available: http://www.westga.edu/~distance/ojdla/fall33/rockwell33.html

Rose, E. (2000). An evaluation of online distance education course databases. *DEOSNEWS, 10*(11).

Shecter, B. (2000, November 23). U of T pulls back from Thomson link. *The National Post* (Toronto),   .

Shorr, P. W. (2000, October 17). Distance education acquires new guidelines: Guidelines aim to help colleges monitor e-courses' quality. *Office.com.* [Online serial]. Available: http://www.office.com/search/office.com/article?ARTICLE=20209

Smith, P., & Dillon, C. L. (1999). Comparing distance learning and classroom learning: Conceptual considerations. *American Journal of Distance Education, 13*(2), 6.

Von Holzen, R. (2000, November). A look at the future of higher education. *Syllabus,* Vol. 14, No. 4, 56.

Watzman, H. (2000, April 28). A virtual Jewish-studies program attracts students of many faiths. *Chronicle of Higher Education,* p. A51.

Whalen, T., & Wright, D. (1999). Methodology for cost-benefit analysis of Web-based tele-learning: Case study of the Bell Online Institute. *American Journal of Distance Education, 13*(1), pp. 22–44.

Young, J. R. (2000a, January 14). Faculty report at University of Illinois casts skeptical eye on distance education. *Chronicle of Higher Education,* p. A48.

Young, J. R. (2000b, January 14). Monograph reassures scholars wary of online teaching. *Chronicle of Higher Education,* p. A51.

Young, J. R. (2000c, March 3). Dispatches from distance education, where class is always in session. *Chronicle of Higher Education,* p. A41.

Young, J. R. (2000d, September 29). Officials from 30 nations seek global coordination in distance education. *Chronicle of Higher Education,* p. A46.

Young, J. R. (2000e, November 24). Kentucky's virtual university creates fund to spur other online-education programs. *Chronicle of Higher Education,* p. A54.

33

Legal Issues in the Development and Use of Copyrighted Material in Web-Based Distance Education

Tomas A. Lipinski
University of Wisconsin—Milwaukee
tlipinsk@csd.uwm.edu

INTRODUCTION

The expansion of education into digital environments is forcing all participants—educators, institutions, students, and proprietors (copyright owners)—to reexamine the nature of ownership and use rights. Although recent case law and legislation indicate future trends, many issues remained unresolved. Further, the developing legal environment suggests that the likely result will not favor the expansion of distance education without a cost, namely, the recognition and satisfaction of proprietary interests not only in monetary terms but also in terms of access. This recognition and satisfaction must also resolve the growing controversy over the ownership and control of faculty-created or -enhanced educational materials used to support the distance curriculum.

FACULTY AND INSTITUTIONAL OWNERSHIP ISSUES

In the development of distance and Internet-based instruction, the issue of ownership under the intellectual property laws appears to fall in the area of content, not processes. Consequently, it is an issue of copyright, not patent. The material created by faculty is often loaded on a course Web site or recorded during a remote broadcast (Borow, 1998). There are three legal factors that impact or underlie the question of ownership:

Prepared by Tomas A. Lipinski, J.D., LL.M., Ph.D., this summary is designed to provide accurate and authoritative information on the subject matter covered. However, this information is *not* provided as a substitute for legal advice. If legal advice or expert assistance is required, the services of a competent legal professional should be retained.

1. The difference between instruction in a "work made for hire" scenario and instruction in an independent contractor setting (the implications of this difference must be fully understood).
2. The teaching exception to the work for hire doctrine as it has been developed in relevant Seventh Circuit U.S. Court of Appeals precedent as well as other persuasive authority.
3. The application of faculty "lecture-note" ownership concepts to Web-based environments.

Understanding the relationship between these factors is also important. The issue of ownership should be addressed by any institution providing distance education, as instructors or faculty members are sure to raise these or related concerns as distance and Web-based instructional modes expand.

Application of the Work for Hire Doctrine

The first question is whether or not the person employed, regardless of title, is an "employee" for purposes of the copyright law. If the person is an employee, then all works created in the course of that employment are considered to be works made for hire (see 17 U.S.C. § 101). If a work is "made for hire," then the employer (the educational institution) and not the person (the faculty member) who created the work is considered the owner of the work (Simon, 1982–1983). The U.S. Supreme Court has addressed this issue and concluded that "the general common law of agency, rather than [ ] the law of any particular State" should control (*Community for Creative Nonviolence v. Reid*, 1989). The Court held that the Restatement of Agency, Second (1958) is also instructive in determining whether or not a person is an employee under general rules of agency. Taken together, the following factors are instructive when making that determination:

The extent of control over the details of the work, including the ability to assign other work to the hired party and the hired's ability to in turn hire and pay assistants.
The distinctness of the occupation or profession of the hired party.
The locality of the work (and whether the work is performed with or without direct physical supervision).
The skill level required.
Which party supplies the instrumentality, tool, or place of work.
The duration of the work or project.
The method of payment (by time or by the entire project), including the provision of employee benefits, and the tax treatment of the hired party.
Whether the work is part of the regular business of the employer.
The perception in the minds of both parties. Whether the principal is in business as a matter of course.

It would appear that most faculty, lecturers, instructors, and teachers are employees for the purposes of the copyright law "work made for hire" doctrine and not independent contractors. Faculty hired to consult in some capacity at another institution (or even at their own institution), during summers, for example, might fall into independent contractor status for purposes of that consultation.

Independent Contracting Models

Since faculty would, for purposes of the copyright law, be considered employees, faculty work product falls under the work for hire doctrine, with ownership in the work created belonging to the school, university, or employer. However, this does not end the discussion. A faculty member may also be considered an independent contractor, even if performing duties similar to his or her employee duties and for the same employer (see *Avtec Systems, Inc. v. Pfeiffer*, 1992, 1994, according to which a software developer owns programs created outside of the normal course of employment, and *Sherrill v. Grieves*, 1929, which involves faculty ownership of scholarly work; see also Wadley & Brown, 1999). However, this exception should not be relied upon by faculty seeking to have the work product of extracurricular activity classified as their own because of the reality of the all-consuming "publish or perish" environment in higher education (Dreyfuss, 1987; DuBoff, 1984). Although it would seem logical that a member of the mathematics faculty who wrote a mystery novel on the weekends would own the copyright to the book, it is not clear, under a strict reading of the statute, case law, and scholarly reviews cited, that the same person writing an article on algebra on weekends would own that, as it would surely be a "work prepared by an employee within the scope of his or her employment" (see 17 U.S.C. § 101; see also *Marshall v. Miles Laboratories, Inc.*, 1986).

Second, if the independent contractor status of an instructor or faculty member is legally established, the ownership of the work can still reside in the educational institution or the administering entity under an extension of the work for hire doctrine. Thus, work produced by the independent contractor faculty member may be treated as a work made for hire. (Understanding the nuance of this law is essential, as an educational institution may have a policy dictating when an independent contractor work is to be treated as a work made for hire. If the institution does have such a policy, the policy must be reviewed to make sure that it is consistent with the federal copyright law.)

However, this extension can occur only if the following two requirements are met (17 U.S.C. § 101). First, the educational institution or entity and the faculty member must execute a written contract to that effect, and, second, the work must fall within one of nine statutory categories, some of which may apply to the distance or Web scenarios occurring in distance education settings (e.g., a faculty member's development of Web-based instruction under separate agreement as an independent contractor). The categories are as follows: "as a contribution to a collective work, as part of a motion picture or other audiovisual work, as a translation, as a supplementary work, as a compilation, as an instructional text, as a test, an answer material for a test, or as an atlas" (17 U.S.C. § 101; see also *Mast v. Committee on the Status of Women*, 1993).

As noted, some distance and Web-based work may fall into these categories (Daniel & Pauken, 1999; Holmes & Levin, 2000), and this work then could by agreement be treated as work for hire, with ownership belonging to the educational institution or employing entity (assuming that the work was originally subject to the independent contractor rules). On the other hand suppose a computer science faculty member produced a student record management software program through an independent contractor consulting arrangement with his or her university. The program would belong to the faculty member, because any university policy that automatically gave ownership of all works produced with institutional computing facilities to the university would not operate. First, the program was made while the faculty member was an independent contractor, and there was no specific written agreement treating the software otherwise (a general employment contract would not suffice). Second, the work does not fall into one of the nine specific statutory categories.

In independent contractor cases outside the statutory categorization, the most that can be hoped for is an assignment of copyright, or some portion of it, by the faculty member to the educational institution or employing entity. This option could include the sharing of ownership rights between the member and the educational institution. This is the practical effect of contracts or policies that recognize ownership residing with the independent contractor or faculty member but grant certain storage, use, and modification rights to the educational institution or employing entity. For instance, an institution could continue to use a Web site constructed by a faculty member in subsequent offerings of a course for a limited number of years. The ownership or assignment right vested in the faculty member would permit the member to "take" a previously developed Web course to his or her next job and offer the same course based on the same Web site content at the new institution. (Note: In work for hire scenarios, assuming operation of the teaching exception [see below], storage becomes an issue when lectures from a course that is broadcast or streamed are otherwise routinely recorded and stored.)

Lecture Notes and Development of a Faculty Ownership Right

If a faculty member is in fact an employee and his or her work product is thus included within the work for hire doctrine, then precedent (particularly strong in the Seventh Circuit) suggests that there is a recognized "teaching" exception for faculty at institutions of higher education. (See *Hays v. Sony Corporation of America*, 1988; *Weinstein v. University of Illinois*, 1987; Kulkarni, 1995; see also Lape, 1992. Contra, see *University of Colorado v. American Cyanamid*, 1995; *Vanderhurst v. Colorado Mountain College District*, 1998.) Under the academic or teaching exception to the work for hire doctrine, a faculty member would hold the copyright associated with material he or she produced, not the university. One commentator believes that this exception might also extend to the K-12 environment (see Nimmer & Nimmer, 2000, § 5.03[B][1][b][I] n. 31, at 5-17–5-18). Regarding ownership of students' copyrightable works, additional arguments can be made for ownership vesting in graduate teaching assistants, for example. Unlike faculty, students are not employed to teach and research, or at least they are not employees in the same sense that tenure track faculty are employees (Patel, 1996).

The issue of the existence of a teaching or faculty exception to the work for hire doctrine is by no means settled, however. Recent case law supporting such an exception appears only in one federal appellate circuit (covering the states of Wisconsin, Illinois, and Indiana). Furthermore, recognition of the exception goes against the plain language of the statute; instead, it is based on tradition and public policy.

Moreover, recent precedent rejects this exception. In *University of Colorado v. American Cyanamid* (1995), the district court observed that the "[p]laintiffs maintain the Regents are quite obviously the owner, because the article is a 'work made for hire' by the coauthors done within the scope of their employment [footnote to 17 U.S.C. § 201 omitted] (Pls.' Reply Br. Supp. Mot. Partial Summ. J. at 29 n.55). Plaintiffs argue Cyanamid has offered no evidence to rebut such ownership. I agree" (at 1400). Subsequently, the same district court, in *Vanderhurst v. Colorado Mountain College District* (1998), interpreted the scope of the work for hire doctrine:

> It is undisputed that Vanderhurst prepared the Outline on his own time with his own materials. However, there is no genuine dispute that Vanderhurst's creation of the Outline was connected directly with the work for which he was employed to do and was fairly and reasonably incidental to his employment. Further, creation of the Outline may be regarded fairly as one method of carrying out the objectives of his employment. See, RESTATEMENT (SECOND) AGENCY, at 228. I conclude, therefore, that pursuant to the "work for hire" doctrine, as of 1995, any copyright remaining in the Outline did not belong to Vanderhurst. Thus, I will grant defendants' motion for summary judgment on claim eight. (at 1307)

It should be noted that while these cases represent more recent precedent, the cases are from a district court, and if this issue arose in another circuit, the appellate decisions from the Seventh Circuit might have greater weight, though both series of cases would represent persuasive precedent only.

Finally, a faculty member does have a right to deliver course content in a manner of his or her own choosing. This creates a distinction between what is taught and how it is taught (see *Williams v. Weisser*, 1969, citing *Baker v. Seldon*, 1880). Consequently, a faculty member has a copyrightable interest in the lecture notes created to support a teaching endeavor and in the other fixed expressions of that teaching made by others as well. (See Nimmer & Nimmer, 2000, § 5.03: "Thus, if a professor elects to reduce his lectures to writing, the professor, and not the institution employing him, owns the copyright in such lectures" [footnotes 94 and 95 omitted]). This rule would by implication include the recording or other fixation of a faculty lecture by a commercial note-taking service. (See *Williams v. Weisser*, 1969: "We are, however, convinced that in the absence of evidence the teacher, rather than the university, owns the common law copyright in his lectures" [at 544].) It would also extend to a situation in which lectures routinely recorded as a part of the delivery of course content (e.g., simultaneous recording during a distance education broadcast or live Web stream). Since either recorded broadcast lectures or Internet-based instruction involve the fixation of teaching expression, the requirements for a valid copyrightable work are met (i.e., the result is a work of authorship fixed in a tangible medium). (See 17 U.S.C. § 102: "Copyright protection subsists, in accordance with this title, in original works of authorship fixed in any tangible medium of expression, now known or later developed.") Therefore, copyright should logically cover the Web-based equivalent of lecture notes and under the teaching exception vest ownership in the faculty member. The implication is that the subsequent storage and use of that protected expression by the faculty member and the educational institution should be identified. The fact is that, if a broadcast or streamed lecture (or other analogous lecture note material) is recorded using and stored on institutional equipment, a copyrighted work has been created. As a result, the ownership of that work, under the copyright law, belongs to the faculty member, and storage of the work using institutional facilities should be at the direction or under the control of the faculty member.

The Academic Exception and University Copyright Policy

It should also be pointed out that many universities have a copyright policy in place similar to the one at issue in *Weinstein v. University of Illinois* (1987), which defined conditions under which faculty output would be considered a work for hire and when it would be considered to belong to the faculty. Typically, such a copyright policy is considered part of the employment contract with the university. In fact, for public institutions, it may be part of the state's administrative code. According to the policy at issue in *Weinstein*, a state of Illinois faculty member retained the copyright to his or her scholarly output unless the work fell into one of three categories:

> (1) The terms of a University agreement with an external party require the University to hold or transfer ownership in the copyrightable work, or (2) Works expressly commissioned in writing by the University, or (3) Works created as a specific requirement of employment or as an assigned University duty. Such requirements or duties may be contained in a job description or an employment agreement which designates the content of the employee's University work. If such requirements or duties are not so specified, such works will be those for which the topic or content is determined by the author's employment duties and/or which are prepared at the University's instance and expense, that is, when the University is the motivating factor in the preparation of the work. (at 1094)

In light of the "publish or perish" atmosphere of the university setting (with scholarly writing necessary for getting tenure), the district court interpreted the third provision as covering faculty article production. However, the Seventh Circuit disagreed. According to the appellate court, the trial court had misinterpreted the university's work for hire policy. According to the Seventh Circuit, the "work made for hire" policy appeared to apply "more naturally" to administrative reports, e.g., the result of committee work, than journal articles (*Weinstein v. University of Illinois*, 1987, at 1094–1095). Therefore, there is some legal support for the argument that faculty scholarly output, even when it is a tenure requirement, is not within "employment duties," nor prepared at "the University's instance and expense," at least not according to the Seventh Circuit. For faculty at institutions with similar policy language, such language would at least not stand in the way of ownership rights vesting in the faculty.

Another factor to consider is that a university copyright policy may contain language indicating that if the university incurs extraordinary expense in the support or production of faculty output, then the university shall have ownership rights in the works produced. A university may want to argue that its investment in distance education programs would meet these somewhat specious standards. However, the case law from the Seventh Circuit again suggests otherwise. In *Hays v. Sony Corporation of America* (1988), the court commented as follows:

> Although college and university teachers do academic writing as a part of their employment responsibilities and use their employer's paper, copier, secretarial staff, and (often) computer facilities in that writing, the universal assumption and practice was that (in the absence of an explicit agreement as to who had the right to copyright) the right to copyright such writing belonged to the teacher rather than to the college or university. (at 416)

The point can be made that in the technology-infused classroom of the 21st century, as well as in distance education environments, the use of expensive technology should not be seen as "extraordinary" and trigger policy provisions vesting ownership in the institution. The high price of new technology is simply another cost of doing business in the distance education environment, much like the photocopier, the overhead projector, and the computing facilities of the 1970s and 1980s.

USE OF COPYRIGHTED MATERIAL IN DISTANCE EDUCATION ENVIRONMENTS

The design, construction, and use of the digital classrooms and Web sites can easily raise copyright issue. Several rights of copyright owners must be considered: the right to reproduce and distribute the copyrighted work, such as by digitizing materials for use in course website, and the performance or display of the material that occurs during the instructional session. Recent case law suggests an increased aggressiveness on the part of copyright owners to target nonprofit and individual copyright violators. This development may impact nonprofit educational institutions as well. In contrast, recent legislation may operate to shield educators in certain circumstances for the acts of third parties, such as students, or shield an institution against acts of the faculty.

General Liability Issues in Copyright Infringement Litigation

The ease with which material may be posted, framed, or linked to an educational Web site increases the risk of copyright infringement (see Appendix A). Recent litigation suggests that, like unauthorized photocopying or other reproduction in the analog world, unauthorized reproduction (posting or framing) in a digital or Web environment will be considered a copyright infringement (see *Religious Technology Center v. Netcom On-Line Communications Services*, 1995). Furthermore, posting, framing, or linking, besides raising issues of unauthorized reproduction, can bring into play other exclusive rights of the copyright owner, such as the right to display or distribute the work or to make derivative versions of the work (see 17 U.S.C. § 106; *Playboy Enterprises, Inc. v. Frena*, 1993; *Kelly v. Ariba Soft Corp.*)

Direct Copyright Infringement.   There are three types of copyright infringement: direct, contributory, and vicarious. Direct infringement is the most common type of violation of a copyright owner's exclusive rights. This type occurs when a faculty member, for example, posts the copyrighted material of another without permission on a course Web site in excess of any fair use or other statutory giant. Note that direct infringement must occur before a finding of contributory or vicarious infringement can be made. In *Marobie-F v. National Association of Firefighter Equipment Distributors* (1977), a tax-exempt organization that loaded several volumes of the plaintiff's clip art onto its Web site without permission was held to have violated not only the right of reproduction but also the right of display. Framing material from one Web site onto a distance education site may violate the copyright owner's exclusive right of display (*Kelly v. Ariba Soft Corp.*). In the *Marobie-F* case, the use was not a fair use under 17 U.S.C. § 107. Even though the tax-exempt trade organization, like an institution of higher education, was noncommercial, the remaining three fair use factors favored against a finding of fair use (the work was creative in nature, all of the work was taken, and the posting of the clip art impacted negatively on the market for the work).

Framing, including framing content on to a course Web site, can also trigger a claim of direct infringement (see *The Washington Post Co. v. Total News, Inc.*, 1997). The most controversial application of framing gives rise to the unresolved issue of whether the frame creates an unauthorized derivative work (e.g., an edited work [the frame]) based upon a complete original (the framed Web site) (see *Futuredontics Inc. v. Applied Anagramics Inc.*). According to one commentator, a finding of infringement based on this theory is likely: "No final decision on the merits has been issued, but the district court's denial of plaintiff's preliminary injunction motion, as well as its denial of defendant's subsequent motion to dismiss, indicates that such unauthorized framing will quite likely constitute a violation of the exclusive right to prepare derivative works under § 106 of the Copyright Act" (Clarida, 1999, p. 7).

Contributory Copyright Infringement.   Contributory copyright infringement occurs when someone induces or causes or materially contributes to the infringement of another. What if a faculty member referred students to a site where "illegal" copies of Cliff Notes or some other educational support material could be obtained for free? The "referral" might take the form of a live link on a course Web site, a nonactive URL listed in an online syllabus, or a description of how to get to the material. Again, what if an educational institution provides students with technology that can crack a DVD's copyright protection code in violation of the section 1201 anti-circumvention rules discussed below? Such scenarios raise the issue of how much inducement by the educational institution will trigger liability for contributory copyright infringement.

A disturbing development with application to Web environments occurred in the *Intellectual Reserve, Inc. v. Utah Lighthouse Ministry, Inc.* (1999) litigation. In that case, the defendants initially posted copyrighted material without permission on their Web site (about 17 pages, or about 5%, of a 330-page, two-volume handbook). A temporary restraining order was issued to the defendants to cease display of the pages on their Web site. Undaunted in their quest to publicize the inner workings of the Church of Latter Day Saints, the defendants placed a note on their Web site that the handbook was still online. The note included a description (but not an active URL text or a logo link) of how viewers of their site could locate three other sites where the full text of the handbook could be obtained. The defendants also included the text of several e-mails that encouraged browsing of the handbook and urged viewers, once at one of the three full-text sites, to download and send the handbook to others. The court believed that the actions of the defendants went beyond any sense of passive awareness or of providing a mere informational or directory service. The court referred to one incident in particular: "[I]n response to an e-mail stating that the sender had unsuccessfully tried to browse a website that contained the Handbook, defendants gave further instructions on how to browse the material" (at 1295). The defendants were thus found to have materially contributed (contributory infringement) to the infringement by the subsequent visitors (direct infringement) to the three other Web sites where the plaintiff's work was posted.

The defendants did not constitute a commercial entity but were individuals providing information in hopes of stimulating discourse on church policy. What is also significant in this case is the fact that the defendants did not provide the locations of the infringing material through the use of active links. Their directions still required users to manually cut and paste or enter URL information. The message is clear: Do not steer students to a source or site of infringing material, nor encourage students to visit and download the material from the infringing sites. The factor for an educational institution may be one of reasonableness. For example, is it reasonable to suppose that a link from a course Web page or online library catalog to a particular Web site containing over 10,000 digital music files downloadable for free would be a link to an infringing site? The legal standard is "know" or "reason to know." This does not require investigation of every site or source to which students are referred, but common sense suggests that if a site or source is suspect, is should not be referred to.

Recent case law also suggests that some personal uses once thought to be fair uses, such as uploading or downloading music files over the Internet, are in fact infringing. As a result, educational institutions may wish to rethink practices built upon the erroneous assumption that all personal or educational uses are fair uses. In *A&M Records, Inc. v. Napster, Inc.*, which involves the infamous file-sharing technology, an initial motion to dismiss was denied, as the district court concluded that the section 512 immunity provisions (discussed below) were inapplicable, arguing that, because "Napster does not transmit, route, or provide connections through its system, it has failed to demonstrate that it qualifies for the 512(a) safe harbor." In a second opinion, the court concluded that Napster was guilty of contributory and vicarious infringement. As indicated earlier, before a finding of contributory or vicarious infringement may be found, direct infringement (the target of the contributory infringement) must be found. Thus the court considered whether individual users who employed the Napster technology to share copyrighted works were infringing the copyright of song owners. First, the court reviewed various studies on the impact of Napster technology and concluded that there was a negative impact, especially in high traffic areas like college campuses. Second, the court discussed whether, under *Sony Corporation of America v. Universal Studios, Inc.* (1984), Napster technology was capable of "commercially significant noninfringing uses." This is often known as the "staple article of commerce" defense (in *Sony*, a Betamax machine was determined to have significant noninfringing uses, since it can play prerecorded videotapes). In *Napster*, however, the court was not persuaded and found that "any potential noninfringing use of the Napster service is minimal or connected to the infringing activity or both." Proceeding to the four-part fair use test, the court found that, although individuals engaged in the file sharing, it was "not personal use in the traditional sense." This was true for two reasons: First, the scale of the MP3 file sharing using Naptser technology made it a nonprivate use, and, second, unlike the making of a copy for a friend, Napster transfers were made to an "anonymous requester." The second and third factors again, like in the *UMG Recordings v. MP3, Inc.* case, weighed against a finding of fair use, as the works were creative (second factor) and 100% of the works were typically taken (third factor). Finally, various studies demonstrated a negative impact on the market. In addition, the widespread use of Napster created a market barrier to the entry by legitimate players into the Internet file-sharing arena. Using the same four-part fair use test, the Southern District of New York found MP3 liable for similar reasons (see *UMG Recordings v. MP3, Inc.*, 2000).

On appeal to the Ninth Circuit, the appellate court agreed that the individual upload and download by Napster users was not a fair use of the copyrighted recordings. The works were creative and thus this fair use factor weighed against the use, however while the complete songs were used on the system, the court was quick to point out that a complete 100% taking does not necessarily preclude a finding fair use. The court was also convinced that the exchange of music through Napster-file sharing negatively impacted the market for the work. In rejecting the defendant's suggestion that the works on Napster be subject to some sort of compulsory licensing scheme, the court noted that it was the copyright owners right alone to decide how and when to develop additional markets and distribution schemes for its protected music. The most significant portion of the discussion dealt with how the court characterized the personal nature of the use: the peer-to-peer exchanges of copyrighted material. "The recent *A&M records, Inc. vs. Napster, Inc.* litigation also clarified that personal uses that do not involve an offering for sale of the reproduced work might nonetheless be deemed commercial if the copying is repeated and exploitative. So far, making a single digital copy of the work does not rise to the level of the personal yet commercially widespread and anonymous copying involved in the Napster music file-sharing system." (Lipinski, 2002, 39) Even though personal, a use traditionally thought to be fair, it was still considered "commercial," and thus deemed unfair by courts. For this reason the biling sharing was also unlike the time shifting of television programming (recording the program on a Beta tape for later viewing at home) deemed a fair use by the Supreme Court in *Sony Corporation of America vs. Universal Studios, Inc.*

In related development, the rock band Metallica earlier in 2000 had filed suit (*Metallica v. Napster, Inc.*, 2000) against several institutions of higher education (University of Indiana and Yale University) for providing Internet users with the Napster file-sharing software that allowed students at those campuses to download music from the Internet. Yale and Indiana University were dropped from the *Metallica* lawsuit after those schools banned students from using Naptser. "Both corporations and universities must be aware of their potential liability for contributory copyright infringement in this new environment.... Accordingly, prudent universities will be very cautious about permitting Napster use on their networks in the current environment" (Schonfeld, 2000, p. 23). The lesson for educational institutions is clear: Because the acts of students using MP3/Napster or MP3/Napster-like copying and file-sharing technology is direct infringement, the institution or its employees should not do anything to induce or cause, or materially contribute to that infringement by its students.

Vicarious Copyright Infringement. Vicarious infringement is found when one has the "right and ability to supervise the infringing activity and also has a direct financial interest in such activities" (*Fonovisa, Inc. v. Cherry Auction, Inc.*, 1996, at 262). Vicarious liability is imputed from employee to employer (i.e., the employer is responsible for acts of its employee) but not vice versa. Vicarious liability is grounded in the tort concept of respondeat superior, and contributory infringement is founded in the tort concept of enterprise liability. (see *Demetriades v. Kaufmann* (1988): "Benefit and control are the signposts of vicarious liability, [whereas] knowledge and participation [are] the touchstones of contributory infringement" [at 293].) Vicarious liability in employment settings does not require knowledge of the infringement by the vicarious defendant (see Hazard, 2000, ¶ 7.08, at 7-72–7-75). It is also applicable in an independent contractor setting, where the acts of an independent contractor may be imputed to the contracting institution (see *Southern Bell Telephone and Telegraph v. Associated Telephone Directory*, 1985). However, an employment setting is not always required, as was the case in *Fonovisa*, in which a swap meet purveyor was held liable for the infringing acts of booth renters who bought and sold bootleg tapes, or in *Columbia Pictures Industries v. Redd House* (1984), in which a shop owner who allowed customers to view copyrighted video cassettes was held liable for the infringing acts of these customers. What is required is a financial interest from the direct infringing actor to the vicarious infringer where the locus of the infringement acts as a draw for future infringers or in the case of an educational institution, attracts more students, which in turn increases tuition revenue, which a court might conclude establishes the financial nexus necessary for a claim for vicarious liability.

The court in *A&M Records, Inc. v. Napster, Inc.* (2000) also considered whether Napster was responsible for vicarious infringement. It reached this conclusion:

> Although Napster, Inc. currently generates no revenue, its internal documents state that it "will drive [sic] revenues directly from increases in userbase." ... It hopes to "monetize" its user base through one of several generation revenue models noted in the factual findings. ... This is similar to the type of direct financial interest the Ninth Circuit found sufficient for vicarious liability in *Fonovisa*, where the swap meet's revenues flowed directly from customers drawn by the availability of music at bargain basement prices. (at *71–*73) (italics added)

An educational entity might under particular curcumstances described above offer the some impermissible draw to students.

Damage and Liability Limitations Provisions (17 U.S.C. §§ 504 and 512)

An educational institution may be liable for the direct unauthorized posting of copyrighted material by its employees, including faculty (vicarious liability), and by students (contributory liability). (Faculty and students of course remain liable for their own acts of infringement.) However, several provisions of the copyright law may operate to lessen the sting that a successful infringement suit may cause an institution by reducing the damages that may be awarded or by eliminating altogether the monetary relief of the plaintiff.

Section 504 Damage Remission.   Section 504 (17 U.S.C. § 504) States the following:

> The court shall remit statutory damages in any case where an infringer believed and had reasonable grounds for believing that his or her use of the copyrighted work was a fair use under section 107, if the infringer was: (i) an employee or agent of a nonprofit educational institution, library, or archives acting within the scope of his or her employment who, or such institution, library, or archives itself, which infringed by reproducing the work in copies or phonorecords; or (ii) a public broadcasting entity which or a person who, as a regular part of the nonprofit activities of a public broadcasting entity (as defined in subsection (g) of section 118) infringed by performing a published nondramatic literary work or by reproducing a transmission program embodying a performance of such a work.

In short, a qualifying nonprofit educational institution can not be required to pay statutory damages, only the actual (damages) cost of the work infringed. Consider the protection awarded to an infringing educational institution under section 504 in light of the liability of the defendants in the *MP3* litigation cited above. Suppose a university with a music program loaded (reproduced) and made available to students 4,700 CDs on its server (the same approximate number as the defendants in the *MP3* case). At a value of $15 per CD, the university would face damages of $70,500, a far cry from the $17.5 million the *MP3* court hypothesized might be awarded under a statutory damages scheme ($25,000 per work infringed). The catch is that the distance educator would be required to demonstrate a "reasonable belief" that the use was fair. A misinformed or uniformed belief will not suffice. In addition, as the legal landscape in digital environments develops and as compliance programs in educational institutions become more widespread and effective, convincing a court as to the reasonableness of persistent uploading and downloading or the facilitation of those acts by faculty and students will probably become more difficult to establish.

The Online Service Provider (OSP) Passive Conduct Provisions. As part of the 1998 Digital Millennium Copyright Act (DMCA) (Pub. L. No. 105-304, 112 Stat. 2860, codified at 17 U.S.C. § 512), Congress created a new section dealing with the "limitations on liability relating to material online." The subsections of section 512 indicate those circumstances in which a "service provider" (which could be an institution of higher education) will not be held responsible for the infringing acts of third parties. Immunity is never complete under section 512, but the new law eliminates monetary relief including actual damages as a remedy, including costs and attorneys' fees. Certain types of injunctive relief (e.g., removal of infringing material or denial of system access to the infringing employee or student) are still possible. The provisions are complex, and an only a brief overview is presented here (see Appendix B).

In order to seek refuge in the immunity provisions, an educational institution or other OSP must first meet various threshold requirements. For example, the educational institution "service provider" must have "adopted and reasonably implemented" a policy providing that it will police its network and terminate repeat infringer access (17 U.S.C. § 512(i)(1)(A)). Both the legislative history and statutory language are silent as to the content of the policy required and the conditions for determining what constitutes "repeat infringement." As a result, "To ensure that they have adopted and implemented an appropriate policy and, thus, are not denied the benefits of the act's limitations on liability, service providers should document and maintain records of all attempts to implement their policies reasonably" (Kupferschmid, 1999). At a minimum, an educational institution, after adopting a copyright compliance policy, should make every effort to publicize the policy and provide employees with basic education on the copyright law. The process might include postings on all faculty-, staff-, and student-accessible Web pages, documentation, training programs, and some acknowledgement on the part of faculty, staff, and students of their awareness and responsibility to comply with the copyright law.

In general, section 512 provides a limitation on liability for service providers against the infringing acts of third parties in the following situations: transmitting, routing, or providing connections to infringing material (the "transitory digital network communications" or store and forward limitation of § 512(a)); system caching (§ 512(b)); information stored by a user (the "user storage" limitation of § 512(c)); linking or referring users to infringing material (the "information location tools" limitation of § 512(d)); and disabling access to, or removing in good faith, allegedly infringing material (the take-down provisions of § 512(g)). The first two provisions, concern acts—transitory storing and forwarding and caching—that happen automatically. On the other hand, posting (third-party "storage") and linking, the acts covered in the next two provisions, are not temporary or transient. Moreover, they are visible and thus "by their nature allow service providers to intervene" (Dratler, 2000, § 6.01, at 6-11) As a result, elaborate take-down and counter notification provisions accompany the posting and linking subsections of section 512(c) and (d).

In order to take advantage of the subsection 512(c) immunity, the service provider must designate an agent to receive complaints of infringement from copyright owners and coordinate compliance measures. This is not required for the store and forward liability limitation of subsection 512(a), and although not required for 512(b) and 512(d) (the cache and link provisions), it is recommended (Dratler, 2000, § 6.01, at 6-13). Participating in the "registered agent" provisions of course increases the administrative oversight and therefore the cost of the compliance-liability limitation commitment required by the educational institution under section 512. Furthermore, appeal to any provision will require at a minimum that a preexisting compliance policy be in place, as discussed above. In other words, seeking refuge in section 512 requires a before-the-fact copyright compliance program to be in place. The section 512 liability limitation is not something sought after infringement proceedings have commenced.

Special Applications to Higher Education (17 U.S.C. § 512(e)).   Additional immunity is provided for institutions of higher education if certain conditions exist. "This special consideration is embodied in new subsection (e), which provides special rules for determining whether universities, in their capacity as a service provider, may or may not be liable for acts of copyright infringement by faculty members or graduate students in certain circumstances" (H. Rpt. No. 105-796, 1998, p. 74). First, it applies only to faculty or graduate students when "performing a teaching or research function." The higher education environment is unique. This does not mean that is it rampant with copyright infringers. Rather colleges and universities, because of concepts of academic freedom, have less control over faculty than does the average employer over its employees (Dratler, 2000, § 6.06, at 6-139). Thus a strict application of respondeat superior (vicarious liability) should not operate, reducing the responsibility of institutions of higher education for the acts of its employees. (This is also in contrast to the pre-K through 12 environment.) Subsection 512(e) operates to expand the reach of sections 512(a) through 512(d) to treat certain acts of teaching faculty and graduate students as if a third party performed those acts. For purposes of 512(a) and 512(b) (transitory "store and forward" communication and system caching), the institution receives the immunity of those subsections, as the "faculty member or graduate student shall be considered to be a person other than the institution," thus his or her acts are not imputed to the institution. For purposes of 512(c) and 512(d) (storage and information location tools), the knowledge of an infringement is not attributed to the institution. In other words, the knowledge or awareness of an infringing posting or link by a faculty member or graduate student as employee is not imputed to the institution from that faculty member or graduate student; rather, "that determination must be made on the basis of the knowledge or awareness of other employees of the institution, such as administrators and paid professional staff" (Dratler, 2000, § 6.06, at 6-142).

However, in order for the imputation or attribution to not occur and for the section 512(c) liability limitation protect the institution, three conditions must exist. First, within the preceding 3 years the institution must not have received three or more notices of infringement (according to the notice provisions of 512(c)(3)) by the faculty member or graduate student from a copyright owner. Second the institution must be engaged in a compliance program that "provides to all users of its system or network informational materials that accurately describe, and promote compliance with the laws of the United States relating to copyright." Logic suggests that this is more than the repeat infringer policy requirement of sections 512(a)-(d). Finally, the infringing activities must not "involve the provision of online access to instructional materials that are or were required or recommended, within the preceding 3-year period, for a course taught at the institution by the faculty member or graduate student."

> The reference to "providing online access" to instructional materials includes the use of e-mail for that purpose. The phrase "required or recommended" is intended to refer to instructional materials that have been formally and specifically identified in a list of course materials that is provided to all students enrolled in the course for credit; it is not intended, however, to refer to the other materials which, from time to time, the faculty member or graduate student may incidentally and informally bring to the attention of students for their consideration during the course of instruction. (House Report No. 105-796, 1998, pp. 74–75)

In other words, the posting of infringing reading lists, e-reserves, or specifically created digital libraries in support of a particular course will not qualify for subsection 512(e) immunity.

Then, because the faculty member or graduate student is an employee of the institution, his or her infringing acts would be imputed back to the employer under agency principles, and the institution would share liability as a contributory or vicarious infringer.

As with all of the section 512 defenses, the limitation on liability for monetary relief is complete. Thus, section 512(e) limits the types of injunctive relief available to plaintiffs under section 512(j). However, the quid pro quo for this means that injunctive relief aimed at an infringing nonprofit educational institution might go "beyond disabling access to particular material on a specified site . . . [and i]n a proper case, the nonprofit educational institution might even be subject to structural relief designed to correct a chronic or persistent tendency to infringe copyrights" (Dratler, 2000, § 6.06, at 6-146).

PERFORMANCE AND DISPLAY OF COPYRIGHTED MATERIALS IN THE DISTANCE EDUCATION ENVIRONMENT

The performance and display of copyrighted material in distance education settings, whether through traditional broadcast or newer Internet streams or web site access implicates the copyright owner's exclusive rights of performance and display. Educators receive additional use rights beyond fair use in 17 U.S.C. § 110(2). However, these rights are very limited when compared to those enjoyed by teachers in "live" face-to-face teaching encounters.

First, the opening phrase of section 110(2) limits the category of works that may be performed in a transmission to two categories of works: nondramatic literary (e.g. reading from a text) or musical works (e.g. singing a song). Second, the performance or display must be a part of the "systematic instructional activities" of the nonprofit educational institution. For example, section 110(2) might not support the broadcast of copyrighted materials (performance or display) as part of a school's orientation activities or commencement exercises. The legislative history suggests the "concept of 'systematic instructional activities' is intended as the general equivalent of 'curriculums,' but it could be broader in a case such as that of an institution using systematic teaching methods not related to specific course work." (H. Rpt. No. 94-1476, 94th Cong. 2d Sess. 56-57 (1976) (reprinted in 17 U.S.C.A. § 110, Historical and Statutory Notes).) An example could be a portion of text describing how to use a distance technology.

Subsection 110(2)(B) also requires that the "performance of a nondramatic literary or musical work or display of a work" be "directly related and of material assistance to the teaching content of the transmission." The legislative history of the 1976 Act offers little assistance in understanding the second substantive requirement of section 110(2) found in section 110(2)(B). However a recent Senate Report observes that "in the Register's Report [footnote omitted] the dual requirement of *relevance and materiality* connects the copyrighted work to the curriculum, and it means that the portion of the work performed or displayed may not be performed or displayed for mere entertainment of the students, or as unrelated background material." (S. Rpt. No. 107-31, 107th Cong. 1st Sess. 10-11 (2001) (italics added).) Last, under the current language of section 110(2)(C) it is unclear whether the rights granted to educators in section 110(2), allow the transmission over the Internet of a performance or display of copyrighted material under the most prevalent one-to-one distance education model (that is, remote broadcast to individual students at separate locations, e.g., via computers, at their home or work). The text of the statute suggests not. This is so because section 110(2)(c) indicates that a qualifying transmission must be made "primarily" to one of only three categories of locations or persons. First, and of most relevance to the present discussion, section 110(2)(C)(i) indicates that the reception must be made primarily for "reception in the classroom or similar places normally devoted to instruction." The one-to-many mode of the traditional "broadcast" model is reflected by the present formulation of section 110(2) and operates as a significant limitation on many current distance education scenarios, and contrasts with the wide range of rights inuring to an educator in a live class under section 110(1).

Pending legislation is likely to dramatically alter the copyright landscape. S. 487, the Technology, Education and Copyright Harmonization (TEACH) Act of 2001, is a complex piece of legislation and its analysis here is both premature and beyond the scope of this chapter. A thorough analysis is found in Lipinski (2003).

FAIR USE IN EDUCATIONAL SETTINGS

In the distance education environment, digital classrooms and digital libraries raise further issues of copyright liability. Even if section 110 is expanded to allow the display or performance of existing works in digital distance environments (Lipinski, 1999, p. 17), there is still the issue of copying and pasting or otherwise digitally manipulating material and placing it on the Web for distance students to access (Colbert & Griffin, 1998, p. 457). Amendment to the section 112 empheral recordings provision is also contemplated by TEACH but would only apply section 110(2) material not general e-reserves or virtual course libraries.

Creating Digital Libraries and Resources.   It is apparent that publishers are becoming more willing to pursue infringement actions against nonprofits, individuals, and educational institutions, even where the primary market for the protected work consists of schools, libraries, or other nonprofit organizations. In *Hotaling v. Church of Latter Day Saints* (1999), the statute of limitations for infringement based on unauthorized reproduction had passed, the plaintiff claimed that the distribution was ongoing, as the unlawfully copied work was made available to members of the public through the holdings of the church library. The court observed, "[w]hen a public library adds a work to its collection, lists the work in its index or catalog system, and makes the work available to the borrowing or browsing public, it has completed all the steps necessary for distribution to the public" (at 203). Because the library had unlawfully made a complete cover-to-cover copy of one of the plaintiff's books, the distribution of that material was also unlawful. Application of this holding to distance education environments suggests that, once material is posted unlawfully to a course Web site, it would continue to violate the copyright owner's right of distribution for every day it remains on that site.

Another case pertinent to the issues that arise in nonprofit distance education is *Los Angeles Times v. Free Republic* (2000). The *Free Republic* was a bulletin that posted verbatim copies of articles from the *Los Angeles Times* and *Washington Post* for discussion and critique by board members. The court concluded that this copying and posting was not a fair use. Was the *Free Republic* board not unlike the instructor who posts articles as part of a distance education course, then expects the students to provide comment through a course discussion board? Although there is a vast difference between the enrollment of a typical education distance class and the number of users of the *Free Republic*—a handful or several dozen or even several hundred versus 20,000 registered users logging up as many as 100,000 hits per day—this case offers caution for the often routine cutting pasting that occurs in many distance education settings.

First, in looking at the purpose of the use, the district court concluded that, although the use was perhaps noncommercial (supporting the claim that the use was fair), it was also nontransformative:

> [T]he court finds that the non-transformative character of the copying in this case tips the scale in [the] plaintiffs' favor, and outweighs the non-profit/public benefit nature of the purpose for which the copying is performed. This is particularly true since the posting of plaintiffs' articles to the Free Republic site amounts to "systematic . . . multiplying [of] the available number of copies" of the articles, "thereby serving the same purpose" for which licenses are sold or archive charges

imposed. (at 53, quoting *American Geophysical Union v. Texaco, Inc.*, 60 F.3d 913, 924 (2d Cir. 1994)). It could be argued that the non-transformative reposting of newspaper stories on the Free Republic board is not much different from the course pack, e-reserve or reading list creation in which many institutions engage.

Recall that the board was essentially personal and educational in purpose (though perhaps not in a formal sense). The frightening parallel to many distance education scenarios should be obvious.

The second factor favored the defendants, since the nature of the works copied was factual, i.e., news stories. However, since complete copies of the articles were published, the third factor favored the plaintiffs. Also the court questioned whether there was need to post articles in their entirety if the purpose was to encourage discussion of the news and topics of the day (summaries or headlines with citations would suffice). The fourth factor also weighed against a finding of fair use, as the court found the posting of complete articles a substitute for the original work, especially considering the scale of the board service. The court rejected a First Amendment defense as well.

This does not mean that all posting, pasting or other digital manipulation is prohibited under the copyright law. Another instructive case *Kelly v. Arriba Soft Corp.* (2002) also decided by the same appellate court the decided the *Napster case*. In *Kelly*, the plaintiff claimed that the unauthorized use of her photographs violated her exclusive right of reproduction and display. Reproduction, in that the miniaturization of photographs by the defendant onto its web site as part of thumbnail web site index of world wide web photographs was not a fair use, and display, in that the framing of several of the plaintiffs photographs within the defendant's web site was also in excess of fair use. The Ninth Circuit concluded that the former thumbnail miniaturization was a fair use but the full-image frame was not. In both instances, the taking was 100% of the work and the work was creative (the amount factor and nature of work factor). The difference between the two acts was that the appellate court concluded that the thumbnail use was transformative, it created something new, an index. It did not operate as a substitute for the original (the court observed the resolution or image quality of a thumbnail was not equivalent to the original), thus it failed to harm the market for the plaintiff's works, in fact the thumbnail web index directed others to the original web site where the copyrighted works of the plaintiff where located and where potentially additional revenues could be generated for the plaintiff by site visitors. In contrast, the frame was not a fair use display of the plaintiff's photographs on the defendant's web site. By framing the plaintiff's works on their web site the defendant's obviated the need for web site visitor's to ever leave its site and "travel" to the plaintiff's site. The frame then operated as a substitute for the original works-the photographs, on the plaintiff's web site-and thus also negatively impacted the market for her works.

Although the DMCA did amend section 108 to allow certain types of libraries (those that are open to the public and that reproduce materials without indirect commercial advantage, see 17 U.S.C. §108(a)) to digitize unpublished works for purposes of preservation and security (17 U.S.C. § 108(b)) and to digitize published works to replace copies that are damaged, deteriorated, lost, stolen, or in an obsolete format (17 U.S.C. §108(c)), the change should not be read as a general provision allowing widescale digitalization of library collections. The language of the statute also suggests this: The "digital format is not [to be] made available to the public in that format outside the premises of the library." In other words, no remote access to section 108(b) or (c) digitized material is allowed. Further, in the case of works digitized under section 108(c), there is the additional requirement that an unused replacement not be available at a fair price. Section 108(c) is designed to apply to works in the possession of the school, college, or university library that are no longer available in the market place and whose use is compromised by its less than accessible physical condition, i.e., damaged, deteriorated, lost, stolen, or in obsolete format. Libraries are then left with a general section 107 (fair use) defense when digitizing collections or large amounts of material in conjunction with the support of distance education and remote access of materials by students. Furthermore, in amending section 108, Congress cautioned specifically against the extensive digitalization of collections and the provision of remote access to them:

> Finally, the Committee wants to make clear that, just as when section 108 of the Copyright Act was first enacted, the terms "libraries" and "archives" as used and described in this provision still refer to such institutions only in the conventional sense of entities that are established as, and conduct their operations through, physical premises in which collections of information may be used by researchers and other members of the public. Although online interactive digital networks have since given birth to online digital "libraries" and "archives" that exist only in the virtual (rather than physical) sense on websites, bulletin boards and homepages across the Internet, it is not the Committee's intent that section 108 as revised apply to such collections of information. The ease with which such sites are established online literally allows anyone to create his or her own digital "library" or "archives." The extension of the application of section 108 to all such sites would be tantamount to creating an exception to the exclusive rights of copyright holders that would permit any person who has an online website, bulletin board or a homepage to freely reproduce and distribute copyrighted works. Such an exemption would swallow the general rule and severely impair the copyright owners' right and ability to commercially exploit their copyrighted works. Consequently, the Committee intends that references to "the premises of the library or archives" in amended sections 108 (b)(2) and (c)(2) mean only *physical premises*. (Senate Report No. 105-190, p. 62). (italics added)

Most libraries and educational institutions justify making a complete library of electronic materials available to students either through a traditional electronic extension of the library (a so-called e-reserve) or via the distance education Web site directly as a fair use under section 107. However, as the developing case law demonstrates, assuming that all personal, educational, and nonprofit uses are permissible is dangerous indeed. Section 108 "does not permit the usual reserve collection practice of making several copies of the material, assembling them in a folder or notebook, and placing them on reserve for students to check out" (Melamut, 2000, p. 177). Guidelines for single and multiple copying in educational settings do exist (see Guidelines for Classroom Copying in Not-for-Profit Educational Institutions (Classroom Guidelines), reprinted in H. Rpt. No. 94-1476, p. 68). Although many educators believe that these guidelines should apply to any environment (since technological neutrality is supposedly built into the copyright law), if a distance educator is going to analogize his or her reproduction to the reproduction in traditional classroom courses and use a general section 107 fair use defense as articulated in the Classroom Guidelines, then the guidelines must be followed in spirit and letter. Faculty cannot pick and choose which portions of the Classroom Guidelines to use or apply to digital or distance environments. For example, this would mean that the copying under the Classroom Guidelines can in no circumstances "be used to create or to replace or substitute for anthologies, compilations or collective works" or be of "consumables," such as workbooks, exercises, and standardized tests, nor should the copying "be repeated with respect to the same item by the same teacher from term to term," and be limited to nine instances of such "multiple" copying in particular course. These rules apply to single copies made by or for an instructor or to multiple copies made for students. Thus, even if an instructor were to classify an electronic reserve reading list as an assortment of single copies (knowing full well that every student will probably print out every article, allowing publishers to argue that in effect an e-reserve is a multiple copying scenario [but see, Lipinski, 1999, p. 16]), the instructor would still need to conform to the requirements of the existing Classroom Guidelines. This limitation on the amount of e-reserve digitalization that can occur under section 107 may explain why, when the Fair Use Guidelines for Electronic Reserve Systems were proposed in 1976 (reprinted in Bielefield & Cheeseman, 1997, pp. 195–199), the guidelines suggested that "[t]he total amount of material included in electronic reserve systems for a specific course as a matter of fair use should be a small proportion of the total assigned reading for a particular course."

Moreover, relying on these guidelines may offer some hard and fast standards for organizations to operate under, but there is no guarantee that the guidelines are legal safe harbors. The educational "fair use" guidelines that govern classroom coping of print works, music, inter library loan, off-air tape recording, e-reserve or digital multimedia manipulation are not part of the copyright statute, and in that sense may offer only a false safe harbor. (Crews, 2001) In fact, recent dicta in an appellate decision offers an interpretation in direct contrast to the Fair Use Guidelines for Educational Multimedia (Multimedia Guidelines) (reprinted in, Bielefield and Cheeseman, 1997, 92-102) which allows educators and students to incorporate a digital copy of a photograph or a limited audio (thirty seconds) or video (three minutes) clip into an educational multimedia work such as a power point presentation or website. Compare the fair use formulation in the Multimedia Guidelines with the recent language from the *Corley* decision.

> We know of [**77] *no authority for the proposition that fair use, as protected by the Copyright Act, much less the Constitution, guarantees copying by the optimum method or in the identical format of the original.* Although the Appellants insisted at oral argument that they should not be relegated to a 'horse and buggy' technique in making fair use of DVD movies, [footnote omitted] the DMCA does not impose even an arguable limitation on the opportunity to make a variety of *traditional fair uses of DVD movies, such as commenting on their content, quoting excerpts from their screenplays, and even recording portions of the video images and sounds on film or tape by pointing a camera, a camcorder, or a microphone at a monitor as it displays the DVD movie.* The fact that the resulting copy will not be as perfect or as manipulable as a digital copy obtained having direct access to the DVD movie in its digital form provides no basis for a claim of unconstitutional limitation [i.e., vis-à-vis an impermissible restriction on free speech] of fair use. [footnote omitted] (*Universal City Studios v. Corley,* *77-*78) (italics added)

If this shrinking view of fair use comes to dominate the legal landscape then little if any digital content will be subject to fair uses rights of access and use?

Wither Fair Use: The Subsection 1201(d) Anti-Circumvention Exemption. Section 1201 contains elaborate measures designed to protect the technological safeguards that copyright owners develop to shield their works. As stated in 1201(a)(1): "No person shall circumvent a technological measure that effectively controls access to a work protected under this title." Section 1201 was also added to the copyright law as part of the DMCA. However, the so-called anti-circumvention provision did not take effect until October 28, 2000. "Due to controversy surrounding this provision, the prohibition will not take effect for two years while the Librarian of Congress conducts a rule-making process, with public input, to determine the nature and extent of any exemptions that should be made available" (Lazar, 1999, p. 53; see also, Samuelson, 1999). The rule-making process is now complete:

> The Librarian of Congress, on the recommendation of the Register of Copyrights, has announced the classes of works subject to the exemption from the prohibition on circumvention of technological measures that control access to copyrighted works. The two classes of works are: 1) Compilations consisting of lists of websites blocked by filtering software applications; and 2) Literary works, including computer programs and databases, protected by access control mechanisms that fail to permit access because of malfunction, damage or obsolescence. These exemptions are in effect from October 28, 2000, to October 28, 2003.

The recommendations are to be reviewed every 3 years. Additional material may be found at http://www.loc.gov/copyright/1201/anticirc.html.

In one of the first cases to apply section 1201, *Universal City Studios, Inc. v. Reimerdes* (2000), aff'd sub.nom. *Universal Studios, Inc. v. Corley* (2001) the court addressed the use of a program called DeCSS that could be used to de-encrypt (circumvent) digital versatile disks (DVDs) that store feature-length films and other copyrighted material. The district court had little trouble concluding that the DeCSS software was primarily designed to circumvent the DVD encryption software and that people posting or linking to the DeCSS software violated section 1201, but since those provisions were not yet effective by law, the court looked to the anti-trafficking provisions of subsection 1201(b). The court rejected both a First Amendment defense as well as a fair use defense against contributory infringement raised by *Sony* (a defence based on the technology allegedly having a substantial noninfringing use). Considering the legislative history of the provision, the court observed: "A given device or piece of technology might have a 'substantial noninfringing use, and hence be immune from attack under *Sony*'s construction of the Copyright Act—but nonetheless still be subject to suppression under section 1201.' Indeed, Congress explicitly noted that section 1201 does not incorporate *Sony*" (*Reimerdes* at, 323; footnotes omitted). However, although supportable from a legal perspective, the courts application of the DMCA "effectively eliminates the fair use protections" built into section 1201 and "allows copyright owners to put into place encryption measures to preclude fair uses of works" (Ottenweller & Chatterujee, 2000, p. C4). In other words, someone could engage in a fair use but not be able to use prohibited (anti-circumvention) technology to do it, in which case the individual would still violate section 1201 even though not be liable under a general theory of contributory infringement vis-à-vis *Sony*.

The decision of the district court was affirmed on appeal. While the Second Circuit in *Universal City Studios v. Corley*—the name of the *Reimerdes* case on appeal—determined that the DeCSS computer code Corley and his Hacker 2600 associates circulated was speech and like other "computer code, and computer programs constructed from code can merit First Amendment protection" (*Universal City Studios v. Corley*, *48, and cases cited therein), it also characterized the anti-circumvention and anti-trafficking rules as content neutral restrictions on speech subject to a less strict constitutional limitation. It reasoned:

> DeCSS is computer code that can decrypt CSS. In its basic function, it is like a skeleton key that can open a locked door, a combination that can open a safe, or a device that can neutralize the security device attached to a stores's products... At first glance, one might think that Congress has as much authority to regulate the distribution of computer code to decrypt DVD movies as it has to regulate distribution of skeleton keys, combinations to safes, or devices to neutralize store product security devices. However, despite the evident legitimacy of protection against unauthorized access to DVD movies, regulation of decryption code like DeCSS is challenged... because DeCSS differs from a skeleton key in one important respect: is not only is capable of performing the function of unlocking the encrypted DVD movie, it also is a from of communication, albeit written in a language not understood by humans. *Universal City Studios v. Corley*, *59-*60)

Since the anti-circumvention and anti-trafficking rules were content neutral, the restriction of section 1201 need only serve a "substantial governmental interest" and "not burden substantially more speech than is necessary to further that interest". (*Universal City Studios v. Corley*, *63) The court concluded that the standard was satisfied, stating: "Although the prohibition on posting prevents the Appellants from conveying to others the speech component of DeCSS, the Appellants have not suggested, much less shown, any technique for barring them from making this instantaneous worldwide distribution of a decryption code that makes a lesser restriction of the code's speech component." (*Universal City Studios v. Corley*, *63-*64) Another case involving criminal penalties under the DMCA is also pending against Elcomsoft Co. Ltd. (*U.S. V. Elcom, Ltd* 2002), the employer of a programmer who wrote a code that unlocks Adobe Systems Inc.'s password-protected eBooks and PDF files. The prosecution in the case argues that the unlocking code does not impact the fair use right to reproduce the work but since it removes rather than copies—removes the encryption protection-it creates a derivative work and the right to make a derivative work is a right solely within the purview of the copyright owner. (Hoppin, 2002) The trial judge recently rejected a First Amendment challenge to the DMCA on reasoning similar to that employed in *Universal City Studios v. Corley*. The practical consequence of these and other decisions is to place copyright owners' rights ahead of others' personal or civil rights such as free speech. Many commentators have questioned whether the anti-circumvention provisions effectively eliminate the concept of fair use. For example Mutchler (2000) stated: "The fair use doctrine is predominantly market and economy based and therefore must be considered in detail when applying the new and evolving DMCA in a global electronic commerce" (p. 12).

Specific exemptions to the anti-circumvention rules exist in subsection 1201(d), which provides that "[a] nonprofit library, archives, or educational institution which gains access to a commercially exploited copyrighted work solely in order to make a good faith determination of whether to acquire a copy of that work for the sole purpose of engaging in conduct permitted under this title shall not be in violation of subsection (a)(1)(A)." However a work so accessed "may not be retained longer than necessary to make such good faith determination, and may not be used for any other purpose." Further, the exemption shall only apply with respect to a work when an identical copy of that work is not reasonably available in another form."

Suppose a university faculty member or librarian would like to access a copy of a work protected by anti-circumvention technology in order to replace a damaged copy owned by the institution. Without anti-circumvention technology and section 1201 in place, subsection 108(c) would allow the reproduction. However, with the new law, this is prohibited; the faculty or librarian could only access a protected copy to determine whether to acquire a replacement copy. Again, commentators question the practical impact of this exemption:

> What happens when an "identical copy" is available in another form, but the copyright proprietor demands an unreasonable or exorbitant price for authorized access? Under the explicit statutory limitations to the exceptions discussed above, a copy obtained by circumventing technological protection can only be used to evaluate whether to acquire a legitimate copy at the unreasonable or exorbitant price. If correct, this interpretation of the exception would render the "fair use" provisions of the exception to the 1976 Act [such as 17 U.S.C. § 108] a dead letter—precisely the result that Congress apparently intended to avoid by adopting the exception in Section 1201(d). (Dratler, 2000, § 3.04[3], at 3-62).

There has been no litigation of subsection 1201(d) as of the writing of this chapter.

ACKNOWLEDGMENT

Research assistance for the content of this article was provided in part by a grant from the University of Wisconsin—Milwaukee Graduate School Research Committee Award for FY 1999-2000.

APPENDIX A: COMPARISON OF COPYRIGHT INFRINGEMENT CASES

Case	Liability for Direct Infringement by Defendant/Operator	Liability for Contributory Infringement	Liability for Vicarious Infringement
Religious Technology Center v. Netcom On-Line Community Service, 907 F. Supp. 1361 (N.D. Cal. no causation. 1995).	No. Lack of knowledge. Allowed up/download. No causation.	Perhaps. Subsequent knowledge and failure to remove.	No. Lack of financial benefit.
Sega Enterprises of America, Inc. v. MAPHIA, 948 F. Supp. 923 (N.D. Cal. 1996).	No. Did not participate in up/download.	Yes. Knowledge of others participation. Solicited up/download.	Not applicable.
Sega Enterprises, Ltd. v. Sabella d/b/a Sewer Line, 1996 U.S. Dist. LEXIS 20470 (N.D. Calif. 1996).	No. Sold copies, but no actual up/download.	Yes. Had reason to know.	Not applicable.
Playboy Enterprises, Inc. v. Frena, 839 F. Supp. 1552 (M.D. Fla. 1993).	Yes. No actual up/download, but supplied a product, distribution, and display.	Not applicable.	Not applicable.
Playboy Enterprises, Inc v. Webbworld, Inc., 991 F. Supp. 543 (N.D. Tex. 1997).	Yes. More than conduit (*Netcom*), rather like a store (sold images).	Not applicable.	Yes. Subscription revenue based on percentage sales.
Fonovisa, Inc. v. Cherry Auction, Inc., 76 F.3d 259 (9th Cir. 1996).	Yes. Trading in pirated recordings.	Yes. Express encouragement.	Yes. Revenue derived from various fees. Overall commercial design.
Sony Corporation of America Inc. v. Universal City Studios, Inc., 464 U.S. 417 (1984).	No. Time-shifting for personal use allowed.	No. Staple article of commerce or substantial noninfringing use.	Not applicable.
Intellectual Reserve, Inc v Utah Lighthouse Ministry Inc., 75 F. Supp. 2d 1290 (Dist. Utah 1999).	No. Hattowever, visitor to site infringes when copy made in RAM.	Yes. Induce others to infringe by encouraging visit and download from site.	Not applicable.
Universal City Studios v Reimerdes, 82 F. Supp. 2d 211 (S.D.N.Y. 2000) (preliminary injunction); 111 F. Supp. 294 (S.D.N.Y. 2000) (permanent injunction). aff'd sub.nom. *Universal City Studios v. Corley*, 273 F.3d 429 (2d Cir. 2001).	Yes. Trafficking and in the future circomvention. Decoding of DVD video on Internet via DeCSS technology.	Yes. DMCA overrules *Sony*. Direct link w/load, direct link w/click and load, reference to sites w/load plus other material.	Not applicable.
UMG Recordings v. MP3, Inc., 92 F. Supp. 2d 349 (S.D.N.Y. 2000); 2000 U.S. Dist. LEXIS 13293 (S.D.N.Y. 2000) (damages).	Yes. Not a fair use: commercial, space-shift not personal, creative, 100%, derivative market.	Not applicable.	Not applicable.

(Continued)

APPENDIX A: (*Continued*)

Case	Liability for Direct Infringement by Defendant/Operator	Liability for Contributory Infringement	Liability for Vicarious Infringement
A&M Records, Inc. v. Napster, Inc., 2000 U.S. Dist. LEXIS 6243 (N.D. Cal. 2000) (motion to dismiss denied); 2000 U.S. Dist. LEXIS 11862 (N.D. Cal. 2000) (motion for preliminary injunction granted); 2000 U.S. App. LEXIS 18688 (9th Cir. 2000) (stay of enforcement re the injunction granted). aff'd in part, rev'd in part 239 F.3d 1004 (9th Cir. 2001).	Yes. Not a fair use: large scale of up/downloads, anonymous users, creative, 100%, market studies, barriers to entry.	Yes. *Fonovisa* applies. Napster is an Internet swap meet, materially contributes to infringement by others.	Yes. Ability to control and acquire indirect dollars via value and plans to monetize user base.
Metallica v. Napster, Inc., No. 00-0391 (C.D. Cal. April 13, 2000).	Possible. See above.	Possible. See above.	Possible. See above.

Note:* Many case are pre DMCA, section 512. As a result if decesions such as the **Playboy cases, holding online intermediories liable for direct infringement, the online service provides community lobbied conguins to secure statutory protection.

APPENDIX B: LIMITATIONS ON LIABILITY RELATING TO MATERIAL ONLINE (17 U.S.C. § 512)

	Store and Forward (512(a))	Caching (512(c))	Posting (512(c))	Linking (512(d))	Take-down (512(g))*
Nature of action	Transient. Transparent.	Transient. Transparent.	Human volition. Visible.	Human volition. Visible.	Human volition. Visible.
Service provider (SP)	User selected, sent, without SP modification. SP: digital and online. 512(k)(1)(A).	SP selection or modification allowed. SP may include analog. 512(k)(1)(B).	SP selection or modification allowed. SP may include analog. 512(k)(1)(B).	SP selection or modification allowed. SP may include analog. 512(k)(1)(B).	SP selection or modification allowed. SP may include analog. 512(k)(1)(B).
General compliance requirements	Adopt/implement repeat infringer policy and no interference with technical controls. 512(i).	Same.	Same.	Same.	Notice of take-down. 512(g)(2)(A).
Registered agent	Not required.	Not required but recommended (Dratler, 2000, § 6.01, at 6-13).	Required. 512(C)(2).	Not required, but recommended (Dratler, 2000, § 6.01, at 6-13).	
Special compliance requirements	Third party. Automatic. No selection of recipients. Time and access limitation of copy. No modification. 512(a)(1)-(5).	Third-party availability. Third-party direction. Automatic. 512(b)(1)(A)-(C).	No actual knowledge. No financial benefit. Take-down provision. 512(c)(1)(A)-(C).	No actual knowledge. No financial benefit. Take-down provision. 512(d)(1)-(2).	Counter-notification notice and repost. 512(g)(2)(B)-(C).
Additional compliance requirements	None.	See 512(b)(2)(A)-(E).	Designated agent. Notification. elements. 512(c)(2) and (3).	Notification elements. 512(d)(3) incorporating 512(c)(2) and (3).	

*Note: the immunity extended by § 512(g) (immunity for liability arising from an erroneous take-down) is not immunity for copyright liability but for defamation or unfair trade or related offenses; in other words one could not violate another's copyright by removing an infringing work from network display but one could defame another by suggesting that his or her posting (the posting that was taken down) was of a dubious (infringing) nature (see Dratler, 2000, § 6.03[2][a][iii][C]).

COURT CASES

A&M Records, Inc. v. Napster, Inc., 2000 U.S. Dist. LEXIS 6243 (N.D. Cal. 2000) (motion for summary adjudication denied); 2000 U.S. Dist. LEXIS 11862 (N.D. Cal. 2000) (motion for preliminary injunction granted); 2000 U.S. App. LEXIS 18688 (9th Cir. 2000) (stay of enforcement re the injunction granted aff'd in part, rev'd in part, 239 F.3d 1004 9th Cir 2001).

America, Inc. v. MAPHIA, 948 F. Supp. 923 (N.D. Cal. 1996).

Avtec Systems, Inc. v. Pfeiffer, 805 F. Supp. 1312 (E.D. Va. 1992), aff'd in part, rev'd in part and remanded, 21 F.3d 568 (4th Cir. 1994).

Baker v. Seldon, 101 U.S. 99 (1880).

Columbia Pictures Industries v. Redd House, 749 F.2d 154 (3rd Cir. 1984).

Community for Creative Nonviolence v. Reid, 490 U.S. 730, 109 S. Ct. 2166, 2171 (1989).

Demetriades v. Kaufmann, 690 F. Supp. 289, 292 (S.D.N.Y. 1988).

Fonovisa, Inc. v. Cherry Auction, Inc., 76 F.3d 259 (9th Cir. 1996).

Futuredontics Inc. v. Applied Anagramics Inc., 152 F.3d 925 (9th Cir. 1998) (affirming denial of preliminary injunction); and 45 U.S.P.Q. 2d 2005 (C.D. Cal. 1998) (denial of defendant's motion for summary judgment).

Hays v. Sony Corporation of America, 847 F.2d 412 (7th Cir. 1988).

Hotaling v. Church of Latter Day Saints, 118 F.3d 199 (4th Cir. 1999).

Intellectual Reserve, Inc. v. Utah Lighthouse Ministry, Inc., 75 F. Supp. 2d 1290 (Dist. Utah 1999).

Kelly v. Ariba Soft Corp., 280 F.3d 934 (9th Cir. 2002).

Los Angeles Times v. Free Republic, 2000 U.S. Dist. LEXIS 5669 (C.D. Calif. April 4, 2000).

Marshall v. Miles Laboratories, Inc., 647 F. Supp. 1326 (N.D. Ind. 1986).

Marobie-F v. National Association of Firefighter Equipment Distributors, 983 F. Supp. 1167 (N.D. Ill. 1997).

Mast v. Committee on the Status of Women, 815 F. Supp. 1112, 1116–1118 (N.D. Ill. 1993).

Metallica v. Napster, Inc., No. 00-0391 (C.D. Cal. April 13, 2000).

Playboy Enterprises, Inc. v. Frena, 839 F. Supp. 1552 (M.D. Fla. 1993).

Playboy Enterprises, Inc. v. Webbworld, Inc., 991 F. Supp. 543 (N.D. Tex. 1997).

Religious Technology Center v. Netcom On-Line Communications Services, 907 F. Supp. 1361 (N.D. Cal. 1995).

Sega Enterprises, Ltd. v. Sabella d/b/a Sewer Line, 1996 U.S. Dist. LEXIS 20470 (N.D. Calif. 1996).

Sega Enterprises of America, Inc. v. MAPHIA, 948 F. Supp. 923 (N.D. Cal. 1996).

Sherrill v. Grieves, 57 Wash. L. Rep. 286 (D.C. 1929). This court no longer exists; its duties were transferred to the U.S. District Court for the District of Columbia. Anyone looking for this case is advised to look for it in the Copyright Office Bulletin. See 20 Copyright Office Bulletin 675 (Dist. of Columbia Supreme Court 1929).

Sony Corporation of America v. Universal Studios, Inc., 464 U.S. 417 (1984).

Southern Bell Telephone and Telegraph v. Associated Telephone Directory, 756 F.2d 801 (11th Cir. 1985).

UMG Recordings v. MP3, Inc., 92 F. Supp. 2d 349 (S.D.N.Y. 2000) (determining liability); *UMG Recordings v. MP3, Inc.*, 2000 U.S. Dist. LEXIS 13293 (S.D.N.Y. 2000) (determining damages).

Universal City Studios v. Reimerdes, 82 F. Supp. 2d 211 (S.D.N.Y. 2000); 111 F. Supp. 2d 294 (S.D.N.Y. 2000) (permanent injunction); aff'd sub.nom. *Universal Studios, Inc. v.*

Corley, 273 F.3d 429 (2d Cir. 2001), 2001 U.S. App. LEXIS 25330.

University of Colorado v. American Cyanamid, 880 F. Supp. 1387 (D. Colo. 1995).

United States v. Elcom Ltd. 2002 WL 1009662 (N. D. Calif, 2002).

Vanderhurst v. Colorado Mountain College District, 16 F. Supp. 2d 1297 (D. Colo. 1998).

The Washington Post Co. v. Total News, Inc., No. 97 Civ. 1190 (S.D.N.Y. complaint filed Feb. 20, 1997, dismissed after settlement June 5, 1997).

Weinstein v. University of Illinois, 881 F.2d 1091 (7th Cir. 1987).

Williams v. Weisser, 273 Cal. App. 2d 726, 78 Cal. Rptr. 542 (1969).

REFERENCES

Bielefield, A., & Cheeseman, L. (1997). *Technology and copyright law: A guidebook for the library, research, and teaching professions.* New York: Neal-Schuman.

Borow, T. A. (1998). Copyright ownership of scholarly works created by university faculty and posted on school-provided Web pages. *University of Miami Business Law Review, 7*, 149–169.

Clarida, R. W. (1999, October). Linking and framing: the courts have spoken (sort of). *The Intellectual Property Strategist*, p. 7.

Colbert, S. I., & Griffin, O. R. (1998). The impact of "fair use" in the higher education community: A necessary exception? *Albany Law Review, 62*, 437–465.

Crews, K. D. (2001). The Law of Fair Use and the Illusion of Fair-Use Guidelines, 62 *Ohio State Law Journal* 599–702.

Daniel, P. T. K., & Pauken, P. D. (1999, April 1). The impact of the electronic media on instructor creativity and institutional ownership within copyright law. *Education Law Reporter*, pp. 1–20.

Digital Millennium Copyright Act, Pub. L. No. 105-304, 112 Stat. 2860 (1998).

Dratler, J., Jr. (2000). *Cyberlaw: Intellectual property in the digital millennium.* St. Paul, MN: West Group.

Dreyfuss, R. C. (1987). The creative employee and the copyright act of 1976. *University of Chicago Law Review, 54*, 590–647.

DuBoff, L. D. (1984). An academic's copyright: Publish and perish. *Journal of the Copyright Society, 32*, 17–38.

Hazard, J. W., Jr. (2000). *Copyright law in business and practice.* St. Paul, MN: West Group.

Holmes, G., & Levin, D. A. (2000). Who owns course materials prepared by a teacher or professor? The application of copyright law to teaching materials in the Internet age. *Brigham Young University Education and Law Journal*, 165–189.

Hoppin, J. (2002, April 1). Copyright Law Faces Court Test: Will Digital Act Pass Constitutional Muster? *The National Law Journal*, at A17.

H. Rpt. No. 94-1476, 94th Cong. 2d Sess. (1976) (reprinted in 17 U.S.C.A. §110, Historical and Statutory Notes). (Relating to 17 U.S.C. & 110).

H. Rpt. No. 94-1476, 94th Cong. 2nd Sess. 68 (1976). (Reprinted in. *Copyright issues in schools: Learn how to protect yourself and your school from violating copyright law*, Appendix A, pp. 1–4, by M. A. F. Howie, Ed., 1997, Danvers, MA: LRP Publications). (Reprinting the "Guidelines for classroom copying").

H. Rpt. No. 105-796, 105th Cong. 2nd Sess. (1998). (Digital Millennium Copyright Act)

Kulkarni, S. R. (1995). All professors create equally: Why faculty should have complete control over the intellectual property rights in their creations. *Hastings Law Journal, 47*, 221–256.

Kupferschmid, K. (1999, February). Something for everyone. *Intellectual Property Magazine*, no pagination (available in the LEXIS-NEXIS LEGNEW Library).

Lape, L. G. (1992). Ownership of copyrightable works of university professors: The interplay between the copyright act and university copyright policies. *Villanova Law Review, 37*, 223–271.

Lazar, B. A. (1999, March 15). New statute tackles challenging Internet and creativity issues: Digital Millennium Copyright Act arrives. *New York Law Journal*, P. S3.

Lipinski, T. A. (1999). An argument for the application of copyright law to distance education. *American Journal of Distance Education, 13*(3), 7–21.

Lipinski, T. A. (2002, January/February). Librarian's Guide to Copyright for Shared and Networked Resources. N. Waller (Ed.), *Techsource: Library Technology Reports (Expert Guides to Library Systems and Services)*, 38, 1–119. Chicago: American Library Association.

Lipinski, T. A. (2003). Legal Reform in an Electronic Age: Analysis and Critique of the Construction and Operation of S. 487, the Technology, Education and Copyright Harmonization (TEACH) Act of 2001, forthcoming *Brigham Young University Education and Law Review.*

Melamut, S. J. (2000). Pursuing fair use, law libraries, and electronic reserves. *Law Library Journal, 92*, 157–192.

Mutchler, J. H. (2000, October). Circumvention of copyright protection systems. *Intellectual Property Today*, p. 12.

Nimmer, M. B., & Nimmer, D. (2000). *Nimmer on copyright*. Albany, NY: Matthew Bender.

Ottenweller, C. R., & Chatterjee, I. N. (2000, October 16). Courts begin to rule against acts of circumvention, *National Law Journal*, p. C2.

Patel, S. H. (1996). Graduate students' ownership and attribution rights in intellectual property. *Indiana University Indiana Law Journal, 71*, 481–512.

Samuelson, P. (1999). Intellectual property and the digital economy: Why anti-circumvention regulations need to be revised. *Berkeley Technology Law Journal, 14*, 519–566.

Schonfeld, M. (2000, September). Singin' the Napster blues. *The Metropolitan Corporate Counsel*, p. 23 (available in the LEXIS-NEXIS LEGNEW Library).

Simon, T. F. (1982–1983). Faculty writings: Are they "works made for hire" under the 1976 copyright act? *Journal of College and University Law, 9*, 485–513.

S. Rep. No. 105-190, 105th Cong. 2nd Sess. (1998). (Digital Millennium Copyright Act)

S. Rpt. No. 107-31, 107th Cong. 1st Sess. 10–11 (2001).

Wadley, J. B., & Brown, J. L. M. (1999). Working between the lines of *Reid*: Teachers, copyrights, work-for-hire and a new Washburn University policy. *Washburn Law Journal, 38*, 385–453.

34

Strategic Planning
for Distance Education

Ryan Watkins
The George Washington University
rwatkins@gwu.edu

Roger Kaufman
Florida State University
rkaufman@nettally.com

INTRODUCTION

Higher education has recently witnessed an unprecedented expansion by conventional universities to support the distance delivery of instruction. With this, there has been an introduction of new institutions with a sole focus on distance education, accompanied by a developing acceptance of degrees achieved outside of the conventional classroom and campus environment. Each of these shifts has altered the foundational frameworks on which the administration and management of institutions of higher education in the United States and around the world have operated and relied. No longer can we depend on the conventional "wisdom" of classic institutional administration to ensure our success in the future. And as Barker (1993) reminds us, when a paradigm shifts, everyone (even those who have been extremely successful in the past) goes back to zero.

Reacting to the current and upcoming changes in higher education will not, however, guarantee success. And since no institution can accurately predict the future, those that will lead in the upcoming decades will be those institutions that can create the future—those that can create the desired changes and offer learners the knowledge and skills necessary for making a contribution and gaining prosperity (Hamel & Prahalad, 1994; Kaufman, Watkins, & Leigh, 2001; Mitroff, Mason, & Pearson, 1994). In this chapter we suggest a practical and pragmatic framework for the planning and achievement of beneficial results both now and in the future (Watkins, Triner, & Kaufman, 1996). This framework, however, lies beyond the boundaries of the conventional thinking within higher education. It does not always fit with "how we have always done it around here" and will likely challenge many of the "truths" on which many institutions have built their past success. And yet, without a new perspective on defining and achieving success in the new age of distance education, many institutions of higher education will not be able to compete.

THE CALL FOR DISTANCE EDUCATION

When education professionals (trainers, professors, instructors, instructional designers, etc.) hear, "We *need* a distance education program," their first impulse is to search through course curricula to determine which courses can be easily translated into online video, audio, or digital formats. While rarely questioning the requirement and/or usefulness of distance education, "all too often those charged with setting up a distance education system are not given the choice to recommend against it" (Rumble, 1986). Further, Rumble (1986) urged educators to understand that just because there are education problems that may be satisfied by distance education methods, this does not necessarily mean that distance education is the best choice for addressing them. Fortunately, educators today have tools available to them that reduce the possibility of implementing distance education as an inappropriate response to institutional problems or opportunities. Devoting time to a rigorous needs assessment is a practical way of justifying all actions that follow the request for distance education—or any other solution in search of a problem (Kaufman, 2000).

Before your institution elects to invest financial and time resources in a distance education program, a rigorous needs assessment may justify the decision and prepare you to make the difficult decisions that follow (Kaufman & Watkins, 2000; Kaufman, Watkins, & Leigh, 2001; Watkins & Kaufman, 1996). Today's educators frequently feel pressured to implement solutions prior to justifying their actions by showing that all stakeholders are likely to receive some benefit. Like in corporate settings, educational institutions frequently leave few incentives for the educators to step back and analyze all the necessary information before making complex decisions. This lack of effective strategic planning aligned with front-end assessment is unfortunate because, by the time the impact of a possibly ineffective intervention (e.g., distance education) is known, the institution may well have sustained damage and/or the ideal time for addressing the problem/opportunity has passed (Saba, 1999; Watkins, in press; Watkins & Corry, 2002; Watkins & Kaufman, 2002).

PROACTIVE CHANGE

The institutions that will lead distance education in the future will not address the changing realities of education from a reactive perspective. Though common in the two worlds of business and education (Haeckel, 1999), the tactic of waiting to respond to the actions of your competitors can be a death sentence in today's educational marketplace. Yet predicting the future is not a science. So how will leaders in distance education ensure a useful and successful future? They will create it! (See, for instance, Kaufman & Lick, 2000; Lick & Kaufman, 2000–2001).

Proactive change creation moves institutional planning and needs assessment away from a responsive mindset to one focused on adaptability and creation (see Table 34.1). This change in perspective is essential for determining if and when distance education (or any new educational program) may be appropriate for an institution.

Success in the future is likely to be dependent on the ability of an institution to create the future they want, as opposed to reacting what others have produced. As witnessed in many industries throughout the past, organizations that can create the market they want have a definite competitive advantage. In higher education, we can identify a similar trend, with institutions such as the University of Phoenix, UKOU, and Nova Southeastern University creating markets for distance education and then finding success in meeting the desires of those markets.

TABLE 34.1
Change Creation and Change Management

Change Creation	*Change Management*
Proactive	Reactive
Being pursued	Catching up
Setting the standard	Trying to be competitive
Leading	Following
Long-term focus	Short-term focus (quick fixes)
Vision-driven to add value to all stakeholders	Driven by external events
Internal planning for a better future	Externally imposed disruptions
Strategic	Tactical
Focuses on all of the institution plus external clients and society	Focus on parts of the institution
A system approach	A systems approach
Future-creating organization	Responsive and resilient organization
Learning organization	Organizational learning
Works to reinvent a new corporate culture	Works within the current corporate culture

Note. From "Mega-Level Strategy Planning: Beyond Conventional Wisdom," by R. Kaufman and D. Lick, 2000, in *Technology-Driven Planning: Principles to Practice*, edited by J. Boettcher, M. Doyle, and R. Jensen. Copyright 2000. Adapted with permission.

NEEDS ASSESSMENT: A MODEL FROM THE LITERATURE

A pragmatic needs assessment (Kaufman, 1992, 1998, 2000) will identify, prioritize, and justify the closure of societal, institutional, and individual needs (i.e., gaps in results). Although there are many models for conducting a needs assessment,[1] arguably the most fashionable models are those of Rossett (1987),[2] Robinson and Robinson (1995), Mager and Pipe (1997), and Kaufman (1992, 1998, 2000). Each of the models can be used effectively to provide educators with insights otherwise missing from the decision-making process. Though the Kaufman model, in particular, provides a rigorous process that aligns strategic planning, tactical and operational planning, and needs assessment processes with a focus on societal and organizational value added. These alignments, we suggest, can be of great advantage when making and justifying difficult decisions regarding the future of distance education in any institution. The needs assessment procedures suggested below represent a blend of strengths from a variety assessment models yet are structured within the Kaufman framework.

The pragmatic needs assessment we propose for effective needs assessment and decision making are based on three fundamental principles:

Distance learning is a means, not an end. A practical and effective needs assessment differentiates between ends and means. Ends are the results of all that your institution does and delivers. Means are the ways in which results are obtained (Kaufman, 1992, 1998, 2000). Distance learning is a means for achieving institutional results. We should first focus on the ends required by the institution for long-term success (based on their contribution to both the organization and the external stakeholders) before we decide that distance learning is the most effective and efficient means for achieving these ends.

---

[1] See Watkins, Leigh, Platt, and Kaufman (1998) for a comparison of alternative needs assessment models in terms of what they deliver in scope and content.

[2] Though there have been serious challenges to "training needs assessment" based on the fact that, because of their target organizational level, they can be wrong 80–90% of the time. This is a potentially serious problem (Triner, Greenberry, & Watkins, 1996).

All results are not the same. Institutional results can be differentiated depending on their primary client and beneficiary (Kaufman, 1998, 2000). Many institutions are proficient at analyzing their inputs and processes yet have spent far less time differentiating the results they lead to. By differentiating among related results we can ensure that all institutional *products* and *outputs* are aligned with the desired contributions (*outcomes*) of the institution to its external clients and community. Institutions should seek to link the products they produce with the outputs they deliver and the outcomes that result, thus aligning Micro-, Macro-, and Mega-level planning and assessment (Kaufman, 2000; Kaufman, Watkins, & Leigh, 2001).

For effective needs assessment, "need" should be treated as a noun and not a verb. In the context of a needs assessment, the distinction between "need" as a noun and a verb is vital. By electing to refer to a need as a gap in institutional results (a noun), you can avoid the alluring trap of selecting solutions prematurely, such as distance learning. Being able to identify, prioritize, and justify interventions and expenditures on the basis of gaps in results (rather than desired interventions) is the reward for this slight adjustment to your vocabulary. As for those individuals who insist on using "need" as a verb, you will undeniably hear comments like "We need a distance learning program" long before any difference between desired and current results has been identified.

Having stated these fundamental principles, we may begin to discuss the procedures for effectively determining if and when a distance education program may be appropriate for your institution.

STEP 1: IDENTIFY AND ALIGN THE INSTITUTION'S VISION AND MISSION

Step 1 can (but shouldn't) be an "additional task" for many educational institutions. Although most institutions today have multiple mission statements to include in their strategic plan, such as statements of goals, values, principles, and visions (Kaufman, Stith, Triner, & Watkins, 1998), rarely are these the useful documents they could be for directing decision making (Kaufman, 2000). Departments and units often have their own missions, which may or may not be in alignment with the larger institution's vision of the future. How will the mission of a potential distance education program facilitate the vision of the institution? Will the mission of the distance education program be derived from the vision of the institution or will the vision be strained to incorporate the program?

A challenge for educators is not only to identify the missions of departments, schools, colleges, businesses, and so on, but to ensure that all these missions are aligned and contribute to the success of the overarching organizational entity and society at large. Covey (1996) stated that "total organizational alignment means that within the realities of the surrounding environment, all components of your organization—including your mission, vision, values, strategy, structure, systems, individual styles and skills, and especially the minds and hearts of your people—support and work together effectively for maximum performance". For institutions entering a needs assessment, these alignments are essential for defining the desired—or required—results (as well as optimal process efficiency and effectiveness).

If any institutional mission (or even the objective of a distance learning program) does not contribute to the achievement of the overall vision (best set in measurable yet ideal terms), then this mission should be revised before any interventions are implemented. Interventions not linked to the aligned institutional ideal vision and mission objective may lead to inappropriate and/or damaging results (Kaufman, 1998, 2000). The implementation of a distance learning program should instead deliver value-added results for learners and the community. This alignment is what links programs to the attainment of institutional objectives and ensures that they are not implementing solutions to nonexistent problems.

Your institution may be lacking a vision or a mission that sets measurable performance criteria for success (Abrahams, 1995; Byars and Neil, 1987; Covey, 1996; Garratt, 1995; Nanus, 1992; Senge, 1990). If so, then it is an imperative for effective decision making that these be established so all educational programs know where they are going and how to tell when they have arrived. Often institutional and program objectives are not written with measurement criteria included. Measurement criteria will be essential in the third step of the needs assessment, in which needs are prioritized and selected for closure.

Beyond the alignment of the institutional vision and mission, educators should utilize environmental scans and market analyses to validate the direction of the institution (Willis, 1992, 1994) and further ensure that the organization and its clients are consistently moving toward adding measurable value to learners, faculty, and our shared society (Martin, 1993; Parston, 1997; Pava & Krausz, 1995).

STEP 2: IDENTIFY THE NEEDS

Needs are discrepancies between current results and the results required for the accomplishment of the institution's vision, mission, program objectives, and individual and team objectives (Kaufman, 2000). Identifying needs requires both the information obtained in step 1 (the results the institution must accomplish for success in the future) as well as the collection of additional data regarding current performance and the state of the institution. It is common for a needs assessment to both utilize institional data available in existing files, accreditation reports, and other resources, as well as opinion data through the interviews, questionnaires, focus groups, or other procedures to supplement the findings (Willis, 1994, p. 10; see also Willis, 1992). The combination of both "hard" and "soft" data, as well as qualitative and quantitative data, is essential in determining if distance education is right for your institution (see Table 34.2).

The Organizational Elements Model (OEM) can be a useful tool for organizing the information you collect. The OEM differentiates five levels of institutional planning and assessment:

Mega–Planning and assessment whose primary client and beneficiary is society and whose results are termed "outcomes."

Macro–Planning and assessment whose primary client and beneficiary is the institution and whose results are termed "outputs."

TABLE 34.2
Example Data Collections Tools and Techniques for Each Data Type

	Hard	*Soft*
Quantitative	Performance data	Likert-type scale surveys[a]
	Budgets	Performance ratings
Qualitative	Focus groups	Opinion surveys
	Analysis of professional list serve	Individual interviews
	Multi-source performance observations	Single-source performance observations

[a]The results of Likert-type scale surveys are often mistakenly taken as hard data because they are in quantified form. This is a good example of why we should consider data on both dimensions (hard-soft and quantitative-qualitative), for a single dimension may lead to confusion, use of inappropriate statistical techniques, as well as incorrect conclusions.

TABLE 34.3
Examples of Hard and Soft Data in Relation to the Organizational Elements Model

Level	Hard Data	Soft Data
Mega (societal value added)	Ideal vision	Student quality of life
	Student and faculty safety	Continuingtaxpayer satisfaction with education
Macro (organizational payoffs)	Mission objective accomplished	Executive management satisfaction and perceptions of value
Micro (individual and team results)	Operating costs	Individual/team morale and perceptions of value
	Individual/team performance	Learning/learner mastery gains
		Learner satisfaction with what has been learned
Process (methods and means)	Cycle time	Learner "attendence" and participation
	Length of time taken on a course topic	Learner satisfaction with the learning processes
	Number of overheads used in instruction	
	Use of computer-driven instruction	
Input (resources and prerequisites)	Resource availability	Resource adequacy
	Resource functionality	Resource timeliness

Micro–Planning and assessment whose primary clients and beneficiaries are the individuals and teams within the institution and whose results are termed "products."

Process–Planning and assessment whose primary focus is on institutional processes and activities.

Inputs–Planning and assessment whose primary focus is on resources and assets.

With the OEM as a guide, institutional data should be collected that reflect each of the interdependent levels (see Table 34.3 for examples).

Examination of and participation in all five elements of the OEM allow educators to gain a systems view of their institution, external clients, and societal context and realities. Decision makers are not limited to a Macro (organization-wide) view, nor a Micro view (i.e., of sections and/or departments) when they apply the OEM.

The Mega level of the OEM adds a stakeholder, society, that has traditionally been forgotten or assumed in the development of distance education programs (Kaufman, 2000; Kaufman, Watkins, & Leigh, 2001). Not only is society as a whole a beneficiary of that which an institution does and delivers, but for many institutions (especially K-12 schools and universities) society is the primary financial supporter of their efforts. The application of this strategic approach ensures that society is not forgotten in the needs assessment or in the possible implementation of a distance learning program.

STEP 3: PRIORITIZE AND SELECT NEEDS TO BE CLOSED

Prioritizing and selecting the needs—remembering that they are gaps in results—to be closed is essential to the success of any institution. Comparing the cost of closing the gaps and the cost of not closing the gaps will be the center of this analysis. In this step of the assessment, collected data will drive the decision making. The extent to which data are collected and analyzed will have two effects on the quality of the needs assessment: (a) An extended period of data collection can negate the timeliness of the assessment, and (b) not enough supporting

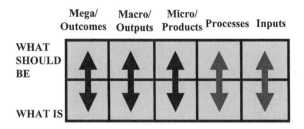

FIG. 34.1. The organizational elements model as it relates to needs assessment. (See Kaufman, 1992, 1998, 2000, and Kaufman, Watkins, and Leigh for a further explanation of the model.)

data can invalidate the results of the assessment. The context of the performance problem (i.e., the reason why distance education is being considered) within your institution should facilitate the balancing of these two variables.

The cost of not closing the gaps is essential consideration in the third step of the assessment and unfortunately is often neglected during application. The cost analysis of problems can keep you from enacting a $10,000 distance learning solution to a $500 performance problem (and economics of scale can further complicate this issue). Providing guidance on the procedures for this analysis is, however, difficult because of the specifics of each institution. A smart starting place for the analysis of the cost of not closing the gaps is to look at the elements previously used to fill in the OEM in step 2 (Kaufman, Watkins, & Sims, 1997). It will be worth your time to at least estimate the costs of each gap between what is and what should be (see Fig. 34.1).

The cost of closing the gaps is more familiar to most educators and educational administrators. To complete this analysis within step 3, you must enter step 4. A Cost-Consequences Analysis (Kaufman & Watkins, 1996; Kaufman, Watkins, & Sims, 1997; Muir, Watkins, Kaufman, & Leigh, 1998) is a tool that provides educators with a coarse-grain examination of the cost of closing the gaps, and keeps the needs assessment within the context of the OEM. The Cost-Consequences Analysis incorporates, as suggested by Rumble (1986), the cost-efficiency, cost-effectiveness, and cost-benefit analyses.

STEP 4: IDENTIFY SOLUTION REQUIREMENTS AND ALTERNATIVE SOLUTIONS

Before you leap forward to the identification of alternative solutions—unfortunately the place where most programs begin—you should define the solution requirements. These requirements will establish the criteria by which each alternative solution will be judged. Specific solution requirements will facilitate the listing of alternative solutions and the selection of the "best" solution(s). The solution requirements identified should include time, costs, available resources, and necessary results.

We suggest that at least two or three alternatives be identified for any intervention. Most problems have more than one possible solution. A distance education program may be a feasible solution for most institutions, but other alternatives exist and should be sought out. Alternative solutions should be identified despite limitations that may bar them from being selected for implementation. In addition, identify the pros, cons, and costs for each possible solution. This is the time to get innovative. Creating an extensive list of alternative solutions is a necessary step on the way toward selecting the most effective and efficient solution. The effort you put into thoroughly analyzing all the possible solutions for any problem will pay off when you make decisions and search for confidence that you made the right decisions.

STEP 5: SELECTING THE SOLUTION(S) FROM AMONG THE ALTERNATIVES

Using the analysis of steps 3 and 4 and ensuring alignment with steps 1 and 2, you now proceed to make a decision. Deciding upon a single solution may or may not be advisable. For many problems or opportunities, a combination of alternatives may yield the best results. Pressures from above (claims that, "we need a distance learning program") and costs alone should not drive the decision but rather, be a piece in a dynamic process. The needs assessment provides you with the essential information for identifying the "right" solution for your institution. Having systematically implemented a needs assessment process will add validity, usefulness, and confidence to your decisions.

The needs assessment process described in this chapter offers several distinct advantages for institutions that implement it with rigor:

1) The process is driven by an ideal vision (Kaufman, 1992, 1998, 2000) at the Mega level.
2) This vision is a statement framed in measurable terms of the kind of world we want to create for tomorrow's child, and it embodies all the elements of a society or community so that institutional planning and assessment can begin where diverse communities find commonality rather than differences.
3) Decisions are based on attaining measurable results for individuals, the institution, and the society or community.
4) The rigor of the process can be adjusted for different contexts and institutional constraints.
5) Information from the assessment will determine performance criteria and evaluation criteria.
6) The process leads toward alignment of all that the institution uses, does, produces, and delivers with valuable results for the society or community.

These advantages are invaluable, especially when a distance education solution has been prematurely prescribed. Since educators are increasing being held accountable for the results of their efforts, time should be taken to assess any performance solution before implementation. In many cases, probably, a distance education solution will be justified when the needs assessment is complete. The accessibility and reduced long-term cost of distance education programs make them viable alternatives for meeting many institutional objectives. A rigorous needs assessment process can provide a level of assurance that a distance education program will both meet these objectives and move the institution and the community toward the achievement of their vision.

When through rigorous needs assessment and strategic planning an institution determines that distance education is the most effective and efficient means for achieved specified results, it will have many good resources available for learning how to complete the tactical planning and successfully implement the new program (see Chapter 40; see also Hamel & Prahalad, 1994; Mitroff, Mason, & Pearson, 1994; Pfeiffer, Goodstein, & Nolan, 1989).

FUTURE RESEARCH IN PLANNING FOR DISTANCE EDUCATION

The recent growth and prosperity of distance education is unlikely to continue into the future if educational institutions are not dedicated to adding value to lives of learners and communities (Kaufman & Watkins, 2000). If any educational institution continues to focus on achieving

TABLE 34.4
An Analysis of Distance Education Delivery Systems

	Conventional Instruction	Classic/Historic Distance Learning	Current Distance Learning	Future Distance Learning
Is it learner, teacher, organization, or society focused?	Teacher and organization focused	Learner focused	Learner and organization focused	Society organization, and learner focused
Is it content driven or driven by the usefulness of what is learned?	Content driven	Content driven	Content delivery driven (see Saba, 1999)	Usefulness driven
Are needs identified? Are needs assessed? Are needs assessed as gaps in result?	Needs assumed	Needs assumed	Needs assumed	Needs formally determined as gaps in results
Are the courses/programs linked to external usefulness? Are the courses/programs linked with other learning opportunities?	Usefulness assumed	Usefulness assumed	Usefulness assumed	Usefulness linked to external value added
Are the courses/programs delivered at an institution or at a remote site, including one's home or workplace?	Institution	Remote site or home	Remote site or home (see Matthews, 1999)	All sites possible (see Welsh, 1999; Moore & Kearsley, 1996)
Are the courses delivered using conventional means, telephone, books, and/or workbooks, video, computer, web? What are the degrees of freedom for the delivery?	Conventional means with some audio-visual support (see Duning, 1987).	Video, telephone, correspondence materials/books and workbooks (see Matthews, 1999; Moore & Kearsley, 1996)	Computer, web, some video	All means possible
Is the content of the courses/programs designed by using a performance system or instruction system process?	Rarely	Rarely	Some of the time	Always
Is there open interactivity between learner and instructor/deliverer? Does the learner get immediate feedback concerning performance?	Some of the time	Rarely	Some of the time	Always when appropriate
Are the courses/programs evaluated for return on investment for the learners, the designers/deliverers, the institution, or society?	Return on investment assumed	Return on investment assumed	Return on investment for learners and sometimes the organization (see Moore & Kearsley, 1996)	Return on investment for all

Note. From "Assuring the Future of Distance Learning," by R. Kaufman and R. Watkins, 2000, *Quarterly Review of Distance Education*, Copyright 2000. Reprinted with permission.

results only at Micro and Macro levels (at best), it will eventually lose out to competitors whose mission is to give learners the skills and knowledge they require to attain long-term success and a high quality of life. Yet, in order for institutional planning to be prepared for these new requirements, the educational paradigms that have brought success in the past must be reviewed to determine their likely effectiveness today and tomorrow.

The transformation of future planning in distance education should be considered within the context of the history of distance education (see Table 34.4). Although some trends are more evident in the literature than others, a composite of planning and assessment within distance education offers many issues demanding research, including these:

What constitutes a useful distance education program?

What constitutes an effective distance education course or degree program?

How do institutions validate decisions regarding the implementation of distance education?

How can educational institutions be responsive and responsible—maintain their adaptability and create the future they and their community desire?

What happens to distance education programs when technologies drive the decision making rather than adding value to the lives of learners?

When distance education is determined to be the "best" solution for an institution, how can it design effective and efficient systems?

How are effective and efficient distance education systems managed.

How can a distance education program or curriculum be shown to add value measurably to internal and external clients.

REFERENCES

Abrahams, J. (1995). *The mission statement book: 301 corporate mission statements form America's top companies.* Berkeley, CA: Ten Speed Press.

Barker, J. A. (1993). *Paradigm pioneers* (Videotape, Discovering the Future Series). Burnsville, MN: ChartHouse Learning Corp.

Byars, L., & Neil, T. (1987, July–August). Organizational philosophy and mission statements. *Planning Review, 15*(4), 32–36.

Covey, S. (1996, March). Principle-centered leadership: Organizational alignment. *Quality Digest*, 21. Available August 11, 2002 at http://www.qualitydigest.com/mar/covey.html

Duning, B. (1987). Independent Study in Higher Education: A captive of legendary resilience? *American Journal of Distance Education, 1*(1), 37–46.

Garratt, B., (Ed.). (1995). *Developing strategic thought: Rediscovering the art of direction-giving.* London: McGraw-Hill.

Haeckel, S. (1999). *Adaptive enterprise: Creating and leading sense-and-respond organizations.* Boston: Harvard Business School Press.

Hamel, G., & Prahalad, C. K. (1994). *Competing for the future: Breakthrough strategies for seizing control of your industry and creating the markets of tomorrow.* Boston: Harvard Business School Press.

Kaufman, R. (1992). *Strategic planning plus: An organizational guide* (Rev. ed.). Newbury Park, CA: Sage.

Kaufman, R. (1995, August 31). If distance learning is the solution, what's the problem: Beyond DDSS. DEOSNEWS [Online serial]. www.ed.psu.edu/acsde/deos/deosnews/deosnews5_8.asp

Kaufman, R. (1998). *Strategic thinking: A guide to identifying and solving problems* (Rev. ed.). Arlington, VA: American Society for Training & Development; Washington, DC: International Society for Performance Improvement.

Kaufman, R. (2000). *Mega planning: Practical tools for organizational success.* Thousand Oaks, CA: Sage.

Kaufman, R., & Lick, D. (2000). Mega-level strategic planning: Beyond conventional wisdom. In J. Boettcher, M. Doyle, & R. Jensen (Eds.), *Technology-driven planning: Principles to practice* (pp.   ). Ann Arbor, MI: Society for College and University Planning.

Kaufman, R., Stith, M., Triner, D., & Watkins, R. (1998). The changing corporate mind: Organizations, vision, mission, purposes, and indicators on the move toward societal payoffs. *Performance Improvement Quarterly, 11*(3), 32–34.

Kaufman, R., & Watkins, R. (1996, Spring). Cost-consequences analysis. *Human Resources Development Quarterly,* *7*(1) 87–100.

Kaufman, R., & Watkins, R. (2000). Assuring the future of distance learning. *Quarterly Review of Distance Education,* *1*(1), 59–67.

Kaufman, R., Watkins, R., & Leigh, D. (2001). *Useful educational results: Defining, prioritizing and achieving.* Lancaster, PA: Proactive Publishing.

Kaufman, R., Watkins, R., & Sims, L. (1997). Cost-consequences analysis: A case study. *Performance Improvement Quarterly, 10*(2), 7–21.

Lick, D., & Kaufman, R. (2000–2001). Change creation: The rest of the planning story. *Planning for Higher Education, 29*(2), 24–36.

Mager, R. F., & Pipe, P. (1997). *Analyzing performance problems* (3rd ed.). Atlanta: Center for Effective Performance, Inc.

Martin, R. (1993, November–December). Changing the mind of the organization. *Harvard Business Review,* 81–89.

Matthews, D. (1999, September). The origins of distance education and its use in the United States. *T.H.E. Journal.*

Mitroff, I., Mason, R. O., & Pearson, C. M. (1994). Radical surgery: What will tomorrow's organizations look like? *Academy of Management Executives, 8*(2), 11–21.

Moore, M. G., & Kearsley, G. (1996). *Distance education: A systems view.* Belmont, CA: Wadsworth.

Muir, M., Watkins, R., Kaufman, R., & Leigh, D. (1998). Costs-consequences analysis: A primer. *Performance Improvement, 37*(4), 8–17.

Nanus, B. (1992). *Visionary leadership.* San Francisco: Jossey-Bass.

Parston, G. (1997). Producing societal results. In F. Hesselbein, M. Goldsmith, & R. Beckherd (Eds.). *The organization of the future* (pp.   ). San Fransico: Jossey-Bass.

Pava, M., & Krausz, J. (1995). *Corporate responsibility and financial performance: The paradox of social cost.* Westport, CN: Quorum Books.

Pfeiffer, J. W., Goodstein, L. D., & Nolan, T. M. (1989). *Shaping strategic planning: Frogs, bees, and turkey tails.* Glenview, IL: Scott, Foresman & Co.

Robinson, D. G., & Robinson, J. C. (1995). *Performance consulting: Moving beyond training.* San Francisco, CA: Berrett-Koehler.

Rossett, A. (1987). *Training needs assessment.* Englewood Cliffs, NJ: Educational Technology Publications.

Rumble, G. (1986). *The planning and management of distance education.* New York: St. Martin's Press.

Saba, F. (1999). Planning for distance education: Too much focus on delivery systems? *Distance Education Report, 3*(4), 5.

Senge, P. M. (1990). *The fifth discipline: The art and practice of the learning organization.* New York: Doubleday-Currency.

Triner, D., Greenberry, A., & Watkins, R. (1996). Training needs assessment: A contradiction in terms. *Educational Technology, 36*(6), 51–55.

Watkins, R., (in press). Determining if distance education is the right choice: Applied strategic thinking in education. *Computers in the Schools.*

Watkins, R., & Corry, M. (2002). Virtual universities: Challenging the conventions of education. In W. Haddad and A. Draxler (Eds.), *Technologies for education: Potentials, parameters and prospects* (pp.   ). Paris: UNESCO.

Watkins, R., & Kaufman, R. (1996). An update on relating needs assessment and needs analysis. *Performance Improvement, 35*(10), 10–13.

Watkins, R., & Kaufman, R. (2002). Is your distance education program going to accomplish useful results? In M. Silberman (Ed.), *The 2002 training and performance sourcebook* (pp. 89–95). Princeton, NJ: McGraw-Hill.

Watkins, R., Leigh, D., Platt, W., & Kaufman, R. (1998). Needs assessment: A digest, review, and comparison of needs assessment literature. *Performance Improvement, 37*(7), 40–53.

Watkins, R., Triner, D., & Kaufman, R. (1996). The death and resurrection of strategic planning [Review of *The Rise and Fall of Strategic Planning*]. *International Journal of Educational Reform, 5*(3), 390–393.

Welsh, T. (1999). Implications of distributed learning for instructional designers: How will the future affect the practice? *Educational Technology Magazine, 39*(2), 41–45.

Willis, B. (1992). *Effective distance education: A Primer for faculty and administrators.* Fairbanks, AK: University of Alaska.

Willis, B. (1994). *Distance education strategies and tools.* Englewood Cliffs, CA: Educational Technologies Publications.

35

Distance Education Leadership: An Appraisal of Research and Practice

Michael F. Beaudoin
University of New England
mbeaudoin@mailbox.une.edu

A new role for the professoriate in the new millennium has been recognized and encouraged, especially as technology-assisted instruction has proliferated and changed the way teachers and students interact and the manner in which educational entities must now do business to meet the demands of a digitized society. The literature describing the rapid evolution of distance education delivery systems over the past 20 years has frequently categorized it into three stages, from correspondence education to technology-assisted education to networked education. Although examples of all three stages currently exist, a consistent theme is that we are now witnessing dramatic changes in how instruction is designed and delivered over time and space. With this dynamic becoming more pervasive, faculty are being admonished to be more receptive and adaptive to opportunities for playing exciting new roles in the distance education arena.

But it seems we have not yet paid adequate attention to new roles required of leaders within institutions offering distance education. Schools and colleges in the new century need leaders who have reflected on their experiences and internalized an understanding of their own capacity to lead. This should apply no less to those in leadership roles in distance education settings within those institutions. The intended purpose here is to look at the role of leadership in distance education settings, examine recent research and writing in this area, and identify research lacunae needing further investigation; offer insights and suggestions for "best practices" to those involved in or aspiring to leadership roles; and generate increased interest in the study of distance education leadership.

For purposes of this chapter, leadership, as distinct from managerial functions, is defined as a set of attitudes and behaviors that create conditions for innovative change, enable individuals and organizations to share a vision and move in the appropriate direction, and contribute to the management and operationalization of ideas. It is possible to play a leadership role without neccesarily being an expert in the field. A university president or elected public official who endorses, articulates and facilitates distance education goals crafted by others can have a widespread impact (e.g., William Rainey Harper, founding president of the University of Chicago, and Gov. William Leavitt of Utah, who was instrumental in the creation of the Western Governors University). It is also important to note here that effective leadership practice is not confined to those in adminstrative roles; indeed, there are leaders without portfolio who, as influential thinkers and theorists, have had a significant effect on their organizations and the field.

However persuasive the arguments might be that fundamental changes are occurring in the digital age that will profoundly impact the academic workplace, many still believe that there are too many alarmists who insist that the teaching/learning environment must be dramatically restructured, and they point out that the academy has been educating the citizenry in essentially the same fashion throughout other significant periods of change. But the issues to be addressed in order to remain competitive today are not quite so simple anymore. Institutional decision makers need to be informed and enlightened enough to ask fundamental questions that could well influence their institution's future viability. How many faculty will we be needed in 10 years? Will the notion of classrooms survive? Is the present structure of the institution viable? Will teachers and students need to meet on campus anymore? Can the organization's decision makers respond to new competitors?

The changing context of education and the aggressive encroachment into this domain by the powerful forces of digital commerce make it impossible to ignore these questions. The confluence of competition, cost, technology, and new consumer demands has insinuated new rules of engagement into a historically placid environment that has derived its strength from tradition rather than change. This set of circumstances is going to force all academic enterprises to rethink their place and purpose not just in philosophical terms but in very pragmatic ways as well. Indecision and immobility during these tumultuous times could prove fatal to a number of institutions, and it is the presence of effective distance education leadership in such an uncertain milieu that could well make the difference between success or failure.

Whether or not it embraces the trend, the academy is shifting from a campus-centric to a distributed education model, and although the administrative and instructional infrastructures that presently characterize most of our institutions will not necessarily disappear, they will be utilized in different ways. Those who dismiss this as a passing phase perhaps do not recognize how pervasive these changes already are even within their own institutions, however mainstream they may still appear to be. In increasing numbers, students now simply want access to learning resources and an accepted credential to verify their learning, both commodities that have typically been aggregated and self-contained on a campus. But because distance education technologies now make it possible for students to get what they need while geographically separated from a fixed location and with less human mediation, educational administrators continue to carry the burden of a bureaucracy and a physical plant that are becoming increasingly outmoded and costly.

Thus, as the boundaries and distinctions between traditional and so-called nontraditional education are blurring, there is a need for leaders able to function effectively in both contexts, and because many distance educators are among the few who have already moved within these overlapping circles, they are well positioned to play key roles. Many, having succeeded to some extent in "institutionalizing" open and distance education, are now able to move from the margins to the mainstream of their organizations and assume new roles. However, for those now willing to enter, or who are thrust, into this milieu, is it readily apparent what attitudes are best suited to manage these distance education endeavors, what techniques are effective in directing this burgeoning phenomenon, and what type of leadership might be most appropriate to move the field to its next phase? It seems that we have yet to offer much guidance to educational administrators on how they can best contribute to this inexorable trend in their midst.

Certainly, we have chronicled the activities and accomplishments of several early pioneers as correspondence study was incorporated into the extension units of a few institutions, and we have recognized and recorded the efforts of a few influential activists, such as Lord Perry of Walton and Charles Wedemeyer, who advanced the acceptance of this new form of educational practice. Eventually, some of those who began teaching in this mode and who directed the first distance education units established at a few bold institutions reflected on those early experiences and began to articulate ideas and ideologies around the practice of teaching and learning at a distance. Based on their observations and experiences, a new body of literature gradually took form, mostly around pedagogical issues.

As the field took shape as a separate and distinct area of academic activity and academic inquiry and more programs began to emerge, experientially based accounts of program activities and accomplishments proliferated. Great efforts were made during this era to legitimize distance education by offering evidence that it was comparable to classroom-based instruction. As new technologies rapidly emerged to facilitate delivery through a variety of media, increased attention was given to analyses of which delivery system was most effective in aiding teachers to teach and learners to learn and of the impact of certain delivery systems on the nature of the interaction between teachers, students, and the medium they utilized. Some attention was also given to case studies of various approaches to the planning and management of selected programs, both successful and unsuccessful ones, and to evaluation methods appropriate to measure the outcomes and efficacy of these ventures. Yet largely absent throughout this period of research and writing in this emerging field was any focused consideration of the dimension of leadership and its impact on the obvious growth and apparent success of distance education at literally hundreds of institutions worldwide.

Although educational structures often appear to be relatively static, they do gradually accommodate selected change, usually in response to external factors that eventually force decision makers to consider new strategic initiatives. Few institutional leaders today would not acknowledge that technological innovation is perhaps the single most compelling factor driving them toward new organizational structures and new pedagogical models. For many, these represent the most significant change since their institution was established. Despite its seemingly inherent resistance to change and its historical unwillingness to keep pace with the larger society, higher education has itself entered an industrialized phase, and the resulting changes in structure and systems will demand compatible leadership styles, including approaches that have not typically characterized educational management.

Otto Peters (1994), one of the first to make important contributions to distance education theory, believes the industrialization of education is nowhere more evident than in distance education. He has written extensively on how distance education practitioners have necessarily incorporated entrepreneurial elements, such as division of labor, marketing, management, and quality control, that are more typical of operating a business than overseeing an academic enterprise. To be sure, such elements exist in many educational organizations, but they are far less obvious there than in most distance education environments. Indeed, Peters and others have often chosen to establish entirely new and distinct distance education entities based on an industrial model, such as the British Open University, rather than attempt to transform existing institutions. Roy McTarnaghan, founding president of Florida Gulf Coast University, speaks insightfully in an interview in *the American Journal of Distance Education* ("Speaking Personally," 1998) of establishing that distance education institution in 1997, noting that such large-scale endeavors must create a distinctive culture and a clearly articulated mission shared by all stakeholders, especially faculty, if they are to succeed.

Hall (1998) offers a thoughtful analysis of what new institutional structures are emerging within which leaders will be required to function. As traditional and distance education institutions converge, leaders who have been dealing with discreet programs identified with their institutions will now have to manage networked institutions in which proprietary lines between programs and students are blurred and participants shift among multiple formal and informal learning venues, with no single institution as a point of reference. As alliances develop and networking expands to increasingly include for-profit entitities, the mega-university is evolving toward what Hall calls the "meta-university." He argues that bold and creative leadership is required to manage and evaluate these emerging new structures, driven in large measure by networking technology.

Those suggesting ways to attract leaders to the field of distance education and develop their skills might encourage mentoring by senior administrators, attendance at professional meetings, seeking out relevant graduate courses, and keeping current with literature in the field. This latter suggestion—to consult the literature as a source of guidance—presumes that there is a worthwhile body of work available, of course. In the early 1990s, Duning (1990) undertook an in-depth review of the literature on managerial leadership in distance education. At that point, she asserted that this area of research had attracted far less attention than other areas within the field. There have been descriptions of program planning processes, but little examination had occurred of leadership, however defined, within a larger distance education context. Duning also noted that, although there is a substantial body of knowledge about nontraditional settings, it is almost entirely unknown to academe. As might be expected, much distance education literature that does gain attention is denigrated. For example, a report entitled *What's the Difference: A Review of Contemporary Research on Effectiveness of Distance Learning in Higher Education* (1999) (not surprisingly, sponsored by the American Federation of Teachers and the National Education Association, both long-time opponents of distance education and its perceived encroachment into the domain of the professoriate) argues that the overall quality of distance education research is questionable and does not ask the right questions.

In the early 1990s, Duning and others assessing the status of scholarly inquiry into the area of distance education management concluded that the field lacked a theoretical framework to guide our understanding of distance education practices and that, of all the areas of study in distance education, management still appeared to be the most neglected. We now undertake the task of reexamining the status of this vacuum to determine if it has been filled; to ask, if not, why not; and if it has, to consider whether the results constitute a useful contribution to theory and practice in the field.

This author dutifully reviewed more recent literature in the field by conducting a content analysis of titles and abstracts of articles appearing in two American publications during the past four years: *the American Journal of Distance Education* (*AJDE*) and *DEOSNEWS*, an electronic journal, both published by the American Center for the Study of Distance Education at the Pennsylvania State University. Also examined were the 1998 and 1999 issues of a European journal, *Open Learning*, edited by Greville Rumble, and the 1997–1999 issues of *Distance Education*, an international journal published by the Open and Distance Learning Association of Australia.

A look at volumes 10 through 13 of the *AJDE* revealed that, with the conspicuous exception of one issue (Summer 1998), which was devoted entirely to distance education leadership (edited by this author), no writings specifically dealt with activities and outcomes that seemed to have any obvious connection to leadership. Volumes 6 through 10 of *DEOSNEWS* contain only two titles that have any leadership connotations. It is of some interest to note that in one issue there was a review of literature classified as "administration and organization," offering the possibility that leadership would be addressed, even if only tangentially. But this was not the case. Although the titles in the European and Australian journals included several articles related to staff development and the economics of distance education, no articles appeared on the topic being searched. Thus, over a four-year period, several widely read sources of research and writing in distance education theory and practice offer very little indeed on the topic of leadership.

We can optimistically take note, however, of a new journal introduced in January 1999, the *International Journal of Leadership in Education: Theory and Practice*, published by the Taylor-Francis Group (London) and edited by Duncan Waite. Although the first three volumes seem to favor school leadership issues and a few titles suggest the leadership in distance education is rather broadly defined, the journal nonetheless provides a promising new forum and gives distance education practitioners and researchers the opportunity to contribute to a professional publication dedicated entirely to educational leadership.

Another useful device for gauging how popular a specific topic seems to be at a given moment is to conduct a content analysis of presentations at major national and international distance education conferences. A number of these papers eventually find their way into the published literature in the field and can thus serve as indicators of what topics are currently in vogue. Therefore, an examination was undertaken of titles and abstracts of papers presented at the European Distance Education Network, Bologna, Italy (1998); the distance education conference sponsored by the University of South Australia (2000); and the ICDE World Conference on Open Learning and Distance Education in Duesseldorf, Germany (April 2001).

Not unexpectedly, the attention focused on the themes of distance education management in general and leadership in particular was conspicuously thin. The Bologna conference, entitled "Universities in a Digital Era—Transformation, Innovation and Tradition," offered 137 papers and workshops on a wide range of topics, including several within the category of organization and policy. Although a few of these referred to various approaches used to plan and implement particular projects, none directly addressed matters concerning leadership per se. The Australia conference program, entitled "Distance Education—An Open Question?" listed 133 presentations. Again, of these, not one, based on a reading of the abstracts, appeared to address issues related to leadership. One keynote address did discuss technology-driven change in education and did contain a few comments germane to distance education leaders. The world conference in Germany, entitled "The Future of Learning—Learning for the Future: Shaping the Transition," received a total of 624 proposals for presentations. From the large number of offerings, it could be presumed that a few authors would take leadership as their area of special interest. Indeed, several proposals were placed in either the category of strategies and policies or category of management and logistics, and no doubt a reading of their full text would reveal some content related to the leadership theme. (Interestingly, the one session dealing specifically with the topic discussed an online course on the subject of leadership.)

Finally, with respect to the current body of written work, there is, of course, an increasingly steady supply of new books on distance education, many offering a chapter or two on aspects of administration and organization. For example, Moore and Kearsley's (1998) volume on a systems approach to distance education does contain a chapter on administration, with brief but useful discussions on such topics as staffing and planning, but it has nothing specifically on leadership. An examination of new books on open and distance learning reviewed and/or received by the journals noted above yielded no titles that deal primarily with organizing and leading distance education programs. Also, a review of the subject index of 10 prominent books on open and distance education published since 1993 uncovered no listings on the subject of leadership and only two on administration or management.

If the literature on the management in distance education is relatively thin, we can hardly be sanguine about the prospect of finding much on the more specific aspects of leadership in this field. Yet, it is encouraging to observe that there are now occasional volumes appearing that focus on topics that flirt with the leadership theme. For example, a review of the database on Open and Distance Education publications, edited by Keith Harry of the British Open University, listed three book titles devoted to open and distance education leadership and management (Duning, van Kekerix, & Zabrowski, 1993; Freeman 1997; Paul 1990). The most recent addition to this genre is *Leadership and Management in Open and Flexible Learning*, edited by Latchem and Hanna (2001). And although these works are mainly intended to offer strategies for developing and directing open learning initiatives rather than formulating more theoretical constructs, they will certainly help close the gap in the literature on leadership.

In summing up this brief review of scholarly presentations and writing, it should be acknowledged that, within this body of work, there may well be more attention given to leadership than was discoverable by a cursory examination, and no doubt some authors would protest that their contributions do address, at least in part, some dimension of leadership. Even if this protest is legitimate, however at least 70 percent of the work reviewed and noted here falls into the domain of case studies of specific programs (a great many, in fact, use the case study nomenclature in their titles). Furthermore, whether content related to leadership is included or not, we might question the usefulness of this reportage for better understanding leadership theory and practice—or, in truth, any other important aspects of distance education.

We should also inquire at this juncture if the paucity of scholarly material related to leadership in distance education is compensated for, to some extent, by the availability of material in other areas of educational theory and practice, including adult and continuing education, which is closely aligned with distance education. In fact, in this particular area we find a rather impressive range of writings not only on the planning and management of continuing education activities but also on the topic of leadership. Simerly and others have contributed a number of accomplished studies that, in the absence of a more fully articulated body of work on distance education leadership, can be quite useful to distance educators. Simerly (1987) identified the following strategies as critical to effective continuing education leadership, and these seem no less applicable to distance education:

Analyze systems and conduct environmental scans.
Be aware of power.
Manage both conflict and agreement and reach consensus.
Understand the impact of institutional culture.
Function with ambiguity, complexity, and decentralization.
Utilize tactical and strategic planning.
Demonstrate the value of the educational organization to multiple constituencies.

It will be interesting to observe if some contributors to the literature on continuing education will now offer similar insights into distance education where the two types of education intersect. This is quite possible, since many distance education initiatives are spawned within continuing education units, where there is often an entrepreneurial and innovative spirit. Note that, in the area of elementary and secondary school administration, there is now a considerable amount of attention given to leadership topics, and this attention could lead to greater awareness by those in other areas.

One is tempted to conclude, from this review, that the subject of leadership in distance education is being actively avoided in favor of the usual fare—reports and case studies of specific projects and programs that go into excrutiating detail about the life (and sometimes death) of particular initiatives at selected institions. Unfortunately, these accounts seldom offer any useful insights about distance education practice that might be generalized for possible relevance and application in other similar settings, and almost never is there any thoughtful analysis about the impact of leadership (or lack of it) on the outcomes chronicled in these studies.

What are some plausible explanations for this paucity of interest in leadership among distance educators despite the enormous interest in the topic in the corporate sector, as seen in best-selling books and high-priced seminars? First, those researching and writing in the field may just now be getting beyond the phase of single-mindedly pursuing analyses of how distance instruction compares with more conventional methods and how new technologies affect various learning environments. A related factor may be that most of these researchers and writers have been academics and have understandably preferred to focus on pedagogical issues rather than administrative matters.

Second, a reasonable amount of attention has in fact been given to the planning and administration of distance education programs for quite some time. Although most of this work consists of specific case histories, the case-history approach to planning and administration has perhaps been considered adequate to meet the needs of distance educators. Related to this is the fact that the concept of "leadership" is not widely recognized as a separate and distinct element of administrative practice or study. This is especially so outside of the United States. In Germany, for instance, where what is referred to as the "Führer complex" is still prevalent, leadership is not discussed, or at least not studied, in the field of education. Prominent European theorists such as Otto Peters and Bèorje Holmberg have made important contributions to the organization of distance education, but they and others have not identified leadership as a discreet topic for analysis.

Third, there are those who simply dismiss the concept as not especially useful for advancing the study or the practice of distance education. It is seen as an elusive idea that does not readily lend itself to reliable analysis or to a universal set of desirable behaviors safely applicable to the idiosyncracies of each situation. Further, just as some argue that there are no characteristics attributable to distance education that are uniquely its own, they likewise believe that leadership within distance education merits no special scrutiny or analysis as a distinct area of study.

What, ultimately, is the usefulness of the body of work accumulated thus far on the subject of distance education leadership? Although the work that does exist consists mostly of occasional book chapters, conference presentations, journal articles, and "principles of good practice" lists, distance education practitioners currently in or moving toward leadership roles do have a variety of growing resources available to guide their practice. Assuming that there may be some value for the field of distance education if there is increased attention to leadership issues, what can be done to generate more interest in the topic? At the very least, those planning publications and meetings related to distance education could actively solicit contributions on the subject of leadership in distance education and dedicate entire conferences, journal issues, or books to it.

Beyond some useful literature in continuing education, as previously noted, are there resources from other areas of study that could compensate for the lack of interest in the specific topic? We suggest that Donald Schon's (1983) important study of reflective practice has significant implications for distance educators, no less so than for the several professions Schon used to illustrate his theories. Schon made a provocative case for developing mature practitioners by insisting that they actively engage in a process of ongoing systematic reflection on their work during their performance of it rather than at a later point, when they may no longer be able to make appropriate interventions to enhance their effectiveness. This seems an especially worthwhile process for an entire generation of distance education practitioners, who now have substantial personal and institutional experience and are still highly active. By engaging in "reflection in action," these veterans have the opportunity, as Schon aptly described it, to define new truths, not only for their own benefit but for the entire profession as well. This effort and its results have the potential to make important new contributions to the field and offer insights into its leadership.

Is there, in fact, any value in attempting to craft, if not a bona fide theoretical framework for leadership practice that is unque to distance education, at least a set of guiding principles that, at this moment in which distance education has evolved to a new role and status, can well serve its providers and consumers? Those responsible for mapping new directions for moving distance education practice to the next stage of its development might be somewhat heartened by the recent attempts by several groups, including professional associations and accrediting bodies, to define so-called principles of Good practice. The New England Association of Schools and Colleges (1998), for example, has developed and promulgated a "policy for the accreditation of academic degree and certificate programs offered through distance education." These standards for quality are certainly useful in providing suggested criteria by which we can plan new programs and measure what we are doing in such areas as matching technology with needs, providing appropriate student support, implementing evaluation measures, and the like. In the absence of a more precise theoretical framework, such principles do offer, at least, some insights about what constitutes effective leadership practice and how it ultimately impacts the success or failure of our collective efforts. But producing checklists of helpful hints about what to do and what not to do hardly seems adequate to the tasks ahead.

Although the most common way of assessing progress in the development of a body of knowledge in an area of study is to review the literature, it is possible that a brief survey of other activities related to distance education leadership may yield some useful information that could compensate for the apparent paucity of written work on the subject. For example, there are a number of centers for distance education housed at colleges and universities (e.g., the American Center for the Study of Distance Education at Pennsylvania State University) that sponsor symposia, workshops, publications, and programs of study on leadership or on topics that can contribute to our understanding of distance education practice. Also, professional development sessions on distance education administration are increasingly in evidence. Several institutions now offer week-long summer institutes that do, in fact, specifically address distance education leadership (e.g., the Institute for the Management of Distance Education, offered by the Western Cooperative for Educational Telecommunications; see http://www.wiche.edu/telecom/Events/). These are presumably serving a useful purpose in providing experienced and aspiring leaders with insights and guidance. More importantly, a number of institutions, particularly in the United States, now offer certificate and graduate programs of study in distance education, including courses specifically designed to prepare leaders for the field. As just one example, a Master of Distance Education program is offered online by the University of Maryland University College, which also offers a related certificate program in collaboration with Oldenburg University's Center for Distance Education (Germany). This degree program is attracting an international cohort of students and has a waiting list for admission (see http://www.umuc.edu/mde). It is interesting to speculate on what impact these curricula might eventually have in creating a distinct body of work that offers a more theoretical approach to leadership rather than the prevailing emphasis on practical applications of administrative techniques. Preparing candidates for careers specifically in distance education through professional education programs has potentially significant implications as for the first time the field will acquire a new generation of individuals in leadership roles who did not "come up through the ranks" during a period when the field was just emerging as a recognizable and viable area of professional practice. In addition to introducing new leadership styles and strategies in their chosen field, this cohort might contribute important new theoretical perspectives as well.

Having now entered a new century in which the constant advance of technology is likely to present provocative new challenges as well as opportunities, it is tempting to ask if there is perhaps a leadership style that is most appropriate for distance education. Although suggesting a single best approach may be too bold a step, researchers might attempt to identify situations in which distance education leaders are likely to find themselves in the near term and consider general strategies that seem compatible with those situations and likely to be productive. Such strategies might include the following:

Creating more partnerships, including alliances with for-profit companies typically seen as competitors.
Devising meta-university arrangements whose networking structures make parochial interests a handicap.

Reaching for broader markets and taking a truly global view of distance education.
Creating more free-standing virtual entities utilizing asynchronous formats.
Developing more exclusively online delivery systems rather than mixed-media approaches.

Although no particular leadership style may be universally suitable, certainly transformative leadership as described by Bennis and Nanus (1985) remains a particularly compelling model for distance education leaders today. For one thing, organizational practices long entrenched in educational entities urgently require reshaping so that these entities can adapt to environmental changes, most notably the emergence of a worldwide market for students but also the exponential increase in potential competitors for those students. Transformative leaders in education must be capable of helping its stakeholders (e.g., administrators, faculty, students, and trustees) recognize that there are obvious benefits in doing business in new ways and that they can no longer afford the luxury of adopting new ways of teaching and learning in an incremental fashion (a fashion academics are so accustomed to and comfortable with). To be sure, there are no facile formulae that, when be matched with particular settings, will ensure infallible leadership performance; ultimately, a sense of vision, resoluteness, and the ability to operationalize concepts are requisites of success.

Advocates and initiators of distance education need to be seen, by themselves and others, not as mavericks on the fringes of their institutions but rather as contributors who can play a key role in bringing their institution to the next stage of development. This new status among those responsible for "alternative" programs has grown more common as institutional decision makers become aware, often with some alarm, that they may not be as relevant and responsive as their competition to the demands of diverse new market segments seeking access to learning opportunities. Leaders can capitalize on their institution's growing need to remain competitive in a broader arena by demonstrating how distance education offerings, once relegated to the margins, can become central to the institution's strategic planning and essential for the institution's success and even survival in the new global marketplace. And though some might object to appealing to an organization's self-interest as a means of advancing distance education, the fact is that an innovative new idea very often succeeds, not because it is noble, but because it can serve a useful purpose, both for the larger system as well as for its proponents.

Leaders must create conditions conducive to energy, initiative, and innovation in their particular milieu and bring along others above and below them in the organizational hierarchy. This requires, in addition to tranformational leadership, what Hershey and Blanchard (1977) called "situational" leadership, with its ability to diagnose the organization at a particular moment and determine its stakeholders' readiness for moving in a new direction. In fusing these two approaches, the leader diagnoses the organization's situation in the immediate environment and then transforms it as far along the change continuum as necessary using a collaborative style of leadership. In this way, a climate less resistant to and more receptive toward distance education is created, often in an incremental fashion as the situation is gradually transformed.

Since few distance educators have the opportunity to create entirely new free-standing entities exclusively designed for online or other delivery systems but instead labor within institutions positioned somewhere along the continuum between conventional and alternative infrastructures (what might be called a hybrid model), most eventually face the conundrum of whether to promote the notion of a central unit to coordinate distance education activities or at least foster new initiatives. One argument is that, in the absence of a focal point for such endeavors, individual faculty will likely tinker indefinitely and inefficiently on their own with a variety of instructional technology options intended to augment their classroom-based courses but their efforts will not ultimately result in a systemwide adoption of distance education in any comprehensive and cost-effective manner. In addition, those institutions that do incorporate small-scale distance education initiatives but contract out many specialized functions that allow them to retain their existing infrastructure are often seen as suspect because they can conveniently tout their involvement in distance education without any real institutional shift in its direction.

Another view is that an incremental process of increasingly widespread individual initiatives within an institution will eventually lead to a critical mass of participation and ultimately create a demand for more institutional commitment and support. Proponents of this latter strategy maintain that it is the pattern that typifies most institutions' progression toward distance education today and that premature administratively driven initiatives will only generate further faculty resistance and impede any prospects for longer-term change. Bernath (1996) provides interesting insights into this dilemma, using various European models to illustrate the positive and negative forces at play when attempting to integrate distance education into conventional universities. For opinion leaders in distance education, this particular issue can be one of the most critical, and their insights and advice on the best option will test their credibility and influence within their organizations.

To succeed in any of these contexts, a macro view is critical. Distance education leaders must not be overly preoccupied with nurturing their own existing programs and providing the horsepower for only their initiatives; they must also insinuate themselves into the academic mainstream and the inner circle of decision makers responsible for bringing the entire organization to a new place. Distance educators should see themselves, not as protectors and survivors of isolated programs for which they have labored mightily, but as valued strategic partners who can enable the larger institution, often long viewed as the enemy, to catch up with them and emulate their practices and successes. In short, distance education managers should be treated as educational leaders who, through less directing and more motivating, can facilitate the articulation, development, implementation, and stewardship of a vision of learning that is shared and supported by a wider academic community.

Distance education leaders, however, must disabuse themselves of the idea that their programs, even if more widely accepted and adopted within their institutions than in the past, are now accepted as fully legitimate (i.e., equivalent to classroom-based instruction). It is more likely that, in most instances, these alternative delivery methods are simply recognized as an effective means of capturing a larger market share of prospective consumers and generating additional revenues. Distance education leaders can be convincing advocates because colleges and universities, as in the past, must plan their future in a continuing context of uncertainty. Since much of that uncertainty in this era has been brought about by the rapid emergence of instructional technology, this phenomenon positions experienced open learning practitioners to be far more influential in shaping a strategic agenda for the next decade than was usually the case in the past.

If their institutions still do not "get it," then distance education leaders must diligently seek opportunities to convey a sense of urgency that what they currently are doing, perhaps somewhat unnoticed and serving a relatively small proportion of overall enrollments, nonetheless represents a model for replication elsewhere if further institutional growth is to be realized. This requires these leaders to tout past successes. By doing so, they can convincingly cast distance education as a model to be emulated elsewhere in the organization. This is already happening in the area of instructional design, where many faculty may be unaware of or uninterested in just how much learning from a distance is taking place through their own institution but will nonetheless be eager to acquire new technology tools and training to augment their classroom-based courses.

Much of higher education is still characterized by "old millennium" thinking, appropriate for an economy in which decisions on the number of sections for particular courses were based on faculty workloads. In the new economy, where information is the product to be delivered to a broader market in less time and at lower cost, distance education leaders must help their organizations ask the right questions and find their appropriate niche through "new millennium" strategic thinking. In an earlier era, distance educators typically assumed a warrior mentality to advance their cause; today, they can be more effective as brokers facilitating the expansion or replication of programs and services they championed during more contentious times.

Although effective distance education leadership requires a presence and participation in a wider arena, playing a role in the macro environment should not occur at the expense of attending to the details of running distance education programs. The tasks to be overseen by managers of both small and large, new and established programs demand a formidable repertoire of skills that need constant attention and refinement. Needs assessment, market analysis, strategic planning, fitting technology to needs, operationalizing ideas, resource mobilization, introducing online infrastructure, policy formulation, training and support for faculty, collaborating with partners, program evaluation and accreditation, and mentoring the next generation of leaders—all are tasks requiring vigilance and guidance.

The presumed dominance of online teaching/learning environments for the forseeable future raises a further question: Will a particular style of leadership be more effective in this milieu than in earlier ones? Are there any "best practices" for leading distance education initiatives and activities in the online domain? Are some of the complex roles exercised by the previous generation of leaders less relevant now than in earlier periods of the movement? Regardless of the medium in use, it would seem that the roles of conceptualizer, implementor, and evaluator are still viable. Perhaps less critical are the roles of advocate, reformer, and technician, which occupied so much time in the past. Too often, those presiding in decision-making forums engage in long deliberations on complex technological options but bereft of fundamental pedagogical issues. Distance education leaders, whatever other roles they may assume, must always maintain the essential role of educator.

As we conclude this appraisal of leadership in distance education and the study of it, we would do well to briefly examine the distinctive and distinguished leadership of two seminal figures in the field in hopes of identifying those aspects of their personality and practice that contributed most to their near-legendary status. Although we might agree with Otto Peters' characterization of Charles A. Wedemeyer as the great visionary and Lord Perry of Walton as the great pragmatist of distance education, we can also safely state that both shared an overarching leadership trait by emphasizing the implementation of innovation. Wedemeyer had the capacity to conceptualize and synthesize earlier philosophies and emerging new ideas and to articulate their implications and applications. Perry was able to translate those concepts into a new institution, the British Open University, that has had enormous influence on the evolution of much subsequent distance education practice.

Can it be said, too, that Wedemeyer and Perry, along with other leaders, were especially effective in having their ideas adopted around the world because they were charismatic? Certainly yes, at least in the sense of charismatic leadership as defined by Conger and Kanungo (1987), whose list of traits most surely applies to them. In particular, they undoubtedly focused primarily on a vision and mission, developed a unique and inspirational view of the future, empowered and energized others to implement their vision, pressed their organization to continuously improve, widely communicated and lived their vision, integrated congruent values into the culture they were influencing; and profoundly inspired and affected their followers' aspirations.

Now that we have offered a number of attributes for successful leadership, a final caution is perhaps appropriate, particularly for those who may feel best equipped to provide the creative new leadership the field warrants. Paradoxically, it seems that the past experience and longevity of some distance educators actually works against them in providing leadership for a new age of learning. Ever more powerful interactive technology has resulted in the diminution of distance and has also reduced the decision-making window for institutions to respond to a new class of educational consumers willing to spend money to save time. Yet many who may have pioneered distance education at their institutions may still be preoccupied with bridging the distance gap, which effectively no longer exists. Distance education leaders who in the past put their energy into debating the virtues of out-of-classroom learning must now play a more valuable role in facilitating discussions and decisions of much wider scope and more profound consequences for the future of their institutions. There must be a shift in the leaders' focus, from the micro issues surrounding technology and its impact on learners to a macro view of institutions and the impact of technology in this larger context. Thoughtful attention to issues in this wider arena will lead to appropriate action and ultimately impact the teaching/learning process regardless of what technology is utilized.

It is essential that veteran as well as emerging leaders be prepared for these new roles, not just by relying on instinct derived from past experience but also by seeking new insights through greater attention to leadership as a discreet area of study and practice. The potential contribution of distance educators in a widening sphere of influence is too significant at this juncture to relegate to the periphery of others' thinking and of our vision of where we want to go and where we want to take others.

REFERENCES

Bennis, W., & Nanus, B. (1985). *Leaders: The strategies for taking charge.* New York: Harper & Row.

Bernath, U. (1996). Distance education in mainstream higher education: Strategic issues at conventional universities. In *Internationalism in distance education: A vision for higher education* (ACSDE Research Monograph No 10. pp. 45–51) University Park, PA: Pennsylvania State University. (ed. Melody Thompson)

Conger, J. A., & R. N. Kanungo. (1987). *Charismatic leadership: The elusive factor in organizational effectiveness.* San Francisco: Jossey-Bass.

Duning, B. (1990). The literature of management. In M. Moore (Ed.), *Contemporary issues in American distance education* (pp. 30–43). Oxford: Pergamon Press.

Duning, B., van Kekerix, M. J., & Zabrowski, L. M. (1993). *Reaching learners through telecommunications: Management and leadership strategies for higher education.* San Francisco: Jossey-Bass.

Freeman, R. (1997). *Managing open systems.* London: Kogan Page.

Hall, J. (1998). Leadership in accreditation and networked learning, *American Journal of Distance Education, 12*(2), 5–15.

Hershey, P., & Blanchard, K. (1977). *Management of organizational behavior.* Englewoood Cliffs, NJ: Prentice Hall.

Latchem, C., & Hanna, D. (2001). *Leadership and management in open and flexible learning.* London: Kogan Page.

Moore, M., & Kearsley, G. (1998). *Distance education: A systems view.* Belmont, CA: Wardsworth.

New England Association of Schools and Colleges, Commission on Institutions of Higher Education. (1998). *Policy for the accreditation of academic degree and certificate programs offered through distance education.* Bedford, MA: New England Association of Schools and Colleges.

Paul, R. H. (1990). *Open learning and open management: Leadership and integrity in distance education.* London: Kogan Page.

Peters, O. (1994). *Otto Peters on distance education: The industrialization of teaching and learning* (D. Keegan, Ed.). London: Routledge.

Schon, D. (1983). *The reflective practitioner: How professionals think in action.* London: Temple Smith.

Simerly, R. G. (1987). *Strategic planning and leadership in continuing education.* San Francisco: Jossey-Bass.

Speaking personally with Ray McTarnaghan (Interview). (1998). *American Journal of Distance Education, 12*(2), 73–78.

What's the difference? A review of contemporary research in American higher education distance learning. (1999). Washington, DC: American Federation of Teachers; National Education Association.

36

Issues in Organizing for the New Network and Virtual Forms of Distance Education

Andrew Woudstra
Athabasca University
Andrew_Woudstra@vital.athabascau.ca

Marco Adria
University of Alberta
marco.adria@ualberta.ca

The story of Universitas 21 is one that many in the field of distance education watch carefully. Universitas 21 is a group of large and influential universities formed for the purpose, in the words of its Web site, of establishing a "framework for member universities to pursue agendas that would be beyond their individual capabilities, capitalizing on the established reputation and operational reach of each member." The resulting network includes among its goals the development of the following: international curricula; quality assurance for international enrollments; instruction, assessment, and certification of students; an internationally recognized brand for a global network of high-quality universities; and partnership opportunities for major new providers, including corporate universities. The 18 members are from 10 countries and include the Universities of Michigan, Nottingham, Melbourne, and Toronto.

Various international activities have been developing in the partnership, but one in particular involves an e-learning initiative. On November 20, 2000, Thomson Learning, a division of Thomson Corporation, announced an agreement with Universitas 21 to offer degrees, diplomas, and certificates to students completing courses over the Internet ("Thomson Learning," 2000). Thomson Learning would be responsible for course design, content development, testing and assessment, student database management, and language translation for the project. Thomson Corporation had already been devoting major resources to its e-learning initiatives www.thomsonlearning.com and www.thomson.com. The announcement appeared to be part of an effort to extend the collaborative goals of Universitas 21. However, three days after the announcement, the University of Toronto announced rather abruptly that it was not ready to support the venture (Shecter, 2000). The university stated that it was indeed a member of Universitas 21 but that its membership did not imply a relationship with Thomson learning and the distance-learning venture. A spokesperson at the University of Toronto said it was concerned about its brand. For its part, Thomson was clear that it was seeking to associate itself with Universitas 21 because of its brand recognition.

THE CONTINUING "DISRUPTIVE" INFLUENCE OF THE INTERNET

Some research, accompanied by much speculation and theorizing, is being undertaken to explain what is happening in many industries closely tied to what some are calling the "new economy." Christensen and Overdorf (2000) theorize that the characteristics of a technology can be so disruptive that they destroy old industries and businesses and create new ones. Consider the influence of online investing, Internet retailing, Internet reservation systems, and Internet auction sites on the established business practices across many industries. Christensen and Overdorf believe that those organizations that maintain a balanced perspective among resources, processes, and values and consider them all in their strategic adaptation will be best able to cope with disruptive change. They note that none of the minicomputer companies were successful with the personal computer and that only one department store became a leader in discount retailing. Kling (2000) does not establish such a direct causal relationship between technology and change, suggesting instead that an "ecological" view allows the analysis of the complex social context in which information technologies are introduced. He sees technological implementation as an ongoing process rather than a series of one-shot implementations.

Regardless of the question of causality, the Internet is associated with change in many industries and fields, including education. Evidence of this is the creation of new terms such as *e-learning* and *e-education*. Following are some of the broad capabilities of the Internet in relation to organizations ("Survey of E-management," 2000):

It allows a dramatic decrease in the cost of handling and transmitting information. A document that could be express mailed for $25 or faxed for $5 can be e-mailed for pennies.

It uses IP standards that allow almost anyone to access that part of the information stream to which access is not restricted. Markup languages HTML and XML are open standards and allow information and documents to be viewed on the Web and accessed freely. XML has the added feature of indicating the nature of the document in its code.

It makes much more of what management does within the organization visible to the general membership of the organization.

It changes boundaries inside and outside the organization. Collaborating with others becomes easier and less expensive. Linkages within the organization can eliminate internal barriers. For individuals, the boundary between home and work are redrawn, and the boundaries between the individual and the organization become less clear.

Employees can access training from any location at any time. Any organization member from any location can access forms, policies, internal job markets, and other organizational information.

Knowledge management becomes much more efficient with the Internet. Knowledge management involves connecting those who know with those who need to know. It involves converting personal knowledge into organizational knowledge. It involves collaboration both within the organization and with other organizations. A central feature of managing collaboration is less emphasis on the individual project and achievement and more on teamwork. Available software allows individuals to work together on the current version of a project from anywhere that they have access to the Internet.

Effective use of the Internet can improve service and create loyalty, allowing organizations to retain clients. Creating loyalty involves adding extra value. In some situations this means adding a contact point where the person using the service can contact a representative of the organization. It may also mean creating a unique experience for the client.

Organizations and institutions have established various networks as they attempt to implement some of these capabilities. These networks vary in their organizational structures, use of technology, and ownership. They can be virtual extensions of an individual organization using technology to connect with and work with external individuals and entities to perform specific functions or tasks. Alternatively, they can be groupings of independent organizations that have joined together to enter new markets or explore new technologies. Or they can be new ventures formed by member organizations for specific tasks or functions. Some of the networks that have been established recently are well developed conceptually and operationally, whereas others resemble the loosely linked distance education consortia of the past. Some use the Internet intensively to leverage their organizational and operational capacities, whereas others are content to use technology as a simple enhancement of their current operations. Some network members are privately owned corporations, others are publicly held or a private-public hybrid. Here are some prominent and representative examples.

Consortia continue to form. In May 2000, for example, the state of Connecticut allocated $2 million to a partnership of state and private colleges and universities (Klonoski, 2000). The *Connecticut Distance Learning Consortium* was established to deliver credit and noncredit courses to students in the region and to gain a foothold in a wider market. Partners in the consortium include the state's departments of education and higher education, all 12 community colleges in the state, and 16 colleges and universities. Similarly, the *Canadian Virtual University* is a partnership of six small private and public Canadian universities that are collaborating to offer university degrees and certificates through distance education. This is a credit-coordinating arrangement whereby students can choose courses and programs from a seamless set of offerings.

Partnerships between public universities and private companies are being established. The *Global University Alliance* (GUA) was set up to offer distance education to adult learners via interactive Web and database technologies. Its target market is Asia. GUA's commercial partner, NextEd, plans to provide student support services, such as a call center in the local language, along with an advising/admission/registry interface with the home institution and Internet connections. The founding members include several medium-sized universities in Canada, Australia, the United States, and Germany: Athabasca University, the Rochester Institute of Technology, the University of South Australia, and six others. This is an example of a consortium that intends to create and manage common resources, but it is not clear how these resources will actually be shared. As with Universitas 21, the private partner seems to see control of the technology platform as the key to its place in the consortium. However, there are many political and social barriers facing entrants into the Asian market, and these may have been underestimated. Multiple partnerships are evident in this example, with Athabasca University participating in this network as well as in the Canadian Virtual University.

Of the examples given here, *Fathom Knowledge Network Inc.* (fathom.com) is perhaps the most highly developed. It is a virtual network that makes intensive and sophisticated use of the Internet, billing itself as the "premier destination for authenticated knowledge and online learning." Members of the network include elite universities (such as Columbia University and the University of Chicago), along with libraries, museums, and other institutions with a widely recognized reputation (e.g., the British Library, the Victoria and Albert Museum, and Cambridge University Press). Via the network's portal, referrals are made to online courses offered by both members and nonmembers. As noted previously, some institutions have decided to join more than one network, possibly in order to avoid being left out of a strategically important collaborative venture. For example, the University of Michigan, mentioned earlier as a member of Universitas 21, is also a member of Fathom.

Finally, there is Britain's *Open University*, which has avoided entering into a consortium network. Instead, it seems to regard itself as the dominant figure in an emerging "core-ring" structure. It has established Professional Development Europe as a wholly owned subsidiary. Although the exclusive offering of the company is an MBA, Professional Development Europe is involved in delivering other management programs, such as management certificates and doctorates in business administration through links with "sister companies" and universities. These companies and universities are to function as suppliers in a dependent relationship with the university.

These examples illustrate the range of the continuum on which partnering is taking place. In the case of the Connecticut consortium, we see the conventional, loosely coupled, cooperative linking of agencies and institutions that is intended to create a regional base for the delivery of distance education programs. Professional Development Europe, on the other hand, represents the more corporate-style effort of a global organization to create a wholly owned subsidiary for the purpose of catering to an international niche market. The presence of some universities in more than one of these alliances appears to indicate a practice of diversifying strategic options.

What is common to these examples? It is the use of technical and organizational innovations made possible by the wide application of the Internet for the purpose of developing a network organization. The network in each instance is dedicated to encouraging the dynamic use of resources and expertise to address a rapidly expanding and complex market. The expansion of the market seems likely to continue to be international in scope and to extend to more than the adult and higher education sectors. Malaysia's University of Technology is experiencing tremendous growth, with more than 70,000 student enrolments (Cohen, 2000). Similarly, as Thailand's constitution extends free education from 6th grade to 12th grade, more students will be eligible for and demanding higher education. In India, foreign companies and universities are now using distance education to meet the increased demand from students as a consequence of better access to the Internet. At Dr. B. R. Ambedkar Open University, for example, thousands of working students are now studying for their degrees (Overland, 2000).

DISTANCE EDUCATION AND THE EMERGING NETWORK ORGANIZATION

Although there is growing interest in the influence of the Internet on learning and more research on how online courses may be presented, there continues to be a dearth of literature—descriptive, prescriptive, or analytical—on organizing for distance education. Rumble (1986) provided the earliest attempt to map the territory of organizing for distance education, identifying three macro-administrative designs possible for distance education organizations:

1. Single mode, in which distance education is the "core business" of the organization.
2. Mixed mode, in which both traditional teaching and distance education take place within the same organization.
3. Consortium, in which resources, especially teaching resources such as course materials and communications technology hardware, are shared within a region or nation.

More recently, an emerging picture of the convergence of these three modes has been depicted. Dunning (1990) speculated on the integration of campus and distance education. Holt and Thompson examined the effects of information technology on distance learning institutions using a case study (1995) and a strategic framework (1998). Dede (1996) explored the effects of emerging technologies on both distance education and campus-based face-to-face education and developed a three-part conceptual framework encompassing knowledge webs, virtual communities, and shared synthetic environments for enabling distributed learning. Bates (1997) postulated that the Internet and its increasing broadband capacity would encourage the convergence of campus-based organizations and distance education organizations as interactive network-based technologies begin to be used extensively in both.

At the same time, the capability of administrative systems to respond to and shape the convergence of campus-based and distance education initiatives has been questioned. Rumble (1981) examined the economics of distance education and some of the key cost structures found in distance education organizations, suggesting that management across academic and production departments would need to be focused and relatively strong in comparison to that found in traditional educational organizations. Murgatroyd and Woudstra (1989) distinguished between strategic planning, which they saw as a relatively common exercise, and strategic management focused on competencies needed to cope with uncertainty, which they claimed was a more important yet rare process. Woudstra and Powell (1989) examined the use of value-chain analysis in analyzing work processes at a single-mode distance education institution. Finally, Woudstra and Murgatroyd (1992) proposed a design process for distance education organizational structures using concepts based on Handy's (1989) shamrock organization and scenario-planning techniques (Schwartz, 1991; Wack, 1985a, 1985b). The model featured a dedicated core of academic and professional staff, combined with a collaborative network of part-time and contracted academics, professionals, and related organizations.

Over the past decade, the model described in Woudstra and Murgatroyd (1992) was largely implemented in the Athabasca University School of Business. A distinct strategic business unit, the Centre for Innovative Management (CIM), was created in 1993 to offer a for-profit MBA program. Professors in the management studies area at the university had persuaded the CIM's founding director, Dr. Stephen Murgatroyd, that a new degree offered from a new organization could be succcessful given advances in information technology. A relatively small core of academic and professional staff would be responsible for developing and delivering an MBA, contracting to suppliers of services as required. Separate from the rest of Athabasca University, CIM was not hindered by legacy systems of administration or learning technology. The defining pedagogical feature of the Athabasca MBA has been its use of the students' workplace as a source of discussion, assignment, and case material. Students in the program have consistently rated highly the opportunity to use their workplace as a setting for projects and the ability to interact with students from other workplaces for online comment and discussion. The Athabasca University MBA program is a success story. It had over 1,000 registered students in the year 2000 and consistently ranks very high in student satisfaction surveys.

Meanwhile, the undergraduate business program, which remained on the main Athabasca University campus, extensively redesigned its operational model to serve more students more effectively, using financial resources that have increased more slowly than the enrollment rate. Using a Domino/Notes server platform parallel to the one used for the MBA, a call-center model serves some 6,000 students per year. A network of course assistants, academics, markers, and learning facilitators deals with student queries as a team (Adria and Woudstra, 2001).

TRANSACTIONS AND THE NETWORK ORGANIZATION

Thus far, we have considered two related components of the new world of distance education: the Internet, which makes possible innovative organizational structures, and the network distance education organization, which has evolved in some selected cases beyond the traditional consortium model. For faculty, staff, and managers of distance education organizations, there remains the underlying question of what it is about the organizational structure of a network that offers a competitive advantage.

The network organization may be considered as one of three generic models of economic organization (Williamson, 1994). The *market model* of economic organization seeks an exchange relationship with the external environment directly. Transactions in the market model are founded on price. Price provides the basis for establishing the preference of a buyer for a particular seller. The cost of economic transactions can be low as long as the information required to make a transaction is easy to obtain.

The *hierarchy model*, in contrast, is established to facilitate transactions that, if carried out in a market, would carry a higher cost. As Powell (1990) pointed out, "Transactions are moved out of markets into hierarchies as knowledge specific to the transaction (asset specificity) builds up" (p. 297). An organization that has implemented the hierarchy model allows the generic transaction of the market to take place in a more differentiated and specific context. As indicated at the beginning of this chapter, the Internet can reduce the cost of transactions by making richer, more complex, and move up-to-date information available to a larger group of people. It therefore reduces, though does not eliminate, the economic imperative for organizational boundaries. Organizations can become smaller and more focused on core activities while arranging for other organizations to perform peripheral, noncore tasks.

The *network model* is designed to establish transactions among organizational partners that form neither a market nor a hierarchy. Network models "entail more enduring and diffuse connections than markets but more reciprocal and egalitarian arrangements than hierarchies" (Scott, 1998, p. 276). Network transactions possess a different communication tone: "In markets the standard strategy is to drive the hardest possible bargain in the immediate exchange. In networks, the preferred option is use of creating indebtedness and reliance over the long haul" (p. 302). Table 36.1 shows the three models of economic organization, along with their salient characteristics.

The Internet can make the organization and by extension the network more transparent. More organizational members can see a truer picture of what the organization's management or leadership is doing. Individuals can access the network resources from any location at any time. In relation to both its members and its clients, the network organization must create the resources and knowledge repositories that will create and develop loyalty. It must add the extra value for its membership that will bind their loyalty.

The transactions carried out historically by distance education organizations have been accomplished through both the hierarchy and market models of organization. The interactions within the hierarchy of the distance education organization have mainly been for the purpose of achieving a division of labor different from that of the conventional university or school.

TABLE 36.1
Three Models of Economic Organization

Key Factors	Models		
	Market	*Hierarchy*	*Network*
Normative basis	Contract; property rights	Employment relationship	Complementary strengths
Means of communication	Prices	Routines	Relational
Mode of conflict resolution	Haggling; resort to courts for enforcement	Administrative fiat; supervision	Norm of reciprocity; reputational concerns
Degree of flexibility	High	Low	Medium
Amount of commitment among parties	Low	Medium to high	Medium to high
Tone or climate	Precision and/or suspicion	Formal/bureaucratic	Open-ended; mutual benefits
Actor preference or choices	Independent	Dependent	Interdependent

Note. From "Neither Market Nor Hierarchy: Network Forms of Organization," by W. W. Powell, 1990, in B. M. Staw and L. L. Cummings, *Research in Organizational Behavior* (p. 300), Greenwich, CT: JAI Press. Copyright 1990 by JAI Press Inc. Adapted with permission.

This new division of labor was necessary for obtaining resources, realizing development and production capabilities, negotiating contracts with academic staff, and so on.

Distance education organizations have been heavily dependent on a production model. This has meant a more direct recourse to hierarchical structures and ultimately more power for managers than would typically be the case in an educational organization. Rumble's (1986) corollary remains valid, but only partially, in relation to the experience of a decade and a half ago:

> Management [of distance education] . . . needs to ensure integrated decision making across a range of functionally distinct areas. This can be be achieved through joint decision making processes which involve both academics and operational and administrative staff. It is also most likely to be achieved by rational and possibly hierarchical approaches to management, rather than by approaches which tolerate collegiality, politicization and organised anarchy. This does not mean that these latter models are not found in distance education systems. They may be present, but the overall management of the institution must be both stronger and more rationally orientated than is necessarily the case in conventional educational institutions. (p. 181)

These imperatives are fading with the Internet's development as the communications platform and knowledge storehouse for all education organizations. Harrison's (1994) account of the network organization should ring true to many members of distance education organizations, with its description of "core" and "peripheral" jobs and functions:

> According to a central tenet of best-practice flexible production, managers first divide permanent ("core") from contingent ("peripheral") jobs. The size of the core is then cut to the bone—which, along with the minimization of inventory holding, is why "flexible" firms are often described as practicing "lean" production. These activities, and the employees who perform them, are then located as much as possible in different parts of the company or network, even in different geographical locations. . . . [T]he practice of lean production (the principle applies as much to the service sector as to manufacturing) involves the explicit reinforcement or creation *de novo* of sectors of low-wage, "contingent" workers, frequently housed with small business suppliers and subcontractors. (p. 11)

Network organizations in production industries may be considered to fall into four classes: craft industry organizations, industrial districts, strategic alliances, and vertically disaggregated organizations (Harrison, 1994). These classes are of varying relevance to distance education organizations because of the varying degree to which production principles are applied in these organizations. In *craft industries*, for example, such as the construction, publishing, and film and recording industries, projects are the primary mode of production. Each product is unique, and suppliers and subcontractors are in a relationship of personal trust with the contractor.

The *industrial district* is characteristic of German textile firms and the Emilian model of production in Italy. Companies choose to locate in an area because of the "existence of a dense, overlapping cluster of firms, skilled laborers and an institutional infrastructure" (Powell, 1990, p. 309). The districts may be led either by small firms or by a smaller number of large firms.

In a *strategic alliance*, all participants provide technological expertise, managerial expertise, and capital. The strategic alliance model underlies the new distance education. In production industries, strategic alliances have been the domain of big-ticket production companies such as airline manufacturers. Partners enter such alliances in order to respond to technological constraints (i.e., they desire to share the large costs of developing new technologies) and to financial demands (i.e., they desire to reduce the risks of entering new markets). Although strategic alliances are common within the distance education field, the actual sharing of resources has not been in evidence in the alliances established to date. For example, Fathom,

TABLE 36.2
Virtual Organizing: Three Vectors and Three Stages

Vectors and Characteristics	Stage 1	Stage 2	Stage 3
Virtual encounters	Remote experience of products and services. Textbook publishers are creating supplementary Web site links to connect students and professors throughout a course.	Dynamic customization. In place of standard textbooks, instructors now assemble textbooks that suit their styles and objectives. Textbook publishers move to create an organization that can deliver educational solutions for its customers.	Customer communities; user communities. Students and academic groups form and are incorporated and recognized as part of the value delivery system (e.g., Amazon's community of readers, Harley owners group).
Virtual sourcing	Sourcing modules. The Web is pushing the ability to source standard products, linking suppliers and customers and creating savings of 20% to 50%.	Process interdependence. Companies assign responsibilities for functions such as customer service and logistics across organizational boundaries to outside organizations.	Resource coalitions. Organizations become a portfolio of capabilities and relationships. One firm does not dominate all others in the virtual integration network. Each participant balances its leadership position relative to one set of resources, with secondary roles in complementary resources.
Knowledge leverage	Work unit expertise. An organization's ability to make processes effective is supported by groupware, intranets, and communications technology. Case reasoning tools, neural nets, and the Web allow capture and leveraging of knowledge on a global scale.	Corporate asset. Across work units knowledge collection, sharing, and creation are systematically managed. Virtual teamwork programs access expertise remotely to problem-solve in real time.	Professional community expertise.This community is well beyond a focal organization. It leverages the experience and knowledge of professionals, researchers, students, teachers, and practitioners in a comprehensive virtual electronic network.
Target locus	Task units.	Organization.	Interorganizational.

Note. From "Real Strategies for Virtual Organizing," by N. Venkatraman and J. C. Henderson, 1998, *Sloan Management Review, 40*(1), p. 34. Copyright 1998 by the Sloan Management Review Association. Adapted with permission.

the Global University Alliance, and the Canadian Virtual University, as discussed previously, currently market existing courses and programs for their member institutions.

Finally, *vertical disaggregation* has been used by large organizations to keep pace with shorter product life-cycles and rapid technological change. The U.S. automobile industry, for example, has used it as part of a process of "downsizing." Suppliers now compete to provide smaller components of the final product. Vertically disaggregated organizations may be expected to eventually develop in the distance education field, although, as noted above, the strategic alliance model has been the preferred choice to date. Vertical disaggregation is associated with a shortening of the life-cycle of products (including, perhaps, products such as courses and course-development and course-production methods) and with keeping up with rapid and continuous change in information and communications technologies. Traditional campus-based universities are network-based organizations in which a strong administrative structure has been used to create some order and predictability among academics, especially in terms of their patterns of work, and to recruit and organize students. Although academics have come to see the university as a secure "employer," employment security was not among its original goals. Rather, the university was intended to be a safe haven in which discussion and dissent could be freely undertaken and the advancement of knowledge could be pursued in an unhindered manner. Historically, academics have been much more entrepreneurial and more prepared to venture than they are now. That could again be the case if vertical disaggregation continues to occur in both traditional universities and distance education institutions.

The virtual network (which can have a mix of "clicks and bricks") is a type of vertically disaggregated network but may also evolve further to allow even more rapid and flexible adjustment in knowledge-based industries such as education. Virtual organizing, according to Venkatraman and Henderson (1998), can result in a living organization that is multi-organizational in scope and contains customer (student) communities, resource coalitions, and professional communities of practice. Sustained innovation and growth are made possible by virtual organizing. Table 36.2 analyzes virtual organizing across three vectors: virtual encounters, virtual sourcing, and knowledge leverage. It also depicts its progression through three stages of development. Meeting the challenges of moving toward stage 3 will require action in a number of key areas.

Distance education organizations have been more hierarchical than other educational organizations because of the production function. The differentiation of production processes that characterizes distance education organizations has resulted in a more highly differentiated division of labor. In this sense, distance education organizations have been developing the network form of organization both explicitly and implicitly for some time—explicitly through consortia and implicitly through the differentiation of production processes. These organizations must now bind their peripheral suppliers as well as their student groups more closely through the use of virtual organizing practices capable of creating loyalty. The increase in competition in the field of distance education, coupled with continued deployment of new technologies, will encourage a further development of the network model using virtual learning communities.

TOWARD THE STRATEGIC DEVELOPMENT OF THE NETWORK ORGANIZATION IN DISTANCE EDUCATION: COMMUNICATION IN VIRTUAL LEARNING COMMUNITIES

The critical components of networks are know-how, speed, and trust. By considering the economic basis for transactions and the means by which the costs of these transactions are reduced in the network form of organization, we have reviewed the means by which know-how and speed are given central importance in the network. The *economic* basis for network organizations has thus been described as a shift in the site for transactions. The *social* basis for network organizations is a shift in the way relationships between organizations are established and maintained. Personal ties and referrals by friends and associates are typical of network organizations. Communication systems and practices underlie these components. Referrals and ties emphasize the personal nature of a true network, because it is only a personal relationship, as opposed to a hierarchical relationship, that can lead to trust. Trust is the basis for not only network organizations but also online communities.

Handy (1989) and Kanter (1983, 1989, 2001) theorized about the shape of the emerging organization. Kanter, in particular, has studied the nature of innovation in large firms. There is also a growing literature on the virtual organization and its effective organization and management (Davenport & Pearlson, 1998; Drucker, 1985; Townsend, DeMarie & Hendrickson, 1998; Venkatraman & Henderson, 1998; Williams & Cothrel, 2000). Markus, Manville, and Agres (2000) have examined the factors that make a virtual organization successful. Using the open source movement as a base for study, they looked at a variety of open-source models and their methods for considering input, making decisions, and resolving disputes. They argue that virtual organizations tend to be successful when they are characterized by the following:

Mutually reinforcing motivations, with a share or "ownership" for individuals in collective success.

Self-governance, including membership management, rules, and institutions adaptable to individual needs.

The ability to monitor and sanction members' behavior.

Reputation as a motivator, along with control mechanisms and a shared culture.

Effective work structures and processes.

Effective technology for communication and coordination, with norms for its use.

This list of factors is echoed by McWilliam (2000) and Williams and Cothrel (2000). Williams and Cothrel studied four online communities, including About.com, a network of Web sites consolidated under one banner. About.com uses "guides" recruited initially by offering Web site creators a small fee to bring their site under the About.com banner. Guides receive a small share of advertising revenues. They are geographically dispersed and are not About.com employees. The "Community of Guides" is a forum that allows guides to interact with each other and with About.com staff. It is almost entirely virtual and includes e-mail, chats, and bulletin boards. There are training sessions, newsletters, and an ongoing stream of communication from About.com to the guides. Rookie guides are offered peer mentoring. All press releases are circulated to guides before they are distributed to the media. The community features a virtual lounge or water cooler where announcements are posted and where important resources such as contracts, promotional packages, stationery, and archived newsletters can be found. Guides help each other; About.com helps them to do that. Between 25% and 30% of the conversation on the bulletin boards consists of guides helping one another.

The potential for distance education organizations to learn from operations such as About.com seems obvious. *Harvard Business Review* provides an example of a well-developed concept for an online community. The review has created a discussion forum for its readers in which discussions can take place related to individual articles (see http://www.hbsp.harvard.edu/products/hbr/index/html). Authors are encouraged to provide a note to lead off the discussion. After that, people comment on and question the ideas presented in the article. Future research in the pedagogy of distance education should be devoted to developing concepts similar to this one. It is toward the ideal of a committed, decentralized, and dynamic community of scholars and students that the network distance education organization is progressing.

In the hierarchy form of economic organization, a species of trust is enforced by fiat. Information is provided on demand. However, the kind of information and knowledge that is characteristic of network organizations is available only in situations in which the identity of the two participants is a critical factor in making the exchange possible. Communication in the network organization is characterized by trust. Uzzi's (1996) study of network organizations in the New York garment district revealed that trust was not considered by CEOs as a nebulous or unimportant characteristic. Instead, they mentioned it frequently. Referring to other partners, one CEO said, for example, "They're part of the family" (p. 677). Trust in the network is the condition under which partners are willing to exchange *valuable* information and knowledge. Communication in networks shifts, as Powell has observed, from a market emphasis on prices and the hierarchical concern with routines to a focus on relational communication:

> Within hierarchies, communication and exchange is shaped by concerns with career mobility—in this sense, exchange is bound up with consideration of personal advancement. At the same time, intra-organizational communication takes place among parties who generally know one another, have a history of previous interactions, and possess a good deal of firm-specific knowledge; thus there is considerable interdependence among the parties. In a market context, it is clear to everyone concerned when a debt has been discharged, but such matters are not nearly as obvious in networks or hierarchies. (p. 302)

Urban, Sultan, and Qualls (2000) noted that, for the Internet organization, "Trust is built in a three-stage cumulative process that establishes (1) trust in the Internet and the specific Web site, (2) trust in the information displayed and (3) trust in the delivery fulfillment and service" (p. 40). In order to develop trust, individuals must provide information in an unbiased and complete manner, promises must be kept, and help, either in the form of software agents or human resources, must be accessible easily and with no or little delay. Privacy must be assured, and operations should be as transparent to the user as possible. Again, creation of communities of users can be very helpful in building trust. We have noted how effective communities have been for About.com. Communities of customers have been surprisingly valuable to companies such as Harley Davidson. The Harley Owners Group (HOG) is housed at the Harley Davidson Web site and has been a valuable link for the company. For established organizations with brand recognition, transferring brand equity to the new medium can be an effective means of maintaining and building market share.

Trust of the type considered here is different from the variety discussed in the literature on hierarchical organizations (Graen & Uhl-Bien, 1995). Hierarchical organizations establish trust relationships vertically within the organization, whereas the network organization must establish such relationships horizontally. Horizontal relationships across organizations are much more difficult to establish than vertical relationships within the organization. Shared goals and organizational culture, along with financial incentives, encourage trust within the organization. In a network, a relationship of trust must be established progressively, using personal references and contacts, and it must be maintained through processes that encourage formal and informal communication at all levels of the organization.

PRACTICAL AND THEORETICAL IMPLICATIONS
OF THE NEW DISTANCE EDUCATION

We turn finally to the likely challenges faced by practitioners in and theorists of the emerging network distance education organization. The uncertain environment and rapid technological change are creating a new interest in planning and strategy models, as evidenced in recent literature. From general articles on theories of change (Beer & Nohria, 2000) through a survey on models of strategy formation (Mintzberg & Lampel, 1999) to specific prescriptions for strategy formation (Abell,1999; Beinhocker, 1999; Pascale, 1999), recognition of increasing uncertainty and the need to cope with it flows through the management literature. Drucker (1985) noted that resistance to change or entrepreneurial innovation is especially strong in service organizations such as government agencies, labor unions, churches, hospitals, schools, and universities. In the most successful strategic changes, strategy follows structure (Chandler, 1962), but in practice there is most often an existing organizational structure that must adjust to change (Abell, 1999). In these cases, structure will often limit the implementation of a new strategy, causing the implementation to be suboptimal or to fail. The managers of existing organizations wishing to engage in e-education face strong barriers. The tendency of their organizations will be to limit strategic redirection in order to minimize structural change.

The task for managers and advocates of virtual distance education is to devise organizational and management processes that will encourage change and allow it to be measured (Garvin, 1998). Woudstra and Powell (1989) examined the workflow processes in a uni-modal distance education university through the value-chain model. Woudstra and Murgatroyd (1992) postulated factors required to initiate change toward a new organizational format. The "balanced scorecard" (Kaplan & Norton, 1992; 1996) provides an excellent framework for assessing performance and implementing strategies applicable to the education industry (O'Neil, Bensimon, Diamond, & Moore, 1999). Abell (1999) advocated dual-strategy paths for today and tomorrow. Beinhocker (1999) suggested the nurturing of multiple strategies and maintaining options until it becomes clearer which will be successful. Beinhocker used Microsoft as an example, noting that in 1988 Microsoft had initiatives in four operating systems. It eventually focused on Windows, which became the predominant personal computer operating system. However, in 1988 it was far from certain which operating system architecture would prevail, and Bill Gates kept Microsoft's options open.

An organization must be prepared to make a substantial commitment of resources and time if it is serious about learning enough about its portfolio to make future choices. Without commitment, there can be little learning and little development of trust between the organization and internal or external community partners. The organization must also take steps to communicate details of its projects and their success and failure to its members so that they become receptive to innovative change. An existing university—dual mode, single-mode distance, or single-mode traditional—will be best served by developing a portfolio of projects in virtual e-education. Some of these projects might be internal and others might be external. At Athabasca University, a small institution, there are at a minimum three departments with initiatives in online Web-enhanced course delivery. The university has joined two university consortia in distance education, and the Canadian Virtual University is headquartered on its campus. It has numerous one-on-one collaborations domestically and internationally. There will come a point, however, when Athabasca University, like Bill Gates, will have to make some hard decisions about which initiatives to continue.

Beinhocker (1999) and Pascale (1999) both noted that the key to success in an uncertain environment is to be adaptive by diversifying strategic options and creating adaptive systems. Pascale (1999) and De Geus (1997) supported a view of the organization as a living system that, if allowed, will adapt to survive and prosper through experimentation, learning, and seizing the momentum of success. This concept of the living organization is compatible with Ghoshal, Bartlett, and Moran's (1999) new management model, in which facilitating cooperation among people has precedence over enforcing compliance and initiative is valued more than obedience.

Meeting the current challenges of distance education requires new patterns of communication between distance educators and their students. We would point to the following strategies as potentially helpful for distance educators who are considering organizing or reorganizing their operations with the intention of creating a network organization, virtual organization, or virtual community.

First, complementary strengths must be identified and developed cooperatively by partners. Examples of strengths that may be brought to a network by a partner include the disciplinary-specific intellectual capital held by faculty and coded in learning materials, know-how that is specific to the tier, and structural capabilities, such as the capacity to produce course materials or deliver courses continuously. Some distance education organizations have libraries. Others rely on students to use the libraries in their place of residence. Those who have developed libraries have a significant asset that should be identified as a strength. Those who have developed a significant body of courseware should also identify this as a strength. An open-handed, gain-sharing process must be used to create incentives for contributors to participate. Publishing companies (e.g., Thomson Learning) that are moving further into the curriculum process understand this. However, the entire network will have to adopt gain-sharing in some form as participants become more aware of their ability to generate returns from their intellectual capital.

Second, communication methods and practices should be assessed and, if appropriate, changed. Distance education operations that seek exchanges with one another must identify channels of communication that are available most of the time and communication processes that emphasize the relational nature of the network. Because distance education organizations have expertise in establishing communication pathways for their students, they should be able to establish similar pathways for communicating with their partners. Virtual communities use a variety of means, including e-mail, discussion forums, conferences, newsletters, knowledge storehouses, calendars, and shared network storage. The transfer of "fine-grained information" makes the network valuable to the partners. Fine-grained information encompasses both tacit and proprietary knowledge. Tacit knowledge is "know-how" that is generally not codified, that is, published or even expressed verbally (Abrahamson & Fairchild, 1999; Crossan, Lane, & White, 1999; Hirschorn, 1998; Pfeffer & Sutton, 1999). Tacit knowledge must be tapped and members must have a reason to provide it. It is not clear if information systems can codify tacit knowledge, but some organizations are trying to codify it (e.g., fathom.com). A member will contribute or exchange proprietary information if there is seen to be a net benefit from the exchange: "Social relations make information credible and interpretable, imbuing it with qualities and value beyond what is at hand" (Uzzi, 1996, p. 678).

Third, processes of conflict resolution must be given continuing attention. The network organization relies on what Powell (1990) calls "norms of reciprocity." Rather than seeking redress for damages suffered, the network organization attempts to (a) minimize and manage damages and (b) "trade" damages. Minimizing and managing damages involves communication to ensure that the resources of the network are deployed to reduce the scope and extent of damages where they occur and to avoid them in future. Trading damages means recognizing that the network bestows advantages and that these should be set against the disadvantages of membership.

In a well-functioning virtual community, the members participate in making and changing the rules, and the rules they adopt fit their unique needs. They need a set of procedures for discussing and voting on important issues (Markus et al., 2000). In a distance education network, these groups need to be respected throughout the organization's levels. Rules should not be hierarchically imposed. Joint problem-solving arrangements are required to ensure not only that damages do not spread but also that trust and the continuous exchange of information are maintained: "[F]irms that are linked through embedded ties work through problems and get direct feedback—increasing learning and the discovery of new combinations" (Uzzi, 1996, p. 679). Joint problem-solving must be initiated "just in time," overcoming the barriers of geography and organizational hierarchies. Virtual teams are emerging as a method of creating task forces "on the fly" (Boudreau, Loch, Robey, & Straub, 1998; Townsend et al., 1998). These may be used across organizations to ensure that problem solving, damage control, and trust are preserved.

Fourth, flexibility, commitment, an open-ended climate, and interdependence should become common values. Flexibility should be emphasized. However, managers and academics in network distance education organizations should accept that they will have less flexibility in making decisions in relationship to the market. This is because decisions of this kind will now be coordinated with partners and student-customers and freelance or volunteer contributors. Network members or participants should be aware of the need to contribute to the partnership. The degree of commitment is higher than it is outside of the network. A long-term perspective should be adopted toward benefits of membership in the network, along with a flexible approach to operations in the short term. Decisions in the network will have implications for other members. Unilateral actions will not only create the risk of damage to another partner but will likely decrease the level of trust among partners.

Fifth, leadership and governance policies must create a system of checks and balances to distribute power throughout the network. A good example is the U.S. Constitution, with its division of power among the legislative, executive, and judicial branches. Checks and balances keep one branch from overtaking the others. De Geus (1997) advocates creating decision-making impediments that make it difficult to move decisions upward in the organization. If it is obvious that decisions must be made at the appropriate level and attempts to move the decision upward will hurt the organizational member's future in the organization, agreements to make a decision will be more forthcoming.

Sixth, entrepreneurial initiative and innovation should be natural and expected in the network organization. Learning by accommodation (De Geus, 1997), or making internal changes to fit a changing world, is critical to sustaining a healthy, thriving organization. Allowing and encouraging diversity helps accommodation. Use of techniques such as scenario planning helps the organization view possible futures and allows an assessment of their probabilities and the actions necessary to accommodate them.

Seventh, the network organization must systematically evaluate its progress and measure effectiveness. The balanced scorecard is winning wide acceptance in both production and service organizations as an effective framework for capturing the key factors of an organization's success. O'Neil et al. (1999) discussed the adaptation of the balanced scorecard in a major U.S. university.

Researchers considering the likely trajectory of the network organization in distance education should hold an explicit set of assumptions about the conditions under which the network is a preferred model of organizing. Powell (1990) stated that the establishment of a network organization is a response to a situation in which the following is true:

> Sustained cooperation is needed.
> Incentives are required for learning and circulation of information, leading to the quick translation of ideas into action.
> Resources are variable and environments uncertain.
> Means are needed to utilize and enhance intangible assets such as tacit knowledge and technological innovation. (p. 322)

These conditions of existence raise questions about how and why the network organization will continue to be the dominant mode of organizing in the field of distance education. We conclude with some further questions for research.

FUTURE RESEARCH

The trajectory of the network organization is toward "concentration without centralization" (Harrison, 1994). That is, power remains within the largest institutions, while the development of new technologies occurs in smaller organizations, and the risk of entering new markets is shared. Yet most alliances that have developed in distance education have involved partners in the same "tier"—that is, similar in prestige, size, and technological capability. For example, the Canadian Virtual University seeks to create a network of *like* distance education organizations. These organizations are also exclusively Canadian institutions, although we would argue that geographical or national location will increasingly become irrelevant within a given network tier. The core-ring model, in which a dominant organization seeks to establish a disaggregated relationship with organizations that will compete with one another as suppliers, has not yet been realized, although the Open University, as noted earlier, may be seeking such a structure. A question that researchers should therefore consider as these alliances develop is whether a true alliance of equal partners is likely to emerge or whether, as Harrison (1994) suggests is the more common case, a core-ring structure will be formed.

Studies in organization theory and political economy have often considered networks in production industries. The question of how such networks emerge in service industries has been given less attention. Distance education network organizations may be characterized as hybrids of production and service. Even in the age of online learning, the production of course materials retains aspects of the industrial mode of book publishing. Indeed, printed materials remain at the center of most online courses and programs. However, as online, Web-enabled course development and delivery gains acceptability, we will see publishing companies moving further into the curriculum creation and delivery process (see the discussion of Universitas 21 and Thomson Learning at the beginning of this chapter). Printed materials will be accessed electronically rather than in hard-copy form. A distance education organization's services are provided to students, of course, but also to internal organizational groups. Which aspects of a network form of organization are most appropriately applied to the production activities of the distance education organization and which are best used in relationship to service activities? To what extent will the organization outsource the curriculum development process to publishing companies or similar groups?

Network organizations are not a new phenomenon in distance education or in the educational field generally. Educational organizations have traditionally combined their resources and shared knowledge. However, the distance education field has been characterized by more competition than has been the case in other types of education. So, what is really different about the network organization? What boundaries have shifted? What boundaries remain the same? How will virtual organizing affect the nature of the network? Will the distinctions blur between competition and cooperation among network participants?

Distance education organizations have conventionally considered their proprietary knowledge (knowledge that they, wholly own) and their tacit knowledge (implicit in their practices) to be worth protecting at almost any cost. In the network organization, "new connections and new meanings are generated, debated, and evaluated" (Powell, 1990, p. 325). Ongoing personal relationships of trust are required to establish and maintain a web of relational connections whose purpose is the sharing of strategic and operational information and knowledge. In the new distance education, knowledge will become embedded within a virtual network of organizations, individuals, information-sharing forums, and virtual knowledge storehouses.

REFERENCES

Abell, D. F. (1999). Competing today while preparing for tomorrow. *Sloan Management Review, 40*(3), 73–81.

Abrahamson, E., & Fairchild, G. (1999). Management fashion: Lifecycles, triggers, and collective learning processes. *Administrative Science Quarterly, 44*, 708–740.

Adria, M., & Woudstra, A. (2001). Who's on the line? Managing student interactions in distance learning using a one-window approach. *Open Learning, 16*(3), 249–261.

Bates, A. W. (1997). The impact of technological change on open and distance learning. *Distance Education, 18*(1), 93–109.

Beer, M., & Nohria, N. (2000, May-June). Cracking the code of change. *Harvard Business Review*, 133–141.

Beinhocker, E. D. (1999). Robust adaptive strategies. *Sloan Management Review, 40*(3), 95–106.

Boudreau, M. C., Loch, K. D., Robey, D., & Straub, D. (1998). Going global: Using Information technology to advance the competitiveness of the virtual transnational organization. *Academy of Management Executive, 12*(4), 120–28.

Chandler, A. (1962). *Strategy and structure: Chapters in the history of the industrial enterprise.* Cambridge, MA: M.I.T. Press.

Christensen, C. M., & Overdorf, M. (2000, March-April). Meeting the challenge of disruptive change. *Harvard Business Review,* 66–76.

Cohen, D. (2000, July 14). Hong Kong's boom in distance education may be a sign of what's to come in Asia. *Chronicle of Higher Education,* p. 50.

Crossan, M., Lane, H., & White, R. (1999). An organizational learning framework: From intuition to institution. *Academy of Management Review, 24,* 522–537.

Davenport, T. H., & Pearlson, K. (1998). Two cheers for the virtual office. *Sloan Business Review, 39*(4), 51–65.

Dede, C. (1996). The evolution of distance education: Emerging technologies and distributed learning. *American Journal of Distance Education, 10*(2), 4–36.

De Geus, A. (1997). *The living company.* Boston: Harvard Business School Press.

Drucker, P. F. (1973). *Management: Tasks, responsibilities, practices.* New York: Harper & Row.

Drucker, P. F. (1985). *Innovation and entrepreneurship: Practice and principles.* New York: Harper & Row.

Dunning, B. (1990). The literature of management. In Moore, M. G. (ed.), *Contemporary issues in American distance education.* New York: Pergamon Press. pp. 30–41.

Garvin, D. A. (1998). The processes of organization and management. *Sloan Management Review, 39*(4), 33–50.

Ghoshal, S., Bartlett, C. A., & Moran, P. (1999). A new manifesto for management. *Sloan Management Review, 40*(3), 9–20.

Graen, G. B., & Uhl-Bien, M. (1995). Relationship-based approach to leadership: Development of leader-member exchange (LMX) theory of leadership over 25 years: Applying a multi-level multi-domain perspective. *Leadership Quarterly, 6*(2), 219–247.

Harrison, B. (1994). *Lean and mean: The changing landscape of corporate power in the age of flexibility.* New York: Basic Books.

Handy, C. T. (1989). *The age of unreason.* London: Arrow Books.

Holt, D. M., & Thompson, D. J. (1995). Responding to the technological imperative: The experience of an open and distance institution. *Distance Education, 16*(1), 43–64.

Holt, D. M., & Thompson, D. J. (1998). Managing information technology in open and distance higher education. *Distance Education, 19*(2), 197–227.

Hirschorn, L. (1998). *The workplace within.* Cambridge, MA: M.I.T. Press.

Kanter, R. (1983). *The change masters: Innovation and entrepreneurship in the American corporation.* New York: Simon & Schuster.

Kanter, R. (1989). *When giants learn to dance: Mastering the challenge of strategy, management, and careers in the 1990s.* New York: Simon & Schuster.

Kanter, R. (2001). *Evolve! Succeeding in the digital culture of tomorrow.* Boston: Harvard Business School Press.

Kaplan, R., & Norton, D. (1992, January-February). The balanced scorecard: Measures that drive performance. *Harvard Business Review,* 71–79.

Kaplan, R. (1996). *The balanced scorecard: Translating strategy into action.* Boston: Harvard Business School Press.

Kling, R. (2000). Learning about information technologies and social change: The contribution of social informatics. *The Information Society, 16,* 217–232.

Klonoski, E. (2000, May). *$2 million goes to Connecticut online learning* (Connecticut Distance Learning Network press release).

Markus, M. L., Manville, B., & Agres, C. E. (2000). What makes a virtual organization work? *Sloan Management Review, 42*(1), 13–26.

McWilliam, G. (2000). Building stronger brand through online communities. *Sloan Management Review, 41*(3), 43–54.

Mintzberg, H. & Lampel, J. (1999). Reflecting on the strategy process. *Sloan Management Review, 40*(3), 21–30.

Murgatroyd, S., & Woudstra, A. (1989). Issues in the management of distance education. *American Journal of Distance Education, 3*(1), 4–19.

O'Neil, H., Bensimon, E., Diamond, M., & Moore, M. (1999). Designing and implementing an academic scorecard. *Change: The Magazine of Higher Learning, 31*(6), 32–40.

Overland, M. A. (2000, July 14). India uses distance education to meet huge demand for degrees. *Chronicle of Higher Education,* pp. 48–49.

Pascale, R. T. (1999). Surfing the edge of chaos. *Sloan Management Review, 40*(3), 83–94.

Pfeffer, J., & Sutton, R. (1999). Knowing "what" to do is not enough: Turning knowledge into action. *California Management Review, 42*(1), 83–108.

Powell, W. W. (1990). Neither market nor hierarchy: Network forms of organization. In B. M. Staw & L. L. Cummings (Eds.), *Research in organizational behavior* (pp. 295–336). Greenwich, CT: JAI Press.

Rumble, G. (1981). Economic and cost structures. In A. Kaye & G. Rumble (Eds.), *Distance teaching for higher and adult education.* (pp. 220–234). London: Croom Helm.

Rumble, G. (1986). *The planning and management of distance education.* London: Croom Helm.

Schwartz, P. (1991). *The art of the long view.* New York: Double Currency.

Scott, W. R. (1998). *Organizations: Rational, natural, and open systems* (4th ed.). Upper Saddle River, NJ: Prentice-Hall.

Shecter, B. (2000, November 23). U of T pulls back from Thomson link. *Financial Post,* p. C4.

Survey of e-management. (2000, November 11–17). *Economist.*

Thomson Learning partners with Universitas 21 to develop global e-university (Press release). (2000, November 20). Available: http://www.thomsonlearning.com/press/

Townsend, A. M., DeMarie, S. M., & Hendrickson, A. P. (1998). Virtual teams: Technology and workplace of the future. *Academy of Management Executive, 12*(3), 17–29.

Urban, G. L., Sultan, F., & Qualls, W. J. (2000). Placing trust at the center of your Internet strategy. *Sloan Management Review, 42*(1), 39–48.

Uzzi, B. (1996). The sources and consequences of embeddedness for the economic performance of organizations: The network effect. *American Sociological Review, 61,* 674–698.

Venkatraman, N., & Henderson, J. C. (1998). Real strategies for virtual organizing. *Sloan Management Review, 40*(1), 33–48.

Wack, P. (1985a, September-October). Scenarios: Uncharted waters ahead. *Harvard Business Review,* 72–89.

Wack, P. (1985b, November-December). Scenarios: Shooting the rapids. *Harvard Business Review*, 139–150.

Williams, R. L., & Cothrel, J. (2000). Four smart ways to run online communities. *Sloan Management Review, 41*(4), 81–91.

Woudstra, A., & Powell, R. (1989). Value chain analysis: A framework for management of distance education. *American Journal of Distance Education, 3*(3), 7–21.

Woudstra, A., & Murgatroyd, S. (1992). *Responding to change: Designing a flexible learning organization for distance education* (ACSDE Research Monograph No. 4). University Park, Pennsylvania: American Center for the Study of Distance Education, College of Education, The Pennsylvania State University.

Williamson, O. E. (1994). Transaction cost economics and organization theory. In N. J. Smelser & R. Swedberg (Eds.), *The handbook of economic sociology* (pp. 77–107). Princeton, NJ: Princeton University Press; Russell Sage Foundation.

Womack, J., & Jones, D. (1996). *Lean thinking: Banish waste and create wealth in your corporation.* New York: Simon & Schuster.

37

Dynamics of Faculty Participation in Distance Education: Motivations, Incentives, and Rewards

Linda L. Wolcott
Utah State University
linda.wolcott@usu.edu

THE INSTITUTIONAL CONTEXT

Faculty Roles and Expectations

The current growth in distance and online learning occurs at a time when higher education has already been engaged in examining the work of faculty. Over the past decade, there has been widespread discussion about reforming the tenure system and better defining what constitutes scholarship. Together, these forces are reshaping the role and expectations of faculty in higher education.

Statistics continue to show a rise in the number of distance and online courses and increasing use of technology in instruction. For example, the Campus Computing Survey (Green, 2000a) found that "more college courses are using more technology resources" (par. 7) and data "continue to show gains in the use of technology in the classroom and the role of technology to support instruction and learning" (par. 8). With an increase of 46.5% from the previous year in the number of institutions offering one or more college courses online, it is easy to conclude that faculty are increasingly involved in developing, teaching, and managing online courses.

Indeed, teaching at a distance, particularly online, is fast becoming a role expectation, especially for prospective and new faculty. There is mounting pressure from administrators to jump on the online bandwagon and to preserve a niche from edubusiness competitors. Pressure also comes from students who expect faculty to make Web-based materials available. Such expectations have added another dimension to the description of faculty roles. Burbules and Callister (2000) paint an apt picture:

> The image of the solitary teacher/scholar, recruiting a few students to come to campus to study as apprentices, teaching a few large-section courses to keep the credit-hour averages up, and going home at night to work on that Major Book, is fading from the scene; individuals may aspire to this

549

life, and a few may be fortunate enough to attain it—but it can no longer be the sole professional role that new academics prepare themselves for. (p. 282)

In their new professorial role, faculty will likely "spend less time 'professing' and more time on educational process matters" (Massy, 1998, p. 15), work more collaboratively with teaching peers and professional staff, and function increasingly as a mentor and facilitator focusing on student learning and assessment (Plater, 1995). To this, we can add the emerging role of faculty members as entrepreneurs, marketing their intellectual property online and beyond their institution in a marketplace perceived to have no bounds.

The shift in emphasis brings with it concomitant changes in the nature of faculty work. The use of technologies alone has implications for pedagogy as well as for workload. The Web, with its graphical and asynchronous features, for example, changes both the form of presentation and the dynamics of instructional communication with and among the students. Distance teaching involves faculty in new modes of producing and delivering instruction that often result in a public record of their pedagogy. Digital technologies introduce new formats for the production, publication, and dissemination of faculty scholarship—and time becomes an even greater premium.

The new and added dimensions of faculty work bring us back to the debates about tenure and the nature of scholarship. Accommodating faculty time and effort associated with distance teaching, the creation of online instructional materials, and digital scholarship challenges the existing system for acknowledging and rewarding faculty for their teaching, research, and service.

Reward Systems

During the 1990s there was considerable discussion about the institutional reward system in higher education. Boyer (1990), for example, was a herald in raising concerns about the nature of scholarship and the changing role of the professoriate. Others (e.g., Diamond, 1993; Edgerton, 1993; Fairweather, 1993; Mingle, 1993; "Work of Faculty," 1994) examined the existing reward structure, including institutional values, faculty expectations, workload, and tenure practices. They were especially critical of a reward system that relied on extrinsic rewards (Lonsdale, 1993) and traditionally rewarded research while undervaluing the efforts that faculty put into teaching. Reformers urged a realignment of institutional priorities and values, recognition for the scholarship of teaching, and more flexible promotion criteria.

Institutions have been slow to change well-entrenched practices. However, the impact of information technologies on teaching and learning has added a new urgency to the debate. Green's (2000b) Campus Computing Survey identified faculty rewards and recognition among persistent problem areas. Although few institutions have had policies that address alternate forms of scholarship or reflect the dimensions of faculty roles associated with distance education (U.S. Department of Education, 1997), discourse on policy issues is increasing. A case in point is the recent activity on campuses centering on the issue of intellectual property rights and the development of related policies. (For an in-depth discussion of intellectual property and copyright, see Chapter 33.)

The lack of inclusive policies has caused particular difficulties for distance education faculty. It is widely accepted that developing and teaching distance education courses takes a considerable investment in time and energy (some say more than conventionally taught courses). Further, activities associated with distance teaching represent an alternate form of scholarship that is not yet well recognized nor credited. Should faculty members who have the desire and enthusiasm for teaching with technology put the time and effort into distance education when it does not earn them credit toward tenure and/or advancement in rank? Already disadvantaged in terms of institutional rewards for teaching, faculty stand to be disproportionately unrewarded for their involvement in distance education.

Indeed, in a climate of institutional self-examination, it is appropriate that many are beginning to ask questions about incentives and rewards for faculty participation in technological innovations. Why do faculty participate in distance education? What motivates or hinders them? What are institutions doing to encourage and acknowledge involvement? These are not insignificant questions. In their report on technology in higher education, the Academy for Educational Development foresaw the importance of a supportive rewards structure for both the faculty and the institution:

> A change in the reward system for faculty is critical. Most faculty now take on using technology as an extra task. Even if technology applications are part of an institution's program, most promotion and tenure systems make no provision for rewarding a professor who experiments with or uses technology to reach students either on or off campus. Faculty members need performance-based merit increases and promotions that include recognition of activities in using technology as well as in publishing.... Until these alternate methods of delivering instruction are accepted as integral parts of the academic process and faculty are rewarded accordingly, little expansion in the use of technology on campuses will occur. (McNeil, 1990, pp. 4–5)

Throughout the past decade, we have been reminded that the success of distance education lies with faculty who are both motivated to invest in innovative practices and adequately rewarded for doing so (Beaudoin, 1990; Dillon & Walsh, 1992; Olcott & Wright, 1995; Wolcott, 1997). Today, similar sentiments resound with renewed urgency as C. Peter Magrath, president of the National Association of State Universities and Land-Grant Colleges, recently admonished: "In the 21st century, public service and outreach must become a central obligation of the university, and the culture and the rewards system must reflect this—not in rhetoric, but in reality" (as cited in Hardi, 2000 par. 3).

Ultimately, the issue is one of cultural change, and it is with the preceding discourse as background that this chapter examines research on the culture of the institutional reward system with respect to distance education. The purpose of the chapter is to provide a state-of-the-art review of research on faculty participation in distance education and associated incentives and rewards.

REVIEW OF RESEARCH

As a nascent field of inquiry, distance education is without a broad theory base of its own (McIsaac & Gunawardena, 1996; Moore & Kearsley, 1996). Faculty development issues such as participation, recruitment, and retention are areas in which theory is lacking. Several works, however, are notable for advancing our understanding of motivation as well as the institutional context within which it is set. Works by Dillon and Walsh (1992) and Olcott and Wright (1995) have set the stage for studying faculty motivation and participation in distance education.

Dillon and Walsh's literature review stands as a seminal work concerning research about faculty issues in distance education. Their review of 24 studies included findings relating to barriers to participation, faculty motivation, and institutional incentives. They concluded that institutions lack commitment to and support for distance education, intrinsic factors motivate faculty to teach at a distance, and faculty perceive that distance teaching is not rewarded. Overall, they faulted the literature for its lack of quantity and quality and for failing "to view faculty development within the framework of a system which supports both professional development (i.e., faculty development) and the organizational development (i.e., improving the institutional environment for teaching and decision making)" (p. 18). Despite its shortcomings, the research they cited has laid the foundation for further inquiry.

Olcott and Wright (1995) took up the challenge issued by Dillon and Walsh and proposed the missing framework, noting further that "[faculty] resistance [to participation in distance education] has been due, in large part, to the lack of an institutional support framework to train, compensate, and reward distance teaching faculty commensurate with those in traditional instructional roles" (p. 5). They conceptualized faculty involvement in distance education from an institutional perspective and offered an "expanded view" of participation that places faculty at the center. Designed to increase participation, the framework emphasizes a central leadership role for faculty and underscores the critical support and advocacy role of administrators. The four concentric rings that surround the faculty at the core of their model depict the infrastructure required for developing a supportive institutional environment. Incentives, financial support, rewards, resources, policies, and institutional commitment are factors that figure prominently in the support framework. Together with the work of Dillon and Walsh, Olcott and Wright's conceptualization is frequently referenced in studies that examined barriers to and incentives for faculty participation in distance education.

Research in the area of distance education draws from and builds upon theory from related disciplines. In relation to faculty participation, several frameworks have been helpful for examining faculty motivation and participation. The work of Rogers (1995) has been particularly influential. His theory about the adoption and diffusion of innovations helps to explain how the characteristics of an innovation shape faculty decisions to adopt it and the rate at which it is adopted. He delineated five innovation attributes to predict adoption: relative advantage, compatibility, complexity, trialability, and observability. Based on these characteristics, chances of adoption are increased when the innovation is perceived to be better than the idea or practice that preceded it; it is consistent with the adopter's needs, experiences, and values; it is easy to understand or use; it can be tried or experienced on a limited basis; and results can be seen.

Although Lonsdale (1993) noted that there is no definitive model that explains motivation of academic staff, theories of work motivation provide the background for beginning to understand factors that contribute to faculty participation. In this highly dynamic and evolving field, there are numerous theories that attempt to explain motivation in the workplace. Landy (1989) identified five broad classes: need, instrumentality, comparison, goal-setting, and reinforcement theories. Instrumentality theories have been useful in explaining motivation and the interrelationships among effort, performance, and satisfaction. Landy describes the logic underlying these theories: "We usually decide to engage in the activity if it will provide us with something of value. In that sense, the activity is *instrumental* in achieving some valued outcome" (p. 379).

The study of incentives and rewards in the work environment has its roots in expectancy theory (Vroom, 1964) and equity theory (Adams, 1964). Expectancy theory (also referred to as expectancy/valence theory and valence, instrumentality, and expectancy theory) posits that an individual considers the probability that his or her effort will lead to a particular outcome (expectancy); that the outcome has value; and that, once attained, the outcome will lead to other desired and valued outcomes (instrumentality). The expectancy measured against the value placed on the outcomes (valence) determines the individual's motivation to perform. In other words, effort leads to performance, performance leads to outcomes, and valued outcomes lead to satisfaction.

Equity theory assumes that an individual assesses the value of an outcome (e.g., a promotion, merit pay, or other form of recognition) against the value of what he or she has put into the activity (e.g., expertise and time). The resulting ratio of inputs to outcomes is compared with the perceived ratio of similar efforts and outcomes of others to assess the equity of the situation.

Neumann and Finaly-Neumann (1990) describe the theory at work in an academic setting:

> Faculty members enter work situations and make various investments in as well as contributions to the university. The university is expected by faculty members to provide a supportive environment that facilitates the realization of these investments (skills, abilities, and needs) and a work compensation system that is equitable in rewarding these contributions. To the extent that the university is perceived to provide a supportive environment and an equitable reward system, faculty commitment is likely to increase and vice versa. (pp. 77–78)

Two of a growing number of theories and models of work motivation, expectancy theory and equity theory illustrate the complex interplay among the variables that lead to effort, performance, and satisfaction. Understanding the dynamics of motivation and the interrelationships among incentives and rewards in the context of distance education is central to providing a supportive institutional environment. Some researchers have begun to draw from this wealth of insight to guide their inquiry into faculty participation.

This review builds on the foundation laid by Dillon and Walsh's review of faculty issues and examines pertinent works published or presented since 1992. To identify recent research for inclusion, online searches were conducted of the ERIC database, *Education Abstracts, Dissertation Abstracts International*, and *ProQuest Digital Dissertations* in addition to online journals such as the *Online Journal of Distance Learning Administration*, and the *Journal of Asynchronously Learning Networks*, and online databases including Distance Education Online Symposium.

For inclusion in the review, literature had to meet the following criteria:

- The work was empirical. That is, it was based on the collection of data and reported the results of qualitative or quantitative data analysis.
- The work addressed higher education in the United States and involved faculty members who taught courses in distance education programs that used electronic technologies such as interactive television, audio- and/or videoconferencing, or online/Web-based delivery.
- The work focused on higher education faculty and their reasons for participating or not participating in distance education, factors that encouraged or deterred participation, or institutional rewards and returns for participation.

Twenty-three studies that met the above criteria were located and are addressed in this review. These works reviewed include seven published articles, nine dissertations, and seven conference papers. The review examines and synthesizes research aimed at answering the following questions about higher education faculty and their involvement in distance education: Why do faculty get involved? What enables them to participate (or hinders them)? What encourages or discourages them? What do they get out of it?

Barriers to Participation

Since the Dillon and Walsh (1992) review, Olcott and Wright (1995) looked further at barriers to participation, referring to them as "institutionally embedded disincentives" (p. 8). In fact, the literature has continued to identify barriers to faculty participation in distance education. Clark (1993) categorized such barriers as "administrative, technical, economic, and student support obstacles to distance teaching" (p. 30). For this review, barriers are defined as and limited to (a) factors found in the environment or institutional context and (b) attitudes and perceptions held by individual faculty that deter them from teaching courses by distance.

Environmental and contextual barriers are those associated with the institutional setting; they are policies and practices typically outside the control of the individual. Contextual barriers commonly involve the inadequacy or absence of some aspect of institutional support. They include lack of incentives (Bolduc, 1993; Halfhill, 1998; Jackson, 1994; Ndahi, 1999), lack of rewards (Jackson, 1994; Montgomery, 1999; Ndahi, 1999), lack of administrative or technical support (Bebko, 1998; Betts, 1998; Halfhill, 1998; Montgomery, 1999; Ndahi, 1999; Rockwell et al., 1999; Schifter, 2000b; Wolcott & Haderlie, 1995), lack of adequate information (Montgomery, 1999; Ndahi, 1999); lack of training (Ndahi, 1999; Schifter, 2000b), lack of adequate compensation (Wolcott & Haderlie, 1995), and lack of clear commitment to or policy on distance education (Bebko, 1998; Halfhill, 1998; Ndahi, 1999).

There is considerable research in which barriers are enumerated; however, many of the factors identified in the literature as barriers are considered to be disincentives for the purpose of this review. Disincentives are associated with the characteristics of distance teaching and with individual costs and benefits perceived to derive from participation. Though they both function to impede involvement, disincentives are distinguished from barriers and are reviewed in a subsequent section of this chapter.

Research has identified attitudes and perceptions that act as barriers and play a major role in decisions to adopt distance education and its technologies for teaching. For example, a negative image of distance education deterred participation among some faculty (Bebko, 1998; Halfhill, 1998). Clark (1993), in seeking "to estimate the receptivity of faculty" (p. 20) to distance education and the media and methods used, found that, overall, faculty held positive attitudes toward the concept. Their attitudes toward personal use of distance education in their programs were more negative. However, Bebko's (1998) research helps to understand the origins of faculty receptivity. She reported that the faculty members at the two institutions she studied were more likely to decide to use distance education technology if they held the following beliefs:

> (1) that technology-based distance education can produce a quality learning experience, (2) that technology-based distance education will better address student needs, (3) that they personally are capable of developing and/or delivering effective technology-based distance education, and (4) that it is to their advantage to develop and/or deliver technology-based distance education. (p. 97)

Faculty also expressed fears and feelings of inadequacy that acted as deterrents. Such attitudes spoke to the faculty's uncertainty and concerns for changes in the status quo and included fears associated with the use of technology (Jackson, 1994), the fear of being displaced (Halfhill, 1998), and the fear of losing autonomy or control over the teaching and learning process (Halfhill, 1998; Jackson, 1994). Fears and uncertainty regarding the tenure and promotion process and job security were also common, as Bebko (1998) and Halfhill (1998) discovered.

Faculty surveyed by Montgomery (1999) scored low in relation to the "barrier" factor she identified. She interpreted this to mean that they lacked confidence in their ability to overcome barriers, the most frequently cited of which related to issues of information and effectiveness. Faculty expressed the belief that they did "not know enough about distance education to be comfortable teaching with it" and did "not feel it would be an effective teaching method for [their] field" (pp. 169–70). These faculty members were not alone in feeling poorly informed (see also Betts, 1998).

Many studies of perceptions of and barriers to distance education look to Rogers' (1995) theory of diffusion of innovation for a conceptual framework. Using the innovation-decision model, Northrup (1997) examined faculty members' perceptions of and their decisions to use distance education as a medium of course delivery. She found that faculty held positive perceptions of distance education. With respect to the five innovation attributes, she concluded that the perception that faculty could experience distance education on a limited basis (i.e., the trialability attribute) was a significant factor in influencing them to adopt distance education. The faculty members studied by Ndahi (1999) were also heavily influenced by trialability, but they were also more likely to use distance learning technology if they found that the technology was easy to understand and use.

The attitudes of one's colleagues appear to be influential in decisions about involving oneself in distance education. Walsh (1993) found that peer and personal experience influenced attitudes toward technology-based distance education, but no single variable explained attitudinal differences. Rather, he concluded, "attitude is comprised of a series of interrelated factors: exposure; peer influence; barriers and incentives to engaging in distance education; and opportunity and support for teaching a distance education course" (p. viii). Montgomery (1999) applied Walsh's attitudinal differences model and found support for four of the elements: exposure, peer influence, incentives, and opportunity. Further, she extracted three factors—which she labeled *vision, effectiveness*, and *barriers*—that accounted for the majority of variance in explaining faculty attitudes toward technology-based distance education.

In applying the theory of planned behavior, Halfhill (1998) found faculty attitudes to be predictive of their intention to participate. Specifically, faculty members' "perception of the attitudes held by important peers coupled with their assessment as to their eventual success are more important factors leading to intention than their own personally-held attitudes" (p. 116). This conclusion is supported by Montgomery (1999), who concluded that peers were "the greatest and most influential source of information" (p. 168). Findings relating to contextual barriers and to individual attitudes and perceptions point to the importance of a supportive institutional infrastructure for and a commitment to distance education.

Faculty Motives for Participation

Psychological definitions of motivation identify two types: intrinsic motivation and extrinsic motivation. The former has an internal origin; an individual derives satisfaction from performing or being associated with a particular activity because it appeals to his or her values or fulfills a personal need or drive (i.e., motive). In other words, engaging in the activity is reward in itself. Extrinsic motives, on the other hand, are associated with benefits received from a source other than the activity. The individual is moved to action in response to the prospect of an external benefit or reward. The majority of research on faculty participation has focused on why faculty do or do not participate and factors that encourage or discourage them. In this section, we review findings pertaining to individual influences and personal reasons for choosing whether or not to become involved in teaching distance education courses.

Intrinsic Motives.   Research continues to support previous findings by Taylor and White (1991) that faculty members are motivated to teach in distance education programs more by intrinsic than extrinsic reasons. Others, specifically Betts (1998); Miller and Husmann (1999); Rockwell et al. (1999); and Wolcott (1997) reached the same conclusion. In many cases, a particular attribute of distance teaching holds an inherent appeal, such as the opportunities distance education affords underserved or geographically disadvantaged students.

The studies examined for this review have many motivating factors in common. Wolcott and Betts (1999) classified five types of intrinsic motives: personal or socially derived satisfactions, personal or professional growth, personal challenge, altruistic, and career enhancing. Similarly, four groups of influences emerged from Schifter's (2000b) factor analysis, including intrinsic motives and personal needs.

Intrinsic motives have consistently been at the top of the list of factors most influential in faculty decisions to participate in distance education. For example, participants in Betts' (1998), study most frequently cited intrinsic reasons: to reach new audiences, to develop new ideas, to use new technologies, intellectual challenge, and overall job satisfaction. In modifying and administering Betts' survey at another institution, Schifter (2000b) observed the same primary motivators. Among the nonparticipators surveyed, intrinsic motives figured prominently as factors that would motivate them to participate in the future, though the influence was less strong for the nonparticipators polled by Betts. The majority of factors that were found by both Betts and Schifter to have motivated participators (or had the potential to motivate them to continue and/or increase their participation) were intrinsic factors.

Results are similar across a variety of disciplines and institutions. Faculty studied at two midwestern institutions by Rockwell et al. (1999) identified the following intrinsic or personal motives: providing innovative instruction, applying new teaching techniques, self-gratification, and fulfilling a personal desire to teach. Developing distance education courses and programs appealed to the agricultural science faculty and extension educators at the 42 universities surveyed by Jackson (1994) because doing so was an effective way to reach larger audiences and provided the opportunity to increase public interest and meet public requests for information. Industrial and technical educators from 20 universities were motivated to participate because they saw an opportunity to improve their teaching, provide students greater access to education, and increase enrollments (Ndahi, 1999). Community college faculty rated self-fulfillment, the enjoyment of teaching, professional challenge (Miller & Husmann, 1999), and making courses more accessible to students (Kirk & Shoemaker, 1999) as their most motivating factors. The need for increased flexible access to higher education opportunities for the changing student population (Bebko, 1998), satisfying demonstrated students needs (Halfhill, 1998), and feeling that students would benefit (Montgomery, 1999) are additional examples of student-centered factors that were intrinsically motivating for faculty.

Extrinsic Motives.   Schifter (2000b) identified a group of factors she labeled extrinsic motives. They included the expectation by the university that faculty would participate, a requirement by the department, and support and encouragement from individual departments as well as from the institution. However, none of these factors was included as a strong motivator identified by the faculty. In fact, few cases of participation have been attributed to extrinsic motives.

One exception is found among the community college faculty studied by Kirk and Shoemaker (1999), who reported that the prospect of being extrinsically rewarded with more money, equipment, or release time figured as a strong motivator influencing them to participate. And contrary to the distance education participators she studied, Betts' (1998) nonparticipators listed extrinsic factors that they speculated would motivate them to participate. An increase in salary and monetary support such as overload pay or a stipend ranked the highest. However, the preponderance of evidence, such as that reported by Wolcott (1997), Betts (1998), and Wolcott and Betts (1999), indicates that faculty members who are involved in distance teaching are not in it for the money.

Least motivating, extrinsic reasons typically tend to be at the bottom of the lists of influencing factors. For example, reasons such as being required to participate (Kirk & Shoemaker, 1999) or the anticipation of rewards such as merit pay, tenure, and promotion credit (Miller & Husmann, 1999) were rated low by the faculty surveyed. Similar findings led Betts (1998) to conclude that "extrinsic factors ... did not have a significant effect on faculty participation in distance education" (p. 9). Overall, Wolcott and Betts (1999) observed that "just as intrinsic factors amounted to reasons to participate, external factors were often reasons not to" (p. 44).

Differences among faculty motives add another dimension to the dynamic of participation. Unlike the faculty in research universities, the community college teachers surveyed by Miller and Husmann (1999) saw distance teaching as part of their job, and this perception mitigated the influence of external pressures. Consistent with motivation theory, Kirk and Shoemaker (1999) further observed that the motives of their subjects varied with their personal characteristics and demographics such as career stage. They also noted differences by age and prior experience, concluding that "extrinsic rewards tended to be a greater motivator for younger versus older instructors" (p. 315) and that instructors with prior experience teaching online were more motivated than were the inexperienced instructors by the challenge of online teaching, their interest in computers, and their desire to make courses more accessible to students. Similarly, Rockwell et al. (1999) reported that faculty members, having taught at a distance, were more likely to be motivated by a personal desire to teach and by self-gratification than were their non-distance-teaching colleagues.

The research also reveals differences between faculty motives to participate and what administrators believed motivated or would motivate their faculty. For example, although faculty participators in Betts' (1998) study cited intrinsic reasons, the deans thought extrinsic motives were more powerful. They speculated that faculty would participate if offered monetary support, an increase in salary, credit toward tenure and promotion, and release time. Again, in Schifter's (2000b) study, the list of the top five motivators cited by faculty (including distance education participators and nonparticipators) did not include any extrinsic motives. Administrators, however, believed that "faculty [were] more motivated by things they could 'get' by participating in distance education (e.g., more money, personal credit, and reduced load) than factors that might be more beneficial to the program or students" (p. 8). Rockwell et al. (1999) also found that "administrators were more likely to see 'monetary awards' . . . as an incentive than were the teaching faculty" (p. 6), and faculty members "exclusively teaching undergraduate level courses" more so than those teaching graduate level courses. They also noted "faculty were more likely to see 'developing effective technology skills' . . . as an obstacle than were administrators" (p. 5).

Incentives

Incentives appear to play a major role in faculty decisions regarding participation. Indeed, the lack of incentives has been considered a barrier to institutional growth in distance education (U.S. Department of Education, 1997). When present, however, incentives can facilitate faculty involvement. Shattuck and Zirger (1993) concluded that, along with tradition, incentives were a driving force behind faculty participation among the engineering faculty they surveyed.

In a general sense, an incentive is "an external stimulus which energizes behavior and/or gives it direction" (Ramachandran, 1994, p. 213). In the context of this review, incentives are factors that encourage or facilitate faculty involvement. They have the effect of lowering barriers and enabling participation because they are perceived to satisfy a faculty member's particular goal or personal need. What functions as an incentive for one person may be quite different from that which motivates another—or the same individual under a different set of circumstances. Although incentives can be viewed as the converse of barriers, there may be only a shade of difference between them. Evidence provided by the research suggests that if the absence of a factor presents an obstacle to participation, its presence may act as an incentive. As Montgomery (1999) observed, "Incentives and deterrents are two sides of the same coin as far as faculty are concerned" (p. 165).

Incentives that have been identified with respect to distance education appear to be of several types: (1) situational aspects or characteristics of the work environment that facilitate participation, (2) inducements offered by the institution expressly to entice faculty to participate, and (3) intrinsic rewards returned for participation.

Certain aspects of the institutional or work environment may encourage faculty to participate in distance education programs. For example, Bebko (1998) identified seven influences that she labeled "strong enhancers." Among them were several situational characteristics whose presence heightened the attraction of distance education and influenced faculty to become involved in teaching distance courses. These included the availability of "technology training and technical assistance for students, a framework for student to student support systems, [and] student-friendly student services," along with "competition with other institutions, and collaboration with and beyond the institution" (p. 95). Having a supportive department head proved to be a situational factor that enabled participation (Halfhill, 1998; Wolcott, 1997), as did the involvement of good faculty, departmental commitment, enlightened administrators, and a well-developed support system (Wolcott & Haderlie, 1995).

Typically, we think of incentives as having an external origin. For example, institutions traditionally offer inducements such as bonus pay to encourage a particular behavior or activity valued by the organization. A major category of extrinsic incentives relates to the issues of workload and salary. Wolcott and Haderlie (1995) found that inducements can take many forms, including workload adjustments such as release time, a modified or reduced teaching assignment, double credit for distance teaching, or a mini-sabbatical; the opportunity to teach the distance education course as part of one's assigned teaching load rather than as an overload; and additional compensation or an overload stipend. Supplemental compensation was one of the most frequently offered incentives identified by Kambutu (1998). However, he found that over 50% of the institutions he surveyed did not offer incentives such as release time, extra compensation, and favorable workload policies. Other inducements included the availability of course development funds (Jackson, 1994; Wolcott & Haderlie, 1995), travel or equipment funds (Wolcott & Haderlie, 1995), and adequate staff support and time to plan (Jackson, 1994).

Schifter (2000a) looked at compensation practices and incentives for both developing distance education courses and teaching them. For developing courses, the incentive provided most often was payment of the faculty members' Internet service provider. Incentives almost never provided for course development were payment for graduate assistants and payment for faculty overload. The provision of funds for a teaching assistant ranked as the incentive that was provided least often. Schifter concluded, as had Wolcott and Haderlie in 1995, that practices vary widely among institutions. Further, she concluded that "compensation and incentives are only marginally better for developing a distance education course than for teaching one," that compensation and incentives "are not needed at institutions where development and teaching a DE course is expected and part of the culture," and that "where development and teaching a DE course is encouraged and supported by administration, but not expected, campus culture . . . and precedence may provide answers to differences" (p. 11).

Though less direct than other incentives provided by the institution, the availability of instructional support services for distance teaching can encourage participation. However, neither Wolcott and Haderlie (1995) nor Lee (2000) found evidence that institutional support services were widely available to promote professional growth and to improve teaching among distance education faculty specifically. The most widely available support services were workshops and seminars, instructional consultation, and materials production (Wolcott & Haderlie 1995). Occasional support was found in the form of site facilitators, instructional designers, teaching assistants, and graders. There was little evidence of mentoring.

The nonparticipators surveyed in Schifter (2000b) listed incentives that, if available, would influence them to participate, and among them was technical support provided by the institution. The faculty in Betts' (1998) study also indicated that their institution could do more to encourage faculty to participate in distance education, such as providing more information about distance education and offering technical training and support. Likewise, Ndahi (1999) found that "86% of the respondents would like their institution to provide more incentives for teaching a distance class" (p. 29). However, Kambutu (1998) documented that services were not necessarily available to or provided for faculty teaching at a distance.

The third category of incentives is more subjective. These incentives represent perceived personal returns on investment (i.e., intrinsic rewards). In the quid pro quo terms of expectancy theory, intrinsic rewards are the personally valued outcomes returned for the faculty member's participation. Getting back something of value that would enhance professional growth or career development was one type of outcome that functioned as an incentive. For example, faculty were enticed by professional development opportunities offered by distance education and found it to be instrumental in improving their teaching skills and adding resources to their classroom instruction (Wolcott & Haderlie, 1995). Other faculty members found that participation in distance education afforded them the opportunity to make industry contacts and increased their visibility and reputation in their field (Wolcott & Betts, 1999). The expectation of some type of recognition from administrators was an incentive for some (Jackson, 1994).

Faculty also drew satisfaction from the opportunity to boost their department's enrollments and extend its influence and to reach a particular segment of the student population, such as adult learners. These, together with career-enhancing perquisites, were intrinsic rewards also identified by Wolcott and Betts (1999).

Disincentives

Although some aspects of distance teaching may act as incentives, others can militate against it. Unlike the environmental factors labeled herein as barriers, disincentives relate to the costs of or lack of benefits from choosing to participate in distance education. Wolcott and Betts (1999) divided disincentives into two categories, inhibitors and demotivators: "Inhibitors refer to those aspects or characteristics of distance teaching that relate to the cost of involvement. Demotivators are factors that represent the lack of benefit perceived to result from involvement. Both types of factors reduce personal motivation and pose a barrier to participation" (p. 43).

A number of factors identified in the literature as barriers fit the definition of an inhibitor. One of the most common inhibitors, for example, is the extra demand on time. Almost universally, faculty expressed the concern that distance teaching costs them too many hours. Specifically, time requirements associated with preparing courses (Halfhill, 1998; Jackson, 1994; Ndahi, 1999; Rockwell et al., 1999; Wolcott & Betts, 1999) and learning new teaching or technological skills (Betts, 1998; Halfhill, 1998; Ndahi, 1999; Wolcott & Haderlie, 1995) surfaced as major disincentives.

Rockwell et al. (1999) observed differences in the perception of disincentives between tenured and nontenured faculty. Time taken from research, training requirements, assistance or support needs, and developing effective technology skills were each perceived as less of an obstacle by nontenured faculty members than by the tenured faculty. Wolcott (1997), in contrast, described the risk to junior faculty when distance teaching robs them of the time needed for research and publishing activities that are more highly valued and rewarded.

In addition to the lack of time, faculty in a number of studies cited several professional concerns among the factors that either did or would inhibit them from participating. Other inhibitors included concerns about workload (Betts, 1998; Halfhill, 1998; Wolcott & Haderlie, 1995) and the quality or academic rigor of courses in which face-to-face interaction was absent (Betts, 1998; Halfhill, 1998). Similar inhibitors were found by Schifter (2000b) and were among the detractors identified by Bebko (1998).

Other disincentives relate to the perceived lack of benefit from participating in distance education. One of the most prevalent demotivators was the lack of consideration accorded distance teaching in annual, promotion, and tenure reviews (Wolcott, 1997). Schifter's factor analysis (2000b) identified a group of demotivators, which she labeled inhibitors, that were essentially perceived lacks. They included lack of release time, lack of merit pay, lack of monetary support for participation, lack of grants for materials or expenses, and the lack of career advancement resulting from participation in distance teaching. Betts (1998) explored the latter demotivator in greater detail. She found that the majority of faculty members and deans saw little or no career advantage to be gained from distance teaching.

Wolcott and Betts (1999) examined the concept of equity in relation to the faculty's perceived return on investment. Their conclusions illustrate the dynamics of motivation:

> Internal motivation was a characteristic of those who were involved in distance education; they valued outcomes that returned personal satisfaction, and they sought them in distance education. Although the exchange was not always perceived as equitable when measured against external rewards, the benefits of participation in relation to personal motives outweighed the cost in terms of time and amount of work invested. . . . When the costs of distance education represented more than the faculty member was willing to invest, they became a disincentive to participation. (pp. 46–47)

Rewards for Distance Teaching

Rewards provide the formal and informal means through which institutions acknowledge faculty for their efforts. As with motives, rewards can be intrinsic or extrinsic in nature. The term typically calls to mind some tangible return for good performance. However, rewards neither have to be material nor large to be valued. As noted in the previous section, individuals may draw considerable satisfaction from their involvement in activities that return a valued outcome irrespective of its size.

Indeed, for many, teaching is its own reward; there is an abundance of anecdotal evidence to confirm that distance teaching can be a rewarding experience for faculty. However, the question of whether distance teaching is rewarded is one that has recently become the subject of inquiry. Although the majority of faculty (distance education participators and nonparticipators alike) surveyed in Betts' (1998) study felt that participation in distance education should not be rewarded differently, studies strongly suggest that it is inadequately rewarded (see Kambutu, 1998; Wolcott, 1997). Clark (1993) reported that faculty members were evenly divided between those who thought that their participation would be adequately rewarded and those who did not. Faculty who doubted that they would be adequately rewarded cited the following reasons: inadequate financial compensation, the extra workload, lack of rewards, concerns relating to research and publication, and distrust of administrators. Indeed, the lack of adequate rewards has been shown to be a personal disincentive as well as a barrier to institutional development in distance education (U.S. Department of Education, 1997).

Although the issue of rewards is an emerging topic of discussion, little research has dealt directly with faculty rewards for distance teaching. In examining institutional practices, researchers have noted few instances of formal rewards and recognition. For the most part, distance education has not been formally rewarded through advancement in rank, tenure, or merit pay (Wolcott, 1997). Informal recognition can come in a number of forms, ranging from pats on the back to more formal acknowledgements such as an award. Few examples of formal recognition practices have been identified, although faculty members reported that a casual " 'at a boy" or token of appreciation were welcome forms of informal recognition (Wolcott, 1997). Wolcott also found that, indirectly, faculty felt recognized when administrators would "brag publicly" or receive attention for their distance education programs.

Few have studied rewards in depth. Wolcott (1997) took an institutional perspective and interviewed chief academic officers, distance education administrators, and faculty at four research universities. Drawing on theories of work motivation, she examined the relationship between distance teaching and the institutional reward system. She described a culture in which distance education held a marginal status; in which it was not highly valued, well rewarded, or highly correlated to the tenure and promotion process; and in which rewards were dependent on the commitment of the academic unit and its head. Questioning specifically, "How do reward processes such as tenure and promotion accommodate distance teaching in institutions that, by tradition, emphasize research" (p. 4), she found that faculty received little credit for developing and teaching distance education courses, that the support of the institution and department head was critical, and that participation in distance education posed a risk to the junior, nontenured faculty.

Wolcott's work continued with the development and validation of a scale designed to assess faculty beliefs about rewards for distance teaching. Preliminary results (Wolcott, 1999) provide additional evidence that faculty are intrinsically motivated to participate in distance education; underscore the importance of commitment and support, especially on the part of the department chair or head; and raise issues regarding the equity of rewards and return on the faculty member's investment in distance teaching.

As the ultimate extrinsic reward at research institutions, tenure is the holy grail of an academic career, and as the nursing faculty members studied by Bodenbender (1998) urged, participation in distance education is deserving of professional recognition and needs to be considered in the promotion and tenure process. Yet Kambutu (1998) noted that, among the majority of administrators, distance teaching did not receive consideration during promotion and tenure decisions and was not recognized by departments and senior faculty members—nor did administrators think it important to recognize it. He concluded that "distance instruction is not instrumental in attaining some of the extrinsic rewards valued by faculty such as workload policies that recognize distance teaching, career promotion, tenure, and status in the institution" (p. 146).

The situation is different for community college faculty. As with their university counterparts, the faculty members surveyed by Miller and Husmann (1999) did not get involved in distance teaching to earn credit toward tenure and promotion. However, among the community college faculty whom Kirk and Shoemaker (1999) studied, "chances of being promoted" and "public recognition by supervisor" were strong motivators for instructors, especially those who had a greater knowledge of the Internet than did their colleagues.

As distance education becomes more widespread and integrated into the academic culture, teaching at a distance seems to be gaining acceptance as a valued activity. Recently, Schifter (2000a) found that 43% of the 160 institutions represented in her survey reported that participation in distance education was applicable toward tenure and promotion. According to the respondents, "Teaching a DE course is treated just like any other teaching assignment, service or professional development [activity]" (p. 4).

CONCLUSION

Until recently, faculty issues have been largely ignored in distance education research (Dillon & Walsh, 1992). Although faculty participation has been an issue of interest among distance education administrators, research has been sparse over the past two decades. Studies have focused mostly on obstacles to participation and factors that encourage faculty to participate. From a research perspective, there has been less interest in faculty motivation. Perhaps as a result of rapid growth in online instruction and its impact on faculty work, researchers have begun to expand their coverage and practitioners have picked up the theme in the popular literature. Empirical studies relating to faculty participation have increased, as evidenced by a flurry of research activity in the late 1990s. However, the current research shows a continued interest in and emphasis on barriers and incentives.

The body of research suffers from a confusion of terms that has made a comprehensive synthesis of findings difficult. Researchers have made little attempt to define concepts or to distinguish among terms such as *motive, incentive*, and *barrier.* The major challenge in reviewing the research literature has been to operationally define constructs and assign relevant findings to them. In an attempt to clarify and ground the terms, this review has drawn from the field of psychology as well as the fields of management and organizational behavior to understand the distinctions between the concepts of barrier, motive, incentive, disincentive, and reward.

Recently, both Saba (2000) and Perraton (2000) have been critical of the research in distance education for its atheoretical approach. "Research questions are rarely posed within a theoretical framework or based on its fundamental concepts or constructs" (Saba, 2000, pp. 2–3). Much of the research relating to faculty motivation and participation is, likewise, shallowly anchored in the theoretical foundations of distance education or related disciplines. Although researchers have acknowledged the antecedent work of Dillon and Walsh (1992), Olcott and Wright (1995), and Rogers (1995), few have made references to theory outside of the field. With a few exceptions (Betts, 1998; Kirk & Shoemaker, 1999; Wolcott, 1997; Wolcott & Betts, 1999), the wealth of theory in the area of management and organizational psychology has been neglected.

In proposing a timely research agenda, Perraton (2000) faulted existing research for emphasizing the application of distance education while largely ignoring its context. Issues relating to motivation cannot be fully understood without considering the institutional context, yet research on faculty participation is only beginning to expand the examination into the surrounding environment. The present findings about factors that enable and deter, encourage and discourage, and punish and reward can lead us to inferences about the institutional climate and culture. But again, few studies have ventured beyond the task of identifying barriers and incentives to consider those factors in the complex and dynamic culture that is higher education.

Perraton (2000) also noted that research that informs the development of policy is particularly rare. In the collective findings about faculty participation, policymakers can find a wealth of information to inform their decision making. Though few, the studies, when taken together, offer several common conclusions with easily identifiable policy implications. For example, findings continue to remind us that faculty motivation is predominantly intrinsic; it should be obvious to policymakers that there is little utility in continuing to offer monetary incentives to promote participation among the early adopters. The "second-wave" faculty—those who are more wary of new technologies, according to Brown and Floyd (1999)—may be enticed by the prospect of financial gain but may be equally motivated by the offer of individual assistance and technical support in learning to use the novel technologies. In either case, research findings should encourage institutional policymakers to look beyond extrinsic incentives and rewards to those that have been shown to have a greater appeal to faculty.

To illuminate the context and be useful in informing policy, research often requires approaches of a qualitative nature. The majority of the studies that met the criteria for this review used survey methods to identify barriers to and inducements for faculty participation in distance education. Several researchers (Bebko, 1998; Bolduc, 1993; Wolcott, 1997; Wolcott & Betts, 1999) applied qualitative methods involving interviewing and document analysis; a few (Halfhill, 1998; Rockwell et al., 1999) combined quantitative and qualitative data collection techniques. Research intended to provide an understanding of the institutional culture and its influences on faculty motivation should employ in-depth methods, such as the use of case studies.

The preponderance of survey methods may be attributed to the fact that most of the studies have been conducted as doctoral dissertation research. Lacking the experience and resources to conduct more intensive investigations, the student researchers have likely relied on less expensive and time-consuming methods to tap an accessible population. The absence of a solid grounding in theory remains a concern, however, as does the small number of researchers looking into faculty issues. We should be optimistic that, as the field continues to mature, researchers will expand their theoretical perspectives and methods of inquiry as well as the scope of their investigations.

One of the keys to successful distance education programs continues to be the participation of the institutions' best faculty. Though limited in number and scope, research studies to date tell us that faculty participation hinges on their being intrinsically motivated and feeling equitably rewarded for their efforts. We have a sense of why faculty members participate and what initially motivates them to so do. We know less about recruiting faculty, about attrition among distance education faculty, or, more important, how to sustain faculty motivation. What, for example, are appropriate strategies for recruiting faculty of different ranks and career stages? How do institutions respond to changing motivations over time? What is the efficacy of particular incentives and rewards? What factors are associated with retention of distance education faculty?

We have a fairly good understanding of the types of motivational practices within institutions, including the incentives, compensation practices, workload assignments, and rewards provided for distance teaching. But as yet, we know little about institutional policies and how practices and policies affect faculty participation and motivation. Are new forms of digital scholarship acknowledged and credited toward merit, promotion and tenure? Do intellectual property policies encourage innovation and fairly reward faculty for their contributions? Are institutional commitments to distance teaching and learning reflected in policies and criteria for recognition and reward? The field could also benefit from knowing more about the effectiveness of institutional support services in enhancing motivation. Specifically, to what extent are faculty development activities such as training, mentoring, and instructional design services instrumental in motivating and supporting distance teaching faculty?

In closing, we should acknowledge that the research on faculty participation and motivation has taken place under the assumption that distance teaching typically represents an add-on to the traditional faculty role. In such a scenario, questions regarding workload, barriers, incentives, compensation, and rewards are important to raise. However, as distance education merges into the main stream of higher education teaching and learning, some participation issues may become moot. Indeed, do incentives, recruitment, and retention matter if distance teaching becomes a common function of the typical faculty role? Brian Hawkins (2000), president of EDUCAUSE, predicts that "the new marketplace will be associated with new models of faculty motivation" (p. 70). Yet in the new world of e-learning, it is likely that policy issues such as appropriate and equitable rewards will remain important to faculty.

The rapidly changing landscape accentuates the need for the field to frame its inquiry in a broader context. Researchers should tie their investigations to existing theory and look to related disciplines for theoretical approaches that could advance the field. There are promising directions in the area of organizational behavior and industrial psychology; for example, traditional work motivation theories are yielding ground to research on goal-setting and personal efficacy (Landy, 1989). It might also prove informative to apply models from management theory to distance education work environments. Neither should investigations ignore theoretical ground broken within the field of distance education. Already widely referenced, the institutional support framework proposed by Olcott and Wright (1995), for instance, deserves testing.

Researchers should also consider the larger higher education context when addressing faculty issues. They should connect with conversations about the scholarship of teaching, intellectual property, workload, faculty pay, and tenure reform. The issues become nearly inseparable as the information technology revolution makes distance education issues those of mainstream higher education. However, the revolution is only partly technological, as we are reminded by Munitz (2000): "It is also cultural, and therein lies both the threat and the promise for today's institutions of higher education as they make hard decisions about mission, priorities, and money" (p. 18). To realize the promise of distance education, we must understand faculty motivation, and that means understanding the culture in which the faculty work. Research on motives, incentives, and rewards for distance teaching can help institutions in making those hard decisions.

REFERENCES

Adams, J. S. (1964). Inequity in social exchange. In L. Berkowitz (Ed.), *Advances in experimental social psychology* (Vol. 2; pp. 267–299). New York: Academic Press.

Beaudoin, M. (1990). The instructor's changing role in distance education. *American Journal of Distance Education, 4*(2), 21–29.

Bebko, P. R. (1998). Influences upon higher education faculty use of distance education technology (Doctoral dissertation, Florida Atlantic University, 1998). *Dissertation Abstracts International, 59(02A)*, 0427.

Betts, K. S. (1998). Factors influencing faculty participation in distance education in postsecondary education in the United States: An institutional study (Doctoral dissertation, The George Washington University, 1998). *Dissertation Abstracts International, 59(07)*, 2376A.

Bodenbender, K. D. (1998). Baccalaureate and graduate nursing faculty attitudes towards and perceptions of interactive television teaching (Doctoral dissertation, University of Iowa, 1998). *Dissertation Abstracts International, 59*(09A), 3413.

Bolduc, W. J. (1993). The diffusion of digital compressed video-interactive in a university environment, 1988–92: A case study (Doctoral dissertation, Florida State University, 1990). *Dissertation Abstracts International, 54*, 4294A.

Boyer, E. L. (1990). *Scholarship reconsidered: Priorities for the professoriate*. Princeton, NJ: Carnegie Foundation for the Advancement of Teaching.

Brown, D. G., & Floyd, E. S. (1999, Winter). Faculty development: Building university programs that capture faculty enthusiasm for computers and learning. *Multiversity* [Online], 5 pages. Available http://www.wfu.edu/~brown/MultiversityBestPracticeBrown_Floyd.htm.

Burbules, N. C., & Callister, T. A. (2000). Universities in transition: The promise and the challenge of new technologies. *Teachers College Record, 102*(2), 271–293.

Clark, T. (1993). Attitudes of higher education faculty toward distance education: A national survey. *American Journal of Distance Education, 7*(2), 19–33.

Diamond, R. M. (1993). How to change the faculty reward system. *Trusteeship, 1*(5), 17–21.

Dillon, C. L., & Walsh, S. M. (1992). Faculty: The neglected resource in distance education. *American Journal of Distance Education, 6*(3), 5–21.

Edgerton, R. (1993). Re-examination of faculty priorities. *Change, 25*(4), 10–25.

Fairweather, J. S. (1993). Academic values and faculty rewards. *Review of Higher Education, 17*(1), 43–68.

Green, K. C. (2000a). *The Campus Computing Project*. Available: http://www.campuscomputing.net/summaries/2000/index.html

Green, K. C. (2000b). *Campus computing, 2000: The 2000 national survey of information technology in U.S. higher education* [PowerPoint slides]. Available: http://www.campuscomputing.net/archive/Green-cc2000.PDF

Halfhill, C. S. (1998). An investigation into factors influencing faculty behavior concerning distance learning instruction using the theory of planned behavior (Doctoral dissertation, University of Central Florida, 1998). *Dissertation Abstracts International, 59(11A)*, 4113.

Hardi, J. (2000, March 31). Land-grant presidents call for new "covenant" with state and U.S. governments. *Chronicle of Higher Education* [Online]. Available: http://www.chronicle.com/weekly/v46/i30/30a04101.htm

Hawkins, B. L. (2000, November-December). Technology, higher education, and a very foggy crystal ball. *EDUCAUSE Review*, 65–73.

Jackson, G. (1994, February). Incentives for planning and delivering agricultural distance education. *Agriculture Education Magazine*, 15–16.

Kambutu, J. N. (1998). A study of selected administrators' self-perceptions concerning the available support services and extrinsic rewards for distance education at the 67 land-grant institutions in the United States (Doctoral dissertation, University of Wyoming, 1998). *Dissertation Abstracts International, 59(09A)*, 3318.

Kirk, J. J., & Shoemaker, H. (1999). Motivating community college instructors to teach on-line: An exploration of selected motivators. In *Instructional Technology* (pp. 310–317). (Proceedings of the 1999 AHRD Conference, Arlington, VA, March 3–7, 1999). Baton Rouge, LA: Academy of Human Resources Development. (ERIC Document Reproduction Service No. ED 431 942)

Landy, F. (1989). *Psychology of work behavior* (4th ed.). Belmont, CA: Wadsworth.

Lee, J. (2000). Institutional support for distance education among higher education institutions. Unpublished doctoral dissertation, Utah State University, Logan.

Lonsdale, A. (1993). Changes in incentives, rewards and sanctions. *Higher Education Management, 5*, 223–235.

Massy, W. F. (1998). Understanding new faculty roles and work patterns. In *Technology and its ramifications for data systems: Report of the Policy Panel on Technology* (pp. 15–19). Washington, DC: National Postsecondary Education Cooperative. (ERIC Document Reproduction Service No. ED 424 829)

McIsaac, M. S., & Gunawardena, C. (1996). Distance education. In D. H. Jonassen (Ed.), *Handbook of research for educational communications and technology* (pp. 403–437). New York: Macmillan.

McNeil, D. R. (1990). *Wiring the ivory tower: A round table on technology in higher education.* Washington, DC: Academy for Educational Development. (ERIC Document Reproduction Service No. ED 320 555)

Miller, M. T., & Husmann, D. E. (1999). Faculty incentives to participate in distance education. *Michigan Community College Journal, 5*(2), 35–42.

Mingle, J. R. (1993). Faculty work and the cost/quality/access collision. *Trusteeship 1*(5), 11–16.

Montgomery, C. J. (1999). Faculty attitudes toward technology-based distance education at the University of Nevada, Las Vegas (Doctoral dissertation, University of Nevada, Las Vegas, 1999). *Dissertation Abstracts International, 60*(09A), 3222.

Moore, M. G., & Kearsley, G. (1996). Distance education: A systems view. Belmont, CA: Wadsworth.

Munitz, B. (2000, January-February). Changing landscape: From cottage monopoly to competitive industry. *EDU-CAUSE Review*, 12–18.

Ndahi, H. B. (1999). Utilization of distance distance learning technology among industrial and technical teacher education faculty. *Journal of Industrial Teacher Education, 36*(4), 21–37.

Neumann, Y., & Finaly-Neumann, E. (1990). The reward-support framework and faculty commitment to their university. *Research in Higher Education, 31*(1), 75–97.

Northrup, P. T. (1997). Faculty perceptions of distance education: Factors influencing utilization. *International Journal of Educational Telecommunications, 3*, 343–358.

Olcott, D., & Wright, S. J. (1995). An institutional support framework for increasing faculty participation in postsecondary distance education. *American Journal of Distance Education, 9*(3), 5–17.

Perraton, H. (2000). Rethinking the research agenda. *International Review of Research in Open and Distance Learning* [Online serial], *1*(1). Available: http://www.irrodl.org/content/v1.1/hilary.pdf

Plater, W. M. (1995). Future work: Faculty time in the 21st century. *Change, 27*(3), 22–33.

Ramachandran, V. S. (Ed.). (1994). *Encyclopedia of human behavior.* San Diego, CA: Academic Press.

Rockwell, S. K., Schauer, J., Fritz, S. M., & Marx, D. B. (1999). Incentives and obstacles influencing higher education faculty and administrators to teach via distance. *Online Journal of Distance Learning Administration* [Online serial], *2*(4). Available: http://www.westga.edu/~distance/rockwell24.htm

Rogers, E. M. (1995). *Diffusion of innovations* (4th ed.). New York: The Free Press.

Saba, F. (2000). Research in distance education: A status report. *International Review of Research in Open and Distance Learning* [Online serial] *1*(1). Available: http://www.irrodl.org/content/v1.1/farhad.pdf

Shattuck, K. L., & Zirger, A. J. (1993). Faculty incentives for outreach engineering education programs. Unpublished manuscript, University of Florida, College of Engineering, Outreach Engineering Education Program.

Schifter, C. C. (2000a, June). *Distance education faculty incentives and compensation: An exploratory study.* Paper presented at the meeting of the National University Teleconferencing Consortium, Toronto.

Schifter, C. C. (2000b, June). *Faculty participation in distance education: A factor analysis of motivators and inhibitors.* Paper presented at the meeting of the National University Teleconferencing Consortium, Toronto.

Taylor, J. C., & White, V. J. (1991). Faculty attitudes towards teaching in the distance education mode: An exploratory investigation. *Research in Distance Education, 3*(3), 7–11.

U. S. Department of Education, National Center for Educational Statistics. (1997). *Distance education in higher education institutions* (NCES 98-062). Washington, DC: Author.

Vroom, V. H. (1964). *Work and motivation.* New York: Wiley.

Walsh, S. M. (1993). Attitudes and perceptions of university faculty toward technology based distance education (Doctoral dissertation, University of Oklahoma, 1993). *Dissertation Abstracts International, 54*, 781A.

Wolcott, L. L. (1997). Tenure, promotion, and distance education: Examining the culture of faculty rewards. *American Journal of Distance Education, 11*(2), 3–18.

Wolcott, L. L. (1999, April). *Assessing faculty beliefs about rewards and incentives in distance education: Pilot study results.* Paper presented at the meeting of the American Educational Research Association, Montreal, Canada. (ERIC Document Reproduction Service No. ED 435 271)

Wolcott, L. L., & Betts, K. S. (1999). What's in it for me? Incentives for faculty participation in distance education. *Journal of Distance Education, 14*(2), 34–49.

Wolcott, L. L., & Haderlie, S. (1995, August). The myth of dangling carrots: Incentives and rewards for teaching at a distance. In *Proceedings of the 11th Annual Conference on Teaching and Learning at a Distance* (pp. 307–312). Madison, WI: University of Wisconsin-Madison.

Work of faculty: Expectations, priorities, and rewards. (1994, January-February). *Academe*, 35–48.

38

Evaluating Distance Education Programs

Melody M. Thompson
The Pennsylvania State University
mmt2@outreach.psu.edu

Modupe E. Irele
The Pennsylvania State University
mei106@outreach.psu.edu

INTRODUCTION

As with any other educational activity, distance education programs must be subjected to periodic evaluations. Monitoring the value and effectiveness of programs is necessary to (a) justify the initial investment of resources; (b) ensure that goals are being met; (c) guide improvement of both processes and outcomes; and (d) provide a basis for decisions to continue, expand, or discontinue programs. Unfortunately—and again as with other educational activities—evaluation of distance education programming is too often poorly designed and/or underfunded; it is more of an afterthought than an integral part of planning and implementation.

WHY EVALUATE? THE CONTEXT FOR EVALUATION

The global educational context is changing rapidly. Programs, institutions, and societies need to make significant decisions as to how they wish to influence or shape the changes that are occurring and/or be shaped by them. Intentional, planned, and thoughtful responses depend on the availability of sufficient actionable information, however. Evaluation activities are a vital source of such information.

Distance Education Past: Evaluation as the Basis for Acceptance

For years, within traditional institutions the impact of distance education programming on the institutional system as a whole was small (although the impact on individual lives was often great). Since the impact was minimal, the monitoring and evaluation of distance education programming tended to be of interest to the parent institution primarily as a means of ensuring that such programming did not detract from the reputation enjoyed by its traditional programming.

For this reason, decades of evaluation studies focused on demonstrating that distance education programs were "as good"—that is, that students learned as much in them—as resident instruction programs. The primary approach used was the media-comparison study, which pitted classroom-based instruction against technologically mediated instruction. Comparable outcomes were documented in hundreds of such studies. A comprehensive overview of this literature can be found in *The No Significant Difference Phenomenon* (Russell, 1999) and *The Effects of Distance Learning* (Moore & Thompson, 1997). A critique of such studies and their findings is offered by the Institute for Higher Education Policy (1999) in *What's the Difference? A Review of Contemporary Research on the Effectiveness of Distance Learning in Higher Education.*

Institutions dedicated to distance education made a similar attempt to demonstrate parity with traditional institutions. They, like distance education programs within traditional institutions, fought for credibility from established entities that undervalued nontraditional study—and therefore distance study. Thus, whether the distance education program was offered by a traditional institution or an institution specializing in such programming, its evaluation was defensively focused on presenting data that would allow its continued existence, if only on the margins.

Distance Education Present: Evaluation of a Transformative Phenomenon

But now the situation has changed. Distance education, thanks to the power and reach of the World Wide Web, has been "discovered." Recast as "online learning" or "e-learning," it has moved from the shallows into the mainstream—at least into the mainstream of media attention. Titles of articles appearing in educational and popular publications herald the advent of a new era in learning and demonstrate the extent to which a once-obscure, little-known, and little-respected phenomenon—distance education—has captured the attention of the educational world:

How the Web Is Revolutionizing Learning
Campus Revolution: How IT Is Changing the Teaching/Learning Environment
The Power of the Internet for Learning: Moving from Promise to Practice
Harvard U. Offers Online Course "Tastings" to Its Alumni
Cyber Cafes to Boost Learning
States Struggle to Regulate Online Colleges That Lack Accreditation
Digital Diploma Mills: The Coming Battle over Online Instruction
Rethinking the Role of the Professor in an Age of High-Tech Tools
Distance Learning: Promise or Threat?

Distance education is no longer on the margins of the educational system, tolerated as long as it conforms and defers to the "real thing" (i.e., resident instruction). It is no longer an alternative primarily for nontraditional students but is being incorporated into programs serving traditional campus-based students as well. As the article titles above illustrate, this movement from the margins into the mainstream of institutional education has resulted in a new image for distance education. Depending on one's perspective, it has become either a shining promise or a looming threat, either of which has the potential to transform the traditional educational environment.

Judith Eaton (2000), president of the Council for Higher Education Accreditation, reinforces this point when she states that distance education, "however unintentionally," challenges the "core academic values . . . central to the history and tradition of higher education"

(p. 1). Although a challenge to tradition may have either negative or positive results—threat or promise?— the extent of the current challenge underlines its potential impact. For example, the U.S. Department of Education's National Center for Education Statistics (NCES) recently reported that "from 1994–95 to 1997–98 the number of distance education degree programs increased by 72% [and] that more than 1.6 million students were enrolled in distance education courses in 1997–98" (Institute for Higher Education Policy, 2000, p. 5), and enrollments have soared since that report was published. International growth is likely to be even more dramatic. As the level of global Internet users increases—one estimate suggests the number will reach 638 million by 2004—the international demand for online education will likewise increase. Moe and Blodget (2000) note that, given both the increasing demand and the limited access to high-quality postsecondary education in many parts of the world, there could be as many as 40 million online students by 2025.

Given this increasing prominence and the potentially transformative effects of new forms of distance education on the existing educational enterprise, performing rigorous evaluation and research studies has become imperative. As Bates (2000) points out, because of

> the rapid speed with which new technologies for teaching are infiltrating even the most cautious and conservative of universities, and the lack of experience in the use and management of such technologies, the case for researching and evaluating the applications of these new technologies is obvious (p. 198).

Even more important than doing evaluation is doing evaluation right, that is, asking the right questions and then using the answers appropriately. Ehrmann (1997b) notes that it "takes just as much effort to answer a useless question as a useful one" (p. 1), but we cannot afford to be asking useless questions. Only thoughtful and focused examination of distance education programming, especially in its newest forms, will reveal whether, and under what conditions, the adoption of these innovations will be the fulfillment of the promise or the threat.

Although the current headlong rush to move this little understood but potentially transformative educational phenomenon into the mainstream is resulting in increased, often impatient, demands for evaluation information, evaluation studies must reflect rigorous planning and execution rather than unconsidered adoption of past approaches to evaluating traditional or distance programs. Only through careful planning and implementation can evaluation studies provide the information necessary to ensure that whatever transformation occurs is intentional rather than accidental, directed rather than haphazard.

WHAT IS EVALUATION?

The terms *evaluation*, *assessment*, and *research* often are used interchangeably, but each has a different meaning, function, and value for understanding the operations and outcomes of distance education programs.

Evaluation and Assessment

Stufflebeam (1999), in his treatment of educational program evaluation, defines evaluation as "a study designed and conducted to assist some audience to measure an object's merit and worth" (p. 3). In educational contexts, evaluation studies are implemented to examine and report on the strengths and weaknesses of programs, policies, personnel, processes, products/outcomes, and organizations to improve their effectiveness (American Evaluation Association, as cited in Saba, 2000, p. 1). Evaluation encompasses both expected and unexpected occurrences and involves making judgments about their merit and worth (Chambers, 1995; Institute for Higher

Education Policy, 1999; Rowntree, 1992; Stufflebeam, 1999; Thorpe, 1996). Thus, the focus of evaluation is always on the "value" of some aspect of programming to a group or groups of stakeholders: society, institutions, students, employers, and so on.

Assessment, on the other hand, attempts to determine the objective level of some variable of interest: test score, interaction level, response time, and so on (Joint Committee on Standards for Educational Evaluation, 1994). Assessment, with its focus on measuring "what is," is a subset of evaluation (Rowntree, 1992). It is a valuable tool in the larger evaluation activity, which has as its focus comparison to some previously determined standard—"what should be." Assessment asks "How much?" whereas evaluation asks "Is it good enough?" and "If not, why not?"

Some activities conducted in the name of evaluation lack the focus on merit or value. Stufflebeam (1999) characterizes as pseudo-evaluations those activities that are motivated by a desire to project a specific view of a program regardless of its actual worth. Practices such as using biased surveys or releasing only positive findings may advance particular agendas by seeming to support the claims of excellence necessary to secure sponsor support, but these practices should not be classified as evaluation. Not only do they mislead stakeholders, but they also make the information gathered useless for making planning decisions or program improvements.

Research

Both assessment and evaluation are focused on practical examination of programs to discover what works and what needs to be improved as the basis for effective management and planning decisions (Bates, 2000; Lockee, Burton, & Cross, 1999). Research studies, on the other hand, generate hypotheses from theory and then gather data as the basis for accepting or rejecting the hypotheses. They are intended to develop a deep understanding of particular aspects of a phenomenon through rigorous examination of relevant variables.

This chapter focuses on evaluation rather than research. Readers interested in research in distance education may find useful McIsaac and Gunawardena's (1996) "Distance Education" and the discussion of research issues, designs, and constructs in Lockee, et al.'s (1999) "No Comparison: Distance Education Finds a New Use for 'No Significant Difference.'"

Purposes of Evaluation

Evaluative studies are conducted to answer questions of interest to stakeholders. Thus, the focus of an evaluation will vary with the informational needs of each stakeholder or stakeholder group, although most evaluation activities have more than one purpose. Common purposes include justifying the investment of resources, examining issues of quality and effectiveness, measuring progress toward program goals, establishing a basis for improvement of both program processes and outcomes, and providing a basis for strategic decision making.

Justification of Investment

Extensive monetary and staff resources are necessary to develop high-quality distance learning programs, especially those designed and delivered with high levels of technical, instructional, and student-service support. Although such programs may not in themselves be more expensive than traditional instruction—indeed, when "brick and mortar" costs (for buildings and grounds) and convenience benefits are factored in, distance learning programs may be comparably or less expensive (Bates, 2000; Thompson, 1994; Whalen & Wright, 1999)—they do in most cases represent new costs that ultimately must be justified.

Such is particularly the case when distance programs are "grafted" on to a traditional educational institution where the standard for both format and effectiveness is resident instruction and where competition for resources is almost always fierce. In this environment, evaluative measures that provide return-on-investment information offer a basis for judging the program's productivity or value to the institution in economic terms (Stufflebeam, 1999).

Measuring Progress Toward Program Objectives

Probably the most prevalent motivation for conducting evaluation activities is to gather information about the extent to which program objectives are being met. Demonstrating that objectives have been met can be important in justifying program costs and establishing credibility for distance education within the larger institution or educational system, particularly when these goals are important to or reflect the mission of the larger system.

As Moore (1999) notes, within an educational system the most important of these goals is the achievement of learning objectives. However, other goals, such as maintaining cost-effectiveness or increasing educational access, also are legitimate foci for monitoring and evaluation.

The value of objectives-focused evaluations is dependent on both the clarity of program objectives and the flexibility with which the evaluation is designed and implemented. According to Cyrs (2001), "without the specification of objectives, there are no criteria on which to base an evaluation" (p. 1). Moore (1999) takes the argument even further, stating that "whether or not evaluators can show that the project was effective will ultimately depend on how well the objectives of the project have been stated" (p. 2).

Clearly stated objectives are a necessary but not sufficient criterion for effective evaluation. A too-narrow focus on stated objectives can "lead to terminal information that is of little use in improving a program" (Stufflebeam, 1999, p. 12) or for judging the program's merit or value; it also runs the risk of crediting objectives that in themselves have little merit or value (Stufflebeam, 1999).

These limitations can be overcome by broadening the focus to include an assessment of the correspondence between program objectives and participants' assessed needs, a search for unanticipated side effects and an examination of the program processes as well as its outcomes (Stufflebeam, 1999). To count as evaluation rather than merely monitoring or assessment, there must be an attempt to go beyond the question "Did the program do what it set out to do?" to "Did achieving the program's objectives give value to the stakeholders?"

Measuring "Quality" and/or "Effectiveness"

Measuring "quality" and "effectiveness" is another commonly stated purpose. The term *quality* is generally used to refer to program characteristics and processes (technological infrastructure, student services, etc.), whereas *effectiveness* more usually refers to outcomes (learning outcomes, participant satisfaction, etc.).

It is important to realize that, without referents, the terms *quality* and *effectiveness* are meaningless. Cyrs' comment in the previous section can be rephrased to state that "without the specification of standards, there are no criteria on which to base an evaluation of quality." The appropriate overarching questions for a distance education program are not "Is this a quality program?" and "Is this an effective program?" but rather "Does this program meet accepted and articulated standards of quality?" and "Is the program effective in particular ways in meeting specific goals of stakeholders?"

Until recently, there were few standardized criteria for distance education quality or effectiveness other than those imposed by the continued, usually institution-specific demands for evidence of parity with traditional educational programs. As Duning, Van Kekerix, and

Zaborowski (1993) point out, "Universally accepted measures do not exist. Even where documentation of outcomes can offer a basis from which to develop approaches to quality assurance, this information is routinely dismissed in favor of long-held views about how education is best conducted" (p. 191). Thus, the term *quality distance education program* has been used to refer to programs that replicate as closely as possible the institution-specific features, services, and assumed outcomes of traditional resident programs (Chambers, 1995; Ehrmann, 1997b; O'Shea, Bearman, & Downes, 1996).

In the absence of more appropriate criteria for the evaluation of quality and effectiveness, activities with this purpose become either so general as to provide no useful guidance or so specific as to be limited to "a very small and temporary universe" (Ehrmann, 1997b, p. 1). Happily, a number of groups are working on the development of distance education program standards that cut across contexts and represent best practices in a number of areas. These emerging standards will help to focus and rationalize distance education evaluation, with great benefits for the field as a whole. Specific sets of standards and guidelines are discussed below in "Development of Standards for Distance Education."

Providing a Basis for Improvement

Closely related to tracking progress toward goals and measuring quality and/or effectiveness is a focus on improving programs. The former activities both rest on the implied assumption that any gaps discovered by evaluation activities between programs and desired goals or standards will trigger efforts toward improvement.

Moore (1999) views the component of action as inherent in the concept of evaluation and as following naturally from assessment or "monitoring" activities: "Evaluation . . . is the process of analyzing the feedback data gathered by the monitoring system, reviewing it, and making decisions" (p. 1) that will lead to improved materials, methods, processes, and outcomes. Moore notes further that a good monitoring and evaluation system provides administrators with data on instructor, student, and/or system problems "while there is still enough time to take remedial action" (p. 1).

The quotation above raises the issue of timing and suggests the question of formative versus summative evaluation. According to Cyrs (2001), "Formative evaluation is conducted formally and informally through a course/program to provide corrective feedback to the stakeholders that need the data" (p. 2). Summative evaluation, on the other hand, "takes places at the end of a course or program. These data are used to re-design a course or program. This type of evaluation includes attitudes toward the course/program as well as learning outcomes. In addition, summative evaluation would include administration of the program/course" (p. 2).

Formative and summative evaluation approaches can be combined effectively to provide the basis for program improvement in a number of areas.

Informing Institutional Strategic Planning and Decision Making

As noted in the first section, distance education is no longer on the margins of higher education. Whether promise or threat (or both), it is converging with traditional education in ways that have the potential to be transformative for both. However, as Bers (1999) points out, to date strategic planning for distance education "is taking place as a separate process from more comprehensive or traditional planning" (p. 73).

The changing internal and external factors affecting higher education today suggest that successful and rewarding institutional "mainstreaming" of distance education will result, not from its conformity to the dominant direction of the current mainstream, but rather from both new and established entities together "dredging a new mainstream" (Miller, 1990, p. 211)— that is, creating a more flexible and powerful extension of the knowledge and teaching resources of educational institutions to meet the lifelong learning needs of individuals regardless of time or place.

Watkins and Kaufman (2003, this volume) cite Barker's contention that "when a paradigm shifts, everyone (even those who have been extremely successful in the past) goes back to zeros." In deciding how to most effectively incorporate the power and promise of distance education into long-term plans on either an institutional or societal level, everyone may begin at zero, but those with the right kind of information—actionable data from evaluation and research—will have the tools to move intentionally and confidently into the future.

Evaluation studies that focus on issues of access, equity, learning effectiveness, and organizational impact can provide the basis for assessing the ability of distance education programs to forward an institution's values and vision. When the information from these studies is combined with that gained from long-term research studies that rigorously examine the effect of distance education on all parts of the educational system (learners, faculty, institutions, and society), distance education initiatives can be purposefully integrated into strategic plans to promote the intended goals of the institution.

THE "HOW TO'S" OF EVALUATION: EVALUATION CHOICES AND MODELS

Below we present an overview of selected literature on the process of evaluating distance education programs. We draw on both face-to-face education and distance education resources that provide a foundation for evaluation best practices.

Making Evaluation Choices

An evaluator is faced with a number of choices in planning and implementing an evaluation project. He or she must clarify the stakeholders' information needs, and determine what specifically will be evaluated, choose the most appropriate data collection methods and tools, and decide on a reporting format that gets the right information into the right hands.

Purpose and Focus of the Evaluation

To obtain reliable, valid evaluation information, evaluators must begin with a clear understanding of the purpose and focus of the evaluation. They must begin with questions such as "Who are the stakeholders?" "What do they need to know?" and "How will the data be used?" (Cyrs, 2001). As part of the planning phase, evaluators should gather feedback from stakeholders to clarify the purpose and focus of a particular evaluation activity, which will be based in large part on program and institutional priorities. Probably the most common mistake made by evaluators is to try to answer too many questions with one evaluation activity or to try to answer very general questions. Ehrmann (1997a) suggests that "the most difficult challenge in [thinking] about doing a study is the process of figuring out what to study" (p. 6).

Evaluation Data Collection Methods and Tools

Matching the purpose and focus to the appropriate approach or tools is the evaluator's second challenge. Moore and Kearsley (1996) identify a range of data collection methods, including participant observations, questionnaires, interviews, online monitoring of responses, and advance prototyping or pilot testing. To this list, Cyrs (2001) adds surveys, student personal diaries, learning assessment instruments (tests, essay questions, portfolios, etc.), and product assessment criteria.

Reeves (1995) has developed a wide range of evaluation tools, including an anecdotal record form that collects the "human story," an expert review checklist for gathering feedback on particular aspects of a program, a focus group protocol, an implementation log for collecting information on the actual versus planned use of program features, and a user-interface rating form for assessing the design of an interactive instructional product's interface with the student. His "evaluation matrix" is an integrating tool that helps evaluators assess the advantages of each individual tool listed above for answering particular evaluation questions.

Evaluation Reports

Just as evaluators make choices about the process of evaluation, they also need to make decisions about the final product of the evaluation activity: the evaluation report. *The Program Evaluation Standards* (Joint Committee on Standards for Educational Evaluation, 1994) suggests criteria relating to several aspects of evaluation reporting:

> Report clarity. Evaluation reports should clearly describe the program being evaluated, including context, purposes, procedures, and findings so that essential information is provided and easily understood.
> Report timeliness and dissemination. Significant interim findings should be disseminated to allow timely use.
> Disclosure of findings. The full set of evaluation findings, along with a description of pertinent limitations, should be made accessible to the persons affected by the evaluation and those with expressed legal rights to receive the results.
> Impartial reporting. Reporting procedures should fairly reflect the findings, avoiding distortion caused by personal feelings or biases.

The American Evaluation Association's (1995) "Guiding Principles for Evaluators" further notes that, although "evaluations often will negatively affect the interests of some stakeholders, evaluators should . . . communicate [their] results in a way that clearly respects stakeholders' dignity and self-worth" (p. 7).

Reeves (1995) notes that the long reports written by many evaluators are seldom read. To increase the likelihood that an evaluation report will ultimately have an impact on institutional decision-making, he suggests formatting the report in easy-to-consume "chunks" of information in four sections: (1) an attention-getting headline, (2) a description of the major issues related to the headline, (3) a presentation of data related to the issues, and (4) a bottom-line recommendation or summary of the findings.

Comprehensive Evaluation Models

A number of sources offer useful and comprehensive guides to evaluation. In particular, two resources based on traditional education provide extensive advice that is applicable to distance education as well. These are described in the following section.

Models from Traditional Education

Foundational Models for 21st Century Program Evaluation (Stufflebeam, 1999) builds on decades of evaluation theory and professional practice, including the work of evaluation luminaries such as Tyler, Cronbach, Scriven, Guba, and Lincoln. In the book Stufflebeam reviews 22 alternative evaluation approaches, sorting them into those that are "best to take along" into the 21st century and those that "would best be left behind" (p. 1). The 20 "keepers" are sorted into three broad categories: questions/methods-oriented evaluation approaches, improvement/accountability-oriented evaluation approaches, and social agenda–directed (advocacy) approaches.

To help evaluators choose approaches appropriate to their particular contexts and purposes, Stufflebeam treats the 22 approaches in depth, analyzing each in terms of 10 descriptors: (1) advance organizers, (2) main purposes, (3) sources for the questions asked, (4) representative questions, (5) methods employed, (6) evaluation professionals associated with the type of study, (7) others who have extended the approach, (8) key considerations in choosing the approach, (9) strengths of the approach, and (10) weaknesses of the approach. Numerous other documents and tools related to program evaluation are available on the Web site of the Evaluation Center at Michigan State University (http://www.wmich.edu/evalctr/), which Stufflebeam directs.

The Program Evaluation Standards, developed by the Joint Committee on Standards for Educational Evaluation (1994), offers four categories of standards for program evaluation: utility standards, feasibility standards, propriety standards, and accuracy standards.

Of particular interest is the derivative document "What the Program Evaluation Standards Say About Designing Evaluations," which synthesizes advice from "hundreds of practitioners in education and evaluation" (Joint Committee on Standards for Educational Evaluation, 1994, p. 1) regarding the design of evaluations. This document focuses on a number of key aspects of evaluation design: stakeholder identification, evaluator credibility, information scope and selection, values identification, practical procedures, formal agreements, complete and fair assessments, program documentation, purposes and procedures, information sources, validity of information, reliability of information, analysis of quantitative information, analysis of qualitative information, justifiable conclusions, impartial reporting, and metaevaluation. For each of these areas the authors offer "best practices" suggestions and guidelines keyed to program standards in each of the four areas (i.e., utility, feasibility, propriety, and accuracy). This document and information about other derivative documents in this series are available online at http://www.wmich.edu/evalctr/jc/DesigningEval.htm.

Models Specific to Distance Education

Over the years, a number of experienced distance educators have developed evaluation approaches that focus exclusively on distance education. The work done in this area by Flagg (1990, as cited in Saba, 2000), Duning et al. (1993), Ehrmann (1997b; 1999a; 2001), Bates (2000), and Cyrs (2001) is representative.

Flagg (1990, as cited in Saba, 2000, p. 1) focuses specifically on formative evaluation as a tool for making midcourse corrections. He offers seven steps for planning and implementing a formative evaluation:

(1) Clarify; state the purpose of the evaluation study.
(2) Select and specify recipients of the evaluation information.
(3) List evaluation questions.
(4) Indicate the overall scheme or "paradigm" of the evaluation.
(5) Select data collection strategy and measurement tools.
(6) Identify respondent samples.
(7) Select evaluation setting and procedure.

Saba (2000) suggests that, although administrators should be involved in all seven steps proposed by Flagg, the last five steps are "technical in nature" and would be best carried out by experienced evaluators.

Duning et al. (1993) approach the evaluation of distance education from the perspective of "assessing and maintaining quality" (p. 187). They begin their discussion with a myth and its corresponding reality:

Myth: Quality in telecommunications-based education is a matter of combining traditional instructional standards with assessments of technical accessibility, reliability, and interactivity.
Reality: The potential reach and instructional impact of educational telecommunications systems require measures of quality that speak to values underlying new relationships with the learner. (p. 187)

Thus these authors neatly integrate the concept of needing new and well-articulated standards in distance education with the concept of value (and values) inherent in any evaluation activity.

Duning et al. (1993) suggest that distance learning systems can and should be evaluated at three levels: the functional, the managerial, and the instructional or ethical. They identify the functional level with the technical-design activities involving equipment requirements or specifications as well as the technical support staff. The managerial level focuses on the extent of success in fostering and managing necessary relationships inside and outside the organizational structure of the program. These relationships may be with other organizational units or with faculty, learners, or others crucial to the implementation of the program. Finally, the ethical level focuses on program outcomes. The ethical dimension of this level is reflected in the choices that are made in deciding what to measure and what these decisions show about the values of the institution. As the authors put it, "We become what we measure" (p. 197).

Operationalizing distance education program evaluation at the functional, managerial, and ethical levels "necessitates development of credible standards of quality grounded in benchmarks" for learner satisfaction and achievement, instruction, student support services, and integration of institutional values. Throughout *Reaching Learners Through Telecommunications*, Duning et al. (1993) offer clear guidance on how to establish context-appropriate benchmarks for quality that can serve as the basis for rigorous, value-based program evaluations.

Ehrmann (1997a, 1997b, 1999a, 2001) has contributed extensively to the literature on distance education evaluation. As the director of the Flashlight Project, a program of the American Association of Higher Education's Teaching, Learning, and Technology (TLT) Group, he has spearheaded the investigation of evaluation issues from a variety of perspectives and has taken a leading role in developing a comprehensive "Tool Kit" to guide evaluators of distance education programs.

Ehrmann (1999a) builds his evaluation approach around the idea that distance education has and enables general goals that can be isolated and closely studied:

Enabling important new content to be taught.
Changing who can learn.
Improving teaching and learning activities.
Lowering or controlling the costs of teaching and learning activities.

Using the metaphor of a flashlight, which illumines a small area brightly, he suggests that evaluators begin with a general, usually "almost incoherent" question of interest in one of these areas and then transform it from a formless "blob" to a focused evaluative "triad." Ehrmann uses the term *triad* to refer to a focused question or set of questions crafted to examine (1) a particular technology or method (e-mail, paced instruction, etc.) in relation to (2) a particular practice enabled by that technology or method and (3) a desired program outcome.

The next step in the process is to ask questions in five related areas:

(1) The technology per se.
(2) The use of the technology for the activity.
(3) The activity per se.
(4) Whether and how the activity is contributing to the desired outcome.
(5) The outcome per se.

The Flashlight Project has developed a number of services and tools to help evaluators implement their own focused evaluation studies. The 500-item Current Student Inventory, for example, is a set of questions that relates areas 1, 3, and 5 to a number of teaching and learning issues:

Active learning.
Collaborative learning.
Using time productively.
Rich and rapid feedback.
Engagement in learning.
Faculty-student interaction.
High expectations for all students regardless of learning style.
Cognitive and creative outcomes.
Accessibility.
Positive addiction to technology.
Prerequisites for using technology.
Time on task.
Respect for diversity.
Application to the real world.

An overview of this and other Flashlight resources is available at http://www.tltgroup.org/resources/index.html.

Bates (2000) begins with the assumption that past approaches to and questions about distance education evaluation are no longer relevant to the current context. From his perspective, a continued focus on the relative effectiveness of distance delivery compared to face-to-face instruction is "frankly a waste of time" (p. 198). Like Duning et al. (1993) and Ehrmann (1997b), he challenges evaluators to focus not on similarities to traditional education but rather on differences, particularly on different or new learning outcomes enabled by technology-mediated distance education.

Bates' ACTIONS model focuses attention on "a wider range of factors than the ability of technology to replicate classroom teaching" (p. 200). The acronym ACTION represents seven factors to be considered in evaluating the effectiveness of different instructional technologies:

Access and flexibility.
Costs.
Teaching and learning.
Interactivity and user-friendliness.
Organizational issues.
Novelty.
Speed.

For each of these factors, Bates suggests appropriate evaluation and research questions.

In addition to his focus on the instructional effectiveness of technologies, Bates examines evaluation issues relating to software applications, learner impact (beyond learning outcomes), academic technology organization and management, and cost-benefit analyses. He suggests the need for carefully designed evaluation studies focused on answering questions in all of these categories and identifies important areas for study within each.

Cyrs (2001) offers evaluators guidelines for developing and implementing distance learning program and course evaluations for audio, video, data, and print programs. He focuses on 10 areas to guide evaluation of all forms of distance education:

The purpose of the evaluation.
The question to be answered.

Formative and summative evaluation.
Types of evaluation instruments.
Course design.
Course administration.
Learning outcomes.
Delivery technology(ies).
Presentation skills of instructor.
Learning environment.
Sample evaluation criteria and rating scales.
Use of different teaching (communication) strategies.

Within each area, Cyrs suggests relevant questions useful for focusing the evaluation on specific elements of the course or program. Cyrs also provides additional evaluation criteria relevant to courses and programs delivered via the World Wide Web. Specific considerations include class size, the balance between synchronous and asynchronous activities, instructor response time, ease of site navigation, and opportunities to interact with peers and the instructor.

Focusing on Costs

The models described above provide the basis for a comprehensive approach to evaluating the multifaceted activity that we call distance education. Some authors, however, have focused more narrowly on one specific element of distance education, cost, and have proposed models for evaluating the costs related to distance education.

The cost structures of distance education are more complex than those of face-to-face instruction because they are derived from a wider range and combination of factors. Beyond simple analyses of monetary cost, other considerations such as learning outcomes and their expected value for learners, employers, and other stakeholders need to be taken into account (Moore & Thompson, 1997; Rowntree, 1992). Because of this complexity, many distance education evaluators have adopted a cost-benefit approach when evaluating the costs of distance education programs.

Distance education costs are driven by fixed and variable costs, the technologies used, the production and delivery systems employed, the number of students served, and the length of time the teaching materials can be used (Bates, 1995). Benefits may be categorized into three groups: benefits that are performance driven (e.g., learning outcomes), those that are value driven (e.g., access, flexibility, or ease of use), and societal or value-added benefits (e.g., decreased unemployment and potential for new markets) (Bates, 1999; Chute, Thompson, & Hancock, 1999).

A clear understanding of costs relative to benefits requires an understanding of the relative importance of each cost variable for decision-making. Evaluators will ask a number of questions, including "Will technology-based course materials be used for long enough to justify the costs of production, with sufficient numbers of students to reduce costs?" and "Will the cost of achieving superior learning gains negatively impact students' access?" Answers to questions such as these are likely to reveal wide variability in the strategies used by organizations to achieve their objectives. For example, an organization with the objective of collaborative learning in a live environment may integrate technologies that allow for socializing, such as interactive satellite, rather than limit itself to less expensive asynchronous technologies or media, such as e-mail.

Several studies from the literature provide cost-benefit approaches to evaluating distance education costs. Dillon, Gibson, and Confessore (1991) offer a systems-modeling approach based on cost categories that can be generalized across systems. By highlighting the relationship between categories, the model allows a cost comparison of five alternative technology systems and an analysis of the best match between the desired level of interaction, the available budget, and a specific delivery system.

At Washington State University, administrators and faculty evaluated the cost per student per week in creating course materials using different technology approaches. They found that, though the Web-based model was the most expensive in terms of total costs, it was much less expensive than an alternative modular approach in terms of cost per student; in addition it had lower developmental costs and resulted in better learning gains (Ehrmann, 1999b).

The University of British Columbia is conducting an ongoing project that uses several models to evaluate the costs and benefits of telelearning (Bates, 1999). These models are based on cost per student study-hour, which, according to Daniel (1996), best captures the volume of activity and number of students and provides the best comparison between costs of different technologies.

Inglis (1999) questions the emphasis on the cost-benefit approach in a distance education environment that is now so heavily influenced by the World Wide Web, with its associated high development costs. Like Rumble (1997), he argues that an activity-based costing approach in which costs of discrete educational activities are evaluated separately allows a focus on those variables that have the greatest impact on costs.

The *Flashlight™ Cost Analysis Handbook*, developed by the TLT Group of the American Association of Higher Education, applies activity-based costing to analyze how educational uses of technology consume a variety of resources, including time, money, and space. The intent of the model is to provide a basis on which institutions can "improve the way current activities use resources, to forecast resource use by proposed new activities, or to report on total costs (Ehrmann, 2001).

An alternative to the two approaches described above is a model developed by Jewett (1999) as part of the Technology Costing Methodology (TCM) project conducted jointly by the Western Interstate Commission for Higher Education and the National Center for Higher Education Management Systems. Jewett's cost simulation model, BRIDGE, compares the costs of two approaches to institutional expansion, one based on adding more face-to-face courses and the other on adding a mix of face-to-face and distance education offerings:

> The BRIDGE model compares the projected operating and capital costs of two campuses over a period of years. Both campuses are assumed to begin with the same initial FTE, academic programs, and physical facilities. Both grow by the same amount of FTE over a given period of years. One campus accommodates all of its FTE in classroom-type (lecture/lab) instruction. The other campus accommodates its FTE in a changing mix of classroom, live broadcast, and asynchronous network type courses. The values for initial (beginning) FTE, ending FTE, and the length of the growth or simulation period are specified by the user. The final mix of FTE for the mediated campus among classroom, live broadcast, and asynchronous courses is also specified by the user.

Interested readers can download a copy of BRIDGE from http://www.calstate.edu/special_projects/mediated_instr/Bridge/index.html.

The ultimate goal of the TCM project is to develop an authoritative methodology and related procedures for calculating instructional technology costs both within an institution (to guide resource decisions) and across institutions (to legitimately compare different instructional or technological approaches). The resulting *Technology Costing Methodology Handbook* will benefit legislatures, state governing boards, state coordinating boards, and federal agencies in strategic planning and decision making. Updates on the progress of the TCM project are available at http://www.wiche.edu/telecom/projects/tcm/.

CURRENT AND FUTURE TRENDS IN DISTANCE
EDUCATION EVALUATION

Development of Standards for Distance Education

> How can a teaching/learning process that deviates so markedly from what has been practiced for hundreds of years embody quality education? (Institute for Higher Education Policy, 1999, p. 7)

Convincingly answering the question above has been the goal of distance education evaluators for decades. It has also been the source of considerable frustration. Throughout this chapter we have cited authors frustrated by the difficulty of conducting meaningful evaluations in the absence of appropriate and clearly articulated standards for distance education programs and processes. This situation has been exacerbated by the fact that distance education has generally been compared with and asked to "measure up" to resident instruction, itself an activity "too easily satisfied with surrogate measures of its performance" (Pew Higher Education Research Report, as cited in Duning et al., 1993, p. 188).

Over the past five years, several organizations have attempted to develop standards for distance education practice that could guide the development, delivery, and evaluation of distance education programs and processes in a rapidly changing educational environment. Examples include the following:

Distance Learning Evaluation Guide (American Council on Education, 1996)
An Emerging Set of Guiding Principles and Practices for the Design and Development of Distance Education (Pennsylvania State University, 1998)
ADEC Guiding Principles for Distance Teaching and Learning (American Distance Education Consortium, 2000)
Principles of Good Practice for Electronically Offered Academic Degree and Certificate Programs (Western Cooperative for Educational Telecommunications, 1999)
Principles of Good Practice: The Foundation for Quality of the Electronic Campus of the Southern Regional Education Board (Southern Regional Education Board, 2001)
Quality on the Line: Benchmarks for Success in Internet-Based Distance Education (Institute for Higher Education Policy, 2000)
Best practices for Electronically Offered Degree and Certificate Programs (Regional Accrediting Commissions, 2000)

These guidelines are generally consistent in their focus on issues related to course design, learning outcomes, technology, learner and faculty support, institutional commitment, and assessment and evaluation. However, the question remains as to the ultimate impact such documents will have on distance education practice and evaluation. Is there any evidence of current influence or future impact?

Moving Standards into Practice

The research report *Quality on the Line* (Institute for Higher Education Policy, 2000), which contains published benchmarks or quality indicators developed by a variety of organizations involved in distance education, asks among other questions, "Are the benchmarks viewed as essential to quality on-line education by faculty, students, and administrators?" and "To what extent are the benchmarks being implemented in educational institutions?"

The researchers examined these questions using a case-study approach involving six institutions. Benchmarks were grouped into seven categories:

(1) Institutional support.
(2) Course development.
(3) Teaching/learning process.
(4) Course structure.
(5) Student support.
(6) Faculty support.
(7) Evaluation and assessment.

The report noted that "quality benchmarks were considered with great care and embraced by every institution that participated" (p. 13). However, of the 45 benchmarks originally identified from the literature, 13 were omitted from the subsequent list of recommended benchmarks because of the low importance ratings given them by the study respondents. The study also identified several benchmarks that generally were rated as very important but scored relatively low in terms of actual implementation:

A documented institutional technology plan.
Faculty incentives and institutional rewards.
Specific time expectations for students and faculty.
Technical assistance and training for students.
Technical assistance and training for faculty.
Evaluation and assessment.

The findings of *Quality on the Line* indicate that distance educators and higher education institutions are taking guidelines and standards for high-quality distance education seriously and are in most cases incorporating them into their distance education programs. The few disparities between reported importance and level of implementation are themselves useful in identifying areas for future examination and improvement.

Standards and Institutional Accreditation

Compelling evidence that emerging standards for distance education are having an impact on evaluation can be found in the fact that the guidelines published in the *Principles of Good Practice for Electronically Offered Academic Degree and Certificate Programs* (Western Cooperative for Educational Telecommunications, 1999) have been incorporated into the evaluation guide developed for use by all eight regional accrediting agencies for higher education institutions. This action was intended "to address concerns that . . . accreditation standards are not relevant to . . . distributed learning environments, especially when . . . experienced by off-campus students" (Regional Accrediting Commissions, 2000, p. 1).

Perhaps of even greater importance in terms of both current practice and future impact is the following statement, which reflects a new awareness of the changing place of distance education in American higher education: "Electronically offered programs both support and extend the roles of educational institutions. Increasingly they are integral to academic organizations, with growing implications for institutional infrastructure" (Regional Accrediting Commissions, 2000, p. 2). This recognition of electronically mediated education and its articulation in a document that will guide distance education program evaluation throughout American higher education will perforce have a profound impact on distance education practice and evaluation in the years to come.

CONCLUSION

The convergence of distance education and traditional education is at once the educational community's most exciting possibility and its biggest challenge. The excitement comes from the opportunity to extend knowledge and teaching resources to new populations of learners regardless of time or place while at the same time revitalizing and enhancing those resources through the new pedagogical approaches enabled by powerful communications and data technologies. The challenge comes in melding an innovative, rapidly changing area of practice with complex and firmly established structures built on "traditional institutional hallmarks" of quality (Regional Accrediting Commissions, 2000, p. 2).

This challenge is reflected clearly in the area of evaluation. In the quotation we cited earlier in this chapter—"We become what we measure"—Duning et al. (1993) concisely point to one of the most important questions facing the educational community today: "What do we want to become?" Answering this question will be facilitated by a careful and creative application of the concepts of integration and balance to our evaluation activities.

Ewell (1998) introduces the concept of integration in his discussion of the refocusing that needs to occur in relation to program evaluation. Most evaluations today are conducted in order to comprehensively examine all aspects of a program, as in regional institutional evaluations, or to examine one or more elements in depth, as in most of the formative or summative evaluations conducted by programs themselves. What is missing, Ewell notes, is "attention to how disparate aspects of the institution or program actually fit together," a focus on the relationships among "various functions in light of their intended and actual contributions" toward intended goals (p. 4). Such a focus is important not only at the institutional level but at the national and perhaps international levels as well: Evaluations "of single institutions operating in isolation from one another become increasingly problematic" as learning resources and processes become "de-institutionalized" (p. 5).

Readers of Moore and Kearsley (1996) will recognize in these comments their idea of a systems view of the educational enterprise. However, the educational community, both within single institutions and as a whole, has yet to envision the "new mainstream," the transformed system that will result from the convergence of two previously disparate forms of education.

Decisions regarding the evaluation of distance education programs—decisions that reflect the values held by institutions and societies—can play an important part in shaping this system. The coming transformation will occur more rapidly than some are comfortable with and too slowly for others; it is in the transition process that the concept of balance becomes a key to eventual success. Balancing stakeholder priorities, balancing risks and returns, and balancing innovation and tradition will need to be done with judgement, dedication, and good will if we are to realize the promise of an educational enterprise that seamlessly integrates the best of distance and traditional education.

REFERENCES

American Council on Education. (1996). *Distance learning evaluation guide*. Washington, DC: Author.

American Distance Education Consortium. (2000). *ADEC guiding principles for distance teaching and learning*. Available: http://www.adec.edu/admin/papers/distance-teaching_principles.html

American Evaluation Association. (1995). Guiding principles for evaluators. *New Directions for Evaluation, 66,* 19–26. Available: http://www.eval.org/EvaluationDocuments/qeaprin6.html

Bates, A. W. (1995). *Technology, open learning and distance education*. London: Routledge.

Bates, A. W. (1999). *Developing and applying a cost-benefit model for assessing telelearning.* (NCE-Telelearning Project No. 2.3). Available: http://research.cstudies.ubc.ca

Bates, A. W. (2000). *Managing technological change. Strategies for college and university leaders.* San Francisco: Jossey-Bass.

Bers, T. (1999, Fall). The impact of distance education on institutional research. *New Directions for Institutional Research, 103*, 61–78.

Chambers, E. (1995). Course evaluation and academic quality. In F. Lockwood (Ed.), *Open and distance learning today* (pp. 342–343). London: Routledge.

Chute, A., Thompson, M., & Hancock, B. W. (1999). *The McGraw-Hill handbook of distance learning: An implementation guide for trainers and human resources professionals.* New York: McGraw-Hill.

Council for Regional Accrediting Commissions with assistance from The Western Cooperative for Educational Telecommunications (2000). Best practices for electronically offered degree and certificate programs. Boulder, CO: Author. Available: http://www.wiche.edu/telecom/Article.htm

Cyrs, T. E. (2001). *Evaluating distance learning programs and courses.* Available: http://www.zianet.com/edacyrs/evaluate_dl.htm

Daniel, J. (1996). *Mega-universities and knowledge media: Technology strategies for higher education.* London: Kogan Page.

Dillon, C. L., Gibson, C. C., & Confessore, S. (1991). The economics of interaction in technology-based distance education. In *Proceedings of the Seventh Annual Conference on Distance Teaching and Learning* (pp. 40–45). Madison, WI: University of Wisconsin-Madison.

Duning, B. S., Van Kekerix, M. J., & Zaborowski, L. M. (1993). *Reaching learners through telecommunications.* San Francisco: Jossey-Bass.

Eaton, J. S. (2000). *Core academic values, quality, and regional accreditation: The challenge of distance learning.* Washington, DC: Council for Higher Education Accreditation.

Ehrmann, S. C. (1997a). *The Flashlight Program: Spotting an elephant in the dark.* TLT Group, One Dupont Circle, NW, Suite 360, Washington, DC, 20036-1110 Flashlight Program. Available: http://www.tltgroup.org/programs/elephant.html

Ehrmann, S. C. (1997b). *What does research tell us about technology and higher learning?* TLT Group, One Dupont Circle, NW, Suite 360, Washington, DC, 20036-1110 Flashlight Program. Available: http://www.learner.org/edtech/rscheval/rightquestion.html

Ehrmann, S. C. (1999a). *Studying teaching, learning and technology: A tool kit from the Flashlight Program.* TLT Group, One Dupont Circle, NW, Suite 360, Washington, DC, 20036-1110 Flashlight Program. Available: http://www.tltgroup.org/resources/fstudtool.html

Ehrmann, S. C. (1999b). *What do we need to learn about technology use in education?* TLT Group, One Dupont Circle, NW, Suite 360, Washington, DC, 20036-1110 Flashlight Program. Available: http://www.tltgroup.org/resources/fquestions.html

Ehrmann, S. C. (2001). *Evaluation and assessment: Articles and related url's.* TLT Group, One Dupont Circle, NW, Suite 360, Washington, DC, 20036-1110 Flashlight Program. Available: http://www.tltgroup.org/resources/farticles.html

Ewell, P. T. (1998). *Examining a brave new world: How accreditation might be different.* Washington, DC: Council for Higher Education Accreditation. Available: http://www.chea.org/Events/Usefulness/98May/98_05Ewell.html

Inglis, A. (1999). Is online delivery less costly than print and is it meaningful to ask? *Distance Education, 20*(2), pp. 220–239.

Institute for Higher Education Policy. (1999). *What's the difference? A review of contemporary research on the effectiveness of distance learning in higher education.* Washington, DC: Author.

Institute for Higher Education Policy. (2000). *Quality on the line. Benchmarks for success in Internet-Based Distance Education.* Washington, DC: Author.

Jewett, F. (1999). *Evaluating the benefits and costs of mediated instruction and distributed learning: Cost simulation model (BRIDGE).* Available: http://www.calstate.edu/special_projects/mediated_instr/Bridge/index.html

Joint Committee on Standards for Educational Evaluation. (1994). *The program evaluation standards: How to assess evaluations of educational programs.* Thousand Oaks, CA: Sage.

Joint Committee on Standards for Educational Evaluation. (1994). What the program evaluation standards say about designing evaluations. Thousand Oaks, CA: Sage. Available: http://www.wmich.edu/evalctr/jc/DesigningEval.htm

Lockee, B. B., Burton, J. K., & Cross, L. H. (1999). No comparison: Distance education finds a new use for "no significant difference." *Educational Technology, Research and Development, 47*(3), 33–44.

McIsaac, S. M., & Gunawardena, C. (1996). Distance education. In D. H. Jonassen (Ed.), *Handbook of research for educational communications and technology* (pp. 403–437). New York: Simon & Schuster Macmillan.

Miller, G. E. (1990). Distance education and the curriculum: Dredging a new mainstream. In M. G. Moore (Ed.), *Contemporary issues in American distance education* (pp. 211–220). Oxford: Pergamon Press.

Moe, M. T., & Blodget, H. (2000). *The knowledge web: Part 1. People power: Fuel for the new economy.* New York: Merrill Lynch.

Moore, M. G. (1999). Monitoring and evaluation. *The American Journal of Distance Education, 13*(2), 1–5.

Moore, M. G., & Kearsley, G. (1996). *Distance education. A systems view.* Belmont, CA: Wadsworth.

Moore, M. G., & Thompson, M. M. (1997). *The effects of distance learning* (Rev. ed.). University Park, PA: Pennsylvania State University, American Center for the Study of Distance Education.

O'Shea, T., Bearman, S., & Downes, A. (1996). Quality assurance and assessment in distance learning. In R. Mills & A. Tait (Eds.), *Supporting the learner in open and distance learning* (pp. 193–205). London: Pitman.

Pennsylvania State University. (1998). *An emerging set of guiding principles and practices for the design and development of distance education.* University Park, PA: Author.

Reeves, T. (1995). *Evaluation tools.* Available: http://mime.marc.gatech.edu/MM_Tools/evaluation.html

Rowntree, D. (1992). *Exploring open and distance learning.* London: Kogan Page.

Rumble, G. G. (1997). *The costs and economics of open and distance learning.* London: Kogan Page.

Russell, T. L. (1999). *The no significant difference phenomenon as reported in 355 research reports, summaries and papers: A comparative research annotated bibliography on technology for distance education.* Raleigh, NC: North Carolina State University, Office of Instructional Telecommunications.

Saba, F. (2000). Evaluating distance education programs. *Distance Education Report, 4*(4), 1.

Southern Regional Education Board. (2001). *Principles of good practice. The foundation for quality of the Electronic Campus of the Southern Regional Education Board.* Available: http://www.sreb.org/student/srecinfo/publications/principles.asp

Stufflebeam, D. L. (1999). *Foundational models for 21st century program evaluation.* Kalamazoo, MI: Western Michigan University, The Evaluation Center.

Thompson, M. (1994). Speaking personally with Alan Chute. *The American Journal of Distance Education, 8*(1), 72–77.

Thorpe, M. (1996). Issues of evaluation. In R. Mills & A. Tait (Eds.), *Supporting the learner in open and distance learning* (pp. 222–234). London: Pitman.

Watkins, R., & Kaufman, R. (2003). Strategic Planning in Distance Education. In J. Moore & W. G. Anderson (Eds.), *Handbook of Distance Education* (pp. 503–514). Mahwah, NJ. Lawrence Erlbaum Associates.

Western Cooperative for Educational Telecommunications. (1999). *Principles of good practice for electronically offered academic degree and certificate programs.* (Balancing Quality and Access project). Available: http://www.wiche.edu/Telecom/projects/balancing/principles.htm

Whalen, T., & Wright, D. (1999). Methodology for cost-benefit analysis of Web-based tele-learning: Case study of the Bell Online Institute. *The American Journal of Distance Education, 13*(1), 22–44.

V

Different Audiences in
Distance Education

39

The Involvement of Corporations in Distance Education

Diana G. Oblinger
North Carolina State University
dgobling@unity.ncsu.edu

Sean C. Rush
IBM Corporation
scrush@us.ibm.com

CORPORATIONS AS CONSUMERS OF DISTANCE EDUCATION

Corporate Universities

Corporations are involved with distance education for a variety of reasons and in multiple ways. Many corporations operate distance education organizations for their own employees in order to provide up-to-date information and ensure that they maintain the competitive advantage and productivity associated with skilled workers. Sometimes corporations provide education for customers. Well-informed customers make better product selections and tend to be more satisfied. Corporations are also involved in distance education as a business per se. This involvement ranges from providing venture capital to offering products or services that allow others to engage in distance education.

Today's corporate universities function as strategic umbrellas for meeting the total educational requirements of companies; they provide education, training, and human resource development, often tailored to specific business needs. Corporate universities can be found in all sectors—finance, information technology, manufacturing, professional services, and so on. Some corporate universities are entirely based within a single company whereas others may involve partnerships or outsourcing arrangements. Beyond providing training and education, corporate universities are ideal places for team building and for developing corporate culture (Anderson, 2001).

IBM provides an example of the variety of activities that could fall under a corporate university umbrella.

The IBM Global Campus offers almost 1,000 distributed learning offerings, including Web-based courses.

IBM Global Services Institute provides distributed learning training to new employees in the services business segment.
Distributed learning programs, such as Sales Compass for IBM sales professionals, provide just-in-time, just-enough training on products, solutions, and industries.
GoingGlobal provides traveling IBM employees with helpful cultural information for doing business in any one of 57 different countries.
Web sites such as Video JukeBox offer audio and video presentations for both live and playback learning events. (*IBM Global Learning*, 1999)

In many cases, corporate universities award joint degrees with traditional universities, but they are not themselves accredited. For example, the Bank of Montreal offers an MBA degree through a joint program with Dalhousie University. Bell Atlantic Learning Center also offers joint degrees with a consortium of 23 universities in New England (Morrison, 2000).

Worries about how corporate universities and e-learning would fare in a time of economic downturn have proven to be unfounded. A recent survey indicated that 54% of corporate training managers and executives feel the sluggish economy will have no affect on e-learning program budgets (EdNET Week Headlines, 2001). In fact, in difficult economic situations, the rationale for e-learning is more compelling than ever, and e-learning is projected to grow rapidly. According to the American Society for Training and Development (ASTD), the average U.S. company is training more of its employees than ever before, and the fastest growing area of corporate training by far is e-learning (e-Learning, n.d.).

Another source of stability for corporate universities during cost-containment cycles derives from their source of funds. Over the last few years, a number of corporate universities have migrated from being cost-centers to revenue producers. Corporate University Xchange estimates that 25% of corporate universities receive funding from outside the organization (e.g., external sales). This percentage is expected to increase to 43% by 2003. Most indicate that the funds will be derived from marketing courses to customers and/or suppliers as well as to state and/or federal government agencies (Corporate University Xchange, 2001).

Motorola University, perhaps the best-known corporate university, offers a series of solutions to those outside the company. Working adults can take courses from Motorola University at any of its sites in 13 countries. In addition to courses and conferences, the university provides consulting services aimed at helping others plan and implement a corporate university (e.g., advice on operations and outsourcing) or improve the performance of an existing corporate university (Motorola Corporate University, 2001). PeopleSoft provides another example. PeopleSoft combined its internal university with its education services unit; now PeopleSoft University markets courses to the company's clients. In fact, the company has set up more than 200 classrooms worldwide, with a computer for every student and the possibility of individual mentoring from the company's tutors (Authers, 2001).

Although corporate universities may seem to compete with traditional higher education institutions, few if any companies are in contest with academia. Corporate universities are not seeking to be as rigorous as traditional universities or provide as broad an education (Morrison, 2000). Rather, 62% of corporate universities currently have alliances with four-year colleges—a number that is expected to rise. Fifty percent plan to offer degrees in business/management, engineering/technical, computer sciences, or finance/accounting in partnership with a college or university. Over 70% of the corporate universities surveyed indicated they would grant continuing education credits in similar job families (Corporate University Xchange, 2001). Rather than traditional subjects, corporate universities tend to focus on fostering managerial competence, providing task-oriented education, and instilling the corporate culture. For example, the Borders Group has installed a Click2Coach training system to help train employees on how to handle calls that come through the Border Call Centers. The Web-based system can play back recorded calls while a screen-capture feature tracks rep access moves online (Swanson, 2001). Eighty-two percent of corporate universities are used to acculturate their own employees (Twigg, 2000).

Corporate universities are not restricted to the United States. Although Europe has fewer corporate universities (around 100, compared with 2,000 in the United States), many European firms have established training centers that are the equivalent of a corporate university. ABB, the Swedish-Swiss manufacturing group, and ABN Amro, the Anglo-Dutch banking group, have both set up "academies." BAE Systems, the British aerospace group, and Suez, the French utilities company, call their learning centers "universities." Germany has seen the emergence of corporate universities in the last decade, founded by firms such as Bertelsmann, DaimlerChrysler, Deutsche Bank, and Lufthansa. Whereas some are run as internal business units, others are operated as subsidiaries and profit centers (Andresen & Irmer, 1999).

Some European firms are establishing more innovative structures than are typical of U.S. corporate universities. Union Fenosa is a Spanish utility and telecom conglomerate that employs 16,000 people on five continents. Last year it invested 21 million Euros in a corporate university in partnership with the Spanish government and Iese, a Barcelona-based business school. The university will educate internal staff and customers. So far, 35,000 customers in 54 customer companies are using its management module (Cribbs, 2001).

Multinational corporations face the challenge of training or educating workers in many countries. Increasingly, these firms are turning to e-learning. An example is McDonald's, which has 28,000 restaurants in 120 countries. McDonald's trains 1.5 million employees worldwide. In fact, it trains so many people that it has surpassed the U.S. Army as the nation's largest training organization. Hamburger University trains 5,800 students each year and develops additional training for employees worldwide. Courses are taught in 23 languages. Although it has used classroom training and CD-ROMs, McDonald's plans to roll out a major e-learning initiative over the next few years. Using e-learning, the company hopes to customize training to every culture in which it operates. It estimates that e-learning will reduce training time by 40% to 60% and that just-in-time learning will double employee retention rates for the material. In addition, the company plans to implement a "learning content management" system that will enable it to register, document, and train students automatically; monitor performance through specialized reports; and control and update the content as necessary (Gotschall, 2001).

Customer Education

Corporations use e-learning for more than training their own employees. In fact, some of the most valuable training that a company pays for may be directed, not toward its employees, but toward its customers. Increasingly, corporations are using e-learning to educate external parties central to a company's success, such as customers, suppliers, and partners. For example, instead of an instruction manual explaining how to operate an item, customers may be provided e-learning access so they can learn online. Not only can this type of customer support be more effective and efficient, but the company can collect data about its customers this way.

The Internet allows corporations to disseminate information quickly and cost-effectively, thus ensuring that customers, suppliers, and partners will be equipped with the most up-to-date information. Customers will be more informed about products and services, enabling them to make more educated (and potentially an increased number of) purchasing decisions. Suppliers will be equipped with a better understanding of their clients' needs, allowing for better service. Partners will gain additional insight into their affiliates, enabling them to work with them more efficiently and effectively (Moe, 2000, pp. 234–235). On average, 10% of a corporate university's curriculum is targeted at external clients such as customers and suppliers (*Customer Education Research Consortium*, Customer n.d.).

A relatively recent change is for companies to use education to generate revenue for the corporate university while simultaneously reinforcing the company brand. In what some term eduCommerce, companies such as IBM are using online educational offerings as a strategic opportunity to strengthen customer relationships and acquire new customers (*Customer Education Research Consortium*, n.d.). In fact, a growing number of corporate universities are operating as profit centers, providing customized training programs to outsiders for a fee. For the most part, corporate university courses offered to customers and suppliers focus on technical areas such as software coding, semiconductors, product repair, and total quality management (*Customer Education Research Consortium*, n.d.).

GartnerGroup predicts that by 2003, 40% of e-learning activities will be aimed at customers (Aldrich, 2000). Customers are more likely to make a purchase (especially a large or complex one) when they are more informed about the product or service. And customers may be more willing to spend time to take a course if it is paid for by someone else. A number of companies offering free online education, like Dell Computer, 3Com, and Charles Schwab, are betting that customers will be. Each company offers extensive learning opportunities through its Web sites in an attempt to make customers more comfortable with their purchases.

Even those courses that are not directly aimed at selling a product or service benefit the company by strengthening brand names and creating goodwill among clients (or potential clients). As products and services grow increasingly complicated, e-learning will become a larger component of developing brands and maintaining customer relationships (Ruttenbur, Spickler, & Lurie, 2000, p. 72).

MOTIVATIONS FOR DISTANCE EDUCATION

Competitiveness

The major rationale for business and industry to be involved in education, whether on-site or at a distance, is competitive advantage. The quality and skill of the workforce is a key factor in a company's marketplace advantage ("National Commissions," 2000). In an economy with 4.0% unemployment, an underdegreed adult population, and a huge percentage of the new jobs created requiring higher skills (85% by 2005), corporate learning has never been more important.

Further, as human capital becomes the chief source of economic value, education and training will become lifelong endeavors for the vast majority of workers. It is currently estimated that on average 50% of an employee's skills become outdated within 3 to 5 years. Seventy percent of Fortune 100 companies cite the lack of skilled workers as their top barrier to sustained growth. Speed and responsiveness are important as well. When time to competency is minimized, the organization's competitiveness is improved. As a result, employers increasingly view training and lifelong learning as important to maintaining and enhancing business success ("National Commissions," 2000).

Mergers are undertaken to enhance competitiveness, yet melding different corporate cultures, procedures, and systems is difficult at best. Many have used a corporate university to inculcate a common culture and vision throughout the organization. Another factor driving the growth of corporate universities is the shortened life cycle for products and services. Corporate universities, such as Dell University, are responsible for new product orientation, among other things (DeVeaux, 2001).

Productivity

Motorola calculates that every $1 it spends on corporate learning translates into $30 in productivity gains within 3 years (Moe, 2000, p. 227). General Motors (GM) provides another example. GM sponsors a technical education program that delivers distance degrees to employees. The program, begun in 1984, delivers company-sponsored degrees from the bachelor's through the doctorate from universities such as Carnegie Mellon and Purdue. The company reports that the program saved it $46.2 million by increasing the bottom line through educational efforts ("General Motors," 2001).

Similar sentiments are widespread. A recent survey of corporate training executives found the following:

> One-third of those surveyed said a comprehensive learning program has helped their organization to improve the bottom line, create organizational efficiencies, and move faster to market with new products.
> Nearly 50% said their corporate learning program will have an increased impact on their organization's ability to serve customers within the next 3 years.
> More than 40% think an enterprise-wide learning program has been an important factor in recruiting and retaining quality employees; 58% believe the impact will be even stronger in the next 3 years.
> Eighty-four percent said senior-level management has become more committed to e-learning programs in the last 12 months ("More Than Half," 2001).

Recruitment and Retention

Corporation-sponsored education helps businesses attract and retain employees. Over 50% of companies that are publicly traded mention in their annual reports that they invest in education and training as a way to attract and retain employees ("More Than Half," 2001). In an economy where unemployment is at an all-time low and human capital has unprecedented importance, retaining good employees is critical.

Recruitment and retention are global issues. FedEx Europe established FedEx Quality University, a global learning system with a virtual campus, to retain employees. More than 140,000 worldwide employees have access to the content. When FedEx employees cannot find a suitable course in the Quality University, they can take a course from an outside source. Xerox has adopted a similar strategy. To meet the needs of the 19,000 European workers (from 35 countries, speaking 15 languages), Xerox established a virtual university—the Virtual Learning Environment. The impetus came from the company's need to develop and retain good employees (*Learning European Style*, 2001).

The returns from improving employee retention are tangible. Industry sources suggest that the cost of a lost employee is 1 × annual wages plus benefits. Consider a hypothetical company that has 1,000 employees and is experiencing 30% turnover. Using $30,000 for the average wage and benefits package, a 50% improvement in retention could add $4.5 million to the bottom line (Moe, 2000, p. 301).

Cost Savings

Particularly for large companies, there may be significant cost savings where wide-scale online education can replace face-to-face instruction:

> Three years ago it cost Novell $1,800 for a 4-day certification course that now costs $700 to $900 over the Web. (This comparison does not capture the costs of the employee's travel, lodging, or time away from the job.)
> Hewlett Packard saved $150,000 in outside testing costs alone through online learning.
> The FBI's National Security Division saved $2 million when it developed a distance-learning course to replace one full week of training at the FBI Academy (Moe, 2000, p. 233).

IBM estimated that, in 1999, it realized over $100 million from cost savings on travel and living expenses, as well as other types of cost avoidance, by going to online education (*IBM Global Learning*, 1999). Plus, estimates are that the company has been able to provide five times as much content at one third of the cost with e-learning (Hall, 2000).

Cost savings for mid-sized corporations are also possible. SCT University provides an example. The company's professionals use live, interactive Web collaboration not only for SCT University courses but also for team meetings, sales demonstrations, quarterly market unit meetings, and training and orientation for new employees. SCT has 3,400 employees in 29 countries. SCT University has proven extremely cost-effective. In 1998, prior to its launch, the company educated a maximum of 350 students at a time in physical classrooms. With the virtual university, SCT can educate 16,156 people at one time, 85% of whom are trained via e-learning. The cost per learner has dropped from $2,000 in 1998 to just $44.50 in 1999 (Gotschall, 2001).

CyberU.com is one of several companies that provide training services for small and medium-sized businesses that lack the resources a large company might have to create its own program. These learning portals are analogous to an Amazon.com for online learning. Most small companies spend about $700 per year on training for one employee. If the employee takes one instructor-led course for $500 and buys a few books or videos, that consumes the entire training budget. At a learning portal, one can purchase 5 to 10 courses for $700. It is much more cost-effective for employees. For example, Made2Manage Systems, an application service provider, has launched a new virtual university system to serve courses to employees inside manufacturing companies. The new system, called Time2Learn, will deliver courses in areas such as price scheduling, job order rework, data refining, job order queues, and purchasing order queues (*New Subscription Based Education Program*, 2001). These e-learning sites also offer assessments, transcripts, and even management reports. Other sites include eMind.com, GeoLearning.com, and Click2learn.com (Hall, 2000a).

According to *Training Magazine*, corporations save between 50% and 70% when they replace instructor-led training with the electronically delivered equivalent. Housing and travel costs account for the majority of the savings (Hall, 2000b). Convenience improves because people don't need to travel or block out several days for a class. It is efficient because a course can be completed in half the time, and retention can be just as good or better than with instructor-led training. The immediacy of online learning drives retention of information that is frequently far superior to that achieved with traditional forms of corporate learning.

For example, Ninth House offers TV-sitcom-like simulations. The half-hour programs re-construct business situations that teach leadership, project management, and communication skills. Trainees take charge of the events in the simulations, and their choices dictate the outcome. The courses are said to increase the knowledge that workers retain by 50% over traditional classroom training. Further, the 2 to 4 hours of online instruction can replace 2-day seminars (*Companies Embrace e-Training*, n.d.). Other studies have indicated that retention of certain subject matter may be up to 250% greater with e-learning than with the classroom-based model (Moe, 2000, p. 233). It is worth noting that these benefits are available to organizations of any size, and learning portals make it easy to access thousands of courses (Hall, 2000a).

However, not all corporations are moving learning from the classroom to the Web. Many prefer a blend of face-to-face and online instruction. For example, IBM's e-learning division, Mindspan Solutions, offers an in-house training program for IBM managers that uses the Web for 75% of learning activities. The remaining 25% of the "Basic Blue" management training takes place face to face. The "Basic Blue" program provides on-the-spot and soft skills training to 4,500 managers. E-learning events include online collaboration, simulations, job aids, and short courses (*Training That Goes the Route*, 2001). Another example is provided by Babson

College, which has developed a custom version of their MBA degree for hybrid online and face-to-face delivery at Intel sites in Santa Clara, California, and Portland, Oregon ("Babson College," 2001).

Market Size and Growth

In response to competitive pressures, American companies have increased their spending on training over the last 5 years. The average U.S. company is training more of its employees than ever before, more dollars are going to technical skills training than any other type of training, and e-learning is gaining momentum. Other pertinent facts include these:

The average company is training 78.6% of its employees.
The top 10% of companies surveyed are training 98.4% of their employees.
The top 10% of companies surveyed spent an average of $1,655 on training per eligible employee, compared with $677 for the average survey respondent.
The largest share of spending on training went to training in technical processes and procedures (13%), with professional skills next (11%). Interpersonal communication, new employee orientation, and IT skills followed (9% each).
The use of e-learning averages 8.4% for small companies. Large companies are increasing the percentage of training delivered via e-learning, which went from 12.3% in 1998 to 13.8% in 1999 (*ASTD Releases*, 2001).

Overall, the corporate education market is huge. U.S. corporations with over 100 employees budgeted approximately $62.5 billion for training in 1999. This compares with $48.2 billion in 1993 (*e-Learning and Knowledge Technology*, 2000). Individual corporation figures are impressive as well. Each year General Electric spends $500 million on training and education. IBM spends $2 billion. The global corporate and government learning market measured over $280 billion in 1999 and is expected to grow to over $365 billion by 2003 (Moe, 2000, p. 238).

Corporate University Xchange, a U.S. corporate education research and consulting group, estimates that over the past 15 years the number of corporate universities has grown from about 400 to some 2,000. It predicts that the number of corporate universities will exceed 3,700 by the end of the decade. The average budget is $17 million. On average, 4,000 employees are trained each year, with 39 hours of training per employee per year, compared with 8 hours in 1999. An average of 23% of employees have their training delivered via technology; this figure is expected to rise to 50% by 2003 (Anderson, 2001).

Corporate America's adoption of e-learning has come at a much more rapid pace than in higher education. For example, IBM launched its corporate university more than 3 years ago, making it available to all 307,000 employees. Initially, 10% of the programs were computer-based, but today almost 37% of its education is in the form of e-learning (Anderson, 2001).

This trend may be driven by the simple fact that companies are finding it is the only way they are able to keep their workforces up to date in a business environment in which an organization must be able to turn on a dime (Ruttenbur et al., 2000, p. 66). IDC projects that U.S. Web-based corporate learning will expand rapidly, from $1.1 billion in 1999 to $11.4 billion by 2003, representing a compound annual growth rate of 79% (Moe, 2000, p. 233).

Although instructor-led training currently represents more than 70% of delivered training, this percentage is expected to fall to 35–40% by 2004. Replacing it is technology-based training, the largest component of which will be e-learning (Ruttenbur et al., 2000, p. 68). According to *Training Magazine*, 36% of online training is delivered through platforms that allow students to interact with their instructor and with each other; 64% of trainees only interact with the computer. In 1999, CD-ROMs were the leading method of computer-based training (37%), followed by intranets (25%). Web-based training accounted for 13% of all training delivered through the use of a computer (*e-Learning and Knowledge Technology*, 2000).

Companies in Europe, Asia, and South America are embracing e-learning as well. Experts estimate that the European market is 12 to 18 months behind the U.S. market in terms of the adoption of e-learning; however, it is catching up quickly. IDC predicts that the worldwide corporate e-learning market will exceed $23 billion by 2004, representing a compound annual growth rate of 68.8% from 1999 through 2004. North American will account for two thirds of that growth, but Western Europe will experience the fastest growth rate (97.2%), followed by Japan, Latin America, and the Pacific ("e-Learning," n.d.).

CORPORATIONS AS SUPPLIERS OF DISTANCE EDUCATION

e-Learning Companies

Corporations are also providing the distance education structure for other organizations, such as traditional universities. The activities of these organizations range from providing specific products and services to outsourcing the entire operation. There are a number of possible groupings for this emerging market.

There are several leading for-profit educational entities that have begun to move into the e-learning market. Many of these for-profit universities are targeting the individual professional learner, including degree completion students. Examples of for-profit universities include the University of Phoenix, KaplanCollege, DeVry University, and Capella University.

Another segment of the for-profit educational market focuses on training rather than education. The companies involved tend to target corporate learners. They include entities such as SmartForce, Ninth House Network, and DigitalThink. These training companies use a variety of training delivery methods (synchronous and asynchronous) and media, ranging from customized to off-the-shelf courseware.

Another category of e-learning providers blend academic content with corporate structures. These firms aggregate content from academic institutions, professional associations, or training companies; enhance and digitize the content; then distribute it. Some provide a comprehensive collection of content, whereas others are more vertically focused. Most initially targeted corporate learners, but they are now moving into the lifelong learner and MBA markets as well. Examples include Unext.com (partners include Columbia, the University of Chicago, and the London School of Economics) and Fathom.

These firms are organized and provide education in a different way than traditional colleges and universities. For example, Fathom was created in 1999 by Columbia University as a consortium of content providers dedicated to providing learning opportunities on a broad range of subjects for lifelong learners. Fathom provides:

Lectures, interviews, articles, performances, and exhibits by faculty, researchers, and curators from member institutions.
Reference content spanning all disciplines and fields of study.
Trails, a unique way of organizing content thematically.
Online courses from Fathom partners.
Recommended readings.

Two distinctive features of Fathom are "trails" and the ability to immediately purchase books, journals, periodicals, and articles that are directly related to subjects in which users are most interested. Trails connects articles from different disciplines through common topics, where various trails intersect. At each intersection, the site gives users the option of either continuing to read articles along the original trail or jumping to a different route (Carlson, 2000). For example, from an article on women in medicine, one can choose to continue on the trail of "History of Science" or switch trails to "History of Medicine," "Women in the Workplace," or "Redefining the Roles of Women." Trails are an attempt to put knowledge in context and provide a multidisciplinary way of looking at a subject. Fathom expects to make a profit by selling books and marketing online courses.

Fathom's course providers are diverse: Columbia Interactive and the BBC, Kaplan College, New School Online University, SmartForce, UCLA Extension, the University of British Columbia, XanEdu, Syracuse University, and others.

Portals represent another category of firms providing educational products and services. Portals provide a central location for purchasers to browse a wide variety of e-learning products, most of them typically developed by third parties. Portals aggregate, host, and distribute content for significant numbers of users, making them cost-effective, efficient, and convenient learning solutions. The process of selecting learning materials is streamlined since it is handled by the portal. With the right set of tools, employees can manage their professional development and update their credentials using corporate databases (Moe, 2000, p. 254). There are a growing number of portals, including Click2learn.com, CyberU.com, KnowledgePlanet.com, Learn.com, eMind.com, and SmartPlanet.com.

Corporate Involvement in Noncourse Components of the Learning Environment

Higher education encompasses a variety of processes, such as admissions, learner support, assessment, advising, and credentialing. Historically, higher education institutions had no option but to provide all these services for students. Today, there are a growing number of new entrants to the education market that can augment or replace services traditionally provided by institutions, from admissions to tutoring.

e-Admissions

There are several firms that now provide online admissions for students and institutions. Embark.com is an application service provider (ASP) that provides recruitment and enrollment services to over 350 higher education institutions. Estimates are that Embark has more than one million registered users, 10–15% of whom are outside the United States. ASPs such as Embark provide users with a single source, online system that simplifies the process of identifying potential colleges as well as applying to them. Embark has databases for careers, majors, colleges, and scholarships. Students can register to be recruited by multiple institutions (Embark, 2000). Other providers of e-admission services include XAP and CollegeNet.

e-Commerce

Students and their institutions buy and sell things. Student Advantage (www. studentadvantage.com) is a large student membership organization that provides an online marketplace for students. It is designed to help students save money on a variety of products, whether offered online or offline. It has proprietary commerce relationships with nearly 50 national retailers and businesses, including AT&T, Amtrak, Staples, Textbooks.com, and Tower Records. It also provides news, discussions, a scholarship search database, and academic research tools. Student Advantage has over one million student members from 3,000 colleges and universities.

e-Procurement

Beyond e-learning and e-commerce, firms specializing in e-procurement are focusing on higher education. HigherMarkets is an example of firms that create online purchasing systems for colleges and universities. The rationale for moving to e-procurement is to reduce transaction costs, saving both time and money. A traditional purchase requisition costs $150 to process. With e-procurement, the costs range from $10 to $15. Additional efficiencies and price discounts could lead to an additional 10% in savings.

e-Library

One of the challenges associated with anytime, anyplace education is providing access to library materials and services. This past year, several e-library offerings have emerged. For example, Questia offers library service allowing students to access roughly 70,000 titles by keyword. Students must pay $20 a month for Questia's service. Among the benefits offered, students will be able to cut and paste content into their papers, and the service will automatically create footnotes and hyperlink the footnotes of papers that are submitted online, allowing professors to check references easily (*Digital Library Company*, 2000).

Another e-library firm is Ebrary (www.ebrary.com). It provides a search engine, ebrarian™, to help users find what they need. Through ebrary libraries can provide users with access to content and a range of tools such as definitions, explanations, translations, biographies, and map locations. There is an annual license fee that is based on institution size and library type.

Supplemental Content Providers

Historically, students have used a variety of study guides and supplementary material to aid them. Cliff Notes is a classic example. There are several online supplemental content providers who offer materials ranging from traditional study notes to video-based online tutorials.

An example of a new entrant that provides study aids and supplemental educational material is PinkMonkey. Launched in 1997, PinkMonkey is a free study site that has the largest collection of chapter summaries available on the Internet (109 Barron's Booknotes and 171 MonkeyNotes™). Its study guides are comprehensive online textbooks. The company generates revenue primarily through Internet advertising and sponsors. Within four months after the site was launched, over 110,000 students had enrolled as members (PwC, 2000a).

A different model is provided by Thinkwell (www.thinkwell.com), which uses as a tag line "the next-generation textbook." The Thinkwell text is a CD-ROM set accompanied by a Web site that Thinkwell customizes to a specific class. The CD-ROM set includes video tutorials. The customized Web site contains accompanying illustrated notes, exercise problems, animations, and a threaded discussion forum. Material is sequenced to fit the instructor's syllabus. Citing the fact that many students avoid reading textbooks, the company suggests replacing the traditional print textbook with Thinkwell's multimedia approach, which uses video, animation, and graphics to bring content to life. For example, students can watch Thinkwell's video tutorials at home so during class they can work on problems and applications, hold discussions, or do case studies.

Custom Books, Print-on-Demand, and e-Books

Although they have existed for several years, e-books and their educational counterparts, e-textbooks, are becoming more widely used.

An increasing number of firms are becoming involved with e-books (i.e., books that can be downloaded onto devices that display the text). Major companies, such as Microsoft, Time

Warner, and Simon and Schuster are aggressively targeting the e-book market. Random House recently agreed to split e-book royalties 50-50 with authors, representing a significant increase over the share authors receive on print books (*Plot Thickens*, 2000).

Advising and Tutoring

There are many critical educational components that are found outside the "classroom." Advising and tutoring are among them. Students need access to information that allows them to make good decisions on career paths, majors, and specific courses. Some may need the assistance of tutors and mentors as well.

Smarthinking.com supplements the academic support of traditional institutions. Its virtual learning assistance center provides trained tutors (e-structors) and independent study resources available around the clock in subjects such as mathematics, economics, accounting, statistics, and psychology. Smarthinking offers one-on-one learning support, help with last-minute questions before an assignment deadline or exam, and long-term support to encourage students to become stronger writers and better reasoners. It also provides an online writing lab for all courses, grammar and brainstorming help desks, and independent study resources.

Tutor.com is a leading provider of education referral services, with over 18,000 tutors available in 375 subject areas. Through its site, students can search for online tutors or face-to-face ones available in the learner's geographic area. Independent tutors and instructors register to become members of Tutor.com's national registry, a professional organization that provides resources, referrals, and a proof of background check for those seeking tutors (PwC, 2000b).

Learners can view Tutor.com's database of thousands of instructors free of charge. Tutors are available by discipline and subspecialty. Students may select from among tutors based on their credentials and whether or not they are certified. Online sessions use a specially developed virtual classroom application that includes text chat and whiteboard capabilities.

Although we might think of tutoring and mentoring as mainly for younger students, they are playing an increasingly important role in corporate education as well. An online tutor or mentor not only can serve as a resource to answer questions but also can provide feedback and advice, keeping the student involved and motivated to complete the course. For example, when employees at Sun Microsystems were asked to complete a self-paced online course without the help of a tutor, only 25% finished. However, when given the same assignment and access to a tutor through e-mail, telephone, or online discussion group, 75% completed the corporate training (Moe, 2000, p. 242).

Testing and Assessment Services

Although external testing and assessment may be better accepted in the corporate market, several firms have targeted testing and assessment services for education. Some services are provided on-site; others are available online.

Question Mark Corporation (http://www.questionmark.com) provides products and support services for education and training in both corporations and academic institutions. The company sells and supports software that allows users to write, deliver, and mark surveys, tests, questionnaires, and tutorials. Applications include academic tests, product knowledge tests, attitude surveys, personnel evaluations, and self-paced study guides that can be administered over the Web. To complement the applications, Question Mark also provides education to help users understand issues associated with computerized assessments, different levels of evaluation, and best practices for developing and deploying exams.

Prometric (http://www.prometric.com), which offers technology-based testing and assessment services, focuses on large-volume tests. Its network consists of over 4,800 computer-based testing service centers in 136 countries. With additional capacity provided by mobile computer-equipped testing facilities, Prometric has delivered more than six million tests in over 136 countries. Based on experience with tests such as the GRE, GMAT, and TOEFL, Prometric helps educational organizations convert to technology-based assessment. A number of benefits of computer-based testing are cited, including the ability to score tests immediately, allowing for the inclusion of simulations of real-life situations, and matching questions to the ability of the test taker.

Financing Distance Education Through Venture Capital

The potential of e-learning for training and education has attracted the attention of private investment firms. Venture capital investors provided $1.1 billion of funding to training companies in 1999; Web-based training companies attracted 55% of that private investment ("National Commissions," 2000).

During the first quarter of 2000, venture capital activity rose. More than $1 billion in venture capital was invested in education start-ups. But when the stock market began to fall, venture capital activity slowed. In the second quarter of 2000, education start-ups attracted only $814 million. The decline in investment has paralleled the downturn of the general stock market. As the outlook for the economy and stock market improves, venture capital activity is predicted to pick up again. In aggregate, education entrepreneurs have received more than $2.9 billion in private investment during 2000, 15% more than the $2.5 billion invested in 1999. Over the past two years, $5.5 billion of private capital has been invested in education and training markets, far exceeding any previous rates of venture capital investment in education (Evans, 2001).

About a dozen companies have played active roles in education investments. During 2000, the 10 leading education investors made 66 investments into start-ups, representing roughly 30% of the education and training deals. The year also saw the emergence of the "Big Four" strategic investors: Kaplan, Knowledge Universe, Pearson, and Sylvan Ventures, with 26 equity investments. The key investment themes for 2000 were Web-based courseware tools, enterprise systems for colleges and universities, and e-libraries (Evans, 2001).

CONCLUSION

Corporations are involved in distance education in a number of ways. Many find distance education of their own workers a competitive necessity. Some have created their own corporate universities to provide this education and training; others rely on educational portals. Irrespective of the source, predictions are that corporate spending on education and training will grow as business competitiveness and economic strength become increasingly predicated on a skilled workforce.

Some corporations are providing distance education to the traditional higher education market; others specialize in training. Irrespective of the target market or business model, corporations and higher education institutions are blending content and expertise to create new types of organizations.

Corporations also provide venture capital and specific products and services to higher education's distance education efforts. Products take the form of networks, computers, and applications. Services range from online admissions to tutoring to e-books.

Although higher education and corporate education each have unique characteristics, they also share many elements. As education continues to be more important, the complementarity of higher education and corporate education will grow.

REFERENCES

Aldrich, Clark. (2000, July). Customer-focused e-learning: The drivers. Available: http://www.learningcircuits.org/jul2000/aldrich.html

Anderson, L. (2001, March 26). Business education: Tailor-made for lifelong learning. *Financial Times.* Available: http://globalarchive.ft.com/globalarchive.articles.html

Andersen, M., & Irmer, A. (1999, November-December). Corporate universities in Germany: First experiences. *Corporate University Review.* Available: http://www.traininguniversity.com/magazine/articles/Germany.asp

ASTD Releases its 2001 state of the industry report. (2001, March 26). Alexandria, VA: American Society for Training and Development. Available: http://www.astd.org/CMS/templates/index.html

Authers, J. (2001, March 26). Economy causes concern. *Financial Times.* Available: http://globalarchive.ft.com/globalarchive/articles.html

Babson College to design custom MBA in entrepreneurship for Intel Corporation. (2001, February). *Virtual University Gazette.* Available: http://www.geteducated.com/vug/feb01/newcorp0201.htm

Carlson, S. (2000, November 15). Web company founded by Columbia U opens a "beta version" of its site. *Chronicle of Higher Education.* Available: http://chronicle.com/free/2000/11/2000111501u.htm

Chen, Y. (2000, November 13). Booktech.com builds momentum in custom content delivery. *The Education Economy.* Available: http://www.eduventures.com/news/education_economy/archive/education_economy_68.cfm

Companies embrace e-training. (n.d.). Available: http://mu.motorola.com/newsclip.shtml

Corporate University Xchange. (2001). *Survey of corporate university future directions.* Available: http://www.learningestore.com/corpu?ssp=%2Fcatalog%2Fproducts_search_detail.saba&id=prdct000000000001380&price=500

Cribbs, G. (2001, March 26). Innovation sets the trend. *Financial Times.* Available: http://globalarchive.ft.com/globalarchive.articles.html

Customer Education Research Consortium: Customer training the next frontier. (n.d.). Available: www.corpu.com/research_services/index.html

DeVeaux, P. (2001, February). An interview with Jeanne Meister. *e-learning Magazine.* Available: http://www.elearningmag.com/issues/feb01/life.asp

More than half of corporate training executives surveyed say sluggish economy will have no impact on e-learning program budgets. (2001, May 11). *EdNET Week Headlines.* Available: http://hellerreports.com/dte/lead05-11.html

Digital library company plans to charge students for access. (2000, November 15). *Edupage.* Available: http://listserv.educause.edu/cgi-bin/wa.exe?A2=ind0011&L=edupage&D=1&H=1&O=D&F=&S=&P=561

Plot thickens as electronic books move more into the mainstream. (2000, November 21). *Edupage.* Available: http://listserv.educause.edu/cgi-bin/wa.exe?A2=ind0011&L=edupage&D=1&H=1&O=D&F=&S=&P=761

E-learning: A strategic imperative for succeeding in business. (n.d.). *Fortune.* Available: http://www.timeinc.net/fortune/sections/e-learning/e-learning.htm

E-learning and knowledge technology: SunTrust Equitable Securities. (2000, March). Available: www.maisie.com/reports/e-learnO.pdf

Embark. (2000). Unpublished slides.

Evans, T. (2001, March). *Venture capitalists seek reality, revenues and rational business models.* Boston: Eduventures, Inc.

General Motors Technical Education Program saves company $46.2 million. (2001, May). *Virtual University Gazette.* Available: http://www.geteducated.com/vug/may01/newcorp0501.htm

Gotschall, M. (May, 2001). E-learning: A strategic imperative for succeeding in business. *Fortune.* Available: http://www.timeinc.net/fortune/sections/e-learning/e-learning.htm

Hall, B. (2000a). Building competitive advantage through people and technology. *Forbes.* Available: http://www.forbes.com/specialsections/elearning/e-04.htm

Hall, B. (2000b). Corporate drivers of e-learning. *Forbes.* Available: http://www.forbes.com/specialsections/elearning/e-03.htm

IBM Global Learning recognized by Corporate University Xchange. (1999, April 26). Available: http://www-3.ibm.com/services/learning/global/news/NEWS_12096.html

Learning European style. (2001, January). New York: Corporate University Xchange. Available: http://www.corpu.com/about/news/training_jan01.html

Moe, M. (2000, May 23). *The knowledge web.* New York: Merrill Lynch.

Morrison, J. (2000, July-August). Corporate universities: An interview with Jeanne Meister. *The Technology Source.* Available: http://horizon.unc.edu/TS/vision/2000-07.asp

Motorola Corporate University. (2001). Available: http://mu.motorola.com/corporate.shtml

National commissions, studies focus on questions about e-learning. (2000, November). *WorkAmerica,* 3–7.

New subscription based education program launched by Made2Manage Systems. (2001, February 8). Indianapolis, IN: Made2Manage Systems. Available: http://www.made2manage.com/news/2_08_01.asp

PwC. (2000a, March 31). An overview of North Carolina Corporate Universities. Unpublished manuscript, University of North Carolina.

PwC. (2000b, Summer). Case studies on e-learning Vendors and innovative partnerships. Unpublished working notes, University of North Carolina.

Ruttenbur, B. W., Spickler, G. C., & Lurie, S. (2000, July). *e-Learning: The engine of the knowledge economy*. Morgan Keegan & Co. Memphis, TN.

Swanson, S. (2001, February 12). Borders adds online training to call centers. *Information Week*. Available: http://www.informationweek.com/824/border.htm

Training that goes the route: Experts laud IBM Mindspan Solutions. (2001, April 11). Available: http://www.lotus.com/news/news.nsf/public/E5D7EFCF362C18D0852569F5005AFAE8

Twigg, C. (2000, September 1). Sorting the spin. *The Learning MarketSpace*. Available: http://www.center.rpi.edu/LForum/lm/Sept00.html

40

Planning and Managing Distance Training and Education in the Corporate Sector

Zane L. Berge
University of Maryland, Baltimore County
berge@umbc.edu

> One way to view management's role is that managers must constantly align and realign the strategic plan of the organization so that mission-critical functions match the core capabilities and core competencies of the enterprise.

If we begin to analyze the above statement, we find several concepts that need to be explored: *strategic plan, mission-critical functions, core capabilities*, and *core competencies*. Distance education forces managers to think of each of these in new ways. Even how strategic planning is accomplished successfully in the global economy of the 21st century is different from in the past.

Managers and leaders who are charged with distance training and education functions decide on what courses and programs to produce and what media and infrastructure will be used to implement these programs. Their decisions are guided by the organizational mission and by business needs, usually determined by market research or policy. This means aligning projects *and* programs that involve distance training and education activities with strategic plans. Put simply, managers are using distance training and education to solve business problems through managing and planning. That said, we are only beginning to identify in useful ways what capabilities and competencies are needed in distance training and education.

GLOBAL ECONOMY IS CHANGING HOW WE DO BUSINESS

Our global society is moving into the Knowledge Age, where technology dictates that we will live, work, and learn differently than we did in the Industrial Age. The new age demands more skills, knowledge, learning, and re-learning. What is mission critical to an organization often changes, because what is important in today's society seems ever changing. The transition from an industrial economy to a knowledge-based economy has companies competing to control

TABLE 40.1

Shifts in the Economy

Old Economy	New Economy
One set of skills	Lifelong learning
Labor vs. management	Teams
Business vs. environment	Encouragement of growth
Security	Risk taking
Monopolies	Competition
Plant, equipment	Intellectual property
National	Global
Status quo	Speed, change
Top-down	Distributed

intellectual assets, not physical assets (McCrea, Gay, & Bacon, 2000). We could spend the rest of the chapter discussing the mega-trends affecting society and the economy: globalization, technology, outsourcing, consolidation, demographics, and branding. Table 40.1 lists some overall changes being felt within most larger organizations (Moe, Bailey, & Lau, 1999). With the increased rate at which the amount of information doubles, it is essential that the right information reaches the right people when it is needed (Ruttenbur, Spickler, & Lurie, 2000, p. 10).

Many changes have to do with philosophy and in turn organizational culture. For instance, it use to be that university students could, for the most part, in 4 years or 4 years plus graduate work, expect to gain the skills and knowledge necessary to prepare them for a lifetime of work in their chosen field. Of course, today's university educators do not harbor any illusions. Each professor knows that it is increasingly important to teach students how to learn so that the effects of the ever decreasing half-life of knowledge can be mitigated through lifelong learning. The same is true of learners in the workplace:

> A consideration of training at a distance forces a re-examination about the ways people learn and are trained (Albright & Post, 1993). Corporate employees in the future will need to take control of their own growth and development, demanding training time and money as part of their rewards for supplying their services. Adult education principles of self-directed and life-long learning will become a major part of compensation packages. Collective bargaining agreements in the future will probably require levels of training for employees that do not exist today. Companies desiring a competitive advantage will "jump on the band wagon" and establish policies and procedures to take advantage of distance learning to deliver these services.... The rapidly changing workplace of the future will demand that trainers move toward this vision with a spirit of adventure. Training professionals at all levels will need considerable imagination, common sense and creativity to cope with the changes that undoubtedly await us. Corporate success depends upon having and keeping talented people. The shortage of such people is widely accepted, and training (including distance education), at long last, is beginning to be recognized as part of the solution. (Dooley, Dooley, & Byrom, 1998, p. 353)

Occurring along with these changes in how training and education is perceived are cultural changes throughout the organization and the people associated with it (see Table 40. 2). For instance, as more employees have technology systems at home and as pressure increases for individuals to take control of their own learning throughout their lifetime, there can be a blurring of the distinction between what is learning and what is work.

Employees know that they must continuously learn or be at a competitive disadvantage personally in the marketplace, and they therefore demand the organization support their learning.

TABLE 40.2

Shifts in Training

Old Economy	New Economy
Four-year degree	Forty-year degree
Training as cost center	Training as competitive advantage
Learner mobility	Content mobility
Correspondence and video	High-tech multimedia centers
One size fits all	Tailored programs
Just-in-case	Just-in-time
Isolated learners and learning events	Ongoing virtual learning communities

McCrea et al. (2000) state that management's mission is to develop an "enterprise-wide process of continuous and globally distributed learning that directly links business goals and individual learning outcomes" (p. 16). Although the concept of "just enough" training may be useful (Zielinski, 2000), there is no such thing as just enough learning.

BUSINESS NEEDS FOR DISTANCE TRAINING AND EDUCATION

Having a strategy that links distance training and education to the organization's business goals is important (Galagan, 2000; Chapter 34 of this volume). There are compelling reasons for distance training and education in the workplace. Reasons for which organizations are turning to distance training include the ability of such training to broaden the exposure of employees to nationally and internationally recognized experts, reduce costs (e.g., time to market, travel expenditures, and time spent in training), and lower the opportunity costs of lost productivity.

Significant Business Needs

Essentially, one can view distance training as serving three significant business needs:

1. Meeting the challenge of uncommon organizational change.
2. Sustaining competitive advantage.
3. Achieving organizational goals.

Meeting the Challenge of Uncommon Organizational Change.   Short of bankruptcy, there may be no business event that serves as a stronger catalyst for change than a corporate merger. The cultural context in which people work is made clear when a merger juxtaposes different cultures and challenges everyone to change and grow. For example, Friend and Hepple (2001) described the merging of SBC's regional telecom training centers as follows:

> Working across time zones with widely varying systems, practices, and cultures challenged the merged SBC. Eliminating redundancies resulted in savings for the CFL and its SBC internal clients. However, staffing varied continuously through restructuring, job changes, outsourcing, and new hiring. As employee experience levels fluctuated, the need for faster, more effective, and more flexible training had never been greater. (p. 52)

Another type of tumultuous change can come from a mandate, whether from a government authority or the organization's chief executive. The disruptive cultural and organizational consequences of mandate being handed down are one of the principal reasons distance education has found success in meeting training and educational needs within many organizations.

Sustaining Competitive Advantage.   We have entered the Knowledge Age, and the new economy requires a continuously learning workforce. Rapid technological change and a core of knowledge workers who stay abreast of the change are considered key to sustaining a competitive advantage in the marketplace. As organizations invest in building learning systems that contribute to individual and corporate success, distance training and education will set the standard.

Achieving Organizational Goals.   Because the global economy, in conjunction with technological advancements, is changing the way business is transacted, competition for markets and customers continues to present a significant challenge. Distance training and education is looked upon as a way of investing in people throughout the organization and thereby aiding the pursuit of organizational goals.

Key Business Drivers

The key drivers pushing business units to use distance training and education include these:

The cost to the employer.
The lack of time available to trainees and trainers.
The fast pace of change and the reduction in development-to-delivery cycles, which allow ever smaller window for training.
The need to train large numbers of employees.
The need to train employees who are spread across a wide geographic area.
Reduced training budgets (despite increased training needs).
The need to become a learning organization.

The Cost to the Employer.   There are often high costs associated with having most training delivered in the traditional classroom. If trainers are not on-site, line managers must fund travel budgets and assume the loss of productivity during employees' travel time. With traditional training methods, companies generally spend more money, up to two-thirds of the training expenses, on transporting and housing trainees than on actual training programs (Mottl, 2000; Urdan & Weggen, 2000). Alternatives include outsourcing and having trainers travel to the trainees, which could and reduce overall training costs. The impact on the trainers, however, is often too great (Howard, 2001; Latten, Davis, & Stallings, 2001).

Lack of Time.   Although cost is a major issue for the organization, lack of time is a critical factor for the employees. Finding the time to improve technical skills while concurrently attending to business deliverables on short development-to-delivery cycles often seems impossible to everyone concerned (Branch, Lyon, & Porten, 2001).

Short Development-to-Delivery Cycles.   By the time training is designed, developed, and scheduled, the employee no longer needs it (Dobbs, 2000). As competition and demand in today's society reduce development-to-delivery cycles, there is a smaller window for training to occur. Latten et al. (2001) described the situation their company faced:

Our client base was quickly surpassing the existing training infrastructure. Mergers and organizational changes were creating an environment where key business decisions were being made faster than ever. The result, an increased demand for training as a result of new business strategies and processes. The need for training to reach growing numbers of participants, faster and in their place of business was at an all time high. We knew that traditional classroom training was not a possible solution for meeting the current business challenges. Both cost and reduced cycle times were obstacles that traditional classroom training could not easily address. (p. 164)

In many cases, learning opportunities have to be modular, just-in-time, and highly relevant to compete with other tasks and opportunities that are critical to the success of the organization (Rogers & Becker, 2001). Many organizations face mergers, mandates, and increased business from other sources, with the result that new initiatives occur faster than ever. As project timelines accelerate to meet the growing demand, there is less time to build trainer expertise and less time to reach larger numbers of trainees (Latten et al., 2001).

High Numbers of Employees.   Large organizations are especially challenged by the need to provide training to a large workforce at a reduced cost and with limited resources. Training at national or regional facilities becomes impossible when thousands or hundreds of thousands of employees need to be trained uniformly but quickly (Wankel, 2001).

Training Employees in a Wide Geographic Area.   When there are a great number of employees to train, especially when they are dispersed geographically, equitable training delivery is difficult and costly.

Distance training and education, beside making economic sense, allows training content to be offered in convenient, adult-sized bites rather than in week-long sessions at remote locations. Persons charged with training can target specific audiences regardless of geographic location or make subject matter experts available based on need rather than ease of access to location (Dessinger & Conley, 2001; Walker, 1998).

Reduced Training Budgets.   Budgets continue to be squeezed, and managers are required to do more with less. Payne and Payne (1998) described such a scenario at the Federal Aviation Administration:

> The FAA's technical training budget was cut by Congress from over \$135M in 1992 to just over \$77M in 1996, a 43% decline (Federal Aviation Administration, 1997). This dramatic reduction in the training budget resulted in the number of FAA students receiving technical training declining from over 28,000 to just over 16,000, a corresponding drop of 41% (Federal Aviation Administration, 1997). A congressional mandate during this same period caused the FAA to go through a downsizing activity that reduced the size of the agency by 11%. This downsizing asked fewer FAA employees to do more during an era of a severely constrained and a continually declining training budget as the mission of the Agency did not change. The problem the FAA faced was finding ways to reduce the overall cost of providing training while increasing the training opportunities for employees. The FAA needed to solve this problem in a manner that was not prohibitively expensive in its start-up costs and that could begin to show a return on the investment almost immediately. (p. 202)

Need to Become a Learning Organization.   As mentioned earlier, university professors know they cannot teach students all that they will ever need to know in a given field. Workplace organizations are starting to understand that the same thing is true about training. This is why Peter Senge's work on "learning organizations" has resonated as it has (Senge, 1990; Zemke, 1999). At the heart of the learning organization is a change in philosophy from instruction and training to learning—and a key element in distance training is the students' taking responsibility for their own learning. Workers who neglect to invest in their own intellectual capital do so at their own risk, because they can no longer rely on a single set of skills for a lifetime of work (Ruttenbur et al., 2000). So, employees today demand that organizations continually invest in their professional development (McCrea et al., 2000, p. 11). All this changes significantly the roles and functions of both instructors and learners.

PLANNING AND MANAGING DISTANCE TRAINING AND EDUCATION

Responsibilities

Those responsible for planning and implementing a distance education program face both pedagogical and organizational challenges. The management team must systematically analyze organizational needs. It must include at least one person with a high rank to champion technology-enhanced learning (the person's rank must match, in terms of organizational level, the strategic goals for the training program). The team must also have a person or persons in charge of infrastructure and support services and other managers and staff with a stake in promoting successful technology-enhanced learning. The management team's charge may include the following:

Identify the business purposes and goals of initiating and supporting a distance learning program.

Collect and summarize information on current distance education programs and the strategic plans of various business units considering the use of distance training and education.

Evaluate strategies and technologies for delivering distance education programs (in terms of their advantages, disadvantages, and costs) and reach agreement on which strategies and technologies will be proposed.

Define what is needed to deliver technology-enhanced learning programs effectively, including equipment and facilities, competencies and training, policy development and cultural change.

Investigate successful models at other organizations.

Specify needs and incentives for instructors, designers, and developers who become involved in developing and implementing technology-enhanced learning.

Estimate costs and resource commitments.

Identify potential barriers to successful implementation of the recommended strategies and technologies and suggest how to manage these.

Establish a process for reviewing new technologies and other aspects of distance programs at least annually to assess their potential for improving the delivery of distance training and reducing associated costs.

Report findings and recommendations to senior decision-makers.

Define needs for particular academic programs. (University of Kansas Medical Center, 1996)

Obstacles

There are many individual barriers to distance training and education. Based on survey responses, a subsequent factor analysis clustered the 64 barriers into the following 10 factors:

1. Administrative structure.
2. Organizational change.
3. Technical expertise.
4. Social interaction and quality.
5. Faculty compensation and time.

6. Threatened by technology.
7. Legal issues.
8. Evaluation/effectiveness.
9. Access.
10. Student support services. (Muilenburg & Berge, 2001)

Administrative Structure.   Lack of credibility for distance education within a particular administrative structure and lack of money can be problems for distance education. Competing with or using new business models can cause difficulties, too. When partnerships are formed between different units within an organization or between different organizations, lack of agreement on such issues as revenue sharing, regulations, tuition and fees, scheduling, FTEs, and issuance of credits can become an obstacle to distance education.

Organizational Change.   Most organizations are resistant to change. Without a shared vision for distance learning, a strategic plan, and key players within the organization who are knowledgeable and supportive of distance learning, implementing a distance learning program is a slow and difficult process. Difficulty in convincing stakeholders of the benefits of distance learning, the often slow pace of implementation, and the lack of an identifiable business need are all barriers to distance education.

Technical Expertise, Support, and Infrastructure.   It is difficult to keep up with the fast pace of technological change. Many instructors lack the knowledge and skills to design and teach distance learning courses, yet their organizations lack support staff to assist with technical problems, develop distance learning course materials, or provide distance learning training. Technology-enhanced classrooms or laboratories and the infrastructure required to use them may not be available.

Social Interaction and Quality.   Participants in distance learning courses can feel isolated due to absence of person-to-person contact. Some educators and students are uncomfortable with the use of student-centered and collaborative learning activities on philosophical grounds or because these methods represent a change from the traditional social structure of the class-room. There are concerns about the quality of distance learning courses and programs, the students' possible lack of prerequisite skills and knowledge, the outcomes of student learning, and the testing and assessment of learning outcomes.

Faculty Compensation and Time.   In all stages of design, development, and evaluation, distance education courses almost always require a greater time commitment than face-to-face education with the same instructional objectives. Therefore, faculty compensation, incentives, workload, and release time become important issues if the current compensation system is based on classroom teaching. Lack of grants to fund distance learning projects is also a problem.

Threatened by Technology.   Some instructors fear that an increase in the use of distance learning technologies may decrease the need for teaching faculty. Feeling intimidated by technology may also lessen an instructor's sense of competence or authority. Either or both of these psychological factors may lead instructors to feel that their job security is threatened:

> Trainers (line evaluators, contractors, and Institute staff) perceived their classroom days were over. They had relished the role of "sage on the stage" and were reluctant to relinquish that gratifying identity. With technology perceived as the "enemy" in human interaction and spontaneity, many felt the joys of interacting with peers and colleagues would rapidly decline in this new medium

reminiscent of the "high tech, low touch" theory. They struggled to envision the possibilities of building positive educational relationships online or through video conferencing. (Longnecker, 2001, p. 99)

Legal Issues.   The increasing use of the Internet to deliver distance education raises concerns about copyright, fair use policies, intellectual property rights, and problems such as piracy, hackers, and viruses.

Evaluation/Effectiveness.   There is concern over the lack of research supporting the effectiveness of distance learning as well as the lack of effective evaluation methods for distance learning courses and programs.

Access.   Many students do not have access to courses offered via newer technologies such as the Internet. Some instructors also lack access to the necessary equipment and courses.

Student Support Services.   The provision of student services such as advisement, library services, admissions, and financial aid is critical to the success of any distance learning program. There are also concerns about how to monitor the identity of distance learning students.

STAGES OF ORGANIZATIONAL CAPABILITY

When considering the distance delivery of training and education and viewing the organization collectively, it is useful to think of the "stage" that the move toward distance education is at. As with any innovation, the process usually looks like two steps forward and one back:

> The promise of distance learning remains unfulfilled in many organizations. In spite of many good intentions, extensive pilots and trials, and a great deal of perception building efforts, these organizations fail to recognize some key planning and implementation steps that can make the difference in "Sustaining Distance Learning." (Howard, 2001, p. 270)

Schreiber (1998) presented a model describing stages of organizational maturity (or capabilities) with regard to the delivery of distance training and education:

Stage 1. Separate or sporadic distance learning events occur in the organization.
Stage 2. The organization's technological capability and infrastructure can support distance learning events. When distance education events occur, they are replicated through an interdisciplinary team that responds to staff and management needs and makes recommendations regarding the organization and management of distance learning among the workforce.
Stage 3. The organization has established a distance learning policy, procedures are in place, and planning occurs. This means that a stable and predictable process is in place to facilitate the identification and selection of content and of technology to deliver distance training.
Stage 4. Distance training and education has been institutionalized in the organization in such a way that policy, communication, and practice that are aligned and business objectives are being addressed. The business unit has established a distance education identity and conducts systematic assessment of distance training events from an organizational perspective.

Of course, these stages represent points along a continuum; the stages an organization moves through when planning to institutionalize distance training and education are neither linear nor discrete. Although it is convenient to describe an organization as being at a particular stage, this does not mean that all elements from earlier stages are absent, nor that all units within the organization are at that same stage.

In general, success early in stage 1 is achieved by using effective project management processes. Later, in late stage 1 and in stage 2, the emphasis shifts to *program* management. In late stage 2 and stage 3, along with the continuation of program management, a good amount of organizational development and cultural change efforts are necessary to sustain distance training and education implementation and use at the organizational level. Stage 4 involves using effective strategic planning to guide cultural change and resource reallocation and linking program planning and perspectives to organizational strategic planning and perspectives. Keep in mind that there are often two levels of analyses. Activities, processes, and work, such as evaluation and marketing, occur at the program level, and these same functions appear at a higher, organizational level.

Not all organizations, perhaps not even most organizations, should consistently strive toward achieving a higher stage of technology use or totaling integrating distance education into the way business is conducted. There is nothing wrong with an organization's distance training and education being a series of events or one or more separate programs. Program implementation initially relies on sound project management, and regardless of whether the organization changes to a more integrated stage of distance training or not, solid program planning and program management will always to be keys to program effectiveness and efficiency. What matters most is that the appropriate level of distance education capability is strategically planned for at the appropriate organizational level and that the allocation of resources matches that level of capability.

LINKING THE ORGANIZATIONAL PERSPECTIVE
TO DISTANCE TRAINING PROGRAMS

Strategic planning consists of all the means that an organization can use to redefine itself and to realize a plan. Since the fundamental objective of a strategic plan is to chart a course from where the organization is now to where it wants to be at an agreed point in the future (i.e., at the end of the planning cycle), knowing the current stage of organizational capability would be useful for identifying barriers to the implementation of distance training and education to be on the lookout for.

The overarching goal of strategic planning is to create a common vision of the desired future within the organization while ensuring that performance objectives are integrated into operations and strategies and that training provides those involved with the skills they need (Watkins & Callahan, 1998). One way to view such planning is as a systematic way of identifying and capitalizing on the strengths within the enterprise. At the same time, planning is done to identify and provide for the needs of the organization (this includes identifying and overcoming barriers). Serious consideration must be given to the critical strengths (core competencies and core capabilities) and to the barriers (both perceived and real) that will arise during the implementation of distance training and education.

There is a variety of strategic planning models that have been described for business, nonprofit, and educational organizations (see, e.g., Bean, 1993; Burkhart & Reuss, 1993; Cafferella, 1994; Goodstein, Nolan, & Pfeiffer, 1992). Regardless of the particular model or process an organization uses for such planning, major issues that must be planned for include educational process, student recruitment and enrollment management, higher education development and student development services, human resources, research, information, physical

Program Perspective: Project/Program Management	Tools for Change	Organizational Perspective: Strategic Planning
Exercising professional responsibility	*Budget*	Integration with the organizational mission and vision
	Infrastructure	
Engaging relevant contexts		Guiding beliefs/principles
	Communication	
Designing the program		External environmental scan
Managing administrative aspects	*Workforce development*	Internal organizational strengths
	Policy	

FIG. 40.1.   Linking the program perspective with an organizational perspective: Using project and program management, tools for change, and strategic planning.

planning and development, financial management and planning, national role, collaboration, and institutional culture (Pienaar, Brink, & Barsby, 1999). Strategic planning is defined not by a methodology, a process, or a system but by the entire context and system in which it occurs:

> [Strategic planning] could be considered a concerted effort to achieve an ensemble of decisions and actions which form and guide an organization to be what it is, to do what it does and to know why it does it (Bean, 1993). By utilizing a future-looking approach, strategic planning emphasizes the future implications of decisions made in the present. (Hache, 1998 n.p.)

With a clear vision of the future of the organization, strategic planning is used to create and define the environment—with its boundaries and parameters—in which distance training and organizational learning will take place. The idea is to create a mission and objectives, gather extensive data, analyze and diagnose information regarding the internal and external environment, and decide on the strategies, actions, and evaluations that have a high chance of success in implementation while avoiding expensive pitfalls (Albrecht & Bardsley, 1994). The tools used to link strategic planning to program management include communication systems and management of those systems, budgeting, infrastructure, workforce development, and revisions to policies and procedures (see Fig. 40. 1).

Communication

Distance training and education depends on the marriage of computer and communication systems. It should be managed as a system in which the communication aspect of the technologies is emphasized. The technologies most often associated with distance learning include print, audioconferencing, audiographic teleconferencing, interactive compressed video teleconferencing, computer-mediated conferencing, and video teleconferencing using satellite, broadcast, cable, and fiber transmission media. The technologies typically used in corporate distance learning settings emphasize "conferencing capabilities," which underscores the communication dynamic that is typically encountered in classroom settings (Wagner, 2000).

Establishing a Budget

The organization must decide what equipment and resources are considered infrastructure and what are considered operational expenses. A review of cost analyses for all distance training programs may show that a program will appear to lose money if technology infrastructure costs are included in the program budget. Still, a program budget, to give a true indication of costs, must cover all areas, including support services (e.g., instructional development, registration, and materials development), infrastructure, and instructor training and development (Berge & Schrum, 1998). Essentially, the budget and resource allocation issues in distance training and education involve course design or course purchase, course development and delivery, learner support, and administration of the program.

Determining Functional Infrastructure

Some infrastructure resources and functions should be common to all distance training, and others are more useful when decentralized. Although decentralization may appear to unnecessarily duplicate efforts and costs, it may more closely align expertise with program needs. Centralization of services may allow managers of all distance training and education programs more direct access to top decision-makers and encourage a more efficient use of resources. The risk is in overburdening specific programs with bureaucracy and overhead while not meeting specific program needs. Generally, centralization is favored for the following functions: marketing, instructional design and development support, technology help desk and infrastructure, professional/faculty development, evaluation, promotion and incentive structures, and registration.

Workforce Development

It is hard to imagine anything more important to program implementation than recruiting and retaining expert trainers and support staff. Are all instructors equally suited to teach in distance training and education programs? The answer is generally no. Would it be wise to begin with a small cohort of willing trainers? If time and energy are spent in training this cohort, and it is given support for its development and implementation, its successes will often inspire others.

In some organizations, an initial group of enthusiastic instructors have been trained in effective distance teaching methods, and the individuals in this group then become mentors for the next group of instructors. Ongoing support is given to these instructors through workshops, online discussion groups, and strategic feedback. Occasionally, an instructor works as an apprentice to a practitioner teaching a distance course during one term and then, during the following term, is mentored as he or she practices what was learned.

A timeline is helpful to new distance training instructors as they begin to conceptualize their tasks. Answers to the following questions and the availability of specific training as needed will go a long way toward retaining new distance instructors: What business needs are being targeted? At what point should the syllabus be in place? What materials need to be developed and tested? Is the hardware and software already in place and functional? What are the options when something goes wrong?

Revising Policies and Procedures

The management team can provide leadership in policy revision and remove barriers to the mainstreaming of distance training and education. Each incentive or disincentive, the reporting and accountability structures, and the determination of major resource allocations have a role in changing the organizational culture. Leadership is required to nurture the necessary changes in the social, political, economic, and training/educational environment. Several critical issues unique to program planning for distance training are likely to emerge.

Policies and procedures are normally framed within organizational policies or outside mandates. Such policies are tools for leading an organization in ways that are thought by management to be useful—either in defining a vision or orchestrating cultural change within the organization. A key to ensuring that mandates or missions are carried out and that organizational policies are implemented is to develop a strategic plan. This plan becomes one of the primary instruments of organizational policy and provides the framework for allocating and managing resources and accommodating organizational change and development (World Bank, n.d.).

CONCLUSION

In the global economy of the 21st century, learning organizations are under increasing pressure to show that training and professional development are directly contributing to their profitability. Further, they are being forced to do this at a time when employees are often scattered around the world and when bringing them to a central location and keeping them from their jobs for extended periods of time is no long an option, either from a cost perspective or a time-to-market standpoint. This chapter has focused on the organizational perspective while hinting at the dramatic changes to the roles and functions of instructors and learners that are occurring.

Distance training and education provided by an organization is essential for improving the performance of employees. In fact, to remain competitive, every organization will have to place more emphasis on distance learning. Furthermore, for distance training and education to be effective, the organization will have to engage in sound planning and management.

REFERENCES

Albright, R. C., & Post, P. E. (1993). The challenges of electronic learning. *Training and Development, 47*(8), 27–29.

Albrecht, R., & Bardsley, G. (1994). Strategic planning and academic planning for distance education. In B. Willis (Ed.), *Distance education: Strategies and tools* (pp. 67–86). Englewood Cliffs, NJ: Educational Technology Publications.

Bean, W. (1993). *Strategic planning that makes things happen.* Amherst, MA: HRD Press.

Berge, Z. L., & Schrum, L. (1998). Strategic planning linked with program implementation for distance education. *CAUSE/EFFECT, 21*(3), 31–38.

Branch, A., Lyon, A., & Porten, S. (2001). Hewlett-Packard's Regional Training Center: Site Information & Learning Centers (SILC). In Z. L. Berge, (Ed.), *Sustaining distance training: Integrating learning technologies into the fabric of the enterprise* (pp. 235–254). San Francisco: Jossey-Bass.

Burkhart, P. J., & Reuss, S. (1993). *Successful strategic planning: A guide to nonprofit agencies and organizations.* Newbury Park, CA: Sage.

Cafferella, R. S. (1994). *Planning programs for adult learners: A practical guide for educators, trainers and staff developers.* San Francisco: Jossey-Bass.

Dessinger, J., & Conley, L. (2001). Beyond the sizzle: Sustaining distance training at ford motor company dealerships. In Z. L. Berge (Ed.), *Sustaining distance training: Integrating learning technologies into the fabric of the enterprise* (pp. 178–198). San Francisco: Jossey-Bass.

Dobbs, K. (2000). Who's in charge of e-learning? *Training, 37*(6), 54–58.

Dooley, L. M., Dooley, K. E., & Byrom, K. (1998). Distance training under construction at H. B. Zachry Company. In D. A. Schreiber & Z. L. Berge (Eds.), *Distance training: How innovative organizations are using technology to maximize learning and meet business objectives* (pp. 351–368). San Francisco: Jossey-Bass.

Federal Aviation Administration, Training Program Office, AHR-14. (1997). *Survey of educational technology.* Washington, DC: Department of Transportation, AHR-14.

Friend, N., & Hepple, T. (2001). Lessons from merging SBC's Regional Telecom Learning Centers. In Z. L. Berge

(Ed.), *Sustaining distance training: Integrating learning technologies into the fabric of the enterprise* (pp. 48–69). San Francisco: Jossey-Bass.

Galagan, P. A. (2000, May). Getting started with e-learning: An interview with Dell Computer's John Cone about pulling the big lever. *Training and Development, 54*(5), 62–64.

Goodstein, L. D., Nolan, T. M., & Pfeiffer, J. W. (1992). *Applied strategic planning: A comprehensive guide.* San Diego, CA: Pfeiffer & Co.

Hache, D. (1998, Summer). Strategic planning of distance education in the age of teleinformatics. *Online Journal of Distance Learning Administration, 1*(2). Available: http://www.westga.edu/~distance/Hache12.html

Howard, B. (2001). Supporting an enterprise distance learning program at NYNEX. In Z. L. Berge (Ed.), *Sustaining distance training: Integrating learning technologies into the fabric of the enterprise* (pp. 270–290). San Francisco: Jossey-Bass.

Latten, S., Davis, M., & Stallings, N. (2001). Sustaining distance education and training First Union: Transitioning from the classroom. In Z. L. Berge (Ed.), *Sustaining distance training: Integrating learning technologies into the fabric of the enterprise* (pp. 164–177). San Francisco: Jossey-Bass.

Longnecker, J. L. (2001). Attracting, training, and retaining instructors for distance learning at the U.S. General Accounting Office. In Z. L. Berge (Ed.), *Sustaining distance training: Integrating learning technologies into the fabric of the enterprise* (pp. 85–105). San Francisco: Jossey-Bass.

McCrea, F., Gay, R. K., & Bacon, R. (2000, January 18). *Riding the big waves: A white paper on the B2B e-learning industry.* Thomas Weisel Partners SanFrancisco/NewYork/Boston/London. Available: http://www.onlinelearning2000.com/elearningWeisel.pdf

Moe, M. T., Bailey, K., & Lau, R. (1999, April 9). *The book of knowledge: Investing in the growing education and training industry.* (Report No. 1268). Merrill Lynch & Co., Global Securities Research & Economics Group, Global Fundamental Equity Research Department.

Mottl, J. N. (2000, January 3). Learn at a distance: Online learning is poised to become the new standard. *InformationWeek Online.* Available: http://www.informationweek.com/767/learn.htm

Muilenburg, L. Y., & Berge. Z. (2001). Barriers to distance education: A factor analytic study. *American Journal of Distance Education, 15*(2), 7–24.

Payne, L. W., & Payne, H. E. (1998). Interactive video teletraining in the Federal Aviation Administration. In D. A. Schreiber & Z. L. Berge (Eds.), *Distance training: How innovative organizations are using technology to maximize learning and meet business objectives* (pp. 201–222). San Francisco: Jossey-Bass.

Pienaar, H., Brink, C., & Barsby, T. (1999). Strategic planning framework: Strategic direction. Available: http://www.uct.ac.za/general/stratpl2.htm

Rogers, N. E., & Becker, S. L. (2001). From training enhancement to organizational learning: The migration of distance learning at the American Red Cross. In Z. L. Berge (Ed.), *Sustaining distance training: Integrating learning technologies into the fabric of the enterprise* (pp. 329–350). San Francisco: Jossey-Bass.

Ruttenbur, B. W., Spickler, G., & Lurie, S. (2000, July 6). *e-Learning: The engine of the knowledge economy.* Morgan Keegan & Co. Available: http://outland.masie.com:8080/reports/elearning0700nate2.pdf

Schreiber, D. A. (1998). Organizational technology and its impact on distance training. In D. A. Schreiber & Z. L. Berge (Eds.), *Distance training: How innovative organizations are using technology to maximize learning and meet business objectives* (pp. 3–18). San Francisco: Jossey-Bass.

Senge, P. M. (1990). *The fifth discipline: The art and practice of the learning organization.* New York: Doubleday.

University of Kansas Medical Center. (1996, January). Charge to the distance education strategies and technologies planning team. Available: http://www.kumc.edu/de_strategies/charge.htm

Urdan, T. A., & Weggen, C. C. (2000). Corporate e-learning: Exploring a new frontier. W. R. Hambrect & Co. Available: http://www.wrhambrecht.com/research/coverage/elearning/ir/ir_explore.pdf

Wagner, E. D. (2000, Fall). Emerging technology trends in e-learning. *Line Zine* [Online serial]. Available: http://www.linezine.com/2.1/features/ewette.htm

Walker, S. (1998). Online training costs and evaluation. In D. A. Schreiber & Z. L. Berge (Eds.), *Distance training: How innovative organizations are using technology to maximize learning and meet business objectives* (pp. 270–286). San Francisco: Jossey-Bass.

Wankel, M. J. (2001). The United States Postal Service's integration of distance training and education initiatives to meet organizational goals. In Z. L. Berge (Ed.), *Sustaining distance training: Integrating learning technologies into the fabric of the enterprise* (pp. 291–311). San Francisco: Jossey-Bass.

Watkins, K., & Callahan, M. (1998). Return on knowledge assets: Rethinking investments in educational technology. *Educational Technology, 38*(4), 33–40.

World Bank. (n.d.) *Global Distance Educationet.* Available: www.globaldistancelearning.com/Management/Benefits/effectiveness.html

Zemke, R. (1999). Why organizations still aren't learning. *Training, 36*(9), 40–49.

Zielinski, D. (2000). Can you keep learners online? *Training, 17*(3), 64–75.

41

Web-Based Continuing Professional Education: Uses, Motivations, and Deterrents to Participation

Kathy J. Perdue
Certified Public Accountant
Office@kathyperdue.com

THE CURRENT STATE OF WEB-BASED CONTINUING PROFESSIONAL EDUCATION

Beginning in the 1970s, many professionals engaged in providing services to the general population were required by the state government to participate in continuing professional education. This mandating of continuing education is a result of accelerating technological advances combined with social pressures to ensure professional competency and performance (Phillips, 1978). In addition to participation in mandatory continuing education, many other professionals elect to participate in continuing professional education for purposes of knowledge acquisition. For many professions, such as certified public accountants (CPAs), physicians, and lawyers, successful completion of continuing professional education requirements is necessary to retain a state government–issued license to practice.

Web-based Continuing Professional Education

The constant and ever-quickening pace of change in the world today dictates that practicing professionals engage in a process of lifelong learning. As various researchers (Nowlen, 1988; Queeney & English, 1994) have determined, significant factors contributing to this demand include the following:

- the explosion of information,
- the changing nature of knowledge,
- increasing organizational complexity,
- the drive to maintain excellence and to remain competitive,
- the public's demand for professional accountability,
- compulsory relicensure,

- the threat of malpractice litigation,
- rapid development of new technologies, and
- shifts in governmental regulatory patterns.

All of these factors combined to place a growing demand on professionals to be involved in quality lifelong learning.

Houle (1980) indicates that mandatory continuing professional education is often the alternative selected by legislative and administrative entities to address the issue of public reliance on professionals. The alternative of recredentialing has received significant resistance from professionals themselves. Not surprisingly, given the significant investment of time and resources that such a requirement involves, the greatest deterrent to pursuing mandatory or additional continuing professional education is the professional adult learner's inability to allocate time for education activities (Queeney, 1995). This is also the case in other adult education arenas (Darkenwald & Merriam, 1982; Scanlan, 1986; Valentine & Darkenwald, 1990). As a result, independent study options including correspondence courses, satellite, teleconferencing, compressed video, cable television, interactive computer, and other distance learning modes have come to be seen as attractive alternatives to traditional classroom-bound training (Verduin & Clark, 1991). The option of utilizing Web-based training—that is, taking advantage of multimedia and computer networking to mediate and support instruction when teachers and learners are separated in place and/or time (Simoff & Maher, 1997)—as a means of accommodating mandatory continuing education requirements is becoming increasingly available to professionals (Carlozzi, 1998; Nacinovich, 1998).

Research concerning continuing education via distance education is in its early stages. It consists primarily of a few descriptive studies of multiple professional groups (Scalter, 1990; Grundnoski, 1992) conducted before the Web became popular as an education medium. One empirical study conducted for the Georgia Society of Certified Public Accountants by Perdue and Valentine (1998) found that respondents believe distance education, including use of the Internet, is an effective way to learn. In addition, the study found that the vast majority of respondents reported having adequate access to the technology necessary for participation in a variety of distance education activities. However, with the exception of text-based distance education, the percentage of respondents actually *using* distance education for continuing professional education was minimal.

Over the 20-year period beginning in 1971, 52 of the 54 legal jurisdictions that issue CPA licenses mandated continuing professional education for relicensure (Streer, Clark et al., 1995). In the year 2000, these requirements were still in place (American Institute of Certified Public Accountants, 2000). The mandating of continuing professional education for CPAs—and the attendant expected windfall of new customers—almost immediately spurred continuing professional education providers to evaluate advancements in education delivery. Three of these studies have applicability to this research. First, a study of Ohio CPAs by Kreiser, Baird, and Michenzi (1989) suggested that accountants have a preference for live interactive courses and significant concerns with respect to cost containment and the available variety of continuing professional education topics. Three years later Seay and Watson (1992) conducted a telephone survey of the American Institute of CPAs, the National Association of Accountants (now the Institute of Management Accountants), and the Institute of Internal Auditors. At that time none of these professional organizations had current or future plans to offer continuing professional education via satellite or two-way interactive television, technologies that were then becoming popular. Seay and Watson were able to identify one firm that averaged two to three satellite continuing professional education courses per year in conjunction with several state CPA societies. However, concerns about costs, logistics, and uncertainty about a new approach were reasons most frequently cited for not pursuing delivery of continuing professional education via telecommunication. Finally, a recent study by Ernst & Young (Kahan, 1997) found that continuing professional education delivered via the Internet, audio and videotapes, and CD-ROM has been favorably received by practitioners. The study found practitioners who took courses on interactive, multimedia continuing professional education products performed far better on-the-job than those attending seminars and conferences and were able to finish their work at a faster pace. Thus it would seem that time has brought about changes in providers' and practitioners' attitudes about what constitutes "appropriate" and "preferred" education technology.

Researchers generally acknowledge that Web-based learning has a useful role in continuing professional education, particularly for knowledge workers. "Knowledge workers" are individuals who earn a living by critically analyzing available information for relevance and value and applying creativity in order to create new knowledge. In a rapidly changing and open information society, knowledge workers have to act ever more quickly if they are to keep abreast of change. As a result, the most useful training delivery system would be one that is distributed rather than centralized, allowing for learner control of time and place. This implies the use of technology-based training delivery systems (Romiszowski, 1997).

REVIEW OF RESEARCH

Participation research has a long history in adult education. There are basically three topics that researchers address in this arena: 1) What is the extent of participation? 2) What motivates learners to participate? and 3) What deters learners from participating? The remainder of this chapter is devoted to addressing these three areas.

Use of Web-Based Continuing Professional Education

Several studies in the late 1990s have researched the use of Web-based continuing professional education. In studying ways in which physicians kept current with new knowledge, Lott (1994) found the least used and least liked types of continuing medical education focused on educational methods generally associated with self-directed learning including video or audio programs, self-assessment programs, and computerized activities. In a study to assess the readiness of practicing physicians for the use of computer-based continuing medical education, Khonsari (1995) found that the respondents' attitudes were systematically related to specific factors. These factors were age, majority of practice, level of board certification, years of practice, location of practice, level of experience and familiarity with computer applications (specifically computer-based distance continuing medical education), and the preferred methods of receiving information. On average, respondents' attitudes were slightly to moderately positive toward computer-based continuing medical education. Hayden (1996) analyzed attitudes of physicians and nurses toward computer-based distance learning in emergency medicine. Hayden found greater than 90% of the respondents indicated a willingness to engage in online computer-based continuing medical education programs, particularly those meeting state licensing board criteria for credit toward license renewal. Hayden also found clear user preference emerged for various online services, such as real-time consultations.

Hatfield's research (1996) on the effectiveness of distance education technologies in the delivery of public school continuing professional education indicated that continuing professional education could affect the techniques and practices of teachers. However, Hatfield found the method of delivery may have little influence on effectiveness. In a study addressing the use of computer-based distance education in continuing education, Atwood (1998) found 73.6% of university and college continuing education units were offering some type of computer-based distance education. However, findings in the study indicate the use of traditional classroom-based methods is continuing within computer-based distance education.

For at least one kind of knowledge worker, CPAs, the most useful delivery system would also be interactive. Although the American Institute of Certified Public Accountants and the National Association of State Boards of Accountancy require two hours of self-study to receive one hour of continuing professional education credit, each one hour of self-study on an *interactive* self-study course counts for one hour of credit (American Institute of Certified Public Accountants and National Association of State Boards of Accountancy, 1998). Given the requirement facing most CPAs that they complete an average of 40 hours of continuing professional education per year, combined with the flexibility inherent in technology-based training delivery, multimedia continuing professional education courses would seem to hold a definite allure for CPAs. In theory, multimedia courses inject fun, increase retention, and provide convenience into significant, recurring, educational requirements (Nacinovich, 1998). In reality, multimedia vendors report a tepid response at best to the technology. According to Nacinovich, the earliest provider of multimedia continuing professional education courses to CPAs offered its first course in 1993. Five years later, the vendors estimate that 50% of their customers have taken at least one multimedia course. Less than 10% of another major vendor's 25,000 customers have ordered 1 of the 58 available multimedia CD-ROM courses. Other organizations offering continuing professional education courses to CPAs also indicated poor market reception. In a study of the continuing professional education needs of certified management accountants, Foy (1998) found little use or acceptance of the many self-study forms of continuing professional education such as computer-based training, audiotapes, and others. This was insightful since lack of time to complete continuing professional education was a significant concern for most of this population.

Motivation for Participation in Web-Based Continuing Professional Education

The concept of motivation, as well as the concept of deterrents, is central to most theoretical frameworks of participation in adult education (Rubenson, 1977; Cross, 1981; Darkenwald & Merriam, 1982). Using Scanlan's (1986) definition of deterrents *to* participation as reasons contributing to an adult's decision *not to* engage in learning activities, motivation would be "a reason or a group of reasons contributing to an adult's decision to engage in learning activities." In discussing Web-based education specifically, Keller and Burkman (1983) defines motivation as the choices people make concerning experiences they will approach or avoid and the degree of effort they will exert in that respect.

Houle (1980) notes that more than half of continuing learning in the professions is self-directed, so professional education programs should build on, encourage, and complement self-directed learning. Because a majority of continuing learning in the professions is self-directed, a challenge to preprofessional education is to encourage and support self-direction so that more students become lifelong learners (Houle, 1980; Knox, 2000). One trend in the 1990s changing the face of continuing professional education was the increasing number of programs being offered in distance education formats by universities and professional associations (Cervero, 2000).

Piper (1990) investigated the elements of engineers' professional practices that influence their attitudes toward and their participation in continuing education activities. Piper concluded that participation was influenced by the interaction of three factors: engineers' beliefs about the exertion of effort leading to the successful completion of a continuing education activity, their beliefs about the realization of awards resulting from participation, and the value that they placed on those rewards. Piper stated that all three factors had to be perceived favorably for high participation rates to occur.

There is little empirical research at the current time specifically addressing motivations to participation in Web-based continuing professional education. Nevertheless, the distance education and continuing professional education literature does provide limited anecdotal information.

Several projects during the 1990s researched adult learners in general and their motivations for participating in Web-based education. In studying respiratory care practitioners' participation intentions for completing a baccalaureate degree through distance education, Becker (1995) found learners intending to use distance education felt they would have more interaction with their classmates, need to be on campus less, receive more prompt instructor feedback, have more flexible schedules, and find media-oriented learning more engaging. They also felt that future employers, family, coworkers, and friends would view their decision to use distance education positively. Digilio (1998) studied characteristics of older adult learners and the reasons that Web-based instruction provides the flexibility to meet the needs of adult learners. Based on a review of the literature, Digilio stated that adult learners experience different constraints, motivations, and learning styles than traditional college students, and distance learning technologies have the potential to overcome many of these constraints. In studying adult learners enrolled in a Web-based distance education course, Lim (2000) conducted a study to develop a predictive model for satisfaction of adult learners participating in Web-based distance education courses and found that attitude toward computers was a predictor variable for participation in Web-based distance education courses.

Also during the 1990s, several studies of continuing professional education using distance education technologies were conducted. In 1992, McGee studied self-directed learning among emergency room physicians and reviewed methods of learning utilizing computer, cable television, computer-assisted instruction, computer bulletin boards and forums, and video conferences. The findings indicate they were cost-effective and facilitated wider communication both nationally and internationally (McGee, 1992). In a study of participation in distance continuing professional education by working engineers, Noyes (1998) identified the strongest facilitators to participation in distance education as affordable learning, easy access, course schedule, class during work time, and flexible makeup opportunities. In studying the potential of listservs for continuing professional education, Medley (1999) stated the use of listservs facilitates international programs that provide vehicles for stimulation of new ideas and global concerns. Wilson and Bagley (1999) evaluated distance learning materials through a national survey of 1,000 British pharmacists and focus groups of 40–50 and found high users were motivated and undeterred by design issues mentioned by mid and low users. The most highly valued aspects of distance education were portability, storability, and relevant topics. Garrison and Anderson (1999) argue for an approach to distance education called "little distance education" that is consistent with the traditional goals and values of creating knowledge through a critical community of learners.

While not specifically identified as motivations to participation in distance education, features of Web-based education provide positive incentives for professionals to participate. Khan (1997) has synthesized the literature to develop the following list of key features: interactive, multimedial, open system, online search, device-distance-time independent, globally accessible, electronic publishing, uniformity worldwide, online resources, distributed, cross-cultural interaction, multiple expertise, industry supported, learner-controller, convenient, ease of use, online support, authentic, course security, environmentally friendly, nondiscriminatory, cost-effective, ease of coursework development and maintenance, collaborative learning, formal and informal environments, online evaluation, and virtual cultures. These features either individually or combined could provide motivation for professionals to participate in Web-based education.

In one empirical research project recently conducted, Thomas-Goodfellow, Perdue, and Valentine (2001) studied motivations to Web-based continuing professional education for

TABLE 41.1

Top Eight Motivators for Respiratory Therapists ($n = 110$)

Rank	Item	M^*	SD
1	Web-based CPE courses fit into my busy schedule better than regularly scheduled classes.	5.25	1.00
2	Web-based CPE courses let me learn at any hour of the day or night.	5.22	1.11
3	Web-based CPE courses eliminate the need for travel.	5.09	1.19
4	With Web-based CPE courses I can start a course on the specific date that I find most convenient.	5.06	1.10
5	Web-based CPE courses let me learn at the location I find most convenient.	5.04	1.09
6	Web-based courses save me time.	4.99	1.15
7	Web-based courses make it possible to locate course topics not available in my area.	4.99	1.12
8	Web-based courses save me money.	4.95	1.25

*Based on a 6-point Likert scale (1 = strongly disagree to 6 = strongly agree).

respiratory therapists. A survey instrument containing 16 motivations to participate in Web-based continuing professional education was developed based on Khan's Web-based education features (Khan 1997). A rank listing of these motivators revealed the top eight included items for respiratory therapists relating to time constraints, scheduling, and access. The top eight items providing the greatest motivation for respondents' participation in a Web-based continuing professional education are depicted in Table 41.1.

Deterrents to Participation in Web-Based Education

As previously stated, the concept of deterrents is central to most theoretical frameworks of participation in adult education (Rubenson, 1977; Cross, 1981; Darkenwald & Merriam, 1982). Scanlan (1986) defined deterrents to participation as "a reason or group of reasons contributing to an adult's decision *not* to engage in learning activities" (p. xi). Valentine and Darkenwald (1990) refined the definition of deterrent to be one that "suggests a more dynamic and less conclusive force, one that works largely in combination with other forces, both positive and negative, in affecting the participation decision" (pp. 30–31). Darkenwald and Valentine (1985) state "that an individual's decision not to participate in organized adult education is typically due to the combined or synergistic effects of multiple deterrents, rather than one or two in isolation" (p. 187).

In the earliest empirical deterrent work in adult education, Scanlan and Darkenwald (1984) identified six deterrent factors impacting on participation in continuing education labeled Disengagement, Lack of Quality, Family Constraints, Cost, Lack of Benefit, and Work Constraints. Further empirical work conducted by Darkenwald and Valentine (1985) found six factors that deter the general public from participating in organized adult education: Lack of Confidence, Lack of Course Relevance, Time Constraints, Low Personal Priority, Cost, and Personal Problems. Additional deterrence work was done much along the same lines, but varying by the population studied (Martindale, 1986; Hayes, 1987; Davis, 1988; Weischadle, 1988; Reddy, 1991).

The Internet as a learning environment gives the learner the choice of where and when to study. Facilitated by technology, it also permits individual interactions with the instructor and other learners as well as participation in group discussions (Webb & Street 1997). There is limited literature specifically addressing deterrence for Web-based continuing professional

education. In a 1998 study of barriers to participation in distance continuing professional education by working engineers, Noyes identified barriers to participation as job/family constraints,
work/family interference, lack of desired courses and degree options, poor course advising and
homework feedback (Noyes, 1998). General writings about Web-based education contain references to factors that clearly deter individuals from participating or continuing to participate
in Web-based education. Those most frequently cited in the literature are related to interaction
and technical capability (Khan, 1997; Owston, 1997; Webb & Street, 1997; McCormack &
Jones, 1998).

As Simoff and Maher (1997) have noted, one considerable drawback of the current design
of Web-based courses is the loss of interactivity and the single direction flow of the majority of information. The chief aspect of lack of interactivity is the loss of physical cues that
(nonblind/deaf) adults are used to having available to help in interpreting the context of dialogue. In addition, asynchronous communication can make it difficult to track the progress
of a conversation, determine if other participants have received a student's contribution, and
assess if that contribution has been interpreted in the manner in which the student intended.
One outcome of Simoff and Maher's research is an awareness of the necessity for an increased
time commitment to address the level of interaction desired (McCormack & Jones, 1998).

Technical capability can be as large a barrier to participation in Web-based education as
the loss of interactivity. Having the capability to participate in Web-based learning requires
appropriate computer systems, communication connectivity, and personal technical knowledge
(Khan, 1997; Webb & Street, 1997; McCormack & Jones, 1998). For Web-based learning to
be more effective than irritating, it is necessary to have sufficient memory for multiwindows
and multitasking. The lack of these has been cited as a significant barrier to participation in
electronic-based distance education (Mak & Mak, 1995).

An additional barrier is the lack of adequate communication connectivity. Without reliable
access to the Internet, participation in Web-based learning can be impossible. And without
sufficient modem speed to prevent frustratingly long download periods when accessing sound,
video, and graphics, Web-based learning, while do-able, can *feel* impossible (Filipczak, 1995;
Dillon, 1997; Owston, 1997; McCormack & Jones, 1998). Not surprisingly, Gantz (1997)
reported that according to an International Data Corporation survey, the biggest obstacle to
Web-based training is providing reliable and fast access to users. Unfortunately, efforts to
alleviate these barriers frequently run up against another, equally daunting barrier: economics;
it can be extremely expensive to acquire an appropriate computer and communication system
(Filipczak, 1995; Dillon, 1997; Owston, 1997; McCormack & Jones, 1998).

Even when the barriers above can be overcome, there still remains the issue of comfort with
technology. Eastmond (1995) stated that adult learners found becoming comfortable with technology to be critical to their success in electronic learning. Filipczak (1995) agreed, indicating
that "learner success depends on technical skills in computer operation and Internet navigation, as well as the ability to cope with technical difficulties" (p. 112). Other significant issues
associated with personal technical knowledge include a learner's mistrust of the unknown,
difficulties in comprehending the constantly changing capabilities of emerging technology,
and high initial expectations for commercial quality and tailored delivery courses (Lockheed
Idaho Technologies Co., 1995). Each of these can easily be a deterrent to participation in the
full potential of Web-based continuing professional education.

An empirical study by Perdue and Valentine (2000) developed a survey instrument to
gather data from a systematic sample of members of the Georgia Society of Certified Public
Accountants (CPAs) in order to obtain information concerning their perceptions of Web-based
continuing professional education. This study concentrated on identifying phenomenon that
would deter CPAs from participating in Web-based continuing professional education. The
purpose of the study was to identify the relative importance of deterrent items to participation

TABLE 41.2
Top Eight Deterrents for Certified Public Accountants ($n = 444$)

Rank	Item#	Item	M^*	SD
1	17	I prefer hearing CPE lectures in person rather than reading them on a *computer screen.*	4.20	1.55
2	57	It has never occurred to me to participate in Web-based CPE courses to complete my CPE requirements.	4.03	1.80
3	16	I prefer face-to-face interaction with the *instructor* rather than electronic communication used in Web-based CPE courses.	4.01	1.59
4	13	I prefer traditional classroom instruction over Web-based CPE courses.	4.00	1.53
5	18	I prefer hearing CPE lectures in person rather than hearing them through a *computer speaker.*	3.93	1.58
6	15	I prefer face-to-face interaction with my *peers* rather than electronic communication used in Web-based CPE courses.	3.89	1.59
7	14	I prefer using printed materials over the kind of electronic materials (e.g., computer screens, E-mails) used for Web-based CPE courses.	3.86	1.51
8	41	I am concerned that I don't know how to evaluate the quality of a Web-based CPE course before enrolling in it.	3.79	1.65

*Based on a 6-point Likert scale (1 = strongly disagree to 6 = strongly agree).

in Web-based continuing professional education, determine if there was a more parsimonious explanation using factors underlying these deterrent items, and examine the relationship between personal and professional variables and the deterrent factors identified.

Using a ranking of all deterrent items, the relative importance of individual deterrent items was determined. Taken together, the research suggests that some of the deterrent items were relatively more important than others in deterring CPAs from participating in Web-based continuing professional education. It is interesting to note the highest-ranking items for these CPAs relate to concerns about the specifics of electronic education and electronic interaction. This is attitudinal in nature and tends to make a statement of a desire for protection of how they have always completed their continuing professional education requirements.

The top eight items provide the greatest deterrence to respondents' participation in a Web-based continuing professional education and are depicted in Table 41.2. Of those top eight items, seven involve educational methodology preferences.

Factors Underlying the Deterrent Items

While a rank listing of the individual deterrent items indicated their relative importance in their power to deter participation in Web-based continuing professional education, factor analysis was used to group individual deterrent items into categories. This allowed for the identification of four factor constructs underlying the deterrent items on the survey. As Table 41.3 illustrates, mean item means for the four factors ranged from 1.82 to 3.80 on a 1 (strongly disagree) to 6 (strongly agree) point scale.

Factor I: Concerns About the Quality of Course Offerings.   The second most powerful factor (as measured by mean ratings) in terms of its power to deter participation is concerns about the quality of Web-based continuing professional education. Professionally, CPAs are concerned about the relevancy and accuracy of Web-based course content, the inability to

TABLE 41.3
Mean Ratings of Four Deterrents Factors for Certified Public Accountants

Rank	Factor	Factor Name	Mean	Minimum	Maximum
1	II	Concerns about Electronically Mediated Communication	3.80	2.75	4.20
2	I	Concerns about the Quality of Course Offerings	3.03	2.42	3.80
3	IV	Concerns about the Availability of Necessary Personal Resources	2.15	1.83	2.31
4	III	Concerns about Access to Technology-Associated Resources	1.82	1.55	2.03

obtain printed materials or course recommendations from other CPAs, and the issue of how long a Web-based course would take to complete. This supports Gantz (1997) and Hawkins (1997) who state that the biggest obstacles to Web-based education are the accuracy of course content and the richness of the offerings. The CPAs also expressed concerns about the quality of security in submitting financial or personal information and written comments over the Internet in order to participate in a Web-based course. This supports claims made by Wiesenberg and Hutton (1995) that learners participating in Web-based education were anxious about putting their written word out on the Internet due to the uncertainty of how it would be used in the future. It also supports Nguyen, Tan, and Kezunovic (1996) and McCormack and Jones (1998) who state that learners' concerns about the security of the Web is a significant challenge to overcome.

CPAs also expressed concerns that electronic discussions would lack focus and could be misinterpreted, they don't know how to evaluate the quality of a Web-based course, and Web-based courses might not provide immediate feedback. Concerns about the perception of the quality of course offerings to others include the value placed on Web-based courses relative to other forms of continuing professional education and concerns about the documentation of continuing professional education and acceptance of those credits by their State Board of Accountancy or other administrative agency.

Factor II: Concerns About Electronically Mediated Communication. The derived factor with the largest mean deals with concerns about electronically mediated communication. This factor's mean is twice as high as the CPAs concern about access to the needed technology-associated resources. Collectively, the variables suggest a resistance to change among respondents. Specifically, they suggest a resistance to change in the way that continuing professional education has been traditionally conducted. This resistance is reflected as a rejection of electronically mediated interpersonal communication. This indicates that CPAs clearly prefer face-to-face interaction with instructors and their peers over the electronically mediated communication used in Web-based courses. This supports previous studies by Moore and Kearsley (1996) asserting that interaction is of critical importance in education facilitated at a distance. It also supports assertions by Simoff and Maher (1997) and Webb and Street (1997) that the loss of interactivity is a considerable challenge in the design of Web-based courses.

Also present are concerns about the use of electronic communication extended to all facets of its use as an educational medium. The CPAs polled in this study prefer hearing lectures given in traditional classroom settings over listening to lectures spoken through a computer speaker or reading them on a computer screen. They also prefer print materials to e-mail. This is in agreement with McCormack and Jones (1998) who argue that students brought up on force-feeding education methods may have difficulty in adapting to any new method of education. In short, they prefer traditional modes of educational communication to the electronically mediated variety. In general, most respondents don't believe that Web-based continuing professional education courses have sufficient advantages to justify using them for continuing professional education. This supports the previous study by Perdue and Valentine (1998) that indicated that while these CPAs had the technology-associated resources, they prefer holding onto the status quo.

An examination of the relationship between concerns about electronically mediated communication and the personal and professional variables begins to tell us that this deterrent operates in different ways for different groups of people. The older a CPA is, the more he or she is deterred from participation in Web-based continuing professional education by his or her concerns about electronically mediated communication. Older CPAs are more apt to have a preference for doing things the old way. Males seem to be different from females in regard to their concerns about electronically mediated communication. Males are more deterred by their concerns about electronically mediated communication than are females. Females appear to be more open to the use of Web-based courses. This is inconsistent with the literature (Mason & Kaye, 1989; Canada & Brusca, 1991; Starr, 1997) that states females tend to participate in technology at a slower rate than their male counterparts. The longer a CPA had held his or her certification, the more apt he or she is to have concerns about electronically mediated communication and to be concerned about the availability of necessary personal resources. CPAs prefer doing things in an established manner.

Factor III: Concerns About Access to Technology-Associated Resources.   The derived factor with the least power to deter CPAs from participating in Web-based continuing professional education is concerns about access to technology-associated resources. With the lowest average items mean, this factor indicates the lack of participation in Web-based continuing professional education courses is not principally related to difficulty in accessing necessary technology-associated resources. This is congruent with findings of earlier research by Perdue and Valentine (1998) that most CPAs have the technology-associated resources necessary to participate in Web-based continuing professional education.

The content of this factor is best reflected in three types of resources: Web-based technology-associated resources themselves, the financial resources necessary to obtain Web-based technology, and the specialized knowledge resources necessary to utilize Web-based technology. While the literature reflects lack of access to technology as a significant barrier to participation in Web-based education (Filipczak, 1995; Lockheed Idaho Technologies Co., 1995; Mak & Mak, 1995; Wulf, 1996; Gantz, 1997; Khan, 1997; Owston, 1997; Webb & Street, 1997; McCormack & Jones, 1998), CPAs indicate, by and large, that they have access to the technology required. This is in contrast to the literature and indicates that the importance of this barrier is specific to the population.

It is also interesting to note that CPAs, an extremely cost-conscious group of professionals, do not perceive that the cost of acquiring the needed technology as important in their willingness to participate in Web-based continuing professional education. Again, this is in conflict with the literature that indicates cost is a major barrier to Web-based education (Lockheed Idaho Technologies Co., 1995; Dillon, 1997; Owston, 1997; McCormack & Jones, 1998). This difference may be explained by the adoption of technology by CPAs in order to perform their professional duties.

Factor IV: Concerns About the Availability of Necessary Personal Resources.   The second least powerful derived factor in terms of its power to deter participation concerns the availability of necessary personal resources. Only the factor identified as concerns about technology-associated resources had a lower average items mean. Collectively, the variables suggest CPAs perceived themselves as having the personal resources necessary for participation in Web-based continuing professional education.

The content of this factor includes both internal characteristics and external constraints. Concerns about personal characteristics included respondent fears that they lack the patience to learn how to use the Web for a Web-based continuing professional education course and the confidence necessary to participate in Web-based continuing professional education courses. The CPAs indicate they have the patience and confidence to participate in Web-based continuing professional education. This fails to support the literature indicating that the lack of personal characteristics is a barrier to participation in Web-based education (Eastmond, 1995; Filipczak, 1995; Romiszowski, 1997; McCormack & Jones, 1998). This is partially explained by the level of education and work experience CPAs have received by the time they achieve their certification and by the detailed nature of the work they have selected to perform as their profession.

Concerns about constraints focused on issues external to the respondents and included the lack of time to learn how to use the Web and the lack of skill to download the computer software needed to participate in Web-based continuing professional education courses. Similar to their perceptions on personal characteristics, the CPAs indicated these personal constraints do not deter them from participation in Web-based continuing professional education. This again fails to support the literature claiming lack of time to learn how to use the Web and lack of necessary technical skills deter participation in Web-based education (Filipczak, 1995; Wulf, 1996; Webb & Street, 1997; McCormack & Jones, 1998). CPAs believe they have the skill set to participate in Web-based continuing professional education.

An examination of the relationship between concerns about the availability of necessary personal resources and the personal and professional variables begins to tell us that this factor also operates in different ways for different groups of people. The older the CPAs are, the more they are deterred from participation in Web-based continuing professional education by their concerns about the availability of necessary personal resources. This is inconsistent with Rogers' (1995) writings in which he asserted that early adopters of innovations are not different from later adopters in terms of age. Also, years certified as a CPA is a relevant characteristic in the power of concerns about the availability of necessary personal resources to deter their participation in Web-based continuing professional education.

FUTURE RESEARCH

As the 21ˢᵗ century begins, both the concept of "professional" and the concept of "continuing professional education" are in transition. In addition, the characteristics of "future profession-als" are changing dramatically from those of the previous generation. These emerging trends will impact on participation in Web-based education.

Trend 1—Globalization of Professions

As providers of preservice education for professionals, higher education institutions have recognized that globalization has impacted on traditional policies and procedures for delivery of that education. The literature on graduate and professional education reflects the trends of internationalization of the curriculum and growth in interdisciplinary education (Kezar, 1999). Teichler (1999) suggested that research on the relationships between higher education and the world of work should be based on anticipation of likely changing conditions in the future to include trends toward a lifelong learning society and toward a global labor market.

Burbules and Callister (2000) investigated the transition of universities in terms of two interrelated sets of changes: globalization and the incorporation of new information and communication technologies. They found that these changes are having significant influence on the knowledge activities of research, publication, and pedagogy. Jarvis (2000) concluded that all education is in the superstructure of society and that in order to respond to the demands of the new infrastructure of global society, higher education will have to change quite radically in both its provision and the manner in which it provides learning opportunities. One response to the needed adaptation to a global environment is the increase in the number of institutions seeking global accreditation. These forms of accreditation provide a system of standards and evaluation that is applied commonly among institutions or programs on a global basis. Inevitably, traditional, nationalistic methods of quality assurance will make way for global forms of public protection and education quality (Lenn, 1996).

Specific professional groups, such as lawyers, have recognized and reacted to the globalization of their workplace environment. Trubek, Dezalay, Buchanan, and Davis (1994) discussed the future of the legal profession as it relates to global restructuring and the law. Their findings indicate that internationalization of legal fields is occurring with the creation of transnational legal arenas. In the medical arena, Spallek, Berthold, Shanley, and Attstrom (2000) studied the global community of dentists. They demonstrated in a survey-based research study that there is an interest in the dental community for a worldwide quality assurance evaluation criteria for online dental continuing professional education courses.

The accounting profession has gone one step further. In addition to striving for international standards, an international credential has been proposed that is global in reach, portable from one country to another, includes global standards for competency and ethics, and requires a commitment to continuing learning. It is broadly based with holders expected to come from a broad range of disciplines, including among others, accounting, business law, information technology, engineering, and business administration. Four professional accounting institutions in the United States, Canada, Australia, and New Zealand are proposing this new international credential for business professionals. In order to compete in the global, knowledge- and technology-driven marketplace, international accounting bodies would create and monitor global standards for performance competencies, examinations, ethical standards, and continuing education. The defining aspect of the proposed professional credential is that it is global and allows the holder to provide services seamlessly across international borders (American Institute of Certified Public Accountants, The Canadian Institute of Chartered Accountants et al., 2000; Reeb & Cameron, 2000).

Trend 2—Redefinition of Continuing Professional Education

The primary rationale by licensing authorities for continuing professional education is to strive for a high level of quality in the services provided by professionals to members of society. This has been traditionally accomplished through continuing professional education lectures describing well-defined problems and prescribed solutions. Practitioners and continuing educators are proposing a new model of education that is embedded in the practitioners' environment. Mott (2000) stated that "a model of continuing professional education, of learning from and within practice, would help ensure more effective career practitioners and improved professional practice for society" (p. 24).

The current argument for continuing professional education to take place in the practitioner's environment is based on assertions that merely updating professionals' knowledge does not allow them to know how to deal with ill-defined issues of the real world (Wilson, 2000). This has significant implications for the incorporation of distance education as a means of facilitating 1) the location of learning in the professional's environment and 2) the timing of learning at any time of the day or night. Instructional technologies now allow professionals to customize their lifelong learning process by researching information or interacting with peers and/or experts while remaining in their practice location.

Trend 3—Future Professionals

An important trend to recognize is the changing characteristics of the future workforce, a portion of whom will become professionals. According to Tapscott (1999b), there are an estimated 88 million people in the United States and Canada who are between the ages of 2 and 22. The term he applies to this segment of the population is the Net Generation. Unlike the 85 million baby boomers of the previous generation who grew up with the passive media of television, the Net Generation is the first to grow up surrounded by digital media. Tapscott contends this group will force many significant changes in society, including changes in education. To the portion of this generation with access to technology, the Internet has resulted in assertiveness and self-reliance in using technology to explore and discover new knowledge. This generation prefers the interactive entertainment of the Web and understands they can control what they access rather than having content pushed at them. Consequently, this generation will want to learn in an interactive mode rather than a broadcast mode.

Hay (1999) stated that third millennium educational administrators must recognize the societal trend of the Net Generation and adapt to new modes of learning. With the Internet as the learning environment, digital media shifts the learning experience from 1) linear to hypermedia learning, 2) instruction to construction of knowledge, 3) teacher- to learner-centered education, 4) absorbing to synthesizing material, and 5) school-time to customized lifelong learning (Tapscott, 1999a). Glenn (2000) indicated that business educators are addressing the learning needs of Generation Net students by employing different methodologies than previously utilized. These methods include self-directed learning, interactive environments, assignment selection, and multiple forms of feedback. Jones (2000) indicated that strategies to address Generation Net learning needs include learning through doing, using real-world context, and emphasizing both acquisition and use of information.

As we begin the 21st century, the three trends discussed previously will impact on participation in Web-based continuing professional education. It is too soon to judge the full impact of these trends, but it is reasonable to expect the impact to be significant. Further research will be required to study how these trends will affect future participation, specifically in terms of the future extent of use, motivations for, and deterrents to Web-based continuing professional education.

REFERENCES

American Institute of Certified Public Accountants. (2000). Statement of standards for continuing professional education (CPE), American Institute of Certified Public Accoutants.

American Institute of Certified Public Accountants and National Association of State Boards of Accountancy. (1998). *Digest of state accountancy laws and state board regulations.* New York: American Institute of Certified Public Accountants.

American Institute of Certified Public Accountants, The Canadian Institute of Chartered Accountants et al. (2000). *The XYZ concept: Turning knowledge into value.* New York: American Institute of Certified Public Accountants.

Applegate, L. M., Cash, J. I. Jr. et al. (1988). Information technology and tomorrow's manager. *Harvard Business Review, 66*(6), 128–137.

Atwood, J. B. (1998). *The use of computer-based distance education in continuing education.* Orlando: University of Central Florida, 120.

Baird, M. (1995). Training distance education instructors: Strategies that work. *Adult Learning, 7*(1), 24–26.

Becker, E. A. (1995). *Test of Fishbein and Ajzen's theory of reasoned action with respiratory care practitioners' intentions to complete their baccalaureate degree through distance education.* Madison: The University of Wisconsin, 176.

Burbules, N. C., & Callister, T. A. Jr. (2000). Universities in transition: The promise and the challenge of new technologies. *Teachers College Record, 102*(2), 271–293.

Canada, K., & Brusca, F. (1991). The technological gender gap: Evidence and recommendations for educators and computer-based instruction designers. *Educational Technology Research and Development, 39*(2), 43–51.

Care, W. D. (1995). Helping students to persist in a distance education program: The role of the teacher. Paper presented to the Faculty of Nursing University of Manitoba, Winnipeg Manitoba, Canada, January 1995.

Carlozzi, C. L. (1998). Learning for the future. *Journal of Accountancy, 186*(1), 42–44.

Cervero, R. (2000). Trends and issues in continuing professional education. *New Directions for Adult and Continuing Education, 86*(Summer), 3–12.

Cross, K. P. (1981). *Adults as learners: Increasing participation and facilitating learning.* San Francisco: Jossey-Bass.

Darkenwald, G. G., & Merriam, S. B. (1982). *Adult education: Foundations of practice.* New York: Harper & Row.

Darkenwald, G. G., & Valentine, T. (1985). Factor structure of deterrents to public participation in adult education. *Adult Education Quarterly, 35*(4), 177–193.

Davis, L. J. (1988). *Deterrents to bank managers' participation in continuing education.* New Brunswick: Rutgers.

Digilio, A. H. (1998). Web-based instruction adjusts to the individual needs of adult learners. *Journal of Instruction Delivery Systems, 12*(4), 26–28.

Dillon, N. (1997). Internet-based training passes audit. *Computerworld, 31*(44), 47–48.

Eastmond, D. V. (1995). *Alone but together: Adult distance study through computer conferencing.* Cresskill, NJ: Hampton Press.

Filipczak, B. (1995). Putting the learning into distance learning. *Training, 32*(10), 111–118.

Foy, N. F. (1998). Continuing professional education needs of NYNEX Certified Management Accountants and implications for the Institute of Certified Management Accountants' mandates. New York: Columbia University Teachers College, 327.

Gantz, J. (1997). Web-based training can help IT organizations. *Computer World, 9*(July), 37.

Garrison, D. R., & Anderson, T. D. (1999). Avoiding the industrialization of research universities: Big and little distance education. *American Journal of Distance Education, 13*(2), 48–63.

Glenn, J. M. (2000). Teaching the Net generation. *Business Education Forum, 54*(3), 6–14.

Grundnoski, A. T. (1992). *A descriptive study of attitudes and behavior toward professional continuing education by distance means within five professional groups in Marquette County, Michigan.* East Lansing: Michigan State University.

Hatfield, G. M. (1996). *The effectiveness of distance education technologies in the delivery of public school continuing professional education (educational technology).* Norman: The University of Oklahoma, 102.

Hawkins, D. T. (1997). Web-based training for online retrieval: An idea whose time is coming. *Online, 21*(3), 68–69.

Hay, L. E. (1999). Where are you going in the next millennium? *School Business Affairs, 65*(12), 17–21.

Hayden, J. W. (1996). *Computer-based distance learning in emergency medicine: An analysis of attitudes between physicians and nurses.* Memphis: University of Memphis, 160.

Hayes, E. R. (1987). *Low-literate adult basic education students' perception of deterrents to participation.* New Brunswick: Rutgers.

Houle, C. O. (1980). *Continuing learning in the professions.* San Francisco: Jossey-Bass.

Jarvis, P. (2000). The changing university: Meeting a need and needing to change. *Higher Education Quarterly, 54*(1), 43–67.

Jones, C. L. (2000). Reaching and motivating N-Gen students. *Business Education Forum, 54*(3), 4.

Kahan, S. (1997). CPE reaching cyberspace. *Practical Accountant, 30*(1), 45–49.

Keller, J., & Burkman, E. (1983). Motivational design of instruction. In C. M. Reiguluth (Ed.), *Instructional design theories and models: An overview of their current status* (pp. 386–434). Hillsdale, NJ: Lawrence Erlbaum Associates.

Kezar, A. J. (1999). *Higher education trends (1997–1999): Graduate and professional education.* Washington, DC: Office of Educational Research and Improvement.

Khan, B. H. (1997). Web-based instruction (WBI): What is it and why is it? In B. H. Khan (Ed.), *Web-based instruction.* (pp. 5–18). Englewood Cliffs, NJ: Educational Technology Publications.

Khonsari, L. S. (1995). *A survey of physicians' attitudes toward distance computer-based continuing medical education.* Tampa: University of South Florida, 155.

Knox, A. B. (2000). The continuum of professional education and practice. *New Directions for Adult and Continuing Education, 86*(Summer), 13–22.

Kresier, L., Baird, B., & Michenzi, A. (1989). Mandatory CPE: What do practitioners prefer? *The Practical Accountant* (May), 59–62.

Lenn, M. P. (1996). The globalization of accreditation. *The College Board Review, 178*(July), 6–11.

Lim, C. K. (2000). *Computer self-efficacy, academic self-concept and other factors as predictors of satisfaction and future participation of adult learners in Web-based distance education.* Boca Raton: Florida Atlantic University, 140.

Lockheed Idaho Technologies Co. (1995). *A study of advanced training technology: Emerging answers to tough questions.* Washington, DC: U.S. Department of Energy.

Lott, D. R. (1994). *Diffusion of medical innovation to Pennsylvania's rural physicians (distance education).* College Park: The Pennsylvania State University, 234.

Mak, L., & Mak, S. (1995). *Web in action: Applications and hesitations.* Paper presented at the First Australian World Wide Web Conference, New South Wales, Australia.

Martindale, C. J. (1986). *Factors deterring air force enlisted personnel from participation in voluntary adult education programs offered through education services centers.* Auburn: Auburn University.

Mason, R., & Kaye, A. (Eds.). (1989). *Mindweave: Communications, computers and distance education.* Oxford: Pergamon Press.

McCormack, C., & Jones, D. (1998). *Building a web-based education system.* New York: Wiley Computer Pub.

McGee, J. (1992). *Self-directed learning among emergency room physicians.* New York: Columbia University Teachers College, 237.

Medley, M. D. (1999). The potential of listservs for continuing professional education. *Journal of Continuing Higher Education, 47*(2), 25–31.

Moore, M. G., & Kearsley, G. (1996). *Distance education: A systems view.* Belmont: Wadsworth.

Mott, V. W. (2000). The development of professional expertise in the workplace. *New Directions for Adult and Continuing Education,* (86), 23–31.

Nacinovich, M. (1998). CPE: Lights, camera, action? *Accounting Technology, 14*(3), 38–43.

Nguyen, A. T. A., Tan, W., & Kezunovic, L. (1996). *Interactive multimedia on the world wide web: Implementation and implications for the tertiary education sector.* Paper presented at the Second Annual World Wide Web Conference, Goldcoast, Australia.

Nowlen, P. M. (1988). *A new approach to continuing education for business and the professions: The performance model.* New York: Macmillan.

Noyes, R. (1998). *A study of barriers and facilitators to participation in distance higher education by working engineers.* Norman: The University of Oklahoma, 234.

Owston, R. D. (1997). The world wide web: A technology to enhance teaching and learning? *Educational Researcher, 26*(2), 27–33.

Perdue, K. J., & Valentine, T. (1998). Beliefs of certified public accountants toward distance education: A statewide Georgia survey. *The American Journal of Distance Education, 12*(3), 29–41.

Perdue, K. J., & Valentine, T. (2000). Deterrents to participation in web-based continuing professional education. *The American Journal of Distance Education, 14*(1), 7–26.

Phillips, L. E. (1978). Consumer Groups and the CEU. In H. B. Long and C. B. Lord (Eds.), The continuing education unit: concept, issues, and use: initiated and approved by the National University Extension Assoication (pp. 77–94). Athens, GA: University of Georgia Center for Continuing Education.

Piper, J. E. (1990). *Engineers who continue to study: The relationship of selected factors to participation/non-participation in continuing education.* College Park: University of Maryland College Park, 168.

Queeney, D. S. (1995). *Assessing needs in continuing education.* San Francisco: Jossey-Bass.

Queeney, D. S., & English, J. K. (1994). *Mandatory continuing education: A status report.* Columbus, OH: ERIC Clearinghouse on Adult, Career, and Vocational Education.

Reddy, K. B. (1991). *Perceived deterrents to participation in compensatory education by educationally disadvantaged adult South Africans.* Cornell: Cornell University.

Reeb, W. L., & Cameron, M. (2000). *Adding value to the profession: The proposed global credential.* American Institute of Certified Public Accountants.

Rogers, E. M. (1995). *Diffusion of innovations* (4th ed.). New York: Free Press.

Romiszowski, A. J. (1997). Web-based distance learning and teaching: Revolutionary investion or reaction to necessity? In B. H. Khan (Ed.), *Web-based instruction* (pp. 25–37). Englewood Cliffs, NJ: Educational Technology Publications.

Rubenson, K. (1977). *Participation in recurrent education.* Paris: Center for Educational Research and Innovations.

Scalter, K. (1990). *An investigation of national and international approaches to teleconferencing in continuing and distance education.* Boston: Boston University.

Scanlan, C. L. (1986). *Deterrents to participation: An adult education dilemma.* Columbus, OH: ERIC Clearinghouse on Adult, Career, and Vocational Education, The Ohio State University.

Scanlan, C. S., & Darkenwald, G. G. (1984). Identifying deterrents to participation in continuing education. *Adult Education Quarterly, 34*(3), 155–166.

Seay, R. A., & Watson, J. D. (1992). Telecommunications: An emerging opportunity for continuing professional education. *The Ohio CPA Journal,* (February), 16–19.

Simoff, S. J., & Maher, M. L. (1997). *Web-mediated courses: The revolution in on-line design education.* Paper presented at the Third Australian World Wide Web Conference, Lismore, New South Wales, Australia.

Spallek, H., Berthold, P., Shanley, D. B., & Altstrom, R. (2000). Distance education for dentists: Improving the quality of online instruction. *The American Journal of Distance Education, 14*(2), 49–59.

Starr, C. (1997). *New technologies and women.* Montreal, Quebec, Canada: The Janus Project Workshop.

Streer, P. J., Clark, R. L., & Holt, M. E. (1995). Assessing the utility of continuing professional education for certified public accountants. *Research in Accounting Regulation, 9,* 211–222.

Tapscott, D. (1999a). Educating the net generation. *Educational Leadership, 56*(5), 6–11.

Tapscott, D. (1999b). *Growing up digital: The rise of the net generation.* Boston: McGraw-Hill Professional Publishing.

Teichler, U. (1999). Research on the relationships between higher education and the world of work: Past achievements, problems and new challenges. *Higher Education, 38*(2), 169–190.

Thomas-Goodfellow, L., Perdue, K. J., & Valentinem, T. (2001). Respiratory therapist and the world wide web: Going online to satisfy continuing professional education requirements. *Respiratory Care Education Annual, 10,* 3–13.

Trubek, D. M., Dezalay, Y., Buchanan, & Davis. (1994). Global restructuring and the law: Studies of the internationalization of legal fields and the creation of transnational arenas. *Case Western Rserve Law Review, 44*(2), 407–498.

Valentine, T., & Darkenwald, G. G. (1990). Deterrents to participation in adult education: Profiles of potential learners. *Adult Education Quarterly, 41*(1), 29–42.

Verduin, J., & Clark, T. (1991). *Distance education: The foundations of effective practice.* San Francisco: Jossey-Bass.

Webb, G., & Street, M. A. (1997). *A theoretical framework for internet-based training at Sydney Institute of Technology.* Paper presented at the Third Australian World Wide Web Conference, Lismore, New South Wales, Australia.

Weischadle, M. A. P. (1988). Effects of attitudes and deterrents on participation in continuing education by real estate professionals. New Brunswick: Rutgers.

Wiesenberg, F., & Hutton, S. (1995). *Teaching a graduate program using computer mediated conferencing software.* Paper presented at the annual meeting of the American Association for Adult and Continuing Education, Kansas City, MO.

Wilson, A. L. (2000). Professional practice in the modern world. *New Directions for Adult and Continuing Education, 86*(Summer), 71–79.

Wilson, V., & Bagley, L. (1999). Learning at a distance: The case of the community pharmacist. *International Journal of Lifelong Education, 18*(5), 355–369.

Wulf, K. (1996). Training via the internet: Where are we? *Training and Development, 50*(5), 50–55.

42

Distance Education in the U.S. Air Force

Philip J. L. Westfall

Air Force Institute for Advanced Distributed Learning,
Department of the Air Force
philip.westfall@atn.wpafb.af.mil

INTRODUCTION

The Air Force has used distance learning (DL) since 1950. The need to leverage new instructional technologies and to expand the use of DL to meet readiness requirements and keep training and education costs down has led to the independent development of a variety of DL programs. While the Air Force has a mature print-based DL program, the last ten years have seen a rapid expansion of DL programs using interactive television (ITV), computer-based instruction (CBI), and online courses. Each school within the Air Force developed most of its DL courses independently, with no central management. With DL receiving increased attention from the leadership in the Department of Defense (DOD), in 1995 the Air Force formed the Air Force Distance Learning Office (AFDLO). Its mission was to serve as the focal point for implementation of DL policy and emerging DL technology. In this capacity, it coordinated and facilitated DL across the Air Force and developed a DL roadmap for the future. As a result of this roadmap and the 2000 reorganization of HQ Air University, the Air Force greatly expanded AFDLO's responsibilities. In February 2000, the AFDLO merged with the Extension Course Institute and became the Air Force Institute for Advanced Distributed Learning (AFIADL). The AFIADL is located in Montgomery, Alabama, at the Gunter Annex of Maxwell Air Force Base (AFB) and is part of the Air University, a Directorate of the Air Education and Training Command (AETC). The AFIADL brought three separate DL mission areas into one organization: (1) the Extension Course Institute, (2) the Air Technology Network Program Management Office, and (3) the Air Force implementation of the Advanced Distributed Learning Initiative (ADLI) and emerging DL technology.

PROGRAMS AND INITIATIVES

Extension Course Institute

The Extension Course Institute (ECI) was established in 1950 as the Air Force's only correspondence school. The institute's original mission was to provide voluntary nonresident courses for both active duty and reserve Air Force personnel. Since 1950, more than 13 million airmen have taken these DL courses, furthering their careers while acquiring job-critical knowledge and skills. Today, with a staff of both civilian and military personnel, the institute supports formal training and educational programs of the Air Force, Air National Guard, and Air Force Reserve. The institute provides over 450 career-broadening courses (at the low cost of $42 per student) to people throughout the Department of Defense and to civil service employees in all federal agencies. This translates to more than 255,000 course offerings every year. These courses are known for their instructional excellence and have always exceeded the standards of both the Distance Education & Training Council and the American Council on Education. Over the years, the institute's mission has undergone several major changes. In 1963, the institute became an essential and mandatory part of a large number of on-the-job-training programs when it started providing self-study materials for the specialty knowledge portion of the Air Force's official upgrade training program. In 1969, the Extension Course Institute was given the additional mission of providing study reference materials used in preparation for specialty knowledge testing for the enlisted personnel promotion system. In February 2000, the institute was brought under the management of the AFIADL and continues essentially intact as the Extension Course Program (ECP).

The ECP operates in a fully automated environment. Course development, production, distribution, the registrar, and student administration functions are managed on a sophisticated system consisting of nearly 400 PCs and a mainframe. To profit from rapidly growing technological capabilities, the ECP is enhancing its efficiency and productivity by procuring advanced computer systems and software. The new equipment and software should greatly enhance AFIADL's ability to meet the needs of the Air Force for better training at a better price. Students will experience better service and enjoy lessons that are more current. All of these ECP improvements will contribute to increased Air Force readiness.

The quality of ECP's correspondence courses is maintained through internal efforts, of course, but additionally, the Distance Education and Training Council (DETC) has traditionally accredited the program, and it undergoes periodic review by the Air University Board of Visitors. The American Council on Education also evaluates the ECP courses for credit recommendations in upper baccalaureate, lower baccalaureate, and vocational areas. This program assists graduates of these courses to continue their education and pursue degrees at non-DOD institutions.

Since 1993, the ECP has incorporated computer-based instruction into its curricula. The trend is to convert more print courses to multimedia where more interactivity is required. The CBI programs are forwarded to the students in the form of diskettes or compact disks with supplementary hard copy of printed reference materials.

Air Technology Network

Using interactive television (one-way video over satellite with multipoint audioconferencing) for distance learning began in 1991. The Secretary of the Air Force for Acquisition gave funding that year to the Air Force Institute of Technology (AFIT—also a school within the Air University) at Wright-Patterson AFB to quickly reduce the backlog of students that required courses for certification on the then newly designed career field progression. Located near

Dayton, Ohio, AFIT is the Air Force's graduate engineering school. It also offers professional continuing education in acquisition and civil engineering. It was the acquisition program, however, that brought satellite to the rest of the Air Force and led to the creation of the Air Technology Network (ATN). A Center for Distance Education (CDE) was created, and there, the planning for the development of a digital video satellite network was patterned after the pioneering efforts in digital technology of the National Technological University of Ft. Collins, Colorado. The CDE took the idea one step further by conceiving and developing a network that would be interoperable across the federal government; it was dubbed the "Government Education and Training Network" (GETN). CDE collaborated with the Army Logistics Management College (ALMC) at Ft. Lee, Virginia, to use the same satellite service provider to establish the first multiservice, distance learning network. The Army had been using an analog network for several years but saw the promise of digital technology, so ALMC agreed to have its existing satellite network retrofit to the same digital technology the Air Force was adopting. Through use of government-wide contract vehicles provided by the federal government's General Services Administration, GETN has grown from these first two broadcast centers (at AFIT and ALMC) in 1993 to 15 digital-Ku-band satellite uplink broadcast centers, with over 20 video channels available, reaching over 1,300 fixed-dish downlink sites located throughout the continental United States, Alaska, Hawaii, and Puerto Rico. GETN currently broadcasts approximately 11,000 hours per year. Within the Department of Defense, the other agencies using GETN are the Air National Guard, the Air Force Reserve, the Defense Equal Opportunity Management Institute, the Defense Logistics Agency, the Army National Guard, and the U.S. Navy. The following civilian government agencies currently use GETN: the Federal Aviation Agency, the Department of Energy, the U.S. Courts, the Department of Justice, the U.S. Coast Guard, the Environmental Protection Agency, the U.S. Fish & Wildlife Service, and the National Park Service.

The advantages of a single network are obvious: GETN allows the various user agencies to share distance learning programs and use common facilities. Additionally, the Army National Guard provides a listing of other satellite programs that may be of interest to the government community but that are on other satellites that are analog. These programs are rebroadcast on GETN, adding even more distance learning programs to the community of users.

As for the ATN, it has grown to a network of 5 broadcast Centers and 250 ITV classrooms. The Air Force's ATN can broadcast any GETN program to a total of 10 sites in Germany, England, and Italy, and 5 more sites at AF installations in Korea and Japan. ATN now broadcasts over 3,500 hours per year, and has reached over 17,000 students who have successfully completed its courses. These interactive television courses range from a few days to a semester in length and cover subjects such as contracting and acquisition management; environmental management; safeguards and security; aircraft maintenance and repair; professional military education; professional continuing education; parenting; communication; Air Traffic Control and related courses; diversity; equal opportunity training (EOT); and law, medicine, chaplaincy, and management and leadership courses.

ATN is very cost-effective. With respect to out-of-pocket costs for putting a course on the air, there are usually no development costs. The time to convert an existing lecture-based course to on-the-air can be as little as three months. Delivery costs vary somewhat from school to school, but using actual costs for one of ATN's biggest users reveals that cost-avoidance or savings can be as much as 96%. For example, AFIT's School of Systems and Logistics' current in-residence costs for a typical 60-hour course is $370,000 for 200 students. By satellite, it is only about $13,000—that is under 4% of the costs of inresidence. More important is the total cost to the Air Force of doing business over satellite. If the costs of personnel and other overhead are added to these out-of-pocket costs, and then one compares ATN's total costs with only the per diem and travel of TDY, it is still remarkably favorable: $225 per student day in residence compared to just $47 per student day using ATN. That means that ITV is under 21% of the costs of in residence. For FY00, the cost-avoidance estimate for all courses combined was over $7.5 million.

Today, the ATN and its Program Management Office are part of AFIADL. Its operation

- meets a vast number of educational objectives,
- preserves academic quality,
- is cost-effective,
- is geographically unconstrained,
- is interactive,
- is responsive to frequent changes,
- offers tenfold increase in student throughput, and
- permits interoperability with other government agencies.

GETN has the capacity to store and forward digital video programs as well as datacast Internet protocol courseware to servers and desktops across the world. GETN, therefore, will not only offer its traditional ITV courses, but also will become the bypass technology to the public Internet to offer distance learning *anytime, anywhere, anyway.*

The Advanced Distributed Learning Initiative

The Office of the Secretary of Defense (OSD) is leading the effort known as the Advanced Distributed Learning Initiative (ADLI). The ADLI is a structured, adaptive, collaborative effort between the public and private sectors to develop the standards, tools, and learning content for the future DL environment. The effort seeks to make DL available "anytime, anywhere" through the use of the Internet. The ADLI envisions high-quality, cost-effective, network-centric, asynchronous instruction. It primarily consists of a learning management system and a reference model for the development of shareable content. The sharable content object reference model (SCORM), which is still in its developmental and prototyping stages, sets the standards for the development and sharing of instructional modules in a networked environment. The Air Force is an active participant in OSD's vision, which is captured in the *DOD Strategic Plan for Advanced Distributed Learning, 30 Apr 99.* As DL technologies mature and become cost-effective, eligible Air Force courses will be converted to ADLI format to exploit positive return on investment.

The AFIADL strategy is to pursue emerging network-based technologies; create common standards that will enable reuse and interoperability of learning content; lower development costs; promote widespread collaboration that can satisfy common needs; enhance performance with next-generation learning technologies; work closely with industry to influence the commercial-off-the-shelf product development cycle; and establish a coordinated implementation process. The ADLI is designed to deliver efficient and effective high-quality learning continuously to DOD personnel *anytime, anywhere.* The ADLI end-state envisions universal use of instructional components that are characterized by:

- *accessibility* from any location, remote or local;
- *interoperability* between all ADLI instructional platforms, media, and tools;
- *durability* to withstand base technology changes without significant recoding or redesign;
- *reusability* between applications, platforms, and tools; and
- *cost-effectiveness* to provide significant increases in learning and readiness per net increment in time or cost.

The Air & Space Learning Network Initiative

Air & Space Learning Network (ALN) will be a learning management system (LMS) that will tie all distance learning program support through a single portal. ALN will be an Air Force learning portal. It will be an enterprise-level learning management support system accessed through the AF portal. The ALN will also have the functionality of an indexed search engine encompassing education, training, performance support, exercise, modeling, and simulation domains. The ALN will be a centralized, single log-on, one-stop shopping "system of systems" for the education, training, performance support, exercise, modeling, and simulation environments. The ALN will be a "system of *learning* systems"—directly related to and in support of enterprise-level AF learning. ALN will provide one-stop shopping for Air Force-related education, training, and instructional information, services, and systems through a standard interface that promotes ease-of-use and efficient account management. ALN will be both mission-centric and student-centric, and comply with or apply evolving DOD and industry learning standards and best practices, such as the SCORM. The ALN functionality will include enterprise learning management, decision support, curriculum management, learner support, knowledge management, electronic performance support, and learning data warehouse and repository. It will support all forms of DL and in-residence technology insertion, all from a centralized enterprise location with shared services and resources. ALN will implement, to the maximum extent possible, key elements of knowledge management and electronic performance support systems in support of Air Force learning.

AFIADL TODAY

The Air Force Institute for Advanced Distributed Learning's entire focus is distance learning. According to the DOD Implementation Plan for ADL, "ADL is an evolution of distributed learning (distance learning) that emphasizes collaboration on standards-based versions of reusable objects, networks, and learning management systems, yet may include some legacy methods and media." AFIADL's mission, as stated in its strategic plan, is to "promote, deliver, and manage ADL [distance learning] for our aerospace forces." AFIADL functions to create an Air Force environment that recognizes the value of distance learning. It works with OSD and sister services to review best practices in industry and academia. AFIADL is the Air Force focal point for implementation of DL policy and DL emerging technology. Currently, AFIADL is prototyping learning management systems and SCORM-conformant courses, developing electronic testing, and supporting efforts to resolve infrastructure, bandwidth, security, and firewall policy issues. AFIADL is stepping up to its charter to lead the Air Force in coordinating a strategic plan to implement distance learning wherever and whenever practical. Its chief responsibilities are to:

- obtain senior leadership support,
- develop DL plans,
- represent AF in all levels of DOD,
- develop ALN,
- establish instructional processes and standards,
- improve education and training efficiencies where practical and cost-effective,
- improve customer support,
- explore and prototype research and evaluation function,
- publish instructional technology standards,

- modernize information management,
- facilitate development of DL manpower standards,
- advocate requirement priorities,
- develop contractor support,
- apply ADLI to the Extension Course Program,
- improve the efficiency of ATN, and
- expand DL opportunities via ATN.

It is generally known in the DL community that the DOD's strategy is to focus on Web-based instruction through its ADLI. Although AFIADL is focusing on the ADLI as its flagship strategy of the future, AFIADL's programs are currently being delivered by CBI, ITV, and print. Through its distance education programs (the Extension Course Program and the Air Technology Network), AFIADL delivers education at a distance by developing, publishing, and distributing or broadcasting over 400 courses for professional military education, professional continuing education, career development programs, and specialized courses to Air Force war fighters and war fighting support personnel worldwide. AFIADL also distributes study materials to eligible Air Force enlisted personnel in support of the Weighted Airman Promotion System (WAPS). The four major content areas are briefly described below.

Professional Military Education Courses

The professional military education courses are taken by both commissioned and noncommissioned officers. These courses, of which there are currently 36, teach leadership, management principles, techniques of effective communication, problem solving, analysis of professional reading materials, international relations, national decision making, and defense management. The courses give students the broad skills and knowledge they need to be effective leaders at various stages in their careers. AFIADL offers PME via print, CD-ROM, and Internet media.

Professional Continuing Education Courses

Professional continuing education courses meet the professional continuing educational (PCE) needs primarily of two career fields in the Air Force: acquisition management and civil engineering. There are currently 52 courses that vary in length from one week to one academic quarter. The primary audience is composed of officers and middle-management civil service employees. These courses are developed by Air University schools outside of AFIADL, but those that are developed for interactive television are provided through the Air Technology Network. These courses, therefore, come under the accreditation guidelines of the DETC.

Career Development Courses

Career development courses (CDCs) constitute the largest portion of the institute's curricula. There are currently 394 courses, which are primarily print based. These self-study courses help enlisted personnel complete the specialty knowledge portion of their on-the-job-training program. Enlisted personnel must complete CDCs successfully at various stages to advance in their careers. CDCs are also available on a voluntary basis to others for career broadening. The institute offers CDCs in a very wide variety of career fields. Students enroll individually through their Base Education Services Office.

Specialized Courses

These courses provide valuable information and career-broadening knowledge to individuals in a variety of career fields. Today, AFIADL offers 27 specialized courses in such areas as aircrew operations, general military training, medicine, civil engineering, security police, contract law, finances, logistics plans, supervisor safety, public affairs, weather, and chaplaincy programs.

AFIADL AND THE FUTURE OF DL MEDIA

The focus on DL does not mean the end of the traditional classroom. In fact, out of about 1,500 active AETC in-residence courses, it is expected (based on a contracted evaluation) that only about 120 may be eligible for conversion to DL. The Air Force, therefore, will still have traditional classrooms for courses that should not be converted to DL formats. Whereas the requirement for traditional classrooms may be reduced, traditional methods will still play a vital role in necessary categories such as Basic Military Training. The end result is that the Air Force will add value to the total education and training system by providing more courses to a greater number of students.

Print

Print will continue to be used extensively. Whereas there is a DOD drive to convert most if not all DL to online, AFIADL will not select media that are less than optimal to reach its many learning objectives. Print still offers the most effective way for students to read large amounts of text. Those using online or CBI media for reading report a decrease in reading speed and retention. Additionally, it is truly the only anytime, anywhere medium. DOD firewalls, cost of development of PC-based courses, and lack of bandwidth assures this medium a long future in DL. It will continue to be used as a supporting medium for most courses, whether they are ITV, audioconferencing, CBI, or online. As soon as technology and quality control permits, some text materials will be delivered electronically for on-site printing and binding.

Satellite

The use of ITV is growing due to increasing availability and ease of converting classroom programs to DL. All development is done quickly and in house, which makes ITV an attractive and cost-effective medium. Satellite has been used exclusively for ITV so far, but with the advancement of digital technologies, the bandwidth once used for synchronous video will be used as a bypass technology to the Internet. Current firewall restrictions within the DOD, and the current bandwidth limitations on terrestrial networks, make the use of satellite for datacasting an attractive alternative. Additionally, there is a DOD initiative to distribute asynchronous video content across military installations to avoid transportation of celluloid films. AFIADL is working with DOD to use its ATN to distribute digitally converted films to any military installation that uses the GETN. Use of satellite technology for DL in the federal government is currently in a state of growth (less than dramatic, however), so it continues to have a future as a viable DL medium, at least for the near term (this decade). The cost of satellite delivery, however, will very likely continue to grow from year to year, and bandwidth may become less available. Add to the equation an expanding terrestrial infrastructure with reduced usage charges, and the use of geosynchronous satellites may not be as attractive tomorrow as it is today.

CBI

The AFIADL's CD-ROM courses will continue to be used due to the number of courses already developed. CBT offers richer multimedia and interaction than (asynchronous) online courses. CBI is very portable, and courses that exclusively used print have been supplemented by CD-ROMs for added interactivity. With the development of datacasting, many of these courses will be available for delivery by satellite to local servers without having to modify them to meet the constraints of public Internet delivery. It is expected, however, that with time and funding, many of these legacy CD-ROM courses will migrate to SCORM standards.

Advanced Distributed Learning Initiative

The AFIADL has just begun piloting SCORM-conformant courses. It is anticipated across DOD that Internet delivery will be the DL medium that will experience the most extensive growth. As increased funding becomes available, the AFIADL will work closely with its ADLI partners to develop courses in conformity with SCORM standards. As these standards are being considered across industry, it may to have a bright future. Internet-based courses will be more efficiently developed and shared across the DOD; but they are not a panacea. While it offers interchangeability and availability, there are still significant hurdles to overcome and many questions not yet answered. "Granulating" all instruction, as the SCORM requires, may result in many, if not most, learning objects having to be extensively retooled to be usefully integrated in any given course. While the focus is on "sharability," the author has never received a satisfactory answer to the question of how much course content needs to be shared. Intelligent tutoring, often associated with the ADLI, will be a facet of Internet-based instruction, but costs and development time will continue to be substantial despite the expected cost-efficiency of the SCORM. Courses that require synchronous video instruction, or require the reading of large amounts of text, may not be suitable for online delivery in the near term.

CONCLUDING REMARKS

AFIADL has developed a strategic plan and is marshalling the resources necessary to expand its programs to enhance the Air Force's readiness by leveraging the latest and existing technologies in a cost-effective blend of DL media. In a nutshell, AFIADL supports a blended-media approach. Its fundamental principle in DL is that learning objectives and cost drive media selection. It is axiomatic at AFIADL that no single DL medium is a panacea. Its vision statement below includes a qualifier to the popular mantra, "anytime, anywhere":

Excellence in Advanced Distributed Learning . . . Right Way, Any Time, Any Where

REFERENCES

Air Education & Training Command. (2000, Aug.). *AETC ADL Implementation Plan*. Available with limitations from Randolph AFB, TX: AETC/DOS.

Air Force Institute for Advanced Distributed Learning. (1999, Aug.). *The Distance Learning Roadmap*. Available with limitations from Maxwell AFB–Gunter Annex, AL: AFIADL/XR.

Air Force Institute for Advanced Distributed Learning (2001, Mar.). *Strategic Plan*. Available with limitations from AFIADL/XR. Maxwell AFB–Gunter Annex.

Air Force Institute for Advanced Distributed Learning. (2001, May). *Air Force Advanced Distributed Learning Vision* (draft). Available with limitations from Maxwell AFB–Gunter Annex, AL: AFIADL/XR.

Air Force Institute for Advanced Distributed Learning. http://www.maxwell.af.mil/au/afiadl.

Air Technology Network Program Management Office. http://atn.afit.af.mil.

Government Education & Training Network. (http://getn.govdl.org)

Office of the Deputy Under Secretary of Defense (Readiness). (2000, May). *Department of Defense Implementation Plan for Advanced Distributed Learning*. Available with limitations from ODUSD(R) Defense Pentagon, Washington D.C.

Office of the Under Secretary of Defense for Readiness & Training. (1999, April). *Report to the 106th Congress: DOD Strategic Plan for Advanced Distributed Learning*. Washington, DC: OASD/RA (RT&M), Defense Pentagon.

DISCLAIMER

Whereas descriptions of AFIADL's programs were drawn directly from available documents published by AFIADL, the views expressed in this chapter are those of the author and do not reflect the official policy or position of the U.S. Air Force, Department of Defense, or the U.S. government. This chapter, however, has been reviewed for factual accuracy by the AFIADL and the Air University Public Affairs Office.

43

The U.S. Marine Corps Distance Learning Program

Steven M. Jones
United States Marine Corps
DL Center
jonessm@mitre.org

Wanda Mally
United States Marine Corps
DL Center
mallyw@tecom.usmc.mil

Larry A. Blevins
United States Marine Corps
DL Center
blevinsla@tecom.usmc.mil

James E. Munroe
United States Marine Corps
DL Center
munroeje@tecom.usmc.mil

We will deliver world-class training and education via a Marine Corps Learning Network enabling Marines to learn via the appropriate media, when and where learning is most needed. The learning experience will be part of a Marine's career long learning continuum that supports the operational readiness of the Total Force and prepares Marines to meet the challenges of tomorrow.

—Steven M. Jones, LtCol USMC (ret),
United States Marine Corps DL Center (DLC)

To help the U.S. Marine Corps meet new challenges in instructional and information technologies with increased flexibility, the Marine Corps Combat Development Command's (MCCDC) Training and Education Command (TECOM) developed the Training and Education Modernization Initiative (TEMI). The objective of this initiative is to maximize the Corps' limited training and education resources by restructuring current institutional training, improving our training design/development and training management processes, introducing technology into classrooms, and capitalizing on modern distance learning (DL) technologies. Professional military education (PME) programs will also benefit from this initiative as current distance education courses are enhanced through the application of advanced/emerging information technologies.

BACKGROUND

Reviews of our training and education processes several years ago revealed problem areas that significantly impact operational readiness.

- Student loads frequently exceed formal school seat capacity resulting in large pools of Marines awaiting training (MAT).

- Initial resident-skill training pipelines are increasingly long and have increased the training component of the manpower investment account and decreased manning in the operating forces.
- The Marine Corps' current focus on resident formal school attendance as a prerequisite for military occupational specialty (MOS) qualification is too rigid and contributes to mismatch problems for the Marine Corps Reserves.
- Further, the current Marine Corps Institute (MCI) paper-based correspondence courses are not closely linked to resident skill-training curricula and do not contribute to MOS qualification.
- Existing nonresident PME courses, which include soft-skilled courses such as leadership and military history, are based primarily on resident PME curricula and are not optimized for DL.

The TEMI is an attempt to correct many of these deficiencies through a comprehensive review and restructuring of Marine Corps' training and education processes. Restructuring includes improving instructional design, development, delivery, and education and training management processes. The scope of commitment to training and education modernization spans a total force that is 210,048 strong, consisting of 173,142 active duty Marines and 37,906 reservists. For many government agencies, global organizations, and other branches of the military, these numbers may seem small, but the size of the Marine Corps training and education population is only one of a number of key factors in the overall challenge to educate and train our Marines. Other important considerations such as our focus on leadership skills and restrictions imposed by geographic distribution of our troops during war and peacetime help define the Marine Corps' need for far-reaching, high-impact, cost-effective training and education programs.

DL is a major component of the TEMI. DL technology has the potential to dramatically change the way we train and educate Marines. Just as modern weaponry has changed warfare, DL technology is transforming Marine Corps training and education from a centralized, formal school-based, instructor-centered environment to a more distributed, learner-centered approach. Our investment in technology is being driven by operational readiness requirements and focuses on improving both the effectiveness and the efficiency of the training and education programs provided to Marines worldwide.

Opportunities

Why should the Marine Corps embrace DL and modern training technologies? First, there is tremendous momentum across industry, academia, and the services to exploit modern technology to improve instruction and increase opportunities for access. Recent advances in technology have made DL an increasingly viable option to deliver courses on demand, with minimal regard to time and distance. Second, Executive Order 13111, signed by the president on January 12, 1999, emphasized the exploitation of technology for delivering training and education across the entire federal government. Both Congress and the Secretary of Defense tasked the services, during the Quadrennial Defense Review, to increase the use of DL, where possible, in order to reduce the cost of institutional training and education programs. Finally, DL has the potential to "level the playing field" for our reserve forces by providing them with increased opportunities for training and education. Expanded use of DL helps reduce resident training time and training education costs and increases educational opportunities for all Marines.

The Marine Corps is exploring various advanced technologies to develop and deliver learning products *just-in-time*, when and where Marines most need them. Marines can expect to use a Marine Corps intranet, the Internet, learning resource centers (LRCs), interactive multimedia instruction (IMI), video teletraining (VTT), and embedded training (ET) to master new skills and learn. DL technologies have the potential to yield significant savings; however, they are costly to initiate, requiring a substantial up-front investment and must be well planned and coordinated.

The cost of technology has highlighted the importance of a coordinated approach to research, development, acquisition, and life cycle management. Some acquisition programs are consulting training design specialists early in the requirements definition phase to reduce the cost of training and align it with existing Marine Corps training standards. The continued partnership between the acquisition force, manpower, and training has the potential to achieve significant life cycle cost-efficiencies for major Marine Corps equipment procurements in the future.

Many promising technologies are still under development and require further study to ensure that each will be a cost-effective solution to the Marine Corps' growing training and education requirements. Likewise, the partnership between acquisition, manpower, and training is in its infancy and must be cultivated. Moreover, cultivating partnerships with our sister services is important as the Corps attempts to leverage its investment to meet Marine Corps specific requirements and defray the cost of implementing new technology. The future of Marine Corps training and education will be shaped by how we take advantage of these new technologies and emerging partnerships.

Modernization Tenets

Training and education is an investment in operational readiness. Restructuring of existing programs must focus on enhancing operational readiness by making training and education more effective and more efficient. The basic tenets of the TEMI are:

- Training and education are a core responsibility of the service.
- Operational readiness is the primary consideration for implementing training and education programs.
- Marine Corps training and education is standards based.
- A Marine's educational experience is part of a career-long learning continuum supporting the operational needs of the total force.
- Technology will be leveraged to improve the effectiveness and efficiency of Marine Corps training and education.
- DL will increasingly be used to meet future Marine Corps training and education requirements.
- The Marine Corps will leverage other Department of Defense (DOD) and governmental agency instructional technology efforts.

Current Uses of DL in the USMC and DOD

While the focus in Marine Corps training and education is to teach skills and knowledge, we also teach intangible knowledge and decision-making skills through professional military education courses that have a morale component—even some spirituality. Such intangible knowledge and skill areas, such as leadership and strategic planning, are not necessarily priorities in the typical education and/or commercial arenas.

The Marine Corps has to also consider other significant factors in our approach to training and education strategies, such as how the Corps differs from sister services in terms of tasking, physical environment, and so on. Deployment is a good example: Because the Marine Corps spends a great deal of time at sea, we particularly need the portability that DL has to offer.

Finally, the Marine Corps places emphasis on educating its young Marines in "life skills." The average 25-year-old has already developed academic skills such as math, reading, spelling, balancing a checkbook, and the like, but many young Marines still need support in these areas and DL is a viable way to meet this requirement.

Although the Corps differs from sister services in these and other areas, we have still learned a great deal from them. What we know of adult learners has had a positive influence on the way we model our instruction. Data and approaches used by the U.S. Army Headquarters Training and Doctrine Command have shown us what motivates learners, barriers to distance learning, and in general, how adults learn. We use these and other factors to discern the best instructional strategies when producing a course (Abell, 2001).

DL has been a normal part of Marine Corps training and education programs for over 80 years. Using paper-based media, various programs from skill training to PME, provided by the MCI, have met our evolving training and education needs. These correspondence courses, delivered asynchronously, are the foundation of our DL programs today. However, the emphasis on this type of delivery means is rapidly changing. During FY97, the MCI began developing its first multimedia DL courses for both CD-ROM and Internet delivery. Currently there are seven IMI courses completed with students enrolled in them. An additional 12 IMI courses are in under development. The Marine Corps has also completed one VTT course and has an additional four under development. As training reviews are accomplished and additional subject matter is determined suitable for DL delivery, the number of courses will grow exponentially.

The Office of the Secretary of Defense (OSD) and the White House Office of Science and Technology Programs (OSTP) have collaborated to develop the advanced distributed learning (ADL) initiative. The purpose of the ADL initiative is to ensure access to high-quality education and training materials that can be tailored to individual learner needs and can be made available whenever and wherever they are required. This initiative is designed to accelerate large-scale development of dynamic and cost-effective learning software and to stimulate an efficient market for these products to meet the education and training needs of the military and the nation's workforce in the 21st century. Distributed learning will accomplish this through the development of a common technical framework for computer and net-based learning that will foster the creation of reusable learning content as "instructional objects." ADL partnerships between the federal government, private-sector technology suppliers, and the broader education and training community will be the means for formulating voluntary guidelines that meet common needs. By making learning software accessible, interoperable, durable, and reusable, the ADL initiative ensures that academic, business, and government users of learning software gain the best possible value from the materials they purchase. Success of the ADL initiative will be measured by the extent to which (1) consumers are able to purchase high-quality learning software less expensively than they do today; (2) the size of the learning software market increases; and (3) producers of learning software can achieve a higher return on their investments. The Marine Corps is an active participant in the ADL initiative.

Why Expand the Use of DL in the Marine Corps Today?

There are a number of reasons why the Marine Corps is rapidly expanding the use of DL as a form of instructional delivery.

- We can no longer afford to do business as usual. The challenge today is to meet increased training and education requirements in spite of cuts in funding, manpower, and training facilities. While resources are decreasing, requirements for training and education are increasing. An increasingly younger force, new equipment, changing missions, and MOS mergers mean increased training and education requirements. DL offers the Marine Corps a way to meet these emerging requirements.

- A second reason is that the other military services, which provide training for approximately 63% of our MOSs, are expanding their use of DL over the next several years. If the Marine Corps does not develop a similar capability, we will reduce the training opportunities for our Marines in the future.
- The use of DL can reduce the cost of traditional training and education while still meeting training and education needs. Using network and CD-ROM distribution in DL can significantly reduce the distribution costs associated with conventional paper-based courses. Offering a course via DL reduces travel and per diem costs.
- Adopting DL can also provide widespread access to training and education resources. For example, it can significantly increase student throughput. The Air Force Institute of Technology (AFIT) increased student throughput from 300 to 3,000 for its acquisition planning and analysis course by converting it to a DL format. The Naval Postgraduate School is pursuing a similar course of action for several of its graduate education programs. Finally, the National Guard Bureau is developing comprehensive DL programs to increase training for thousands of guardsmen across the United States.

The Shift From the Instructor-Centered Paradigm to the Learner-Centered One

The Marine Corps strategy for success in the DL arena is to align itself with the overall cultural shift toward learner-centered training and education technologies. We recognize the need to develop systems that enable us to reach more Marines with better and more-focused training and education programs in the future. In keeping with the commandant's planning guidance, the DL aim is to extend learning beyond the boundaries of the traditional classroom by exploiting technology. Technology has matured to the point where we can now deliver world-class interactive instructional materials using multiple media formats without regard to time, space, or distance. Moreover, the rapid growth of the Internet has changed our perception of information sharing, electronic commerce, delivering instruction, and collaborative learning. Academia, government, and industry are using this medium to train and educate the modern workforce. The Marine Corps is also using Internet-based technologies to deliver interactive learning products and to facilitate a collaborative learning environment.

Due to the rapidly changing technological landscape and the desire to achieve and maintain interoperability, the Marine Corps uses instructional technologies and information systems based on open-system architectures and industry-standard protocols. Further, our DL systems conform to the requirements of the defense information infrastructure (DII) common operating environment thereby increasing our chances for seamless interoperability among the services.

Current and future DL programs are learner centered rather than instructor centered. They are being designed specifically with the distance learner in mind. DL solutions will be network delivered where possible. We are exploiting the power of the Internet to distribute and track computer-based IMI. Realizing that a robust infrastructure is required to support the network-based learning environment, we are developing interim hybrid solutions using a combination of Internet, CD-ROM technology, and traditional paper-based DL courses until the enterprise network can adequately support network delivery. We will support network-based learning with robust videoconferencing and teletraining capabilities leveraging on existing service and government video networks.

Finally, Marine Corps DL will encourage the development of artificial intelligence, intelligent agents, intelligent tutoring systems, performance support, and embedded training technologies to reduce the requirement for equipment- specific training in the future.

ORGANIZATIONAL ROLES TO SUPPORT USMC DL

The DL program is supported by the following organizational components: the DL center (DLC), formal schools, and base learning centers. These components conform to a three-tier approach for DL. Each component corresponds to an echelon within the Marine Corps and has specific roles and responsibilities at that level. The components of the DL functional structure are physically connected via the Marine Corps Enterprise Network (MCEN), forming the Marine Corps DL Network (MarineNet).

The DLC is an organization within the TECOM, Quantico, Virginia, which is under the operational control of the commanding general (CG) TECOM. Its mission is to design, develop, and implement DL solutions together with the sponsors of Marine Corps training and education programs. The DLC provides a consolidated Corps-wide online catalog of DL products, to include a VTT listing accessible through the Internet. The DLC also manages master DL manpower data, ensuring that complete and accurate information on enrollments, completions, and qualifications are passed to the Marine Corps Total Force System (MCTFS). The organization that handles these enrollments is the Marine Corps Institute. MCI serves as the production arm of the DLC and provides Corps-wide standardization, certification, and quality control for all DL efforts.

The formal schools are functional area proponents that provide content and subject matter expertise for the development of DL products and courseware for training and education under their purview. Multimedia course development and maintenance are outsourced to commercial development firms.

The base learning centers are the primary locations for delivering DL courseware to Marines in a given geographic area. The base learning centers are comprised of a DL application server suite with one or more interconnected learning resource centers (LRCs) and VTT centers. The number of LRCs and VTT centers within a geographic region depends on the size of the region and the population supported by the base, station, or site. The base learning centers provide local DL account management, storage, and distribution of electronic courseware to all Marines and any other authorized user connected to the base network.

THE NATURE OF THE MARINE CORPS DL SYSTEM

DL Content Development

An integral part of the Marine Corps TEMI is a comprehensive review of each of the formal training tracks. TECOM conducts detailed training reviews for each of the Marine Corps' institutional training courses at regular intervals. The objectives of the training review process are: (1) design a comprehensive MOS training concept, (2) identify essential job performance competencies and supporting tasks for MOS qualification, (3) design a training progression model that meets career-track requirements for each MOS, and (4) redesign courses as appropriate to incorporate both resident and DL to achieve MOS qualification within established resource guidelines.

This detailed training review process is not an insignificant effort. It requires time and dedicated effort on the part of all stakeholders to develop relevant and cost-effective training solutions for each of our MOSs and presents us with an opportunity to significantly enhance Marine Corps training.

Once the curriculum reviews are completed, the formal schools design and develop resident instruction and provide subject matter expertise for the development of DL products to support the new training progression models and curricula. The implementation of revised integrated curricula varies depending on the complexity and subject matter. However, the target is to deliver new training and education solutions within 9 to 12 months of commencing the review process.

Paper-based courses of instruction and job aids are being produced in accordance with the *MCI Style Guide*. All forms of computer-based instruction are developed in accordance with the *Marine Corps IMI Style Guide*. Using best practices in screen design and computer-based instruction employed by Shneidermann (Ikegulu, 1998) and other professionals in the field of human-computer interface (HCI) design, we have employed human-computer interface design standards that capitalize on direct manipulation and menus, affording our students a well-rounded, integrated environment. These design standards have also been incorporated into templates and fully documented, so that the courseware, while sometimes developed by different vendors, all has the same look and feel for the Marine Corps user community.

In a number of cases, we include a metaphor or an extended metaphor to construct effective mental models for the learner. This approach is in line with the practices of cognitive psychologists, who note that information is better retained by the learner if he or she is allowed to construct a memory link between the new information (being learned) and past experience (Ritchie & Hoffman, 1997).

The annual DL program course development goal is 12 courses (7 MOS skill, and five PME) between FY 02 and FY 07. DL course development priorities are published annually.

DL Infrastructure

MarineNet uses the MCEN and the DII to connect Marine Corps bases and stations and the 194 reserve sites across the country. An open-system architecture is used to ensure interoperability between Marine Corps and other service DL and communications systems and platforms. VTT centers supporting MarineNet conform to DOD-mandated standards to ensure interoperability with other DOD systems.

The primary access to MarineNet occurs at the local level through the base learning centers. Dedicated DL servers are required for each base and serve multiple "tenant" schools and LRCs. The server resources provide the storage capacity for all electronic training material accessed through workstations aboard the base, as well as the necessary management tools to monitor student progress, monitor network utilization, determine courseware availability, and maintain statistical information.

The LRC is the primary access point for DL courseware for those Marines who do not have access to computer workstations. The LRC is a client-server local area network (LAN) system connected to the base network backbone. Each LRC can accommodate approximately 20 simultaneous users. Automated electronic classrooms (AECs) are also being fielded to selected schools. AECs are dual-purpose facilities that serve as both technologically enhanced resident classrooms during scheduled training hours and LRCs during unscheduled times. Approximately 62 LRCs and 36 AECs are being fielded as part of the DL program in addition to the workstations already connected to the Marine Corps enterprise network.

The VTT centers provide the capability to conduct DL using the latest video teleconferencing (VTC) technologies. The centers have a 2-way video and 2-way audio (2V/2A) capability and accommodate 15 to 20 students. The system conforms to all DOD standards and guidelines and is capable of multipoint conferencing with all VTT centers DOD-wide. The MarineNet VTT systems leverage the existing Marine Corps Satellite Education Network (MCSEN) and the Navy Learning Network VTT capabilities. During FY02 the MCDLP absorbed the MCSEN system and additional VTT sites at both active and reserve locations. The MarineNet VTT also merged with the Navy Learning Network system which significantly expanded learning opportunities for DL students.

Deployable LRCs (DLRC) are being fielded in FY03 to provide operational units with the capability to access DL resources while these units are deployed. This small self-contained, *ruggedized* client-server network will have the same capability as a fixed site LRC. Further, it will have the capability to connect to shipboard or external Transmission Control Protocol/Internet Protocol (TCP/IP) networks. The system is composed of a server suite and 20 client workstations. Courseware is uploaded onto the deployable server before deployment and student progress data is passed via a satellite link to a central learning management system located at the DL center. Operations and maintenance for the DL infrastructure are handled through commercial contract support.

The issue of developing content that can be supported on our infrastructure is addressed early in our course development process—during the analysis stage involving the media feasibility study for each course. Riley (1997) describes some of the (hardware) issues associated with Web-based DL that impact the DL product, including bandwidth issues. We highly emphasize the up-front analysis phase of our courses that "weeds out" those potential DL candidates that are not really candidates at all. Further, we look at the content of existing courses to determine if they are suitable for conversion to DL—looking at issues such as content stability (how often it is likely to change in a given amount of time).

Learning Management System

Another critical component of the DL program is the enterprise-wide learning management system (LMS) that manages courses and students in a distributed environment. The Marine Corps has partnered with the Navy's chief of naval education and training (CNET) to provide a viable learning management solution. The system is extremely flexible in order to support our mobile population of active duty, reserve, and civilian Marines for online registration, tracking, and assessment. The system provides an alternative registration and assessment capability for traditional DL courses and serves as the secure gateway for new online DL courseware and materials. The system is accessible through MarineNet and the conventional Internet.

Instructor Development and Support

DL is a new operating environment for Marine Corps instructors and curriculum developers. Exposing our instructors, training developers, and senior leaders to emerging DL instructional technologies helps them overcome the normal apprehension associated with applying new methods and training concepts. Accordingly, instructor development and support are critical factors to the overall success of the DL program. The DLC and the instructional management schools, which are located at Camp Pendleton and Camp Lejeune, develop instructor training programs and provide technical support to facilitate the expansion of DL capabilities at the Marine Corps formal schools. The training programs include information on the instructional design process, implementation of DL instructional technologies, and project management.

COSTS AND BENEFITS OF DISTANCE LEARNING

Establishing a viable DL program is resource intensive and requires a significant up-front investment in order to build the necessary infrastructure that enables access for all Marines and Marine Corps civilian personnel. The Marine Corps DL program received initial program funding in FY99 to establish a representative architecture and complete the pilot initiative. The DL program competed successfully for additional funding in FY00 and received acquisition

Milestone III approval in April 2000. In order to reduce the overall cost of the program, several ongoing initiatives and programs are being leveraged including:

- Base Telecommunications Infrastructure (BTI)—This initiative upgrades the telecommunications network infrastructure aboard every base and station between FY97 and FY02.
- Marine Corps Satellite Education Network (MCSEN)—MCSEN is an existing video-conferencing network available aboard major Marine Corps bases and stations. MCSEN is currently devoted to voluntary off-duty education and the academic skills program. MCSEN is funded. MCSEN would merge into the DL program in FY02.
- Total Army DL Program (TADLP)—The TADLP will provide the Marine Corps with additional DL courseware and training opportunities including access through the Army's Doctrine and Training Digital Library (ADTDL), the Training Network (TNET), and Satellite Education Network (SEN).
- National Guard Bureau's (NGB) Distributed Training Technology Program (DTTP)—The DTTP establishes a robust DL infrastructure across all 50 states and is a funded initiative. The Marine Corps and NGB are exploring collaboration opportunities for the future.
- Navy DL Programs—CNET is providing assistance with IMI development and connectivity through the CNET's Navy Learning Network.

Justification for DL program funding was based upon several basic assumptions: first, that the overall training modernization initiative, of which DL is a part, can successfully reduce institutional training time. This notion is called training buy-back. Using the training buy-back strategy, the Marine Corps is able to shorten some traditional resident training tracks, thereby reducing the manpower investment account.

- Marines who finish training sooner can be sent to the operating forces, thus improving operational readiness.
- Shorter resident training tracks enable the Marine Corps to increase the frequency and throughput, reducing the number of Marines awaiting training in pools.
- Finally, increased use of DL can reduce travel and per diem expenditures.

These underlying assumptions drive the DL investment strategy. The pilot initiative was fully funded to properly assess and validate the DL communications architecture, course development, and management processes. The pilot helped shape the future direction of the DL program. The MOS training tracks that provide the greatest opportunity for training buy-back have been reviewed first and appropriate DL products are being developed. DL procurements and fielding plans are closely aligned with MCEN upgrades. All computer hardware components are procured and managed under the Marine Corps common hardware suite initiative at the Marine Corps Systems Command. The Marine Corps seeks every opportunity to leverage other service and federal government DL programs that fit into the MarineNet concept and DL architecture in order to achieve economies and increase access.

The scope of the Marine Corps approach to DL is not limited to critical factors such as return on investment and training time alone. There are other factors that we can and should also evaluate four or five years from now to determine the success of today's DL program. These include whether:

- the Marine Corps is better prepared due to DL;
- low density–high demand positions are being filled at a greater rate;

- we are able to retain more Marines in the force because we've been able to reduce the traditional time away associated with resident courses; and
- there is an increase in the number of Marines for a given MOS that is traditionally short.

These examples would represent our way of "time-shifting" training, giving Marines an incentive to go into MOS areas that give them more options for training, without causing them to travel away from their work site and their families.

MOVING FORWARD: BUILDING ON WHAT WE'VE ACHIEVED AND WHAT WE'VE LEARNED

The following paragraphs describe areas of Marine Corps education and training that have been positively impacted by the DL program. They represent a few of our "success stories."

Basic Electronics Course

Most enlisted Marines who are chosen for MOSs in the communications and electronics field are sent to entry-level training at Marine Corps Communication Electronics School (MCCES) in Twenty-nine Palms, California. One of the first courses they might attend is the basic electronics course (BEC). This is a "feeder" or prerequisite course designed to provide students with the basic concepts of electricity, electronics, digital logic, computer operation, and basic electronic construction techniques, for further training in the maintenance of telecommunications or electronics equipment and qualification in the 2800 or 5900 MOSs. This course provides technical instruction in the fundamental concepts of electronic theory common to all Fleet Marine Force communication-electronics equipment. Topics include electrical and electronic principles, direct and alternating currents, passive and active components, solid state devices, analysis of properly operating circuits, generic use of test equipment, techniques and quality control of soldering, concepts of basic digital circuits, and techniques of logical troubleshooting. Personnel and equipment safety, including electrostatic discharge safeguards, are stressed throughout the entire course.

The BEC is technical in nature and contains concepts and theories that are difficult for many Marines to comprehend. Prior to 1997, the failure rate of the course was as high as 46%, that is, almost half of the students did not pass the course the first time through and had to take the course again.

But in 1997, MCCES and DLC implemented a solution that infused technology into the BEC classroom. The solution involved the purchase of a modular, computer-based electronics training system with interactive hardware and software. The system purchased from Lab-Volt Systems, Inc., incorporates a comprehensive series of boards that take the student from the basics of AC/DC circuits to advanced studies in microprocessors and communications. Today, the failure rate of the BEC is an astoundingly low 6%.

MCAVRET

In the late 1990s, the Marine Corps was experiencing significant losses of aircraft and personnel in the AV-8 Harrier jet community. In 1998, a review panel was organized to investigate the reason(s) for the losses. The first annual Harrier Review Panel (HaRP) report confirmed that the reduced number of staff noncommissioned officers (SNCO) and noncommissioned officers (NCO) in the Harrier aircraft maintenance MOSs was adversely affecting the ability of experienced supervisors to thoroughly mentor first-term Harrier maintenance personnel.

The HaRP concluded that increasing the experience level in Harrier squadrons would reverse this situation, improve maintenance capability, and increase mentoring opportunities to assure future maintenance capability was adequate to meet the operational needs of the Harrier community.

VMAT-203 (a harrier training squadron) Fleet Replacement Enlisted Skills Training (FREST), located at Marine Corps Air Station (MCAS) Cherry Point, North Carolina was given the task to develop career-level courses for the following MOSs: AV-8 Harrier aircraft mechanic, fixed-wing aircraft airframe mechanic, fixed-wing aircraft safety equipment mechanic, aircraft communication and navigation weapons systems technician, and aircraft electrical systems technician. The FREST teamed with Naval Air Warfare Center Training Support Division (NAWCTSD) in Orlando, Florida, and the DL center to develop a family of pilot courses for the MOSs with the purpose of achieving three goals:

- Develop advanced career-level courses that will challenge, stimulate, motivate, and *train* young second-tour Marines.
- Insert proven current technology into the instructional strategy and use it to take the training *to* the Marines at their home base.
- Combine the first two goals to make a meaningful contribution to Harrier readiness and safety.

The resulting program was called the Marine Corps Aviation Readiness Enhancement Training (MCAVRET) Program. VMAT-203 FREST delivered the first prototype course in September and October 2000 using point-to-point video teletraining (VTT) technology. The MCSEN system was used to link MCAS Cherry Point and MCAS Yuma, Arizona. Using MCSEN for VTT presentations enabled FREST instructors at Cherry Point to conduct training at both sites simultaneously. Feedback from the students was tremendously positive and the pilot was deemed a success.

Taking training to the Marines had two benefits: it reduced the time the Marines were away from work and their families, and it eliminated the cost associated with travel. VTT technology will continue to be exploited for the remainder of the Harrier maintenance MOSs. Using VTT as a delivery method for the MCAVRET program is one of several first steps the DL center is taking to transition Marine Corps training and education to meet the existing challenges.

Terrorism Awareness

Nearly every Marine completes the MCI course *Terrorism Awareness for Marines*, originally published in paper-based format as part of the Marine Corps program to combat terrorism. The course was converted to IMI in 1997 and addresses the basics of terrorism and provides procedures for minimizing an individual's susceptibility to terrorist attack at work, at home, while traveling, and on liberty. Also presented are effective measures Marines can use if taken hostage by a terrorist group.

In 1998, the DLC conducted an internal, limited-scope test with Marine students. The informal test focused on two areas: time required to complete the IMI course and IMI course final examination scores. The results of the test were compared to the Marine Corps average that was computed from historical data based on paper-based enrollments. The results showed that by taking the IMI version of terrorism awareness, the time required to complete the course was reduced from 11 hours to 6 hours, while the average exam scores rose from 85% to 92%! We saw firsthand that the IMI version was more efficient and more effective than the paper-based version.

Personal Financial Management

Most Marines complete the MCI course *Personal Financial Management*, originally published in paper-based format to assist Marines in their management of personal financial matters. The course was converted to IMI in 1997 and includes topics such as the collecting and safeguarding of important papers, veterans benefits, insurance policies, military retirement, and so on. Again, in 1998 the DLC conducted an internal, limited-scope test focusing on the same two areas: time required to complete the IMI course and IMI course final examination scores. Again, the results showed that by taking the IMI version of *Personal Financial Management*, the time required to complete the course was reduced from 7 hours to 4 hours, while the average exam scores rose from 83% to 93%.

On the Horizon . . .

Courses related to information technology tend to produce a good return on investment. Some of the content currently in development includes subjects such as public key infrastructure (PKI) overview and information assurance (IA) awareness training. The estimated cost-avoidance for courses like these promises to be in the millions of dollars annually.

Other Success Stories: "Let the Numbers Speak for Themselves!"

In FY01, we experienced a fivefold increase in the number of hours of Web- or CD-ROM–based interactive multimedia instruction in development, 300 hours compared to 61 hours in FY00, and anticipated that our trend for growth would continue.

Although the Marine Corps has its own DL goals and expectations, it refuses to live a stove-pipe existence. Just recently, we strengthened our commitment in training and education by partnering with the Navy to make nearly 1,000 e-learning courses available through MarineNet with content ranging from the latest networking and office automation technologies to critical business skills and soft skills needed for effective personal and business communication.

Each month, the number of Marine distance learners increases, as we continue to see a rapid rise in the number of visits to the learning resource centers. Just in the month of May (2001) alone, nearly 5,000 Marines visited the LRCs to access our courseware online. But we don't find these numbers surprising because nearly 85% of all course enrollments are online.

Challenges

To fully realize the potential of DL, the Marine Corps must deal with several significant challenges.

- First, we must overcome resistance to change. DL establishes a new learning environment and changes the way we will train and educate in the future. This change will meet resistance due to lack of experience with developing effective DL solutions, unfamiliarity with the technology, and the perception that DL will eliminate jobs or diminish resident instruction. Lack of personal experience is prevalent among the DL nay-sayers.
- Second, we must establish incentives for DL programs that are tied to promotion or advancement opportunities. Incentives will likely be the catalyst for rapid expansion of the current DL initiatives.
- Third, providing effective mentoring and maintaining cohesion in a distributed training environment is challenging. The shift to student-centered learning must be balanced with a team training approach that is mentored and proctored by senior leaders. This shift

in learning methods will not occur overnight but will instead require several years to implement.

- Fourth, not every Marine learns at the same pace using this approach. Some Marines require a more structured learning environment and increased interaction to facilitate learning. Any training and education solution that is developed must be able to accommodate alternate learning methods and schedules. The key ingredient will be to establish an environment in the unit that is conducive to learning and to provide the proper leadership to ensure that DL programs are totally accepted and completed.

Issues regarding Internet access aboard Marine Corps bases and stations must also be addressed and resolved prior to realizing the full benefit of DL. A 1997 study by the Army Research Institute revealed that more than 70% of the officers and just over 30% of the enlisted soldiers had regular Internet access. The Army has identified lack of Internet access for soldiers as a critical barrier to success in its DL program. While the Marine Corps has not conducted a similar study, it seems similar percentages would apply to the Marine Corps. For DL to fully succeed, Marines must have significantly greater access to the Marine Corps network and the Internet.

Finally, the Marine Corps' high operational tempo makes finding time to train and educate very difficult. Finding this time represents perhaps the greatest challenge to leaders, trainers, and educators in the information age. DL programs cannot be relegated to off-duty hours. If the Marine Corps is to realize the full potential of these new instructional delivery methods, we must schedule training and education events into normal duty hours.

The new Marine Corps DL program expands on the earlier work of the MCI by developing integrated training and education programs for initial skill and skill progression training that lead to MOS qualification and enhance current distance education programs. The DL program is a funded total force program supporting both the active Marine Corps and the Marine Corps Reserve. Implementing comprehensive DL programs is a complex undertaking and involves developing innovative solutions in the following major technology domains:

- Instructional content,
- Delivery infrastructure,
- Instructional management systems for delivering courses,
- Management of students in a distributed environment, and
- Instructor training and support.

The DL program offers solutions in each technology domain and is being implemented in two phases—a pilot phase (FY97–99) and a program expansion phase (FY00–05).

The pilot effort was initiated to study infrastructure, process, and resource requirements to successfully establish a viable DL program. Lessons learned from the pilot effort are being used to shape the DL program so that our limited resources can be effectively focused on establishing a flexible Corps-wide DL capability in the future. A major part of implementing the USMC DL program is establishing the Marine Corps learning network or MarineNet infrastructure. MarineNet is the wide-ranging initiative that provides the supporting infrastructure and access points to enable the delivery of world-class training and education to all Marines.

The objective of the TEMI, and specifically the implementation of DL, is to provide better and more effective training with fewer resources. Initiating modern instructional technologies to both deliver DL and enhance our resident school training presents significant challenges. Meeting our goals of reducing training pools, training time, and training structure while providing better and more efficiently delivered instruction to our Marines is only part of the challenge. Shifting to a learner-centric from an instructor-centric approach to learning, ensuring computer literacy, making limited time available for Marines to train via DL, and overcoming institutional resistance to change present challenges of an equal or even greater magnitude.

REFERENCES

Abell, Millie. (2001). *Soldiers as distance learners: What Army trainers need to know*. From the World Wide Web http://www.tadlp.monroe.army.mil/abell%20paper.htm.

Ikegulu, Patricia R. (1998). *Effects of screen designs in CBT environments*. (ERIC Document Reproduction Service No. ED 428 757).

Riley, Peter C. (1997). *Designing, developing and implementing WWW-based distance learning*. Paper presented at the Inter-service/Industry Training, Simulation and Education Conference (I/ITSEC) 19th, Orlando, FL, December 1–4, 1997. (ERIC Document Reproduction Service No. ED 415 345).

Ritchie, Donn C., & Hoffman, Bob. (1997). *Using instructional design principles to amplify learning on the world wide web*. (ERIC Document Reproduction Service No. ED 415 835).

44

Distance Learning in the U.S. Army: Meeting the Readiness Needs of Transformation

Michael W. Freeman
Computer Sciences Corporation
mfreema7@csc.com

The United States Army has a well-earned reputation as the premier training organization in the world. The Army has also long been a proponent of training innovations to foster improved effectiveness and efficiency of providing ready soldiers and units. Army doctrine considers training to be the linchpin of organizational performance as evidenced by the following quote from Army regulations:

> Good training is the key to soldier morale, job satisfaction, confidence, pride, unit cohesion, esprit de corps, and combat effectiveness. (Department of the Army, 1981)

Distance education has the potential to dramatically enhance Army organizational performance by increasing personnel qualifications in the unit and reducing the impact of skill decay by making training available when and where required. It is widely recognized as the method of choice for reducing costs, increasing flexibility, increasing access, and increasing the number of learners reached. The potential for savings to the military services is tremendous, with the Army providing training to over 335,000 students annually in residence (Program Management Office, The Army Distance Learning Program, 1999).

The current Army training concept has its roots in the traumatic post-Vietnam downsizing of the Army, the accompanying reductions in defense budgets, and the end of the draft in the 1970s. Those daunting challenges required soldiers to be more highly skilled while the systems became more cost-effective.

In response to these challenges, the Army adopted a philosophy of tightly integrating institutional and unit training with the primary goal of improving effectiveness on the job. This systems approach to training was used to focus training on successful performance to job standard and to decentralize execution to the units. The performance orientation placed emphasis on soldiers being able to do the tasks required to established standards.

Reduction in manpower and time available to formal Army schools meant many of the skills once taught in schools would have to be learned in units and on the job. To meet these requirements, the Army began a program to use technology to develop and implement training extension courses or TEC. These courses were concentrated on critical job tasks and delivered with synchronized slide projectors and tape recorders. While very basic and static in design and delivery, the TEC program set the tone and intent for all Army distance learning programs to follow (Chapman, Lilly, Romjue, & Canedy, 1998).

The primary modernization goal of the Army is digitization of processes and organizations to achieve information dominance. The ability to conduct predeployment, mission-specific training under the tutelage of skilled subject-matter experts can result in faster preparation for contingencies and can also level the playing field for reserve component and geographically remote organizations and learners by providing a standardized learning experience without walls or barriers (Freeman, Wisher, Curnow, & Morris, 1999). However, to take advantage of the myriad of new digital systems, soldiers must be prepared to operate them effectively (Murray, 2000).

The first goal of The Army Distance Learning Program (TADLP) is to increase Army readiness to deploy and fight. In order to do this, the Army program must provide professional education and training on demand to wherever soldiers are located. This includes permanent assignment locations and temporary locations in both developed and austere environments. It also includes soldiers' work sites and, for selected events, their homes.

The second goal is to establish a system to deliver standardized training. The plan is to deliver training from proponent schools to soldiers via a "telecommunications common operating environment." Increasing the availability of training while maintaining standardization of learning outcomes is especially important for an organization with a worldwide mobile workforce of over 1.25 million full- and part-time technicians and professionals. Accordingly, the Army has pioneered many distance education approaches and established programs to provide distance education services. However, the rapid development of enabling technologies and the transformation of the Army into a more agile Information Age force requires continuing critical review of current programs and methodologies in light of emerging needs (U.S. Army Public Affairs Office, 2001).

The U.S. Army Training and Doctrine Command (1998, p.) defines distance learning as:

> delivering standardized training using multiple media and technologies when and where it is needed. It includes providing individual, collective, and self-development training to Army members and units. Distance learning may involve student-instructor interaction in both real time (synchronous) and non-real time (asynchronous).

BACKGROUND

The current Army distance learning program has its genesis in the challenges faced by the force during the drawdown after the Cold War and during preparation for deployment to the Gulf War. Some of the Army's units and individuals experienced significant problems in attaining collective readiness for deployment. A large number of the issues encountered were the result of the difficulties with attaining and maintaining individual competency in a widely dispersed environment (Office of the Under Secretary of Defense for Personnel and Readiness, 1999).

After the 1991 Gulf War, the Army underwent a drawdown and change of strategic focus. The myriad of ensuing worldwide missions resulted in more short-notice deployments away from home, reduced training budgets, and increased reliance on reserve components. Army missions increased by over 300%. The existing Army training and education system was unable to respond to emerging and rapidly changing requirements. It was an industrial-age system of episodic learning where soldiers were trained in basic tasks followed by working in a deployable unit. Unit assignment was then followed by advanced training before further work assignment.

The requirement for on-demand continuous learning to take care of short-term missions combined with declining resources to support in-residence training dramatically reduced both the relevance and effectiveness of the system. Additionally, the bureaucracy associated with the system required extended time to produce effective training. The time and resource requirements resulted in limited relevance to a combat force increasingly saddled with short notice and contingency requirements. In response to these challenges, the Army selected a course of action with the goal of distributing quality training to a soldier's unit rather than requiring the soldier to travel to a central training site (U.S. Army Training and Doctrine Command, 1999).

By way of background, the Army is really three interrelated organizations: the regular Army, the Army Reserve, and the Army National Guard. Each is pursuing distance learning in a coordinated manner. The regular Army is composed of approximately 480,000 full-time soldiers. Many are deployed overseas, but all need to acquire and maintain military skills and knowledge. The Army Reserve is composed of approximately 205,000 part-time soldiers who train 39 days per year. They are widely dispersed across the country, meeting and training one weekend per month at a local reserve center and meeting for two weeks of full-time training. The Army National Guard has more than 350,000 members who also meet 39 days per year and have 2 weeks of full-time training.

IMPLEMENTATION

The Army distance learning program is intended to provide access to technology and courseware. The current plan provides over 800 relatively high-bandwidth, interconnected classrooms or digital training facilities (DTF). These DTFs are located throughout the United States and the world with the goal of providing a facility within 50 miles of every soldier's work location. The high-bandwidth DTFs provide seating for 12 students (for reserve component locations) to 16 students (for regular Army locations). As of October 2000, over half of soldiers are within 50 miles of a facility, achieved primarily through placing priority on areas with the highest population density. The plan for the complete system is for 95% of the potential students to be within 50 miles of a DTF.

The development of the Army's distance learning program is broken into six increments or blocks. The technologies and methodologies planned for implementation in each block is provided in Table 1. Each Block provides progressive capabilities primarily in the methods and technologies used for synchronous courseware delivery, asynchronous courseware delivery, collaborative tools, course management and provision of e-mail. Additionally, Block 5 provides transportable DTFs to serve deployed forces in remote sites and Block 6 provides distributed training simulations (Program Management Office, TADLP, 2000). Each Block 1 DTF provides a PC, modular computer furniture, and raised floor for future networking for each student and a classroom manager. Synchronous courses are provided through a room based H.320 video conferencing system with two 32-inch monitors and microphones for students. The videoconferencing system is connected through a dedicated, leased line to a central network control station and then to other systems. The classrooms are extensively renovated to provide standard configurations and layouts. In Block 1, the PCs in the classroom are standalone and not networked so asynchronous courseware is provided on CD-ROMs. Block 1 began in fiscal year (FY) 1998 and was replaced by Block 2 in FY 2001.

TABLE 44.1
TADLP Implementation

	Block 1	Block 2	Block 3	Block 4	Blocks 5 & 6
Synchronous Courseware Distribution	Room Video-teletraining–Switched H.320	Room Video-teletraining–Switched H.320	Room Video-teletraining–Switched H.320	Desktop Video-teletraining–Internet Protocol	Desktop Video-teletraining–Internet Protocol
Asynchronous Courseware Distribution	Compact Disk	Compact Disk/Network	Compact Disk/Network	Compact Disk/Network	Compact Disk/Network
Learning Management	Legacy Only	Legacy Only	DL/Legacy	DL/Legacy	DL/Legacy
E-mail	No	Yes	Yes	Yes	Yes

Block 2 includes networking the classrooms and providing the necessary desktop management, system administration, and application monitoring. The existing Block 1 classrooms will undergo retrofitting of network access and new networked classrooms will be established. In Block 2, asynchronous courseware distribution will move to the wide area network and Internet. In this block, synchronous courseware will remain on the dedicated, leased video lines. Messaging and collaboration tools are planned for adoption to provide student-to-student and student-to-instructor interaction to include standardized e-mail address, chat, and message boards. Block 2 is scheduled from FY 2001 to FY06.

Development of Block 3 began in FY00 and provides an automated learning management system. This system envisions course and classroom management and automated testing and interfaces with personnel systems.

Block 4 is planned to converge the separate data and video transport systems into a single network. It will also provide video-on-demand in local classrooms and synchronous delivery of courseware to the desktop using H.323 Internet Protocol services.

Block 5 is intended to provide deployable components. These portable classrooms will be provided to forward deployed units to provide professional and on-demand readiness training. They may also be used to handle surge requirements at unit home stations.

Block 6 is planned to provide distributed training simulations.

CHALLENGES

The Army distance learning program originally focused on providing education and training to the right place at the right time primarily by providing access to technology, courseware, and learning management. Since Army networks were immature, the method selected to provide access to technology was to establish geographically fixed classrooms with standardized packages of video training and computer equipment installed. These relatively high-cost, dedicated, high-bandwidth fixed facilities jump-started the program and provided an end to end management solution to ensure interoperability of software and communications.

In this initial implementation of the program, synchronous events are conducted through high-end videoteletraining using leased, dedicated communications lines. Asynchronous courseware was initially distributed only on CD-ROM with selected courses available over the wide area network. Legacy systems are used to manage student enrollment, tracking, and management. The chief advantages of this approach are the use of familiar technology and methodology, standardization and ease of configuration management at the end points and network control sites, and relatively quick establishment of a physical presence at customer locations. The chief disadvantages of this approach are the limitation of emerging and innovative distance learning methods, mismatch of availability of classrooms and courseware, and commitment to synchronous video. The high cost and relative inflexibility of constructing and maintaining fixed facilities consumes an extraordinary percentage of available funds.

Since custom courseware is much more difficult to develop and field than the off-the-shelf hardware for the classroom facilities, early blocks of the program have an apparent mismatch in content compared to hardware available. Waiting so long in the program to provide a student management system that addresses distance learning challenges could result in reduced student access to training and low utilization of classrooms. Classrooms were significantly underutilized early in the program and this could continue until the program matures.

Standardization of classroom hardware and limited funding for technology replacement resulted in the earliest fielded classrooms in the most critical locations relegated to the least capable hardware. Future distance learning operations could be hampered by the problem of aging hardware even as the delivery networks, courseware, and student management systems mature.

POTENTIAL RESEARCH

Innovative tools for improving training and learning continue to evolve and expand. The proliferation of Web courseware technologies, as well as the addition of innovative technologies to deliver content to remote sites, multiplies the opportunities and challenges facing training environments (Gray, 1999). The effectiveness of these new training approaches and technologies, however, must be assessed and rapidly assimilated into practice to maximize return. The Army should establish a training laboratory program to rapidly assimilate best of breed, emerging methodologies, and technologies into operational use. Also, the unique opportunities that the military training culture offers in measuring training effectiveness should be considered in any evaluation conducted in military settings (Curnow & Wisher, 2000).

The Army is striving to transform itself into a distributed, networked, collaborative fighting force. The proliferation of low-cost personal computers capable of rendering high-quality graphics, adoption of international standards for multimedia conferencing, and the ubiquity of network access have resulted in the opportunity for the Army to train as it fights by creating affordable, effective, networked training environments. These training environments should provide the opportunity for knowledge-based, mentored, collaborative training of all soldiers, teams, and units to include operations, maintenance, and leadership functions.

Since the best way to train a distributed, collaborative force is in a distributed, collaborative training environment, the training doctrine for all echelons of the Army should be executed through a distributed, collaborative network. That network should also provide for a family of low-cost augmentations/interfaces to enable learning interactions. The Army should leverage investments and increase access now by delivering distance learning over and to administrative and strategic command and control systems. For example, since current command and control networks are not robust enough for high-bandwidth real-time events over single media, the Army should ensure simultaneous access for all learners, regardless of bandwidth service, by using hybrid environments that distribute the communication load over multiple, low-bandwidth communications media. These training environments are especially applicable for real-time collaborative coaching of leaders, operators, and maintainers.

Of special concern is the development and fielding of a comprehensive, seamless learning management system reaching across all domains and locations. This learning management system should incorporate cognitive modeling, prognostics, and recommended remedies to create mass customization of the learning experience based on situation, learning styles, and available technologies. This should also enable the equivalent of an electronic training job book containing the status and history of cognitive performance for each soldier, team, and unit (ASB, 2001).

The Army could also benefit from research in the four key areas described by the National Institute of Standards and Technology (1999) in its report on adaptive learning systems. These areas are courseware development, modes of delivery, search and retrieval, and efficient performance support.

In the research area of courseware development, focus should be on how the Army can develop interoperable and reusable course content in an efficient, cost-effective manner. The importation and transformation of legacy course data should also be addressed.

For research into modes of delivery, the focus should be on how the Army can accommodate and enable synchronous and asynchronous collaboration for both content development and instructional use. Also important is research into methods of distributing content widely to increase access while also providing flexible accommodation to support different learning needs.

Search and retrieval research should address the need of the Army to provide powerful, highly interactive methods of supporting trainers, students, and organizations with complex information acquisition and management tools. Also required is the capability to package and tailor the resulting outputs precisely to the environments and limitations of the user.

Investigations of efficient performance support should be designed to determine how the Army can provide robust and reliable applications for providing on-demand assistance to learners regardless of location or task. This support must also be tailored to meet the needs of both the academic and real-world performance environment (National Institute of Standards and Technology, 1999).

CONCLUSION

Distance learning has the potential to increase unit readiness by providing critical training for individuals, crews, and leaders as and where needed. This on-demand learning has the potential to dramatically enhance organizational performance by increasing personnel qualifications in the unit and reducing the impact of skill decay. The ability to conduct predeployment, mission-specific training under the tutelage of skilled subject-matter experts can result in faster preparation for contingencies. However, in order to achieve its potential the Army's distance learning program must increase access while delivering needed skills and knowledge.

The key to developing and sustaining a relevant, responsive, accessible Army distance learning system is a robust research program resulting in integration of best practices and technologies. This program should seek a balance between selected basic experimental research and a wider plan of applied research to provide focused solutions to Army challenges. To this end, organizations and individuals seeking to support the Army's initiatives should pursue a research program that provides the framework to rapidly assimilate best of breed, emerging methodologies, and technologies into operational use.

DISCLAIMER

The views expressed in this chapter are solely those of the author and not those of Computer Sciences Corporation, the Department of the Army or any entity with which the author is affiliated.

REFERENCES

Army Science Board (ASB). (2001). *Technical and tactical opportunities for revolutionary advances, Army science board 2000 summer study.* Washington, DC: Department of the Army, Office of the Assistant Secretary of the Army for Acquisition, Logistics and Technology.

Chapman, A. W., Lilly, C. J., Romjue, J. L., & Canedy, S. (1998). *Prepare the Army for war: A historical overview of the Army training and doctrine command, 1973–1998.* Fort Monroe, VA: Headquarters, U.S. Army Training and Doctrine Command.

Curnow, C. K., & Wisher, R. A. (2000). *Reconciling reaction and outcome measures in distributed learning environments.* Paper presented at the American Educational Research Association Conference, New Orleans, LA.

Department of the Army. (1981). *Army regulation 350-1, Army training.* Washington, DC: Department of the Army.

Freeman, M., Wisher, R., Curnow, C., & Morris, K. (1999). Down the digital dirt roads: Increasing access to distance learning with hybrid audiographics. *Proceedings of the 1999 Interservice/Industry Training Simulations and Education Conference* (pp. 52–61). Arlington, VA: National Training Systems Association.

Gray, S. (1999). Collaboration tools. *Syllabus, 12*(5), 48–52.

Murray, B. (2000). General says Army's weakest links are bandwidth and training. *Govt Computer News,* (April 24), 41–42.

National Institute of Standards and Technology. (1999) *ATP focused program: Adaptive learning systems.* http://www.atp.nist.gov/atp/focus/als.htm.

Office of the Under Secretary of Defense for Personnel and Readiness. (1999). *Department of Defense strategic plan for advanced distributed learning.* Washington, DC: Department of Defense. Available at: http://www.adlnet.org.

Program Management Office, The Army Distance Learning Program (PM TADLP). (1999). *Memorandum dated 27 April 1999, Subject: Acquisition strategy, the Army distance learning program (TADLP) modernized training system.* Fort Belvoir, VA: Department of the Army.

Program Management Office, The Army Distance Learning Program. (2000). *The Army distance learning program brochure.* Fort Monroe, VA: Department of the Army. Available at: http://www.tadlp.army.mil/brochure.pdf.

United States Army Training and Doctrine Command. (1998). *Total Army distance learning master plan.* Fort Monroe, VA: United States Army Training and Doctrine Command. Available at: http://www.tadlp.monroe.army.mil/supportingdocuments.htm

United States Army Training and Doctrine Command (TRADOC). (1999). *The Army distance learning program (TADLP), operational requirements document (ORD).* Fort Monroe, VA: United States Army Training and Doctrine Command.

U.S. Army Public Affairs Office. (2001). *The Army budget fiscal year 2001.* News Release No. 00-005. Washington, DC: U.S. Army Public Affairs Office. Available online at: http://www.dtic.mil/armylink/news/Feb2000/r20000207fy2001grntopbill.html

45

Community Colleges and Distance Education

Christine Dalziel
Instructional Telecommunications Council
cdalziel@aacc.nche.edu

It is no wonder distance education has transformed the way courses are taught at community colleges and universities around the world. Distance learning has expanded educational opportunities for employees who need to enhance their job skills but don't have the time to attend a traditional face-to-face classroom; for mothers who want to earn their college degrees while caring for their children at home; and for students in rural areas, where geography prevents them from traveling to and from campus. International students can also take advantage of the wide variety of online courses offered by colleges and universities in the United States without having to obtain a visa or leave town.

The latest data from the National Center for Educational Statistics (2000) show enrollment in distance learning courses based on new electronic technologies increased by 72% at public two-year colleges from 1995 to 1998, and by 204% at public four-year universities. Public two-year colleges increased their number of different distance learning courses by 99% from 1995 to 1998, while public four-year universities increased their offerings by 104%.

The Instructional Telecommunications Council defines distance education as "the process of extending learning, or delivering instructional resource-sharing opportunities, to locations away from a classroom, building or site, to another classroom, building or site by using video, audio, computer, multimedia communications, or some combination of these with other traditional delivery methods" (Gross, Gross, & Pirkl, 1994). The Department of Education uses a similar definition.

Although community colleges have offered distance learning programs to students for many reasons since the mid-1970s, the successful ones have done so to serve new audiences in their community and extend the traditional open-access mission of the college—to provide affordable access to higher educational opportunities to all students, regardless of their educational, financial, or ethnic background.

Students are demanding distance learning opportunities for many reasons. Most are busy and don't have time to travel to campus to attend traditional face-to-face classes. Those in rural areas live too far from campus or would like to take a course that is not offered at their local college. Many distance learning students have responsibilities at home or are disabled. Others cannot attend a regular face-to-face class because they travel too much, work in the military, or are confined to prison. High school seniors often take advantage of concurrent enrollment courses offered at a distance from their local community college since technology allows them to take these advanced placement courses without having to travel across town. Other students just find the courses convenient—the two courses they need to graduate are offered at the same time or the class conflicts with an internship opportunity. College administrators find most students take a mixture of face-to-face and distance learning classes.

Distance learning courses are ideal for older, working students. These learners are more likely to succeed than younger students because they tend to be more motivated and self-disciplined. For example, they will work through the coursework in a timely manner and not leave it all until the end of the semester. The technology also allows these students to complete their coursework at the end of their working day. Since 60% of community college students are more than 21 years old, it makes sense that 2-year institutions have led the way in offering distance learning opportunities to their students.

Many college administrators choose to offer distance learning courses because they are afraid their college will become redundant if it doesn't "keep up with the Joneses." This fear is legitimate as technology has removed the geographic monopoly colleges have traditionally enjoyed. Rather than having to attend the college down the road, students can use a computer and modem to enroll in college-level courses offered in the next state. Colleges are increasingly competing for students with other nonprofit colleges and universities, for-profit institutions, and corporate training facilities.

Those colleges and universities that don't understand the elements required to facilitate a quality distance learning program often receive a rude awakening. They jump into distance learning to save money since they figure they won't have to finance the "bricks and mortar" of on-campus classrooms. Others think they can convince faculty to teach twice as many students for less pay. Most of these endeavors fail when faculty refuse to be overworked and improperly trained, while students get frustrated and drop out of the distance learning courses because the college hasn't invested in providing the technological support or services they need to succeed. Implementing a quality distance learning program often requires high up-front costs to purchase the new technology, hire support personnel, pay for proper faculty training programs, and finance course development. Successful programs often report hiring more faculty to respond to the rising popularity of distance learning courses.

A LITTLE HISTORY

Community colleges have offered students telecourses, or high-quality preproduced video programs, since the mid-1970s. Students learn from a series of twenty-six 30-minute video segments. The college often arranges with its local PBS or cable access channel to broadcast the programs so students can watch the course material live or tape the segments for later viewing. Increasingly, colleges have made the tapes available in the college library so students can check them out or rent them from a local video store. Other community colleges mail students a complete set of the tapes and retrieve them at the end of the semester. The college assigns an instructor to guide the students through the course material. A textbook and detailed study guide usually accompany the program, and students communicate regularly with the professor via phone, by audiobridge, or increasingly by e-mail. Students also meet on campus for face-to-face study sessions with the professor or fellow classmates or to complete science lab assignments. Most colleges require students to come to campus or go to a designated testing center to take a proctored midterm and final exams.

Since the early 1970s community colleges have also used instructional television technologies, such as ITFS (instructional television fixed service), to teach students at remote locations in real time. These courses are popular in rural settings where small groups of students attend classes at branch campuses and participate in the live interactive courses with a professor who teaches via compressed or full-motion video from a central hub or location. The courses are virtually the same as face-to-face classes since they take place live and are highly interactive.

ONLINE COURSES

The Internet revolutionized distance learning in the mid-1990s. Many community colleges rushed to produce and offer their students online courses as soon as the prices for computers came down for both the college and students who study from their home, dorm room, workplace, or anywhere else. Easy-to-use online course management software became affordable and made it easier for colleges to teach their faculty to develop customized online courses. Community colleges have taken advantage of this medium that encourages asynchronous communication among students, teachers, and their peers via e-mail, file transfer, and course chat rooms.

At its most basic, an online course consists of a Web site that includes the syllabus, notes from the professor, a list of reading and written assignments, and links to other Web sites. As the price for broadband connections comes down, colleges have begun experimenting with including animation, video clips and streaming audio and video to provide students with more exciting learning environments.

Most community colleges limit online course enrollment to 20 to 30 students due to the high volume of e-mails, which means student-to-teacher and student-to-student interaction can take place at anytime of the day or night. Faculty often complain that, although they love the increased student involvement, they are inundated with e-mails and have to control their time so they don't get burned out.

Since e-mail communication is primarily text based, distance learning faculty have found students respond with more thoughtfully written questions and comments, which fosters the pedagogical ideal of writing-across-the-curriculum. Online courses provide a great educational medium for shy or disabled students since they are more likely to e-mail a question or comment to their professor or fellow classmates rather than risk the embarrassment of standing up in a face-to-face classroom. Online courses are ideal for students who live in different time zones since the communication is asynchronous. The Web also allows students to consult with experts from around the world and delve independently into tangential aspects of the subject area they are studying.

ACCREDITATION

In early 2000, the eight regional accrediting commissions[1] endorsed the "Best Practices for Electronically Offered Degree and Certificate Programs," a systematic approach to applying "well-established essentials of institutional quality to distance learning" (Western Cooperative

---

[1] Commission on Higher Education, Middle States Association of Colleges and Schools—info@msache.org; Commission on Institutions of Higher Education, New England Association of Schools and Colleges—cihe@neasc.org; Commission on Technical and Career Institutions, New England Association of Schools and Colleges—rmandeville@neasc.org; Commission on Institutions of Higher Education, North Central Association of Colleges and Schools—info@ncacihe.org; Commission on Colleges, The Northwest Association of Schools and Colleges—pjarnold@cocnasc.org; Commission on Colleges, Southern Association of Colleges and Schools—webmaster@saccoc.org; Accrediting Commission for Community and Junior Colleges, Western Association of Schools and Colleges—accjc@aol.com; Accrediting Commission for Senior Colleges and Universities, Western Association of Schools and Colleges—wascsr@wascsenior.org.

for Telecommunications, 2000). This document was designed to help institutions plan for distance learning activities and provide a self-assessment framework for those colleges that are already offering distance learning courses. "For the regional accrediting associations they constitute a common understanding of those elements that reflect quality distance education programming. They are intended to inform and facilitate the evaluation policies and processes of each region." (Western Cooperative for Telecommunications, 2000).

In many ways these guidelines should convince any distance learning skeptics that colleges are applying the same rigorous pedagogical scrutiny to their distance learning programs as they are to their traditional face-to-face course offerings. Maintaining regional accreditation status is of vital importance to higher education institutions. Not only is the college's reputation at stake, but also the institution must be accredited to offer students federal financial aid and/or receive government grants.

The guidelines state that the distance learning program must be consistent with the college's educational role or mission. The curriculum must be faculty-driven and the college must provide appropriate staffing and technical assistance to ensure the course is top-notch. There should be an appropriate amount of synchronous or asynchronous interaction among the students and faculty to ensure the desired educational outcomes are realized. Consequently, there should be a correlation between the number of students and the amount of interaction educators and students expect to receive. The guidelines also ask colleges to provide distance learning students with the corresponding student services they need to help them succeed in their educational program.

STUDENT SUPPORT SERVICES

Most colleges and universities that offer distance learning courses are addressing the challenge of offering comprehensive online support services to students so they do not have to come to campus to complete administrative tasks or take advantage of the educational services the college makes available to its on-campus students. Today's students have been raised on the Internet and e-commerce. They expect to be able to register, choose their classes, and purchase books in an online environment. They can easily go elsewhere if the college they want to enroll in does not offer them the convenience online services bring.

The 2000 Campus Computing Survey (Green, 2000) surveyed 469 two- and four-year public and private U.S. colleges and found that more institutions have increased the number of services they offer their students on their Web sites.

- 76.1% offer online undergraduate applications (55.4% in 1988).
- 83.1% have an online course catalog (65.2% in 1998).
- 35.5% have an online or electronic library reserve system (17.9% in 1998).
- 55.5% offer one or more full online college courses.

Most college and university Web sites include the information students need to apply for financial aid or obtain other educational grants or financing. This is often the most frequently visited section of the college Web site since students are looking for ways to finance their higher education. Finding the necessary funding plays a pivotal role in their decision to attend college, and a comprehensive financial aid Web site may be one of the institution's most effective recruitment tools. The Web site must be accurate due to the complex nature of financial information and timely so students can meet the required application deadlines.

National Association of College Stores (NACS) research indicates that, on average, students make 5 online purchases annually, spend $330, and have bought items online in the past 2 months (National Association of College Stores, 2001). Many community college online bookstores offer textbook reservation systems so students can order textbooks online to pick up when they visit the bookstore or receive via mail. Many faculty also prefer to submit their textbook adoption requests online. College bookstores also often make college merchandise available to students and alumni for online purchase.

Many colleges and universities provide some sort of online library services to their distance learning students. Colleges should aim to offer students the same access to library services in an online environment as they do for those who are able to physically visit the library. The ideal library will provide a variety of online services so distance learning students can renew or order books, documents, or other materials online; submit a question to a reference librarian; order books via interlibrary loan; and access electronic reserves, online databases, electronic books, full-text journals, and relevant Web sites. However, administrators should keep in mind that electronic databases can be frustrating to distance learners if they show a wide variety of resources they cannot access off-campus.

Often the online college library provides a portal for other online student services, such as counseling, academic advising, and tutoring. These services often generate the personal connections many distance learners need to overcome any feelings of alienation or isolation from the college that result from their geographic location or busy lifestyle. Sandra Miller, director of the Learning Assistance Center and Support at Atlantic Cape Community College, writes that interacting with tutors and other administrators can often help students from feeling lost and enhance their sense of personal involvement with the institution. This sense of belonging is often necessary to help students stay motivated and get through their educational program (Dalziel & Payne, 2001).

Every student needs to have adequate technical expertise to successfully complete a distance learning course. As online courses become more mainstream, administrators find that students from a variety of educational and technical backgrounds are interested in taking courses at a distance. Students need to know how to use the network properly, how to install and operate the modem and software if necessary, and how to send and receive e-mail messages. Many colleges have 24-hour help desks (with answers provided by phone or e-mail) to accommodate questions from students.

Most colleges require their online students to attend an on-campus orientation session or make the training video available in the college library. Others have developed elaborate online teaching tools to serve those who need to learn at a distance because they cannot come to campus for whatever reason. They need to make sure their students are able to use the technology, can work independently, and are not just looking for an "easy A" when they really need to learn in a face-to-face environment.

Those who are not familiar with distance learning are often extremely concerned about evaluation and testing. How can you ensure the person who takes a test or writes a paper is the same student who enrolled in the class? For this reason most community colleges require their distance learning students to travel to campus or a designated location to take their midterm and final exams in a proctored testing center. Many distance learning faculty grumble that instructors in face-to-face classes do not require their students to show them a photo ID before taking a test. They cannot guarantee an enrolled student wrote his or her own term paper. Distance educators often take extra steps to get to know their students, through e-mail communications or writing assignments at the beginning of the term to determine a student's writing style. Nevertheless, cheating exists, and colleges are searching for ways to protect against any fraud or dishonesty.

STATEWIDE VIRTUAL NETWORKS OR COLLABORATIONS

Most states have created, or are beginning to develop, statewide virtual networks or collaborations where students can find all of the distance learning course offerings in their state listed on one Web site.[2] These networks take on various sizes, distance learning delivery formats, and student service options.

For example, two- and four-year institutions participate in the Illinois Virtual Campus,[3] while only two-year technical colleges belong to the Georgia Virtual Technical Institute.[4] The Electronic Campus of Virginia[5] offers a variety of distance learning course delivery options while, as its name implies, Colorado Community College Online[6] only includes online courses.

Collaborations exist at all levels. For example, the colleges within the Virtual College of Texas have developed articulation agreements so students can sign up with a home institution and automatically receive credit for the courses they take from another college in the network. The colleges in the Michigan Community College Virtual Learning Collaborative[7] pool their resources and receive minigrants from the Kellogg Foundation to develop courses and programs that will be offered on their network. In 1999 the Maryland Higher Education Commission created the Faculty Online Technology Training Consortium, to fund faculty training at the 20 participating colleges of Maryland Online.[8]

The administrators of these networks face many challenges, including deciding how the network will be structured, funded, and governed; coordinating program and curriculum development; determining how the network of colleges will deliver student services; developing common forms and articulation agreements; formulating course assessment procedures; and arranging for common faculty training programs.

CHALLENGES—BRIDGING THE DIGITAL DIVIDE

While educators at community colleges have been on the front lines providing educational opportunities to nontraditional students, they are continually concerned about excluding access to online courses from those who cannot afford high-end computers or monthly Internet accounts. Their mission to provide open-access education is key and community colleges are concerned by the widening gap that persists between the information "haves" and "have nots," as the Department of Commerce reported in 1999.[9] National statistics show many Americans are still being left behind in the new Information Age, particularly those who reside in economically disadvantaged, predominately minority, and/or rural communities.

---

[2] See http://www.itcnetwork.org for a list of these statewide collaborations.

[3] See http://www.ivc.illinois.edu/.

[4] See http://www.gvti.org/.

[5] See http://www.vacec.bev.net/.

[6] See http://www.ccconline.org/.

[7] See http://www.mccvlc.org/.

[8] See http://www.marylandonline.org/marylandonline/resources_fr.html.

[9] "Falling Through the Net: Defining the Digital Divide" reports that:

Between 1997 and 1998, the divide between those at the highest and the lowest education levels increased 25 percent and the divide between the highest and the lowest income levels grew 29 percent. Households with incomes of $75,000 or higher are more than twenty times as likely to have access to the Internet than those at the lowest income levels and more than nine times as likely to have a computer at home.

Rural areas are less likely to be connected than urban areas. Regardless of income level, those living in rural areas are lagging behind in computer and Internet access. At some income levels, those in urban areas are 50 percent more likely to have Internet access than those earning the same income in rural areas.

See http://www.ntia.doc.gov/ntiahome/fttn99/contents.html.

Most community colleges provide these students with access to computer labs on their campuses, so they can participate in online courses, search the Web for educational materials, or research job opportunities. Others are experimenting with providing students with computers through leasing arrangements or low-cost loans for their eventual purchase.

Although online courses have seen a surge in popularity, many argue telecourses will continue to be popular as long as the so-called digital divide exists. Telecourse students only need to have access to a television and VCR to view the course material. Dallas TeleLearning, a major telecourse producer, reports that their telecourse enrollments are holding steady, primarily because colleges that are new to the field find telecourses to be a cost-effective way to offer distance learning opportunities to their students. Carolyn Robertson, the director of distance learning at Tarrant Community College District in Fort Worth, Texas, estimates that although all of their online classes have filled up in two weeks at most (and sometimes two days), nearly half of their 13,000 distance learning students from summer 2000 to spring 2001 were telecourse enrollments.

There is a lack of national figures for the number of telecourse students, but Michael Fregale at the PBS Adult Learning Service estimates that 500,000 students enrolled in PBS-distributed telecourses in the 1999–2000 academic year, while more than 5 million students have enrolled in their courses since 1981. PBS estimates that colleges generate approximately $100 million a year in tuition each year from telecourses. Similarly, although they only serve students at 200 colleges, RMI Media Productions, Inc., an educational multimedia distributor, rents 18,000 telecourses directly to students each year. These numbers represent only a fraction of the total number of students who are enrolled in telecourses, since many colleges distribute their telecourses for broadcast on their local cable access channels or to students directly through their college library.

FACULTY TRAINING

To teach quality, educationally sound distance education courses, faculty need to know how to use technology to incorporate different types of learning media to create a complete educational package that makes sense to their students. At the simplest level, instructors need to know how to post their syllabi to a designated course Web site and use e-mail to communicate with their students. More experienced distance learning instructors enhance their Web sites with hyperlinks, charts, photographs, or videoclips to illustrate ideas, or use chatrooms to create class discussions or facilitate student-to-student interaction.

Community colleges with quality distance learning programs have recognized the need to train their existing faculty, who are often uncomfortable using new technologies, so they can use proven pedagogical techniques to teach students in a completely different way. The instructor is no longer a "sage on the stage," but a mentor and coach who often communicates one-on-one with students who are learning at their own pace in an asynchronous environment.

In 1998, Kristen Betts did an extensive survey of 1,001 faculty at George Washington University and found that the lack of release time, lack of technical support from their institution, and concern about workload prevented many instructors from getting involved in distance learning (Betts, 1998). It is unreasonable to expect faculty to take on new initiatives without a high level of institutional support. The need for colleges to offer their teachers enhanced training in educational technologies will only expand as student demand for online courses increases and distance learning becomes a mainstream teaching tool.

"Will New Teachers Be Prepared To Teach In A Digital Age?," a 1999 study funded by the Milken Family Foundation and conducted by the International Society for Technology in Education, found that teacher preparation programs, "while well-intentioned, are not providing the kind of training and exposure teachers need if they are to be proficient and comfortable integrating technology with their teaching."[10]

Community colleges have been involved in training preservice teachers—those who are planning to teach at the K-12 and postsecondary level—to use these wonderful new technology tools in their classrooms, regardless of whether the learning takes place on site or at a distance. Many teachers save money on their tuition by attending classes at community colleges to learn the latest cutting-edge technologies and then transferring to four-year institutions to complete their education degrees. In Illinois, 67.4% of public university graduates who received a bachelor's degree in education in 1997 took more than half of their classes at a community college.[11]

UPDATING THE COPYRIGHT ACT OF 1976

So distance education can achieve its full potential, Congress must update Section 110 of the Copyright Act of 1976 so educators can use the same copyrighted material in a digital environment as the law allows teachers to use in a face-to-face classroom. If a professor finds material that would perfectly illustrate a point in that day's lecture, the law allows him or her to perform or display the copyrighted material in a face-to-face, but not in a distance learning, classroom. This restriction prevents distance educators from being flexible, hinders their ability to be responsive to student needs, and takes an element of spontaneity away from their courses. Often after determining who owns the copyright for a certain work, requests to use the material in an online setting are met with refusals from the copyright holder, exorbitant price demands, or no response at all.

To correct this discrepancy in the copyright law, Congress must enact legislation that implements the recommendations contained in the *Report on Copyright and Digital Distance Education* released by the Copyright Office in May 1999. These recommendations would extend to distance education the current educational exemptions Congress wisely gave face-to-face instructors in 1976. These recommended changes would also protect the legitimate rights of publishers. A revision of the copyright law based on these recommendations would go a long way toward maximizing the effectiveness of online education.

CONCLUSION

Distance education will continue to be popular among students at community colleges, as it was in the early 1970s when administrators were struggling to document what they already experienced in the distance learning classroom—that teaching at a distance is a viable, effective means of education that will continue to grow and prosper.

As the prices for high-end computers come down and bandwidth limitations are no longer a concern, more educators will use the Internet to transmit a variety of media to an increasingly diverse student population who come from a variety of income levels. Technology provides faculty the vehicle so they can incorporate all kinds of video, music, photographs, text, or other educational materials into their own learning modules to create a unique learning package.

To comfort the fears of distance learning skeptics, administrators should view this use of technology as a means to an end. Some students will always need to learn in a face-to-face environment. Most high school students need to leave home after they graduate to experience the independence, diversity, and free flow of ideas a college campus environment brings, almost

---

[10]See http://www.mff.org/edtech/.
[11]University/Community College Shared Data Files.

as a right of passage. However, distance education serves those students who prefer to learn on their own time or have no other choice but to learn at a distance.

REFERENCES

Betts, K. S. (1998). *Factors influencing faculty participation in distance education in postsecondary education in the United States: An institutional study.* Unpublished doctoral dissertation, The George Washington University. UMI Dissertation Services, Report #9900013.

Dalziel, C., & Payne, M. (Eds.). (2001). *Quality enhancing practices in distance education: Student services.* Washington, DC: Instructional Telecommunications Council.

Green, K. R. (2000). The 2000 campus computing survey. Retrieved August 2, 2001, from the World Wide Web: http://www.campuscomputing.net/.

Gross, R., Gross, D., & Pirkl, R. (1994). *New connections: A college president's guide to distance education.* Washington, DC: Instructional Telecommunications Council.

National Association of College Stores. (2001). Student watch campus market research. *Online Shopping II* (8), 8–9.

National Center for Educational Statistics. (2000). *Distance education at postsecondary education institutions: 1997–98.* Washington, DC: Department of Education.

Western Cooperative for Telecommunications. (2000). Best practices for electronically offered degree and certificate programs. Retrieved July 14, 2001, from the World Wide Web: http://www.wiche.edu/telecom/.

46

Virtual and Distance Education in American Schools

Tom Clark
TA Consulting
taconsulting@yahoo.com

HISTORICAL TRENDS AND CURRENT STATE OF THE FIELD

From Independent Study to Virtual Learning

The virtual school movement at the turn of the 21st century is in many ways an outgrowth of the independent study high school movement that began in the 1920s. Although it is a counterintuitive thought for many, it would appear that in 2001, independent study programs still enroll more students in K-12 courses via distance education than all of the technology-based methods combined. Over 30 regionally accredited colleges and universities provided high school courses via independent study in 2000–2001. Most offered a full curriculum, and at least seven had high school diploma programs. By 2001, at least five offered all essential courses in their high school diploma program online through a virtual school, as well as continuing their independent study options. The learning and support infrastructures of these virtual school efforts build directly upon the long experience of these schools in their independent study high school programs.

The role of independent study programs as the forerunner of virtual schools is nowhere more apparent than at the University of Nebraska-Lincoln (UNL). The university began a supervised correspondence study program in 1929. The university's Independent Study High School won state accreditation for its diploma program in 1967 and regional accreditation through the North Central Association in 1978 (Young & McMahon, 1991). In spring 1996, the university was the first organization to obtain federal funding to build a virtual school through its CLASS Project. The university's Department of Distance Education used a $2.5 million proof of concept funding from the U.S. General Services Administration and a five-year, $17.5 million U.S. Department of Education Star Schools Program grant to develop custom software and build a complete Web-based high school curriculum. In 1999, the University of Nebraska-Lincoln shifted its focus to a unique approach to attaining sustainability, building on its experience in spinning off private companies from its research-and-development efforts. Through an exclusive licensing agreement, a newly established corporation, Class.com, marketed the university's online high school courses. As federal funding ended in 2001, Class.com and the Department of Distance Education parted ways. Ownership of the CLASS software became nebulous, and Class.com ported its courses to a commercial platform, continuing to pay royalties to the university, while UNL's Department of Distance Education began developing its own courses and had a partial core curriculum available once again in 2002.

Many years earlier, Nebraska's supervised correspondence study effort appears to have been the first federally funded K-12 distance education program. In 1932 Nebraska received a $5,000 grant from the Carnegie Foundation for curriculum enrichment in small high schools, through continued implementation of its supervised study method (Broady, 1932). Pilot funding from Carnegie led to what was an enormous federal grant at the time for an educational program—$100,000 a year for 10 years from the federal Works Progress Administration, or WPA (Young & McMahon, 1991).

Supervised Correspondence Study.   From the beginning, a key way high school independent study differed from postsecondary independent study was in the use of supervision. The Nebraska plan for enriching the curriculum of small high schools through a supervised extension service has become the model for much of Nebraska's subsequent work in supervised independent study and even in the virtual school program marketed today by Class.com. In supervised correspondence study, "the local high school secures the lessons, provides periods in the regular school day for study, supervises the pupils' work, and returns the lessons to the correspondence study center" which prepares and grades the lessons (Broady, Platt, & Bell, 1931, p. 9).

This plan had its basis in an earlier experiment. Superintendent Sydney C. Mitchell devised the Benton Harbor Plan for supervised vocational correspondence study in 1923 (Mitchell, 1923). Mitchell conceived it as a method "For the Ninety Percent" who were at risk of not finishing high school, hence the title of his groundbreaking 1923 article. He saw expanding vocational curricula during the school day as a way of reaching these at-risk learners. The plan required local adult supervision throughout the course of study and other support structures intended to help guarantee high completion and retention rates.

From 1923 to 1930, over 100 high schools started supervised correspondence study programs (Harding, 1944). Prior to 1929, Mitchell's Benton Harbor Plan and most other high school programs relied primarily on vocational programs from for-profit proprietary correspondence study firms. In 1929, the University of Nebraska became the first university to use supervised correspondence study, based instead upon a mix of vocational and academic high school courses from its university correspondence study department. "Supervised correspondence study may serve either or both of two distinct purposes in education," Mitchell wrote in 1939. "In either case, the techniques of administration are similar" (p. 12).

Growth of Independent Study.   Independent study is the term commonly used by universities since the 1960s to describe their style of correspondence study. The University Continuing Education Association (UCEA), founded in 1915 as the National University Extension Association (NUEA), represents mainly colleges and universities with outreach functions including independent study for K-12, college, and noncredit audiences. The sole member institution offering high school but not college courses by independent study is the North Dakota Division of Independent study, part of the state department of education. Six other states have nonuniversity-based independent study divisions but are not UCEA members. Most UCEA members also belong to the American Association for Collegiate Independent Study (AACIS). Vocational institutions use the term *home study* to describe their type of independent study

(Moore & Kearsley, 1996). The Distance Education and Training Council (DETC), formerly the Home Study Council, acts mainly as a clearinghouse and accrediting body for vocational independent study opportunities. Five of the eight private high schools accredited by DETC in 2001 offered full diploma programs.

Some colleges and universities without high school independent study units offer K-12 distance learning through various technologies. Michigan State University offers Advanced Placement (AP) courses, in part through the Michigan Virtual High School, a program of the free-standing Michigan Virtual University. A number of colleges and universities participate in satellite-based videoconferencing consortia or use compressed video to deliver high school and concurrent enrollment courses, discussed in a later section.

There has been limited experimentation with elementary-level correspondence study through the years. Montana's department of education used it during the World War II gasoline shortage (Haight, 1944). Many independent study high school programs grant limited admission to their programs for junior high students. Independent study has continued to make quiet contributions to K-12 distance learning. The Portable Assisted Study Sequence (PASS) Program is a good example. Begun in 1978 by Parlier High School in California, PASS used competency-based credits and portable learning (independent study) packets to help migrant students complete high school. By the mid-1980s, PASS had been adopted in 13 states, enrolling over 4,000 students in nearly 7,000 courses and allowing them to earn over 1,000 semester credits, with 806 achieving high school graduation (Morse, Haro, & Herron, 1986). PASS is still a component of many migrant education programs across the nation.

Estimating the Scope of K-12 Distance Education

It is difficult to estimate the scope of K-12 distance education. Overall high school enrollments in high school independent study, in terms of unique individuals enrolled and total course enrollments, have been tracked consistently over time by UCEA, but there have not been efforts to systematically track enrollments by home study, videoconferencing, and other K-12 distance education methods at the national level. While the U.S. Department of Education has begun to systematically study the scope of postsecondary distance education, no such efforts are apparent at the K-12 level. Adding to difficulties in estimating scope is dual enrollment. High school students have participated in dual-enrollment opportunities through independent study, telecourses, videoconference courses, and Web-based courses designed for lower division college students, but postsecondary institutions do not track these enrollments systematically.

Some efforts have been made to track the growth in technologies used for distance education or supplemental technology-enhanced education. The last national study of all school technologies by the U.S. Department of Education was in fall 1996. It found little growth from the previous year, except in Internet and computer access. Since then, the department has focused on study of access to computers and the Internet. Two for-profit firms, Quality Education Data (QED) and Market Data Retrieval, cover technology access in schools but have had a similar focus on computers and the Internet in recent years. In 1998, QED's national survey of schools showed a growth in use of satellite TV equipment from 1 to 20% between 1991 and 1998 but a slowing growth rate by 1995. A stable 76% of schools were using cable TV in annual surveys from 1995 through 1997. Only about 3% of all public schools, including 6% of high schools, owned videoconferencing equipment in 1996–1997 (Quality Education Data, 1998). These results were similar to those reported in the fall 1996 Department of Education survey. Technologies may vary substantially by school size and location. About 40% of K-12 unit schools, typically the smallest and most rural districts, reported use of satellite television in 1999 (Howley & Harmon, 2000).

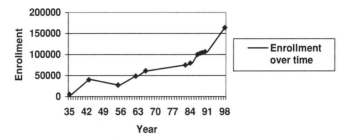

FIG. 46.1.   NUCEA Independent Study High School Course Enrollments, 1935–1998.

Figure 46.1 shows the continued growth of high school independent study. The NUEA began tracking academic high school study by correspondence in its member institutions in 1929. Bittner and Mallory (1933) bemoan the "difficulty of securing uniformity in methods of counting students and enrollments" (p. 270). The first numbers graphed in Fig. 46.1 are for 1934–1935, when 75% of enrollments were at the University of Nebraska-Lincoln. The steady growth of supervised correspondence study continued during World War II, when a teacher shortage and early enlistment spurred a jump in high school enrollments. The United States Armed Forces Institute (USAFI), affiliated with the University of Wisconsin, acted as a broker for high school completion and other independent study educational opportunities for soldiers from 1942 through 1974 (Gooch, 1998). After the war, high school enrollments in NUEA institutions dropped until the mid-1950s, when they resumed a steady upward trend. The NUEA continued to track enrollments, as it became the National University Continuing Education Association (NUCEA) in the 1960s, then the UCEA in the 1990s. After slower growth in the 1970s, enrollments increased 40% in the 1980s (NUCEA, 1991) and a similar rate in the 1990s, reaching 164,000 in 1997–1998, according to Pittman (2000), a chronicler of the American independent study movement. In the 1990s, a majority of high school independent study programs were seeing enrollment declines, offset by enrollment increases in the largest programs. Some universities phased out or downsized their high school programs. The leader in high school enrollments was Texas Tech University Independent School District, which had not actively pursued a virtual school option by 2001.

Emergence of the Virtual School

The emergence of virtual schools for K-12 learners in the late 1990s represents the latest in an ever-accelerating series of technological advances in the field of K-12 distance education. Clark (2001) identified and surveyed a "peer group" of 44 regionally accredited or state approved U.S. K-12 schools that offered Web-based instruction in 2000–2001, achieving a 73% response rate. Here a virtual school was defined as a regionally accredited or state-approved school offering one or more Web- or Internet-based K-12 courses. Identifying the total universe of virtual schools is complicated by the fact that many schools offer a course or two through a consortium or from an external provider, granting credit locally. For example, the VHS consortium reported 3,000 course enrollments in courses shared by 170 schools in 2000–2001, with each participating school offering at least one online course. Of the schools responding to the 2001 survey, all reported offering high school courses online in 2000–2001, and a surprising 51% said they offered middle school courses as well. A majority developed at least some of their own courses. Most were counting course enrollments only, making it difficult to provide any reliable estimate of how many unique individuals were enrolled. Counting course enrollments according to standard high school Carnegie units is necessary to estimate full-time equivalent students served for program funders. Responding schools reported at least 24,000 K-12 online course enrollments. This number is, of course, still far fewer than the course enrollment figures for high school independent study.

Virtual K-12 schools may be grouped in many ways. As seen in the previous section, they may be part of or an outgrowth of independent study high school programs at universities. Some are sponsored or sanctioned as statewide by state governments or state departments of education, while others are virtual charter schools with a statewide reach. Numerous local and regional education agencies have developed online schools, mainly to supplement local course options. Private for-profit and nonprofit schools have developed online courses and programs to serve academic and vocational curricula. Virtual schools developed by public and private consortia and nonprofit organizations have also had a national impact. Course, content, and platform providers, many of them for-profit corporations, also play a critical role in virtual school development.

Some authors made prescient statements about virtual schools during the "pre-Web" era. In December 1987, Morten Paulsen, a Norwegian distance education expert, penned an article entitled "In Search of a Virtual School." Referring to both K-12 and postsecondary education, Paulsen asserted, "the virtual school will dominate future distance education. It is possible to create a virtual school around a computer-based information system . . . at present, computer conferencing is the only technology that can serve as a basis for creating a virtual school" (pp. 71–73). Paulsen believed that in contrast to previous distance learning systems, computer conferencing systems had the capability to handle the professional, didactic, administrative, and social tasks necessary to run a virtual school. Other authors expressed similar ideas, but the technology was not ready.

In the 1980s and 1990s, many schools used computer-based or computer-aided instruction methods for supplemental drill and practice and individualized instruction. Computer conferencing emerged, in which computer users could exchange information by "e-mail" or interact in real time. During the 1990s, the main focus in K-12 schools was getting on the Internet. Berge and Collins (1998) compiled descriptions from the field of the supplemental use of Internet technologies in a wide variety of K-12 "online classroom" contexts. They characterized these K-12 activities as a form of computer-mediated communication, or CMC. Computer networking at the school building, district, regional, and statewide levels has been used to integrate technology into the curriculum, perform administrative tasks, and provide online resources and supplemental distance learning activities for students and teachers since the late 1980s (Eisenberg, 1992). Multimedia tools also emerged in the 1980s and 1990s that could be used to create highly interactive and engaging content and instructional methods in computer-based environments. All of these technologies and approaches helped set the stage for the virtual school movement.

By 1994, there were already several virtual school experiments underway. Many of the early virtual schools combined Internet tools such as e-mail, chat, and FTP with computer-aided instruction techniques to deliver mainly text-based online instruction. The Utah Electronic High School began in 1994 as a broker for a blend of technology-delivered high school courses from in-state and out-of-state providers. It was housed in the state department of education, an approach subsequently used by many statewide virtual schools.

Federal and state funding has played a major role in the growth of the virtual school movement, beginning with the spring 1996 to the University of Nebraska-Lincoln documented earlier. That fall, a federal grant helped launch the Hawaii E-School, the first state-level, state-operated virtual school using only online instruction. In 1997, the Concord Consortium's Virtual High School project received federal funding. Just as the Western Governors University jump-started interest in virtual universities, these high-profile projects helped raise similar interest in virtual schools. The Florida Virtual School, originally the Florida Online High

TABLE 46.1
State-Sanctioned State-Level Virtual Schools: Operational Model and Year Founded

Free-Standing School	Operated by a Consortium, State Education Agency or Partner	Primarily Operated by State Education Agency	
Florida (1997)	Arkansas (2000)	Utah (1994)	Kentucky (2000)
Michigan (2000)	Illinois (2001)	Louisiana (2000)	North Dakota (2000)
	Alabama (1999)	New Mexico (2001)	West Virginia (2000)
	Oklahoma (2002)	Hawaii (1996)*	Idaho (2002)*

*Hawaii re-established as a charter school in 2000; Idaho established as a charter school in 2002

School was begun that same year as a cooperative effort between two Florida school districts funded through a state grant. A second wave of virtual schools began appearing in 1999.

By August 2002, at least 14 states had virtual schools in operation that were officially recognized by the governor, legislature or state education agency as 'the' statewide virtual school (see Table 46.1). Florida and Michigan have a freestanding statewide virtual school funded through a legislative line item, but other statewide schools typically are operated by the state education agency or by a consortium that includes this agency. Many other states had funded online Advanced Placement course enrollments in their states but did not characterize their efforts as a "statewide" virtual school. Most notable of these is California's University of California College Prep initiative. In Oklahoma, a statewide pilot project called VISION (Virtual Internet School in Oklahoma Network) was funded by the legislature in 2001 to offer online math courses in elementary and secondary schools. Some states seem unsure about pursuing a statewide virtual school option.

Virtual charter schools are another emerging state-level phenomenon. The Hawaii E-School, one of the first statewide virtual schools, transitioned to Hawaii E-Charter in 2001 as its federal funding ended. The Idaho Virtual High School, which began instruction in summer 2002, is a state-operated charter school in which financial apportionment per pupil to local school districts from general education revenue is based upon student completions of the school's virtual courses, resulting in a net neutral effect on school funding. Most virtual charter schools, however, are operated by local or regional education agencies. Some states allow operation by nonprofits, such as eCOT, the Electronic Classroom of Tomorrow, Ohio's largest charter school, with about 2,800 enrollments, and by for-profit entities. One of the longest-running charters is Basehor-Linwood Virtual Charter School, established by a Kansas public school district in 1997. In Kansas, participation in statewide virtual charter school activities is at the discretion of local districts. In most of the 38 states with charter school legislation, state aid follows the student to the district operating the charter school. In Pennsylvania, legislation requires the district of a student's residence to pay directly for attendance at the state's seven virtual charter schools, even for homeschoolers not previously registered in district. This led to a lawsuit by the Pennsylvania Schools Boards Association (2001) on behalf of districts refusing to pay for unexpected bills for which they cannot budget. The main target audience of the virtual charter schools is homeschoolers. In spring 1999, an estimated 850,000 students nationwide were being homeschooled (U.S. Department of Education, 2001a), an estimate some consider conservative. A new for-profit school called K12, headed by former Secretary of Education William Bennett, was established to operate virtual charter schools for early elementary grade homeschoolers in Pennsylvania and four other states through agreements with existing districts. This new virtual school builds on the experience of private schools serving elementary homeschoolers through independent study supervised by a parent.

Many local education agencies have also opened virtual schools mainly intended to provide alternative or supplemental education for in-district students and to reach out to homeschoolers in their states. Mindquest is an online diploma program for adults and young adults who have left school, administered by the Bloomington, Minnesota, public schools. The Internet Academy, operated by the Federal Way, Washington public schools, serves primarily in-district homeschool students. HISD Virtual School in Houston, Texas, provides online AP courses and a full middle school curriculum. Some are offering online summer school courses for the district's students, such as Spring (Texas) ISD's eBranch. Some regional education agencies, such as Virtual Greenbush in Kansas, provide access to virtual courses, mainly from external providers, as one of their many services to districts.

A wide range of for- and nonprofit and private K-12 schools have also entered the virtual education market. Virtual private schools primarily serve homeschoolers. A few are accredited by one of the six regional accreditation agencies or have approval as a recognized diploma-granting educational program through a state education agency. Accredited virtual private schools include the Keystone Virtual High School, part of Keystone National High School, one of the oldest proprietary high schools in the nation, and the nonprofit Christa McAuliffe Academy, which emphasizes individualized instruction via courseware delivered over the Internet, with personal mentoring and weekly cohort classes online. Other regionally accredited schools include Laurel Springs School and WISE Internet High School. Many private schools offer evidence of accreditation by an alternative accreditation body, but those obtaining high school diplomas from these schools may face challenges in establishing their equivalency with diplomas from regionally accredited or state-approved schools in seeking employment or university admission. However, many of these providers offer excellent resources for parents conducting homeschool instruction, who already faced those issues. Well-known providers include the International High School and the Willoway Cybershool.

Consortia are also playing an important role in the growth of virtual schooling. The best known of these is the Concord Virtual High School, founded in 1997 by the Hudson (Massachusetts) public schools and the Concord Consortium, now operated by the nonprofit VHS Inc. The VHS, Inc.(R) is a unique cooperative in which schools across the nation have contributed a "netcourse" and in return received 20 student enrollments in courses offered by consortium member schools. Based on the success of the VHS model, other virtual schools such as the long-running Cyberschool in Eugene, Oregon, and the Colorado Online School Consortium have adopted similar approaches. Many consortia are extending existing "P-16" dual-credit partnerships via on-site or videoconference-based courses to the Web, such as Lewis and Clark Community College in Illinois and the Connecticut Distance Learning Consortium. Two multi-state consortia of state governments, AP Nexus in the southeast and the Western Consortium for Accelerated Learning Opportunities, seek to expand access to Advanced Placement online courses in member states.

Course, content, and platform providers, many of them for-profits, also play a critical role in the growth of the virtual school movement. Many virtual schools today are basically "portals" that obtain their Web-based courses from vendors or other virtual schools, but a majority use external provider software and delivery platforms to develop their own courses or co-develop courses with external providers or other schools. A limited number have created custom software and delivery platforms, such as Nebraska CLASS, briefly profiled earlier. Course providers such as the for-profits Class.com and Apex Learning and the nonprofit Florida Virtual School have become builders and operators of virtual schools, working with local districts. Some for-profit providers of course development and delivery platforms have added a focus on K-12 to their primary focus on postsecondary education markets.

Audio-Based K-12 Distance Education

The first major electronic media used in distance education, educational radio, saw limited use in U.S. K-12 education, especially in the 1920s and 1930s. It was used mainly for supplemental instruction. Gordon (1931) conducted music instruction by radio for Wisconsin schools and in 1930 conducted a simple comparative study of 25 music classes receiving instruction by radio versus an equal number studying conventionally, with the same materials. Barresi (1987) notes that while the study would not withstand "the rigorous scrutiny of today's researchers" (p. 266), it gave Gordon the opportunity to test K-12 instructional materials designed for radio. Radio still has many supplemental uses in U.S. K-12 education, mainly as an object of study rather than an instructional delivery method (Ninno, 2000). Educational telephone has also had limited applications in K-12 education. Statewide educational telephone networks such as Wisconsin's ETN began to appear in the late 1970s, serving mainly continuing and community education purposes. Some universities experimented with audioconferencing, supplemented by videotape or other media, for K-12 instruction. Schmidt, Sullivan, and Hardy (1994) report the use of audioconferencing by the UT Telelearning Center to successfully teach an Algebra I course for remedial purposes to migrant students at a growing number of sites. The audioconferencing portion of the Learn Alaska Network may be considered its only successful component, providing programming for K-12 and other audiences in remote areas (Bramble, 1988). Audioconferencing and computer conferencing led into a variety of low-bandwidth networking technologies in the 1980s, such as freeze-frame video, audiographics, and Videotex (Hudson & Boyd, 1984). For example, the Northeastern Utah Telelearning Project used audiographics to deliver high school courses among five rural high schools (Miller, 1989). Contact North built an audiconferencing network in Northern Ontario, with a focus on providing college preparatory courses (McGreal & Simand, 1992). Audioconferencing was used as a key component in later technologies with widespread applications in K-12 education, such as satellite and network-based videoconferencing.

Video-Based K-12 Distance Education

A variety of video-based media have been used for distance education in schools. Elsewhere in this volume, Wisher and Curnow describe large-scale empirical studies on the use of instructional film and television in the K-12 classroom. Through its Sixth Report and Order in 1952, the Federal Communications Commission (FCC) reserved TV channels for educational use, facilitating the creation of a national network of educational stations. Later rulings reserved space for education on cable TV and direct-to-home satellite systems. The Communications Act of 1934, establishing the FCC, did not reserve educational frequencies for radio.

K-12 educational television programming began in 1933 at the University of Iowa over Experimental Visual Broadcasting Station W9XK, with supplemental 15-minute evening broadcasts to groups of children, such as Boy Scouts seeking to meet merit badge requirements. About 389 such programs were broadcast between 1932 and 1939 (Kurtz, 1959). This early tradition of out-of-school educational broadcasting for children was continued through popular programs such as *Sesame Street* and *3-2-1 Contact* on PBS stations beginning in the 1970s. Supplemental in-school experiences have also been a major focus. In 1998, about 80% of U.S. public television stations provided educational services to elementary or secondary schools (Corporation for Pubic Broadcasting, 1999). In general, the use of educational broadcast television in the United States for full courses designed for K-12 learners has been rare. In Canada, provincial networks have provided both supplemental broadcasting and full courses for K-12 learners. Kuplowska (1987) evaluates four K-12 courses offered by TVOntario.

Satellite Videoconferencing. Satellite videoconferencing also emerged in the mid-1980s as a method of providing high-quality video-based instruction without the use of terrestrial transmitters. It represented an evolution from airplane-based transmitters, such as the Midwest Program on Airborne Television Instruction, launched in 1961 by Purdue University to provide supplemental telecasts to K-12 learners in six Midwestern states (Smith, 1961). Ten years after the first satellite was placed in a stationary geosynchronous orbit around the earth, the Applications Technology Satellite F (ATS-F) series was used in 1973 to telecast pilot programs for K-12 educators (Grayson, Norwood, & Wigren, 1973). In 1985, the first national satellite network created to serve K-12 education was founded. The TI-IN Network was privately operated and delivered courses and staff development programming developed at Education Service Center 20 in San Antonio, Texas. By 1986, it had 150 receive sites in 12 states and offered 18 high school courses and staff development opportunities (Pease & Tinsley, 1986). Similar networks operated by universities, state education agencies, and consortia were developed to serve national and state-level audiences. In 1988, these educational satellite networks began to receive federal funding to support their programming through the U.S. Department of Education's Star Schools Program, which may be considered the first modern-day federal funding for K-12 distance education (Kirby, 1998). Small and rural school districts have shown the greatest continuing interest in these curriculum-expanding opportunities, as evidenced by figures presented previously.

The emergence in 1989 of the for-profit Channel One led to controversy. A commercial satellite provider that offers a video news magazine for grades 6–12 via dedicated satellite receivers in schools, Channel One interlaced advertising with content. However, studies did appear to indicate positive impact, as detailed later in this chapter. In the late 1990s, as satellite direct-to-home commercial TV systems emerged to compete with cable TV systems for television viewers, they forged partnerships similar to Cable in the Classroom, an initiative begun by the cable TV industry in 1989. These partnerships allow commercial cable and satellite providers to fulfill FCC requirements through public interest programming channels and free access to copyright-cleared content for schools. Some satellite education networks are providing programming for these new satellite-based public interest channels offered by commercial providers. New technologies allow the use of satellite networks as Internet backbones, linking directly into school networks and allowing the sharing of digital information such as video on demand. Doubtless new K-12 applications will emerge from these innovative uses of a "mature" technology.

From 1987 through 1999, Hezel Associates annually documented distance learning activities in all 50 states. Their last report (Hezel Associates, 1998) is probably the best overall descriptive source on networking activity at all educational levels, including terrestrial and satellite networks. Beginning in the 1980s, terrestrial videoconferencing networks were established with a succession of technologies. Closed-circuit educational telecommunications networks using compressed or full-motion videoconferencing systems for two-way video, two-way audio emerged in the early 1990s and began replacing systems based on microwave closed-circuit telecasts and Instructional Television-Fixed Service microwave broadcasts. Hundreds of small videoconferencing networks appeared at the K-12 level, linking schools at the district, regional, and state levels, and consortia of all levels of educational institutions. These networks are used for distance education and supplemental learning, in-service training, and meetings (Bosak, 2000). Planning for statewide networks can be traced at least to the mid-1970s. Most statewide networking efforts have involved separate or bundled services for voice, video, and data and include computer networks linking K-12 schools.

Early educational networks, such as the Education Network of Maine in 1989, combined two-way video via microwave with microwave broadcasts (ITFS) or compressed video to outlying sites. The Utah Education Network, serving both K-12 and higher education, came online in 1991 using a microwave backbone and compressed video to other sites. Oregon's EDNET, begun in 1989, consisted of satellite, compressed video, and computer networks. Later networks used fiber optic technologies. The Iowa Communications Network is the most extensive and unique example. This state-owned and financed network connects over 700 two-way full-motion video classrooms in K-12 schools and other mainly nonprofit facilities, including almost every high school in the state. Sites are generally required to use compatible equipment and follow a central network design. Costs of network use are subsidized. Similar statewide networks were built in the mid-1990s, usually with private financing and ownership by the regional telephone company, such as the Maryland Information Highway and the North Carolina Information Highway. The Georgia Statewide Academic and Medical System, using analog compressed video, was funded in 1992 through legislation applying overcharges by the regional telephone company to network construction. Later regional and statewide networks, such as the Illinois Century Network, have been overlays of existing regional or local videoconferencing networks.

There has been declining interest in adding new capacity to statewide and regional video networks in recent years. Subsidies for local schools are decreasing and line costs increasing. Meanwhile, the focus has moved to computer-based online learning. Martin (1993) found that schools that obtained satellite downlinks through a 1998–1990 Star Schools grant to 35 Oklahoma schools generally continued to receive programming after grant-funded support ended, although about half reported a decrease in use from the first year of operation. Some satellite education networks ceased to offer K-12 courses during the 1990s. For example, Oklahoma State University's Advanced Placement Physics by Satellite was taken off the air in 1997 due to rising costs (OSU, 2001). Its K-12 Academy continues with videotapes and online courses. However, many videoconference networks and satellite education networks continued to serve stable or growing numbers of K-12 participants.

Distance and Virtual Professional Development for K-12 Educators

In addition to providing direct K-12 instruction, distance learning systems from independent study to the Internet have played an important role in the provision of professional development programming for K-12 educators (Schmidt & Faulkner, 1989).

Those interested in a recent comprehensive overview of distance education designed for K-12 educators may wish to consult *Teaching and Learning at a Distance* (Simonson, Smaldino, Albright, & Zvacek, 2000). Distance learning for preservice teacher education and in-service professional development has a long history in the United States. The first teachers or normal college to offer correspondence study appears to have been Western State Normal School (later Western Michigan University) in Kalamazoo, Michigan, beginning in 1905 (Bittner & Mallory, 1933). Maul (1929) identified 59 of 157 teacher's colleges and normal schools responding to a 1928 survey as offering college courses by correspondence. Today hundreds of postsecondary institutions offer courses via distance learning for K-12 educators, and some offer online degree programs in education. These courses and programs are applicable toward initial and special certification, recertification, administrative certifications, and advanced degrees in education or teaching content areas. The use of videotaped or live broadcasts of "best practice" classrooms to instruct preservice educators in teaching techniques (for example, Merkley & Hoy, 1985) is an example of the supplemental use of distance education methods in preservice educator training.

Shortages of certified teachers have led to a focus on distance education programs for the alternative certification for educators working with temporary licenses, including elementary, secondary, and special education teachers. In California, CalStateTeach was developed by

California State University to provide online courses for alternative certification of K-8 teachers with emergency credentials (Shaker, 2000). In general, K-12 educators must be licensed by a state in order to work in its schools. Many states are creating new certification requirements as part of education reform. Competency-based recertification approaches are replacing approaches that merely require the accumulation of university credits. In addition, many local districts have policies for increased pay tied to advanced degrees or certificates.

For online professional development providers to be successful, they must build on existing staff development activities and networks, with a focus on improving teaching and learning, not on the technology (Killion, 2000). External providers supplement the efforts of staff development infrastructures within local and regional education agencies. Regional universities are the traditional providers of college credit courses applicable to recertification, but distance and virtual learning allows access to new providers. Online staff development systems can complement data-driven assessment of training needs and support teachers in their individualized professional development portfolios.

Schrum (1992) describes an early Internet-based professional development course designed to introduce teachers to technology and distance learning methods. The most common topic for online professional development appears to be technology and its integration in the classroom, although there are also well-established examples of online professional development specific to core content areas.

Factors in the Current State of K-12 Distance and Virtual Learning

Some of the factors affecting the current state of K-12 virtual and distance education include demographic factors, attitudes in society and schools, education market forces, access and equity issues, and federal and state support and policies.

Demographic Factors.   As noted earlier, participation in K-12 distance education courses delivered by satellite appear highest in rural and small schools. Over half of the schools participating in the Concord VHS, a virtual school collaborative, have enrollments under 800 students (U.S. Department of Education, 2000a). K-12 student populations have continued to grow in many states, taxing conventional school facilities and resources. However, it is not clear that distance learning has been an important factor in directly addressing shortages of educational facilities in these states. Conventional K-12 schools play an important role by supervising children as their parents work, a role that virtual schools cannot play. Most students in Web-based and video-based courses offered by state-approved or regionally accredited schools appear to be taking their courses as part of regular instruction within a public school (Clark, 2001). Instead of replacing conventional schools, virtual schools have expanded curricular options and extended teaching resources for students in those schools, while also expanding options for homeschool students.

Attitudes in Society and Schools.   The attitudes of parents and community members play an important role in determining K-12 student participation in distance and virtual learning. As Iowa developed its statewide education network in the mid-1990s, an important goal was to obtain community support through public relations efforts and a focus on network use in K-12 education (Sorensen & Sweeney, 1994). These efforts may help explain the continuing financial support of Iowans in building what became the largest statewide videoconferencing network. A national Phi Delta Kappa poll of 1,108 adults (Rose & Gallup, 2001) shows that 30% of respondents approved allowing students to earn high school credits over the Internet without attending a regular school, compared with 41% who approved of homeschooling. The authors felt that this showed that the public "is less willing to embrace cyberspace instruction" than homeschooling (p. 42). However, those surveyed were not asked about students earning credits over the Internet while attending a regular school, which appears to be at least as common an arrangement in practice. Schools are responsive to local public demands for education reforms like integrating the latest technology into education, but slow to institutionalize such changes. Only reforms with deep-rooted constituencies tend to persist. Cuban (1998) has long noted the limited and unimaginative use of available technology by classroom teachers. Teachers are mainly concerned with using instructional methods they see as practical and effective within traditional school structures. These structures often work against interdisciplinary, distributed uses of technology and provide limited technology support for teachers. Only 23% of a national sample of students in "high-tech" schools surveyed in 2001 reported using computers at least 5 hours a week in school (*Education Week*, 2001).

Education Market Forces.   As described earlier in this chapter, many for-profit vendors are participating in the development of virtual schools. For these for-profit companies, K-12 distance and virtual learning is part of a multibillion-dollar education market in which the interests of venture capitalists and shareholders must be weighed along with those of students, parents, and local communities. A significant portion of the technology investments in schools has come through in-kind donations from technology vendors. These for-profit organizations work closely with state and local education agencies and play a role in public policymaking and planning.

Access and Equity Issues.   Access to distance education and educational technology has been seen by states and the federal government as a way in which schools can address important equity issues. Coupled with issues of curriculum equity and equitable support structures for distance learners, these inequities in technology access and use have serious implications for those seeking to provide equal access to virtual schooling via the Internet.

Support for technology infrastructure building at the local, regional, and state levels is one way policymakers have sought to equalize educational opportunities. By 2000, 98% of U.S. schools had Internet access, compared to 35% in 1994 (U.S. Department of Education, 2001b). This rapid rise can be attributed in part to the Education rate (E-rate) program, a federal program to develop Internet infrastructure in schools and libraries. Established in 1996, by 2001 it had provided $5.8 billion in support to E-rate applicants. Gaps in access to educational technology persist in schools but have narrowed. For example, the ratio of students to Internet-connected computers in 2000 was 9 to 1 in the poorest schools, where it had been 17 to 1 only a year earlier. However, the ratio was 6 to 1 for students in low-poverty schools. The latest in a series of special reports on technology in schools (*Education Week*, 2001) highlight inequities in how computers are used to educate children, rather than inequitable access to computers. The report finds that poor children, minority students, girls, low achievers, students learning to speak English, children with disabilities, and youngsters who live in rural areas may not benefit equally from computer access. Some researchers have studied technology access for special populations, such as the compliance of distance learning systems with the Americans with Disabilities Act (Meyen, Lian, & Tangen, 1998) and barriers to technology access for K-12 learners with disabilities (U.S. Department of Education, 2000b).

Support structures for K-12 distance learners in multiple-site courses can vary considerably. For example, Moore, Burton, and Dodl (1991) found considerable variability in local standards and qualifications for satellite education facilitators in a statewide project. Curriculum equity has become a rallying point for those seeking to redress historical inequities in education (Hill, 2000). The virtual school movement has been fueled in part by a lawsuit against the state of California over access to Advanced Placement high school courses that can increase college opportunities for K-12 learners. A number of state departments of education have used a portion of their federal AP funding to purchase services from virtual school AP providers and incorporated these AP courses into their statewide virtual schools in part to address curriculum equity issues. Tushnet and Fleming-McCormick (1995) reported on an evaluation of projects funded through the Star Schools Program that found participating rural schools more likely to achieve equity objectives through satellite-based distance learning than high-minority and low-income urban schools. Urban high-need schools face challenges in making effective use of distance education. The TEAMS project of the Los Angeles County Office of Education, funded through the federal Star Schools Program, is frequently cited as an example of supplemental distance learning successful with urban K-12 learners (Majdalany & Guiney, 1999). Another curriculum equity issue is the use of distance learning in academic tracking. In a 1984 survey, only 25% of school counselors at small high schools in Texas reported recommending correspondence study to students needing additional credits, and most correspondence students they referred were D and F students (Barker & Petersen, 1984). On the other hand, a later survey of principals at small Texas schools showed that 80% limited enrollment in satellite videoconferencing courses to A and B students (Barker, 1987). However, vocationally oriented high school correspondence study has been shown to reduce dropout rates and increase GED completion for school leavers (Bucks County Public Schools, 1972). In the 1980s, computer-based drill and practice became a common tool in working with at-risk learners, and Internet-based alternative schools have emerged as a strand in the virtual school movement.

Federal and State Support and Policies.   The federal government has traditionally seen educational technology and distance learning as tools for use in education reform and school improvement efforts. In the United States, K-12 education is locally controlled but governed at the state level with some federal assistance (Clark & Else, 1998a). Canadian K-12 education is similarly governed at the provincial or territorial level (MacKeracher, 1984). A number of federal grant programs have supported the development of K-12 and virtual learning in the United States, as is evident in projects described earlier in this chapter. States have provided "pass-through" grants through federal education reform programs used for widespread experimentation at the local and regional level and have developed state-level initiatives for education networks and technology in support of educational reform. Federal grants spurred the development of the first large-scale uses of supervised independent study and virtual or online study. Future federal support for such innovations may be targeted more directly to high-need school districts. The educational technology programs of the U.S. Department of Education are proposed for consolidation into state block grants by the Bush administration, with formula application to districts serving low-income populations replacing competitive grant proposals.

Perhaps the most well-known federal policy document focusing on K-12 distance learning in the United States is *Linking for Learning* (Office of Technology Assessment, 1987). It contains case studies, contractor reports, and analyses of technological and policy options. Defining distance education in terms of electronically delivered instructional activities, including supplemental classroom experiences via telecommunications, the authors concluded its use in K-12 education had increased dramatically over the past five years. They noted that state education agencies could act both as gatekeepers and catalysts and that federal and state regulations significantly affected the development of distance education. The report called for supportive policies, more research and evaluation to show effectiveness, stronger dissemination efforts, expansion of infrastructures, and support for teachers involved in distance education. The report of the Web Based Education Commission (2000) made similar recommendations across all education levels, with a focus on expanding access to Internet technologies.

State mandates on the compulsory nature of K-12 education and seat-time requirements for state aid to local districts have helped sustain the supervised independent study method, and other distance learning methods such as group-based videoconference courses, to the present day. State departments of education provide state-level approval of programs and diplomas, sometimes applying seat-time or other requirements that private or university-based virtual schools cannot meet. Distance teacher certification is a continuing issue. Moore and Kearsley (1996) cite England (1991), who found that only 37% of state education agencies responding to a survey allowed out-of-state K-12 teachers to teach distance students in their state without obtaining in-state certification. While no more recent state-by-state distance teacher certification studies are apparent in the literature, some states have developed certification reciprocity agreements applicable to distance learning. However, many distance education providers continue to work around this issue by assigning a local teacher as supervisor who becomes the teacher of record or training in-state teachers to teach sections of their courses.

Several researchers have attempted state-by-state reviews of K-12 distance education policies and practices, mostly in the 1980s and early 1990s. Moore and Kearsley (1996) cite a number of state-level inventories or other resource studies leading to recommendations for policies or regulations supporting the statewide development of distance learning systems. They state that "eventually, statewide systems will have to be created" (p. 185) due to the advantages of economies of scale. However, while some states have sought to create unified "one-stop" access to their various distance learning infrastructures, the components continue to be operated by different agencies. With a few exceptions, states that have begun state-level virtual schools have done so as parallel efforts, unconnected to video-based or independent study distance learning programs. Thomas (2000) reviews policy issues related to virtual school courses and offers questions for discussion by policymakers. The Educational Technology Cooperative of the Southern Regional Education Board (2000) has provided a list of *Essential Principles of Quality for Web-Based Courses for Middle and High Schools.*

EMPIRICAL RESEARCH EVIDENCE IN THE K-12 SECTOR

Scope of K-12 Distance Education Research

As mentioned previously, distance education is considered herein to be formal learning where teacher and learner are separate during a majority of instruction. Available knowledge derived from empirically based evidence appears to be more limited in K-12 distance education than in postsecondary education for several reasons. First, there is simply less formal distance education at the K-12 level than the postsecondary level. Second, most empirical research is conducted at universities, where college student populations are more readily available. Third, when distance education is studied in the schools, a descriptive approach is often taken. Fourth, some of the best empirical research in K-12 distance education is conducted for unpublished doctoral dissertations. Since many of these new PhDs are not seeking tenure at research universities, they do not follow up with extensive publications to more broadly disseminate their research. A limited number of unpublished dissertations are cited herein, in research areas where there is little other empirically based evidence. In addition to quasi-experimental methods typical in K-12 distance education research, some researchers are now obtaining empirically defensible results by using inductive methods to analyze data from case studies and interviews. They use coded ethnographic and naturalistic data to identify patterns and trends and triangulate multiple data sources to increase the validity and reliability of their findings.

Williams, Eiserman, and Quinn (1988) conducted a review of research and evaluation studies of distance education programs for elementary and secondary school children in the 50 states. They concluded that little credible evaluation data was being collected to test the quality of these programs. A number of evaluation studies of K-12 distance education projects are apparent in the literature. While many are quite comprehensive, the focus is typically on project improvement and reporting progress, rather than on demonstrating impact. Schools often have multiple projects or initiatives underway at the same time, and isolating out the effect of a single treatment is difficult.

Through the 1990s, installing technology infrastructure and getting on the Internet was a major focus in K-12 education. Considerable research, some of it empirically based, has focused on evaluating the impact of investments in technology. The U.S. Department of Education (2000a) summarizes 13 such technology investment studies from 1996 through 2000. Reflecting the interest of K-12 educators and policymakers in practical advice and examples, there has been a great deal of descriptive or developmental research in recent years on the uses of technology in schools to improve teaching and learning.

Research on Academic Success

A perennial issue in K-12 distance learning has been whether distance learners achieve outcomes at least equal to conventional learners. The focus of education stakeholders on improved standardized test scores has been a driving force here. However, standardized academic content area tests do not measure all significant learning impacts (Hawkes, Cambre, & Lewis, 1999). Smith and Dillon (1999) observe that in most studies comparing distance learning with conventional learning, the learning strategies or methods used within the distance learning and conventional courses are not the same, so that there is not really a simple comparison of delivery methods. Rather than advocating studies that control for both media and method, they call for studies that use achievement and other outcomes to demonstrate the most effective combinations of instructional methods and media. In doing so they build upon the work of Kozma and others. Kozma (2000) summarizes a number of major technology interventions and the variety of alternative research methodologies used to demonstrate their effectiveness, noting that many of the technology treatments are "naturally and intentionally confounded" (p. 10). Curriculum, teaching, assessment, and technology components of the design cannot be disentangled for study in isolation. Threlkeld and Brzoska (1994) review a sample of studies from secondary and college levels in terms of types of media and instructional variables such as interactivity; learner motivation, characteristics, and support; instructor elements; and cost variables, and reach similar conclusions.

It is within this context that studies of comparative achievement are presented. Their main value for the field continues to be one of building credibility for distance and virtual education to external audiences, but they can also assist in studying relatively more successful or less successful ways in which distance learning can be applied in K-12 education. While studies of student success have usually included comparative research on the academic achievement of conventional and distance learners, they have also included study of student attitudes and motivation and other elements that may help explain success. A few of the more comprehensive or rigorous studies of K-12 academic achievement are described below.

According to Cavanaugh (1999), "distance education research has not been subjected to repeated review and synthesis, especially in regards to K-12 education" (p. 5). To address this limitation in the field, this researcher conducted a meta-analysis of 19 recent comparative studies of the academic achievement of K-12 distance learners. In meta-analysis, researchers try to gauge through an "effect size" how much of the difference between the scores of two groups cannot be explained by the variability of scores within each group. Meta-analyses summarize the effects found in a group of rigorous studies.

After identifying hundreds of potential studies through an extensive literature search on the Internet, Cavanaugh narrowed the list to 59 studies published between 1980 and 1998

TABLE 46.2

Results of 421 Comparisons Between Instructional Television and Conventional Teaching

Educational Level	No Significant Differences	Television More Effective	Conventional More Effective
Elementary	50	10	4
Secondary	52	24	16
College	152	22	28
Adult	24	7	2
All levels	308	63	50

Source: Chu and Schramm (1975), p. 7.

involving 929 K-12 learners. These studies had an experimental or quasi-experimental design that provided quantitative outcomes from which effects could be estimated. After eliminating studies with insufficient data or problems with rigor, Cavanaugh and her research team arrived at a sample of 19 studies. Twelve of the 19 studies selected were of K-12 courses taught by distance education, while the remainder studied the use of distance learning technologies as a supplement or enhancement to regular classroom activities.

Doctoral students at the University of South Florida acted as coders of the characteristics of each study, achieving 85% interrater agreement. The dependent variable, academic achievement in a content area, was indicated by achievement measures administered in conjunction with a distance learning treatment, either pre-post or post only. Treatment variables coded included duration and frequency of instruction, delivery system, and student characteristics such as ability level and grade in school. Differences between control and experimental posttest mean scores were divided by the average standard deviation to yield Cohen's effect size. In studies with multiple achievement measures or samples, effect sizes were found for each and then averaged. Adjustments were made for bias in sample sizes. The weighted mean effect size across the 19 studies was 0.147 (SD = .69). This result indicates a marginal advantage for distance learning or no significant difference. It signifies a gain of about .147 standard deviation unit for a student at the 50th percentile when learning through distance education or using distance learning technologies supplemental to regular classroom instruction rather than conventional classroom study.

A fairly strong positive effect size (0.489) was found for the 6 studies involving learners in grades 3–8, while a neutral effect size (−0.011) was found for the 13 studies involving students in grades 9–12. In the three studies dealing with foreign language, achievement of distance learning students was significantly lower than that of conventional students. As Cavanaugh notes, "distance education courses for foreign language instruction should be evaluated very carefully" (p. 19).

Previous meta-analyses and compilations also concerned the use of distance learning technologies in K-12 learning. A compilation of 421 comparative studies of instructional television and conventional teaching by Chu and Schramm (1975) included 64 studies at the elementary level and 122 at the secondary level. Overall, about three in four studies showed "no significant difference."

Only 6% of elementary-level studies favored conventional study, compared with 13% at the secondary level. While 16% of studies favored instructional television at the elementary level, 20% did at the secondary level. At the college level, 14% favored conventional study, while only 11% favored instructional television. Chu and Schramm concluded that "by and large, instructional television can be more easily used for primary and secondary students than for college students" (p. 6). In comparative studies of the effectiveness of computer-assisted instruction versus conventional education, Kulik, Bangert, and Williams (1983) found an effect size of .32 for students in grades 6–12, while Kulik, Kulik, and Bangert-Drowns (1985) found an average effect size of .47 for studies involving students in Kindergarten through fifth grade. Since the focus here is on K-12 distance education rather than supplemental technology uses, other meta-analyses are not highlighted here.

Correspondence Study.   In his doctoral dissertation, Childs (1949; published in NUEA, 1960), studied 1,800 Nebraska high school students enrolled in conventional study and 1,250 enrolled via correspondence study, who were given an exam in a particular topic area after finishing equivalent courses in that topic. On average in most areas tested, the correspondence students scored significantly higher than conventional students of equal age and ability level, based on matching by IQ and GED tests. A few studies were identified on supervised correspondence study at elementary levels. Gleason (1961) randomly selected high-achieving seventh and eighth graders in southeast Wisconsin to participate in supervised correspondence study through the University of Wisconsin Extension. Based upon the results of his research, he recommended enrollment of eighth-grade students under certain conditions. Dyson (1980) found that correspondence instruction in reading served to maintain or improve word recognition over the summer for first through third graders in an Illinois public school, with learning gains significantly higher for these participants than participants in a control group. K-12 distance education, in which full courses are delivered at a distance, has been traditionally conducted at the high school level. However, many virtual schools now offer online middle school courses and some offer elementary school courses online (Clark, 2001).

Audiographics.   An alternative program using audiographics in a summer program with eighth graders at risk of dropping out showed mixed results (McBride, 1990). Ryan (1996) studied the effectiveness of secondary study by audiographics of Canadian K-12 students, through comparisons of experimental and control groups in terms of academic achievement at the time of initial instruction and the success of both groups in postsecondary education, finding no significant differences in outcomes. The attitudes of secondary students in northern Ontario taking courses by audiographics were compared with students at remote sites showing no differences in attitudes from those at the host site with the teacher (McGreal, 1994). Hobbs (1990) conducted a study of student outcomes and other factors across three technology systems in use in North Dakota in 1990, for audiographics, satellite instruction and two-way video instruction.

Satellite One-Way Video.   Russell (1991) found no significant differences in achievement by satellite students in relation to the technical knowledge and practices of remote site facilitators. This researcher hypothesized that variations in student achievement across sites were due to a combination of factors. Martin and Rainey (1993) found no difference between the attitudes of students enrolled in a satellite course in anatomy and physiology at seven high schools toward the subject matter when compared with a control group of students studying conventionally in the same schools (total $N = 98$). There were different teachers in the experimental and control groups, although identical curricular materials were used. There were no differences in pretest scores, but the experimental group scored significantly higher in a posttest. The locally developed pre- and posttests were identical and had good internal consistency. Dees (1995) and Larson (as reported in Larson & Bruning, 1996) conducted similar studies of high school courses using one-way video satellite delivery, yielding opposite results. Larson studied 102 students enrolled in a satellite practical pre-college mathematics course in 21 rural Nebraska high schools, compared with an equivalent number of students enrolled in three traditional pre-calculus classes at a single high school. The study found that the satellite students had more positive attitudes about mathematics, but significantly lower scores on a college mathematics placement test. Dees compared 36 students enrolled in satellite AP chemistry with a control group of 36 students at 6 Illinois schools enrolled in a traditional AP chemistry course. Compared to the conventional students, the satellite students scored significantly lower on a pretest designed by the satellite AP instructor but significantly higher on a posttest, the American Chemical Society's 1990 High School Advanced Chemistry Exam. Gray (1996) studied two groups of students enrolled in Detroit public schools who studied first-year Japanese conventionally ($N = 72$) or via satellite ($N = 16$). The two student groups were demographically equivalent, although prior grade point averages were high for the distance learning group. The distance learning group scored significantly higher than the conventional group on both the satellite course provider and conventional course exit examinations. Controlling for differences in prior grades, the distance learning students performed as well or better than the conventional students.

Interactive Two-Way Video.   Olivieri (1994) studied the social environment of K-12 classrooms in two courses offered over the two-way video Mississippi Fibernet 2000 network, an educational telecommunications network, using the Trickett and Moos Classroom Environment Scale (CES). The results indicated that communication and interaction within and between sites was important, electronic mail increased the level of interaction, and there was more competitive behavior within than between sites. Hinnant (1994) used a quasi-experimental design to evaluate student outcomes in Mississippi Fibernet 2000. The researcher found no significant differences in learning achievement between students in classes using two-way full-motion video and those in conventional courses. Students participating in compressed video classes rated video quality significantly lower than those participating in broadcast quality full-motion video. Burkman (1994) alternately taught high school psychology classes at two high schools at host and remote sites over a two-way video, two-way audio network, giving pre- and posttests for two instructional units. The Dunn and Dunn Learning Style Inventory was used to categorize students. Overall, there were no significant differences in achievement, although students categorized as requiring more teacher motivation tested lower on average when they were at the remote site than when their site was the host site. Students at both sites generally held positive attitudes toward interactive television instruction. Libler (1991) studied students in classes at six remote sites and the host site (total $N = 85$) in a high school physics class delivered over an interactive television system. Students at the remote sites scored lower on a national content area examination, whether or not their site had certified teachers acting as on-site facilitators. Student achievement and student attitudes toward interactive television were similar at remote sites with a certified teacher acting as facilitator and at sites with no facilitator at all. Students generally held positive attitudes about the content area and slightly more positive than negative attitudes toward interactive television.

Sisung (1992) studied three sections of a high school humanities course taught by the same teacher, with 29 students studying conventionally and 15 at the host site or single remote site of an interactive television course. Students at the host site watched and interacted with the teacher via monitors at the front of the classroom, making the host site experience very similar to the remote site one. Student outcomes measured were found to be equivalent, including motivation, attitudes according to the Dolan and Enos School Attitude Measure, and exit exam scores. Video analysis showed more off-task behavior by students in the conventional classroom than in the host or remote site distance learning classrooms. Wick (1997) studied 76 students enrolled in interactive television courses at 7 Minneapolis high schools. This researcher found no significant difference in scores between on-site and remote site students but significant differences in student attitudes, with on-site students seeing distance learning as more interesting than conventional courses and remote site students preferring traditional classes. Downs and Moller (1999) report doctoral research by Downs, who used naturalistic techniques to study issues in a high school course offered from a host site to two remote sites on a two-way video network, finding that some participating students perceived barriers to social interaction across sites and that some had privacy concerns related to network use. Students at remote sites held less positive attitudes toward some aspects of a high school course via two-way interactive videoconferencing, with host site students reporting more positive attitudes about personal contact with the teacher, teacher feedback, and perceived learning (Learmont, 1990).

Distance learning technologies are far more commonly used for student enrichment in K-12 schools than for direct K-12 instruction. Here a face-to-face instructor is using distance learning technologies to supplement or enhance the course of regular instruction. The difference can be blurred, since schools typically assign a local teacher of record for any full course offered during the instructional day at a distance to a student registered in a K-12 public school, in order to meet seat-time requirements for continued state funding.

Elementary school applications of distance learning technologies have usually been supplemental in nature and not distance education by definition and, therefore, receive less emphasis in this summary of distance education research. Several researchers have sought to evaluate the effectiveness of satellite-based student enrichment programs for elementary classroom students (for example, Crowley, 1994; Mananers-Gonzales, 1995). A study of 1,500 middle and high school students who viewed a Channel One commercial news magazine in comparison with an equal number who did not indicated that scores on current events tests were 5 to 8% higher for viewers (Johnston, Brezinski, & Anderman, 1994).

Academic Persistence.   Student motivation and persistence in K-12 distance learning have long been a subject of study. According to Young and McMahon (1991), the University of Nebraska documented annual completion rates in high school courses from 1932 to 1990 of between 65 and 75%. While the University of Nebraska was successful in achieving high completion rates through a well-planned supervised study program for high school students, it was the exception, not the rule. In 1956, Childs and the other researchers representing the Division of Correspondence Study of the NUEA found that about 58% of students enrolling in high school courses at 24 NUEA member institutions actually completed them. However, for those who completed and submitted one lesson, the completion rate rose to 69% (Childs, 1966). This study is especially interesting in that so many institutions shared their completion rates. DiSilvestro and Markowitz (1982) found that learning contracts with high school and postsecondary independent study students were increased completion of initial assignments but had little effect on course completion rates. One of the few studies in the 1990s focusing on K-12 student persistence in distance learning was performed by Laube (1992), who surveyed 351 secondary correspondence education students in British Columbia, achieving a 52% response rate. Analysis showed significant relationships between completion of courses and the setting of educational goals, regular time for study, and positive attitudes toward academic tutors.

Equitable Access and Participation.   The research on equitable access and participation in distance education has been mainly descriptive or anecdotal in nature and is reported in the earlier section of this chapter describing the current state of the field. In K-12 education, a major focus has been on describing levels of access to technology infrastructure and relative levels of participation by minority, urban and rural, and disadvantaged learners. Major sources of data have included national surveys of schools and reports by state and federal grantees. Some authors have summarized the literature on equity issues for distance learning and provided recommendations on how to ensure equity (for example, Campbell and Storo, 1996), but when research-based studies have been conducted on equity issues in technology-enhanced K-12 learning, they have rarely been specific to K-12 distance education courses.

Teachers and Teaching.   There is limited empirical research specifically focused on K-12 teachers and teaching in distance education courses, although it has been an aspect of some studies of student outcomes in K-12 distance education and evaluative studies of distance learning systems. Many researchers have studied preservice and in-service postsecondary teacher education courses delivered via distance education methods, but these studies are not reported in this chapter.

Larson and Bruning (1996) focus on student outcomes, but also studied the impact of satellite-based mathematics instruction on 21 certified mathematics teachers acting as co-instructors at remote sites. Reflective logs, observations, and semistructured interviews were used throughout the course. Teachers held positive attitudes, saw the resources provided as being of high quality, and used new teaching strategies both in the satellite course and other courses they taught. Fast (1995) studied interaction in a high school Russian course delivered from a host site to two remote sites via interactive television. Discourse analysis was used to gather empirical evidence to study the claims in the literature that foreign language instruction via multisite distance learning was inherently deficient due to a lack of sufficient interaction among teachers and participants. Fast found interaction by students to negotiate meaning was limited, appearing only when the teacher used methods that encouraged it. Video feedback played a more important role than audio feedback in giving context to linguistic input. Results suggested that when effectively used, interactive television could be an effective mediator for multisite interaction in foreign language courses. Barker and Patrick (1989) conducted content analysis of transcripts and videotapes of five hours of instruction by satellite television instructors in computer science, art history, and sociology. They studied the frequency of 12 observable teaching behaviors derived from the literature. Although 90% of instructional time was classified as teacher dialogue, a variety of student-teacher interactive behaviors commonly considered to be good instructional practice were observed. Miller and Miller (2000) found that secondary agriculture teachers in Iowa appeared uncertain about teaching over the Iowa Communications Network citing barriers such as scheduling and difficulties conducting laboratory and field experiences. The addition of more local network classrooms did not appear to increase interest in network use among these teachers.

Research on Infrastructure and Policy.   Most of the research in this area could also be categorized as descriptive in nature. In 1996, Clark and Else (1998b) surveyed all high school principals with classrooms on the Iowa Communications Network about policy issues related to effective use of the Network for educational purposes. They asked how important it was to address certain policy issues to ensure effective network use, and how well these issues were currently being addressed. The greatest gaps between perceived importance and current status were on issues commonly cited for satellite-based networks, such as incompatibility of school daily schedules and academic calendars among participating sites. Other issues were unique to two-way video networks, such as barriers related to course sharing arrangements and the need to train many teachers for network use.

Some studies use empirical techniques with qualitative data. Kirby and Driscoll (1997) describe a rigorous case study approach used in Kirby's doctoral research to study three sites in the same interactive television high school physics course. It was found that the site facilitator assumed supporting roles for planning and instruction and primary roles for classroom management and climate, depending on local climate factors. Analysis by Kirby of the distance education system using an instructional systems perspective confirmed the importance of all system components working together to maximize course outcomes at the macro (course design) and micro (lesson design and utilization) levels. Johnson (1996) studied the implementation of distance learning via two-way video networks in Wisconsin secondary schools where high school students were enrolled in interactive television courses, using Yin's case study approach. Open-ended structured interviews with distance education coordinators from 25 districts yielded three case study districts considered successful in implementing distance education. Through case study methods, Johnson found the involvement of the distance education coordinator, school administrators, and teachers critical in building the necessary broad-based support for implementation.

SUGGESTIONS FOR FURTHER RESEARCH IN THE FIELD

Learner Outcomes

Research on Methods to Demonstrate the Impact of Distance and Virtual Learning on K-12 Student Academic Performance.   This is still the key issue in the eyes of many state and national policymakers nearly 80 years after the introduction of supervised high school correspondence study. Multiyear programs with rigorous, well-funded evaluation research designs are needed to demonstrate such impact. These evaluations should measure progress in academic outcomes by K-12 learner cohorts over time that is attributable to program treatments involving distance and virtual learning. Process skills like information literacy and engagement in learning are important products of technology integration into the K-12 curriculum and should be systematically studied. However, these process skills will only be considered relevant by policymakers if they can be linked to actual impact on academic outcomes and long-term beneficial outcomes in college, work, and life.

Delineation of Factors That Increase Success Rates for All K-12 Learners in Their Distance and Virtual Learning Experiences.   Completion rates are a perennial issue in K-12 distance learning. Research on academic outcomes should include research on completion rates and the factors critical to student completion. Some of the best research on this topic, still relevant today, was performed by Childs and others associated with the independent study high school movement beginning in the 1930s. Online Advanced Placement courses have to some extent reintroduced the rigor of study associated with academic high school correspondence courses. Learners needed skills in pacing, reflection, text comprehension, and writing to succeed in independent study high schools. How do these "independent study" skills compare with the skills needed for success in the virtual school?

Research on the Most Effective Uses of Specific Electronic Media in Combination With the Most Impactful Instructional Methods in K-12 Distance Learning.   Study of effective combinations of media and methods is relevant to ongoing efforts by state governments to created educational networks that aggregate new and existing electronic media such as online virtual learning, two-way terrestrial video networks, satellite videoconferencing networks, and video on demand. States should consider the most cost-effective approaches to educational networks in support of teaching and learning, based on the research, rather than grounding decisions about media and methods in political considerations or popular interest in new technologies.

Equitable Access and Participation

Continuing Research on the Impact of K-12 Distance and Virtual Learning on Underserved and Underrepresented Populations.   Without proactive measures, underserved and underrepresented populations will participate and succeed at unequal rates in distance and virtual learning. State-designated and other virtual schools may increase apparent

AP access and broaden the curriculum for urban, small, and rural schools, but virtual schooling also has the potential to exacerbate differences in access to and participation in quality education. As in the first independent high school study in 1923, remedial and vocational education is becoming a focus for some virtual school efforts. Relatively few virtual schools, on the other hand, are proactively preparing elementary students in underperforming schools for success in rigorous online high school courses. How can distance learning help close the achievement gap for these learners?

Research on Factors That Increase Online Advanced Placement (AP) Course Completion, Exam Sitting, and Pass Rates for Underserved and Underrepresented Learners. For several reasons, Advanced Placement courses are playing an important role in the growth of virtual schools, especially state-sponsored virtual schools. College opportunities for underserved and underrepresented K-12 students can be greatly impacted by AP success. Facilitating success in these courses, especially for minority and underrepresented learners, is a critical issue that will help address the achievement gap, indicating a research need deserving special emphasis.

Teaching and Learning

Research on the Broad Impact of Distance and Virtual Professional Development on K-12 Schools. Distance learning for practicing teachers has helped address the perennial issue of staffing small and rural schools with qualified teachers. Will it have an impact more broadly on schools as teachers seek to meet new recertification requirements and align curricular content to new state standards? Which combinations of staff development media and methods have the most impact on teaching?

Research on Best Practices in Distance and Virtual Professional Development and Its Integration Into Existing In-Service Programs. There is the danger that well-planned local K-12 staff development efforts will be short-circuited by pressures to move to large-scale externally provided staff development not attuned to local needs. Study of the effective integration of online staff development in local efforts could lessen resistance of both local staff developers and national experts in the field to the introduction of online staff development.

Study of the Effectiveness of Supplemental Technology Resources. A burgeoning supply of teaching and learning resources for supplemental use in regular classroom instruction is available via the Web and other media. Supplemental resources can also aid a teacher in instructional management, standards-based instruction, and other areas critical to improving teaching. While these supplemental experiences often cannot be strictly defined as distance or virtual learning, their effectiveness should be studied, given the great extent of local state and federal funding devoted to them and their potential impact on teaching and learning.

Infrastructure and Policy

Research on the Relationship Between Educational Technology Infrastructure and Success in Distance and Virtual K-12 Learning Initiatives. In the last two decades, many states and districts made heavy investments in educational telecommunications networks for voice, video, and data, undertaking a variety of unique approaches. How do these infrastructures impact distance learning for K-12 education and staff development? Which approaches have provided the greatest benefits at the lowest costs?

Research on the Relationship Between Educational Policy and Success in Distance and Virtual K-12 Learning Initiatives.   Federal policy has supported the development of a number of federal programs and state pass-through programs that seek to use distance and virtual learning to improve the quality of K-12 education. States and districts have long used distance learning to seek to mitigate trends toward consolidation of small and rural schools and to address issues of equitable access to education. The evidence suggests that the impact of these efforts has been important but relatively limited in the context of K-12 education overall. What impact will the shift away from discretionary educational technology grant programs to a new federal emphasis on formula-based technology block grants to states have on student learning at the local level? How can local, state, and national policy best support distance and virtual learning initiatives that have a broader impact?

Research on the Impact of "Virtual Education" on Traditional Education Providers. In the new "education economy," distance and virtual learning may affect the market share of universities and other education agencies in teacher education, staff development, and distance study for K-12 learners. Learners and schools have an ever-widening array of options. How can traditional providers compete and collaborate in this new environment? What should be their relationship with the new providers? What is the best path for schools in blending old and new external relationships to improve teaching and learning?

REFERENCES

Barker, B. O. (1987). *An evaluation of interactive satellite television as a delivery system for high school instruction.* Paper presented at the annual meeting of the Southwest Educational Research Association, 10th, Dallas, TX, January 29–31, 1987. (ERIC Document Reproduction Service No. ED 277 534)

Barker, B. O., & Patrick, K. R. (1989). Instruction via satellite television: An exploratory analysis of teacher effectiveness. *Research in Rural Education, 5*(3), 31–36.

Barker, B. O., & Petersen, P. D. (1984). *A research report of small high schools in the United States in regards to curricular offerings, micro-computer usage, and correspondence courses.* Salt Lake City: Brigham Young University, Division of Continuing Education. (ERIC Document Reproduction Service No. ED 239 825)

Barresi, A. L. (1987). Edgar P. Gordon: A pioneer in media music education. *Journal of Research in Music Education, 35*(4), 259–274.

Berge, Z. L., & Collins, M. P. (Eds.). (1998). *Wired together: The online classroom in K-12.* Cresskill, NJ: Hampton Press.

Bittner, W. S., & Mallory, H. F. (1933). *University teaching by mail; A survey of correspondence instruction conducted by American universities.* New York: Macmillan.

Bosak, S. (2000). Videoconferencing comes of age. *American School Board Journal, 187*(6), 48–50.

Bramble, W. J. (1988, Winter). Distance learning in Alaska's rural schools. *Learning Tomorrow, 4,* 241–256. (ERIC Document Reproduction Service No. ED 302 210)

Broady, K. O. (1932, February). Supervised correspondence study given new impetus. *Nebraska Education Journal.* Abstracted in Perlham, P. D. B., *Teaching by correspondence: An annotated bibliography* (p. 13). Sacramento: California State Department of Education, 1936.

Broady, K. O., Platt, E. T., & Bell, M. D. (1931). *Practical procedures for enriching the curriculums of small schools.* Lincoln: University of Nebraska.

Bucks County Public Schools. (1972). *Supervised independent study program. Annual report.* Doylestown, PA: Bucks County Public Schools. (ERIC Document Reproduction Service No. ED 072 213)

Burkman, T. (1994). An analysis of the relationship of achievement, attitude, and sociological element of individual learning style of students in an interactive television course (Doctoral dissertation, Western Michigan University, 1994). *Dissertation Abstracts International, 55*(06), 1533A.

Campbell, P. B., & Storo, J. (1996, December). Reducing the distance: Equity issues in distance learning in public education. *Journal of Science Education and Technology, 5*(4), 285–295.

Cavanaugh, C. S. (1999). *The effectiveness of interactive distance education technologies in K-12 learning: A meta-analysis.* Tampa: University of South Florida. (ERIC Document Reproduction Service No. ED 430 547)

Childs, G. B. (1949). A comparison of supervised correspondence study pupils and classroom pupils in achievement in school subjects (Unpublished doctoral dissertation, University of Nebraska, Lincoln). Abstracted in *An annotated bibliography of correspondence study 1897–1960* (p. 173). Washington, DC: National University Extension Association, 1960.

Childs, G. B. (1966). Review of research in correspondence study. In C. A. Wedemeyer (Ed.), *The Brandenburg memorial essays on correspondence instruction: II* (pp. 126–140). Madison, WI: University of Wisconsin Extension.

Chu, G. C., & Schramm, W. (1975). *Learning from television: What the research says* (Rev. ed.). Washington, DC: National Association of Educational Broadcasters.

Clark, T. (2001). *Virtual schools: Status and trends*. Phoenix, AZ: WestEd/Distance Learning Resource Network. Retrieved October 1, 2001, from http://www.dlrn.org/virtualstudy.pdf.

Clark, T., & Else, D. (1998a). *Distance education, electronic networking, and school policy*. Fastback 441. Bloomington, IN: Phi Delta Kappa. (ERIC Document Reproduction Service No. ED 425 711)

Clark, T., & Else, D. (1998b). Distance education policy and Iowa schools: A survey of administrators. In N. J. Maushak, and L. Manternach-Wigan (Eds.), *Addendum to the encyclopedia of distance education research in Iowa* (pp. 9–23). Ames, IA: Iowa State University.

Corporation for Public Broadcasting. (1999). Elementary and secondary educational services of public television grantees: Highlights from the 1998 station activities survey. *CPB Research Notes*, No. 116. (ERIC Document Reproduction Service No. ED 428 746)

Crowley, T. W. (1994). Evaluation of Educational Service District 101's elementary level young astronaut satellite course (Doctoral dissertation, Gonzaga University, 1994). *Dissertation Abstracts International, 56*(2), 0520A.

Cuban, L. (1998, Winter). High-tech schools and low-tech teaching: A commentary. *Journal of Computing in Teacher Education, 14*(2), 6–7.

Dees, S. C. (1995, January). An investigation of distance education versus traditional course delivery using comparisons of academic achievement scores in Advanced Placement chemistry and perceptions of teachers and students about their delivery system (Doctoral dissertation, Northern Illinois University, 1994). *Dissertation Abstracts International, 55*(07), 1756A.

DiSilvestro, F. R., & Markowitz, H., Jr. (1982). Contracts and completion rates in correspondence study. *Journal of Educational Research, 75*(4), 218–221.

Downs, M., & Moller, L. (1999, December). Experiences of students, teachers, and administrators in a distance education course. *International Journal of Educational Technology, 1*(2), 1–13.

Dyson, M. (1980). *Teaching reading by correspondence to children with reading defects*. Paper presented at the annual International Convention of The Council for Exceptional Children, 58th, Philadelphia, PA, April, 1980, Session B-1. (ERIC Document Reproduction Service No. ED 196 249)

Education Week. (2001, May 10). *Technology counts 2001: The new divides*. Special Report.

Eisenberg, M. B. (1992). *Networking: K–12. ERIC digest*. Syracuse, NY: ERIC Clearinghouse on Information Resources. (ERIC Document Reproduction Service No. ED 354 903)

England, R. (1991). *A survey of state-level involvement in distance education at the elementary and secondary Levels*. Research Monograph Number 3. State College, PA: Pennsylvania State University, American Center for the Study of Distance Education.

Fast, M. G. (1995). *Interaction in technology—mediated, multisite, foreign language instruction*. Paper presented at the annual meeting of the American Educational Research Association, San Francisco, CA, April 18-21, 1995. (ERIC Document Reproduction Service No. ED 385 231)

Gleason, G. T. (1961). *Correspondence study for superior achieving elementary students*. Milwaukee: University of Wisconsin-Milwaukee, Correspondence Study Department.

Gooch, J. (1998). *They blazed the trail for distance education*. Madison: University of Wisconsin Extension. Retrieved May 14, 2001, from the Distance Education Clearinghouse Web site: http://bluto.uwex.edu/disted/gooch.htm.

Gordon, E. B. (1931, February). An experiment in radio education by radio broadcasting. *School Life*, 104–105.

Gray, B. (1996). Student achievement and temperament types in traditional and distance learning environments (Doctoral dissertation, Wayne State University, 1996). *Dissertation Abstracts International, 57*(4), 1549A.

Grayson, L. P., Norwood, F. W., & Wigren, H. E. (1973). *Man-made moons: Satellite communications for schools*. Washington, DC: National Education Association.

Haight, R. C. (1944). Elementary education by correspondence. *School Management, 13*, 307.

Harding, L. W. (1944, May). Correspondence instruction. *Education Digest, 9*, 8–11.

Hawkes, M., Cambre, M., & Lewis, M. (1999). The Ohio SchoolNet telecommunity evaluation results: Examining interactive video adoption and resource needs. Oak Brook, IL: North Central Regional Educational Laboratory. (ERIC Document Reproduction Service No. ED 433 003)

Hezel Associates. (1998). *Educational telecommunications and distance learning: The state-by-state analysis, 1998–99*. Syracuse, NY: Hezel Associates.

Hill, D. (2000). Test case. *Education Week, 19*(25), 34–38.

Hinnant, E. C. (1994). Distance learning using fiber optics: A study of student achievement and student perception of delivery system quality (Doctoral dissertation, Mississippi State University, 1994). *Dissertation Abstracts International, 55*(10), 3164A.

Hobbs, V. M. (1990). *Distance learning in North Dakota: A cross-technology study of the schools, administrators, coordinators, instructors, and students.* Denver, CO: Mid-Continent Regional Education Laboratory. (ERIC Document Reproduction Service No. ED 328 225)

Howley, C. B., & Harmon, H. L. (2000). K-12 unit schooling in rural America: A first description. *Rural Educator, 22*(1), 10–18.

Hudson, H. E., & Boyd, C. H. (1984). Distance learning: A review for educators. Austin, TX: Southwest Educational Development Laboratory. (ERIC Document Reproduction Service No. ED 246 872)

Johnson, C. F. (1996). Distance education: Factors that affect implementation in secondary schools (Doctoral dissertation, University of Wisconsin, Madison, 1996). *Dissertation Abstracts International, 57*(4), 1550A.

Johnston, J., Brezinski, E. J., & Anderman, E. M. (1994). Taking the measure of channel one: A three year perspective. Ann Arbor, MI: University of Michigan, Institute for Social Research. (ERIC Document Reproduction Service No. ED 371 712)

Killion, J. (2000, Summer). Log on to learn. *Journal of Staff Development, 21*(3), 48–53.

Kirby, E. (1998). Administrative issues for high school distance education. *Online Journal of Distance Learning Administration, 1*(2). Internet-only journal. Retrieved May 14, 2001, from http://www.westga.edu/~distance/jmain11.html.

Kirby, J. E., & Driscoll, M. (1997). Facilitator and student roles and performance in a high school distance education course. Paper presented at the annual meeting of the American Education Research Association, Chicago, IL, March 27, 1997. (ERIC Document Reproduction Service No. ED 406 966)

Kozma, R. (2000). Reflection on the state of educational technology research and development. *Educational Technology Research and Development, 48*(1), 5–15.

Kulik, J. A., Bangert, R. L., & Williams, G. W. (1983). Effects of computer-based teaching on secondary school students. *Journal of Educational Psychology, 75*(10), 19–26.

Kulik, J. A., Kulik, C. -L. C., & Bangert-Drowns, R. L. (1985). Effectiveness of computer-based education in elementary schools. *Computers in Human Behavior, 1*(1), 59–74.

Kuplowska, O. (1987). Distance education activities at TVOntario: Evaluation results. *Media in Education and Development, 20*(3), 88–90.

Kurtz, B. E. (1959). *Pioneering in educational television, 1932–1939.* Iowa City: State University of Iowa.

Larson, M. R., & Bruning, R. (1996). Participant perceptions of a collaborative satellite-based mathematics course. *American Journal of Distance Education, 10*(1), 6–22.

Laube, M. R. (1992, January). Academic and social integration variables and secondary student persistence in distance education. *Research in Distance Education, 4*(1), 2–9.

Learmont, O. D. (1990). Affective differences between host-site and remote-site distance learners participating in two-way interactive television classrooms for high school course credit (Doctoral dissertation, Wayne State University, 1990). *Dissertation Abstracts International, 52*(2), 0516A.

Libler, R. (1991). A study of the effectiveness of interactive television as a primary mode of instruction in selected high school physics courses (Doctoral dissertation, Ball State University, 1991). *Dissertation Abstracts International, 52*(6), 2116A.

MacKeracher, D. (1984). An Overview of the Educational System in Canada. Toronto: TVOntario, Office of Development Research. (ERIC Document Reproduction Service No. ED 323 970)

Majdalany, G., & Guiney, S. (1999). *Implementing distance learning in urban schools.* ERIC/CUE Digest, No.150. New York, NY: ERIC Clearinghouse on Urban Education. (ERIC Document Reproduction Service No. ED 438 338)

Mananers-Gonzales, P. (1995). Elementary distance learning: Factors affecting the adoption of telecommunications technology as perceived by administrators (Doctoral dissertation, Northern Arizona University, 1995). *Dissertation Abstracts International, 52*(5), 1605A.

Martin, C. M. (1993). Oklahoma's Star Schools: Equipment use and benefits two years after grant's end. *American Journal of Distance Education, 7*(3), 51–60.

Martin, E. D., & Rainey, L. (1993). Student achievement and attitude in a satellite-delivered high school science course. *American Journal of Distance Education, 7*(1), 54–61.

Maul, C. (1929). Administrative practices in correspondence study departments of teachers colleges and normal schools. (Unpublished masters thesis, University of Kansas, Lawrence). Abstracted in Perlham, P. D. B., *Teaching by correspondence: An annotated bibliography* (p. 41). Sacramento: California State Department of Education, 1936.

McBride, R. O. (1990). Telelearning: An evaluative study of a computer-based, interactive audio and graphics long-distance learning system for secondary education (Doctoral dissertation, Georgia State University, 1990). *Dissertation Abstracts International, 51*(3), 0730A.

McGreal, R. (1994). Comparison of the attitudes of learners taking audiographic teleconferencing courses in secondary schools in northern Ontario. *Interpersonal Computing and Technology Journal, 2*(4), 11–23. Internet-only journal. Retrieved May 14, 2001, from www.emoderators.com/ipct-j/1994/n4/mcgreal.txt.

McGreal, R., & Simand, B. (1992). Problems in introducing distance education into Northern Ontario secondary schools. *American Journal of Distance Education, 6*(1), 51–61.

Merkley, D., & Hoy, M. P. (1985). Teacher-on-television: A new mode of preservice classroom observation. *Phi Delta Kappan, 66*(5), 373–374.

Meyen, E. L., Lian, C. H. T., & Tangen, P. (1998). Issues associated with the design and delivery of online instruction. *Focus on Autism and Other Developmental Disabilities, 13*(1), 53–60.

Miller, G., & Miller, W. (2000). A telecommunications network for distance learning: If it's built, will agriculture teachers use it? *Journal of Agricultural Education, 41*(1), 79–87.

Miller, G. T. W. (1989). Using high technology in education—The Northeastern Utah Telelearning Project. *Rural Special Education Quarterly, 9*(4), 33–36.

Mitchell, S. C. (1923, June). For the 90 per cent. *School Review,* 439–444.

Mitchell, S. C. (1939). *Supervised correspondence study for individual pupil needs.* Scranton, PA: International Textbook Company.

Moore, D. M., Burton, J. K., & Dodl, N. R. (1991). The role of facilitators in Virginia's electronic classroom project. *The American Journal of Distance Education, 5*(3), 29–39.

Moore, M. G., & Kearsley, G. (1996). *Distance education: A systems view.* Belmont, CA: Wadsworth Publishing Co.

Morse, S. C., Haro, L., & Herron, P. (1986). *The P.A.S.S. program.* San Diego: Interstate Migrant Secondary Team Project. (ERIC Document Reproduction Service No. ED 269 193)

National University Continuing Education Association. (1991). Independent study program profiles 1989–1990. Final report. Washington, DC: NUCEA, Research and Evaluation Committee. (ERIC Document Reproduction Service No. ED 328 723)

Ninno, A. (2000). Radios in the classroom: Curriculum integration and communication skills. *Educational Media and Technology Yearbook 2000, 25,* 70–73.

Office of Technology Assessment. (1987). *Linking for learning: A new course for education.* Washington, DC: OTA, U.S. Congress.

Oklahoma State University. (2001). *K12 distance learning academy.* Retrieved May 14, 2001, from the Oklahoma State Extension Web site: http://extension.okstate.edu/k12.htm.

Olivieri, K. C. (1994). The social environment dimensions of a fiber optic distance education network as defined by high school teachers, facilitators, students, and staff in the rural south (Doctoral dissertation, Mississippi State University, 1993). *Dissertation Abstracts International, 54*(7), 2545A.

Paulsen, M. F. (1987, December/January). In search of a virtual school. *T. H.E. Journal,* 71–76.

Pease, P. S., & Tinsley, P. J. (1986). *Reaching rural schools using an interactive satellite based educational network.* Paper presented at the annual conference of the National Rural and Small Schools Consortium, Bellingham, WA, October 7-10, 1986. (ERIC Document Reproduction Service No. ED 281 681)

Pennsylvania School Boards Association. (2001, April 23). PSBA files lawsuit on cyber school payments. Retrieved May 14, 2001, from the Association's Web site: www.psba.org/CyberSchs/cyberlawsuit.html.

Pittman, V. (2000). Waiter, there's a school in my university! *Journal of Continuing Higher Education, 48*(1), 46–48.

Quality Education Data. (1998). *Technology in public schools (16th ed.).* Denver, CO: Quality Education Data.

Rose, L. C., & Gallup, G. (2001, September). The 33rd annual Phi Delta Kappa/Gallup poll of the public's attitudes toward public schools. *Phi Delta Kappan,* 41–58.

Russell, F. K. Jr. (1991). Receive-site facilitator practices and student performance in satellite-delivered instruction. In *Proceedings of Selected Research Presentations at the Annual Convention of the Association for Educational Communications and Technology,* Orlando, Florida, February 13-17, 1991. (ERIC Document Reproduction Service No. ED 335 011)

Ryan, W. F. (1996). The distance education delivery of senior high mathematics courses in the province of Newfoundland and Labrador (Doctoral Dissertation, Ohio University, 1996). *Dissertation Abstracts International, 57*(7), 2841A.

Schmidt, B. J., & Faulkner, S. L. (1989, Fall). Staff development through distance education. *Journal of Staff Development, 10*(4), 2–7.

Schmidt, K. J., Sullivan, M. I., & Hardy, D. W. (1994). Teaching migrant students algebra by audioconference. *American Journal of Distance Education, 8*(3), 51–63.

Schrum, L. (1992). *Information age innovations: A case study of online professional development.* Paper presented at the annual conference of the American Educational Research Association, San Francisco, CA, April 20-24, 1992. (ERIC Document Reproduction Service No. ED 346 849)

Shaker, P. (2000). *CalStateTEACH: The origins and emergence of a state university distributed learning teacher education program.* Paper presented at the annual meeting of the American Association of Colleges for Teacher Education, 52nd, Chicago, IL, February 26-29, 2000. (ERIC Document Reproduction Service No. ED 440 062)

Simonson, M., Smaldino, S., Albright, M., & Zvacek, S. (2000). *Teaching and learning at a distance: Foundations of distance education.* Upper Saddle, NJ: Prentice-Hall.

Sisung, N. (1992). The effects of two modes of instructional delivery: Two-way forward-facing interactive television and traditional classroom on attitudes, motivation, on-task/off-task behavior and final exam grades of students enrolled in humanities courses (Doctoral dissertation, University of Michigan, 1992). *Dissertation Abstracts International, 53*(11), 3880A.

Smith, M. H. (Ed.). (1961). *Using television in the classroom: Midwest program on airborne television instruction.* New York: McGraw-Hill.

Smith. P. L., & Dillon, C. L. (1999). Comparing distance learning and classroom learning: Conceptual considerations. *American Journal of Distance Education, 13*(2), 6–23.

Sorensen, C., & Sweeney, J. (1994). *Iowa Distance Education Alliance. Final evaluation report. Abbreviated version.* Ames, IA: Iowa State University, Research Institute for Studies in Education. (ERIC Document Reproduction Service No. ED 389 060)

Southern Regional Education Board. (2000, August). Essential principles of quality: Guidelines for web-based courses for middle and high schools. Atlanta, GA: Educational Technology Cooperative, Southern Regional Education Board. Retrieved May 14, 2001, from the Board's Web site: http://www.sreb.org/programs/edtech/webbased/srebpubs.asp.

Thomas, W. R. (2000). *Web courses for high school students: Potential and issues.* Atlanta, GA: Southern Regional Education Board. Retrieved May 14, 2001, from the Board's Web site: http://www.sreb.org/programs/edtech/webbased/srebpubs.asp.

Threlkeld, R., & Brzoska, K. (1994). Research in distance education. In B. Willis (Ed.), *Distance education: Strategies and tools* (pp. 41–66). Englewood Cliffs, NJ: Educational Technology Publications.

Tushnet, N. C., & Fleming-McCormick, T. (1995). Equity issues in the star schools distance learning program. *Journal of Educational Computing Research, 13*(2), 173–183.

U.S. Department of Education. (2000a). *e-learning: putting a world class education at the fingertips of all children.* Washington, DC: U.S. Department of Education, Office of Educational Research and Improvement.

U.S. Department of Education. (2000b). *What are the barriers to the use of advanced telecommunications for students with disabilities in public schools?* Washington, DC: U.S. Department of Education, National Center for Education Statistics. (NCES 2000-042)

U.S. Department of Education. (2001a). *Homeschooling in the United States: 1999–2001.* Washington, DC: U.S. Department of Education, National Center for Education Statistics. (NCES 2001-033)

U.S. Department of Education. (2001b). *Internet access in U.S. public schools and classrooms: 1994–2000.* Washington, DC: U.S. Department of Education, National Center for Education Statistics. (NCES 2001-071)

Web Based Education Commission. (2000, December). *Report of the Web Based Education Commission to the President and the Congress of the United States.* Washington, DC: The Commission. Retrieved May 14, 2001, from the Commission's Web site: http://interact.hpcnet.org/webcommission/index.htm.

Wick, W. R. (1997). An analysis of the effectiveness of distance learning at remote sites versus on-site location in high school foreign language programs (Doctoral dissertation, University of Minnesota, 1997). *Dissertation Abstracts International, 58*(2), 0360A.

Williams, D. D., Eiserman, W. D., & Quinn, D. W. (1988). Distance education for elementary and secondary schools in the United States. *Journal of Distance Education, 3*(2), 71–96.

Young, R. G., & McMahon, M. (1991). University-sponsored high school independent study. In B. L. Watkins & S. J. Wright (Eds.), *The foundations of American distance education: A century of collegiate correspondence study* (pp. 93–108). Dubuque, IA: Kendall/Hunt.

VI

The Economics of Distance Education

47

Modeling the Costs and Economics of Distance Education

Greville Rumble
Independent Consultant
greville.rumble@btinternet.com

The costs of educational technology are of increasing interest to academics, government, international agencies, and development agencies. The relatively new discipline of the economics of education, initiated in the United Kingdom by Vaizey (1958) and in the United States by Schultz (1961), focused on attempts to quantify the economic benefits of, and the efficiency of public expenditure on, education. In parallel, the application of technology to education came to be seen as a way of lowering the costs of education (Jamison, Suppes, & Wells, 1974, p. 57). The use of technology would, it was argued, change the production function, offering what Wagner (1982, p. ix) later described as "a mass production alternative to the traditional craft approach." The scene was therefore set for academic economists to take an interest the in possible impact of technology on educational costs.

COSTING DISTANCE EDUCATION

Broadly one can identify four generations of distance education systems:

- *correspondence systems* (referred to below as Class I systems),
- *educational broadcasting systems* (Class II systems),
- *multimedia distance education systems* (Class III systems), and
- *online distance education systems* (Class IV systems).

These distinctions are not, of course, as clear-cut in practice as typologies of distance education make them appear. Nevertheless, they offer a useful framework within which to consider the costs of distance education in its various "ideal" forms.

It was the development of capital-intensive, big-budget Class II and III systems that forced governments and aid agencies to ask how much these systems would cost, at the same time as the providing institutions sought to derive methods that would help explain their costs to funding agencies. Ultimately three lines of inquiry emerged:

- From the mid-1970s until about 1982, a series of international conferences on the costing of educational technology took place (see UNESCO, 1977, 1980; Klees, Orivel, & Wells, 1977; Eicher, Hawkridge, McAnany, Mariet, & Orivel, 1982). Drawing on work undertaken progressively by Orivel (1975, 1977), Jamison, Klees, and Wells (1976, republished 1978), Jamison (1977), Klees and Wells (1977), and Eicher (1977, 1978a, 1978b), by the early 1980s the methodological issues had been agreed on, and it was left to Eicher et al. (1982) and Orivel (1987) to synthesize the work. However, although this work addressed the costs of a wide-range of technologies, in practical terms the cost functions developed applied most closely to the Class II systems, which were then the focus of international efforts.
- Also from the mid-1970s, a series of studies sought to explain the operating costs of the distance teaching universities (Smith, 1975; Rumble, 1976, 1981, 1982; Wagner, 1977; Snowden & Daniel, 1980; Muta, 1985; Muta & Sakamoto, 1989; Muta & Saito, 1993, 1994; Pillai & Naidu, 1991, 1997). These studies generally aimed to show that the distance teaching university in question was (a) more cost-efficient than traditional universities in the same country, and/or (b) would achieve economies of scale if only it were allowed to expand. By and large this work failed to address the costs of the constituent technologies of the distance teaching universities, choosing rather to take the media mix as a given. As such they could be criticized for failing to seek more cost-efficient methods through the exploration of the costs of different technology strategies (c.f. Mace, 1978).
- Finally, the costs of developing Class IV systems began to receive attention from the late 1980s (Rumble, 1989, 2001; Phelps, Wells, Ashworth, & Hahn, 1991; McGraw & McGraw, 1993; Arizona Learning Systems, 1998; Bacsich et al., 1999; Bartolik-Zlomislic & Bates, 1999; Bartolik-Zlomislic & Brett, 1999; Inglis, 1999; Rumble, 1999; Whalen and Wright, 1999a, 1999b; Bakia, 2000). In the process a whole new generation of people is beginning to grapple with issues of cost methodology and the problem of applying costing techniques to online learning (see, for example, Bacsich et al., 1999).

MODELING THE COSTS OF DISTANCE EDUCATION

The basic cost function for educational television systems developed by Jamison, Klees, and Wells (1978, pp. 93–98) suggested that the total costs (TC) of a system were made up of the costs (C) of a number of functions:

$$\text{TC} = C_C + C_P + C_T + C_R \qquad \text{(Eq. 1)}$$

where the subscripts C, P, T, and R refer to central, programming, transmission, and reception respectively (Equation 1). Each of these constituent components C_C, C_P, and so on are further broken down into separate cost functions that reflect the determining variables that drive costs. Among the main system variables identified (Jamison, Klees, & Wells, 1978, p. 94) are the number of students, the number of hours of programming each year, the area of the region to be served, the number of pages of printed material for each student, the number of students who share a receiver, the fraction of the reception sites located in nonelectrified areas, and the number of reception sites. Among the cost variables identified are the cost of project planning and start up, central administration, the production facility (land and buildings), and the production equipment; the annual cost of program production; the cost of the transmission facility (land and buildings); the annual cost of power, maintenance, and operating personnel for a transmitter capable of covering the area served; the cost of one receiver; the cost of related reception equipment (e.g., antennae) for reception sites; the cost of building modifications for television reception; the cost per reception site for power generation equipment (required for television only in nonelectrified areas); the cost of electric power per reception site per hour (using power lines); the cost of electric power per reception site per hour using local power generation equipment or batteries; the cost per hour for maintenance at each reception site; and the cost of a book per page (Jamison, Klees, & Wells, 1978, pp. 94–95). All capital items were annualized for a given number of years (which varied depending on the nature of the capital item) using the standard annualization factor, a(r, n) and an appropriate social discount rate (r).

The approach initially used by those modeling the costs of the distance teaching universities was much simpler. Basically just three variable, cost-inducing outputs were identified: the number of courses in development/production; the number of courses in presentation; and the number of students. Capital costs were ignored. Wagner's (1977, pp. 370–371) cost function explaining the costs of the British Open University (Equation 2) is a good example of the approach taken:

$$E = \alpha + \beta_n C_n + \beta_p C_p + \delta S \qquad \text{(Eq. 2)}$$

where

E = the total recurrent expenditure
α = the total fixed costs of the enterprise
β_n = the average variable cost of development/production per standard course equivalent per year
C_n = the number of standard course equivalents in development/production in any year
β_p = the average variable cost of presentation per standard course equivalent per year
C_p = the number of standard course equivalents in presentation in any year
δ = the average variable cost per full-time equivalent student per year
S = the number of full-time equivalent students

PROBLEMS WITH THE MODELS

All these models basically assume that the total costs of a system are made up of a combination of fixed and variable costs. Fixed costs are those that do not vary with any change in the level of activity; variable costs do change. The total costs of a system (T) will thus be equivalent to the sum of the fixed costs (F) plus the variable cost per unit of activity (V) times the volume of activity (X):

$$T = F + VX \qquad \text{(Eq. 3)}$$

Such models are seriously weakened by the fact that they do not specify "the fundamental variables, which affect costs, in sufficient detail to be of practical value to people who are trying to prepare an operating budget for an institution" (Rumble, Neil, & Tout, 1981, p. 235). With each technology having its own cost structure, and with empirical studies showing wide variations in the actual cost of technologies (see below), it is clear that the models would need to be much more sophisticated to capture the actual factors driving costs. For example, the development, production, and delivery costs of a course vary depending on the mix of media, and the models ought to reflect this. Similarly, in the case of student costs, while many of the costs of student support are driven by the number of individual students in the system, some of them are driven by the number of student course enrollments and others by the number of student groups. The idea that there is an average course with an average cost per course, or an average student with an average cost per student, is a fiction. At best the models provide us with a crude, aggregated, approximation of costs.

More significantly, all the models treat overhead costs as a fixed cost that is then allocated to students in an attempt to derive an average student cost, such that the average cost per student (A) is equal to the variable cost per student (V) plus a "share" of the overhead costs (F):

$$A = V + F/S \qquad \text{(Eq. 4)}$$

Even Rumble's models of the costs of the Universidad Estatal a Distancia in Costa Rica and the Universidad Nacional Abierta in Venezuela (Rumble, 1981, pp. 385–386; 1982, pp. 129–130), which attempted to correct some of these weaknesses by taking account of other factors such as the number of organization/managerial units managing academic programs, the number of local study centers, the number of broadcasts, and so on, do not capture the fundamental variables driving costs *in sufficient detail* to make them useful as tools for a real understanding of costs.

A further problem with some of the models is that they do not take account of capital costs. The models developed by Jamison, Klees, and Wells did this, but those used to cost the distance teaching universities did not. Economists are generally agreed that the costs of capital tied up in projects need to be taken into account (Jamison, Klees, & Wells, 1978, p. 32; Perraton, 1982, p. 6; Wagner, 1982, p. 89; Levin, 1983, pp. 68–69). This is generally done using the annualization equation which "annualizes" capital costs by estimating an average of the combination of depreciation and interest on the undepreciated portion over the life of the facility (Equation 5):

$$a(r,n) = \frac{r(1 + r)^n}{(1 + r)^n - 1} \qquad \text{(Eq. 5)}$$

where $a(r,n)$ is the annualization factor, n is the life of the capital equipment, and r is the prevailing rate of interest. It is worth noting, however, that quite small changes in the rate of interest and the lifetime assumptions made will have significant implications for the total cost of the project. However, the use of interest rates to assess the relative cost of public projects involving capital elements does not, in Eicher's view, rest upon a sound theoretical basis for public finance decisions (because such decisions rarely in fact involve a choice between spend and investment for income growth) (Eicher, 1978b, p. 13). However, it is difficult to see how a true comparison of costs between a highly capital-intensive and a less capital-intensive option can be obtained without taking at least the annualized capital cost into account, and this the cost functions developed by Smith (1975) and those who followed him failed to do.

Another problem affects those distance education projects that are embedded in dual-mode institutions (i.e., institutions that teach both by traditional and by distance means). The problem arises because some of the costs of the two approaches may be shared because of the existence of what are called joint products. A *joint product* is one of two or more products in which, initially, a single stream of inputs goes in until a "separation point" is reached, after which the products are acted on separately. For example, academics may develop a course and then teach one version by traditional class-based means and another version by distance means; or a series of lectures delivered in class may be videotaped and subsequently used in a distance program. Equally, some of the overhead costs of the institution will support the distance program, and some the off-campus program, and will therefore need to be apportioned across the products if only for pricing purposes. Rumble (1997, pp. 65–70) identified no less than six different approaches used to attribute development costs to joint products in mixed-mode institutions and two approaches to attribute delivery costs. Such variations can radically affect the level of reported costs in systems and can be used both to manipulate data provided to funding bodies and to "justify" different pricing decisions.

FACTORS DRIVING COSTS IN EDUCATION

In practice, the identification of drivers affecting costs in distance education systems has developed over the years to embrace a range of factors, many of which are interrelated. What is difficult is to put cost figures to these drivers.

Technology Choice

Technology choice has a significant effect on both total and average costs. A summary of the current evidence follows.

(a) Face-to-Face Teaching.   Face-to-face teaching in lectures (any audience size), seminars (small- to medium-sized group teaching), and tutorials or supervisions (one-to-one or one-to-two) involves relatively low fixed costs but, particularly in the case of small- and medium-sized group teaching, incurs a rapid increase in student variable costs because increases in student numbers and hence group numbers have to be matched with increases in staff numbers. The average student:staff ratio can vary enormously. In the UK higher education, for example, a feature of the past 30 years has been an increase of the average number of students per member of staff. This has had a major effect on the cost structure of campus-based higher education in the UK. As Scott (1997, p. 38) comments,

> the massification of British higher education is demonstrated [by] the sharp reduction in unit costs. Overall productivity gains of more than 25 per cent have been achieved since 1990. . . . This pattern, which exactly matches the expansion of student numbers, closely follows the cost curves in other countries where mass higher education systems developed earlier than in Britain. *It supports the claim that mass systems have a quite different economy from that of élite systems.* (my italics)

Generally speaking, where few students are involved, face-to-face teaching may be the cheapest option. This is because student numbers are too small to warrant investment in learning materials. However, depending on the technology choice, distance education can be more cost-efficient than traditional approaches for large numbers of students, but any attempt to provide a significant amount of face-to-face contact will create a very expensive system.

(b) Technology in Distance Education.   Distance education systems are generally said to have high fixed costs but low variable costs per student. Each technology has its own cost structure. As evidence accumulated, so analysts attempted to generalize their findings in ways helpful to decision makers. In the mid-1990s, Bates (1995, p. 5) indicated that print, audiocassettes, and prerecorded Instructional Television were the only media that were relatively low cost for courses with populations of from under 250 students a year to over 1,000 student a year. In addition, radio was also likely to be low cost on courses with populations of 1,000 or more students. Other media, such as good quality broadcast television, preprogrammed computer-based learning, and multimedia are much more expensive.

The problem with such generalizations is that technology costs are in practice susceptible to wide variations. The NBEET study found a range in the production costs of a 30-minute videotape of from Australian $1,000 to A$39,000 (NBEET, 1994, pp. 36, 37). The range of costs in computer-based teaching was also very great (p. 37). Bates (1995, p. 197) gave a cost range of from Canadian S2,600 to S21,170 per student hour for the development of online teaching materials. Arizona Learning Systems (1998, pp. 13–14) suggested costs of from US$6,000 to $1,000,000 for a three-unit Internet course, depending on the approach used. The cheapest approach involved the presentation of simple course outlines and assignments; more expensive options included the provision of text ($12,000), text with reference materials ($18,000), images ($37,500), audio and video ($120,000), simulations ($250,000), and virtual reality ($1,000,000).

The problem arises in part because a whole range of organizational and working practices impact on the actual cost of the technology as it is used *in particular circumstances* (see below). There may also be problems because costs in one system may not be directly comparable with those in another. For example, some systems have access to facilities (for example, study center space or transmission time) at preferential rates; in other cases costs that in one system fall on the institution's budget may in another be passed onto the students, so that comparisons based on *institutional* budgets are misleading. It is very important, when one comes to compare the costs of one system with another, to be clear about the precise nature of the model being used and to understand how this can affect cost comparisons.

(c) Conclusions.   The main message to emerge from these studies is that there are a great many caveats that have to be made to any statement about the costs of technology within education. The problem is that the cost of a given technology is not just driven by the hardware and software costs of that technology but by other factors—of which the working practices underpinning the use of the technology is perhaps the most important.

Using Existing Materials

The costs of developing courses can be brought down by developing "wrap-around" materials to accompany existing textbooks and other materials, thus "transforming" them into a distance course by commodifying traditional lectures (by, for example, videotaping them) for later use and by buying-in material developed elsewhere by another supplier (Rumble, 1997, pp. 87–91). Certainly the additional costs of videotaping lectures and reusing them for subsequent generations of students can be very low indeed (Fwu et al., 1992). Studies suggest, however, that the cost advantages of buying-in materials can be overestimated. Although this may be a cheaper option for low student numbers, payments to the providing institution mean that it can be cheaper to develop one's own materials—with Curran (1993, p. 21) suggesting that the break-even point at which this is true can be as low as 123 students on a course.

Working Practices

Much of the information that we have on the costs of technologies is derived from particular case studies. Although analysts frequently counsel against assuming that the costs in one system will be similar to those in another, the urge to generate guidance for policymakers often leads to an assumption that the cost experience of one institution will transfer to another. Underlying this assumption is a belief that technology determines the social sphere (that is, the organizational structures, hierarchies, and work roles) within which it is used. Particular levels of costs are then thought to be a natural outcome of the sociotechnical conditions engendered by a given technology. While technological determinism has now been discredited (c.f. Grint & Woolgar, 1997, pp. 11–14 for a resumé of the arguments), the perspective has a long history and was still being advocated in the 1960s and 1970s (Bell, 1960, 1973; Kerr, Dunlop, Harbinson, &

Myers, 1964; Blauner, 1964). Blauner (1964, p. 6), for example, maintained that "the most important single factor that gives an industry a distinctive character is its technology."

A technologically determinist approach to distance education would naturally be embedded in the literature, manifesting itself in assumptions that it is the technology itself that determines the structures of distance education systems. There is some evidence of this in recent literature. Thus Daniel (1996, p. 15) cites McGuinness's (1995) claim that *"technology, distance learning* and *global networks* for scholars and students *are transforming institutional practices* in ways that may make current institutional structures and governmental policies obsolete" (my italics). Elsewhere Daniel (1996) suggests that what he calls the mega-universities (that is, universities that have distance teaching as their primary activity and in excess of 100,000 active enrollments [p. 29]) "operate differently from other universities in many ways, not least in the way they have redefined the tasks of the academic faculty and introduced a division of labor into the teaching function" (p. 30). He goes on to claim that *"changes in technology transform* the *structures* of industries" (p. 80, my italics). Further, this is a continuing process since "it is clear that *new technologies*, such as computer conferencing and the Internet, *will change* the format of university courses taught at a distance" (p. 130, my italics). In point of fact, of course, the relationship of technology to structure, work roles, skill levels, and so on is not simple, not constant across settings and firms, and not determined by the technology itself but by management. This does not negate the fact that technology can be used by management to reduce costs and that technology change may be accompanied by organizational change.

This kind of technological determinism can blind managers to the very real variations in the way in which technologies are used in practice and to the wide range of costs that result. In fact, the way in which work is organized around a given technology, and the way in which human resources are engaged in the enterprise (including the use of casual as opposed to core labor), has a profound effect on costs (Rumble, 1997, pp. 83–87).

(a) The Organization of Academic Labor.   Many distance teaching systems have industrialized the organization of materials development, production, and delivery, thus breaking with the traditional craft approaches that characterize traditional education (Peters, 1967, 1973, 1983, 1989). The overall task of teaching can thus be divided into its constituent roles—curriculum design, instructional design, content preparation, materials development, and production (all tasks that themselves may require a number of specialisms), tutorial backup, continuous assessment, and examination script marking. These roles can be given to different people, in part reflecting the need to access specialist knowledge and skills, and in part because the very nature of the system would make it difficult for one person to undertake all of the tasks (e.g., to both develop all the materials and teach and assess all the students on a large-scale course). Most large-scale systems have a division of labor between those who develop the materials and those who support and assess the students. However, where student course numbers are low, individual academics may both develop the materials and teach the students (Rumble, 1986, pp. 127–129). Those who believe that the industrialized model reduces academic autonomy and control over the teaching process and thus degrades academic work (e.g., Campion & Renner, 1992; Raggatt, 1993) see this model as particularly attractive. It is one of the reasons why online teaching models are thought to be so attractive—though in fact any system that involves both the development of online materials and the support of online students is likely to begin to move toward a division of labor if course student numbers increase beyond the support capacity of a small group of academics.

The organization of the course development process—and the way in which it is planned and controlled—also varies greatly. Course authors can work on their own, with an editor (the author-editor or transformer model), in small groups, or in large course teams (Rumble, 1997, pp. 83–86)—the latter being an expensive way of developing materials (Perry, 1976, p. 91).

What is feasible is in part determined by the way in which the curriculum has been divided and the content organized. Small modules or courses, and those based more heavily around existing texts and materials, allow much greater scope for individual academic control, while large modules and those involving a great deal of specially developed materials are likely to require a big team effort. In general the use of consultants can bring down costs significantly (Rumble, 1997, p. 87).

(b) Contracting of Academic and Support Labor.   The division of academic labor has been accompanied by another feature—the use of short-term and piece-work contracts. The nature of the employment contract is a crucial factor in determining costs. Course developers may be hired on permanent, full-time contracts *of* service to develop course materials. This is the most costly option, with a potential long-term commitment (to holiday, sick, and study leave) up to retirement age. Alternatively, they can be hired on short-term temporary contracts *of* service that limit the long-term liability of the employer; or as consultant authors and materials' developers on contracts *for* service, essentially paid piece-rates for their output. This latter option is relatively cheap. As for the tutors that support the students, many of them are employed on piece-work rates, paid by the hour for their class tutoring or by the script in respect of assignment and examination scripts marked.

In mixed-mode institutions course developers may teach on-campus students as well as develop materials. In some systems staff who have a full teaching load on campus are bought out to help develop distance teaching materials, either to develop a version of their own existing on-campus courses or a new course (Rumble, 1986, pp. 131–133; 1997, pp. 81–83). However, this does not always happen, with the result that staff may be reluctant to get involved in mixed-mode operations (Ellis, 2000).

Nonacademic work—for example, editing, illustration, and the like—can also be given to consultants, while whole functions such as printing and the production and transmission of broadcasting may also be outsourced, either to a single supplier or to a number of suppliers. Whether outsourcing actually saves money will depend on circumstances including the relative transaction costs of in-house versus outsourced work and the extent to which outside providers can offer a price that is competitive.

The Curriculum

The number of courses on offer is also an important variable. The more courses that are offered, the greater the investment in developing, maintaining, and remaking the course materials will be. The number of courses offered depends in part on the number of awards or qualifications on offer, the range of subjects offered within those qualifications, and the extent to which students can choose elective courses as opposed to being restricted to mandatory courses.

The number of years over which courses are presented, and the frequency with which materials have to be remade, will also affect costs. All content dates with the passage of time but in some subject areas (e.g., computing) knowledge dates extremely quickly, while in other subjects changes of legislation, societal change, and changes in academic interests and the impact of research on the subject all result in the need to update courses.

The Number of Learners

All commentators recognize that the number of students enrolled in a system is a crucial factor affecting both total system costs and average student costs. Media and technology choice will have a bearing here, given that some technologies lend themselves to economies of scale while others do not. Systems that provide considerable support to students generally deliver significantly less in the way of economies of scale than those providing little or no support.

It is generally assumed that the more students a distance learning system has, the lower the average cost, and this is broadly so. This has led many distance education systems to seek to expand their student numbers year on year. There is, however, a problem with this. What distance educators seem to do in many ways parallels the wasteful practices of the post-World War II American automobile industry (see Johnson, 1992, pp. 44–46) by assuming that the high overhead costs inherent in distance education can be controlled by expanding student numbers to position oneself to sell places on courses at a lower rate than more traditional institutions. Thus, the emphasis is placed on driving expansion fast enough to cover overhead costs that are, to a considerable extent, caused by scale and complexity, and that are deemed to be fixed and hence beyond control. But most the economies of scale are reaped early on in expansion. The nature of the average cost curve is such that the more students there are in the system, the harder it becomes to achieve significant economies of scale. The pursuit of expansion in itself may cause costs to rise.

Thought must also be given to the number of students at individual course level. For any given student population, the more courses on offer, the lower the average course population. However, students will rarely if ever be distributed equally across the courses. It is much more likely that the 80:20 rule will apply, with 80% of the students enrolled on something like 20% of the courses, so that one can expect a few courses have very high student populations and a large number to have relatively few students in them. Planners thus need to consider the likely student population on each course and bear this in mind in selecting the media to be used on each course.

Organizational Structures

Two things are worth noting about the cost studies undertaken to date. Firstly, most of them focus on the costs of single-mode systems, either large-scale educational broadcasting systems (Class II systems), or medium to large multimedia distance education systems (Class III systems). Second, where cost comparisons are made between the costs of traditional and distance education, the comparison is between the costs of these large-scale systems and the costs of traditional approaches to education. Relatively fewer studies have either looked at or compared the costs of distance-based provision *within* the context of mixed-mode institutions teaching both on campus by traditional means and off campus by distance education (exceptions include Wagner, 1975; Deakin University, 1989; Coopers & Lybrand, 1990; Taylor & White, 1991; Ansari, 1992; Makau, 1993; Cumming & Olaloku, 1993). Intriguingly, some of these studies suggest that mixed-mode institutions may achieve even lower costs per student than do distance teaching institutions—an issue that Rumble (1992; 1997, pp. 152–159) has examined. Using evidence derived from Taylor and White (1991), Rumble (1992) argues that, given the relatively low costs of producing videotaped versions of lectures and simple printed lecture notes around guided reading, it does not cost much to develop resource-based learning packages that can be used by on-campus students. Indeed, many campus-based institutions are doing this already to lower their teaching costs. Once they have done so, they can then use the same materials to teach off-campus students, often at a lower costs than that attained by many of the purpose-built distance teaching institutions. Hallak (1990, p. 200) and Renwick (1996, pp. 59–60) also suggest that lower costs may be possible; the Committee of Scottish University Principals (1992, pp. 34–9, 41) was unable to come to a conclusion; and Daniel (1996, pp. 32, 68) believes the competitive advantage lies with the mega-universities. This is an area for further research.

CONCLUSIONS

As mentioned above, one outcome of the earlier work was general agreement on the methodology to be employed in costing educational technology and distance education projects. Unfortunately, these methods have their foundations in 20th-century management accounting systems. Such systems have difficulty in dealing with multiproduct systems because (a) they take little or no account of variations in the design of courses and the levels of service offered to different students (e.g., students on different courses or having different educational and support requirements), but instead assume a standard course model and standard student incurring average direct costs; (b) they often fail to identify the real drivers of costs; and (c) they allocate overheads to products by largely arbitrary means (see Johnson & Kaplan, 1987, for a critique of 20th-century management accounting systems).

The failure to recognize the wide variation in costs of products and services to students, and the failure to identify the cost drivers actually pushing costs, means that most of the studies cited in this article, and all the models identified, are of limited use in helping decision makers understand the real behavior of costs in distance education systems. This largely invalidates the use of simple cost functions to project forward total system costs in situations where student numbers are increasing or being reduced, or where curriculum, organizational, technological, and process change is under way. These are very real drawbacks and limit the value of the studies in terms of the practical advice that can be gained from them to guide future decision making.

On the other hand, these difficulties should not detract from the fact that in very many cases the average cost per student or graduate in Class I, II, and III distance learning systems is less than the average cost in classroom-based systems. So, while distance education is not *necessarily* a more cost-efficient option, it often is, and it is this that rightly makes it an attractive proposition for politicians, governments, educational leaders, and training providers.

Two worries remain, however. First, it is not yet clear what the relative costs of Class IV (computer-based/virtual classroom) distance education systems will be. There are worrying indications that such systems require more input from teachers than Class I, II, and III systems, not least because they enable greater interactivity between teachers and students.

Bates (2000, p. 127) suggests, first, that the cost of providing online student-teacher and student-student interaction tends to be lower than the cost of providing traditional face-to-face support, and that is because "a good deal of the students' study time . . . is spent interacting with the pre-prepared multi-media material, so the teacher needs to spend less time per student overall moderating discussion forums compared with the total time spent in classroom teaching" (p. 128), and second, "the online costs still have to be added to the costs of prepared multimedia materials" (p. 128), and this pushes the total costs of online Class IV systems above those of correspondence (Class I) and multimedia (Class III) systems.

One of the interesting features of electronic moderating could be the moderator's experience of the time it takes to support students electronically. In face-to-face tuition there is a clear cost control mechanism in place—the timetable. The same is not true of online teaching, where the pressure is to respond to students' queries rapidly and individually. Tolley (2000, p. 263) recounts her experience as a tutor on the "correspondence" and "online" versions of an Open University course. On the version of the course with scheduled tutorials, she estimated she spent 42 hours (10 hours preparation, 17 hours teaching, 15 hours sent preparing and sending tutorial related mailings), though this excluded her (unpaid) travel time to the tutorials (12 hours) and the unrelated time she spent marking assignments. On the online version, she spent 120 hours excluding assignment marking. In other words, her workload more than doubled. In addition, working online had a "dramatic effect" on her telephone bill. Crucially she was not paid for the additional time she spent. When tutors begin to demand to be paid for the increased workload, some chickens may come home to roost, either in demands for increased pay, or in a reluctance to take the job. This suggests that the first of Bates' claims is debatable—and that the costs of online teaching may be more expensive than costs for Class I, II, and III systems.

Annand (1999) suggests that it is these costs that may in the end constrain the extent to which large-scale distance teaching universities can adopt online technologies. Arizona Learning Systems (1998, p. 20) reports that "All providers of Internet courses...have reported that this direct communication [between teachers and students] takes more time than preparation and delivery of a classroom lecture and the corresponding contact with students." These faculty workload costs have pushed the typical direct cost per course enrollment of an Internet course (US$571) above that of traditional classroom instruction ($474), but they suggest that faculty workload will be reduced through improved support and processes. Arizona Learning Systems projects that measures such as the development of academic help desks could result in unit costs falling to $447 (1998, p. 7). In some cases colleges have restricted course enrollments in order to bring instructor time down (1998, p. 22). Arizona Learning Systems (1998, p. 24) suggests that the average cost per course enrollment should fall as enrollments rise. For a simple text course unit costs would fall from $782 per enrollment with 10 students to $453 with 500 enrollments, and for a multimedia course with images, the cost per enrollment would be $1,496 with 10 students, falling to $467 with 500 students (1998, p. 24).

Second, it may be that flexible learning strategies within campus-based systems actually yield a more cost-efficient option than pure distance teaching systems—particularly those that use expensive media mixes (i.e., Class II and III systems). There is considerable scope here for further research, but as Rumble (2001) shows, there are very significant areas of cost that need to be taken into account, and the best strategy for decision-makers at this point in time is to treat any suggestions that on-line teaching will bring the costs of education down with considerable caution.

REFERENCES

Annand, D. (1999). The problem of computer conferencing for distance-based universities. *Open Learning, 14*(3), 47–52.

Ansari, M. M. (1992). *Economics of distance higher education*. New Delhi: Concept Publishing Company.

Arizona Learning Systems. (1998). *Preliminary cost methodology for distance learning*. Arizona Learning Systems and the State Board of Directors for Community Colleges of Arizona.

Bacsich, P., Ash, C., Boniwell, K., & Kaplan, L., with Mardell, J. and Caven-Atack, A. (1999). *The cost of networked learning*. Sheffield: Sheffield Hallam University, Telematics in Education Research Group.

Bakia, M. (2000). *The costs of ICT use in higher education. What little we know*. Mimeo. Washington, DC: The World Bank, Education Technology Team, Human Development Network.

Bartolik-Zlomislic, S., & Bates, A. W. (1999). Assessing the costs and benefits of telelearning: A case study from the University of British Columbia. Available at http://det.cstudies.ubc.ca/detsite/framewhat-index.

Bartolik-Zlomislic, S., & Brett, C. (1999). Assessing the costs and benefits of telelearning: A case study from the Ontario Institute for Studies in Education of the University of Toronto. Available at http://det.cstudies.ubc.ca/detsite/framewhat-index.

Bates, A. W. (1995). *Technology, open learning and distance education*. London: Routledge.

Bates, A. W. (2000). *Managing technological change. Strategies for college and university leaders*. San Francisco: Jossey-Bass Publishers.

Bell, D. (1960). *The end of ideology*. Glencoe, IL: The Free Press.

Bell, D. (1973). *The coming of post-industrial society*. New York: Basic Books.

Blauner, R. (1964). *Alienation and freedom*. Chicago: Chicago University Press.

Campion, M., & Renner, W. (1992). The supposed demise of Fordism: implications for distance education and higher education. *Distance Education, 13*(1), 7–28.

Committee of Scottish University Principals. (1992). *Teaching and learning in an expanding higher education system*. Edinburgh: CSUP.

Coopers and Lybrand in association with the Open University. (1990). *A report into the relative costs of open learning*. Milton Keynes: The Open University.

Cumming, C., & Olaloku, F. A. (1993). The Correspondence and Open Studies Institute, University of Lagos. In H. Perraton (Ed.), *Distance education for teacher training* (pp. 349–377). London: Routledge.

Curran, C. (1993). Scale, cost and quality in small distance teaching universities. In H. Siggard Jensen and S. Siggard Jensen (Eds.), *Organization, technology and economics of education. Proceedings of the COSTEL Workshop, Copenhagen, 11–12 January 1993.* Copenhagen: n.p.

Daniel, J. S. (1996). *Mega-universities and knowledge media. Technology strategies for higher education.* London: Kogan Page.

Deakin University. (1989). *Further investigations into activity costing in a mixed mode institution.* Canberra: Department of Employment, Education and Training, Commonwealth of Australia.

Eicher, J.-C. (1977). Cost-effectiveness studies applied to the use of new educational media. In *The economics of new educational media* (pp. 11–26). Paris: The UNESCO Press.

Eicher, J.-C. (1978a). Quelques réflexions sur l'analyse économique des moyens modernes d'enseignement. A paper presented to the International Conference on Economic Analysis for Education Technology Decisions, University of Dijon, Institut de Recherches sur l'Economie de l'Education, 19–23 June 1978.

Eicher, J.-C. (1978b). Some thoughts on the economic analysis of new educational media. In *The economics of new educational media. Vol. 2: Cost and effectiveness* (pp. 9–21). Paris: The UNESCO Press.

Eicher, J.-C., Hawkridge, D., McAnany, E., Mariet, F., & Orivel, F. (1982). *The economics of new educational media. Volume 3: Cost and effectiveness overview and synthesis.* Paris: The UNESCO Press.

Ellis, E. M. (2000). Faculty participation in the Pennsylvania State University World Campus: Identifying barriers to success. *Open Learning, 15*(3), 233–242.

Fwu, B.-J., Jamison, D., Livingston, R., Oliveira, J., Skewes-Cox, T., & VanderKelen, B. (1992). The National Technological University. In G. Rumble and J. Oliveira (Eds.), *Vocational education at a distance: International perspectives* (pp. 117–130). London: Kogan Page.

Grint, K., & Woolgar, S. (1997). *The machine at work. Technology, work and organization.* Cambridge: Polity Press.

Hallak, J. (1990). *Investing in the future. Setting educational priorities in the Developing World.* Paris: UNESCO, International Institute for Educational Planning and Pergamon Press.

Inglis, A. (1999). Is online delivery less costly than print and is it meaningful to ask? *Distance Education, 20*(2), 220–239.

Jamison, D. T. (1977). *Cost factors in planning educational technology systems.* Paris: UNESCO, International Institute for Educational Planning.

Jamison, D. T., Klees, S., & Wells, S. (1976). *Cost analysis for educational planning and evaluation: Methodology and application to instructional television,* Washington, D.C.: U.S. Agency for International Development.

Jamison, D. T., Klees, S. J., & Wells, S. J. (1978). *The costs of educational media. Guidelines for planning and evaluation.* Beverly Hills: Sage Publications.

Jamison, D. T., Suppes, P., & Wells, S. (1974). The effectiveness of alternative media: A survey. *Review of Educational Research, 44*(1), 1–67.

Johnson, H. T. (1992). *Relevance regained: From top-down control to bottom-up empowerment.* New York: The Free Press.

Johnson, H. T., & Kaplan, R. S. (1987). *Relevance lost. The rise and fall of management accounting.* Boston: Harvard Business School Press.

Kerr, C., Dunlop, J. T., Harbinson, F. H., & Myers, C. A. (1964). *Industrialism and industrial man.* London: Oxford University Press.

Klees, S. J., Orivel, F., & Wells, S. (1977). *Economic analysis of educational media. Final report of the Washington Conference, 2–4 March 1977.* Paris/Washington: UNESCO, US AID, ICEM, EDUTEL.

Klees, S. J., & Wells, S. J. (1977). *Cost-effectiveness and cost-benefit analysis for educational planning and evaluation: Methodology and application to instructional technology.* Washington, D.C.: U.S. Agency for International Development.

Levin, H. M. (1983). *Cost-effectiveness: A primer.* Beverly Hills: Sage Publications.

Mace, J. (1978). Mythology in the making: Is the Open University really cost-effective? *Higher Education, 7*(3), 295–309.

Makau, B. (1993). The external degree programme at the University of Nairobi. In H. Perraton (Ed.), *Distance education for teacher training* (pp. 316–348). London: Routledge.

McGraw, B. A., & McGraw, K. L. (1993). The performance support system as a training solution: Cost/benefit considerations. *Journal of Instructional Delivery Systems, 5*(3), 7–19.

McGuinness, A. C. (1995). The changing relationships between the states and universities in the United States. *Higher Education Management, 7*(3), 263–279.

Muta, H. (1985). The economics of the University of the Air of Japan. *Higher Education, 14*(5), 269–296.

Muta, H., & Saito, T. (1993). Economics of the expansion of the University of the Air of Japan. In Asian Association of Open Universities (Ed.), *Economics of distance education. AAOU VIIth Annual Conference 1993.* Hong Kong: Open Learning Institute of Hong Kong.

Muta, H., & Saito, T. (1994). Comprehensive cost-analysis of the University of the Air of Japan. *Higher Education,* *28*(3), 325–353.

Muta, H., & Sakamoto, T. (1989). The economics of the University of the Air of Japan revisited. *Higher Education,* *18*(5), 585–611.

NBEET (National Board of Employment, Education and Training). (1994). *Costs and quality in resource-based* *learning on- and off-campus. Commissioned Report no. 33.* Canberra: Australian Government Publishing Service.

Orivel, F. (1975). Standard tables for cost measurement. In *The economics of new educational media* (pp. 26–35). Paris: UNESCO.

Orivel, F. (1977). Cost analysis in educational technology: Practical problems. In *The economics of new educational* *media. Volume 2: Cost and effectiveness* (pp. 22–35). Paris: The UNESCO Press.

Orivel, F. (1987). *Analysing costs in distance education systems: A methodological approach.* Dijon: Université de Bourgogne, IREDU. Mimeo.

Perraton, H. (1982). *The cost of distance education.* Cambridge: International Extension College.

Perry, W. (1976). *Open University. A personal account by the first vice-chancellor.* Milton Keynes: Open University Press.

Peters, O. (1967). *Des Fernstudium an Universitätn und Hochschulen.* Weinheim: Beltz.

Peters, O. (1973). *Die didaktische Struktur des Fernunterrichts Untersuchungen zu einer industrialisierten Form des* *Lehrens und Lernens.* Weinheim: Beltz.

Peters, O. (1983). Distance teaching and industrial production. A comparative interpretation'. In D. Sewart, D. Keegan, and B. Holmberg (Eds.), *Distance education: International perspectives* (pp. 95–113). London: Croom Helm.

Peters, O. (1989). The iceberg has not melted: Further reflections on the concept of industrialization and distance teaching. *Open Learning, 4*(2), 3–8.

Phelps, R. H., Wells, R. A., Ashworth R. L. Jr., & Hahn, H. A. (1991). Effectiveness and costs of distance education using computer-mediated communication. *The American Journal of Distance Education, 5*(3), 7–19.

Pillai, C. R., & Naidu, C. G. (1991). *Cost analysis of distance education: IGNOU.* New Delhi: Indira Gandhi National Open University, Planning Division.

Pillai, C. R., & Naidu, C. G. (1997). *Economics of distance education. The IGNOU experience.* New Delhi: Indira Gandhi National Open University.

Raggatt, P. (1993). Post-Fordism and distance education—A flexible strategy for change. *Open Learning, 8*(1), 21–31.

Renwick, W. (1996). The future of face-to-face and distance teaching in post-secondary education. In *Information* *Technology and the future of post-secondary education.* Paris: OECD.

Rumble, G. (1976). *The economics of the Open University.* A paper presented to the Anglian Regional Management College/Organization for Economic Co-operation and Development "International Management Development Programme for Senior Administrators in Institutions of Higher Education," Danbury, Essex, 1976–77. Milton Keynes: The Open University, Academic Planning Office.

Rumble, G. (1981). The cost analysis of distance teaching. Costa Rica's Universidad Estatal a Distancia. *Higher* *Education, 10,* 375–401.

Rumble, G. (1982). The cost analysis of learning at a distance: Venezuela's Universidad Nacional Abierta. *Distance* *Education, 3*(1), 116–40.

Rumble, G. (1986). *The planning and management of distance education.* London: Croom Helm.

Rumble, G. (1989). On-line costs: Interactivity at a price. In R. Mason and A. Kaye (Eds.), *Mindweave. Communication,* *computers and distance education* (pp. 146–165). Oxford: Pergamon Press.

Rumble, G. (1992). The competitive vulnerability of distance teaching universities. *Open Learning, 7*(2), 31–49.

Rumble, G. (1997). *The costs and economics of open and distance learning.* London: Kogan Page.

Rumble, G. (1999). The costs of networked learning: What have we learnt? Paper presented to the FLISH99 (Flexible Learning on the Information Superhighway) Conference, Sheffield Hallam University, Sheffield, UK, 25–17 May 1999. Available at http://www.shu.ac.uk/flish/rumblep.

Rumble, G. (2001). The costs and costing of networked learning. *Journal of Asychronous Learning Networks, 5*(2), 75–96. Available at http://www.aln.org

Rumble, G., Neil, M., & Tout, A. (1981). Budgetary and resource forecasting. In A. Kaye and G. Rumble (Eds.), *Distance teaching for higher and adult education* (pp. 235–270). London: Croom Helm.

Schultz, T. (1961). Investment in human capital. *American Economic Review, 51,* 1–17.

Scott, P. (1997). The postmodern university? In A. Smith and F. Webster (Eds.), *The postmodern university? Contested* *visions of higher education in society.* Buckingham: Open University Press.

Smith, R. C. (1975). A proposed formula for Open University expenditure in a plateau situation. Internal paper, June 1975. In *Review of academic staff working group: Report of a group to the Department of Education and Science* *and to the Council of the Open University.* Milton Keynes: Open University.

Snowden, B. L., & Daniel, J. S. (1980). The economics and management of small post-secondary distance education systems. *Distance Education, 1*(1), 68–91.

Taylor, J. C., & White, V. J. (1991). *The evaluation of the cost-effectiveness of multi-media mixed-mode teaching and learning*. Canberra: Australian Government Publishing Service.

Tolley, S. (2000). How electronic conferencing affects the way we teach. *Open Learning, 15*(3), 253–265.

UNESCO. (1977). *The economics of new educational media*. Paris: UNESCO.

UNESCO. (1980). *The economics of new educational media. Volume 2: Cost and effectiveness*. Paris: The UNESCO Press.

Vaizey, J. (1958). *The costs of education*. London: Faber.

Wagner, L. (1975). Television video-tape systems for off-campus education: A cost analysis of SURGE. *Instructional Science, 4*(2), 315–332.

Wagner, L. (1977). The economics of the Open University revisited. *Higher Education, 6*(3), 359–381.

Wagner, L. (1982). *The economics of educational media*. London: The Macmillan Press.

Whalen, T., & Wright, D. (1999a). Cost-benefit analysis of Web-based tele-learning. Case study of the Bell Online Institute. University of Ottawa, Faculty of Administration.

Whalen, T., & Wright, D. (1999b). Methodology for cost-benefit analysis of web-based tele-learning: Case study of the Bell Online Institute. *The American Journal of Distance Education, 13*(1), 24–44.

48

Cost-Effectiveness of Online Education

Insung Jung
Ewha Womans University, Korea
insung_jung@yahoo.com

COST-EFFECTIVENESS OF EARLY DISTANCE EDUCATION

There is a relatively large body of literature discussing the costs and benefits of distance education across technologies and in a variety of contexts. In general, the literature has shown that "distance education can be more cost-effective than face-to-face education and that costs are predominantly dependent upon student enrollment and the fixed costs of course development and delivery" (Cukier, 1997, p. 138).

Capper and Fletcher (1996) analyzed previous studies on cost-effectiveness of distance education and identified factors influencing costs in distance education. Those factors include number of courses offered (since the cost of developing a course is one of the major expenses in distance education, the most cost-efficient approach is to offer fewer courses for larger numbers of students), frequency of course revision, type of media used, type and amount of student support, and attrition rate. They concluded that even though cost-effectiveness of distance education is supported in most of the studies, costs vary substantially from one situation to another and are influenced by a number of factors. Generally cost-effectiveness of distance education increases as the number of students increase and the number of courses declines.

A substantial number of studies analyzed in Capper and Fletcher's (1996) report supported cost-effectiveness of distance education. A study that was conducted in Sri Lanka showed that distance education was by far the most cost-effective—4.5 to 6 times more cost-effective than residential training programs offered in colleges of education or in in-service teacher training programs. The main reason for this cost-effectiveness of distance education was that the teachers in the distance education programs continued with their full teaching loads, whereas the other groups did not. As appeared in this study, savings on salary costs and travel costs for program participants have been reported as one of the main sources of cost-effectiveness of distance education.

There were cost-effectiveness studies that focused more on effectiveness of distance education than on the costs and analyzed general cost-effectiveness of distance education via

717

various technologies. Early cost-effectiveness studies on videoconferencing reported substantial cost-benefits (Showalter, 1983; Hosley & Randolph, 1993; Trevor-Deutsch & Baker,
1997). Even though its costs were higher than other classroom-based programs, interactive
satellite-delivered training courses were found to be cost-effective due to increased enrollments, increased student access to quality programs and resources, and other benefits (Ludlow,
1994).

Hall (1997) compared CD-ROM–based training to classroom-based training in a high-tech
company and reported that over the 3-year pilot period, costs for the CD-ROM–based course
were 47% less than those for classroom-based courses. Moreover, the improved instructional
design, a variety of instructional models, and other strategies contributed to more effective
learning and reduced training time.

After analyzing a series of studies on cost-effectiveness of distance education, Moore and
Thompson (1997) found that cost-effectiveness depended more on costs in relation to education
value, rather than on costs alone. Moreover it is indicated that as technologies are rapidly
evolving and costs related to these technologies also change drastically, difficulties arise in
predicting costs of a certain technology. Thus, as Hezel (1992) has suggested, a question of
"is the educational outcome worth the cost?" is more appropriate than the question of asking
comparative costs between distance education and traditional face-to-face education.

With these considerations in mind, Moore and Thompson (1997) reported several studies on
cost-effectiveness of technologically mediated instruction using various technologies in a variety of contexts. As early examples of the studies, reports of Christopher (1982) and Showalter
(1983) were analyzed. Christopher found that the Teleteach Expanded Delivery System was
more cost-effective than resident instruction for providing training to Air Force students at
remote sites. Showalter reported a 55% cost-benefit in delivering continuing education to professionals via an audioconferencing system. The cost-benefits of audioconferencing were also
reported in some other studies in K-12 context (Schmidt, Sullivan, & Hardy, 1994).

In addition, studies that specifically compare cost-effectiveness of a distance education
course via videoconferencing to a traditional classroom-based course were reported. Those
studies emphasized substantial savings through decreased travel costs by bringing training to
the workplace (Moore & Thompson, 1997).

While these studies are useful in providing a comparative look at identifying the costs and
effectiveness of media-mediated courses, not much research has been conducted to assess cost-
effectiveness of online education. Even in the studies of cost-effectiveness of online education,
"costs of development or costs born by students" are often excluded, and "these studies often
use competing methodologies, making them difficult to compare" (Bakia, 2000). Because of
the relatively small number of studies and methodological limitations of cost-effectiveness
studies, findings from these studies need to be viewed as suggestive rather than definitive.

COST-EFFECTIVENESS OF ONLINE EDUCATION

Many educators or decision makers believe that the primary benefit of online education is
that costs can be distributed over a large number of students, resulting in economies of scale
for educational institutions (Kearsley, 2000; Inglis, 1999; Whalen & Wright, 1999). It is assumed that large student enrollment would increase revenue and lower the cost per student and
operating expenses.

While the possibility of reducing the costs appears to be one of the main factors that motivates decision makers to adopt online education, two other factors also seem to be important:
improving the quality of students' learning experience through various types of online interaction and increasing access (Inglis, 1999). From the student's perspective, online education

means increased opportunities for interaction with other students and instructors and for wider access to a variety of multimedia resources and experts worldwide. As discussed in several articles (Relan & Gillani, 1997; McDonald & Gibson, 1998; Salmon, 1999), online technologies are known to be capable of providing an interactive learning environment that supports people in communicating with others in different places and time zones to fulfill their education or training needs. The Internet, as one of these online technologies, is viewed as an innovative distance education approach for delivering instruction to learners in different places and/or different times and for improving learner-learner, learner-instructor interaction. Related research and case studies show that a virtual education via the Internet provides an opportunity to develop new learning experiences for learners by managing self-directed learning and sharing information and ideas in a cooperative and collaborative manner (Hiltz, 1994; Daugherty & Funke, 1998; Jonassen, Prevish, Christy, & Stavrulaki, 1999).

Cukier (1997) argued the importance of including educational values of online education such as increase in educational access and improvement in interaction among learners in analyzing cost-effectiveness. She summarized four of the cost-benefit methodologies examined in the previous studies and provided an integrated methodology for the cost-benefit analysis of network-based learning. Four approaches to cost-benefit analysis include a value-based approach, a mathematical modeling approach, a comparative approach, and a return on investment approach.

A value-based approach considers the pedagogical needs and values of an educational institution in analyzing cost-benefits of online education. For instance, an educational institution that sees small-group interaction as important learner experience will be more likely to view interaction as a benefit to be analyzed whereas an institution whose goal in adopting online education is to reach as many students as possible will view expansive delivery and limited interaction as benefits in introducing online education. A mathematical modeling approach focuses on the costs and benefits that can be easily quantifiable. For example, a study that examines both the costs and benefits of videoconferencing used in two different ways will be interested in cost assessments for the teleconferencing, the costs savings resulting from remote delivery in two ways (where the instructor travels to the students and where the students travel to the instructor), and benefits of each method. In this study, cost-benefits of videoconferencing in two different delivery situations will be quantified for comparison.

Cukier (1997) explains that a comparative approach can be used in a situation when the same course is delivered using different technologies, for example, comparing online education with traditional face-to-face instruction. A return on investment approach attributes an economic value to benefits and seeks to measure monetary gains of adopting a new medium as a delivery means.

The proposed approach to cost-benefit analysis of online education, called an integrated approach, focuses on integrating major concepts in these four previous approaches. When this integrated approach is adopted, analyses of costs must address categories of capital and recurrent costs, production and delivery costs, and fixed and variable costs. And when estimating benefits of online education, performance-driven benefits such as learning outcomes, cost savings, students/teacher satisfaction, and opportunity costs; value-driven benefits such as flexibility, access, interaction, user-friendliness, and adaptability of materials; and value-added benefits such as reduction in capital investment, reduction in pollution, increased job creation, new business opportunities, reductions in social community costs, and creation of secondary markets must be analyzed. Cukier emphasized that the analysis of costs and benefits should be conducted separately and the approach should be multileveled. But costs and benefits will ultimately be evaluated subjectively.

Based on Cukier's (1997) frameworks of cost-benefit analysis, six case studies have been conducted by the NCE-Telelearning project team in Canada and two of them are available online. Cost measures assessed in the two case studies (Bartolic-Zlomislic & Bates, 1999; Bartolic-Zlomislic & Brett, 1999) include 1) capital and recurrent costs, 2) production and delivery costs, and 3) fixed and variable costs. The cost structure of each technology is analyzed and the unit cost per learner is measured. The costs assessed in Bartolic-Zlomislic and Brett's study did not include overhead costs as these were unknown. Benefit data include 1) performance-driven benefits, 2) value-driven benefits, and 3) societal or value-added benefits. Both quantitative and qualitative data were collected and included students, faculty and staff, and administrator perspectives.

A case study by Bartolic-Zlomislic and Brett (1999) analyzed costs and benefits of an entirely online graduate course at the Ontario Institute for Studies in Education of The University of Toronto in changing the software from Parti, a UNIX-based mail and conferencing software, to WebCSILE, a Web-based software. The results of the study project that their online program will make a small notional profit of $1,962 (Canadian currency) per year during five years and 19 students will be needed to break even. It concludes that it is possible to develop highly cost-effective online courses within a niche market, at relatively moderate cost to learners. It also recognizes that despite the change in software from Parti to WebCSILE, the largest cost of the online course is tutoring and marking time spent by the instructors due to the nature of the course that emphasized active online discussions. These costs could be lowered if the format of the course was changed to less constructivistic environment. The instructors and students reported that additional skills to the contents of the course were learned, such as computer and writing skills. A case study from the University of British Columbia (Bartolic-Zlomislic & Bates, 1999) also reported similar results. The researchers found that the annual break-even enrollment based on the projected costs and revenues over 4 years was 44 students.

The paper by Inglis (1999) is an attempt to examine the costs of shifting from a print-based course to an online course and to seek the rationales for moving to online delivery. Inglis showed that online delivery was less economical, when measured on a cost per student basis, than print-based deliver for four different intake levels (50/100/150/200 students). The distribution costs (such as ISP charges and individual support) for online courses represented a major component of overall costs. The author predicted that while there is an appreciable likelihood that the costs of mounting the subject online would be considerably higher than the estimates given in this paper, the likelihood of the costs being lower is small. The results of this study, in part, reflect the fact that in traditional print-based distance education most of the economies of scale that are obtainable in the design, development, and delivery stages have already been obtained. Several strategies to balance costs with benefits in online education are suggested.

There are other empirical studies that specifically compare the cost-benefits of an Internet-based distance course to traditional face-to-face courses. A study conducted by the Rochester Institute of Technology compared the operational costs of asynchronous instruction using a variety of online technologies including e-mail, Internet, Web materials, and telephone conferencing in traditional classrooms and distance courses. Given the exclusions of planning and production costs and investments in technical infrastructure, the study reported cost-effectiveness of asynchronous instruction used in distance courses. It also found that faculty used equal or more time in distance courses and reported using their time differently (Bakia, 2000).

Another study conducted by Whalen and Wright (1999) reports that Web-based training has higher fixed costs than classroom-based training but these higher course development costs are offset by lower variable costs in course delivery. In general, Web-based training is more cost-effective than classroom teaching mainly due to the reduction in course delivery time and the potential to deliver courses to a larger number of students in Web-based training. Asynchronous teaching on the Web showed cost-effective compared with synchronous teaching on the web because of the cost of having a live instructor and the greater student salary costs due to the extra time required to deliver the course. Also, the online education platform costs affected cost per course due to the different license fees and upgrading costs across the platforms. The amount of multimedia content in the courses was a significant factor in costs.

A report of cost-effectiveness of online courses in Korea National Open University (Jung & Leem, 2000) shows that the development and delivery costs for online education decrease over time (cost per online course was US$12,768 in 1998 and US$7,902 in 1999). And when compared with a traditional distance education course that used TV and textbook, an online course had higher completion rate (55.2% in the traditional course and 93.1% in the online course) and thus lower cost per completer. The students in two different courses show significant differences in learning achievement and technology literacy level.

While the studies reviewed above provide some ideas about cost-effectiveness of online education, we still need "a firm understanding of the cost-drivers" (Bakia, 2000, p. 52) of online education programs and more rigorous effectiveness data in various learning contexts to make a firm conclusion on cost-effectiveness of online education. From the studies reviewed in this section, we understand that the scale, design, and production quality, an institution's pedagogical value, and rapidly changing costs of hardware and software all influence cost-effectiveness of online education. Some studies have focused on identifying more specific factors affecting cost-effectiveness of online education. The following section introduces their tentative findings.

Factors Affecting Cost-Effectiveness of Online Education

After analyzing previous studies on cost-effectiveness of ICT in higher education, Bakia (2000) concludes that "the most obvious obstacles (in implementing online education in developing countries) include prohibitive internet connection costs and inadequate technical infrastructures. Several factors suggest that the use of ICT in education, at least in the short-term, will be relatively more costly in developing countries, even if Internet access were readily available and affordable" (p. 52). Besides factors associated with technical infrastructure, several other factors that affect cost and/or effectiveness of online education are identified in previous studies.

- Number of students in a course (Capper & Fletcher, 1996)
- Number of courses offered (Capper & Fletcher, 1996)
- Amount of multimedia component in online courses (Whalen & Wright, 1999)
- Amount of instructor-led interaction (Whalen & Wright, 1999; Inglis, 1999)
- Type of online education platforms (Whalen & Wright, 1999; Inglis, 1999; Bartolic-Zlomislic & Bates, 1999; Bartolic-Zlomislic & Brett, 1999)
- Choice of synchronous versus asynchronous online interaction (Whalen & Wright, 1999)
- Completion rate (Jung & Leem, 2000)

Moreover, some cost-saving strategies were identified in case studies. Online education systems often require a huge database system of online courses and materials. Since the cost of developing a database is high, most online education institutions have experienced financial difficulties in establishing a large database for their students. As a strategy to reduce the cost in operating online education, many institutions have "unbundled" educational functions— such as online course development, distribution, tutoring, assessment, general administrative affairs and learner supports (Farrell, 1999)—which are increasingly shared among specialized institutions.

Unlike analog systems, digital databases can be linked through computer networks, shared globally, revised by users, and then transformed into meaningful knowledge. The Cyber Teacher

Training Center in Korea, for example, is establishing a database of online teacher training programs in cooperation with other Korean teacher training institutions. Online training programs in this database can be used, revised, and implemented in different ways by different centers, and sharing allows each training center to reduce its costs for program development (Jung, 2000).

Another example is the Instituto Tecnológico y de Estudios Superiores de Monterey (ITESM) in Mexico. ITESM is a 27-campus university system with more than 78,000 students throughout Mexico and Latin America. Using the IBM Global Campus—an integrated system that provides Internet access, tools to design online courses, and other databases—ITESM draws on resources outside its system and offers more than 2,500 distance learning courses to students throughout the hemisphere (World Bank, 1998). With the Internet and a comprehensive intranet connecting its campuses and a distributed learning system called Lotus LearningSpace, educational resources developed by each instructor can be shared, students can interact collaboratively with other students and have direct access to instructors as well as library resources, and instructors can update their courses as needed. By sharing educational resources and providing additional classes and curricula without incurring the capital investment costs of building new campus facilities, immediate savings were reported.

Partnerships reduce the burden to online education institutions by distributing costs across partners. An example of a sound partnership is the one between Boston College and the government of Ireland (Jung, 2000). In collaboration with other business partners, these two entities are developing technology resources for both K-12 and higher education in a project called Schools IT2000. This project aims to integrate ICTs into Ireland's school system; Boston College provides much of the infrastructure and creates curricular materials, and Telecom Eireann provides Internet access (Oblinger, 1999).

By forming appropriate partnerships with businesses, online education institutions diminish their investment risks. Collaborations with education institutions can also be mutually advantageous by permitting the exchange of technology and human resources and the sharing of courses. Each institution can develop online courses in its areas of specialization and exchange access to those courses with its partner institutions. Partnerships can also be formed with education institutions or companies in foreign countries.

Cost-effectiveness of online education can be achieved either by reducing the costs or improving the effectiveness of online education. Recent studies in the cost-effectiveness of online instruction seem to focus more on identifying factors affecting learning process, satisfaction, and achievement in online instruction than on comparative cost-effectiveness of online courses over traditional courses. Instructional design, social, and students' personal factors have been identified as three major factors contributing to success in online learning (Jung & Rha, 2000).

Instructional design factors such as flexible course structure, quick and frequent feedback, visual layouts, and multiples zones of content knowledge influenced online interaction and learner satisfaction (Vrasidas & McIsaac, 1999; McLoughlin, 1999), and thus improved effectiveness of online education. For instance, McLoughlin (1999) attempted to present an approach to the design of a culturally responsive Web environment for Indigenous Australian students and to illustrate how cultural issues and decisions were incorporated into pedagogical design of an online course. He found that design strategies such as providing the multiples zones of content knowledge, adopting participatory course structure, and creating dynamic online learning communities were effective in improving students' learning and satisfaction.

Social factors also affect the effectiveness of online learning. Anderson and Harris (1997) identified factors predicting the use and perceived benefits of the Internet as an instructional tool. Interpersonal interaction among learners and social integration were among the most influential factors. This result is supported by another study conducted by McDonald and Gibson (1998). In addition, the study of Gunawardena and Zittle (1997) reveals that social presence exhibited by participants contributed more than 60% of learner satisfaction with computer conferencing courses. Specifically, Gunawardena and Zittle examined how effective social presence—the degree to which a person is perceived as real in mediated communication environment—as a predictor of overall learner satisfaction in a computer-mediated conferencing system. Extensive analyses of previous studies on social presence theory were provided at the beginning of the paper. They also provided construct validity and internal consistency of the instrument that was used in the study and contained 61 items measuring social presence, active participation in the conference, attitude toward computer-mediated communication, barriers to participation, confidence, perception of having equal opportunity to participate in the conference, adequate training, technical skills and experience using conference, and overall satisfaction. The results of the study reveal that social presence contributes about 60% of learner satisfaction with computer-conferencing courses. It is suggested that design strategies that enhance social presence need to be integrated in computer-mediated learning environments in order to improve the effectiveness of online education.

Students' personal factors also play an important role in online learning. For example, students' prior knowledge with technology or subject affected learning in online courses (Limbach, Weges, & Valcke, 1997; Wishart & Blease, 1999; Hill & Hannafin, 1997). Limbach, Weges, and Valcke (1997) conducted two studies in law content domain to explore a relationship between certain student characteristics and the preference for a specific study mode in print-based and in electronic learning environments. The results of the first exploratory research identify that about 75% of the students preferred a theory-based study mode and this preference seemed to be related to higher learning experience with this study mode. The second experimental research shows that even though the students indicated a more diverse preference for certain study modes in contrast with the first research, there was more preference for the theory-based study mode in a printed delivery learning environment mainly due to the greater experience and prior knowledge students had with this approach. This article clearly indicated that it is desirable to consider student variables in designing distance learning environments to provide students with the possibility to opt for a specific study mode and delivery mode and thus to improve effectiveness of distance education.

In addition, Biner, Bink, Huffman, and Dean (1995) found several personality factors such as self-sufficiency, introversion, and relative lack of compulsiveness were related to achievement among the telecourse students. Learners being autonomous individuals constructing their own knowledge (Laffey, Tupper, Musser, & Wedman, 1998; Bullen, 1998; Naidu, 1997; Jonassen et al., 1999) and being actively involved in their learning (Shneiderman, Borkowski, Alavi, & Norman, 1998; Hillman, 1999) also tended to maximize their own learning.

Given the fast development of information and communication technologies, we can expect that online technology will bring changes in forms of teaching-learning and educational institutions at all levels throughout the world. It is thus important for educators and policymakers to understand the factors affecting effectiveness so strategies can be appropriately explored to improve overall cost-effectiveness of online education.

FUTURE DIRECTIONS

As indicated above, a relatively small number of studies have been conducted to investigate cost-effectiveness of online education. Moreover, there are methodological limitations of those cost-effectiveness studies so that the findings from these studies need to be viewed as suggestive rather than definitive.

More valid and reliable empirical data are needed on issues of costs and learning improvement for definite conclusions on the cost-effectiveness of online education. Some specific questions for future studies on cost-effectiveness include:

- Does standardization of the online program format reduce costs without diminishing the quality of education and/or decreasing online interactions?
- How much can online resource sharing improve the cost-effectiveness of virtual education? How do different design strategies of online courses affect cost-effectiveness?
- What are possible ways of improving cost-effectiveness, while maintaining high interactivity?
- How can economies of scale be achieved in specific contexts?
- How often must online education courses be updated or revised to maximize cost-effectiveness?

The increased number of technology options have brought more opportunities than before for distance education. Online education programs offer possibilities that would not otherwise be available because of costs, time, or location constraints, especially to working adults. In addition, traditional institutions that have never provided distance education are now able to use online technologies to increase the flexibility and openness of their programs. Even though most agree that advanced technologies have made education and training more flexible and open, many learners still are unable to access the necessary technologies. There is a fear that the gap between the "haves" and the "have-nots" has widened and continues to do so. Issues of removing or lessening the disparity of access need to be addressed in cost-effectiveness studies of online education.

Educators and researchers must also continue to explore more sophisticated means of improving quality and cost-effectiveness of online education. In this regard, future studies should address areas such as:

- Instructional strategies: What are the effective design strategies to help learners maintain and manage their learning goals and processes while browsing online resources?
- Strategies for active involvement: How can we assist learners to more actively process information and construct meaningful knowledge?
- Motivational strategies: How can virtual education motivate the learner?
- Strategies for guidance and feedback: What are the most effective and efficient means of providing guidance and feedback to learners during their learning process?
- Testing strategies: What are the most effective testing strategies in virtual education to ensure that learners have integrated the designed knowledge and skills?

Some of these questions have been answered. For example, in comparing two different instructional design strategies for Web-based training courses for corporate employees in Korea, Jung and Leem (1999) reported that a Web-based course that adopted design strategies to provide specific guidelines to self-directed learning appeared to be more effective than a course that provided a more open-paced problem-based learning environment. The Web-based course, which presented content in small chunks, provided specific guidelines to help learners manage their everyday learning schedule and provided opportunities for self-examination through various types of checklists. Its completion rate was 93.4% and the average grade was 85%. In another Web-based course, each learner was asked to solve authentic problems individually, using various online resources. Later, students collaborated with other learners to improve individual solutions. The completion rate for that course was 72% and the average grade was 62%. It was determined that a course that required active online discussion and individual research for Web resources without specific guidelines was somewhat inappropriate in a corporate training context in Korea.

Yet another example is a study that explored motivational strategies for online education. As introduced above, Gunawardena and Zittle (1997) reported that "social presence"—the degree to which a person is perceived as a real person in the media-mediated learning environment created by instructors was a strong predictor of learner satisfaction—and thus, motivation—in a computer conference.

Not much empirical research has been conducted to explore the effects of specific design strategies on students' learning and motivation. Future research should examine effective design strategies to develop quality online education courses in a variety of learning contexts and thus to improve cost-effectiveness of online education.

REFERENCES

Anderson, S. E., & Harris, J. B. (1997). Factors associated with amount of use and benefits obtained by users of a statewide Educational Telecomputing Network. *Educational Technology Research and Development, 45*(1), 19–50.

Bakia, M. (2000). Costs of ICT use in higher education: What little we know. *TechKnowLogia, January/February*, 49–52. Available at http://www.techknowlogia.org/.

Bartolic-Zlomislic, S., & Bates, A. W. (1999). Assessing the costs and benefits of telelearning: A case study from the University of British Columbia. Available at http://research.cstudies.ubc.ca/.

Bartolic-Zlomislic, S., & Brett, C. (1999). Assessing the costs and benefits of telelearning: A case study from the Ontario Institute for Studies in Education of the University of Toronto. Available at http://research.cstudies.ubc.ca/.

Biner, P. M., Bink, M. L., Huffman, M. L., & Dean, R. S. (1995). Personality characteristics differentiating and predicting the achievement of televised-course students and traditional-course students. *The American Journal of Distance Education, 9*(2), 46–60.

Bullen, M. (1998). Participation and critical thinking in online university distance education. *Journal of Distance Education, 13*(2), 1–32.

Capper, J., & Fletcher, D. (1996). *Effectiveness and cost-effectiveness of print-based correspondence study*. A paper prepared for the Institute for Defense Analyses. Alexandria, VA.

Christopher, G. R. (1982). The Air Force Institute of Technology—The Air Force reaches out through media: An update. In L. Parker & C. Olgren (Eds.), *Teleconferenicng and electonic communications* (pp. 343–344). Madison, WI: University of Wisconsin-Extension.

Cukier, J. (1997). Cost-benefit analysis of telelearning: Developing a methodology framework. *Distance Education, 18*(1), 137–152.

Daugherty, M., & Funke, B. (1998). University faculty and student perceptions of Web-based instruction. *Journal of Distance Education, 13*(1), 21–39.

Farrell, G. M. (1999). Introduction. In G. M. Farrell (Ed.), *The development of virtual education: A global perspective*. London: The Commonwealth of Learning.

Gunawardena, C. N., & Zittle, F. J. (1997). Social presence as a predictor of satisfaction within a computer-mediated conferencing environment. *The American Journal of Distance Education, 11*(3), 8–26.

Hall, B. (1997). *Web-based training: A cookbook*. New York: John Wiley & Sons.

Hezel, R. T. (1992). Cost effectiveness for interactive distance education and telecommunicated training. In *Proceedings of the Eighth Annual Conference on Distance Teaching and Learning* (pp. 75–78). Madison, WI: University of Wisconsin-Madison.

Hill, J. R., & Hannafin, M. (1997). Cognitive strategies and learning from the World Wide Web. *Educational Technology Research and Development, 45*(4), 37–64.

Hillman, D. C. A. (1999). A new method for analyzing patterns of interaction. *The American Journal of Distance Education, 13*(2), 37–47.

Hiltz, S. R. (1994). *The virtual classroom: Learning without limits via computer networks*. Norwood, NJ: Alex Publishing Corporation.

Hosley, D. L., & Randolph, S. L. (1993). Distance learning as a training and education tool. Kennedy Space Center, FL: Lockheed Space Operations Co. (ERIC Document Reproduction Service No. ED 335 936).

Inglis, A. (1999). Is online delivery less costly than print and is it meaningful to ask? *Distance Education, 20*(2), 220–239.

Jonassen, D., Prevish, T., Christy, D., & Stavrulaki, E. (1999). Learning to solve problems on the Web: Aggregate planning in a business management course. *Distance Education, 20*(1), 49–63.

Jung, I. S. (2000). Korea's experiments in virtual education. *Technical Notes, 5*(2). Washington, D.C.: World Bank.

Jung, I. S., & Leem, J. H. (1999). Design strategies for developing web-based training courses in a Korean corporate context. *International Journal of Educational Technology, 1*(1), 107–121.

Jung, I. S., & Leem, J. H. (2000). *Comparing cost-effectiveness of web-based instruction and televised distance education.* A paper prepared for the Institute of Distance Education of the Korea National Open University. Seoul, Korea.

Jung, I. S., & Rha, I. (2000). Effectiveness and cost-effectiveness of online education: A review of literature. *Educational Technology.*

Kearsley, G. (2000). *Online education: Learning and teaching in cyberspace.* Belmont, CA: Wadsworth.

Laffey, J., Tupper, T., Musser, D., & Wedman, J. (1998). A computer-mediated support system for project-based learning. *Educational Technology Research and Development, 46*(1), 73–86.

Limbach, R., Weges, H. G., & Valcke, M. M. A. (1997). Adapting the delivery of learning materials to student preferences: Two studies with a course model based on "cases." *Distance Education, 18*(1), 24–43.

Ludlow, B. L. (1994). A comparison of traditional and distance education models. In *Rural partnerships: Working together.* (ERIC Document Reproduction. Service No. ED 369 599).

McDonald, J., & Gibson, C. C. (1998). Interpersonal dynamics and group development in computer conferencing. *The American Journal of Distance Education, 12*(1), 7–25.

McLoughlin, C. (1999). Culturally responsive technology use: Developing an on-line community of learners. *British Journal of Educational Technology, 30*(3), 231–244.

Moore, M. G., & Thompson, M. M. (1997). The effects of distance learning: revised edition. *ACSDE Research Monograph, 15.* Penn State University.

Naidu, S. (1997). Collaborative reflective practice: An instructional design architecture for the Internet. *Distance Education, 18*(2), 257–283.

Oblinger, D. G. (1999, Winter). Strong links: Multiversity. *IBM Magazine.*

Relan, A., & Gillani, B. B. (1997). Web-based instruction and traditional classroom: Similarities and differences. In B. H. Khan (Ed.), *Web-based instruction* (pp. 41–46). Englewood Cliffs, NJ: Educational Technology Publications.

Salmon, G. (1999). Computer mediated conferencing in large scale management education. *Open Learning, 14*(2), 34–43.

Schmidt, K. J., Sullivan, M. J., & Hardy, D. W. (1994). Teaching migrant students algebra by audioconference. *The American Journal of Distance Education, 8*(3), 51–63.

Shneiderman, B., Borkowski, E. Y., Alavi, M., & Norman, K. (1998). Emergent patterns of teaching/learning in electronic classrooms. *Educational Technology Research and Development, 46*(4), 23–42.

Showalter, R. G. (1983). *Speaker telephone continuing education for school personnel serving handicapped children: Final project report* 1981–82. Indianapolis: Indiana State Department of Public Instruction, Indianapolis Division of Special Education. (ERIC Document Reproduction Service No. ED 231 150)

Trevor-Deutsch, L., & Baker, W. (1997). *Cost/benefit review of the interactive learning connection.* University Space Network Pilot. Ottawa, Canada: Strathmere Associates International Ltd.

Vrasidas, C., & McIsaac, M. S. (1999). Factors influencing interaction in an online course. *The American Journal of Distance Education, 13*(3), 22–36.

Whalen, T., & Wright, D. (1999). Methodology for cost-benefit analysis of Web-based telelearning: Case study of the Bell Online Institute. *The American Journal of Distance Education, 13*(1), 23–44.

Wishart, J., & Blease, D. (1999). Theories underlying perceived changes in teaching and learning after installing a computer network in a secondary school. *British Journal of Educational Technology, 30*(1), 25–42.

World Bank (1998, April). *Latin America and the Caribbean: Education and technology at the crossroads. A discussion paper.* Washington, D.C.: World Bank.

49

A Comparison of Online Delivery Costs with Some Alternative Distance Delivery Methods

Alistair Inglis
Victoria University of Technology
alistair.inglis@vu.edu.au

There is a great deal of interest, both within institutions and within the higher education sector generally, in how the costs of online delivery compare with the costs of well-established methods of delivery. This is apparent from the number of studies being carried out at the institutional level and within the sector (Bacsich et al., 1999; Bartolic-Zlomislic & Bates, 1999a, 1999b; Inglis, 1999; Jewett, 1998; Morgan, 2000).

Understandably, institutions should be interested in the impact that the shift to online delivery is going to have on costs, given the pace at which that change is occurring. However, coming to an understanding of how the costs of the new methods of delivery compare to the costs of existing methods of delivery involves more than keeping account of actual costs. It involves gaining an understanding of the factors that have the capacity to have a major impact on cost relativities and understanding the extent of that impact. Through achieving such an understanding it is then possible to anticipate how particular changes in a delivery model are likely to impact overall costs of delivery and therefore the viability of programs. Without that understanding, detailed information on the actual costs of individual programs may simply lead to greater confusion.

THE DRIVE FOR INCREASED PRODUCTIVITY

The importance that educational institutions are placing on developments in the areas of online learning, at least at the higher education level, is indicated by the degree of interest that has been shown in the National Learning Infrastructure Initiative (NLII) that has been sponsored and promoted by EDUCAUSE (formerly EDUCOM). The rationale for the NLII was initially set out in a white paper that explained the necessity for taking a more systemwide approach to use of new learning technologies in terms of the economic imperatives facing educational authorities (Twigg, 1994).

The case that Twigg presented for making the shift to new learning technologies was based on the need for future governments to achieve economies in the provision of postsecondary education. Twigg argued that the growth in population and the disappearance of old jobs and the creation of new jobs would lead to a substantial growth in lifelong learning. This increase in demand for postschool education would place so much economic pressure on governments that they would be forced to respond by looking for ways to cut the cost of education. Twigg's analysis is supported by others who have studied the economics of higher education (see, for example, Arvan, 1997). The National Learning Infrastructure Initiative was put forward as the answer to achieving more with less.

TWIGG'S MODEL

Twigg argued that the ways to reduce costs are to reduce the need for direct faculty intervention and to make savings in buildings and plant. Both of these outcomes could be achieved, she said, by increasing students' abilities to locate and use learning resources. Twigg argued that, when implemented, the National Learning Infrastructure would "increase access (via the network), improve quality (through the availability of individualised interactive learning materials) and contain costs (by reducing labor intensity in instruction)" (Twigg, 1994).

The means by which Twigg saw savings being achieved was not, therefore, simply through a shift from face-to-face to online learning, but more particularly through a shift from classroom-based to resource-based learning. This argument is spelt out in much greater detail in Twigg (1996).

THE DISTINCTION BETWEEN CLASSROOM-BASED AND RESOURCE-BASED MODELS OF COURSE DELIVERY

Inglis, Ling, and Joosten (1999) pointed out that distance education programs, including distance education programs delivered online, differ according to whether they adopt a classroom-based or a resource-based model of delivery. Classroom-based learning is learning that takes place through dialogic interaction between student and tutor and student and student. Resource-based learning is learning that takes place through interaction between the student and self-paced instructional materials (see Table 49. 1). Most examples of distance education programs combine elements of both classroom-based and resource-based learning. However, it is the manner in which these types of learning are combined that determines the model of delivery that is being used. In the case of the classroom-based model, learning is centered around group activities. Such resource materials as are used serve the purpose of supporting and extending those group activities. In the case of the resource-based model, learning occurs through interaction between the learner and the learning materials.

TABLE 49.1

Examples of Delivery Methods Employed in Classroom-Based and Resource-Based Models of On-Campus, Traditional Off-Campus, and Online Modes

	Classroom-Based	*Resource-Based*
On-campus	Tutorials	Computer-assisted instruction
	Seminars	Computer-managed learning
Traditional delivery	Audio teleconferences	Print-based self-instructional packages
	Videoconferences	Broadcast television and radio
Online delivery	Asynchronous learning networks	Web-based delivery
		Multimedia packages
		Streaming video and streaming audio

The reason for drawing this distinction between classroom-based and resource-based models of delivery is that the differences between these two models are critical to the economics of distance education delivery. It helps in understanding the economics of online delivery if one first has a grasp of the way in which the economics of teaching at a distance has served to shape the earlier history of distance education.

THE EXAMPLE SET BY THE UK OPEN UNIVERSITY

The successful establishment of the UK Open University marked a watershed in the development of higher education. Prior to the establishment of the Open University, distance education programs had been characterized by high failure and dropout rates.

The Open University was founded on a vision of offering mature-aged adults from lower socioeconomic groups who had been deprived of the opportunity of gaining a university education a second chance. The Open University used a mode of teaching that was heavily resource-based. The model that the university adopted combined the use of correspondence material, television and radio broadcasts, face-to-face tuition at local study centers, and residential schools. This model was chosen because the students for whom the university would be catering were expected to be working while they were studying and therefore would not be able to attend daytime classes. However, the use of broadcast television and high-quality print packages involved substantial development costs. Nevertheless, the university recognized that its resource-based delivery model also offered considerable potential for economies of scale and that these economies were capable of yielding considerable savings in recurrent costs for the university compared with conventional universities. (Wagner, 1972).

THE IMPORTANCE OF ECONOMIES OF SCALE

The costs of any productive activity may be subdivided into costs that do not increase with the unit of output and costs that do. The former are termed *fixed* costs and the latter are termed *variable* costs. In education, examples of fixed costs include the costs of institutional infrastructure such as buildings and plant and the costs of courseware design and development, while examples of variable costs include the cost of labor associated with tutoring, student support and assessment.

Economies of scale are obtained by spreading the fixed costs over a larger student intake. Ashenden (1987) pointed out that opportunities for obtaining economies of scale arise at two levels. At the course level, economies of scale can be obtained by spreading the fixed costs associated with the design and development of courseware across a larger course intake. At the institutional level, economies of scale are obtained by spreading the costs of the institutional infrastructure needed for delivery of programs across a larger distance education cohort. While Ashenden was referring to the type of print-based distance education practiced in Australia, the pattern he described is capable of being mapped onto cost structures for resource-based online delivery. As in the case of printed-based delivery, economies of scale can be obtained at the course level by spreading the fixed costs of design and development of the Web-delivered resource materials across a larger course intake. Meanwhile, economies of scale can be obtained at the institutional level by spreading the costs of information and communications technology infrastructure needed to support online delivery across a larger total online enrollment.

The immediate success of the UK Open University led to many other countries around the world establishing national single-mode distance education universities based on the Open University model. However, two countries that stand out as not having followed this trend are Australia and the United States.

In Australia, a well-developed system of off-campus education was already in existence at the time that the Open University was established. Even so, a major government inquiry was launched to assess whether an open university should be established in Australia (Committee on Open University to the Universities Commission, 1974). This inquiry recommended against the establishment of an open university and recommended instead the establishment of a National Institute for Open Tertiary Education as a statutory body and the establishment a new regional university with special responsibility for open education. Due to the economic conditions that developed shortly afterward, neither was established. This left the way open for the newly established colleges of advanced education in Australia's dual-sector higher education system to fill the gap in the market. By the early 1980s more than 40 institutions were operating in distance education and there was widespread duplication of courses. Most institutions were unable to capture a sufficient portion of the market to operate efficiently.

Recognition by the statutory authority that was then responsible for overseeing the funding of the higher education sector, the Commonwealth Tertiary Education Commission, of the inefficiencies that such a dispersed system created led to a decade of research into the costs of distance education. At the end of this period, the Australian government legislated to rationalize distance education. However, it did not reduce the number of providers to one. The work by Ashenden's (1987) investigation demonstrated that by adhering to the production values that were accepted in Australia institutions could operate cost-effectively with average course intakes of 50–150 and average total intakes of 3,000. The government therefore designated 8 Distance Education Centres, involving a total of 10 universities.

The fact that the United States did not follow other counties in setting up a national university dedicated to distance education can be explained in cultural terms. The strong tradition that existed in the United States of school leavers moving away from home to begin higher education meant that there wasn't the level of unmet demand for undergraduate places that fuel the growth of distance education elsewhere in the world. When educational institutions in the United States began to move into distance education, they did so not by adopting the resource-based learning model that had been adopted elsewhere in the world, but by extending the classroom-based model beyond the walls of the institutions using the power of the communications media (Twigg, 1996). They created a "remote classroom" model based on two-way videoconferencing and one-way audio, two-way video (Daniel, 1998). Because of the strong U.S. economy, institutions were not faced with such cost constraints as universities elsewhere. Institutions took advantage of economies of scale to recoup the substantial investment costs needed to implement distance education by this mode. However, most did not take the second step of trying to reap economies of scale through a shift to resource-based learning.

Twigg's argument has carried such weight in the U.S. context because of the difference described between characteristics of the U.S. higher education system and the higher education systems in other countries.

Twigg was not the first person to campaign for the adoption of online delivery on economic grounds. A much earlier proponent of technology was Murray Turoff.

TUROFF'S MODEL

Murray Turoff has been one of the pioneers of computer-mediated communication and is widely regarded as the "father of computer conferencing." While working in the office of the president of the United States in the 1960s, he was responsible for the development of the first publicly used computer conferencing system. As professor of computer science at the New Jersey Institute of Technology, he went on to establish the Electronic Information Exchange

System (EIES), a system that was used in industry and education. He has continued to make a substantial contribution to the research into the use of computer-mediated communication.

In 1982 Turoff proposed the establishment of a new institution that would teach online and developed a costing model to demonstrate the viability of the proposal; he has regularly updated that model since (Turoff, 1996). Given Turoff's long-standing advocacy of the role of computer conferencing in business and education, it is only to be expected that the type of virtual classroom he would advocate is one based on the classroom-based model. Turoff argues that in this fast-paced world, by the time that subject matter is sufficiently well understood that it can be presented in the form of learning packages, it is too out of date to be relevant at university level (Turoff, 1997).

Many distance educators would not agree with Turoff's assessment of the limitations of learning packages. The pace at which disciplinary knowledge is expanding varies greatly from discipline to discipline. Even in those disciplines where progress is rapid, distance education providers have found ways of keeping up with development through the implemented just-in-time methods of production. Twigg (1994) argued that what students need to learn is the means by which disciplinary knowledge is accessed. If that is accepted, then the pace at which what students are needing to learn is changing is by no means as rapid as Turoff has claimed, even in disciplines such as computing and law. Nevertheless, it is important to be aware of the philosophical assumptions Turoff makes in order to understand the basis upon which his costing model is derived.

Given what has been said above about the way in which economies of scale are obtained, one would not expect substantial savings to be generated through the adoption of Turoff's model, and indeed Turoff makes no such claims. In setting out his costing, Turoff was not trying to show that it was possible to make substantial savings through making the shift from campus-based to online delivery but that it was possible to deliver programs online at a cost commensurate with delivering the same programs face-to-face. Turoff believed that the purpose of using technology in the delivery of programs in higher education should not be to enable larger class sizes to be supported, nor to increase efficiency, but rather to improve the effectiveness of teaching. Turoff did not seek to achieve savings by such means as relegating teaching to low-paid instructors or by limiting the extent of instructor contact. To ensure that the quality of faculty would be on average higher than in existing institutions, he proposed that instructors be paid generously in comparison with those offered by traditional universities. However, the salaries to be paid to staff are not quite as generous as they appear at first glance, because instructors would be required to provide their own computers, scanners, and pay the costs of communication and well as the costs of development of learning materials.

Where savings are achieved in Turoff's model is in the institutional infrastructure. Computer and communications costs are kept low, principally by requiring students to accept most of these costs. Turoff argued that the $15–20 (U.S. dollars) cost of unlimited network access compared favorably with the cost of travel to a college over a significant distance or the cost of room and board to live on campus. There is already some evidence emerging that students' patterns of attendance at universities are changing as they recognize that the need for attending on campus is diminishing. However, there is a danger in assuming that what applies to some students applies to all.

Interestingly, Turoff's decision to shift the use of funds from the physical plant to faculty also largely eliminates any opportunities that might otherwise have existed for obtaining economies of scale.

Twigg, on the other hand, was predicating her case on the assumption that governments would need to reduce the costs of education. The creation of the National Learning Infrastructure was her solution to how this could be achieved. However, the way in which these savings were to be achieved was through economies of scale. Use of the new learning technologies is the means by which the shift to resource-based learning is accomplished. The argument Twigg advanced for the National Learning Infrastructure was in essence no different from the argument made two decades earlier by champions of the Open University model. That being the case, it is worth asking whether even greater savings could be achieved by switching to print.

THE EDUCATIONAL RATIONALES FOR ALTERNATIVE MODELS

From what has been said above, it should now be evident that the more marked the move to resource-based delivery, the greater the potential for achieving economies of scale and the greater the scope for cost savings. Yet it is important also to consider this question: What effect does changing the mix have on the educational quality of the programs being delivered?

The models proposed by Twigg and Turoff represent the opposite ends of a continuum that ranges across various combinations of classroom-based and resource-based components. In considering how these two complementary approaches to delivery might be best applied, it is necessary to take into account the educational rationales for choosing one or another approach or a combination of the two.

Feenberg (1999) has characterized the difference between these two alternative models of online distance education as being between 'automating and informating' (Feenberg, 1999, p. 2). In describing the difference in this way, Feenberg tries to accentuate the difference between an emphasis on costs and an emphasis on quality. Feenberg acknowledges the opportunity that exists with what he terms an "automated" system to obtain economies of scale but argues that courses produced by a live teacher, which have the advantage of enabling learners to engage actively in dialogue, will be designed in relatively simple and flexible formats.

However, portraying the resource-based learning model as an automated model is something of a shibboleth. Almost nowhere in the world has implementation of the resource-based model been seen to obviate the need for student interaction. In the UK Open University, local study groups is a key feature while in Australia, teletutorials, weekend residential schools, or residential schools are key components. Feenberg acknowledges that prepackaged computer-based materials will supplement the teacher. In acknowledging the legitimacy of the use of these materials, Feenberg accepts that there will be components of either delivery model in which the potential for economies of scale will exist and can be exploited.

While some of the details of Feenberg's argument might be questioned, the issue he raises is certainly a recurrent theme in the literature of online delivery (Harasim, Hiltz, Teles, & Turoff, 1995; Inglis et al., 1999; National Committee of Enquiry into Higher Education, 1997; Turoff, 1997). However, the conclusion this debate leads us to is not that collaborative learning is preferable to material-mediated self-instruction but that the optimum situation is represented by a combination of both approaches.

The purpose to which research on comparative costs needs now to be directed is therefore to understanding how to obtain the most cost-effective combination of delivery strategies. This combination need not, of course, be limited to strategies mediated by the new learning technologies, but could also include the use of more traditional delivery media such as print, where this is appropriate.

WHY COMPARE COSTS?

Research into the costs of delivery of education and training is seldom driven merely by curiosity. It is usually driven by the need of education and training managers for dependable data upon which to base management decisions. The type of research that is undertaken is therefore determined by the types of issues that are uppermost in the minds of managers. Sometimes there may be a political element. However, more commonly the reasons are economic—education and training providers find themselves having to stretch their budgets further and are keen to learn the best way to do this.

Rumble (1999) suggested that some of the reasons why educators worry about costs of online delivery include the need to understand and control costs, to identify costs in order to set prices, to demonstrate increased cost-efficiency and cost-effectiveness, and to justify projects in terms of their costs and benefits, and the fear that the overall cost will be too great for institutions or that the costs imposed on students will be too heavy.

In the period immediately following the establishment of the World Wide Web, many education and training managers saw it as offering a way to achieve substantial reductions in the costs of delivery of programs. Initial interest in the costs of online learning was therefore focused on confirming that the types of savings that were being promised could in fact be obtained. However, this phase has passed. Most education and training managers now realize that the costs of online delivery are somewhat higher than at first believed. However, more importantly, they accept that online learning is here to stay and that, therefore, even if online delivery were to be shown to be not as economical as existing methods, it would still continue to evolve and would become less costly over time. Their primary responsibility as managers is therefore no longer to determine whether their organizations should be considering shifting to online delivery, but rather when and how. The management imperative in relation to online delivery is no longer to reduce costs, but rather to manage costs.

DIFFICULTIES IN MAKING COMPARISONS ON THE BASIS OF ACTUAL COSTS

While it is usual to base comparisons of different modes of delivery on actual costs, this approach runs into a number of difficulties when addressing an international arena.

Actual costs vary considerably from country to country but they don't vary consistently. For example, labor costs are much higher in first world countries than in third world countries. However, the costs of technology and telecommunications are generally higher in third world countries than in first world countries. Furthermore, relative costs are not very stable, being subject to exchange rate variations that at times can be quite large. A variation in the exchange rate between two countries can therefore produce a change in a major cost component that is much larger than the total contributions of minor cost components.

In coming to understand the way in which the costs of different delivery methods compare, it is therefore more important to appreciate the relative impact that different variables have on costs and the way in which they impact costs than to have a detailed knowledge of the actual costs of different cost components for a particular type of project in a particular context.

HOW SHOULD COSTS BE COMPARED?

Recent studies of costs in distance education recognize the importance of adopting an activity-based costing approach (Cokins, 1996) rather than a costing approach based on line items (Rumble, 1986, 1997). However, the fact that institutions have not yet adopted activity-based accounting is one of the major factors that continues to bedevil attempts to investigate relative costs on a systemwide scale (Bacsich et al., 1999).

The adoption of activity-based costing focuses attention on the differences that exist between different phases of a production cycle and numerous models have been proposed for subdividing the phases involved in the delivery of distance education programs by more traditional media (see, for example, Bates, 1995; Rumble, 1997). Bacsich and his colleagues have examined the suitability of several models for costing online delivery and have proposed a new life cycle model comprising planning and development, production and delivery, and maintenance and evaluation phases, which they have attempted to validate by reference to panels of practitioners (Bacsich et al., 1999).

In analyzing the costs of two alternative ways of going about a process it is generally of little value to compare the costs of inputs without comparing the value of the outputs. Comparing inputs without at the same time comparing outputs carries the tacit assumption that the outputs are the same or equivalent. In the case of the delivery of educational programs this is seldom, if ever, the case.

Cost-effectiveness analysis compares costs with outcomes whether or not those outcomes can be measured in financial terms. Cost-benefit analysis compares costs with benefits in economic terms (Moonen, 1997).

Cukier (1997) has pointed out that many published cost-benefit studies in distance education examine costs but not benefits. Studies that do not attempt to compare benefits as well as costs are of limited value in establishing the "big picture." However, it is often the case that before and after conditions are often so different when courses are moved online that finding suitable outcome measures is often quite difficult. In the studies that Cukier reviewed, the types of benefits that were identified included cost savings, opportunity costs, or learning outcomes. Bartolic-Zlomislic and Bates (1999a), drawing on the work of Cukier, assessed the benefits flowing from a joint venture development involving the University of British Columbia and the Monterrey Institute of Technology using a range of outcome measures. These included measures of performance-driven benefits such as student/instructor satisfaction, learning outcomes, and return on investment; measures of value-driven benefits such as increased access, flexibility, and ease of use, and measures of value-added benefits including the potential for new markets.

Bates (1995) argued that the basis on which costs are compared should take into account the purpose for which they are being compared. If this purpose is to decide whether to use a particular technology or if there is a fixed overall budget then it may be most appropriate to use the total cost over the whole of life of the project; if the purpose is to maximize the investment in the production of resource, then the marginal cost of increasing the amount of resource material may be the best measure; if the purpose is to recover the costs of delivery through student fees, then the marginal cost of adding an additional student may be the most appropriate measure; and if the purpose is to compare different technologies then the average cost per student hour is probably the best measure.

An alternative approach to using actual costs for comparing the costs of alternative methods of delivery is to use break-even analysis (Markowitz, 1987) in which the comparison is made on the basis of the time taken to recover the initial investment. This approach is most appropriate for use in situations where all of the initial investment is being recovered through course fees and it is important to know whether investment in the initial development of the course is justified.

As several authors point out, the number of studies that make any attempt to compare the costs of online delivery is small (Bacsich et al., 1999; NBEET, 1994; Rumble, 1999).

WHICH COSTS SHOULD BE COMPARED?

The costs of delivery of distance education programs can be divided up in a variety of ways (Bates, 1995)—for example, into capital and recurrent costs, into fixed and variable costs, and into development and delivery costs. However, what is more important than being able to place costs into their appropriate categories is understanding how the different types of costs interrelate. For it is the ways in which costs interrelate that determines whether, in a particular set of circumstances, one mode of delivery will be less costly than another.

However, even understanding the relationship between different cost components is not, on its own, sufficient because the relationship between different types of costs depends on the measure that is used—whether costs are compared on the basis of overall costs, costs per student per workload hour, costs per student per contact hour, or some other measure. Each of these bases of comparison has the potential to produce a different result. Given this situation, the aim in comparing costs should not be to determine which is the best measure of costs, but to decide which is the best measure for the purpose at hand.

THE IMPORTANCE OF COMPARING LIKE WITH LIKE

If costs are compared without also comparing benefits, a tacit assumption is made that the delivery methods being compared yield the same or similar benefits. However, the more two delivery methods differ, the less it is likely that the benefits will be equivalent.

It is not hard to imagine how existing courses delivered in alternative modes might be directly translated into online versions. For most institutions that are currently heavily involved in distance education, direct translation of existing courses is the obvious and probably preferred first step to moving into this medium. However, simple translation of courses into the online medium is often deprecated because it makes no attempt to take advantage of the attributes of the media (Oliver, 1999).

Moving into the online environment offers possibilities that are not available at acceptable cost via alternative media. These include animation, streaming audio, streaming video, and full color. Advantage can be taken of some of these options, such as color, without appreciably increasing cost. However, the costs of enhancement of the learning environment are typically much higher than the costs of direct translation. The development costs of interactive multimedia products are many times higher than the development costs of print materials designed to support attainment of the same learning outcomes (Bates, 1995). If more traditional methods of delivery are to be compared with augmented forms of online delivery, then any improvement in the effectiveness with which students learn should be treated as an additional benefit and some attempt should be made to measure the economic value of this improvement.

The decision to shift to online delivery may provide the trigger for initiating a major course revision. However, the staff time involved in regular revision ought not to be regarded as an additional cost. Regular revision of courses is an accepted aspect of good practice in the resource-based learning model of distance education. If the timing of the redesign effort is altered by virtue of moving a course online, then only that portion of the development cost attributable to the cycle time of redevelopment ought to be considered an additional cost.

THE CONFOUNDING EFFECTS OF HIDDEN COSTS

A difficulty that arises in trying to compare the costs of online delivery with the costs of other forms of delivery is that there are invariably some costs that remain unaccounted for. These "hidden" costs can distort the basis of comparison. The costs of long-established methods of delivery are usually well understood, whereas the costs of emerging methods of delivery are often not all known. Comparisons of this type therefore tend to understate the costs of newer methods of delivery while fully accounting for the costs of existing methods. The effect is to place new methods of delivery in a more favorable light.

Paul Bacsich and his colleagues at Sheffield Hallam University in the United Kingdom have been trying to quantify the costs of online delivery (Bacsich et al., 1999). They have found that, in the institutions they have studied, many of the costs of online delivery are not being recorded.

Bacsich and his colleagues subdivide hidden costs into three separate categories: institutional costs, costs to staff, and costs to students. Institutional costs are the costs borne by the institution. They include among these the costs of costing, the costs of collaboration, the costs of monitoring informal staff student contact, and the costs of copyright compliance. Staff costs are the costs borne by the staff even though in some cases they should, in principle, be borne by the institution. Among the staff costs, they include the costs of time spent out-of-hours in development of learning materials and the costs of use of privately purchased computers and consumables. Among the costs to students, they point to the costs of ink-jet cartridges needed to print out learning materials.

Bacsich and his colleagues have concluded that there is a pressing need for institutions to start tracking the costs of online delivery. However, he acknowledges that there are a number of quite serious difficulties in trying to do this: academics, management, and administrators were reluctant to consider the use of any form of time sheet to track the extent of the investment of staff time in these activities; institutions were reluctant to acknowledge that staff work overtime; and the ways in which costs are internally accounted for within institutions were inconsistency and nongranularity of internal accounting (Bacsich et al., 1999).

One finds differences of interpretation as to what should be regarded as hidden costs. For example, Morgan (2000) includes as hidden costs the costs of maintaining the central administrative services such as the central finance office and the president's office, the costs of construction and maintenance of Web sites, and the costs of evaluation. Yet many of these are acknowledged and most can be readily quantified in some way. Whether one classifies these as hidden costs is therefore likely to depend on the individual context.

SHIFTING COSTS FROM THE PROVIDER TO THE LEARNER

A special case of hidden costs occurs where costs are shifted from the distance education provider to the learner. Moonen (1994) argued that for costs to be reduced in the log run, some costs must be passed on to the student.

As has already been pointed out, Turoff's costing model assumed that students would accept the costs of communication. Rumble (1999) gives examples that suggest that institutions are moving in the direction of requiring students to assume responsibility for communications charges.

Inglis (1999) found that in comparing the actual costs of offering a print-based course with the expected costs of offering the same course online, communication costs represented a significant proportion of the costs of online delivery.

Furthermore, if the costs of online delivery of resource materials are going to be higher than the costs of print-based delivery, the students may prefer to be given the option of the medium in which they receive their materials.

OTHER COSTS THAT NEED TO BE CONSIDERED
IN A TRAINING CONTEXT

Most of the published research into the costs of delivery of distance education programs has been related to the delivery of programs in higher education. In higher education, costs are borne by the student or the state or both, in a training environment the cost is more commonly borne by the employer. When the focus is shifted to the training environment an additional set of cost factors has to be taken into account. For an employer, the costs of training include not only the costs of the training itself but also the costs of any travel and accommodation required to participate in the training and the cost of the loss of the trainee's time (Moonen,

1997; Ravet & Layte, 1997). Whether such ancillary costs ought to be taken into account in making any cost comparison depends on the standpoint from which costs are being compared. If one is comparing cost from the viewpoint of the training provider, then the costs of travel, accommodation, and lost working time are not relevant. However, if one is comparing the costs from the perspective of the employer, then the magnitude of these ancillary costs tip the balance between online delivery and face-to-face delivery when choosing between training. It is therefore obviously important for the employer to take into account these costs.

COMPARISON OF THE COSTS OF DELIVERY IN A BUSINESS CONTEXT

Online delivery is assuming growing importance in corporate training because of its synergistic relationship with e-business. In the business sector, investment decisions have traditionally been made on the basis of return on investment. Investment in training is treated no differently from other types of investment. In making decisions on investments, businesses are more interested in the benefits that will accrue than just the absolute cost of the investment. Return on investment (ROI) is the principal financial metric used to assess the value of a training investment (Cukier, 1997). ROI may be expressed as the annual profit from an investment after taking into account taxation, expressed as a percentage of the original investment, or as the number of months or years for the cash flow generated by the investment to recover the initial investment.

While ROI can be calculated for an individual investment decision, it is more common for the ROI for different alternatives to be compared. For example, the ROI for online delivery of training may be compared with that of delivery via more traditional face-to-face training.

The way that the expected return is measured is obviously of critical importance in such comparisons. Training managers are apt to measure return in terms of the attainment of training outcomes. However, as Cross (2001) has argued, that as business unit managers judge the worth of training in terms of the improvements in business outcomes attributable to the training investment, astute training managers will estimate returns in business terms.

Both because the business returns to be expected from an investment in training are so dependent on the nature and state of the business and the relationship of the particular training to the activity of the business, and because the staff time and travel costs of training will depend on a business's locations, it is difficult to generalize about the how alternative delivery methods compare. Because of the mounting interest in e-learning and the more hard-headed approach that business managers normally adopt toward investment decisions, one may be inclined to believe that e-learning must be proving cost-effective. However, what may be of greater interest in this connection is that when it comes to investments in e-learning, senior executives of e-business enterprises are relying more on intuition and on financial metrics because their focus is more on growth than on financial returns.

WHAT CONCLUSIONS CAN WE DRAW?

Rumble (1999), in reviewing the findings of the small number of studies that have so far attempted to measure the actual costs of delivering courses online, has highlighted the great disparity in the findings. However, given what has been said here about the impact of economies of scale, the great differences in development costs for different types of delivery options, and the importance of the delivery model, this should not be surprising. However, from an understanding of the way these and other factors impinge on fixed and variable costs it is possible to predict how costs are likely to be impacted by changes in delivery methods and the results of such studies as have been undertaken do broadly correspond with these predictions.

Shifting from a remote classroom model of distance education delivery to a virtual classroom model is likely to result in some increase in overall costs. There is very limited scope for obtaining economies of scale at the course level by moving from on-campus to online delivery. However, because even classroom-based delivery uses institutional infrastructure there is still some scope for obtaining economies of scale at the institutional level. However, variable costs are likely to increase because of the additional time taken to communicate in the written rather than the spoken word while fixed costs are likely to increase because of the additional investment in infrastructure and support services

Shifting from print-based delivery to an online RBL model is unlikely to result in appreciable savings and could also result in an increase in overall costs, once again because of the additional investment in infrastructure and support services that will be required.

In both of the above cases, there is likely to be a significant additional cost to the student of moving online. Telecommunications charges make an important contribution to the overall costs of delivery and most distance education providers in the higher education sector are requiring these charges to be borne by the student. Requiring students to bear the communication costs doesn't reduce the overall costs of online delivery but it may bring the costs to the institution down to a manageable level. In workplace training, it is not readily possible for telecommunications costs to be passed on to the trainee. However, in this context the costs of staff time, travel, and accommodation need to be taken into account in comparing online delivery with face-to-face training and there may therefore still be a net saving to gained in moving to online delivery.

Shifting from the remote classroom model of distance education delivery to an RBL model of online delivery does offer considerable potential for achieving in savings in the costs of delivery. However, the savings will accrue, not from the change in the method of delivery but rather from the change in model of delivery.

In all cases, there will be a substantial impact initially from the start-up costs associated with the establishment of new infrastructure, the development of new procedures, and the creation of new organizational structures for student and staff support.

Nevertheless, the benefits of shifting to online delivery may justify the additional initial investment and any ongoing additional costs. This will particularly be the case where the shift to online delivery offers the opportunity to open up new markets that could not be accessed economically via existing delivery methods. Also, with time, the costs of online delivery are likely to fall as the capacity of networks grows, competition for customers increases, and technology improves. Meanwhile, the costs of existing methods of delivery are likely to remain stable or even increase.

WHAT MORE WOULD IT BE USEFUL TO KNOW ABOUT THE RELATIVE COSTS OF ONLINE LEARNING?

The work by Bacsich and his colleagues aimed at identifying the hidden costs of networked learning may provide a more accurate accounting of the dispersal of funds for online delivery, but it remains to be seen whether the possession of such information will lead to more effective management of institutional resources, at least initially.

In times of rapid change, the ways in which institutions conduct their operations and deploy staff and resources are generally more dependent on political rather than on economic factors. It is only once the new ways of operating have become more stable and predictable that costs begin to play a more decisive role in determining the choices that managers make. The phenomenon that Cross (2001) alludes to in relation to workplace training of managers relying more on intuition in making their decisions in relation to the implementation of online delivery probably applies more generally, if for no other reason than that the paucity of dependable information leaves them with no other choice.

Nevertheless, it is inevitable that education and training managers will continue to maintain a close interest in the costs of online delivery. Keeping costs within acceptable limits is what managers are expected to do. What this suggests is that the type of information that managers, and for that matter teachers, require is information that lets them make choices at the micro level.

The question that managers now want answered is not "Which method of delivery is less costly?" but "How can the costs of delivery best be managed?" In other words, given that the decision has been taken to go online, how can the quality of courses and programs be maintained or increased without at the same time producing an escalation of costs.

What has been argued here is that effective management of costs is more readily achieved if the delivery of courses and programs is conceived of in terms of delivery models rather than in terms of delivery system components and that when considered in these terms, maintenance of the quality of programs and courses is most easily achieved through a blending of resource-based and classroom-based approaches.

Because productivity and costs are likely to become increasingly important issues in education and training, providers in the United States are likely to move more and more toward resource-based learning in order to take greater advantage of the opportunity to obtain economies of scale. At the same time, distance education providers elsewhere in the world will take advantage of conferencing capabilities of networked learning in order to decrease the isolation of distance learners and improve the quality of their learning experience. The combined effects of these trends will be to bring the practice of distance education in the United States and practice of distance education elsewhere in the world into line. From a situation where it is readily possible to distinguish two quite different and often competing approaches of distance education delivery, we will move to a situation where two complementary approaches to distance education delivery are melded into a single hybrid approach.

This phenomenon is likely to start to bring to the surface new costing issues such as:

- How can the melding of classroom-based and resource-based learning optimize the trade-off between costs and quality?
- How can resources best be deployed to take advantage of economies of scale while not adversely affecting the quality of the student's learning experience?
- What are the most effective ways of supporting student-student and student-instructor interaction without at the same time increasing costs?
- What possibilities exist for using the potential of information technologies to reduce the variable costs associated with student support?
- In what ways can improvements in the management of start-up of projects help to contain the initial investment in infrastructure, institutional reorganization, and staff development required to shift from existing methods of delivery into online delivery?
- How are course completion rates and student satisfaction measures impacted by the balance struck between the use of self-instructional courseware and virtual classroom group interaction?

REFERENCES

Arvan, L. (1997). The economics of ALN: Some issues. *Journal of Asynchronous Learning Networks, 1*(1), 17–27.

Ashenden, D. (1987). *Costs and cost structure in external studies: A discussion of issues and possibilities in Australian higher education.* Canberra: Australian Government Publishing Service Evaluations and Investigations Program.

Bacsich, P., Ash, C., Boniwell, K., Kaplan, L., Mardell, J., & Caven-Atach, A. (1999). The costs of networked learning. Sheffield: Sheffield Hallam University.

Bartolic-Zlomislic, S., & Bates, A. W. (1999a). Assessing the costs and benefits of telelearning: A case study from the University of British Columbia. Available at: http://research.cstudies.ubc.ca/.

Bartolic-Zlomislic, S., & Bates, A. W. (1999b). Investing in online learning: Potential benefits and limitations. *Canadian Journal of Communication, 24,* 349–366.

Bates, A. W. (1995). *Technology, open learning and distance education.* London: Routledge.

Cokins, G. (1996). *Activity-based cost management—Making it work.* New York: McGraw-Hill.

Committee on Open University to the Universities Commission. (1974). *Open tertiary education in Australia.* Canberra: Australian Government Publishing Service.

Cross, J. (2001). *A fresh look at ROI, learning circuits.* American Society for Training and Development. Available at: http://www.learningcircuits.org/2001/jan2001/cross.html.

Cukier, J. (1997). Cost-benefit analysis of telelearning: Developing a methodology framework. *Distance Education, 18*(1), 137–152.

Daniel, J. (1998). *Mega-universities and knowledge media: Technology strategy for higher education.* London: Kogan Page.

Feenberg, A. (1999). Whither educational technology. *Peer Review, 1,* 4. http://www.rohan.sdsu.edu/faculty/feenberg/peer4.html.

Harasim, L., Hiltz, S. R., Teles, L., & Turoff, M. (1995). *Learning networks: A field guide to teaching and learning online.* Cambridge, MA: MIT Press.

Inglis, A. (1999). Is online delivery less costly than print and is it meaningful to ask? *Distance Education, 20,* 220–239.

Inglis, A., Ling, P., and Joosten, V. (1999). *Delivering digitally: Managing the transition to the knowledge media.* London: Kogan Page.

Jewett, F. (1998). Case studies in evaluating the benefits and costs of mediated instruction and distributed learning. Available at: http://www.educause.edu/nlii/meetings/orleans97/case.html.

Markowitz, H. Jr. (1987). Financial decision making—Calculating the costs of distance education. *Distance Education, 8*(2), 147–161.

Moonen, J. (1994). How to do more with less? In K. Beattie, C. McNaught, and S. Wills (Eds.), *Interactive multimedia in university education: Designing for change in teaching and learning.* Amsterdam: Elsevier.

Moonen, J. (1997). The efficiency of telelearning. *Journal of Asynchronous Learning Networks, 1*(2), 68–77.

Morgan, B. M. (2000). *Is distance learning worth it? Helping determine the costs of online courses.* Unpublished master's thesis, Marshall University, Huntington, West Virginia.

NBEET (National Board of Employment, Education and Training). (1994). *Costs and quality in resource-based learning on- and off-campus.* NBEET Commissioned Report No. 37. Canberra: Australian Government Publishing Service.

National Committee of Enquiry into Higher Education. (1997). Higher Education in the Learning Society. Available at: http://www.leads.ac.uk/educol/ncihe/docsinde.htm.

Oliver, R. (1999). Exploring strategies for online teaching and learning. *Distance Education, 20*(2), 240–254.

Ravet, S., & Layte, M. (1997). *Technology-based training. A comprehensive guide to choosing, implementing and developing new technologies in training.* London: Kogan Page.

Rumble, G. (1986). *Activity costing in mixed-mode institutions: A report based on a study of Deakin University.* Deakin Open Education Monograph, No. 2. Geelong: Deakin University.

Rumble, G. (1997). *The costs and economics of open and distance learning.* London: Kogan Page.

Rumble, G. (1999). The costs of networked learning: What have we learnt? Papers from the Conference on Flexible Learning and the Information Superhighway. Available at: http://www.shu.ac.uk/flish/rumblp.htm.

Turoff, M. (1996). Costs of the development of a virtual university. *Journal of Asynchronous Learning Networks, 1*(2), 17–27. Available at: http://www.aln.org.

Turoff, M. (1997). Alternative futures for distance teaching: The force and the darkside. Invited Keynote Presentation, UNESCO/Open University International Colloquiem, Virtual Learning Environments and the Role of the teacher, Milton Keynes: The Open University.

Twigg, C. A. (1994). The need for a national learning infrastructure. *Educom Review, 29*(4, 5, 6). Available at: http://www.educause/nlii/keydocs/monograph.html.

Twigg, C. (1996). *Academic productivity: The case for instructional software.* A report from the Broadmoor Roundtable, Colorado Springs, July 24–25. Available at: http://www.educause.edu/asp/doclib/abstract.asp?ID=NLI0002.

Wagner, L. (1972). The economics of the Open University. *Higher Education, 1,* 159–183.

VII

International Perspectives

50

Global Education: Out of the Ivory Tower

Robin Mason
The British Open University
r.d.mason@open.ac.uk

WHAT IS THE PROBLEM?

Every day there are announcements of new companies being formed to market online and distance courses, or new partnerships among existing institutions to broker courses and programs both nationally and internationally. Just like airline companies, universities around the world are partnering up. The World Education Market held in Vancouver in May 2000 was a timely sign: The fair was expressly organized to help universities, training providers, software companies, and representatives from countries with large education needs to meet and form alliances, and it attracted participants from over 60 countries. As the race to form global alliances gathers momentum, a number of academics and commentators on the higher education scene have begun to investigate the reality behind the globalization fever. A number of research studies have already appeared that analyze current trends, applications, and emerging models.

Until this globalizing trend began to take hold, most people viewed education as a charitable activity, which required large inputs of cash from governments and large inputs of thought from academics locked away from the harsh realities of life. The advent of a consumer approach to higher education threatens to abandon the undoubted benefits of the old order in the haste to topple its ivory tower unreality. It is now quite common to hear education policymakers and senior university faculty talking about "market share," and in some cases, making profits or more alarmingly, staying in business.

What exactly does the term *globalization* mean in relation to higher education? Not surprisingly, the concept is used differently by different constituents and other words such as *borderless education, and virtual, online, distributed, and international education* all have somewhat similar designation. Within this family of concepts, at least some of the following

743

elements are usually implied:

- international communications based on telecommunications, information, and media technologies, which facilitate transnational circulation of text, images, and artifacts,
- international movement of students to study in other countries as well as a demand for online courses without a residency requirement in another country,
- increasing multicultural learning environment whether online or on campus,
- increasing global circulation of ideas and particularly Western pedagogical systems and values,
- rise of international and virtual organizations offering Web-based education and training.

In practice, online courses and programs are increasingly attracting students from around the world, and some are even being designed specifically for a global market.

Accreditation

One area in which educational globalization lags behind economic globalization is that of cross-border regulations. While economic globalization is supported by increasing deregulation of financial markets and reductions in tariffs allowing an easy flow of goods and services, the educational counterpart of this—credit transfer—is undeveloped even at a national level in most countries outside the United States, let alone at an international level. If an international system of transferring credit from one university to another were in place, the full floodgates of global higher education would be opened.

What is more likely is that the monopoly on accreditation that universities have enjoyed for centuries will simply be sidestepped by organizations offering courses, information, resources, and educational opportunities that the market is demanding. This is already the case in the area of IT accreditation, where Microsoft certification is valued more highly than a BSC in computing.

Access

Without a doubt, the issue about globalized education that arouses most concern and discussion is access. Those who believe that education is a basic right think that commercialization carries acute risks.

> They argue that education must not only train workers, but also citizens and responsible individuals. Therefore they question not only the effects liberalization will have, which would lead to discrimination against the most disadvantaged countries, groups and individuals, but also the impact a commercial approach will have on the spread of "common values" or respect for the indispensable diversity of learning content and methods, which take into account the language, culture and teaching traditions of the people for whom they are intended. (Hallak, 2000, p. 17)

There are two aspects to the concern about access:

- that those without an IT infrastructure will be disenfranchised, putting higher education even further out of reach and
- that in countries, cities, and wealthy enclaves where access to global online courses is possible, the status of degrees from prestigious Western universities will undermine local and national universities and lead to cultural homogeneity with all the consequent loss of diversity so marked in the plant and animal worlds.

Student Readiness

We know that the technologies are already in place to manage teaching on a global scale—at least for those who have access to electricity, computers, and the Internet. However, the social and psychological fabric needed to underpin education online lags much further behind mere technical provision. Are the potential students of global education ready to be self-directed, self-motivated, and resourceful e-learners?

This chapter looks at the research underpinning these interconnected issues: the drivers behind globalization, the implications of the commercialization of education, the models used by the early adopter programs, and the reaction of those not yet involved. While America is leading the practice of global education, a good deal of the research about the phenomenon comes from those countries most likely to be affected by American domination of a global market in education: Canada, Australia, and the UK.

WHAT IS THE EVIDENCE?

The Destruction of the Ivory Tower

Many critics and observers of the higher education scene in the United States are predicting the death of the university. Brown and Duguid in their influential analysis, *The Social Life of Information*, say, "universities are one of the few institutions that have been around throughout the last millennium... some doubt whether they will make it very far into the next" (2000, p. 208). One of the greatest threats to the traditional university is the rise of other educational providers: corporate universities, private for-profit universities, virtual universities, and a wide range of education brokers. Most of these new providers are businesses and the focus of a business is profit, while the focus of a university is knowledge.

> These companies are in the knowledge business—knowledge for profit—and they are revolutionizing the way we learn at the same time as they are creating a powerful new opportunity for growth in business.... Behind it all looms a gargantuan government-run education system incapable of handling a doubling of knowledge about every seven years. The knowledge revolution will power the new global economy, reshape many of our institutions—particularly education—and touch every aspect of our lives. Business sees the opportunity, and it is driving ahead full speed to realize this vision to adapt to, and profit from, the realities of the new information economy. (Davis & Botkin, 1995, pp. 14–15)

Davis and Botkin's (1995) enchantingly titled book, *The Monster under the Bed: How Business is Mastering the Opportunity of Knowledge for Profit*, sounded one of the early alarm bells for the university sector. Reductions in the funding of public universities, the changing nature of those wanting access to higher education, and above all, the larger social phenomena of consumerization and commodification of knowledge have all contributed to a profound questioning of the role and place of the university in a global economy. Those who have studied the higher education scene in the United States tend to fall into two camps: enthusiasts (e.g., Margolis, 1998) and alarmists (e.g., Luke, 1996). In addition to the fundamental debate over whether the university has a future and indeed, what higher education genuinely should be about, they differ in their conclusions about whether access will be increased or not by technology-mediated delivery.

Van Weigel (2000) argues that e-learning can increase the reach of higher education, but usually does this at the expense of quality. Rich approaches to learning—such as cognitive apprenticeship, collaborative research, critical reflection, and problem-based learning could be readily adapted to undergraduate contexts through Internet-based technologies. He goes on to say:

> Some may contend that undergraduate students are simply not ready for this. To that I respond, How would we know?... By the time they reach college, students have been socialized to expect less and less from education. The adventure of learning has been collapsed to what one gets on the final exam. .... Intellectual risk-taking is only rarely rewarded. (Weigel, 2000, p. 13)

In short, the globalization of education is exacerbating problems in higher education, which have roots much deeper than recent trends of consumerization and Internet technologies. However, the fear is that the focus of change in higher education is too much focused on short-term gain and maximizing revenue at the expense of the longer-term purposes of higher education.

Globalization and Education

One area of serious research is concerned with the way in which global education is a reflection or extension of society's increasing understanding of the interrelatedness and interdependence of the physical world. The development of this global consciousness has been heightened by the spread of global communication systems and particularly the entertainment media. One researcher to study the relationship between global consciousness and education is John Field:

> Distance open learning appears to be uniquely suited to the emerging world order. As borders open up across the globe to traffic of almost every kind, so distance open learning flows increasingly across national frontiers. Once an essential element in nation-building, education is increasingly a commodity, most readily exportable in the form of distance open learning. (Field, 1995, p. 270)

He documents the ways in which, as with other social and political trends, education is increasingly being thought of as a commodity to be shaped according to consumer demand.

Other researchers of the rise of "student-as-consumer" are more positive about its effects—particularly the way in which it is changing the worst aspects of the ivory tower practices of the university. Early studies of the use of computer conferencing note that teachers and course developers are being forced to consider the needs and requirements of learners, and online communication allows students' opinions to be embedded into the learning environment. A British researcher, Richard Edwards, concludes that the globalization of education through the use of telecommunications technologies will empower the learner and force the providers of education to concern themselves with students' real needs, rather than with the transmission of a preestablished canon of knowledge.

> Technologically-mediated knowledge provides the basis for individualising learning in a more complete and active way.... Here distance is subservient to the discourse of open learning and "educative" processes are displaced and reconstituted as relationships between producers and consumers in which knowledge is exchanged on the basis of the usefulness it has to the consumer. It is therefore a discourse of open learning which might be said to more fully govern the practices of those operating at a distance in the postmodern moment, as increased marketisation is introduced into the provision of learning opportunities and mass markets fragment and become more volatile across the globe. (Edwards, 1995, p. 251)

Educators, just like businesses, will have to become more flexible—in their staffing ratios, in their approach to students, and in their considerations of the curriculum. Various structural rigidities of traditional universities will have to be overcome: constraints on what constitutes the academic year, on where credits can be accumulated, and on how courses can be modularized. The kinds of courses that the global consumer is demanding are flexible, adaptable, portable, and interactive (Mason, 1998, p. 7).

Unbundling the Education Process

Many researchers in the field have noted and documented the ways in which universities, in the face of virtual and global expansion, are outsourcing functions and processes that are no longer considered core business.

> Until recently, the university was a self-contained society. Faculty members developed courses and course materials, offered those courses, and assessed student performance. The university provided pre-enrolment, enrolment, financial aid, record-keeping, and transcription services. It also provided instructional support services such as a library, computer labs, bookstore, and student union, complete with clubhouses, dining rooms, and restaurants, and meeting places. Many provided complete housing services. (Dirr, 1999, p. 27)

While few mourn the outsourcing of the food service or even the bookstore and other business and administrative operations, alarm sets in when universities consider unbundling student support and assessment. This is all part of a larger movement toward specialization of function, and for universities it may mean that one supplies content and curriculum design, another supplies assessment or awarding, and a company supplies the marketing, technology expertise, and perhaps capital. As part of an education consortium, this model of focusing on core areas of expertise can be seen as a strength and even a benefit for learners. For global programs, this disaggregation is a necessity.

Studies of Global Education

The United States is the undisputed leader in the field of online education and hence of institutional change. This has prompted governments in the UK, Canada and Australia to commission hefty studies on the danger of their national universities being eroded by U.S. globalized education. Each of these reports is based on extensive research of American activity, literature, and attitudes. All three come to similar conclusions: that their national universities are under threat and that joining the global bandwagon is the only way to survive.

The UK study was entitled *The Business of Borderless Education* (CVCP, 2000) and runs to two volumes. It investigates current policy and practice of noncampus higher education worldwide, but particularly in the United States. A wide range of regulatory issues as well as a number of the leading exemplars of global education are studied in some detail. An extensive list of recommendations covers advice to UK universities, government agencies, research and funding bodies, and quality assurance agencies. U. S. case studies include various corporate universities, for-profit universities, and media and software giants that have education initiatives.

Regarding the success of U.S. globalization, the CVCP study asks:

> Why then has borderless higher education taken off in the United States to a greater extent than in the UK (and elsewhere)? Three key reasons appear to be: a strong tradition of private higher education; devolved accreditation arrangements; and high student fees at mainstream institutions. (2000, p. 84)

It goes on to note that:

> Most for-profit providers, even if not primarily online focused as yet (for example, the University of Phoenix), are not oriented around the residential model (or indeed research model) of the university and thus are not concerned to support a range of subjects or the host of infrastructural, social and recreational facilities common at traditional institutions. . . . Innovative, non-traditional providers stress their commitment to the adult learner, point to pedagogically sound and professionally relevant curricula and exemplary student services. The charge is made that much traditional higher education largely falls on these counts. (CVCP, 2000, pp. 86–87)

Other issues related to global or borderless education are copyright and intellectual property, technology infrastructure, and governance, and these are also investigated in some depth in this UK research. The team of eight researchers, mainly UK academics, was advised by a steering group of representatives of UK Vice Chancellors and Principals. It is no coincidence that, at the same time as the findings from this study were published, the UK government announced that it was funding an e-university initiative to allow British universities to enter the global e-learning business.

The Australian study entitled, *New Media and Borderless Education*, was the first of the three and concluded that:

> There is evidence of a major segmentation of the market, with new providers targeting the lifelong learning cohort (25 years and up). This includes corporate training/education, a domain only partially catered for by traditional universities and a profitable market—being largely self-funded and employer-funded. Continuing and professional education is a component of lifelong learning for those in the workforce. There is a widespread perception that traditional institutions are not meeting the needs of the lifelong learning cohort and that the field is open for new providers to meet market demands. One obvious, and problematic, outcome of this segmentation is that traditional institutions may be left serving the less profitable traditional undergraduate market (18-24), which is largely government-funded or family-funded, in a time when governments are increasingly endeavouring to cut public outlays. Looking further into the future than the medium-term prospects, this arguably represents one of the most significant challenges to, and opportunities for, established higher education providers. (Cunningham et al., 1998, p. xv)

A follow-up study in 2000 conducted by the same team took the most prominent area to emerge from their first report and tackled it in much more depth:

> Corporate providers were considered to be one of the major emerging alternatives to the traditional higher education sector, able to capture profitable niche markets in lifelong learning and vocational training through their ability to deliver more flexible and tailored programmes, and their ability to generate future employment opportunities for their "students." (Cunningham et al., 2000)

The team approached 13 U.S. institutions from among a list of corporate universities, for-profit providers, and virtual universities. Nine on-site visits took place and interviews with various personnel were conducted over several days at each site. In addition, more than a dozen other organizations were the subject of a contextual study, the purpose being to establish a wide range of perceptions about the "business" of education in the United States. Interview protocols were constructed with a view to determining types of learners targeted, use of technology in teaching and learning, governance and staffing issues, courses offered, curricular approaches, challenges faced by the organization and plans for expansion, particularly into overseas markets.

The extent and seriousness of the UK and Australian studies are an indication of the importance with which globalization is viewed by the higher education sector.

The Canadian study was conducted by a firm of consultants for the Council of Presidents of the Public Universities, Colleges and Institutes of Alberta (COP, 2000). While not as extensive a study of the U.S. scene as the UK and Australian reports, it was conducted after them and therefore built on their findings. A particularly valuable part of the study is a taxonomy of business models that encapsulates current distributed learning activity worldwide. The models are based upon the distribution channels used and the nature of collaboration between the partners, as these are two of the key challenges in offering Web-based learning. Six distinct approaches are identified, although the researchers point out that many providers combine elements from several models.

1. Direct Sales/Virtual Universities

   This is the most common but also the most varied model. University of Phoenix and Jones University International are two examples as they offer online learning courses directly to the learner or corporations.

2. Partnership/Joint Venture

   The researchers explain the advantage of partnerships in this way:

   > Although this model is similar to consortia models with collaboration being the attraction of the model, partnerships and joint ventures typically have less cultural drag than do consortia. The effort spent on collaboration between the multiple members in consortia is high while partnerships are more straightforward—members are fewer and roles are typically clearer. (COP, 2000, p. 16)

3. Brand Broker

   In this model an independent broker offers courses designed or delivered from brand-name learning providers. Typically there is an exclusivity agreement that restricts memberships so that the brand is not diluted. Unext.com and Cardean.com are two exemplars.

4. Mall/Aggregator Broker

   This model is primarily a broker's information portal where learners can find appropriate courses—an online yellow pages. The researchers note that so-called mall brokers are realizing that they must provide more than mere listings and leading examples are adding new features to keep browsers returning to the site.

5. Regional Consortia/Associations

   A consortium of multiple providing institutions, sometimes regionally based but increasingly international, share activities, staff, technology infrastructure, and so on to improve efficiency and gain market share. There are many U.S. examples, but two international examples are Universitas 21 and Next Ed.

6. Channel Supplier

   This model takes the form of an individual institution using an existing Web marketing channel to offer courses to a well-defined market. The researchers acknowledge that this is a very new model and only in the developing stage. However, they consider that it is potentially one of the largest growth areas for online learning.

The conclusions of the report are in line with the UK and Australian studies. Two items from the executive summary are:

> Strategy will make the difference. Providers need to position themselves strategically in the marketplace—making conscious choices and trade-offs based upon their missions and abilities. They must clarify what value they offer customers and what their core competencies are.

Collaboration is essential. Collaboration and partnerships are necessary to compete. This is true for regional markets and for international markets. Around the world, business partnerships are occurring between regional institutions, consortia of international institutions, and between the public and private sector. (COP, 2000, pp. 1–2)

The evidence from these three studies points to the same conclusion: that getting into the globalized arena or at least the e-learning business is necessary for survival, and existing universities ignore the trend at their peril. Concerns about the creation of a "have-not" underclass, about which institution accredits the students, and about whether the courses are commodities or learning opportunities are seen as problems to tackle along the way, not as signs that this trend can or should be resisted.

Related Fields of Research

It would be difficult to claim that the globalization of education is a distinct research field—at least not yet. Other, more developed areas of research feed into the studies that do exist and researchers bring varied perspectives and research literature to bear on their analysis and comment on the globalization issue. Related areas of particular significance (some of which are covered in this volume) include:

- institutional change and business reengineering,
- management studies about models of partnerships and consortia,
- approaches to staff development, especially the training of online teachers,
- the pedagogy of online learning, and
- technology and software development to support global course delivery.

WHAT FURTHER RESEARCH IS NEEDED?

There are many aspects of the design and delivery of global education that would benefit from further research. However two stand out as being especially relevant for global education.

The first of these is the issue of student readiness for learning where there is no face-to-face component to the course provision. While this is questionable among American students, it is a much more complex issue when considering students from other countries. There are many variables: age, academic level, previous study, style of learning, and access to the technology of delivery. Early indications are that students who are older, studying at postgraduate level with easy access to a PC, self-confident, and willing to interact with their peers online will be much more successful on global courses than those who begin without these advantages (Macdonald & Mason, 1998). While many local and national online courses have some provision for face-to-face tutorials, courses offered to students all over the world rarely do. Even real-time events online are difficult for a global student body.

Trials and experiments in how to help students become more self-directed as learners are also needed. What works for different types of learner—mentoring, preparatory material, computer-based self-testing exercises, carefully scaffolded learning materials, or combinations of these? Studies need to be carried out across a range of curriculum areas. Students from science backgrounds have different skills, approaches to learning, and habits of studying by the time they reach postgraduate level than their fellow students who have pursued arts subjects. This may mean they have different levels of readiness to engage in online interaction, collaboration, and group work or to sustain motivation without any face-to-face support.

The second issue is closely related to student readiness for online learning. It involves the cultural differences that inevitably arise in online courses with students from many countries, educational backgrounds, and mother tongues. While cultural differences are not unique to global courses or even to online courses, they are much more evident and more difficult to address without the benefit of face-to-face interaction. Two American researchers who have begun to investigate the effect of global courses on students from other cultures are Gayol and Schied. They note:

> Content selection, visual design, central planning, language, teaching-learning routines, accreditation, academic prestige of the originating site, are all centralized textualities which might work together as an assimilationist or exclusionary pedagogy. (Gayol & Schied, 1997, p. 12)

Edwards and Usher's new book, *Globalisation and Pedagogy*, establishes a firm research base for the study of the significance of globalizing processes for education and pedagogy:

> At a time when learners are themselves subject to great changes in their sense of identity under the influence of economic, political and cultural change, there is therefore a question as to whether, for instance, the humanistic notions of learner-centredness provides us with the categories to "make sense" of learners. As with learners, so with learning. If identity is becoming subject to different forms of experiencing with the influence of globalising processes, then the ways in which learners are engaged may also need re-evaluating. (Edwards & Usher, 2000, p. 53)

Among the very earliest research studies of cultural issues in online courses is a special issue of the journal, *Distance Education*, May 2001. One of the articles in this issue explains the background to this new research area:

> We believe that because we are responsible for delivering courses to a global population we need to endeavour a) to ensure that those students who bring other, non-UK, cultural and linguistic experiences to our courses should not be disadvantaged, and b) to explore ways in which we may transform the cultural basis of these courses so that they more fairly reflect the plurality of backgrounds of the participants. (Goodfellow, Lea, Gonzalez, & Mason, 2001, p. 67)

Many of the studies in the special issue are written by practitioners who base their research on interviews with students, analysis of conference interactions, experiments with cross-cultural online collaborations, and feedback from tutors who teach global student groups. Designing courses for a global student body is an area that has received very little attention, and most practitioners are operating in a research vacuum.

Related questions that need addressing across a range of disciplines, levels, and institutions are:

- How can courses prepared for students of one culture and educational paradigm work successfully for students unfamiliar with the language and educational practices of another country?
- How can the support mechanisms developed by one institution be spread globally and still offer all students an equal education?
- How can online technologies produce the same quality of learning environment for students from a range of cultural backgrounds as that of the cherished campus experience?

In short, apart from the profound implications that global education is having on the evolution of the university, there is the more practical question of "Does it work?" Quality assurance, student support, and agreement about best practice on global courses are areas that need to be underpinned by research on the new phenomenon of global education.

Researching the future is not as easy as studying the past. Scare mongering and sales talk often substitute for careful analysis in this debate about the university in the global Information Age. Nevertheless, there are researchers who are tackling specific aspects of the problem. If it is an irresistible direction for universities, it is better that we understand it than that we merely decry it.

REFERENCES

Brown, J. S., & Duguid, P. (2000). *The social life of information.* Boston: Harvard Business School Press.

COP. (2000). Business models of distributed learning. An interim report to the council of presidents. Available at: http://www.standing-stones.com/e-cave/links_by_business_models.htm.

Cunningham, S., Tapsall, S., Ryan, Y., Stedman, L., Bagdon, K., & Flew, T. (1998). *New media and borderless education: A review of the convergence between global media networks and higher education provisions, 97/22.* Canberra: Department of Education, Training and Youth Affairs.

Cunningham, S., Ryan, Y., Stedman, L., Tapsall, S., Bagdon, K., Flew, T., & Coaldrake, P. (2000). *The business of borderless education.* Draft final report. Canberra: Department of Education, Training and Youth Affairs.

CVCP. (2000). *The business of borderless education: UK perspectives.* Available at: http://www.universitiesuk.ac.uk/bookshop/

Davis, S., & Botkin J. (1995). *The monster under the bed: How business is mastering the opportunity of knowledge for profit.* New York: Simon and Schuster.

Dirr, P. (1999). Distance and virtual learning in the United States. In G. Farrell (Ed.), *The development of virtual education: A global perspective.* Vancouver: Commonwealth of Learning.

Edwards, R. (1995). Different discourses, discourses of difference: Globalisation, distance education and open learning. *Distance Education, 16*(2), 241–255.

Edwards, R., & Usher, R. (2000). *Globalisation and pedagogy. Space, place and identity.* London: Routledge/Falmer.

Field, J. (1995). Globalisation, consumption and the learning business. *Distance Education, 16*(2), 270–283.

Gayol, Y., & Schied, F. (1997). *Cultural imperialism in the virtual classroom: Critical pedagogy in transnational distance education.* Presented at the 18th ICDE World Conference, *The new learning environment: A global perspective,* June 2–6, 1997, Pennsylvania State University, USA.

Goodfellow, R., Lea, M., Gonzalez, F., & Mason, R. (2001). Opportunity and e-quality: Intercultural and linguistic issues in global online education. *Distance Education, 22*(1), pp. 65–84.

Hallak, J. (2000). Guarding the common interest, education: The last frontier for profit. *The Unesco Courier,* November.

Luke, T. (1996). *The politics of cyberschooling at the virtual university.* Available at: http://www.edfac.unimelb.edu.au/virtu/luke.htm.

Macdonald, J., & Mason, R. (1998). Information handling skills and resource based learning. *Open Learning, 13*(1), 38–42.

Margolis, M. (1998). Brave new universities. *First Monday,* 3. Available at: http://www.131.193.153.231/issues/issue3_5/margolis/index.html.

Mason, R. (1998). *Globalising education. Trends and applications.* London: Routledge.

Weigel, V. (2000 Sept/Oct). E-learning and the tradeoff between richness and reach in higher education. *Change, 33*(5), 8–13.

51

Culture and Online Education

Charlotte N. Gunawardena
The University of New Mexico
lani@unm.edu

Penne L. Wilson
The University of New Mexico
plwilson@unm.edu

Ana C. Nolla
The University of New Mexico
ananolla@unm.edu

This chapter examines the significance of culture and its impact on communication and the teaching and learning process in online courses and programs. We begin with a definition of *culture* and explore theoretical constructs that explain cultural variability in behavior and communication. Then, we look at how culture influences perception, cognition, the teaching-learning process, and the diffusion of online education. We conclude with a discussion of research issues in cross-cultural studies and the implications for future online education research. We borrow significantly from research conducted in the field of cross-cultural psychology, intercultural communication, and the emerging body of research on intercultural computer-mediated communication (CMC). While our discussion has implications for distance education in general, we relate our discussion and examples to the emerging field of online education.

DEFINITION OF CULTURE

The meaning of *culture* is a complex and difficult concept to define in a formal sense, although many definitions of culture exist. According to Branch (1997), "Culture is regarded as the epistemology, philosophy, observed traditions, and patterns of action by individuals and human groups" (p. 38). More than this static definition, however, are the concepts that culture is constantly changing and that individuals belong to more than one culture, some voluntarily and some involuntarily. Not only is culture an abstract concept of self and group, "it also consists of a distinctive symbol system together with artifacts that capture and codify the important and common experiences of a group" (Wild, 1999, p. 198). Trompenaars and Hampden-Turner (1998) explained that the essence of culture is not what is visible on the surface, and Hall (1998) added that "culture hides much more than it reveals and, strangely enough, what it hides, it hides most effectively from its own participants" (p. 59). Hall (1998) distinguished between manifest culture (which is learned from words and numbers) and tacit-acquired culture (which is not verbal but is highly situational and operates according to rules that are not in awareness, not learned in the usual sense but acquired in the process of growing up or simply being in different environments). If culture is diverse, changing, and concrete as well as abstract, the implications for its potential impact on communication at a distance become increasingly complex.

For the purpose of this chapter, we would like to adopt the definition of culture put forward by Matsumoto (1996), who perceived culture as: "the set of attitudes, values, beliefs, and behaviors shared by a group of people, but different for each individual, communicated from one generation to the next" (p. 16). As Matsumoto notes, this definition suggests that culture is as much an individual, psychological construct as it is a social construct. "Individual differences in culture can be observed among people in the degree to which they adopt and engage in the attitudes, values, beliefs, and behaviors that, by consensus, constitute their culture" (Matsumoto, 1996, p. 18). As Rogers and Steinfatt (1999) observed, not only do nationalities and ethnic groups have cultures, but so do communities, organizations, and other systems. In the online environment, we are increasingly observing the emergence of networked learning communities, or "cybercommunities" bound by areas of interest, transcending time and space (Jones, 1995, 1997). These communities develop their own conventions for interaction and for what is acceptable and not acceptable behavior online (Baym, 1995).

We use the terms *intercultural communication* to refer to interaction between and among individuals from various cultural backgrounds and *cross-cultural studies* to refer to studies that compare cultural differences in communication phenomena.

THEORETICAL DIMENSIONS OF CULTURAL VARIABILITY

Researchers in the fields of cross-cultural psychology and intercultural communication agree that the major dimension of cultural variability that can be used to explain intercultural differences in behavior is individualism-collectivism (IC) (Gudykunst, 1994; Kagitcibasi, 1997; Matsumoto, 1996; Rogers & Steinfatt, 1999). This dimension has been used theoretically and empirically to explain and predict similarities and differences between cultures (Triandis, 1995; Triandis, McCusker, & Hui, 1990), and there is congruence in the conceptual understanding of IC across cross-cultural researchers around the world (Hui & Triandis, 1986). Other dimensions of cultural variability include power-distance, uncertainty avoidance, masculinity-femininity (Hofstede, 1980, 1984), contextualization (Hall, 1966), and language, an important aspect of cultural identification (Rogers & Steinfatt, 1999).

Individualism-Collectivism (IC)

Matsumoto (1996) noted that IC refers to the degree to which a culture encourages, fosters, and facilitates the needs, wishes, desires, and values of an autonomous and unique self over those of a group. In individualistic cultures, personal needs and goals take precedence over the needs of others. In a collectivist culture, individual needs are sacrificed to satisfy the group. While members of individualistic cultures see themselves as separate and autonomous individuals, members of collectivist cultures see themselves as fundamentally connected with others. According to a 1988 study examining IC on self-ingroup relationships by Triandis, Bontempo, Villareal, Asai, and Lucca, IC differences should vary in different social contexts. People act differently depending on whom they are interacting with and the situation in which the interaction is occurring. A person could have collectivistic tendencies at home and with close friends and individualistic tendencies with strangers or at work. While individuals can be quite collectivist in an individualistic culture, individuals in a collectivist culture can be quite individualistic (Rogers & Steinfatt, 1999).

In the cross-cultural study of self-ingroup relationships mentioned earlier, Triandis et al. (1988) suggested that cultural differences on IC differ in self-ingroup compared to self-outgroup relationships. Individualistic cultures tend to have more ingroups because individuals have more access to ingroups; however, members are not strongly attached to any single ingroup. Members therefore tend to drop out of groups that are too demanding, and their relationships within their groups are marked by a high level of independence or detachment. In collectivist cultures, depending on the effective functioning of the group, a member's commitment to an ingroup is greater. Collectivists keep stable relationships with their ingroups no matter what the cost and exhibit a high level of interdependence with members of their groups. It is important to examine this line of research further in the context of computer-mediated collaborative groups.

One of the well-known studies of IC was conducted by Hofstede (1980, 1984), who analyzed data from employees in an international corporation with sites in more than 50 countries. In addition to IC, Hofstede identified three other dimensions of cultural variability in his study. These dimensions were labeled "power-distance," "uncertainty avoidance," and "masculinity-femininity."

Power Distance

Power distance is the extent to which less powerful persons in a society accept inequality in power and consider it as normal. Power distance is described as either "high-power" distance in countries where individuals of higher status exert undue influence during group communication or "low-power" distance where the status differences among people are less significant and the communication process is more democratic. Matsumoto (1996) suggested a slightly modified version of power-distance called *status differentiation*, the degree to which cultures maintain status differences among their members.

Uncertainty Avoidance

Uncertainty avoidance refers to the value placed on risk and ambiguity in a culture. It is the extent to which the members of a society are made nervous by situations that they perceive as unstructured, unclear, or unpredictable—situations that they therefore try to avoid by maintaining strict codes of behavior and a belief in absolute rights. Countries with strong uncertainty avoidance will have less tolerance for ambiguous situations.

Masculinity-Femininity

Hofstede's dimension *masculinity-femininity* refers to the degree to which cultures foster traditional gender differences among their members. Countries that Hofstede (1986) labeled as masculine strive for maximal distinction between what men are expected to do and what women are expected to do. They expect men to be assertive, ambitious, and competitive and strive for material success, while women are expected to serve and to care for the nonmaterial quality of life, for children, and for the weak. Feminine cultures, on the other hand, define relatively overlapping social roles for the sexes. Feminine cultures stress quality of life, interpersonal relationships, and concern for the weak.

Confucian-Dynamism

In a later study, Hofstede and Bond (1988) identified a factor in Asian cultures that was not accounted for in the previously identified factors of individualism versus collectivism, power distance, uncertainty avoidance, and masculinity versus femininity. *Confucian dynamism*, later called *long-term orientation* by Hofstede (1991), identified individuals as having either a tendency toward future-oriented Confucian teachings—persistence, status-ordered relationships, thrift, and a sense of shame that was called High Confucian dynamism—or toward past- and present-oriented Confucian teachings—steadiness and stability, protection of face, respect for tradition, and reciprocation of greeting, favors, and gifts that was labeled Low Confucian dynamism.

Despite criticisms of Hofstede's dimensions (sample based on a single multinational organization, subjects predominantly middle-class males, neglect of subcultures within various countries, the results being dated as cultures are not static but change over time) and the danger of stereotyping individuals of a particular culture, Ross and Faulkner (1998) recognized that Hofstede's work has made a valuable contribution to intercultural understanding, "Providing insight into what culture is in and of itself" (p. 39). Hofstede's model is one of very few empirically supported frameworks that attempt to explain interpersonal phenomena and communication in terms of observed cross-cultural differences (Barret, Drummond, & Sahay 1996; Bochner & Hesketh, 1994; Cifuentes & Murphy, 2000; Fernandez, Carlson, Stepina, & Nicholson, 1997; Merritt, 2000). Ross and Faulkner (1998) hesitated to rely solely on dimensional information for understanding a particular culture. They believed that dimensional information serves as an excellent guide to approach understanding, but they cautioned against the danger of overgeneralizing or treating it as absolute. They advocated using Hofstede's dimensions with culture-specific approaches that will provide contextual understanding.

High-Context versus Low-Context Cultures

In addition to national differences, cultures can be differentiated along a dimension of contextualization (Hall, 1966, 1976). Hall distinguished between high-context and low-context cultures based on the amount of information that is implied versus stated directly in a communication message. High-context cultures depend upon the contextual clues delivered through indirect verbal messages in order to extrapolate meaning. Low-context cultures, on the other hand, obtain meaning from the information provided by the explicit code of the message itself. This difference in an individual's need for context is especially important when communicating via a text-based online environment. Those from low-context cultures like the United States will be able to obtain information from the code of the text itself while those from high-context societies like Mexico, Japan, or some Native American cultures will need the context to understand the message. Rogers and Steinfatt (1999) observed that in general, a low-context individual often becomes puzzled and frustrated when interacting with people from a high-context culture. Their messages seem incomplete and ambiguous. High-context individuals often hide their feelings to avoid hurting those with whom they might disagree.

TOWARD A MORE COMPREHENSIVE VIEW OF CULTURAL VARIABILITY

Kincaid (1987) showed the shortcomings of Western approaches to understanding cultural differences in communication processes. Miike (2000) pointed out that three important themes emerge that seem to be particularly helpful in establishing an Asian paradigm of communication theory: relationality, circularity, and harmony. The Western value of individuality marks a sharp contrast to the Eastern value of relationality. Interrelatedness and interdependence are much more explicitly recognized in Eastern cultures than they are in Western cultures. In Eastern cultures, the sense of self is more deeply rooted in the web of human relationships and people are highly influenced by their relationships with political systems, economic power, history, religious beliefs, and natural environments. Cicularity refers to transcendence in space and time. It provides a sense of relatedness of the present to the past and the future, and a sense of relatedness of life to the whole of nature. Human beings exist between their past ancestries and their future descendants. Citing Kim's work on Eastern and Western perspectives, Miike (2000) noted that in the East because the universe is seen as a harmonious entity, there is apparent lack of dualism in epistemological patterns. "Easterners" sense-making process and perceptual world are inherently based more on 'between-ness.' This intrapersonal feature may explain partly why, at least through Westerners' eyes, Easterners tend to communicate ambiguously and irrationally" (Miike, 2000, p. 4). Based on this epistemology, Miike (2000) presented three assumptions about communication: (a) communication takes place in "contexts" of various relationships, (b) the communicator is both active and passive in multiple contexts, and (c) mutual adaptation is of central importance as adaptation is the key to harmonious communication and relationships.

As we examine how cultural variability plays a role in international distance education, it is important to remember that "the variation within a culture in terms of situations, individuals, and socioeconomic status may account for as much or more of the variation in intercultural interpretations of messages as does the difference between the cultures of the individuals involved" (Rogers & Steinfatt, 1999, p. 96). In this regard it is worthwhile to consider the model developed by Shaw and Barrett-Power (1998), which provided a detailed and precise mapping of the elements that constitute cultural differences by stressing the importance of considering the impact of both apparent and less visible aspects of cultural differences. The model differentiates between two sources of cultural differences—readily detectable attributes and underlying attributes. Readily detectable attributes are those that can be easily recognized in a person such as age, gender, or national/ethnic origin. Underlying attributes are divided into two categories. The first category (Underlying Attributes I) represents cultural values, perspectives, attitudes, values and beliefs, and conflict resolution styles, which are closely correlated with readily detectable attributes. The second group of attributes (Underlying Attributes II) includes socioeconomic and personal status, education, functional specialization, human capital assets, past work experiences, and personal expectations. These attributes are less strongly connected to nationality/ethnic origin, age, or gender of individuals.

CULTURE AND COGNITIVE PROCESSES

Just as culture influences the way we receive information about the world around us, culture also influences the way we process that information (Matsumoto, 1996). Bruner's (1973) understanding of how culture interacts with human development and biology to define the human condition made a significant impact in the field of psychology, which to a large extent had ignored the influence of culture and the social context on the development of cognitive processes. Members of different cultures, because of the unique demands of living in specific contexts and societies, make sense of their experience in different ways. Bruner, Oliver, and Greenfield (1966) showed that Eskimo children do not exhibit the egocentrism that is a characteristic of American and European children because they depend upon group cooperation to hunt seal or fish in order to survive. Piaget proposed that egocentrism was a universal characteristic of all preoperational children (2–7 years), but his research was based on observations of mostly European and American children (Driscoll, 1994). As a further example, Driscoll (1994) cited a study conducted by Cole and Bruner in 1971, where the ability to make estimates of volume and distance was compared between nonliterate rice farmers from Central Africa and Yale University sophomores. Whereas the Yale students were superior in estimating distance, the rice farmers were more accurate in estimating how much rice was contained in different sized bowls. Cole and Bruner concluded that the results suggest a cultural influence on the manifestation of inherent competence. Inherently, there must be no difference between the two groups in their ability to make estimates, but the demands of their respective cultures have made it more likely for them to develop different manifestations of this ability.

Vygotsky (1962, 1978) believed that it is difficult to understand individual cognitive development without reference to the social and cultural context within which such development is embedded. He claimed that higher mental processes in the individual have their origin in social processes, and that mental processes can be understood only if we understand the tools and signs that mediate them. Because tools emerge and change as cultures develop and change, Vygotsky stressed the importance of historical and cultural perspectives in understanding human mental functions. One basic mental process is the manner in which we categorize or group things into categories. In his research with Dyirbal-speaking Aborigines in Australia, Lakoff (1987) showed how their categorization schemes are markedly different from typical Western thinking. The degree to which thinking is context-bound came to represent for Vygotsky an important indicator of intellectual development.

Perception

Chen and Starosta (1998) affirmed that a person's culture has a strong impact on the perception process and cited Bagby's 1957 research that described the influence of culture on perception. Culture not only provides the foundation for the meanings we give to our perceptions, it also directs us to specific kinds of messages and events. Cross-cultural research on visual perception has shown how culture influences perception. Much of this work is based on research conducted by Segall, Campbell, and Herokovits (1963, 1966), who tested differences in optical illusions.

Chen and Starosta (1998) further observed that perceived meanings of different colors also show the influence of culture. For example, white is a wedding color in the United States, but a funeral color in India where red is a wedding color. They also note that the influence of culture on perception is often reflected in the attributional process. Attribution means that we interpret the meaning of other's behaviors based on our past experience or history.

Thinking Patterns and Expression Styles

Thinking patterns refer to forms of reasoning and approaches to problem solution (Chen & Starosta, 1998). Thinking patterns differ from culture to culture. A logical, reasonable argument in one culture may be considered as illogical and undemonstrated in another culture. In a study that examined the impact of a global e-mail debate on intercultural communication, Chen (2000) noted that differences in thinking patterns and expression styles among participants may affect their perception and utilization of e-mail and intercultural sensitivity. In a debate that took place between American college students studying business and their counterparts in Denmark, France, Germany, Hong Kong, and Turkey, Chen observed that the debate format immediately caused orientation problems for some of the participants. The "debate" itself is a product of low-context culture that requires a direct expression of one's argument by using logical reasoning. American, Danish, and German students participating in the project did not show any difficulty in conducting the e-mail debate, while students in France, Hong Kong, and Turkey were confused by the format. The confusion led to two outcomes. First, students in France, Hong Kong, and Turkey resisted or were reluctant to conduct the communication. Second, when they were required to conduct the e-mail debate, they tried to match their American counterparts by abandoning their own expression styles. In order to improve the format problem in future global e-mail communication, Chen (2000) suggested that a format suitable for both high- and low-context cultures be designed. He suggested that a regular exchange of information regarding one or several course related topics could be used to replace the debate format. Students should be encouraged to freely share their ideas and opinions from their cultural perspective without being confined by rigid communication formats.

Kaplan's (1966) study explained the differences in thinking patterns reflected in five different language systems: English, Semitic, Oriental, Romance, and Russian, and Ishii (1985) pointed out the differences in thought patterns that exist between Americans and the Japanese. He cited a Japanese work by Shigehiko Toyama who contends that Anglo-Americans think in "line" while Japanese think in "dots." Along these same lines, Ishii suggested that the concepts of the American "bridge" and the Japanese "stepping stone" reflect the patterns of thought characteristic of each culture. Using the American "bridge" model, the speaker or writer organizes his or her ideas and tries to send them explicitly and directly, as if building a bridge from point I to point II. Using the Japanese "stepping stone" approach, the speaker or writer organizes his or her ideas and sends them implicitly and indirectly, as if arranging stepping stones from point I to point II. Sometimes the arrangement itself is not clear and the listener or reader must infer or surmise the intended meaning. Ishii observes that the distinction between these two rhetorical patterns may be supported by Hall's discussion of high-context and low-context cultures. The Japanese "stepping stone" pattern is an example of high-context communication while the "bridge" pattern is an example of low-context communication.

The differences in thinking patterns can lead to misunderstanding in intercultural communication, especially when that communication takes place in a computer-mediated context, which lacks the nonverbal cues of face-to-face communication.

Language

Language is a very important part of cultural identification (Rogers & Steinfatt, 1999). It represents a different way of thinking as well as a different way of speaking, and cognition is mediated and influenced by language (Gudykunst & Asante, 1989; Pincas, 2001). Matsumoto (1996) noted that culture influences the structure and functional use of language, and as such language can be thought of as the result or manifestation of culture. Language also influences and reinforces our cultural values and worldview. "The cyclical nature of the relationship between culture and language suggests that no complete understanding of culture can be obtained without understanding the language, and vice versa" (Matsumoto, 1996, p. 266).

The Sapir-Whorf hypothesis postulates that language shapes our thinking, beliefs, and attitudes. Whorf (1998) observed that the grammar of each language is not merely a reproducing instrument for voicing ideas but rather is itself the shaper of ideas, the program and guide for people's mental activity, for their analysis of impressions, for their synthesis of their mental stock in trade. The categories and types that we isolate from the world of phenomena are organized by our minds, and this means largely by the linguistic systems in our minds. Whorf noted that languages dissect nature and classify items of experience differently. The class corresponding to one word and one thought in one language may be regarded by another as two or more classes corresponding to two or more words and thoughts. As an example, he pointed out that the Eskimo language has three words for "snow" while the English language contains a single word.

Matsumoto (1996) demonstrated how one aspect of language, self-referents, exemplifies the cyclical relationship between language and culture. In American English we generally use one of two words, and their derivatives, to describe ourselves when talking to others—"I" and "we." In Japanese, what you call yourself and others is totally dependent on the relationship between you and the other person, and often it is dependent on the status differential between the two people. Matsumoto (1996) explained that, "by using the complex system of self—and other—referents in the Japanese language, a person's system of thought and behavior becomes structured over time to reflect the culture" (p. 270).

Nonverbal Communication

Verbal language is just one aspect of communication. Another large and important part of communication is nonverbal communication, including facial expressions, tone of voice, posture, dress, and so on. Just as spoken language differs from one culture to another, so does nonverbal behavior. Matsumoto (1996) noted that the problem in intercultural communication is that these nonverbal languages are silent. He further observed that there is a substantial base of cross-cultural research in the areas of gaze and visual attention, interpersonal space, and gestures, to inform us of how culture influences these aspects of the communication process.

CULTURE AND COMMUNICATION IN THE ONLINE ENVIRONMENT

Hall (1998) claimed that culture is communication. "The essence of any culture is primarily a system for creating, sending, storing, and processing information. Communication underlies everything" (p. 53). In the online context that communication takes place through a computer-mediated environment, by which people create, exchange, and perceive information using networked telecommunications systems that facilitate encoding, transmitting, and decoding messages. Online conferences or computer conferences use this medium either in a synchronous (real-time) or asynchronous (delayed-time) format. Three attributes of CMC, time-independence, text based communication, and computer-mediated interaction (Harasim, 1990), influence the way individuals communicate in groups. Each of these attributes has strengths and weaknesses that can detract from or add to the complexity of the communication.

Most computer conferences are based on asynchronous (not real-time) communication. Asynchronous group interaction increases opportunities for member input but communication anxiety, the feeling experienced when one's message is not answered or referenced (Feenberg, 1987), may be a concern, along with lack of immediate feedback, which makes it difficult to determine if the receiver has understood the message.

Text-based communication contributes to more reflective interaction (Harasim, 1990) and can free people from the bonds of physical appearance and enable communication at the level of ideas (Harasim, 1993). It incorporates the cognitive benefits of writing (Garrison, 2000). However, many of the nonverbal and contextual cues generally rich in relational information are absent in CMC. Harasim (1993) cited research that shows that the reduced cues in text-based messages make it difficult to resolve conflicts of ideology or interest. However, field research in CMC often reports more positive relational behavior and has indicated the development of "online communities" and warm friendships (Walther, 1992; Baym, 1995). Kollock and Smith (1999) noted that these online communities differ in important ways from face-to-face communities. The comparative anonymity provided by the text-based system has shown to create interpersonal distance that allows less vocal or introverted participants "space" and opportunity to contribute, resulting in an equalizing effect of participation (Hartman et al., 1995; Olaniran, 1994). A cross-cultural study we conducted on group development and group process (Gunawardena et al., 2001) found that the text-based system equalized status differences in a high-power distance society like Mexico. However, because of the premium on text-based communication, those who feel that they are not good writers or for whom the language of the conference is not their native language may feel disinclined to participate.

Computer-mediated communication is interactive and encourages involvement. While the online environment is particularly appropriate for collaborative learning approaches because it emphasizes group interaction, individuals who do not wish to interact in a group space or who have poor computer skills are less likely to participate.

Feenberg (1993) described his experience with silence in the Western world during an initial online course offered by the Western Behavioral Sciences Institute to students scattered between Caracas, Philadelphia, and San Francisco:

> One teacher offered elaborate presentations that resembled written lectures. While interesting, these had the undesirable effect of reducing the participants to silence. In a face-to-face classroom teachers can determine from subtle clues whether students' silence signifies fascination or day-dreaming. But silence on a computer network is unfathomable; it is intensely disturbing to address the electronic void. Hence the "communication anxiety" of conferencing participants, especially those with leadership roles. . . . Later we understood that it takes far more nerve to admit confusion and ask for clarification in a written medium than face-to-face. The lack of tacit cues such as raised eyebrows or puzzled looks proved fatal to this teaching style in the online environment. (p. 191)

When the teacher established a communication model, laid down explicit ground rules for discussion, posed problems and asked questions illustrated by examples, the students started talking. Without a reassuring communication model, participants are fearful of writing the wrong thing and withdraw into the perfect silence of a blank screen. Feenberg (1993) argued that most online groups need a familiar framework adapted to their culture and tasks, otherwise "they are repelled by what might be called contextual deprivation" (p. 194). Social rules and conventions of communication are vital to understanding the norms according to which we carry out conversations and judge others. For instance, cultural variations in the use of silence might well lie behind some lack of participation in online discussions. As Ishii and Bruneau (1994) pointed out the Japanese culture nurtures silence, reserve, and formality, whereas Western cultures place more value on speech, self-assertion, and informality. They conclude that whereas verbal communication plays a very important role in promoting intercultural as well as interpersonal understanding we should recognize that the ultimate goal-stage of communication—interpersonally or interculturally—may be communication through silence.

The learned conventions of turn-taking are universal but differ in detail from culture to culture, for example in the degree to which overlapping talk is tolerated. For the most part, the one-speaker-at-a-time structure predominates and people adjust their turn-taking patterns as they negotiate role relationships, power relationships, or institutionalized procedures. Deviant users are called "disruptive," "irrational," "undisciplined," or even "unintelligent." Comparative studies of non-native and native English conversational discourse have become a rich territory for exploration of how culturally specific assumptions and strategies vary in cross-cultural encounters (Driven and Putts, 1993). Cross-cultural pitfalls in greetings and leave-takings are well known but exist equally in all pragmatic acts such as requesting, apologizing, complimenting, approving, and so on. Neither the content nor the forms of speech acts can be straightforwardly transferred from one language to another. We see how cultural assumptions affect all aspects of interaction in any speech event, whether spoken or written.

In normal speech communities, conventions of use develop naturally over time. For efficiency in online education, they are best established by the course designers in advance and made an aspect of the study skills for online work. Van der Linde's (1997) guidelines to ensure effective communication in multicultural school situations can be adapted to the online learning environment. The primary guideline recommends that the participants acknowledge the various cultures within the environment and develop flexibility in communication. "During communication people must set aside all reservations if they are to understand the other party fully" (p. 10). Additional suggestions include: (1) using a facilitator, (2) avoiding ambiguity,

(3) communicating expectations, (4) providing feedback, (5) being sensitive to verbal (textual) nuances, and (6) building a relationship with the online community.

CULTURE AND THE DIFFUSION OF TECHNOLOGICAL INNOVATIONS

In his landmark study on the diffusion of innovations, Rogers (1995) argued that the adoption of technological innovations has failed because the diffusion process did not take into account the cultural beliefs of the local communities. "An important factor regarding the adoption rate of an innovation is its compatibility with the values, beliefs, and past experiences of individuals in the social system" (p. 4). This is an important point to keep in mind as educational institutions develop online courses that are offered in sociocultural contexts different from the one in which they were developed.

The educational culture that is transmitted can be very different from the educational culture that adopts the program and can become a dominating force. Whose ideas are being shared or incorporated into the local culture or frame of reference? How will this incorporation affect the local culture?

This implies the need to collaborate with local educational institutions or organizations when developing international online courses. Bates (2001) offered three models of international online distance education and observed that there are many benefits to be gained by working in partnership with institutions in different countries. Some of these benefits are cultural adaptation; assistance with student recruitment, tutoring, and assessment; local accreditation/qualification; and contributions to content and program design to ensure local relevance.

Rogers and Steinfatt (1999) discussed the consequences of the rapid growth of the Internet and the capability of U.S. businesses and media to export news and programs with images of U.S. culture throughout the globe. They note that developing nations see themselves as victims of a one-way flow of communication. They see these cultural influences as a continuation of the previous colonial system through a monopoly of information resources available only to wealthy nations. Nations of Latin America, Africa, and Asia wonder if this new communication technology will give them a voice or whether their disadvantaged communication situation will be worsened. According to Bates (2001):

> English (or perhaps more accurately American) is at the moment by far and away the most predominant language in terms of the international delivery of online education, although there is also a growing number of programs in Spanish being delivered across borders in Latin America. (p. 128)

Fairclough (1989) observed that language is no longer seen as a neutral instrument free of values or power relations. On the contrary, it is embedded with intentions of others. "International discourse communities are forming concepts (mostly in English) that represent and provide frameworks for the ideologies of different communities of practice" (Pincas, 2001, p. 41). There are clear disadvantages of working in another language in online courses when students have to contribute toward collaborative assignments or participate in discussion forums with those for whom English is the first language (Bates, 2001). Global universities are faced with the choice between continuing to expect all students to adjust to traditional English-Western academic values and uses of language or changing their processes to accommodate others, perhaps moving toward workplace and lifelong learning demands for education that are credit-worthy for experiential rather than academic reasons (Pincas, 2001).

In every cultural context, there will be issues that need to be dealt with when new ideas or ways of doing things are implemented. Bellman, Tindimubona, and Arias (1993) noted that despite strong interest in Africa for computer networking, there is a serious problem often referred to as "the last mile." This is a combination of national government policies that restrict transborder flows of information and local-level politics within and between institutions that restrict usage either by refusing access to the technology or by making access too difficult for easy use. In high-power distance societies it is often the case that access to technology filters down the power ladder and those who need it most such as students may have the least access to it.

Before implementing online educational projects in different cultural settings, needs assessments should be conducted to determine receptivity to distance learning modes via communications media. A study by Anakwe, Kessler, and Christensen (1999) examined the impact of cultural differences based on the concepts of individualism and collectivism on potential users' receptivity toward distance learning using a sample of 424 students enrolled in two northeastern universities. This study found that individualists' motives and communication patterns are in synch with distance learning as a medium of instruction or communication, whereas collectivists' motives and communication patterns shun any form of mediated instruction or communication. They noted that program developers should identify ways to alleviate the shortcomings collectivists face in any form of mediated communication network. Citing Nakakoji's 1993 work on cross-cultural considerations in designing human-computer interaction, Collis (1999) noted that cultures differ on willingness to accommodate new technologies, acceptance of trial-and-error in terms of computer use, differences in expectations for technical support, preferences for precision versus browsing, preferences for internal versus system/instructor control, and differences for tolerance of communication overlaps and interruptions.

CULTURE AND THE ONLINE TEACHING LEARNING PROCESS

Discussing his experience teaching international online courses, Bates (2001) pointed out cultural differences that influence the online teaching learning process. There is a tendency in "Western' " courses from the United States, Britain, Canada, and Australia to encourage critical thinking skills, debate, and discussion, where students' views are considered important and where the views of teachers can be legitimately challenged and student dissent is even encouraged. In other cultures there is a great respect shown by students for the teacher, and it is culturally alien to challenge the teacher or even express an opinion on a topic:

> In our online courses there appears to be major differences between ethnic groups in their willingness to participate in online forums, and these differences seem to be independent of skill in conversing in a foreign language. We reward through grades students who participate actively and work collaboratively through discussion forums, and this will seriously disadvantage students for whom this is an alien or difficult approach to take, even for those willing to work in this way. I therefore find myself wondering to what extent I should impose "Western" approaches to learning on students coming from other cultures, while acknowledging on the other hand that this "new" or different approach may have attracted them to the courses in the first place. (Bates, 2001, p. 129)

Drawing on the work of Henderson (1996) and Reeves (1992), Collis (1999) discusses factors that might differ among different cultures in interactive technology-based teaching and learning. For example: Pedagogical Philosophy (Instructivism versus Constructivism), Goal Orientation (Sharply focused versus Unfocused), Role of Instructor (Teacher Proof versus Equalitarian Facilitator), Value of Errors (Errorless Learning versus Learning from

Experience), Motivation (Extrinsic versus Intrinsic), Accommodation of Individual Differences (Nonexistent versus Multifaceted), Learner Control (Nonexistent versus Unrestricted), and Co-operative Learning (Unsupported versus Integral). While the distinctions may not always be bipolar as indicated in this example, they highlight the numerous factors where cultural variability might be observed in the teaching-learning process.

Cultural schemata can affect how students will behave in particular instructional situations (Driscoll, 1994). Driscoll cited an example of one of her doctoral students from Taiwan who found his schema for multiple-choice tests to be inappropriate for taking tests in the United States. He was accustomed to selecting more than one response on multiple-choice items and did not realize that in the United States only one answer would be considered correct. In discussing how the cultural context influences student learning, Nelson-Barber and Estrin (1995) showed that in "Native communities" children are usually expected to learn through observation and direct experience rather than from explicit verbal instruction. Concepts to be learned are seen as interconnected, and skills are learned in a meaningful context. This is a reflection of Pincas' (2001) explanation that classroom events have always been seen to match the educational schemata of the local community because of the interaction between the school environment and its surrounding culture.

CULTURE AND INSTRUCTIONAL DESIGN

According to McLoughlin (1999), "Culture and learning are interwoven and inseparable" (p. 232). Course designers must be aware of the diversity of the reachable group of learners and the diversity of culture-based learning styles that is possible within that group. Dunn and Griggs (1995) from their extensive research on learning styles concluded that each cultural group tends to have some learning style elements that distinguish it from other cultural groups. However, they point out that a consistent finding in research is that individuals within a family, classroom, or culture have unique learning style preferences that differ from those of their siblings, parents, peers, and cultural group. They stated that instructors need to be aware of three critical factors: (1) universal principles of learning do exist, (2) culture influences both the learning process and its outcomes, and (3) each individual has unique learning style preferences that affect his or her potential for achievement. Discussing learning styles research and supporting the culturally diverse distance learner, Sanchez and Gunawardena (1998) pointed out that when trying to accommodate a variety of learning styles in instructional design, it is best to design alternative activities to reach the same objective and give the students the option of selecting from these alternatives those which best meet their preferred learning style. They also stress the importance of providing a delicate balance of learning activities that provide opportunities to learn in preferred ways and activities that challenge the learner to learn in new or less preferred ways. "The variety of learners, cultures, and learning styles presents a challenge—and variety itself becomes the solution" (p. 61).

Because cultural influences on the teaching and learning process are complex, one must consider the cultures of all those involved in the process: course designers, teachers, and students. Initially, course designers and instructors should consider the culture from which they themselves come. Designers and instructors are not objective; each of them has his or her own view of the world and means of acting within it based on the multiple cultures within which each of them exists. They bring to the design and delivery task a set of values, attitudes, and societal norms that influence and determine the way in which instructional material is created and how it is evaluated. It is important to recognize that instructional approaches in a particular educational setting are "embedded in a cultural context of beliefs, expectations, and values. These do more than support the (instructional) techniques. They are a part of them"

(Jin & Cortazzi, 1998, p. 786). The artifact or instructional product the designer produces "embodies cultural influences such as the instructional designer's world view, their values, ideologies, culture, class and gender, and their commitment to a particular design paradigm" (Wild, 1999, p. 198).

In order to design culturally appropriate online courses, designers and instructors must first develop cultural sensitivity or awareness. Powell (1997b) defines this awareness as

> the ability to be sensitive to the existence and legitimacy of other cultures; understand and accept other cultures, and view cultural phenomena from the perspective of both the culture in which they occur and another culture usually (that of the viewer). (p. 6)

Reeves specifies that this sensitivity should include "attention to the values, orientations, learning styles, language factors, and traditions of learners from diverse cultural and ethnic backgrounds, as well as those with special educational needs" (1997, p. 27).

Once the designers and instructors have developed this sensitivity to cultural pluralism, they can then be disposed to preparing culturally sensitive technology-based instruction materials for culturally pluralistic learners that consider the following additional accumulated factors and variables as compiled from Powell (1997a, 1997b), Reeves (1997), Collis (1999), and McLouglin (1999):

- Setting and context
- Historical perspectives
- Ethical perspectives
- Values and attitudes
- Socioeconomic environment
- Social roles and relationships
- Task or relationships in social networks
- Diversity within groups
- Static or variable course construction
- Internal or external learner control expectation
- Levels of control for the individual student
- Variety of activities to address different learning styles
- Variety of opportunities for interaction
- Variety of evaluation methods

As McLoughlin (1999) has observed "culturally appropriate design clearly demands management of a complex set of interrelated factors" (p. 233).

When designing, we must attempt to understand that the instruction is being created for use in technology-based instructional formats. Chen, Mashhadi, Ang, and Harkrider (1999) stated, "Technology appears to make everything transparent, whilst, in fact it is conveying and shaping both private and public understanding" (p. 221). McLoughlin (1999) reminds us that the technology is itself a cultural amplifier that transforms the nature of human productivity. It can also quantitatively change the process of cognition and amplify the cultural dimensions of communication, task analysis, and problem solving (p. 232).

Chen et al. (1999), drawing from Stoney and Wild's 1998 study, pointed out that in designing culturally appropriate Web-based instruction,

> the interface designer must be aware how different cultures will respond to issues of the layout of the graphical interface, images, symbols, colour and sound, inferring that culture itself cannot be objectified unproblematically as just another factor to be programmed into a learning course. (p. 220)

Such apparently simple issues of layout and format become increasingly complex as the plurality of learners increases. Furthermore, "It should also be born in mind that although people invent technology, technology in turn shapes people" (Chen et al., 1999, p. 221).

In discussing her experience with the creation of WWW-based course support sites, Collis (1999) suggested guidelines that designers can use to accommodate culture-related differences. These guidelines suggest that when designing for a diverse audience, flexibility and variety are prime factors. Drawing from the work of Henderson, McLoughlin (1999) expands the idea by proposing a multiple cultures model of instructional design. This is characterized by a design paradigm, which endorses multiple cultural realities or zones of development. Essentially, this approach is a form of "eclectic paradigm," which entails designing learning resources that allow variability and flexibility while enabling students to learn through interaction with materials that reflect multiple cultural values and perspectives, include multiple ways of learning and teaching, and promote equity of learning outcomes by combining mainstream and nonmainstream cultural interests.

In drawing conclusions about two Web-based, project-based instructional courses involving diverse populations, Chen et al. (1999) suggested that social interactions among team members, teacher support, and school culture are important considerations. Therefore, in addition to flexibility, variety, and multiple cultural values and perspectives, designers and instructors must carefully consider the concept of interaction. Chen et al. proposed that social and cultural understanding need to be explicit and up front, before participants are able to build the online networks of trust upon which effective communication and learning is based. Furthermore, they state, "an effective learning environment involves more than the use of technology—culturally mediated social interaction and perseverance towards a shared vision is an essential part of the learning process" (p. 228).

It is also important to remember that simply providing an opportunity for interaction within the Web-based environment is not enough. "Productive interactions amongst learners depend upon a backlog of common experience and a mutual recognition that experience is indeed held in common" (Crook and Light, 1999, p. 192). These meaningful opportunities for interaction not only between a teacher and student but also among students often provide the motivation for students to complete a Web-based course (Witherow, Bromber, and Johnson, 2001).

Recognizing the importance of studying online group interaction and development from a cross-cultural perspective, Gunawardena et al. (2001) conducted a research study employing a mixed-model design to examine if there are differences in perception of online group process and development between participants in Mexico and the United States. Survey data indicated significant differences in perception for the norming and performing stages of group development. The groups differed in their perception of collectivism, low power distance, femininity, and high-context communication. Country differences, rather than age and gender differences, accounted for the differences observed. The differences between the Mexican and U.S. groups in how they viewed the relationship between teacher and students was reflective of Hofstede's (1986) findings on power distance. However, the results indicated that even in high-power distance countries like Mexico, the anonymity provided by the online environment may play a role in creating a more democratic learning environment. Focus group participants identified several factors that influence online group process and development: (1) language, (2) power distance, (3) gender differences, (4) collectivist versus individualist tendencies, (5) conflict, (6) social presence, (7) time frame, and (8) technical skills.

Pincas (2001) addressed several issues that international educators must consider as they plan global online courses. One important issue is how to contextualize their courses in such a way as to reduce misunderstanding. Furstenberg, Levet, English, and Maillet (2001), urged online teachers to try to make culturally hidden semantic networks explicit by structuring course discussions around enabling students to situate themselves in relation to others, to perceive similarities and differences in personal opinions and reactions within the group, and to start identifying the many and complex factors influencing their attitudes so that they may become aware of how the content and manner of what they say is relevant to their immediate situation and to a given context. Pincas (2001) noted that in most cases where students are working in an international context, they need to find a balance between adapting to different social and cultural interactions in English, while maintaining a secure sense of self as a member of their national culture. Learning is a crucial part of the process of developing a "professional self" and now has to occur in very new environments, which do not reflect the local culture in familiar ways. Pincas stressed that we are on very difficult terrain when we attempt to measure the values of our diverse students by our assessment methods. Performance criteria can be defined in terms of expected learning outcomes when these can be expressed as precise knowledge. But when outcomes are defined in terms of attitudes to learning, and cultures differ as to what is worth learning, the criteria may not be based on universal conceptual categories.

Goodfellow, Lea, Gonzalez, and Mason (2001), in their investigation into the ways that cultural and linguistic differences manifest themselves in the offering of a global online MA program, report four dimensions of difference between participants on the courses: "cultural otherness," "perceptions of globality," "linguistic difference," and "academic convention." Therefore, when developing international online courses it is important to be mindful of the cultural schemata learners may bring to the educational transaction and the expectations they may have of the teaching and learning process.

DESIGNING FOR CULTURAL DIFFERENCES IN ONLINE COURSES: A PROPOSED FRAMEWORK

In this section, we propose a design framework based on our review of the literature and our own research for incorporating cultural relevance into online courses. The framework consists of two parts: the first part describes the institutional context and variables associated with it, and the second part describes issues related to online course design.

In order to address the cultural diversity that is possible within the population of students participating in a global Web-based course, flexibility must be provided within the organization of the course and the interface that will deliver it. Figure 51.1 represents a dynamic educational system, which exists within a global context. Each of the elements—institution, instructor, individual, and group—brings to the course non-negotiable factors that exist within their cultures and negotiable factors that are presented as choices and options within the framework of the course. In a culturally relevant design the most important factors are dialogue and communication. Course design must accommodate dialogue for negotiation of course structure to take place.

The arrows in the diagram represent the dialog that must take place in order for negotiations to take place. The entire framework sits within an environmental context that is key to the design of the course.

Institution

Non-negotiables inherent in the culture of the institution are such factors as the timeline for completion of the course, the standards that must be met to earn a specific grade, the credit that will be issued for the course, and the cost of tuition (Collis, 1999). One of the indications of good course design is clarity of the expectations of the institution. Once the expectations have been defined and set, the non-negotiables may be clarified through dialog. It is also the responsibility of the institution to provide support for the development and delivery of the

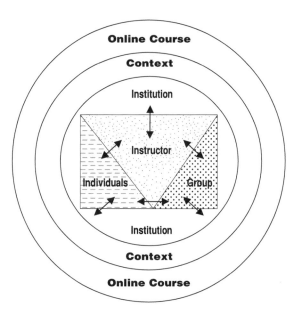

FIG. 51.1.   Negotiables and Non-negotiables in Designing for Cultural Differences.

course including equipment and facilities, support staff to develop the course, research and reference facilities, and monetary resources. The quantity and the quality of this second set of factors can be negotiated with the instructor responsible for delivery of the course and to a limited degree with the individuals and the groups participating in the course.

Instructor and Student

The instructor and the individual student bring to the course a set of non-negotiables inherent in their own cultures. These include language, beliefs, preferred methodologies and learning styles, knowledge and skill base, and attitudes about learning. Because of the global audience in a Web-based course, the course must provide choices and options for the students built around these non-negotiables in order to provide a flexible environment that will meet student needs (Collis, 1999). The interface of the course should allow students to select the colors, navigational patterns, and delivery medium for the course (Marcus & Gould, 2000). Icons used in the interface should be universally understandable like the colors of the stoplight: red for stop, green to go, and amber to slow down. The content of the course should provide student choices of learning through activities and assessments that are provided to meet the students' preferences. These choices can, however, be limited by the instructor in order to push students to expand their learning comfort zone and to successfully process information and acquire skills in a variety of formats (Chen et al., 1999).

Group

Within the course, groups will function to process information and complete activities. If we subscribe to the view that knowledge is socially constructed (Vygotsky, 1978), then group interaction becomes critically important and becomes part of the design. This interaction among students and between students and instructor will provide a forum for the social construction of knowledge and lend social presence to the course (Gunawardena, 1995). Choices of communication channels will provide students the opportunity to discuss information and complete

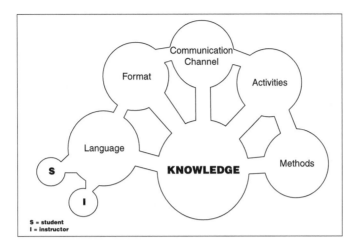

FIG. 51.2.   AMOEBA: Adaptive, Meaningful, Organic, Environmental-Based Architecture for Online Course Design.

projects in both asynchronous and synchronous timeframes. Individuals will negotiate the form and function of the group. In addition, the group, as well as individuals, can negotiate elements of the activities and assessment instruments with the instructor.

This process of negotiation, making choices, and limiting choices within the framework of the non-negotiables will provide a dynamic and flexible course, which can meet the needs of students from a global audience. In order to plan for this dynamic, culturally relevant online learning system, the developer will analyze the needs and characteristics of potential student participants.

Based on those needs and characteristics, the online designer and developer will offer a series of options for a particular instructional situation. In Fig. 51.2, we visualize these options in a flexible, open-ended learning environment that can be molded to the needs identified.

We chose an AMOEBA as the metaphor to describe our course design framework because it is a single-celled organism that can sense, categorize, and act, and can incorporate all life's functions within a multicompartmentalized single cell. It is mobile without a definite shape yet maintains its structure. Most importantly, it has the ability to adapt to its environment. The AMOEBA is adaptive to its environment; it is meaningful because it provides meaningful learning opportunities for students; it is organic because it is alive and can grow, change, and recycle; it is environment-based because it depends upon the environment for nutrition and support; and it is an architectural design built around interrelated component parts that fit together, change shapes, and split off as needed to allow the organism to respond to the environment.

The AMOEBA implies a constructivist and participatory approach toward instructional planning as well as comfort with change and the unexpected. The instructor and the students coexist and coparticipate within the framework of the AMOEBA. An instructor becomes a facilitator and a colearner with the students by involving them in curricular decisions and providing choices as described below:

- **Language Choice** should be provided based on the dominate language of the potential participants and as many other languages as resources will allow. (Wilson, Gunawardena, & Nolla, 2000)
- **Format Choices** will provide the participant choices of colors, icon sets, and organizational and navigational structures that are culturally appropriate and appealing. Marcus

and Gould (2000) point out that metaphors, mental models, navigation, interaction, or appearance of Web sites might confuse or even offend and alienate a user. These authors apply Hofstede's dimensions of culture to examine Web sites in terms of audience. Marcus and Gould (2000) suggest that high-power distance cultures might prefer to see a university Web site that features pictures of institution administrators, faculty members, an emphasis on the structure of the university, and a strong axial symmetry in the layout of information. On the other hand, participants from low-power distance countries will prefer a more asymmetric layout, photos of students of both genders, and site navigation that will give students more control including such features as an option to operate a WebCam to take a virtual tour of the university campus. Then again, higher power distance cultures might use the unique environment of the Web to present a more low-power distance appearance.

- **Communication Channels** choices will provide participants and/or the instructor with the opportunity to select synchronous or asynchronous communication channels. The choice of channels will determine the interactions that will occur among the participants and between the participants and the instructors. Synchronous channels will signal the use of such devices as chat rooms and instant messaging, while asynchronous channels will signal the use of devices like bulletin boards and computer-aided conferencing (Collis, 1999).

- **Activity Choices** will provide a variety of culturally appropriate learning activities and will include choice of group or individual work, research papers, portfolios, and projects, which are offered depending upon the course subject, the needs of the learner, and the parameters as established by the instructor (Collis, 1999).

- **Methods Choices** will provide role options for teachers and students such as students moderating discussions in the place of the instructors and giving one another feedback (Collis, 1999).

- **Knowledge Construction** will result from the completion of activities, using a selected set of methods, and from the interaction among the participants, which may include discussion, consensus building, and/or individual reflection. Thus, the AMOEBA will allow knowledge to be constructed through the interaction of its components.

Since the AMOEBA is presented as an adaptive, meaningful, organic, environmental-based architecture for culturally relevant course design, it has to be stressed that no choice is absolute and that students and instructors may change their options. As the instructor works with the participants, he/she will determine students' comfort zones and try to push them beyond these zones. Students can increase the kinds of activities they can successfully complete, using a variety of methods and, most importantly, build their abilities to work in different languages, formats, and communication channels, thus promoting the global construction of knowledge.

RESEARCH ISSUES AND RECOMMENDATIONS
FOR FUTURE RESEARCH

Our review of the literature has indicated little published research on the cultural aspects of online learning and teaching, a view borne out by some of the authors who have begun research in this area (Branch, 1997; Chen, 2000; Goodfellow et al., 2001; Wild, 1999). Many of the studies we reviewed provided guidelines for practice based on experience and intuition; there were few research-based studies. None of the existing research reached out to explore global perceptions about learning, and the most ambitious were limited to regional online courses. There was, however, a keen awareness of the increased complexity of conducting research on cultural issues in the online context. The conclusions calling for flexibility, variety, and consideration of multiple perspectives suggests that the problem, at this point in time, will only become more complex.

Our own experience conducting a collaborative cross-cultural research study with a group of colleagues in Mexico using a mixed-model design to examine group process and development online (Gunawardena et al., 2001) taught us a great deal about the research process, the value of quantitative versus qualitative methods for studying phenomena related to culture, and the challenges of conducting reliable and valid cross-cultural research studies. Reflecting on our research process, we feel that the greatest challenge to conducting cross-cultural research is finding equivalent samples for comparison in quantitative studies. This problem is echoed by Vijver and Leung (1997) who noted that "Cross-cultural studies often involve highly dissimilar groups. Consequently, groups can differ in many background characteristics, only some of which are relevant to the topic studied" (p. 32). Further, individual differences in cultural groups need to be accounted for so that we do not subscribe to the fallacy of homogeneity (that terms such as "American" connote internal sameness) or the fallacy of monolithic identity (the assumption that individuals in groups have no differential identities) (Stanfield II, 1993). Therefore we recommend that future researchers use a more comprehensive model for comparison such as the one developed by Shaw and Barrett-Power (1998) to understand cultural differences. We only used one aspect of this model in our study and realize the limitation of our selection. Future researchers need to conceptualize identity issues in cross-cultural studies to go beyond simplistic stereotyping and use qualitative methods to understand how people define themselves.

We felt we were able to design the study and interpret the results better because we collaborated with a team of researchers from the two countries and would like to recommend this approach to future researchers. Although the instruments were simultaneously developed by the group of researchers, with the first version developed in English and translated into Spanish and refined, the data indicated minor errors in translation. Another challenge we encountered was construct equivalence, for example the construct "conflict" was perceived differently in the two national contexts. The use of a mixed-method approach employing both quantitative and qualitative data helped us to avoid some of the pitfalls in interpretation of this construct.

Bhawuk and Triandis (1996) provided a review and critique of methodology for studying culture, a good starting point for the beginning researcher. They noted that emics and etics are perhaps the two most crucial constructs in the study of culture because they emphasize two perspectives. Emics focus on "the native's point of view"; etics focus on the cross-cultural scientist's point of view. They also represent the culture-specific and culture-general elements of cultures. The emic approach is predominantly followed by anthropologists who believe that each culture has unique ideas, behaviors, and concepts, and that its uniqueness must be the focus of their study. The etic approach is mainly followed by cross-cultural scientists (both anthropologists and psychologists) who believe that cultures have both specific and universal dimensions and are interested in observing these universals. Bhawuk and Triandis note that similarities between cultures must be established before their differences can be studied, because if a framework of universal constructs is not observed, it is impossible to distinguish a cultural difference from a misperception of the methods. A related methodological issue in the study of cultures is the level of analysis. For example, correlations obtained from individual-level data may not always replicate correlations obtained when cultures or nations are used as the units of observation.

Bhawuk and Triandis (1996) advocated subjective cultural studies, which maximize the advantages of both emic and etic approaches and the use of many methods that converge. They noted that each culture is likely to have its own way of reacting to each method (each method has a unique meaning in each culture), and therefore, a multimethod approach is preferable. They point out the difficulty of conducting experiments in cross-cultural settings as well as the difficulty of using tests such as ability, personality, and attitude tests, because a test usually measures one or, at most, a few variables out of context. They recommend that cross-cultural studies be undertaken by teams of researchers, representing the various cultures being studied. The research strategy should be determined jointly. Then, each investigator should check the cultural appropriateness of the methods in his or her culture, and adjustments in procedure should be made to make all materials culturally appropriate. Gradually, cross-cultural researchers are recognizing the value of interpretive and critical approaches to the study of cultural phenomena over logical empiricist approaches (Martin & Nakayama, 1999).

As the Internet spreads and institutions begin to offer international courses, studies examining cultural issues in the online learning environment will become increasingly important. We would like to encourage researchers to take up the challenge of conducting sound theoretical research studies examining cultural issues in the online environment to guide our future practice.

REFERENCES

Anakwe, U. P., Kessler, E. H., & Christensen, E. W. (1999, July). Distance learning and cultural diversity: Potential users' perspective. *The International Journal of Organizational Analysis, 7*(3), 224–243.

Barret, M., Drummond, A., & Sahay, S. (1996). Exploring the impact of cross-cultural differences in international software teams: Indian expatriates in Jamaica. In J. D. Coelho, W. Conig, H. Bremar, R. O'Callahan, & M. Saaksjarvi (Eds.), Lisbon, portugal. *Proceedings of the 4th European Conference on Information Systems* (ECIS). 347–356.

Bates, T. (2001). International distance education: Cultural and ethical issues. *Distance Education, 22*(1), 122–136.

Baym, N. K. (1995). The emergence of community in computer-mediated communication. In S. G. Jones (Ed.), *Cybersociety* (pp. 138–163). Thousand Oaks, CA: Sage.

Bellman, B., Tindimubona, A., & Arias, A. Jr. (1993). Technology transfer in global networking: Capacity building in Africa and Latin America. In L. M. Harasim (Ed.), *Global networks: Computers and international communication* (pp. 237–254). Cambridge, MA: The MIT Press.

Bhawuk, D. P. S., & Triandis, H. C. (1996). The role of culture theory in the study of culture and intercultural training. In D. Landis and R. S. Bhagat (Eds.), *Handbook of intercultural training* (2nd. ed.) (pp. 17–34). Thousand Oaks, CA: Sage.

Bochner, S., & Hesketh, B. (1994). Power distance, individualism/collectivism, and job-related attitudes in a culturally diverse group. *Journal of Cross-Cultural Psychology, 25*(2), 233–258.

Branch, R. M. (1997, March-April). Educational technology frameworks that facilitate culturally pluralistic instruction. *Educational Technology*, 38–40.

Bruner, J. S. (1973). *The relevance of education.* New York: Norton.

Bruner, J. S., Oliver, R. R., & Greenfield, P. M. (1966). *Studies in cognitive growth.* New York: Wiley.

Chen, A-Y., Mashhadi, A., Ang, D., & Harkrider, N. (1999). Cultural issues in the design of technology-enhanced learning systems. *British Journal of Educational Technology, 30*, 217–230.

Chen, G. M. (2000). Global Communication via Internet: An Educational Application. In G. M. Chen and W. J. Starosta (Eds.), *Communication and global society* (pp. 143–157). New York: Peter Lang Publishing.

Chen, G. M., & Starosta, W. J. (1998). *Foundations of intercultural communication.* Boston, MA: Allyn and Bacon.

Cifuentes, L., & Murphy, K. L. (2000). Images of Texan and Mexican cultures shared in a telecommunications partnership. *Distance Education, 21*(2), 300–322.

Collis, B. (1999). Designing for differences: Cultural issues in the design of the WWW-based course-support sites. *British Journal of Educational Technology, 30*(3), 201–215.

Crook, C., & Light, P. (1999). Information technology and the culture of student learning. In J. Bliss, R. Saljo, and P. Light (Eds.), *Learning sites: Social and technological resources for learning.* New York: Pergamon. Chapter 14, 183–193.

Driscoll, M. P. (1994). *Psychology of learning for instruction.* Boston: Allyn and Bacon.

Driven, R., & Putz, M. (1993). Intercultural-communication. *Language Teaching, 26*, 144–156.

Dunn, R., & Griggs, S. A. (1995). *Multiculturalism and learning style: Teaching and counseling adolescents.* Westport, CT: Praeger.

Fairclough, N. (1989). *Language and power.* London: Longman.

Feenberg, A. (1987). Computer conferencing and the humanities. *Instructional Science, 16*(2), 169–186.

Feenberg, A. (1993). Building a global network: The WBSI Experience. In L. M. Harasim (Ed.), *Global networks: Computers and international communication* (pp. 185–197). Cambridge, MA: The MIT Press.

Fernandez, D., Carlson, D., Stepina, L., & Nicholson, J. (1997). Hofstede's country Classification 25 years later. *The Journal of Social Psychology, 137*(1), 43–54.

Furstenberg, G., Levet, S., English, K., & Maillet, K. (2001). Giving a virtual voice to the silent language of culture: The cultura project. *Language Learning & Technology, 5*(1), 55–102.

Garrison, R. (2000). Theoretical challenges for distance education in the 21st century: A shift from structural to transactional issues. *International Review of Research in Open and Distance Learning, 1*(1). http://www.icaap.org/iuicode? 149.1.1.2.

Goodfellow, R., Lea, M., Gonzalez, F., & Mason, R. (2001). Opportunity and E-quality: Intercultural and linguistic issues in global online learning. *Distance Education, 22*(1), 65–84.

Gudykunst, W., & Asante, M. (1989). *Handbook of International and Intercultural Communication.* Newbury Park, CA: Sage Publications.

Gudykunst, W. B. (1994). *Bridging differences: Effective intergroup communication* (2nd. ed.). Thousand Oaks, CA: Sage.

Gunawardena, C. N. (1995). Social presence theory and implications for interaction and collaborative learning in computer conferences. *International Journal of Educational Telecommunications, 1*(2/3), 147–166.

Gunawardena, C. N., Nolla, A. C., Wilson, P. L., López-Islas, J. R., Ramírez-Angel, N., & Megchun-Alpízar, R. M. (2001). A cross-cultural study of group process and development in online conferences. *Distance Education, 22* (1), 122–136.

Hall, E. T. (1966). *The hidden dimension.* Garden City, NY: Doubleday.

Hall, E. T. (1976). *Beyond culture.* Garden City, NY: Doubleday.

Hall, E. T. (1998). The power of hidden differences. In M. J. Bennett (Ed.), *Basic concepts of intercultural communication: Selected readings* (pp. 53–67). Yarmouth, ME: Intercultural Press.

Harasim, L. M. (1993). Networlds: Networks as social space. In L. M. Harasim (Ed.), *Global networks: Computers and international communication* (pp. 15–34). Cambridge, MA: The MIT Press.

Harasim, L. (1990). Online education: An environment for collaborations and intellectual application. In L. M. Harasim (Ed.), *On line education: Perspectives on a new environment.* New York: Praeger.

Hartman, K., Neuwirth, C. M., Kiesler, S., Sproull, L., Cochran, C., Palmquist, M., & Zubrow, D. (1995). Patterns of social interaction and learning to write: Some effects of network technologies. In M. Collins and Z. Berge (Eds.), *Computer mediated communication and the online classroom: Volume II* (pp. 47–78). Cresskill, NJ: Hampton Press.

Henderson, L. (1996). Instructional design of interactive multimedia: A cultural critique. *Education Technology Research and Development, 44*(4), 85–104.

Hofstede, G. (1980). *Culture's consequences: International differences in work-related values.* Beverly Hills, CA: Sage Publications.

Hofstede, G. (1984). Cultural dimensions in management in planning. *Asia Pacific Journal of Management, 1*(2), 81–99.

Hofstede, G. (1986). Cultural differences in teaching and learning. *International Journal of Intercultural Relations, 10*, 301–320.

Hofstede, G. (1991). *Cultures and organizations: Software of the mind.* London: McGraw-Hill.

Hofstede, G., & Bond, M. H. (1988). Confucius and economic growth: New trends in culture's consequences. *Organizational Dynamics, 16*(4), 4–21.

Hui, C. H., & Triandis, H. C. (1986). Individualism-collectivism: A study of cross cultural researchers. *Journal of Cross-Cultural Psychology, 17*, 225–248.

Ishii, S. (1985). Thought patterns as modes of rhetoric: The United States and Japan. In L. A. Samovar and R. E. Porter (Eds.), *Intercultural communication: A reader* (4th ed.) (pp. 97–102). Belmont, CA: Wadsworth.

Ishii, S., & Bruneau, T. (1994). Silence and silences in cross-cultural perspective: Japan and the United States. In L. A. Samovar and R. E. Porter (Eds.), *Intercultural communication: A reader* (7th ed.) (pp. 246–251). Belmont, CA: Wadsworth.

Jin, L., & Cortazzi, M. (1998). Dimensions of Dialogue: Large classes in China. *International Journal of Educational Research, 29*, 739–761.

Jones, S. G. (1995). *Cybersociety: Computer-Mediated communication and community.* Thousand Oaks, CA: Sage.

Jones, S. G. (Ed.). (1997). *Virtual culture: Identity and communication in cybersociety.* London: Sage.

Kagitcibasi, C. (1997). Individualism and collectivism. In J. W. Berry, M. H. Segall, and C. Kagitcibasi (Eds.), *Handbook of cross-cultural psychology (vol 3): Social behavior and applications* (2nd. ed.) (pp. 2–49). Needham Heights, MA: Allyn and Bacon.

Kaplan, R. B. (1966). Cultural thought pattern in inter-cultural education. *Language Learning, 16*, 1–20.

Kincaid, D. L. (1987). Communication east and west: Points of departure. In D. L. Kincaid (Ed.), *Communication theory: Eastern and western perspectives* (pp. 331–340). San Diego, CA: Academic Press.

Kollock, P., & Smith, A. (Eds.). (1999). *Communities in cyberspace*. New York: Routledge

Lakoff, G. (1987). *Women, fire and dangerous things: What categories reveal about the mind*. Chicago, IL: University of Chicago Press.

Marcus, A., & Gould, E. W. (2000). *Cultural dimensions and global web user-interface design: What? So what? Now what?* Available online at: http://www.tri.sbc/hfweb/marcus/hfweb00_marcus.html.

Martin, J. N., & Nakayama, T. K. (1999). Thinking dialectically about culture and communication. *Communication Theory, 1*, 1–25.

Matsumoto, D. (1996). *Culture and psychology*. Pacific Grove, CA: Brooks/Cole Publishing Company.

McLoughlin, C. (1999). Culturally responsive technology use: Developing an on-line community of learners. *British Journal of Educational Technology, 30*, 231–243.

Merritt, A. (2000). Culture in the cockpit: Do Hofstede's dimensions replicate? *Journal of Cross-Cultural Psychology, 31*(3), pp. 283–301.

Miike, Y. (2000, August). *Toward an Asian standpoint of communication theory: Some initial assumptions*. Paper presented at the Pacific and Asian Communication Association Convention, "Waves of Change: The Future of Scholarship in Communication and Culture," Honolulu, HI.

Nakakoji, K. (1993). Cross-cultural considerations in designing human-computer interaction. *American Programmer, 6*(10), 18–24.

Nelson-Barber, S., & Estrin, E. T. (1995). Bringing Native American perspectives to mathematics and science teaching. *Theory Into Practice, 34*(3), 174–185.

Olaniran, B. A. (1994, February). Group performance in computer-mediated and face-to-face communication media. *Management and Communication Quarterly, 7*(3), 256–281.

Pincas, A. (2001). Culture, cognition and communication in global education. *Distance Education, 22*, 1.

Powell, G. C. (1997a, March-April). Diversity and educational technology: Introduction to special issue. *Educational Technology*, 5.

Powell, G. C. (1997b, March-April). On being culturally sensitive instructional designer and educator. *Educational Technology*, 6–14.

Reeves, T. (1992). Effective dimensions of interactive learning systems. *Proceedings of the Information Technology for Training and Education Conference (ITTE'92)*. Brisbane, Australia: University of Queensland.

Reeves, T. C. (1997, March-April). An evaluator looks at cultural diversity. *Educational Technology*, 27–31.

Rogers, E. M. (1995). *Diffusion of innovations* (4th ed.). New York: The Free Press.

Rogers, E. M., & Steinfatt, T. M. (1999). *Intercultural communication*. Prospect Heights, IL: Waveland Press.

Ross, R., & Faulkner, S. (1998). Hofstede's dimensions: An examination and critical analyis. In K. S. Sitaram and M. Prosser (Eds.), *Civic discourse: Multiculturalism, cultural diversity, and global communication* (pp. 31–40). Stanford, CT: Ablex Publishing Co.

Sanchez, I., & Gunawardena, C. N. (1998). Understanding and supporting the culturally diverse distance learner. In C. Campbell Gibson (Ed.), *Distance learners in higher education: Institutional responses for quality outcomes* (pp. 47–64). Madison, WI: Atwood Publishing.

Segall, M. H., Campbell, D. T., & Herokovits, J. (1963). Cultural differences in the perception of geometric illusions. *Sciences, 193*, 769–771.

Segall, M. H., Campbell, D. T., & Herokovits, J. (1966). *The influence of culture on visual perception*. Indianapolis, IN: Bobbs-Merrill.

Shaw, J. B., & Barrett-Power, E. (1998). The effects of diversity on small work group process and performance. *Human Relations. 5*(10), 1307–1325.

Stanfield II, J. H. (1993). Epistemological considerations. In J. H. Stanfield II and R. M. Dennis (Eds.), *Race and ethnicity in research methods* (pp. 16–36). Newbury Park, CA: Sage.

Stoney, S., & Wild, M. (1998). Motivation and interface design: Maximising learning opportunities. *Journal of Computer-Assisted Learning, 14*, 40–50.

Triandis, H. C. (1995). *Individualism and collectivism: New directions in social psychology*. Boulder, CO: Westview Press.

Triandis, H. C., Bontempo, R., Villareal, M. J., Asai, M., & Lucca, N. (1988). Individualism and collectivism: Cross-cultural perspectives on self-ingroup relationships. *Journal of Personality and Social Psychology, 4*, 323–338.

Triandis, H. C., McCusker, C., & Hui, C. H. (1990). Multimethod probes of individualism and collectivism. *Journal of Personality and Social Psychology, 59*, 1006–1020.

Trompenaars, F., & Hampden-Turner, C. (1998). *Riding the waves of culture: Understanding diversity in global business* (2nd ed.). New York: McGraw-Hill.

Van der Linde, C. H. (1997, Winter). Intercultural Communications within multicultural schools: Educational Management insights. *Education, 118*(2), 191–206.

Vijver, F. v.d., & Leung, K. (1997). *Methods and data analysis for cross-cultural research*. Thousand Oaks, CA: Sage.

Vygotsky, L. S. (1962). *Thought and language*. Cambridge, MA: The MIT Press.

Vygotsky, L. S. (1978). *Mind in society*. Cambridge, MA: The MIT Press.

Walther, J. B. (1992). Interpersonal effects in computer-mediated interaction: A relational perspective. *Communication Research, 19*(1), 52–90.

Whorf, B. L. (1998). Science and linguistics. In M. J. Bennett (Ed.), *Basic concepts of intercultural communication: Selected Readings* (pp. 85–95). Yarmouth, ME: Intercultural Press.

Wild, M. (1999). Editorial. *British Journal of Educational Technology, 30*(3), 195–199.

Wilson, P. L., Gunawardena, C. N., & Nolla, A. C. (2000). Cultural factors influencing on-line interaction and group dynamics. In *Proceedings of the 16th Annual Conference on Distance Teaching and Learning* (pp. 449–456). Madison, WI: University of Wisconsin System.

Witherow, J., Bromber, R., & Johnson, J. (2001, April). *Effective interaction online.* Paper presented at *Education odyssey: 2001*, 12th Annual TELECOOP Distance Learning Conference, Colorado Springs, CO.

52

Globalization and the Reinvention of Distance Education

Terry Evans
Deakin University, Australia
tevans@deakin.edu.au

Daryl Nation
Monash University, Australia
Daryl.Nation@celts.monash.edu.au

Human behavior can be genuinely purposive because only human beings guide their behavior by a knowledge of what happened before they were born and a preconception of what may happen after they are dead; thus only human beings find their way by a light that illumines more than the patch of ground they stand on.

—P. B. and J. S. Medawar, *The Life Science* (1977) quoted in Boorstin (1984, p. 557)

INTRODUCTION

The growth of the Internet has presented institutions and practitioners with a dilemma. On the one hand the capacities of the Internet to provide a powerful array of interactive means for enhancing distance education are a boon. On the other hand, these capacities have been espoused by all educational providers and viewed just as positively to the extent that nowadays no self-respecting university, at least in the developed world, is without a Web presence and online education. Therefore, distance education institutions now find that their boon is also producing a new wave of competitors using forms of quasi distance education.

The resolution of the dilemma rests on rethinking the theory and practice of distance education in relation to the resurgence of constructivist theory and the development of Internet-based educational technologies. Matters such as interaction and dialog, which have had an important place in the theory and practice of distance education, need to be reconsidered and reformulated in this light. Good distance educational design has not only recognized the importance of interaction, but also the importance of students' contexts in influencing their learning. These matters need to be reconsidered in the light of the virtual world that surrounds students' real-world experiences. Active engagement with the resources and facilities of the Web needs to be part of "new distance education." The Web is not just a means to deliver distance education; it also has important influences in other aspects of students' lives. The globalizing potential and consequences of the new distance education need to be understood and recognized within the emerging theory and practice in the field.

Distance education has a rich history of theory and practice. It is important that this history is built upon to formulate a new phase of distance education in a way that incorporates the appropriate strengths and values of the past into a new form of multimedia education at a distance.

THE EMERGENCE OF DISTANCE EDUCATION

Distance education emerged as a descriptor for those forms of institutional education occurring outside the classroom and beyond the campus in the 1960s. By the 1970s, it had achieved broad acceptance and in the 1980s it "arrived" as one of the "flavors of the decade" in education, in higher education especially. International confirmation of this new terminology and status occurred at Vancouver 1982 with the official change of the name of the global peak body from the International Council for Correspondence Education (ICCE) to the International Council of Distance Education (ICDE) (Evans & Nation, 1989c, pp. 7–8; Moore, 1990, p. xiv).

In Australia, the new term was given substance in 1980 with the establishment of the journal *Distance Education* by the Australian and South Pacific External Studies Association (ASPESA). The deliberate intention was to create an international journal "emphasizing research on distance education" (Keegan & Mitchell, 1980, p. vi). There had been other journals and newsletters addressed to members of the field; however, to a large extent, these contained news of activities and events, reports on policy and practice, and professional debates rather than research and scholarship. There had also been reports on research and theoretical discussions but these were on the margins. Notable examples were the *I.C.C.E. Newsletter*, which commenced in 1970; *epistolodidaktika*, sponsored by the European Home Study Council; the *Australian and South Pacific External Studies Association Newsletter*, started in 1974; and *Teaching at a Distance*, produced by the Open University of the United Kingdom (OUUK), which also began in 1974.

While there has been a substantial and sustained development of research in distance education since the early 1980s, this was built upon earlier pioneering efforts of considerable substance and diversity—much of which had been published in Europe, in languages other than English, in the 1960s and 1970s. Börje Holmberg's (1977, 1981, 1985) work has been recognized as the one of the important single contributions in this regard, and it remains of immense significance particularly because he devoted considerable effort to systematic bibliography. Holmberg's work is distinguished by his attention to the relationships between policy, practice, research, and theory.

Charles Wedemeyer's (1981) magisterial *Learning at the Back Door* synthesized a wide range of research and theory in relation to his extensive experience in pioneering the application of educational technologies in the University Extension programs at the University of Wisconsin from the early 1960s (1981, pp. xiii–xvii; Moore, 1990, pp. xv–xvi). This book demonstrated the powerful effects of a critically reflective approach to practice and remains as an object lesson to practitioners and researchers to this day.

During the heyday of the ICDE in the 1980s there was much research and scholarship proceeding in the tradition pioneered by Holmberg and Wedemeyer. The collection *Distance Education: International Perspectives*, edited by David Sewart, Desmond Keegan, and Holmberg (1983), which drew together work from Australia, Europe, and North America, endeavored to set the agenda for further work through judicious sections from the mentors and their acolytes. The rhetoric of its preface offers a paradigm case of the "spirit of the age," which was manifested similarly in many other contexts:

> Distance education, for long the Cinderella of the educational spectrum, emerged in the early 1970s and early 1980s as a valued component of many national educational systems in both developed and developing countries. The foundation of the Open Universities, developments in communications technology and in audio-, video- and computer-based learning, a new sophistication in the design of print-based materials and better support systems for the student learning at a distance, have all contributed to the availability and quality of distance education programs. (1983, p. ix)

In a similar vein, ASPESA sponsored the publication of *Diversity Down Under: In Distance Education*, which offered South Pacific perspectives on developments in policy and practice and contained some attempts to relate these to relevant scholarship and research (Smith, 1984). The First American Symposium on Research in Distance Education held in 1988 at Pennsylvania State University also proceeded in this tradition. It attempted to give some coherence to policy, practice research, and scholarship in the field in North America and spawned *Contemporary Issues in American Distance Education* (Moore with Cookson, Donaldson, & Quigley, 1990).

We do not intend to deal extensively with definitional debates and disputes. However, we do recognize that such disputes exist and that they are integral to policy, practice, research, and theory in the fields central to our theme: distance education and educational technology. Indeed, as we write the practical reminders are chronic and important. In 1999, Monash University's Distance Education Centre was merged into a new Centre for Learning and Teaching Support as part of a new teaching and learning plan that centered on flexible learning as it overarching concept. As Monash entered 2001 distance education disappeared as a mode of enrollment/study to be replaced by off-campus distributed learning. At Deakin University in 2000 discussions and deliberations led the university to propose the establishment of an e-campus as the focus for all its online activities and services. The e-campus is to be a "place" that all students and staff visit as part of their online university life, and it will be the home campus for all those students who are currently designated as off campus. Both Deakin and Monash are, in one sense, dispensing with distance education and, in another, making it even more integral to their organizations.

Doug Shale's (1990) contribution to the First American Symposium canvassed issues related to the reconceptualization of distance education and came to the conclusion that it was useful to retain a relaxed view of the boundaries pertaining to the morphology of distance education and a stricter view of the educational processes inherent in the field. The emphasis must be placed on the social transactions that are inherent in the teaching and learning processes, with a keen and pragmatic eye on the effects of technological changes on institutionalized education. We maintain the "relaxed attitude to nomenclature"; expressed in 1989 and reaffirmed in 2000 (Evans & Nation, 1989b, p. 37; 2000, pp. 160–164). In doing so, we invoke the spirit of Wedemeyer (1981) to remind us of the usefulness of a perspective developed from nontraditional learning and, even more importantly, to deal with the practical and policy problems of the field on the bases of broad-ranging theories and evidence from research. In this regard, we have found it useful to make educational technology central to own work.

THE IMPACT OF EDUCATIONAL TECHNOLOGY

Educational technology was at the center of the renaissance that elevated *distance education* the status of master concept in the 1970s. This recognition was manifested significantly by the decision of the British Open University to create a major division and name it the Institute of Educational Technology (IET). The IET was founded as an academic unit charged with responsibility for devising and maintaining, in concert with academic colleagues in its faculties, a system of teaching and learning that eschewed the classroom as the main context for these activities and was centered on teaching materials. In its operation the system was supported by tutors whose main engagement with their students was through written assignments and occasional face-to-face sessions (Evans & 1993b, 1989a, pp. 237–245, 1989c pp. 6–7, 1993a, pp. 7–10, 1993c. 196–214).

Our involvement in distance education as practitioners stretches back to the early 1970s and this experience convinced us to develop research and theoretical interests in the field from the mid-1980s (Evans & Nation, 1987, 1989a, 1989b, 1989c, 1993a, 1996, 2000). This project has recognized the importance understanding the relationships between practice, research, and theory. It has emphasized the utility of understanding educational endeavors in the context of the cultural, economic, political, and social contexts within which they occur. It has sought to bring to the field insights from social sciences, generally, and sociology, particularly, to challenge and complement a dominant paradigm drawing inspirations from various traditions in educational psychology.

Educational technology has moved to the center of our attention as this project has progressed. Our initial forays into public debate manifested a concern that distance education, under the control of educational technologists, was in danger of becoming a multinational instructional industry that alienated "its students from each other and wider educational and social processes" (Evans & Nation, 1987, p. 49). This narrow or traditional view of educational technology understood it as a movement rooted in behaviorist psychology, often practiced as instructional design, that attempted to program students' learning. Our engagement with educational technology revealed that there were considerable changes afoot within educational technology in both its senses: the tools or media that were being developed for educational purposes and the theoretical and research endeavors driving the changes in material technology (Evans & Nation, 1993b, pp. 196–209).

Our approach has sought to incorporate research and theory from the humanities and social sciences that understand education in its cultural, economic, political, and social contexts. In particular we have drawn extensively on Anthony Giddens, whose theory of structuration attempts to unite an understanding of the individual and society (Giddens, 1984, 1991a, 1991b, 1994, 1998, 1999a, 1999b).

In an attempt to further a constructively critical dialog between educational technologists influenced by constructivism and those proceeding from critical theory, we have turned to Wedemeyer (1981) as a source for the basis of this accommodation. Writing in 1980, Wedemeyer was able to proceed on the basis of decades of practical experience in university extension providing *Learning at the Back Door* to those denied conventional access to university studies. He was the driving force in the Articulated Instructional Media (AIM) project undertaken in the mid-1960s at the University of Wisconsin. He was proud to claim that "this experiment . . . laid the theoretical, academic, technological and operational bases for the creation of the new institutions of open, distance and independent learning" (Wedemeyer, 1981, p. 204), a view supported by others (Moore, 1990, pp. xii–xiv).

Two decades after the publication of his master work, Wedemeyer's principal manifest objective has been fulfilled: distance education in all its guises has entered the mainstream. Its immense value today rests with the strength of its underlying educational philosophy and with the breadth of the theoretical, academic, technological, and operational principles it canvassed and the integrity between them it achieved. This is well illustrated by his address to "technology as means":

The continuing danger in a technologically oriented society and culture is the technology becomes and end in itself. . . . Yet technology usually originates as a means towards some useful or even humanistic end. It is one of the tasks of humanists, educators, and social scientists to resist the evolution of technology to ends, and insist that technology remain only a means. (Wedemeyer, 1981, p. 102)

He proceeded with a reminder that educators had a duty to use technology, according to these principles, and if they failed to do so, the void would be filled by those with instrumental rather than humanistic motives.

Those in distance education and educational technology who espouse constructivist theories and practical approaches could usefully consult Wedemeyer for assistance in coming to terms with those who offer critical or humanistic critiques of constructivism. His work is informed by the antecedents of the "new constructivists," such as Robert Gagné and Jerome Bruner. It is also informed more comprehensively by other work from a variety of other humanities and social sciences and interpreted within an intellectual framework with its basis in the classical American pragmatism of John Dewey and George Herbert Mead. Above all, it is grounded in a quest for policies and practices that make paramount the learning needs of students.

GLOBALIZATION AND DISTANCE EDUCATION

As the deep interrelationship between distance education and technology moves into a new generation (Bates, 1991; Garrison, 1985; Nipper, 1989) with the new educational technologies, then some new and significant interconnections unfold as a consequence. In particular, the new educational technologies, based as they are on computer and communications systems, open new forms of interactive and multimedium distance education to a new world of students (although it should be recognized that the postal system arguably has a broader global reach). However, the computer and communications media also bring to the doorstep of distance education a range of matters that were either nonexistent before or were at least of minor significance. In essence, these matters can be considered under the rubric of globalization and particularly in terms of theoretical explanations of the reflexiveness of social life (for example, Giddens, 1984), which help explain the practical conditions that distance education faces.

Evans (1997) considered the interrelationships between globalization and distance education and he argued for a broad understanding of the term, thus:

Globalisation implies that most people, if not all, are connected more or less contemporaneously with distant events, sometimes whether they like it or not. This "time-space compression" (Giddens, 1994, p. 7) is not just limited to communications and transport, but also to economic activity. The social and cultural implications . . . are intimately connected. (1997, p. 18)

Many would argue that the human experience is altering fundamentally within a globalizing world—that is a world where social, economic, cultural, and political activity is becoming more integrated and less demarcated by distances, national borders, and cultures. It is doing so not just because of the speed and interactivity of new communications media, but also because of the fusion of cultural conditions. For some, in this latter cultural sense, globalization is substantially Americanization in that the dominant influence via the Internet is from the United States. However, this is somewhat of an oversimplification in that prior to the Internet, other media also often reflected a significant American flavor (film, for example). And another predominantly English language nation, the UK, has been globally influential through other media (for example, popular music, television, newspapers) as well. Certainly, it seems that the domination of English as the global language has been further strengthened via the Internet and the Web. As we shall illustrate, these matters are important for theory, practice, and research in distance education.

Toward these ends Edwards, using Robertson's (1992) work, considered the impact of globalization on forms of distance education. He argued that it is not so much the fact of global connections that is important, "but (rather) in the contemporary world there is an intensification of the processes and the awareness of the globe as a single environment" (Edwards, 1994, p. 10). In effect the natural world has always been "globalized," for example, its climate and weather systems have been part of a complex and interrelated "global" system. Historically, it can be shown that from the earliest times humans have sought to explore the margins, and often extend the boundaries, of their territories. Indeed it was in response to the colonization of much of the world by European powers—such as Portugal, Spain, and especially Britain—that the first antecedents of distance education were established (see Bolton, 1986). In effect, human societies, at least for the past two centuries, have been seeking to explore and colonize the "new" world and then to overcome what the Australian historian Blainey (1966) called "the tyranny of distance" between the centers of the colonial powers in Europe and their new colonies. It was always a long technological and cultural struggle with time and distance. It seems that computer and communications technologies have, to the extent that their media allow, fostered a "disrespect" for time and distance, although nature is usually able to impress its diurnal and seasonal rhythms on everyone, everywhere.

The tensions between the globalizing forces of contemporary life and the ways in which people live and learn (Giddens, 1991a, 1991b) can have major implications for open and distance education theory and practice, and for (distance) learners' self-identities (Evans 1989, 1995a, 1995b). Perhaps the best example of this is found in the interrelationships between the developed and the developing world where the possibilities and consequences of the new forms of distance education seem most alluring and yet most threatening. It is first worth noting that the term *developed nation* is misleading. "It conveys," as Evans (in press) suggests, "a sense that the 'developing' is over and that the countries in question have reached a stage of being developed: there is no further room to improve." Contrarily, a fundamental characteristic of a "developed country" is that it is speeding simultaneously along various lines of development . . . it is actually a *compulsively developing* one; one which values change and progress as central in its national culture.(original emphasis) It is as if the so-called developed nations actually have a "compulsive development culture."

Likewise, compared to developed nations, developing nations are not usually developing at the same pace and do not possess a compulsive development culture. Indeed, it could be argued that without some miraculous or equally profound progress, a developing nation is unlikely even to keep pace with the speed of development in the developed world. It has often been considered that appropriate forms of distance education may be able to assist developing nations to leapfrog some developmental stages by taking developed world educational programs and inserting them "in-country." In this way the learners benefit from a standard of program that their own nation's educational infrastructure cannot provide. The are examples of where this has been of general benefit (Perraton, 1993, 2000); however, as Evans (1997) noted, there is a series of "access versus invasion" dilemmas to be broached, especially when distance education is facilitated by the new educational technologies. For example, Papua New Guinea (PNG) is a developing nation that has had a long-standing involvement with distance education at both the school and higher education levels. It has used distance education in attempting to deal with not only the serious needs for education in the country but also to cope with the poor communications, isolation, and remoteness of many of the communities involved. As Guy (1991, 1997) commented the access to developed world distance education courses is not without its invasive consequences, especially in a nation that is founded on over 800 language and cultural groups. However, the current PNG government is not resiling from distance education, but rather sees the new educational technologies as enabling access to education to be provided in even the remotest PNG communities where no electricity, telephone, roads, or airstrips exist. The answer is seen to rest on solar electricity, computers, and satellite communications to enable people to access a world of (distance) education.

The rhetoric of globalization abounds in educational contexts today. The rhetoricians address the two main platforms of educational endeavor: the pedagogical and the curricular. At the pedagogical level educators are encouraged to see their practices as being mediated, usually through electronic communications, along global lines. It is said that communications media, both directly and indirectly, are able take their teaching to learners around the globe, or conversely, they may use global resources via these media, to foster or enhance their own teaching. At the curricular level, it is said that no longer can the teacher just teach about the local, but rather global matters must be covered in order that the learners become knowledgeable global citizens. The rhetoric of globalization has its parallels (if not origins) in the transnational corporations, governments, governmental agencies (especially transgovernmental agencies such as UNESCO and the World Bank), and nongovernmental organizations. Much of the rhetoric is underpinned by the arguments and values of economic rationalism, whereby the worth of individuals, products, and services is determined by their economic value in the (increasingly global) marketplace. However, the consequences for the languages, cultures, and communities involved are difficult to predict other than that they are likely to be profound and, in some respects at least, deleterious.

Developed nations face their own dilemmas concerning the globalizing forces of distance education. There is a reflexiveness embedded in the globalizing forces of (distance) education. As the PNG example illustrates, distance education is not only affected by globalization, but it also operates as a globalizing entity in itself, and in so doing adds its own particular influences. As we have argued previously (Evans & Nation, 1996, pp. 163–165), this is a version of what might be called the "global-local" tension within globalization, which operates through to the level of the individual person. As Giddens (1994) makes clear, the "intensified reflexivity" of globalization creates the conditions for "a world of clever people" where "individuals more or less have to engage with the wider world if they are to survive in it. Information produced by specialists (including scientific knowledge) can no longer be wholly confined to specific groups, but becomes routinely interpreted and acted on by lay individuals in the course of everyday actions" (p. 7). "Clever people" need to be able to read, understand, analyze, and act locally on the basis of their learning:

> Not only does this say something about the need for high levels of education for the population, but it implies that the curricula involved need to reflect both global and local needs. We can also infer that, due to the reflexive, and therefore dynamic, nature of globalization, people need to engage in lifelong education in order to participate fully in social life. (Evans & Nation, 1996, p. 164)

In many respects one might expect that the advent of the new educational technologies has enabled distance education to enter a new plane and become an even more powerful area of theory, practice, and research. However, just as globalization operates reflexively between the local and the global, and just as the "access" to distance education can be an "invasion" for a developing nation, so the new educational technologies present new possibilities for distance education but also, as we argue below, they sow the seeds of the demise of distance education as a field of research, theory, and practice.

WRESTLING THE SCORPION: THE END
OF DISTANCE EDUCATION?

In some respects distance education is a relatively recent area of educational research, theory, and practice. Its name was formalized in the 1970s, although the history of its practices goes back beyond the turn of the 20th century. It has operated under various terms, with probably *correspondence education* being its most enduring predecessor. It can be seen that *distance education* (using this term to cover all its preceding forms) both relies upon, and is a demand of, the modern industrial world. It was this world that provided the means of printing and reproduction and the means of communication and transport to enable distance education to operate. Likewise, it was the ever-expanding developed areas of the world, together with the demands for people with education and training to work and run the newly pioneered areas, that helped to create the need for education and training to occur "at a distance" from where it was provided. The "traditional" forms of face-to-face education were found wanting in most respects, although they did offer some direct and indirect forms of assistance, whether it was through boarding education or through providing the people to develop or support the new distance education.

In this sense it can be seen that the modernization that led to what some call the first generation of educational technologies used in distance education (Bates, 1991; Garrison, 1985; Nipper, 1989) created the opportunities and conditions for its existence. The second generation of audiovisual media supplement or enhance distance education considerably. Arguably, the rise of the large open universities around the world in the last decade or so can be traced to the development of the United Kingdom Open University (UKOU), which itself was inextricably linked to the use of (BBC) radio and television. The impetus the UKOU gave to distance education during the 1970s and 1980s was largely connected to its systems for the development and use of print and audiovisual media, although there were other very significant factors too, not the least of which was the need for greater access to educational opportunities for all people. Things were somewhat different in the United States, which, with exceptions, seemed to remain somewhat immune to these forms of distance education. American distance education typically pursued interactive audio and video links for remote class tuition, rather than the print-based tuition and assessment, supported by other media, that is commonplace in international distance education.

Since the emergence and rise of the computer-based communications technology, distance educators have seen their capacity to provide their wares enhanced. In particular, the database, graphics, word-processing, communications, and multimedia capacities have proven to be untapped reserves for the distance educator. However, the computer-based communications technology scorpion has a sting in the tail that may prove more than just painful for distance education. This is because, despite the size and influence of some of the world's mega universities (Daniel, 1996), distance education has remained a relatively marginal endeavor in educational policy and practice. The traditional universities have increasingly become aware of the importance of computer-based communications technology to their existences, too. Not just for educational purposes directly—although this is probably where the sting will be terminal for distance education—but also for their marketing, business, and administration needs.

Some years ago Smith and Kelly (1987) encouraged a debate as to whether distance education might shift from the "margins to the mainstream" of education. Certainly, there were some clear reasons for thinking that this was a possibility, for example, in that distance education appealed to an important and expanding number of mature-age learners needing to undertake continuing education. However, a decade later Evans, Nation, Renner, and Tregenza (1997) issued a rather different prognosis for distance education. Partly on the basis of their research into reforms in traditional universities, they addressed the Open and Distance Learning Association of Australia's 1997 conference thus:

> We do not wish to romanticise *distance education*, indeed, we remain critical of various aspects. However, the current circumstances lead us to wonder whether it is time for ODLAA members and other fellow travellers to assert themselves on national and institutional policy agendas so that the research theory and practice which has been nurtured over previous years is not lost, and maybe then re-invented, by people who are ignorant of its importance and potential for taking (tertiary) education into the next millennium. (Evans et al., 1997, p. 152)

The problem identified is twofold. Conventional universities were embracing the new educational technologies, in effect, to teach their at-a-distance students without the benefit of the expertise and understanding that decades of research, theory, and practice in distance education could provide.

Additionally, we can see that the sorts of changes that new technology has brought to society, work, and finance more generally has impacted on the nature of education in ways that sting distance education again. As we argued above, distance education itself is a product of modernity. Its forms of administration, production, and distribution are characteristic of modern (Fordist) societies, much in the way Peters (1983) described (somewhat controversially) nearly two decades ago. However, the new technologies and the way that they have been deployed by business, government, and other institutions have yielded significant, and sometimes fundamental, changes to the way work and society operates. Some refer to this new condition as postmodernity or late-modernity. Within this context various forms of education have been spawned that draw, to a greater or lesser extent, from education. These are forms such as, open learning, flexible learning, fleximode, open campus or virtual campus. Edwards (1994, 1997) saw the emergence of open learning and flexible learning as consequences of postmodernity. Likewise, Campion (1992) and Campion and Renner (1991) explained these new configurations in post-Fordist terms. These authors are critical of these shifts in terms of their impact on the quality of education and learning, indeed, Campion (1996) is particularly so. Others, such as Jakupec (1996, 1997), Nicoll (1997), and Kirkpatrick (1997), are similarly critical, especially in terms of seeing these new forms of distance education as being influenced by, or having arisen from, the dominance of "economic rationalist" neo-conservative politics in the 1990s.

These critiques of the various late-modern offshoots of distance education are often founded on the assumption that the types of learning that are fostered by these approaches are likely to be of the repetitive, "banking" kind eschewed by Freire and others in the 1970s (see Freire, 1972). The expectation of the critics is that learning will be reduced to "serving the system" and not be of a kind that empowers learners. These concerns are supported by a good deal of evidence that suggests that new forms of distance education (and many other forms of education and training) are coming under the influence of what we might call "neo–instructional industrialism," that is the old industrial approaches to distance education re-jigged into online forms. This should be seen as a trend to be resisted and avoided; indeed, if distance education is to survive its stings, it will need to be on the basis that it is rejuvenated in a way that uses the new educational technologies to foster dialog and critique. In order to do so it will need to address the challenge of the constructivists who are becoming influential in the design of new forms of distance education. We take up this matter in more detail below.

BEFORE AND BEYOND CONSTRUCTIVISM

Since the early 1990s constructivism has ridden a populist wave to become a fashionable theoretical position on which to build educational practices. For many it seemed to represent a significant, even radical, departure from previous approaches. Certainly this is understandable for those who were trying to break away from largely behaviorist-influenced or behaviorist-derived approaches to educational technology, such as programmed learning, which had gained favor in the 1970s and 1980s. The increasing "technologization" of teaching, learning, and assessment during this period made some educational psychologists with humanist, rather than behaviorist, leanings increasingly nervous.

Constructivism's origins, as is often the case with "modern" theories, have long and deep roots into epistemological histories. Candy (1991) took the view that its origins can be recognized as early the 5th century BC in Greece. However, in terms of current approaches, there were significant contributors to the field in the second half of the 20th century. In psychology, Kelly propounded a form of personal construct theory in the mid-1950s (Kelly, 1955). In sociology, Berger and Luckmann popularized the notion of the social construction of reality in the mid-1960s (Berger & Luckmann, 1967). In educational psychology, Piaget had a profound influence on teacher education and early schooling, which can be seen to reflect and articulate constuctivist ideas (Piaget, 1971). In Australia, Connell's work on the child's construction of politics provides another valuable thread to the notion of construction (Connell, 1971). Arguably, in philosophy, the hermeneutic propositions of Husserl are again congruent with the meaning-making elements of constructivism (Husserl, 1965).

The resurgence in interest in what might be called constructualist thought is largely attributed to Glasersfeld, who added a new "radical" edge to the notion of constructivism (Glasersfeld, 1995). Then, as we have argued, it was the next decade when constructivism took off as a movement. It has been highly popular in science education for children, and to a lesser extent in educational and instructional design for adults, including in distance education. Jegede is a scholar of both science education and distance education, and so it is not surprising that he was among the vanguard of those in distance education who advocated that constructivism be taken seriously for the research and practice of teaching and learning in distance education (Jegede, 1992). However, perhaps the most notable statement in terms of the impact of constructivism on distance education came from Hawkridge (1999). He was the foundation director of the Institute of Educational Technology at the UK Open University (arguably one the most important developments in distance education of the 20th century). He is also an eminent scholar in the field of educational technology.

Hawkridge's statement is based on a review of the state of theory, research, and scholarship in educational technology since the 1970s in an editorial for the *British Journal of Educational Technology*. He identified three challenges that remained to be met:

> First, educational technologists should understand and apply constructivism rather than behaviourism in their development of teaching and learning systems. Second, they should develop systems for teaching and learning that match the opportunities offered by the hardware and software of modern computers and telecommunications, including the Web. Third, they should answer the moral and ethical challenges from those who criticise educational technologists for not caring enough about teachers and students, for not endorsing an emancipatory view of education. (Hawkridge, 1999, pp. 299–300)

This summary grows from earlier analyses by Hawkridge (1976, 1979, 1981, 1983, 1991) in which he reflected critically on the mission of educational technologists, addressed the views of critics, and continued to suggest changes in approaches related to changing conditions in education and society and progress in educational theory and practice. We have addressed these analyses in considerable detail previously (Evans & Nation, 1993a, 1993b, 1996, 2000). However, it is important to note here that some of the challenges to educational technology were also similar to challenges made to aspects of contructivism's earlier forms. For example, Berger and Luckmann's work in sociology lost favor under the weight of Marxist and neo-Marxian critiques of interactionist sociology generally. The absence of notions of social structure (class), power and authority in the individualist theories of social constructionism, symbolic interactionism, and so on rendered them unpopular by the mid to late 1970s. Of course, the structuralist theories were themselves rendered unpopular by the various theoretical positions of postmodernism, poststructuralism, and feminism. Hence, we would argue, that constructivist principles are likely to be only partially successful in achieving Hawkridge's mission. Indeed, they are especially likely to be so if the proponents and exponents of constructivism in distance education and educational technology do not recognize both the useful related work that has been done in and/or through distance education since the early 1970s that was not labeled constructivism, but that represents a relevant and strong base on which to build, and also that constructivism is limited by its weakness in terms of both the recognition of and articulation with social theories.

This is not to deny that the transformation in thinking demonstrated by reconstructed behaviorists is important for the future of distance education (and education more broadly). However, the fact is that most of those espousing constructivism remain unwilling or unable to recognize the need for substantial analyses of the economic, political, and social contexts within which teaching and learning occur and, even more so, they seem unable to grasp the rich potential of investigations from a diverse range of related disciplines. In our view, failing to make these connections will only remake distance education into a softer, individualistic form of instructional industrialism.

Having said this, considerable progress has been made to bridge the paradigmatic chasm between those who can be regarded as instructional industrialists and proponents of critically reflexive education. It is especially noteworthy that Jonassen, an heir to the Gagnéian cognitivist tradition, is an instructive case. A recent publication, written with two colleagues, addressed to aspiring school teachers begins:

> Constructivism is a relatively new idea in education. It is an even newer idea to educational technology. It is so new to some educational circles that some people perceive it as a fad. We think not. Constructivism is an old idea to sociology and art. And as a way of understanding the learning phenomenon it is ageless. People have always constructed personal and socially acceptable meaning for events and objects in the world. ... People naturally construct meaning. Formal educational enterprises that rely on the efficient transmission of prepackaged chunks of information are not natural. They are pandemic. The modern age values understanding less than it does the efficient transmission of culturally accepted beliefs. It doesn't have to be that way. Modernism can support meaning making as well. This book looks at how modern technologies, such as computers and video, can be used to engage learners in personal and socially constructed meaning making. ... *Learning With Technology* is about how educators can use technologies to support constructive learning. In the past, technology has largely been used in education to learn *from*. Technology programs were developed with the belief that they could convey information (and hopefully understanding) more effectively than teachers. But constructivists believe that you cannot convey understanding. That can only be constructed by learners. So this book argues that technologies are more effectively used as tools to construct knowledge *with*. The point of the book is that technology is a tool to think and learn *with*. (Jonassen, Peck & Wilson, p. iii)

We have argued elsewhere that the notion of technology as tool is somewhat impoverished and that technology is more usefully seen as the science, art, and craft of using a tool (Evans & Nation, 1993, 1996). Hence educational technology is the art, science, and craft of educators when they use a tool—be it a computer or chalk—for educational purposes. Notwithstanding this, Jonassen, Peck, and Wilson are espousing what distance educators such as Morgan have named as the new educational technology (Morgan, 1997). Despite the importance of Jonassen, Peck, and Wilson's recognition of the social elements in educational technology, the allegation of the novelty of constructivist ideas in educational theory and practice illustrates the point of weakness we mentioned above in relation to Hawkridge's summation of 30 years of educational technology. Accepting that Jonassen, Peck, and Wilson acknowledged that sociology has an enduring record for espousing the importance of the social construction of knowledge, it would be even more useful if they could point to substantial contributions in this regard, such as those made by Basil Bernstein, Geoffrey Esland, and Michael Young in the late 1960s and early 1970s and given general currency through OU courses in Education (Bernstein, 1971; Esland, 1971; Young, 1971). These contributions have continued to develop and retain their vitality today (for example, Young, 1998). It is worth discussing one of these contributions in more detail, because it illustrates the weakness in terms of both educational technology and science education.

In 1971 Esland identified the potential for educational psychology to create and facilitate the theory and research that could act as a basis for understanding teachers and learners as constructors of meaning. He did so in the course of a study of the emergence of curriculum reforms such as "Nuffield science," which were influenced very heavily by the work of Jerome Bruner and Jean Piaget. From this epistemological perspective, children and adolescents are "little scientists" who can be led to discover what scientists have come to know. Esland's study demonstrated that these reforms to teaching and learning in schools were often founded on the rocks of psychometric approaches in the tradition of behaviorism and Gagné. He noted then the tendency for psychometricians to incorporate Bruner and Piaget's ideas into their models and, in the process, to lose or misunderstand their emphasis on the meaning making capacities of learners. Bruner's early work, with its conformity to the scientism of 1960s and 1970s academic psychology, also contributed to this misunderstanding. His mature work demonstrates much more clearly that an understanding of meaning making is the central aspect of educational psychology and that anthropology, art, literature, music, sociology, and other social sciences all have important contributions to make to any complete analysis (Bruner, 1986, 1990).

For some years we have asserted that the social theorist Anthony Giddens offers a most effective basis for a thoroughly connected understanding of meaning making in economic, political, and social contexts (Evans & Nation, 1996, pp. 163–165; 2000, pp. 164–168). For example, Giddens has continued in the tradition of interdisciplinarity that Bruner valued in the Harvard Department of Social Relations. He has produced some powerful eclectic theoretical works that allow others to analyze, articulate, and explain their own research, reflections, and theorizing in terms that recognize the power of human agency within the changing social, economic, and political conditions. Giddens's understanding of the "reflexivity of modernity" offers a substantial theoretical basis for the learning society that is rapidly becoming the challenge we face as individuals making our way in the world personally, domestically, economically, politically, and socially and as members of organizations (such as educational enterprises) attempting to reform the world (Giddens, 1991a, pp. 36–45). With Kasperson (2000, pp. vi–vii), we agree that many can be bewildered by Giddens's overwhelming style—in his technical works, at least. We remain optimistic, however, that the time has come for his ideas to have a more pervasive influence.

CONCLUSION

The emergence and success of the British Open University in the 1970s signaled that distance education could hold a preeminent part in place in higher education nationally and internationally. As late comers to the field, the British educational authorities were able to draw upon the experience of those in Europe and the New World who had pioneered the establishment of a variety of programs of correspondence education, based in various organizational contexts, in colleges and universities in the late 19th and early 20th centuries. Unlike most of these pioneering programs, the Open University was a single-purpose institution devoted exclusively to educating part-time students whose circumstances or desires meant that they could not attend campus-based programs.

In many respects, the fledgling New World democracies recognized that education had to be taken to their citizens at the pioneering frontiers of their lands. They saw it as necessary and practical to take the classroom to the adults and children, from various religious and cultural backgrounds, who were building the new nations. The initiative for many of these developments was essentially local and/or national, but like most educational endeavors there was always an international element in evidence. These were expressed through the emergence of organizations such as the ICDE and its predecessors. They played an important part in the development of the open university movement in the 1980s. The fact that universities were the focus of many of the developments was also influential, but never so exclusively, in the birth of research and scholarship aimed at understanding and improving policy and practice in the field.

In an age of "hyper (un)reality," in which incantations about the necessity and inevitability of global, mega and/or virtual universities are part of many a cultural, economic, political, and social discourses, it is essential for practitioners, policymakers, researchers, and theorists to maintain educational technologies as a central interest. We have ceased to be surprised that educators and their clients need to be reminded that technologies emerged in the Stone Age and that the "new" communications and information technologies are simply the latest manifestations of a phenomenon that is always integral to education. The preeminent task for practitioners and scholars is to pursue the job of understanding and improving their use on the most substantial scale possible.

From our first involvement in distance education we have valued the confluence of knowledge from practice, research, and theory. Our experiences as undergraduate baby-boomers taught us to privilege the classroom and the campus. Charismatic lecturers, lively seminar groups, raging debates in "the caf," and the "demos" were imagined as the best in the undergraduate experience. Correspondence education was secondhand and second rate for both students and teachers, according to this mentality. Our own experience both confirmed and denied this. Any genuinely critical reflection on the totality of experiences of campus life and classroom-based teaching and learning will soon reveal many flaws. Our approach, centering critical reflections on the practice of ourselves and our colleagues, has been founded on a rich tradition of scholarship developed by pioneers such as Charles Wedemeyer.

It is heartening to realize that this book has given considerable emphasis to contributors who have been willing to value the richness of these traditions in research theory. While it may be imprudent to single out one bearer of this tradition, we believe it is instructive to reflect on recent contributions by Otto Peters (2000, and Chap. 7 in this book). Peters is often misunderstood as "the high priest of industrialized distance education." In fact, he is a practitioner, researcher, and scholar of substantial range and diversity. A close reading of his publications reveals, above all, that any useful understanding of educational endeavors requires a deep consideration of the cultural, economic, and political contexts in which they occur. This remains of paramount importance for the future of distance education and its children.

We remain disappointed that there are still too many practitioners, researchers and theorists in our field, by whatever name we call it, who seem incapable of recognizing the importance of contributions from earlier generations and from a variety of academic callings and approaches. Let the debate continue as we reflect critically during construction of the "new universities" required of the future.

"Tear downs the wall(s)!"

—Waters (n. d. p. 136)

REFERENCES

Bates, T. (1991). Third generation distance education. *Research in Distance Education, 3*(2), 10–15.

Berger, J., & Luckmann, T. S. (1967). *The social construction of reality.* Harmondsworth: Penguin.

Bernstein, B. (1971). On the classification and framing of educational knowledge. In M. F. D. Young (Ed.), *Knowledge and control: New directions for the sociology of education* (pp. 47–69). London: Collier-Macmillan.

Blainey, G. (1966). *The tyranny of distance: How distance shaped Australia's history.* Melbourne: Sun Books.

Bolton, G. (1986). The opportunity of distance. *Distance Education, 7*(1), 5–22.

Boorstin, D. J. (1984). *The discovers.* London: J. M. Dent & Sons.

Bruner, J. (1986). *Actual minds, possible worlds.* Cambridge, MA: Harvard University Press.

Bruner, J. (1990). *Acts of meaning.* Cambridge, MA: Harvard University Press.

Campion, M. (1992). Revealing links: Post-Fordism, postmodernism and distance education. In T. D. Evans & P. A. Juler (Eds.), *Research in distance education 2* (pp. 45–51). Geelong: Deakin University Press.

Campion, M. (1996). Open learning, closing minds. In T. D. Evans & D. E. Nation (Eds.), *Opening education: Policies and practices from open and distance education* (pp. 147–161). London: Routledge.

Campion, M., & Renner, W. (1991). The supposed demise of Fordism: Implications for distance education and higher education. *Distance Education, 13*(1), 7–28.

Candy, P. C. (1991). *Self-direction for lifelong learning: A comprehensive guide to theory and practice.* San Francisco: Jossey-Bass.

Connell, R. W. (1971). *The child's construction of politics.* Melbourne: Melbourne University Press.

Daniel, J. (1996). *The mega-universities and the knowledge media.* London: Kogan Page.

Edwards, R. (1994). From a distance? Globalisation, space-time compression and distance education. *Open Learning, 9, 3*, 9–17.

Edwards, R. (1997). *Changing Places? Flexibility, lifelong learning and a learning society.* London: Routledge.

Esland, G. M. (1971). Teaching and learning as the organization of knowledge. In M. F. D. Young (Ed.), *Knowledge and control: New directions for the sociology of education* (pp. 70–115). London: Collier-Macmillan.

Evans, T. D. (1989). Taking place: The social construction of place, time and space and the (re) making of distances in distance education. *Distance Education, 10*(2), 170–183.

Evans, T. D. (1995a). Globalisation, post-Fordism and open and distance education. *Distance Education, 16*(3), 256–269.

Evans, T. D. (1995b). Matters of modernity, late modernity and self-identity in distance education. *European Journal of Psychology of Education, 10*(2), 169–180.

Evans, T. D. (1997). (En)Countering globalisation: Issues for open and distance educators. In L. Rowan, L. Bartlett, & T. D. Evans (Eds.), *Shifting borders: Globalisation, localisation and open and distance education* (pp. 11–22). Geelong: Deakin University Press.

Evans, T. D. (2002). Policy and planning in the developed countries: Coping with compulsive development cultures. In S. Panda (Ed.), *Planning and management of open and flexible learning* (pp. 13–19 in press). London: Kogan Page.

Evans, T. D., & Nation, D. E. (1987). Which future for distance education? *International Council for Distance Education Bulletin, 14*, 48–53.

Evans, T. D., & Nation, D. E. (1989a). Critical reflections in distance education. In T. D. Evans & D. E. Nation (Eds.), *Critical reflections on distance education* (pp. 237–252). London: Falmer Press.

Evans, T. D., & Nation, D. E. (1989b). Dialogue in practice, research and theory in distance education. *Open Learning, 4*(2), 37–43.

Evans, T. D., & Nation, D. E. (1989c). Introduction. In T. D. Evans & D. E. Nation (Eds.), *Critical reflections on distance education* (pp. 5–8). London: Falmer Press.

Evans, T. D., & Nation, D. E. (1993a). Distance education, educational technology and open learning: Converging futures and closer integration with conventional education. In *Distance education futures: The proceedings of the Australian & South Pacific External Studies Association biennial forum* (pp. 15–36). Adelaide: University of South Australia.

Evans, T. D., & Nation, D. E. (1993b). Educational technologies: Reforming open and distance education. In T. D. Evans & D. E. Nation (Eds.), *Reforming open and distance education* (pp. 196–214). London: Kogan Page.

Evans, T. D., & Nation, D. E. (1993c). Introduction: Reformations in open and distance education. In T. D. Evans & D. E. Nation (Eds.), *Reforming open and distance education* (pp. 7–14). London: Kogan Page.

Evans, T. D., & Nation, D. E. (1996). Educational futures: Globalisation, educational technology and lifelong learning. In T. D. Evans & D. E. Nation (Eds.), *Opening Education: Policies and practices from open and distance education* (pp. 162–176). London: Routledge.

Evans, T. D., & Nation, D. E. (2000). Understanding changes to university teaching. In T. D. Evans & D. E. Nation (Eds.), *Changing university teaching: Reflections on creating educational technologies* (pp. 160–175). London: Kogan Page.

Evans, T. D., Nation, D. E., Renner, W., & Tregenza, K. (1997). The end of the line or a new future for open and distance education? Issues for practitioners, researchers and theorists from a study of educational reform in post-secondary education. In *Open and Distance Learning Association of Australia* (pp. 151–155). Launceston: University of Tasmania.

Freire, P. (1972). *Pedagogy of the Oppressed*. Harmondsworth: Penguin.

Garrison, D. R. (1985). Three generations of technological innovation in distance education. *Distance Education, 6*(2), 235–241.

Giddens, A. (1984). *The constitution of society*. Cambridge: Polity Press.

Giddens, A. (1991a). *The consequences of modernity*. Cambridge: Polity Press.

Giddens, A. (1991b). *Modernity and self-identity: Self and society in the late modern age*. Cambridge: Polity Press.

Giddens, A. (1994). *Beyond left and right: The future of radical politics*. Cambridge: Polity Press.

Giddens, A. (1998). *The third way: The renewal of social democracy*. Cambridge: Polity Press.

Giddens, A. (1999a). *Runaway world*, Reith Lectures 1999, BBC Online Network. http://news.bbc.co.uk/hi/english/static/events/reith_99/default.html

Giddens, A. (1999b). *Runaway world: How Globalization is Reshaping our Lives*. London: Profile Books.

Giddens, A. (2000). *The third way and its Critics*. Cambridge: Polity Press.

Glasersfeld, E. v. (Ed.). (1995). *Radical constructivism: A way knowing and learning*. London: Falmer.

Guy, R. (1991). Distance education and the developing world. In T. D. Evans & B. King (Eds.), *Beyond the text: Contemporary writing on distance education* (pp. 152–175). Geelong: Deakin University Press.

Guy, R. (1997). Contesting borders: Knowledge, power and pedagogy in distance education in Papua New Guineai. In L. Rowan, L. Bartlett, & T. D. Evans (Eds.), *Shifting borders: Globalisation, localisation and open and distance education* (pp. 53–64). Geelong: Deakin University Press.

Hawkridge, D. (1976). Next year Jerusalem! The rise of educational technology. *British Journal of Educational Technology, 12*(1), 7–30.

Hawkridge, D. (1979). Persuading the dons. *British Journal of Educational Technology, 3*(10), 164–174.

Hawkridge, D. (1981). The telesis of educational technology. *British Journal of Educational Technology, 12*(1), 4–18.

Hawkridge, D. (1983). *New information technology in Education*. Beckenham: Croom Helm.

Hawkridge, D. (1991). Challenging educational technology. *Educational Training and Technology International, 28*(2), 1–22.

Hawkridge, D. (1999). Thirty years on, BJET! and educational technology. *British Journal of Educational Technology, 30*(4), 293–304.

Holmberg, B. (1977). *Distance education: A survey and bibliography*. London: Kogan Page.

Holmberg, B. (1981). *Status and trends of distance education*. London: Kogan Page.

Holmberg, B. (1985). *Status and trends of distance education* (2nd rev. ed.). Lund: Lector Publishing.

Husserl, E. (1965). *Phenomenology and the crisis in philosophy*. New York: Harper Torch Books.

Jakupec, V. (1996). Reforming distance education through economic rationalism: A critical analysis of reforms to Australia higher education. In T. D. Evans & D. E. Nation (Eds.), *Opening education: Policies and practices from open and distance education* (pp. 77–89). London: Routledge.

Jakupec, V. (1997). Guest editorial. *Studies in Continuing Education, 19*(2), 95–99.

Jegede, O. (1992). Constructivist epistemology and its implications for contemporary research in distance learning. In T. D. Evans & P. A. Juler (Eds.), *Research in distance education 2* (pp. 21–29). Geelong: Deakin University Press.

Jonassen, D. H., Peck, K. L., & Wilson, B. G. (1999). *Learning with Technology: A constructivist perspective*. Upper Saddle River: Merrill-Prentice Hall.

Kasperson, L. (2000). *Anthony Giddens: An introduction to a social theorist*. Oxford: Blackwell.

Keegan, D., & Mitchell, I. McD. (1980). Editorial. *Distance Education, 1*(1), vi.

Kelly, G. A. (1955). *The psychology of personal constructs*. New York: Norton.

Kirkpatrick, D. (1997). Becoming flexible: Contested territories. *Studies in Continuing Education, 19*(2), 160–173.

Moore, M. G. (1990). Background and overview of contemporary American distance education. In M. G. Moore with P. Cookson, J. Donaldson, & B. A. Quigley (Eds.), *Contemporary issues in American distance education* (pp. xii–xxvi). Oxford: Pergamon.

Moore, M. G. with Cookson, P., Donaldson, J., & Quigley, B. A. (1990). *Contemporary issues in American distance education.* Oxford: Pergamon.

Morgan, A. R. (1997). Still seeking the silent revolution? Research, theory and practice in open and distance education. In T. D. Evans, V. Jakupec, & D. Thompson (Eds.), *Research in distance education 4* (pp. 7–17). Geelong: Deakin University Press.

Nicoll, K. (1997). "Flexible learning"—Unsettling practices. *Studies in Continuing Education, 19*(2), 100–111.

Nipper, S. (1989). Third generation distance learning and computer conferencing. In R. Mason & A. Kaye (Eds.), *Mindweave* (pp. 63–73). Oxford: Pergamon Press.

Perraton, H. (Ed.). (1993). *Distance education for teacher training.* London: Routledge.

Perraton, H. (2000). *Open and distance learning in the developing world.* London: Routledge.

Peters, O. (1983). Distance teaching and industrial production: A comparative interpretation in outline. In D. Sewart D. Keegan & B. Holmberg (Eds.), *Distance education: International perspectives* (pp. 95–113). London: Croom Helm.

Peters, O. (2000). The transformation of the university into an institution of independent learning. In T. D. Evans & D. E. Nation (Eds.), *Changing university teaching: Reflections on creating educational technologies* (pp. 10–23). London: Kogan Page.

Piaget, J. (1971). *Structuralism.* London: Routledge and Kegan Paul.

Robertson, R. (1992). *Globalisation: Social theory and global culture.* London: Sage.

Sewart, D., Keegan, D., & Holmberg, B. (Eds.), (1983). *Distance education: International perspectives.* Beckenham: Croom Helm.

Shale, D. (1990). Towards a reconceptualization of distance education. In M. G. Moore with P. Cookson, J. Donaldson, & B. A. Quigley (Eds.), *Contemporary issues in American distance education* (pp. 333–343). Oxford: Pergamon.

Smith, K. (1984). *Diversity down under: In distance education.* Toowoomba: Darling Downs Institute Press.

Smith, P., & Kelly, M. (Eds.). (1987). *Distance education and the mainstream.* London: Croom Helm.

Waters, R. (no date). *The wall.* No place of publication: Avon, publishers of Bard, Camelot and Flare Books.

Wedemeyer, C. A. (1981). *Learning at the back door: Reflections on non-traditional learning in the lifespan.* Madison: The University of Wisconsin Press.

Young, M. F. D. (1971). An approach to the study of curricula as socially organized knowledge. In M. F. D. Young (Ed.), *Knowledge and control: New directions in the sociology of knowledge* (pp. 19–46). London: Collier, Macmillan.

Young, M. F. D. (1998). *The curriculum of the future.* London: Falmer Press.

53

Distance Education in the Perspective of Global Issues and Concerns

Jan Visser
Learning Development Institute
jvisser@learndev.org

INTERNATIONAL DEVELOPMENT: THE BROAD CONTEXT

The history of international development is more than 50 years old. The origin of its prehistory may be located hundreds of years earlier, when the efforts of navigators and new conceptualizations by scientists started changing our idea of the world and of our place within it (e.g., Boorstin, 1985; Koestler, 1959). Those who had the economic power, and thus had access to the technology of the day, discovered that they were not alone in the world and that other peoples—mostly seen as essentially different and invariably inferior—co-inhabited the planet. Different forms of, often exploitative, cohabitation emerged during colonization. That period ended during the third quarter of the last century. Emancipation and decolonization, largely driven by the formerly oppressed, led to the recognition among those who eventually relinquished power that not everything in the world was right. In fact, it laid bare great inequalities that conflicted with long-held moral convictions—convictions that had, until then, been solely applied (and even then only partially) to the societies of those who held the convictions. Such inequalities, it was realized, were immoral and they threatened stability. A new world order was called for.

Initial ideas about development focused on technology transfer. The world was seen as polarized between *developed* and *underdeveloped* nations (terms that were later replaced by *industrialized* and *developing* nations). A simple rationale underlay the development philosophy. Those countries that saw themselves as developed had little to learn from those that required development; contrariwise, the developed nations felt obliged to share their expertise with those whose different state of development was assumed to have resulted from the absence of such expertise. There was thus a formidable urge on the part of some to teach and an assumed great need on the part of hundreds of millions of others to learn. While the development discourse reflecting this philosophy has become more nuanced over the decades, much of its basic assumptions are still very much alive.

The above remarks provide a backdrop for the subsequent discussion of the development of distance education as a contributing factor to building a better world. The following four statements are offered as an advance organizer for that discussion:

1. The development effort undertaken over the past half century has, to a considerable extent, focused on creating and improving education systems, modeled after those of the industrialized West.
2. Educational needs in developing nations (defined as implied by the previous statement) have been so enormous—compared to the available resources—that traditional modalities to meet them could not be but insufficient. The search for alternatives, including distance education, was a natural consequence of this recognition.
3. The visions underlying the concepts of development and education tend to explain the world, its history, and the possibilities to shape its future in linear terms. They furthermore assume that the knowledge systems of the developed world are superior to local or indigenous knowledge systems. The history of international development of the past half century justifies questioning the validity of these visions.
4. When the international development effort took off, the prevailing global issues and concerns were limited in scope and biased toward the problems that had upset the world during the late 1930s and early 1940s. It took another half century to discover that the world was infinitely more complex than we had ever thought. A more comprehensive picture of global issues and concerns has started to emerge during the last decade of the 20th century. However, we are far from understanding fully how to deal with the implications of those issues from a learning point of view.

SCOPE OF THIS CHAPTER

This chapter looks at distance education in the perspective of global issues and concerns, a topic closely linked to the very reasons why distance education became an important international development issue. I particularly focus on the discrepancy between the established practice of distance education and the overriding purposes for educational development. This leads to a critique of the field as it currently stands, a critique, though, that is equally valid for many other modalities of educational practice.

The above referred critique of distance education is linked to the larger question of the meaning of learning. After an analysis of the development of distance education in the next two sections, I therefore elaborate on the need to revisit the meaning of learning as it relates to the demands of our time. This then allows holding current perceptions of distance education against the light of an enhanced vision of learning, leading, finally, to recommendations about what to emphasize and what to de-emphasize in developing the field further.

TAKING A CLOSER LOOK AT THE PROBLEM

The development of distance education globally, particularly in the developing world, has largely been driven by the desire to overcome the shortcomings of established schooling practices. The literature of the period when distance education started to position itself as a serious alternative to or complement of school-based offerings would often contrast distance education—or, as it used to be called, correspondence education and, in some other cases, radio or TV education—with so-called traditional or conventional education (e.g., Edström, Erdos, & Prosser, 1970; Erdos, 1967; Faure et al., 1972; Perraton, 1976; Young, Perraton, Jenkins, & Dodds, 1980).

Different considerations motivated the emergence of distance education as a significant alternative. Chief among them was the growing awareness of the injustice inherent in the deprivation of a large proportion of the world's population of opportunities to learn commonly available to others.

At the same time there was the expectation that "new media" would usher in an era of until-then-unimagined possibilities to overcome the barriers of the past. In an address to the State Department on August 20, 1971, Arthur C. Clarke expressed it this way: "The emerging countries of what is called the Third World may need rockets and satellites much more desperately than the advanced nations which built them. Swords into ploughshares is an obsolete metaphor; we can now turn missiles into blackboards" (1992, p. 208).

Hope and vision were accompanied by the desire to gather evidence in support of the claims that media, and the instructional design principles underlying their use, could indeed help to overcome the formidable obstacles faced by educational leaders and planners in developing countries. Most notable perhaps was a worldwide research project undertaken by UNESCO's International Institute for Educational Planning in 1965 and 1966 under the leadership of Wilbur Schramm, resulting in the landmark publication of three volumes on *New Media in Action: Case Studies for Planners* and a companion volume on *The New Media: Memo to Educational Planners* (UNESCO: International Institute for Educational Planning, 1967a, 1967b). Other prominent sources reflecting the thinking of that time regarding the educational use of media are Schramm's (1977) *Big Media, Little Media*; Jamison & McAnany's (1978) *Radio for Education and Development*; and Jamison, Klees, & Wells' (1978) *The Costs of Educational Media: Guidelines for Planning and Evaluation*.

During the same period the instructional design field was coming of age with such classics as Gagné's *The Conditions of Learning* (first published in 1965) and Gagné and Briggs' *Principles of Instructional Design* (first published in 1974), giving confidence that the process of making people learn and ensuring that their learning achievements would match their originally identified learning needs could be not only controlled but also managed within a considerably wider range of parameters than those traditionally considered. Particularly, it became clear that that process was not necessarily or exclusively dependent on a human facilitator.

The above factors taken together provided a powerful reason to search for the solution of the world's educational problems in settings beyond those of the conventional schooling practice. Naturally, it also raised questions about the quality of the contemplated alternatives as compared to the traditional practices they were supposed to replace or complement.

Two inadequacies of traditional education are usually highlighted in such sources as mentioned above. Then as well as now, traditional schooling systems cater for only a limited part of the audience they are supposed to serve. This results in great inequity globally regarding how people can see themselves as active participants in a world that is larger than their immediate environment. It led Julian Huxley, Executive Secretary of the Preparatory Commission for UNESCO in 1946, later UNESCO's first director-general, to consider that "Where half the people of the world are denied the elementary freedom which consists in the ability to read and write, there lacks something of the basic unity and basic justice which the United Nations are pledged together to further" (cited in UNESCO, 2000, p. 27). While Huxley recognized that various factors are responsible for such inequity, he saw what was then called "Fundamental Education" (p. 27) as essential to "the wider and fuller human understanding to which UNESCO is dedicated" (p. 27). The problem is far from over. According to the 2000 issue of the World Education Report (UNESCO, 2000), the world total of illiterates still stands at 875 million, i.e., a very significant proportion of the 6 billion inhabitants of our planet. Moreover, the number of children in the primary school age not going to school continues to be of the order of magnitude of 100 million.

However, access to learning opportunities was not the only problem. The other major shortcoming of the schooling system, recognized in at least part of the literature cited earlier (e.g., Faure et al., 1972; Young et al., 1980), had and has to do with the schooling tradition itself, particularly the kind of learning it instills in students, the social consequences of expectations it generates, and the often poor relevance of what is being learned for those who learn and their surrounding development context.

The former of the two deficits constitutes a violation of the fundamental human right to education. That right is specified in Article 26 of the Universal Declaration of Human Rights (Table 53.1). The World Education Report 2000 (UNESCO, 2000) gives ample coverage of how that right and its implications have been perceived and discussed since the Declaration was adopted and proclaimed by the General Assembly of the United Nations on December 10, 1948.

It is important for our discussion that the Declaration links education to "the full development of the human personality and to the strengthening of respect for human rights and fundamental freedoms" (cited in UNESCO, 2000, p. 16). Education, in the view of the Declaration, thus transcends the mere concern with the acquisition of particular skills and pieces of knowledge. Instead, it relates it to the ability to live in harmony with oneself, one's environment, and one's fellow human beings. Consequently, the deficit of the school system should not be interpreted solely in terms of the lack of opportunity to acquire such competencies as the ability to read and write, but rather in terms of how such, and other, abilities "promote understanding, tolerance and friendship among all nations, racial and religious groups, . . . and the maintenance of peace" (UNESCO, 2000, p. 16).

Insofar as distance education strives to overcome the shortcomings of the school systems, it should be judged by the above standards. The primary question to be asked is not how the development of distance education has improved access to and participation in education, and at what cost, but rather: Does distance education contribute to a better world? Put this way, the question also includes concerns about the second major area identified above, the one that motivated the distance education field to see itself as an opportunity, not only to open up possibilities for learning to the as-yet unreached, but equally to do so in ways that would be responsive to questions about the purposes of education, the meaning of learning, and the critique of the existing schooling tradition.

MEANS OR END?

Article 26 of the Universal Declaration of Human Rights represents a rare instance in the development of international discourse about educational policy where an unequivocal reference is made to the purposes of education beyond the scope of particular content concerns.

TABLE 53.1
Article 26 of the Universal Declaration of Human Rights

Article 26
1. Everyone has a right to education. Education shall be free, at least in the elementary and fundamental stages. Elementary education shall be compulsory. Technical and professional education shall be made generally available and higher education shall be equally accessible to all on the basis of merit.
2. Education shall be directed to the full development of the human personality and to the strengthening of respect for human rights and fundamental freedoms. It shall promote understanding, tolerance and friendship among all nations, racial or religious groups, and shall further the activities of the United Nations for the maintenance of peace.
3. Parents have a prior right to choose the kind of education that shall be given to their children.

From: Universal Declaration of Human Rights (1948; cited in UNESCO, 2000)

It advances the perspective that education is not an end in itself, but rather a means toward how we, humans, collectively shape the ways in which we socially organize ourselves, live together, and share the resources of our planet. The terms in which that perspective is formulated reflect the post-World War II concerns of the time when the Declaration was drafted. The ensuing debate and subsequent international frameworks developed over the past half century have consolidated, strengthened, and expanded the original vision of Article 26, allowing it to evolve and become responsive to currently felt global concerns. Sustainable development and poverty eradication are but two of the global concerns that were not explicitly expressed in the original formulation of Article 26, which are now felt to be essential for a stable and harmonious world order.

Particularly the last decade of the past century has seen heightened interest in discussing the purposes of education in the light of global issues and concerns. Those issues and concerns have to do with such matters as our fragile environment; the growth of the world population; our ability to interfere technologically and scientifically with who we are; the depletion of the world's resources; the advancement of peace, not as the mere absence of war, but as a culture, a set of values, attitudes, traditions, modes of behavior, and ways of life (United Nations, 1999); and the impact of pandemic diseases. An impressive range of world conferences—the World Education Report 2000 (UNESCO, 2000) mentions 15 of them, starting with the World Conference on Education for All in Jomtien, Thailand, in 1990 and ending with the World Science Conference in Budapest, Hungary, in 1999—has helped to put the crucial issues of our time on the agenda of the international community, while seeking to understand how education can contribute to addressing them. Two major UNESCO reports produced during the 1990's—*Learning. The Treasure Within* (Delors et al., 1996) and *Our Creative Diversity* (Pérez de Cuéllar et al., 1996)—should be seen in the same light.

This renewed attention to the overriding purposes of education should come as no surprise. For the first time in several million years of hominid development, the human species faces challenges of a magnitude it has never had to deal with before. I have argued elsewhere (J. Visser, 2001), drawing also on the views of authors such as Koestler (1989/1967), Pais (1997), and Sakaiya (1991), how these challenges are part of a context of change patterns that are unique for our time and markedly different from those that characterized the human condition a mere couple of decades ago. They require human beings to be able to function in entirely unpredictable situations. Lederman (1999, April) thus calls for schools to

> look across all disciplines, across the knowledge base of the sciences, across the wisdom of the humanities, the verities and explorations of the arts, for the ingredients that will enable our students to continually interact with a world in change, with the imminence of changes bringing essentially unforeseeable consequences. (p. 3)

It needs no arguing that, by extension, the same rationale should apply to any alternative to the school, such as distance education systems that are being put into place to overcome the shortcomings of the school. However, it would be a mistake to look at the school, and its alternatives, as a panacea for the complex set of problems referred to above or to look at it in isolation. Schooling is not the same as learning. Schooling plays a role, and it can play a much more useful and effective role if it were profoundly reconceptualized, but that role is limited and relative to the role played by other factors that condition the learning environment at large. To appreciate the relative importance of the schooling tradition—including how that tradition is reflected in the practice of distance education—as well as to critically do away with those elements of the tradition that violate the attainment of agreed purposes, we must first develop a more comprehensive picture of what learning is.

LEARNING: THE COMPREHENSIVE PICTURE

One of the greatest impediments to the development of a learning society is the difficulty to overcome the preconceptions about learning with which we grow up (J. Visser & Y. L. Visser, 2000, October). The need to broaden our views of learning has been amply discussed in a series of transdisciplinary debates, promoted and conducted under the auspices of UNESCO and the Learning Development Institute since 1999 (J. Visser et al., 1999; Meaning of Learning [MOL] project, n.d.).

Further insight can be derived through disciplined inquiry into learning as perceived by those who learn. Such inquiry typically focuses on the entire human being or on the activity of an entire collaborative entity in a cultural-historical perspective. It thus involves units of analysis whose order of magnitude by far transcends the habitual research perspective, which tends to focus on learning tasks that are narrowly defined in scope and time and that may involve only very specific learning behaviors assumed to be undertaken by isolated individuals. (A similar point is made by Cole, 1991, regarding the need to redefine the unit of analysis in the study of socially shared cognitions.) Research such as referred to above was reported by Y. L. Visser and J. Visser (2000) in their analysis of so-called learning stories. That research focused on the perceptions about learning from the perspective of individuals. John-Steiner (2000) went beyond the individual level, making the collaborative team or partnership the unit of analysis, in her study of creative collaboration.

The preliminary results reported by Y. L. Visser and J. Visser (2000) indicate that the advance toward meaningful learning should focus on:

- the development of felt ownership of knowledge;
- the emotional integration of any particular learning experience in an individual's perceived lifespan development;
- the generative nature of learning;
- the real-life context as the natural habitat for learning;
- the interaction with the learning of others as a basis for one's own learning;
- the power of learning to turn negative self-perceptions into positive ones;
- the discovery of persistence as a strategy to manage life's challenges.

Such learning was found to be particularly facilitated when initially negative conditions could be transformed into positive challenges; when role models were present or emotionally significant support was available in the environment of the learner; or when there were opportunities for independent exploration of one's learning and metacognition.

Much in the analysis of the above-referred individual learning stories points toward the importance of context, particularly the social, cultural, and historical integration of the learning individual. John-Steiner's (2000) analysis of cases of creative collaboration reinforces, makes more explicit, and enhances that notion. In analyzing her cases, she builds a strong argument against the prevalent cultural model of the solitary creative mind and stresses the principle that "*humans come into being and mature in relation to others*" (p. 187). Interdependence, or social connectedness, is thus a crucial dimension of any learning context, a dimension that needs to be balanced with that of the learner's individuality.

Feldman (2000), shedding foresight on the importance of John-Steiner's work, refers to the search for "balance between individuality and social connectedness" (p. xii) as the central theme of the current century, contrasting it with the past century's focus on "intellectual development that placed the lone seeker of knowledge . . . at the center of the developmental process" (p. ix). Such a shift of focus comes at a good time. The global issues and concerns considered in this chapter are too involved and too complex to be addressed by solo efforts. They call for visions of learning that are built around notions of sustained collaboration and dynamically evolving dialectic relationships between individuals and communities. Such visions have only marginally to do with the content of learning. Rather, they impact on how people learn and therefore on how the learning landscape should be restructured. They are an equally powerful motivation to start thinking differently about learning, "undefining" the concept (J. Visser, 2001), and recasting it as a disposition to dialog—expressed at different levels of complex organization—for constructive interaction with change.

A final important contribution to creating comprehensive visions of learning can be found in the efforts to review significant research findings of the past and present, emanating from different disciplines, with a view to summarizing them in the framework of transdisciplinary major themes. An excellent example of such an effort is the work undertaken by the Committee on Developments in the Science of Learning of the National Research Council (Bransford, Brown, & Cocking, 1999). The Committee identifies five major themes that are important in changing our conceptions of learning. They have to do with: (1) how we develop coherent and accessible structures of information; (2) the ways in which we develop expertise and acquire the capability to solve problems we have never dealt with before; (3) new insights in learning and mental development at the initial stages of the human lifespan; (4) the role played by metacognitive and self-regulatory processes; and (5) the relation between learning and the cultural and community context in which symbolic thinking emerges.

ACHIEVEMENTS TO DATE

Earlier in this chapter I referred to Article 26 of the Universal Declaration of Human Rights as an instance of broad consensus within the international community about the crucial importance of a global concern and the potential role of education—and thus also distance education—in addressing it. Considering that many more such global concerns have lately been added to the shared conscience of humanity, it is of interest to look back and ask ourselves what has been done. What we see is not encouraging.

There is little doubt that considerable achievements in implementing Article 26 mark the more than five decades since the proclamation of the Universal Declaration of Human Rights. The field of distance education can claim credit for at least part of those achievements. However, as the World Education Report 2000 (UNESCO, 2000) points out, surprisingly little of what was achieved reflects a concern with more than increasing the numbers of those who benefit from structured learning opportunities. In the words of the report:

> While . . . there has been a great deal of progress worldwide over the past half century towards implementation of the right to education in terms of access to education, it nevertheless remains that the vision that came to be embodied in Article 26 of the Universal Declaration of Human Rights was not just a quantitative one. It was also a qualitative one concerning the purposes and hence contents of education. (p. 74)

The language of the above quote is confusing as it equates "purpose" and "content." It is important to distinguish between the two concepts. The concept "content" connotes subject-matter knowledge. This may easily be interpreted as a commodity traded between those who possess it, the teachers, and those who wish to acquire it, the students. Content, however, is only one element that may or may not contribute to attaining a particular educational purpose. The following example may elucidate this.

It is sometimes thought that the teaching of subjects such as history and geography can have a potentially important impact on how students will think about and treat their fellow human beings pertaining to other cultures or whose existence is marked by different histories. Such a thought may indeed have motivated the 1949 International Conference on Public Education, which, mindful of the words of the Universal Declaration, recommended "the teaching of geography as a means of developing international understanding" (cited in UNESCO, 2000, p. 77). While I shall be critical, in what follows, of the rather naïve assumptions inherent in this recommendation, it should be noted that this was one of only two International Conferences, held during the 20 years following the adoption of the Universal Declaration of Human Rights, that produced anything reminiscent of the global issues raised in the Declaration.

It is unlikely that the simple introduction of a piece of curriculum, or the restructuring of existing curriculum, in accordance with the above idea, will more than marginally contribute to the earlier-mentioned larger goal of international understanding so long as "teaching" means "transmission of pieces of knowledge." Much more is needed in changing attitudes. Both Bandura (1969) and Gagné (1985) argue that human modeling and practicing of the model are essential. In the case of our example, the content of disciplines like geography and history may be about as relevant to being exposed to models of human behavior, and being encouraged to practice them, as is the content of disciplines such as physics, chemistry, biology, or mathematics.

In fact, as a segment of the traditional school curriculum, the latter set of disciplines may be more adequate, if purposefully taught, in a strategy to contribute to international understanding. Practitioners of the natural sciences and mathematics are known for their disregard of conventions that would limit them in their pursuit of the advancement of knowledge in their field. This is exemplified by how, during the coldest periods of the cold war, there has always been scientific exchange across the so-called iron curtain. Moreover, even as the Nazis rose to power in Europe, and the Second World War ravaged the continent and its scientific community, interests within the latter ensured that after the end of the war, wounds could quickly be healed. Numerous accounts of the lives of scientists and the development of science in the 20th century (see, for instance, Pais, 1991, and Perutz, 1998) describe in detail, and with great attention to the human qualities involved, what was at stake.

The above argument shows that appropriate procedures, involving apparently unrelated content, can very well serve the purpose of developing tolerance and international understanding. The proper teaching of science could bring to life the human models that Gagné (1985) and Bandura (1969) call for. Practicing those models can well be undertaken in the context of collaborative projects across geopolitical and other boundaries among students (sometimes also involving practicing professional scientists) in areas like environmental science. Current technologies facilitate the building of such distributed learning communities.

CHALLENGES AHEAD

The prevailing focus in the rhetoric of distance education has for a long time been on such issues as cost-effectiveness, economies of scale, and parity of esteem, all of them defined with reference to the traditional school context. This has left the thinking about distance education in the fold of the dominant classroom model. Despite the advent of powerful new technologies and the increasing realization that the problems of today are essentially different from yesterday's problems, there is a disturbing lack of imagination in how discourse and practice remain locked up in the conceptions of the past. The abundant use of such terms as *online classroom* and *virtual school* is but one expression of how powerful a place the ideas of school and classroom continue to occupy in our language, and thus our thought processes. Even when new terms are introduced, such as *e-learning*, the reality behind them is often as sadly representative of the unaltered past—cast for the occasion in new molds—as the choice of the term itself is testimony to the absence of creative thinking.

Simonson (2000) calls for strategies that provide "different but equivalent learning experiences" (p. 29) to learners in face-to-face classes and in online classrooms. This so-called equivalency theory, while recognizing the differences in instructional contexts between the two modalities concerned, may do little to promote a fundamental rethinking of what goes on inside the learning space, whether virtual or real, the implicit assumption being that the face-to-face classroom is the norm and that equivalency rather than improvement should be sought.

Contrasting with the above is the sense of critical appreciation of the state of distance education in the world, emanated from a group of 23 experts from around the globe, convened by UNESCO, at a meeting in Karlsruhe, Germany. One of the recommendations made by that group states:

> Now that distance education has reached its desired level of recognition and esteem *vis-à-vis* traditional educational alternatives, time has come for it to take a critical look at itself, asking questions about how existing experience fits in with the requirements of and opportunities inherent in present day society and how it reflects the current state of knowledge about how people learn. It is recommended that such a critical attitude drive any future development in the field of distance education in UNESCO and its Member States. (UNESCO, 2001, February, p. 4)

The group framed its recommendation with particular reference to "the evolving notions of a learning society and of lifespan human development" (p. 4). It furthermore recommended that distance education be seen as "just one modality—or set of modalities—among many others that together shape the learning environment, which is multi-modal and aware of multiple dimensions of human intelligence, at the cognitive, meta-cognitive and affective level" (p. 4).

In connection with the above recommendation, the group of international experts convened by UNESCO devoted particular attention to the opportunities inherent in the currently available technologies. Market forces, rather than considerations about how and why people learn, determine that such technologies will be used. In the absence of clear thinking, their use will likely result in the replication of past practices by new means. At best, this means that nothing changes; at worst it means that with accelerated speed, and more forcefully than ever, bad practices will be consolidated and reinforced. Or, in the words of the report (UNESCO, 2001, February):

> The advent of the Internet and the invention of the World Wide Web have, supplemented by a wide and growing range of multimedia technologies, particularly during the past decade, fundamentally changed the equation of what is and what is not possible. It has particularly created opportunities for the rediscovery of learning as a dialogic and social process through which diverse people join in the creation of dynamic learning communities, collaborating with each other while using their full human potential to continually develop their capacity to stand prepared for an ever-changing world. Such a process is one of shared construction, which, while it may contain linear elements, is greatly enhanced if the learning environment allows building blocks—of different granularity—to be brought in flexibly, as they are needed. The possibility to create, store and subsequently retrieve for use or further processing such building blocks in digital format is an important asset of today's technology. It awaits further exploration, particularly in the context of the [earlier referred] much needed reconceptualization of learning. In this process, the traditional roles of those who learn and those who facilitate other people's learning are bound to change so fundamentally that terms like "student" and "teacher" become less appropriate to designate the actors in the learning environment. The human and social processes that can be created, while using these new technologies to attend in massive ways to the innate human need to learn, can and must take full account of research findings that have redefined learning as a process of participatory construction rather than as individual acquisition. (pp. 5–6)

The group thus recommended the inclusion of experts in communication and information technology in collaborative multidisciplinary partnerships involved in the reconceptualization of learning. Without doing so, it argued,

> there is the great risk that the use of improved technology will only reinforce and consolidate practices that, though unfortunately often part and parcel of established educational practice, have long been recognized to be counter to the development of humanity's critical and creative capacity and of the human ability to confront the complex problems of today's world. (p. 6)

The latter observation resonates with Salomon's (2000, June) criticism of "technocentrism," which "totally ignores some crucial social and human factors" (p. 4). He observes that without taking these factors into account, "virtual distance learning . . . is in danger of yielding virtual results" (p. 4). Salomon thus urges an emphasis on two things: *tutelage* and *community of learners*. The former aspect has received attention in L. Visser's (1998) work on affective communication and in Gunawardena's (1995) work on social presence. The latter aspect has been emphasized by the group of people who gathered initially around the ideas promoted by UNESCO's Learning Without Frontiers (2000) program and who later converged around the vision of the Learning Development Institute (2001).

COMPLEX COGNITION FOR A COMPLEX WORLD

Gell-Mann (1994) refers to learning as a process in which complex adaptive systems, such as human beings, interact with other complex adaptive systems, making sense of regularities among randomness and allowing them to mutually adapt. In a similar vein, the report of the Committee on Developments in the Science of Learning (Bransford, Brown, & Cocking, 1999) affirms that "learning is a basic, adaptive function of humans" (p. xi). To understand that function, and thus the practice of its facilitation, account must be taken of the entire developing transdisciplinary knowledge base that has its roots in such widely diverse disciplines as "cognitive development, cognitive science, developmental psychology, neuroscience, anthropology, social psychology, sociology, cross-cultural research, research on learning in subject areas such as science, mathematics, history, and research on effective teaching, pedagogy, and the design of learning environments" (p. xxi). Broadening our conception of learning is an essential prerequisite if learning is to have relevant meanings in the context of adaptive human behavior regarding the global issues discussed in this chapter.

Learning, then, should be understood to mean more than what is implied by its regular reference to particular desired changes in human performance capability. In a broader sense, which includes the more specific meaning just mentioned, learning can be seen in relation to the unending dialog of human beings with themselves, with their fellow human beings, and with their environment at large, allowing them to participate constructively in processes of ongoing change. In other words, learning must be "undefined." A possible redefinition thus calls for human learning to be seen as "the disposition of human beings, and of the social entities to which they pertain, to engage in continuous dialogue with the human, social, biological and physical environment, so as to generate intelligent behavior to interact constructively with change" (J. Visser, 2001).

Few people would doubt that learning impacts on the human brain. However, that recognition should not be taken to mean that the individual human mind in isolation should be the prime focus of attention for educators, whether at a distance or in the face-to-face mode. Quite to the contrary, it is increasingly recognized—for instance, by the collective of researchers that contributed to Salomon's (1993) explorations into the distributed nature of cognitions—that knowledge is socially constructed as a result of purposeful interaction among individuals in the pursuit of shared objectives that are situated in sociocultural and historical contexts. Views such as those referred to above should perhaps not be seen as new or surprising, as Nickerson (1993) points out. Rather, they are a consequence of the ways in which, for a very long time, formal instructional practice has kept its eye trained on the individual. So strongly has that been the case that the reality of the communities to which those same individuals belong could no longer be seen. What used to be obvious thus became forgotten and now stands to be brought to the forefront again. Nickerson refers in this connection to Ulam (1991), who says: "Sometimes obvious things have to be repeated over and over before they are realized" (p. 303). In this particular case, however, more is necessary than the frequent repetition of the obvious; the obvious must first be resuscitated.

To do so, we must develop a vision of learning that is ubiquitous; unrelated to conditions such as age, time, space, and circumstance of learning individuals; manifests itself not only in the behavior of individuals but at diverse levels of complex organization; and that, in whatever context it takes place, does so as part of a pattern of interrelated learning events occurring in what can best be called a "learning landscape." Cognition is, and has always been, an ecological phenomenon. Being an ecological phenomenon, it is also evolutionary. The two notions are interrelated, as Levin (1999) points out. "Ecological interactions take place within an evolutionary context and in turn shape the ongoing evolutionary process" (p. 46).

Invoking terms such as *ecology* and *evolution* is not an exercise at inventing sophisticated metaphors. Webster's Third New International Dictionary (Gove, 1993) defines ecology as a "branch of science concerned with the *interrelationship* of organisms and their environments, esp. as manifested by natural cycles and rhythms, *community development* and structure, interaction between different kinds of organisms, geographic distribution and population alterations" (my emphasis). The origin of the word is, according to the Encyclopaedia Britannica (1999), the Greek "*oikos*," which means "household, home, or place to live." These descriptions apply as much to the world of learning entities as they apply to the world of living organisms. This should come as no surprise. The capability to make sense of regularity among randomness, which, according to Gell-Mann (1994), is the essence of learning, is also key to any life form's chances of survival in an environment populated with other forms of life.

My use of the term *learning landscape* may be taken to be metaphorical. Like the real landscape, the learning landscape is the result of, on the one hand, the natural—that is ecological—interplay of different learning entities seeking to establish themselves in the midst of others and, on the other, of the consciously planned action on the part of some actors to reshape and adjust what nature tends to produce. I use the term *landscape* deliberately because of its connotations, some of which are more poetic than operational. This, then, brings into play, in addition to the usual parameters of effectiveness and efficiency of the learning environment, also its aesthetic and ethical qualities. The planners and leaders whose actions impact on the learning landscape may well want to consider this extended meaning of the metaphor and look for beauty and harmony in the learning landscape as a major indicator for the quality of the ecology of cognition. It is probably no exaggeration to say that, so far, the work of governmental educational planning agencies, as well as of related entrepreneurial and institutional efforts, to create the infrastructural conditions for the facilitation of learning, leaves considerable room for improvement in terms of the need to be environmentally aware of what else happens in the learning landscape. This observation obviously includes much of the distance education effort as well.

The term learning landscape reflects the idea of "complex cognition," a concept recently proposed by the author at a Santa Fe Institute seminar (J. Visser, 2000, November). Cognition is a complex phenomenon in the sense that it evolves according to the laws that govern the behavior of complex adaptive systems. The conditions that underlie such behavior are well known (see, e.g., Gell-Mann, 1995; Holland, 1995). The stock market, the weather, and biological systems are examples of it.

The notion of distributed cognitions approximates the idea of "complex cognition." However, as Salomon (1993) points out, the meaning attributed to the term *distributed cognitions* varies considerably, depending on the theoretical perspective adopted by different researchers. On one end of the spectrum there is the view that "cognition *in general* should be . . . conceived as principally distributed," the "proper unit of psychological analysis . . . [being] the *joint . . . socially mediated action* in a cultural context" (p. xv). This view contrasts with the common perception that cognitions reside inside individuals' heads. On the other end of the spectrum one finds the conception that "'solo' and distributed cognitions are still distinguished from each other and are taken to be in an interdependent dynamic interaction" (p. xvi). This juxtaposition of views is resolved in the concept of complex cognition, which makes the distinction irrelevant, integrating the diverse points of view in a single notion. Cognition is individually owned *and* socially shared at the same time.

DISTANCE EDUCATION IN THE PERSPECTIVE OF GLOBAL ISSUES AND CONCERNS

I have so far deliberately refrained from focusing on distance education per se. The problem area chosen as a guiding framework for the intellectual pursuits I made reference to, that of the interaction between humanity's capability to deal with global concerns and the development of its capacity to learn, calls for a comprehensive approach that must not be restricted to the field of distance education alone. On the other hand, the question whether distance education may play a crucial role *within* such a comprehensive approach is a relevant one. I explore that question in this final section. While addressing it, I particularly look at what kind of questions need to be asked and what different orientations need to be developed *if* distance education is to play a crucial role.

One of the overall conclusions of this chapter is that the phenomenon of learning is infinitely more involved and complex than assumed in most of our actions to create the conditions that promote and facilitate learning. The earlier referred learning stories research (Y. L. Visser & J. Visser, 2000) suggests that significant learning often takes place rather *despite* than *because* of the conditions we created for it. I contend that this doesn't have to be so—that, in fact, we can be more clever than we seem to be. To employ such enhanced intelligence, our approaches must become bolder and our views more comprehensive.

The global issues and concerns referred to in this chapter—the profound questions about how we live together on our tiny planet and share its resources, sustaining life as we came to know it and became conscious of our place in it, playing our role in, how in time, perhaps, a next phase in its evolution may emerge—find no response in our designed learning systems. Yet, most people share these concerns and feel they can no longer be dismissed or simply be seen as an afterthought of our more specific attempts at developing human capacity. The history of how the educational establishment, including the distance education variety of it, has failed to address such most-crucial challenges as the ones inherent in Article 26 of the Universal Declaration of Human Rights is proof of the fruitlessness of attempts to use our traditional learning systems in an isolated fashion while dealing with global issues and concerns. Such attempts must be undertaken, as urged in the earlier quoted UNESCO report, in a wider framework, namely that of the learning society and of lifespan human development, taking full account of the convoluted ways in which humans learn (UNESCO, 2001, February).

The important question then is: How can distance education contribute to improving the ecological coherence of the learning environment so that it will allow meaningful learning to evolve in response to the crucial global issues and concerns that mark the beginning of the third millennium? The question branches off in a variety of directions, some of which will be highlighted in the following sections. To bring some order in the observations and conclusions that follow, I deal with them, respectively, at the levels of society at large; collaboration among institutions and organizations within society; the organization of specific institutions; and the learning process.

Implications at the Societal Level

At the level of society at large, the responsibility for the creation of the conditions of learning is a distributed one. This view contrasts with the common idea that such a responsibility resides solely or mostly with ministries or departments of education. Obviously, the latter idea comes from the misconception that education and learning are one and the same thing. It is important to make a distinction between the two and to look at the instructional landscape as a sublandscape of the learning landscape.

Instruction is—or should be—a designed way to facilitate learning for specifically defined purposes. The preoccupation with instruction results in a wide variety of instructional opportunities. Within the conception, advocated in this chapter, that society at large is responsible for the totality of learning that goes on within it, the various instructional opportunities should be aware of each other and interconnect with each other. They form, as an organically interlinked whole of designed opportunities to learn, the instructional landscape.

The instructional landscape does not stand on its own. Many other sublandscapes together make up the learning landscape, in a way similar to how Appadurai (1990) describes the dynamics of global diversity in terms of different "scapes." Other sublandscapes included in the learning landscape are, for instance, the media landscape (see Allen & Otto, 1996) and the sociocultural organization landscape, of which the family is part. A truly ecologically functioning learning landscape will be characterized by the smooth integration among all the various sublandscapes—together with their subordinated sublandscapes—that compose the learning landscape.

Because of its potential flexibility and openness, the distance education modality can play an important role in bringing about ecological integration within the learning landscape. Doing so would be a more laudable goal—and a truly more exciting challenge—than the current emphasis on replication, for ever-expanding markets, of outdated learning structures by new means.

Implications at the Level of Interinstitutional Collaboration

While in some parts of the world there may seem to be no limit to the resources that can be brought to bear on addressing the problems of human learning, whosoever takes the trouble to look at the world at large will soon discover that there is an important challenge in creating sustainable solutions that benefit large numbers of people. Sustainability in this context means that the cost of what we do at a particular time will not be charged to a future we are unable or unwilling to visualize or take responsibility for. It should also be noted that solutions that benefit many people do not necessarily have to rely on mass-produced and mass-delivered options.

There is enormous potential for promoting and facilitating learning in the networking of those who have a passion to learn (e.g., Rossman, 1993). This applies to both individuals and institutions. Anything that detracts from the likelihood that interinstitutional collaboration would occur, such as the artificial opposition between learning at a distance and in the face-to-face mode, is thus counter to exploring this potential.

The tendencies of some institutional environments towards expansion (e.g., Daniel, 2000, July), sometimes through the merger with smaller entities, may seem to contribute to creating larger networks. However, there is the risk that the strong presence of large conglomerates reduces the diversity of the learning landscape, thus taking away one of the most powerful resources in the learning habitat. To the extent that the learning landscape functions in ecologically sound ways, in other words, to the extent that diverse sublandscapes are the active ingredients of the learning landscape, such homogenizing forces may be counteracted by heterogeneous dialogues resulting from interaction with different ideological and cultural traditions (Appadurai, 1990).

There may, as yet, not be enough evidence to draw conclusions about how the various tendencies toward globalization will affect diversity. It would be prudent, though, to keep an open eye toward what may be happening and to assess such possible impact on an ongoing basis. It is equally prudent to encourage ways of networking that deliberately thrive on diversity, i.e., multinodal collaboration among institutions that have a distinct identity, as opposed to building networks that are run out of a central node.

Against the backdrop of the above cautionary remarks, I posit that increased networking around the globe is an important condition for the formation of dynamic learning communities that are sufficiently global in outlook to become a basis for learning to live together (Delors et al., 1996) with the global concerns of our time. For this to be possible, collaborating institutions must once again become what they used to be: universities, places of inquiry not limited by the boundaries of bureaucracy and traditional divisions among disciplines. UNESCO's UNITWIN/UNESCO Chairs (n.d.) program is an interesting example in the above regard.

Implications at the Institutional/Organizational Level

The closing observation in the previous paragraph is also the first recommendation under the present heading. The model of monolithic, bureaucratized, and compartmentalized institutions dominates the institutional heritage of the 19th and 20th centuries. Such institutions now find themselves in need of becoming players in a networked environment, often having great difficulty to respond adequately to the challenge.

In using the term *universities* above, I do not intend to restrict my considerations to higher education institutions. The connection between higher education and higher learning—i.e., learning at a higher level of metacognitive awareness and capability—is rather weak, whence the meaning of the adjective "higher" in higher education seems to have little relevance as a qualifying concept for the kind of learning that is promoted by higher education institutions.

To play an effective role in shaping the increasingly networked learning landscape of the 21st century, institutions whose mission is to promote and facilitate learning must enhance their ability to interact constructively with their changing environment. In terms of the redefinition of learning called for in this chapter (see also J. Visser, 2001), this means that such institutions must conceive of themselves as learning organizations. The literature in this area is vast and so well known that there is hardly a need to mention such names as Senge (1990); Argyris (1993); Senge, Kleiner, Roberts, Ross, and Smith (1994); Marquardt (1996); or Hesselbein, Goldsmith, and Beckhard (1997).

The change of attitude implied in becoming a learning organization should go hand in hand with the development of systemic awareness and abilities in the institution, both in terms of its internal processes and with regard to its role vis-à-vis other institutions and the learning landscape at large. It must equally focus on the profoundly human (as contrasted with bureaucratic) mission inherent in fostering learning, a particularly acute challenge for institutions whose traditions are rooted in the philosophy of the industrial era (Peters, 1994). Clearly, this is a change that affects everyone in the institution: students, faculty, administrative staff, as well as management.

Implications at the Learning Process Level

The most important implications are at the level of the learning process. Very little impact on our ability to deal with global issues and concerns is likely to result from our continued preoccupation with knowledge as a thing, as opposed to knowledge as a process. To reorient the learning process away from its habitual focus on acquiring isolated pieces of knowledge, the overriding vision in learning must be on problems (e.g., Jonassen, 1994; Hmelo, 1998; Bransford, Brown, & Cocking, 1999 [particularly Ch. 2]), transdisciplinarity (Nicolescu, 1996; 1999, April), and consilience (Wilson, 1998).

Reintroducing this overriding concern in our conscious efforts to promote the development of human learning does not mean a radical doing away with everything that has to do with disciplines, content-based curricula, or even rote learning of particular facts. There is abundant evidence to support the idea that such things have their relative usefulness. However, that usefulness gets reduced when it is the only focus in learning and when it cannot be embedded in a larger frame of relevance.

The overall focus on problems, transdisciplinarity, and consilience is a vital condition, also, for learning to become, once again, dialog. It is equally a prerequisite for the development of critical thinking, creativity, and the socialization and contextualization of cognition. Moreover, placing students, and those with whom they learn, eye-in-eye with the real world of whole problems and interconnected knowledge and associated emotions regarding those problems, will be most beneficial to bring back yet another important aspect of our humanity in the learning process: the fact that we function with our entire bodies, not just the neocortex.

The challenge to the distance education community in considering the above implications lies in the need to move past the customary rhetoric of cost-effectiveness and economies of scale. Such notions are based on the idea that the existing principles of instruction are adequate and merely require the redesign of the processes of their application to benefit larger audiences in affordable ways. I have tried to argue that the problems with the development of learning in the context of today's challenges are much more complex and fundamental. They require the field to be reinvented. The difficulty in meeting that challenge is rather psychological than substantial. The problems are known and the tools are there.

REFERENCES

Allen, B. S., & Otto, R. G. (1996). Media as lived environments: The ecological psychology of educational technology. In D. H. Jonassen (Ed.), *Handbook of research for educational communications and technology* (pp. 199–225). New York: Simon and Schuster Macmillan.

Appadurai, A. (1990). Disjuncture and difference in the global cultural economy. *Public Culture, 2*(2), 1–24.

Argyris, C. (1993). *On organizational learning.* Cambridge, MA: Blackwell Publishers.

Bandura, A. (1969). *Principles of behavior modification.* New York: Holt, Rinehart and Winston.

Boorstin, D. J. (1985). *The discoverers: A history of man's search to know his world and himself.* New York: Random House.

Bransford, J. D., Brown, A. L., & Cocking, R. R. (Eds.). (1999). *How people learn: Brain, mind, experience, and school.* Report of the Committee on Developments in the Science of Learning, Commission on Behavioral and Social Sciences and Education, National Research Council. Washington, DC: National Academy Press.

Clarke, A. C. (1992). *How the world was one: Beyond the global village.* London, UK: Victor Gollancz Ltd.

Cole, M. (1991). Conclusion. In L. B. Resnick, J. M. Levine, & S. D. Teasley (Eds.), *Perspectives on socially shared cognition* (pp. 398–417). Washington, DC: American Psychological Association.

Daniel, J. (2000, July). *The university of the future and the future of universities.* Paper presented at the Improving University Learning and Teaching 25th International Conference, Frankfurt, Germany [Online]. Available: http://www.open.ac.uk/vcs-speeches/ [2001, March 13].

Delors, J., Al Mufti, I., Amagi, I., Carneiro, R., Chung, F., Geremek, B., Gorham, W., Kornhauser, A., Manley, M., Padrón Quero, M., Savané, M-A., Singh, K., Stavenhagen, R., Suhr, M.W., & Zhou, N. (1996). *Learning: The treasure within.* Report to UNESCO of the International Commission on Education for the Twenty-first Century. Paris, France: UNESCO.

Edström, L. O., Erdos, R., & Prosser, R. (Eds.). (1970). *Mass education: Studies in adult education and teaching by correspondence in some developing countries.* Stockholm, Sweden: The Dag Hammerskjöld Foundation.

Encyclopaedia Britannica. (1999). *Encyclopaedia Britannica CD 99: Knowledge for the information age. Multimedia edition,* [CD-ROM].

Erdos, R. F. (1967). *Teaching by correspondence* (a UNESCO Source Book). London, UK: Longmans, Green & Co Limited; Paris, France: UNESCO.

Faure, E., Herrera, F., Kaddoura, A-R., Lopes, H., Petrovsky, A. V., Rahnema, M., & Ward, F. C. (1972). *Learning to be: The world of education today and tomorrow.* Report to UNESCO of the International Commission on the Development of Education. Paris, France: UNESCO.

Feldman, D. H. (2000). Foreword. In V. John-Steiner, *Creative collaboration* (pp. ix–xiii). New York, NY: Oxford University Press, Inc.

Gagné, R. M. (1970/1985). *The conditions of learning* (1st/4th ed.). New York: Holt, Rinehart and Winston.

Gagné, R. M., & Briggs, L. J. (1974). *Principles of instructional design.* New York: Holt, Rinehart and Winston.

Gell-Mann, M. (1994). *The quark and the jaguar: Adventures in the simple and the complex.* New York: W. H. Freeman and Company.

Gell-Mann, M. (1995). What is complexity? *Complexity 1*(1), 16–19.

Gove, P. B. (Ed.). (1993). *Webster's third new international dictionary of the English language.* Unabridged edition. Springfield, MA: Merriam-Webster, Inc.

Gunawardena, C. N. (1995). Social presence theory and implications for interaction and collaborative learning in computer conferences. *International Journal of Educational Telecommunications, 1*(2/3), 147–166.

Hesselbein, F., Goldsmith, M., & Beckhard, R. (Eds.). (1997). *The organization of the future.* San Francisco, CA: Jossey-Bass Publishers.

Hmelo, C. E. (1998). Problem-based learning: Effects on the early acquisition of cognitive skill in medicine. *The Journal of the Learning Sciences, 7*(2), 173–208.

Holland, J. H. (1995). Can there be a unified theory of complex adaptive systems? In H. J. Morowitz & J. L. Singer (Eds.), *The mind, the brain, and complex adaptive systems.* Proceedings Volume XXII, Santa Fe Institute, Studies in the Sciences of Complexity (pp. 45–50). Reading, MA: Addison-Wesley Publishing Company.

Jamison, D. T., & McAnany, E. G. (1978). *Radio for education and development.* Beverly Hills, CA: Sage Publications.

Jamison, D. T., Klees, S. J., & Wells, S. J. (1978). *The costs of educational media: Guidelines for planning and evaluation.* Beverly Hills, CA: Sage Publications.

John-Steiner, V. (2000). *Creative collaboration.* New York: Oxford University Press, Inc.

Jonassen, D. (1994). Instructional design models for well-structured and ill-structured problem solving learning outcomes. *Educational Technology Research & Development, 45*(1) 65–94.

Koestler, A. (1959). *The sleepwalkers: A history of man's changing vision of the universe.* London, UK: Hutchinson.

Koestler, A. (1989, originally published in 1967). *The ghost in the machine.* London, UK: The Penguin Group.

Learning Development Institute. (2001). Web site of the Learning Development Institute [Online]. Available: http://www.learndev.org [2001, February 26].

Learning Without Frontiers. (2000). Web site of UNESCO's Learning Without Frontiers program [Online]. Available: http://www.unesco.org/education/lwf/ [2001, February 26].

Lederman, L. M. (1999, April). *On the threshold of the 21st century: Comments on science education.* Paper presented at the Symposium on "Overcoming the underdevelopment of learning" (J. Visser, Chair) at the annual meeting of the American Educational Research Association, Montreal, Canada [Online]. Available: http://www.learndev.org/dl/lederman_f.pdf [2001, January 18].

Levin, S. A. (1999). *Fragile dominion: Complexity and the commons.* Reading, MA: Perseus Books.

Marquardt, M. J. (1996). *Building the learning organization.* New York: McGraw Hill.

Meaning of Learning [MOL] project (n.d.). *In search of the meaning of learning* (J. Visser, Chair). Presidential Session at the International Conference of the Association for Educational Communications and Technology, Denver, CO (October 2000) [Online]. Available: http://www.learndev.org/MoL.html [2001, January 26].

Nickerson, R. S. (1993). On the distribution of cognition: Some reflections. In G. Salomon (Ed.), *Distributed cognitions: Psychological and educational considerations.* Cambridge, UK: Cambridge University Press.

Nicolescu, B. (1996). *La transidiciplinarité—Manifeste* (Transdisciplinarity—A Manifesto). Paris: Éditions du Rocher.

Nicolescu, B. (1999, April). *The transdisciplinary evolution of learning.* Paper presented at the Symposium on "Overcoming the underdevelopment of learning" (J. Visser, Chair) at the annual meeting of the American Educational Research Association, Montreal, Canada [Online]. Available: http://www.learndev.org/dl/nicolescu_f.pdf [2001, March 13].

Pais, A. (1991). *Niels Bohr's times, in physics, philosophy and polity.* Oxford, UK: Clarendon.

Pais, A. (1997). *A tale of two continents: A physicist's life in a turbulent world.* Princeton, NJ: Princeton University Press.

Pérez de Cuéllar, J., Arizpe, L., Fall, Y. K., Furgler, K., Furtado, C., Goulandris, N., Griffin, K., ul Haq, M., Jelin, E., Kamba, A., Magga, O-H., Mikhalkov, N., Nakane C., & Takla, L. (1996). *Our creative diversity.* Report of the World Commission on Culture and Development. Paris, France: UNESCO.

Perraton, H. (Ed.) (1976). *Food from learning: The International Extension College 1971–1976.* Cambridge, UK: International Extension College.

Perutz, M. (1998). *I wish I'd made you angry earlier: Essays on science, scientists and humanity.* New York: Cold Spring Harbor Laboratory Press.

Peters, O. (1994). Distance education and industrial production: A comparative interpretation in outline (1967). In D. Keegan (Ed.), *The industrialization of teaching and learning* (pp. 107–127). London, UK: Routledge.

Rossman, P. (1993). *The emerging worldwide electronic university: Information age global higher education.* Praeger studies on the 21st century. Westport, CT: Praeger.

Sakaiya, T. (1991). *The knowledge-value revolution, or, a history of the future.* Tokyo, Japan: Kodansha International Ltd., originally published in 1985 in Japanese by PHP Kenkyujo, Kyoto, Japan as *Chika kakumei.*

Salomon, G. (Ed.). (1993). *Distributed cognitions: Psychological and educational considerations.* Cambridge, UK: Cambridge University Press.

Salomon, G. (2000, June). *It's not just the tool, but the educational rationale that counts.* Invited keynote address at the 2000 Ed-Media Meeting, Montreal, Canada [Online]. Available: http://construct.haifa.ac.il/~gsalomon/edMedia2000.html [2001, January 20].

Schramm, W. (1977). *Big media, little media: Tools and technologies for instruction.* Beverly Hills, CA: Sage Publications.

Senge, P. M. (1990). *The fifth discipline: The art and practice of the learning organization.* New York: Doubleday.

Senge, P. M., Kleiner, A., Roberts, C., Ross, R. B., & Smith, B. J. (1994). *The fifth discipline fieldbook: Strategies and tools for building a learning organization.* New York: Doubleday.

Simonson, M. (2000). Making decisions: The use of electronic technology in online classrooms. *Principles of Effective Teaching in the Online Classroom: New Directions for Teaching and Learning, 84,* 29–34.

Ulam, S. (1991). *Adventures of a mathematician.* Berkeley, CA: University of California Press.

UNESCO. (2000). *World education report 2000—The right to education: Towards education for all throughout life.* Paris, France: UNESCO Publishing.

UNESCO (2001, February). *Report on the UNESCO programme—Learntec 2001.* Report of the international expert meeting held in conjunction with Learntec 2001 in Karlsruhe, Germany.

UNESCO: International Institute for Educational Planning. (1967a). *New educational media in action: Case studies for planners—I, II & III.* Paris, France: United Nations Educational, Scientific and Cultural Organization.

UNESCO: International Institute for Educational Planning. (1967b). *The new media: Memo to educational planners.* Paris, France: United Nations Educational, Scientific and Cultural Organization.

United Nations. (1999). *Declaration and programme of action on a culture of peace,* General Assembly Resolution A/53/243. New York: United Nations.

UNITWIN/UNESCO Chairs. (n.d.). Web site of UNESCO's UNITWIN/UNESCO Chairs program [Online]. Available: http://www.unesco.org/education/educprog/unitwin/index.html [2001, March 13].

Visser, J. (2000, November). *Learning in the perspective of complexity.* Paper presented at the Santa Fe Institute, Santa Fe, NM [Online]. Available: http://www.learndev.org/SantaFe.html [2001, March 10].

Visser, J. (2001). Integrity, completeness and comprehensiveness of the learning environment: Meeting the basic learning needs of all throughout life. In D. N. Aspin, J. D. Chapman, M. J. Hatton, & Y. Sawano (Eds.), *International Handbook of Lifelong Learning* (pp. 447–472). Dordrecht, The Netherlands: Kluwer Academic Publishers.

Visser, J., Berenfeld, B., Burnett, R., Diarra, C. M., Driscoll, M. P., Lederman, L. M., Nicolescu, B., Tinker, R. (1999, April). *Overcoming the underdevelopment of learning.* Symposium held at the annual meeting of the American Educational Research Association, Montreal, Canada [Online]. Available: http://www.learndev.org/aera.html [2001, January 26].

Visser, J., & Visser, Y. L. (2000, October). *On the difficulty of changing our perceptions about such things as learning.* Paper presented at the Presidential Session on "In Search of the Meaning of Learning" (J. Visser, Chair) at the International Conference of the Association for Educational Communications and Technology, Denver, CO [Online]. Available: www.learndev.org/dl/DenverVisserVisser.PDF [2001, September 20].

Visser, L. (1998). *The development of motivational communication in distance education support* (dissertation). Enschede, The Netherlands: University of Twente.

Visser, Y. L., & Visser, J. (2000, October). *The learning stories project.* Paper presented at the International Conference of the Association for Educational Communications and Technology, Denver, CO.

Wilson, O. E. (1998). *Consilience: The unity of knowledge.* New York: Alfred A. Knopf.

Young, M., Perraton, H., Jenkins, J., & Dodds, T. (1980). *Distance teaching for the third world: The lion and the clockwork mouse.* London, UK: Routledge & Kegan Paul Ltd.

54

Leading ODL Futures in the Eternal Triangle: The Mega-University Response to the Greatest Moral Challenge of Our Age

John Daniel
UNESCO
j.daniel@unesco.org

Wayne Mackintosh
University of Auckland
w.mackintosh@auckland.ac.nz

This chapter concentrates on one particularly successful manifestation of open distance learning (ODL), namely the large-scale single-mode providers, which have been called the mega-universities (see Daniel, 1996). Within the context of leading strategic futures in higher education, we argue, first, that the principles of open learning will continue to be the guiding vision for the future of the university and, second, that the large open learning systems of the mega-universities are an important model for the university of the future.

In order to achieve the objectives stated above, the structure of this chapter is based on three main areas of focus that are derived from the following questions:

- *What is the state of tertiary education provision around the world?* When examining the imbalances between global supply of tertiary education and the magnitude of the moral demand for access, it is clear that the imperative of providing a decent education for all is the greatest moral challenge of our age. Thus, distance education will have to play an important role in helping to resolve this crisis.
- *Why have the large open learning systems used by the mega-universities been so successful?* A clearer understanding of the drivers underpinning the success of the mega-universities in conjunction with an extrapolation of what this may tell us about ODL futures will provide insights into how we can start to tackle the looming higher education crisis on our planet.
- *What have we learned from the mega-university experience regarding the future of the university?* Innovations that have the potential for radical transformation in society also very often include the potential for great risks for society. This section draws on the mega-university experience with particular reference to technology futures for the university.

The mega-university experience, as a particular form of distance education practice, has gained a rich and extensive experience in both the highly industrialized and the developing regions of our world. In many respects, the practice of distance education in the mega-university context is unique when compared to other forms of distance education and face-to-face higher education provision. Furthermore, the mega-university, as institution, has the most extensive experience in technology-mediated learning. It is a unique innovation in the higher education sphere with global relevance. The mega-university is consequently an important area of study with particular reference to leading the creation of new strategic futures for the university.

CONFRONTING THE GREATEST MORAL CHALLENGE OF OUR AGE

Global access to tertiary education has grown from 6.5 million enrollments in 1950 to 88.2 million enrollments in 1997 (UNESCO, 2000a, p. 67). This represents a growth of more than 1200% in less than one generation. Although increases in the absolute capacity of higher education provision can partly be ascribed to population expansion, clearly there has also been a philosophical shift from "class to mass" (World Bank, 2000, Introduction).

Although in 1995 a little more than half of the students enrolled for higher education (47 million) were living in the developing world, it is disconcerting to note that only a few industrialized countries report a tertiary gross enrollment ratio in excess of 50%: for example Australia, Denmark, North America, Norway, New Zealand, and countries in Central and Western Europe. For most of the developing world the gross enrollment ratio is below 15% and the average for Sub-Saharan Africa in 1995 was distressingly below 3%. Using demographic projections of the 18–23-year-old cohort Saint (1999, p. 2) pointed out that at least 16 countries in Sub-Saharan Africa will need to *double* current tertiary enrollments in the coming decade just to maintain the existing and unacceptably low gross enrollment ratio. What is more frightening is that the dismal performance of higher education in many parts of the developing world is limited to the traditional age cohort of tertiary education and does not begin to describe the severity of the problem. For instance, these figures do not reflect the blight inflicting the lives of billions of adults falling outside the parameters of the traditional cohort who, for whatever reason, were not able to benefit from a tertiary education. For the majority of these people, the contemporary prerequisites for lifelong learning in the modern economy are an unattainable aspiration. Furthermore, as the tertiary education sector closes for business around the globe today:

- one out of every 4 adults on our planet will still suffer from the bane of illiteracy, which translates to some 900 million people who may never have the privilege of a tertiary education;
- there are 250 million children in the world who will not receive or complete their basic education, which excludes them from the fundamental right of learning and they are destined to be barred from access to a tertiary education that nowadays is generally regarded as a prerequisite condition for gainful employment in our emerging knowledge economy.

Harnessing the forces of the global knowledge economy to ensure that all people of the world get a decent education is the greatest moral challenge of our age. In an ideal world, the university as institution, combined with its traditional values concerning the well-being of society, should be well positioned to assist in tackling the "Education for All" challenge that was articulated recently at UNESCO's World Education Forum in Dakar in April 2000 (UNESCO, 2000b).

However, in the real world, universities are faced with the perplexing task of balancing the tensions of the eternal triangle. That is, to improve quality, cut their costs, and to serve more and more students.

Open distance learning systems, particularly the large mass providers of distance education, have recorded notable successes in managing the dynamics of the eternal triangle. Clearly, distance education will have to play a pivotal role in this future. Complicating matters is the fact that distance education no longer has a distinct and definitive pedagogy and the concept includes a myriad of delivery alternatives capable of effective provision where teaching and learning behaviors are separated in time-space relationships. Today the concept of "distance education" for example, includes the dual-mode systems pioneered by Australia, the distributed classroom models using compressed video that have gained popularity in the United States, the large single-mode open learning systems perfected by the British Open University, and more recently Web-based and Web-enhanced delivery alternatives.

Apart from the rich variety of forms that are used nowadays for providing distance education, we have also experienced phenomenal growth in the use of distance education as method at traditional universities. In 1990 only a small proportion of traditional universities offered courses by distance. Today no self-respecting university president can admit to not offering courses online. If all universities are involved in distance education today, this raises the question whether open universities will be needed in the future. Alternatively stated, what do the open universities offer that is special?

Given the sheer magnitude of the tertiary education crisis, we desperately need mass providers like the mega-universities to operate within the tapestry of alternative forms of university-level provision. Traditional face-to-face delivery and the variety of other forms of distance education will simply not be able to scale up provision to the levels required of the global demand in a manner that is capable of maintaining a sustainable balance among the tensions of the eternal triangle.

Accordingly, this chapter's focus on the mega-universities is considerably more than an intellectual and scholarly analysis of the characteristic features of mass ODL provision. It is also a justified proposal for an important delivery model that is capable of contributing significantly toward the resolution of the greatest moral challenge of our age.

THE DRIVERS UNDERPINNING THE SUCCESS
OF THE MEGA-UNIVERSITIES

The mega-university systems, as one of the most important innovations in higher education of the 20th century, have successfully combined the challenges of access and quality in an approach that can be scaled up in ways that reduce cost without compromising the core social values of the university: for example, promoting the development of the systematic skepticism and intellectual independence of its learners. Before analyzing the reasons underpinning the innovation associated with the mega-universities, it is useful to establish a frame of reference by comparing the learning systems of the mega-universities with the conventional campus model and dual-mode systems.

Under the conventional campus model, individual faculty members carry the responsibility for teaching. They have relative freedom to organize the learning environment regarding the implementation of the curriculum and have considerable latitude concerning how to teach in the classroom and how to assess learners. The campus model is a robust model and does not require too much organization from the part of the university. Quality of provision is therefore variable and this model is extremely difficult to scale up beyond the physical limitations of campus facilities and the threshold number of learners that an individual faculty member can realistically manage.

The dual-mode systems pioneered by the Australian universities have succeeded in expanding access to off-campus students by using distance education methods to augment face-to-face provision. Typically in dual-mode systems, the lecturer responsible for classroom teaching is also responsible for teaching the distance education students. Dual-mode systems have the advantage that learning resources designed for the distance education mode can also be used effectively in the classroom. Therefore, the pedagogical discipline associated with the design of effective distance education resources can have a positive impact on the quality of the pedagogy in the classroom. Furthermore, interaction in the classroom (for example, identifying areas where contact students are struggling), can be fed back into the distance education component of the course. Dual-mode systems do, however, require a more sophisticated organization system from the university. Furthermore, as with the campus model, it is also difficult to scale up the levels of access beyond that which an individual faculty member can cope with.

The distinguishing pedagogical feature of the mega-university is that, instead of giving individual faculty members the responsibility for teaching, they have developed sophisticated learning systems based on innovative divisions of labor where the responsibility for teaching is carried collectively by the organization. The differentiating feature of the large open learning systems is that the institution teaches, whereas in conventional forms of delivery, an individual teaches. This is a radical difference (Keegan, 1980, p. 19). By breaking the traditional lecturer-student bond and designing a total teaching system where the functions of teaching are divided into a range of specializations, the mega-universities have been able to scale up the delivery of quality teaching to levels that are simply not possible in conventional campus-based or dual-mode models.

Who are the mega-universities? The mega-universities are large open universities found in various parts of the world that report enrollments of more the 100,000 students each. In 1999 there were 11 such institutions enrolling approximately 3 million students between them (Daniel, 1999, p. 30), and they are listed in Table 54.1. Today, it is likely that the number of mega-universities has grown and that they could collectively account for 4 million students.

The 100,000 enrollment criterion is an arbitrary cut-off classification. However, the interesting characteristic of these institutions is not primarily their size, but rather the fact that they are all distance education institutions. In other words, the mega-universities were not able to achieve these levels of access and provision using the traditional campus model. Hence, the

TABLE 54.1

Mega-Universities of the World

Name of Institution	Country	Enrollment	Budget $US Million	Unit Cost[6]
China TV University System	China	530,000[1]	1.2[4]	40
Centre National d'Enseignement à Distance	France	184,614[1]	56	50
Indira Gandi National Open University	India	242,000[2]	10	35
Universitas Terbuka	Indonesia	353,000[2]	21	15
Payame Noor University	Iran	117,000[3]	13.3	25
Korea National Open University	Korea	210,578[2]	79	5
University of South Africa	South Africa	130,000[2]	128	50
Universidad Nacional de Educación a Distancia	Spain	110,000[2]	129	40
Sukhothai Thammathirat Open University	Thailand	216,800[2]	46	30
Anadolu University	Turkey	577,804[2]	30[5]	10
The Open University	UK	157,450[2]	300	50

(*Source:* Daniel, 1999, pp. 30–31)

Notes

1. 1994 figure.
2. 1995 figure.
3. 1996 figure.
4. Central (CCRTVU) unit only.
5. Open education faculty only.
6. Unit cost per student as a percentage of the average for other universities in the country (approximate).

pursuit of scale requires the establishment of a learning system. Furthermore, it is not surprising that the largest student numbers and majority of mega-university institutions are working in the developing world, particularly when assessed against the moral challenge facing higher education that was articulated earlier in this chapter.

Strategy is enriched when it is informed by practice, therefore this chapter draws specifically from the experiences of two notable pioneers, namely the University of South Africa (UNISA) and the British Open University (UKOU). It is not possible within the limited scope of this chapter to cover adequately the experiences of each mega-university, and the specific choice of the two institutions is justified as follows:

- UNISA was the first single-mode, distance education university of the world and while breaking new ground in this field, the organization made fundamental errors in the design of components of its open learning system, which it is now steadily correcting. This attests to necessity of designing robust learning systems that fit the unique requirements of mass distance education provision. Furthermore, UNISA is the only mega-university on the African continent and, as a result, has first-hand experience of the unique challenges associated with Sub-Saharan Africa where the tertiary education crisis is rampant. However, UNISA is also riddled with infrastructural complexities that are not replicated in the same magnitude elsewhere in the developing world.
- Many judge the UKOU to be the most important innovation in higher education and open distance learning. Arguably, the most significant achievement of the UKOU is that it was designed as a total learning system from the student outward. Very few institutions have been able to achieve comparable levels of UKOU learner-centeredness. The UKOU also pioneered the first large-scale university system based on the principles of open learning and was instrumental in implementing the course team approach for the design and development of quality learning materials.

Notwithstanding the justifications for the inclusion of the experiences of the two institutions above, there are important links between the history of the two institutions and the lifework of an American visionary, Charles Wedemeyer, whose foresight concerning learner independence helped direct the realization of the principles of open learning in the mega-universities. This is an early example of globalization in distance education where the development of the mega-universities was linked by the thinking and experience from America, South Africa, and the United Kingdom.

The drivers underpinning the success of the mega-universities will be discussed in terms of:

- the vision of open learning that has directed their strategic futures;
- the practical experience gained by operating at scale concerning the key operational elements responsible for its accomplishments; and
- finally the proof in the pudding, by measuring output in terms of the elements of the eternal triangle.

The Compelling Vision of Open Learning

The creation of the UKOU in 1969 was a significant milestone in the evolution of university-level provision. Supported by the political will to increase access to higher education for working adults in Britain and the desire to do this using new mass-media technology, the UKOU was designed as a totally new learning system. Its vision was ambitious. Walter Perry, the founding vice-chancellor of the UKOU, articulated this vision at the inaugural ceremony in 1969 as being "open as to people, open as to places, open as to methods and, finally open as to ideas" (cited in Daniel, 1995, p. 400). The principles of "open learning" do not only refer to the general aim of opening access to higher education more widely, but also refer to openness concerning methods and ideas. This mission statement still inspires the UKOU today and given recent technological developments, the vision could be amplified by adding: to be open as to time and open to the world.

The principles of open learning will continue to be the guiding vision for the future of the university. To illustrate the significance of this statement we return to the time of the creation of the UKOU. The vision of open learning at the UKOU evolved from the foresight of Charles Wedemeyer, who played a significant role in the planning of the new UKOU. Wedemeyer's thinking was influenced by two other distance education prototypes:

- the Articulated Instructional Media (AIM) project that was steered by the vision of Charles Wedemeyer during the period 1964 to 1968; and
- Wedemeyer's evaluation of the UNISA distance teaching system in 1967, which had already been in operation for two decades prior to the creation of the UKOU.

The decisive characteristic of Wedemeyer's interest in distance education is that it was driven by the vision of promoting the fundamental right of learning and was not a whimsical curiosity into the use of technology in education. Wedemeyer placed pedagogy above technology and held the belief that the learner should be the center of the educational endeavor as clearly expressed in the following statement: "Perhaps no tenet of education is more widely held or more frequently expressed than that education must be centred in the individual" (Wedemeyer & Childs, 1961, p. 13).

Deserving particular mention regarding the realization of the vision of open learning is the Articulated Instructional Media (AIM) project, which began in 1964 under Wedemeyer's leadership at the University of Wisconsin. The goal of the AIM project was to find meaningful ways of connecting (i.e., articulating) a variety of communication media for teaching in a distance education setting.

During the period between 1965 and 1969, there were numerous contacts and visits by Wedemeyer to the United Kingdom with senior officials of the foundation team of the UKOU (see Moore & Kearsley, 1996, pp. 25–27). One of the founding director of studies at the UKOU, Walter James, wrote the following to Wedemeyer:

> You bear some responsibility for the emergence of the Open University in this country. It was your talk on Articulated Instructional Media (AIM) that stimulated us to produce at Nottingham the first university course in this country in which television broadcasts and correspondence instruction were integrated; and it was this experience which produced interest in the University of the Air idea. (Cited in Wedemeyer, 1982, p. 24)

Returning to the other mega-university example selected for this chapter, UNISA began teaching at a distance in 1946 and is therefore the oldest single-mode distance-teaching university in the world.

The UNISA prototype is distinctive because it was designed and created before the new epoch associated with the mass communication media. Consequently, the organization has gained valuable experience regarding the fundamental transformation associated with moving from one delivery epoch to the next.

Furthermore, UNISA was conceived and designed to be a university, and was not originally created as an open learning system (whereas the UKOU was designed from its inception to be an open learning system). Through its traditions as a university, combined with the appointment of reputable scholars, UNISA did pioneering work by gaining an academic reputation for the standards and quality of the distance education method, which in the early years was necessary to deconstruct misconceptions of the perceived superiority of the conventional university. The UNISA mega-university prototype was important because, according to Peters:

> Nowhere else was it possible to let correspondence studies mature over the years into an accepted method of university teaching. Nowhere else was it possible for distance-teaching pedagogical routine to be developed so early from a university-based pedagogical experiment. (1998, p. 158)

Wedemeyer's vision concerning the fundamental right to learning, combined with his experiences of the AIM project and evaluation of the UNISA DE system, certainly helped to promote the practical implementation of the principles of open learning in the mega-university experience. Furthermore, Wedemeyer's early work with the idea of a team of specialists used to develop learning resources for distance education was implemented with unprecedented success at the UKOU. Strategists working in the field of innovating new futures in the field of distance education would do well to gain an intellectual grip on the foresight of Wedemeyer's philosophy because it still holds profound relevance today as we move into the digital epoch of educational provision. Accordingly, we argue that the principles of open learning will remain a guiding vision in the evolution of the future of the university.

Key Elements of Operational Success

By providing distance teaching at scale, the mega-universities have established that success in this area must contain the following four elements:

- Excellent multimedia study materials that are designed and developed by multiskilled course teams to promote independent and autonomous learning;
- Individualized support provided to learners by faculty with special training in working with adults to complement the learning resources that are uniform for all learners;
- Good logistics and administration to ensure a high quality of service to the student;
- Faculty members who remain actively involved in research to maintain the intellectual excitement that students find beneficial and attractive in their learning.

The discussion of the four elements listed above should be interpreted from the perspective of the relationship between technology and distance education. Hence, a few cursory remarks about this relationship and the corresponding pedagogical implications are necessary.

The mega-universities have learned that the quality of pedagogy is not necessarily determined by specific technology choices, rather, it is a function of the pedagogical design that the technology implements. Each technology has its own pedagogical requirements. Also when operating at scale, the division of labor is fundamental to the approach, and this produces a better result than having everyone do everything.

The mega-universities have been involved with technology-mediated learning since their inception—the practice of distance education is simply not possible without technical mediation, and traditionally this has been a differentiating feature of distance education when compared to face-to-face provision. The distance education process is a technology in its own right. Consequently, the mega-universities do not necessarily view the new digital technologies from the same foundational perspectives as conventional university counterparts. The experience is one of using technology at scale to provide quality learning and the mega-universities have developed distinct university structures, processes, and specializations effectively to manage the pedagogical applications of technology. However, what is clear with each wave of new technology—and this is particularly the case with emerging digital technologies—is that the levels of organizational complexity and corresponding demands for new areas of specialization are increasing by an unparalleled order of magnitude.

The fact that distance education is a technology in its own right has direct implications for the pedagogical structure of teaching and learning. In fact, the dominant modes of learning in classical distance education are different from conventional face-to-face instruction. This has resulted in the development of specialized distance education skills and a corresponding research base in the design of "interactive texts" as well as advances in the particular pedagogy of simulated communication such as Holmberg's guided didactic conversation (Holmberg, 1995).

The demands for pedagogical specialization with particular reference to digital ICTs will increase in the future, and the organizational requirements for campus-based institutions moving into this field will, in many cases, be considerably more demanding than initially envisaged because of the changes in the fundamental structure of the pedagogy and resultant changes in learning behaviors. Conventional classroom pedagogy will not be able to deliver the goods, and the implementation of course-team development in these environments, incorporating an increasing variety of specializations, will become progressively more important for future success.

We now return to the discussion of the four critical elements of success based on the mega-university experience. First, the innovation associated with the course team: the idea of teamwork in teaching outside the mega-university context is not widespread in university practice, even though many universities may purport to support the ideals of teamwork. Although the traditions of the academy espouse a collegial model, faculty members tend to work independently and institutional reward and incentive practices tend to promote individual scholarship. Perhaps this is one of the reasons why Web-based teaching is being received so warmly by individual faculty because of the perception that it facilitates online teaching by academics working alone. However, the course-team is one of the critical success factors of the open universities. When Lord Perry, the founding vice-chancellor of the UKOU, is asked what he considers to be the key innovation of the organization's success, he will unhesitatingly reply, "the course team."

At the UKOU, the course team is considerably more than bringing together of a range of experts and specialists—it is a culture of scholarship. The course team makes the art of teaching intellectually challenging for members of the team, and this excitement is communicated to the students through the course materials. Teams may vary in size from 3 to 30 members, with faculty members serving as the core and they are joined by instructional designers, media experts, editors, TV producers, and other professionals.

The members of the team do not perform discrete functions, but collectively give meaning to the distinguishing characteristic of distance education namely that the "institution" and not "individuals" teach in open learning systems. This culture of scholarship means critical review. At the UKOU, it is tradition that the first draft of each member of the team gets comprehensively criticized on both academic and pedagogical grounds.

Prior to the 1990s, UNISA did not use a course-team approach for the development of its courses and relied on the pedagogical skills of individual faculty members, not unlike the teaching practice of the campus-based professor. This strategy was not able to compete pedagogically because of the superiority of course-team approach and second, because of the inherent limitations of conventional classroom pedagogy, which was the dominant frame of reference for many UNISA academics.

In 1994, UNISA embarked on a process of fundamental pedagogical transformation, culminating in a revised tuition policy being approved by the university, which incorporates the principles of course-team development. UNISA underestimated the magnitude of the transformation to the team-approach, particularly with regards to changing existing organizational culture to a culture of team-based scholarship. The lesson learned is that universities that are commencing with the organizational transformation—that will be necessitated by shifts to e-learning of any scale—should not underestimate the magnitude of such change. Furthermore the requirements for courseware to be more flexible and to change more rapidly in the future should also not be underrated.

The mega-universities have successfully learned how to carry out distance education at scale, and this is not merely a technological accomplishment. The innovation associated with proper implementation of the scholarship of course-team development has meant that the mega-university is capable of better quality teaching than conventional universities on both academic and pedagogical grounds.

These levels of academic and pedagogical quality require a huge investment, particularly in terms of expensive academic time. The mega-universities seek economies of scale that are needed to spread this substantial investment over large numbers of students. The significant levels of investment to maintain the quality as described here cannot be sustained unless economies of scale can be generated. Furthermore, it is important to remember the moral aspects relating to the fact that the open universities, despite mass-production, provide a quality tertiary education to millions of people, who otherwise may never have had the opportunity to study at a university.

This brings us to the second element responsible for success in open learning systems: the provision of individualized student support by means of a distributed tutor system to mediate the students' study of the materials and providing individualized comments on students' progress. Student support in ODL refers to "the range of services both for individuals and for students in groups which complement the course materials or learning resources that are uniform for all learners" (Tait, 2000, p. 289). Student support covers the cognitive, affective, and administrative needs of the student.

It must be emphasized that the concept of "student support" as it is used here refers to individualized customization for a learner over and above the teaching contained in the mass-produced materials. Therefore, for example, pedagogically innovative learning experiences, which form part of the learning materials, do not fall under the ambit of this definition even though these pedagogical interventions may "support" learners in their learning. The differentiating feature of student support is the individualized customization and consequently, per definition, it cannot be mass-produced in anticipation of the differentiated needs of students. This is not to say that carefully designed learning materials should not cater for differentiated student needs, but, for purposes of this discussion such examples are the outcome of good instructional design and are not examples of student support.

At the UKOU, each student gets strong personal support. The UKOU makes extensive use of part-time faculty and every 20–25 learners are assigned to a dedicated tutor, who feels personally responsible for the progress of each student. Tutors are responsible for maintaining personal contact with their students, grading assignments, and mediating the learning experience. As in the case of good universities, tutors are not engaged to feed students with answers, but to support them in asking good questions and to promote autonomous learning by supporting the search for finding and evaluating the answers to these questions.

Prior to 1994, student support as defined here was not an integral component of the UNISA delivery system.

In response to criticisms regarding the shortcomings of student support in the UNISA system, in 1994 the University instituted a Department of Student Support, which, among other tasks, is also responsible for instituting face-to-face tutorials for UNISA students. In spite of the good work of the Department of Student Support at UNISA, resource constraints have limited the extent of the tutorial support program. Based on statistics reported by this department, the student support initiative has not been able to extend its access above 10% of the registered students of UNISA (Mackintosh, 1999, p. 9). Consequently, providing student support is still a significant challenge in the UNISA delivery system.

The third element underpinning the success of the mega-universities is that huge learning systems rely on good logistics and administration. The magnitude and efficiency required of logistics and administration in the mega-university context astounds visitors from conventional universities when visiting our institutions.

Consider, for example, that UNISA manages the administration of more than 400,000 individual course registrations from a choice of more than 2,000 individual courses. This means setting up and managing administration systems for course registrations and student finances and keeping records of student progress. UNISA uses a semester system, which means that course registrations take place twice a year. UNISA operates its own print-factory, which is said to be the largest under one roof in the southern hemisphere. The print factory prints some 515 million pages per year and is responsible for ensuring that study materials are available on time when students register. UNISA is responsible for warehousing and distributing study materials, printing and despatching tutorial letters during the course of the academic year, as well as managing the submission of assignments and returning these to students once they have been marked.

Clearly, the logistics and administration of mega-universities are of industrial proportions and necessitate division of labor and specialized industrial equipment. Individual faculty members will not be able to administer these levels in a coherent, efficient, and cost-effective way. Furthermore, good logistics and administration relate directly to the levels and quality of service provided to students. As we move forward into the digital era, successful e-services will depend on getting the "services" as well as the "e" right.

Finally, it is important that faculty remain active in research. We have found that this helps to maintain the intellectual excitement in our teaching materials. It is interesting to note that UNISA, since its inception, engaged in the practice of academic research whereas this feature of the UKOU system developed as the organization matured. Furthermore research is a distinguishing feature of the university as institution when compared to some of the "for-profit" universities.

Universities, including the mega-universities, are confronted with a bewildering problem of maintaining the traditions of research as a contribution to society and the good of teaching while juggling the three balls of the triangle.

Measuring Success in Terms of the Eternal Triangle

We have suggested that the perpetual challenge for universities is to effectively manage the tensions of the eternal triangle: to widen access, to improve quality, and to lower costs. Achieving success within the constraints of this straitjacket sounds impossible, but is nonetheless deliverable in varying degrees. We now evaluate the outputs of the mega-universities according to the corners of this eternal triangle.

The mega-universities have performed extremely well on the access dimension of the triangle. Following the values underpinning the philosophy of open learning, the UKOU has led the pack by becoming the first university of considerable size to waive the traditional academic prerequisites for undergraduate study. Although some mega-universities still apply prerequisite requirements (very often dictated by stipulations by the respective ministries of education for subsidy purposes), this opening of access constitutes a huge step forward in deconstructing controlled elitism in higher education.

The enrollment figures of the mega-universities speak for themselves. More than three million learners are studying through approximately a dozen institutions—numbers that would

require more than 100 large campus-based institutions. The mega-universities are global institutions that have demonstrated the capacity to transcend national boundaries in the provision
of tertiary education. The continued experience being generated by the mega-universities to
deal with cultural diversity across national boundaries will become a significant resource when
moving ahead with the global tertiary education crisis.

On the quality dimension we have explained that the mega-universities, by adopting the
scholarship of the course-team approach, are capable of better and more consistent quality of
teaching than conventional universities on both academic and pedagogical grounds. Quality is
an illusive concept, and is best judged using independent assessments of quality. The United
Kingdom has a fierce but comprehensive state-run assessment system for universities.

In terms of the UKOU's research, it ranks in the top third of all UK universities and some
of its research is world leading. In teaching, the UKOU ranks in the top 10%.

The important point here is that, independently rated, with judicious implementation of the
four elements of success discussed in the previous section, the mega-universities are capable
of providing quality teaching and research that compare with the best in the world. There
are simply no grounds to argue that ODL is necessarily second rate education. The mega-
universities, in particular the UKOU, have succeeded in breaking the historic—and insidious—
link between quality and exclusivity in higher education. The exciting news, when measured
against the magnitude of the global tertiary education crisis, is that mega-university technology
is a transferable technology.

The third dimension of the eternal triangle concerns the objectives of cutting costs in higher
education. The achievements of the mega-universities in cutting costs are, first, a result of
the values underpinning open learning systems and second, a consequence of the strategy of
operating at economies of scale. The core value of open universities is to be open to people
and therefore these institutions are extremely reluctant to discriminate against disadvantaged
people by increasing the financial barriers to study. There is a culture in these organizations to
find innovative solutions when faced with the challenges of escalating costs. They are averse to
passing increasing costs on to the students. Secondly, operating at scale, the mega-universities
are able to teach at much lower costs than conventional universities.

Operating at scale does not necessarily mean that the absolute costs of mass provision
are insignificant. In fact, the absolute cost of designing, developing, and teaching a quality
distance education course with adequate levels of student support is considerable. However,
by capitalizing on economies of scale and efficiencies achieved by the division of labor in large
open learning systems, the mega-universities have achieved considerable cost advantages.

Despite the impressive cost savings associated with the mega-universities, it is important to
emphasize that success is determined by the interplay among all the dimensions of the eternal
triangle. This is particularly important for policymakers in higher education to note: although
distance education is an attractive policy alternative because it can provide teaching at lower
cost, unless quality and access are increased in parallel, the strategy will not succeed. Plainly,
in the mega-university context, the three dimensions of the triangle are not discrete variables.
Without sufficient numbers (i.e., access), it will not be possible to build quality learning into
the system, thus resulting in low success rates. This would translate into an inefficient and
expensive system.

LEADING ODL FUTURES

In concluding this chapter, we focus on selected issues pertaining to the future of the university
in general and the mega-universities in particular. We propose that the large open learning
systems of the mega-universities are an important model for the university of the future,

hence we introduce some of the rationales underpinning our thinking within the contemporary dynamics of today's university context.

We observe much controversy and uncertainty in the debate about the future of the university, particularly in the light of the pervasive advances in digital ICTs, and the potential impact of the global knowledge society on the prospects of the university. Some strategists, like Peter Drucker, have cautioned the university community that: "Thirty years from now big university campuses will be relics" (Drucker & Holden, 1997, p. 1745).

We hold a more optimistic view about the future of the university. From the perspective of the mega-university experience, we make four observations that we believe are critical for the future success of e-learning at the university:

- Conventional campuses will always be in demand and the way in which technology futures evolve at these institutions is likely to be different from that at the mega-university. Those planning to provide e-learning at scale will need to recognize these differences and plan accordingly;
- The tensions of the eternal triangle will apply increasing pressure on all universities. However, universities should not abandon their core values in the scurry for economic survival; otherwise, the future of the institution is at risk, despite existing capacity and foresight within the university to build meaningful futures for society;
- Universities will need institution-wide technology strategies to realize the pedagogical potential of the pervasive advances in digital ICTs. If not, the social value of information may be compromized at the expense of the core values of the university;
- With particular reference to technology futures in the developing society context, we must be watchful that solutions do not entrench the digital divide, or even worse widen it. We should also be particularly sensitive to the cultural relevance of imposing past successes of the industrialized world onto these contexts.

First, traditional university campuses will always be in demand. This model creates a protected environment where young people can come to terms with life, while acquiring the disciplines of scholarship and a critical disposition. Digital ICTs will provide opportunities for enriching the quality of the learning experience in ways that were previously not possible in this model. Arguably such a system may still be criticized as being elitist but will still fulfill an important function in society. However, given the principles of open learning, this is not the core market focus of the mega-university.

The mega-universities practice a form of delivery that is, per definition, technology-mediated learning. As a result, they have already had to develop new pedagogical structures and corresponding organizational structures to cater for the specific divisions of labor associated with providing learning at scale. Consequently, the challenges of the mega-universities with regard to digital ICTs are fundamentally different. For example, the mega-universities are not faced with questions of how to integrate traditional university structures and conventional pedagogy with emerging forms of distance education practice. Our challenges, rather, concern how best to integrate the power of digital ICTs when operating at scale. This is a different question.

Even though traditional university campuses will continue to be in demand, we envisage a significant global shift in the proportional composition of campus-based provision versus open learning systems, as the absolute numbers participating in higher education increase across the globe.

Second, entrepreneurial and corporate forces will place increasing pressures on the university as institution to manage the eternal triangle more effectively. Drucker's predictions concerning the demise of the university as we know it are based on the analysis that student demand will not continue to support the increasing costs of conventional campus-based provision and that corporate providers will be able to do a better job in terms of value-for-money in the higher education market.

We believe that society would experience a catastrophic blow should there be any truth in the outcomes of Drucker's prediction. At the same time, we recognize that the university of the future will have to work hard at effectively managing the tensions of the eternal triangle and argue that the mega-university experience is a model worth investigating for the future.

On the positive side, the university is one of society's oldest institutions with origins that can be traced back to *studia generalia*, which were set up in the 12th century, culminating in the foundation of the famous models of Paris and Bologna and acquiring the term *universitas* toward the end of the Middle Ages (Minogue, 1973, p. 12). Despite the universal unifying idea that the concept "university" implies, the survival of the institution over time can be attributed to the evidence that the university "does not exist as a timeless concept, rather it is shaped and evolves in response to its environment" (Brown, 1996, p. 28). The university has survived, and in many respects has thrived, on sharp transformation in our world. The "educational" industrial revolution, as the most significant transformation of the 20th century, is a noteworthy case in point. The mega-university experience—considering for example, its mechanisation of the teaching-learning process, mass-production of learning materials, and high division of labor—clearly demonstrates that the large open learning systems are education's best examples of successfully responding to the industrialization of society without compromising the core values of the university (see for example Peters, 1989, 1996, 1998).

Unfortunately, the foresight of Otto Peters' thinking on the industrialization of education, first published in the 1960s, has become the topic of gross misinterpretation among numerous scholars in the field of education. Many have failed to see that Peters' work was primarily a sociological analysis, which in effect placed large-scale distance education at the forefront of innovation. His work was not an attack on the sanctity of the "idea of the university," by inappropriately linking the metaphor of smoking factories to reducing the core values of the university. Fortunately, the mega-university experience has proved Peters' critics hopelessly wrong.

The mega-university is an important model for the future because it was able effectively to respond to the challenges of industrialization without compromising the ethos and core values of the university. In fact, in many respects, the mega-universities have guaranteed the survival of the core ethos of the university. They still hold and promote the traditions of academic skepticism and encourage their learners to engage and acquire not only the spirit, but also the skills associated with this critical disposition. The open universities did not abolish the traditions of maintaining academic communities of learners and scholars. Instead, they found innovative ways of sustaining this critical feature of university learning.

Third, taking the pervasive advances of digital ICTs into account, universities will need institution-wide technology strategies because individual faculty and departments doing their own thing will not be able to deliver the goods.

The mega-university experience is founded on technology-mediated learning, and, based on our experience, we have found that it is far more important to concentrate on getting the "soft" technologies of people, institutional structures, and processes right, because the "hard" technologies will inevitably change before they are perfected within the system. In other words, university-wide technology strategies should be defined in terms of fundamental pedagogical processes with a clear understanding of how emerging technologies can support these processes. Having said this, we concede that the implementation of technology in higher education is a complicated business.

A considerable component of this complexity can be attributed to the question of whether the emerging digital ICTs have the power to transform radically the landscape of educational provision. When speculating about the impact of each new technology on education, we find no clear-cut answers and we hesitate to provide a definitive answer. Rather, we would prefer to approach this question from the perspectives of both the radicals, who argue that digital ICTs will enable the radical transformation of the landscape of higher education provision around the world, and the sceptics, who ask why the new digital ICTs should be any different from previous postulated but unsuccessful educational technology revolutions.

Both the skeptics and the radicals refer to digital ICTs in their respective positions. Therefore, we must be clear about what we mean with this concept. Digital ICTs, according to Blurton (1999, p. 47) differ from previous ICTs because they are:

- capable of integrating multiple media into single applications; for example, voice, video, and text can be presented simultaneously on a Web-page;
- interactive in the sense that the information technology can control and manage the sequence of communication depending on user or other input, thus incorporating features of "intelligent" communication;
- more open because digital formats can be interpreted by a variety of hardware platforms; for example, a digital audio clip can be heard over the Internet but can also be broadcast over analog or digital radio systems with relative ease.

Obviously, digital ICTs have inherent pedagogical potential, and if successfully implemented in a teaching system would undoubtedly change pedagogical structures and corresponding teaching and learning behaviors (see for example Peters, 1998). This characteristic relates directly to the quality dimension of the eternal triangle. With particular reference to the cost and access dimensions of the eternal triangle, Bond (1997) summarizes three powerful trends that are driving the information revolution:

- *Cost of communicating.* The transmission cost of sending digital data has decreased by a factor of 10,000 since 1975.
- *Power of computing.* Computing power per dollar invested has also increased by a factor of 10,000 since 1975.
- *Convergence.* Using a single binary code system, digital technology is capable of dealing with voice, video, and computer data over the same network; whereas, in the era before convergence, independent carrier technologies were necessary.

In less technical terms this convergence is summarized by a term that Eisenstadt (1995) calls the *knowledge media*. It refers to the convergence of computing and telecommunications, but is a useful concept because it also includes the convergence of recent developments in the learning sciences. The power of the concept is that when looking at convergence in this way, it is easier to see why we may have something that is qualitatively different than what has gone before.

Clearly the knowledge media represent a powerful transformation force in higher education; however, their potential will only be realized if we understand the social value of information. Brown and Duguid (2000, p. 121) make an important point, emphasizing the social value of information, by stating that "knowledge lies less in databases than in its people." Therefore if the knowledge media will succeed in revolutionising education, we will have to do a lot more work to understand how to socialize a technology.

This is not to contend that digital technologies will not make a difference. The UKOU already has more than 110,000 students online from home, as well as another 112,000 schoolteachers (in a separate program) who are using the technology to learn how to implement ICT successfully in the school. There are about 16,000 online conferences going on at any one time. The point being made is summarized by the profound advice, contained in Brown and Duguid's own words:

Our response is not to say that change is wrong or must not happen. We only say again that envisioned change will not happen or will not be fruitful until people look beyond the simplicities of information and individuals to the complexities of learning, knowledge, judgement, communities, organizations, and institutions. That way, it seems more likely that change will reorganize the higher education system, rather than simply disorganizing it. (2000, p. 213)

The research work of Clayton Christensen should also provide useful insights into resolving some of the tensions between the sceptics and the radicals regarding the dissention of whether or not digital ICTs will revolutionize education. Christensen (2000, p. xv–xvii) reveals that new technologies come in two types

First there are sustaining technologies, which improve current practice in an incremental way. Then there are disruptive technologies, which are innovations that initially result in worse product performance but ultimately change the market in fundamental ways to become new mainstream markets. Disruptive technologies cannot be integrated into current operations in a straightforward way.

Considering the existing practice of the mega-universities, currently operating at scale, the new digital technologies are sustaining in some areas, and potentially disruptive in others. They are sustaining where they reduce costs of open learning systems, for example, improved online administration, or where they improve quality of the distance learning experience, for example, improved communication and online learning resources. In other respects, the digital ICTs are potentially disruptive because they could permit distance learning systems to be reconceived from scratch. At this juncture of our experience, we do not have conclusive examples of a reconceived distance learning system, although we recognize that it is perfectly possible. After all, the large open learning systems were created in response to the disruptive technology of the combined effects of open learning and the provision of quality learning at scale.

Finally, the discussion of digital ICTs and the future of distance education may appear to be somewhat removed from the realities of the higher education crisis in developing society contexts. This is particularly evident when basic infrastructure, let alone reliable ICT infrastructure, is virtually nonexistent in many parts of the developing world. When we analyze the access figures to various communications technologies in the developing world, it is understandable why many distance education policy advisors usually recommend that future distance education strategies should be based on first-generation correspondence study (see Table 54.2).

Promoting first-generation correspondence study in developing society contexts is problematic for a number of reasons.

TABLE 54.2

Selected Information and Communications Technology Indicators

	Developing Countries	Industrial Countries	Sub-Saharan Africa	Southern Asia
Estimated main lines per 100 inhabitants (1996)	4.5	42.4	1.4	1.8
Estimated cellular subscribers per 100 inhabitants (1996)	0.58	9.17	0.21	0.04
No of radio receivers per 1000 inhabitants (1996)	185	1005	166	88
No of television receivers per 1000 inhabitants (1996)	145	524	35	55
No of PC per 1000 inhabitants (1996)	6.5	156.3	3[1]	1.2
Estimated No of Internet users per 1000 inhabitants	0.5	17.9	Na	na

(*Source:* UNESCO, 1999)

1. Independent estimate by Jensen (1999, p. 183) and should be used with caution.

na: not available

First, we have already explained that the provision of individualized tutorial support is a critical factor for ensuring the success of open learning systems. However, because of considerable geographical distances and the shortage of suitably qualified tutors in remote locations where the majority of the population of the developing world reside, correspondence study will not be able to achieve the successes reported by the UKOU. Conversely, digital ICTs provide the potential of effectively overcoming the problems associated with providing local tutors.

Second, policy strategies in ODL that use access to ICT infrastructure as a point of departure will not render impressive results. We have to change our policy approach if we are serious about finding sustainable and effective solutions to the educational crisis in developing countries. Rather we should find innovative ways of establishing and sustaining appropriate ICT infrastructure. The practical realities of limited connectivity in developing countries is a seductive policy trap because the magnitude of the problem blinds the vision concerning how the inherent power of digital ICTs can be used to overcome the chasm between restricted access and generating sufficient demand for rolling out sustainable connectivity.

Third, Braga points out that technological developments "are rapidly eroding economic and technical barriers to entry into communication networks. Developing countries can, for example, leapfrog stages of development by investing into fully digitized networks rather than continuing to expand their outdated analog-based infrastructure" (Braga, 1998). There is evidence that, with government commitment and determinism at policy level, developing countries can achieve the ideals of leapfrogging.

Fourth, developing societies should rather adopt a demand-push strategy. That is, create the demand for broad bandwidth applications—infrastructure will then follow because it can now be sustained by the large demand. The implicit capabilities and advantages of digital ICTs for distance learning should be used as a point of departure to ensure that sufficient demand is generated by the ODL applications of these technologies. In this way, sustainability of the new technologies can be promoted because of the economy-of-scale potential associated with mass-demand, rather than waiting for acceptable levels of connectivity before transforming the practice of distance education in these societies.

The critical point here is that the problems experienced in the developing society are significantly different from the experience of the industrialized world. From the outside, it is very easy to misinterpret the potential for digital solutions in distance education when analyzing absolute statistics. Using these approaches, it is very easy to miss pockets of indigenous innovation, which collectively may provide the foundation for culturally relevant solutions in the future. Global best practice must be interpreted within the contexts of local relevance.

The four observations made above, based on the mega-university experience regarding the future of ODL systems, may raise more questions than definitive answers. However, in the traditions of the academy, it is better to acquire the skills of asking the right questions than it is to repeat predetermined answers.

In conclusion, we have stated that we regard the mega-universities as being the most significant innovation in higher education of the 20th century. We agree with Brown's (1998, p. 25) experience that to be effective, invention is not enough, and pioneering work requires invention-plus-implementation. In other words, innovation is invention successfully implemented. The inventions associated with digital ICTs have the potential of radically transforming higher education provision. However, this will require creative solutions, and by creativity we mean the art of designing within the constraints of the eternal triangle. The mega-university experience may provide strategists with a model that is capable of implementing the innovations associated with digital ICTs, but also of scaling-up their implementation so as to capitalize on further gains from successfully managing the tensions of the eternal triangle.

REFERENCES

Bond, J. (1997). The drivers of the information revolution—cost, computing power and convergence. *Public Policy for the Private Sector*. July. The World Bank Group. Online: http://www.worldbank.org/viewpoint

Braga, C. A. P. (1998). Inclusion or exclusion. Will the networked economy widen or narrow the gap between developing and industrialized countries? *Unesco Courier*. December. Online: http://www.unesco.org/courier/1998_12/uk/dossier/txt21.htm

Blurton, C. (1999). New directions in education. In *UNESCO world communication and information report 1999–2000*, (pp. 46–61). Paris: UNESCO.

Brown, G. (1996). 2000 and beyond—the university of the future. In T. Smith (Ed.), *Ideas of the university*. Sydney: Research Institute for the Humanities and Social Sciences, The University of Sydney in association with Power Publications.

Brown, J. S. (1998). Seeing differently: A role for pioneering research. *Research Technology Management, 41*(3): 24–34.

Brown, J. S., & Duguid, P. (2000). *The social life of information*. Boston, MA: Harvard Business School Press.

Christensen, C. M. (2000). (Reprint of 1997 Harvard Business School Press edition). *The innovator's dilemma. When new technologies cause great firms to fail*. New York: HarperBusiness.

Daniel, J. S. (1995). What has the open university achieved in 25 years? In D. Sewart (Ed.), *One world many voices: Quality in open and distance learning*. Vol. 1 (pp. 400–403). ICDE and The Open University: Milton Keynes.

Daniel, J. S. (1996). *Mega-universities and knowledge media: Technology strategies for higher education*. London: Kogan Page.

Daniel, J. S. (1999). (Reprint with revisions). *Mega-universities and knowledge media: Technology strategies for higher education*. London: Kogan Page.

Drucker, P. A. & Holden, C. (1997). Untitled. *Science, 275*(5307), 1745.

Eisenstadt, M. (1995). Overt strategy for global learning. *Times*, Higher Education Supplement, Multimedia Section, 7 April, vi–vii.

Holmberg, B. (1995). *Theory and practice of distance education* (2nd ed.). London: Routledge.

Jensen, M. (1999). Sub-Saharan Africa. In UNESCO, *World Communication and Information Report*, 1999–2000. Paris: UNESCO.

Keegan, D. (1980). On defining distance education. *Distance Education, 1*(1), 13–36.

Mackintosh, W. G. (1999). Perspectives on student learning and the UNISA DE delivery system: An interplay between organisational design, course design and the challenges of student support in open distance learning. Paper prepared for CNED Professional Development Videoconference: Concevoir des dispositifs ouverts et à distance pour l'enseignement du FLE. 30 June 1999.

Minogue, K. R. (1973). *The concept of a University*. London: Weidenfeld and Nicolson.

Moore, M. G., & Kearsley, G. (1996). *Distance education. A systems view*. Belmont: Wadsworth Publishing Company.

Peters, O. (1989). The iceberg has not melted: Further reflections on the concept of industrialisation and distance teaching. *Open learning, 4*(3), 3–8.

Peters, O. (1996). Responses to "Labour market theories and distance education." Distance education is a form of teaching and learning sui generis. *Open Learning, 11*(1), 51–54.

Peters, O. (1998). *Learning and teaching in distance education. Analyses and interpretations from and international perspective*. London: Kogan Page.

Saint, W. (1999). *Tertiary distance education and technology in Sub-Saharan Africa*. Washington D.C.: Working group on Higher Education, Association for the Development of Education in Africa, The World Bank.

Tait, A. (2000). Planning student support for open and distance learning. *Open Learning, 15*(3), 287–299.

UNESCO. (1999). *World Communication and Information Report 1999–2000*. Paris: UNESCO.

UNESCO. (2000a). *World education report 2000*. Paris: UNESCO Publishing.

UNESCO. (2000b). The Dakar framework for action. Education for All: Meeting our collective commitments. Text adopted by the World Education Forum Dakar, Senegal, 26–28 April 2000. Online: http://www2.unesco.org/wef/en-leadup/dakfram.shtm

Wedemeyer, C. (1982). The birth of the open university—A postscript. *Teaching at a distance*, 21, 21–27.

Wedemeyer, C. A. & Childs, G. B. (1961). *New perspectives in university correspondence study*. Chicago: Centre for the Study of Liberal Education for Adults.

World Bank. (2000). Higher education in developing countries. Peril and promise. Washington D.C.: The World Bank.

55

The Global Development Learning Network: A World Bank Initiative in Distance Learning for Development[1]

Michael Foley
The World Bank Institute
mfoley@worldbank.org

This is the story of an evolution in thinking on the impact that knowledge sharing, distance learning, and communications technologies can have on the development agenda. It is a story of learning by doing, of how, by leveraging systems that already existed for one purpose and using them for another as a value added, a whole new way of doing business could be discovered.

In a videoconference in June 1998 Jim Wolfensohn, President of the World Bank, made the following remarks:

> As we look at the challenges of poverty, it is very clear that money alone is not what is needed. We need colleagues who can learn and share experience with each other. Distance learning, obviously is the tool that will enable this and benefit us all.

This statement matched with the wide recognition that the emerging communications technologies were causing a revolution in the world economy, where knowledge was the new currency, where developed nations were moving from being industrial economies to becoming knowledge economies. The concepts of an Information Highway, an information society, a knowledge society were evolving from this revolution. Among development practitioners the role that knowledge and knowledge sharing had in development took on greater importance, to the point that it was seen as the key to development, maybe even more important than finance, grants, or lending.

The World Bank Institute (WBI) was founded over 40 years ago as the Economic Development Institute (EDI), with the mandate to offer a number of knowledge services, including

---

[1] This material has been prepared by the staff of the World Bank. Any findings, interpretations, and conclusions, are entirely those of the authors and not necessarily those of the World Bank, its affiliated organizations, or the members of its Board of Executive Directors or the governments they represent.

courses, seminars, and policy dialogs to client countries of the Bank, which include almost all of the developing countries. It delivered these services in a traditional face-to-face manner, either in Washington, DC, or in a region. This was an expensive process, involving much long-distance travel and hotel costs, and therefore it made sense to explore the potential of communications technologies and distance learning to improve the cost-effectiveness of the service. The problem was that the telecommunications infrastructure in the client countries of WBI were at a very low level of development. In a study carried out by the Academy for Educational Development (AED) in February 1997 it was concluded that approximately $40 million would be needed to build a distance learning network with a global reach, clearly not an option at that time.

However, because the Bank had offices in almost 100 developing countries it had its own needs, for operational and business purposes, for a more robust communications system than the local infrastructures could support. Over the years, the Information Solutions Group (ISG) of the Bank had built a global communications network based on VSAT technology to connect its worldwide offices to headquarters in Washington, DC, and to each other. By 1997 that network was providing fully interactive video, voice, and data services, and Jim Wolfensohn suggested in a meeting that it could be used to deliver some of the courses from Washington, using the local World Bank offices as venues at which the participants could attend. Things moved rapidly at that point. A distance learning unit was formed and staffed in WBI, studios were built in the main building of the Bank, and in September 1998 the World Bank Learning Network (WBLN) was launched.

The shortcomings of a learning network based in World Bank offices were apparent from the beginning. The local country offices were not equipped, or staffed, to be learning centers. All of the computers in the offices were networked inside the firewall of the Bank's intranet and so they could only be used by staff of the World Bank. Therefore only the videoconferencing facility could be used for courses aimed at external clients, a big drawback for courses using a Web element. Besides, using the name "World Bank Learning Network" and using only offices of the World Bank as venues inhibited the growth of the network as a worldwide partnership of program partners, donors, and governments. It was clear that what was needed was an independent network of centers, connected still through the Bank's global satellite infrastructure, at least until a critical mass of centers were built that could support an independent sustainable network. Resources were mobilized within the Bank to set about working with client governments and donors in order to build the Global Distance Learning Network (GDLN). The name was changed later to Global Development Learning Network in order to put the emphasis on the mission rather than the means of the network and without changing the acronym, GDLN. A target was set by the president to get 10 distance learning centers (DLCs) built in the first year. The target was met and in September 2000, the official launch of the GDLN took place with 14 centers taking part.

DESIGN OF THE SYSTEM

At the outset of the project the issue was to design a system, based on adult learning principles and on the appropriate use of technology, that would be at least be as effective as the traditional face-to-face model employed heretofore but that would be:

- more cost effective,
- reach a wider audience, and
- provide content from a wider circle of providers.

The question then was to design a pedagogical scenario and a technology platform that would achieve the objectives desired, with the target audience concerned, and that was cost effective in the circumstances.

There are general principles of good design that can be applied to all distance learning activities, but in practice the specific pedagogical design employed in a particular course will be influenced by:

- the target audience of the activity
- the content or subject matter to be delivered and
- the outcomes or objectives desired.

There are other considerations that affect the design of a delivery system for distance learning that will have profound effects on the design of the learning activities. They are primarily:

- the cost effectiveness of the system,
- the opportunity costs of alternative systems and methods,
- the availability of technology to the provider and to the learners,
- the geographical location of the learners, and
- the comfort level of the learners with any technology that is used.

Each of these factors can be applied to a particular target audience, be they children, postsecondary students, or adults. The resulting criteria of quality design may be very different for each group as we move from pedagogy for children to andragogy (Knowles, 1970) for adults. The design requirements and sociopsychological conditions are quite different for each group so at this stage there is a need to describe the target group that is being discussed. There is also a need to define what areas of content are to be the focus and what outcomes are set for the activities.

TARGET AUDIENCE

The GDLN has as its target group a range that includes decision makers and midlevel career personnel in government, government agencies, NGOs, academia, civil society, and the private sector, the majority of whom are in developing countries. The following is known about these learners in terms of their resources and constraints:

- Participants tend to be midcareer professionals, i.e., adult learners.
- Participants are not computer savvy and they do not have ready access to technology such as computers and the Internet outside of these centers.
- Participants are traditionally educated, albeit, not experienced with self-directed learning.
- Participants are juggling both family and work commitments with professional development activities.

CONTENT

The content area consists primarily of policy issues in the development agenda of the client countries and the related skill sets that would be needed to inform policy, e.g., data collection and measurement, statistical analysis, project management, economic forecasting, and so on.

OUTCOMES

In regard to the desired outcomes, while the ultimate objective is the alleviation of poverty and economic and social development, the outcome of learning activities themselves can be the same as those for face-to-face activities, i.e., increased knowledge on a particular development topic. With the appropriate application of adult learning theory into the design of the learning activities, and with an appropriate use of a range of technologies, the bar can be raised on the level of outcomes achieved. In the early stages of the GDLN much of the debate was centered around the effectiveness or otherwise of distance education compared to face-to-face activities. As with any radical organizational change there was quite a bit of resistance to the move to distance learning, but as will be described later in the chapter that resistance is now largely overcome.

APPLYING ADULT LEARNING THEORY TO THE SYSTEM DESIGN

In designing the pedagogical approaches for GDLN the results of more than 30 years of research on adult learning was applied to the distance learning programs. They have the following criteria:

1. They are based on clearly established learning needs and built around succinct statements of outcome.
2. They are based on a variety of teaching and learning strategies and methods that are activity based such as simulations, case studies, and problem solving exercises.
3. Effective distance learning materials are experiential; they address the learner's life experiences as a point of departure for the learning program and as a continuous reference throughout the process.
4. Quality distance learning programs are participatory in that they emphasize the involvement of the learner in all facets of program development and delivery.
5. Successful distance learning programs are interactive and allow for frequent opportunities for participants to engage in a dialogue with subject matter experts and other learners.
6. Learner support systems are an integral part of any successful distance learning program.

PLATFORM/TECHNOLOGY CHOICE

When it comes to technology or platform choice, any one technology may be able to deliver a quality distance learning experience but the ideal delivery system will rarely be based on a single platform or technology; rather, it will be an integrated mix of methods, technologies, and networks, with their appropriate educational benefits and learner support services.

The actual availability or cost of a particular technology or technologies to the target audience may be one of the primary criteria for media choice, but it is useful to be platform agnostic regarding cost and availability at the outset of designing a delivery system. The system can be designed for maximum pedagogical effectiveness and it can then be modified by applying the cost and availability criteria. In actual practice, of course, all of the elements, cost, effectiveness and availability, are considered at the same time. It is a classic "chicken and egg" situation.

Bates (1995) suggests 12 golden rules for using technology in education and training which apply whatever technologies are being used and whatever the audience, content and objectives are.

1. Good teaching matters. Quality design of learning activities is important for all delivery methods.
2. Each medium has its own aesthetic. Therefore professional design is important.
3. Educational technologies are flexible. They have their own unique characteristics but successful teaching can be achieved with any technology.
4. There is no "super-technology." Each has its strengths and weaknesses, therefore they need to be combined (an integrated mix).
5. Make all four media available to teachers and learners. Print, audio, television, and computers.
6. Balance variety with economy. Using many technologies makes design more complex and expensive, therefore limit the range of technologies in a given circumstance.
7. Interaction is essential.
8. Student numbers are critical. The choice of a medium will depend greatly on the number of learners reached over the life of a course.
9. New technologies are not necessarily better than old ones.
10. Teachers need training to use technology effectively.
11. Teamwork is essential. No one person has all the skills to develop and deliver a distance learning course, therefore, subject matter experts, instructional designers, and media specialists are essential on every team.
12. Technology is not the issue. How and what we want the learners to learn is the issue and technology is a tool.

THE GDLN TECHNICAL PLATFORM

Given that the GDLN has a target group as defined above, and a content aimed at producing good governance and high-quality policymaking in developing countries plus the skill sets to achieve these aims, a technological platform combined with a pedagogical approach designed for quality adult learning was developed. The fact that this technological platform was to a large extent available already through the World Bank's Global Communications Network was crucial to implementing this design. It would have been almost impossible to develop the infrastructure from scratch. This is what makes the network unique; a platform of technologies that was suitable for incremental growth without a large initial investment. What was available was a global VSAT network, which allowed for interactive video, voice, and data to be used for learning activities as well as for the operational and business purposes for which it was designed. If a secondary network could grow as an added value to the existing network until it reached a critical mass then it could be spun off when it was mature, but be protected in its early growth stages. The potential for two-way interactive video, high-speed Internet access, and voice communications, all independent of local telecom conditions through special licensing arrangements and with low-cost tariffs based on UN rates with Intelsat, gave a freedom to design a distance learning system that was unavailable to most providers. The critical mass for the bandwidth requirements was already met by the World Bank's usage. DLCs could be added with incremental purchase of more bandwidth without a large new investment.

The constraints of the availability of the technology and the learners access to it were removed. Pedagogical scenarios could be developed according to best practice of adult learning if local DLCs could be built to support the technologies and the requirements of adult distance learning. The centers were designed to support synchronous video and data conferencing and asynchronous Internet access in two rooms dedicated to these functions. The added bonus of two-way video and data conferencing was that one could deliver from any center to any other center. It was not a distribution model, but an exchange model. Experience and expertise

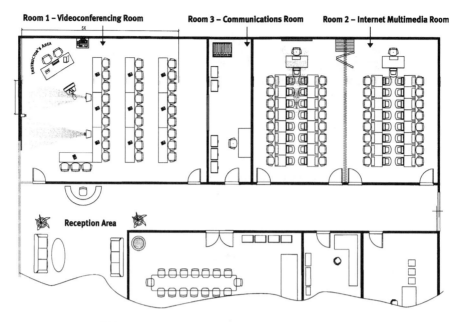

FIG. 55.1.   Typical layout of a Distance Learning Center.

could be exchanged from any center to any other center. The protocols of communication were standard protocols; H320, H323, and T.120 for the synchronous side and TCP/IP for the asynchronous side. The network is currently being converted to Internet Protocol (IP). Any provider with a Web server and an ISDN/T1/Fiber or satellite connection to Washington DC (where the telecommunications hub resides) for videoconferencing could be a program partner. Each center is designed to have the following technical facilities (see fig 55.1):

Videoconferencing Room

- 30 + seats
- A large video projection screen
- A large data projection screen
- A teaching desk at the front of the room equipped with two laptops and a document camera
- 2 cameras, one covering the classroom and one covering the teaching desk
- A videoconferencing CODEC operating at 256Kbps speed

Multimedia Room

- 30 PCs
- 512/64Kbps connection to Internet

Communications

- Video, voice and data by VSAT or fiber through the ISG hub in Washington DC on one of 3 satellites.

FINANCING OF DISTANCE LEARNING CENTERS

The cost of setting up a DLC ranges from $100,000 to $1.5 million, depending on what is already available at a site, on whether a VSAT connection or ISDN is used, and on whether operating costs for the first 3 years are included in the funding. The typical annual operating costs are approximately $250,000 to $350,000 for a VSAT connected DLC. Financing for the centers comes from a range of options: from World Bank loans to donor financing to self-financing. Some examples of donor funding of centers are; the Ukraine center in Kiev is being funded by the Canadian International Development Agency (CIDA); the Bolivian center is being supported by the Spanish government; and the Egyptian center is being paid for by the United States Agency for International Development (USAID). The Japanese government contributed to the funding of the Jordanian center in Amman. In some cases, where an institution already has the facilities for videoconferencing and multimedia, very little extra investment, if any is required. Some institutions, such as Bilkent University in Ankara, Turkey, and others in Latin America have joined GDLN by using ISDN dial-up in the initial stages in order to test the market for the typical GDLN content. This approach allows them to join without further capital investment, although the per minute cost of connecting to GDLN activities is relatively high. When and if the number of activities in which they participate grows substantially they can then consider leasing a connection, by fiber or satellite to the network hub. While currently this hub is in Washington DC, the idea of having a series of regional technical hubs across a number of time zones is being implemented, thus reducing the connectivity cost for an individual institution, and increasing intra regional content exchange. The Paris and Brasilia offices of the World Bank have installed multipoint control units as part of their distance learning facilities. The offices are then linked back to the network operations center (NOC) in Washington, DC, by fiber optic cable. This means that European and Brazilian partners of GDLN have only to connect to the respective regional offices in order to enter the global network.

The terms of the World Bank loans are very favorable, especially for poor countries belonging to the International Development Association (IDA), which is a part of the World Bank Group. An IDA loan is paid back over 40 years, with a 10-year grace period and at an interest rate of 0.75%.

The operational costs of the centers are also funded in a variety of ways that will be described later in this chapter under sustainability.

DEVELOPMENT OF THE NETWORK; GDLN AS A NETWORK OF NETWORKS

While the GDLN, as a telecommunications network, is based primarily on additional capacity of the World Bank's own global satellite network, i.e., a VSAT system providing interactive video, voice, and data on three global beam satellites, it is very rapidly evolving as a network of networks. By partnering with other distance learning networks, on a global, a regional, or a national level, and by interconnecting them technically, the mutual benefit to each network is significant, both in terms of the extended reach to wider audiences and in terms of the richness of content that can be shared.

The British Council has commenced an initiative to build a network of Knowledge and Learning Centers (KLCs) in their offices worldwide and this network has been interlinked with the GDLN network, through the Paris office of the World Bank. The first KLC was opened by Prime Minister Tony Blair in early 2002 in their New Delhi office.

The Japanese government, as part of its commitment to resolving the global digital divide, is building an education and training network called J-Net. Japanese support to GDLN began at the time of the 2000 Okinawa G8 summit when Japan announced the J-Net initiative, with plans to establish 30 core centers around the world.

The first partnering of GDLN with a regional network was with the Monterrey Institute of Technology (ITESM) in Mexico in 1999. By linking their satellite system in Monterrey with the World Bank Institute's studios in Washington, DC, by a fiber connection, courses from WBI were broadcast "live", with interaction by e-mail, to over 100 centers in Mexico and Latin America. Another example of a regional partnership was with the Asociación de Televisión Educativa Iberoamericana (ATEI).

At the national level there is a growing number of examples of the GDLN center in the capital city being connected to an internal national network of the country, typically the high speed research networks of the universities. The GDLN center in Beijing, for example, is being connected to CERNET, the China educational and research high speed network which interconnects the universities of China. The first university in China to join GDLN through this network is Ninxia University.

The Australian academic network, led by the Australian National University, has been linked into GDLN, and AusAID, the Australian aid agency, has committed to support both the establishment of new GDLN centers in Asia and the development of content from Australian knowledge institutions.

EFFECTIVENESS OF THE SYSTEM

As mentioned earlier in this chapter there was some initial resistance to the move to distance learning based on, among other factors, doubts about is effectiveness compared to a face-to-face model. Regardless of the fact that countless studies have demonstrated the "no significant difference" syndrome, it was thought necessary to test the hypothesis with the client group concerned.

A study conducted by WBI (then EDI) demonstrated that a distance learning version of a course on Economic and Business Journalism was as effective as the face-to-face versions of the same course, at least as measured by the participants' satisfaction with the course, its methodology, and its contribution to their professional skills (Bardini, 1998). The course experienced a "dropin" rate as distinct from a "dropout" rate, which is usual with distance learning courses, i.e., the reputation and popularity of the course spread rapidly and there were more participants at the end of the course than at the beginning.

Some aspects of this course, with its delivery spread over a number of weeks to participants who did not have to leave their workplace for more than a half day a week and whose assignments were the actual articles that they were writing for their newspapers, indicated that there was more potential in distance learning than simple knowledge transfer, i.e., that it could have direct results in professional performance and that therefore, to compare it to face-to-face as a measure of its success was perhaps aiming too low.

MOVING BEYOND THE COURSE DELIVERY PARADIGM

With the target group of the GDLN as defined above, early measurements indicate that using DL methods are proving more cost effective to deliver the same course to the same clients than by traditional methods. In other words, the same learning gains were achieved with a greater number of participants for less cost than a face-to-face version of the same content to a similar client group. But is this selling the technology and the pedagogy short? Can more be achieved in terms of impact than just successful course delivery?

An early example of how distance learning can move us from course delivery to a more comprehensive technology enabled development paradigm was the Controlling Corruption "course." It is described below by the senior instructional designer on the course team, Don MacDonald.

CONTROLLING CORRUPTION: TECHNOLOGY ENABLED DEVELOPMENT IN ACTION

Corruption is a serious problem in developing countries, a systemic impediment to sustained economic growth. There is a substantial body of empirical data that shows clear correlations between the growth indicators of impoverished countries (or lack thereof) and indices related to corruption. Previous World Bank attempts to address this issue focused on the regulatory, with strict attention to accountability and transparency policies and practices. But these strategies did not address fundamental cause and effects related to corruption: how to build an accountable, transparent, and self-regulating infrastructure in a developing country that will control corruption.

The emphasis turned to training, capacity building, and technical assistance approaches. These programs were targeted to high-level ministry officials from around the world who were brought to World Bank headquarters for a 10-day program. The course agenda was built around a daily nine hours of lectures/discussion covering a variety of topics related to consequences of corruption in developing economies. But these instructor-led, lecture-based programs did not achieve expected results. A new approach was tested at the World Bank, where a more learner centered curriculum was developed that used a blend of learning methodologies and technologies. After protracted discussions with distance learning and adult learning specialists, however, course subject matter experts were persuaded to entirely rethink their approach to the delivery of this program.

The new curriculum consisted of the following attributes:

1. A move to a more learner-centered and action-oriented curriculum. Course designers and subject matter experts were asked to think not in terms of the information that needed to be transmitted in order to understand corruption, but rather, what individuals working in government ministries needed to know in order to actually control corruption. The program agenda focused on actions that need to be implemented in order to control corruption and the skills that participants need to learn in order to take these actions.
2. Instead of a global focus, with a broad invitation to all client governments of the World Bank to attend a conference-like setting, it was decided to instead focus on select countries. The initial program was targeted to seven countries in Sub-Saharan Africa: Benin, Ethiopia, Ghana, Kenya, Malawi, Tanzania, and Uganda. Invitations were sent to key ministerial personnel in these countries who were asked to attend and to participate in the program as a team, with a mandate to address corruption issues in their respective countries.
3. The overall goal of the program was to enable each country team to develop a comprehensive action plan to control corruption in their respective countries. The specific objectives and program agenda focused on the skills required by the country teams to design, develop and implement a country action strategy to control corruption.
4. Finally, the curriculum was delivered using a blended approach that included a combination of a traditional, face-to-face workshop approach, followed by a regular series

of seminars convened by videoconferencing technology. There was also a substantial amount of print materials developed to support country teamwork, and over the course of time, e-mail communications were added to support the preparation of the strategy paper for Durban.

The blended and technology assisted aspects of this course offer critical "lessons learned" for related development learning projects.

- The face-to-face encounter is valuable in terms of building a sense of team among participants.
- Videoconferencing sessions allow participants to return to their respective countries but still continue with the learning. Twice a week sessions over a month, which addresses topics introduced at the face-to-face session, allow participants to test and apply new concepts within the context of their own country and at the same time, share experiences with other country teams. The videoconferencing sessions also allow for participation by other members of a country ministry who were unable to attend the face-to-face sessions. In addition, videoconferences facilitated the preparation of a common strategy paper representing the views of the participating country teams.
- Internet approaches (Web sites, list servs, discussion forums, email) are being developed to support future roll outs of the program, which will further strengthen the intracountry collaboration that seems a critical feature of success for this curriculum. (MacDonald 199)

SUSTAINABILITY, THE MARKET, AND PROGRAMMING

Refining the mission and focus of GDLN

At the outset of the GDLN initiative, the DLCs were planned to be financially self-sustainable after a three-year buildup period, at least covering their operating costs. The costs included the annual cost of connectivity to the satellite, the total of which is shared among the centers; the staffing costs; maintenance of equipment; rent to the host institution; and so on. While the costs vary somewhat between centers and regions of the world, an average hourly cost of operating the videoconferencing room in each center was calculated and agreed to be $200 per hour (including connectivity cost). A number of models of cost recovery were developed during the first year of operation, based on the different financial arrangements that the program providers would make with the DLCs. Some providers were willing to provide the content free of charge to the DLCs, others would require an income for the content, while others were prepared to not only provide the content free to the DLC, but also were willing to pay the operating costs as well, thus ensuring that the participants had free access to the activity. Out of these varied conditions four scenarios were developed:

Participation in activities is categorized into either (a) Open Access, for which the DLCs will market the activity and invite participants through open marketing, and (b) Select Access, for delivery to a specific audience identified by the program partner.

1. Open Access—No Cost Recovery
   - The program partner provides the activity free of any charges to the DLC.
   - The DLC markets the activity and invites participants.
   - The DLC sets participant fees to recover the DLC costs.

- An activity agreement is negotiated; however, there are no financial transactions processed in the GDLN account between program partner and DLC.
- The program partner pays the videoconference setup fees through the GDLN account.
2. Open Access—Cost Recovery to Program Partner from DLC
   - The program partner provides the activity with the expectation of recovering costs; these costs are negotiated in the activity agreement.
   - The DLC markets the program, invites participants, and provides the distance learning facilities and related services.
   - The DLC sets participant fees to recover the DLC costs and program partner costs.
   - The program partner pays the videoconference set-up fees through the GDLN account.
   - The DLC pays the agreed cost recovery to the program partner through the GDLN account.
3. Select Access—No Cost Recovery
   - The program partner rents the facility and reimburses the cost of other services the DLC will provide as agreed in the activity agreement.
   - The program partner identifies the target audience.
   - The participants attend free of charge.
   - The program partner pays for facility rental, related services such as printing and refreshments, and the videoconference setup fees, through the GDLN account.
4. Select Access—Cost Recovery to Program Partner Directly from Participant Fees.
   - The program partner rents the facility and reimburses the cost of other services the DLC will provide, as agreed in the activity agreement.
   - The program partner identifies the target audience that is to be invited.
   - The program partner sets a participation fee that will cover both the program partner's activity and the DLC costs.
   - The program partner pays for facility rental, related services, and the videoconference setup fees, through the GDLN account.

How sustainability can be achieved will differ between countries and regions. In middle income countries, such as those in parts of Eastern Europe, Latin America and Asia, the ability of the participants, or of their employers, to pay for courses will be much greater than would obtain in the poorer countries of Africa. Letting the market determine the success of failure of a DLC may lead to GDLN deserting the very countries where there is most need. "Following the money," i.e., operating only where there is an ability to pay for services may be appropriate for a private-sector enterprise, but the GDLN was not set up with a profit motive as an objective. One could also foresee, if we followed the market, that the nature of the curriculum, the learning programs themselves, would change from pure development topics to courses and services that served a financially elite few, for example, MBAs from prestigious Western universities or training programs from the world's leading management consultancies.

The question of sustainability has exercised the minds of GDLN staff since the inception of the initiative, and now, after 2 years of full operation, the issues are becoming clearer and more refined strategies are being put in place. The following principles are driving these strategies:

- The GDLN is a development network with a niche role in the supply of knowledge services in support of development strategies.
- Its primary target audience, or clientele, is development practitioners, decision makers, and agents of change in government departments, government agencies, NGOs, academia, civil society, and the private sector.

- GDLN is a public good and therefore, needs to be financed by more creative ways than merely leaving it to market forces.
- GDLN is a partnership of multilateral development agencies and lending institutions, bilateral donors, centers of expertise, developing countries, and the DLCs.
- The learning programs are to be based on the development strategies of these partners and respond to the learning needs of the partners involved.
- GDLN is a network of networks. While it is primarily based on the global communications network of the World Bank, it is being linked to other distance learning networks in regions and countries.
- As a public good, the GDLN will most likely remain a part of the World Bank's telecommunications network and not be spun off as an independent entity.
- Outcomes and impact are the key criteria of the success of its activities.
- The varying economic and social conditions in different regions of the world will be reflected in the strategic approaches adopted in these regions in terms of appropriate content and development of the network. GDLN is not a one-size-fits-all.

WHAT IS THE MARKET?

Like any school, discipline, or business, a decision is made to operate in a particular market and to specialize in this area. This can be determined by the *process* or by the *content*. For GDLN it can be technology-based distance learning (process) or development knowledge (content). If the niche is selected according to process, then any content would do, as long as it is in a distance learning format and it has a market in the targeted countries. If this path is followed by GDLN, all that will be achieved is the establishment of a series of sustainable small distance learning enterprises in a number of countries, and not in the poorest. This may be the job of the private investment banks or of the private sector. It is not the job of the World Bank. The core mission of GDLN has to be defined according to the niche content that is being offered, i.e., learning services for development, mainly in the policy area. This is generally agreed upon at this stage, but it has significant implications for the business plan and the operating procedures of GDLN, especially in the way that needs are assessed, content is developed, and programming is sought.

A NEEDS DRIVEN NETWORK—TWO TYPES OF NEEDS

While it is almost a truism to say that programming in any network should be needs driven as opposed to supply driven, there will always be an element of ready content from providers for which there is no stated need. The market analysis performed by the DLCs will determine whether some supply is needed or not. Therefore offerings of content from providers will be welcomed and the acceptability or not will be determined by the DLC management in each country.

However, the strategy of the program developers, those who have the responsibility of finding the content of learning activities for the network, will be to base most of the content on the stated needs of the countries in the partnership. But first there must be agreement on what kind of needs can best be fulfilled with the GDLN.

When educators discuss learning needs they generally refer to the learning needs of the individual, and adult educators talk about a portfolio of credits related to an individual's career and personal development. While this is laudatory, if we only address individual learning needs, then the impact of GDLN will be dissipated into a series of unconnected courses of benefit only to individual people. The DLCs, operating as small businesses, may succeed financially with this model, but the opportunity to seriously influence the development agenda of the host country will be missed.

Experience has shown that we can go beyond simple individual learning gains from courses to actual outcomes that are generated by groups of people in a country and that move the development process forward. An example is the curbing corruption course—the outcome of which was a series of national strategy documents completed by seven African countries. The real benefit of GDLN will be apparent when the learning activities are tied to *country* knowledge gaps, the existence of which hamper the formulation and implementation of development strategies and their related programs. Another way of looking at country learning needs is to look at:

1. The stated development strategies of the client countries. In the case of the World Bank and its work with countries these strategies are expressed in the Comprehensive Development Framework (CDF) documents, the Country Assistance Strategies (CAS), the Poverty Reduction Strategy Papers (PRSPs) of each country. These documents have been produced by the countries themselves in association with the World Bank.
2. The operations of the lending institutions, and thereby linking lending with learning.
3. The development agendas of the donor agencies.

Achieving this will require more than a simple system of course delivery by distance learning. There is no doubt that GDLN can deliver quality courses. It will continue to do so, and as the network grows the cost effectiveness of the system will increase. However, a key element for success of the network and of its member centers is that the content will be demand driven, based on country and regional needs as determined by the countries themselves in association with aid agencies and lending institutions. As the needs are tied to key development outcomes the list of learning activities will become more programmatic in nature, rather than be merely a list of random and unrelated courses. The power of the network as an engine of development will emerge because the pedagogy and technology utilized will enable action learning to take place in the context of real-life programs and it will enable them to be developed and implemented. The development agencies will be able to link their funding programs with capacity-building learning activities tailored to the program objectives and delivered to the stakeholders in the program, throughout the life of the program, and beyond it. Instead of attempting to increase the impact of learning activities to an indeterminate level, an impact objective, or at least an outcome objective, can be set a priori and then learning strategies can be designed to achieve that objective. We can move the paradigm from distance learning course delivery to what can be called technology-enabled development.

The role of the individual DLCs within the network of GDLN can be to act as one of the prime engines for development impact within their own countries, especially in the poorest countries where there are limited alternative sources of expertise. In middle-income countries this role would be less dramatic. In poor countries the DLCs can act as more than simple distance learning centers. They can become knowledge centers for development action in their countries. They would be key focal points for the harnessing of international knowledge and experience related to their host countries' development strategies, working alongside and in partnership with local learning and research institutions. These strategies and related programs are developed by the governments in association with local civil society, international and local NGOs, multilateral development banks, and bi-lateral donors.

The role of the DLCs is to work with these players to discover the knowledge and skill gaps within the teams mandated to implement the programs. Some of those gaps will require technical assistance from experts outside of the country and this is the area on which GDLN needs to focus, to find the expertise from the program partners that would fill these gaps.

PROCESSES

How can this be made to work, in a systematic businesslike fashion? How do programs of learning activities and knowledge-sharing activities that will be relevant, will fulfill needs, and will contribute to the development agenda be found?

As mentioned above, much of the current GDLN programming is supply driven. What needs to happen is to get it to be demand driven. How? Are needs assessments required? Yes, but more proactive strategies are required in order to build a curriculum of learning activities. Is there a requirement for curriculum development then? Yes, but what is needed is more than a series of courses in a curriculum. What is needed is the right knowledge at the right time to help development practitioners do their job more efficiently and effectively. What is needed is the development of communities of practice. "The most important thing that we learned was that communities were the heart and soul of the whole thing (knowledge management)" (Barth 2001). Development strategies need to be tied with the appropriate learning strategies, and knowledge management and knowledge sharing is at the core of the process.

The program of GDLN should be proactively built rather than be the result of passively reacting to supply. Many of the tools to define the program already exist. On a broad level they could be the United Nations Millennium Development Goals. As already mentioned, in the case of the World Bank they are the Comprehensive Development Frameworks (CDF), the Country Assistance Strategies (CAS), and the Poverty Reduction Strategy Papers (PRSPs). Every development agency has its own strategies and policies on which to base its programs of assistance to developing countries. These programs can be the baseline from which much of the technical assistance and training is planned. This technical assistance and training can become the basis of the curriculum of GDLN.

The business case for this model of GDLN is based on the principle that the "user" must pay for the service, but the "user" must be defined. It may be the individual participants in the programs, but if the programs are based on the development strategies of the countries concerned, then the learning activities will be seen as a public good and therefore the "user" in this case can be defined as whoever has the agenda for wanting the activity to happen. This may be the government of the country or one of the development agencies working in partnership with the government, and they should be expected to pay the costs involved.

STRATEGIES FOR PROGRAMMING—A KNOWLEDGE MANAGEMENT PROCESS

Moving from a supply-driven model to a demand-driven one, and basing activities on programs rather than on courses, the roles of those involved in program development for GDLN, such as the GDLN Services Team and the management of the DLCs, become much more proactive in the areas of needs assessment and program design, in sum, in the area of Knowledge Management.

This approach will bring GDLN much closer to the operations side of the donor and lending agencies, because the training content of GDLN will be based on the needs of the client countries in relation to the successful implementation of their funded projects. The program developers will then work more closely with:

- Governments of client countries.
- Country or regional directors of the development and lending agencies.
- Chambers of Commerce and other civil society organizations in client countries.

By applying Knowledge Management principles and systems to the knowledge requirements for the operations and projects, training needs will emerge, which in turn will be the opportunity of learning program developers to find the corresponding expertise. They will do this, not by an open ended call for course proposals, but by actively seeking suppliers for the specified training, advisory services, or knowledge sharing activities that have been identified. The GDLN is beginning to be regarded by some development agencies as a tool for the implementation of their aid programs and they are providing the funding to support not only the content development but also the operational costs of the DLCs in the countries concerned. The managers of development programs can build in a learning plan at the program planning stage, and GDLN will be seen as one tool for its implementation. The technical assistance aspect of projects can also include learning and advisory services, some of which can be delivered through GDLN, with a budget to cover the costs involved. The GDLN and the DLCs that make up its core can then be perceived as service providers to the development process, and not as charities to be subsidized.

THE FUTURE; PARTNERSHIPS AND GDLN AS A "NETWORK OF NETWORKS"

It has been argued, with some justification, that GDLN is aimed at the elite, not the financially elite admittedly, but the power elite. It is also generally agreed in development circles that development will only work if he there is a concordance between top-down and grass roots involvement. The challenge to GDLN is to be able to complete the circle by reaching the grass roots. Currently GDLN centers are in capital cities, close to government and centers of power and much of the effort of the GDLN teams is to ensure that this primary network is operating effectively and in a sustainable fashion. The next stage in the growth will be to extend the network to areas outside capital cities, using a variety of networks and technologies. This is already happening, e.g., the China network mentioned above, and in Ethiopia, where a secondary national training network is being planned. In middle income countries partnerships are being formed with already existing national and regional networks, e.g., in Ecuador and Brazil.

The use of secondary national networks will require some new approaches to both content and to pedagogical design. Domestic networks, new ICTs such as digital audio broadcasting, and two-way Internet services, provided in a public/private partnership, are seen as an essential future development of GDLN. While the GDLN centers themselves are relatively expensive, there are some models already developed of "GDLN-Lite" versions, which can reach out to the edge of isolated and rural areas, in conjunction with regional and national strategies for distance learning.

GDLN is a work in progress, lessons are being learned, and policies and strategies are changing accordingly. Input to this most exciting development in distance learning is welcome.

REFERENCES

Bardini, M. D. (1998). *Economics and business journalism: Kenya distance learning course.* EDI Evaluation Studies Number ES99-19. Report to the World Bank Available at http://www.worldbank.org/wbi/evaluation/journalism.pdf

Barth, S. (June 2001). The knowledge bank. Interview with Stephen Denning. *Knowledge Management* magazine. Available at http://www.destinationcrm.com/km/dcrm_km_article.asp?id=858

Bates, A. W. (1995). *Technology: Open Learning and Distance Education.* London, Routledge.

Knowles, M. S. (1970). *The modern practice of adult education: Andragogy versus pedagogy.* New York: Association Press.

MacDonald, D. (1999). Internal report to WBI Management on "Controlling Corruption" course.

Wolfensohn, J. D. (June 1998). Videoconference World Bank.

Author Index

Page numbers not in parentheses refer to the reference lists at the end of each chapter. Those numbers in parentheses refer to citations in the text.

H

Q

R

Subject Index